DICTIONARY
OF
AMERICAN LIBRARY
BIOGRAPHY

DICTIONARY OF AMERICAN LIBRARY BIOGRAPHY

Edited by Bohdan S. Wynar

Libraries Unlimited, Inc., Littleton, Colo. - 1978

LIBRARIES UNLIMITED, INC.
P.O. Box 263
Littleton, Colorado 80160

Library of Congress Cataloging in Publication Data

Main entry under title:

Dictionary of American library biography.

    Includes bibliographies and index.
    1. Librarians--United States--Biography.
I. Bobinski, George Sylvan. II. Shera, Jesse
Hauk, 1903-   III. Wynar, Bohdan S.
Z720.A4D5   020'.92'2 [B]   77-28791
ISBN 0-87287-180-0

Table of Contents

94756

Contributors

ABBOTT, John C. Director, Lovejoy Library, Southern Illinois University at Edwardsville
Raymond Cazallis Davis

ABELL, J. Richard. Head, History and Literature Department, Public Library of Cincinnati and Hamilton County, Ohio
Nathaniel Dana Carlile Hodges

ADAMS, Virginia M. Curator of Special Collections, Providence Public Library, Rhode Island
Clarence Edgar Sherman

ANDERSON, Margaret. Assistant Professor, Faculty of Library Science, University of Toronto
Henry Evelyn Bliss, George Herbert Locke

ASH, Lee. Library Consultant, Bethany, Connecticut
Pierce Butler

BASSETT, Robert Julian. Head, Reference/Documents Department, University of Tennessee/Knoxville Library
William Herman Jesse

BAUMANN, Charles H. University Librarian, Eastern Washington University, Cheney
Angus Snead Macdonald

BEATTY, William K. Professor of Medical Bibliography, Northwestern University Medical School, Chicago
George Edwin Wire

BERKELEY, Dorothy Smith. (Retired), Charlottesville, Virginia
John James Beckley (with Edmund Berkeley)

BERKELEY, Edmund. (Retired), Charlottesville, Virginia
John James Beckley (with Dorothy Smith Berkeley)

BERNEIS, Regina F. Librarian, School of Librarianship, Western Michigan University, Kalamazoo
Ralph Munn, Effie Louise Power

BIDLACK, Russell E. Dean, School of Library Science, University of Michigan, Ann Arbor
Rudolph H. Gjelsness

BLACK, Jeannette D. Curator of Maps (retired), John Carter Brown Library, Brown University, Providence, Rhode Island
Lawrence Counselman Wroth

BLAZEK, Ron. Associate Professor, School of Library Science, Florida State University, Tallahassee
George Burwell Utley

BOAZ, Martha. Dean, School of Library Science, University of Southern California, Los Angeles
Mabel Ray Gillis, Harriet Emma Howe (with John Taylor Eastlick and Laurel A. Grotzinger), *William Setchel Learned, Althea Hester Warren*

BOBINSKI, George S. Professor and Dean, School of Information and Library Studies, State University of New York at Buffalo
James Bertram, Andrew Carnegie, William Isaac Fletcher, Alvin S. Johnson

BONN, George S. Professor of Library Science Emeritus, University of Illinois at Urbana-Champaign
Anne Morris Boyd

BRADLEY, Carol June. Music Library, State University of New York at Buffalo
George Sherman Dickinson, Otto Kinkeldey, Oscar George Theodore Sonneck

BRANSCOMB, Lewis C. Professor of Thurber Studies, Ohio State University, Columbus
Ervin Harold Pollack (with Roy M. Mersky), *Ernest Cushing Richardson*

BRAUNAGEL, Judith. Assistant Professor, School of Information and Library Studies, State University of New York at Buffalo
Mary Lemist Titcomb

BREIVIK, Patricia Senn. Dean of Library Services, Sangamon State University, Springfield, Illinois
Milton James Ferguson, Frank Pierce Hill

BRESIE, Mayellen. Director, Harold R. Yeary Library, Texas A&I University at Laredo/Laredo Junior College
Paul Joseph Foik

BRODERICK, John C. Chief, Manuscript Division, The Library of Congress
John Russell Young

BROWN, H. Glenn. Chief Reference Librarian and Emeritus Professor of Bibliography, Brown University, Providence, Rhode Island
Henry Bartlett Van Hoesen

BROWN, Ralph Adams. Distinguished Teaching Professor of American History, State University of New York, College at Cortland
James Kendall Hosmer, Victor Hugo Paltsits, Clifford Kenyon Shipton

BRYAN, Alice I. Professor Emeritus, School of Library Service, Columbia University, New York
Robert Devore Leigh

BRYAN, James E. Director (retired), Newark Public Library, New Jersey
John Boynton Kaiser

BYAM, Milton S. Director, Queens Borough Public Library, Jamaica, New York
Francis Regis St. John

CABEEN, S. K. Director, Engineering Societies Library, New York
Harrison Warwick Craver

CARL, Herbert A. Administrative Librarian (retired), Office of Libraries and Learning Resources, U.S. Office of Education, Washington, D.C.
Ralph McNeal Dunbar

CASEY, Marion. Department of History, University of Richmond, Virginia
Charles McCarthy

CHENEY, Frances Neel. Professor Emeritus, School of Library Science, George Peabody College for Teachers, Nashville, Tennessee
Margaret Hutchins

CHILDS, James Bennett [deceased]. Honorary Consultant in Government Document Bibliography, The Library of Congress
Charles Martel (with John Y. Cole)

CHRISTOPH, Peter R. Associate Librarian, New York State Library, Albany
Henry Augustus Homes

COHEN, Morris L. Librarian, Harvard Law School Library, Cambridge, Massachusetts
Miles Oscar Price (with Meira G. Pimsleur)

COLE, John Y. Planning Office, The Library of Congress
Charles Martel (with James Bennett Childs),
Herman Henry Bernard Meyer, Daniel Alexander Payne Murray,
George Herbert Putnam, Ainsworth Rand Spofford,
John Gould Stephenson

COLSON, John Calvin. Assistant Professor, Department of Library Science, Northern Illinois University, DeKalb
Henry Eduard Legler, Lutie Eugenia Stearns

CONAWAY, Charles William. Assistant Professor, School of Library Science, Florida State University, Tallahassee
Lyman Copeland Draper

CORY, John Mackenzie. Director, The New York Public Library
Franklin Ferguson Hopper (with Lawrence P. Murphy)

COSTELLO, Joan M. Librarian, Osterhout Free Library, Wilkes-Barre, Pennsylvania
Hannah Packard James (with Edward G. Holley)

CRAMER, C. H. Dean and Professor of History Emeritus, Case Western Reserve University, Cleveland
William Howard Brett, Linda Anne Eastman

CRAWFORD, Helen. Associate Professor Emeritus and former Librarian, Middleton Health Sciences Library, University of Wisconsin—Madison
Rachel Katherine Schenk

CROUCH, Keith. Chief Librarian, Royal Military College of Canada, Kingston, Ontario
Charles Henry Gould

CURLEY, Arthur. Associate Director, Detroit Public Library
Margery Closey Quigley

CUTLER, Wayne. Associate Professor, Department of History,
Vanderbilt University, Nashville, Tennessee
Justin Winsor (with Michael H. Harris)

CVELJO, Katherine. Associate Professor, School of Library and
Information Sciences, North Texas State University, Denton
Frederick Winthrop Faxon, Douglas Crawford McMurtrie (with
Marilyn Domas White), *Donald Goddard Wing*

DAIN, Phyllis. Professor, School of Library Service, Columbia Univer-
sity, New York
*Edwin Hatfield Anderson, John Shaw Billings,
Harry Miller Lydenberg*

DALE, Doris Cruger. Associate Professor, Department of Curriculum,
Instruction, and Media, Southern Illinois University, Carbondale
Mary Eileen Ahern, Clement Walker Andrews

DALLIGAN, Alice C. Chief, Burton Historical Collection, Detroit
Public Library
Adam Julius Strohm

DALTON, Jack. Director, Library Development Center, Columbia
University, New York
Harry Clemons

DANTON, J. Periam. Professor Emeritus, School of Library and
Information Studies, University of California, Berkeley
LeRoy Charles Merritt

DAVIS, Donald G., Jr. Associate Professor, Graduate School of
Library Science, University of Texas at Austin
*Arthur Elmore Bostwick, Florence Rising Curtis,
Josephine Adams Rathbone*

DEADERICK, Lucile. Director, Knoxville-Knox County Library,
Tennessee
Mary Utopia Rothrock

DIKEMAN, Robert K. Assistant Professor, Graduate School of Library Science, Louisiana State University, Baton Rouge
Evan J. Crane

DILLON, Lisa deGruyter. Extension Librarian, Alpha Regional Library, Spencer, West Virginia
William Torrey Harris (with Francis L. Miksa)

DINNAN, Leo T. Director, Wayne County Federated Library System, Wayne, Michigan
Walter Herbert Kaiser

DOBBS, Kimberly W. Executive Officer, Law Library, The Library of Congress
Bernard Richardson Green

DOUGLASS, Robert R. Professor Emeritus and Dean (retired), Graduate School of Library Science, University of Texas at Austin
Esther Laverne Stallmann

DOWDEN, Keith. Assistant Director, Resources and Reference Services, Purdue University Libraries, West Lafayette, Indiana
John Helenbeck Moriarty

DOWNS, Robert B. Dean of Library Administration Emeritus, University of Illinois at Urbana-Champaign
Arthur Monroe McAnally, Phineas Lawrence Windsor

DUNKIN, Paul S. [deceased]. Professor, Graduate School of Library Service, Rutgers—The State University of New Jersey, New Brunswick
Esther June Piercy

EASTLICK, John Taylor. Associate Dean, Graduate School of Librarianship, University of Denver
Ralph Theodore Esterquest, Harriet Emma Howe (with Martha Boaz and Laurel A. Grotzinger)

EDMONDS, Anne C. Librarian, Mount Holyoke College, South Hadley, Massachusetts
Flora Belle Ludington

ELLINWOOD, Leonard. Head (retired), Humanities Section, Subject Cataloging Division, The Library of Congress
David Judson Haykin

ERICKSON, Rolf. Head, Circulation Services Department, Northwestern University Library, Evanston, Illinois
Theodore Wesley Koch

ESTABROOK, Leigh. Assistant Professor, School of Library Science, Simmons College, Boston
Ezra Abbot

FASICK, Adele M. Associate Professor, Faculty of Library Science, University of Toronto
Anne Carroll Moore

FENSTER, Valmai R. Lecturer, Library School, University of Wisconsin–Madison
Mary Emogene Hazeltine

FOCKE, Helen M. Professor Emeritus, School of Library Science, Case Western Reserve University, Cleveland
Alice Sarah Tyler

FOOS, Donald D. Dean, Graduate School of Library Science, Louisiana State University, Baton Rouge
Aksel Gustav Salomon Josephson

GAMBEE, Budd L. Professor, School of Library Science, University of North Carolina, Chapel Hill
Frederick Morgan Crunden, Asa Don Dickinson,
Mary Salome Cutler Fairchild, Samuel Swett Green,
Caroline Maria Hewins

GAMBEE, Ruth R. Catalog Librarian (retired), University of Michigan Law Library, Ann Arbor
Nicholas-Alexandre-Marie Vattemare

GLEAVES, Edwin S. Director, School of Library Science, George Peabody College for Teachers, Nashville, Tennessee
Francis Keese Wynkoop Drury

GOFF, Frederick R. Honorary Consultant in Early Printed Books, The Library of Congress
Robert William Glenroie Vail

GOODWIN, Jack. Bibliographer for the History of Science and Technology, Smithsonian Institution Libraries, Washington, D.C.
Cyrus Adler

GORDON, Dudley. Professor Emeritus, Los Angeles City College; Curator, The Lummis Home, Los Angeles
Charles Fletcher Lummis

GORDON, Martin K. Reference Section, History and Museums Division, Headquarters, United States Marine Corps, Washington, D.C.
Patrick Magruder

GRANNIS, Chandler B. Formerly Editor-in-Chief, *Publishers Weekly*, New York
Frederic Gershom Melcher

GROTZINGER, Laurel A. Professor, School of Librarianship, Western Michigan University, Kalamazoo
Adelaide Rosalie Hasse, Harriet Emma Howe (with Martha Boaz and John Taylor Eastlick),
Alice Bertha Kroeger, Margaret Mann,
Isadore Gilbert Mudge (with John N. Waddell),
Katharine L. Sharp

GWINN, Nancy E. Information and Publications Officer, Council on Library Resources, Washington, D.C.
George Watterston

HAAS, Marilyn L. Reference Librarian, Lockwood Memorial Library, State University of New York at Buffalo
Winifred Gregory Gerould, Orville Augustus Roorbach

HANSEN, Ralph W. Chief Librarian of the Acquisition Department and University Archivist, Stanford University Libraries, California
Nathan van Patten

HARDING, Thomas S. Librarian Emeritus, Washburn University of Topeka, Kansas
Carleton Bruns Joeckel, McKendree Llewellyn Raney

HARLAN, Robert D. Professor and Associate Dean, School of Library and Information Studies, University of California, Berkeley
Helen Elizabeth Haines

HARMELING, Sister Deborah. Head Librarian, Mount St. Mary Seminary of the West, Norwood, Ohio
Thomas Jefferson (with Michael H. Harris),
John Langdon Sibley (with Michael H. Harris)

HARRIS, Michael H. Professor, College of Library Science, University of Kentucky, Lexington
Benjamin Franklin, Chalmers Hadley (with
Trina E. King and Edward D. Starkey),
Thomas Jefferson (with Sister Deborah Harmeling),
Charles Coffin Jewett, John Langdon Sibley (with
Sister Deborah Harmeling),
George Ticknor, Justin Winsor (with
Wayne Cutler)

HARVEY, John F. St. Johnsbury, Vermont
*James Thayer Gerould, Francis Lee Dewey Goodrich,
Hans Peter Luhn, Harriet Dorothea MacPherson*

HASKELL, John D., Jr. Editor, Committee for a New England Bibliography, Boston
Appleton Prentiss Clark Griffin

HAYES, Catherine D. Assistant Director of Libraries, University of Rochester, New York
Donald Bean Gilchrist

HEALEY, James S. Director, School of Library Science, University of Oklahoma, Norman
John E. Fogarty, William Eaton Foster

HELD, Ray E. Associate Professor Emeritus, School of Library and Information Studies, University of California, Berkeley
James Louis Gillis

HENCH, John B. Editor of Publications, American Antiquarian Society, Worcester, Massachusetts
Clarence Saunders Brigham

HENKLE, Herman H. Executive Director and Librarian (retired), John Crerar Library, Chicago
Jens Christian Bay

HERRING, Billie Grace. Associate Professor, Graduate School of Library Science, University of Texas at Austin
Alice Sinclair Harrison

HICKEY, Doralyn J. Professor, School of Library and Information Sciences, North Texas State University, Denton
Paul Shaner Dunkin

HODGES, Margaret. Professor, Graduate School of Library and Information Sciences, University of Pittsburgh
Elva Sophronia Smith

HOLLEY, Edward G. Dean, School of Library Science, University of North Carolina, Chapel Hill
Wilberforce Eames (with W. Davenport Robertson), *Charles Evans, Hannah Packard James* (with Joan M. Costello), *Otis Hall Robinson*

HUMPHRY, John A. Executive Director, Forest Press, Lake Placid Education Foundation, Albany, New York
Hiller Crowell Wellman

IMMROTH, John Phillip [deceased]. Associate Professor, Graduate School of Library and Information Sciences, University of Pittsburgh
James Christian Meinich Hanson

JACKSON, Eugene B. Professor, Graduate School of Library Science, University of Texas at Austin
Bill Milton Woods

JOHNSON, Andrew F. Librarian, Pacific Northwest Collection, University of Washington Libraries, Seattle
Charles Wesley Smith

JOHNSON, Herbert F. Librarian of Oberlin, Oberlin College Library, Ohio
Azariah Smith Root

JOHNSON, Mary Frances K. Professor, Library Science/Educational Technology Division, University of North Carolina at Greensboro
Mary Teresa Peacock Douglas

JONAH, David A. John Hay Professor of Bibliography Emeritus; Librarian and Director Emeritus, Brown University Libraries, Providence, Rhode Island
Harry Lyman Koopman

JONES, Virginia Lacy. Dean, School of Library Service, Atlanta University, Georgia
Susan Dart Butler, Sadie Peterson Delaney

JORDAN, Casper LeRoy. University Librarian, Atlanta University, Georgia
Samuel W. Starks

JOSEY, E. J. Chief, Bureau of Specialist Library Services, New York State Education Department, Albany
Charles Bunsen Shaw, Edward Christopher Williams

KALTENBACH, Margaret. Associate Professor Emeritus, School of Library Science, Case Western Reserve University, Cleveland
Herbert Simon Hirshberg, Hannah Hunt (with John A. Rowell)

KARLOWICH, Robert A. Assistant Professor, Graduate School of Library and Information Science, Pratt Institute, Brooklyn, New York
Mary Wright Plummer (with Nasser Sharify)

KASER, David. Professor, Graduate Library School, Indiana University, Bloomington
Randolph Greenfield Adams, Eileen Roach Cunningham

KELLY, Richard Edward. Editor, *Episcopal Churchfacts from Western New York*, Diocese of Western New York, Buffalo
Charles Knowles Bolton

KENNEDY, Frances. Executive Secretary, Oklahoma Library Association; Director Emeritus, Oklahoma City University Library
Allie Beth Dent Martin

KING, Trina E. Indexer, H. W. Wilson Company, New York
Chalmers Hadley (with Michael H. Harris and Edward D. Starkey)

KINGERY, Robert E. Coordinator (retired), Community Relations Services and Personnel Recruiting, Dayton and Montgomery County Public Library, Ohio
Electra Collins Doren, Paul North Rice

KINGSBURY, Mary E. Associate Professor, School of Library Science, University of North Carolina, Chapel Hill
Mary Frances Isom, Marie Shedlock

KLINE, Nancy M. Map Librarian, University of Connecticut Library, Storrs
Ena Laura Yonge

KODA, Paul S. Curator of Rare Books, University of North Carolina, Chapel Hill
George Parker Winship

KRASH, Ronald D. Director, General Library, State Library of Pennsylvania, Harrisburg
Thomas Lynch Montgomery

KRAUS, Joe W. Director, Illinois State University Library, Normal
William Beer, Reuben Brooks Poole

KRUMMEL, D. W. Professor, Graduate School of Library Science, University of Illinois at Urbana-Champaign
William Stetson Merrill (with William Landram Williamson), *Charles Benjamin Norton, Stanley Pargellis*

LAUGHER, Charles T. Special Collections, Dalhousie University Library, Halifax, Nova Scotia
Thomas Bray

LIBBEY, David C. Assistant Professor, Division of Library Science and Instructional Technology, Southern Connecticut State College, New Haven
Andrew Keogh

LOGSDON, Richard H. Professor, Department of Library Science, Queens College, City University of New York, Flushing
Anita Miller Hostetter

LOGSDON, Robert L. Acting Head, Division for the Blind and Physically Handicapped, Indiana State Library, Indianapolis
Charles Everett Rush

LOOMIS, Koert C., Jr. Editorial Staff, Libraries Unlimited, Inc., Littleton, Colorado
Walter Stanley Biscoe (with Bohdan S. Wynar),
John Hall Jacobs (with Bohdan S. Wynar),
Malcolm Glenn Wyer (with Bohdan S. Wynar)

LORD, Clifford L. Director, New Jersey Historical Society, Newark
Reuben Gold Thwaites

LOWRIE, Jean E. Director, School of Librarianship, Western Michigan University, Kalamazoo
Casper Carl Certain, Alice Louise LeFevre

LOWY, Beverly R. Library Director, North Bellmore Public Library, New York
Margaret Clara Scoggin

LYMAN, Helen Huguenor. Professor, Library School, University of Wisconsin—Madison
Frank Avery Hutchins

MARSHALL, John David. Middle Tennessee State University Library, Murfreesboro
William Wayne Shirley

McDONOUGH, John. Manuscript Historian, Manuscript Division, The Library of Congress
John Silva Meehan

McDONOUGH, Roger H. New Jersey State Librarian Emeritus, Princeton
Sarah Byrd Askew

McGUIRE, Alice Brooks [deceased]. Associate Professor, Graduate School of Library Science, University of Texas at Austin
Lucile Foster Fargo

McMULLEN, Haynes. Professor, School of Library Science, University of North Carolina, Chapel Hill
Jennie Dorcas Fellows, Frederick Leypoldt

McSWAIN, Mary Brown. Librarian (retired), Graduate School of Library Science, University of Texas at Austin
Julia Bedford Ideson

MERSKY, Roy M. Professor of Law and Director of Research, School of Law, University of Texas at Austin
Ervin Harold Pollack (with Lewis C. Branscomb)

MICKEY, Melissa Brisley. Corporate Librarian, Kraft, Inc., Glenview, Illinois
Cornelia Marvin Pierce

MIELE, Madeline F. Market Research Manager, R. R. Bowker Company, New York
Richard Rogers Bowker

MIKSA, Francis L. Associate Professor, Graduate School of Library Science, Louisiana State University, Baton Rouge
Charles Ammi Cutter, John Eaton,
William Torrey Harris (with Lisa deGruyter Dillon),
Samuel Foster Haven, Charles Alexander Nelson,
Stephen Buttrick Noyes, Alexander Joseph Rudolph,
Frederic Vinton

MILLER, Marilyn. Associate Professor, School of Library Science, University of North Carolina, Chapel Hill
May Hill Arbuthnot

MOHRHARDT, Foster E. Consultant, Council on Library Resources, Washington, D.C.
Verner Warren Clapp

MONROE, Margaret E. Professor, Library School, University of Wisconsin—Madison
Jennie Maas Flexner, Patricia L. Bryan Knapp

MOORE, Mattie Ruth. Director of Library and Media Services (retired), Dallas Independent School District
Alice Rebecca Brooks McGuire (with
Claud Glenn Sparks)

MORTON, Florrinell F. Professor Emeritus, Graduate School of Library Science, Louisiana State University, Baton Rouge
Essae Martha Culver

MURPHY, Lawrence P.   Special Assistant to the Director, The New
     York Public Library
          Franklin Ferguson Hopper (with John Mackenzie Cory)

NORELL, Irene P. Associate Professor, Division of Library Science,
     San Jose State University, California
          Hannah Logasa

OEHLERTS, Donald E. Director of Libraries, Miami University,
     Oxford, Ohio
          Alfred Morton Githens, Charles Follen McKim,
          Henry Hobson Richardson, Edward Lippincott Tilton

PALMER, Roger Cain.   Lecturer, School of Library Science, University
     of Michigan, Ann Arbor
          Charles Frances Dorr Belden

PARKER, Wyman W. Librarian Emeritus, Wesleyan University,
     Middleton, Connecticut
          Arthur Fremont Rider

PAULSON, Peter J.   Director, New York State Library, Albany
          James Ingersoll Wyer

PIMSLEUR, Meira G.   Acquisitions Librarian (retired), Columbia Uni-
     versity Law Library, New York; Editorial Assistant, Oceana
     Publications, Dobbs Ferry, New York
          Miles Oscar Price (with Morris L. Cohen)

PLATOU, Mary Jane. Assistant Librarian for User Education, State
     University of New York, Agricultural and Technical College, Delhi
          Bessie Graham

PLOTNIK, Arthur.   Editor, *American Libraries*, Chicago
          Halsey William Wilson

POND, Patricia B. Associate Dean, Graduate School of Library and
     Information Sciences, University of Pittsburgh
          Mary Evelyn Hall

POWELL, Lawrence Clark. Professor in Residence, Graduate Library
     School, University of Arizona, Tucson
          Edith Margaret Coulter, John Edward Goodwin,
          Sydney Bancroft Mitchell

PRICE, Paxton Pate. Executive Director, St. Louis Public Library, Missouri
Charles Herrick Compton

RICHMOND, Phyllis A. Professor, School of Library Science, Case Western Reserve University, Cleveland
Lucile M. Morsch

RINEHART, Constance. Professor, School of Library Science, University of Michigan, Ann Arbor
Julia Pettee

ROBERTSON, W. Davenport. Librarian, National Institute of Environmental Health Sciences, Research Triangle Park, North Carolina
Wilberforce Eames (with Edward G. Holley), *Henry Harrisse*

ROHDE, Nancy Freeman. Assistant Professor, Library School, University of Minnesota, Minneapolis
Gratia Alta Countryman

ROONEY, Paul M. Director, Buffalo and Erie County Public Library, Buffalo, New York
Walter Lewis Brown, Theresa Hubbell West Elmendorf

ROSCOE, Sandra. Assistant Reference Librarian, University of Chicago Library
Joseph Sabin, Lloyd Pearsall Smith

ROTH, Elizabeth E. Keeper of Prints, The New York Public Library
Frank Weitenkampf

ROWELL, John A. Professor and Director, School Library Media Program, School of Library Science, Case Western Reserve University, Cleveland
Hannah Hunt (with Margaret Kaltenbach)

SABINE, Julia. Supervising Librarian (retired), Art and Music Department, Newark Public Library, New Jersey; Special Assistant to the Director, Munson-Williams-Procter Institute, Utica, New York
Beatrice Winser

SAMORE, Ted. Professor, School of Library Science, University of
Wisconsin—Milwaukee
Matthew Simpson Dudgeon

SASSÉ, Margo. Audio-Visual Coordinator, San Diego Mesa College,
California
Anne Thaxter Eaton, Minerva Amanda Lewis Sanders,
Caroline Burnite Walker

SCHIFF, Judith A. Chief Research Archivist, Manuscripts and
Archives, Yale University Library, New Haven, Connecticut
Addison Van Name

SCHUMAN, Patricia Glass. President, Neal-Schuman Publishers, Inc.,
New York
Clara Whitehill Hunt

SELDEN, Bernice. Library Consultant, writer of books for teenagers,
New York
Ernestine Rose

SHAPIRO, Ruth. Formerly Headquarters Librarian, American Library
Association, Chicago; Executive Secretary, Milwaukee Council for
Adult Learning
Miriam Downing Tompkins

SHARIFY, Nasser. Dean and Professor, Graduate School of Library
and Information Science, Pratt Institute, Brooklyn, New York
Mary Wright Plummer (with Robert A. Karlowich)

SHERA, Jesse H. Dean Emeritus, School of Library Science, Case
Western Reserve University, Cleveland
Ralph Albert Beals, Sidney Herbert Ditzion,
Margaret Elizabeth Egan, Mortimer Taube

SHIELDS, Gerald R. Assistant Dean, School of Information and
Library Studies, State University of New York at Buffalo
David Horace Clift

SHOVE, Raymond H. Professor Emeritus, Library School, University
of Minnesota, Minneapolis
Frank Keller Walter

SHUMAN, Bruce A. Associate Professor, School of Library Science, University of Oklahoma, Norman
Carl Bismarck Roden

SINNETTE, Elinor Des Verney. Consultant, Unesco, Nairobi, Kenya
Arthur Alfonso Schomburg

SITTIG, William J. Technical Officer, Research Department, The Library of Congress
Thorvald Solberg

SLAVENS, Thomas P. Professor, School of Library Science, University of Michigan, Ann Arbor
Charles Ripley Gillett

SMITH, Elizabeth W. Lecturer, School of Information and Library Studies, State University of New York at Buffalo
Josephus Nelson Larned

SMITH, Jessie Carney. University Librarian and Federal Relations Officer, Fisk University, Nashville, Tennessee
Arna Wendell Bontemps

SMITH, Susan Seabury. Professor Emerita, School of Library and Information Science, State University of New York at Albany
Martha Caroline Pritchard

SOLOMITA, John. Deputy Director, Queens Borough Public Library, Jamaica, New York
Harold Walton Tucker

SPARKS, Claud Glenn. Dean, Graduate School of Library Science, University of Texas at Austin
William Warner Bishop, Alice Rebecca Brooks McGuire (with Mattie Ruth Moore)

STARKEY, Edward D. College Librarian, Urbana College, Urbana, Ohio
Chalmers Hadley (with Michael H. Harris and Trina E. King)

STEVENS, Jane E. Assistant Professor, School of Library Service, Columbia University, New York
Bertha Margaret Frick

STEVENS, Norman D. University Librarian, University of Connecticut, Storrs
John Cotton Dana, Edmund Lester Pearson,
Ralph Robert Shaw

STEVENS, Rolland E. Professor, Graduate School of Library Science, University of Illinois at Urbana-Champaign
Julia Wright Merrill

SULLIVAN, Howard A. Assistant Director of the Libraries, Wayne State University, Detroit
George Flint Purdy

SULLIVAN, Peggy A. Assistant Commissioner for Extension Services, Chicago Public Library
Sarah Comly Norris Bogle, Frederick Paul Keppel,
Robert MacDonald Lester, Carl Hastings Milam

SWANK, R. C. Professor, School of Library and Information Studies, University of California, Berkeley
Donald Coney

TABB, Winston. Congressional Research Administrator, The Library of Congress
George Franklin Bowerman

THOMPSON, Lawrence S. Professor of Classics, University of Kentucky, Lexington
Charles Harvey Brown

THOMPSON, Susan Otis. Assistant Professor, School of Library Service, Columbia University, New York
Richard Heston Shoemaker

TRYON, Jonathan S. Associate Professor, Graduate Library School, University of Rhode Island, Kingston
Reuben Aldridge Guild

TUCKER, Florence Ray. Research and Grants Coordinator, Detroit Public Library
Henry Munson Utley

TURNER, Harold M. Bronxville, New York
Joseph Green Cogswell

VANN, Sarah K. Professor, Graduate School of Library Studies, University of Hawaii, Honolulu
Melvil Dewey, Jacob Schwartz, Jr.,
Evelyn May Seymour

VINCE, Thomas L. Librarian and Curator, Hudson Library and Historical Society, Hudson, Ohio
Burton Egbert Stevenson

VORMELKER, Rose L. Adjunct Professor, School of Library Science, Kent State University, Ohio
Marilla Waite Freeman, Linda Huckel Morley,
Catherine Ruth Savord

WADDELL, John N. [deceased]. Assistant Professor, School of Library Service, Columbia University, New York
Isadore Gilbert Mudge (with Laurel A. Grotzinger)

WARNER, Lee H. Associate Curator, Historic Tallahassee Preservation Board, Florida
Joseph Lewis Wheeler

WESSELLS, Michael Butler. Researcher, Battelle Columbus Laboratories, Columbus, Ohio
John Edmands, Frederick Beecher Perkins,
Bernard Christian Steiner, Earl Gregg Swem

WHITE, Marilyn Domas. Assistant Professor, College of Library and Information Services, University of Maryland, College Park
Belle da Costa Greene,
Douglas Crawford McMurtrie (with Katherine Cveljo)

WHITMORE, Harry E. Assistant Professor, School of Library Science, University of Michigan, Ann Arbor
Minnie Earl Sears

WIEGAND, Wayne A. Assistant Professor, College of Library Science, University of Kentucky, Lexington
Henry James Carr, William Coolidge Lane,
Klas August Linderfelt

WILLIAMSON, William Landram. Professor, Library School, University of Wisconsin—Madison
William Stetson Merrill (with D. W. Krummel),
William Frederick Poole

WINCKLER, Paul A. Professor, Palmer Graduate Library School, Long Island University, Greenvale, New York
Charles Clarence Williamson

WINGER, Howard W. Professor, Graduate Library School, University of Chicago
Leon Carnovsky

WOOD, Raymund F. Professor Emeritus, Graduate School of Library and Information Science, University of California at Los Angeles
Ina Donna Coolbrith

WOODWARD, Daniel H. Librarian, Huntington Library, Art Gallery, and Botanical Gardens, San Marino, California
George Watson Cole

WOOLLS, Blanche E. Associate Professor, Graduate School of Library and Information Sciences, University of Pittsburgh
Frances Jenkins Olcott

WRIGHT, Lillian Taylor. Head, Technical Services, Blazer Library, Kentucky State University, Frankfort
Thomas Fountain Blue

WYNAR, Bohdan S. President, Libraries Unlimited, Inc., Littleton, Colorado
Walter Stanley Biscoe (with Koert C. Loomis, Jr.),
John Hall Jacobs (with Koert C. Loomis, Jr.),
Malcolm Glenn Wyer (with Koert C. Loomis, Jr.)

YOUNG, Arthur P. Assistant Dean and Associate Professor, University of Alabama Library, University, Alabama
Daniel Coit Gilman

YOUNG, Betty. Head, Circulation Department, East Campus Library, Duke University, Durham, North Carolina
Lillian Baker Griggs

YOUNGS, Willard O. Librarian Emeritus, Seattle Public Library, Washington
Judson Toll Jennings

Preface

R. G. Collingwood, in the opening pages of his *The Idea of History*, addresses himself to the nagging question of the purpose of history and concludes that "history is for human self-knowledge." It is important to us, he argues, to know what we are, first as human beings and second as the kind of individual each of us is. But no one knows what it is to be a human being until he knows what human beings have done. Eric Fromm has said that man himself is the most important creation and achievement of the continuous human effort the record of which we call history. History, then, is the record of the collective actions and thoughts of human beings working and thinking either as individuals or together in societies. "There is properly no history; only biography," wrote Ralph Waldo Emerson.

What Collingwood and the others have said of the individual is also true of societies, institutions, and professions. All of these have left records that tell us what they are and what their potential for the future can be. All of these are the result of individuals working together and, most important for us, leaving behind them a record, both graphic and artifactual, of their efforts, their successes, failures, and their dreams and aspirations. Without record, there can be no history.

The history of librarianship is important to us for the reasons that Collingwood has set forth. We cannot know ourselves as a profession until we know what we have done and, from that record, we learn what we can do and what we are. Library history is necessary to our professional self-knowledge, and it is written in the lives of those men and women who have practiced it, have thought and written about it, and have given it vitality and life.

Librarianship, like all other social innovations and movements, reached its present professional state after centuries of development, trial and error, action and reaction. American librarianship as we know it today is the culmination of generations of human endeavor. Thus, one can say of library history, as Thomas Carlyle has said of history generally, that it "is the essence of innumerable biographies." Yet, everyone working in the field of library history has been hampered by the paucity of reliable information concerning those dedicated men and women who, throughout their lives, made librarianship an essential element in the communication system of contemporary society. Immersed in the records of others, we have neglected our own. It is the purpose of the *Dictionary of American Library Biography* (DALB) partially to correct this hiatus in our professional knowledge. Obviously, these biographies cannot be definitive, but they at least set some signposts along the way to guide the footsteps of the future investigator. If biography is the stuff of which history is made, here is some of the substance essential to an appreciation of our professional antecedents.

A TRIBUTE TO COOPERATIVE EFFORT

The *Dictionary of American Library Biography* contains thoroughly researched, original biographical sketches of 302 outstanding men and women who, in large measure, founded and built this country's free public libraries, assembled monumental university and research collections, started school and special libraries, initiated pioneering ideas in library education, constructed irreplaceable bibliographic tools, forged national, regional, and state professional associations, and introduced to the library profession the philosophical concepts, innovative methods, and technology necessary to construct a solid foundation for our present library and information networks.

Envisioned by its Editorial and Advisory Board members as a major contribution to library history, DALB remained only a cherished plan until individual members of the library profession accepted the challenge of researching, writing, and refereeing the over 300 biographical sketches. Without the unselfish efforts of its contributors, this major project would not have become a reality. DALB, probably the first biographical dictionary of its kind for any professional group in the United States, is a tribute to the cooperative efforts of over 200 people dedicated to the idea that the history of librarianship is important to the profession. This historical study of library leaders and their accomplishments makes it possible to gain a proper historical perspective and to interpret and appreciate the profession's present resources and their origins.

Entries are arranged alphabetically by the surname of the biographee. In almost all cases, the narrative begins with a summary of the subject's family background and educational career. The largest portion of the sketch is devoted to the biographee's career activities, highlighting major contributions to or influence on librarianship in its many forms. Professional associations, publications, and other pertinent data are presented, as is an analysis of the biographee's role in library history. In many instances, the biographical sketches are either the first or the most considerable study yet made of the individual, drawing not only upon existing scholarship but sometimes upon exhaustive original research. Occasionally, in addition to purely historical documentation, a biographical sketch contains personal elements, reflecting the fact that the biographer knew the biographee (and, in some cases, quite well). Such personal reminiscences, and quotations from contemporaries or obituaries, represent contributions to the existing record, lifting the biography out of the wooden narration of facts and providing a more human picture of the subject, but never at the expense of pertinent information.

To provide additional references, each biographical sketch concludes with a bibliography noting biographical listings and obituaries, books and articles about the biographee, and primary sources and archives, if known. Occasionally, when the DALB biographer has had access to sources that might not have been available to earlier biographers, we have been able to correct misinformation appearing in standard sources. On the other hand, we must admit that we have not always been able to provide all of the information that might have been desirable—most often, of course, for the earlier figures.

Mention should be made of some of the more troublesome editorial questions that have followed us throughout the preparation of the volume. The question of racial terminology was naturally among them—specifically, whether to use Negro, Afro-American, or black, since social customs have changed over the years. Following consultation with members of the Advisory Board and others, we decided to use the terms Negro and Afro-American, since those were commonly accepted in the historical context of the biographees. In the supplements to DALB, the term "black" will be used, reflecting current usage, since biographees included in the supplements will be primarily those who died after June 30, 1976. Other editorial decisions related to the use of Dr., Mr., Mrs., and Miss. In some cases, academic titles could not be verified and others were honorary. Based on the practice of the *Dictionary of American Biography*, such titles as Dr. were omitted. The appellations Mr., Mrs., and Miss were also not used.

SELECTION CRITERIA

Details of the evolution of selection criteria, which matured through long discussion, are presented in the section describing the history of DALB and the procedures used in compiling it. Great care has been taken in choosing the candidates for inclusion, in appointing a knowledgeable board of advisors, in selecting qualified authors for the biographies, and in choosing referees to authenticate the sketches. The decision was soon reached that DALB should emphasize figures of national importance, based on the following criteria: contributions of national significance to library development; writings that influenced library trends and activities; positions of national importance (presidents of the American Library Association and Librarians of Congress were automatically included); major achievements in special fields of librarianship; significant scholarly, philanthropic, legislative, or governmental support or activity that affected American libraries. To ensure proper historical perspective, only those people deceased as of June 30, 1976, were considered for inclusion.

Such a policy, however, raises the vexing problem of defining what is meant by "national influence" or "professional distinction." Certainly no editor would think of omitting such names as Melvil Dewey, Charles A. Cutter, Charles Coffin Jewett, or Richard Rogers Bowker, whose accomplishments are already reasonably well documented in library literature. Thus, the selection of the fifty or so most prominent figures in American librarianship was, relatively speaking, an easy task. However, one of the great values of a biographical dictionary of this kind is that it can reach beyond the obvious. Considering the infancy of the biographical literature of librarianship, we felt that we should attempt to make available information about prominent librarians who are less widely known and whose library contributions are not widely documented. Despite their lack of renown, such people exerted a substantial influence on library science. It was up to the contributors to DALB and to the Editorial and Advisory Boards to rediscover such historically important figures, whose names have been obscure to our profession at large until this time.

Yet, the question of when regional influence becomes national in impact remains basically unanswered and unanswerable to any degree of certainty. The vigorous discussions held among Editorial and Advisory Board members on individual cases illustrate the difficulty of the problem. (These discussions were carried on through both correspondence and actual meetings of those members present at ALA Midwinter and Annual Conferences.) Thus, librarians who may have been innovative in some field or procedure that later had national importance are included, while others, who did fine work in a region or city but whose work was not innovative in that same sense, are not to be found in DALB.

Beyond those included in this book, a large number of librarians exists whose influence did not extend beyond the local scene but whose professional lives touched and influenced, in very important ways, the people who knew and worked with them. Such librarians may have been omitted over the vigorous protests of those who felt, quite rightly in many instances, that their particular mentors had suffered neglect. These borderline cases caused a number of lengthy and sometimes heated discussions, as is pointed out in the section on history and procedures. Votes by Advisory Board members, and further verification, usually from the biographee's geographical area, were determining factors. For the omissions, we express regret; indeed, we ourselves have had to accept such omissions, recognizing the demands of editorial necessity.

Librarians' natural bias for the printed word was also a factor in deciding whom to include, but again, it was not the single standard by which achievement was judged. Obviously, less documentation is available concerning the careers of earlier figures in librarianship than on the careers of our contemporaries (as is noted in several sketches), but this does not lessen the importance of these early figures to the profession. Rather, the burden of finding and interpreting a wide range of available documentation falls more heavily on library historians, for they cannot rely upon long lists of publications and official positions to determine the actual professional influence of given individuals. Thus, the present volume represents the consensus of the Editorial and Advisory Boards as to the identity of those leaders and innovators most directly responsible for the current state of librarianship in the United States.

HISTORY AND PROCEDURES

The *Dictionary of American Library Biography* had its origins at the January 1973 ALA Midwinter Conference in Washington, D.C., where Bohdan S. Wynar invited George S. Bobinski and Jesse H. Shera to collaborate with him on the project. By the June 1973 ALA Annual Conference, an Advisory Board of librarians, library historians, and scholars had been formed, and specific criteria and procedures had been worked out. During this time, names of potential biographees and biographers were suggested by members of the Editorial and Advisory Boards to make up an initial list. George Bobinski, after compiling lists of biographees, began contacting prospective biographers late in the summer of that year.

The first tentative list of biographees for DALB, compiled in May 1973, consisted of 138 names. By July of that year, the list had grown to 303 names, and (with the addition of even more names in October 1973 and in February 1974) the second tentative list eventually consisted of 506 names. The following sources proved to be the most valuable in compiling the lists, but even they were not exhaustive: *Dictionary of American Biography*, *National Cyclopaedia of American Biography*, the "Library Hall of Fame" (which appeared in the March 15, 1951, issue of *Library Journal*, marking the 75th anniversary of ALA), Cannons's *Bibliography of Library Economy*, lists of past presidents of ALA and former Librarians of Congress, *Biography Index*, and Michael Harris's *Guide to Research in American Library History*. Members of the Advisory Board and people not directly connected with the project also suggested names during the period when lists of potential biographees were circulated for reactions.

Another problem was the selection of authors with the requisite scholarly and literary abilities to treat their subjects thoroughly. Potential biographers could often be identified on the basis of theses, dissertations, monographs, or journal articles they had previously written about potential DALB biographees. In other cases, the task was not so easy, and, in July 1974, the Editorial Board asked for assistance from library school faculty members specializing in library history. In a few instances, it even became necessary for the Editorial Board to concentrate on the biographee's geographic area by contacting local librarians and requesting recommendations for potential biographers. Thus, the contributors include librarians, library historians, and a few people from outside the library profession.

Some delays were experienced when sketches did not arrive as expected. In a few cases, new biographers had to be found and given adequate time in which to research and write. Unfortunately, some biographers who were themselves worthy of inclusion in DALB died early in the progress of the *Dictionary*. Biographies of them had to be prepared as well, and thus we have the situation that some people who contributed sketches to DALB themselves became the subjects of sketches. Any prominent figure in librarianship who died following the cut-off date of

June 30, 1976, and any figures for whom sketches did not become available for publication will be included in supplemental sketches, to be published as discussed below.

By July 1975, the Editorial and Advisory Boards chose, after careful deliberation, 309 names for inclusion (an additional 215 having been considered but not chosen). That August, a general newsletter describing the project was sent out to announce that publication was intended for 1976, to coincide with the centennial of the founding of the American Library Association and the bicentennial of the United States. Yet, the very procedures established by the Boards to ensure comprehensive coverage and to discover errors of fact or emphasis became the stumbling block that prevented the completion of the project as scheduled.

In addition to being read by at least two Editorial Board members, each sketch was sent to outside volunteer readers (referees) who had specialized knowledge of the biographee. In a majority of cases, people who contributed sketches were generous enough with their time to serve as referees for other sketches as well. Their comments (of varying length and utility) were then taken under consideration by Bohdan Wynar and the Libraries Unlimited editorial staff. Occasionally, a referee would submit a new version of a sketch; at other times, new versions were requested when an existing sketch proved inadequate to the purposes and standards of DALB. Some sketches were reviewed as many as five times, a few (of lesser-known figures) were reviewed once or twice; some were reviewed soon after receipt in 1975, others during 1976 and the first half of 1977. However, the comprehensive review did take place as the project originators had desired, in spite of the extra time entailed by this concern for accuracy of fact and interpretation.

Perhaps the most vexing problem in assembling DALB and bringing it to completion was the question of retaining or omitting sketches of "borderline" cases—that is, people whose achievements, while considerable, were found upon close examination to have been duplicated in kind by librarians in other cities or regions. Thus, while "builders," they were not leaders when compared with others of larger, more certain national achievement. Well over 50 such sketches were found to exist in the DALB files. The reasons for questioning the inclusion of a particular sketch ranged from the biographee's real lack of definable national achievement to the author's concentration on interpretation, reminiscence, or flattery (with a concomitant lack of historical data). In over 20 cases, subjects were found to have been less impressive in actual professional contributions than in word-of-mouth reputation, but this became clear only when the completed sketch of that person was examined.

Thus it was that the second DALB newsletter was issued in November 1976, with coding indicating that certain sketches still needed initial review while others had been reviewed and found wanting for the purposes of DALB. Notes of protest and agreement concerning sketches marked as "drop" or "possible drop" came in immediately; deficiencies in some sketches were remedied, while others were still found not to justify their subjects' inclusion, even after repeated attempts to gain more information. After consultations with and votes by members of the Advisory Board, approximately 60 percent of those sketches previously scheduled for dropping were retained, once high factual accuracy and literary quality had been provided by the original or a second biographer and their true importance had been properly documented and emphasized.

One group of people who have been given very limited coverage includes private book dealers and collectors as well as the founders of large private libraries. In general, the collectors and dealers include people who may have had tangential relationships with libraries but who were more concerned with private individual relationships with books than with public access to and use of them. The founders of large private libraries present a problem of a different sort, in that these libraries have become, in many cases, national treasures; yet the interest of the persons funding such enterprises may have been excited only to the extent that they provided funds and hired someone knowledgeable to direct the use of those funds. Hence, no sketches of Pierpont or J. P. Morgan, John Jacob Astor, or Henry E. Huntington appear in DALB, since their lifelong interests and activities were, in essence, outside of librarianship. Sketches do appear, though, of Belle da Costa Greene, Joseph G. Cogswell, and George Watson Cole (the first librarians, respectively, of the institutions established by the Morgans, Astor, and Huntington), since these were the people whose expert knowledge was responsible for those unique collections.

The publication of supplementary sketches should remedy any errors of judgment and, at the same time, allow for continuous updating of DALB until such time as a second volume might be deemed necessary and feasible. Those supplementary sketches will be published in the *Journal of Library History*, the most appropriate vehicle for such an on-going venture, and they will be in essentially the same format as those in DALB itself. One of the early sketches to be published will be of John Phillip Immroth, whose premature loss to the profession is much to be regretted but for whom no adequate sketch was available. Others will follow as appropriate, with the selection of biographees and their biographers to be made by the Editorial Board.

In addition to the problem of whom to include, another editorial question involved the length of each biographical sketch. The original letters inviting contributors specified lengths of sketches (ranging from 1,000 to 6,000 words), but such assignments of space were necessarily estimates based on limited initial knowledge of the biographee. Upon receipt of all of the sketches in the Libraries Unlimited editorial office, each sketch was evaluated as to the length of its narrative and the relative importance of the biographee vis-à-vis the established giants in the profession (Dewey, Cutter, Poole, etc.). Since this task could be performed only after all the sketches had been assembled and read as a unit, some sketches were found to be too long, others too short, and allocations of space had to be revised. Occasionally, biographers overzealous for their subject presented manuscripts much too long, while, on the other hand, subjects for whom a limited amount of information was available have shorter sketches than we might have wished.

Part of the work of the Libraries Unlimited staff involved the verification of facts that were questioned by authors, referees, or the staff members themselves. Among the sources used to verify information were: *Dictionary of American Biography*, *Dictionary of National Biography*, *National Cyclopaedia of American Biography*, *Who Was Who in America*, *Who's Who in Library Service* (all editions), *Notable American Women 1607-1950*, *Current Biography*, *Contemporary Authors*, *New York Times Obituary Index*, *Pioneering Leaders in Librarianship*, *An American Library History Reader*, the *ALA Membership Directory*, the *ALA Yearbook* (1976, 1977), Cynthia Cummings's *Biographical-Bibliographical Directory of Women Librarians*, the *Encyclopedia of Library and Information Science*, and Elizabeth Stone's *American Library Development 1600-1899*, as well as numerous specialized studies (from article- to book-length) of both individuals and institutions (often noted in the text).

The division of responsibilities among the members of the Editorial Board should be explained here. Jesse Shera contributed his knowledge of American library history and his experience as an author and editor. He wrote a number of biographies and assisted in the stylistic revision of others. When invitations to biographers were originally sent out, his sketch of Ralph A. Beals exemplified the format to be followed.

George Bobinski had primary responsibility for this project during the period January 1973 through the summer of 1976. He identified and compiled lists of prospective biographees and made the early decisions on inclusion and the length of each biography. He assumed responsibility for inviting initial contributions, received the original sketches, did initial follow-up work when sketches had to be reassigned, and, by the summer of 1976, had assembled over 300 biographies.

The coordination of the work of over 200 contributors into a final product lay with Bohdan Wynar, who was responsible for the actual editorial work. These editorial responsibilities included reviewing all sketches submitted, locating referees, advising biographers on needed revisions of their sketches, supervising the rewriting of numerous biographies, and ultimately inviting some alternate biographers. He also developed a consistent format for the biographies, established bibliographic guidelines, and directed the Libraries Unlimited editorial staff toward the goal of producing a volume that we hope adheres to high standards of both literary clarity and factual accuracy.

Members of the Advisory Board assisted initially in selecting biographees and later voted on "borderline" cases. Acting as individuals, they contributed sketches, reviews, and performed other functions as well during the course of the project.

Though their association throughout was a happy one, the members of the Editorial and Advisory Boards were not always in agreement on the decisions that were made. If politics is "the art of compromise," surely the same can be said for the editing of a biographical dictionary, and, as the work progressed, our cumulative respect for the editors of the *Dictionary of National Biography* (DNB), that standard against which all subsequent undertakings of its kind have come to be measured, grew apace. None of us anticipated that we would achieve the level of excellence exhibited by the DNB, but the critics should be reminded that, in every sense, this undertaking was a truly pioneering work devoted to scholarly ideals, pursued as far as possible in emulation of the standards already set for us.

As this book lies before us, a thing of paper, print, and cloth, it engenders by its very physical existence a sense of finality. But the task should not be considered finished until appropriate recognition can be given to those devoted librarians whose names are not writ large in the annals of librarianship. Is remembrance to be conferred only upon those who held high professional office, or engaged in recondite research, or spawned numerous professional articles or books? Another biographical work, a "who was who" of librarianship, is needed to recognize properly those unspectacular but devoted spirits who by precept and example pushed librarianship forward and taught a rising generation what professional librarianship should be.

ACKNOWLEDGMENTS

As was pointed out earlier, DALB would not exist were it not for the collective efforts of the contributing authors. These people, scattered in locations from New England to Hawaii, worked in many cases under less than ideal conditions. In several instances, primary sources were lost and secondary material was difficult to locate or to trace. Often, the writing of sketches involved original research, sometimes of a very extensive nature, in order to achieve a fresh perspective on people and events. It should also be pointed out that the work of some people on DALB will not be readily apparent, as they have verified facts (without asking for credit), have corrected wrong information (again, with no thought of acknowledgment), and have written sketches that were not included in DALB once the final selection of biographees had been completed. To these people, whose names appear below, special thanks are due. Truly, then, the *Dictionary of American Library Biography* has resulted from the collective efforts of a large group of women and men, to whom the library profession is greatly indebted.

The extensive services rendered by a few of the contributors do stand out, though, as being of special importance to the final shape of the book. These people worked over a long period of time, contributing far more than might have been expected of even the most generous of scholars, reviewing sketches, suggesting revisions, verifying existing information, supplying additional information, checking bibliographic citations, and keeping us abreast of the most current research in library history. This involved a considerable investment of their energies and time (and occasionally, personal funds), and without them, DALB would be much the poorer. Therefore, we extend very special appreciation to Thomas S. Harding, Michael H. Harris, Edward G. Holley, Sarah K. Vann, and Wayne A. Wiegand.

Other contributors were able to take time from crowded schedules to help us at various stages of the project, or on specific problems of particular difficulty, and we thank here Russell E. Bidlack, John Y. Cole, Donald G. Davis, Jr., Budd L. Gambee, Laurel A. Grotzinger, Haynes McMullen, Claud Glenn Sparks, Norman D. Stevens, William L. Williamson, and Raymund F. Wood for their fine efforts on behalf of DALB.

Of course, numerous other people (many of whom were already biographers for DALB) made individual contributions to this pioneering effort. They drafted sketches of "borderline" cases so that the biographees' contributions could be determined; they also verified facts, served as referees for sketches, volunteered information, and, in general, assisted in countless ways in the completion of the volume before us. To these people, we are deeply grateful: William K. Beatty, Regina F. Berneis, Martha Boaz, John Boll, Robert E. Booth, Lewis C. Branscomb, Miriam R. Braverman, Patricia Senn Breivik, Maynard Brichford, John D. Bruckman, Charles E. Bunge, William H. Carlson, Edwin Castagna, Larry G. Chrisman, John Calvin Colson, John P. Comaromi, Katherine Cveljo, Mathew F. Dee, C. Edwin Dowlin, Robert B. Downs, Paul Z. DuBois, John Taylor Eastlick, Rolf Erickson, Charles W. Evans, Valmai R. Fenster, Fred Folmer, Donald D. Foos, Thomas J. Galvin, Rhoda Garoogian, Guy Garrison, Arrell M. Gibson, Marc Gittlesohn, Margaret Goggin, Herbert Goldhor, Harold Goldstein, M. Nabil Hamdy, Robert D. Harlan, Sister Deborah Harmeling, J. S. Hartin, John F. Harvey, Emily Waddell Havard, Virginia Haviland, Herman H. Henkle, Billie Grace Herring, Peter Hiatt, Doralyn J. Hickey, Millicent S. Huff, John Phillip Immroth, Eugene B. Jackson, Sidney L. Jackson, Ray C. Janeway, Virginia Lacy Jones, Casper LeRoy Jordan, Helen B. Josephine, E. J. Josey, Margaret B. Kaltenbach, Richard Edward Kelly, Trina E. King, Paul S. Koda, John C. Larsen, Irving Lieberman, Jean E. Lowrie, Morton J. Merowitz, Francis L. Miksa, Nancy E. Miller, Michael Ochs, Donald E. Oehlerts, Katherine Oller, Wyman W. Parker, Caswell Perry, Patricia B. Pond, Lawrence Clark Powell, Harry Ransom, Pat Rea, Sarah Rebecca Reed, Phyllis A. Richmond, William C. Robinson, Julia Sabine, Paul Saenger, Ted Samore, Mary Esther Saxon, Elizabeth Schumann, Nasser Sharify, Spencer Shaw, Stuart Sherman, Louis Shores, Bruce A. Shuman, Clara Sitter, William J. Sittig, Rolland E. Stevens, Lewis F. Stieg, Peggy A. Sullivan, Dennis Thomison, Lawrence S. Thompson, Ellis Tucker, Thomas L. Vince, Rose L. Vormelker, Michael Butler Wessells, Marilyn Domas White, Paul A. Winckler, Sheila Winship, Karen Wittenborg, Blanche E. Woolls, Lubomyr Wynar, Arthur P. Young, Betty Young, Willard O. Youngs.

We also wish to extend thanks to the countless librarians and others with whom we had correspondence on a limited scale. It is, of course, impossible to list them all, but they, too, have contributed in no small way to DALB.

The staff members of several libraries were helpful in verifying information: Penrose Library at the University of Denver; University Libraries at the University of Colorado; and, especially, the Denver Public Library.

Finally, special acknowledgment should be given to the editorial staff of Libraries Unlimited, some of whom devoted over a year to the preparation of DALB. The work of coordinating revisions, referee comments, and other corrections of sketches was ably handled by K. C. Loomis, Jr. He was also primarily responsible for initial copy editing, daily correspondence, record keeping, and assisting with mailings and newsletter preparation. Final copy editing, final proofreading, and coordination of proof checking by biographers was done by Ann J. Harwell. The book design and typesetting are the work of Judy Caraghar; because of her technical expertise, the final proofreading and the correcting of typeset copy were greatly simplified. The name index was prepared by Mary Mitchell. Christine Wynar read many biographical sketches and provided editorial advice. Roberta Depp assisted in verification of some bibliographical data, as did Pam Fisch. The cover and jacket designs are by David Miles.

George S. Bobinski   Jesse H. Shera   Bohdan S. Wynar

ABBOT, EZRA (1819-1884)

Ezra Abbot, son of Ezra and Phoebe Abbot, was born in Jackson, Maine, on April 28, 1819. He received both his baccalaureate (1840) and his master's degree (1843) from Bowdoin College, after which he taught high school for several years in Maine. Abbot married Emily Everett, but they had no children.

In 1848, Abbot moved to Cambridge, Massachusetts, where he taught at the city's high school. Although he remained in that position for only one year, the experience provided the foundation for his *A Classed Catalog of the Library of the Cambridge High School with an Alphabetical Index*, published in 1853, in which he developed the subject classification scheme that he was later to apply at the Harvard College Library. In the preface to this work, Abbot expressed the concern for organization and classification of materials that was to be a major focus of his professional career. "It is hoped," he remarked, "that the use of a classed catalog may promote the formation of those habits of investigation and research which are essential to success in the pursuit of truth ... that [the student] may thus be encouraged to examine and think for himself" (p. vi).

From 1849 to 1852, Abbot held his first library position at the Harvard College Library, and during this time he began the Library's alphabetico-classed catalog. He then moved to the Boston Athenaeum, assuming the post of assistant librarian from 1854 to 1856 and once again bringing his unique skills to bear by introducing an accession catalog to the Athenaeum. At the same time, Abbot began his long association with the American Oriental Society, for which he acted as secretary from 1853 until his death.

When the job of Harvard College librarian became vacant, Abbot submitted his name for consideration by the Harvard Corporation and provided letters of support from a number of esteemed librarians, including George Livermore, Charles Folsom, Charles C. Jewett (q.v.), and William F. Poole (q.v.)—all of whom indicated unqualified enthusiasm for Abbot's candidacy. Poole, who worked with Abbot at the Athenaeum, noted,

> My deliberate opinion ... is, that Mr. Abbot is the most complete and accomplished bibliographer of whom I have any personal knowledge, and I doubt whether a young man of superior or even equal attainments in the profession can be found in this country. His amiable manners, ripe scholarship and extensive knowledge of books emminently qualify him to be the librarian of a large college library.

The only other candidate seriously considered for the position was John L. Sibley (q.v.), who had been assistant librarian for 20 years. Shortly before the appointment was made in April 1856, a number of letters were submitted in Sibley's name. The tone of most of these was reflected in one missive that began "I am not insensible to some of Mr. Sibley's deficiencies...." The details of the academic politics surrounding the selection of the Harvard College librarian have, unfortunately, not been recorded. When the appointment was made, John Sibley received it. In a compromise (the exact nature of which is also unrecorded), Abbot was designated as "Assistant Librarian with Exclusive Authority in Classifying and Cataloging the Books" at a salary of $1200 per annum.

The next sixteen years, under Sibley, were Abbot's most productive as a librarian, bibliographer, editor of books on the New Testament, and author of articles in such journals as *Christian Examiner*, *Unitarian Review*, *Bibliotheca Sacra*, *North American Review*, *Journal of the Society of Biblical Exegesis*, and *Journal of the Oriental Society*. In keeping with his letter to the Corporation regarding his candidacy for librarian, Abbot concerned himself "with the books which the library has *not*" and with using "the best means in his power to secure a supply of the deficiency." In a letter to President Hill (June 29, 1867), he stated that the "great need of the Library is a permanent fund of $150,000 together with ample provision for making the books purchased as useful as possible by being promptly and thoroughly catalogued under both authors and subjects." To begin the fund, he offered $100 out of his pocket, pointing out that "a man does not grow rich in Cambridge on $1400 a year." In 1860, he hired a young assistant, Charles A. Cutter (q.v.), who was later to write Abbot's obituary in *Library Journal*.

Abbot's major bibliographic work, *Bibliography of Works Relating to the Nature, Origin, and Destiny of the Soul*, was published in 1863 as an appendix to Alger's *Critical History of the Doctrine of a Future Life*. The revolution in Scripture scholarship from text to form criticism has diminished the value of Abbot's work to contemporary scholars. The esteem with which he was held by his contemporaries, however, was reflected in the honors bestowed upon him during his life. In 1861, he was elected to membership in the American Academy of Arts and Sciences, and in 1871, to membership in the New Testament Revision Company. He received honorary degrees from Harvard (A.M., 1861, and S.T.D., 1872), Yale (LL.D., 1869) and Bowdoin (LL.D., 1878). The University of Edinburgh invited him to receive the D.D., but he died before it was conferred. In 1872, Abbot became Bussey Professor of New Testament Criticism and Interpretation at the Harvard Divinity School, a position he held until his death in Cambridge, Massachusetts, March 21, 1884.

An obituary in the April 5, 1885, *Literary World* stated,

There was a fine fitness in his name; he was the Ezra of his times. There was a fine fitness in his look, which was rabbinic—a tall, slender, stooping heavy-haired man, whose figure was an impersonation of severe thought, with keen eyes which looked out at you furtively for an instant before his face lit up at recognition with the radiance of the soul within.

Biographical listings and obituaries—Cutter, Charles A. [Obituary]. *Library Journal* 9, No. 4:59-60 (April 1884); *Dictionary of American Biography* 1 (Benjamin Wisner); *National Cyclopaedia of American Biography* 4; *Quinquennial File*, Harvard University archives; *Who Was Who in America*, Historical Volume (1607-1896). **Books and articles about the biographee**—*Ezra Abbot*. Cambridge: Harvard Divinity School, 1884. **Primary sources and archival materials**—Letters from and about Abbot, and his papers and lectures are contained in the Harvard University archives.

—LEIGH ESTABROOK

ADAMS, RANDOLPH GREENFIELD (1892-1951)

Randolph G. Adams was born in Philadelphia on November 7, 1892, the son of prominent attorney John Stokes and Heloise Zelina Root Adams. He once wrote of his family: "My father was the son of a Kentucky judge who married a Philadelphia Quaker; my mother was the daughter of a Connecticut Puritan who married a girl who was mostly French. (It would take a psychologist to make anything of that.)"

Adams attended the Episcopal Academy and the University of Pennsylvania, where he was graduated Phi Beta Kappa in 1914. He went to Europe that summer and was in Berlin when World War I began. Repatriated through Holland, he took an assistantship in history at his alma mater in 1915, became a fellow in history at the University of Chicago in 1916, and entered the United States Army as a private on June 7, 1917. Ten days later, he was married to Helen Newbold Spiller, also of Philadelphia. Discharged a second lieutenant on May 15, 1919, following service with the Quartermaster Corps in France, Adams returned to the University of Pennsylvania as a Carnegie Fellow in international law and was awarded the Ph.D. degree in 1920.

In the same year, Dr. Adams was appointed assistant professor of history at Trinity College (now Duke University) in North Carolina, where he remained for three years. During this period, he saw the publication of his doctoral dissertation, *Political Ideas of the American Revolution*, and he prepared a textbook, *A History of the Foreign Policy of the United States*, which was first issued in 1924. It was also during this time that he began to emerge as a scholar of unusual interest and promise in the area of rare books. It was allegedly Adams's boyhood acquaintance with the Philadelphia industrialist-collector A. Edward Newton that first stimulated his taste for books, a taste that the young professor

nourished by calling on dealers, librarians, and curators of special collections during his visits to other cities.

In June 1923, the William L. Clements Library, with its great holdings of rare and irreplaceable books and documents concerning American history, was opened at the University of Michigan in Ann Arbor. At the time of opening, however, its donor, a retired Bay City manufacturer who also served as a regent of the University, had not yet settled upon a satisfactory director. Upon the recommendation of George Parker Winship (q.v.), librarian of Harvard University, Clements interviewed Randolph Adams and, much impressed by Adams's knowledge of Americana, recommended to his fellow regents that he be appointed director of the Clements Library and professor of history. Adams accepted the appointment and held the post with distinction until his death in 1951. Under his leadership, the Clements Library flourished and was soon recognized as one of the greatest repositories of American history in the nation.

Adams was a controversial figure among both scholars and his fellow librarians. Supported always by the regent-donor of his library, Adams insisted upon interviewing everyone who sought access to the rarities in his custody to assure himself that they had both sufficient need and adequate appreciation of them. Many were turned away annoyed, and others who were ultimately allowed admittance were often miffed at his questioning of their right of access. But Adams staunchly adhered to the notion that a reader can have no rights; he can have only privileges. "A library," he wrote, "is a place where there may be a book, which, under certain circumstances, he may have earned the right to consult or read," and the curator is the sole arbiter of who does and who does not deserve the privilege. In a period of egalitarian ascendency, this concept of the role of the curator was understandably questioned, and Adams found himself called upon frequently to explain and defend it, both at home at the University of Michigan and abroad in the scholarly community.

"Our function," he explained, in speaking of the Clements Library, "is to collect the thing set down at the time the event took place, by a participant." Accordingly, the Library soon possessed such notable corpuses of manuscript material as the British Headquarters Papers of General Thomas Gage and of Sir Henry Clinton, the papers of Lord George Germaine and of Nathanael Green, and many similar closely related collections. Book holdings were enhanced through the acquisition of such treasures as the 1663 "Eliot Indian Bible," the *Dotrina Breve* printed by Juan Pablos in Mexico City in 1540, and Thomas's *The Valley of the Mississippi Illustrated*. He concentrated his efforts on bringing together fine collections and competent curatorial staff to match the graceful Renaissance structure which housed the William L. Clements Library rather than striving to increase the Library's use.

The library world especially took umbrage at Adams's restrictive attitudes and engaged him in frequent colloquies on the matter, debates in which Adams was ever an effective adversary. In 1937, in the *Library Quarterly*, the Clements director published an essay entitled "Librarians as Enemies of Books," a trenchant piece that served as the rallying point of the decade for all bookmen persuaded of the efficacy of Adams's position. In this essay, which has been six times reprinted, Adams animadverted upon a main orientation which he felt had then taken over the profession. He wrote:

> The librarian, we are told at each successive presidential address given before the American Library Association or its ganglia, is no longer a curator of books—he is an administrative official and a promoter of adult education. . . . It may even be said that the collector is picking up the mantle of scholarship dropped by the librarian as the latter ascends into the heaven of efficiency. This is entirely proper, as the book collector is often a man of feeling and sentiment, characteristics which are in danger of being trained out of the modern librarian.

Such statements, however, although they aroused ire among librarians, were probably salutary and did much to remind them that a stewardship of books was, if not the only, at least one of the essential elements of their responsibility to society. Adams's remarks were also understandably welcome to the rare book and bibliophilic community, which was coming to feel increasingly beleaguered by these new administrator-librarians. That community recognized him immediately as an effective spokesman for its creed of the supremacy of books.

Although Professor Adams remained a prolific author throughout his life, he was not a highly productive scholar in the usual sense. In addition to the two books mentioned earlier, he published two books for young people—*Gateway to American History* (1927) and *Pilgrims, Indians and Patriots* (1928)—both of which originated as essays prepared for the education and entertainment of his two sons, Richard Newbold and Thomas Randolph (who subsequently became librarian of the John Carter Brown Library). His A. S. W. Rosenbach Lectures in Bibliography at the University of Pennsylvania in 1938 were published the following year under the title *Three Americanists: Henry Harrisse, Bibliographer; George Brinley, Book Collector; Thomas Jefferson, Librarian.* In addition, he wrote many essays for the library, history, and bibliographic press—including substantial contributions to the *Dictionary of American Biography* and the *Dictionary of American History*—and he prepared many scholarly bulletins for the William L. Clements Library. A complete listing of his published works extends to 147 items.

Honors of many kinds came to Professor Adams. In 1929, he was appointed visiting professor of international relations at St. Andrews University in Scotland. In 1938, Albion College conferred upon him an honorary Doctor of Laws degree, and in the same year, as has been indicated, he was the Rosenbach Fellow. In 1940 and 1941, he was called to the presidency of the Bibliographical Society of America. He was also elected to membership in the American Library Institute, the American Antiquarian Society, the Grolier Club, and the exclusive Katholepistemiad Club at the University of Michigan. He was an adviser to Princeton University's project for publishing the papers of Thomas Jefferson (q.v.) and served also as a director and trustee of the Franklin D. Roosevelt Library, Inc., in Hyde Park, New York.

Tall, dark, and slim, Professor Adams pursued gardening as his favorite non-literary activity, although he disdained most sports and amusements. "He utilized his free time chiefly in informational reading or informational conversation," reports his sometime colleague, Howard H. Peckham. "His only digression was detective novels late at night. This kind of devotion to his work led to one of his famous observations, 'Contract bridge is the idiot's substitute for research.'" It may also have contributed to his untimely death in Ann Arbor on January 4, 1951, of heart disease, from which he had suffered for some time.

Biographical listings and obituaries—*Current Biography* (1943); *National Cyclopaedia of American Biography* 42; Paltsits, Victor Hugo. "Randolph Greenfield Adams." *Bibliographical Society of America News Sheet* 71:3-4 (May 15, 1951); Storm, Colton. "Randolph Greenfield Adams." *Antiquarian Bookman* 7:1097-98 (March 24, 1951); *Who Was Who in America* III (1951-1960). **Books and articles about the biographee**—Haugh, Georgia C., comp. *A Bibliography of Randolph G. Adams with an Introductory Memoir.* Ann Arbor: William L. Clements Library, 1962; [Peckham, Howard H.] "Randolph G. Adams, by a Former Colleague." *Michigan Alumnus* 57:310-17 (August 11, 1951).

—DAVID KASER

ADLER, CYRUS (1863-1940)

Cyrus Adler was born in Van Buren, Arkansas, in 1863, to Samuel and Sarah Sulzberger Adler. An A.B. degree earned from the University of Pennsylvania (1883) was followed by an A.M. (1887), and by a Ph.D. in Oriental studies (1887) from Johns Hopkins University, where he then became an instructor in Semitic languages.

On a recreational trip to Washington, Adler met several Smithsonian Institution officials and became honorary assistant curator of Oriental antiquities in the United States National Museum, as well as fulfilling several international exposition commissions for the Smithsonian. G. Brown Goode, assistant secretary of the Smithsonian, was so impressed by Adler's learning, efficiency, and personality, that in 1893 he offered Adler the position of Smithsonian Librarian, although Adler's only library experience consisted of having cataloged a few private libraries during his student days. Two of these catalogs were published and exemplify the bibliographical art of the period.

The Smithsonian Library that Adler undertook to administer was divided between the Smithsonian Deposit at the Library of Congress and working libraries in various Smithsonian buildings. Staff was short, backlogs were enormous, and space allocated was inadequate both at the Library of Congress (then in the Capitol Building) and in the Smithsonian buildings on the Mall. Adler soon obtained more space and more staff at the Institution, although overcrowding at the Library of Congress was not relieved until the move into its new building in 1897. Despite his lack of training and experience in librarianship, however, Adler demonstrated a remarkable grasp of the principles and practices of library work. Under Adler, library procedures, particularly in serials recording, were modernized and much backlog was eliminated. Bound serial sets were transferred and consolidated as necessary to insure completeness either at the Smithsonian itself or in the Smithsonian Deposit at LC.

Adler initiated an employees' lending library at the Smithsonian which operated successfully for many years until the District of Columbia Public Library was opened. Also an active member of the American Library Association, he presented papers at its annual meetings of 1896 and 1897.

Adler's greatest contribution to librarianship during his Smithsonian years was helping to create, and then vigorously fostering, the *International Catalogue of Scientific Literature.* Indeed, the *Catalogue* might never have come into being without the efforts of Adler and John Shaw Billings (q.v.). At the Smithsonian, Adler established and directed the *Catalogue*'s U.S. office, fought for appropriations and, in years when no government money was appropriated, carried on the work using Smithsonian private funds.

In 1895, Adler was appointed assistant secretary of the Smithsonian while continuing to act as librarian, a promotion that formalized the close working, as well as personal, relationship that had grown up between Adler and Samuel P. Langley, secretary of the Smithsonian.

Throughout Adler's adult life, he pursued several careers at the same time. During his Smithsonian years, he commuted weekly to New York in connection with the Jewish Publication Society, as editor of

the *American Jewish Year Book* and as president of the Board of Trustees of the Jewish Theological Seminary. As a member of the Board of Trustees of Gratz College, he traveled regularly to Philadelphia, where he met and married Racie Friedenwald in 1905. They were to have a daughter, Sarah.

In 1908, Adler resigned from the Smithsonian to become first president of Dropsie College for Hebrew and Cognate Learning in Philadelphia, where he organized the library along the same lines as the Smithsonian Library—a central collection with separate sectional libraries relating to special subjects. After donating much of his personal library to the new institution, he actively solicited books and money for it from his many friends and succeeded also in obtaining the Lesser Collection and the Joshua I. Cohen Library, both of which he had cataloged as a student at Johns Hopkins.

With his usual ability to fill several positions at once, Adler became, albeit reluctantly, acting president of the Jewish Theological Seminary in New York (1916) while continuing as president of Dropsie, and in 1924, he became permanent head of both institutions until his death. Adler had begun collecting books and manuscripts for the Seminary as early as 1902, so with him as Seminary president and Professor Alexander Marx as director of libraries, the Seminary rapidly acquired one of the foremost Jewish libraries in the world. Adler summarized his library philosophy in an address at the dedication of the new library building in 1930:

We shall ask you to look upon this Library not as a perfect thing or a finished thing, but as a beginning. To paraphrase the statement of one of the great museum directors, a perfect library is a finished library and a finished library is a dead library. I hope that we shall always be growing.

Adler was appointed to the Board of Trustees of the Free Library of Philadelphia in 1908 and was president of the Board from 1925 to 1939. He was presented the key to the Library's new building in dedicatory ceremonies in 1927, although with customary modesty Adler credited the new building to John Ashurst, Free Library librarian. Adler had been the quietly effective mover in securing the necessary funding, however, and was later to express great pride in the unusual experience of having a goodly sum left over from the building fund.

In addition to his formal positions, Adler was a prolific writer, editor, and lecturer, was the founder of the American Jewish Historical Society, and was an advisor to all Presidents of the United States from William McKinley to Franklin D. Roosevelt. His autobiography, *I Have Considered the Days* (1941), is as witty, charming, interesting, and modest as Adler himself must have been. Previously, his friends had had Adler's *Lectures, Selected Papers, Addresses* privately printed (1933) in honor of his seventieth birthday, and this included a bibliography of his writings. His other publications included pieces on John Ashurst of the Free Library of Philadelphia (eulogy, 1932), the relation of Richard Rush to the Smithsonian (in *Smithsonian Miscellaneous Collections*, 1909), and Samuel P. Langley (Smithsonian *Annual Report* for 1906). He also contributed bibliographic pieces to the field of Oriental studies.

Adler died in Philadelphia on April 7, 1940. He was a devout Jew, and Jewish interests were of great importance to him, but he was never parochial. His friendships were wide, international, and never limited by racial or religious considerations. In the closing page of his autobiography, Adler stated his "philosophy of life and action: To go on doing the best I can in any and every circumstance that arises, to be loyal to the traditions of my people and my family, to keep, in fact, so busy doing that I have no time to be a philosopher." How well he succeeded is perhaps best summed up in Franklin Roosevelt's tribute to Adler on his seventieth birthday, "Yours has been a rich and full career of varied activity and great usefulness ... you have touched life at many angles and whether in spiritual, civic, or cultural activities your labors have ever been directed to the happiness of others and the well-being of the community." To which I would add only that Adler's community was the community of all mankind.

Biographical listings and obituaries—*National Cyclopaedia of American Biography* 41; [Obituary]. *New York Times*, April 8, 1940, p. 1; *Who Was Who in America* I (1897-1942). **Books and articles about the biographee**—Neuman, Abraham A. *Cyrus Adler, a Biographical Sketch*. Philadelphia: Jewish Publication Society of America, 1943/5703; Temkin, Sefton D. "Adler, Cyrus." *Encyclopaedia Judaica*. New York: Macmillan, 1971. Vol. 2. **Primary sources and archival materials**—Adler, Cyrus. *I Have Considered the Days*. Philadelphia: Jewish Publication Society, 1941; Smithsonian Institution. *Annual Reports*, 1893-1909. Adler's papers are divided between the American Jewish Historical Society, Waltham, Massachusetts (6 cartons, 1887-1934), and the Smithsonian (Libraries—2 cartons, 1896-1908; Archives—International Catalogue of Scientific Literature *Records*, 3 cubic feet, 1893-1933).

—JACK GOODWIN

AHERN, MARY EILEEN (1860-1938)

Mary Eileen Ahern, the one and only editor of *Public Libraries*, was born on a farm in Marion County near Indianapolis, Indiana, on October 1, 1860. She was the second of three children of William and Mary O'Neil Ahern, both natives of Ireland. After being graduated from Spencer, Indiana, High School in 1878 and Central Normal College, Danville, Indiana, in 1881, she then taught in the public schools of Bloomfield, Spencer, and Peru, Indiana.

Her library career began April 1, 1889, when she became assistant state librarian of Indiana, a position she held until 1893. The report of the librarian, Jacob P. Dunn, for 1891-1892 comments on the valuable cataloging work that Ahern did during this period. In 1893, she became state librarian, having been elected by the State Legislature for a two-year term, and she served in that position until 1895, when her party was defeated at the polls.

In 1889, she called a meeting of librarians to establish the Indiana Library Association, and she served as its secretary and guided its activities for seven years, from 1889 to 1896; she was president in 1895. During her two years as state librarian, knowing she would not be re-elected, Ahern campaigned to have the State Library transferred to the State Board of Education so that it would be less "used as a shuttle-cock in the political game of battledore." In July 1895, finding herself out of a job, she decided to go to library school.

In 1895-1896 she attended the Library School of the Armour Institute of Technology in Chicago. While a student at the Armour Institute, she was offered the editorship of a new journal (to be called *Public Libraries*). The offer was made by a committee of two librarians and two officials of the Library Bureau, who had reached the consensus that a new periodical designed to serve small public libraries was necessary. Herbert Davidson of the Library Bureau agreed to finance the magazine, and Mary Eileen Ahern accepted the mantle of editor. It was the beginning of a long and fruitful career.

The first issue of *Public Libraries* appeared in May 1896. Because of failing eyesight, Ahern relinquished her editorial work in 1931 at the age of 71. So closely had the periodical been associated with her that, by general consent, it came to an end with her retirement. Melvil Dewey (q.v.) said in his final tribute to her:

Libraries under another editor cd never be just the same. From the 1st number her personaliti has been stampt on her magazine & ther is a fitting digniti in marking her retirement by clozing her 36 volumes as a stori completed. The editor has laid down her fasil, efisient & sumtyms militant pen but we all hope that her voice for meni mor years will be heard in librari consel in which she has so long playd so prominent a part.

Stricken with arteriosclerotic heart disease, she died at the age of 77 on Sunday, May 22, 1938, on a train near Atlanta, Georgia, while on her way back to Chicago from Orlando, Florida.

The 36 volumes of *Public Libraries* (changed to *Libraries* in 1926) serve as a permanent memorial to Ahern. Besides editing it for all those years, she contributed many articles to it, several of which were published accounts of speeches she had given. She spoke on the responsibilities of being a trustee before the Indiana Trustees Association (*Public Libraries*,

April 1924), on the opportunities of the school librarian before the library section of the State High-School Conference at the University of Illinois in Urbana (*Libraries*, April 1928), and on goals and ideals for a state library before the National Association of State Libraries in New Haven (*Libraries*, November 1931). Even when on vacation, she visited libraries, and after a winter trip to Florida in 1930, she wrote about the libraries of Florida (*Libraries*, May 1930).

In its second year of publication, *Public Libraries* was made the official organ of the Illinois Library Association and remained so until the periodical ceased publication in 1931. Mary Ahern was thrice president (1908, 1909, and 1915) of the Illinois Library Association, and served as chairman of numerous committees as well. Her presidential address in 1915 dealt with the debits and credits of twenty years of library work in Illinois. At the 1922 meeting of the Illinois Library Association, she delivered a paper on library progress in Illinois, and at the 1925 meeting she talked about the relationship of the library trustee to the public.

She spoke at library conferences all over the country. At the 1925 meeting of the California Library Association, she lectured on the law of balance in relation to librarianship. At the 1926 meeting of the Wisconsin Library Association, she talked about library developments in Wisconsin. Not only did she attend and speak at conferences on librarianship, but in 1924, she addressed the twentieth annual conference on children's reading in Grand Rapids, Michigan, discussing what the library can do for the foreign-born child.

Mary Ahern joined the American Library Association in 1897. She served on the ALA Council for almost twenty years and was chairman or a member of many important committees. She attended over forty ALA conferences and had a perfect record of attendance from 1893 to 1931.

In 1928, she welcomed members and friends of ALA to the fiftieth annual conference in West Baden, Indiana, with an opening address on the developments of librarianship in the Midwest. She talked about the many new opportunities for women in librarianship: "The swing toward the choice of women for positions of full power and emolument has not swept around a large arc of the library circle, but the segment included is growing larger and the sense of power and responsibility is growing steadily, growing stronger, for men and women too." Although she was a militant advocate of the role that women could play in librarianship and encouraged many women to enter the field, for some unknown reason, she did not support suffrage for women.

In 1896, the Board of Directors of the National Education Association granted permission for the formation of a Library Department within the Association, and Ahern served as secretary for the years 1897 and 1900-1905. At the 1903 meeting in Boston, she delivered a paper entitled "Library Instruction in the Normal School: What May Be Accomplished by Definite Instruction in the Normal Schools." This was a topic in which she was deeply interested, and in 1905, she joined with Melvil Dewey and others in a five-member committee to supervise the writing of a report by Elizabeth G. Baldwin to a joint committee representing ALA and NEA on "Instruction in Library Administration in Normal Schools."

Ahern believed very strongly in the library as an educational factor and wrote two major articles on the subject, one in *The Chautauquan* (August 1903) and one in *The Elementary School Teacher* (January 1905). Of the six articles dealing with libraries that appeared in the annual reports of the U.S. Commissioner of Education from 1911 to 1916, Ahern wrote the one for the 1913 report entitled "Library Activities During 1912-13."

She was, as well, one of the 44 charter fellows of the American Library Institute, held the position of secretary from 1912 to 1916, and served on its Board until 1927. At the Institute's 1911 meeting in New York, she presented a paper on working conditions in libraries, and at the 1917 meeting, she delivered an historical résumé of the Institute's first years. Then in 1920, she presented a memoir of Charles Henry Gould (q.v.) at the meeting in Atlantic City. Finally, she wrote a review of the Institute's first 25 years, which was published in *Libraries* (July 1931).

In addition to her membership in these professional groups, she was a member of the Illinois Women's Press Association, the Chicago Library Club, the Chicago Women's Club, the Women's City Club of Chicago, and the Fortnightly Club of Indianapolis.

In 1897, she went to England for the Second International Library Conference and for the celebration of the twentieth anniversary of the Library Association. As R. R. Bowker (q.v.) reported it, she "astonished our English brethren by showing them how large and how able a proportion of librarianship across the sea consisted of American sisters."

During 1917-1918, she was a member of the Illinois Advisory Committee of the Women's Council of National Defense and had charge of the ALA's campaign to secure funds in Illinois, Michigan, and Wisconsin. Having been in charge of publicity for the Library War Service of ALA in France during the first six months of 1919, she wrote of her wartime experiences from Paris in an article in *Library Occurrent* and delivered a brief paper on her experiences in France at the 1919 meeting of the Library Department of NEA. She went abroad again in 1927 to study the organization and administration of French and British libraries.

The last issue of *Libraries*, December 1931, contained "A Parting Word," in which she discussed her years as editor, saying: "I have laid my stone in the building of library service in the first third of the twentieth century, and where and when others have found it a helpful stepping-stone, I shall still abide in the work they are able to accomplish because of that stone, and so, as editor of PUBLIC LIBRARIES and LIBRARIES, 'Ave! Salve!'" This same issue carried many tributes to her from her Chicago colleagues and from librarians in many parts of the country. The tributes speak of her as an incorruptible woman of strong convictions with a large gift of sympathy and human understanding. She was witty, exhilarating, clever, and keen on storytelling. The 36 volumes of *Public Libraries* earned for Mary Eileen Ahern the gratitude of the entire library world.

Biographical listings and obituaries—*National Cyclopaedia of American Biography* A; *Notable American Women* 1 (Harriet D. MacPherson); [Obituary]. *ALA Bulletin* 32:380 (June 1938); [Obituary]. *Library Journal* 63:455 (June 1, 1938); [Obituary]. *Chicago Daily Tribune*, May 24, 1938, p. 12; [Obituary]. *New York Times*, May 25, 1938, p. 23; *Who Was Who in America* I (1897-1942). **Books and articles about the biographee**—Bowker, R. R. "Women in the Library Profession." *Library Journal* 45:635-40 (August 1920); Dale, Doris Cruger. "Covering the Library Beat from West Baden to Great Britain: The One and Only Editor of *Public Libraries* Magazine." *American Libraries* 7:124 (March 1976); Dewey, Melvil. "A Notable Record." *Libraries* 36:438 (1931); Faxon, Frederick W. "Our Frontispiece." *Bulletin of Bibliography* 12:125 (May-August 1925); "A Library Hall of Fame for the 75th Anniversary." *Library Journal* 76:466-72 (March 15, 1951); Wright, Ida Faye. "Illinois Librarians in 'A Library Hall of Fame.'" *Illinois Libraries* 34:3-6 (January 1952). **Primary Sources and archival materials**—Ahern, Mary Eileen. "A Letter of Historical Interest." *Library Occurrent* 11:79-81 (July-September 1933).

—DORIS CRUGER DALE

ANDERSON, EDWIN HATFIELD (1861-1947)

Through quiet but forceful leadership of several of the foremost library institutions of his day, Edwin Hatfield Anderson exerted a powerful if indirect influence over librarianship. As the first librarian of the Carnegie Library of Pittsburgh, he shaped it into a many-faceted agency embodying the latest ideas and ideals of community service; as New York state librarian and director of the New York State Library School, he revitalized the State Library and stabilized the school; as director of the New York Public Library, he guided one of the great libraries of the world through a time of prodigious growth. He was an able administrator with the gift of finding and training promising men and women who shared his high standards of service and could put them into practice. Anderson was born on September 27, 1861,

in Zionsville, Indiana, seventh of ten children of Philander (a physician) and Emma A. Duzan Anderson and spent his early years on the Kansas-Oklahoma border. He graduated with an A.B. from Wabash College in Indiana (1883) and, after reading law, writing for newspapers, and teaching school, he entered the only library school in the United States, Melvil Dewey's (q.v.) New York State Library School at Albany. He attended from October 1890 to May 1891, when lack of money forced him to cut short his studies; from January to May 1891, he also worked as librarian of the Young Men's Christian Association in Albany. As of June 1891, he started work as a cataloger at the new Newberry Library in Chicago; the following December 22, he married Frances R. Plummer of Chicago, daughter of Jonathan Wright Plummer and Hannah Ann Ballard Plummer and sister of Mary Wright Plummer (q.v.), who became a distinguished library educator and writer. Edwin and Frances Anderson had two adopted daughters, Charlotte W. and Cecile W.

The 1890s were a propitious time for a young man of vigor and ability to make his way as a librarian, especially a young man as attractive, genial, and intelligent—and as fond of a good joke—as Edwin Anderson. There was soon to be enormous expansion of library services, particularly in urban centers, a trend accelerated by the philanthropy of Andrew Carnegie (q.v.), with whom Anderson's career was to be associated. In May 1892, he left Chicago to become librarian of one of Carnegie's first library benefactions, the Carnegie Free Library, opened in 1889 in Braddock, Pennsylvania, site of a Carnegie steel works near Pittsburgh. Three years later, Anderson was called to an important new post that gave him a chance to develop his ideas on a large scale, the librarianship of the Carnegie Library of Pittsburgh, soon to open as the central part of a cultural center in Schenley Park that encompassed an art museum and music and lecture halls as well.

When Anderson arrived in Pittsburgh in April 1895, there was an edifice but no library. He had to create the library. He quickly recruited staff members from all over the United States, and by November, when the library opened, 16,000 volumes stood ready for public use, together with a complete dictionary card catalog and a catalog in pamphlet form listing some 9,000 titles. This accomplishment heralded several of the many outstanding features of the Carnegie Library of Pittsburgh: an excellent staff, a comprehensive, well-selected collection, and a distinguished cataloging department that produced, besides dictionary catalogs in both card and book form, a complete printed classed catalog in book form (originated by Anderson but published in 1907 after his departure). Also issued were annotated book lists that were sold widely and, in 1903, in cooperation with the Cleveland Public Library, a printed catalog card service for children's books.

These and other services exemplified Anderson's belief in the public library's duty to offer convenient access to good books (the means, in his view, of popular enlightenment), and to provide scholarly publications and specialized information for those who needed them. He built an excellent, varied collection of reference works, with reference service by trained librarians, and was quick to see the value of having strong holdings in science and technology in an industrial center like Pittsburgh. As a result of Anderson's urging, Andrew Carnegie donated funds to buy such materials, which in 1902 formed the basis for a Department of Technology, the first such public library division in the country. Under Anderson's vigorous direction, the central building proved almost at once inadequate; in 1899, his arguments for expansion convinced Carnegie to supply the money for a new wing. Anderson also devoted a good deal of time to designing and then developing the six branches that were constructed under his supervision, and to planning a seventh.

Children's services, not envisioned by the library's founders, were another of Anderson's innovations in Pittsburgh. Convinced that the best hope for society lay with its children, who could be made into citizens "capable of governing and being governed" and whose lives could be ennobled through reading "good books" (as he said in the Carnegie Library of Pittsburgh's *6th Annual Report*, for the Year Ending Jan. 31, 1902, p. 25), he established children's departments in the central building, in the branches, and out in the neighborhoods. Home libraries, deposit stations, reading clubs, storytelling sessions, summer playground activities, work with schools, and mothers' groups were organized. In order to have properly trained personnel for this work, Anderson started in 1900 a training class which, the next year, became the Training School for Children's Librarians, predecessor of the Carnegie Library School (supported by Carnegie from 1903 to 1916).

Under Anderson's leadership, the Carnegie Library of Pittsburgh grew into a model institution of its kind. He worked quietly, with reserve, but forthrightly; he knew how to get on with the trustees and to earn the confidence of a man like Carnegie. Thus, he managed to become part of the intellectual community of Pittsburgh, which was useful in gaining support for library programs and keeping abreast of the interests of scholars and scientists. Active also in professional organizations, he served as president for 1901-1902 of the Keystone State Library Association and as a member for 1903-1904 of the Pennsylvania Public Records Commission and Historical Archives Commission.

After nearly ten years, having had enough of Pittsburgh and of library work and being in ill health, Anderson resigned as of December 1, 1904, to try zinc and lead mining in Missouri. A year superintending his mining properties restored his health and his interest in librarianship, and he returned east to take up, in January 1906, Melvil Dewey's former positions as director of the New York State Library and of the New York State Library School. Besides reorganizing the State Library, strengthening its collections, putting its catalogs in better order, and improving public services, Anderson began planning a new building (soon to be desperately needed as a result of the Capitol fire of 1911). Library extension work was strengthened, and the quarterly journal *New York Libraries* was started in October 1907. At the Library School, which had suffered a crisis with the departure of Dewey and his two strongest faculty members, Anderson was a steadying force. Though not there long enough to leave a great impress, he did introduce more flexibility and variety into the curriculum and employed as instructors more practicing librarians (including himself) than Dewey had. His concept of librarianship was expressed in a short essay on "Men in Library Work" (which he wanted to encourage) in his 1907 *Report* of the Library School: "They [young men] have known nothing of [librarianship's] opportunities for executive and administrative ability, for real scholarship, for high social service, of its educational relations and significance" (p. 217).

The following year Anderson opened the annual meeting of the New York Library Association, of which he was then president, with a characteristically realistic view of public libraries:

The library's position will be determined by what we do, not by what we say, its value is in direct proportion to the efficiency of those who manage and serve it. . . .

"Reading maketh a full man." It is upon the recognition of this fact that the library idea is founded. It is of the profoundest interest to all that the human product should be as perfect as possible. Literature is the record of human experience and we can scarcely conceive of the development of the finished human product without discriminating and continuous reading of that record. It is this discriminating reading that our public libraries are designed to promote. If they succeed only in part we need not speculate about their place in the educational scheme. Of their usefulness we are sure, and in America there will always be a place for the useful. [Quoted in *New York Libraries* 1:178-79 (Jan. 1909).]

On June 1, 1908, Anderson had moved to such an institution, one upon which he could bring to bear all his experience and which would provide a congenial environment for his talents and interests. He would be assistant director of the nation's leading public library in its leading city, the New York Public Library, which combined under one management two library systems, a research library (then called the Reference Department) and a circulating library network (then called the Circulation Department). With a grand new central building under construction (mainly for the Reference Department), with 25 branches recently opened, and with 15 more in the works (all but one built with Andrew Carnegie's money), and with the population, wealth, and cultural and intellectual life of New York City burgeoning, the Library stood on the verge of a great era.

The director, the brilliant and strong-minded, but by then old and ill, John Shaw Billings (q.v.), needed help in managing what had become a very large, complex institution. Billings especially needed aid in overseeing all of the new construction and in dealing with the municipal government (which supplied the sites, books, and operating expenses for the Carnegie branches and the funds for building, equipping, and maintaining the central building). Though apparently nothing was said, it was clear that the assistant director had to be capable of eventually succeeding Billings as director, and it is not likely that at the age of 47 Anderson would have come to New York without such a prospect. With his flair for administration, his strong personality, executive ability, genial manner, and commitment to library service of high quality and grand scope, Anderson proved himself a fitting candidate for the directorship, to which he was appointed by the trustees as of May 14, 1913, after Billings's unexpected death the previous March.

Anderson remained director for 21 years, presiding over the largest and most used public library in the world during a time of growth and change, and through the shortages of the First World War, the inflation of the post-war years, and the rigors of the Great Depression, as well as the vicissitudes of New York City government and politics. From 1913 to 1934, when Anderson retired, the Reference Department's holdings grew from over a million to more than two million volumes, and the Circulation Department's holdings grew by nearly 75 percent, to well over a million. In 1934, over four million people (double the number from 1913) came into the central building, where four and a half million publications were consulted; eleven and a half million books went through the Circulation Department (as compared with eight million in 1913); the staff increased by a third (from 1,046 in 1913 to 1,556). The divisions in the Reference Department expanded, and the number of branches grew to 46; there were also 11 sub-branches and the Library for the Blind. Early in Anderson's directorship, the Municipal

Reference Library and the Manuscript Division were established; later came the Picture and Theater Collections. Children's work under Anne Carroll Moore (q.v.) became renowned, and young adult work as a special service was begun, as was the pioneering readers' advisory service under Jennie M. Flexner (q.v.). Arthur Schomburg's (q.v.) collection of Negro history and literature was acquired and deposited in the 135th Street Branch, which was being developed as a cultural community center for Harlem; the Bronx Reference Center was opened; the 58th Street Branch was built into the famous Music Library; extension work, including the use of book wagons in outlying districts, was expanded; the research collections were inventoried and shelflisted for the first time; information services in the main building were developed; innovative research in preservation of library materials was carried on. Soon after Anderson became director, space problems in the central building became apparent and then acute, to be relieved somewhat by the purchase of an annex in 1933 but nevertheless leading to the imposition, reluctantly, of restrictions on student use of the research collections.

Anderson was proud of all this activity and growth, especially as it took place in an institution that served the public without question. He was fond of comparing the New York Public Library with the Library of Congress and the British Museum: it had fewer resources but far greater and more varied use and relatively little public subsidy. For Anderson, as for his staff, the New York Public Library was the popular university that he had envisioned a public library to be back in his Braddock days, and they all shared the satisfaction of participating in a great democratic enterprise and felt for it extraordinary loyalty.

It was for nurturing this spirit that Anderson is best remembered. Though he was responsible for and knowledgeable about all of the Library's complex operations and devoted much time to finances, relations with city authorities, policymaking, and general administration, his unique strength, by all accounts, was in developing a staff that some librarians thought was the finest in any public library in the United States. A corps of well-qualified librarians, both men and women, was to him crucial to achieving his aim of offering the best and most efficient library service in the world. This principle, much in evidence throughout Anderson's previous library career, was brought to full fruition at the New York Public Library. Though an advocate of library school training (see his "Training for Library Service," *Library Journal*, May 15, 1924, pp. 462-66), he had a flexible approach, so that the staff there included many persons with library experience or library education, or both, and some with only subject or language proficiency. However, all had the potential for excellence and all balanced each other to produce a blend of special competencies and knowledge and efficient administration. Anderson could perceive the capacity for growth and leadership in people, give them scope to develop, and allow them to move as far, as fast, and in as many directions as they could. As one retired librarian put it, there was the chance to do things. It was to this environment as much as anything else that the New York Public Library owed its pre-eminence, both in Anderson's time and beyond. Anderson's own high standards served as model and impetus (see his *Conditions, Plans, and Ideals*, The New York Public Library, 1914, for an idea of his approach to library service).

He also saw a need at the Library for a professional library school and convinced Andrew Carnegie to underwrite the New York Public Library Library School, which opened in 1911 with Mary Wright Plummer as principal, and soon rose to front rank in professional library education. By the mid-twenties, the influential Carnegie Corporation report on library education, written by Charles C. Williamson (q.v., an early Anderson recruit at the New York Public Library), recommended university affiliation for library schools. Anderson, skeptical as he was of this principle, was instrumental in the 1926 transfer of the New York Public Library Library School to Columbia University and its merger with the New York State Library School to form Columbia's School of Library Service.

Through the Library School and through the staff development program, Anderson was responsible for training not only numerous fine librarians in the New York Public Library system but also many others who went on elsewhere to become leaders in the profession. Those who stayed constituted a virtual learned society and faculty of public education, working under Anderson's two highly respected chiefs, Harry M. Lydenberg (q.v.), the great collection builder and head of the Reference Department, and Franklin F. Hopper (q.v.), the genial head of the Circulation Department, each of whom succeeded him, in turn, as director.

With close associates, Anderson was loquacious, charming, and full of humor, and he could be friendly and helpful to young recruits. (At the Century Association in New York, the well-known literary club, he was considered a charming conversationalist.) Otherwise, he was somewhat aloof and reserved. Always exacting and impatient of slowness or insincerity, he became more so as he grew older. A perfectionist, he held himself to the same standards of hard work and excellence as he did others. He was straight-backed in both physique and character, which showed in the strong jaw of his handsome face. The carefully written letters that he sent from the Library often show a tendency to plain speaking and sometimes a touch of snobbery: he was conscious of his own worth and of the worth of his institution.

In his prime, Anderson was a superb administrator. By the late 1920s, when he was past 65 and ailing, he was no longer so effective. There being no retirement system yet at the Library, the trustees dealt with the situation in the same way their predecessors had done with Billings: they appointed an assistant director, Harry Lydenberg, in 1928. Six years later Anderson resigned, effective November 1, 1934. He was named director emeritus and retired on a pension awarded on an ad hoc basis. The Board's regard for him was high enough that Lewis Cass Ledyard, Board president during much of Anderson's tenure as director, bequeathed to him $40,000 (along with an equal sum to Lydenberg and two million dollars for the Library) in "grateful appreciation" for "devoted and efficient service" and "loyal and faithful co-operation" in the Library's interest (see Ledyard's letter to Lydenberg dated Aug. 2, 1932 in the Lydenberg Papers at NYPL). Anderson lived in retirement with his wife in Dorset, Vermont, and at the end of his life, in Williamsburg, Virginia; he died peacefully in his eighty-sixth year at the home of one of his daughters in Evanston, Illinois, on April 29, 1947.

Anderson had been active in the American Library Association, of which he was president in 1913-1914 (his inaugural address was published in the July 1914 *Library Journal*), and he was friendly with many librarians of his day. He had also served as president of the New York Library Association (1907-1908; see "Library Week at Lake George," *New York Libraries*, Jan. 1909), the New York Library Club (1910), and the New York State Library School Association (1896-1897 and 1912-1913). He was awarded several honorary doctorates, and, in recognition of the New York Public Library's services to the ethnic communities of New York, he was decorated by the governments of Rumania and Czechoslovakia.

Apart from official reports and letters, Anderson did not write very much. He appreciated scholarship and encouraged it in his staff, but he was not a scholar himself; he kept up with and readily put to use new ideas, but he was not an originator of them. His great strength was as an executive, in putting concepts to work and in inspiring young librarians to fulfill their potentials for creative leadership and service.

Biographical listings and obituaries—*Dictionary of American Biography* Supp. 4 (Edward G. Freehafer); *National Cyclopaedia of American Biography* D [contributor notes that this contains errors]; [Obituary]. *New York Times*, May 1, 1947; *Who Was Who in America* II (1943-1950); *Who's Who in Library Service*, 1st ed., 2nd ed. **Books and articles about the biographee**—Dain, Phyllis. *The New York Public Library: A History of Its Founding and Early Years*. New York: The New York Public Library, Astor, Lenox and Tilden Foundations, 1972; Hopper, Franklin F. "Edwin Hatfield Anderson."

Bulletin of the New York Public Library 51:389-90 (June 1947); Lydenberg, Harry M. "Edwin Hatfield Anderson, 1861-1947." *ALA Bulletin* 41:258-59 (Aug. 1947); Lydenberg, Harry M. "Edwin Hatfield Anderson Stressed Personal Factors." *Library Journal* 72:1288-89 (Sept. 15, 1947); Lydenberg, Harry M. *History of The New York Public Library, Astor, Lenox and Tilden Foundations.* New York: The New York Public Library, 1923; Metcalf, Keyes D. "Six Influential Librarians." *College & Research Libraries* 37:337-39 (July 1976); Metcalf, Keyes D. "Tribute to Dr. Edwin H. Anderson." *New York Libraries* 14:150-51 (Nov. 1934); Rhodes, Isabella K. Discussion in The New York State Library School. *Register, 1887-1926.* New York, 1959. **Primary sources and archival materials**—As far as can be determined, there is no body of Anderson papers available. The archives of the New York Public Library should be consulted for letters (especially one to NYPL Trustee George L. Rives dated May 5, 1913) and other documents by him, as should the minutes of the Board of Trustees. See also the annual reports and other publications of the Carnegie Free Library of Braddock, the Carnegie Library of Pittsburgh, the New York State Library, and the New York State Library School (especially *The First Quarter Century of the New York State Library School, 1887-1912*, Albany, 1912). The Lydenberg papers at NYPL contain folders devoted to Anderson, and the contributor also used personal interviews with several former NYPL librarians.

—PHYLLIS DAIN

ANDREWS, CLEMENT WALKER (1858-1930)

Clement Walker Andrews, the first librarian of the John Crerar Library, was born on January 13, 1858, in Salem, Massachusetts, the son of Joseph and Judith Walker Andrews. His father was a banker and merchant who served as a brigadier general in the Massachusetts Militia before and during the Civil War; his mother was prominent in philanthropic work. Educated at the Boston Latin School, Clement Walker Andrews received his A.B. degree from Harvard University in 1879, graduating with honors in chemistry, and his A.M. degree in 1880 from the same university. The honorary degree of LL.D. was conferred upon him by Northwestern University on June 14, 1911.

His first two years after graduation were spent in the laboratory of Carter, Densmore & Company, manufacturers of Carter's ink. In 1883 he became an assistant and a year later an instructor in organic chemistry at the Massachusetts Institute of Technology. During the twelve years that he was at M.I.T., Dr. Andrews pursued the two careers of chemist and librarian. In 1885, he was placed in charge of the William Ripley Nichols Chemical Library. In 1887, he began cataloging the M.I.T. collections, and he was appointed librarian of the Institute Library two years later. With the cooperation of the faculty, he systematized the work of the previously independent departmental libraries. In 1891-1892, he had full charge of the laboratory work in organic chemistry, and in 1892, he was elected secretary of M.I.T.'s Society of Arts and appointed editor of its publication, the *Technology Quarterly and Proceedings.*

Gradually his library and bibliography work began to take precedence over his work in organic chemistry, and the scientist became librarian.

In 1895, at the age of 37, Andrews was called to Chicago by the directors of the John Crerar Library to organize this new institution. Established by the will of John Crerar as a free public library, the Crerar Library, upon the unanimous decision of the directors, was to specialize in scientific and technical literature. Andrews served as librarian (he did not like to be called director) until January 24, 1928, when he retired due to ill health. At this time, the directors of the Library adopted a resolution making him librarian emeritus.

He died of a paralytic stroke at the age of 72, after an illness of three years. Andrews never married. An old bachelor, he lived with three others a life of social semi-retirement, but he was well known and liked throughout the library profession. In his later years, he was something of a recluse, whether at Chicago or at Melvil Dewey's (q.v.) Lake Placid South. He was buried in Salem, Massachusetts.

During his administration, the John Crerar Library grew from nothing to more than half a million volumes with a staff of over sixty assistants. In directing the Crerar Library, which was first housed in rented quarters in the Marshall Field building at Wabash Avenue and Washington Street, Andrews was always guided by the collective opinions and practices advocated by the American Library Association. He once cited Melvil Dewey as an example of one who had achieved administrative success through fearless devotion to an ideal, and he adopted the Dewey Decimal Classification system for the Crerar Library. A classed catalog, supported by an author-title catalog and a subject index, became the center of the reference unit.

Andrews brought to the selection of materials at the Crerar Library his practical experience in science and technology, a mastery of Greek, Latin, and the Western European languages, and broad European travel. J. Christian Bay (q.v.) reports that Andrews had an unfailing instinct for reference sources that were needed in the Library, and, "as late as 1926 he purchased a periodical still left on his original list of desiderata from 1895, and its purchase closed the accession of a group which rarely if ever can be acquired in this age."

Under the leadership of Andrews, the Crerar Library grew in prestige to become a worthy parallel to the Newberry Library. In 1921, Dr. Andrews had the satisfaction of seeing the Crerar Library established in its own building on the corner of Michigan Avenue and Randolph Street, planned and built according to his specifications.

His annual reports during his 32 years as director of the Crerar Library are part of his chief written memorial, the more widely known part being editorial in nature. While at M.I.T., he compiled and edited *A List of the Scientific Periodicals in the Libraries of the Massachusetts Institute of Technology, April, 1887.* While in Chicago, he edited *A List of Serials in Public Libraries of Chicago and Evanston, Corrected to January, 1901.* Other writings appeared in both chemical and library periodicals. His first published article in the field of librarianship was on technical collections in public libraries (*Library Journal,* January 1895), and many of the articles he wrote were descriptions of the work of the John Crerar Library.

Another group of writings consists of papers presented at the meetings of the American Library Institute and the American Library Association, which were published in *Library Journal* and other library periodicals. At the annual meetings of the American Library Institute, of which he was one of the 44 charter fellows, and president from 1922 to 1924, he spoke on the printing and sale of catalog cards, a practice the Crerar Library had instituted before the Library of Congress did so. He spoke as well on cooperation among libraries, on the economics of library architecture, and on the functions of the American Library Institute.

Papers delivered at ALA conferences were: his presidential address on the use of books; a rationale for the centralization of university libraries; and a paper on classification, in which he discussed some of the innovations and changes in the Dewey Decimal Classification carried out at the Crerar Library. In July 1897, Andrews read a paper on American printed catalog cards at the Second International Library Conference in London. He reported briefly on this and other international meetings held that year at the 1898 ALA conference at Chautauqua, New York.

In addition to speaking at professional conferences, he was invited to deliver an address at the cornerstone-laying ceremony of the William Rainey Harper Memorial Library of the University of Chicago in 1910. At that time he addressed himself "to a simple presentation of the services which the Harper Memorial Library ought to render to the University and the problems which it has to solve in so doing." He also wrote for *Public Libraries,* which was edited by his colleague, Mary Eileen Ahern (q.v.).

Andrews had a keen appreciation of history and literature. He spoke often of the great New England poets and quoted authors, ancient and modern. His favorite poem was "The Chambered Nautilus" from *The Autocrat of the Breakfast Table,* by Oliver Wendell Holmes. He said to J. C. Bay on one occasion: "This poem epitomizes pretty well my philosophy of life, they might read it at my funeral." He was a member of the Cobden (honorary member),

Harvard, Onwentsia, University, Caxton, and Chicago Library clubs.

Andrews freely contributed his professional talents to the Illinois Library Association and the ALA. He joined ALA in 1890, and attended 34 annual conferences. Besides considerable committee service (for years he chaired the Finance Committee), he was on the Executive Board for eight years, was first vice-president for 1905-1906, and was president in 1906-1907. As an ex-president, he served on the Council for many years.

Andrews was a dignified man with a beard and a moustache. He was a hard worker, library work being both his vocation and avocation, and evenings and Sunday afternoons often found him at his desk. He had a fine mind and in discussions and conversations reached conclusions quickly, sometimes too quickly. Gertrude Forstall recollected in 1931 that "he had not the patience to impart information necessary to slower minds. . . ."

A memorial resolution that the Board of Directors of the John Crerar Library adopted at his death described his unusual qualities as human being and as librarian:

> The fundamental organization, the practices and methods instituted under our authority by Dr. Andrews, have stood the test of time and change. His influence in our community, through his efforts toward an ideal realization of the best library service, was very great. Respected among his professional contemporaries and recognized with honor in their collective work, he gave an unusual example of true historical continuity of a life work which he ever regarded as a high privilege.

After his death on November 20, 1930, tributes were printed in *Libraries* (January 1931) from his three fellow Chicago librarians: Theodore Wesley Koch (q.v.), Northwestern University Library; Carl B. Roden (q.v.), Chicago Public Library; and George B. Utley (q.v.), Newberry Library. Utley said: "He has left us an example of loyal unselfish service to his chosen vocation which is a pleasant memory and an inspiration to those who follow."

Biographical listings and obituaries—*National Cyclopaedia of American Biography* 14; [Obituary]. *Chicago Daily Tribune,* November 21, 1930, p. 18, col. 2; [Obituary]. *Libraries* 36:15-17 (January 1931); [Obituary]. *Library Journal* 55:961 (December 1, 1930); *The Twentieth Century Biographical Dictionary of Notable Americans,* Vol. 1. Boston: The Biographical Society, 1904; *Who's Who in America* 16 (1930-1931). **Books and articles about the biographee**—Ahern, Mary Eileen. "Honor from His Fellow Citizens." *Libraries* 33:131-32 (March 1928); Bay, J. Christian. "In Memorian: Dr. Clement Walker Andrews, 1858-1930." *The John Crerar Library Quarterly* 2:5-8 (Supplement) (1930). Reprinted in essentially the same form in: "Dr. Clement Walker Andrews, 1858-1930." *Libraries* 36:1-5 (January 1931); "Clement Walker Andrews: Librarian, 1858-1930." In his *The Fortune of Books; Essays, Memories* *and Prophecies of a Librarian*. Chicago: Walter M. Hill, 1941, pp. 192-198; "The First Librarian: Clement Walker Andrews (1858-1930)." In his *The John Crerar Library, 1895-1944: An Historical Report*. Prepared under the Authority of The Board of Directors by The Librarian. Chicago: The Library, 1945, pp. 83-90; Brown, Charles Harvey. "Clement Walker Andrews, 1858-1930." In Emily Miller Danton, *Pioneering Leaders in Librarianship, First Series*. Chicago: American Library Association, 1953, pp. 1-12; Dickinson, Sarah S. "Early Memories." *John Crerar Library Quarterly* 11:15-16 (April-June 1931); Faxon, Frederick W. "Our Frontispiece." *Bulletin of Bibliography* 11:97 (September-December 1921); Forstall, Gertrude. "Recollections of the J. C. L." *John Crerar Library Quarterly* 11:19-21 (July-September 1931).

—DORIS CRUGER DALE

ARBUTHNOT, MAY HILL (1884-1969)

On August 27, 1884, May Hill was born to Frank and Mary Elizabeth Seville Hill in Mason City, Iowa. She received her baccalaureate degree from the University of Chicago in 1922 and her master's degree from Columbia University in 1924. On December 17, 1932, she married Charles C. Arbuthnot, head of the Economics Department of Western Reserve University.

May Hill Arbuthnot's contributions to teacher education and the study of children's literature were diverse. In 1961, Western Reserve University (now Case Western Reserve) conferred upon her the degree of Doctor of Humane Letters, honoring her as teacher, scholar, writer, and lecturer. She held memberships in Phi Delta Kappa, Pi Lambda Theta, and Delta Kappa Gamma.

She began her career at Superior (Minnesota) State College in 1912, where she was a training teacher. In 1918, she joined the faculty of the Ethical Culture School in New York City. From that position, she went in 1922 to Cleveland, Ohio, as principal of the Cleveland Kindergarten-Primary Training School. Five years later, under her direction and leadership, the Training School became a part of the School of Education at Western Reserve University. During her years in Cleveland, she also established the first nursery schools in both the city and the state of Ohio, and in 1929, she opened the University Nursery School on the campus of Western Reserve. This nursery school became a successful model of a laboratory for teachers, doctors, nurses, parents, and others concerned with child development. Arbuthnot retired in 1950 from active teaching but devoted the next few years to writing and lecturing about literature for children.

In the later years of her life, many honors were bestowed upon her. In 1959, the Women's National Book Association honored her for distinguished achievement in the world of books with the Constance Lindsay Skinner Award. In 1964, the Catholic Library Association awarded her its Regina Medal in formal recognition of her "continued distinguished

contribution to the field of Children's Literature." Three months before her death on October 2, 1969, Scott, Foresman and Company, publisher of most of her books about children's literature, and the Children's Services Division of the American Library Association announced an honor lectureship to be presented in her name. The May Hill Arbuthnot Honor Lectureship allows for the annual selection of an outstanding author, critic, librarian, historian, or teacher of children's literature to prepare a paper "which shall be a significant contribution to the field of children's literature." In her acknowledgment of the honor, she stated the philosophy that kept her a popular speaker about children's literature, "I am a strong believer in the efficacy of direct speech, the spoken word. For poetry, it is the only way and for more people than we bookish ones like to admit, it is the best way. That is, a forthright vigorous lecture can set fire to a piece of literature that had failed to come to life from the printed page."

Her contributions in the fields of childhood education and children's literature were substantial. Thousands of American children learned to read from the "Basic Curriculum Readers" which she co-authored with William S. Gray of the University of Chicago. Most of these children probably remember them as the "Dick and Jane" books.

Many more thousands of children benefited indirectly from her enthusiasm for and knowledge of children's literature. Her classes in children's literature were popular, she was a sought-after speaker throughout the country, and for years she was review editor, first for *Childhood Education* and later for *Elementary English.*

Perhaps the most widely known of her books is *Children and Books*, first published in 1947 (5th edition, rev. by Zena Sutherland, 1977). In this text for children's literature courses, she brought together her deep concern for the healthy complete development of children, her love of good books, and her belief that good books can assist children in meeting their developmental needs. The philosophy throughout this book is that teachers, librarians, and parents can and should influence children to "a joyous appropriation and use of worthwhile books."

She enlivened her philosophy further in a series of anthologies that attempted to bring together by literary genre excellent examples of fine literature and good advice on its selection and use with children. These anthologies include: *Time for Poetry* (rev. 1968 with Sheldon L. Root), *Time for Fairy Tales* (rev. 1961), *Time for True Tales and Almost True* (1953), *Time for Biography*, with Dorothy M. Broderick (1968), *Time for Stories of the Past and Present*, with Dorothy M. Broderick (1969), *Time for New Magic*, with Mark Taylor (1971), *Time for Old Magic* (1970), and *Time for Discovery*, with Evelyn

Wenzel (1971). A bibliography, *Children's Books Too Good to Miss*, now in its sixth edition (1971), *Children's Reading in the Home* (1969), and the general *Arbuthnot Anthology of Children's Literature* (rev. 1976 by Zena Sutherland), have all been used widely in college courses and by other adults concerned with children's reading.

Friends valued her for her enthusiasm, honesty, integrity, and curiosity about all of life's experiences. Her drive and commitment belied her small stature; Dorothy Broderick wrote of her after her death,

> She was a great lady, and in the words of today's generation "she was tough." She worked with and for children all her life, but escaped the malady of herself becoming childish. She never stopped growing. She was tiny physically, a giant in every other way.... If there was one single reason over all others for loving her, it was this: she felt strongly and she thought clearly. When it came to important things, she never let her feelings keep her from thinking tough. Call it what you will: integrity or intellectual honesty. She had it.

May Hill Arbuthnot often expressed her belief in the importance of libraries and librarians to children. More important, however, she provided leadership in urging adults to assume their responsibilities to see that good books were placed in the hands of children. Her philosophy and her high standards for children's literature were important in the years when American book publishing for children became so prolific. An apt assessment of her contribution is provided by Zena Sutherland in her preface to the fourth edition of *Children and Books* (1972):

> It would be impossible to express adequately the gratitude I feel to May Hill Arbuthnot. Everyone who works toward the goal of bringing to children the undying pleasure of a love for books knows that hers was a permanent contribution to children's literature. Her knowledge, her enthusiasm, her practical common sense, and her boundless imagination have guided countless parents, teachers, librarians, and students. All of these qualities are evident in *Children and Books*, and it has been a joy and a challenge to adapt her work to today's needs. Her death brought an abrupt end to plans to work together, but May Hill Arbuthnot is still with us in her books, a wise and blithe spirit.

Biographical listings and obituaries—*Contemporary Authors*, Vol. 9, 1st revision; [Obituary]. *Library Journal* 94:4198 (November 15, 1969); *Who Was Who in America* V (1969-1973). **Books and articles about the biographee**—Adrienne, Sister M. "The Sixth Regina Medal Award." *Catholic Library World* 36:17 (September 1964); Corrigan, Marie C., and Adeline Corrigan. "May Hill Arbuthnot." *Catholic Library World* 35:337-39 (Feb. 1964).

—MARILYN MILLER

ASKEW, SARAH BYRD (1863-1942)

Sarah Byrd Askew was born on February 15, 1863, in Dayton, Alabama, the youngest of three daughters of Samuel Horton and Thyrza Pickering Askew. (The reported birth date of 1877 was a polite fiction, as discovered when her death certificate was filed.) When Sarah was three years old, her mother died and her father married Kittie Reeves. They eventually had six daughters and a son.

Sarah was educated at the Dayton Academy until the family moved to Atlanta, Georgia, when she was thirteen. There she grew up near the home of Joel Chandler Harris, which seems to have inspired her permanent love for the famous "Br'er Rabbit" stories that she later narrated to large audiences. In Atlanta, she also was graduated from high school, went to business school, and became a stenographer.

Askew's interest in library work was first sparked during an extended visit with her sister in Cleveland, where she met William Howard Brett (q.v.), director of the Cleveland Public Library. Impressed by Brett's enthusiasm for librarianship, she accepted his offer of a temporary appointment in one of Cleveland's branch libraries. Once working, she was immediately absorbed in this new field and realized that she had found her life's work. With Brett's encouragement, she went to Brooklyn to enroll in the Pratt Institute Library School in 1903.

Upon completing her studies at Pratt in 1904, Askew returned to the Cleveland Public Library as an assistant. She had been there for only a few months, though, when she was invited to organize the newly created New Jersey Public Library Commission (forerunner of the Library Development Bureau, which is now an integral part of the New Jersey State Library). At the time of her appointment in January 1905, when she was almost 42 years old, only 66 public libraries existed in the entire state. She was instructed to "get libraries going." A measure of her effectiveness is the fact that there were 316 local libraries in New Jersey at the time of her death. In 1909, she briefly changed jobs, succeeding John M. Roger as reference librarian in the New Jersey State Library until 1912, but in 1913 she returned to the Public Library Commission, where she stayed for the remainder of her life. She was its secretary from 1930 on.

An evangelist for public libraries, Askew frequently rode trucks or drove her own horse and buggy into the small towns of New Jersey in order to arouse citizen interest in public library development. Realizing that enough local libraries could not be organized to reach all of the state's citizens, she began to consider establishing libraries on a county-wide basis. People were captivated by her magnetic personality, and the public library movement in New Jersey began to gain momentum. Throughout her career, she remained an adroit politician and wisely gained the wholehearted support of, among others, the State Federation of Women's Clubs, the PTA, the State Teachers' Association, state and local grange groups, and many others for her library plans.

Subsequent to her return to the Public Library Commission in 1913, she continued her library development efforts, working with every civic group she could reach. Her vision of county library systems, with mobile units bringing library services to people in small towns and rural communities, was exciting, practicable, and organizationally sound. Then, in 1920, the New Jersey Legislature passed the necessary enabling legislation allowing the establishment of county-wide libraries. Under Askew's guidance, 12 of the state's 21 counties eventually established county libraries in accordance with this legislation. When the citizens of Burlington County voted on the question of establishing the first county library in New Jersey in 1920, the measure was passed by a two-to-one margin and was, in Askew's words, "the most thrilling professional experience I can remember."

Her work for county libraries had been interrupted in 1917 by United States entry into World War I, because New Jersey was filled with servicemen there for basic training prior to overseas assignment. Askew's imagination was fired by the challenge of bringing books to these thousands of men, and she became head of the New Jersey Library War Service from 1917 to 1919. As such, she organized a statewide program to supply books to the 42 military camps, stations, and hospitals within New Jersey's borders, and, since nearly all of the camps were embarkation points for overseas duties for the servicemen, she also ensured that books went to the troopships and then to the front lines. Book service to men in camp hospitals was carried out under her personal direction.

Then, following her successes in the 1920s with county libraries, which included her planning a Model-T truck to carry books to isolated areas (thus anticipating today's bookmobiles), came the Great Depression of the 1930s. This afforded Askew yet another opportunity to help people, since libraries could help people to identify and capitalize on their respective talents. Also, in concert with the Works Progress Administration (after 1939, the Work Projects Administration), she was able to place hundreds of individuals in useful library jobs. Because of the training they received on these library projects, a great many of these people were later placed on library payrolls.

When World War II broke out, Askew again became involved in service to her country. She actively took part in organizing the Victory Book Campaign and soon had books moving steadily into the military camps of New Jersey and beyond. Since the Public Library Commission was represented on the State Defense Council, it supplied information services and bibliographies and also helped plan the role of libraries in the state's defense program. Askew was, of course, heavily involved until she began a long hospitalization.

Sarah ("Sallie") Askew was small, with blue eyes and red hair, and her speech was softly slurred with a Southern accent. Her sister described her as "quicksilver"; to the writer, she was a great actress who just happened to become a librarian.

Early in her career, Askew had also recognized the need for practical library training courses. Thus, in 1906, she established a summer school where librarians of small, rural libraries could, as she put it, "learn to do a better job." She was also active in professional organizations, serving as president of the New Jersey Library Association (1913-1914 and 1939-1940), vice-president of the American Library Association (1938-1939), chairperson of children's reading for the National Congress of Parents and Teachers (1924-1929), and a member of the Trenton (New Jersey) Board of Education (1923-1933). She contributed frequently to professional publications, and she wrote one brochure, *The Man, the Place and the Book* (1916), in which she described the beginning of a library in a remote New Jersey fishing village.

Askew's outstanding contributions to the state and nation were widely acknowledged. In 1930, when the New Jersey College for Women (now Douglass College of Rutgers University) was to confer its first honorary degree, hers was the one name unanimously suggested. The citation read in part,

> Apostle of the gospel of good reading for all people and of the public library as an essential element in the educational service of every enlightened community; distinguished for wit and wisdom in public address; idolized by her associates in every library in New Jersey; through whose enthusiastic, tactful and persevering efforts the State she loves with such rare devotion has advanced to foremost rank in the extent and efficiency of its public libraries.

In 1956, the new library building of Paterson State College was named the Sarah B. Askew Library.

After a long hospitalization for cancer, Sarah Askew died in Trenton, New Jersey, of bronchopneumonia on October 20, 1942. She was buried in the family plot in Atlanta, Georgia.

Biographical listings and obituaries—*Notable American Women*; [Obituary]. *Library Journal* 67:962 (November 1, 1942); *Who Was Who in America* II (1943-1950). **Books and articles about the biographee**—*New Jersey Library Association Newsletter*, Sept. 1961; Severns, Hannah. "Sarah Byrd Askew, 1863-1942." In Emily Miller Danton, ed., *Pioneering Leaders in Librarianship, First Series.* Chicago: American Library Association, 1953, pp. 13-21; Smith, E. L.

"Sarah Byrd Askew." *Library Journal* 67:944-45 (November 1, 1942). **Primary sources and archival materials**—Consult the records of the New Jersey Public Library Commission and the death record in the State Department of Health (where her birth date is established as 1863). Too, the author of the article in *Notable American Women* agrees with this contributor that the birth date was indeed 1863 and not 1877.

—ROGER H. McDONOUGH

BAY, JENS CHRISTIAN (1871-1962)

The *Library Journal* for June 1, 1962, carried the following brief notice of the death of J. Christian Bay: "Jens C. Bay, Emeritus Librarian, John Crerar Library, Chicago, died April 11 at the age of 91. Mr. Bay was an authority on the history of the Middle-West, and was well-known as a medical reference librarian." In those 91 years, J. Christian Bay did, indeed, become a leading expert on the history and bibliography of Western America, was a notable medical librarian, served until his seventy-fifth year as librarian of one of the world's leading scientific libraries, and died one of the ablest bookmen among American librarians.

Jens Christian Bay was born in Rudkobing, Denmark, a village on the island of Langeland, October 12, 1871. From the natural world of his native Denmark and from his study of botany at the University of Copenhagen from 1887 to 1892, he gained the scientific background that served him in all of his professional career.

In 1892, Bay came to the United States, where he first worked at the Missouri Botanical Garden cataloging botanical illustrations, reviewing botanical literature, and studying. After two years, he moved to Des Moines, Iowa, to serve as bacteriologist for the Iowa State Board of Health until 1897. This was followed by an abortive experience as a teacher in a private school. By his thirtieth birthday, he was at the Library of Congress, where he began a library career that was to last nearly half a century.

The tour of duty at the Library of Congress lasted five years, and in that period he worked on early editions of the LC classification schedules for Class G (Geography, Anthropology, etc.) and Class L (Education), and wrote the first edition (1904) of the Class R schedules (Medicine), contributions still of service to American libraries. Like many other librarians who had the good fortune to work at LC, even for a limited time, he developed a lifelong attachment to that Library, and, characteristically for Bay, a deep affection for and loyalty to Herbert Putnam (q.v.), the Librarian of Congress.

His classification work attracted the attention of Clement Walker Andrews (q.v.), librarian of the John Crerar Library in Chicago, and in 1905 Bay was invited to Crerar to serve as classifier in that already well-known, rapidly growing science library. In 1909, he was appointed medical reference librarian, serving until he succeeded Andrews, first as acting librarian in 1927, during Andrews's long illness, and then as librarian in 1928.

Generally speaking, a close identity develops between a great library and its chief administrator, but in the case of Bay and the Crerar Library, the relationship was more one of symbiosis. Bay's primary interests were scholarly rather than administrative, however. Because of his age and his other interests, the quality of his management deteriorated in later years; but this also happened as a result of World War II and the government's heavy demands for manpower, especially from the classes of young graduates. The federal government's demands for scientific information were especially burdensome during this period, and those staff members not affected by the draft were doubly taxed in their work. Bay, however, continued the depth and breadth of his intellectual interests until long after retiring as librarian in 1946, two months after his seventy-fifth birthday.

For the full measure of this complex man, one must view the character and scope of his published writings. With a remarkable command of English as well as French, German, Danish, and the other Scandinavian tongues, he showed a phenomenal familiarity with literature (from Danish poetry through the English novel), accounts of Western exploration, botany, medicine, and the history of science. And his productiveness resulted in an average of three or more publications each year throughout his adult life, well into his years as an octogenarian. More than 150 entries for his writings are in volume 40 of the *National Union Catalog Pre-1956 Imprints*. The bibliography of Bay's writings at the time of his seventieth birthday, issued by his assistant librarian, Kanardy Taylor, lists 160 items; and his complete published writings exceeded that number by a substantial margin.

His ability to pursue bibliographic activity with intensity was exhibited early in three indexes that required not only expert knowledge of the subject matter, but infinite care and patience: the *Index Emendatus ad Halleri Bibliotheca Botanica* (1908), of the classic eighteenth century bibliography of botany by Albrecht von Haller; the index to volumes 26-100 (1843-1910) of *Flora, oder allgemeine botanische Zeitung*; and a typescript index (1911) to the elephant folio of John James Audubon's *The Birds of America*. Through the years, he also compiled numerous bibliographies for publications.

Bay was, in another facet of his writing, a productive biographer. One might conclude that a primary root of his interest lay in the strong attachment he developed for individuals with whom he associated, among whom were William Trelease, eminent American botanist; Christian Fenger, noted Chicago physician; J. C. M. Hanson (q.v.), giant among early American librarians; and his own predecessor at Crerar Library, Clement Walker Andrews. Beyond personal acquaintances, however, he wrote studies of Albrecht von Haller, "medical encyclopedist"; George Washington, "citizen and farmer"; Conrad Gesner, "the father of bibliography"; and Henry Lewis, author of the Mid-Western classic, *Das illustrierte Mississippithal*, of which Bay edited a reprint edition. His studies also ranged into commentaries on such literary classics as *Hamlet, The Pickwick Papers*, and *Uncle Tom's Cabin*.

Over many years, Bay prepared an annual Christmas book, published by the Torch Press in Cedar Rapids, Iowa, in which many of the studies mentioned above appeared. One pleasing item in the series was his *Biography and Biographies, Hints and Indications* (1948). The series also included four items that deserve special mention because of their high quality as selective bibliography. These were: *A Handful of Western Books* (1935); *A Second Handful . . .* (1936); and *A Third Handful . . .* (1937); and *Journeys and Voyages to Nature; A Survey of One Hundred Books* (1950). Each of these little volumes reflects the extraordinary range of his familiarity with diverse fields of interest. One small quotation is typical of the fluidity with which he leads the reader from one notable book to another.

> *Whaling* books are numerous. None, I think, can compare with Edmund Fanning's repeatedly printed *Voyage to the South Seas* (1823) and especially with Wm. Scoresby's *Journal of a Voyage to the Northern Whale Fishery*. Other accounts may seem pretty monotonous but like numerous sketches and descriptions of sea life by Louis Becke, teem with curious and penetrating descriptions of the wonders arising from oceans and remote shores and islands far away.

No biographical sketch of Jens Christian Bay can be adequate that does not mention his passion for collecting books. In the course of his lifetime, he gathered two distinguished collections, both of which now enrich Midwestern libraries. The first is the "J. Christian Bay Collection of Western Exploration," purchased by the Missouri State Historical Society Library in Columbia, Missouri, and the second is a collection of some 14,000 volumes now in the Margaret I. King Library at the University of Kentucky (described by Lawrence S. Thompson in the paper cited below).

Bay died on April 11, 1962, in Elmhurst, Illinois, where he had made his home for more than thirty years, and is buried in Mount Emblem Cemetery in that city. His wife, Dora Detjen Bay, and one son preceded him in death, and two sons and two daughters survived him.

Biographical listings and obituaries—*Kraks Bla Bog* (Denmark), 1960; *National Cyclopaedia of American Biography* 50; [Obituary]. *Library Journal* 87:2115 (June 1, 1962); *Who Was Who in America* IV (1961-1968). Books and articles about the biographee—Taylor, Kanardy L. *J. Christian Bay at Seventy: A Review and a Bibliography*. Chicago: The John Crerar Library, 1941; Thompson, Lawrence S. "Jens Christian Bay, Bibliologist." *Libri* 12:320-30 (1963). Primary sources and archival materials—Bay, Jens Christian. *The Fortune of Books; Essays, Memories and Prophecies of a Librarian*. Chicago: Walter M. Hill, 1941.

—HERMAN H. HENKLE

BEALS, RALPH ALBERT (1899-1954)

Ralph Albert Beals was born March 29, 1899, at Deming, New Mexico, the son of Nathan A. and Alice Seeley Beals. He received his baccalaureate degree from the University of California at Berkeley in 1921 and served as secretary to the president of the University from 1921 to 1923. Receiving his master's degree in English from Harvard University in 1925, he remained at Harvard as an assistant in English until 1928. From 1928 to 1933, he was an instructor in English at New York University. He married Alice B. Stone on June 12, 1928, and they had one daughter, Mary Druitt Beals.

In 1933, he left New York University to become assistant to the director of the American Association for Adult Education, a position which he held until 1939, when he resigned to pursue work for the doctorate at the Graduate Library School of the University of Chicago.

His decision to enter librarianship was largely due to the influence of Frederick Keppel (q.v.), then president of the Carnegie Corporation of New York. Keppel, who had provided substantial grants in support of libraries and library education, had become concerned because a number of major university library positions had been given to non-librarians; his inquiries into the cause thereof brought the response from university administrators that there were no trained librarians who were qualified for the responsibility. Keppel, therefore, set out to attempt to remedy the situation by providing support for promising young people to attend library school. Beals was his first and only "experiment," and an extremely successful one it was.

Beals's decision to become a librarian was further encouraged by his growing disillusionment with the adult education movement. While in California, he had received the certificate of the Riverside Library School which, in its day, had an excellent reputation. Moreover, during his one year in the army, in 1918, he had served as camp librarian at one of the military installations in the Southwest, so Keppel's suggestion to pursue library work was not an entirely new idea.

Fortunately, Dean Louis Round Wilson at Chicago possessed the acumen to perceive Beals's potential, so he was enrolled at the institution on the Midway in the autumn of 1939, and it was at that time that our lasting friendship began. In one academic year, Beals completed all the requirements for the doctorate except the writing of the dissertation, which, because of subsequent preoccupation with professional affairs, was never completed.

The doctorate always eluded him, much to his chagrin. Two attempts at a dissertation at Harvard had to be abandoned, after a substantial investment in time and labor, because the subjects were discovered to have been preempted by others. In the spring of 1954, he was notified by President John S. Millis of Western Reserve University that he had been elected to receive the honorary degree of Doctor of Humane Letters at the June convocation as part of the ceremonies honoring the fiftieth anniversary of that university's School of Library Science. By June, however, his health had deteriorated and his physician would not permit him to make the trip to Cleveland. He was notified that the degree would be conferred following his recovery; no one guessed at that time that the trip would never be made. It was a last cruel irony.

Having completed his residency at Chicago, Beals was appointed by Clara Herbert as assistant director of the Public Library of the District of Columbia. In this position, which he held from 1940 to 1942, he played a major role in developing the plans for the new library building. In the spring of 1942, he was invited by Robert Maynard Hutchins, on the recommendation of Louis Round Wilson, to assume the directorship of the University of Chicago Library. He left Washington that spring, convinced that he would not accept the position if it were offered to him, but returned from Chicago with a signed contract, because of his profound admiration for Hutchins and what he was attempting to accomplish. He remained at Chicago from 1942 to 1946, and during the last year, he was dean of the Graduate Library School as well as director of the University Library. These years were all too short, both for librarianship and for library education. Of Beals's arrival in Chicago, Hutchins subsequently wrote:

He took a very solemn, not to say dim, view of the situation. How could it be otherwise? ... The combination of poor accommodations and poor organization had greatly depressed the faculty.... He went about his task in his quiet way. He was humorous, most often at his own expense; he was persistent; he was clear. The first thing he did was to change the attitude of the faculty about the Library. He did this mostly by the charm and force of his personality.... He improved the library service. He worked out sensible and

efficient relationships with the departmental libraries. Since he could not solve the problem of space, he set himself to mitigate its worst effects. He devoted himself to expanding the microfilm collections of the University. He took the lead in the discussions that resulted in the foundation of the inter-university center for little used books that has meant so much to the universities of the Middle West.

Hutchins goes on to say that Beals's influence was not limited to the library but was felt throughout the University. He was an active and influential contributor to the bi-weekly deans' meetings, and he revitalized a tired library staff with his vision and sense of purpose.

The same qualities of leadership that characterized Beals as a librarian were evident during the one short year that he was dean of the Graduate Library School, which had fallen into a measure of disarray during the years of World War II. From 1942 to 1945, Dean Carleton B. Joeckel (q.v.) had kept the school going despite the severe handicap of a reduction in both faculty and students due to the demands of wartime service. Nevertheless, a number of students who were not taken into the armed services were able to complete the work for their degrees without any lowering of standards. Furthermore, Joeckel retained the services of Professors Pierce Butler (q.v.) and Leon Carnovsky (q.v.), both of whom continued to render yeoman service under Beals. Beals then initiated a curriculum revision aligned to his conception of what a professional education should be, and one cannot but wonder what the benefits to librarianship and library education would have been had he remained at Chicago for the rest of his life. As a teacher, he was a master of the Socratic method, squarely in the tradition of Hutchins, Mortimer Adler, and Scott Buchanan. He did not tolerate fools at all, and he could browbeat a student unmercifully when he thought the situation so required. The first lesson his students had to learn was to stand up to his relentless logic, and this was not an easy assignment.

In the spring of 1946, Beals was invited by Morris Hadley, chairman of the Board of Trustees of the New York Public Library, to accept the directorship of that distinguished institution. The decision was, perhaps, the most difficult of his entire career. He did not want to leave Chicago, though the prospect of an opportunity to develop library programs for the general public as well as for the serious scholar did attract him. Eventually, Beals reached a decision to reject the New York offer, though during an hour-long conversation with Hadley he outlined some twelve conditions that would have to be met if he were to accept. In less than 24 hours, Hadley and the mayor of New York had agreed to all the terms, and

Beals felt obligated to go. I was with him when the final call came through; he was stunned, visibly shaken, and kept repeating, "I never thought they could do it." When I inquired if this meant that he would leave, he replied, "I am afraid it does."

"The same calm, quiet clarity," wrote Hutchins, "that made him effective in the University [of Chicago] made him a great leader in the greatest of public libraries. . . ." He revitalized the New York Public Library as he had that at the University of Chicago. During his regimen, the per capita appropriation by the city was doubled, the book stock of the Circulating Department was lifted out of its deteriorating condition, library salaries were substantially improved, and the Reference Department, which was dangerously close to deficit financing because of inflation and faltering support, was enriched by a sustained drive for contributions from business, industry, and foundations. Administratively, the Circulation Department and the Reference Department, which previously had operated as virtually separate institutions, were brought together in a new and harmonious relationship.

But Beals's influence and effectiveness extended beyond the boundaries of Manhattan to the entire state of New York. He was president of the New York Library Association and assumed leadership in securing state aid for New York libraries. His name was one of six submitted by the American Library Association as acceptable candidates for Librarian of Congress at the time of Luther Evans's resignation in July 1953, though, of course, Verner Clapp (q.v.) was the profession's first choice. At the time of his death in 1954, the *New York Times* said editorially, "The people of this city have lost a good neighbor and the library profession an able and inspiring leader."

He had been elected to membership in many distinguished literary and scholarly organizations: Phi Beta Kappa, the Bibliographical Society of America, the Institute of Graphic Arts, the New York Historical Society, the Caxton Club, the Grolier Club, the Coffee House Club, the Century Association, and the English Horticultural Society, in addition to the usual professional library associations. He held the Order of St. Olav, first class, from the King of Norway for his work in the restoration of the library of the University of Oslo. From 1946 to 1949, he was a member of the U.S. National Commission for UNESCO, and from 1940 to 1950, he served on the New York Governor's Commission of State Library Aid.

The bibliography of his writings is regrettably brief, for he wrote, as well as spoke, with distinction. Only three books bear his name. With M. E. Barnicle and J. S. Terry, he edited *Readings in Description and Narrative* (1930) and *Aspects of Post-Collegiate Education* (1935); with Leon Brody he edited *The Literature of Adult Education* (1941). Also, from 1937 to 1938 he edited, in association with Morse Cartwright, the *Journal of Adult Education.* Most of these, as their titles suggest, were the work of others rather than his own.

Of his individual essays, two stand out as being particularly notable, both for style and for content: "The Librarian as Anthologist," in *D.C. Libraries* (January 1941) and "Implications of Communications Research for the Public Library," in *Print, Radio, and Film in a Democracy*, edited by Douglas Waples (also 1941). The latter essay is notable for the development of Beals's tripartite classification of library literature into glad tidings, testimony, and research. The former essay is one of the most beautifully written statements of the role of the librarian that this writer has yet encountered; only the essays of Archibald MacLeish can rival it. It should be reprinted in a less fugitive form. The frequency with which Hutchins asked Beals to review Hutchins's own writings prior to their presentation or publication bears witness to Beals's sense of literary style and his critical acumen.

Unfortunately, Beals never formalized his philosophy of librarianship, though there can be little doubt that he had one. Thus, any such frame of reference must be inferred from the limited number of his writings. One can certainly say, however, that he believed implicitly in the library as an engine of scholarship, a major source for the dissemination of knowledge, and an agency for the promotion of taste. Fear of charges of censorship never deterred him from eliminating those books that he thought intellectually unworthy of a place on the library's shelves. Though he was most widely hailed as an administrator, for him the managerial aspect was always subordinate to the ends of scholarship, in its popular as well as its academic sense.

He was a tall, gaunt man, almost ascetic in appearance, who spoke always with perfect syntax, usually in complete sentences, and whose conversation was occasionally illuminated by an epigram. "If I am a good administrator," he once told me, "it is because I have long legs and big ears. A good administrator must go a lot of places he does not want to go, and listen to a lot of things he does not want to hear." Again, when I told him that our 11-year-old daughter had taken me to task for being so impolite as to argue with him at table during a Sunday dinner at his home, he replied, "Tell Mary that intellectuals are never so happy as when they appear least so to others."

It is not easy to assess objectively a man who has been such a powerful influence in one's professional philosophy as Ralph Beals has in mine, so the task might best be left to another. Again to quote Hutchins as a witness:

I wanted Ralph Beals because he was a university man. By that I do not mean that he had graduated from a university. He was a university man in the sense that he knew what a university was. . . . The University of Chicago was an exciting place, but it never seemed quite the same after 1946.

Many of us could say the same for the library world after Beals's death on October 14, 1954.

Biographical listings and obituaries—*Current Biography* (1947, 1954); *National Cyclopaedia of American Biography* 40; [Obituary]. *New York Times*, October 15, 1954, p. 23; *Who Was Who in America* III (1951-1960). Books and articles about the biographee—Hutchins, Robert M., and others. *Ralph A. Beals, 1899-1954.* New York: The New York Public Library, 1955. Primary sources and archival materials—Beals's papers are divided between the archives of the University of Chicago and the New York Public Library.

—JESSE H. SHERA

BECKLEY, JOHN JAMES (1757-1807)

John Beckley was born in England on August 4, 1757, but little is known of his family or of his early education. At age eleven, he came to Virginia as a scribe for John Clayton, clerk of court for Gloucester County and Virginia's best known botanist. He lived in Clayton's home and continued his education and training under Clayton's guidance until the latter's death in 1774. He married Maria Prince of New York City and had one surviving child, Alfred, later a general, who founded and named Beckley, West Virginia.

Following Clayton's death, Beckley remained in Virginia, studying law and serving as clerk for a great many of the committees which characterized this pre-Revolutionary period. In 1777, at the age of twenty, he was elected clerk of the Virginia Senate. In 1779, he replaced Edmund Randolph as clerk of the Virginia House and took over Randolph's law practice when the latter was elected to the Continental Congress.

Beckley was elected to the Williamsburg Lodge of Freemasons and to the founding chapter of Phi Beta Kappa, then in its third year. An extremely active member of the honor society, he helped to design their seal and was influential in its establishment as a national rather than a local society, drawing up the charters for Harvard and Yale universities. When the seat of Virginia government was moved from Williamsburg to Richmond, Beckley became involved in the government of the newly incorporated city, as one of the first twelve councilmen and as the second mayor, serving three terms in that office while still in his twenties.

With the establishment of the federal government in New York in 1789, Beckley was elected the first clerk of the House of Representatives, and he served until 1797, then again from 1801 until his death.

Thomas Jefferson (q.v.) referred to him as the most able clerk in the United States, and other prominent figures concurred. In his political sympathies, Beckley was an ardent "Democratic-Republican," closely associated with Jefferson, Madison, Monroe, and other leaders of the party which was the ancestor of the modern Democratic Party, despite the then-common name of Republican. When the federal government moved to Philadelphia, Beckley became active in city, state, and national politics, campaigning vigorously for Jefferson and other Republican candidates and causes. Extremely active in his opposition to Federalists in general, and to Alexander Hamilton in particular, he became well known as both a speaker and a political writer. In the latter capacity, he worked closely with James Monroe, Philip Freneau, Benjamin Franklin Bache, and William Duane. As was the custom of the time, his writing was published under pseudonyms such as "The Calm Observer" and "Americanus." The effectiveness of his writing can be judged from the fact that the Federalists resorted to a highly irregular early election in order to remove him from office in 1797.

While he must surely have expected Federalist retaliation, his defeat was a very critical matter for Beckley. He had many family responsibilities in England and in Virginia, and his wife, her mother, and her brother were with him in Philadelphia. He had acquired extensive land grants in Western Virginia, Kentucky, and elsewhere, but land was very difficult to sell and there were taxes to pay. The threat of debtors' prison was real indeed. Governor McKean of Pennsylvania came to his rescue in 1800 when he appointed Beckley clerk of the Philadelphia Mayor's Court and clerk of the Orphans' Court for the county.

When Philadelphia Republicans celebrated the inauguration of Jefferson in March 1801, the orator chosen for the great occasion was John Beckley, long known both for his ability as a speaker and for his intense loyalty to Jefferson. It was rather generally assumed that he would be one of the new President's early appointees to some important national post, but he was not. In December 1801, he was re-elected clerk of the House, and the Beckleys moved to Washington. As in Richmond, Beckley became involved in the government of the new city. In 1805, he was one of nine men elected to the Second Chamber.

Although Jefferson had not given Beckley an appointment, he eventually applied for a part-time one. When the Congressional Library was established, he decided that he could perform the duties of librarian in addition to those of clerk. Congress had had its own reference library for many years, managed jointly by the secretary of the Senate and the clerk of the House, so Beckley was not inexperienced in such matters. He applied to James Madison for the post, and on February 5, 1802, the *National Intelligencer* announced: "The PRESIDENT of the United States has appointed **John Beckley Librarian** of the two Houses of Congress." It was hardly a major appointment—he would receive the munificent sum of two dollars per day!

Beckley worked with a joint congressional committee, with advice from Jefferson, in purchasing additional books for the Library. He prepared the first catalog of the Library's holdings and had it published by his friend William Duane in 1802 (with a supplement in 1803). He also encouraged American writers, such as his friend Dr. Benjamin Rush, to deposit copies of their works in the Library.

He had to contend, however, with sundry problems. When he had requested the appointment, he had assumed that he could use some of the clerical assistants employed in his office as clerk of the House and had done so. Unfortunately, one of these clerks, Josias Wilson King, who had been appointed by the Federalists in 1797, had also sought the post of librarian and worked for Beckley until he was fired in 1805. He then prepared a memorial to Congress accusing Beckley of having promised to share the salary of librarian with him and failing to do so and also of neglecting the Library. A congressional committee investigated the charges and declared them to be without foundation. In recent years, King's charges have apparently been the basis for accounts indicating that Beckley neglected his duties as librarian, but there appears to be no factual basis for this view. In spite of limited budget and inadequate housing, the Library grew and attracted favorable comment from such visiting dignitaries as Baron Von Humboldt and Charles Willson Peale.

Beckley died April 8, 1807, in Washington. Although he was our first Librarian of Congress, he will be remembered primarily as a political figure, having received high praise as a party organizer, a sort of unofficial national party chairman. He introduced various campaign practices and strategies, variations of which are still employed today. He played an important part in establishing Republican party principles and in bringing that party to power.

Books and articles about the biographee—Berkeley, Edmund, and Dorothy Smith Berkeley. *John Beckley: Zealous Partisan in a Nation Divided.* Memoirs of the American Philosophical Society, Volume 100. Philadelphia, 1973; Berkeley, Edmund, and Dorothy Smith Berkeley. "The First Librarian of Congress—John Beckley." *Quarterly Journal of the Library of Congress* 32:83-117 (1975).

—EDMUND BERKELEY
—DOROTHY SMITH BERKELEY

BEER, WILLIAM (1849-1927)

William Beer was born in Plymouth, England, on May 1, 1849, the son of Gabriel and Harriet Ferguson Beer. He never married. He attended the Plymouth Grammar School and studied in Paris from 1872 to 1878, when he returned to England to study mining at the College of Physical Science at Newcastle-upon-Tyne (later King's College, Durham University). In 1879, he joined a stained glass manufacturing company. His interest in libraries began early in his career, for at the age of twenty he became a director of the Cottonian Library in Plymouth and had collected a library of Newcastle imprints, which he donated to the public library upon his emigration to America.

Nevertheless, in Newcastle, mining was his first concern. He chose to come to North America in 1884, and after a period of travel in Canada and the United States, he found employment with mining companies in Opechee, Michigan, in 1886 and 1887. In May 1889, he again expressed interest in libraries and attended his first American Library Association conference in St. Louis, registering simply as "William Beer, Leadville, Colorado." In July, 1890, he was appointed librarian of the public library of Topeka, Kansas.

As Beer described his work at Topeka in an article in the *Library Journal* (April 1892) he emphasized library service to the workingman. He inaugurated a series of university extension lectures on electricity and had reading lists of the books available in the city's libraries prepared. He hoped "to get the right to speak in every trade lodge in the city and explain to the carpenter, the painter, and the blacksmith what they can find on our shelves of a helpful character." He also served as secretary of the Kansas State Library Association. Late in 1891, he accepted the librarianship of the Howard Memorial Library in New Orleans, and on December 1 he assumed his new duties.

Established with an endowment from Annie T. Howard in 1882, the Howard Memorial Library was comfortably situated in an H. H. Richardson-style (q.v.) building. A reference library specializing in Southern history and literature, it was, in fact, the only library consistently available to the Louisiana public at that time. Beer enthusiastically immersed himself in the task of developing an outstanding library, using his vacations for intensified book-hunting expeditions to investigate Louisiana material in every library and bookstore he could manage to visit. In 1894, for example, he visited 60 libraries and nearly 100 bookstores in the Eastern states, and, in his 1895 annual report, he claimed that his acquisitions in London, Rotterdam, the Hague, Amsterdam, Leyden, Berlin, Paris, Dresden, Brussels, and Antwerp made the Library's collection of Louisiana history "incontestably the finest in the world." The American Historical Association invited him to prepare a

Louisiana bibliography for its 1895 annual report, but unfortunately he never managed to complete the project.

In 1896, he was also appointed librarian of the Fisk Free and Public Library, and for the next ten years he served as librarian of both institutions. Formed from two inactive libraries in the city, the Public Library opened on January 18, 1897, in new quarters on the second floor of St. Patrick's Hall (within five blocks of the Howard Memorial Library). Cooperation between the two libraries was encouraged by both the librarian and Frank T. Howard, president of the Public Library Board and secretary of the Howard Memorial Library. Finding lists of books were issued by classes until a complete catalog was published in 1900. By 1903, the Library had an annual budget of $28,000, had been designated to receive a Library of Congress depository card set, and had qualified for a Carnegie gift of $350,000 toward the construction of a main building and three branches. An architectural competition for the main building was held in 1905, and the successful architect was announced in February 1906. Beer may well have worked himself out of a position, because in 1905, the Library Board determined to elect a librarian who could give his undivided attention to the Public Library. On April 19, 1906, Beer resigned.

The Howard Memorial Library, of course, regained a full-time librarian, and thenceforth Beer's energy and ingenuity were put to the test in stretching a book budget that seldom exceeded $500 a year. Careful and persistent soliciting of gifts and exchanges with other libraries accounted for a large proportion of the books acquired. In 1892, the Library became a selected depository for U.S. government publications, and the Smithsonian Institution and the Carnegie Institution of Washington also placed the Library on their mailing lists soon after. Beer secured important publications from foreign governments during trips to Europe in 1895, 1902, 1905, 1911, 1912 and 1913, and to Mexico and Cuba in 1906. Many of the books acquired on these trips were relegated to the basement, awaiting the attention necessary to add them to the active collection. However, the attention never came, and Beer's successor, Robert J. Usher, estimated there were 100,000 volumes on hand in 1928; a sizeable collection still remained for sorting in 1948.

From 1891 to 1911, Beer was the region's foremost representative to professional library organizations. As a member of the American Library Association from 1889, he attended fifteen conferences and presented papers at many of them. He was as well a fellow of the Library Association and served as a member of the National Advisory Board for the Special Libraries Association from its inception. In Louisiana, he established a Travelling Library

Association in 1897 (27 years before the State Library inaugurated extension services) and served as the second president of the Louisiana Library Association. He was also a member of the Bibliographical Society, the Grolier Club, the Bibliophile Society, the Caxton Club, and a founding member of the Bibliographical Society of America. He was equally at home with fellow members of the Société des Américanistes, the American Historical Association, the American Economic Association, the Mississippi Valley Historical Association, and the state historical societies of Louisiana, Mississippi, and Texas.

A glance through his correspondence file shows that Beer came to be a source of information for a great range of scholars and writers. The files include letters from Reuben Gold Thwaites (q.v.) in search of Jesuit materials, Walter L. Fleming investigating the history of Reconstruction, James Franklin Jameson requesting letters of introduction to French and Italian libraries, Charles Evans (q.v.) at work on his *American Bibliography*, Clarence S. Brigham (q.v.) preparing his *Bibliography of American Newspapers*, the American novelist Winston Churchill seeking historical background for *The Crisis*, and Theodore Roosevelt at work on his *Winning the West*.

Beer's own writings, which included 85 items published between 1889 and 1923, are characteristically bibliographical notes and texts of historical documents, reports on library problems to professional library periodicals, and articles and contributions to encyclopedias and books on the history of New Orleans and Louisiana. His *Checklist of American Periodicals*, reprinted from the *Proceedings of the American Antiquarian Society*, his unsigned bibliography of Louisiana French literature in the *Cambridge History of American Literature*, and bibliographies of Charles Gayarré and Grace King were among his more important publications. His greatest satisfaction, however, was in passing information to others. His discovery in France of seven early letters from John J. Audubon to his father, published in Francis H. Herrick's *Audubon, the Naturalist* (New York: D. Appleton and Company, 1917, vol. 1, pp. 154-155) is an example.

Two descriptions of Beer give some indication of his contemporary reputation. First, Anatole Le Braz, the French novelist, wrote after a visit to New Orleans in 1917:

> Là officie l'homme du monde qui, avec le vicomte de Villiers du Terrage, possède le mieux l'histoire de la colonisation française aux bouches du Mississippi. D'ailleurs, sur quoi ou sur qui M. William Beer n'est-il pas renseigné? Ce Celte de la Cornouaille anglaise a mené longtemps une vie toute celtique, c'est-à-dire un peu errante et, en apparence, décousue. Jeune, il a eu soif de l'univers, et il n'y a pas une route du globe, où il

ne se soit hasardé, pas une, non plus, où il n'ait, en dépit du proverbe, ramassé quelque mousse: ses connaissances sont sans limites, comme sa serviabilité. Devenu sédentaire en vicillissant il s'est retiré dans une bibliothèque à son goût, dont il est le volume le plus rare, le plus attachant et, si je ne m'abuse, le plus consulté. [*Revue des Deux Mondes* LI:324 (May 15, 1919)]

Edward Laroque Tinker's recollections for the Bibliographical Society of America describe him affectionately in his later years:

A brush of gray hair shot straight up from his forehead like a cockatoo's comb, and an accentuated hawk-nose overhung a clipped moustache and a neatly pointed gray beard. Bushy eyebrows overshadowed tired eyes, misty-irised with age, and his whole appearance suggested a sleepy bird of prey; but this predatory impression was most misleading, for in reality he was a very kindly but caustic old gentleman who derived the keenest pleasure from presenting to someone a book or pamphlet he or she really desired and had long sought. Indeed, he had in a superlative degree that priceless quality in a good librarian—a passing for placing the right books in just the right hands, where they would become the most effective tools for creative work.

At the time of his death on February 1, 1927, in New Orleans, William Beer was remembered by few librarians, although the editors of historical and bibliographical journals published appreciative obituaries. He outlived many of his contemporaries, seeing a time when the antiquarian and the bookman were held in less esteem. He left no new concepts of librarianship, no great scholarly publications; he neither sought nor attained high office in the professional organizations. Yet if his influence was not national in scope, neither was it merely local. He developed what was then the major reference library of the South Central states and attracted scholars from all parts of the country to make productive use of it. He organized the New Orleans Public Library and established an early experiment in library extension service in Louisiana. In a region where libraries lagged behind those of the East and the Midwest, he represented Southern libraries to the professional, bibliographical, and historical societies of the country with scholarly distinction.

Biographical listings and obituaries—*Dictionary of American Biography* 2; *Who Was Who in America* I (1897-1942). **Books and articles about the biographee**—Kraus, Joe W. "William Beer and the New Orleans Libraries, 1891-1927." *ACRL Monographs*, No. 1 (January 1952). Includes a bibliography of Beer's writings; "Our Frontispiece: William Beer." *Bulletin of Bibliography* XII (May-August 1923). Tinker, Edward Laroque. "William Beer, 1849-1927." Bibliographical Society of America *Papers* XX:77-84 (1926). **Primary sources and archival materials**—Beer's papers are in the Howard-Tilton Memorial Library, Tulane University, New Orleans.   **—JOE W. KRAUS**

BELDEN, CHARLES FRANCIS DORR (1870-1931)

"He realized that as it is the privilege of the people to go to the Library, so it is the duty of the Library to go to the people . . ." stated the resolution of the trustees of the Public Library of the City of Boston upon the death of their director.

Charles F. D. Belden was born in Syracuse, New York, on October 5, 1870, the son of Francis Crapo and Jennie Maude Wright Belden. When he was five, the family moved to Niagara Falls; subsequently, Belden received his high school education at Buffalo. In 1895, he was graduated with an A.B. from Harvard and remained to begin studies at Harvard Law School, where Dean Ames suggested that he initiate work on a catalog of the Law School Library while completing requirements for a law degree. After being graduated in 1898, Belden returned to Niagara Falls, took the bar examination, and was admitted to the bar of the state of New York.

As he was about to begin practice, Harvard offered to make him secretary of the law faculty, a position that Belden accepted and held for three years. In 1902, he was appointed assistant librarian of the Law Library, and in the ensuing seven years, he completed work on the *Catalogue of the Library of the Law School of Harvard University*, published in two volumes in 1909.

Belden headed the Boston Social Law Library in 1908 until, in 1909, he was appointed state librarian of Massachusetts. Charles K. Bolton (q.v.) recalled,

His death takes me back to a morning in 1909 when I first met him at the Social Law Library. The State Library was in need of a director. When I left Mr. Belden I called up Horace G. Wadlin of the Boston Public Library, and suggested Mr. Belden for the State position. Mr. Wadlin came at once to the Athenaeum, we visited Mr. Belden, and then he went to Governor Draper. In less than an hour from my first acquaintance with Mr. Belden he became State Librarian.

In 1909, Belden was also appointed chairman of the Free Public Library Commission of Massachusetts (a position he held until his death), which was instrumental in extending public library services to all sections of the state.

During the eight years that Belden served as state librarian, he was also president of the Massachusetts Library Club (1911-1913) and of the National Association of State Librarians (1911-1912). In addition, he supervised the preparation of *Hand-List of American Statute Law* (1912).

Then, on January 26, 1917, the trustees of the Boston Public Library elected Belden as librarian. During his stewardship, the Boston Public increased its collections by one-third, doubled its circulation, increased the number of branch libraries, and added several important special collections (the Defoe collection, the Lewison bequest of Washingtoniana, and the Sabatier collection of Franciscan literature). Belden, described by one colleague as "informal, friendly, easy to approach," was rewarded for his competent leadership when the trustees changed his title from librarian to director in 1923.

At the 1925 Seattle convention of the American Library Association, Belden was elected president, and during the fiftieth anniversary convention held in Atlantic City in 1926, Belden delivered his presidential address, "Looking Forward." He spoke of the coming need for "specialists in the varied fields of library work and administration." He also stressed the importance of applying research techniques to librarianship, the role of the library as "every man's university," the desirability of cooperative ventures among libraries, and the roles of the products of new technologies (recordings and films) and services (photostat and radio chats) in libraries. Belden's most important literary work, "Libraries: Public and Private (1890-1928)," appeared as a chapter in volume five of Albert Bushnell Hart's *Commonwealth History of Massachusetts.*

Belden's accomplishments were recognized with two honorary degrees (M.A., Harvard, 1926, and Doctor of Letters, Boston University, 1930), honorary memberships in four foreign library associations, and medals from the cities of Ravenna and Rome.

Belden married Anna Marian Blackwell on May 26, 1908, and they had four children. He died on October 24, 1931, and an obituary prepared by Edward H. Redstone concluded, "his friends and admirers throughout the country will remember him as the kindly, sympathetic, and lovable friend, loyal in his friendships and devoted to his principles."

Biographical listings and obituaries–"Charles Francis Belden." *More Books* 6:321-26 (October 1931); *National Cyclopaedia of American Biography* 23; *Who Was Who in America* I (1897-1942). **Books and articles about the biographee**–Bolton, C. K. "Charles F. D. Belden." *Library Journal* 56:1009 (December 1, 1931); Redstone, E. H. "Memorial of Charles F. D. Belden." N.A.S.L. *Proceedings* (1931-32), pp. 22-23.

–ROGER CAIN PALMER

BERTRAM, JAMES (1872-1934)

From 1886 to 1917, Andrew Carnegie (q.v.) donated $41,033,850 to 1,412 communities in the United States for the erection of 1,679 public library buildings. Although almost everyone in librarianship is aware of Carnegie's benefactions, few know of the important role that James Bertram, Carnegie's secretary, played in this library philanthropy.

James Bertram was born in Corstorphine, Scotland (now part of Edinburgh) on March 17, 1872. After graduation from a business school, he worked in a variety of posts with railroads in Scotland and South Africa and as secretary of two mining companies in South Africa. He was forced to return to Scotland for reasons of health and, while convalescing there, was advised by a former teacher to apply for the position of private secretary to Andrew Carnegie (who visited and lived part of each year in Scotland at his Skibo Castle). Bertram received the appointment and remained as private secretary from 1897 to 1914 and as secretary of the Carnegie Corporation (founded by Carnegie in 1911 to carry on his philanthropy) from 1911 until his death in New York City on October 23, 1934.

As Carnegie's private secretary, James Bertram was the real power behind the library benefactions. Carnegie provided the funds and set up the general guidelines; Bertram put them into action. Except for the early gifts up to 1896 (fourteen buildings to six communities), Carnegie was not personally involved in the day-to-day details and decisions regarding building grants. These were the responsibility of James Bertram, and he handled them with careful scrutiny, dispatch, and loyalty to his superior.

The procedure for obtaining a Carnegie public library building grant was fairly simple. The mayor and council of a community in need of a library structure had to promise to provide a site and pledge to support the new library through local taxation in an annual amount that would be at least 10 percent of the sum given for the library building (which was usually based on about $2.00 per capita of local population).

It was James Bertram who answered all letters of inquiry, who examined all applications and statements of promise for building sites and support, and who then followed through on each grant (often for a period of many years) until the building was finished and dedicated. One must examine the actual files to appreciate the magnitude of this task. Some 40 reels of microfilm at the Carnegie Corporation offices in New York City contain approximately 50,000 pieces of correspondence and documents, an average of 30 items for each of the 1,412 communities receiving and 225 communities requesting but not receiving building grants. Both Carnegie and Bertram firmly believed in simplified spelling, and all of Bertram's correspondence was written in this form.

Bertram has been well characterized by various contemporaries. Frederick P. Keppel (q.v.), a former trustee and president of the Carnegie Corporation, paid tribute to his integrity, picturesque personality, and dauntless courage. Durand Miller, who once worked for Bertram, recalls him as being thrifty, very religious (a staunch Presbyterian), inclined to be irritable, rather brusque in manner, and short and direct in speech. To Robert M. Lester (q.v.) another contemporary Carnegie Corporation employee, Bertram was a devoted, meticulous Scot who made a religion out of the Carnegie spirit of giving. Frank P. Hill (q.v.), in the only biographical source we have about James Bertram, described him as methodical and sure of his ground. Brevity was a strong trait. He never used a paragraph when a sentence would do, and a word often took the place of a sentence.

These personal qualities were frequently reflected in the Carnegie library correspondence. Bertram's letters were extremely businesslike and at times abrupt and even rude. He often lacked tact and assumed that communicants had done their homework, understood the mechanics of obtaining Carnegie library funds, and would find his short, terse notes to be self-explanatory and clear. Judging from their replies, most applicants accepted Bertram's vagueness and impatience with tactful grace by writing polite letters of inquiry or by quietly acceding to a curt order. Almost all contacts Bertram had with the library world were through correspondence. Although he never attended a library conference, one observer attributed his aloofness to a desire to maintain a strictly impersonal and disinterested attitude toward each and every applicant.

James Bertram's position was difficult because he had to decide on the disposition of a vast sum of money and see that it was properly expended, since every dollar had to be well spent. He judged proposals strictly on their merit. Personal relations or considerations never influenced his judgment. No worthy applicant was to be rejected, and yet, no unworthy one was to be accepted. As a result, some felt that Bertram was inconsiderate, austere, legalistic, and overly critical, but those who knew him well characterized the man as sympathetic, sincere, kindly, logical, practical, fair-minded, and socially affable. He was a hard-working secretary who did his job to the best of his ability, and there is no indication that Carnegie ever disapproved of his secretary. On the contrary, he rewarded Bertram with a life trusteeship at $5,000 per year in the Carnegie Corporation and provided him with a $10,000 annuity in his will.

James Bertram not only played an important role as the executor of Carnegie public library building philanthropy, but he was also one of the earliest—if not the earliest—codifiers of standards for public library architecture in the United States. By 1907, Bertram had become aware that most of the buildings being built with Carnegie funds were poorly designed and inadequate, and that his guidance and control were needed. There was little knowledge of what was good library architecture, so Bertram began to request that plans be submitted to him for approval. In 1911, after consultation with the library and architectural experts of the time, he compiled and had printed *Notes on Library Building*, which was then sent to each community obtaining a grant as a guide for its building. This leaflet decried architectural elaboration and offered basic principles and

outline sketches, all of which led to a more open, flexible, and less expensive structure. But it still left every community with a great deal of freedom to plan its own library interior as it liked, within these few reasonable bounds, and to design the exterior as it pleased, as long as it kept away from expensive columns, portals, stairways, and domes. This was the beginning of modern library architecture, and many of the principles are still in effect.

James Bertram did his work efficiently but quietly—so quietly, in fact, that he has never received the recognition he deserves in American library history as an important force in the development of public libraries and public library architecture in the United States.

Biographical listings and obituaries—*Who Was Who in America* I (1897-1942). Books and articles about the biographee—Bobinski, George S. *Carnegie Libraries: Their History and Impact on American Public Library Development.* Chicago: American Library Association, 1969; Hill, Frank P. *James Bertram: An Appreciation.* New York: Carnegie Corporation, 1936; Lester, Robert M. *Forty Years of Carnegie Giving.* New York: Scribner's, 1941. Primary sources and archival materials—For correspondence to Bertram and by him, see the Carnegie Library Correspondence (forty microfilm reels) at the Carnegie Corporation offices in New York City.

—GEORGE S. BOBINSKI

BILLINGS, JOHN SHAW (1838-1913)

John Shaw Billings was called by his biographer, Fielding Garrison, "perhaps the most versatile American physician of his time" (in *Biographical Memoirs*); he was also probably the most versatile librarian that the United States has produced and certainly one who achieved the most eminence in the scientific community. His scientific interests and accomplishments ranged widely—vital and medical statistics, public and military health, sanitary engineering, medical education, hospital construction, medical history, the organization of scientific societies and scientific research. In creating the monuments for which he is best known among librarians—the Surgeon-General's Library (later the National Library of Medicine), its *Index-Catalogue* and the *Index Medicus*, and the New York Public Library—Billings contributed to almost every aspect of modern librarianship. He was an outstanding member of the generation of librarians that founded the library profession in the United States and one of the great bibliographers and librarians of all time.

The third child and only son of James and Abby Shaw Billings, both descendants of English settlers, John Shaw Billings was born in Cotton Township, Switzerland County, Indiana, on April 12, 1838. Of his parents' five children, only he and his younger sister Emma survived. The family moved to New York State briefly, then to a farm on Narragansett Bay, Rhode Island, and, when John Shaw Billings was about ten years old, back to Indiana, where his father ran a country store in Allensville; later they seem to have lived in nearby Oxford, Ohio. An incessant reader and assiduous student, Billings gave up his share of the family property to his sister so that he could go to Miami University in Oxford, from which he graduated in 1857 with the second honor in his class. The next year, he worked in order to earn enough money to enroll in the autumn of 1858 in the Medical College of Ohio in Cincinnati, where, laboring in the dissecting rooms and clinics of local hospitals. he eked out a very bare living until his graduation in 1860 with an M.D. degree.

In order to graduate, he had to write a dissertation, a "melancholy duty" that, he recalled, educated him to the difficulty of penetrating the medical literature. His frustrating hunt for material convinced him of several things: that far too much time and labor had to be expended in searching through numerous poorly indexed books for items on a subject (in this case the surgical treatment of epilepsy); that there existed over one hundred thousand volumes of medical books and journals but no library in the United States where most of them could be found; and that in order to make reasonably sure of having seen all of the relevant literature on a subject, one had to go to the great capital cities of Europe. In the *Cincinnati Lancet-Clinic* [n.s. XX (1888), 297], Billings said,

> It was this experience which led me when a favorable opportunity offered at the close of the war, to try to establish, for the use of American physicians, a fairly complete medical library, and in connection with this to prepare a comprehensive catalog and index which should spare medical teachers and writers the drudgery of consulting ten thousand or more different indexes, or of turning over the leaves of as many volumes to find the dozen or so references of which they might be in search.

Billings was referring to the Civil War, whose outbreak in 1861 cut short his plans for a civilian medical career. Until he received his commission in the United States Army Medical Corps, in the examination for which he did brilliantly, he served as a contract surgeon for the Army in Washington. There he met and married (on September 3, 1862) Katherine Mary Stevens, daughter of a former United States Congressman, Hestor Lockhart Stevens. By then his commission had come through (on April 16, 1862) and he had accepted an appointment as first lieutenant and assistant surgeon on July 16, 1862. In the Army, he quickly showed surgical skill and originality, organizational and executive ability, and courageous devotion to duty, in recognition of which he was given responsible positions and brevetted captain, major, and lieutenant-colonel. First he

administered field hospitals and performed battle surgery; in August 1863, he was ordered to New York City. After commanding several Army hospitals, he was sent on February 1, 1864, to lead an expedition to Ile à Vache, near Haiti, to rescue freed salves stranded there in consequence of an ill-considered scheme of colonization. On March 29, 1864, Billings again joined the field, as acting medical inspector of the Army of the Potomac; four months later, he returned to Washington on sick leave, after which he was assigned to the medical director of the Army of the Potomac to work on the field reports that were eventually embodied in the *Medical and Surgical History of the War of the Rebellion.* The following December 27, he was transferred to the Surgeon-General's Office, to remain for 31 years as lieutenant-colonel and deputy surgeon-general, until his retirement from the Army on October 1, 1895.

Initially he was concerned with demobilizing Army hospitals and medical personnel, and it was not until the fall of 1865 that the small library of the Surgeon-General's Office came informally under his charge as one of his miscellaneous duties. Official assignment to supervise the library, along with the museum, came much later, on December 28, 1883. In his work at the library, the combination of his scientific interests, bookish inclinations, and concern for the communication of medical knowledge resulted in what William Welch, at the 1913 memorial meeting for him at the New York Public Library, called "probably the most original and distinctive contribution of America to the medicine of the world."

With the ultimate aim of advancing medicine in general and American medicine in particular, Billings wanted to encompass in the library "the entire field of medical and surgical literature" and to form "an excellent foundation for a national medical library that shall be worthy of the name, and put the writers and teachers of this country on an equality with those of Europe so far as accessibility to the literature of the subject is concerned." (See his article "Medical Libraries in the United States" in Part I of the 1876 U.S. Bureau of Education publication, *Public Libraries in the United States of America.*) From a mere 1,800 volumes in 1865, he increased the collection to 40,000 books and 40,000 pamphlets in 1876; by 1878, every important current medical journal was being received, and the library contained more than 75 percent of such journals ever published. By 1895, steady acquisition, including strong gift and exchange activities, had brought the collection to 308,445 pieces, the largest medical library in the Western Hemisphere and one of the half dozen largest in the world.

Though this was a considerable achievement, Billings's uniquely creative work went beyond a mere accumulation of resources to the actual provision of bibliographical access. Up to his time, medical bibliographies had been the product of individual effort and were without provision for keeping abreast of current publications. As a type, they could not cover the exponentially growing, varied literature, including many new journals, spawned by the new scientifically and clinically oriented medicine and required by practitioners who could no longer depend on a few texts and their own experience. Billings conceived a scheme of access modern in both content and execution: a system of retrospective and current bibliographical control accomplished on a corporate basis.

The first element in his system was the *Index-Catalogue* of the Surgeon-General's Library, presented in preliminary form in a *Specimen Fasciculus* in 1876 and then published in its first series in sixteen volumes over sixteen years, from 1880 to 1895. A single-alphabet list of authors, subjects, and titles of the monographic and serial collections of the Surgeon-General's Library, including entries for parts of larger works, the *Index-Catalogue* was the work of Billings and his principal assistant, Dr. Robert Fletcher, with Billings himself indexing journals; much of the routine labor was done by the library staff, mainly uneducated soldiers trained by him and Fletcher. Though it was intended to display the contents of only one library—and that not completely—rather than the entire medical literature, the excellence of the collection Billings had amassed (together with the expert choice of materials listed), the overall accuracy of the entries, the convenience of the dictionary arrangement, and the inclusion of analytics, made the *Index-Catalogue* an unprecedented comprehensive index to the world's medical literature. "No undertaking in bibliography of the same magnitude dealing with a special subject had ever been issued, and its extraordinary value," Sir William Osler said at the memorial meeting after Billings's death, "was at once appreciated all over the world."

As a companion to the *Index-Catalogue*, Billings and Fletcher edited, on a private basis, beginning in 1879 and continuing until 1898 (with Fletcher carrying on alone from 1895), the *Index Medicus*, a monthly classified index to the contents of current medical publications, with annual author and subject indexes. Successive series of the *Index-Catalogue* and the *Index Medicus* provided, until the advent of new bibliographies, complementary retrospective and current access to the Surgeon-General's Library's holdings and thus to much of the existing medical literature. A final part of Billings's system was a liberal loan policy to make the material itself available to physicians all over the country. Books would be lent to individual physicians either indirectly through request from a library or directly through a system of monetary deposits. Another service by Billings and Fletcher was the supplying of information to inquirers, in person and by mail; the volume of such replies reached as much as two thousand a year. Within the Surgeon-General's Library, however, for all of Billings's concern with bibliography and systemization, he and Fletcher, relying on their prodigious memories, failed to institute schemes for internal control and efficient storage and retrieval of library materials. For example, the classification system for books was idiosyncratic, there were no call numbers, and books were not listed in a permanent, well-maintained, complete card catalog.

The systems that they did work out formed a foundation for the mid-twentieth century leadership and innovation by the Library (as of 1956, officially the National Library of Medicine that Billings had envisioned years before) in both medical bibliography and the dissemination of materials through the use of modern technology, most notably the computer and reprographic devices. Billings himself, moreover, contributed to the development of the computer. An accomplished statistician, he was consultant and editor for vital statistics for the United States Census from 1880 through 1910. While working on the 1880 census, he suggested to Herman Hollerith, a young assistant, that he devise a machine to tabulate population data that had been punched on cards. Hollerith's resultant machine, used in the 1890 census, was eventually (and with Billings's encouragement) the basis for the company that later became International Business Machines and made the Hollerith card ubiquitous.

During his years in Washington, Billings was involved in many other projects whose importance brought him to national and international prominence. He reorganized the Marine Hospital Service, wrote influential reports on Army hospitals and hygiene and, in 1893, became professor of military hygiene in the new Army Medical School at Washington. An acknowledged authority in the newly established field of public health, he was vice-president from 1879 to 1882 of the short-lived National Board of Health and founder of the American Public Health Association. Though he planned the interior of the new Surgeon-General's Library and Museum, opened in 1887, he was much more deeply occupied from 1875 to 1889 with the design of the new Johns Hopkins Hospital, a utilitarian structure bearing the stamp of his practicality and of his influential ideas on hospital construction, ventilation, hygiene, and medical education. As medical advisor to the hospital's trustees, he wrote a series of classic reports and was also closely concerned with the development of the new Johns Hopkins Medical School. His advice and services were greatly in demand; he also wrote numerous papers, gave speeches and lectures in the

United States and abroad, and participated in the activities of scholarly and scientific groups. Though not alienated from library circles, he does not seem to have been deeply engaged with them before 1896.

In 1895, through the influence of his friend, the neurologist and novelist S. Weir Mitchell, had come an offer that drew Billings from the Army to the offices of chief of the University Hospital, professor of hygiene, and director of a new Laboratory of Hygiene at the University of Pennsylvania in Philadelphia. Almost immediately he had another call, again on Mitchell's recommendation, to start a new career, at the age of 58, as chief of the new New York Public Library, an institution of much greater scope, both actual and potential, than the Surgeon-General's Library.

The New York Public Library was the product of the consolidation in May 1895 of the Tilden Trust and two privately endowed reference libraries, the once-great Astor Library and the Lenox Library, a conglomeration of special collections. At that time New York City (until 1898 comprising only Manhattan, the Bronx, and Richmond, and afterwards Brooklyn and Queens as well) had special and academic libraries but no general library, popular or research, commensurate with its size, wealth, and culture. The Astor's still large and useful collection was inadequately cataloged, indifferently managed, and badly crowded, and both it and the Lenox desperately needed, besides the funds that the merger brought, an infusion of energy, competence, and foresight and a reversal of their reputation for being snobbish and inconsiderate of the public. As for circulating libraries, a scattered group of independent local libraries offered varied services; they were dependent for operating expenses on usually inadequate appropriations from the municipal government.

The men who engineered the consolidation of the Astor-Lenox-Tilden foundations wanted to develop the finest research library in America, the equal of the British Museum or the Bibliothèque Nationale, a goal that required for its achievement a leader of rare quality, a latter-day Panizzi. They found him in John Shaw Billings. He, in turn, could not refuse the challenge. On January 15, 1896, the trustees of the New York Public Library appointed Billings superintendent in chief, a title changed to director three months later. He came to New York half-time until June, with a leave during the summer to attend the international conference on indexing scientific literature in London, where as an American delegate he contributed to the creation of the *International Catalogue of Scientific Literature*. (The work in America on the *Catalogue* was primarily the result of the efforts of Billings and Cyrus Adler [q.v.] of the Smithsonian Institution.) In September, Billings began full-time work in New York at a salary said to

be the highest ever paid to the head of an American library. The appointment elicited widespread approval and at once gave stature to the New York Public Library.

Billings's standing in scientific and professional circles, as well as his excellent character and his concurrence in the trustees' ambitions for the Library, allowed him to establish with them the kind of close, harmonious, and mutually respectful relations unusual at that time. This group of wealthy, sophisticated lawyers and businessmen highly esteemed and rarely contradicted his advice and opinions, however difficult he became as he grew older. In matters of policy and planning, as well as internal library administration, Billings was the major force, though acting with the trustees' knowledge and consent. This relationship presaged the modern ideal of a library board as primarily a policymaking body working with a strong librarian who was trusted to run the library with little or no interference.

Billings rapidly set to work to forge the Astor and Lenox Libraries into a first-rate, unified, research library useful to the scholars, scientists, writers, and other seekers of information and knowledge in the New York metropolitan area. This meant giving attention to administrative reorganization, rearrangement of space, implementation of new rules and services for readers, strengthening the staff, and expansion of cataloging and acquisition programs—a range of concerns wider than he had had at the Surgeon-General's Library.

The great card catalog was begun, including entries for periodical articles that Billings himself would select from piles of journals he would take home each night. Because of the press of arrears and new accessions, he could not apply the same standards of completeness and accuracy as he had for the *Index-Catalogue*, and the creation of a shelflist was postponed, the only serious omission in his administration that his protégé and biographer Harry M. Lydenberg (q.v.), could find. Another expression of Billings's practical approach was the unique classification system he devised, based on the nature of the collections, the needs of readers, and the arrangement of a new central building, where most of the materials would stand in stacks closed to the public. He also launched the monthly *Bulletin of The New York Public Library* in January 1897, a useful vehicle for bibliographical enterprises when the bibliographical tools that would be commonplace half a century later were still undeveloped or nonexistent.

Billings also carried his interest in collection building to New York. Already famous as a bibliographer and all his life an omnivorous reader, he knew books of all kinds and was well acquainted with the book trade. No matter what else he was involved in, he would scan booklists and catalogs, select materials, inspect new accessions, arrange exchange agreements, and, as he did for the Surgeon-General's Library, beg gifts from anyone he could. Continuing the original Astor Library policy, he aimed at a well-rounded, useful collection of materials for study in most fields, especially modern publications, though he did leave extensive collection in certain special subjects to other local libraries. Alert to the growth of the new social sciences and science and technology, he developed the serial and documents holdings in those fields into outstandingly strong collections; in 1897, he set up the first formal documents unit in a large American public library. In establishing the unique Jewish Division and the Slavonic Division, both of which became outstanding intellectual resources, Billings responded to the interests of the large East European Jewish population of New York City. Under his administration came the first public print room in New York and the first in any public library (the Library of Congress excepted) in the United States. Together with an interest in ephemera and hospitality to materials on all sorts of subjects (and despite certain lacunae), these activities laid the basis for the catholic acquisition policy that distinguished the research collections of the New York Public Library through the years.

The accomplishment in New York by which Billings is perhaps best known, and which overshadowed his other equally important work there, was the central building, opened in 1911. This massive marble pile, its neo-French Renaissance exterior designated a landmark by the New York City Landmarks Preservation Commission in 1967, and its lavishly embellished interior in 1974, was the masterpiece of architects John M. Carrère and Thomas Hastings. As a library, however, it was very much the creation of Billings, the utilitarian planner. Carrère and Hastings won the commission because they submitted a design that would best meet the functional, practical specifications written by Billings and at the same time be an impressive public monument and symbol of municipal largesse. Billings first sketched and then elaborated the interior layout, based on his conception of the library as serving three categories of readers—the popular, the serious, and the specialist. He circulated his ideas (including the innovation, for American libraries, of the main reading room placed on the top floor, at the rear and above the stacks) to prominent librarians and other persons for comment. The response was on the whole positive, with librarians especially delighted by his functional approach and by the then unusual circumstance of a librarian being given a key role in architectural planning.

Billings's involvement with the central building continued through all phases of planning, construction, outfitting, moving, and opening. Indeed, much

of his work prior to 1911 was directed toward that day when finally the collections and staff would move to what seemed to be a commodious new building. But use increased much more quickly and demands made upon the building became more complex than Billings had envisaged, so that only a few years later readers, staff, and collections became cramped for space.

By that time, the New York Public Library had evolved into two gigantic, virtually autonomous units, the research library (then the Reference Department) and the branch system (then the Circulation Department), a peculiarity that Billings had a hand in creating. For various reasons, New York City never had had (until 1970) a large central, popular circulating collection of books and other materials. At the turn of the century, the requirement seemed to be, instead, a unified system of branches to cater to local communities' needs for educational and recreational materials. Billings saw early that this would mean the eventual merger of all the independent circulating libraries and the construction of a network of branch buildings, their operations to be supported by city funds. He realized, too, that for practical and political reasons, the New York Public Library would have to be involved. It is a measure of his devotion to duty that, beginning in late 1899, with the new central building under way and the research library reorganized, and when various pressures had built up for decisions to be made about the circulating libraries, Billings threw himself into the problem, one in which he had had little interest and no experience. All of his life, he had been immersed in scholarly, scientific, and medical matters, and had, besides, a rather cool, unsentimental view of the masses and of the moral and social good accomplished by free access to books. At the same time, he did believe in popular libraries as an educational force important to a democratic society, and he thought that a research reference library would not be incompatible with a popular lending one and that both could be managed by the same board of trustees and director.

After the consolidation of the New York Free Circulating Library into the New York Public Library in 1901 and the consequent establishment of its Circulation Department, Billings persuaded the steel magnate Andrew Carnegie (q.v.), then retiring from business and searching for a field for large-scale philanthropy, to give $5,200,000 to construct branch libraries in New York City, with the provision that the city would maintain them at not less than 10 percent of his gift. This was Carnegie's most spectacular benefaction up to then and the beginning of his wholesale library giving. The result for the New York Public Library was that most of the independent libraries in Manhattan, the Bronx, and Richmond came into its Circulation Department, and Carnegie's money enabled the erection of forty branches in the three boroughs under its aegis; further, the municipal government committed itself for the first time to the support of a popular library system in perpetuity. Billings then left the operation of this system to its chiefs, though retaining responsibility for it and keeping himself informed about it. Interested in and knowledgeable about children's literature, he was especially proud of the efforts of Anne Carroll Moore (q.v.), head of children's services, to build a distinguished central collection and community-oriented programs in the branches. The children's work, together with work with schools, the blind, the foreign-born, and community organizations and the provision of "travelling" book collections for hundreds of institutions and individuals all over the city, as well as the ordinary circulation of books in the branches, made the New York Public Library one of the best, as well as the largest, popular library systems in the world.

The administrative organization of the New York Public Library, with two massive library systems under his control, reflected Billings's pragmatism (as well as the peculiar historical conditions of their founding) in being rather idiosyncratic and without distinct lines of demarcation and authority. He kept a good deal of the management in his own office; his administrative style was strong, individualistic, and demanding, yet it gave scope for staff members' own individuality. Especially in the early days when the library was small and needed to overcome a legacy of administrative weakness, he concerned himself with many details. Though staff development was not Billings's strongest contribution, he did give attention to personnel matters; indeed he had to, as from the time he arrived in 1896 to his death in 1913, the staff grew from 42 to almost a thousand. He started an apprentice program (progenitor of the Library School, opened in 1911), formulated consistent personnel policies, and tried to attend to employees' welfare as best he could at a time when there were no pensions or other social security programs. In certain cases, his judgment of people was such as to make enduring contributions to the New York Public Library and to librarianship in general. For example, he singled out, among others, the young Harry Lydenberg, to whom he would pass on the heritage of great book collector and who eventually would himself be director. In 1908, Billings surrendered some of his administrative duties to an assistant director, Edwin Hatfield Anderson (q.v.), who would be his successor.

At the New York Public Library, the venture of his late years, Billings, with the help of trustees and staff, organized and supervised a comprehensive, mammoth system of reference and circulating libraries—collections, services, buildings—that in overall structure, organization, and policies retained for years afterwards the strong impress of his ideas. To the extent that the New York Public Library played a leadership role among American libraries and developed as a national and international cultural resource of first rank, his work had an even wider impact.

At the same time, Billings had kept up his interests and activities in scientific, scholarly, and professional affairs. From 1893 to 1903, he served on the Committee of Fifty studying the physiological aspects of alcoholism; he planned the Peter Bent Brigham Hospital in Boston and acted as consultant from 1905 to 1908; he helped to organize the Carnegie Institution of Washington and from 1903 to his death, was chairman of the board. Elected president of the American Library Association in 1902, he announced in his presidential address Andrew Carnegie's gift, proffered at his (Billings's) advice, of $100,000 to endow the Association's Publication Board. He also secured the revival of *Index Medicus* (from 1903), with Fletcher as editor-in-chief.

During his very last years, Billings retired somewhat from public view and became on his own admission old, cranky, and sometimes unreasonably intractable. He had suffered for years from serious, painful illnesses (cancer of the lip and renal and biliary calculi), and the death of his wife in 1912 was a keen blow. In March 1913, he underwent a fourth major operation, from which he did not recover. He died of pneumonia on March 11, a month before his seventy-fifth birthday. Funeral services were held in the Georgetown church were he had been married 51 years before, and he was buried with military honors at Arlington; both the New York Public Library and the Johns Hopkins Hospital held memorial meetings, and there were numerous notices of his death. Five children survived him: Mary Clare, twins Kate Sherman and Jessie Ingram, John Sedgwick, and Margaret Janeway. Another child had died in infancy.

During his life, Billings received much recognition. He and Weir Mitchell were said to have been the two best-known American physicians abroad, and he was awarded honorary degrees from the world's greatest universities, including Oxford, Edinburgh, and Dublin. Besides his chairmanship of the Carnegie Institution and the presidency of the American Library Association, he served as president of the Philosophical Society of Washington, the American Public Health Association, the Congress of American Physicians and Surgeons, and the New York Library Club, and as vice-president of the American Statistical Association and treasurer of the National Academy of Sciences. The Royal College of Physicians of Ireland and the Royal College of Surgeons of Ireland elected him an honorary fellow, and he held memberships in some forty other scientific societies. His retirement from the Army was marked by a banquet in Philadelphia, where it was announced that his portrait was to be hung in the Surgeon-General's Library; he was also given $10,000 contributed by physicians in the United States and Great Britain in acknowledgement of his services to medical scholarship. The trustees of the New York Public Library presented him with several expressions of their regard: an unofficial gift of $20,000 from a few of them, a pension fund, and an oil portrait of him to hang in the new central building. His friend Mrs. Anna Palmer Draper, a benefactor of American science who died in 1914, bequeathed to the New York Public Library $200,000 for a "John S. Billings Memorial Fund" for the purchase of books for the research collections.

The many tributes to Billings dwell almost as much upon his character and qualities of mind as on his achievements. Vigorous, self-confident, commanding, yet courteous, modest, calm, and reserved, with a tall, powerful build, keen blue eyes, drooping mustache, and deep voice, Billings was a dominating, impressive figure. He was considered a paragon of sobriety, integrity, sincerity, reliability, loyalty, fairness. His broad knowledge, strong character, clear mind, good sense, and phenomenal capacity for work inspired admiration and emulation. Details of method concerned him less than results and essentials, which he could acutely sense, a trait upon which much of his many-sided success depended but which was coupled with impatience with ineptitude and incompetence. His was a decisive and forceful rather than a conciliatory nature. Strong-tempered and strong-willed, he did not like to be contradicted or have his decisions questioned. Yet despite his somewhat remote, cool manner and tendency to imperiousness, he had the capacity for warm friendship and the charm and wit to bind people to him with ties of affection, respect, and even worship. And until his late years, he remained open to new ideas and realistic about a changing world. He was not without contradictions: an advocate of individualism, he spent 33 years in the Army and worked all his life for organizations concerned with public services; dispassionate toward the lower classes, he labored to provide educational and health services for them, if only for the benefit to the rest of the society that their well-being generated; sharing somewhat the ethnic prejudices of his class and time, he was able to work with all kinds of people and to build wide-ranging library collections for their use.

Biographical listings and obituaries—Concise sources of information about Billings are: the biographical articles in the second volume of *Dictionary of American Biography*, by Walter F. Willcox (who notes an important article by Billings not listed in the revised Hasse bibliography), and in the *Encyclopedia of Library and Information Science*, by Frank Bradway Rogers; obituaries in the *Bulletin of The New York Public Library* (17 [April 1913], 307-312), and *Library*

Journal (38 [April 1913], 212-213); and the entry in *Who Was Who in America*, Vol. I, 1897-1942, which, however, has an incorrect birth date. **Books and articles about the biographee**—Billings's major short writings are brought together in *Selected Papers of John Shaw Billings, Combined with a Life of Billings*, by Frank Bradway Rogers (n.p.: Medical Library Association, 1965). This collection also includes a short biography, a comprehensive bibliography of works about him, and a revised version of Adelaide Hasse's "Bibliography of the Writings of John Shaw Billings," which was first published in the standard biography by Fielding H. Garrison, *John Shaw Billings, a Memoir* (New York: G. P. Putnam's Sons, 1915). Garrison's book includes generous excerpts from Billings's journals, letters, and speeches, a genealogy of the Billings family compiled by Billings's wife, a copy of his official military record, and three portraits of him at different ages. A second, shorter biography is Harry M. Lydenberg's *John Shaw Billings, Creator of the National Medical Library and Its Catalogue, First Director of The New York Public Library* (American Library Pioneers, I; Chicago: American Library Association, 1924). Lydenberg's *History of The New York Public Library, Astor, Lenox and Tilden Foundations* (New York: The New York Public Library, 1923) has information on Billings, as does Phyllis Dain's later analysis, *The New York Public Library: A History of Its Founding and Early Years* ([New York]: The New York Public Library, Astor, Lenox and Tilden Foundations, 1972), whose extensive notes and bibliography supplement the materials listed in Rogers' compilation. Dorothy M. Schullian and Frank B. Rogers, "The National Library of Medicine," *Library Quarterly* (28 [Jan., April 1958], 1-17, 95-121), provides background for Billings's work at that institution. Among many short pieces on Billings are S. Weir Mitchell, "Biographical Memoir of John Shaw Billings, 1838-1913," and Fielding H. Garrison, "The Scientific Work of John Shaw Billings," published together as National Academy of Sciences, *Biographical Memoirs* 8 (August 1917), 373-416. The proceedings of the memorial meeting at The New York Public Library (The New York Public Library, *Memorial Meeting in Honor of the Late Dr. John Shaw Billings, April 25, 1914* [New York: 1913]) contain appreciations of him by prominent men and women who knew him well. John F. Fulton in *The Great Medical Bibliographers: A Study in Humanism* (Philadelphia: University of Pennsylvania Press, 1951) and Estelle Brodman in *The Development of Medical Bibliography* (Medical Library Association, Publication, No. 1; n.p.: Medical Library Association, 1954) evaluate Billings's place in the history of medical bibliography. **Primary sources and archival materials**—The major corpus of John Shaw Billings's personal papers is in the Manuscript Division of The New York Public Library; this includes personal and professional correspondence, various writings, lecture notes, and other materials. Correspondence with Billings's grandson, John Shaw Billings, failed to yield information about any other extant collection. There is much Billings material in the archives of The New York Public Library and in the minutes of the library board and its committees. The National Library of Medicine has considerable Billings manuscript materials, mostly official library correspondence but also some personal letters. The National Archives contain papers pertaining to Billings's service with the United States Government, and there are some papers in the Library of Congress, the University of Pennsylvania Library, the Johns Hopkins University Library, and the University of Rochester Library. The New York Public Library's annual *Reports*, as well as the contents of its *Bulletin*, also indicate Billings's activities there.

—PHYLLIS DAIN

BISCOE, WALTER STANLEY (1853-1933)

Walter Stanley Biscoe, "colej clasmate, associate and frend" of Melvil Dewey (q.v.), was born on February 14, 1853, one of four sons of the Reverend Mr. Thomas Curtis and Ellen Elmore Lord Biscoe. Educated in Worcester, Massachusetts, public schools, Biscoe was graduated Phi Beta Kappa from Amherst (B.A., 1874). He had also been awarded the Strong Prize (in Greek) and the Walker Prize (twice, for mathematics, beating out Dewey both times). Biscoe then tutored at Amherst for a year and later became librarian of the Taunton, Massachusetts, Public Library (1875-1876). Returning to Amherst as both Walker instructor in mathematics (1876-1878) and assistant librarian (1876-1879, succeeding Dewey), he received his M.A. there (1877).

Also upon his return, Biscoe began a professional association with Melvil Dewey that would last until the latter's death in 1931. The first edition of the *Decimal Clasification and Relativ Index* appeared in 1876. In the thirteenth edition (1932), Dewey's comments about Biscoe (originally in the second edition [1885]) still stand, clear evidence of his continuing debt to this reserved, meticulous, self-effacing man: Biscoe's was throughout "the most extended and valued assistance."

Dewey departed for Boston in 1876. Biscoe, still at Amherst, became acting librarian in 1879, but he responded to Dewey's call to Columbia College (later University) in 1883, at first to help reclassify the College's Library and later to help establish the new School of Library Economy (1887). Hired as catalog librarian, Biscoe also helped with the second and third (1888) editions of the *Decimal Clasification* (DDC) and taught in the School as well (1887-1889). Upon Dewey's forced resignation from Columbia and subsequent move to the New York State Library at Albany, Biscoe followed. Officially catalog librarian (1889-1895) and then senior librarian (1896-1929), he also taught in the then New York State Library School (1889-1926). His chief claim to a place in library history, however, remains his DDC work, which he did in Albany after Dewey had removed to Lake Placid (1906). Biscoe retired in 1929.

Dewey, involved in many other projects, sought trusted subordinates to whom he could delegate authority for new DDC editions. He found them in May Seymour (q.v.) and Dorkas Fellows (q.v.), editors successively of Editions 4 to 13; but Biscoe was responsible for theoretical projections of DDC structure as well as for the more immediate problems of locating new subjects in each new expansion. Both Seymour and Fellows consulted him regularly, but Fellows soon recognized the truth in what Dewey had written to her (July 27, 1921): "Of cours yu wil hav to hav a lot of patience to worry the help yu need out of Biscoe. . . ." She visited Biscoe personally to force pronouncements from him rather than wait for written replies that might never arrive. His slowness, however, was probably the result of the combination of his duties at the State Library and his chronic concern for tidying up even the smallest details as much as it was a personal trait. Dewey recognized this problem but also left him fairly much on his own with the DDC, a mark of both his respect for the man's talents and his well-founded belief that Biscoe would remain faithful to Dewey and his ideas.

Rather than a static memorial, Biscoe saw the DDC as a dynamic, flexible tool designed (and changed) to serve "all kinds of people for all kinds of purposes." Rejecting the notion that classification schemes should be organized from a particular, restricted viewpoint, he wrote (*Library Journal* 23:611 [November 1898]):

We all agree (and Mr. Dewey perhaps most of all) that the Decimal classification is not perfect; but we must look for something less one-sided, something more in sympathy with varying needs and thought ... before change is made. I am inclined to think that far too much stress is laid on the logical grouping. There is too much of a feeling that the classification must represent the present condition of the world's belief as to the inter-relations of the various subjects. I prefer to regard it as a vast series of pigeon-holes in which subjects are placed and to which the alphabetic index is the guide.

Biscoe's special contribution to the DDC was the "Biscoe Time Table," his plan for sub-arranging books under classes by publication/copyright date over the period 1000 B.C. to 2000 A.D. (see his "Chronological Arrangement of Books on Shelves," *Library Journal* 10:246-47 [1885] and Dewey's explanation in DDC, 11th edition, pp. 30, 984-85). This was one of four possible arrangement schemes under class numbers, but Dewey felt it to be especially valuable in "syence and useful arts," where study of the "historic development of subject" might prove illuminating.

Active in the New York Library Association, Biscoe was vice-president of the group twice (1893-1894, 1901-1902). He belonged as well to the American Library Association and the Bibliographical Society of America. His few non-DDC writings include the reminiscence "As It Was in the Beginning" (*Public Libraries* 30:72-80 [1925]).

Biscoe never married, but when the Deweys were in Albany, he lived with his sister across the street from them. After his retirement, he worked on a biographical project (*10,000 Eminent Americans* [or *100,000*; both titles are reported]); however, all of his files, notes, and manuscripts were incinerated when his apartment building burned. Walter Stanley Biscoe died, some days later, on December 22, 1933.

Biographical listings and obituaries—*Biographical Record of the Alumni and Non-Graduates of Amherst College*

(Classes '72-'96), 1871-1896. Compiled and edited by William L. Montagne. Amherst: Carpenter and Morehouse, Princeton, 1901, Vol. II, p. 37; *Biographical Record of the Graduates and Non-Graduates, Centennial edition 1821-1921.* Edited by Robert S. Fletcher and Malcolm O. Young. Amherst: The College, 1927, p. 335. **Books and articles about the biographee**—Comaromi, J. P. *The Eighteen Editions of the Dewey Decimal Classification.* Albany, N.Y.: Forest Press, 1976; Dawe, G. *Melvil Dewey: Seer; Inspirer; Doer, 1851-1931.* Lake Placid, N.Y.: Lake Placid Club, 1932.
                                        —BOHDAN S. WYNAR
                                        —KOERT C. LOOMIS, JR.

BISHOP, WILLIAM WARNER (1871-1955)

William Warner Bishop, eldest child of William Melancthon and Harriette Anna Warner Bishop, was born at Hannibal, Missouri, on July 20, 1871. Seven years later, when her husband died, Harriette Bishop moved with Warner and his two sisters to Detroit.

Warner Bishop attended the University of Michigan, graduating as a Phi Beta Kappa member with the A.B. degree in 1892 and the master's degree a year later. Circumstances never permitted his earning a doctorate, a fact he regretted throughout his lifetime; but he was awarded honorary doctoral degrees from Miami University (1926), Oberlin (1928), New York University (1928), Columbia University (1930), University of Western Ontario (1932), Ohio Wesleyan College (1937), the National University of Ireland (1938), and Catholic University of America (1939).

Bishop wished to make a career teaching the classics. After an unhappy year at Missouri Wesleyan College (1893-1894), he became an instructor of Greek and Latin in the Academy of Northwestern University (1894-1895), then joined the faculty of Garrett Biblical Institute as instructor in Greek and assistant librarian. During four years in Chicago, he became acquainted with librarians prominent in the city and with William Rainey Harper, president of the University of Chicago, who employed him to teach Greek at Chautauqua assemblies in the summers of 1896, 1897, and 1898. Two Chicago colleagues, George E. Wire (q.v.) and Anderson Hopkins, became not only friends but also mentors. Wire, of the Newberry Library staff, instructed him in library routines, and Hopkins, of the Crerar Library, guided his thinking about the larger issues of librarianship.

At the end of the summer of 1898, Bishop went on a fellowship to the American School of Classical Studies in Rome, a move he later called (in the January 1949 *Library Quarterly*) an effort "to get out of library work." Upon his return in 1899, however, fate continued to deny him the opportunity to devote his life to scholarship in New Testament Greek or Christian archaeology. The only acceptable position available was that of librarian and Latin teacher at the Polytechnic Preparatory School in Brooklyn, a post he occupied until 1902.

In New York he came under the influence of Mary Wright Plummer (q.v.), head librarian and director of the Library School, Pratt Institute. Plummer asked him to present a series of lectures to library school students (1902, 1903, 1907, 1908), and it was she who recommended him for the position as head cataloger at Princeton in 1902.

When he joined the staff of E. C. Richardson (q.v.) at Princeton, he began work as a full-time librarian, at last abandoning ambitions to be a classics scholar. As cataloger (1902-1905) and as reference librarian (1905-1907), he developed in knowledge of library work; but perhaps even more importantly, through Richardson's reports of his own travel abroad and his work in the American Library Association, Bishop broadened his conception of the librarian's role, laying foundations for his own prominence in national and international library affairs in later years. In 1905, Bishop married Finie Murfree Burton, whom he had met at Chautauqua in 1897. They had one child, William Warner Bishop, Jr.

Bishop spent the years 1907-1915 as superintendent of the Reading Room at the Library of Congress. Under Herbert Putnam (q.v.), that Library was a progressive, enlightened operation, but Bishop's job did not provide a congenial milieu in which he could grow and utilize his full abilities. When he was offered the position as director of the University of Michigan libraries, it had irresistible appeal, and he returned to Ann Arbor in 1915 to remain until his retirement in 1941.

Throughout his long career, Bishop wrote 290 items. Omitting book reviews and various reports, they deal primarily with cataloging and classification, reference work, the Library of Congress, academic library service and administration, and national and international cooperation in library work. For the most part, the pieces appeared in periodicals, but a few books should be cited: *Practical Handbook of Modern Library Cataloging* (1st edition, 1914; 2nd edition, 1924); *Cataloging as an Asset* (1916); *The Backs of Books and Other Essays in Librarianship* (1926); *Essays Offered to Herbert Putnam by His Colleagues and Friends on His Thirtieth Anniversary as Librarian of Congress, 5 April 1929*, edited with Andrew Keogh (q.v.) (1929); *Carnegie Corporation and College Libraries, 1929-38* (1938); and *A Checklist of American Copies of "Short-Title Catalogue" Books* (1st edition, 1944; 2nd edition, 1950). By his writings and numerous speeches, Bishop was able to further the adoption of enlightened practices in libraries in the early part of the twentieth century.

He joined the American Library Association in 1896, becoming serial number 1435 on the rolls of the twenty-year-old organization. Bishop enjoyed the discussions at meetings, but even more he relished the opportunities to meet the people who were the leaders. It was a lifelong characteristic that he sought to meet the people in authority, to be "on the inside." ALA *Proceedings* show that he delivered several papers at annual meetings, became a member of Council in 1912, a member of the Committee on International Relations in 1915, chairman of the College and Reference Section in 1917, and chairman of the Cataloging Rules Committee in 1917. He had been active in ALA, but even he was surprised to be nominated and elected president in 1918, relatively early in his career. He conjectured in a letter to M. Louise Hunt (June 9, 1920) that it was because of his former association with Putnam; the Library War Service under Putnam was in full swing, and an ALA president was needed who could work harmoniously with him. At the time of the annual conference in 1919, at which Bishop presided, he tried to set the stage for forward-looking post-war organizational activities as the climax to a year of creative leadership of American librarians and bold support for ALA War Service activities.

Whatever his accomplishments as president, the office prepared him for more than two additional decades of service to ALA in various important capacities. In addition to his formal appointments—Council, Executive Board, Board of Education for Librarianship, Commission on the Library and Adult Education, chairman and member of various committees—the executive secretary and others in authority frequently asked for his informal advice, thus magnifying his voice in organization affairs and influencing ALA policies and the course of subsequent events in the library world. He became the champion of the scholarly element in American librarianship, counterbalancing the orientation of ALA toward public librarianship.

In the area of international intellectual cooperation, he was ALA's chief representative for nearly twenty years. Before 1941, he had no equal among American librarians in this area of endeavor. In an era when activities of an international character were, as Carl H. Milam (q.v.) wrote to him (May 13, 1927), "just about the biggest thing in the ALA program," he served as chairman of the Committee on Library Cooperation with Other Countries (1921-1924); chairman of the Executive Board's Sub-Committee on Foreign Affairs (1925-1926); member of the Committee of Twenty-Five on the Celebration of the Fiftieth Anniversary, of its Executive Committee of Nine, and chairman of a sub-committee for the organization of the international conference aspects of the celebration (1923-1926); personal emissary to foreign governments and library organizations; chairman of the Committee on International Relations (1926-1934) and committee member (1935-1937); and consultant to the Board on International Relations (1942-1949). Appointed in 1928 by the

Executive Board as the first American representative to the International Federation of Library Associations and its executive body, the International Library Committee, he retained the appointment until 1945, serving as president of the international organization from 1931 to 1936.

Foster Mohrhardt described Bishop (*Wilson Library Bulletin*, November 1957) as "our first international librarian" on the basis of Bishop's involvement in matters of intellectual cooperation as a representative of ALA. However, his international activities also grew out of his affiliation with several other organizations. One of the most significant and interesting of his many activities was his service as principal adviser to the Vatican Library in its reorganization project, financed by the Carnegie Corporation, beginning in 1927. In an effort to increase the usefulness of the Vatican Library to scholars from all parts of the world, the Corporation decided to send to Rome "an American librarian of highest competence, familiar with every phase of the problems of library administration . . . for the purpose of organizing a thoroughly modern plan of classification and cataloging for those great collections" (see letter to Bishop from Nicholas Murray Butler, dated December 17, 1926). The American, assisted by a delegation of two or three persons, was to serve as counsellor to the Vatican Library staff and to demonstrate methods of successful library administration.

Bishop accepted the assignment and first visited the Vatican Library in early 1927 to make a preliminary survey of the problem, report to the Corporation, and recommend a plan of operation and a budget. The plan he formulated, which was carried out under his direction over the succeeding years, involved preparation of catalogs for the priceless manuscript collections, the systematic classification and cataloging of the collection of printed books, an inventory of incunabula, acquisition of new equipment, and an expansion of physical quarters. In 1928, on a second visit to the Vatican, Bishop took a party of expert catalogers (J. C. M. Hanson [q.v.], Charles Martel [q.v.], William M. Randall, and Milton L. Lord). A code of cataloging rules, invaluable as an aid to international cooperation in the library field, was developed during the 1928 visit and later published as *Norme per il cataloge degli stampati*. Bishop visited Rome six times between 1927 and 1934. In the course of his Vatican work, he became close friends with Monsignor (later Cardinal) Eugène Tisserant, the chief assistant in the Library. As well, he had several audiences with Pope Pius XI, who had himself been a librarian for thirty years before becoming Pope. The international understanding and good will fostered by the collaborative work under Bishop's direction at the Vatican can hardly be exaggerated.

Bishop can be credited with the leading American role in the founding of the International Library and Bibliographical Committee in 1927-1928 (re-named International Federation of Library Associations [IFLA] in 1929) and its early work. He was the first ALA representative, and at the organizational meeting in 1928 was elected a vice-chairman. Marcel Godet, the representative from Switzerland, described (in *William Warner Bishop, a Tribute*, 1941) the impact Bishop made at meetings of the organization:

> Grisonnant, la barbiche en pointe, avec ses yeux gris-bleu au regard ferme et droit, il avait l'air sérieux qu'on peut attendre d'un bibliothécaire formé dans la théologie, mais on sentait vite, sous sa gravité, un caractère foncièrement bienveillant, simple et humain, qui conquérait la sympathie. Sa compétence, les judicieuses propositions qu'il présenta au nom de l'Association américaine—notamment celles tendant à la constitution de sous-commissions—lui valurent d'emblée une place importante au sein du Comité dont il fut nommé premier vice-président.

In 1931, he was elected the second president of IFLA and presided at the Second World Congress of Libraries and Bibliography in Madrid in 1935. He resigned as IFLA president in 1936, but he remained the ALA representative on the International Library Committee, the governing board, until 1945.

In numerous other ways, as well, Bishop was involved in international intellectual cooperation. For instance, as a member of the League of Nations Library Planning Committee from 1928 to 1937, he was an adviser on the library building and library affairs of the League. The extent of his influence in worldwide development of libraries through his promotion of international exchange of librarians and students from Europe, Asia, New Zealand, Australia, Latin America, and elsewhere could be assayed only if one could measure the effects on the altered lives of the individuals and their influence on the institutions for which they worked and on the course of librarianship in their native countries.

Bishop was able to serve the profession in the United States as a foundation adviser for a longer period of time, more continuously, and more effectively than any other librarian of his day. Primarily, he worked with the Carnegie Corporation of New York. When, in the early 1920s, the Corporation turned its interest from library buildings to other aspects of support for librarianship and libraries, it included among its philanthropies the donation of grants to selected colleges for purchase of books. Bishop served as chairman of a series of advisory groups created to aid in making these gifts. Composed of experts from the fields of education and librarianship, the groups he chaired extended their service from 1928 through 1943, as they supervised 302 grants totalling about $2,600,000 to four-year liberal arts colleges, junior colleges, teachers' colleges, colleges for Negroes, state colleges, and technological colleges.

The tangible and intangible benefits resulting from Carnegie grants made under Bishop's chairmanship were numerous. The higher standard of teaching made possible by the new books and the increased awareness of college administrators of the problems and potentialities of their libraries were not measurable; but the development of the first qualitative standards for libraries in four-year colleges and junior colleges, the compilation of Shaw's well-known *A List of Books for College Libraries* (Chicago: ALA, 1931) and Mohrhardt's *A List of Books for Junior College Libraries* (Chicago: ALA, 1937), and the body of doctrine on college libraries (including four books) developed during the projects were tangible effects. The four books were William M. Randall's *The College Library* (Chicago: ALA, 1932); James T. Gerould's *The College Library Building* (New York: Scribner's, 1932); William M. Randall and F. L. D. Goodrich's *Principles of College Library Administration* (Chicago: ALA, 1936); and B. Harvie Branscomb's *Teaching with Books* (Chicago: Association of American Colleges, 1940).

Bishop's further association with the Carnegie Corporation's work with libraries included responsibility for a demonstration of good service in dental libraries; participation in influencing the Corporation to award scholarships for advanced study of library science (1929-1942); and supervision of a grant to the University of Michigan to support an experiment in microphotography as a bibliographical medium. Of Bishop's service for the Carnegie interests, Frederick P. Keppel (q.v.), Carnegie Corporation president in 1941, said, "It is my considered judgement that William Warner Bishop has exerted a deeper and a more salutary influence on what may be called the Carnegie Library tradition than any other single individual. . . ." (in *William Warner Bishop, a Tribute*).

Bishop's work with national and international library organizations and with philanthropical foundations was spectacular, but his service as director of libraries at Michigan and as chairman of the Department of Library Science were his main interests through the years 1915-1941. A thorough scholar himself, skilled in languages and personally acquainted with American and European bookdealers, he built a collection of materials that was not only one of the largest in the country but also one of the best-selected for research purposes.

He became a librarian in an era before formal training in librarianship was common, but he was strongly convinced of the need for such training. Instruction in library science under his guidance moved from an undergraduate summer program to the status of a major library school at Michigan. His chief contribution to education was perhaps his insistence on a scholarly approach everywhere to education for the profession; his unique contribution was the revelation to students through his many outside activities of the broad horizons of library work.

A man of bulky proportions, Bishop had bright blue eyes and a white goatee. He was conservative in dress, a Victorian gentleman who carried a cane throughout his life. Governed by a code of behavior he had learned as a child, he seemed a little pompous, stilted, tense, and aloof to some observers. Still, those contemporaries whom he chose as friends and a group of younger "protégés" found him to be kind, considerate, and fair. He was a man whose exterior appearance and manner hid feelings that he expressed only with great difficulty, even to intimates. Everyone who knew Bishop was impressed with his complete integrity in moral matters. As an administrator he was a stickler for details and order but appreciative of honest effort and careful work. Someone has said that at times he seemed to "pontificate" at the University of Michigan Library. Nevertheless, the faculty and the library staff respected him as a person, as an administrator, and as a scholar.

At the time of Bishop's retirement, Robert M. Lester (q.v.), secretary of the Carnegie Corporation, eulogized him for his "honesty, fair dealing, tact, wisdom, and unbelievable store of information." Lester continued, "He has set an example, for over forty years, of how a librarian can be a scholar, an administrator, an educator, a gentleman, and a fisherman." Indeed, the nature of librarianship in 1941 had been shaped in no small part by Bishop's activities and achievements since his entrance into the profession in 1895. Bishop died on February 19, 1955.

Biographical listings and obituaries—*Who Was Who in America* III (1951-1960). **Books and articles about the biographee**—Lester, Robert M. Speech in honor of William Warner Bishop. Ann Arbor, Michigan, May 22, 1941; Sparks, Claud G. "William Warner Bishop, a Biography." Ph.D. dissertation, University of Michigan, 1967. Complete bibliography included; *William Warner Bishop, a Tribute.* New Haven: Yale University Press, 1941.

—CLAUD GLENN SPARKS

BLISS, HENRY EVELYN (1870-1955)

Henry Bliss was born January 29, 1870, in New York City. His parents, Henry Hale and Evelina Matilda Davis Bliss, were both descendants of colonial English families, and during the years of Henry's early childhood the family seems to have divided its time between New York and the New Jersey estate owned by the Davis family. Until the age of eleven, Henry was educated at home by his mother. Later, he had a series of governesses who tutored him in French, Latin, arithmetic and history, and not until 1883 did he begin school—a grammar school in New York. Two years later, he entered the department of classics at

the College of the City of New York, beginning an attachment to this school that, except for three years (1888-1891), was to find him studying and then working there until his retirement in 1940. He left CCNY in 1888, without taking the degree, partly because his father was urging him to go into business, and partly because he was unhappy with his program of study. He then spent three years in the New York business world and a few months teaching, but when, in 1891, he was offered the deputy librarian's position at CCNY, he accepted it immediately. Eventually he moved up the administrative ladder to become head of Department Libraries (1925), and then associate librarian (1928), holding the latter position until he retired.

In 1901, Bliss married a member of the Hunter College faculty, Ellen de Koster. They had two daughters (one of whom died in 1918) and two sons. Mrs. Bliss died of cancer in 1943, and after her death, Bliss moved to Pasadena, California, to be near his surviving daughter and her family. In 1947, he went to live in Florida, remaining there until 1952, when he moved north and spent the last three years of his life in Plainfield, New Jersey. Plainfield was near his publishers, the H. W. Wilson [q.v.] Company, and within an easy bus ride of the major research collections of the Northeast. Until shortly before his death in 1955 he made frequent trips to New York, to confer with his editors, to avail himself of library facilities, or to meet his friends.

Bliss began his library career having had no formal training in librarianship, and indeed, without having obtained a college degree. His early duties involved him in extensive contact with both faculty and students, providing advice to those in search of materials. It was not long before he discovered that the various classification schemes then available for library materials (Dewey's, Cutter's Expansive Classification, and the LC system) achieved neither of the two goals he would have demanded. They did not accommodate materials in the new, expanding disciplines of science and technology or those being tagged as social sciences. Not only were their structures inadequate for these disciplines, but even when they could be twisted to be used, the library materials classified according to these systems were not arranged in the collection in the way that would be most useful to the needs of the users. The greater part of Bliss's professional life was spent developing a classification system based on the principle that the arranged order of the materials held in a library collection should be the order that users found most expeditious, and, if necessary, the order should change to reflect changes in the style and format of the various disciplines. Also included in Bliss's thinking was the corollary of the above principle—that the arrangement of the various disciplines should reflect their relationship to each other, so that those most closely linked should be found together.

In a conversation with Eugene Garfield a year or so before his death, Bliss admitted to having been frustrated in his early attempts to master all human knowledge, which he had sought to do through the study of mathematics. As he began his library career, he was convinced that the only way to achieve even limited mastery of knowledge was to determine the relationships between subjects, the key to which lay in devising a proper classification scheme for knowledge as an organized whole.

His first major published work, *The Organization of Knowledge and the System of the Sciences* (Holt, 1929), found him defining the organization of knowledge in this fashion:

> . . . [it] comprehends not only the *mental* processes, the development of concepts and the conceptual synthesis of knowledge, but also the *intellectual* correlation and systematization of valid knowledge, from the simpler social synthesis of common experience and elementary education to the more complex conceptual systems of science and philosophy.

Bliss's mathematical background is evident throughout the work, as he used words and expressions with a careful, almost mathematical, precision. He did not, however, view the organization of knowledge as having a rigidly defined state, but as pliant, adapting to changing views and ideas. Thus, the classification scheme would not be permanent, but *relatively* so, designed to reflect the consensus of at least *one* generation of thought.

Although Bliss was not writing solely for librarians in this first book, as its dedication tells us, he was a librarian himself, and was therefore concerned with the arrangement of subject matter in libraries. Indeed, the theoretical concepts developed by Bliss have influenced many other classification systems. One of the basic principles advocated by Bliss was the idea of "consensus." To use his own words, "Knowledge should be organized in consistency with the scientific and educational consensus, which is relatively stable and tends to become more so as theory and system become more definitely established in general and increasingly in detail." Thus, according to Bliss, the most important part of the classification scheme was its order of basic and subordinate classes, determined by the scientific and educational consensus of educational requirements in the various branches of knowledge. In other words, the classes and schedules should arrange recorded knowledge in the order that has been found to be satisfactory by the expert scholars in a given discipline. The more closely a library classification reflects this consensus, the more efficient and flexible this classification scheme will be.

The order of classes is based on three major principles: collocation of related subjects, subordination of special to general, and graduation of specialty. By collocation of related subjects, Bliss means placing closely related subjects in close proximity in the classified sequence—e.g., chemical technology is collocated with chemistry, plant pathology with plant eugenics, etc. By subordination, Bliss means placing related subjects according to the principle of decreasing extension, so that the general subject is followed by the more specific subject. Graduation by specialty, proceeding from the more general to the more specific, means that "the generalizations and laws of each more general science are true in some measure of all the more special sciences. . . . But the laws or truths of the more special sciences rarely apply to the more general sciences or solve their problems." The notation of the scheme uses the alphabet in its full English form of 26 letters as the base for all classification by knowledge, reserving arabic numerals for considerations of form. An outline of the scheme is given below:

1–9	Anterior numeral classes (for special collections)	
	A. Philosophy and General Science	P. Religion, Theology, and Ethics
	B. Physics	Q. Applied Social Sciences
	C. Chemistry	R. Political Science
	D. Astronomy, Geology, Geography	S. Law
	E. Biology	T. Economics
	F. Botany	U. Arts: Useful Arts
	G. Zoology	V. Fine Arts
	H. Anthropology	W-Y. Literature and Language
	I. Psychology	Z. Bibliology, Bibliography, Libraries
	J. Education	
	K. Social Sciences	
	L-O. History, Social, Political and Economic, including Geography	

This discovery of the principle of the accurate collocation of subjects was described by Berwick Sayers some four years after Bliss's death as having heavily influenced later classification study. Sayers saw as purely common sense the notion of devising a classification scheme to reflect the order and relationship of the various parts of a discipline as determined by a consensus of the researchers needing its material, as well as the idea of subdividing from the general to the more specific.

Fairly early in his career at the CCNY Library, Bliss got a chance to put his ideas into actual practice. During the period 1905-1908, City College moved to a new campus and the library had new, larger quarters. One result of the move was that Bliss was allowed to reclassify the collection along the lines of his own principles. It may have been as an aid to working out a new scheme that he enrolled, in the summer of 1903, in the only class of library training he ever took, the course in classification taught by William Fletcher (q.v.) at Amherst. At some point that summer, he also discussed classification with the developer of the Expansive Classification scheme, Charles A. Cutter (q.v.), then director of the Forbes Library.

While reclassifying the CCNY Library, and working out a full-scale classification system of his own, Bliss was writing many articles for a wide range of journals, from the *Philosophical Review* and the *Philosophy of Science* on the one hand to the *Educational Review* and *Library Journal* on the other. He was also active in attending professional meetings and workshops, especially if they focused on classification or bibliography. In his articles and speeches for librarians, he stressed the practical aspects of classification. The existing schemes, he demonstrated frequently, took no account of the organization of modern science, and because they showed so little respect for the disciplines, they were bringing on the profession of librarianship the scorn of the learned. "Scientists would derive more benefit from library classifications if they had more respect for them; and they might have, if the D.C. had evinced more regard for science," he wrote in a 1912 article in *Library Journal*, shortly after the seventh edition of the Decimal Classification had appeared. The alphabetical organization of subjects that it encouraged, and that he felt to be entrenched in American librarianship, mangled, separated and distorted the sciences, demonstrating total disregard for the current consensus of intellectual thought. Most outspoken in his condemnation of the Dewey Decimal system, perhaps because it was being so widely adopted and he despaired of dislodging it without great effort, Bliss reserved final judgment on Cutter's Expansive Classification and the Library of Congress system. Later, he was to be more outspoken against the defeats of each of these.

Although firmly convinced, as a result of his own research and efforts (and in part his opinions must have been tested against those of the scholars who used his library collections), that his own formulations were more practical and relevant to current needs of library users than were other classification systems, he also argued that no system need expect to be permanent. Addressing the 1913 Kaaterskill Conference of the ALA, he said that a good system should last a century, but that he also felt that "a good library should be willing to reclassify if necessary, at least some of its collections two or three times in a century." The most important point to remember was that one should be in step with the consensus of the order of scientific thinking, and if this meant reclassifying materials from time to time to make their use more convenient to the research

scholar, then Bliss was ready with advice to librarians on the proper use of labels to be pasted on the books with the new classification numbers. Library practice needed to consider, he felt, the most efficient way to change the records. Were he alive today, he would doubtless be pointing out the relative ease with which computers could handle the reclassifying and record changing, since they could even print out the new white labels.

Although Bliss had developed a scheme to allow reclassification of the CCNY Library, and had sent off a skeletal outline of a full plan for the consideration of E. C. Richardson (q.v.) at Princeton by 1910, he had had insufficient time to get a fully organized plan ready for publication. When President Mezes of CCNY, heard about his project and its potential international applications to bibliography, he arranged for Bliss to have a leave of absence to complete his work, and the years 1922-1924 saw Bliss working full time on the development of his "Bibliographic Classification." By June 1924, he had prepared both a draft work on the organization of knowledge and a classification scheme, and two manuscript volumes were ready for publication by December. However, not until John Dewey had both written an introduction to it and given the work high praise did Henry Holt decide to gamble on the one book, *The Organization of Knowledge and the System of the Sciences* (1929). Bliss had even more trouble finding a publisher for the other manuscript, *The Organization of Knowledge in Libraries*, but when the ALA Publishing Board demanded that he pay them a subsidy to cover publishing costs, Bliss offered the work to the H. W. Wilson Company, which brought it out in 1933. From this point on, Wilson was Bliss's publisher.

In 1953, Wilson published the final volume of the fully expanded tables of the Bibliographic Classification. Bliss's schedules were as adaptable to consensus on the organization of knowledge as he could make them, and they offered alternative locations so that materials could be arranged exactly in accord with the demands their particular users made on them. But the sciences themselves were expanding, and one of the complaints that Bliss had earlier voiced against Dewey's system was that it could not be revised to cope with new subdivisions in the disciplines. In order to ensure a continual updating of his own scheme, he arranged for the publication, with himself as editor, of the *Bliss Classification Bulletin.* Until his death in August 1955 he supervised this bulletin, which Wilson published. The *Bulletin* is now published by the Bliss Classification Association in Great Britain, where over thirty libraries use the Bibliographic Classification for their materials.

At one period in his life, all of Bliss's spare time seems to have been devoted to his classification work, but his prolonged leave of absence from regular duties in the 1920s took care of that problem, leaving time for many interests and hobbies of diverse types. He was a co-editor of the *City College Quarterly* while working at the Library, and was active in such professional organizations as the American Library Association, the Special Libraries Association, and, to a lesser extent, the Library Association of Great Britain. He also belonged to the British Poetry Society and was a poet in his own right. In 1937, he brought out a volume of poetry entitled *Better Late Than Never.* Among his other interests were gardening, cabinetmaking, and hiking.

Although troubled by deafness, Bliss did not confine himself in the years immediately prior to his death to work on the *BC Bulletin* or on his memoirs. He was fascinated by the new developments in documentation and the new electronic machinery that was being used to handle documents and data. His interest in the machines was heightened because he knew that, using the device of coordination included in his Bibliographic Classification, he could organize collections of periodical articles, as well as books.

Bibliographic Classification has not been widely adopted in the United States, in part perhaps because it appeared after both the Dewey system and the LC system (with its ready-made cards and catalogs) were firmly established. Faced with what would have been monumental reclassification problems, despite Bliss's earlier arguments as to how simply this could be handled, most librarians did not seriously consider using it. Besides his own library at CCNY, only one other American library has so far adopted the Bibliographic Classification—the library of the Southern California School of Theology at Claremont, which began using it in 1958, finding that it best suited their needs and that none of the other major schemes were as useful. Outside the United States over fifty libraries in Britain, Nigeria, Australia, and New Zealand have adopted the system.

Regardless of the reception (in terms of use) that the Bibliographic Classification received from the library profession, there seems to be agreement that, for a system designed mainly by one man, it is a formidable achievement. Bliss died on August 9, 1955.

Biographical listings and obituaries—*Current Biography* (1953, 1955); *Who Was Who in America* V (1969-1973). **Books and articles about the biographee**—Borchardt, D. H. "The Bibliographic Classification of Henry Bliss: An Interpretation." *Australian Library Journal* 7:123-27 (October 1958); Borchardt, D. H., *et al.* "University of Tasmania Library in a State of Bliss." *Australian Library Journal* (April 1955):48-52; Garfield, Eugene. "A Memorable Day with Henry E. Bliss." *Wilson Library Bulletin* 48, No. 4:288-92 (December 1974); Mills, Jack. "Bibliographic Classification." In Allen Kent and Harold Lancour, eds., *Encyclopedia of Library and Information Science.* New York: Marcel Dekker, 1969. Vol. 2, pp. 368-80; Mills, Jack. "The Bliss and Colon Classifications." *Library Association Record* 53:146-53 (May 1951); Sayers, W. C. Berwick. "In Appreciation of the Bibliographic Classification." *Wilson Library Bulletin* (May 1954):765-66, 774. See also the relevant chapters on Bibliographic Classification in his *Introduction to Library Classification* and *A Manual of Classification*; Shell, Elton E. "The Use of Henry E. Bliss's Bibliographic Classification at the Southern California School of Theology." *Library Resources and Technical Services* 5, No. 4:290-300 (Fall 1961); Tee, Lim Huck. "The Bibliographic Classification of Henry Evelyn Bliss: An Assessment." *Malayan Library Journal* (July 1962):149-55.

—MARGARET ANDERSON

BLUE, THOMAS FOUNTAIN (1866-1935)

Thomas Fountain Blue, second child and first male child of former slaves, was born March 6, 1866, at Farmville, Virginia. He attended Hampton Normal and Agricultural Institute from 1885 to 1888, then taught school in Virginia. He enrolled in Richmond Theological Seminary in 1894, graduating with the degree of Bachelor of Divinity in 1898. The title of his graduating oration was "Woman, a Silent Force in Ameliorating the Condition of Humanity."

Thomas F. Blue married Cornelia Phillips Johnson of Columbia, Tennessee, on June 18, 1925. To this union were born Thomas F. Blue, Jr., in 1926, and Charles Johnson Blue in 1929. Harold F. Brigham, Indiana State Library, Indianapolis, Indiana, remarked in a letter dated July 1, 1955, that "Mr. and Mrs. Blue constituted an ideal team, both on the job and in their personal lives. She possessed qualities which complemented those of her husband. Together they were a strong team in the library, home and community."

The year 1905 marked the beginning of his career as a pioneer black librarian, when he was appointed branch librarian of the Western Colored Branch of the Louisville Free Public Library, which opened on September 23, 1905. (There was one immediate forerunner in this category in Galveston, Texas, where a small branch for colored patrons was opened on January 11, 1905.) Andrew Carnegie (q.v.) increased an original grant to Louisville with a sum designated specifically for the establishment of a satisfactory system of branches. In a letter to the head librarian of the Louisville Free Public Library, Carnegie wrote that he was "greatly pleased to hear of the splendid success of the library movement in Louisville and especially of the department provided for colored people." The *Louisville Courier-Journal* reported on July 27, 1905, that Thomas F. Blue was "well educated, having graduated from one of the best colleges and was well qualified for the position."

In May 1909, the Louisville Free Public Library Trustees voted to establish a second colored branch library in the eastern portion of Louisville. On September 10, 1913, the trustees recommended that Thomas F. Blue be given joint directorship of the

Western and Eastern Colored Branch Libraries, and these deliberations were confirmed on September 11, 1913. The Eastern Colored Branch Library was opened on January 28, 1914. From then on, the Colored Branch Libraries expanded services to include classroom collections, deposit stations, story hours, book review sessions, library apprentice education, and an additional branch located in Central High School. A logical promotion greeted Thomas F. Blue on March 12, 1919, when he was appointed head of the Colored Department of the Louisville Free Public Library.

Review of the literature will show more written about Blue than by him. He was a prepared and ordained minister who never held a pastorate, but who delivered thought-provoking sermons at churches of such varied denominations that many people never knew he was a member of a Baptist church. Likewise, he was invited to give keynote speeches at several national, regional, or black library conferences. Many of his papers have survived in manuscript form and may be read in the private library of his home. Chief among the latter are: "Training Class at the Western Colored Branch," delivered when the American Library Association convened in Detroit, in June 1922, where he was the only black in attendance and the first black to have a place on its program; "Arousing Community Interest in the Library," delivered as the opening speech at a conference of black librarians held at Hampton Institute, March 1927; he also read a paper on "The Library as a Community Center" at the same conference. "Making the Library Known to the Community" was the topic of his paper delivered at the dedication ceremonies of the new Fisk University Library, Nashville, Tennessee, November 1931. His key concepts involved linking the library to the community and the reciprocal linking of the community to the library. Writings about Blue appeared frequently in the *Southern Workman*, and there have been vivid references to him in *Library Journal*, *Special Libraries*, *Opportunity*, and other publications.

The major contribution of Thomas F. Blue, if one can be isolated from several outstanding ones, was his development and leadership of the Library Apprenticeship Training Program for black library personnel. During most of his career, there were no facilities in the South for training black librarians. Several cities sent black persons to Louisville for apprenticeship training; Atlanta, Birmingham, Chattanooga, Cincinnati, Evansville, Houston, Knoxville, Louisville, Memphis, and Nashville were the main cities to do this, but only women were sent. Apprentice classes were conducted with the assistance of department heads from the main Louisville Free Public Library. Blue was looked upon as a pioneer in training black librarians, and apprentices were taught and tested on classification, cataloging, and general library logistics.

Blue focused zealously on meticulous records, high quality, community interest, varied services, and professional responsibility. Among the varied services attributed to his pioneering leadership are promoting the library as a center from which to radiate many influences for general betterment, holding exhibitions to enhance cultural development, sustaining the open shelf system, providing meeting rooms for service-oriented community clubs, managing classroom collections and library stations in support of the public schools, holding open-to-the-public book reviews, a children's story hour, sponsoring the Frederick Douglass Debating Club and Negro History Week, lending aid to the organization of out-of-state libraries, and circulating lists of fundamental books to developing libraries in other cities.

Blue was called to military service during two wars. He served as YMCA secretary of the Sixth Virginia Regiment Volunteers, stationed at Camp Poland and Camp Haskell in the Spanish-American War. Immediately following this, he was the first regular civilian secretary of the Louisville Colored Branch YMCA, until appointed to library services by the Louisville Free Public Library in 1905. Blue was granted a leave-of-absence in 1918-1919 to do Army YMCA work at Camp Zachary Taylor.

In addition to his interest in people, Blue shared active membership in the American Library Association, the Negro Library Conference, the Special Committee of Black Ministers of Louisville, the Louisville Chapter of the Association for the Study of Negro Life and History. Thomas F. Blue was tall, slim, immaculate, and photogenic; as an indication of his sense of humor, he kept a record of humorous comments that he overheard at branch libraries and other frequented places. Throughout his career, he generated unique library techniques that became part of basic library theory and that initiated specialized phases of library services. He died on November 10, 1935. On November 20, 1935, the Louisville Free Public Library Board of Trustees passed a resolution documenting its esteem for so renowned a pioneer librarian.

Biographical listings and obituaries—*Who's Who in Colored America*. 3rd ed. Ed. by Thomas Yenser. Brooklyn: Thomas Yenser, 1930, 1931, 1932. **Books and articles about the biographee**—Curtis, Florence Rising. "The Contribution of the Library School to Negro Education." *Library Journal* 51:1088 (December 1926); Gleason, Eliza Atkins. *The Southern Negro and the Public Library*. Chicago: The University of Chicago Press, 1941; Jackson, Wallace Van. "Some Pioneer Negro Library Workers." *Library Journal* 64:215-17 (March 1939); *Libraries and Lotteries; A History of the Louisville Free Public Library*. Compiled by Workers in the Service Division of the WPA in the State of Kentucky. American Guide Series. Cynthiana, Ky.: Hobson Book Press, 1944; "Personal Notes." *Southern Workman* 37:126 (February 1909); Shores, Louis. "Negro Library Conference Held." *Library Journal* 56:40 (January 1931); Shores, Louis. "Public Library Service to Negroes." *Library Journal* 55:150-54 (February 1930); Wilkins, John. "Blue's 'Colored Branch': A

'Second Plan' That Became a First in Librarianship." *American Libraries* 7:256-57 (May 1976); Wright, Lillian T. "Thomas Fountain Blue: Pioneer Librarian, 1866-1931." Master's thesis, Atlanta University, 1955; Yust, William F. "Louisville Free Public Library Building." *Library Journal* 34:398 (September 1909). **Primary sources and archival materials**—The pamphlets *Colored Branch* (1909, 1910, 1912), *Colored Branches* (1915), and *Colored Department* (1927), all published by the Louisville Free Public Library, provide first-hand accounts of services offered.

—LILLIAN TAYLOR WRIGHT

BOGLE, SARAH COMLY NORRIS (1870-1932)

Sarah C. N. Bogle was born November 17, 1870, in Milton, Pennsylvania, to John Armstrong and Emma Ridgway Norris Bogle. After six years with a private tutor, Sarah Bogle attended Miss M. E. Stevens' school in Germantown, with a year at the University of Chicago and extensive travel completing her education. As Sarah Vann has recorded:

> With an abundance of energy and intelligence, she felt the need for disciplined stimulation, and in 1903, at thirty-two, she entered the library school of Drexel Institute in Philadelphia. After graduating in 1904, she spent three years as librarian at Juniata College in Huntingdon, Pa., where her executive skills helped bring about the completion of a library building.

For less than a year (1909), Bogle worked at the Queens Borough (New York) Public Library. She then went to the Carnegie Library of Pittsburgh, first as a branch librarian, and later as head of the children's department and principal of the library school for children's librarians there. Juniata College awarded her an A.M. degree in 1917.

In 1951, when the editors of *Library Journal* (March 15, 1951) selected Bogle as one of forty persons to be named to a Library Hall of Fame in honor of the seventy-fifth anniversary of the American Library Association, they offered this terse review of her career and her contributions to librarianship:

> Developed library work with children at Pittsburgh. Fine efforts to raise the professional standards and guide library schools made her nationally influential. Showed in Paris what an international library school could mean to the profession.

> Carnegie Library Pittsburgh 1911-17; principal, Carnegie Library School, 1911-20; secretary A.L.A. Board of Education for Librarianship, 1924-32; director, Paris Library School under A.L.A., 1924-29.

Bogle's career was associated most closely with education for librarianship and with the American Library Association, and in those activities she achieved a wide acquaintance and universal respect from colleagues and others who observed and appreciated her work. Her interests in the international

aspects of librarianship were also provided an outlet there. Throughout her later years, however, she retained a great interest in library work with children and made some efforts to keep in touch with that area of the profession.

Having worked in the public library of Pittsburgh and having administered the Carnegie Library School, Bogle brought to the American Library Association in 1920 a broad background and a variety of interests. Her position at ALA headquarters in Chicago was inadequately described by the *Library Journal*; she was the assistant secretary for the Association, working closely with its secretary, Carl H. Milam (q.v.), from 1920 until her death. Before joining the staff, she had frequently attended ALA annual conferences and had been a member of the ALA council from 1917 to 1920. She had also been president of the Association of American Library Schools, 1917-1918.

Her appointment at ALA predated Milam's, and she was some years his senior, but the two developed an effective teamwork with a notable absence of friction and competition. They complemented each other well in interests and competencies. Milam was aware of her "genius in human relations," and it was put to good use both in contributing to the morale of the headquarters staff and in seeking funds for the various projects that the Association wanted to undertake in those post-war years.

Bogle was credited with having gotten the funds for the Paris Library School, and she was a major force in its short-lived history. In 1923, she received a three-month leave with pay from ALA "to organize and conduct a summer library school in Paris and to make certain investigations concerning the need for library training." The first two years of the school were funded by $50,000 from the American Committee for Work in Devastated France, and the school's target audience was to be French people who wished to prepare for librarianship. Students from other countries were also attracted, with 184 from 19 countries represented in 1927. John D. Rockefeller, Jr., contributed $37,500 to the school in 1926, but he and others urged ALA to find additional permanent support from other sources. Bogle worked heroically to accomplish this and investigated the possibility of having an American university take over the administration of the school, but without success. In 1929, the school had to be counted as "an early victim of the economic disasters."

Although Mary Parsons became resident director of the school in Paris, Bogle followed an exhausting travel schedule, administering the school through voluminous correspondence and one or more European trips a year. She combined this travel with such responsibilities as representing ALA at the International Library Committee meeting in Stockholm in 1930. She also had carried out some work directly for other agencies, such as a survey of library needs for the Virgin Islands, which she conducted for the Carnegie Corporation in 1929.

This active period was also the time when the Association was moving into the area of accreditation of library education programs, and the major responsibility for that activity was also Bogle's. The Temporary Library Training Board and its successor, the Board of Education for Librarianship, both demanded much of her time and attention. In a plaintive note written in 1925 to Harriet Howe (q.v.), the ALA staff member who handled much of the work related to the Board of Education for Librarianship, its chairman, Adam Strohm (q.v.), wrote: "Lastly, when does the Col. House of the A.L.A. return to her neglected A.L.A. wards?"—thereby comparing the peripatetic Bogle with Woodrow Wilson's aide, who also dealt with a great variety of responsibilities.

C. C. Williamson's (q.v.) 1923 report, *Training for Library Service*, gave impetus to the development of more formal library education programs in the United States. ALA's Temporary Library Training Board was established that same year with support from the Carnegie Corporation, which had also underwritten the Williamson report. Within the profession, there were confusion and disagreement about whether library education programs could and should be conducted in public libraries, whether correspondence courses should be encouraged or permitted, and how faculties for library education programs might be prepared and deployed. Bogle's own experience as a library educator and as principal of the Carnegie Library School had fitted her well to be the tactful, forceful exponent of some of the ideas and principles enunciated by the two Boards. Her staff expanded during this period, with Lucile F. Fargo (q.v.) joining her and Harriet Howe in 1926. In that year, the Board of Education for Librarianship took on the responsibility of administering the Carnegie Corporation grants to existing library schools. There were some problems in having the same Board decide which schools should get grants and whether or not programs should be accredited, but Bogle's integrity and objectivity were undoubtedly points in her favor when there was controversy about allocation of grants or accreditation of programs. Another indicator of the scope of the problem was that in the ten-year period after 1919, the number of schools offering thirty or more hours of library science increased from 15 to 31.

Other activities grew from the ALA's emphasis on library education. Bogle worked with Tommie Dora Barker on a study of library schools and the need for library education in the South. She was instrumental in calling a meeting of the presidents and librarians of Negro colleges and universities to discuss prospects and plans for library education for Negroes, one outgrowth of which was the financing of the Hampton Institute Library School program by the Rosenwald Fund. Bogle was very effective in working with foundation directors and others whose financial support was important. Frederick Keppel (q.v.) of the Carnegie Corporation admired her greatly and often sought her judgment on other library-related projects, while also assisting her in some that she proposed to him.

Contemporaries noted something of the grande dame in Bogle's manner, though photographs of her show little that is distinguished. However, her bearing and grooming gave her a memorable air of elegance, and the awe which she aroused in many is reflected in a comment made by Louis Round Wilson in an interview conducted almost forty years after her death: "her judgment of men, I thought, was an excellent judgment. She was about the most able person I've met in librarianship."

As a representative of the Association, Bogle frequently spoke to professional groups and contributed articles to professional journals. She wrote in a straightforward style, most often describing the status quo of some aspect of librarianship or suggesting action on a favored proposal. One posthumous article in the Indian publication *The Modern Librarian* (1933) showed her open view of school library development and her ability to condense information for a foreign audience:

School libraries are operated under many forms of organization and administration.... Training for school librarianship is likewise unstandardized but the tendency is toward the requirement of training adequate in content and professional in character.

Bogle died of cancer on January 11, 1932, after a long illness, and was buried in Milton, Pennsylvania, the town of her birth. In the early stages of her disease, she maintained some secrecy about her condition, answering forwarded mail from a hospital in New York. She returned to Chicago and attempted to return to work in the summer of 1931, but within weeks she was again hospitalized in New York. As she wrote to Keppel on November 26, "being an old cracked cup is not a pleasant experience." For her, who had been active in so many professional activities and who was always planning and working toward the future, it must have been especially unpleasant.

In a time when few women achieved prominence even in a profession in which they predominated numerically, Bogle stood out as a unique personality. Unlike many of the others, such as Mary Wright Plummer (q.v.) or the earlier Caroline Hewins (q.v.), she worked with the Association on a national level more than with any single library or library education program. Bogle's interests were even international in scope, as her work with the Paris Library School demonstrates. Even working as assistant to the fairly colorful Milam, she maintained her own personality while remaining loyal to him. Everett O. Fontaine and others credit her with preventing a threatened withdrawal of the College and Reference Section from ALA by declining to serve as its secretary if it should withdraw. Fontaine thought that "her loyalty to the principle of a unified library effort prevailed, and perhaps she should be credited, in part at least, with having prevented this rupture."

Biographical listings and obituaries–*Notable American Women* 1 (Sarah K. Vann); [Obituary]. *New York Times,* January 12, 1932; *Who Was Who in America* I (1897-1942). Books and articles about the biographee–Craver, Harrison W. "Sarah C. N. Bogle. An Appreciation." *ALA Bulletin* 26:488-90 (1932); Fontaine, Everett O. "People and Places of the Milam Era." *ALA Bulletin* 58:363-71 (May 1964); "A Library Hall of Fame for the 75th Anniversary." *Library Journal* 76:466-72 (March 15, 1951); Sullivan, Peggy. *Carl H. Milam and the American Library Association.* New York: H. W. Wilson, 1976.
　　　　　　　　　　　　　　–PEGGY A. SULLIVAN

BOLTON, CHARLES KNOWLES (1867-1950)

Charles Knowles Bolton was born November 14, 1867, in Cleveland, Ohio, the only child of Charles Edward (1841-1901) and Sarah Elizabeth Mary Knowles Bolton (1841-1916). Both his paternal and his maternal ancestors were of English descent and had settled in New England during the early colonial period. Bolton's father received his B.A. and his M.A. from Amherst College. Prominent as a businessman, philanthropist, writer, lecturer and Republican politician, he served as mayor of East Cleveland. Bolton's mother, a graduate of the Hartford Female Seminary, was devoted to such causes as religion, education, temperance, the welfare of animals, and social reform, subjects on which her writings earned her prominence as an author. Having rather substantial wealth, the Boltons were able to travel widely, while maintaining their large residence in East Cleveland.

Young Bolton thrived in this environment. Markedly studious, he graduated from Cleveland Central High School (now East Technical High School) and entered Harvard University in 1886, receiving his B.A., cum laude, in 1890. After a graduation trip to England, he worked briefly for S. S. McClure, soon to be well known as founder of *McClure's Magazine,* and then, in November 1890, accepted the position of assistant at the Harvard University Library. There he remained until December 1893, when he became librarian of the Brookline Public Library, in suburban Boston. His successful demonstration of administrative abilities, his active role in a number of organizations, and his many books and articles attracted attention, and he was barely in his thirties when, in 1898, he was appointed librarian of the Boston Athenaeum.

In this position, Bolton later wrote, his chief goal was to make the Athenaeum "a pleasant place in which to read and work." He considered it "the finest type of club, with intellectual, cultivated surroundings." Incorporated in 1807 as a proprietary library, it has played a conspicuous intellectual and social role, its directors and visiting patrons having included a great many prominent figures.

The seventh to hold the position of librarian, Bolton continued in that capacity for 35 years. Under his leadership, the collections grew from approximately 190,000 volumes to approximately 325,000 volumes. The present building, erected between 1847 and 1849 at 10½ Beacon Street, also changed to a considerable extent. Between 1913 and 1915, it was reconstructed, fireproofed, and substantially enlarged, work that Bolton succeeded in carrying forward while notably maintaining service to the library's patrons. From 1907 to 1920, concurrent with his position as librarian, Bolton served on the faculty of Simmons College, where he taught courses in library history and administration.

Contentedly, he watched the years pass. "I think that I can say that I have really been doing the kind of work that I should have chosen to do in the place I should have chosen to be," he said in 1923. "I very much enjoy growing older," he commented a few years afterwards. In March 1933, he resigned the post of librarian. For a brief period, from 1935 to 1936, he came out of retirement to accept the position of supervisor ("non-relief," as he was wont to say) of the Works Progress Administration's *Survey of Early American Portraits in New England and New York.* Bolton's retirement was hardly a period of inactivity. Always an energetic man, he continued his scholarly pursuits until a few days before his death, in his early eighties, and only an acute loss of hearing, in his late seventies, compelled him to relinquish his active roles in a host of organizations.

Bolton participated in many of the leading cultural organizations of New England, such as the American Antiquarian Society, the Massachusetts Historical Society, and Boston's Museum of Fine Arts. An active Episcopalian, he served as senior warden of "the Old North Church" during the period of the building's splendid restoration. He was chairman of the Shirley Republican Committee and frequently was a delegate to the state Republican Convention.

Dedicated to research and writing, Bolton produced many books over the years from the 1880s to the 1950s. Although he wrote plays, poetry, and studies in library science, politics, and education, his most consequential works are in history, genealogy, and heraldry, most notably dealing with colonial New England and in particular with the genealogy of the Bolton family. His *Bolton's American Armory* is still a standard source, one of several of his writings that remain in print. In addition to his books, he wrote articles for leading historical, library science, and church periodicals, among others.

In 1897, when he was 30, Bolton married Ethel Stanwood, then 24 and a graduate of Wellesley College. A Bostonian, Ethel Bolton shared her husband's background and activities, both as author and as active participant in organizations. They had two sons, Stanwood Knowles and Geoffrey.

The Boltons owned a house in Brookline and a 96-acre estate, Pound Hill Place in Shirley. Bolton relished the life of the gentleman farmer and, following his retirement, he sold the Brookline house. At Pound Hill Place, the Boltons amassed, through inheritance and purchase, a large collection of books and antiques. They enjoyed a wide circle of friends and acquaintances and their doors were always open to visitors. Clifford Kenyon Shipton (q.v.), a neighbor, friend, and fellow historian, recalled that Pound Hill Place was "a literary focus" where "Sunday afternoon tea usually found out-of-town visitors … drawn by friendships which the Boltons had made in the myriad fields of their interests." Through an extensive correspondence, Bolton communicated with individuals in many parts of the world.

On May 19, 1950, Bolton died at the Community Memorial Hospital, in Ayer, Massachusetts. Three days later, he was buried in the Bolton family plot at Shirley Center Cemetery. A fine example of the scholar-librarian, he had made important contributions to his several fields and had given to thousands of individuals the benefits of knowing "a kind heart and brilliant mind."

Biographical listings and obituaries–*American Ancestry*. Albany, N.Y.: Joel Munsell's Sons, 1888. Vol. III; *American Authors and Books, 1640 to the Present Day*. 3rd ed., rev. by Irving Weiss and Anne Weiss. New York: Crown, 1972; *National Cyclopaedia of American Biography* 1; [Obituary]. *Athenaeum Items*, No. 49 (1950); [Obituary]. *The Boston Daily Globe*, May 20, 1950; [Obituary]. *The Christian Science Monitor*, May 20, 1950; [Obituary]. *The New England Historical and Genealogical Register* CIV (1950); *Reports of the Harvard College Class of 1890* (1890-1940); *Who Was Who in America* III (1951-1960). **Books and articles about the biographee**–"Librarian Authors." *Library Journal* 56:797 (October 1, 1931); Shipton, Clifford Kenyon. "Charles Knowles Bolton." *Proceedings of the Massachusetts Historical Society* LXX (1957).

–RICHARD EDWARD KELLY

BONTEMPS, ARNA WENDELL (1902-1973)

Arna (born Arnaud) Wendell Bontemps, poet, author and librarian, was born in Alexandria, Louisiana, on October 13, 1902. The oldest of two children, he was the son of Paul Bismark Bontemps, a brick and stone mason and subsequently a minister, and Maria Carolina Pembroke Bontemps, who taught in the public schools prior to her marriage. When

Bontemps was 3½ years old, the family moved to Los Angeles, where they considered the educational opportunities for the children to be greater, and where the father looked toward increased opportunities for employment, having been oppressed by economic conditions in the South at that time.

Young Bontemps received his preparatory education from San Fernando Academy, which he attended from 1917 to 1920; the A.B. degree from Pacific Union College in 1923; and the A.M. degree from the Graduate School of Library Science, University of Chicago, 1943. He was awarded an honorary L.H.D. degree from Morgan State College in 1969 and the same degree from Berea College in 1973. Both in 1938 and in 1942, he was a Rosenwald fellow. He was granted a Guggenheim fellowship for creative writing in 1949 and again in 1954, further confirmation of his status as one of America's pioneer black authors and librarians.

His love for books and libraries became a part of his life early and had a noticeable effect on him throughout his lifetime and his career. Bontemps recalled that he "came to himself" while in the children's reading room in the branch library in Los Angeles. From that time, he lived and worked in an atmosphere of books. With school and college days behind him in California, and with a small sheet of adolescent poetry in his suitcase, Bontemps hurried to New York in search of employment, unaware of the exciting upsurge of creativity in the black community there that came to be known as the Harlem Renaissance. Although he considered a medical career, and although the musical impulse recognized earlier in his family was also prominent in his mind, he dismissed the possibility of a career in either of these fields and accepted a teaching post at the Harlem Academy, where he remained from 1924 to 1931.

On August 26, 1926, Bontemps married Alberta Johnson, whom he met in New York while teaching at the Harlem Academy. They had six children: Joan Marie, Paul Bismark, Poppy Alberta, Camille Ruby, Constance Rebecca, and Arna Alex.

During his teaching days, Bontemps also carried on his literary work, writing poetry, short stories, novels, and history, many of which works were well received. He also met and worked with the major figures of the Harlem Renaissance, including Langston Hughes, Jean Toomer, James Weldon Johnson, and Countee Cullen. His career in private school teaching continued, however, as he moved to Huntsville, Alabama, in 1931, and taught at Oakwood Junior College until 1934. In 1935, Bontemps and his family moved to Chicago, where he accepted a teaching position in the Shiloh Academy, remaining in that position for three years.

With the Julius Rosenwald Fund fellowships which he received in 1938 and in 1939, he engaged in creative writing and travel in the Caribbean.

Because his career in writing began before he entered the library profession, Bontemps has been regarded frequently as a "writer turned librarian." His reason for entering librarianship was "I thought it was right for me." After engaging in graduate work in English at the University of Chicago, he discarded the idea of continuing with the doctorate in English because the effects of the Depression on the job market were still very much present, particularly for English teachers. Thus, the idea of librarianship seemed to come at a time when Bontemps could take full advantage of it.

Earlier, Bontemps had struck up an acquaintance and friendship with James Weldon Johnson, professor of creative writing at Fisk. When Johnson died in 1938, Fisk was without a scholar to fill this post. Later on, Fisk found itself without a head librarian, as its former librarians Louis Shores and Carl White had moved on to other positions, and Neil Van Heusen had died. Thomas Elsa Jones, the president of Fisk, approached Bontemps about a combined creative writing and library post. Bontemps, though, felt that his lack of experience, coupled with the absence of a library science degree, would lead him to difficulty with other librarians at Fisk. In his determination to bring Bontemps to the campus, the Fisk president appointed an acting librarian and did not fill the position permanently until Bontemps could receive his degree. Upon receiving a fellowship, Bontemps entered the Graduate Library School at the University of Chicago, receiving his degree in December 1943, four months after he came to Fisk. The joint position was never realized, however. Bontemps found that the position of librarian was full time and left no time for teaching creative writing. He asked to be relieved of the teaching aspect of the position and, as a result, he did not teach creative writing at that time. "I'm awfully glad I didn't," he remarked, although he could not know that nearly thirty years later he would direct a writers' workshop at Fisk.

Bontemps saw his accomplishments in building the collections at Fisk as both personally important and important to scholarship in general. He secured a gift from the E. R. Alexanders to form the E. R. Alexander Collection, a financial boost during a time of limited funds. With a grant from the General Education Board, he was able to make purchases of early materials on the black experience that are now recognized as classics in the field. Additionally, he was able to enlarge greatly the Negro collection that had been started at the time of Fisk's founding in 1865 and had been built up especially by Arthur A. Schomburg (q.v.), when he was curator of the collection from 1929 to 1931. His long, close association

with Langston Hughes resulted in the establishment of a Langston Hughes Collection, and the papers of such Harlem Renaissance figures as Jean Toomer, James Weldon Johnson, Charles S. Johnson, and Countee Cullen also came to Fisk. Too, he was active in collecting secondary as well as primary materials, and Fisk thereby built up one of the outstanding small college libraries in the country, particularly with regard to materials detailing the black experience.

Bontemps retired from his post in 1964. For one year following, he served as director of university relations and acting librarian at Fisk, until a new librarian could be appointed. Bontemps was 64 years old and wanted to take a sabbatical "while I thought it was a little more hopeful." He then accepted an invitation to teach a course in black history at the University of Illinois, Chicago Circle. Illinois also wanted him to introduce courses in black literature, one of the areas that he long had been promoting. It was his belief that "the black experience is seen better through the literature than through the history." As he examined the curricular offerings in the schools, in the colleges, and in black studies programs during the 1970s, Bontemps concluded that the literature predominated. "And I think that I was the one who initiated the emphasis," he remarked.

His position as lecturer and curator of the James Weldon Johnson Collection at Yale, which he assumed in 1969 and continued to 1971, enabled Bontemps to continue his productivity in a more precise phase of librarianship, working with a special black collection that had a continuing interest for him. It also enabled him to share his writing talents with others through the lectures that he gave at Yale and elsewhere. Despite the fact that he reached the mandatory retirement age while at Yale in 1971, Bontemps had a standing invitation to return to Chicago Circle; but he chose instead to return to Fisk in Nashville, where he began writing his autobiography.

Bontemps produced scores of works, including novels, poetry, plays, books, biographies, histories, and anthologies. His first published item, a poem entitled "Hope," appeared in *Crisis* in 1924, about the time of his move to New York. *God Sends Sunday*, which appeared in 1934, was his first novel; and, while certain literary historians used that work to mark the end of the Harlem Renaissance, for the author, it marked the beginning of a succession of experiments with a variety of literary forms. *God Sends Sunday* was read very little during the Depression year in which it appeared; however, the work went through various dramatic and musical adaptations, culminating in a musical comedy titled *St. Louis Woman*, on which he had the collaboration of Countee Cullen, himself a Harlem Renaissance writer.

Bontemps's major writings included *Golden Slippers: An Anthology* (1941); *Father of the Blues*, by W. C. Handy (edited by Bontemps, 1941); *Black Thunder* (1936, reissued 1968); *We Have Tomorrow* (1945); *Story of the Negro* (1948); *The Poetry of the Negro, 1746-1970* (co-edited with Langston Hughes, 1949); *Chariot in the Sky* (1951); *Story of George Washington Carver* (1954); *Lonesome Boy* (1955); *The Book of Negro Folklore* (an anthology co-edited with Langston Hughes, 1959); *Frederick Douglass: Slave-Fighter-Freeman* (1959); *One Hundred Years of Negro Freedom* (1961); *American Negro Poetry* (1963); *Personals* (1963); *Famous Negro Athletes* (in collaboration with Jack Conroy, 1965); *Anyplace But Here* (1966); *Hold Fast to Dreams* (1969); *Great Slave Narratives* (anthology, 1969); *Free at Last: The Life of Frederick Douglass* (1971); *Young Booker: Booker T. Washington's Early Days* (1972); and *The Harlem Renaissance Remembered: Essays Edited with a Memoir* (1972).

Bontemps proved that the two careers make a favorable blend and that librarians can be creative writers and scholars. His writings, and particularly his children's works, helped fill a void in literature, since there were few black characters in early literature. He enjoyed writing for children for a number of reasons:

> children are very loyal readers; they stay with you; they respond. . . . There is a new generation of them every year, so that the book stays in print. . . . The children tell other youngsters who just follow them the next year that "you ought to read the *Fast Sooner Hound*; that was good. . . ." So the result is that you have a book that will last. . . . It's always gratifying for a writer to write anything that lasts. So much writing has such a short life. When you have a book that has been in print for 40 years, it makes you feel awfully proud.

His anthologies and other compilations, pulling together important works by black writers, made them available in a single source. Also, his influence was felt by young writers throughout his career. Earlier, he had persuaded such writers as Langston Hughes and Countee Cullen to write children's works, which they did, and quite successfully. Jack Conroy commented on his efforts in this regard when he said:

> When I visited Paul Breman in London shortly before he issued *Personals*. . . , I was reminded again of Arna's unceasing efforts to help other writers. . . . I learned that Arna had interested him in an edition of Fenton Johnson's "W. P. A. Poems," the manuscript of which I had given him so long ago. It never materialized in print, or hasn't to this date, but its very existence, as Arna notes in his preface to our *Anyplace But Here*, did Johnson a lot of good.

Bontemps's love for the Harlem Renaissance never weakened. His lectures in later years often centered on this theme and found full expression in *The Harlem Renaissance Remembered*, to which he added a memoir (1972). Here he reflects on his experiences and interactions with many of the Renaissance figures, giving a first-hand account of the writers and artists. He was also an avid sports fan, and his interest in sports probably stimulated him to write *Famous Negro Athletes*, one of his most successful works.

His influence on young writers was felt even through his last years, as he conducted writers' workshops at Fisk (1971-1973). Indeed, after he returned to Fisk, he was called upon by the entire Fisk community to give his services, and at the same time, the nation was looking to him for wisdom and leadership in areas of black literature and culture. Thus, in his later years, Bontemps was able to effect without difficulty what he had struggled to accomplish in earlier years, when publishers rejected works with black characters and when the nation's interest in black literature was less noticeable.

The Alexander Pushkin Prize was awarded to Bontemps in 1926 for his poem "Golgotha Is a Mountain" and again in 1927 for his poem "The Return." He received the Crisis Poetry Prize in 1927 for his poem "A Nocturne at Bethesda." In 1932, he was awarded the *Opportunity* (*Journal of Negro Life*) short story prize for "A Summer Tragedy," and in 1956 he received the Jane Addams Children's Book Award for *Story of the Negro*. The Society of Midland Authors awarded Bontemps the Dow Award in 1967 for his book *Anyplace But Here*. Yet, the honors Bontemps received extended beyond those awarded to him for his creative works. In 1948, he was elected to membership in PEN, the International Association of Writers. The Library of Congress named him honorary consultant in American Cultural History in 1972. He was also a member of the Authors League of America and the Dramatists Guild.

Bontemps is well remembered also for his even temper, his good nature, his warm, friendly, positive approach. When asked if he considered himself an even-tempered person, he replied, "Well, I think that I can see things as a whole a little better than some of the people I've worked with. But I think that's just all the result of the way that I grew up, and my environment." For example, while others have found W. C. Handy, whose biography Bontemps edited, cantankerous and difficult, Bontemps found him creative, and a wild and curious genius. "I can back off and sort of see his situation," he remarked. Regarding collaboration on a project, he remarked that "it is not difficult when people know each other and know how the other thinks, and [have] a desire to be harmonious." In specific reference to Langston

Hughes, he remarked that, if they found areas in which their thoughts ran a little differently, they simply did not work in those areas but chose areas in which they had a broad similarity of outlook.

His appearance complemented his personality. Bontemps had creole features and was of medium height with a stocky build (he weighed around 175 pounds in his later years). His face always reflected his kind and gentle nature, his graciousness, while his greying hair helped give him a distinguished appearance. His gentleness and warmth were present whether he was administering to the library needs of Fisk, lecturing to groups, or telling stories to children. His ability to tell the history of the Fisk Jubilee Singers, for instance, often put the listener back into the period of history of which he spoke and enabled him to capture the feeling of that day.

The qualities of Arna Bontemps as writer, lecturer, and librarian are well preserved not only in his numerous works, in documents written about him, and in the library collections that he built, but in the hearts of those who knew him and worked with him. The scholarship, creativity, and humanitarianism that he brought to his library work will long serve as an example to future librarians. He died June 4, 1973.

Biographical listings and obituaries—Contemporary Authors 1, 41; Current Biography (1946); Who Was Who in America V (1969-1973); Who's Who in the World, 2nd ed. Books and articles about the biographee—Conroy, Jack. "Memories of Arna Bontemps: Friend and Collaborator." American Libraries 5:602-606 (December 1974); Jones, Virginia Lacy. "Arna Bontemps, 1902-1973." Publishers Weekly 96:2038 (July 1973). Primary sources and archival materials—Black Oral History Interview with Arna Bontemps, January 9, 1972, by L. M. Collins. Transcript, Fisk University Library, Fisk University, Nashville, Tennessee; Black Oral History Interview with Arna Bontemps, July 14, 1972, by Ann Allen Shockley. Transcript, Fisk University Library, Fisk University, Nashville, Tennessee; Bontemps, Arna. The Harlem Renaissance Remembered. New York: Dodd, Mead, 1972; The bulk of Bontemps's personal papers are at Syracuse University, while other personal papers and those from his position as University Librarian at Fisk are housed at Fisk University.

—JESSIE CARNEY SMITH

BOSTWICK, ARTHUR ELMORE (1860-1942)

Arthur Elmore Bostwick was born March 8, 1860, in Litchfield, Connecticut, the only son of David Elmore and Adelaide McKinley Bostwick to survive infancy. His father, a physician with general practice, died when Bostwick was twelve years old, leaving his determined mother with sole responsibility of raising him.

Bostwick benefitted from the intellectual heritage and the natural attractions of Litchfield, and he indulged in several pastimes—sleighing, skating, following circuses, trainhopping, "winding wreaths of evergreen at Christmastime for the little Episcopal church" (where his mother played the organ), "attending trials diligently" at the county courthouse, and reading old periodicals and books in the garret of the family home, which housed lodgers from time to time. Young Bostwick also travelled to Philadelphia for the Centennial Exposition and to New York for theatrical performances, edited the Litchfield Institute's school paper for two years, and worked (in his mother's place) in the Litchfield Circulating Library. He took the Yale entrance examination in June 1877.

At Yale, Bostwick distinguished himself not only in his studies of physics (he was the first recipient of the Silliman Fellowship in physical science), but also as editor of the Yale Daily News, Class Day historian, and as an enthusiastic patron of the arts and sports. Two years after earning the B.A. degree and admission to Phi Beta Kappa (1881), Bostwick received the Ph.D. in physics, the only Ph.D. awarded by Yale University in 1883. He appeared headed for a career in college teaching, but that door closed at Yale after one year on a temporary appointment. Bostwick, needing some security in light of his recent engagement to be married, then accepted appointment as a high school teacher in Montclair, New Jersey, where he lived for the next 25 years. In June 1885, he was married to Lucy Sawyer; they had three children—Andrew Linn, Esther, and Elmore McNeill.

Bostwick found that two years of high school teaching were enough to discourage him, although as he wrote, he "always enjoyed communicating any special knowledge . . . to those who are interested in acquiring it." In 1886, through connections with his cousin, John D. Champlin, he joined the editorial staff of Appleton's Cyclopedia of American Biography in New York City. Thereby doubling his salary, he was able to retain the family home in Montclair and further develop his writing abilities. After two years, the Appleton project ended, and he joined Champlin in producing the one-volume Young Folks' Cyclopedia of Games and Sports (1890). In addition, from 1890 to 1894, he successively helped edit Forum magazine; A Standard Dictionary of the English Language (1893), edited by Isaac K. Funk and Adam W. Wagnalls; and the science section of Literary Digest, a responsibility he discharged until 1933. In each of these endeavors, his knowledge of the physical sciences and his literary talent complemented each other well.

In 1895, Bostwick became chief librarian of the New York Free Circulating Library, again at the behest of his cousin. His former employer, William H. Appleton, was a founder of the Library and current chairman of the library committee. Admitting that his "ignorance of library administration and library methods was complete" and that he was entering the profession at the top, Bostwick nevertheless resolved to succeed. He also acknowledged that his library education would involve continuous commitment, which explains in part his later ambivalence about supporting the exclusive prerogatives of library schools for professional training. Bostwick entered librarianship under exciting circumstances. The concepts of circulating library and reference library had recently been joined (1895) by the establishment of the New York Public Library, a system of separate branch libraries linked to the endowed collections of the older, private Astor and Lenox libraries, along with the Tilden Trust—all under the general directorship of John Shaw Billings (q.v.). Bostwick's apprenticeship was to supervise a half-dozen branch libraries, where he soon inaugurated the open-shelf arrangement and consolidated extension service for schools.

From 1899 to 1901, he directed the new Brooklyn Public Library, which New York City had just acquired. Here, Bostwick supervised the transition from private to public support, implemented the branch concept, promoted open shelves, established children's collections and an apprenticeship program, supported a travelling library, and stimulated a five-fold circulation increase. But in 1901, he returned to the New York Public Library, to his old job, now retitled chief of the Circulation Department.

The 1895 reorganization, however, took time to be realized. Small circulating libraries received encouragement to join the system as branches through a 5.2 million dollar donation that Andrew Carnegie (q.v.) designated specifically for the erection of branch buildings (ultimately about 65 in all). Bostwick matured professionally during this exciting eight-year period in New York. He not only supervised the vast building program, with many branches often opening simultaneously, but

> began children's rooms and a training class, initiated cooperation with the public schools, and provided foreign language books for the swelling immigrant population, whose reading needs he met with rare understanding. By 1909 he was overseeing the largest circulation library in the world, with forty-one branches and an annual circulation of 6,500,000 volumes.

He became an effective spokesman for "the library as an instrument of popular education" in contrast to Billings who, with his military bearing, viewed a library as "a reference institution for scholarly use." However, Bostwick's growing philosophical breach with his chief did not prevent his swift rise to national recognition in his profession. Prior to his service as president of the American Library Association (1907-1908), he was president of the New York Library Club (1897-1899) and the New York State Library Association (1901-1903); he became a fellow of the American Library Institute in 1906. By 1909, however, the situation prompted him to accept the directorship of the St. Louis Public Library upon the resignation of his old friend Frederick M. Crunden (q.v.).

From 1909 to the end of his life, the "transplanted Easterner," as Bostwick referred to himself, made St. Louis his home. He served as librarian until 1938 and thereafter as associate librarian. His "fine administrative and organizational ability, his flair for experiment, his liberal views (he refused to stop the circulation of German books during World War I), and his experienced community-mindedness" all contributed to the St. Louis Public Library's national stature. After a new main building was occupied in January 1912, Bostwick concentrated on developing the library's influence on the city—during peace and prosperity, and during war and depression. When he "retired" in 1938, the trustees noted that branches had grown from four to nineteen, that circulation had more than tripled (to over three million volumes), and that he had instilled loyalty in the staff.

Bostwick's St. Louis years included several specific achievements, but they ended amid the economic woes of the 1930s, which blunted further growth. Among his accomplishments were the successful retention of the library's share of tax funds, in spite of a vigorous campaign by the mayor to divert them into a general fund; the reclassification of the collection from the system devised by William T. Harris (q.v.), former school superintendent, to a Decimal Classification; and the establishment of the "St. Louis Plan" of providing duplicate copies of current titles by charging borrowers a cent or two per day (once a book was paid for, it was transferred to the circulating collection). The Depression strained both Bostwick's ingenuity and that of his staff. As the assessed valuation of property declined, so did the revenues devoted to the Library. The income for 1938, for example, was over $100,000 less than it had been in 1929. The book budget for 1939 had shrunk to $50,000, whereas a decade earlier it had been $90,000.

During his retirement, Bostwick reflected comfortably on his past in his engagingly written autobiography, *A Life with Men and Books* (1939), from which most of his quotations in this sketch are taken. His life story, spanning the period between Melvil Dewey's (q.v.) apogee and World War II, is one of few such reminiscences in print. Ever a cultured gentleman, Bostwick was no stranger to intellectual society. He read several languages, enjoyed reading mathematical works and music scores for pleasure, and relished the performing arts, travel, and social gatherings. His wide reading, including detective stories, was well known. He reached his stride in St. Louis, which he came to love and passionately defend against its critics. In the words of Margery Doud, a colleague, he was called upon to address many groups and clubs and in time became a member of many leading organizations. He was tall and of commanding presence. His face, though grave in repose, lighted up instantly in conversation or when he addressed audiences. He added distinction and authority to any gathering he attended and was soon very much a part of the intellectual life of St. Louis.

Among the groups to which he belonged were the New England Society (president, 1911), Contemporary Club, St. Louis Art League (president, 1920), Society of St. Louis Authors, St. Louis Branch of the League of Nations Non-Partisan Association (president, 1924-1933), St. Louis branch of the Foreign Policy Association (president, 1927), Missouri Welfare League (president, 1926-1936), and the St. Louis Archeological Society (president, 1915). His social organizations included the Authors Club (New York), Artists' Guild, Town and Gown, and the Round Table (a prestigious dinner club). As Charles H. Compton (q.v.), his assistant and successor, has written, "to the discerning he was the first citizen of St. Louis."

Bostwick's formal affiliations in librarianship present a wide spectrum of interests including, in addition to those already mentioned, being a delegate to the Copyright Conference (1905-1906) and the presidency of the Missouri Library Commission (1911-1917). Besides his ALA presidency (1907-1908), he also served on the War Service Committee (1917), the Publishing Board (1909-1921; president, 1918-1921), and the Library Survey Committee (chairman, 1922-1929). He made numerous surveys himself in various parts of the country, including the Boston Public Library, the Oakland Public Library, and the St. Paul Public Library. He consulted on the building of libraries at Jacksonville, Florida; Tuxedo Park, New York; and Mobile, Alabama; and he advised on the plans for the Sterling Library at Yale University. He was well received both as a public speaker and as an ambassador of the profession.

In one of his crowning experiences, he visited China in 1925 as an ALA representative under the auspices of the Chinese Association for the Advancement of Education; after that, he served as an honorary director of the Library Association of China. In 1929, he was an ALA delegate to the International Library Conference held in Rome and Venice, at which Mussolini delivered the welcoming address and at which he himself read a paper on "The Public Library in the United States."

Bostwick was also involved with higher education, as a member of the New York State University Council (1904) and a participant in institutes and forums at Washington University, from which he received the honorary LL.D. in 1932. Since the St.

Louis Public Library maintained a library school from 1917 to 1932, Bostwick also assumed responsibility in the Association of American Library Schools, serving as president in 1932-1933 (the final year of the school's accreditation) and earlier as chairman of the Committee on Relations between AALS and the ALA Board of Education for Librarianship (1928-1932). He delivered addresses at most of the accredited schools.

Bostwick's range of official responsibilities within and without the profession was complemented by a continual flow of publications. These included some two hundred articles and obituary tributes, seven book reviews, and thirteen revealing letters to editors—all within a wide variety of media. Besides the works he edited or jointly authored, he wrote nineteen books, manuals, and pamphlets—among which the most noteworthy were *American Public Library* (four editions between 1910 and 1929), *Popular Libraries of the World* (1933), and his autobiography (1939). He edited the *Classics of American Librarianship* (ten volumes, 1914-1933), *Doubleday's Encyclopedia* (eleven volumes, 1938), and, until his death, *American Library Pioneers* (four volumes, 1924-1942). (Joseph A. Boromé compiled a complete bibliography of his work in 1944.)

To employees, professional colleagues, and individuals who knew him well, Arthur Bostwick was a unique individual with a rare combination of excellent training, developed talents, and natural abilities. James I. Wyer (q.v.) summarized his impression thus: "When to Industry and Versatility are, as with Arthur Bostwick, joined a keen mind, a trained power of analysis, clear thinking, lucid writing, and engaging address, the result is bound to be a striking, exhilarating, almost a spectacular career." Others, such as Anne Carroll Moore (q.v.), regarded him "as guide, philosopher, and friend with a special flair for experimentation in methods and a keenness of observation and power of analysing a situation that presented a constant challenge to be up and doing in whatever field one might be serving."

The 1938 tribute of the St. Louis Public Library Board of Directors was recognized as accurate when read by the entire profession:

the tremendous range of information at his command, his scientific outlook, his freedom from prejudice, the openness of his mind to all points of view, and his wide and intimate knowledge of books. . . . keen interest in all things, a robust joy in life and new experience, a sense of humor that never fails him, and an innate simplicity in his manner and attitude toward others.

Margery Doud, who spent the greater part of her professional life with Bostwick, appraised him thus:

Had he gone to Johns Hopkins, as he almost did when that institution awarded him a fellowship, after his graduate work at Yale, Dr. Bostwick would probably have been lost to the library world and might have become one of the great nuclear physicists. But no matter what field he had entered, he would have brought to it the same basic contribution he brought to librarianship—the liberal open mind, the scientific outlook and clarity of perception, the love of books and faith in their power to educate.

Looking back over his own life, he wrote, "I realize that it has always been focused on one thing—the production and distribution of print—the writing and editing of books and periodicals and making them widely available through the work of libraries."

A stately, reserved, distinguished-looking man, Bostwick impressed some "as if he would send in a riot call if anyone presumed to slap him on the back," according to Keith Kerman of the *St. Louis Post-Dispatch.* He was a progressive Republican in politics and an Episcopalian by church affiliation. While his autobiography deliberately omits much mention of his wife and family, he was devoted to both; Lucy was a cheery companion to him at home and on the road. Although the Bostwicks lived in only two localities, he owned a succession of residences in Montclair and St. Louis; after his wife's death in 1930, he moved to an apartment-hotel with his elder son. Only the younger son survived him, however.

Bostwick died in Oak Grove, Missouri, of auricular fibrillation on February 13, 1942, three weeks before he would have been 82. His ashes were buried in the New East Cemetery in Litchfield—the village of his youth which always gave him, in his words, "such a lift of heart." Allan Angoff succinctly summarized the lasting contribution of the scholar-librarian in 1951 when he wrote, "He set up the love of books as one of the most important requirements for librarianship at a time when it was much more fashionable to emphasize new techniques—and that is an immense contribution whose importance today is even greater than when Bostwick lived." That legacy is treasured even more highly in the 1970s.

Biographical listings and obituaries—*Current Biography* (1942); *National Cyclopaedia of American Biography* 14; [Obituary]. *New York Times,* February 14, 1942, p. 15; *Who Was Who in America* II (1943-1950). Books and articles about the biographee—Boromé, Joseph A. "A Bibliography of Arthur Elmore Bostwick 1860-1942." *Bulletin of Bibliography* 18:62-66 (January-April 1944); Compton, Charles H. *Twenty-Five Crucial Years of the St. Louis Public Library, 1927 to 1952.* St. Louis: St. Louis Public Library, 1953; Dain, Phyllis. *The New York Public Library: A History of Its Founding and Early Years.* New York: The New York Public Library, 1972; Davis, Donald G., Jr. *The Association of American Library Schools, 1915-1968: An Analytical History.* Metuchen, N.J.: Scarecrow Press, 1974; Doud, Margery. "Recollections of Arthur E. Bostwick." *Wilson Library Bulletin* 27:818-25 (June 1953); Doud, Margery. "Arthur E. Bostwick." In *Pioneering Leaders in Librarianship,* edited by Emily Miller Danton. Chicago: American

Library Association, 1953, pp. 22-23; Moore, Anne Carroll. "Arthur Elmore Bostwick, 1860-1942, Citizen of the World." *ALA Bulletin* 36:210-11, 220 (March 1942). **Primary sources and archival materials**—Bostwick, Arthur E. *A Life with Men and Books.* New York: H. W. Wilson, 1939. Consult also the archives of the St. Louis Public Library for Bostwick's papers and other related documents.

-DONALD G. DAVIS, JR.

BOWERMAN, GEORGE FRANKLIN (1868-1960)

George Franklin Bowerman was born September 8, 1868, on his father's farm in Farmington, Ontario County, New York, the first of six children born to Quaker parents, Jarvis R. and Anna Ewer Bowerman. He attended country schools in Farmington and Mendon and, having "from [his] reading early formed a desire for a higher education instead of staying on the farm," went to live with relatives in Honeoye Falls so that he could attend high school there. Since the principal of the school, however, was "a drunken sot who spoke ungrammatically and was a rather boorish person," Bowerman persuaded his father to move to Lima so that George could enroll in the Genesee Wesleyan Seminary, from which he graduated in 1888, the first member of his family to obtain a high school degree.

That same year he entered the University of Rochester, from which he received his baccalaureate degree in 1892, having paid for his education by working in the college library, in a local bookstore, and on the family farm. Later, he was chosen for honorary membership in Phi Beta Kappa, and in 1913, George Washington University conferred on him the honorary degree of L.H.D. Since none of the librarians with whom Bowerman had come in contact had "made sufficient impression on [him] to lead [him] to adopt the profession of librarianship," he applied for a job as a recruiter of fruit tree salesmen and remained in this job for nearly a year.

Bowerman's long career in librarianship began in 1893, when he went to the Chicago World's Fair to meet Melvil Dewey (q.v.), that "remarkable but eccentric man," who was in charge of New York's educational exhibit at the Fair. Dewey immediately employed the young man to grade Regents' examination papers and, a few weeks later, approved his transfer to the New York State Library, so that Bowerman could work full time as a reference librarian while earning his B.L.S. degree from the New York State Library School (1895). He worked for a year as a reference librarian at the Reynolds Library in Rochester, then returned to the New York State Library, where he again worked as a reference librarian from 1897 to 1898.

Because they knew that he was unhappy in Albany, two fraternity brothers arranged for Bowerman to join them at the *New York Tribune,* where he worked as the biographical and educational editor from 1898 to 1900. He spent most of his time writing obituaries and editing the reports of the *Tribune*'s campus stringers, and when the paper experienced financial difficulties, he left to become a biographical editor of the *New International Encyclopedia.* By this time, however, he had decided finally to make a career of librarianship and successfully applied for the chief librarian's position at the Wilmington (Delaware) Institute Free Library, where he served from March 19, 1901, to September 1, 1904.

Though Bowerman, in retrospect, often thought of his years in journalism as a detour from his true calling in librarianship, he also felt that his *Tribune* editorials in support of the appointment of Herbert Putnam (q.v.) as Librarian of Congress in 1899 were probably very influential in his own appointment as head of the District of Columbia Library in 1904. No doubt Putnam's recommendation helped, but "the intelligent forcefulness of his personality" was what impressed the trustees, who in commendation thereafter often referred to his persuasiveness, his boyish enthusiasm, and his "bouyant friendliness."

Bowerman arrived in Washington in the fall of 1904, at the age of 36. And it is a testament to his vision and energy that when he retired on September 30, 1940, after two extensions of his term by President Franklin D. Roosevelt, the Public Library of the District of Columbia was recognized as one of the preeminent public libraries in this country.

In all important respects, the story of George Bowerman's career is the story of the development of the D.C. Public Library. The library was created by an Act of Congress in 1890, but the building was not opened to the public until January 11, 1899. When Bowerman took charge nearly six years later, the library building was not yet fully occupied, the staff was small and poorly trained, and no clear course of development had been propounded. When he left, a new central library was under construction, staff, borrowers and appropriations had been increased by factors of five to ten, and Washingtonians could boast of their renowned and vital public library.

To a degree, of course, one would expect a significant increase in statistics during Bowerman's 36-year tenure. Such expectations might not, however, take into account problems unique to Washington. The peculiarity to note is the fact that residents of Washington, until 1974, were totally disenfranchised; they had no power to create a library, to raise taxes for its support, or even to accept Andrew Carnegie's (q.v.) offer to build a library. The library could come into being only with the consent of Congress, and all of its financial support had to be wrested from the congressional appropriations committees in annual battles so strenuous that they often sent Bowerman home to recuperate after his testimony. The task was especially grueling because

Congress, having its own great library entirely at its disposal, was slow to recognize that the general populace could not and did not have its choice of books delivered directly to the door.

By all accounts, however, Bowerman was more than equal to these battles, succeeding not only in having his appropriations increased from $36,000 to $548,000 during his years as head of the D.C. Public Library, but also in persuading Congress to enact the two major pieces of legislation of which Bowerman, as chief lobbyist, was supremely proud: the Retirement Act of 1920, which brought his librarians into the federal employees' retirement system, and the Classification Act of 1923, which removed librarians from the clerical to the professional federal employee ranks.

Bowerman's conception of the function of a public library is clearly expressed in his definition of a library as the "university of the people." Guided by this principle, he immediately tore all the iron bars off the windows of the central library to let in the (literal and symbolic) light. He fought for the creation of twelve branch libraries, distributed books to more than 180 public and private schools, hospitals, government agencies, etc., and quickly opened the Library's registration rolls to residents of the Maryland and Virginia suburbs and to temporary residents of Washington. Abetted by Theodore Noyes, editor of the prestigious *Washington Star* and president of the Library's trustees for half a century, he aggressively advertised the Library's services, drawing so many new readers to the Library that catalogers often had to be drawn from their work to assist readers. He took special pride in promoting the use of non-fiction by recruiting specialists in fields such as technology, sociology, fine arts, music, Washingtoniana, etc., to stimulate the "robust" reading that he so robustly advocated.

Bowerman also enthusiastically promoted work with children, arguing repeatedly for the professional training of children's librarians and for their treatment within the profession as experts in a vital field, not as subprofessionals engaged in frivolous activity. But the primary motive even for this emphasis was again Bowerman's larger concept of the library as educational center, a notion that led directly to his great involvement in the adult education movement and to his observation that "library work for children is . . . a phase of adult education." The fervor with which Bowerman fought Congress for funds and battled with the superintendent of the District schools for a larger share of the educational "pie" is more easily understood if one keeps Bowerman's conception of the public library clearly in mind. For Bowerman, this philosophy was such a major impetus in his life and career that his anguish over his inability (before 1923 especially) to pay trained librarians sufficiently well to retain them clearly represents not the desire of a bureaucrat for self-aggrandizement, but the fervent belief of this humanist that "reading frees man" and that failure to support the library was as foolhardy as failure to support hospitals and a police force.

Bowerman considered himself fortunate to live long enough to see many of his dreams come to fruition. But even at 72, in his retirement message, he outlined much work still to be done, remarking that the trustees were probably glad to have him retire "in order to keep [him] from outlining a still larger program."

Because of his own frustration at being voteless, and because of his long acquaintance with Susan B. Anthony, Bowerman was an indefatigable supporter of the women's suffrage movement, marching in suffragette parades, urging the appointment of women to his board of trustees and glowing with satisfaction at the selection of a woman, Clara Herbert, as his successor at the D.C. Public Library.

Bowerman was an active member of the American Library Association, serving as treasurer in 1906, as chairman of its Commission on Civil Service Relations, and as a member of its bookbinding and classification of librarians committees for many years. He served as a vice president of the International Congress of Librarians in Brussels (1910), and was a member of the Delaware State Library Commission (1901-1904), of the District of Columbia Library Association (president, 1906-1907), of the Religious Education Association (president of the Library Department), of the Literary Society of Washington, of the National Cathedral Library Committee, and of the (Washington) Cosmos Club. Bowerman was an avid walker, and he delighted in travel, journeying to Alaska, Central America, Mexico, Russia, and (nine times) Europe.

Bowerman's first book was *A Selected Bibliography of the Religious Denominations of the United States* (1896). He wrote frequently for *Library Journal*, *Library Quarterly*, the *Journal of Adult Education* and other professional journals, and collected many of these essays and addresses in *Censorship and Other Papers* (1931), which also contains a fairly comprehensive bibliography of his articles and speeches written prior to that date.

Bowerman's first wife, Sarah Newcomb Graham, whom he married on June 13, 1901, was killed in 1935. At his death on August 6, 1960, he was survived by his second wife, Joy Louise Webster, whom he had married on June 1, 1937. There were no children of either marriage.

Biographical listings and obituaries—*National Cyclopaedia of American Biography* 14; [Obituary]. *The Washington Post*, August 8, 1960; *Who Was Who in America* IV (1961-1968). **Primary sources and archival materials**— Consult Bowerman's *Some Memories, Facts, Figures and*

Events in My Life (privately printed, 1956) as well as his annual reports to the Commissioners of the District of Columbia. See also the scrapbooks on the history of the now Martin Luther King Public Library in that Library's Washingtoniana Division.

—WINSTON TABB

BOWKER, RICHARD ROGERS (1848-1933)

Richard Rogers Bowker, publisher, author, editor, businessman, library advocate, and political reformer —whose name is inseparable from the history of book publishing and librarianship in the United States—was born September 4, 1848, in Salem, Massachusetts. He was the only son and eldest of the two children of Daniel Rogers and Theresa Maria Savory Bowker. His biographer, E. McClung Fleming, describes him as a Yankee Puritan, a background of which Bowker was proud. Bowker was known as a man who always persisted in devising solutions to difficult problems after others conceded defeat, and this persistence inspired his colleagues in cultural, business, and political spheres.

Daniel Bowker and his family lived and prospered in Salem until the depression of 1857 and the hard times that followed forced him to move to New York, where he experienced another series of business disasters. The family had to abandon plans to send Richard to Harvard College, where two hundred years before an ancestor had been president. Instead, Bowker enrolled in the Free Academy, which was to become the City College of New York by the time of his graduation (1868).

As a student, Bowker displayed leadership characteristics, as well as an interest in journalism, reform, and politics. He was the founder and editor of the *Collegian*, one of the first college newspapers in the country, and he not only managed the paper, but did reporting, proofreading, make-up, and other practical tasks. In addition, he is credited with establishing a student senate, the first effort at student government in an American educational institution. He obtained the school's charter for a Phi Beta Kappa chapter, although he was not admitted to it because the school's president perceived rebellious behavior on Bowker's part. Nevertheless, Bowker graduated fifth of eight honor students.

Bowker's college newspaper work brought him into contact with professional journalists, and after reporting on his City College commencement for the newly founded New York *Evening Mail*, he was employed as its city editor. Within a year, he became the paper's literary editor, the first such editor for a New York daily.

Through his work and his numerous contributions to such publications as the *Cosmopolitan*, the *Herald*, the *New York Tribune*, the *London Athenaeum*, and *Scribner's Monthly*, he came to know and be known to the leading literary figures of the period. As a result, Frederick Leypoldt (q.v.) asked him to write an ambitious review, "Literature in America in 1871," for the third edition of his *American Catalogue and Weekly Trade Circular*. The article noted the dominance of such philosophers and poets as William Ellery Channing, Whittier, and Longfellow and reported that three quarters of the novels, and "those of highest merit," were written by women. When Leypoldt's *Publishers' Weekly* appeared in 1872, Bowker became a frequent contributor. In 1875, disgusted with the internal intrigues and financial mismanagement of the *Evening Mail*, he joined Leypoldt as a full-time editor of *Publishers' Weekly*, thus beginning a lifelong association.

Publishers' Weekly was the creation of Frederick Leypoldt, a dedicated bibliographer, who had immigrated to America in 1854 from Stuttgart, Germany. After several years in the bookstore business, he had formed a publishing company with Henry Holt, later the founder of Holt, Rinehart, and Winston. This partnership lasted only two years, however, for Leypoldt was eager to pursue his own publishing interest—book trade bibliography. Initially, his efforts were directed to the expansion of the *Literary Bulletin*, Leypoldt and Holt's monthly circular listing new U.S. and foreign publications. The first issue of the expanded *Bulletin* appeared as *Publishers' Weekly* on January 18, 1872. At the time Bowker joined him, Leypoldt's company produced several publications that were to become cornerstones of American bibliography and that were the predecessors for many of the books, journals, and reference guides still in existence. The company published the *Literary News*, a monthly review of current literature; the *Index Medicus*, a monthly key to medical literature; reading guides and library aids; an annual compilation of publishers' catalogs; and, most important to Leypoldt, weekly, monthly, and annual lists of books published. The annual bibliography eventually appeared as the *American Catalogue*, and an annual *Education Catalogue*, listing available textbooks, was also published.

At first, Bowker's main responsibility was editing the *Weekly*'s general book news section. Gradually, however, he took on more of the business and editorial responsibilities as Leypoldt centered his attention on bibliographic services. Together they made *Publishers' Weekly* a journal of record and a clearinghouse for opinions and discussions leading toward more professional standards within the book industry. Bowker brought a strong managerial hand to the company and an active voice to social and political issues in the book world. He believed in

cheap books, provided they are honest books, well made, and fairly paying the man who sells them; . . . that the interests of the trade and the interests

of the public are identical in the long run; . . . that one publisher has [not] the right to take the fruits of another's labor by "jumping the claim" even if that publisher is not protected by law; . . . the full remuneration of authors, foreign and American; . . . international copyright; . . . that the makers of books should [not] be used by the makers of type to keep the materials of bookmaking at a higher tariff than books, themselves; . . . that the most liberal administration of the postal department best pays.

Book distribution, postal reform, and international copyright were the subjects of Bowker's editorials. He took part in organizing the American Book Trade Association and also campaigned for a joint book trade exhibit at the Philadelphia Centennial.

Meanwhile, *Publishers' Weekly* had begun to cover the activities of a new public library movement. By 1876, however, a small column was not enough to report all the news and changes in that growing field. Bowker and Leypoldt met with Melvil Dewey (q.v.)—then a young librarian at Amherst College—and the three men planned a professional journal and a national library organization. On September 30, 1876, the first issue of the *American Library Journal* appeared, designed to "collate for the librarian every view and fact which may be of use or interest to him in his work." Leypoldt was listed as publisher; Bowker, general editor; Dewey, managing editor; and Charles A. Cutter (q.v.), bibliographic editor. One month after the journal was published, the American Library Association was founded, and the plan for its organization was based on Bowker's experience in founding the American Book Trade Association.

In the beginning, neither the bibliographies nor *Library Journal* was financially successful. Because of Dewey's unreliability and librarians' lack of interest in subscribing, the firm was losing money. In a letter to Bowker several years later, Mrs. Leypoldt described her feelings at the time:

I never believed in the *Library Journal*, because I knew it would not pay. . . . I disapproved of the *management* of the *American Catalogue*; I *denounced* the borrowing of money on *false pretences*, for any fool could see that the *Catalogue* would take much longer to bring out than was stated to the Publishers that gave the money. The *Index Medicus* I thought was a Literary Medical Paper and I had been told Mr. Leypoldt had been guaranteed against loss, so I said nothing until I saw the first number, and when I found it was merely an *index*, consequently only of use to writing doctors, I opposed that and have quarrelled that it should be given up for many months. . . . I believe in the *Publishers' Weekly*. I always said you would make it pay. . . .

In 1878, with his resources spread over a wide range of publications, Leypoldt was forced to sell *Publishers' Weekly* to Bowker for $5,000. His financial condition failed to improve, and in 1884, overworked and deeply in debt, he died.

Leypoldt's untimely death forced Bowker to decide his exact relationship with *Publishers' Weekly*, which he had purchased out of a desire for a profitable investment rather than with any intention of permanently working with the book trade organ. In fact, in 1880, when Bowker had accepted an editorial position in London from Harper's, he had leased the *Weekly* back to Leypoldt, fully expecting the older man to buy back the publication.

Now *Publishers' Weekly* was without a managing editor, and unless someone were found to take over the entire operation—the bibliographic publications as well as the magazines—Leypoldt's life work would be ended. Bowker thus decided to resume the editorship of *PW* and lease *Library Journal* and the other publications from Mrs. Leypoldt. Eventually, in 1914, they incorporated the firm as the R. R. Bowker Company.

After becoming *PW* editor once again, Bowker aggressively entered the battle for an international copyright law as chairman of the Executive Committee and vice president of the American Copyright League. A member of both the authors' and publishers' organizations, Bowker was liaison between the various parties interested in a copyright law, and almost every issue of the magazine, and all the journals to which Bowker contributed regularly—the *New York Tribune*, the *Mail*, and *Harper's Weekly*—carried his crusading essays in favor of a copyright treaty. In 1891, these and other efforts came to fruition when President Harrison signed the first U.S. copyright law. Bowker's writings were collected into an influential book, *Copyright, Its Law and Its Literature*, edited by Thorvald Solberg (q.v.), and Bowker later published his own *Copyright, Its History and Its Law* in 1912.

Bowker resumed his library activities and is said to have done more than any other man of the time to develop library professionalism. In addition to working with the American Library Association, he was proud of his part in inducing President William McKinley to appoint a professional librarian, Herbert Putnam (q.v.), rather than a political figurehead, as Librarian of Congress in 1899. Bowker was also influential in the merging of many branches into the Brooklyn Public Library, and he served as trustee and director of the Library from 1889 until his death in 1933. His other activities in librarianship included helping to found the New York Library Club (1885) and serving as its first president, as well as being the first president of the New York State Library

Association. He lectured at Pratt Institute's Free Library, advised the City College Library, and established a library for his fraternity on that campus. He played an important role in initiating the Free Reference Library of the Brooklyn Museum and served from 1904 to 1918 as president of the Stockbridge, Massachusetts, Library Association. He also subscribed $10,000 to the Library of Congress Trustee Fund for bibliographic services and helped to reorganize the Vatican Library and the Library of the League of Nations.

He continued to write for *Library Journal* and urged librarians to play a part in bringing about a more enlightened society, including involvement in international affairs. He wrote: "Probably no class of people are more desirous of putting aside questions of race and birth and breeding, in the best democratic fashion, than are librarians. . . . their mission is to make good Americans out of all classes of material, whether of bad Americans or good importations."

Bowker was energetically and devotedly involved in the work of the American Library Association. A photograph taken in 1918 in Saratoga Springs shows the elegant Mr. Bowker with snow-white beard and mustache, looking every inch the scholarly and literary figure, seated with ten former presidents of the Association he helped organize—including Dewey, Putnam, and Arthur E. Bostwick (q.v.). Bowker repeatedly declined the presidency of ALA, because he believed the position should be held by a professional librarian. He was, however, a member of its Council and in 1926, in recognition of its great indebtedness to him, the organization elected him honorary president for the fiftieth anniversary year.

Bowker suffered from weak eyesight for many years of his life. By 1901, his approaching blindness hampered him seriously, and he was nearly totally blind by 1910. However, he had been married to Alice Mitchell in Brookline, Massachusetts, on January 1, 1902, in a ceremony conducted by Edward Everett Hale, and she helped him vigorously in his work. He continued as editor of both *Publishers' Weekly* and *Library Journal*, and through his firm and efficient management, his company grew. A number of new titles were added to the catalog, including books today known as *Publishers Trade List Annual*, *Bookman's Glossary*, *American Library Directory*, and *American Book Trade Directory*. In addition, he was responsible for the first systematized bibliography of U.S. government publications, the earliest list of state publications, and the first listing (1899) of the publications of America's scientific and literary societies. For the second edition (1908) of the state publications list, Bowker traveled to many state capitals and did much of the actual bibliographic work himself.

Bowker's role in American politics has been over-shadowed by his achievements in the publishing and literary fields. He was, however, a dedicated and indefatigable leader in the liberal movement. He organized groups, lobbied, wrote, and spoke out through every medium available to him on the strug-gles for free trade, civil service reform, civic educa-tion, ballot reform, anti-machine politics, anti-imperialism, prison reform, adult education, and a myriad of other social and political causes, all based on his belief in the basic goodness and perfectability of man. He wrote,

> the chief work of the Christ spirit in history [was] to develop humanity into the fullness of life, to bring the mass of men out of that mere existence that is scarcely more than a living death; to bring each man, high or low, out into a greater life than the men of his place in the world enjoyed before him.

As early as 1868, Bowker was asked to join the American Free Trade League, and through it he became associated with Carl Schurz, Samuel J. Tilden, William Cullen Bryant, Horace White, and other leading liberals of the time. He was the leader in organizing the Mugwumps, an independent Republi-can group influential in defeating the corrupt Ulysses S. Grant administration in 1880, and in getting Grover Cleveland elected President in 1884.

Bowker was always known as a man of staunch integrity. He saw himself as a public servant when he served as vice president of the publicly franchised Edison Electric Illuminating Company of New York (1890-1899). He supported limiting overcapitaliza-tion, instituting profit-sharing plans for employees, and refusing pressure to give different rates to favored customers. He combined great interest and ability in the mechanical developments of the electrical indus-try with his talent for business efficiency in devising systems for handling the rapidly developing asso-ciated Edison companies. He adapted the company's accounting system to the Dewey Decimal Classifica-tion for books, which made possible the rapid scanning of the total figures. This same system was adapted by some other firms and was still the basis of Edison practice thirty years later. Another aspect of library practice that he applied to handling accounts was the card ledger system, which eliminated the cumbersome books that were difficult to handle and caused much waste of paper because they had to be rewritten every year. During the nine years he was administrating the growing electrical industry, he was responsible for building plants and extending the underground copper conducting system from 67 to 200 miles, necessitating the installation of over 500 miles of cables, and thereby providing electricity to most of New York City for the first time.

The bibliography of Bowker's writings is extensive and the range of his interests is apparent in the titles of some of his publications: *Of Work and Wealth* (1883), *Economics for the People* (1886), *A Primer for Political Education* (1886), *Civil Service Examina-tions* (1886), *Electoral Reform* (1889), *The Arts of Life* (1900), *Of Business* (1901), and many others.

Richard Rogers Bowker died on November 12, 1933. That the publishing and library professions owe him a great debt is without question. The bibliog-raphies and directories published by the company that bears his name made books and periodicals more accessible to readers, booksellers, publishers, and librarians in this country than ever before. To sum-marize his place in the development of the social and cultural history of his time, Allan Nevins says, in the introduction to the Fleming biography:

> No one who knew Mr. Bowker could doubt that his was one of the finest spirits of his time. He has paid a certain penalty for the many-sided range of his labors; had he been less versatile, had his ardor for efficiency, liberalism, and reform been con-fined to fewer channels, he might have made a deeper if narrower impression. But the United States needed and will always need men of his wide reach of public interests and unquenchable zeal in lending a hand to diverse useful endeavors.

Biographical listings and obituaries–*Dictionary of American Biography*, 1st Supp. (Irving Dilliard); [Obituary]. *Library Journal* 58:1001-12 (Dec. 1, 1933); [Obituary]. *Publishers Weekly* 124:1763, 1764-68 (Nov. 18, 1933); [Obituary]. *Wilson Library Bulletin* 8:222-23 (Dec. 1933); *Who Was Who in America* 1 (1897-1942). **Books and articles about the biographee**–Fleming, E. McClung. *R. R. Bowker: Militant Liberal*. Norman: University of Oklahoma Press, 1952; Landau, Robert A. "Bowker, Richard Rogers." In *Encyclopedia of Library and Information Science*. New York: Marcel Dekker, 1970, Vol. 3. **Primary sources and archival materials**–His manuscripts, letters, and pieces of verse are largely contained in the collection given to the New York Public Library–a collection that consists of 158 manu-script containers of diaries and journals, 17 containers of letter books, and 8 chests of scrapbooks and clippings. Other portions of his writings and memorabilia were given to the Library of Congress, the Stockbridge Massachusetts Library, and the Brooklyn Public Library.

–MADELINE F. MIELE

BOYD, ANNE MORRIS (1884-1974)

Anne Morris Boyd was born on January 13, 1884, in Arcola, Illinois, to Wilson Porter and Emma Wyatt Boyd. After her first year of college (University of Kentucky, 1900-1901), financial conditions made it necessary for her to find employment, so she became a teacher in a small school in central Illinois. There she realized the power of books on children's lives, and she decided to become a children's librarian. During these early teaching years, she also spent Saturdays and vacations as an assistant in the local public library. From its librarian and its Board of Trustees she received encouragement to go back to college and to take up library work as a career. While at James Milliken University in Decatur, she took the few library courses offered and was an apprentice-assistant in the Decatur Public Library. Then, with an A.B. from Milliken (1906, in English and history) and her library training, Boyd became the librarian of the Kansas State Agricultural College in 1906.

She remained in Kansas until 1908, at which time she went to the St. Louis Public Library (1908-1909) and then to the Decatur [Illinois] Public Library (1909-1910). Her alma mater in Decatur then hired her as librarian (1910-1913). She next went to White-water, Wisconsin, as librarian of the State Normal School (1913-1917). Finally, at the University of Illinois, she earned her B.L.S. (1918) and found the professional home with which she was to maintain association until her retirement. She began at Illinois as an instructor and rose to professor of library science in 1949.

She "became enamored of government publications," as she put it, while she was in Kansas at her first full-time library job and she had to sort, classify, and catalog a basement full of them. This hands-on experience with government publications aroused her interest in and appreciation for their content, which led eventually to a library school course, a teaching manual, and a reference-textbook that went through three editions.

Her first actual publication was *Exit Miss Lizzie Cox: A Bibliotherapeutic Tragedy* (one-act play, 1926). Her lasting contribution to librarianship, however, was with *United States Government Publications As Sources of Information for Libraries* (1931). A second edition was issued ten years later, and in 1949, it appeared as *United States Government Publications* (revised by Rae Elizabeth Rips). From 1935 to 1953, she issued annual reading lists for the University's Agriculture Extension service. Her article "Personnel and Training for Reference Work" appeared in *The Reference Function of the Library*, edited by Pierce Butler (q.v.) (1943, pp. 249-66). Her early articles and reviews appeared in professional journals, at first on children's literature, and later, on government publications, reading, reference service, and publishing.

Book selection, though, was her abiding interest, and her course at Illinois on that topic was celebrated not only for its broad, user-oriented professional content but also for its stimulating introduction to the whole world of books, thereby helping students to read critically and with appreciation. In the late 1940s, after a revision of the Library School curriculum, Boyd also developed and taught a comprehensive course on the library in the social order.

Active in professional organizations, she served on the ALA Council twice (1931-1936, 1939-1943) and as president of the Association of American Library Schools (1945). She was also vice-president

(1928-1930) of the Illinois Library Association, and a member of the American Association of University Women, the Association for Adult Education, and the Bibliographic Society of America.

In faculty meetings and in discussion groups, she was ready with pertinent comments and ideas for improvement and change, and she was alert to and interested in new courses and newer methods of teaching. Failing eyesight and poor health led to a disability leave in September 1949 and to her retirement in January 1952. Upon her retirement, she was appointed professor of library science, emerita. The Decatur Public Library dedicated its Anne M. Boyd Room on April 12, 1959, and on May 29 of that year, she received from Milliken University its Alumni Merit Award. The Alpha Chapter of Beta Phi Mu (at Illinois) established the Anne Boyd Award in 1960 to be given each year to the outstanding graduating library science student.

Boyd was a member of the University of Illinois Library School faculty for 32 years, and it has been said that the students during those years thought of her as perhaps its most beloved and respected teacher. She died on October 24, 1974, at Champaign, Illinois. Known widely to the library profession for her long-standard book on United States government publications, Anne Boyd is best remembered by University of Illinois Library School students and faculty as an inspiring teacher, a helpful and well-informed colleague, an avid reader, a sympathetic friend, a gracious hostess, and withal a librarian dedicated to high professional standards, one who could develop enthusiasm and respect for library work in all those she touched.

Biographical listings and obituaries—*Who's Who in Library Service*, 1st ed., 2nd ed. Books and articles about the biographee—"Anne M. Boyd Award." University of Illinois Library School Association *News Letter*, Spring 1961, p. 8; "Librarian Authors." *Library Journal* 56:797 (October 1, 1931); "Library School News: Miss Boyd Retires." University of Illinois Library School *Alumni News Letter*, May 1950, pp. 5-6; Slanker, Barbara Olsen, ed. *Reminiscences: Seventy-five Years of a Library School*. Urbana: Graduate Library School, University of Illinois, 1969, pp. 44, 52, 87, 91, 108.

—GEORGE S. BONN

BRAY, THOMAS (1658-1730)

Thomas Bray was born in Marton, Shropshire, England, in 1658 (though 1656 is often cited). His family was poor but of good standing in the community. Thomas probably would have been denied an education save that his interest in and aptitude for learning brought him to the attention of Edward Lewis, vicar of Chirbury, a town three miles from Marton. Lewis possessed a remarkable collection of chained books and encouraged the young scholar to use them.

Lewis encouraged Bray's parents to send him to Oswestry Grammar School to prepare for a university education. He entered All Souls College Oxford in March 1674 as a *puer pauper*, supporting himself by menial service to the fellows. He was graduated with a Bachelor of Arts degree in 1678, but could not immediately afford to remain at the College as a fellow, which was necessary if he wished to proceed to his Master of Arts degree. Much later, he took his M.A. degree from Hart Hall (1693). In 1696, largely because Governor Nicholson and the Council of Maryland thought it would improve his position with the colonial clergy when Bray arrived there, he advanced to the degrees of Bachelor of Divinity and Doctor of Divinity from Magdalen College.

Bray was ordained a deacon in 1681 and appointed to a parish near Bridgnorth, in Warwickshire, where he soon came to the attention of Sir Thomas Price of Park Hall. Price made him his chaplain and secured for him the living of Lea Marsten (or Marson). Living nearby was a staunch nonjuror, John Kettlewell, vicar of Coleshill, who had been presented that living by Simon, Lord Digby. Through his friendship with Kettlewell, Bray was asked to preach the annual assize sermon. Lord Digby was in the audience, and so impressed was he with the young priest's dedication that he recommended him to his brother William, who offered Bray the living at Over Whitacre. While he was at Over Whitacre, Bray married, but nothing is known of his wife save her name, Elenor. She bore him two children, Goditha and William, and the vestry records show she died in 1689. Goditha eventually married a rich upholsterer named Martin, supported many of her father's schemes, and was financially responsible for the publication of the earliest biography of her father, *Public Spirit*, said to have been written by Bray's friend and executor, Samuel Smith.

In 1690, William Digby presented Bray with the rectory of Sheldon, made vacant when the Reverend Digby Bull refused to take the oath of allegiance to the King. Bray continued to hold that living until his death in 1730, although a curate served the parish for a number of years.

Some writers believe that the publication in 1696 of his *Catechetical Lectures* brought Bray to the attention of Bishop Compton of London and influenced the Bishop to appoint Bray as his commissary to the colony of Maryland, but a study of Bray's own accounts shows that he was already engaged in work for Maryland in the fall of 1695, when he appointed a curate for Sheldon and moved to London. It is more probable that Bray came to the attention of Compton through his friendship with Bishop Lloyd and the Digbys.

Henry Compton had been concerned with the spiritual welfare of the American colonies from the time he first took office. In 1689, he had appointed James Blair as commissary for Virginia. When he offered the appointment of commissary for Maryland to Bray in 1696, the latter accepted on the condition that Compton and the other bishops support his plans to provide libraries for all the missionaries. The conditions were accepted, and Bray went ahead with his plans. Circumstances did not permit him to begin his actual service in America until nearly four years later, but in the interim he was far from idle, as he began to select the missionaries and build up the libraries for the New World. His success impressed Governor Nicholson, for in a letter to the Bishop of London written on April 30, 1697, he suggested that Bray be made commissary for New York, Pennsylvania, and New England as well as for Maryland.

As the missionary plans went forward, Bray found that the clergy in England were also in need of books, so he began his work for the erection of parochial libraries in England and Wales, as outlined in his *Essay towards Promoting All Necessary and Useful Knowledge*. By 1697, sixteen libraries had been sent to Maryland, seven had been set up in other colonies, and the foundation for six others had been laid. Bray himself arrived in Maryland in March 1700.

Originally, Bray had planned to provide libraries for all of the parishes of Maryland, but as he learned of the extensive cultural poverty of all of the people in the colonies, he enlarged his plans to provide for one large library in the chief city of each province, the provincial or general library, and a smaller collection, the parochial library, for each of the colonial parishes. A third type of library, the layman's library, would contain books that could be loaned by the minister, and a large collection of pious books and tracts that were to be given free to the people.

From 1695, when Bray first accepted the position of commissary, until 1704, when he presented his final report to the Society for the Propagation of the Gospel in Foreign Parts, he was successful in establishing provincial libraries at Boston, New York, Philadelphia, Annapolis, Charleston, and Bath, North Carolina. He provided 39 parochial libraries, of which 29 were located in Maryland, although each of the other colonies had at least one such library. Finally, he provided over 35 layman's libraries and sent over 35,000 religious books and tracts to the colonies for free distribution. Much of his colonial work was done *in absentia*, however, for he returned to England in 1700, seeing a chance to be more effective in raising funds if he were in England.

Attached to a memorial of Bray's, published in 1700, were two suggestions that indicate his desire to facilitate the dissemination of reading matter and improve and add to the libraries already established in America. Had these suggestions been followed, the libraries he established might have lasted longer; from later developments in the library field, it is obvious that he was a century or more ahead of his time. His first suggestion required that the libraries communicate reciprocal catalogs of their holdings in order "to lend what one may be provided with different from the other." The second, that a small annual subscription be provided by interested persons, with the books so purchased subsequently available to the subscribers "divided and shared by lot among them," later became a part of the subscription library movement of the eighteenth century, helping to facilitate the procurement of new books.

Since he personally established the foundations of a library system in America, there is little doubt that had Bray returned to the country as commissary, he would have kept the colonial libraries alive. If the flourishing religious societies in England had supplied him with books, funds, and the time to return to America, his surprisingly modern ideas might have led to an American public library movement in the eighteenth century. Because Bray could not return, however, his beloved libraries were forced to struggle on alone, depending on occasional benevolence from England for their very existence, with expansion and reciprocal communication existing only within the pages of his own writings.

That Bray's work was continued in America down to the eve of the Revolution tells a great deal about the colonial needs for reading matter still too difficult and expensive to acquire in America. Literally thousands of letters from the colonists and their ministers, preserved in the archives of the Society for the Propagation of the Gospel in Foreign Parts, testify to the fact that the Americans were desperately in need of books during the eighteenth century. Bray and the societies he founded did a remarkable job in providing the colonists with the books and libraries they desired.

During the same years that he was providing books, libraries, and missionaries to the colonies, he was also instrumental in securing the passage of a bill for the establishment of the Church of England in Maryland, and was active in founding the Society for the Promotion of Christian Knowledge and the Society for the Propagation of the Gospel in Foreign Parts. The Act of Establishment remained in force throughout the entire colonial period, and the societies founded by Bray remain in existence today, still active in publishing, education, and missionary enterprise—a tribute to his zeal and thoroughness. In addition, Bray provided libraries in the West Indies, on the coast of Africa, established 61 libraries in England and Wales, 10 on the Isle of Man, and several in the Highlands of Scotland.

Indifference on the part of those in power often caused the benefits of these libraries to be lost to the people. Although Bray was gratified to see legislative protection given to the libraries in three of the colonies during his lifetime, he failed in his attempts to procure public support for growth and development. The establishment of the true public library had to wait upon the shift of support from private benevolence to public funds which came in the latter half of the nineteenth century.

Thomas Bray's library concepts were surprisingly modern, quite in advance of his time. Had he been born 100 years later, he would have been in the thick of the movement for the development of public libraries. In his own time, and through his own labors, a stream of the finest reading matter then available filtered into America. Because of his own activities, and those of the religious societies he founded, Bray deserves credit for serving as one of the greatest single cultural influences at work in the American colonies during the eighteenth century. He died on February 15 (*DNB* date; *Who Was Who in America* gives February 26), 1730.

Biographical listings and obituaries—*Dictionary of National Biography* (Concise edition), Vol. 1; *Who Was Who in America*, Historical Volume (1607-1896). **Books and articles about the biographee**—Laugher, Charles T. *Thomas Bray's Grand Design*. Chicago: American Library Association, 1973; Smith, Samuel. *Public Spirit: Illustrated in the Life and Designs of the Reverend Thomas Bray*. London: J. Brotherton, 1746; Thompson, Henry. *Thomas Bray*. London: S.P.G., 1954.

—CHARLES T. LAUGHER

BRETT, WILLIAM HOWARD (1846-1918)

By modern personnel standards, William Howard Brett was not qualified to be a librarian; he had no college degree or professional experience at the time of his appointment at the Cleveland Public Library. He was the son of idealistic parents, his father, Morgan Lewis Brett, being a descendant of John Alden who came west with his wife, June Brokaw Brett, to Trumbull County in eastern Ohio to participate in a short-lived utopian experiment, the Trumbull Phalanx, similar to Brook Farm in Massachusetts. Young Brett was born in Braceville, Ohio, on July 1, 1846. Disenchanted with the experiment, Morgan Brett and his family settled in Warren in a modest house on a narrow street facing what was then a clean and limpid Mahoning River. The son loved books, learned to read on his own before he began his formal schooling, and at age fourteen, became librarian of his small school collection. The fines provided the salary, an early and impressive example of the incentive system.

After two college years (at Western Reserve College and the University of Michigan), Brett ran out of money and went to Cleveland, where he worked for ten years as a knowledgeable and successful salesman for Cobb and Andrews, the largest bookstore west of Philadelphia. In 1884, he was offered the position as librarian of the Cleveland Public Library, but no one on the Board of Trustees had more than a vague idea as to what the qualifications of a librarian should be. One member, opposed to the appointment, said he could get a bookkeeper for a great deal less than it would be necessary to pay Brett—and "what was a librarian but a bookkeeper?" Fortunately the other Board members, admitting their ignorance about the proper credentials for a librarian, did think that one should *know* as well as *keep* books.

Brett hesitated, as he had family obligations, the library at that time was not nearly so prestigious as Cobb and Andrews, and the small salary was no inducement (he began at $2,100 in 1884, and he was receiving $7,000 when he died in 1918). He finally took the new position because he felt he could render a larger service in the public library, whatever the cost in labor and remuneration might be.

In the post that he held for 34 years, the only thing the poorly qualified Brett did was to achieve international renown for his library and himself. An innovator, he either initiated or adopted enthusiastically the open shelf, children's libraries, extension work in branches and in schools and industrial plants, a cumulative index to periodicals, a catalog that was a marvel, departmentalization of the Library, and the development of a library school. Serving his peers professionally, Brett was president of the American Library Association for the 1896-1897 term. He also organized and became the first president of the Ohio Library Association.

In the United States the open shelf was initially introduced in small libraries; in 1890, Brett was the first director of a metropolitan library with enough fortitude to inaugurate the practice. Critics were convinced that the innovation would produce general pandemonium as well as the loss of books. In a discussion of free access at the conference of librarians held in London in 1877, the opposition included Melvil Dewey (q.v.), soon to become the patron saint of classification. A British librarian was certain that the open shelf could only be introduced "in praise of anarchy," while an American colleague would not consider the idea because it would "muss up" those books that were not stolen. In the face of this barrage, Brett went straight ahead; the result was that circulation doubled, fewer books were lost, and a smaller staff was required to hover over the bookcases.

Brett supported the open shelf because of his faith in humankind and his belief that borrowers must be presented with a maximum choice. From his bookstore experience, he understood fully the value of direct handling of books by customers and that borrowers in libraries must be relieved of the high counters, which were formidable barriers, if a real choice was to be offered to them. Before the institution of free access to books, potential readers could consult a shelf list and make out a call slip. When the book came, they saw it for the first time and frequently found it a disappointment, with the result that several call slips were required before the patron was reasonably satisfied. The call slips sometimes provided amusement for librarians—particularly when puzzled would-be readers asked for any book by "anon" or when a despairing man would write "please pick out a good love story for my wife." Brett knew that most people who entered a library had at best one or two books in mind. In Brett's opinion "in so far as he [a borrower] compared books and exercised his judgment in reaching a choice, he was educating himself." In this regard, the "open alcoves of the free library" would become "broad highways"; he was in essential agreement with the fundamental observation that the objective of a library was "not how to make people wise, but how to make them want to be."

Brett also believed that borrowers not only should be trusted but challenged to prove their integrity. He did not think those entering a library should be treated as were the undergraduate borrowers at Harvard in the mid-nineteenth century, when a student was "made to leave his cloak and cap at the door, so they might not serve to conceal his spoils. . . . he entered and left with a character hanging over him as bad as that of a suspected pickpocket. . . ."

Brett was horrified by the prevailing opinion that a librarian was a fellow who kept people from getting the books they wished, for in his judgment, it was not free access to the shelves that needed to be justified; instead it was *any* restriction by a librarian. He felt that the most important thing about the open shelf was the appeal it made to a sense of honor. His opponents had made the point that if temptation was put in the way of book borrowers, thievery would be the result. Brett had no use for this argument:

Personally I have not much use for the kind of honesty that depends on lack of opportunity; I think that to give . . . access to the shelves is equivalent to saying, we believe you will take care of these books, we believe you will steal them. Most people respond to this. . . . There is no doubt there is the temptation, they would like to carry the books away, and every time they don't do it they are a little more honest than they were before.

This was ultimate faith in the innate decency and honesty of mankind, but Brett had it.

The open-shelf system made it easier for borrowers to find books and magazines suitable to their tastes. So too did a guide to periodicals, a new classification system, a divisional organization, and a useful catalog.

When Brett became librarian, there was no up-to-date guide to periodicals, so he developed and published one. As a result, the Cleveland Public Library distributed in 1896 the first quarterly issues of the *Cumulative Index to a Selected List of Periodicals*, making immediately available the contents of upwards of one hundred periodicals; this index was ultimately published, under other auspices, as *Readers' Guide to Periodical Literature*. In the esoteric but useful field of classification, Melvil Dewey's decimal system was then new and but partially developed. Brett was impressed by its advantages and adopted—or rather adapted—the system because he could improve on it in a number of ways beneficial to public libraries.

He also introduced the flexible library based on divisional lines. The long-accepted plan had been to separate only circulating and reference books. Questions went to the reference department, where the same assistant might find it necessary to answer queries on metallurgy, summer resorts, or Christian theology. No one could possibly be an expert on all three, but the divisional system provided the answer. Brett began it in 1890; however, he was hampered by lack of space until 1913, when he completed the transformation—with all books divided by subject department in the main library. This meant that the same assistants were responsible for the same class of books day after day, developing a competence in the field that enabled them to order books with greater wisdom and to answer reference questions with more certainty of knowing, or being able to find, the answer. This organizational concept has always been associated with Brett's name, and its adoption in other cities followed in due course.

For easy reference, Brett produced a comprehensive catalog (numbering 1,407 double-columned pages) of the titles, authors, and subjects of all books in the Cleveland Library. This enabled a potential borrower to find a book of which the author, title, or subject was known—and to ascertain what the library possessed that was pertinent to his enquiry. Its production represented a supreme effort, since Brett had to know what was in every one of the 32,000 volumes then in the library. Published in 1888, it turned out to be a *tour de force* that two decades later was still serving many other libraries as a prototype and tool.

But Brett's real contribution was in his empathy for people—both readers and library staff. He enticed readers through the open shelf, through schools and branches, and by introducing children for the first time to what libraries had to offer. Although he was not the first to think of books for children, Brett was one of the first to develop attractive rooms for the young and to inaugurate an academic program to train librarians who specialized in children and their

reading needs; as a result he is sometimes spoken of as "the greatest children's librarian."

In the absence of a large and attractive central library (not built until after his death), he took books to readers through a variety of extensions: branches, schools, home libraries for children, deposit and delivery stations in municipal and commercial establishments—and municipal fire houses. With the help of the "good St. Andrew" Carnegie (q.v.), the steel magnate from Pittsburgh, who gave $600,000, more than twenty branch libraries were established. Altogether, Brett brought the number of book outposts, quite beyond the main library, to the impressive figure of 648. His vision was that "of every man's library, every woman's library, even every little child's library—holding in its rich stores of printed wealth the wisdom of the world with its special messages for each."

To provide vocational preparation which he had not enjoyed, Brett began his training program with classes at the Library. In 1904, he became the first dean of the Library School at Western Reserve University—a superlative one even though he possessed no college diploma. With the help of Carnegie (who gave $100,000) *and* the Cleveland Public Library, the School just managed to survive financially while Brett was its dean (1904-1918), and in time, it would establish an estimable national reputation. By 1968, more than thirty members of the staff of the Cleveland Public Library had been members of the School's faculty, almost ninety had served as lecturers and consultants, and the first four deans of the School had been associated with the Cleveland Library in some capacity.

Through training and his own example, Brett developed a remarkable *esprit de corps*. John G. White, the noted bibliophile who was a Library trustee for many years, would say that the city of Cleveland got more from its library than did any other metropolis, and that the reasons were Brett and his successor, Linda Eastman (q.v.). He averred that these two made the ultimate contributions not only by their labors but by creating a spirit among employees that was altogether admirable because of its self-sacrificing character. In White's opinion, the zeal of the staff was the greatest asset that the library possessed; the institution had both heart and soul because the entire staff offered a sympathetic understanding.

Brett was forward-looking and progressive in relation to so many philosophies and practices of his era that it is surprising to find him in a traditional—even a conservative—role on the question of the selection of books. He was on the right wing in the case of novels and what is sometimes designated as "light literature," and on the additional question of what constitutes loyal reading in wartime. The issue of "light literature" was the only one on which Brett and John G. White did not see eye to eye. White's range of reading extended all the way from the Bible and the Koran to Diamond Dick, and he was disturbed by the number of volumes secreted in what he called the "oubliettes" in the librarian's office, where they were seen by no one. Brett also believed it was a library's obligation to practice a rigid censorship in wartime, and he did so after the United States entered World War I. His support for wartime censorship stemmed from a paradox: Brett, a quiet and self-effacing individual who could not bring himself to kill a fly or a caterpillar, found wars both necessary and fascinating. In 1865, the last year of the American Civil War, Brett reached the age of eighteen, and after learning to play the fife and drum, enlisted as a musician, was captured by Morgan's Raiders, and taken as a prisoner to Kentucky. This unsatisfactory experience did not diminish his infatuation for military life, however. In 1918, at the age of 72, he hoped that he might be permitted to go overseas with the American Expeditionary Force—this time as librarian rather than musician.

Brett died in triumph and in tragedy. The triumph was the magnificence of his life work. The tragedy was that in August 1918, the 72-year-old librarian, attempting to board a street car in front of the Library, was cut down by an automobile driven by a drunken driver; the same automobile narrowly missed Linda Eastman. This irresponsible tippler almost succeeded in wiping out the two greatest librarians in the history of the Cleveland Public Library. He was survived by his wife Alice Allen Brett, whom he married in 1879, and five children.

Some believe that Brett had actually delivered his own inspirational valedictory two months before his death in a commencement address to the class of 1918 of the Library School at Western Reserve University. He had closed his presentation by quoting the last words of Sir Richard Grenville, the English naval hero and cousin of Sir Walter Raleigh, whom Brett greatly admired. Grenville, who died courageously in the course of a naval battle, had said:

> Here die I, Richard Grenville, with a joyful and quiet mind, for that I have ended my life as a true soldier ought to do, that hath fought for his country . . . religion and honor. Whereby my soul most joyfully departeth out of this body and shall always leave behind it an everlasting fame as a valiant and true soldier that hath done his duty as he was bound to do.

Biographical listings and obituaries—*Dictionary of American Biography* 3 (Linda Anne Eastman); *Who Was Who in America* 1 (1897-1942). **Books and articles about the biographee**—Cramer, C. H. *Open Shelves and Open Minds: A History of the Cleveland Public Library.* Cleveland: The Press of Case Western Reserve University, 1972; Eastman, Linda A. *Portrait of a Librarian: William Howard Brett.* Chicago:

American Library Association, 1940; Vitz, Carl. "William H. Brett." In John David Marshall, ed., *An American Library History Reader: Contributions to Library Literature.* Metuchen, N.J.: Scarecrow Press, 1961.

                                                    —C. H. CRAMER

BRIGHAM, CLARENCE SAUNDERS (1877-1963)

Clarence Saunders Brigham was born in Providence, Rhode Island, on August 5, 1877, to John Olin and Alice Saunders Brigham. His brother, Herbert Olin Brigham (1875-1959), was also a librarian, serving from 1903 to 1937 as state librarian of Rhode Island and for twenty years afterwards as librarian of the Newport Historical Society. For college preparation, Clarence Brigham attended the English and Classical School in Providence, and from there, he went on to Brown University, graduating in 1899 with the A.B. degree and a Phi Beta Kappa key. Brown, his alma mater, awarded him an honorary master's degree in 1909 and the honorary Litt.D. in 1934. Clark University, located in his adopted community of Worcester, Massachusetts, conferred on him the same degree in 1948. Brigham married Alice Louise Comstock on November 12, 1910, and they had one daughter, Elizabeth Comstock Brigham. Alice Brigham died November 17, 1958.

Immediately after graduating from Brown, Brigham was hired as assistant librarian at the college. He became librarian of the Rhode Island Historical Society in 1900 and served in that position until 1908. He was elected to membership in the American Antiquarian Society (AAS) in October 1905. His appointment as AAS librarian followed in October 1908. Brigham was essentially the fourth librarian at AAS, replacing Edmund Mills Barton. Brigham held the newly created post of director of the Society from 1930 to 1959 and—most unusual—served as president as well from 1955 until his retirement in 1959.

Brigham held membership in numerous scholarly, professional, and bookmen's organizations in addition to AAS, including the Massachusetts Historical Association, American Historical Association, American Library Association, Bibliographical Society of America, the Club of Odd Volumes in Boston, and the Grolier Club in New York. He was a trustee of the Worcester Art Museum and a member of the board of management of the John Carter Brown Library.

During Brigham's long (51 years) association with the American Antiquarian Society—as librarian, director, and president—that organization abandoned its backwater role as preserver of miscellaneous collections of imprints, archaeological artifacts, and antiques, and became one of the preeminent independent historical research libraries in the United States. Brigham was not equally adept at or interested in all of the librarian's functions. His special genius was as a collector of rare books, a delineator of the library's scope, and a bibliographer. Practical cataloging chores he left to associates such as Avis G. Clarke, Dorothea N. Spear, and his successor as librarian, Clifford K. Shipton (q.v.).

It is striking how many of the goals of Brigham's long career were charted at the time he became head of the Antiquarian Society in 1908, and how much the rest of his long and remarkable life was devoted to seeing to it that those plans were realized. Construction of the new Antiquarian Society building—its third home apart from the residence of Isaiah Thomas, who founded it in 1812—was begun just about the same time that Brigham came to the Society as librarian. A half-century later he wrote, "The library building today, except for additions of bookstacks and changes in the dome, is identically the same as when it was built. Never was a building constructed more ideally satisfactory for a research library. In forty-five years there has not been a structural change made or desired." Much the same could be said for his conception of the stewardship of the Antiquarian Society and his confidence in that conception. If the collections in the library be likened to the building that housed them, there might have been additions to the stacks and superficial changes in the dome, but the basic structure of the collections remained much the same as Brigham and other caretakers of AAS had outlined them years before.

The policy that guided the AAS was outlined in his first annual report as librarian, submitted in October 1909—a report that Shipton, Brigham's successor, likened to "a trumpet of revolution which must have shaken the dust out of the folios on the most distant shelves." The policy, in the philosophical spirit of the twentieth century, emphasized specialization. George Parker Winship (q.v.), then librarian of the John Carter Brown Library, and other members of the AAS delimited much of the future direction of the library in 1907. Brigham took this policy, very much his own, and made it an operating principle. Most basically, Brigham said, the new policy was: "To strengthen those departments of the library which are already strong, to obtain material for which the Society is a proper custodian and to reject that which does not come within our scope." In practical terms, this meant a concentration on acquiring everything printed before 1820 in what is now the United States—books, pamphlets, broadsides, newspapers, magazines, and ephemera—and a determined policy of acquisitions within certain fields extending beyond that basic chronological limit, such as almanacs, bookplates, children's literature, American fiction, and American newspapers.

A eulogist once wrote of Henry E. Huntington that he was "the greatest book collector of his day in this period of giants in that field." As an institutional collector, Brigham was hardly less of a giant than Huntington, for whom he occasionally bought books privately. Brigham once rejected the notion that the nineteenth century had been the "golden age of book-buying." He knew better, for, through careful and systematic searching of book catalogs and other sources in the now better-organized antiquarian book market, he managed to acquire in his first four years in Worcester more than twice the number of early American imprints that Isaiah Thomas—one of the leading collectors of his day—had managed to accumulate in thirty years. Brigham also knew well the ways in which collectors and their collections could be cultivated. Friendships with such persons as A. S. W. Rosenbach, Thomas W. Streeter, d'Alté A. Welch, and others paid dividends in both the short and long runs.

Brigham's scholarship was partner to his bookmanship, and most of his scholarly accomplishments were either completed or at least conceived in the early years of his tenure in Worcester. While still librarian at the Rhode Island Historical Society, Brigham was asked by the Council of the Antiquarian Society to prepare an edition of the *British Royal Proclamations Relating to America 1603-1783.* This he agreed to do, and his work (volume 12 of the Society's *Transactions and Collections*, 1911), in part, led him to be selected as librarian of AAS.

Similarly, his scholarly and collecting interest in the engravings of Paul Revere began early. When Brigham came to Worcester, the AAS owned only a few of Revere's engravings. Brigham began collecting, mounted an exhibition of Revere's graphics as early as 1912, and eventually accumulated for AAS the best collection of the artist-patriot's work in the world. Brigham's painstaking bibliographical scholarship was fully revealed in the handsome, fully illustrated volume, *Paul Revere's Engravings* (Worcester, 1954).

Brigham's greatest scholarly contribution, *History and Bibliography of American Newspapers 1690-1820*, likewise had an early genesis. The first installment of his preliminary census of newspapers (covering the states from Alabama through Indiana) appeared in the Society's *Proceedings* for October 1913. The work appeared serially, in eighteen installments, through the *Proceedings* for April 1927. The compiler welcomed additions and corrections, his intention being to hold the material standing in type until it could be revised and gathered together in a volume. As it turned out, the task took decades—and two volumes—to accomplish. Not until 1947, after the exchange of hundreds of letters with newspaper repositories and thousands of miles of travel to examine or re-examine newspaper files, and the relaxation of wartime paper controls, did the *History and Bibliography* appear in book form. The *History and*

Bibliography of American Newspapers was a remarkable achievement. If one allows for the fact that not all early newspapers have remained at the libraries where Brigham located them, the work is still an indispensable and accurate bibliography.

Brigham also encouraged bibliographical scholarship in others. At times, he even acted the part of "broker," eagerly assisting the work of a person he thought capable of getting a specific bibliographical chore done, while discouraging work of another, who to him was less qualified, in the same field. Indeed, one of his protégés, d'Alté A. Welch, once paid tribute to Brigham for "his remarkable genius for stimulating younger men to bibliographical endeavor."

"Mr. Brigham," as staff and visitors called him, was a charming host at the Antiquarian Society. Well-dressed, an inveterate pipe smoker, and blessed with a remarkable memory, he made one feel privileged to be visiting his library. At his home, about a mile from the library and a block from the Worcester Club, Brigham entertained bibliophiles from around the world, including Calvin Coolidge, president of AAS from 1929 to 1933. Brigham's circumstances were comfortable—he once claimed he gave more money for books in one year than the Antiquarian Society gave him for salary—and he ordinarily spent one winter month or so each year in Florida or Cuba.

Brigham retired as both director and president of the American Antiquarian Society in 1959. Shortly before that, he sponsored the publication of his memoirs, *Fifty Years of Collecting Americana for the Library of the American Antiquarian Society* (Worcester, 1958). During the first year of his "so-called retirement," Brigham came to the library daily and prepared "Additions and Corrections" to his newspaper bibliography (published in the Society's *Proceedings*); he also completed for publication the work of his recently deceased assistant librarian, Dorothea N. Spear, *Bibliography of American Directories through 1860* (Worcester, 1961). Clarence Saunders Brigham died August 13, 1963, and is buried in Swan Point Cemetery in Providence.

Biographical listings and obituaries—*Current Biography* (1959, 1963); [Obituary]. *New York Times*, August 14, 1963; [Obituary]. Worcester *Evening Gazette*, August 14, 1963; *Who Was Who in America* IV (1961-1968); *Who's Who in Library Service*, 1st ed., 2nd ed. Books and articles about the biographee—*Clarence Saunders Brigham 1877-1963.* Worcester, 1963; Wolf, Edwin, II, and John F. Fleming. *Rosenbach: A Biography.* Cleveland and New York, 1960; Worcester *Evening Gazette*, June 18, 1934; Sept. 29, 1959. Primary sources and archival materials—American Antiquarian Society, Correspondence (MSS); American Antiquarian Society, *Proceedings*, 1905-1963; *Twenty-eighth Annual Catalogue of the English & Classical School, 63 Snow Street, Providence, R.I. 1891-92.* Providence, 1891; *Twenty-seventh Annual Catalogue of the English and Classical School, 63 Snow Street, Providence, R.I. 1890.* Providence, 1890.

—JOHN B. HENCH

BROWN, CHARLES HARVEY (1875-1960)

Charles Harvey Brown was born December 23, 1875, in Albany, New York, the son of James H. and Mary E. Smith Brown. He married Julia W. Heath on January 16, 1909, and they had two sons, Charles H. and Robert H. Brown.

Since he was the son of a Methodist minister, it was natural that he should enter Wesleyan University, where he graduated in 1897 with a B.A. He was given a position as assistant librarian and remained in Middletown two more years to earn the M.A. degree with a thesis *On the Potential of a Polyhedron of Uniform Density.* Not quite four decades later, Wesleyan awarded him an honorary Litt.D. for noteworthy achievement as librarian of a great scientific collection.

When he took the B.L.S. from the New York State Library School in 1901 and held his first professional appointment at the Library of Congress for the next two years, he was in the midst of men and women who would make American library history in the twenties and thirties. As reference librarian at the John Crerar Library from 1903 to 1909, he acquired an enduring respect for the noble collection of scientific literature formed by Clement W. Andrews (q.v.); this collection was to be a model for much of his work at Iowa State in developing a second great science library in the Midwest. Ten years at the Brooklyn Public Library (1909-1919) as assistant librarian instilled into him a principle he often cited to colleagues: "It makes no real difference what kind of a library you are in—public, college, or special. The satisfaction of patrons is the one really important thing in all of them."

Though he was too old for military duty in World War I, Brown was with the U.S. Navy Library Service from 1919 to 1922. He often recalled this experience with characteristically fierce patriotism. Yet he was always able to put himself in the position of others. In 1946, when I showed him a copy of a captured document with a list of Nazi Party members in Gau Charlottenburg, including the name of his old friend, Albert Predeek, director of the Berlin Technische Hochschule Library until its destruction in 1944, he simply remarked, "Well, wasn't your grandfather a member of the Klan?"

Brown was called to Ames in 1922 and found a new building well under way. In the monumental, inflexible tradition of the Widener Library and its immediate epigoni, the building itself has been a continuing vexation and challenge to all of its librarians. The new librarian had already envisioned substantial quantitative and qualitative growth of the collections at Iowa State and was bitterly disappointed when the size of the west wing was reduced on the argument that the space would never be used. Five years later, outside storage was necessary. In 1940, Brown arranged for the construction of a nearby storage facility, one of the few in this period that provided continuing access to books, as he shunned the idea of dramatizing spatial limitations with boxing.

His first job at Iowa State was to assemble a competent staff for the library of an institution that was rapidly becoming a major research center. In 1924, he employed Ralph Dunbar (q.v.), later the first director of the Office of Education's Division of Library Service. He literally brought up Robert W. Orr, who came to the library as a student in 1926. Orr absorbed so much of Brown's bibliothecal wisdom that he was able to enter Columbia's master's program without a professional degree, and he succeeded Brown in 1946. Of the other highly competent people Brown lured to Ames, Eugene H. Wilson, subsequently both librarian and acting president (June-August 1969) of the University of Colorado, should be mentioned. Brown, like many of his male contemporaries, was never convinced that women had the capability for active leadership in library administration. He secured able and sometimes brilliant ladies for service at Iowa State, but they knew their place. William Warner Bishop (q.v.) gave this writer warm endorsement for a position at Ames in 1940 as "a youngster who can soon replace one of those women."

Brown always insisted that his reference librarians go to any length to answer a question ("There is no reference question that is foolish or has no answer," he often said). But he was also keenly aware of the need for bibliographical training and instituted a required non-credit course in the use of the library for undergraduates and a course in specialized scientific bibliography with one hour of credit for graduate students. A major by-product of this program was to secure instructional rank for all professional staff members by 1940, a very early date compared to trends in other university libraries.

In 1922, there were 90,000 volumes in the library of an institution serving virtually all fields of pure and applied science except human medicine. Brown's first step was to initiate reclassification from DDC to LC, not to ape Bishop at Michigan but in the conviction that the change was in the best interest of superior library service. Since the library was relatively well funded, he was able to acquire fine runs of scientific serials that he could simply remember from his days at the Crerar. Later he was to refine the methods of selection with intensive studies of the most frequently cited journals in various fields, culminating in his well-known study, *Scientific Serials* (1956; ACRL Monograph, 16). By using the valuable publications of the Agricultural and Engineering Experiment stations, the *Iowa State Journal of Science*, and the *Proceedings* of the Iowa Academy of Science, Brown,

together with two of his closest associates, Frances Warner and Grace Oberheim, could acquire by exchange thousands of serial titles unknown in libraries with less aggressive acquisition policies. The volumes in the library numbered over 300,000 at the end of Brown's tenure.

Brown was at the forefront of local, state, national, and international professional activities. The book talks by staff members over WOI, the college's radio station, developed into a "book club" that once had several hundred volumes circulating to many a remote prairie farmstead. It has often been said that Brown was one of the moving spirits in the founding of the Association of Research Libraries, but unfortunately, his correspondence has not been preserved. As chairman of the ARL Serials Committee, he went to Germany in 1935 to confer with publishers and officials about the high price of German periodicals. As a partial consequence of his visit, there was a 25 percent reduction in the price of German serials that were exported, a percentage that was soon thereafter applied to all German publications bought by American libraries and individual scholars. More important, Brown made warm friendships with such men as Predeek and Georg Leyh, dean of German university library directors at the time, and gained a perspective that was to be invaluable during the war years and in his international service after retirement. The high point of his career as an internationalist came, though, in 1947, when he and Verner Clapp (q.v.) went to Japan at General MacArthur's invitation to organize the National Diet Library. Subsequently he and Clapp went to the mainland to visit Chinese university libraries.

Brown's term as ALA president in 1940-1941 was filled energetically. Cognizant of his reputation for frank and even occasionally abrasive remarks, and sensitive about the growing discontent within ACRL (with which he was largely sympathetic), he always had the preliminary drafts of his letters, speeches, and reports examined by staff members at Ames. The integrity of the ALA during his tenure as president was his primary concern, and he was dedicated to maintenance of the status quo. However, he had many doubts about deficiencies within the headquarters organization and pointed out several situations that were later detailed in Ralph Shaw's (q.v.) Activities Committee report at the end of the decade.

As in the case of *Scientific Serials*, Brown's extensive contributions to library literature were largely the result of practical experience and the needs of the Iowa State College Library. His first major work was the library section of the *Survey of Land-Grant Colleges and Universities* (Office of Education *Bulletin*, 1930, no. 4; 2v.). His study of *Circulation Work in College and University Libraries* (1933), jointly written with H. G. Bousfield, pegged down many a fundamental that endures even the age of mechanization.

Had Brown not been dedicated to library administration, he would have earned a secure niche in library history through his work as a teacher and consultant. He taught regularly at Columbia's summer school from 1933 through 1938, and in his retirement he served at Illinois, Florida, and Louisiana State. His death occurred on January 19, 1960.

Brown was a tall man, bald at a relatively early age, and his slight stoop accentuated rather than detracted from an impressive appearance. A faint trace of a speech defect commanded the close attention of his students, staff, and colleagues. Basically authoritarian in his notions about library administration, he was gravely disturbed in later years about trends towards greater staff participation in decision-making, although his strength as an administrator was tempered by a keen sense of the time for flexibility. Throughout his professional and personal life, he cultivated the ideals of accuracy and truth acquired in his mathematical training. He developed that basic strength so much admired by Plutarch, "character is habit of long duration."

Biographical listings and obituaries—*National Cyclopaedia of American Biography* 46; *Who Was Who in America* III (1951-1960). Books and articles about the biographee—"Essays in Honor of Charles Harvey Brown." *College and Research Libraries* VIII, no. 3, pt. 2 (July 1947). Includes a full bibliography of his writings. Orr, Robert W. "Charles Harvey Brown." *The Library at Iowa State* XIV:42-53 (1960).

—LAWRENCE S. THOMPSON

BROWN, WALTER LEWIS (1861-1931)

Walter Lewis Brown was born in Buffalo, New York, on January 4, 1861. His father was James C. Brown, a Buffalo attorney who for a number of years was deputy superintendent of public instruction for the State of New York, and his mother was Margaret Grieg Bullions Brown. Brown received his early education in the public schools of Buffalo, then completed his formal education in the Albany Academy, where his maternal grandfather taught.

In 1877, when Brown began his library career with the Young Men's Association Library at the age of sixteen, there was no publicly supported circulating library in the city of Buffalo. The Grosvenor Library, opened in 1871, was receiving city funds, but it was for reference use only. The circulating library was the Young Men's Association, a private subscription library founded in 1836.

In April of the year in which Brown joined the staff, Josephus Larned (q.v.) became the superintendent of the Young Men's Association Library. Almost immediately, Larned undertook to classify the YMA Library in the new Dewey Decimal Classification, the first complete application of the Dewey system in a large, general library. Brown recalled later how he spent a year or more pasting labels in books, while Mr. Larned cataloged them.

Brown stayed with the Young Men's Association for about five years, then left to take a job with the Peter Paul Company, local booksellers, stationers, and printers, remaining in their employ until he rejoined the YMA staff in 1897.

By then the Library, to avoid confusion with the Young Men's Christian Association, had changed its name to the Buffalo Library. When the Buffalo Library, a private association, entered into an arrangement with the city of Buffalo in 1897 to form the publicly supported Buffalo Public Library, Brown was chosen vice-librarian to serve under Henry Livingston Elmendorf, who succeeded Larned in the same year. Again Brown was present at one of the key events in the history of Buffalo libraries—the transfer from private to public support. Public support had become a necessity when the State Legislature removed the tax-exempt status from the Iroquois Hotel, which was owned by the Buffalo Library and which had made a profit that determined the Library's solvency, and Brown was one of the staunch supporters of the proposal for a free public library.

Brown's career in the Buffalo Public Library was in a period of great growth. In 1898, the first full year of public support, the number of books in the Library was 123,988 and the circulation was 768,028. In 1930, the last full year before Brown's death, the book collection had increased to over 575,000 and the circulation had passed 3,000,000.

When Henry L. Elmendorf, the librarian of the Buffalo Public Library, died July 8, 1906, Walter L. Brown was appointed librarian. According to contemporary Buffalo newspapers, the other person considered by the Library Board for this appointment was Elmendorf's widow, Theresa West Elmendorf (q.v.), who was appointed vice-librarian. She had had a distinguished career as deputy librarian and then librarian of the Milwaukee Public Library from 1880 to 1896, the year in which she married H. L. Elmendorf.

Although Brown himself was not a library school graduate, having acquired his training through the older method of apprenticeship, he was keenly aware of the need for more highly trained library personnel. This was especially true during the decade following World War I, when there was a shortage of recruits, especially of men. Therefore, he cooperated with Augustus H. Shearer, librarian of the Grosvenor Library, in establishing a library training program, which in 1920 became the Department of Library Science of the University of Buffalo, with Shearer as director. For 22 years this department served as the local library school, with most of its graduates joining the staffs of the two public libraries and the new University of Buffalo Library, as well as many smaller libraries in the western New York region.

After Brown became librarian of the Buffalo Public Library, many changes occurred (including his marriage to librarian Margaret Bruce McCabe on September 11, 1909). In 1906 the Library had three branches, and four more were opened in the pre-World War I period. After the War, eight new branch buildings were opened between 1925 and 1929.

Brown expanded the Library's work with the Buffalo public schools, depositing small selected book collections in classrooms; this system, first established by Elmendorf, became known as the "Buffalo Plan." Service in the main building also changed. Departmentalization had been exclusively by function (reference, periodicals) or age (children). In 1929, Brown opened a subject department specializing in technology, with a person of appropriate subject background in charge. A Students' Room, offering service to high school students, was opened the same year. Another idea put into effect during Brown's tenure in the twenties was the Readers' Bureau, which supplied a custom-tailored advisory service to readers who wished to read systematically in order to achieve special objectives.

Walter Brown was very active in library associations. In 1906, the same year in which he became librarian of the Buffalo Public Library, he served as president of the New York Library Association. He was a life member of the American Library Association and a member of the ALA Council when he was elected first vice-president in 1915. He served as president in the year 1916-1917, and during his term, he took a leading part in the organization of library service for the armed forces in this period of preparation for war. He chaired the ALA Headquarters Building Committee in 1928.

When he reached the age of seventy, in January 1931, Walter Brown asked for and received permission to serve as librarian of the Buffalo Public Library beyond the compulsory retirement age, but ill health forced him to reconsider, and on October 10, he submitted his resignation to the Library Board to be effective November 1. Before the Board had time to act on his resignation, he died on October 16, 1931.

Biographical listings and obituaries–*National Cyclopaedia of American Biography* 24; [Obituary]. Buffalo *Courier Express*, October 17, 1931, p. 1; [Obituary]. Buffalo *Evening News*, October 17, 1931, p. 1; *Who Was Who in America* I (1897-1942). Books and articles about the biographee–Bartlett, Lucius. "Our Frontispiece: Walter L. Brown." *Bulletin of Bibliography* 14:65-66 (January-April 1931); Buffalo *Courier Express*, October 10, 1931, p. 1; Buffalo *Evening News*, July 14, 1906, p. 1.

—PAUL M. ROONEY

BUTLER, PIERCE (1886-1953)

Pierce Butler was born to John Pierce and Eva C. Whipple Butler on December 19, 1886, in Clarendon Hills, Illinois. Receiving a Ph.B from Dickenson College in 1906, he taught for one year at a Virginia military academy, then began two years of study (1907-1909) at the Union Theological Seminary. He returned to Dickenson for an A.M. (1910), and that same year received a B.D. from Hartford Theological Seminary. A resident fellow in medieval history at Hartford from 1910-1912, in that last year he obtained his Ph.D. there and was ordained a deacon in the Protestant Episcopal Church as well.

In 1916 he became a reference assistant at the Newberry Library in Chicago. The following year he was promoted to head of the Order Department and served also as bibliographer and custodian of the John M. Wing Foundation on Typography, continuing in those capacities until 1931. His first major book, *A Check List of Books Published in the Fifteenth Century* (rev. ed., 1924) was published by the Newberry Library.

Butler's years at the Newberry also saw his marriage to Ruth Lapham in 1926, and his reinstatement as an Episcopal deacon in 1927 (he had resigned as a deacon in 1922). He also overlapped careers during this time, for he began lecturing part-time at the University of Chicago on the history of printing in 1928. Then, in 1931, he joined the faculty of the Graduate Library School at Chicago, remaining there until his retirement as a professor in 1952.

During his Chicago years, Pierce Butler made an impression on cultural thought and the philosophy of librarianship far beyond his own modest expectations. Through his penetrating and best-known work, *An Introduction to Library Science* (1933), he "provided the first extended exposition of an approach to library education which was [only then] being introduced in the curriculum and research program of the new Graduate Library School at Chicago" (Asheim). For Pierce Butler, the world of the book and of print, and the concept of communication, forced the modern thinker to assume the weight of centuries of intellectual development. He believed that the scholar's purpose was to recognize and interpret the social history of the mind in terms that would validate it for our own age. Thus, Butler thought of the past as an urgent message to be translated to his students and transmuted into practical lessons for their professional action every day. His students and readers will always remember his cogent ability to link the new scientific approach to both the intellectual and technological problems of librarianship (1930-1950, especially) and the broad understanding and deep appreciation of the humanistic tradition that motivated his course work, his mind, and his spirit, and that showed in his writings with such persuasive fervor.

In the bibliography of his writings one scans such titles as "Bibliography and Scholarship" (1922); "The Library, a Laboratory or a Warehouse?" (1927); "Fifteenth Century Editions of Arabic Authors in Latin Translation" (1933); "The Literary History of Scholarship" (1937); his major book, *The Origin of Printing in Europe* (1940); "Scholarship and Civilization" (1944); "Librarianship As a Profession" (1951); "The Cultural Function of the Library" (1952); and "The Life of the Book" (1953). The character of these writings emphasizes Butler's concern with the cultural tradition; dozens of other publications and reviews further indicate the depth of his social, historical, and bibliographical knowledge, all of which reveal the broadest vision of scholarship.

Wilhelm Munthe, in writing of Butler's *An Introduction to Library Science*, said:

Dr. Butler employs a universally valid process of philosophical reasoning in an attempt to show it is impossible to understand a social institution like the library without scientific investigation of the social, psychological, and historical problems that attach themselves to it. . . . Butler's little book is the first attempt at a scientific synthesis of library science in its various aspects, and a step on the road toward a philosophy of librarianship. Some day it may rank among the classics of the library profession. (B. Berelson, ed., *Education for Librarianship.* Chicago: American Library Association, 1949, pp. 53-54)

As a man, Pierce Butler lived the model life of a modern Christian priest (which many people did not know he really was). His kindnesses to his students stretched from restrained petulance towards the intellectually lazy ones to avuncular consideration of the greatest concern. His indifference to scheduled responsibilities was countered by his characteristic charity and benevolence toward all. When some of his favorite ideas about the intellectual relationships of scholarship and librarianship were challenged in the storm of theory that frequently raged among the faculty at the Graduate Library School, he never intentionally offended or hurt a single individual with whom he disagreed, nor did he appear to feel that aspersions on his own theories were without some merit.

Physically, Pierce Butler was neat about his person, rotund, and short. He could appear to be seriously attendant in class, but those who knew him well learned to judge when he was listening or when he had slyly turned off his hearing aid (he was

intensely deaf) in order to appreciate his own thoughts instead of student papers. As a lecturer, he inspired the recollection of antiquity and bred in his students a curiosity about the purpose of past history and librarianship in their own times. Pipe-smoker, and connoisseur of all manifestations of quality, he was a charming and loquacious raconteur who enjoyed the simplest or most sophisticated humor and never hesitated to tell jokes about himself, preening delightfully when his listeners responded.

Although the Butlers had no children, their social life in Chicago included university colleagues and their families, students, and the vast community of friends that Butler made as associate to the rector of St. Paul's Church, Kenwood (where he was, late in life, elevated to the priesthood in 1940), and at St. James's and St. Chrysostom's, where he served later. He belonged to the American Library Association, the Bibliographical Society of America, the Gutenberg Gesellschaft (Mainz), the Chicago Society of Typographic Arts, the Masons, and Alpha Chi Rho. His clubs were the University and the Caxton.

During the 24 years of his association with the youthful Graduate Library School at the University of Chicago, Pierce Butler served under six deans: George A. Works, Louis Round Wilson, Carleton B. Joeckel (q.v.), Ralph A. Beals (q.v.), Clarence Faust, and Bernard Berelson. Each was a man of positive opinions, and the proof of Butler's versatility was that he commanded their respect and maintained excellent relations with all of them, without in any way compromising his own integrity or his strongly held convictions.

Through his writings, particularly the *Introduction to Library Science*, which has been frequently reprinted and remains one of the most frequently required readings in library schools, Pierce Butler continues to exert a very considerable influence over the thinking of modern librarians, and he must be considered one of the modern profession's greatest intellects. He died March 28, 1953, as the result of injuries sustained in an automobile accident.

Biographical listings and obituaries—*Who Was Who in America* III (1951-1960); *Who's Who in Library Service,* 1st ed., 2nd ed.   Books and articles about the biographee—Ash, Lee. "Tribute to Pierce Butler." *Library Journal* 78, No. 10:826 (May 15, 1953); Asheim, Lester. "Preface" to *Introduction to Library Science,* by Pierce Butler. Chicago: University of Chicago Press, 1967; Bell, Bernard Iddings. "Pierce Butler, Professor and Priest." *Library Quarterly* 22, No. 3:174-76 (July 1952); "Bibliography of Pierce Butler." *Library Quarterly* 22, No. 3:165-59 (July 1952); Carnovsky, Leon. "Pierce Butler, 1886-1953." *Library Quarterly* 23, No. 3 (July 1953); Komidar, Joseph S. "Pierce Butler, 1886-1953." *Libri* 4:171-72 (1954); Pargellis, Stanley M. "Pierce Butler—A Biographical Sketch." *Library Quarterly* 22, No. 3:170-73 (July 1952).

—LEE ASH

BUTLER, SUSAN DART (1888-1959)

Susan Dart Butler was born in 1888 in Charleston, South Carolina, the daughter of John Lewis and Julia Pierre Dart. She attended the Avery Normal Institute in Charleston, South Carolina, and the Normal Department of Atlanta University in Atlanta, Georgia, and received some training in librarianship at Hampton Institute in Hampton, Virginia.

Her interest in establishing public library service for Negroes in Charleston, South Carolina, was influenced by her parents' love for books and reading. Her father completed his college work at Atlanta University in 1876 and was graduated in 1882 with the B.D. degree from the Newton Theological Seminary in Newton, Massachusetts. An ordained Baptist minister, he was the pastor of the Morris Street Baptist Church in Charleston, South Carolina. Before marriage to the Reverend Mr. Dart, her mother was a school teacher in Washington, D.C.

The Reverend and Mrs. Dart developed an extensive library in their home for their own reading and that of their five children and their friends' children. In addition to his home library, the Reverend Mr. Dart equipped a room next to his study in the church to be used as a library for young Negro men in the community. In the Dart home, Negro children gathered regularly for Mrs. Dart to tell stories to them and to borrow books from the home library. In order to provide education for Negro children who could not attend the overcrowded public schools for Negroes, the Darts erected on their own land a six-room building known as Dart Hall, in which they established an elementary school. In this building, they also taught older girls to sew, and older boys were at first instructed in blacksmithing and later in printing.

When Susan Dart completed her studies at Atlanta University, her mother insisted that she go to the McDowell Millinery School in Boston, Massachusetts. She made a conscientious effort to comply with her mother's wishes to have a career in millinery work, and for five years she was successful in this vocation. However, her interest in education and librarianship prevailed.

In 1912, she married Nathaniel Lowe Butler, a native of Boston, and returned to Charleston, where her husband went into the real estate business. They were to have a son, Nathaniel L. Butler, Jr. After the death of her father and her son, Susan Butler began to devote her time to the civic, religious, and educational work started by her father. She assembled in Dart Hall the family library and her father's books and made the collection available to readers three days a week. Regular story hours were held for children. High school students used the materials more than other groups. In an effort to learn how to organize and administer a library, she traveled throughout the South to visit college and public libraries that served Negro patrons, talking with many library leaders to get information and ideas. After her travels, her first step was to organize a group of public-spirited women to focus public attention on the need for a public library for Negro citizens, and to urge the city to provide financial support for the library. In the meantime, church groups and women's clubs collected books and raised money to help purchase books. The library was maintained at Susan Butler's expense.

In 1925, she learned, through an interracial committee of the Young Women's Christian Association, that the Rosenwald Fund was interested in promoting public library service for Negroes in the South. She organized an interracial committee of women, of which she served as chairman, to investigate the possibilities of securing help from the Rosenwald Fund to start a public library, to pressure the city to provide financial support, and to collect books from every available source.

By 1927, the book collection had grown and interest in the library on the part of all citizens had been generated, and the library was having an impact on the cultural and educational life of Negroes, especially young people. Also in this year, Edwin Embree, president of the Rosenwald Fund, unexpectedly visited her in the Dart Hall Library. He was pleased with the collection, which covered a broad scope of subjects, and with the program Susan Butler was implementing for children and young people. While in the city, Embree discussed a five-year plan for the development of the Library with the Charleston County officials. After several years of planning and negotiating with the Rosenwald Fund and the Carnegie Corporation, these organizations gave $95,000 on a matching basis for the establishment of the Charleston County Free Public Library. As her contribution, Susan Butler gave the county the use of Dart Hall for the library building for one dollar a year.

As a result of her efforts and the agreement reached with the Rosenwald Fund, on January 1, 1929, the Charleston County Free Library began serving all citizens. In July of the same year, the Dart Hall Branch of the Charleston County Free Library opened. During the first year, Butler served as the children's librarian. In the summer of 1932, she went to Hampton Institute Library School in Hampton, Virginia, to take courses in library science. When she returned, she became the librarian of the Dart Hall Branch Library. The library programs were at first centered on children. Later, a "Great Books" discussion program was initiated for adults, monthly book review programs were held, and bookmobile service was provided for Negro schools within a thirty-mile radius. The branch library became the focal point for materials by and about Negroes.

In addition to pioneering in the establishment of library service for Negroes in Charleston, South Carolina, Susan Butler was a leader in a number of other organizations, all of which worked toward similar goals, to raise the cultural and educational levels of Negroes. She was an active member of the Librarians' Section of the South Carolina State Teachers' Association and the Young Women's Christian Association. She was one of the founders of the South Carolina Federation of Women's Clubs, of which she was the historian. She assisted with the Boy Scouts and the Girl Scouts and served on the Charleston County Board of the American Red Cross. She was on the Board of Directors of the local Boys' Club and of an orphanage in Cayce, South Carolina. She also used her contacts with these organizations to promote the establishment of the Hall Branch of the Charleston County Free Library.

In May 1957, Mrs. Butler retired at the age of 69, after serving as branch librarian for 26 years. The Charleston County Library Board and citizens expressed their gratitude to her for the great service she had rendered to the community. On this occasion her remarks included the following statement:

It has given me great pleasure to watch the progress that children and adult patrons of the library have made. Some of the children have graduated from high school, finished college, and have returned home with college and even more advanced degrees. During the years from 1931 to 1957, I have tried to serve the children and adults of Charleston County, helping them to help themselves by reading and using good books. Many of the students who grew up in the community using Dart Hall are teaching in Charleston today. They have contributed through the years to a fund for the purchase of professional books required by the Extension Department of South Carolina State College. A collection of several hundred books valued at more than $5,000 was donated to Dart Hall Library by teachers for their use. . . .

Susan Butler was one of many Negro women who pioneered in their respective communities throughout the South to establish public library service for Negroes. Two years after her retirement, she died on June 24, 1959. Her work in Charleston, South Carolina, served to guide and inspire others who were working toward the same goals.

Books and articles about the biographee—Bolden, Ethel. "Susan Dart Butler: Pioneer Librarian." Master's thesis, School of Library Service, Atlanta University, 1959.

—VIRGINIA LACY JONES

CARNEGIE, ANDREW (1835-1919)

Andrew Carnegie, often referred to as the "Patron Saint of Libraries," made new library buildings available to hundreds of communities all over the world. He donated $56,162,622 for the construction of 2,509 library buildings throughout the English-speaking parts of the world. More than $41,000,000 of this amount was given for the erection of 1,679 public library buildings in 1,412 communities of the United States. Another $4,283,000 was given towards the construction of 108 academic library buildings in the United States. After 1911, library grants were made by the Carnegie Corporation rather than by Andrew Carnegie personally, although he was president of the Corporation until his death in 1919.

Actually this library philanthropy was only a small part of Carnegie's benefactions. More than $333,000,000 (90 percent of his fortune) was spent by the Steel King for what he termed "the improvement of mankind." The range of his philanthropy was great and varied, from the Simplified Spelling Board, the more than 7,000 church organs, and the Carnegie Hero Fund, to the Carnegie Institute in Pittsburgh, the Carnegie Institution of Washington, the Foundation for the Advancement of Teaching, and the Carnegie Endowment for International Peace. Although the gift of library buildings seems small in comparison, it was perhaps the most dramatic and influential in that it affected millions of people. It also captured the imagination of Americans everywhere so that to this day the public is still generally aware of Carnegie's library philanthropy.

Andrew Carnegie was born in a weaver's cottage on November 25, 1835, in Dunfermline, Scotland. Because of the rapid industrialization of the textile trade, his father was forced to sell out his business; Carnegie's formal education came to an end, and the family moved to the United States in 1846. They settled in Allegheny, Pennsylvania, a suburb of Pittsburgh. Carnegie's first job (at the age of thirteen) was that of a bobbin boy for $1.20 per week. After one year, he became a messenger boy for a local telegraph company, where he taught himself the art of telegraphy. Thomas Scott, superintendent of the Pittsburgh division of the Pennsylvania Railroad, hired him as a private secretary and personal telegrapher, and Carnegie took Scott's place when the latter was eventually promoted. In 1861, after Scott became assistant secretary of war, Carnegie helped organize the military telegraph department.

Carnegie had wide business interests while associated with the Pennsylvania Railroad from 1853 to 1865. He bought into the Woodruff Sleeping Car Company and introduced the first successful sleeping car on an American railroad. During 1862, he invested in what turned out to be a major oil development in western Pennsylvania. The following year, he helped form the Keystone Bridge Company, which successfully and profitably began to replace wooden railroad bridges with structures made of iron.

After he became involved in a small iron-forging company in Pittsburgh, Carnegie gave up his position with the railroad in 1865 to devote more time to his own business interests. For the next 36 years, he built up the Carnegie Steel Company until it was sold to J. P. Morgan in 1901 for nearly $500,000,000. Then, at the age of 66, healthy, alert, and keenly interested in politics and literature, Carnegie retired and devoted the rest of his life to philanthropy and the securement of international peace. He had married Louise Whitfield in 1887, and their daughter Margaret was born in 1897. Bronchial pneumonia caused his death on August 11, 1919.

Most biographers attribute Carnegie's success to his genius for organization, the shrewdness of his business judgment, his ability to select the proper men for the jobs to be done, his faith in the United States as a land of business opportunity and growth, and his policy of expanding during the periods of economic depression. A minority of biographers have characterized him as greedy, ruthless, and a cruel taskmaster.

A memorandum found among Carnegie's papers after his death revealed that as early as 1868, at the age of 33, he had made plans to use the surplus of his income for the benefit of others. But it was not until 1889 that he formally declared his philosophy of the trusteeship of wealth or, as it came to be called, the Gospel of Wealth. In his first essay on the subject, "Wealth," Carnegie declared that wealthy men were to live without extravagance, provide moderately for the legitimate needs of their dependents, and then consider the remainder of their fortunes as surplus funds which they, as trustees, should distribute in their lifetime for the best promotion of welfare and happiness of the common man. The main consideration was to help those who would help themselves— but only to assist, and never or rarely ever to do all, because neither the individual nor the group was improved by almsgiving. The best and most aspiring poor of the community had to be stimulated to improve themselves. The millionaire, as a trustee for the poor, was entrusted with the increased wealth of the community and was able to administer it far better than the community could or would.

In his second essay, "The Best Fields for Philanthropy," Carnegie lists, in order, seven fields to which the wealthy could devote their surplus: universities, libraries, medical centers, public parks, meeting and concert halls, public baths, and churches. The best gift that could be given to a community was a free

library, "provided the community will accept and maintain it as a public institution, as much a part of the city property as its public schools, and, indeed, an adjunct to these."

Why did Andrew Carnegie select libraries to be among his first and foremost benefactions? One reason was given by a friend of the philanthropist, who said that all of Carnegie's gifts were dedicated to causes and movements with which he was especially concerned. Even his most intimate friends could seldom persuade him to give large sums to anything in which he was not personally interested or of which he had not made a personal study.

Libraries and books seemed to be of special concern to Carnegie. His father had led his fellow weavers in Dunfermline to pool their contributions for the purchase of books and delegated one of their number to read aloud while the others worked. This collection became the first circulating library in the town, and Carnegie frequently spoke with pride of his lineage as the son of a library-founding weaver. (Thus, it was to the town of Dunfermline that Carnegie gave his first library, in 1881.) While Carnegie was still a working boy in Pittsburgh, a Colonel Anderson of Allegheny established in 1850 the J. Anderson Library of Allegheny City to furnish reading for the mechanics and workingmen in the trades. Young Andrew wrote a letter to the newspaper requesting that the library be opened to all working boys, and he was invited to use it. In later years, he recalled awaiting Saturday afternoons with intense longing, "and it was when reveling in the treasures which he opened to us that I resolved, if ever wealth came to me, that other poor boys might receive opportunities similar to those for which we were indebted to that noble man." Less than ten years after he made this statement, Carnegie began his library-giving on a grand scale.

Carnegie's confidence in the value of free libraries as a wise object of philanthropy may also have been stimulated by earlier and contemporary library philanthropists. He praised Ezra Cornell for beginning the distribution of his wealth by establishing a public library in Ithaca, New York, in 1857. He also had a high regard for Enoch Pratt's gifts to Baltimore of $1,000,000, with a requirement that the city pay 5 percent of this sum annually to the library trustees for the development of the main library and branches. Carnegie felt that the 37,000 registered borrowers of the Pratt Library were of more value to Baltimore, to the state, and to the nation than all of the inert, lazy, and hopelessly poor in all of the United States. Perhaps Carnegie's library philanthropy was also influenced by his business background. He once told an audience that, far from being a philanthropist, he was making the best bargains of his life. For instance, when he gave a city money for a library building, he succeeded in obtaining a pledge that the city would furnish the site and maintain the library forever. The city's investment was greater than his, and as he said, "This was not philanthropy but a clever stroke of business." To all of these motivations must be added one with which Andrew Carnegie was frequently charged. His accusers claimed that he built libraries as monuments to himself for posterity.

The procedure for obtaining a Carnegie public library building grant was fairly simple. The mayor and council of a community that needed a library structure had to promise to provide a site and had to pledge to support the new library through local taxation in an annual amount that would be at least 10 percent of the sum given for the library building (which was usually based on about $2.00 per capita of local population). James Bertram (q.v.), Carnegie's private secretary, was in charge of the day-to-day operations of the benefactions and in a sense was the real power behind them. Carnegie provided the funds and set up the general guidelines; Bertram put them into action.

The importance of Carnegie library philanthropy lies in its perfect timing, as it came during the best possible period—the height of library expansion in the United States. Beginning in the 1890s, states began to play active roles in organizing public libraries in each community. The need for library buildings was desperate, and Carnegie's gifts helped to fill the void, for the provision of new buildings created an avid interest in and enthusiasm for libraries in their early, crucial years of development.

An important factor in further stimulating public library development was the publicity and advertising resulting from these beneficences. Although the public library, by the beginning of the twentieth century, was generally accepted and approved as a worthy agency, it was, nevertheless, often confronted with a lack of understanding and appreciation and even with indifference. Carnegie dramatized the value of libraries. Here was a famous millionaire who believed that libraries were important and who gave millions for their support. Carnegie and the Carnegie Corporation provided the incentive for each community to obtain a library for its populace, and the rivalry among some towns to outdo one another was still another factor. In the long run, Carnegie made more libraries and books available to more people than anyone before him, and he helped speed the momentum of the public library movement.

Carnegie's initiative also stimulated other library benefactions. During the 1890s, more than $10,000,000 were donated for libraries by philanthropists. From 1900 to 1906, 3,099 individual contributions, totaling more than $24,000,000, were made to libraries, and almost half of this amount was expended for buildings and sites. But, more importantly, Carnegie's philanthropy widened the acceptance of the principle of each local government's responsibility for the public library. The method of giving was not perfect, for the sites selected were often poor and the 10 percent support pledge was sometimes broken, or more often, not surpassed. Nevertheless, the pledge was a wise provision. It placed indirect pressure on governmental bodies and the public to accept the organization and maintenance of the public library as a governmental service.

In library architecture, too, Carnegie provided a stimulus, though derogatory comments are often heard about Carnegie library architecture. These remarks, however, usually refer to the older libraries, built before Carnegie and the Corporation became involved in architectural control. The short architectural memorandum issued by James Bertram in simplified spelling in 1911 was composed of the best library opinion of the time on the subject. Indeed, the memorandum marked the beginning of modern library architecture, and many of the principles are still in effect today.

But one must be careful not to give Carnegie philanthropy all the credit for the growth of the public library. At times, some commentators imply that Carnegie practically founded the entire public library movement, or that without him it would long have rested on a plateau with little further development. On the contrary, the public library system of the United States was expanding under its own power before Carnegie's generosity started on a "wholesale" basis in 1898. In just twenty years, the number of public libraries had grown from 188 in 1876 to 971 with 1,000 volumes or more in 1896. Actually, about two-thirds of the communities receiving funds for one or more Carnegie library buildings already had a free public library or were in the process of organizing one when the Carnegie gift was offered. Yet many had just been organized or were being organized as a result of the stimulation of Carnegie benefactions and with the hope of obtaining new buildings. To be sure, the incentive of Carnegie's gifts was enough to accelerate the library movement—the approximately 188 public libraries in 1876 jumped to 3,873 by 1923.

Andrew Carnegie's philanthropy continued to benefit public libraries and librarianship long after the formal termination of building grants. This extended library philanthropy is still in evidence to this day, and in many ways is even more important than the original bequest of Carnegie buildings. The Carnegie Corporation, which took over Carnegie's philanthropy program, has been so identified with libraries that many people have assumed it was operating solely for the benefit and control of libraries and librarians. Following World War I, however,

Corporation trustees did not resume gifts of money for buildings. Instead, during the period 1917-1925, they organized a series of conferences to determine the manner and means by which the Corporation might be of assistance in improving library services and training.

In 1918, the Corporation asked Charles C. Williamson (q.v.) to make a study of library training. His report recommended that librarians should receive their education in a university rather than in a training school sponsored by a public library. Williamson also recommended the establishment of a graduate library school for advanced study, a national accrediting and certification system for library schools, and numerous fellowships. A monumental work, the study resulted in a complete revision of the curriculum in library schools.

A Carnegie Corporation-sponsored study in 1924 by William S. Learned (q.v.) centered on the library's role as a medium for spreading information. It called for expanded services to be provided by the American Library Association, and for local and regional experiments and demonstrations leading to better ways of getting books to the people. Then in 1926, the Corporation embarked on a ten-year "Library Service Program," for which the trustees approved $5,000,000 in financial support. The aim of this program was to strengthen the library profession by underwriting the activities of the American Library Association, by improving training opportunities, and by supporting certain centralized library services and projects.

Andrew Carnegie had already provided $100,000 in endowment funds to the American Library Association in 1902, and the Corporation gave $549,500 for the general support of the Association from 1924 to 1926. In 1926, it added $2,000,000 in endowment funds. During this period, the Corporation also provided financial assistance to the Library of Congress and to bibliographic centers and regional catalogs, such as those at the Denver and Philadelphia public libraries. Gifts for the endowment and support of library schools and for the establishment of the first graduate library school at the University of Chicago totaled $3,359,550. The Corporation provided fellowships for library training and also sponsored conferences, studies, and publications. Additionally, the Corporation funded demonstrations of methods and techniques for bringing books to people of all ages who were living in rural areas far from the major population centers.

Following World War II, during which the Corporation's library philanthropy was for the most part in a state of suspension, the trustees and officers evolved a new Corporation grant program in which library interests no longer had a major emphasis, although library grants were not excluded. In fact, although the number of grants and the amount expended did decrease, those which were made were of great importance.

The Corporation provided $212,170 to the Social Science Research Council for the Public Library Inquiry. The idea of studying the library's actual and potential contribution to American society was suggested by the American Library Association, and the appraisal was made in sociological, cultural, and human terms. The overall report was published in 1950, with specific studies being issued in twelve volumes between 1949 and 1951. The most significant finding was the poor status of the American public library outside the major cities. There was a superabundance of small, poorly financed, independent local libraries with inadequate book stocks and reference services. The Public Library Inquiry discovered that 65 percent of all libraries were in small towns of less than 5,000 and spent less than $4,000 per year. The survey suggested the organization of larger library systems and the concentration of state and federal library aid for the encouragement of such systems. The small libraries could and should continue to serve the communities that organized them, but they should also be related to surrounding libraries in regional systems with common pools of books and other materials, specialized personnel available for guidance, and centralized reference and processing services.

Again, in 1956, financial assistance from the Carnegie Corporation helped the American Library Association to formulate and publish what popularly became known as the Public Library Standards. The Public Library Inquiry discovered the failings of the public libraries; the Standards presented what they should be doing by setting up minimum guidelines of good service. Public libraries were urged to cooperate, federate, or consolidate into library systems for better library service.

In 1956, a grant of $50,000 was made to the School of Library Science at Western Reserve University for the study of a new curriculum in library training in the light of modern cultural and technological developments.

The Corporation's financial support of demonstration centers for extension of library service in rural areas, of the Public Library Inquiry, and of the Standards was an important factor in bringing about federal aid for public libraries. The Library Services Act (P.L. 597, 84th Congress), signed into law in 1956, was designed as a five-year program to demonstrate improved public library services in areas with populations of less than 10,000 people and nonexistent or inadequate library service. The Act was extended in 1960 for five additional years, then in 1964, it was amended and renamed the Library Services and Construction Act (P.L. 88-269). Benefits were extended to urban as well as to rural areas, and for the first time, funds were not limited to operation and maintenance but could be expended for construction.

Building on the foundation laid by the social libraries, public libraries in the United States have had four important phases of growth. The public library enabling laws, beginning in the 1850s, were the first stimulus. Carnegie's gifts to public libraries were the second. A third major stimulus could well be said to be the library activities of the Carnegie Corporation. In the 1960s, we began to experience the fourth—that of the stimulus of federal support. This latest development came about, to some extent at least, as the result of the influence of Andrew Carnegie and the Carnegie Corporation's library activities. Carnegie's benefactions have, in truth, played a major role in American public library development and have had a significant impact in all areas of American librarianship.

Biographical listings and obituaries—*Who Was Who in America* I (1897-1942). **Books and articles about the biographee**—Bobinski, George S. *Carnegie Libraries: Their History and Impact on American Public Library Development*. Chicago: American Library Association, 1969; Hendrick, Burton. *The Life of Andrew Carnegie*. Garden City, N.Y.: Doubleday, 1932, 2 vols. **Primary sources and archival materials**—Carnegie, Andrew. *Autobiography of Andrew Carnegie*. Boston: Houghton, 1920; Carnegie, Andrew. *The Gospel of Wealth and Other Timely Essays*. Edward C. Kirkland, ed. Cambridge, Mass.: Harvard University Press, 1962; Carnegie Corporation of New York. *Carnegie Corporation Library Program, 1911-1961*. New York: Carnegie Corporation, 1963. Correspondence to Carnegie and by him is contained in the Carnegie Library Correspondence (40 microfilm reels) at the Carnegie Corporation offices in New York City.

—GEORGE S. BOBINSKI

CARNOVSKY, LEON (1903-1975)

Leon Carnovsky was born in St. Louis, Missouri, on November 28, 1903, to Isaac and Jennie Stillman Carnovsky. His father had been a Talmudic scholar, but when the family emigrated from Lithuania they opened a grocery store in St. Louis. Young Carnovsky attended St. Louis public schools and also frequented the local branch of the St. Louis Public Library with the encouragement of his bookish parents. After completing high school, he worked for two years as a secretary in a St. Louis firm that manufactured pistons and piston rings. Competent as a secretary (as evidenced by the rapid and rhythmical clicks emanating from his faculty office typewriter in later years and the shorthand notes he took), he was encouraged by his superior to enter the University of Missouri. He received an A.B. from the University of Missouri in 1927 with a major in philosophy and a minor in sociology. After graduation, he entered the training class of the St. Louis Public Library and worked there

as an assistant, moving in 1928 to a position as assistant to the librarian of Washington University. Awarded a fellowship with an annual stipend of $1,500 at the newly opened Graduate Library School of the University of Chicago in 1929, he earned his Ph.D. there in 1932. In the same year, he joined the faculty of the School as an instructor, advancing through ranks to professor in 1944.

He remained at Chicago teaching, editing, and carrying out research until his retirement in 1971, when he moved to Oakland. He taught courses in public libraries, research methods, education for librarianship, and comparative librarianship. His course for beginning library school students, "The Library and Society," was both broad and profound. From 1943 to 1961, he was the managing editor of *The Library Quarterly*. Interspersed with his work at Chicago, of course, were many shorter assignments carried out abroad, in England, Germany, France, Italy, Israel, Greece, and Japan, and some work as a visiting professor at Berkeley, Syracuse, and Columbia.

Early in his career, he established a reputation as a perceptive surveyor of libraries and library problems. He collaborated with E. A. Wight in the 1936 report *Library Service in a Suburban Area*, the Westchester County study. In 1939, he was director of the appraisal staff for the survey of the Cleveland Public Library. *A Metropolitan Library in Action: A Survey of the Chicago Public Library* was published with C. B. Joeckel (q.v.) in 1940. He conducted surveys of over a dozen libraries and participated as a team member in others, such as the survey of library education he prepared for *Libraries and Librarians in the Pacific Northwest* (1960). UNESCO engaged him to survey library education in Israel and Greece, resulting in *Report of a Programme for Library Education in Israel* (1957) and *A Library School for Greece* (1962). His report on Israel provided the blueprint for the Graduate Library School of Hebrew University, as J. Rothschild, its director, acknowledged in a letter of January 1, 1976. He was also interested in foreign students in America, and his last published survey was *The Foreign Student in the American Library School* (1972).

Much of his most influential writing appeared in journal articles published between 1931 and 1972. These were always clearly written and logically constructed, and they were often reprinted. Perhaps his most frequently reprinted article was "The Obligations and Responsibilities of the Librarian Concerning Censorship" (from *Library Quarterly*, January 1950, pp. 21-32), illustrating a concern emanating partly from his philosophical background and partly from his experience as chairman of the ALA Intellectual Freedom Committee. Added to his articles written for journal publication were the speeches he gave in response to frequent invitations. In his last year as an active professor, for example, he was invited to address the biennial conference of the Australian Library Association at Sydney in 1971.

As managing editor of *The Library Quarterly*, he was, as William Haygood said, "meticulous, discriminating, imaginative, and entirely devoted to ... scholarly standards." He was, and more. All who worked with him on the *Quarterly* remember the passionate devotion he lavished on every detail of journal production—the recruiting and evaluation of manuscripts, the elimination of obscurities in manuscripts going to the copy editor, proofreading, and finally, the care of the subscribers. Not to be disregarded in his editing are several volumes of the proceedings of Graduate Library School Conferences that he organized: *The Library in the Community* (with Lowell Martin, 1944); *International Aspects of Librarianship* (1954); *The Medium-sized Public Library* (with Howard Winger, 1963); *The Public Library in the Urban Setting* (1968); and *Library Networks* (1969).

Leon Carnovsky gazed on his surroundings from dark brown eyes through thick lensed glasses that could not obscure a frank and engaging countenance. Except for a fringe of dark hair, he was bald, a state that he reached early, according to Peggy Sullivan, whom he once told that his appearance was unaltered after the age of twenty. Well muscled, as a result of hiking, bird watching, and swimming, he swung easily along the avenues, his head topped by a fedora in spring and autumn, a straw hat in summer, and a dark beret in winter.

He had many hobbies. One was fishing, pursued during vacations in Wisconsin and Michigan, and throughout the year he kept an aquarium at home. He loved plants and flowers, and the last time this writer saw him (at his home in Oakland in July 1975, when his fatal illness was already long upon him) he directed me from his wheelchair to see the flowers on his nineteenth-floor balcony. He enjoyed music—symphonies, ballets, operas, and oratorios. Often he hummed passages from Handel. The stage was in his family, to say the least, and he was for many years an ornament in a play-reading group in Hyde Park, a fiercely partisan crowd that would like to claim his memory. He took part in the Quadrangle Club Revels, the annual review formerly staged by the faculty club and sometimes directed by his wife, Marian Carnovsky. The ballad he composed and sang (in a costume featuring a red leather cap) about Abe, the 57th Street newspaper vendor, has long been remembered. He also wrote much occasional verse, contributing regularly for faculty birthday celebrations held over a cake and pot of coffee in a back room.

His book collection, "Alice in Translation," began on his first European trip in 1934, when he acquired his first translated version of *Alice in Wonderland*. The collection grew to over fifty examples, which he gave to the University of Chicago Library when he retired.

Leon Carnovsky married Marian Satterthwaite, librarian and author of a book about public libraries, in August 1939. Sharing common intellectual and social interests, they made their home in Hyde Park a lively gathering place where they entertained visiting scholars such as S. R. Ranganathan and Preben Kierkegaard, among others, as well as colleagues, students, and neighborhood friends. Marian died in January 1965. In June 1967, Carnovsky married Ruth French Strout, a colleague at the Graduate Library School, and they continued together the tradition of gracious hospitality and stimulating conversation. He had no children, but at his death on December 6, 1975 (in Oakland), he was survived by his widow, a brother, Morris Carnovsky, the famous actor, and three sisters, Gertrude, Esther, and Deborah.

From 1932 to 1971, he was a member of the faculty of the Graduate Library School, always a worthy example of enlightened and humane scholarship both within and without the academy. His more than 160 publications were written in a crisp, clear prose style, and are often cited by others in the field. One of the architects of library and community survey techniques, he was also a distinguished editor. He supported the work of library associations, serving as president of AALS, 1942-1943, and serving as chairman of the ALA Intellectual Freedom Committee and of the Committee on Accreditation. ALA honored him with the Melvil Dewey Medal in 1962 and the Joseph W. Lippincott Award in 1975. He was an inspiring teacher, delivering well-organized lectures in a clear and resonant voice. In brief, he was a great professor in his time.

Biographical listings and obituaries—*A Biographical Directory of Librarians in the United States and Canada*, 5th ed.; [Obituary]. *American Libraries* 7:11 (June 1976); *Who's Who in Library Service*, 1st ed., 2nd ed., 3rd ed., 4th ed.; *Who's Who in World Jewry* (1972). **Books and articles about the biographee**—"The Brothers Carnovsky: A Profile, a Monologue." *University of Chicago Magazine* 72:2-7 (January/February 1970); Haygood, William Converse. "Leon Carnovsky: A Sketch." *Library Quarterly* 38:422-28 (October 1968); Schlipf, Frederick A. "Leon Carnovsky: A Bibliography." *Library Quarterly* 38:429-41 (October 1968).

—HOWARD W. WINGER

CARR, HENRY JAMES (1849-1929)

"Watchful care, constant attention, foresight, and unremitting work." When Henry J. Carr cited these characteristics as qualities necessary for efficient library performance in his July 4, 1901, presidential address to the American Library Association, he was consciously summarizing his own principles as a professional librarian.

Born on August 16, 1849, to James Webster and Jane D. Goodhue Carr in Pembroke, New Hampshire, Carr entered elementary school in nearby Manchester in 1855. When he was sixteen, his family moved to Grand Rapids, Michigan, where his father established a lumber company. Young Henry enrolled at Grand Rapids Central High School, but after a year he decided to quit. From 1866 to 1878, he served as an accountant and cashier in several commercial offices in Grand Rapids and Chicago.

In 1878, Carr entered law school at the University of Michigan. While pursuing his legal training, he enrolled in the bibliography and elementary library science courses offered by Raymond C. Davis (q.v.), the University's librarian. Davis sparked a latent interest in Carr, and although Carr completed law school and was admitted to the bar of Kent County on April 19, 1879, he never practiced in the legal profession. Instead, he attended the third conference of the fledgling American Library Association in the summer of 1879 and became member number 215. Though Carr continued to work as an accountant, his interest in librarianship increased.

In 1886, the Grand Rapids Board of Education fired its public librarian without prior notice—the third such action by the Board. The move, which reflected characteristic indifference by elected officials regarding library matters, annoyed many townspeople. Carr himself had criticized the Board in March 1877 for being "too political" and spending "too much of its time in personal contacts and fighting for individual interests and opinions." However, William Frederick Poole (q.v.), who was librarian of the Chicago Public Library, blamed weak and inefficient librarians for the dismal situation. But regardless of who was at fault, the Grand Rapids Public Library was still without leadership. When the Board finally directed its Library Committee to find a qualified individual for the vacant post, Committee members conducted the search by personally visiting other libraries and writing to officers of the American Library Association. In these conversations and correspondence, the name that surfaced most frequently was Henry J. Carr. On February 20, 1886, the Board acted on recommendation of its Library Committee and unanimously selected Carr as public librarian of Grand Rapids. Carr accepted the appointment a week later and, despite misgivings about his future employers, he assumed his duties on March 7.

This year, 1886, was an important year in Carr's life for another reason. On May 13, he married D. Edith Wallbridge, librarian of the State Library of Illinois at Springfield, who had graduated from Hillsdale College in 1878. They had met at an ALA conference, and after a four-year courtship she consented to marriage. Following the ceremony, she returned with Carr to Grand Rapids, where she abandoned her professional career to become a housewife.

His success in the profession of librarianship made Carr more ambitious, and he built his reputation quickly. Two years after he assumed his first administrative post, the Grand Rapids *Eagle* praised him as "one of the most competent men in the country to care for and manage a public library." By 1890, he had converted 13,500 low-circulating, poorly cataloged volumes into 22,600 high-circulating, effectively cataloged volumes. Even the process of moving the entire facility from a Grand Rapids office building to the second floor of the new City Hall building in 1888 caused only minor ripples in the library's smooth operation.

The experience at Grand Rapids had been exciting, but by 1890, Carr chafed for a new professional challenge. In August, St. Joseph, Missouri, offered it to him. The Missouri Legislature had enacted a free public library law in 1885, modelled on the very successful one that had spurred the establishment of numerous public libraries in Illinois. Because St. Joseph was the first city in Missouri to benefit from the law, city fathers sought a highly qualified person for the chief librarian's post. Convinced that Henry J. Carr fit their needs, they offered him the position. Carr accepted on one condition—that he be free to leave the St. Joseph area once the library was properly organized and running efficiently. When the city fathers agreed to this stipulation, Carr presented his resignation to the Grand Rapids Board of Education and moved to St. Joseph in October. Five months later, he opened the St. Joseph Public Library with a core collection gleaned from a former subscription library. By the summer of 1891, however, he had honed the library's operational efficiency to such a level that he was ready to move on.

Public officials in Scranton, Pennsylvania, had just laid the cornerstone for the new Albright Memorial Library Building, and members of the Library's Board of Trustees were seeking a competent administrator to organize it before it opened that fall. Carr's reputation was already national, and when the Board extended him an invitation to become chief administrator of the new library in August 1891, he immediately accepted—this time without conditions. He indicated he was ready to settle, and he remained as public librarian in Scranton until his death 38 years later.

As his life became more stable, Carr increased his involvement in professional organizations. He had served as treasurer of the American Library Association from 1886 to 1893, and thereafter became recorder (1894-1895), vice-president (1895-1896), secretary (1898-1900), and finally president

(1900-1901). He also served as vice-president and president of the Pennsylvania Library Club, and as president of the Keystone Library Association (1907-1908). He was a fellow of the American Library Institute from its inception in 1905. Carr published numerous minor articles on classification, catalog duplicating, library furniture, reference list indexes, book borrowing, fines, and the application of commercial accounting principles to library bookkeeping. While his impact on the library profession was not major, it was nonetheless constant.

Carr's attendance at ALA conventions was religious, and his record enviable. In his fifty-year membership, he missed only eight conferences. Edith Carr accompanied her husband to 33 conferences and developed her own identity within the Association by annually compiling the ALA Necrology. She also supervised many social functions at the conventions and on one occasion arranged a stately dinner honoring ALA "pioneers"—those members who had joined the organization prior to 1900. At the 1924 convention, the ALA membership showed its appreciation for the Carrs' loyal service by presenting them with a loving cup.

In June 1926, Carr fell in the library and crushed a vertebra. He remained in poor health until his death on May 21, 1929. He was buried in a Grand Rapids cemetery beside his mother and father.

Biographical listings and obituaries—"Henry James Carr." *Bulletin of the Grand Rapids Public Library* 25:49-51 (May-June 1929); *National Cyclopaedia of American Biography* 12; *Who Was Who in America* I (1897-1942). **Primary sources and archival materials**—Letters from and to Carr are contained in four boxes located in the American Library Association Archives at the University of Illinois.

—WAYNE A. WIEGAND

CERTAIN, CASPER CARL (1885-1940)

C. C. Certain, as he is better known to school librarians, is famous for his important role in developing the first school library standards—*Standard Library Organization and Equipment for Secondary Schools of Different Sizes* (ALA, 1920)—popularly known as the "Certain Standards." Although Certain was primarily an English teacher, his impact on school librarianship is undisputed.

Casper Carl Certain was born in Huntsville, Alabama, in 1885 (the precise day is unknown). He received his B.S. from Alabama Polytech in 1906 and, while serving both as registrar and an instructor in English (1906-1911), he completed the requirements for his E.E. at that same school (1907). He later received an A.M. from Columbia (1923). He was a member of Phi Delta Kappa. At Birmingham's Central High School, Certain was head of the English Department from 1911 to 1915 and returned to Alabama Polytech as a professor of rhetoric from 1915 to

1916. He then moved to Detroit, first as head of the English Department of Cass Technical High School (1916-1918), then as English Department head and assistant principal at Northwest High School (1919-1921), and finally as associate director for language education in the Detroit Public Schools (1921-1923). He eventually became supervisor of public school libraries for Detroit.

During some summers, he taught methods of teaching English—at the universities of Alabama (1915), Utah (1924), and Wisconsin (1926). He also surveyed high school libraries in the South for the U.S. Bureau of Education in 1917 and the English offerings of schools in Hope Farm, New York (1917), and Flint, Michigan (1920-1921). He was director for English education for the Army Education Corps from 1918 to 1919.

The "Certain Standards" grew out of Certain's work as chairman of the Committee on Problems of High School Libraries of the National Education Association's Department of Secondary Education. Also, he was vice president of the NEA Library Department for 1916-1917 and president for 1917-1918, during which time the standards were in preparation. In preparing the standards, Certain chaired a committee of 23 members (comprised of fourteen librarians and nine other educators) representing both the NEA and the North Central Association of College and Secondary Schools. The standards, which were based upon research, including regional surveys of high school libraries beginning in 1915, are remarkably contemporary, especially in their espousal of the "media center" concept.

Following the 1920 report on secondary school libraries, an article entitled "Empirical Basis for Scientific Standards in School Libraries" (in *Junior-Senior High School Clearing House*, 1931, pp. 206-15) listed eighteen items on which he based his survey. The score card resulting from this survey was to be used for a more definitive set of high school library standards, emphasizing organization and administration on the one hand and library service and use on the other, and recognizing that the revised standards should be both qualitative and quantitative. Most of these criteria are included in today's standards and guidelines.

Not only was Certain the promoter of secondary school libraries, but he chaired the joint committee from the NEA's Department of Elementary School Principals and the American Library Association's School Librarians Section that produced a report on *Elementary School Library Standards* (ALA, 1925). A man ahead of his time in many respects, he promoted the concept that "modern [1925] demands" upon the public school presuppose adequate library service; that an essential consideration is that the books and materials be readily available when needed *and* under the direction of a library staff which is part of the school organization. He promoted the use of all kinds of materials (slides, films, maps, etc.), insisting that all teaching materials should be available to students and faculty.

In an article discussing "Some Sociological Sidelights Upon the School Library" (*School and Society*, September 15, 1923), Certain pointed out

> elements of a social character that grow and strengthen under proper conditions of administration.... A knowledge of the great working classifications of books, with attendant confidence in the availability and accessibility of library materials so classified, is undoubtedly one element. There is no need to push ahead in line, to shove someone else aside; every one will be served in good time. The materials are easily accessible; they are available without loss of time. Other elements are respect for public property, association within groups where like needs are felt, common methods of satisfying needs and forms of group conduct determined by the purposes of individuals with common or related ends in view.

Certain's concern for the individual is manifested over and over, and much of what he wrote is applicable today. Yet he continually argued against "smug individualism" and noted the need for balance between the individual and group or social life.

In 1924, his strong plea for administrators to develop elementary school libraries was the impetus for this type of service in the United States. Said Certain (in *Elementary School Journal*, January 1924, p. 358), "without systematic attention, tens of thousands of books which teachers clamor for when presenting requisitions will in many cases be neglected and permitted to go unused by these same teachers.... a constant effort must be put forth to make known to the teachers and the principal the printed materials with which they are concerned and which they need in work and recreation." Commenting (in that same article, p. 364) on a survey that he made of 35 elementary school libraries in Detroit, Certain concludes,

> First, only a person with special training can fulfill the many functions described and, second, no school can reach its highest efficiency until it provides for the systematic and broad use of reading materials which the presence of a trained librarian insures. That instruction has traditionally been altogether in the hands of classroom teachers ought not to blind boards of education or superintendents to the imperative need in a modern school for a more extensive use of reading materials. If this need is recognized, there will naturally follow the transformation of the study-room into a library and the assignment of the supervision of the library to a trained librarian.

Certain continued to be active after the publication of the Certain standards. He was an active member of the ALA Education Committee from 1919 to 1925 and was involved in the publication of the series of five *School Library Yearbooks.* He served as chairman of the committees on library standards of the Department of Secondary School Principals and the Department of Elementary School Principals and as chairman of the ALA school library section. He became the first supervisor of public school libraries in Detroit and is credited with the establishment of elementary school libraries in that city. For the National Council of Teachers of English, he served as treasurer (1914-1915/1915-1916) and as auditor (1922-1923). Finally, he served as founder and editor (1924-1940) of the *Elementary English Review.* (His wife, Julia Lockwood Certain, became editor following his death.)

It was said of C. C. Certain after his death on December 18, 1940, in Detroit, that "nothing was impossible—no wrong too deeply stretched to be routed, no cause too hopeless to be rescued—for he was without fear" (editorial in *Elementary English Review*, January 1941, p. 28). School librarians, and indeed the whole library profession, can be grateful to this educator who took up the cudgel for strong school library programs for all children and young people and who believed in a strong professional library staff.

Biographical listings and obituaries—*Leaders in Education* (1932). Books and articles about the biographee—"Casper Carl Certain, 1885-1940" [editorial]. *Elementary English Review* 18:27-28 (January 1941); Gambee, Budd L. "Standards for School Media Programs, 1920: A Lesson from History." *American Libraries* 1:483-85 (May 1970).

—JEAN E. LOWRIE

CLAPP, VERNER WARREN (1901-1972)

Verner W. Clapp was an internationalist and an individualist who displayed these characteristics even from birth. He was born of American parents in Johannesburg, Transvaal, Union of South Africa, on June 3, 1901. His mother, Mary Sybil Helms Clapp, was the daughter of a Danish mining engineer, and his father, George Herbert Clapp, was a native of Dover, New Hampshire, assigned to Johannesburg on business. In 1905, after the Boer War, the family returned to the United States to reside in Poughkeepsie, New York, where Verner attended public schools until his graduation. Following high school, he matriculated at Trinity College in Connecticut, earning his baccalaureate degree in 1922. His professional colleagues, who later knew him as an inveterate walker, were not surprised to learn that he had been captain of his college track team.

The career-shaping move in his life was made in 1922, when he followed his college graduation with a summer position at the Library of Congress. With the exception of the year 1922-1923, when he pursued graduate work in philosophy at Harvard, Washington was to be his home for the remainder of his life. Here, too, he met Dorothy Devereux Ladd, whom he married on August 24, 1929. They had three children: Nancy Priest, Verner Warren, and Judith Ladd.

Describing the beginning of his career and his choice of librarianship as a profession, Verner said:

In 1922 I was doing graduate work at Harvard and that summer I went to Washington where my parents were then living and looked around for a summer job. I applied at the Library of Congress and got a temporary post as a cataloger in the Manuscript Division. During that three months vacation I cataloged three separate collections. ... I later found out that the man for whom I substituted usually turned out in a year somewhat less than a third of what I turned out that summer. In any case I had a good time, learned a lot about the intimacies of history, and became fascinated with the work. Consequently, becoming disenchanted with philosophy at Harvard the next year, I reapplied at the Library of Congress in 1923, thinking then that I would put in a year there before deciding on a profession. But I never did turn to any other, so that is the beginning of the story.

My first regular job at the Library of Congress was as a reference assistant in the main reading room. I had no qualifications for the job whatsoever except a simple B.A. and I had had no library experience except my stint during the summer. They turned me loose and I began to explore this extraordinary institution into which I had fallen. I used to take myself to the stacks and to the other divisions of the library, and I got in a year or so an education in library work which I would say—well, I will say—was second to none. This may be boasting, but nobody has had it so good since then.

The Reading Room was indeed a unique school, since it was the center for all services to readers including congressmen and their staffs. Clapp's professional library career was within one institution, the Library of Congress. During his 33 years at the Library of Congress, he had a breadth, depth, and sophistication of experience that could not have been duplicated in any other single library or group of libraries. Although, as noted earlier, he felt that his early work in LC was a unique "education in library work," he often voiced a regret at not having had library school training. He told an interviewer:

As you may know, I did not go to library school myself. I have always regretted this ... [and] I have two reasons for this: one, of course is the acquisition of technical information that is picked

up much more rapidly in a teacher-learner relationship, but also there is a second factor, dealing with what I might term professional memory. I think membership in a profession is an important thing, and students who go through a library school share the communal professional memory of failures and successes even at the outset of their careers. They are quickly exposed to participation and discussion about libraries and librarianship. I had to acquire all this separately, and when I see people becoming librarians, especially in the top ranks, only in name and position, I feel there is something wrong. It is that preliminary sharing in communal professional experience which I regret most in my lack of library school training.

Although this statement indicates the sensitivity, the keen analysis, and the modesty that were always typical of Verner, it would be misleading to assume that there was anything lacking in his professional education, competence, training, or "professional memory." The variety and intensity of training that he received during his years at LC were far beyond what any student could have acquired in any library school course.

His wide interests and breadth of knowledge marked him early at the Library as the outstanding new member of the staff. He was tapped by Herbert Putnam (q.v.) in 1928 to originate a special service to Congress called the "Congressional Unit," which was the basis of what has become the Congressional Research Service, one of the outstanding library information services in the world. It was Verner Clapp who laid the groundwork and established the scope of service to be provided by this division. In 1931, Verner became special assistant to the superintendent of the Reading Rooms and in 1937, assistant superintendent of the Reading Rooms. As assistant superintendent, he also was responsible for the Books-for-the-Blind program, and he directed the expansion of Braille and Talking Book services. He also stimulated the establishment of Regional Lending Libraries, which would provide special books and services to the blind throughout the entire country. During the 1940s, under Archibald MacLeish (1939-1944), he was promoted to increasingly important positions, including director of the Administrative Department (1940-1943), director of the Acquisitions Department (1943-1947), and, starting under Luther Evans (1945-1953), chief assistant librarian from 1947 to 1956. He was acting Librarian of Congress during 1953-1954 (prior to the appointment of L. Quincy Mumford) and on other occasions during the absences of the Librarian of Congress.

During World War II, he was responsible for setting up protective measures for the most priceless LC holdings, including the Declaration of Independence, the Constitution of the United States, and the

Articles of Confederation. Added to these was the Magna Carta, which had been sent here from Britain for safekeeping.

In a library as large and as complex as the Library of Congress, it is usually difficult to isolate the contributions of an individual. Verner Clapp is an exception, and his contributions have been notable and identifiable. Beginning in the 1940s, he brought a new emphasis to the Library's acquisition program through internal organization and by the opening of new sources abroad. This led at the end of the war to his stimulation of the Cooperative Acquisitions Project, enabling LC to acquire for itself and 112 other American research libraries a total of two million European publications that had not been obtainable during the war years. Thus, as part of his duties as director of the Library of Congress Mission in Germany (1945-1947), he negotiated the release from Leipzig, in the Russian zone of occupied Germany, of books stockpiled by German booksellers for American libraries on pre-war orders.

In a paper prepared for the Library of Congress Professional Association, Marlene Morrisey of LC summarized his impact on the Library of Congress:

In helping to shape the Library's reorganization in the early 1940s he argued eloquently for a functional organization, including the breaking down of the former Reading Rooms Division into a stack service, a book service, and a circulation service.... He put order into the fiscal controls and budgeting procedures. He wrote parts of the Library's first statement on grievance policy and procedures and led discussions with staff representatives about them. He favored required discussions between supervisors and employees about staff performance because, in his words, "much ill feeling can be avoided if the employee has an opportunity to discuss his shortcomings and his work with his rating officer." ... He recommended the establishment of a permanent inventory staff to assure prompt and systematic reading of the book shelves. He worked out arrangements with the Museum of Modern Art for the selection of motion picture films for the permanent collection of the Library. He translated the Library's acquisitions policies into actual buying of books. He was an advocate of interlibrary cooperation in the microfilming of extensive runs of library materials, with LC serving as a clearinghouse for this purpose. He argued for Library of Congress leadership in development of basic and broad bibliographical tools for the use of scholars in all fields of learning. He developed plans for a U.S. national bibliography.... He participated in the initial revision of the Copyright Act. He was concerned about the atmospheric conditions essential for protection of the Library's treasures, and it was

largely at his instigation that the National Bureau of Standards, in collaboration with the Libbey-Owens-Ford Glass Company, undertook studies that led to the development of the Thermopane-helium process for preserving historic documents.

Speaking at Verner's memorial service, the Librarian of Congress, L. Quincy Mumford, said that although Verner had resigned from the Library in 1956, he

never really left.... In the ensuing years, Verner gave moral as well as financial support through the Council on Library Resources to the national library that he loved so dearly. We always believed that he was part of the Library despite his physical absence. We mourn his loss at the Library of Congress, but we rejoice that he walked our way. We are not only better librarians—we are better human beings because of this journey.

He left to accept an unprecedented opportunity to participate in the shaping of a new era of librarianship. Becoming president of the Council on Library Resources in September 1956, he was in charge of a new foundation made possible by a Ford Foundation grant of $5,000,000. During his presidency (1956-1967), the Ford Foundation made grants to CLR totaling $13,000,000. The Council's charter stated that the foundation was established

for the purpose of aiding in the solution of problems of libraries generally and of research libraries in particular, conducting research in, developing and demonstrating new techniques and methods, and disseminating through any means the results thereof, and for making grants to other institutions and persons for such purposes; and for providing leadership in and wherever appropriate, coordination of efforts (1) to develop the resources and services of libraries and (2) to improve relations between American and foreign libraries and archives.

This broad, encompassing charter was the type of challenge that Verner Clapp welcomed and for which he had unique qualifications of imagination, interest, experience, practicality, and energy. The projects that he initiated or supported covered every aspect of librarianship, as well as activities in archives, copyright, documentation, paper making, and publishing.

At the time of Clapp's retirement as CLR president in 1967, Whitney North Seymour, chairman of the Council's Board of Directors noted:

Mr. Clapp has made the Council on Library Resources significant throughout the world. His imagination, ingenuity and extraordinary fund of information have enabled him to give precise and significant counsel concerning library problems on both sides of the Atlantic. Grants made under his administration have already profoundly influenced library development. The multi-volume *National*

Union Catalog of Manuscript Collections, compiled by the Library of Congress with financial assistance from the Council, is one of the many projects in which he has taken a personal interest. He also has an expert knowledge of scientific developments affecting libraries and helped to stimulate research at the W. J. Barrow Research Laboratory in Richmond, Virginia, that led to the development of a permanent/durable type of paper.

His interests were so broad and his knowledge so extensive that one is baffled in trying to highlight his accomplishments. He had an abiding hope that publications in microform might find common acceptance by individuals as well as libraries. His interest and support gave an unprecedented impetus to the use of microfilm and microfiche.

One of his last projects was the development of a successful Cataloging in Publication program through LC. It is primarily a result of Clapp's vision and perseverance that this service is available today, providing libraries, publishers, and others with regular LC catalog card information as an integral part of the printed book. Libraries throughout the world now have, as a result of this program, opportunities for accelerated service and notable savings.

As Lee Grove of the Council on Library Resources pointed out:

Verner Clapp was invited to head the council. With characteristic enthusiasm he plunged into the work. It was work ideally adapted to him, for it offered opportunity to seek solutions to problems challenging his beloved profession, and it offered scope to his inventive, imaginative mind. It had long been his habit, when he wished to talk with a colleague, to jump up and go to him, rather than to invite him to his office. In the years at the council he has frequently jumped up, been tireless in going to men and meetings; asking, listening, suggesting. This and the encyclopedic knowledge of the library world derived from omniverous reading have resulted in achievements by the council too numerous to catalog here.

His extralibrary activities and services probably exceeded in importance those of any other American librarian. In 1945, he served in San Francisco as an advisor to the United Nations Conference. The library and information services that he organized became the foundation of the present U.N. Library in New York. In 1946, he served as a member of the U.S. delegation to the preparatory meeting of UNESCO in London and was active in UNESCO's library and bibliographic affairs until 1953.

Following his European post-war achievements, he was chairman (1947-1948) of the U.S. Library Mission to Japan, which included Charles H. Brown (q.v.) of Iowa State College and himself. Within two intensive months, they developed a detailed plan for a major national library including legislative reference, bibliographic, and other services. A major achievement was Clapp's advice and guidance for the legislative procedure that established the National Diet Library.

From 1954, he served as director—and from 1960 until his death, as president—of Forest Press, Inc., the publisher of the Dewey Decimal Classification. A trustee of the Lake Placid Club Education Foundation from 1955 until his death, he also was a trustee of Trinity College (Washington, D.C.) in 1970-1972.

The impact of his creative ideas was felt in his work on committees relating to the National Union Catalog, MARC, Cataloging in Publication, copyright, the National Advisory Commission on Libraries, and the Science Information Council.

Fortunately Verner Clapp was made aware of the respect and admiration that his colleagues and friends had for him. There were notable formal evidences—national and international. The American Library Association selected him for three notable awards: the Melvil Dewey Medal, the Lippincott Award, and its highest honor—Honorary Life Membership. The Association of Research Libraries developed for him a unique award—the "Librarians' Librarian." The Special Libraries Association presented him shortly before his death with a "Special Citation." The Japanese government, aware of his work in designing the National Diet Library and its efficient service to the Diet, gave him one of his most cherished honors in 1968, when he was decorated in Tokyo with the Order of the Sacred Treasure.

Upon his retirement from the Library of Congress, his fellow workers and friends established at LC the Verner W. Clapp Publication Fund, which provides a means for issuing facsimiles of historic and rare materials in the Library of Congress.

The bibliography of Verner Clapp's writings from 1933 to 1971 includes over 200 items, with a range of subjects that only partially indicates the breadth of his interests—abstracting, archives, bibliography, biography, communication, copyright, documentation, education, history, libraries, management, microform, optics, paper, reprography, research, technical information, the United Nations and UNESCO. His last articles were on preservation, book paper, Cataloging in Publication, and networks. In many of these fields, he was regarded as a foremost authority. Significant among his publications are *Library of Congress Bibliographical Survey: A Report Prepared for Unesco* (1950); *The Future of the Research Library: A Windsor Lecture in Librarianship* (1964); and *Copyright—A Librarian's View* (1968).

Verner's membership in various organizations only underscores the multiplicity of his interests and abilities. Among the memberships were those in the American Antiquarian Society; the American Association for the Advancement of Science; the American Institute of Graphic Arts; the American, Canadian, and District of Columbia Library Associations; the American Society for Information Science; the bibliographic societies of both America and Canada; the Abstracting Board of the International Council of Scientific Unions; the National Microfilm Association; and the Special Libraries Association. He was also elected to Phi Beta Kappa and was a member of the Cosmos Club and Grolier Club.

Only on rare occasions have memorial meetings been authorized by the Library of Congress. But in honor of Verner Clapp, the Coolidge Auditorium provided a proper setting for homage paid by his friends and colleagues. Frederick H. Wagman of the University of Michigan said:

> I should like to speak of his qualities of mind and character that made me among so many others proud to be his friend. Foremost among these, it seems to me, was his integrity, his deep commitment to justice and honesty, and to the preservation of our civil liberties. . . . Verner did not believe with Meister Eckhart that "in silence man can most readily preserve his integrity." He seized the first opportunity that offered itself to speak before a public and well-publicized forum in Washington attacking the evils inherent in the then-operative loyalty program. Of the many who felt as we did, Verner was one of the very few government officials who had the courage to speak out and do so forcibly.

As a result of his breadth of interests, depth of scholarship, and inquiring mind, Verner was often referred to as a Renaissance man. Marlene Morissey of the Library of Congress reported:

> Mr. Clapp's enthusiasm for sharing with others was evident in every aspect of his life. Devoted to and proud of his family, he often entertained colleagues and friends at home. It was not unusual to hear him discuss at a single social gathering the complete history of copyright legislation in this country and the disciplinary measures imposed on recalcitrant deck attendants in the 1920s. On one occasion he reeled off almost verbatim the British wool laws of the fifteenth century and explained the legal requirement of all-woolen shrouds in order to protect the woolen industry. He regaled a meeting of the Librarian's Conference after his return from a Maine vacation by reporting on his personal research on and observation of the love life of birds nesting nearby.

Once answering a question about which book had influenced him most, Verner cited Herodotus'

History, saying, "This man has conjured up pictures of a world so far back in time that we cannot imagine even the physical effort of moving about in it."

Longinus, in the fourth century B.C., in describing a contemporary, could have been anticipating Verner W. Clapp:

> He talks where necessary, does not make all his points in a monotonous series and has the power of characterization seasoned by simplicity and charm. Then he has an untold store of polished wit, urbane sarcasm, well-bred elegance, supple turn of irony, clever satire, plenty of pointed ridicule and an inimitable fascination. Nature endowed him fully with the power of telling a tale fluently and winding his way through a description with facile inspiration.

On paper, Verner Clapp retired twice—once from the Library of Congress and next as president of the Council on Library Resources. Although he left the presidency of CLR, he continued as a full-time consultant until his death on June 15, 1972. Until the last, his interests were in new ideas, new projects and new activities. Thus, we also knew him as an amateur bookbinder and a flutist. When I last saw him in the hospital, he had become interested in painting and was trying to meet the requests of the nurses and staff for still life paintings of the flowers in his room.

Biographical listings and obituaries—*A Biographical Directory of Librarians in the United States and Canada*. 5th ed.; *Contemporary Authors* 37; *Current Biography* (1972); *The New York Times Biographical Edition* 3; *Who Was Who in America* V (1969-1973); *Who's Who in Library Service*, 1st ed., 2nd ed., 3rd ed., 4th ed. **Books and articles about the biographee**—*Verner W. Clapp, 1901-1972: A Memorial Tribute.* Washington: Library of Congress, 1977. **Primary sources and archival materials**—Clapp's papers are held in the Library of Congress.

—FOSTER E. MOHRHARDT

CLEMONS, HARRY (1879-1968)

Harry Clemons was born in Corry, Pennsylvania, on September 9, 1879. He received his B.A. degree (1902) from Wesleyan University, M.A. degrees in 1905 from both Princeton University and Wesleyan University, and the Litt.D. (1942) from Wesleyan. He also studied at Oxford in 1906-1907, and at the Columbia University School of Library Service during the summer of 1927. He married Jeannie Cooper Jenkins on May 21, 1918, and they had two children, Henry Jenkins and Emily Barber.

From the beginning of his career he divided his time between teaching and librarianship. He was a student assistant in the library at Wesleyan in 1902-1903, an instructor in English at Princeton from 1904 to 1908, and reference librarian at Princeton from 1908 to 1913, when he went to China to become head of the English Department at Nanking University (1913-1920). He was appointed librarian of that institution in 1914 and remained in this position until 1927, with time out during 1918-1919 as the ALA's War Service representative with the American Expeditionary Forces in Siberia and again in 1922, for a brief period in the Chinese section of the Library of Congress. Upon his return to the United States following the Nanking incident in 1927, he became librarian of the University of Virginia, a position he held until retirement age in 1950, when he became the University's consultant in library resources.

Clemons first entered librarianship in a somewhat oblique fashion. He arrived at Princeton as a graduate student and instructor in English in 1904, the year that Woodrow Wilson introduced his preceptorial system at the University. Following Clemons's return from a year's study at Oxford (1906-1907) Wilson, concerned about the library's role in his preceptorial system, persuaded Clemons that his newly acquired familiarity with Oxford's tutorial system qualified him to perform the work that the new system would require of the library. Both Wilson's and Clemons's conception of his role can be inferred from Clemons's first report as librarian of the University of Virginia twenty years later, written just four months after his arrival there:

I am inclined to regard the Reference Division as preeminent among the means of library service. Such a division has not existed as such at this Library.... Yet it is just at this point that a library which has the advantage of location at the University of Virginia ought to be able to attain a degree of cultural service, of scholarly dignity, and of intellectual force which would place it, by these standards, not at the foot but at the head of any list of American university libraries.... The recommendation is, to be honest, only a start towards the organization of such a Division. The personnel and the functions of the Reference Division would need to receive the most careful thought. What I have, tentatively at least, in mind is a staff of three, two being men with academic standing in the University Faculty ... equipped to offer undergraduate and graduate courses in bibliography and the history of books and libraries ... qualified to aid the research workers and authors among the Faculty, to guide the students to a practical knowledge of library resources, to inculcate worthy standards of general reading, and to cooperate with the reference work of the Extension Department of the University. They should be in the words of Emerson, "Professors of Books"....

Before going to Virginia, Clemons spent the years 1913-1927 (with the exceptions noted above) in Nanking, China, as both English teacher and librarian. He also produced a short book from his war experiences. In his foreword to *The A.L.A. in Siberia*, a small volume of letters written by Clemons during his War Service tour, H. B. Van Hoesen (q.v.) says, "His friends at Nanking give such reports of him as 'It is difficult to speak in moderation of the work which Clemons has accomplished for the University; Mr. Clemons has done an appalling amount of work ... inspiring students with his own high ideals and his correctness in the use of English.'" That little volume of letters is a revealing and delightfully witty series of reports, and it shows as well as anything he ever wrote those qualities that his friends cherished—his understanding, his patience, his equanimity, his sense of humor, and above all his ability to make the most of what was available without complaining about what was not. He was to need and to display all these qualities at Virginia.

In his first report, he had shown his full understanding of the University's needs, had unfolded a new conception of a library for his colleagues, and had aroused interest in and support for his building program. Before he could launch his plan, however, the Great Depression was upon the country. Characteristically, he took advantage of it to add staff members he could not have added in other days. During the period when funds were not available even for planning a building, he also involved an extraordinary number of faculty, students, staff, other librarians, architects, and alumni in the step-by-step planning to such good effect that, when funds were finally available, he was ready to move. During the same period, he launched a total recataloging and reclassification program, took advantage of Depression prices and foundation grants to lay the ground work for the research library he had in mind, awakened the citizens of the state and the University's alumni to its library needs, and attracted an extraordinary group of donors and devoted admirers. The details of his accomplishments can be read between the lines of his *The University of Virginia Library, 1825-1950; Story of a Jeffersonian Foundation.* His words would have it that the work was all done by members of his staff.

At Virginia, his method for quietly accomplishing "appalling amounts of work" soon became obvious to his awed colleagues. He came to his office at eight o'clock each morning and worked an open-door, leisurely six-hour day, during which he was freely available to all comers. Then, at two o'clock, he took lunch, a four-hour nap, and a light meal, returned to his desk at eight o'clock in the evening, and worked regularly until two o'clock each morning. At that hour it was light refreshment again, some reading, and four hours of sleep. He maintained this schedule for the 23 years he was librarian and continued it in his productive retirement, with Sunday mornings out for church and, at rare intervals, a day away from town on library business.

During the Princeton years, Clemons had been joint editor with Morris William Croll of John Lyly's *Euphues: The Anatomy of Wit* and *Euphues & His England.* In his preface to the volume, Croll comments that Clemons "devoted scrupulous care to the production of the text—the first text of the *Euphues* in modern spelling and punctuation." This scrupulous care was to be found in each of the thousands of letters he wrote—always handwritten for his secretary in a hand that never ceased to combine firmness and elegance—as well as in the attention he gave to every suggestion, every memorandum to or from his office, and every detail of the operation of the library. He was not forever looking over the shoulders of his associates. Far from it. It is hard to imagine a working situation that provided greater freedom, one in which any suggestion brought forward was likely to receive more courteous attention, a situation in which one's proposals were so often met with, "How can I help you?"

Clemons succeeded so well in conveying to his staff his feeling about the role of the Library that Jefferson's biographer Dumas Malone, in writing of the staff and the Library, was able to say:

> ... there is more sunlight in [the University of Virginia Library], more warmth and courtesy and sheer human kindness, than is commonly encountered. Many have contributed to this spirit, of course, but the person most responsible for it is Harry Clemons, who with unerring instinct seized upon the best traditions of Virginia and of Jefferson and reincarnated them in an institution.

His eagerness to make the resources of the Library available wherever they were needed led him to provide a home for statewide extension library service, a service that he developed until the Virginia State Library was able to take it over some years later, and, when he began the reclassification of the collections, he prepared an extra card of every title, as a matter of course, for the National Union Catalog at the Library of Congress. His openhanded generosity in making the Library's resources available to the Jefferson Writings project at Princeton led Julian Boyd to express his pride in "the country that could produce such magnanimity of spirit at the head of an important institution."

Because Harry Clemons did almost all of his work quietly at home, few librarians outside Virginia knew him. This was unfortunate because he was, in Malone's words, a "scholar without pedantry, a courtly gentleman without tinge of pomposity." Following his death in Charlottesville, Virginia, on August 30, 1968, he was buried there in the University Cemetery.

Biographical listings and obituaries—*Contemporary Authors* 13; [Obituary]. *Library of Congress Information Bulletin* 27:541-42 (September 5, 1968); *Who Was Who in America* VI (1974-1976); *Who's Who in Library Service*, 1st ed., 2nd ed., 3rd ed. **Books and articles about the biographee**—Malone, Dumas. "Foreword" to Harry Clemons, *The University of Virginia Library, 1825-1950.* Charlottesville: University of Virginia Library, 1954. **Primary sources and archival materials**—The Clemons papers are in the Alderman Library, University of Virginia, where the local newspaper and the University student newspapers also carry a running account of his activities (1927-1965). Clemons's book, *The A.L.A. in Siberia*, contains additional information.

—JACK DALTON

CLIFT, DAVID HORACE (1907-1973)

"Skeeter" was the family nickname for the blond, slight figure of a boy, eldest of six born to Charles Lawson and Mary E. Tomlin Clift on June 16, 1907, in Washington, Kentucky. His voice and speech patterns always reflected the soft drawl of the region, and his manner throughout his life time was of a courtliness of another time. But there was tempered into this demeanor an impish way of teasing. And his eyes would betray the delight he found in being able to confound or disarm an associate. He loved to play "dollar poker" using the serial numbers on paper money as the hand, and his devastating insouciance (poker face) established him as champion among his peers.

Horst Eunestus, secretary of the German Libraries International Relations Office, recalled an example of Clift's ability to confound:

> When David and I had lunch during the IFLA [International Federation of Library Associations] meeting in Frankfurt I remarked on his wearing two wristwatches, one on the left and one on the right. He confirmed my guess that one would indicate German and the other Chicago local time and then he pulled out a pocket watch announcing the Moscow time.

Clift was the most avid reader in a family dedicated to the activity. His sister recalls that he was well known for fanning out over long distances, going from farm to village home seeking books and magazines to read, and throughout his career, his baggage always contained books for reading and books to be left as gifts. Holidays and birthdays in the family always brought gift books from him. His choice of subject was eclectic, but he reserved a special fondness for spy fiction.

By the time he had finished high school in 1925, Clift had decided to attend the University of Kentucky just down the road in Lexington. There was not much money, so he boarded at the Lexington home of family friends while taking on every part-time job he could find, including such Clarence

Buddington Kelland classics as jerking sodas and pulling taffy in a candy store. By his junior year, he was able to land a student assistant position in the University library. This opened the door to other possibilities, including summer work for two seasons at the Lexington Public Library. It was probably during this period that the youth with a passion for reading found his heart and soul.

With the help of a loan from the Masonic Order of De Molay, Clift entered the Columbia University School of Library Service in 1930. He was able to obtain student work in the University library until he completed his bachelor's degree in library science by mid-1931.

He went right to work in one of the most famous rooms in contemporary library history, Room 315 of the New York Public Library. Keyes D. Metcalf, then junior assistant to the chief of the Reference Department, recalls the occasion:

> We never had anyone at the New York Public Library from the University of Kentucky, and we were not quite sure that David would work out, but it soon became evident that he was one of the best reference workers that we ever had, this in spite of the fact that within five years around his time, Quincy Mumford, Robert Downs, Ed Freehafer, and many others were working at the same desk. David had a way of satisfying the public and dealing with difficult problems.

In 1933, he married a vivacious and outspoken children's librarian whom he had met in school at Columbia. Eleanore Flynn worked at the Brooklyn Public Library, where she eventually became head of the Central Children's Room while Clift was located at the Fifth Avenue and 42nd Street landmark. They moved to the most fashionable and at the time most inexpensive location for New York's young professionals, Greenwich Village, and their apartment was the center for a tightly knit group of friends and professional peers in and around the city. The Clifts always seemed to have people in for conversation; debates on the composition of the very dry, upright martini; a session of poker; and the type of shop-talk dear to librarians everywhere. Most fondly remembered by intimates were the annual tributes to the Kentucky Derby, complete with juleps, toasts to Kentucky, friendly bets, and several lusty choruses of "My Old Kentucky Home." Colleagues felt that justice had run its course when David Clift was made an honorary colonel on the staff of the Governor of Kentucky in 1957.

Charles Dorsey, a hometown friend of Clift, was launching an engineering career in New York during this period. He recalls that "this period of [David's] life may have been one of the happiest: in retrospect, it seems it was carefree. In such a group, Dave was at his genial best. His friends all esteemed and respected him, and they loved him dearly."

David Clift, with his distinctively gentle and seemingly unobtrusive methods of expediting and solving problems, came to the attention of Charles C. Williamson (q.v.), director of the Columbia University Library, who successfully recruited Clift as his assistant in 1937. Frederick G. Kilgour, then an assistant at Harvard College Library who was attending Columbia University Library School during the summer months, said that "it was difficult to tell whether it was Dave or Dr. Williamson running the library. Of course, both were and they worked together harmoniously." Those five years at Columbia, then, honed the executive abilities and management skills that distinguished David Clift's career.

In 1942, Clift was drafted into the Army and assigned to a hospital, where he was an orderly. Edward C. McDowell, a friend from University of Kentucky days, reports that Clift was soon assigned to the Office of Strategic Services (OSS), Interdepartmental Committee for the Acquisition of Foreign Acquisitions. Clift became deputy to the executive director, Frederick G. Kilgour, and they found themselves having to build an organization and devise procedures from not even whole cloth. Their work provided information for about a dozen separate operations within the OSS, and here again, unobtrusive diplomacy and personnel skills were brought to bear, as the staff grew to approximately 140 people.

Service completed, David Clift was honorably discharged with the rank of lieutenant and immediately accepted appointment as associate librarian at Yale University in 1945. He utilized the additional skills and training that he had garnered in service to design a personnel program, including a position classification and pay plan that became an admired model for many university library systems. The plan remained effective at Yale until the mid-sixties. At this time, in addition to his personnel talents, Clift also was developing his ability to discern trends and problems in the operations of libraries. His experience as a fellow of Yale's Trumball College in 1948 sharpened his skill in communicating library problems to those outside of the profession.

It was also during this period that the American Library Association was undergoing another reorganization uproar, set off by that era's "Young Turks." The Final Report of the Fourth Activities Committee, issued at the Midwinter Meeting in 1949, delineated the conditions of an association that had limped through the Depression of the thirties and had shriveled during the war years of the forties. The Report stated:

> During the last few years, we have discontinued our statistical service; we have reduced the public

library services and the placement services; and we have been faced with the imminent elimination of our International Relations Office and our National Relations Office [forerunner of the current Washington Office]; discontinuance or curtailment of some of the few remaining professional services rendered by the association have been under discussion. . . . [We] have consistently, over the last few years, overspent both our budget and our income. To make the paradox even more confusing, we under pay our staff—both in clerical and the professional grades . . . comparable to what we recommend for others.

Carl Milam (q.v.), after a tumultuous, 28-year reign as ALA's executive secretary, had left under pressure from the "Young Turks" and was serving as librarian for the United Nations. In 1949, at that Midwinter Meeting, his name appeared as the sole candidate for the presidency of ALA, a situation that triggered a divisive donnybrook. Many felt that Milam was a threat to plans for reorganization and were fearful of a return of the autocratic Milam control of the Association. After late hours and heated debate, an opposition candidate, Clarence Graham, was nominated and went on to defeat Milam.

The Association of College and Research Libraries was threatening to pull out of ALA, as had the Law and Special Libraries during Milam's regime. The membership was insecure and the headquarters' staff morale was almost non-existent. Someone was needed who could guide the Association through a major reorganization and bring a feeling of harmony and purpose to the membership while such changes were taking place. It was then that David Clift's name came up. He was noted for his organizational ability, his knowledge of personnel practices, and most particularly for his seemingly unobtrusive methods, which created a feeling of harmonious administration. It took some pleading on the part of his colleagues, many of whom were part of the "Young Turks" movement, but Clift finally took up the challenge and accepted the executive secretary position being happily vacated by John Mackenzie Cory (who served from 1948 to 1951).

On September 4, 1951, David Clift crossed the threshold of the moldering McCormick Mansion in Chicago, which had long since seen better days both as a fashionable residence and as offices for the American Library Association. His slim, slight stature and his affection for bow-ties and light-color suits gave him a much younger image than his 44 years. He had always had this problem of looking much younger than his years, and while he was assistant to the director at Columbia, he had become so concerned about being mistaken for a student that he tried a moustache for a brief period. He had no need for such affectation in Chicago.

The staff was crowded into the old building on Huron Street. Conditions were primitive by current standards, the main method of distributing mail and memos being a wicker basket that was raised and lowered by means of a rope within the ornate stairwell. The membership stood at 19,701 and the general funds budget for that year was $191,129. When Clift retired, a new building (completed in 1963) stood in place of the old mansion. The membership had grown to 30,592 and the general funds budget for that year was $2,262,971. During his tenure, ALA had received approximately $15 million in grants, making possible the establishment of standards, advances in professional library education, astounding changes in library service to schools, the establishment of the "core collection" concept for college and university acquisitions, the creation of *Choice* as a respected book review periodical for undergraduate collections, a change in the official ALA journal from primarily a journal of record to a more modern magazine called *American Libraries*, a series of nationwide adult education programs conducted by libraries, the establishment of goals for public library service, and the development of the concept of intellectual freedom in library service. This is not to slight the successful drives to involve the federal government in support and assistance programs for all types of libraries, plus influential activities in classification, cataloging, documentation, and technology.

In 1951, however, the outlook was bleak. In one of his rare direct reports to ALA Council, David Clift commented that after his first five months he could concede that "this is, indeed, going to be an experience," and he subtly referred to the philosophy which sustained his twenty years, "If we weren't incurable optimists, we wouldn't be at ALA headquarters."

Where others might have seized the opportunity for self-aggrandizement and legend-building, David Clift moved quietly and with a subtlety that superficial observers sometimes mistook for timidity or weakness. When asked once, just a few months before his retirement, what he felt was required of an executive director at ALA, his answer was short and to the point. He said it was to administer the policies decided by the membership and to leave the leadership to those elected by the membership. And a close look at his career at ALA bears him out. He reorganized the demoralized staff at ALA headquarters and created an equitable pay-plan that attracted able and dedicated staff. He provided an atmosphere that respected the individual and allowed for creative growth but not domination by headquarters. But it was in his dealings with the leaders of the profession, both within the political structure of the association as well as without, that marks his particular contribution as conciliator to librarianship.

Verner Clapp (q.v.) was one of Clift's confidants and consequently part of an intimate circle of advisors that were not really a "rump cabinet," but a group seeking his advice. And Clapp isolated that quality at one time when he was asked to describe Clift in action:

> David Clift has the ability to assure you, by a confiding smile, not even accompanied by a wink, that he understands you completely and is on your side; that he is on to the other guys, and although he may have to give in to them, he is doing so for reasons which are subordinate to his own preferences. Add to this a consistent optimism under all inconveniences and adversity ... openmindedness on every opinion and every holder of an opinion, and freedom from envy, jealousy, animosity, and rage.

This is in contrast to the personality of Carl Milam, who was not always tolerant of other opinions and who gave rise to comments like Joseph Wheeler's 1949 statement that he felt at times like "figuratively at least, wanting to kick [Milam] in the shins." Admittedly, the pressures upon the executive director of an association like ALA can be punishing. But, when dealing with the varied egos of long-established administrators of libraries, Clift never publicly revealed an impatience with posturing and pompousness, not to mention incompetence. Because of this, he was able to serve as a conciliator and to encourage consensus. After 26 years of Milam, this was a welcome and healing change for ALA.

He wasn't just born with a knowledge of what was needed in the administration of a library association. He came to ALA with experience behind him as president of the New York Library Club (1941-1942) and the Connecticut Library Association (1950-1951). His international knowledge had begun when he served as acting chief of the Library of Congress Mission to Germany (1945-1946). As the ALA executive director, he headed the delegation of U.S. librarians in a study tour of the Soviet Union in 1961, and he was a member of the delegation that studied the libraries in the Federal Republic of Germany in 1963. He served as a delegate to the International Federation of Library Associations (IFLA) from 1964 to his retirement in 1972. And he was a most active and concerned member of the trusteeship to the American Library in Paris (1969-1972). He was as well a contributor to the First Japan-U.S. Conference on Libraries and Information Science in Higher Education in Tokyo, 1969.

As was his due, David Clift received many honors in his lifetime. From the University of Kentucky he received a Founders Day Award for Distinguished Service (1957) and a Distinguished Alumni Centennial Award (1965), and he was named by Duke University to its Library's Board of Visitors. The ALA honored him three times, first with the Joseph W. Lippincott Award for distinguished library service (1962), and then with an Honorary Life Membership (1972) and the title of executive director emeritus (1972). He was also elected to membership in Delta Sigma Pi and Alpha Beta Alpha (honorary).

Perhaps David Clift's most lasting contribution to librarianship will be in the growth and development of the concepts, defense, and promulgation of intellectual freedom as the *sine qua non* of the profession. No lengthy treatise bears his name, no fiery speeches echo through some ancient hall; Clift did not work that way. When he came to ALA, the Library Bill of Rights had just been adopted three years before, and its ideas were slowly beginning to catch on with the profession. The idea that libraries and librarians have a moral obligation to provide materials and services free from governmental or special-interest-group pressures for control or removal was uncomfortable for many. But in the heat of the Senator Joseph McCarthy years in the early fifties, when ideological insecurity and attack by innuendo threatened library collections everywhere, the concept of intellectual freedom strengthened. One example of that move toward conviction was the adoption of the Freedom to Read Statement.

Theodore Waller, long-time friend and nationally known publisher, commented on the 1953 Westchester Conference and the role David Clift played in the adoption of that document. "There are few developments in our complex world which can be traced to the initiative of one man," Waller said; "Clift, and an intimate collaborator or two, but Clift got the idea ... and did much of the orchestrating."

During the years that followed, it was Clift's "orchestration" that led to the creation of an Office for Intellectual Freedom, a unit unique among educational associations and societies in the United States. That very visible unit, under the direction of Judith F. Krug (Clift's selection), has provided continuity and coordination of ALA's activities for this emerging concept of librarianship. He fostered the climate that nurtured the creation of the Freedom to Read Foundation, an arm of the Association that allows for the establishment of legal precedents in intellectual freedom practices in libraries. And it was his careful guidance that led ALA into the area of assistance for those under attack in defense of intellectual freedom, in addition to those involved in personnel administration disputes through the adoption of the "Program of Mediation, Arbitration and Inquiry" in 1971.

He understood and respected ideas and had faith that the good of which the human soul is capable will prevail. Miriam L. Hornback, Clift's executive assistant, attributes a short piece to David as being the essence of the man:

> I am the Book. I can aid and instruct you. I can enrich your life. I can also annoy and irritate you. I can be dangerous.
>
> I can, sometimes make you think. I have been mistreated and I have suffered. I have been burnt. Yet, I have survived. I am perhaps, the only imperishable thing upon this earth because I am the essence of Man's dreams and Man's spirit. Since I am ageless, I am for all ages of time, and all ages of Men. I am not without needs. I need to be nurtured by Man, not for my sake, but for his. Do not let me be put aside nor suffer me to banishment and darkness. Darkness cannot contain me for long, but darkness imposed upon me leaves Mankind blind.

Charles Dorsey noted that David Clift's "heart and soul were dedicated to the profession." That heart and soul left him sitting peacefully on the Chicago-bound plane at the Kennedy Airport in New York on October 12, 1973. He had just returned from his final trip to Europe, collecting data for a study of comparative librarianship. David's sister, Mrs. Cecil O. Baber, was comforted by the circumstances of his death. "He died doing what made him happy," she said. "I'm afraid that he wasn't feeling well when he made his last trip, but nevertheless he went, which is what he wanted." He returned to his beloved Kentucky for the last time and was buried in Maysville on October 16, 1973.

That is the quiet heritage this man left to librarianship. It is a deep dedication and love of the profession. He wrote and published little, but his direction of the activities of the American Library Association provided a strength and continuity desperately needed following an economic depression and the debilitation of war. Grace Stevenson, his long-time associate executive secretary at ALA, succinctly and rightly says of David H. Clift, "he was never selling a bill of goods—or himself—just libraries."

Biographical listings and obituaries—*Biographical Directory of Librarians in the United States and Canada*, 5th ed.; *Current Biography* (1973); "In memoriam." *Newsletter on Intellectual Freedom* 23:3 (No. 1); *Who Was Who in America* VI (1974-1976); *Who's Who in Library Service*, 1st ed., 2nd ed., 3rd ed., 4th ed.   **Books and articles about the biographee**—[Contributor's note]. *Library Quarterly* 31:401 (October 1961); "Two Decisive Decades—Tribute to an Emeritus." *American Libraries* 3:701 (July-August 1972); Waller, Theodore. "David H. Clift—A Very Partial Profile." *American Libraries* 3:702-711 (July-August 1972); "A Welcome to David H. Clift." *ALA Bulletin* 45:249 (1951).   **Primary sources and archival materials**—Personal correspondence with Mrs. Cecil O. Baber, Mrs. Grace Stevenson, Mrs. Miriam L. Hornback, Mr. Ranson L. Richardson, Mr. Theodore Waller, Mr. Charles M. Dorsey, and Mrs. Eleanore Clift was utilized by the contributor. Some material is held in the ALA archives at the University of Illinois, Urbana.

—GERALD R. SHIELDS

COGSWELL, JOSEPH GREEN (1786-1871)

Joseph Green Cogswell was born on September 27, 1786, in Ipswich, Massachusetts, the son of Francis and Anstis Manning Cogswell. After attending the Latin grammar school in Ipswich, he went to Phillips Exeter Academy, and then entered Harvard at the age of sixteen, being graduated from there in 1806.

The next ten years gave little hint of the field in which he would ultimately distinguish himself. Restless and venturesome, he signed immediately after graduation as supercargo on a merchant ship bound for Calcutta and was gone for a year. Back in Boston in 1807, he studied law for the next two years under Fisher Ames and Judge William Prescott. But in 1809, breaking off his studies, he went to southern Europe, where he engaged in a series of business ventures, none of them successful. Then in 1811, he returned to Boston, this time to finish his studies and even to give signs of being ready at last to settle down.

On April 17, 1812, he married Mary F. Gilman, daughter of the New Hampshire governor, John T. Gilman, and they made their home in Belfast, Maine, where he started a law practice. But the period of domesticity was short lived. Mary Cogswell died early the next year, and that was the end for Cogswell of both married life and the law.

Returning to Harvard in 1813 as a tutor in Latin, he stayed there until 1815, when the chance came to go on business for a friend for a year in southern Europe, most of it in Marseilles. He returned home to Ipswich for a brief interlude, then, late in 1816, was off again for Europe, this time to study, a fact that made this trip the pivotal move of his life.

Cogswell had chosen to study at Göttingen University, where his two brilliant young friends, Edward Everett, aged 22, and George Ticknor (q.v.), 25, were already deeply immersed in their own studies. Everett was preparing himself to occupy the newly endowed Samuel A. Eliot chair in Greek literature at Harvard. Ticknor, on leave from the law, was there only, so far as he then knew, to gratify a passion for scholarship (Cogswell was bringing him news of his appointment as the first Smith Professor of French and Spanish Literature at Harvard). Arriving with Cogswell was a fourth young American, George Bancroft, who was later to distinguish himself as an historian but who, like Everett, was then preparing himself to teach the classics at Harvard.

It was no coincidence the four had all chosen Göttingen. Young as it was, less than a century old, it was already the leading center of learning in the Western world because of the mode of scholarship practiced there. Born of the German enlightenment and men like Leibnitz, and thus aggressively anti-doctrinaire, it stressed a wholly rational, disinterested approach to knowledge. Guaranteed his academic freedom, the Göttingen scholar was to take nothing for granted, in biblical study no more than in the sciences. His findings gained credibility only as they were solidly anchored in the evidence.

It was a method, naturally, that made a strong library indispensable, and Göttingen had such a library, almost as far-famed as the university it served. The collection numbered about 200,000 volumes, or more than a third (by Cogswell's later calculations) of the total resources in print. But size was the least of the library's eminence. Nothing went on the shelves that did not bear a defensible relationship to the University's research programs. In short, it was strictly a working library.

At first, Cogswell knew the library only as a student. Ticknor, Everett, and Bancroft were all working in the classics, and he, taking advantage of the University's broad program of electives, worked in mineralogy, botany, the modern arts, and more. But the course of study hardly mattered. Regardless of field, the whole strategy at Göttingen was to generate inquiry among students and thereby to get them into the library pursuing their own independent studies, thus producing scholars.

Nor was any strategy more likely to succeed with the little American contingent, whose only formal education to that point had treated them like schoolboys, locking them into a narrow, prescribed curriculum with assigned readings from assigned textbooks. Intellectually stifling, the method also made a library less than useless. Now, their minds set free, they kept the library in a state of daily siege, and none more so than Cogswell, a prodigious worker once his mind and energies were engaged.

Even so, the idea of becoming a librarian might never have occurred to him but for Ticknor, who was quick to recognize highly developed bibliographic instincts in others. He was also deeply committed to the development of American libraries, then in a badly impoverished state. Moreover, though five years younger than Cogswell, he exerted a powerful influence on the older man. Thus, at Ticknor's prompting, Cogswell added librarianship to his other studies, and an accomplished librarian was soon in the making.

In the absence of formal library education, the Göttingen library was the best training ground of the day. Incipient and seasoned librarians alike came to study the principles and practices employed there. Cogswell's own instructor was the second librarian, George Behnecke, who had himself trained under the great Christian Gottlöb Heyne, the library's presiding genius for nearly fifty years and the man with whom modern research librarianship may properly be said to have begun.

To give Cogswell an immediate exposure to the range, depth, and physical arrangement of the collection, Behnecke started him at the shelves. Next, for the plan of bibliographic organization, they went to the three catalogs, alphabetic, manuscript, and *Realkatalog*, giving special attention to the last. Forerunner of the subject catalog, the *Realkatalog* (filling 150 folio volumes by then) served both as bibliographic guide and index to the collection, and as such, was an invaluable tool for librarian and researcher alike. Finally, Behnecke introduced Cogswell to all other branches of the operation, including administration. Thus he emerged with a knowledge of the library art that few other Americans possessed.

Nor did his education end when he left Göttingen on November 22, 1817. He studied other European libraries, notably those in Paris, and he also wrote on the subject. Deeply concerned over the backward state of American cultural resources, he contributed two lengthy articles ("On the Means of Education and the State of Learning in the United States" and "The State of Learning in the United States of America") to *Blackwood's Edinburgh Magazine* for its issues of February and March, 1819, respectively. Still more, he managed to expand the American resource with two important acquisitions for the Harvard Library.

On excursions from Göttingen to Weimar, Cogswell had made a warm friend of the aging Goethe, who in his appreciation presented Harvard with a complete set of his works in 39 volumes. With this gift as a base, Harvard later built an extensive Goethe collection which, in turn, became the nucleus of a superb collection of German literature. But a far richer prize was the second acquisition. With money supplied by the wealthy Boston merchant Israel Thorndike, Cogswell was able to buy the great collection of Americana gathered by C. D. Ebeling, historian and city librarian of Hamburg. Priced at $65,000 and amounting to some 3,200 volumes and 10,000 maps and charts, it gave Harvard one of the world's strongest collections in its field.

Coming home rarely equipped in 1820 to serve the cause of American library development, Cogswell lacked only the opportunity, and that was soon forthcoming. Harvard needed a new librarian. After ten frustrating years in the post, the able Andrews Norton was resigning it. Meantime, Everett and Ticknor, by then thoroughly entrenched in their professorships, had been actively intervening to secure it for Cogswell. As a result he was offered the post, and in 1821, not without misgivings, he accepted it.

On its face, the opportunity could hardly have been improved on. Though still small and provincial, light years from Göttingen in academic aim and program, Harvard was nonetheless the oldest, most distinguished seat of learning in the country. As such, it was the obvious place for the creation of a strong research library on the Göttingen model, and the foundation was there—20,000 volumes greatly enhanced by the addition of the Goethe and Ebeling acquisitions, not to mention the books bought by Ticknor in support of his courses. There was also Ticknor himself, close friend, as knowing and committed as Cogswell, and therefore sure to be a valuable ally. The opportunity thus deserved his best efforts and soon received them. Early in 1822, Ticknor wrote to a friend:

> Cogswell is doing much good in the library, reforming it utterly, and will, I am persuaded, when he has finished its systematic catalogue, and shown its deficiencies, persuade people to do something serious towards filling it up.

Again the following October, he wrote:

> The library is in fine order. It is arranged on the same plan with that at Göttingen, though for want of books the subdivisions are much fewer at present, and the catalogues are made out in the same way, so that all possible future additions will require no alteration in any part of the system.

But while Cogswell was working his transformation, he was also running into problems. To realize his aim, "the collecting of a rich treasure of learning for future ages to draw upon," he had counted on a liberal book budget. But he had not reckoned sufficiently with the men who held the purse strings, the Harvard Corporation. With meagre funds at their disposal and with a decidedly limited view of the value of research libraries, they were anything but inclined to budget for "rich treasures of learning." The money, therefore, was not forthcoming (indeed, the annual book budget would seldom exceed $400 for another fifty years). Accordingly, Cogswell, never long on patience, resigned in disgust early in 1823.

Ticknor wished he would persevere, as he had finished his systematic catalog and put the library "in fine shape." If he would only carry on, Ticknor was sure "all things would turn out right." But these were idle wishes. Cogswell had had enough. Besides, his enthusiasms had already turned elsewhere. In 1824, he and George Bancroft, similarly frustrated at Harvard, were starting a boys' boarding school, modeling it on the German *Gymnasium*, with the aim of teaching "more thoroughly than has ever been taught among us." Round Hill School failed, however, in 1834.

The next year he ran another boys' school in Raleigh, North Carolina, but he soon found Southern ways uncongenial. His pupils, for example, thought nothing of wearing their hats indoors. In 1836, he moved to New York City, where he spent the next three years in the home of his friend Samuel Ward, as tutor to his sons. Thereafter, he bought an interest in the *New York Review*, becoming its co-proprietor and editor and contributing one lengthy article, "National Education." But with the April 1842 issue, he abandoned that activity, too. Meantime, his days as librarian were drifting further and further behind him.

But if the old purpose to create a great library had lain dormant, it was by no means dead. All it needed for a swift revival was money, and for that he had already been cultivating no less a prospect than the old fur trader, John Jacob Astor. Sick and lonely among his millions, Astor craved good company, which Cogswell was only too happy to provide. So close an association did he make it, in fact, that he soon became known as "Astor's train-bearer and prime minister." Nor did he lose any time broaching to Astor the idea of memorializing himself with a great city library.

Astor took kindly to the idea at once. Promising an endowment, he encouraged Cogswell to begin planning the library and even advanced him a little money to start buying books. But as time went on, Astor proved more liberal with promises than with money, and in 1842, it almost cost him the association. To hunt down materials for the *History of Spanish Literature* he was writing, Ticknor needed a skilled book agent in Spain, and to that end he had used his considerable influence to secure Cogswell the post of first secretary to the U.S. legation in Madrid. Cogswell had only to pack up and go. But Astor was more than equal to that emergency. He simply added force to the same old promises, and, to Ticknor's keen disappointment, Cogswell elected to stay on.

But finally, in 1848, the end came for Astor, and then he showed himself more generous in death than life. When his will was opened, it bore a codicil, written in 1839, providing for the endowment of a library in New York City that "should be subject only to such controls and regulations as the trustees may from time to time exercise and establish." It was not a vast sum. As America's richest man, Astor could have done far better. But it was enough, and now it only remained for Cogswell to go to work.

The need for such a library as he planned was daily becoming more acute. By mid-century America's long period of cultural colonialism was well behind it. A proud native literature had developed. So, too, under the impetus of men like Jared Sparks, George Bancroft, and William Prescott in history, and Asa Gray, Louis Agassiz, and Benjamin Silliman in science, an American scholarship was rapidly developing. Yet to support scholarly investigation the nation had only five libraries—Harvard, Yale, the Boston Athenaeum, the Library Company of Philadelphia, and the Library of Congress—with as many as 50,000 volumes each. Single libraries in Europe had more than all five combined. To conduct research, therefore, one had to be rich enough, like Ticknor or Prescott, either to import his own library or to go abroad. But now, shortly, the scholar would have a third alternative.

As Cogswell went to work, his model remained the Göttingen library. In the Astor Library, the same utilitarian principles would apply: no rarities for their own sake, but strictly a working collection, gathered to support research in all fields of knowledge but with its leading strengths in science and technology and American history.

Such was the model and such the Library rapidly became. Already 62 years old when the Astor endowment finally came through, Cogswell drove himself as if time might run out on him at any moment. Every phase of the project occupied him: the incorporation, organizing the board of trustees (his friends Fitz-Greene Halleck and Washington Irving became members, the second as chairman, and for a voice in policy decisions he had himself named a trustee as well as superintendent), planning the building, compiling the catalogs, and buying the books.

In the book-buying alone, he performed prodigies. Having been careful first to check the holdings of other New York City libraries for their strengths and deficiencies, he went to Europe in 1848, and on that one trip he bought 20,000 volumes as remarkable in range and depth as in quantity. For Charles Coffin Jewett (q.v.), librarian of the Smithsonian, who was just then completing the first American library survey, they already constituted "a superb collection," and the opening of the library was still four years away.

Once opened, in 1854, the Library became a source of much civic pride as well as an instant tourist attraction. The location alone, within the Astor enclave on Lafayette Street, would have made it interesting. But the building made it far more so, on the outside a large red brick structure in the early Renaissance style and on the inside, large halls with lofty ceilings, galleries, alcoves where the books were shelved running around the perimeter, and big reading tables in the center. Altogether it made a show of unaccustomed magnificence for New Yorkers of the 1850s. Finally, there were the books themselves—80,000 of them by then. Cogswell was sure they comprised "the first library of so considerable extent that has ever at once been called into existence," and not surprisingly, considering the need, it was put to immediate use.

Cogswell's achievement, however, did not win undiluted praise. Astor's will had encouraged New Yorkers to expect a truly public library open to all without restriction. But the actuality fell far short of that. Compelled by the charter to admit anyone fourteen years and older, Cogswell did so grudgingly, making the books hardly more accessible than the contents of a bank vault. No books could leave the library, and only patrons with the most impeccable scholarly credentials were allowed access to them in the alcoves. As Cogswell explained, "it would have crazed me to have seen a crowd ranging lawlessly among the books and throwing everything into confusion."

The same attitude extended to reading materials. He regarded *Punch*, the *London Illustrated News*, and the novels of Cooper, Scott, and Dickens as "trashy," valuable only as they kept the boys "orderly and quiet." Reading them was better than "spinning street yarns." But they were trash nonetheless, and Cogswell "never wanted to see a reader who does not come for a valuable purpose."

The attitude made an interesting contrast with that of his friend Ticknor, and at an especially interesting juncture. At the very time that Cogswell was driving to bring the Astor Library into being, Ticknor was doing the same with the new Boston Public Library. The two libraries opened the same year, in fact. But there all similarity ended. Though an uncompromising elitist himself in many ways, Ticknor was a revolutionary in his ideas of public library service. Where Cogswell would cheerfully have excluded working people, the young, and the poor and, in fact, used various strategies within the charter to do so, Ticknor used all his considerable ingenuity to attract them. He kept the library open long hours, loaded the shelves with popular books, and against much opposition, insisted on circulating them freely into the poorest homes.

Still, Cogswell's exclusionary practices took little from the total achievement. As it was, he did a good deal to democratize library access. By creating America's first modern reference library, he brought the resources for learning into the public domain, a fact the U.S. Bureau of Education clearly acknowledged in its landmark report of 1876 on American public libraries. The report called the Astor Library, by then a collection of 100,000 volumes, "a rare blessing both to this metropolis and to the whole American public."

Cogswell remained superintendent until 1861. Then, at the age of 75, he felt he could no longer bring to the post the energy it required, so he resigned. It was not, however, the end of his services to the Astor. For the next five years he worked on a supplement to the catalog, completing it in 1866. Having retired to Boston, he also paid the Library one final visit in June 1871 to advise on the selection of a new superintendent. The following November 26 he died and was buried in Ipswich.

Biographical listings and obituaries—*Dictionary of American Biography* 4 (William C. Lane); *National Cyclopaedia of American Biography* 11; *Who Was Who in America*, Historical Volume (1607-1896). **Books and articles about the biographee**—Dain, Phyllis. *The New York Public Library: A History of Its Founding and Early Years.* New York: New York Public Library, 1972; Long, Orie W. *Literary Pioneers: Early American Explorers of European Culture.* Cambridge, Mass.: Harvard University Press, 1935; Lydenberg, H. M. "A Forgotten Trail Blazer." In *Essays Offered to Herbert Putnam.* New Haven, Conn.: Yale University Press, 1929. **Primary sources and archival materials**—Ticknor, Anna Eliot, ed.

Life of Joseph Green Cogswell As Sketched in His Letters. Cambridge, Mass.: Riverside Press, 1874.

—HAROLD M. TURNER

COLE, GEORGE WATSON (1850-1939)

A pioneer of modern humanistic bibliography and the first librarian of the Huntington Library was born at Warren, Connecticut, on September 6, 1850, the son of Munson and Antoinette Fidelia Taylor Cole. George Watson Cole attended Phillips Academy at Andover, Massachusetts, clerked for a lawyer, and was admitted to the bar in 1876. He then practiced law until 1885, when he turned to a library career.

In 1888, he was graduated from the Columbia College School of Library Economy, where he met Melvil Dewey (q.v.). After working in libraries in Fitchburg, Massachusetts (1885-1886), and Brooklyn, New York (1886-1887), he became the assistant to William F. Poole (q.v.) at the Newberry Library, Chicago (1888-1890). He served as librarian of the Free Public Library, Jersey City (1891-1895), and then undertook bibliography and worked in the Lenox Library, New York, under the guidance of Wilberforce Eames (q.v.). His landmark publications came soon afterwards: the *Catalogue of Americana in the Library of the Late E. Dwight Church of New York* (1907; 5v.) and the *Catalogue of English Literature and Miscellanea in the E. Dwight Church Library* (New York, 1909; 2v.).

Henry E. Huntington purchased the magnificently cataloged Church library in 1911, and four years later, at age 65, Cole began a retirement career which, in some respects, was his most important: he served as librarian for Huntington from 1915 until 1924. Until 1920, Huntington's books and manuscripts were in New York City, most of them in storage after shipment from abroad. With the completion of a library building in San Marino, California, in 1920, Cole took charge of shipping the collection westward, organizing a staff, and preparing research tools to provide access to the most comprehensive private library ever assembled on British and American history and literature.

Cole's bibliographical work continued after his final retirement in 1924, his major publication being the *Catalogue of the Wymberley Jones de Renne Georgia Library* (1931; 3v.). Over the years he also contributed to Pollard and Redgrave's *Short-Title Catalogue of Books Published in England ... 1475-1640* (London, 1926).

In his later years, Cole was distinguished in appearance, with white hair, mustache, and beard. Early photographs of the Huntington Library staff support the conclusion that in looks, age, and interests, Huntington and his first librarian were kindred spirits. Huntington's employment of Cole was certainly a logical sequel to his practice of buying complete collections and thereby acquiring the fruits of the original collector's intelligence and taste: with the Church library, he also acquired its bibliographer.

There are several important typescripts by Cole in the Huntington Library. Characteristic is a report he prepared in 1924 on the Library as it had grown during the nine years of his tenure—an enlightening and exciting account of some of the greatest book collecting in all of library history. During this period, Huntington acquired the Frederick R. Halsey library of English and American literature (1915), the A. S. Macdonald collection of Californiana and the Britwell Americana (1916), the great Bridgewater (English) collection begun in the sixteenth century (1917), the W. K. Bixby manuscripts of English and American literature and history (1918), the Robert A. Brock collection of early American history and the Henry R. Wagner collection of Western Americana (1922), publisher James T. Fields's archive (1922), the Loudon papers on English and American history, the Battle Abbey manuscripts, the Eames collection of American imprints (1923), and several large blocks of incunabula. That Cole's knowledge and experience had a major influence on Huntington's imaginative collecting is unquestionable.

In recognition of his accomplishments, Trinity College (Hartford) awarded Cole an honorary Doctor of Humane Letters degree in 1920. Cole was a member of the American Antiquarian Society, an honorary member of the Bibliographical Society of London, president of the Bibliographical Society of America (1916-1921), and a member of the Grolier Club. He died at his home in Pasadena, California, on October 10, 1939.

Biographical listings and obituaries—*National Cyclopaedia of American Biography* 16; [Obituary]. *Library Journal* 64:867 (Nov. 1, 1939); [Obituary]. *Library Service News* 9:8 (Dec. 1939); [Obituary]. *News Sheet of the Bibliographical Society of America* 53-4:3 (Sept. 15-Dec. 15, 1939); *Who Was Who in America* I (1897-1942). **Books and articles about the biographee**—Bliss, L. E. "George Watson Cole." *Pacific Bindery Talk* 12:35-37 (Nov. 1939); Carew, Harold D. "Toiler in the Vineyard of Books." *Touring Topics*, February 1929, pp. 32-34, 48-49; "A List of the Printed Productions of George Watson Cole, 1870-1936." *Bulletin of Bibliography* 15:183-86 (May-Aug. 1936); 16:11-12 (Sept.-Dec. 1936); 16:32-35 (Jan.-April 1937); Thompson, Lawrence S. "George Watson Cole, 1850-1939." *Grolier 75.* New York: Grolier, 1959. pp. 54-56.

—DANIEL H. WOODWARD

COMPTON, CHARLES HERRICK (1880-1966)

Charles H. Compton, born in Palmyra, Nebraska, on October 24, 1880, was the third child of Orville and Hannah Jane MacAfee Compton. His parents migrated from Auburn, New York, to spread the gospel, inasmuch as his father was a Presbyterian home missionary. Charles Compton finished his elementary grade school years in Lincoln, Nebraska, where the family had moved when his father took a new pastorate, and where, at age thirteen, Compton began his working career, starting as a Western Union messenger for $12 a month.

Because the University of Nebraska was a local institution and he could save money by living at home, he enrolled there and graduated in 1901. Working summers on a nearby farm, he met his future wife, and he and Ruth Rogers were married by his father in 1908. In his last year at the University, he was one of three men in his class elected to Phi Beta Kappa.

From university graduation until 1905, Compton spent his time working at several different jobs: in a shoe store, selling subscriptions to the Lincoln newspaper, selling insurance, and even peddling stereopticon slides for Underwood and Underwood in Montana.

Without directly realizing it, Compton had come under the influence of his sister, who worked at the University of Nebraska Library. Finding librarianship appealing, he saved money and went to Albany, where he enrolled under Melvil Dewey (q.v.) in the New York State Library School in 1905 and where he forged friendships with many persons who later emerged as library leaders. His roommates were Chalmers Hadley (q.v.), Louis Bailey, and Arne Kildal, a visiting Norwegian. Compton found Dewey to be funny, but at the same time, called him the only genius ever produced by the American library profession. Compton's teachers included James I. Wyer (q.v.), vice director of the school, labeled by Compton as the best teacher he had. He found lecturer Sarah B. Askew (q.v.), of the New Jersey State Library, an inspiration on rural library service extension, and John Cotton Dana (q.v.) was a lecturer who possessed an "intriguing personality." Between his first and second years of training Compton took a combination position—librarian and bookkeeper—at the Albany YMCA in order to finance the remainder of his professional education.

Upon graduating with a B.L.S. in 1908, Compton returned to the Midwest and started his career as librarian for the University of North Dakota, where he centralized the library administration and wrested control of library book ordering from the faculty.

In 1910, Compton headed west again, this time to Seattle, where he spent the next ten years as reference librarian at the Public Library of Seattle. His responsibilities grew with the addition of more departmental supervision assigned him by his chief librarian, Judson T. Jennings (q.v.). Too, a dictum of Jennings's impressed him greatly, and he later used it to good personal advantage: "use sufficient care in selection of staff and [the librarian] need not do much else."

Until the outbreak of World War I, Compton spent his years at Seattle making a name for himself in public relations for the Library. It was an additional assignment to which he applied great imagination and tremendous energy. Circulation at Seattle grew significantly as a result of his program, he took to writing articles about his successful methods, and the *Saturday Evening Post* even gave him a laudatory editorial.

After America entered the war, Compton was called to Washington for assistance with the ALA's Library War Service and worked under Herbert Putnam (q.v.), side by side with other leading American librarians such as Carl Milam (q.v.), Joseph Wheeler (q.v.), and William Howard Brett (q.v.). Compton was in charge of selecting and purchasing books for the Army and Navy.

For a while, after returning to Seattle, he was placed in charge of the Library as temporary replacement for the chief, who went overseas as a war librarian. By this time, the Comptons had two sons, Paul and Kenneth.

Another leave of absence became necessary from 1919 to 1920. Compton was appointed as assistant to Carl Milam in a short-lived national program entitled Enlarged Program Campaign, conceived as a follow-up to the Library War Service and administered by ALA. Headquartered in New York City, the campaign was supposed to result in an expansion and increase of library importance in the lives of Americans. "Good Books Make Good Citizens" was the title of one pamphlet widely distributed throughout the country. Compton and Milam never lost their enthusiasm for the background principle and the national drive, but some critical librarians killed the movement.

Compton returned to Seattle but left several months later to become assistant librarian, under Arthur Bostwick (q.v.), at the St. Louis Public Library in 1921. Thus, it was at age 41 that Charlie Compton, after a few years of association with some of his profession's "greats," and after having achieved some fame on his own merits, joined a big library and was assigned as assistant to a prominent librarian. Compton was a thin man, small in stature, with a quiet personality. His associates described him as a conservative man with a good sense of humor. He was a deep thinker, soft-spoken and even-tempered.

His secretary characterized him as a man dedicated to his profession, next in personal importance to his devotion to his family. Harry C. Bauer, long-time librarian friend at the University of Washington, corroborates this by saying "books, reading and libraries" were his principal concerns. Here was a man who was known for his thoroughness, integrity and

COMPTON COMPTON

deep loyalty, and who had an archival type of mind that relieved the prominent Bostwick of administrative details so that he could write his books and represent the profession in the widest, even international, circles. Compton's approach to his new and influential responsibilities combined modesty and compassion. During the years of the Great Depression, he never relented in his efforts to secure staff pensions, and he employed the first black professional librarian for St. Louis. For all his sympathy and understanding, however, his secretary, who had to relay to him occasional public complaints about service, quoted him as saying that "to work in a library you need a skin thick as an elephant."

Although Compton maintained a warm home life, he was also active in St. Louis community affairs to the extent that the St. Louis Newspaper Guild honored him in 1950 with its Page One Civic Award. He was a charter member of the Adult Education Council, which also recognized him through a gift set to the Library of *The Great Books of the Western World.* He helped establish a suburban public library in Webster Groves, to whose first Board of Trustees he was appointed (and elected vice-president).

He continued his active participation in ALA affairs and was directly responsible, because of concern for his St. Louis staff, for the establishment of the Association's Committee on Salaries. During his eleven years of chairmanship of the Committee, an annual series of comparative figures published in the *Bulletin* led to salary improvements across the country. From 1927 to 1930, he chaired another small ALA committee to examine the critical charges brought against ALA by John Cotton Dana. Their 1930 investigation resulted in the First Activities Committee Report.

Compton succeeded Gratia A. Countryman (q.v.) as ALA president for 1934-1935 and adopted as his principal presidential objective the establishment of a federal library agency plus federal aid to libraries. ALA's goal was to raise $100 million for rural library development. He and Carl Milam, by that time ALA executive secretary, talked to several departmental secretaries in Washington, where they received encouragement and help from John Studebaker, U.S. Commissioner of Education. But a dissident element in ALA criticized the scheme and secured postponement of ALA's promotion of it. During his presidency, Compton was also the Association's representative at the 1935 International Library Congress held in Spain. This international visit impressed him with the greater progress made in England and the Scandinavian countries with public library service than here in the United States.

Back again in St. Louis, he resumed his leadership in the Missouri Library Association, which he had served as president, as well as chairman of the Legislative Committee, for twenty years. During that term of office and afterward, he was uncommonly effective. He and his committee saved the State Library Commission from extinction by the Legislature, and when the state constitution was rewritten, he was instrumental in securing insertion of a section explicitly committing the state to public library development and financial support. Then, on March 1, 1938, Compton was appointed librarian of the St. Louis Public Library, and Bostwick, who had resigned as head, was made associate librarian.

Compton then wrote a series of articles. Published later as a book entitled *Who Reads What?*, these were based on research of reader interest in Thomas Hardy, the Greek classics, George Bernard Shaw, Carl Sandburg, Mark Twain, and William James. His earlier book, *Fifty Years of Progress of the St. Louis Public Library* (1926), was followed by *Twenty-five Crucial Years of the St. Louis Public Library* (1953). Over the years of his tenure, he conducted surveys as well of the public libraries in St. Louis, Louisville, Grand Rapids (Michigan), Lexington (Kentucky), and Nashville.

Charles H. Compton closed his career as a librarian by retiring October 24, 1950, on his seventieth birthday. He was appointed librarian emeritus by the Board of Directors, which published a resolution calling attention to Compton's state legislative achievements, the successful local library tax increase election, the inauguration of bookmobile service, and the establishment of an educational film department. They honored him in 1958 by naming an annex to the Main Library after him, and again with another separate resolution at the time of his death.

But three years before his retirement, an event occurred that gave him his purpose for the remaining years of his life. Great Books discussions came to St. Louis in 1947, and Compton mobilized all of the educational institutions of St. Louis to promote the idea. He chaired the sponsoring committee, co-conducted a group, and promoted the program until his death. Ray Wittcoff, who sold Compton on the idea of having the St. Louis Public Library sponsor the program, told him that his role was indispensable to the enthusiastic St. Louis adoption of Great Books discussions. Compton modestly replied: "Whatever I did was minor; what it did for me was to give me new life."

Meanwhile, he published two more books, *Memories of a Librarian* (autobiography, 1954), and *William James, Philosopher and Man* (1957). Compton died on March 16, 1966.

Biographical listings and obituaries—*Who's Who in Library Service*, 1st ed., 2nd ed., 3rd ed., 4th ed. Books and articles about the biographee—Bailey, L. J. "Salute to Charles H. Compton." *Library Journal* 71:780-81 (June 1946); Bauer, H. C. "Charles Herrick Compton." *ALA Bulletin* 48:139-44 (March 1954); Hadley, C. "Salute to Charles

Herrick Compton." *Library Journal* 71:779-80 (June 1946); Nourse, L. M. "Charles Herrick Compton, 1880-1966." *ALA Bulletin* 60:723-26 (July-Aug. 1966). **Primary sources and archival materials**—The records of the Seattle and St. Louis public libraries contain some archival material, and additional information can be found in Compton's autobiography, *Memories of a Librarian* (1954).

—PAXTON P. PRICE

CONEY, DONALD (1901-1973)

The man primarily responsible for the stature of the libraries of the University of California was born February 21, 1901, at Jackson, Michigan, to Glenn E. and Eunice Frances Diffenbaugh Coney. Receiving his baccalaureate degree from the University of Michigan in 1925, Donald Coney married Dorothy Bell Pettit on July 2 of that same year. They were to have two sons, Donald John and Richard Bell. Coney, having worked in the Michigan library during his student days, continued that work through receiving his A.M. in library science there in 1927.

After professional qualification, he served first as librarian of the University of Delaware (1927-1928). Then he was assistant librarian of the University of North Carolina under Louis Round Wilson (1928-1931), eventually becoming professor of library science and assistant director of the School of Library Science at North Carolina (1931-1932). From there, he moved to Chicago as supervisor of technical processes at the Newberry Library (1932-1934), and as lecturer in library administration at the University of Chicago (1933-1934). He then accepted, at age 34, the directorship of the University of Texas Library, where he served with distinction until 1945. His tenure at Texas witnessed the first application of a computer to library operations—specifically, the work of the Circulation Department under Ralph Parker. When Coney then became university librarian and professor of librarianship at the University of California at Berkeley, his work there until his retirement in 1968 and his death in 1973 was to fulfill his career.

Those 23 years at Berkeley encompassed the great period of growth of the University of California and its libraries. The Library grew from about 1,300,000 volumes to more than 3,000,000, and its career staff grew from about 175 to well over 400. Don Coney was one of the important reasons Berkeley achieved high distinction among the universities of the world, for he created the University Library as it is known and appreciated today, and it remains his achievement.

Coney's interest in the University, however, was by no means limited to its libraries. As a member of the Buildings and Campus Development Committee, he was influential in the conception and design of many of the major new buildings on the campus, such

as the Student Union, Hertz Hall (music), Zellerbach Auditorium, the Art Museum, Wurster Hall (environmental design), and the Moffitt Undergraduate Library. Still more important was his creation of a rich cultural program for the University. In 1955, Clark Kerr, then chancellor at Berkeley, appointed him chairman of the Committee for Drama, Lectures and Music, whose name he soon changed to the Committee for Arts and Lectures—CAL. Travis Bogard, present chairman of the Drama Departments, recalls that

> under his guidance, the Berkeley campus developed as one of the leading dance centers in the western United States; in lectures, films and theatre, the offerings were exceptional in their range and quality; in music, programs of comparable merit could only be found in a major metropolis. He served as chairman until 1970, two years after his retirement. Without exaggerating it can be said that he was the principal architect of the cultural program for which the Berkeley campus is justly famous.

Clark Kerr attributed to Donald Coney the present cultural attractiveness of the University, because of "his great leadership, devotion, taste and discrimination." I myself remember that, in his monitoring of this program, he rarely missed a performance. Also, students at Berkeley who take pleasure in the graphic arts will remember him for his part in the development of the Graphic Arts Loan Collection in the Library, a circulating collection of more than 800 original prints by artists from the sixteenth to the twentieth centuries.

Coney was also vice-chancellor for administration (1955-1956), when this and similar positions were being rotated among distinguished faculty. From time to time, he was a member of various administrative committees, and he was active with the Faculty Club as well. He was also, during his entire career at Berkeley, a working professor in the School of Librarianship and a wise and witty member of the University-wide Library Council—the cooperative organization of the library directors of all UC campuses.

Off campus, Coney was among the most influential university librarians of his generation. He published little, but he wrote and spoke well, with humor and great good sense. And he recruited, trained, and sent out from Berkeley to larger careers such people as Douglas Bryant of Harvard, John Mackenzie Cory of the New York Public Library, Melvin Voigt of the University of California at San Diego, Russell Shank of the Smithsonian Institution, Marion Milczewski of the University of Washington, and Frank Lundy of the University of Nebraska.

During his early years at Berkeley, Coney was engrossed in the national problems of acquiring foreign research materials that had failed to reach our libraries during World War II. He became a member of the Council of the American Library Association and was advanced to the Executive Board in the early 1950s. I served with him on the Board during the hectic years of the Cresap, McCormick, and Paget management survey and the subsequent reorganization of ALA. Also, in the ALA, the Association of Research Libraries, the Association for Asian Studies, and the California Library Association, he fulfilled multitudinous tasks in such areas as joint importations, cooperative microcard and microfilm projects, the National Union Catalog, the Farmington Plan, the Library Technology Project, the acquisition of South, South East, and Far East Asian resources, research library mobilization, and cooperative access to newspapers and other serial publications.

Publicly and professionally, Coney was open and articulate, and he was administratively efficient. Clark Kerr, as his chancellor, said that, among all the deans at Berkeley, Don Coney was always best prepared at budget time. Despite the complexity of his organization, he ran a tight ship, knew the details, and had the answers. Indeed, while the Library was in fact celebrating its 2,000,000th and 3,000,000th acquisitions, Don was presenting the most persuasive and well-documented tales of impending woe and disaster if the budget were not hugely increased. Kerr asked, with an appreciative smile, how things in Don's library could have been getting better and better and worse and worse at the same time. In committees, Don was consummately skillful. He was shrewd, rational, and searching, and he never lost his keen, sly sense of humor. As Lawrence Clark Powell put it, he was "dry but never dull."

Kerr cherishes the memory of his first day as Berkeley's chancellor. His predecessor, Robert Gordon Sproul, had not yet turned over to him the problems of the University; so, at his new office, he found only one item of business on the clean desk before him—a problem fabricated by Coney. The problem was that dogs in the main library were licking water from the drinking fountains, that the Library staff had protested having to share the fountains with the dogs, and what was he, as the new chancellor, going to do about it—in effect, not having anything else to do.

As a person, Don Coney was intensely private; he hid his heart, so to speak, in his pocket, where no one could find it and when it was hurt, the hurt would never show. I never knew him to defend himself against any personal attack, even though his last years at Berkeley were deeply troubled. He was genuinely self-effacing, as witnessed by the fact that even at his death, on February 10, 1973, only a very few of his most intimate friends knew that he was seriously ill. He was not only embarrassed by personal compliments to himself but was also sparing in his

compliments to others. Some of his colleagues who could not reach him wrongly viewed him as being cold and detached; but those who could reach him and who enjoyed his kindness knew otherwise.

Also, Don Coney was one of the most honestly and broadly cultured people I have ever known. He disliked travel, especially by plane, but I have the most happy memories of when, as librarian at Stanford, I shared many long train rides with him to conferences in the East. These were times when I learned not only about his stature in the library world but also about his extraordinary literacy and fine taste for the arts. He never flaunted his love of either books or the arts, but he did read voraciously and did indeed enrich the cultural, and some of the physical, climate of the Berkeley campus, while raising his Library to a balanced position of eminence among the university and research libraries of the world.

Biographical listings and obituaries—*A Biographical Directory of Librarians in the United States and Canada,* 5th ed.; "DC, 1901-1973." *CU News* 28:1-2 (Feb. 1973); *Who's Who in America* 34 (1966-1967); *Who's Who in Library Service,* 1st ed., 2nd ed., 3rd ed., 4th ed. Books and articles about the biographee—Powell, Lawrence Clark. *Fortune and Friendship.* New York: R. R. Bowker, 1968. Primary sources and archival materials—Personnel files of the University of California at Berkeley.

—RAYNARD C. SWANK

COOLBRITH, INA DONNA (1841-1928)

The poet laureate of California, who was also a librarian and who was known in the English-speaking world as Ina Coolbrith, was born on March 10, 1841, in the Mormon capital of Nauvoo, Illinois. The third child of Don Carlos and Agnes M. Coolbrith Smith, she was given the name of Josephine (in honor of her uncle, Joseph Smith, the prophet and founder of the Church of Jesus Christ of Latter Day Saints) Donna (in honor of her father, Don Carlos Smith, Joseph's youngest brother). She was never to know her father, for he died of pneumonia only five months after her birth. The widowed Agnes remained with her daughters in Illinois for five more years, during which time her two brothers-in-law, Joseph and Hyrum, were murdered while being held in the jail in Carthage, Illinois. Agnes Smith and her children were not part of the Mormon exodus to Utah, for she had recently remarried, joining her fortunes with those of a journalist, William Pickett, who took her and her family in 1846 to St. Louis.

Josephine Donna (called Ina in her home—the name was pronounced Eye-na by her family) was ten years old when her mother and step-father decided to join a wagon train going from St. Louis to California. Wandering in the desert east of the Sierra Nevada range, the group luckily encountered the famous scout Jim Beckwourth, who took them over a new pass. He noticed ten-year-old Josephine walking beside her parents' wagon, reached down and placed her on his saddle just in front of himself as they neared the summit, so that she would be the first person to cross over the new pass. "There, little girl," he said, "there is California. There is your kingdom."

Josephine grew to young womanhood in Los Angeles, where at the age of fifteen she was already contributing poems to the Los Angeles *Star*. On April 21, 1858, at age seventeen, she became the bride of Robert Carsley. The marriage did not last long, however. In October of 1861, her husband, returning from a business trip to San Francisco, seems to have been overcome by a jealous rage and tried to kill her. Friends of the family disarmed him, wounding him in the process. But Josephine Carsley felt herself unable to live any longer with a man who had tried to kill both her and her mother, and on December 26, 1861, she became one of California's first divorcees.

About this time, her step-father decided to move the family to San Francisco, and Josephine accompanied them, changing her name so as to drop the unhappy memories of both Smith and Carsley from her life. In the spring of 1862, she arrived in San Francisco as Miss Ina Donna Coolbrith. Already enjoying a minor reputation as a poet, she was not long in becoming a steady and important contributor to the newly founded *Overland Monthly*. Indeed, so frequent were her poetic contributions that she, Charles Warren Stoddard, and editor Bret Harte became known as the "Golden Gate Trinity."

During the years from 1862 to 1874, Ina Coolbrith lived in San Francisco, but in 1874, she accepted a position as librarian of the Oakland Library Association and moved to that city to live. Her "family" at this time consisted of her ailing mother, her orphaned nephew and niece, and Calle Shasta, the Indian girl whom her friend Joaquin Miller had sired while he lived among the Modocs some sixteen years earlier.

The Oakland Library Association gave way, in May 1878, to the Oakland Free Library, one of the first to be established in California under the terms of the Rogers Free Library Act of March 18, 1878. Ina Coolbrith's duties, besides acting as city librarian, were primarily those of a readers' adviser. In this capacity, and with her reputation as a poet reaching national and even international levels, she gave cultural advice and intellectual stimulation to a whole generation of writers and artists, the best known of whom are Joaquin Miller (Ina persuaded him to adopt the name of Joaquin, and she gave him hints on how to write verse), and, later on, Jack London, Isadora Duncan, and Mary Austin.

Besides acknowledging their intellectual indebtedness, many of her patrons of those years remembered her unusual beauty. Isadora Duncan wrote, in *My Life* (1927), her recollections of her life in Oakland: "The librarian was a very wonderful and beautiful woman, a poetess of California. . . . She had very beautiful eyes that glowed with burning fire and passion." And another former patron of the Library, now a school teacher wearing a religious habit, recalling her school days in Oakland, wrote: "Why, we girls used to come to the library just to look at her—she was so beautiful."

Despite her popularity and her efficiency in operating the city library, on September 26, 1892, she was served with a summary notice of dismissal from her position, after eighteen years of devoted and capable service. Although there was a state-wide furor in the press about these "star chamber" proceedings, the Oakland Board of Trustees, while admitting there were no charges against her, refused to budge from their position, relenting only so far as to extend the dismissal date from three days later to three months later. The motives for the dismissal seem to have been primarily financial. The Board believed that the assistant librarian could run the library well enough, and that they could save Coolbrith's salary. Her letter of resignation, written "under protest," was accepted on October 4, and on December 31, 1892, Ina Coolbrith, at the age of 51, found herself unemployed.

During the next few years, Coolbrith devoted herself to literary pursuits, among them the selecting and publishing of a second collection of her verse, which came from the press in October 1895, with the title *Songs from the Golden Gate*. This volume and her earlier collection, *A Perfect Day* (1881), form the basis for her reputation as a poet, though they are far from being a complete collection of her total output. She was the author of approximately 340 poems, some of them several hundred lines in length, including a few that were never published but exist only in manuscript form among her papers.

The sales of her book, however, were not sufficient to provide her with a steady income. One of her admirers once gushed, "Oh, Miss Coolbrith, our whole family just lives on your poems!" "How nice," she smiled in return, "that is more than I was ever able to do." In January of 1898, she was named librarian of the Mercantile Library in San Francisco, a position she held until the end of 1899, when she was invited to be the librarian of the Bohemian Club, the all-male literary club of which she was already an honorary member (one of only three or four women so honored during the 100-odd years of the Club's existence). The Great Fire of April 18, 1906, destroyed Ina Coolbrith's home, as well as her place of work, the Bohemian Club, and she also suffered the loss of an almost completed manuscript, a literary history of California based on her personal recollections of all the people she had known—Harte, Stoddard, Miller, London, and all the rest. In addition, though the loss was not known to her at the time, all the remaining unsold copies of her book, *Songs from the Golden Gate*, were also destroyed.

Most families in burned-out San Francisco soon found new homes, with financial aid from the Red Cross or some other source. But Ina Coolbrith's prominence prevented this, and a variety of special funds were set up, some with disastrous results, to provide her with a new home. Eventually she did acquire both land and a house, in San Francisco, and she moved into the house in December 1909. On May 16, 1910, she was elected president of the newly founded Pacific Coast Women's Press Association. During her presidency, plans were made for the Association to sponsor an "authors' congress" in 1915 as part of the proposed Panama-Pacific International Exposition in San Francisco. This was agreed to, and Coolbrith was named president of the Executive Committee, a full-time task, even though she was still nominally librarian of the Bohemian Club, and did indeed work part of the day in the Club's new quarters.

It was during this Congress of Authors and Journalists, on June 29, 1915, that Senator James D. Phelan, as part of a secretly hatched plot, departed from the announced program to say some words of praise for the poetry of Ina Coolbrith, and then, to her complete surprise, to ask Benjamin I. Wheeler, president of the University of California, to step forward and to crown Ina Donna Coolbrith with the traditional crown of bay leaves, as the first poet laureate of California. The governor had already approved the designation, confirmed later by the Legislature in Senate Concurrent Resolution No. 24 (April 26, 1919), the final wording of the act being ". . . the title of Loved Laurel-Crowned Poet of California."

Death came to Ina Coolbrith on February 29, 1928, only ten days before her eighty-seventh birthday. She had lived to see her position as a librarian vindicated, as city after city in California wrote into its municipal laws provisions that would prevent future summary dismissals of librarians or other city officials. Many of her poems had been set to music, and her great ode, "California," had been choreographed and presented as a pageant. Various cities had declared "Ina Coolbrith Days," when her poems would be read in public, or set to music and sung. Nor did the honors cease with her death. A few years later, a park in San Francisco and a branch library in Oakland would be named for her, as well as a mountain peak in the Sierra Nevada, one that overlooks the Beckwourth Pass through which she had first entered California.

During the last years of her life, Ina Coolbrith had much to be proud of. Her verse had made her name known all over the English-speaking world; her unjust dismissal from the Oakland Library had become a landmark case in the long fight for security of employment for civil service employees; she had been awarded honorary degrees; Luther Burbank had named a flower for her; city mayors had named "days" in her honor; and above all, she had been crowned poet laureate of California, the first woman to be so honored in the whole United States.

She had won her "kingdom" with her pen, and she had reigned therein as a literary queen; but since she had never been formally retired from her last position, as librarian of the Bohemian Club, it is true to say that she was a professional librarian in California for almost all of her adult life. It was perhaps with this thought in mind that she could say to a newspaper reporter, less than three years before her death, "I am prouder of being the first public librarian in California than I am of being its first woman author, for I think public libraries have been a greater help to people."

Biographical listings and obituaries—"Brief Genealogy of Don Carlos Smith, His Wife, Agnes Moulton Coolbrith, and Their Children." *Utah Genealogical and Historical Magazine* 26:105 (July 1935); *National Cyclopaedia of American Biography* 13; *Who Was Who in America* I (1897-1942). **Books and articles about the biographee**—Clark, F. H. "Libraries and Librarians of the Pacific Coast." *Overland Monthly* 18:449-64 (Nov. 1891); Conmy, Peter Thomas. *The Dismissal of Ina Coolbrith as Head Librarian of Oakland Public Free Library, and a Discussion of the Tenure Status of Head Librarians.* Oakland: Oakland Public Library, 1969; Rhodehamel, Josephine D., and Raymund F. Wood. *Ina Coolbrith: Librarian and Laureate of California.* Provo, Utah: Brigham Young University Press, 1973. (Includes bibliography); Stevens, Ivalu D. *A Bibliography of Ina Donna Coolbrith.* Sacramento: California State Printing Office, 1932; Wood, Raymund F. "Ina Coolbrith: Librarian." *California Librarian* 19, no. 2:102-103, 132 (April 1958). **Primary sources and archival materials**—Coolbrith's papers are divided among the Bancroft Library of the University of California at Berkeley, the Huntington Library, and the Oakland Public Library.

—RAYMUND F. WOOD

COULTER, EDITH MARGARET (1880-1963)

Edith Margaret Coulter was born at Salinas, California, in the heart of Steinbeck's Long Valley, on October 30, 1880, one of two daughters of an English father and a Scottish mother, William Story and Elizabeth Mabel Coulter. She and her older sister Mabel (who also became a librarian) were among the first women students at the newly founded Leland Stanford Junior University. There Edith majored in German and history and, after graduation in 1905, went on to the two-year course in the New York State Library School at Albany. There her classmates included Fremont Rider (q.v.), Carl Fitz, Chalmers Hadley (q.v.), and Charles H. Compton (q.v.). Her roommate, Beulah Cross, was also to play an important role in Coulter's subsequent career.

Upon graduating in 1907, Edith Coulter returned to California as a cataloger in the Berkeley Public Library, and soon thereafter, she took a position as supervisor of periodicals in the library of her alma mater. In the meantime, Beulah Cross had married Harold L. Leupp, the assistant librarian of the University of California. In 1911, the Leupps persuaded Coulter to leave Stanford for a senior librarian position at Berkeley. Four years later, she became head of the Reference Department, and in that demanding and rewarding post for the next thirteen years, she gained the knowledge of books and people that made her a great library educator.

Coulter's transition from teaching librarian to library school teacher was gradual. In the summer of 1912, the University first offered instruction in librarianship, and Coulter taught the summer reference courses. She did the same in 1913 and 1915. In 1918, the Department of Library Science was established, with her as lecturer. Too, she earned an M.A. in history at the University in 1924. In 1926, the Graduate School of Librarianship was established at Berkeley. In 1927-1928 Coulter, on a sabbatical leave, visited the principal libraries of the United States and Europe, and in the spring semester, she took a temporary position as a lecturer in the School of Library Service at Columbia.

Returning to Berkeley after this experience, she soon formed, with Director Sydney B. Mitchell (q.v.) and cataloging instructor Della J. Sisler, a powerful triumvirate that eventually raised the Berkeley school to high stature and wide influence. By 1946, she had been advanced to the rank of professor. Her rise was by the traditional route of teaching, professional service, and publication, in all of which she attained distinction. She taught reference work with erudition leavened by dry humor, and students were held by her authority as well as by a certain elfin charm. Also, on the predominantly masculine Berkeley campus, Edith Coulter proved an effective spokeswoman for her few feminine colleagues.

Midway in her career at Berkeley, Coulter discovered unmined riches in the Bancroft Library, a treasury of source material on the West. Pictorial Californiana became her province, and from 1937 to 1952, she edited several volumes of travellers' views and maps for publication by the University Press and the Book Club of California. Her major compilation was *Guide to Historical Bibliographies* (University of California, 1935). She served as chairwoman of the Publications Committee of the latter organization and was on its Board of Directors from 1948 to 1957. To precise knowledge, she brought taste and style.

Edith Coulter was also active in professional organizations. A member of the California Library Association, she served as its secretary in 1916. From 1924 to 1925, she was president of the College and Reference Section of the American Library Association, and she served on the ALA Council from 1928 to 1933. In the American Association of Library Schools, she was president for the 1942-1943 term.

Edith Coulter was respected for her judgment and honored for her research. The California Historical Society made her a fellow in 1959. In 1960, Mills College awarded her an honorary doctorate of letters, and in 1961, she received the ALA's Isadore Gilbert Mudge award for distinguished work in reference librarianship. A lectureship in her name was founded in 1947 by the alumni of the library school and continues to be given annually at the conference of the California Library Association.

After retirement in 1949 as professor emerita and until her death, Coulter came faithfully to her office in the University Library to work on bibliohistorical research projects. She was not too busy to welcome her former students, numbering in the hundreds, who came to thank her for her lasting gifts to them. Her interests were manifold, her sympathies humane. She moved easily along the continuum of history from Sir Francis Drake, who sailed the California coast in 1578, to John Steinbeck, who also was born in Salinas.

Although her step slowed, her shy sweet smile never faded. Edith Coulter died suddenly, without any lingering illness, on January 27, 1963, in her eighty-third year. Her example lives for those who can profit from it.

Biographical listings and obituaries—[Obituary]. *College & Research Libraries* 24:163-64 (March 1963); [Obituary]. *Library Journal* 88:989 (March 1, 1963); [Obituary]. *Wilson Library Bulletin* 37:622 (April 1963); *Who's Who in Library Service*, 1st ed., 3rd ed. **Books and articles about the biographee**—[Biographical sketch]. *Library Journal* 89:2528 (June 15, 1964); Madden, Henry Miller. "Edith M. Coulter: In Remembrance." *California Librarian* 24:97-103 (April 1963); Parker, W. E. "Chronological List of the Writings of Edith M. Coulter." *California Librarian* 24:103-104 (April 1963); Powell, Lawrence Clark. *The Example of Miss Edith M. Coulter.* Sacramento: California Library Association, 1969.

—LAWRENCE CLARK POWELL

COUNTRYMAN, GRATIA ALTA (1866-1953)

Gratia Alta Countryman was born November 29, 1866, at Hastings, Minnesota, the daughter of Levi and Alta Chamberlain Countryman. She received her baccalaureate degree from the University of Minnesota in 1889, planning to be a teacher, but Herbert Putnam (q.v.) persuaded her to apply for a position at the Minneapolis Public Library, which was to open soon under his direction. Deciding to try library work for a year, she began on October 1, 1889, what was to be a lifelong career with that library. After one year, she was promoted to head of the catalog department, and two years later, in 1892, she was appointed assistant librarian to James K. Hosmer (q.v.), who had just succeeded Putnam. In 1904, she succeeded Hosmer as chief librarian, a position she held until her retirement at the age of seventy in 1936, when she was made librarian emeritus.

In his last annual report, written in 1903, Hosmer wrote:

As regards my chief assistant, Miss Gratia A. Countryman, I will only say this: At my coming, Herbert Putnam ... committed her to me with commendation quite unqualified. To this commendation, I ... give unqualified endorsement. The Board has shown its sense of Miss Countryman's deserts [sic] by committing to her the guidance of the institution. Well endowed by nature, thoroughly equipped by education, specially trained and vouched for by the most skillful master of our profession, minutely familiar with this institution, which indeed her care and counsel have done very much to shape, what can be expected for her but the best success.

Hosmer's prediction of success for Gratia Countryman was prophetic. She immediately began to make changes, expanding the Library's services to reach more and more people. In the more than thirty years she directed the Library, service expanded not only into all areas of the city, but into Hennepin County as well, with county residents being served beginning in 1915, and the Hennepin County Library being established in 1922, with Gratia Countryman as county librarian. At the end of her career, she was able to realize with satisfaction that most of her ideas had become fact.

Community-conscious, socially concerned, forward-looking, an educator, social worker, missionary, leader—all are terms that have been used to describe Gratia Countryman. Her vision of library service was expressed in the many speeches she gave, the journal articles she wrote, and especially in her annual reports. The first annual report she submitted included the following view of what a library is for:

A public library is the one great civic institution supported by the people which is designed for the instruction and pleasure of all the people without age limit, ... rich and poor, ... educated and uneducated, without culture limit. ... It should be "all things to all men" in the world of thought. ... The library should be a wide-awake institution for the dissemination of ideas, where books are easily accessible and readily obtainable. It should be the center of all the activities of a city that lead to social growth, municipal reform, civic pride and good citizenship. It should have its finger on the pulse of the people, ready to second and forward

any good movement. ... It should be a quiet retreat for the scholarly man, and the most inviting and hospitable of places for the ordinary reader or casual visitor. ... It is obvious that if a library is to perform its function of elevating the people, it will need to adopt methods other than buying a fine collection of books and housing them in an attractive building and then waiting in a dignified way for the people to come. The scholarly and studious will come as surely as the needle turns to the north, but the others will wait until the library goes to them. ... How to reach the busy men and women, how to carry wholesome and enjoyable books to the far-away corners of the city, how to enlist the interest of tired factory girls, how to put the workingman in touch with the art books relating to his craft and so increase the value of his labor and the dignity of his day's work—these are some of the things which I conceive to be my duty to study, if I would help this public library to become what it is for.

All of these ideas and more she put into action.

Her activities on behalf of libraries were not confined to Minneapolis, however. Early in her career, she recognized the value of library systems and the need for state aid to libraries if library service was to be extended to more and more people. After working with three legislatures, and rallying support from women's groups and influential citizens throughout the state, she was given much of the credit for the passage in 1899 of legislation which provided a means whereby communities throughout the state could start and maintain their own libraries. That same legislation also established a state library commission and travelling libraries for service to rural districts. She was influential in the passage of similar legislation in the state of Wisconsin as well. Then, from 1899 to 1918, she served as recording secretary of the Minnesota Library Commission.

Gratia Countryman was active in professional and civic affairs both locally and nationally. The organizations to which she belonged, a number of which she helped organize, showed a wide range of interests, including the usual professional associations as well as governmental, civic, social service, educational, and cultural groups. Locally, she served as first president or chairman of a number of organizations. Nationally, she was elected a fellow of the American Library Institute in 1906 and remained a member until 1942, and she served in a number of capacities in the American Library Association, including the presidency in 1933-1934. In 1935, she was an ALA delegate to the Second International Library and Bibliographic Congress in Madrid. Even after retirement, she remained active, serving as chairman of the Legislative Committee for the Library Planning Board and directing a newspaper-indexing project for the Minneapolis Public Library for three years.

Her many activities brought her a number of honors. She was elected to Phi Beta Kappa as a student, and after her retirement, she was elected to membership in Delta Kappa Gamma, national honor society for women in education. In 1931, she was given the Civic Service Honor Medal by the Inter-Racial Service Council for her work with the foreign-born, being the first woman to receive this honor. In 1932, the University of Minnesota awarded her an honorary master's degree, again the first such degree given by the institution to a woman as well as the first to one of its own graduates.

That Gratia Countryman had high ideals for the library profession and firm convictions as to what good library service should be is evident from her writings. She saw the need to raise the public's consciousness about the vital role the library could play in American life and the need for state and federal support to link libraries in state and national networks. Her bibliography contains more than fifteen journal articles; a pamphlet, *Library Work as a Profession* (published by the Woman's Occupational Bureau of Minneapolis); and an article on "Librarianship" in *Vocations Open to College Women* (a bulletin published by the University of Minnesota).

Gratia Countryman died in Duluth, Minnesota, on July 26, 1953. She had never married, but, pioneer that she was, she did adopt a son, Wellington, an unusual step for a single woman at that time.

Long after her retirement and for years after her death, those who had known or worked under Gratia Countryman still thought of her as representing the Minneapolis Public Library. A capable administrator who commanded both respect and affection, a severe task-master and sympathetic friend, she was an inspiration to her staff, a number of whom went on to important library positions in other parts of the country. A small woman with a warm smile, low voice, firm and gracious manner, she was also outspoken and forthright, efficient and businesslike, decisive and fearless. Her strong, impressive personality along with her drive to improve library service helped earn her a reputation as a pioneer in professional librarianship.

Biographical listings and obituaries—*National Cyclopaedia of American Biography* E; *Who Was Who in America* III (1951-1960); *Who's Who among Minnesota Women, 1924.* Compiled and published by Mary Dillon Foster, 1924; *Who's Who in Library Service*, 1st ed., 2nd ed.; *Who's Who in Minnesota, 1941.* Minneapolis: Minnesota Editorial Association, 1942. **Books and articles about the biographee**—Casey, Genevieve M. "Gratia A. Countryman." *Wilson Library Bulletin* 11:688-89 (June 1937); Dyste, Mena C. "Gratia Alta Countryman, Librarian." Master's thesis, Library School, University of Minnesota, 1965; Potter, Greta Lagro. "Cratia Countryman, Pioneer." *Wilson Library Bulletin* 28:470-71 (Feb. 1954); Starr, Augusta. "Gratia Countryman, 1866-1953." *Minnesota Libraries* 17:195-96 (Sept. 1953). **Primary sources and archival materials**—The Minneapolis Public Library has an extensive collection of clippings on Gratia Countryman, a scrapbook, and "Memory Book of Fact and Fancy." The Annual Reports (1899-1936) and the minutes of the Library Board meetings contain additional information. Her papers are held by the Minnesota Historical Society (St. Paul), and the University of Minnesota Archives include information on her as a student and an alumna.

—NANCY FREEMAN ROHDE

CRANE, EVAN JAY (1889-1966)

Evan Jay Crane, of the large family of George W. and Minnie B. Crane, was born February 14, 1889, in Columbus, Ohio. On September 30, 1914, E. J. Crane married Mary Marie E. Grant. To this union two children, Grant and Martha, were born. After the death of his first wife, he married Helen R. Gaine on August 10, 1943. Crane died in 1966 and was survived by his wife and two children.

E. J. Crane attended Ohio State University and received his B.A. degree in 1911. Upon his graduation, he joined the staff of the fledgling publication *Chemical Abstracts* as an associate editor. Late in 1914, Crane became acting editor and in 1915, was named editor, a position he held for 44 years until his retirement in 1958. He also served as the first director of the Chemical Abstracts Service from its inception in 1956 until his retirement. Although Crane formally retired in 1958, he never ceased to serve the publication and the organization he so successfully guided. At the time of his death, he was still actively writing and abstracting material for publication.

When E. J. Crane assumed the editorship of *Chemical Abstracts* in 1915, the American chemical industry was coming of age and establishing its independence from European-based research. However, chemical literature was in a chaotic state further complicated by vague and confused nomenclature. Prior to Crane's editorship, the annual subject index relied on the wording of the titles and whatever compound names the author had used in the article. Also authors' names were not rigorously checked for possible confusions in spelling, etc. With the annual indexes for Volume X and the first Decennial Index, a carefully classified subject entry list replaced word indexing, and an entire unified system of nomenclature had been devised so that the large numbers of chemical compounds appearing in the literature could be indexed coherently without scattering entries, this being done according to an alphabetical list of compound families. The author indexes were improved through a system of checking and rechecking authors' names. An annual formula index was added with Volume XIV and a numerical patent index with Volume XXIV. These achievements were coupled with Crane's progress in the area of chemical nomenclature, both of which have proven invaluable to science libraries and to science divisions within general libraries.

In 1937 when A. E. Marshall presented the Society of the Chemical Industry's Chemical Industry Medal to E. J. Crane, he characterized *Chemical Abstracts* and its editor "as the vital working tool of the chemical profession which has changed chemists from Lilliputians to Gullivers in the field of science." Today, the indexing system first developed by Crane and his associates remains the standard that other scientific abstracting and indexing services throughout the world strive to emulate.

E. J. Crane was not only a skilled editor but an effective manager. During his tenure, the *Chemical Abstracts* physical facilities were expanded from a single room in the McPherson Chemical Laboratory to its own spacious building with over 200 employees. This facility, too, was overflowing due to the ever-increasing growth of the chemical literature.

Under Crane's direction, *Chemical Abstracts'* goal of obtaining complete, quality, and timely coverage of the chemical literature was never compromised. During World War II, he set up a staff of abstractors that operated in Switzerland under the most trying conditions. After the War, with the cooperation of General Douglas MacArthur, an active team of abstractors was organized to cover for *Chemical Abstracts* much of the wartime Japanese literature which had been unavailable in the years 1941-1945. Anthony Standen, who wrote the Diamond Jubilee history of the American Chemical Society, said, "*Chemical Abstracts* . . . does an all but perfect job of covering all the new work that is published in chemistry in the entire world. It boils all this information down to a bare minimum to a point where further boiling would inevitably result in loss of yield, and publishes it with exceedingly few mistakes. *And it comes out on time.*"

Early in his career, E. J. Crane recognized a basic problem of science information service—that of coupling the bibliographic awareness function of the abstracting and indexing services with an effective document delivery system through the use of the research libraries. In 1908, *Chemical Abstracts* published its first *List of Periodicals Abstracted by Chemical Abstracts*. The *List* and its subsequent revisions served several functions: 1) to help the user of *Chemical Abstracts* identify the complete titles of materials cited by abbreviated title; and 2) to provide the user with a list of publishers and addresses for the abstracted material. Beginning with the 1922 edition, the usefulness of the *List of Periodicals* was greatly enhanced by the inclusion of data listing selected libraries which currently received the abstracted publications. The *List of Periodicals Abstracted by Chemical Abstracts*, under the editorship of E. J. Crane, stands alone as the first major union list covering not only the literature of chemistry and chemical technology, but much of the entire field of science and technology as well.

In addition to his stewardship of *Chemical Abstracts*, E. J. Crane was a leader in the effort to organize and refine chemical nomenclature. In 1918, he became the chairman of the American Chemical Society's Committee on Nomenclature, Spelling, and Pronunciation. During his years of service, he was a member of numerous national and international organic and inorganic nomenclature commissions. In 1959, Crane was appointed to be a U.S. State Department delegate to UNESCO's Paris Conference on Abstracting. He assisted in the founding of the American Chemical Society's Division of Chemical Literature and became its first chairman in 1958. From 1954 to 1960, Crane was the United States representative in chemistry to the Abstracting Board of the International Council of Scientific Unions. In 1958, he served as the chairman of the first meeting of the National Federation of Science Abstracting and Indexing Services.

E. J. Crane proudly said on numerous occasions that he held only two degrees: B.A. and C.A. In 1938, however, his alma mater, Ohio State University, in recognition of his contributions to the betterment of science and his fellow man, bestowed on him the honorary degree of Doctor of Science. Crane also received numerous awards and citations for his work in scientific abstracting and indexing. The American Section of the Society of Chemical Industry (London) awarded him its Chemical Industry Medal in 1937. The American Chemical Society, at its Diamond Jubilee Meeting in 1951, presented him with its highest award, the Priestly Medal. In 1953, Crane received the Austin M. Patterson Award for documentation in chemistry from the Dayton, Ohio, section of the American Chemical Society.

Crane was also an avid author. He published 80 articles; 32 of these were published in the leading chemical periodicals and serials, and the remaining 48 appeared in their entirety in *Chemical Abstracts*. In 1927, he published, with Austin M. Patterson, *A Guide to the Literature of Chemistry* (John Wiley and Sons, Inc., 1927; later revised with Austin M. Patterson and Eleanor B. Marr, 1957). In 1959, he edited *CA Today—The Production of Chemical Abstracts* (American Chemical Society, 1959). Between 1930 and 1966, Crane also wrote 110 numbers of *The Little CA*, a publication sent to the many abstractors and employees of *Chemical Abstracts*.

E. J. Crane was not only a literature chemist but an active participant in community affairs. In 1924, he was elected mayor of Upper Arlington, a Columbus, Ohio, suburb. He was also a long-term member and past president of the Rotary International Club of Columbus.

In August 1958, *Chemical and Engineering News* paid tribute to E. J. Crane's lifetime of service to the chemical literature by stating that "if there is one man that could be called the keeper of the keys to the wealth of the chemical industry, that man would be Evan Jay Crane, who has literally devoted his life to unlocking doors to chemical knowledge." Crane died on December 30, 1966, at the age of 77.

Biographical listings and obituaries—"CA's E. J. Crane Dead at 77." *Chemical and Engineering News* 45:18 (Jan. 9, 1967); "Evan Jay Crane 1889-1966." *Journal of Chemical Documentation* 7:62-63 (May 1967); *Who Was Who in America* IV (1961-1968). Books and articles about the biographee—"Evan Jay Crane." *Chemical and Engineering News* 36:80 (Aug. 4, 1958); Kenyon, Richard L. "Evan Jay Crane—Editorial." *Chemical and Engineering News* 45:5 (Jan. 9, 1967); Patterson, Austin M. "An Appreciation of E. Jay Crane—Guest Editorial." *Chemical and Engineering News* 25:3561 (1947); "Top Chemical Abstractor Receives Top Chemical Award." *Chemical and Engineering News* 29:4272 (1951).

—ROBERT K. DIKEMAN

CRAVER, HARRISON WARWICK (1875-1951)

Harrison Warwick Craver, born August 10, 1875, in Owaneco, Illinois, was the son of Harrison Eugene and Caroline Ernestine Weirauch Craver. He was graduated from Rose Polytechnic Institute at Terre Haute, Indiana, in 1895 with a Bachelor of Science degree in chemistry. (That institution also awarded him an honorary Doctor of Science degree in 1933.) He married Adelaide Nevins Martin, herself a librarian, on June 17, 1902. The Cravers had no children.

Following his graduation from college, Craver worked as an expert chemist for the steel companies of Kirkpatrick and Company, and later, Shoenberger Steel Company in Leechburg and Pittsburgh, Pennsylvania, and Graham, Virginia. It was in 1900 that he became interested in technical literature and was brought to the attention of Andrew Carnegie (q.v.), who was himself interested in establishing a technology department in the Carnegie Library of Pittsburgh. Craver worked at this for two years in 1900 and 1901, after which he went back to industry for one year with the Allegheny Iron and Steel Company in Brackenridge, Pennsylvania. In 1902, he returned to the Carnegie Library of Pittsburgh as technology librarian, and he was advanced to the position of librarian of the entire Library in 1908. In 1917, he left that institution to become director of the Engineering Societies Library in New York City, a position he held until his retirement in 1945, after which he remained as consulting librarian to that Library until his death on July 27, 1951.

Harrison W. Craver was a pioneer in the field of technical libraries. Until his employment by the Carnegie Library of Pittsburgh, virtually no collections of consequence in the field of technology existed anywhere in this country. His own interests in assembling such a collection coincided with those of Carnegie and the management of the Library, and during his tenure as head of the Technology Division (and later as librarian of the Library), he completed what men of science regarded as one of the world's finest collections of works on the subjects of technology and business.

When Craver came to the Engineering Societies Library in 1917, each of the libraries of the four founder societies—American Society of Civil Engineers, American Institute of Mining Engineers, American Society of Mechanical Engineers, and American Institute of Electrical Engineers (now IEEE)—was kept as a separate collection. He determined to combine them into a single unified collection with one catalog. He also decided that the most useful and efficient type of subject catalog was a classified one using the Universal Decimal Classification (UDC) scheme. To assist in this major cataloging operation, in 1919, he hired Margaret Mann (q.v.) from the Carnegie Library of Pittsburgh to be the head of the Cataloging Department at the Engineering Societies Library. Because there were then no available English editions of the UDC schedules, he personally translated them from the French for internal use at the Engineering Societies Library. (See his "Report on Cataloging to the Library Board of the Library" for June 17, 1919.)

Wanting to make the Engineering Societies Library the premier library of the country in the fields of engineering and technology, Craver personally approved all additions to the collection, and during his tenure, no material was added that did not meet his high standards of permanent value. Many of the principles he established in the early days of the Engineering Societies Library are still being followed today. (See Craver's "The Role of the Library in Engineering Education and Research," in *Inauguration of Oliver C. Carmichael as Chancellor of Vanderbilt University*, Nashville, 1938.)

Craver was very active in professional library associations throughout his career and had a strong influence on many of his confrères. He served on the ALA Council (1909-1917, 1924-1931) and on its Executive Board (1913-1917) and was president of the Association in 1937-1938. He was also a member of the Newcomen Society, the History of Science Society, and a fellow of the American Association for the Advancement of Science. Too, he was president of the Keystone Library Association in 1908-1909 and of the New York Library Club in 1921-1922, and he served for many years as a trustee of the Great Neck Public Library in Long Island, New York.

Biographical listings and obituaries—[Obituary]. *Library Journal* 76:1295 (Sept. 1, 1951); *Who Was Who in America* III (1951-1960); *Who's Who in Library Service*, 1st ed., 2nd ed. Books and articles about the biographee—Tarnow, William H. "The Engineering Societies Library: A History of Its Origins and Early Development 1852-1928." Brookville, N.Y.: Graduate Library School, Long Island University, 1967. 2v. in 1; United Engineering Trustees, Inc., New York. [Citation]. "To Dr. Harrison W. Craver in Commemoration of His Twenty-Five Years of Distinguished Service as Director of the Engineering Societies Library." New York, 1942. IV.

Primary sources and archival materials—The files at the Engineering Societies Library for 1917-1951.

—S. K. CABEEN

CRUNDEN, FREDERICK MORGAN (1847-1911)

Frederick Morgan Crunden was for over thirty years librarian of the St. Louis Public Library, and in that position, was also a leader in the public library movement in the United States. He was born September 1, 1847, in Gravesend, England, to Benjamin Robert and Mary Morgan Crunden, of Saxon, Welsh, and French ancestry. When Frederick was very young, the family moved to St. Louis, but shortly thereafter, his father died. The boy was brought up by his mother, a woman of great determination and ability, who saw that he was educated in the St. Louis public schools. He amply fulfilled his mother's faith in him by graduating from high school in 1865 as valedictorian of his class and recipient of a scholarship to Washington University.

An excellent student, Crunden pursued the "arts and sciences" curriculum, securing his Bachelor of Arts degree in 1868 and his Master of Arts in 1872, while teaching to support himself at the University. Following his graduation, he became a teacher and principal at the Benton and Jefferson schools in St. Louis, and finally at the University itself, where he taught mathematics and elocution. During his years as student and teacher, Crunden had evinced an interest in libraries, which probably led to the next step in his career.

In 1876, differences between the Board of Managers of the St. Louis Public School Library and the librarian, John J. Bailey, reached a crisis point, and Bailey was removed from his position at the beginning of 1877. The Board selected as his successor Frederick Morgan Crunden, then 29 years old and vacationing in Colorado for his health. Possibly the Board wished to take advantage of Crunden's abilities in a less strenuous position than that of teacher, and, knowing his bibliographical inclinations, decided on the position of librarian as a solution. In any case, upon his return, Crunden became secretary of the Board and librarian on January 17, 1877. Ironically, the newly formed American Library Association protested his appointment in the *American Library Journal* of February 1877, condemning the St. Louis officials for dismissing Bailey and replacing him with a young man without library experience. However, this opinion was soon reversed as Crunden rose to become one of ALA's most prominent members.

The Public School Library of St. Louis had been established by a private library society in 1865, but state legislation enabled the city School Board to contribute up to $5,000 annually for its support. Subsequently its management was transferred to the School Board, which contributed gradually increasing amounts over the years. Still it remained a quasi-private library, with borrowing privileges limited to those who paid their $4-a-year memberships, although teachers and their students were admitted free. Then in 1874, the reading room was opened, free, to all. When Crunden became librarian in 1877, the Library had 5,772 registered borrowers, 10 employees, a book budget of $4,800, and about 40,000 volumes. It was housed on the second floor of a building also containing the Board of Education and a public night school.

Crunden immediately went to work with an enthusiasm that never left him during his long tenure in the Library. In keeping with the prevalent library philosophy of the time, he sought to make the Library a free public library removed from the aegis of the School Board, with an adequate budget, and housed in a suitable building of its own. But none of these developments came about swiftly or easily.

The word "school" was removed from the name of the Library, and by 1885, membership fees were lowered to $2 for adults and $1 for those under 18 years. Crunden was largely responsible also for drafting and getting through the Missouri legislature an act enabling communities to tax themselves, upon approval of the local voters, to establish free public libraries (1885). After a vigorous campaign by Crunden and his supporters to educate the voters of St. Louis, the city finally took advantage of this opportunity in 1893 to pass, by a six-to-one margin, the proper legislation to transform the Library into a true "free public library." At the same time, the Library was moved into new quarters on the sixth and seventh floors of the building of the Board of Education, an improvement over the old quarters but still far from the suitable building that Crunden desired. Happily the newly constituted Library was a demonstrable success, for within a year, registrations had increased four-fold and circulation had risen three and one-half times. The Library was thus on its way to becoming one of the major urban library systems of its day.

Crunden was an efficient and dynamic administrator. He took personal interest in his staff as well as in their professional development, which resulted in good morale. He publicized the Library vigorously through the press, posters, his own speeches, and the literary readings for which he and his wife were widely known. Yet, despite the separation of the Library from the School Board, Crunden was also a leader in the movement for greater cooperation between public libraries and schools, working with ALA and the National Education Association to promote school libraries.

The St. Louis Public School Library had emphasized service to children and schools before Crunden, but he continued and enlarged upon this tradition. As early as 1870, the Library had had no lower age limit for children. Bailey had given spirited book talks in the schools, and Crunden, with his rhetorical gifts, did likewise. Too, a librarian was placed in charge of the "children's alcove" in 1894, a children's room was established in 1897, and extensive services were provided to schools. Foreign language collections for immigrants were one of Crunden's special interests, and the German residents in particular were said to have been highly impressed by the quality of the German language books. More generally, Crunden's interest in sociology, political science, literature, and dramatics was an important factor in building up the Library's collections in these areas.

Crunden had the wide ranging interests so desirable in a public librarian. Hence, he was active in many organizations, which enabled him to understand his community better and, at the same time, to publicize the Library. A partial list of these memberships indicates the scope of his concerns: St. Louis Academy of Science, Missouri Historical Society, St. Louis Artists' Guild, Round Table, University Club, McCullough Dramatic Club, and the Single Tax League.

However, Crunden's national and international reputation was probably due largely to his active participation in the library profession. Despite his early rebuff, he joined the American Library Association in 1878 as number 129. He was a member and enthusiastic supporter of the elite American Library Institute and the first president of the Missouri Library Association, but it was for ALA that his most important work was done. He became a councillor of ALA in 1882 and remained in that position for most of his life. In addition to serving on innumerable committees, he was also vice-president in 1887-1888, president in 1889-1890, and a life member. At the ALA meeting in 1893, during the World's Columbian Exposition in Chicago, he contributed a paper on "The Executive Department; Supervision, Building, Finances." In London in 1897, at the Second International Conference of Librarians, he was a vice-president and read a paper on the role of the library in education. The climax of his work for ALA came in 1904, however, when he served as host librarian for the ALA meeting and exhibits at the Louisiana Purchase Exposition in St. Louis. On this occasion he worked indefatigably, and possibly to the detriment of his health, to set up as an ALA exhibit a "model," functioning branch of the St. Louis Public Library in the Missouri building.

Crunden wrote extensively for the St. Louis press and for national magazines, but most influentially for the library periodicals. His first article for *Library Journal* was "Duplicates for Pay" (January 1879), and thereafter, this periodical carried many of his articles and papers, as well as countless items about his work in St. Louis and for ALA. His series, "How Things Are Done in One American Library,"

appeared in the English publication *The Library* from 1899 to 1901, and he had intended to use it as the basis for a book on library administration that remained unfinished at the time of his death.

On June 13, 1889, Crunden married Kate Edmondson, an English woman with considerable dramatic talent who was a great help to him in the social amenities of his professional life. Together they gave well-attended evenings of literary readings, and they cultivated leading actors of the time, who often provided the library staff with free tickets and gave lectures at the library. The Crundens' only child, Frederick Edmondson, died in infancy.

Crunden, warm and outgoing, made many friends, especially among his own staff members and his colleagues at ALA. Convivial and witty, he enjoyed social gatherings. Typically he compiled an "ALA Songbook" for the conference of 1890 at Fabyan's (in the White Mountains), and he couched his observations on the classification controversy in the form of a parody of Gilbert and Sullivan's "Lord Chancellor's Song."

Crunden was quite serious about getting a new library building, however, even though voters twice rejected attempts to finance one. Finally, in 1901, Crunden applied to Andrew Carnegie (q.v.) for funds for this purpose and a million dollars was promised— one-half for a main building and one-half for branch buildings—provided that the city guaranteed a suitable location and an annual income of $150,000. This time the vote was more than seven to one in favor of a new building, and Crunden immersed himself in plans for construction. Many people felt that these exertions, combined with his ALA work at the fair in St. Louis in 1904, contributed to his physical collapse in 1906, when he suffered what may have been a stroke. His mind was left a blank. He rallied occasionally, though, and during one of these moments, he was able to examine the Cass Gilbert plans for the new building. In the hope that he might recover, Crunden was allowed to continue as the nominal head of the Library until 1909, when he retired. He was succeeded by Arthur E. Bostwick (q.v.) of New York, who was also to become a leader in the American public library movement and continue the Crunden tradition at St. Louis. On October 28, 1911, Frederick Morgan Crunden died at St. Luke's Hospital, where he had been confined for five years. Funeral services were held in the Unitarian Church and were followed by cremation.

The palatial building that was the culmination of his dream was opened in January 1912, with elaborate ceremonies in the main hall, featuring Herbert Putnam (q.v.), Librarian of Congress, as speaker. Speakers paid tribute to Crunden, and words from one of his speeches were carved in stone on the new building: "Recorded thought is our chief heritage from the past, the most lasting legacy we can leave for the future. Books are the most enduring monument of man's achievements. Only through books can civilization become cumulative." Comparing Crunden and Carnegie (also quoted in the building's stone), Melvil Dewey (q.v.) said, "One gave a million dollars, the other gave his life."

In 1904, the St. Louis Public Library opened a Frederick Morgan Crunden Branch, which served until the building was sold in 1954. In 1961, St. Louis named a second branch in memory of Crunden, and it continues in service to the present. Mrs. Crunden died on July 19, 1945, and left a bequest of $5,000 to the St. Louis Public Library. In 1954, when a new young people's room was opened at the central library, each of the books bore a bookplate reading, "The Frederick Morgan Crunden Collection of Books for Young People, given by Kate Edmondson Crunden in memory of their son Frederick Edmondson Crunden."

Biographical listings and obituaries—*The Book of St. Louisans.* St. Louis: St. Louis Republic, 1906; *Dictionary of American Biography* 4 (Stella M. Drum); *National Cyclopaedia of American Biography* 6; [Obituary]. *Library Journal* 36:569-70 (Nov. 1911). (Includes "A Tribute from Melvil Dewey"); *Who Was Who in America* I (1897-1942). **Books and articles about the biographee**—Bostwick, Arthur E. *Frederick Morgan Crunden; a Memorial Bibliography.* St. Louis: St. Louis Public Library, 1914; Compton, Charles H. *Fifty Years of Progress of the St. Louis Public Library: 1876-1926.* St. Louis: St. Louis Public Library, 1926; Doane, Bertha. "Frederick M. Crunden, Library Statesman." *Wilson Library Bulletin* 29:446-49 (Feb. 1955); Hyde, William, and H. L. Conrad, eds. *Encyclopedia of the History of St. Louis.* New York: The Southern History Co., 1899. Vol. 1; Moody, Katherine T. "As It Was in the Beginning." *Public Libraries* 30:138-42 (March 1925). **Primary sources and archival materials**—The St. Louis Public Library's archives are located in the Library's Gardner Rare Book Room and are at present largely unsorted. One box of Crunden papers, however, includes correspondence, broadsides advertising his readings, and 172 pages of typed copies of newspaper articles covering the period from the late 1860s to 1911. The Library's *Annual Reports* and a sporadically published, variously named bulletin from those years provide additional information.

—BUDD L. GAMBEE

CULVER, ESSAE MARTHA (1882-1973)

Essae Martha Culver, the youngest of four daughters and two sons, was born in Emporia, Kansas, on November 15, 1882, to Joseph Franklin and Mary Murphy Culver. The family moved to Phoenix, Arizona, upon the death of Judge Culver, and there Essae graduated from high school. She received the Bachelor of Letters degree from Pomona College (Claremont, California) in 1904. She entered Pomona with the expectation that she would prepare for teaching. Her mother had been a teacher, two sisters and one brother were teachers, and even her father had taught before entering the legal profession. Essae firmly rejected teaching as a career for herself,

however. Upon graduation, she accepted the position of assistant librarian at the College, leaving it to attend the New York State Library School in 1908.

Upon completion of her professional study at Albany, she had to make a difficult choice between two available positions—one at a university and the other at a public library. Her decision to accept the latter set the pattern of her library career and determined the nature of her major contribution to librarianship. From 1909 to 1912, she served as librarian of the Salem, Oregon, Public Library, and during vacation periods, she visited travelling library stations for the Oregon State Library. From 1912 to 1925, she was, successively, librarian of the Glenn, Butte, and Merced County libraries, and library visitor for the California State Library.

It was during these California years that Milton J. Ferguson (q.v.), California state librarian, came to know her and her capabilities. In 1925, when asked as president of the League of Library Commissions to make recommendations for an executive secretary to the Louisiana Library Commission, he suggested Essae Martha Culver. Upon the recommendation of the League of Library Commissions, Louisiana had been chosen for a Carnegie Corporation grant to demonstrate a program of state-wide library development. The grant, originally for three years, but later extended to five, was to be administered by the Louisiana Library Commission, under the general supervision of the League. Thus, Culver came to Louisiana in July 1925 to plan and implement this project. She found on her arrival tremendous problems, but problems for which her Oregon and California experiences had eminently prepared her. Fortunately for Louisiana, she also found challenges and opportunities for creative librarianship sufficient to persuade her to make what she had accepted as a short-term assignment the final chapter of her professional career.

In 1925, Louisiana had a fairly adequate permissive library law, but only five free public libraries had been established under the law, none of which served rural people. The state also had a legally constituted Library Commission, to which strong appointments had been made, but it had no physical facilities and no library or staff with which to work. Only as a result of the grant were there funds with which to operate, and, with the appointment of Essae Culver, the beginnings of a professional staff. Academic libraries were weak, and school libraries were almost non-existent. Only one other trained librarian was at work in the state, and no library training programs existed on a permanent basis.

Essae Culver's approach to these problems was two-pronged. She saw as her first responsibility the development of a strong central reference library to serve both the state government and borrowers throughout the state, either through their libraries, or, where no libraries as yet existed, directly. Paralleling this responsibility, she saw it as the Commission's responsibility to encourage the establishment of public libraries through which every citizen of Louisiana could be reached. The state's population distribution and its unique system of parish (i.e., county) government made the parish the logical unit of service. Eventually, larger units of service would be required and would become feasible, but that is a much later chapter.

Recognizing that voters who had little or no experience with libraries could hardly be expected to vote upon themselves a tax to support libraries, she developed a plan for demonstration libraries. Under this plan, the Library Commission, upon request of the local governing body and at minimal expense to the parish, would set up and administer for a specified time (usually a year) a demonstration library. Near the end of the demonstration period, a tax election would be called to determine whether the library would be continued with local support. It is for this demonstration method of library extension that Culver is best known, and it is perhaps her greatest contribution to library practice.

Beyond these developments for which she had direct responsibility, from the outset she saw her role and that of the Commission as one of concern for libraries of all types—school, academic, and special, as well as public—and for library education programs which would prepare the personnel to staff these libraries. One of her first efforts was to encourage the development of a strong school library program within the State Department of Education, and largely through her influence, Louisiana was one of the first Southern states to appoint a school library supervisor. She was influential also in the securing of a General Education Board grant under which the Library School of Louisiana State University was established in 1931.

When Essae Culver retired in July 1962, after 37 years of service, with the title of state librarian emeritus, she could look with much pride upon progress in all aspects of library service, for much of which she was directly responsible, and in all of which she had played an important part. The major task of achieving state-wide coverage with parish and regional libraries, despite floods, the worldwide Great Depression, and wars, was virtually completed. Those few parishes still without libraries were awaiting their demonstrations, plans for which were already on the drawing boards. The State Library, as the Commission had become in 1946, with expanded responsibilities, was now handsomely housed in its own building on the State Capitol grounds. More importantly, it had become a strong reference center in its own right and a backup source for the network of parish and regional libraries serving the state.

Essae Culver's success had been due in large part to her skill in working with people individually and in organized groups. In a state and at a time when politics seemed to be pervasive (this was the Louisiana of Huey Long until his assassination in 1935), she had found it possible to work with political leaders and governing bodies at all levels, while keeping libraries always apolitical. She had enlisted the aid of lay groups such as the Home Demonstration Councils, the Federation of Women's Clubs, and the various men's service clubs in support of libraries. She had initiated the Citizen's Library Movement and utilized it effectively as a citizens' lobby. She had made maximum use of her own Commission members and of the parish library trustees as spokesmen for libraries.

Her influence and leadership in professional library organizations had been strong at state, regional, and national levels. She had served as president of the Louisiana Library Association in 1928-1929, the Southwestern Library Association in 1936-1938, the League of Library Commissions in 1931-1933, and the American Library Association in 1940-1941. Her inaugural address, given at the Boston ALA Conference and entitled "A Call for Action," was exactly that—a call for "a continuing campaign for the eradication of the bookless portions of America." This was the campaign that she had been waging in Louisiana since 1925 with telling success, and that she would continue to wage in her state, her region, and the nation so long as she lived. The slogan she proposed for ALA in her address, "Deeds Not Words," was one by which she conducted her own campaigns, and one that quite well describes the manner of her performance.

Academic honors came to her from the two institutions with which she was most closely associated. Her alma mater awarded her the L.H.D. in 1954; she was the first Pomona alumna to be so honored. Louisiana State University conferred upon her the Litt.D. in 1959 at the dedication of its own new library building. Also, in 1959, the American Library Association awarded her its highest honor, the Joseph W. Lippincott Award, citing her for "providing the world of librarianship with a remarkable and inspired example of library leadership," and referring to her work as that of a "consummate librarian—one who has brought to the task administrative genius, political acumen, and a measureless capacity for sustained effort."

Both in recognition of her contribution to library development and as an incentive to its members to follow her example, the Louisiana Library Association established in 1962, on the occasion of her retirement, the Essae M. Culver Award for distinguished service to librarianship.

Following her retirement, and until her death on January 3, 1973, Essae Culver continued to make her home in Baton Rouge, leaving it from time to time for visits to family and friends, for professional meetings, and for the foreign travel for which she had so little time during her busy working years. For the most part, however, she spent her retirement years enjoying music, books, football, and, most of all, the companionship of her friends.

Biographical listings and obituaries—*Current Biography* (1940); [Obituary]. *American Libraries* 4:217 (April 1973); [Obituary]. *Library Journal* 98:825 (March 15, 1973); *Who's Who in Library Service*, 1st ed.   Books and articles about the biographee—"Announcing the Joseph W. Lippincott Award 1959 for Distinguished Service to Essae M. Culver." *LLA Bulletin* 22:75 (Fall 1959); "Citation for University Honors: Essae M. Culver." *LLA Bulletin* 22:106 (Winter 1959); Currier, Lura G. "The Lengthened Shadow." *ALA Bulletin* 53:35-37 (Jan. 1959); Dixon, Margaret, and Nantelle Gittinger. "The First Twenty-five Years." *LLA Bulletin* 13:36-48 (Spring 1950); Ferguson, Milton J. "A Quarter of a Century After." *LLA Bulletin* 13:35-36 (Spring 1950); Fontaine, Sue. "Talk of Many Things." *LLA Bulletin* 25:59-63, 83 (Summer 1962); Richardson, Cary J. "Pomona Honors Essae M. Culver." *LLA Bulletin* 17:131-32 (Fall 1954); "Tributes for Essae Martha Culver." *LLA Bulletin* 25:65-66 (Summer 1962).

—FLORRINELL F. MORTON

CUNNINGHAM, EILEEN ROACH (1894-1965)

Eileen Roach was born on March 28, 1894, in Baltimore, Maryland, the only daughter of Joseph and Caroline Ferguson Roach. Her father was a physician, and in later life, Eileen Cunningham often attributed her interest in medicine to her childhood recollections of Walter Reed, William Osler, and other professional acquaintances of her father.

The young girl's formal education was limited, but she later liked to recall the rigorous instruction she received during her girlhood from her tutors and governesses. Instruction was supplemented by travel, and after the age of ten, she spent three summers in Europe gaining facility in languages. She attended the Roland Park School for Girls in Baltimore and enrolled for a limited time during World War I in the Johns Hopkins University, where her primary interest was chemistry.

Writing in 1947, Eileen Cunningham described the period from 1918 to 1923 as follows:

Later on when my father lost most of his money and I needed to do something practical I made use of my language training and my knowledge of science ... to do bibliographies and translations for persons doing medical research at Johns Hopkins. This work was a very interesting and profitable experience ... because I learned how to become a research worker in a medical library before I ever thought of becoming a librarian.

Eleanor Steinke, a colleague in later life, has observed that Cunningham's library career was marked throughout by her foremost concern, gained during

this period, for the needs and problems of the library user. Also during this period, she organized and classified a large collection of reprints for the Department of Anatomy at Johns Hopkins.

On July 2, 1923, Eileen Roach was married to a promising young physician in that department, Robert Sydney Cunningham. In 1925, Dr. Cunningham became head of the Department of Anatomy at the Vanderbilt University Medical School, and the couple moved from Baltimore to Nashville, Tennessee. In 1926, Eileen Cunningham was appointed research assistant in the Medical Library there; the following year she became its assistant librarian; and in 1929, she was named Vanderbilt University medical librarian, a post she was to hold for 27 years. Under her direction, the Medical Library of Vanderbilt University flourished and, within a decade, was recognized as "the largest medical school library in the South." She also taught medical bibliography there beginning in 1930, and was designated professor of medical library science in the Medical School in 1949. Her marriage, however, did not last, and she and her husband were divorced, childless, in 1938.

Cunningham attended her first meeting of the Medical Library Association in 1927, beginning a vigorous life of service to the broader profession that was to continue for more than three decades. Although the responsibilities and committee assignments that she accepted in the MLA seem innumerable, ranging over virtually all areas of the field, she had three key interests, each of which had been more or less presaged by her early life and training: 1) a concern for the problems of journal literature, 2) activities on the international scene, and 3) work toward a satisfactory classification scheme for medical literature.

An early exponent of the value of well-indexed and abstracted medical journal literature, Eileen Cunningham became the first chairman of MLA's Committee on Periodical and Serial Publications in 1932. Largely through work initiated by this group, a deputation including Cunningham waited upon a number of Nazi officials in Germany in 1937 in a successful bid to have German periodical publishers modify pricing practices that discriminated against libraries. In the same year, she became chairman of IFLA's Committee on Periodicals and Serial Publications, a post which she filled effectively for two decades thereafter.

Cunningham's international service began in 1935, when she attended the Second International Congress on Libraries and Bibliography in Madrid. During the subsequent quarter-century, her trips abroad were numerous and varied. Perhaps most important among her foreign assignments were her surveys of the medical libraries of Colombia and Mexico for the Rockefeller Foundation, her efforts to reorganize the medical faculty library at the Universidad Mayor de San Marcos in Lima, and her work establishing and operating from 1958 to 1960 the Basic Medical Sciences Institute Library in Karachi, under an ICA contact with Indiana University.

It was probably the "Cunningham Classification," however, that made the Vanderbilt medical librarian's name most widely recognized. Prepared initially in 1927 for her local use only, Eileen Cunningham's *Classification for Medical Literature* soon became widely used and went through five editions by 1967, becoming the all-time bestseller of the Vanderbilt University Press. Completed at a time when most medical libraries were seeking better ways of organizing their collections, the "Cunningham Classification" was most used worldwide until the National Library of Medicine system gained supremacy in the 1950s. The Cunningham scheme was the first to be arranged according to the standard medical school curriculum, with preclinical sciences first, organic systems of the body next, then clinical subjects, with paramedical fields last.

By 1949, Eileen Cunningham could be called "perhaps the best-known medical librarian in the world." Two years earlier, she had become the third woman ever to be elected president of the Medical Library Association, and she had just been designated the first recipient of the MLA's Marcia C. Noyes Award "for outstanding achievement in the field of medical library science." A bibliography of her published works extends to more than fifty items.

Cunningham's work at Vanderbilt, however, always came first. Sometime-colleague Mildred Crowe Langner captured the overwhelming energy of this intrepid lady in the following sentences:

> Her dedication to her work and her meticulous attention to detail were unbelievable. She labored long into the early morning hours and was a most familiar sight to harried physicians as they burst into the library seeking answers to critical questions any time between midnight and dawn. Her desk was always a catastrophic horror with papers reaching almost to the ceiling and covering chairs and parts of the floor, and she loved it that way. How she ever made order out of such chaos is unfathomable.

> Her persistence, her vitality, drive, and insatiable energy had to be seen to be believed, and when seen they were most overpowering. Just talking with her sometimes could be so enervating as to produce complete exhaustion. One would have to retire for rest and replenishment, only to return to the fray from which she had not yet departed and where she was still going strong, buoyed up by the excitement of the struggle and the absolute enjoyment she obtained from any kind of intellectual clashing of wills and opinions.

It all took its toll. In the spring of 1956, she was hospitalized with fatigue and decided to retire on July 1. She kept busy thereafter, however, in professional matters, doing volunteer work, and with such hobbies as bridge, dancing, cooking, and gardening. Ever a gracious hostess, she entertained often and with great charm. Even in age, she was beautiful and vivacious, quick to smile, and an affable, ready conversationalist. On the evening of September 21, 1965, while fulfilling responsibilities as a volunteer secretary to the Nashville chapter of the United Nations, Eileen R. Cunningham suffered a coronary thrombosis and died that night.

Biographical listings and obituaries—Langner, Mildred C. "Obituary: Eileen Roach Cunningham." *Medical Library Association Bulletin* 54:93-95 (Jan. 1966); *Who's Who in Library Service*, 1st ed., 2nd ed., 3rd ed. Books and articles about the biographee—Fitzgerald, W. A. "Mrs. Cunningham Retires." *Tennessee Librarian* 9:7-8 (Oct. 1956); Glasgow, Vicki L. "The Contributions of Eileen R. Cunningham to Medical Librarianship." M.S. in L.S. research paper, The University of North Carolina, 1971; "Medical Library Association. Citations of Honorary Membership." *Medical Library Association Bulletin* 48:474-75 (Oct. 1960). Primary sources and archival materials—Primary materials are in the possession of Mrs. Mildred C. Langner, head librarian of the University of Miami School of Medicine Library, and in the Medical Center Library at Vanderbilt University, Nashville.

—DAVID KASER

CURTIS, FLORENCE RISING (1873-1944)

Florence Rising Curtis was born September 30, 1873, at Ogdensburg, New York, one of at least two daughters of General Newton Martin and Emeline Clark Curtis. She attended Wells College (Aurora, New York) from 1891 to 1894 and although in the class of 1896, she graduated with diploma from the New York State Library School in 1898.

She then held a succession of positions: as assistant librarian, Diocesan Lending Library, All Saints Cathedral (Albany, New York, 1895-1896); as assistant at the Osterhout Free Library (Wilkes-Barre, Pennsylvania, 1894-1897); as librarian and secretary at the state Normal School (Potsdam, New York, 1900-1906); and as librarian of the Atheneum Library (Saratoga Springs, New York, 1906-1908). From 1908 to 1920, she served as an instructor and assistant professor at the University of Illinois, where she worked with Phineas L. Windsor (q.v.), Ernest J. Reece, and others. She completed her formal education during these years, earning the B.A. and B.L.S. degrees from Illinois (1911) and the M.A. degree from the University of Minnesota (1917).

During her Illinois years, Curtis developed a commitment to education for librarianship that motivated her in the years to come. With almost missionary zeal, she served as the first secretary of the Association of American Library Schools (1915-1921), first under James I. Wyer (q.v.) and then under five annually chosen presidents who were administrators of library schools. The major burden of establishing the new organization fell on Miss Curtis's shoulders. Her duties included circulating drafts of constitutional documents, evaluating institutional applications for membership, and keeping the various presidents faithful to their responsibilities.

Her desire for service and education then led to her experiences overseas as an instructor at the government preparatory school and the Honan Agricultural College, Kaifeng, China (1920-1921) and at the Philippine Normal School, Manila (1921-1922). Following her return to America, she was assistant director of the Drexel Institute Library School (1922-1925), under Anne W. Howland.

In 1925, Curtis became director of the new Hampton Institute Library School, which was dedicated to stimulating library development and professional training among Negroes. Here she not only re-established her earlier ties with the library school association, but she rigorously campaigned for her cause, which was less popular in the inter-war decade than in the mid-1970s. Wallace Van Jackson, a Hampton alumnus and later librarian of Atlanta University, summarized her contribution:

> During her period of service at Hampton more than 150 students came under her influence, and she carried the program of library extension to every state in the South. Largely as the result of her foresight and hard work scores of Negro schools and colleges have been accredited by regional agencies because, although she was primarily interested in libraries, she used her influence and energy to improve the whole educational program of the schools she visited. Miss Curtis was a familiar visitor at conferences and meetings of administrators of Negro schools during the period of service at Hampton.

Most of her public professional career and her written contributions came during her Hampton Institute years. She held membership in the Virginia Library Association and the National Association of Teachers in Colored Schools. Although a member of the American Library Association, she did not hold major office. She published two brochures: *The Collection of Social Service Material* (1915) and *The Libraries of the American State and National Institution for Delinquents, Dependents, and Defectives* (1918). She also contributed articles to library periodicals from 1910 through 1938, the most important of which were: "The Contribution of the Library School to Negro Education" (*Library Journal*, Dec. 1, 1926), "Colored Librarians in Conference" (*Library Journal*, April 15, 1927), "Librarianship as a Field for Negroes" (*Journal of Negro Education*, Jan. 1935), and "Community Service of the Library School" (*Southern Workman*, April 1938).

She was an optimistic, hard-working, singleminded library educator who inspired those who knew her—colleagues and students alike. Her loyalty was a marked attribute. As a non-paternalistic white woman dedicated to the improvement of opportunities for other races, she practiced what few others even preached at the time. In the words of one of her graduates, "her many friends among Anglo-Saxon, Negro, Chinese, and Philippino [sic] groups attest to her qualities of sincerity and unprejudiced acceptance of all persons as human beings of basic worth regardless of race, religion or status." In 1939, Hampton Institute closed its library school rather than let lack of funds dilute the quality of the training offered. Two years later, Atlanta University established its library school, continuing the mission of the former school.

Curtis always thought of her home as Ogdensburg, and spent summers there, but she wintered with her sister in Richmond, Indiana. She died there on October 6, 1944. Her religion was Unitarian; her vision was worldwide. Said one of her eulogizers: "I wish to express our heartfelt thanks for her life among us and register the hope that many other librarians will follow her example of interracial good will to the end that America may practice as well as preach democracy."

Biographical listings and obituaries—New York State Library School Association. *New York State Library School Register, 1887-1926*. New York, 1959; [Obituary]. *Library Journal* 69:1060 (Dec. 1, 1944); *Who Was Who in America* II (1943-1950); *Who's Who in Library Service*, 1st ed., 2nd ed. Books and articles about the biographee—"Accredited Library School Histories: Hampton." *Library Journal* 62:27 (Jan. 1, 1937); Davis, Donald G., Jr. *The Association of American Library Schools, 1915-1968: An Analytical History*. Metuchen, N.J.: Scarecrow Press, 1974; Jackson, Wallace Van. "Florence Rising Curtis." *Library Journal* 69:1060 (Dec. 1, 1944). Primary sources and archival materials—Curtis's public papers are located in the archives of the Association of American Library Schools (University of Illinois, Urbana) and the Trevor Arnet Library, Atlanta University Center (Atlanta, Georgia).

–DONALD G. DAVIS, JR.

CUTTER, CHARLES AMMI (1837-1903)

Charles Ammi Cutter was born on March 14, 1837, in Boston, the son of Caleb Champney and Hannah Biglow Cutter. At a very early age he was sent to live with his grandfather, Ammi Cutter (1777-1850) and three maiden aunts in West Cambridge, Massachusetts. There he was provided with a strong Unitarian religious atmosphere and as he grew up, he was encouraged to develop his scholarly abilities. In 1851, after attending the Hopkins School, he moved with his aunts to Cambridge. He attended Harvard College (A.B., 1855), and the Harvard Divinity School (B.D., 1859), where he distinguished himself by winning the Bowdoin Prize Dissertation competition in 1857. Although his schooling served primarily to prepare him for the Unitarian parish ministry, Cutter did not pursue that possibility in earnest. He was introduced to librarianship when, between 1857 and 1859, he served as the student librarian for the Harvard Divinity School. Besides his regular duties, he and a fellow student wrote a new catalog for the collection and completely rearranged the books on the shelves. This first experience in library management also brought him into contact with Ezra Abbot (q.v.), the assistant librarian of the College library. After graduation and a period of tutoring, independent study, and occasional preaching, he joined the Harvard College library staff in May 1860 as Abbot's assistant.

This period in Cutter's life (which continued until the end of 1868) was important both professionally and personally. In 1863, he married Sarah Fayerweather Appleton and during the next five years, three sons were born to them, substantially increasing a household which included Cutter's two surviving aunts as well as one of his wife's sisters and her husband. The need, therefore, to supplement his income gave him added impetus to pursue a wide variety of scholarly endeavors beyond his College library work. He indexed scholarly works, compiled catalogs, gave assistance as a bibliographical expert (most notably to Joseph Sabin [q.v.] on the latter's *Dictionary of Books Relating to America*), and worked for a period as a special cataloging assistant at the Boston Public Library. He also began his literary career by contributing articles and book reviews to the *North American Review* and the *Nation* on literary, bibliographical, and library topics. His writing for the *Nation* continued thereafter for more than thirty years and demonstrated his interest as a library expert in the *Nation*'s crusade for national cultural renewal.

The Harvard situation during the 1860s provided Cutter with an excellent apprenticeship in librarianship, especially under Abbot's able tutelage. Sharing with Abbot personal and scholarly attitudes, Cutter learned from his mentor the systematic basis of a library's bibliographical system. He helped Abbot plan Harvard's influential alphabetico-classed card catalog, and he himself supervised its day-to-day construction. By the end of 1868, Cutter's knowledge of cataloging, his administrative skills, and his personal scholarly attainments were of such repute that he was offered the position of librarian of the prestigious Boston Athenaeum.

The Athenaeum had gained a notable reputation in antebellum literary America. Together with Harvard, it functioned as a focal point for the influential Boston-Cambridge intellectual community. Cutter assumed the Athenaeum post on January 1, 1869, and was subsequently re-elected to that position for each of the next 24 years. He continued the tradition of scholarly, cultured librarianship that the institution already possessed, but he added to it his own systematic understanding of administrative priorities.

The first half of Cutter's tenure at the Athenaeum (1869-1880) was a period of great success for him. His work reflected a broad and systematic view of librarianship. Although he concurred with the Athenaeum's sense of its cultural mission, he succeeded in expanding the Library's service goals. He revived the Library's *List of Additions* as an annotated, serially published guide to the "best" literature, and in 1879, he began syndication of the publication to encourage library advancement through cooperative ventures. He was firmly convinced that the Library was a system in which all elements and processes were interdependent. He rigorously evaluated and improved book access and circulation procedures, and systematically planned for the housing requirements of the Library. Obvious improvements at the Athenaeum increased the trustees' confidence in his judgment, and by the end of this initial period he worked with relative independence, especially in the selection of materials. By 1880, after two sizeable bequests had been received, the library profession regarded the Athenaeum as one of the pre-eminent examples of library progress.

One of Cutter's major accomplishments was the Athenaeum's printed dictionary catalog, published in five volumes between 1874 and 1882. As the first of its kind, the *Catalogue of the Library of the Boston Athenaeum* incorporated Cutter's own sophisticated system of interrelated entries. Cutter published the rationale and methodology in two parts in the U.S. Bureau of Education's "Special Report" on public libraries in 1876. Part I contained his report on "Library Catalogues" and Part II held his *Rules for a Printed Dictionary Catalogue*. The two documents became highly influential among nineteenth-century cataloging guides. By 1904, the *Rules* had been reissued in three more editions.

In 1876, Cutter joined Melvil Dewey (q.v.) and others in the establishment of the American Library Association and the *Library Journal*. He enthusiastically supported Dewey's ventures in cooperation and standardization and helped Dewey with the *Journal* by contributing articles and by writing the "Bibliography" sections. He also participated in the Association's cooperative projects, where his influence was particularly strong in efforts at cooperative cataloging. In fact, the Athenaeum became a developmental and experimental center for the work of the Cooperation Committee, of which he was chairman and Dewey the energetic secretary. Certainly, Cutter was deeply influenced by Dewey's book classification system, which spurred him to develop his own shelf classification system for the Athenaeum. By 1880, he was circulating not only the preliminary schedules, but also the first copies of his "Author Tables." The latter, eventually issued in three separate formats, are now known as the "Cutter Numbers" and are used for arranging books alphabetically by author. (See *C. A. Cutter's Two-Figure Author Table*, *C. A. Cutter's Three-Figure Author Table*, and *Cutter-Sanborn Three-Figure Author Table*, all in the Swanson-Swift revisions and all published in Chicopee, Massachusetts by Huntting, 1969.)

During the second phase of Cutter's years at the Athenaeum (1880-1893), much of his successful work continued. He completed the Athenaeum's catalog in 1882, and funds previously devoted to it provided for a large expansion of the book collections. Cutter also continued to develop his classification system, but conversion of the library's collections to the plan eventually took more than ten years. At the same time, clouds began to gather on the horizon of Cutter's professional and personal life.

First, Cutter's relationship with Melvil Dewey changed significantly. In 1880, a distressing imbroglio involving Dewey's Readers' and Writers' Economy Company, Cutter, and other librarians who had invested both time and money in it, led not only to a considerable loss of money for Cutter, but also to strained relations between the two men. For the first time, competition between them surfaced in the promotion of their respective shelf classification systems.

Second, a struggle for leadership within the ALA developed that deeply affected him. Because of the events of 1880, Dewey lost esteem among other library leaders and his influence within the Association was temporarily impaired. For a period of time in the early 1880s, he withdrew from the active leadership that he had displayed during the Association's first four years. Cutter, along with other, sometimes older and less aggressive leaders, exercised closer control over the Association's business. Cutter continued to serve on various committees and eventually became the Association's president (1887-1889). In 1881, he succeeded Dewey as the editor of the *Library Journal* and remained in that post until 1893. There, and in the pages of the *Nation*, he served as a spokesman for the official Association leaders of the 1880s. The older group, generally conservative in their approach to the role of the profession, stressed the influential role of individual librarians in promoting an enlightened democracy. They saw librarianship as a profession of moral leadership and persuasion. But Dewey, from his new vantage point in New York, chaffed at the ALA's subdued leadership. He represented a new breed of leaders who, while not foregoing the ideals of moral leadership, wished to exercise forcefully the organizational power of the Association to achieve those ends expediently. During the mid- and late 1880s, Dewey's

open criticisms and promotions of specific programs brought about a muted but unmistakable struggle for power over the Association's leadership.

Cutter found himself in the middle of the conflict, sometimes giving measured support for Dewey, particularly in the development of library education, and sometimes serving as a mediator between Dewey and others. Increasingly, however, even he found himself voting against Dewey's most aggressive proposals. In 1892, the picture changed significantly. Dewey's growing support brought him the presidency of the Association and the power to effect far-reaching changes, and Cutter and other leaders who had opposed Dewey's moves found themselves with greatly lessened influence in organizational deliberations.

Finally, developments in Cutter's personal life and in his Athenaeum work also contributed to a darkening picture. In 1883, Phillip, his second son, died, and in 1886, the second of his three aunts who had lived with the Cutters through the years also passed away.

At the Athenaeum, gradual changes in the makeup of the Board of Trustees led to a conflict over Cutter's administrative ideals. The older trustees had welcomed the way in which Cutter had brought the Athenaeum into the mainstream of American library leadership, seeing it as an expansion of the service role of the institution. Some of the newly elected trustees of the 1880s, however, had a more limited perspective concerning the role of the institution. Wishing to preserve the Library more completely for its own patrons, they criticized many of Cutter's organizational changes as unnecessary extravagances and worked to curtail Cutter's administrative activity. Early in 1892, the largely subdued conflict broke more clearly into the open and led to the trustees' unofficial censure of him. Feeling that the situation had become intolerable, Cutter began looking for a new position. In 1893, he refused his re-election to the Athenaeum's post but had no other position in hand. His frustration in securing another position was further compounded by the ALA's leadership struggles. The entire situation became so severe that, by late 1893, he and his wife retreated to Europe where he hoped, in his own words, "to get away from libraries." (See his article in the September 1894 *Library Journal*, "European Libraries: The Bibliothèque Nationale and the British Museum.") Withdrawing from the American library scene, he relinquished the editorship of the *Library Journal* and remained in Europe until late the following summer.

In 1894, Cutter returned to the United States to become librarian of the newly established Forbes Library in Northampton, Massachusetts. While in Europe, he had responded to the request of the Forbes trustees to buy books for them, and, when they subsequently offered him the librarian's post, he accepted it with enthusiasm. He assumed the position at a salary considerably lower than what he had received at the Athenaeum, but he remained convinced that the trustees of the Forbes would extend him the freedom to build a library according to the best principles and practices extant. During the last decade of his life, Cutter devoted himself entirely to the task, though not without renewed personal struggle. Blessed with a large book fund, he built the Forbes collection to 90,000 carefully selected volumes. But the trustees' generosity in collection development did not extend to administrative funds, and Cutter found himself unable to make significant progress in cataloging and classification. However, his efforts to make the Library an instrument of cultural uplift led him to develop one of the first large circulating collections of art reproductions and music. He started a branch library program and also attempted to serve special kinds of users by beginning, among other things, a medical collection and an extensive children's program. Nevertheless, the lack of funds prevented him from hiring highly trained personnel for these programs, and those people he trained himself regularly left the Forbes for better-paying positions elsewhere.

Meanwhile, Cutter continued to labor on his shelf classification system. He had begun a revision of the Athenaeum's system by the late 1880s and, between 1891 and 1893, had published the first six schedules of his better-known *Expansive Classification* (*Expansive Classification, Part 1: The First Six Classifications*, Boston: C. A. Cutter, 1891-1893). But he was unable to apply it completely to the Forbes collections. Nor could he complete the seventh and final "expansion," which proved to be a massive undertaking. His frustration was compounded because he alone had to supervise its publication and promotion, and because he found it impossible not to introduce changes in its structure, particularly in the area of science and technology. In the late 1890s, he also began to revise his *Rules*. Although a fourth edition was published posthumously in 1904, it too was incomplete at the time of his death and gave evidence of his struggle with what he felt were discordant themes in cooperative cataloging.

Cutter participated in professional activities, but more often on the state and local, than on the national, level. In 1891 he had helped establish the Massachusetts Library Club, and in 1898 served as the first president of the new Western Massachusetts Library Club. He traveled to Europe in 1897 to the Second International Library Conference and to the meetings of the Institut Internationale de Bibliographie, making a special effort at that time to promote his Expansive Classification. He was very active in lecturing, especially at the new library schools, Drexel and Pratt.

As the years progressed, Cutter showed evidence of fatigue. The death of his last aunt in 1896 and of another son, Gerald, in 1898 added to his burdens. Despite the frustrations, however, his enthusiasm for library work rarely flagged. In the spring of 1903, he nearly died of pneumonia. After prematurely returning to work in the summer, he was again taken ill, and he died suddenly on September 6 while on a driving trip with his wife.

Charles Cutter's impact on the library profession has taken several forms. His most lasting achievement was in the organization of library materials. He developed a format for the dictionary catalog that has profoundly influenced library systems of bibliographical organization. His dictionary catalog, his *Rules for a Printed Dictionary Catalogue*, and his activity in ALA committees on cataloging provided the impetus for the general discussion of author-title and descriptive cataloging before 1900. His theoretical work on catalog subject access, although not received with the same enthusiasm, provided the basis for subsequent catalog subject heading practice. He also produced two shelf classification systems. Although the better-known *Expansive Classification* remained incomplete, it substantially influenced the Library of Congress classification system and advanced the idea of enumerative schemes in general. (It should be noted that *Expansive Classification, Part 2: Seventh Classification* was edited after Charles Cutter's death by his nephew, William Parker Cutter.)

Cutter presented his Expansive Classification, his life's work, at the Second International Library Conference in London (see its *1897 Transactions and Proceedings*, p. 84). In his talk, he discussed the gradations in the scheme:

It consists of seven tables of classification of progressive fulness, designed to meet the needs of a library at its successive stages of growth. The first table has few classes and no subdivisions. It is meant for a very small collection of books. The second has more classes and some subdivisions, but retains all the old classes with their previous marks. This is intended for the small collection, when it has swelled so much that it must be broken up into more parts. Now, the books which are put into the new classes must, of course, have new marks; but those in the old ones remain as they are—their marks need no change. In this way we go on, gradually increasing the number of classes and sub-classes, and yet in each transition from the simpler to the more complex scheme preserving all the old notation; so that there is only the absolutely necessary amount of alteration. It is as if an indestructible suit of clothes were made to grow with the growth of the youth who wears them. He would not have to go to a tailor now and then to get a new suit. So the rapidly-growing library does not have to get an entire rearrangement every ten or fifteen years, with entirely new class-marks. Passing through the third, fourth, fifth, and sixth, it comes finally to the seventh, which is full and minute enough for the British Museum, with a capacity of increase that would accommodate the British Museum raised to the tenth power; for there might be an eighth and a ninth and a tenth table, if need be. From this adaptation to growth comes the name *expansive.*

The first classification (for "the smallest library") consists of eight main classes. In the second classification ("For a library that has grown larger"), Cutter uses 15 main classes (G for Geography and Travels, L for Physical Sciences, M for Natural History, etc.). The third classification has even more classes and subdivisions, and in the fifth, the whole alphabet A-Z has been applied and all main classes are set out. The following table shows the full range of the system:

A.	General works
B.	Philosophy, Psychology, Religion
C.	Judaism and Christianity
D.	Ecclesiastical history
E.	Biography
F.	History, and Allied studies
G.	Geography and travels
H.	Social sciences (general), Statistics, Economics
I.	Sociology, Education
J.	Political science, Civics, Government
K.	Law
L.	Natural sciences, Math, Physics, Chemistry, Astronomy
M.	Natural history, Biology
N.	Botany
O–P.	Zoölogy, Anthropology, Folklore
Q.	Medicine
R.	Technology
S.	Engineering
T.	Fabricative arts
U.	Combative and preservative arts
V.	Athletic and recreative arts, Theatre, and Music
W.	Art
X.	Philology
Y.	Literature
Z.	Book arts (incl. Literary history)

As with many other classification schemes, Cutter's provides form divisions (designated numerically from 1 through 9—e.g., 1 Theory, 2 Bibliography, etc.) to be applied throughout the system. Additionally, he provides a table of localities with decimal notations, this consisting of a series of numbers (11-99) and a list of countries and places, to be used mainly for division of Geography and History. (If, for example, 45 is the number for England and D is Church History, then D45 is English church history.) The Expansive Classification is, then, a system of mixed notation consisting of capital letters (basic classes), small capital letters (subjects), and numerals. Cutter himself explained the progression in the introduction to the scheme (p. 7):

The [notation] consists of two parts (a) the *class mark*, which shows in what class the book belongs and (b) the *book mark*, which distinguishes that book from other books in the same class. The class mark in the series of classifications set forth here . . . [consists of]: *a letter*, which may be followed by one or more letters when the class is a subject (as History, Philosophy, Science, the Arts), or a kind of literature (as fiction, drama, poetry); a *single figure*—to distinguish books written in a certain form (as dictionaries, encyclopedias, etc.) from other works in the same class; *two figures*—to distinguish books relating to a place (as America, Africa, etc.) from other works in the same class.

For example, F is the class letter of History and 35 is a local number for Rome, so Gibbon's *Decline and Fall of the Roman Empire* has the number F35·G35 (G35 is the author number for Gibbon). Since certain combinations of letters were reserved for subjects, Cutter could provide a short notation for certain aspects of a particular discipline—e.g., chemical analysis, LOS (L—Science and Arts; LO—Chemistry; LOS—Analysis, chemical).

It should be noted, though, that contrary to Cutter's claims (as above), EC does not expand consistently without notational change from the first to the seventh classification schedule. Equally important, however, is the fact that it is unlikely that any library would expand from the first classification to the seventh.

As noted previously, the system also included "Cutter numbers," used most commonly now to allow alphabetical subdivision under individual class numbers. (They are part of the book number but not part of the class number.) This and the use of some EC features in formulating the Library of Congress Classification comprise two of Cutter's continuing contributions to librarianship.

Charles Ammi Cutter was slight of build, of medium height, and wore spectacles because of his severe nearsightedness. His bearded countenance and his occasional absentmindedness, the latter due to his habit of becoming lost in the work at hand, often gave the impression of scholarly aloofness. He used relentless logic in presenting his views aggressively and forcefully in the appropriate forum. During public discussion of library problems, he became known for his ability to state precisely both problems and their possible solutions. Guided by rigorous personal standards, he was not content to allow either his work or the work of others to escape close and exacting scrutiny. At the same time, he did not hesitate to offer sometimes harsh but always incisive criticism of views that he felt wrong or foolish. These attributes made him an imposing and perhaps even threatening figure to those whose grasp of literary matters was neither as comprehensive nor as exacting. In working with others within the profession, many of whom desired more expeditious handling of library matters even at the risk of being less thorough, he must have appeared at times as a difficult, albeit authoritative, colleague.

Those who were close to him, however, found an engaging person. He was a shy, essentially private person, but he was also an intensely warm and understanding friend. He had a playful spirit that expressed itself in a delightful humor, notably to his friends, often ironical concerning himself and punctuated by puns and dry wit. His spirited, although not expert, dancing became humorously celebrated within ALA. He also enjoyed hiking and boating and often invited others to join him. His lifelong interest in French language and culture and in art history reflected his deep sense of esthetic values. His personal attributes suggest an almost childlike sincerity in his approach to life, as he looked for ultimate solutions in library matters but acted always without pretense. Not political by nature, he appeared vulnerable to those who were. Yet, the confidence of others in his sincerity often cast him into a mediating role between others who were more volatile.

Cutter was by nature a systematizer of library ideals. On a theoretical level, he gained his greatest satisfaction from supplying systematic solutions to problems rather than from the limelight of personal leadership. This characteristic, however, has often been overshadowed by his personal attributes or by the lasting utility of the tools that he left behind. Furthermore, because this approach was ingrained in his work, he neither philosophized about it, nor took pains to make it explicit. He simply assumed it was the necessary counterpart to any scientific approach to library problems.

The source for Cutter's approach was his exposure to the Boston-Cambridge antebellum intellectual milieu. The Scottish Realism that formed the basis of his Unitarian schooling emphasized the rational analysis of mental phenomena and the basic harmony of man and nature. Although not explicitly discussed by Cutter, these two concepts were basic to his understanding of library processes and librarianship. The first provided Cutter with a view of the process by which man came to know reality. A system of access to man's knowledge, and particularly a subject system, had to reflect that process. Hence, buried within his rules for cataloging and implicit in his classification system is an appreciation for man's learning processes. The idea of harmony was much more pervasive. Through its pursuit, one perceived truth, the ultimate sense of existence and beauty, and fostered inner culture. Enculturation of this sort was

possible for anybody who desired it enough because it was in fact, mankind's naturally endowed "common sense." Reading was the principal means by which man could achieve that goal. And it was the scholar—one who perceived or was in pursuit of the truth of that harmony—who exemplified the highest form of reading.

For Cutter, librarianship was a lifelong missionary endeavor to awaken or to strengthen the enculturation of man. Bibliography, one of Cutter's earliest interests, was more than simply listing books. It was, rather, seeking out the "best" books by authors who rigorously strove to reach truth. Inferior books lacked evidence of that rigor and appealed only to man's lower faculties. Providing catalog or shelf access systems was also a method by which a librarian could further the same goal. Besides increasing access, such tools also served as teachers. They enabled the librarian to evaluate the materials presented and, in the case of subject systems, introduced the patron to the larger relationships of reality and therefore helped him perceive the harmony of all. This made the dictionary catalog a finely woven fabric of relationships that provided the patron with a "scholarly" approach to the use of knowledge. Catalogs could be simplified (for instance, for children) but not with a lesser goal. Cutter was always troubled by shoddy cataloging, especially when cataloging methods subverted what he thought were the greater purposes of librarianship.

These views, combined with his earlier work with a cultural and scholarly patronage at Harvard and the Boston Athenaeum, initially led Cutter to a rigid outlook on library users. But his association with public librarians in the ALA and finally his own venture into the public library field in the last decade of his life led him to modify his earlier perceptions of users. Although he never questioned the library's goals, he softened his attitude toward the reading of light fiction, introduced concessions to conform to patrons' habits in using catalogs, and expanded his efforts to reach out to the minds of the public. Three years before he died he wrote in an article on "Should Libraries Buy Only the Best Books, or the Best Books That People Will Read?" (*Library Journal*, February 1901): "The whole history of libraries in the past century may almost be condensed into one sentence: They *were* the libraries of the one fit reader; they *are* the libraries of the million unfit as well as the one fit."

Biographical listings and obituaries—*Dictionary of American Biography* 5 (Frederick W. Ashley); *National Cyclopaedia of American Biography* 13; "Necrology." *Library Journal* 29:C197 (Dec. 1904); [Obituary]. *Nation* 77:229 (Sept. 17, 1903); [Obituary]. *Springfield Daily Republican*, Sept. 8, 1903; *Who Was Who in America* I (1897-1942). **Books and articles about the biographee**—"As It Was in the Beginning." *Public Libraries* 29:236-40 (May 1924); Cutter, Benjamin. *A*

History of the Cutter Family of New England. Revised and enlarged by William Richard Cutter. Boston, David Clapp & Son, 1871; Cutter, William Parker. *Charles Ammi Cutter.* Chicago: American Library Association, 1931. (American Library Pioneers, No. 3); Foster, William E. "Charles Ammi Cutter: A Memorial Sketch." *Library Journal* 28:697-703 (Oct. 1903); Foster, William E. "Five Men of '76." *A.L.A. Bulletin* 20:312-23 (Oct. 1926); Green, Samuel Swett. "Biographical Sketches of Librarians and Bibliographers, III: Charles Ammi Cutter, 1837-1903." *Bulletin of Bibliography* 8:59-60 (July 1914); Green, Samuel Swett. *The Public Library Movement in the United States, 1853-1893.* Boston: Boston Book Co., 1913; Holley, Edward G. *Raking the Historic Coals; The A.L.A. Scrapbook of 1876.* Beta Phi Mu, 1967; Immroth, John Phillip. "Charles Ammi Cutter." *Encyclopedia of Library and Information Science.* New York: Marcel Dekker, Inc., 1971, v. 6, pp. 380-87; Immroth, John Phillip. "Expansive Classification." *Encyclopedia of Library and Information Science.* New York: Marcel Dekker, 1972, v. 8, pp. 297-316; Kent, Frederic H. *He Served His Own Generation; A Sermon in Memory of Charles Ammi Cutter....* Northampton, Mass.: 1903?; Little, Agnes E. "Charles Ammi Cutter, Librarian at Forbes Library, Northampton, Massachusetts, 1894-1903." Master's thesis, University of North Carolina, 1962; Miksa, Francis L. *Charles Ammi Cutter: Library Systematizer.* Littleton, Colo.: Libraries Unlimited, 1977. Contains a biography of Cutter, a large selection of his writings, and a complete bibliography; Miksa, Francis L. "Charles Ammi Cutter: Nineteenth Century Systematizer of Libraries." Ph.D. dissertation, University of Chicago, 1974; Miksa, Francis L. "The Making of the 1876 Special Report on Public Libraries." *Journal of Library History* 8:30-40 (Jan. 1973); Morse, Clarence R. "A Biographical, Bibliographical Study of Charles Ammi Cutter, Librarian." Master's thesis, University of Washington, 1961; Solberg, Thorwald. "Some Memories of Charles Ammi Cutter." *Library Journal* 28:769-70 (Nov. 1903); Wikander, Lawrence E. *Disposed to Learn: The First Seventy-five Years of the Forbes Library.* Northampton, Mass.: The Trustees of the Forbes Library, 1972. **Primary sources and archival materials**—Cutter's personal papers were destroyed soon after the death of Mrs. Cutter in 1933. Papers relating to his professional work may be found in the Melvil Dewey papers (Columbia University Library) and the Richard R. Bowker papers (New York Public Library) and in the collections of the Houghton Library, the Harvard University Archives, the Boston Athenaeum, and the Forbes Library (Northampton, Massachusetts).

—FRANCIS L. MIKSA

DANA, JOHN COTTON (1856-1929)

1. Read.
2. Read.
3. Read some more.
4. Read anything.
5. Read about everything.
6. Read enjoyable things.
7. Read things you yourself enjoy.
8. Read, and talk about it.
9. Read very carefully, some things.
10. Read on the run, most things.
11. Don't think about reading, but
12. Just read.

■ ■ ■

Those famous twelve rules about reading, emphasizing personal selection, aptly sum up the approach to librarianship taken by John Cotton Dana who, although he came late and without formal training to librarianship, was one of America's most influential librarians and who, perhaps more than any other person, helped shape the concepts and practices of urban public libraries in the United States.

Of English, French, and Scottish descent, John Cotton Dana was born in Woodstock, Vermont, on August 19, 1856, the third of five sons of Charles Dana, Jr., and Charitie Scott Loomis Dana. His grandfather had opened a general store in Woodstock in 1802, which his father was running at the time of Dana's birth. A scholar, with honorary M.A.'s from Dartmouth College and the University of Vermont, Charles Dana raised his sons in a New England atmosphere with an emphasis on education and reading. Throughout his life, despite interests that often were to carry him far away from Woodstock, Dana was to maintain strong ties with it, and with his family, and was to spend many summers there. When he died, on July 21, 1929, at St. Vincent's Hospital in New York, of acute toxemia following an operation some time before, Dana's body naturally was returned to Woodstock for burial.

Educated initially at home and in the local schools, Dana enrolled at Dartmouth College in 1874. He was a good student and was elected to Phi Beta Kappa, but Dana also found time for other activities. He was a member of the track team, a member of the Psi Upsilon fraternity, the speaker at his Class Day and commencement exercises, and, in his junior year, editor of *The Aegis*, a humorous classbook.

Dana then returned to Woodstock to begin the study of law in the office of French and Southgate. At this time though, his health was threatened by tuberculosis. Seeking a drier climate, he went to Rico, Colorado, where in May 1880 he joined Frank Wadleigh Gove, a Dartmouth classmate who was then a deputy United States land and mineral surveyor. Although admitted to the Colorado bar later that year, Dana worked primarily as a surveyor with Gove for the next two years.

Dana returned briefly to Woodstock in the spring of 1882 (following his mother's death the previous summer) before moving to New York City. There he lived with his brother Charles, a doctor, while studying law again and serving briefly as a tutor. In May 1883 he easily passed the New York State Bar exam, but, finding it difficult to obtain a legal position and again threatened by ill health, in March 1884, Dana left for Fergus Falls, Minnesota, where another college friend, William D. Parkinson, resided. From there he soon moved to Ashby, Minnesota, where he practiced law and became, for a time, editor of the local newspaper, *The Ashby Avalanche.* In July 1884, he received word of his father's death, an event that troubled Dana because he had always relied heavily on his father for advice.

Restless and unhappy in Minnesota, Dana returned to Colorado in September 1884, where he joined his cousin, Edward Sabine, who was running a real estate business in Colorado Springs. In the spring of 1885, Dana joined a surveying party of the Colorado Midland Railroad and, in 1887, he moved to Glenwood Springs as a surveyor for the railroad and later as a construction superintendent. While there, he preached briefly in a Unitarian church, where he met Adine Rowena Waggener, a native of Russellville, Kentucky, whom he married on November 15, 1888. They were to have no children.

Dana had also begun to write. On February 16, 1889, an article by him, "The Public School," in *The Denver Arbitrator*, questioned the quality and relevance of public education and brought Dana much attention. Since the superintendent of the Denver School Board at that time was Aaron Gove, the brother of Dana's friend, the article helped lead to Dana's appointment, in May 1889, as the first librarian of the Denver School District No. 1 in the newly opened East Denver High School.

This library, which later became the Denver Public Library, was created under a newly enacted state law allowing school boards to levy taxes for the purchase of library books for public use. It opened with about 2,000 volumes, three reading rooms—including one for women—and Dana as librarian. He immediately set about publicizing the Library and within the first six months had circulated over 6,000 volumes. By 1893, the Library numbered about 23,000 volumes and attracted over 1,000 visitors daily. Dana had already concluded that the Library's mission was "the spread of ideas," and he brought to librarianship the intensity of his New England upbringing.

Dana developed collections that he thought would be of use to the citizens of Denver, including business material, picture files, and other ephemeral material. He also developed, in conjunction with the Colorado Medical Association, a medical collection that later became the nucleus of the Denver Medical Library. Dana also simplified borrowing procedures; established open shelves; opened reference shelves to the public; provided classroom collections for the schools; in September 1894, established the first separate children's room in the United States; began a training class for library assistants in 1893; published a monthly magazine (*Books*); started museum collections and exhibits; kept the library open from 9 to 9 every day; and otherwise pushed and promoted libraries and library use. By 1896, the annual circulation of the Library averaged four volumes per capita.

The isolation of Denver, Dana's growing sense of ambition and capability, and signs of trouble led to

his departure. Although a popular local figure, Dana was personally attacked for acquiring "goldbug" literature at a time when free silver was a dominant local cause. He vigorously defended his right to stock and circulate literature on both sides of this topic, just as he was to oppose vigorously attempts to remove German material from the Free Public Library at Newark during World War I. Finally, while Dana had supported the Denver Mercantile Library, which the Denver Chamber of Commerce had established in 1885 to serve the public, the Chamber of Commerce began to attack the extravagance of the School Board in supporting a public library from tax funds.

Feeling he could accomplish more elsewhere, Dana became an active candidate for positions at Brooklyn, Buffalo, and Springfield, Massachusetts. Ultimately he accepted the position of librarian of the City Library of Springfield and submitted his resignation to the Denver School Board effective December 31, 1897.

The City Library of Springfield presented new challenges. When he began work there in 1898, Dana found a large, established library with a collection of about 100,000 volumes, but one with serious physical barriers to its easy use. With both a Board of Directors and a staff somewhat resistant to his ideas, Dana faced the task of changing existing habits and patterns to make the Library a strong social force in the community. Problems of physical access to the Library were soon solved by the installation of an elevator and the removal of several other barriers to use. Children's use was encouraged, a loan collection of pictures was established, business material was purchased, training classes were instituted, and other policies and practices that had proved so successful at Denver were adopted. Dana himself spent much time selecting material in order to make the collections more useful to the community; he became particularly involved in the expenditure of a $90,000 bequest for materials in economics and the social sciences that came to the Library with the David Ames Wells Economic Library.

The fact that the directors of the City Library Association were also the directors of the Art Museum and the Museum of Natural History had initially attracted Dana to Springfield. He thought that he had a right to run the museums as well as the Library and he also wanted them to play a greater social role. This brought him into direct conflict with G. W. V. Smith, a wealthy private collector and curator of the Art Museum, whose views were more traditional. Because of a conflict over Sunday openings of the Art Museum, Smith threatened to give his private collection to Buffalo and there was dissension among the Board of Directors.

Dana was becoming increasingly unhappy with his situation; however, his reputation was also bringing him many inquiries about other positions. He was approached by Brooklyn, Boston, and the New York Free Circulating Library. The chairman of the Board of Directors at Springfield, Samuel Bowles, editor and publisher of *The Springfield Republican*, urged Dana to stay and, for a brief time, he did. When the situation did not improve, Dana resigned on December 18, 1901, to accept the position of librarian of the Free Public Library of Newark, New Jersey, succeeding Frank P. Hill (q.v.), a friend and fellow Dartmouth graduate (1876).

When interviewing Dana in Springfield, Richard C. Jenkinson, of the Newark Board of Trustees, had remarked to him that "Newark is not a book reading community, not a library center." Dana's reply was "Let us make it both." When he took up his duties at Newark on January 15, 1902, Dana proceeded to do just that.

Dana spent the rest of his life at Newark and developed perhaps the most outstanding American urban public library of the time. At Newark, Dana found a new library building, a strong collection, and a strong staff, including Beatrice Winser (q.v.). A Newark native, Miss Winser had graduated from the Columbia Library School in 1889, had worked at Newark since her graduation and had become, in 1900 under Hill, assistant librarian. She was to remain in that capacity throughout Dana's career at Newark and was ultimately to succeed him as librarian. Dana and Winser immediately formed a strong and lively partnership. Details of the administration and operation of the Library were left directly in her hands, so with Winser in control of the Library's daily operations, Dana was free to concentrate on other matters. He wrote, planned policies, devised new plans, and used his creative imagination, his ability to see broad relationships, and his skill in communication and interpretation to concentrate on the development of the wide aspects of librarianship and to bring leadership to the Free Public Library of Newark.

Dana quickly applied the basic ideas and practices that he had developed and implemented at Denver and Springfield and within ten years had put virtually all of them into effect at Newark. Some were expanded; for example, the simplified borrowing procedures that he had first instituted at Denver were to lead to the development of the Newark Charging System, which for many years was the system used by a majority of the public libraries in the United States. Some new services, such as foreign language collections for Newark's many non-English speaking residents and the development of branch libraries, he had not tried at Denver or Springfield, but these were basically extensions of Dana's concept of making the Library as useful as possible.

Three major developments marked his career at Newark. The first was intense publicity to bring the Library to the attention of the people. Through *The Newarker* (a Library publication started by Dana), newspaper columns, billboards, and every other possible means, Dana advertised the Library and its work. At the national as well as the local level, in the general press as well as in library periodicals, the Free Public Library received frequent favorable mention. Probably no other American librarian ever made greater use of print than did Dana and certainly not as effectively as he did. The fact that the American Library Association chose to name an award the John Cotton Dana Publicity Awards testifies clearly to the emphasis that he, especially at Newark, placed on public relations, and to the extremely successful job that he did in this respect. Of course, Dana had much to advertise. When he came to Newark the collection numbered about 79,000 volumes, and about 20,000 registered borrowers borrowed annually about 315,000 volumes. By 1928, when the collection had grown to almost 400,000 volumes, over 90,000 registered borrowers were borrowing almost 1,800,000 volumes a year.

Second, and perhaps his most notable accomplishment, was the establishment of what is now the Newark Business Library. At Denver and Springfield, Dana had actively sought to acquire material, much of it considered ephemeral and out of scope by other libraries, of value to the local business community and to promote its use. At Newark, the opportunity arose to bring this idea to fruition. Its development was the result of the excellent use that Dana was able to make of his staff. Sarah B. Ball, the librarian of the newly established Branch No. 1 located in the business district, remarked to Dana concerning the heavy use that the branch was receiving from business men, adding "Why not change the name of this branch to Business Men's Branch and begin collecting everything we can find relating to business?" Dana replied, "You have described something I have long wanted to do! Now we will go ahead with it!" With the vigorous support of Dana, and of Jenkinson of the Board of Trustees, the Business Branch flourished, but it was, in large measure, Ball's energy and enthusiasm and her ability to work closely with the business community that were responsible for the phenomenal success of the branch, which soon served as a model for other special libraries.

Finally, Dana's career at Newark was marked by his increasing interest and accomplishments in museum work. There were no museum facilities in Newark in 1902, for that city was culturally overshadowed by New York. Dana set out to change that. In 1903, he organized one of the first notable exhibits of American art, thus beginning support for American art which was carried through in his museum work. He was also especially attracted by industrial design, and he organized exhibits featuring designs in industry. His view that "beauty has no relation to age, rarity or price" led him to an exhibit of glassware, all of which had been purchased for less than $1 per piece in local stores. Then in 1905, he opened a Science Museum on the Library's fourth floor, and continued his pressure for more museum space and staff.

In 1908, Dana borrowed from George T. Rockwell, a Newark pharmacist, a collection of Japanese porcelain, prints, and silk for exhibit in the Library. It was so well received that Dana was able to persuade the mayor and Council to purchase the collection and to entrust it to the Newark Museum Association, formed on April 29, 1909, with Dana as its secretary. On January 25, 1913, Dana was appointed the Association's first director, holding that position, as well as his Library post, until his death.

Dana's continued interest in the idea of a museum led to the suggestion that, in conjunction with Newark's 250th anniversary in 1916, a Memorial Building should be constructed to house a museum and an auditorium. Dana, on the Executive Committee organizing the celebration, urged that the building be located in the central part of the city where it would be easily accessible. A majority of the site committee, perhaps because of some institutional or personal financial interest, proposed a more remote site. Dana resigned from the committee and the ensuing controversy, in which Dana was strongly supported in the press by Wallace Scudder of *The Newark News*, who had also resigned from the committee, effectively blocked the building of a museum at that time. In 1922, the City Commissioners finally bought land for a museum in the center of the city, and Louis Bamberger, a local businessman, financed most of its construction. On March 17, 1926, the Newark Museum of Art, Science, and Industry, near the Free Public Library, was finally opened, culminating Dana's efforts to bring museum service to Newark.

In every possible way, Dana sought to bring libraries and museums to the attention of the people of Newark and to make them useful adjuncts of their daily life. The *New York Sun* remarked of Dana, in an editorial, "It's a dull day in Newark, N.J. on which John Cotton Dana does not find a way to make the public library more useful. . . . If Newark's population does not attain intellectual predominance over all the other people in the United States, its failure cannot fairly be laid at the door of the public library where Dana holds forth."

Dana was a prominent national figure and always maintained an active interest in local, state, and national library associations and organizations. He was president of the Colorado Library Association in 1895-1896. At Springfield, he helped organize the Western Massachusetts Library Club. While at Newark, he was an active member and twice (1904-1905 and 1910-1911) president of the New Jersey Library Association, as well as an active member, vice president (1903) and president (1906) of the New York Library Club.

In 1892, he was appointed to the Endowment Committee of the American Library Association, thus beginning a long and often stormy relationship with that Association. In 1894, he was elected to the Executive Board and the vice-presidency. He was chairman of the local committee for the Denver Conference in 1895 and at that Conference was elected president. In 1896, he was elected to a six-year term on the Council. Dana served on many ALA committees, including the State Aid to Libraries Committee of the State Library Section; the Committee on Cooperation with the National Education Association; the Constitutional Revision Committee, whose appointment he had suggested while he was president; the Committee on Library Training; the Committee on Relations with the Book Trade; the Committee on Bookbuying; the Committee on Publicity; and the Committee on an Exhibit at the Panama-Pacific Exposition at San Francisco in 1914.

He soon, however, became probably the severest critic that the ALA has ever had and frequently attacked the Association's leadership and policies. He saw ALA as a potential power for good in the library world but felt that it was not accomplishing all that it could. Although he had been dissatisfied with the Association earlier, much of his concern was brought about by problems surrounding the organization of the Special Libraries Association.

Shortly after the formation of the Business Branch, Sarah Ball began to develop contacts with other librarians engaged in special library service. Her contacts with Anna Sears, of the Merchants' Association Library in New York, eventually led to Sears's suggestion that a regional association be formed. Dana suggested that it should be a national association and, at his direction, Ball and Sears sent out letters of invitation to various special librarians, asking them to attend a meeting at the ALA Conference at Bretton Woods, New Hampshire, in 1909. On July 2 of that year, Dana addressed a general session of the Association, and he spoke briefly of the difficulties in developing special collections in libraries. He then invited those interested in addressing such concerns to meet with him, and on that same day the Special Libraries Association was formed, with Dana its first president. At the Mackinac Island Conference in 1910, he sought to achieve the new Association's incorporation within ALA, and the failure of that move only heightened Dana's dissatisfaction with ALA.

He remained an active ALA member but continued to be outspoken. In 1919, he served, with his friend Frank Hill, on the Committee on the Enlarged Program. Hill and Dana, who had not favored locating the ALA headquarters in Chicago initially, wished to reopen this perennial question but withdrew the suggestion at the urging of other members of the Committee. This topic was struck from the text, but a copy of the unrevised index, with reference to this question still in it, was inadvertently distributed, creating a minor controversy. The proposed program also called for a comprehensive library survey, an idea which Dana opposed as a waste of time, and he did not hesitate to make his views widely known. Other differences arose, and the issues at question were not resolved. Finally, Dana and Hill resigned from the Committee and, at that time, Dana wrote:

> I do not feel moved to transfer from my own duties as a librarian and a director of a museum, time and thought and energy to work which is exacting and relatively thankless under the best conditions for an enlargement and enrichment of the field and for an advancement of the standing of an organization whose members find it impossible to stand together thereon.

Subsequently Dana became a more severe and frequent critic, often using his contacts with newspapers to carry the battle to that field, which frequently irritated the supporters of the Association. He remarked of his relationship with ALA, "I have been for years, now and then, the down-right critic of the A.L.A. During these same years I hope I have been of assistance to the A.L.A. in all its good work. My criticism is what I am remembered for, I assume, and I cannot help feeling that I have been, not infrequently, unfairly judged concerning it."

Dana also participated in civic activities in Denver, Springfield, and Newark, seeing in such activities an excellent means of establishing the library as a social force. At Denver, he became, in 1896, secretary, as well as librarian, to the School Board, and also served as president of the Dartmouth Alumni Association of the Great Divide and of the Artists' Club, serving for a time as chairman of its Council. At Springfield, he emphasized the close association of the Library with other organizations but was, perhaps, not there long enough to make the kind of impact that he was to make in Newark.

At Newark, Dana played an important role in the life of the community, and much of what he accomplished for the Library and later for the Museum resulted directly from his political ability and influence. In 1906, he chaired a committee of the Newark Board of Trade, which led to his chairing the newly formed Interurban Association of Northeastern New Jersey, a group which eventually helped form the Port of New York Authority. He also suggested to Mayor Jacob Haussling a City Plan Commission, which was organized in 1911 and on which he served for four years.

Above all, Dana was a prolific writer, and his over 500 writings on all aspects of librarianship and museum work were of great significance. Much of his writing was designed to assist others in putting into practice the ideas that he had developed in using library collections. The most important of these was his *Library Primer* (1896), an amalgamation of articles he had published based mainly on his Denver work. In its time one of the major tools on library organization, this work went through six editions (the last in 1920). Dana's most lasting writings, including his ALA presidential address of 1896, "Hear the Other Side," appeared in a collected volume, *Libraries; Addresses and Essays* (1916). Of all of his writings, "Hear the Other Side" best sums up Dana's thoughts on librarianship. In that early speech, he spoke first of the failure of most public libraries and librarians to be of any real value. Then he spoke of what the individual librarian could do to change that situation, touching on his favorite themes of personal growth, community activity, participation in ALA, service to social and cultural organizations as well as to the business community, and publicizing the library and its work. "Keep these thoughts in mind," he concluded, "and you will see how essential it is . . . that every smallest library be an effective educational machine, and that every humblest librarian be an active, enthusiastic, intelligent worker."

Dana was a man of many other interests. His lifelong interest in printing began with participation in the writing and publishing of an amateur magazine, *The Acorn*, in Woodstock in 1872-1873, continued with his editorship of *The Ashby Avalanche*, and carried over to his library career. At Newark, disappointed with the quality of the printing the Library was receiving, Dana secured a Washington printing press, which he himself often used. He even printed a brief testimonial to the art of printing, which he attributed to an early printer named Cardelius. This attracted some attention, and several humorous letters, written by his friends under pseudonyms, appeared in *The Nation* before Dana wrote to admit that he had made up the text. These were later turned into a pamphlet *Who Was Cardelius?* (1909).

From 1908 until his death, Dana maintained an active role in The Elm Tree Press, which his family operated in Woodstock, where his brothers Edward and Joseph did most of the actual work. "The Librarian's Series," which included Edmund Lester Pearson's (q.v.) *The Old Librarian's Almanack* (1909), edited by Dana and his friend Henry W. Kent, for many years secretary of the Metropolitan Museum of Art, was published there, as was a later series of pamphlets, also edited by Dana, on "Modern Library

Economy As Illustrated by the Newark, N.J., Free Public Library." That Press also published an edition of the poems of Horace and a neglected Latin classic, *Copa*, which Dana edited with his brother Charles.

Dana also avidly used other tools of all kinds. At both Newark and Woodstock, he maintained an extensive carpenter's shop where, in addition to making tables and chairs, he designed and built model boxes to carry and display museum objects as well as a simple device to move display cases. Summers at Woodstock were spent farming, and Dana described with particular pride a windmill he constructed there. Always interested in organizations, he served for two years as a member of the Executive Committee of the Windsor County Fair.

His interests were wide and varied and, although he refused to accept honorary degrees from Dartmouth, Princeton, and Rutgers, his directorship of the Deutscher Werkbund and honorary membership in the Chinese Library Association gave him the greatest pleasure. He was also a member of the Century Club of New York, the American Association for Adult Education, the American Numismatic Society, the Medieval Academy of America, the Vermont Botanical and Bird Club, the New Jersey Audubon Society, the International Advertising Association, and the Japan Society.

"The First Citizen of Newark," as Dana fondly came to be known, was a remarkable personality, as all who came into contact with him attested. Slender and long-legged, with a tall, slightly-stooped frame, his broad forehead, close cropped moustache, and dark, luminous, piercing eyes gave him a strong appearance, and he was almost always the natural focus of attention at meetings. In his speech Dana was quiet and, while not slow, was not an impulsive speaker. When he spoke in public, his manner was conversational, and he was, above all, a good listener. He was gracious, modest, unassuming, and had a charming personality. Thus, while his staff often found it difficult to keep up with the pace which he set, they generally liked and appreciated him.

Melvil Dewey (q.v.) said of Dana, "Sometimes he was so far ahead of his associates that they thought he himself had lost the path. Now and then his keen sense of humor led him to take a rise out of other librarians by saying or writing things just to 'stir up the animals.' " Few other American librarians have done the latter so often or so well.

Biographical listings and obituaries–*Dictionary of American Biography* 5 (George Harvey Genzmer); *National Cyclopaedia of American Biography* 22 (Frank Kingdon); Sabine, Julia. "Dana, John Cotton." In *Encyclopedia of Library and Information Science*. New York: Marcel Dekker, Inc., 1971. Vol. 6; *Who Was Who in America* I (1897-1942). Books and articles about the biographee–Hadley, Chalmers. *John Cotton Dana, a Sketch*. Chicago: American Library Association, 1943; Johnson, Hazel A. "John Cotton Dana." *Library Quarterly* 7:50-98 (1937). Includes comprehensive bibliography of Dana's writings; Kingdon, Frank. *John Cotton*

Dana, a Life. Newark, N.J.: Newark Public Library and Museum, 1940. Primary sources and archival materials– Most of the Dana papers are located in the Newark Public Library; smaller quantities relating to his career in those places are in the Denver and Springfield Public Libraries; much personal material is held by the Woodstock (Vermont) Historical Association, located in the Dana homestead.

–NORMAN D. STEVENS

DAVIS, RAYMOND CAZALLIS (1836-1919)

Raymond Cazallis Davis, librarian of the University of Michigan General Library from 1877 to 1905 and a pioneer in formal education in bibliography and the use of libraries, was born June 23, 1836, on a saltwater farm in the town of Cushing, Maine. There he attended the district school from the age of four until he was twelve. From his early boyhood, he developed a lifelong interest in reading and literature.

Following the death of his mother (Katherine Young Davis) in February 1849, he joined his sea captain father (George Davis) in a two-year voyage around the world. The events of this experience were later described in Davis's only published book, *Reminiscences of a Voyage around the World* (Ann Arbor, 1869). The sea continued to be an important part of his life, and years later, in retirement, he wrote a number of stories and sketches based upon his ocean experiences, several of which were published in *Fore 'n' Aft*.

Following his return in 1851, Davis, now fifteen, enrolled in a school in New Hampshire with the intention of preparing himself for a nautical career. Soon, however, he was persuaded to prepare for college, and in 1855, drawn in part by "the youthful love of adventure" and a desire to study French under Louis Fasquelle, he entered the University of Michigan. His friend and patron, Claudius B. Grant, later thus described Davis upon their first acquaintance: "It is no exaggeration to say that he was the most conspicuous member of that class. In height, fully six feet two inches, erect, manly bearing, with a kindly and intelligent face and withal of modest demeanor. He was at once recognized by us all as a young man of more than ordinary parts."

Health problems pursued Davis most of his life. As a boy he was the victim of a pair of mishaps to which he later ascribed a lifelong "low vitality" and varicose veins, which eventually affected his "locomotion." Toward the end of his second year at Michigan, he suffered a "nervous breakdown," which forced him to withdraw from the University. For the decade 1857-1867 he was effectively precluded from extended intellectual labor. During that difficult time, he acted "as a sort of minute man for relatives and neighbors who were making short voyages along the coast," made several attempts at teaching which were aborted by a return of "confusion of mind," and engaged in several other minor enterprises.

By 1867, Davis felt himself sufficiently recovered to undertake again serious intellectual activity. In the summer of 1868, he received a letter from his friend Grant, now a rising figure in state and university affairs, informing him that he could have an appointment as assistant librarian of the University of Michigan. Davis accepted and commenced his duties in October. Rapidly establishing himself as a great favorite among students and as an effective librarian, he had his salary doubled the following year. Following a long dispute over finances between Davis's chief, Andrew Ten Brook, and the Board of Regents, the Board in 1872 appointed Davis librarian commencing with the year 1873-1874, Ten Brook being allowed to stay on for a year. However, there was considerable sympathy for Ten Brook in the University community, and Davis, who appears to have had no part in the controversy, withdrew his acceptance. Again, for five years, he became "a sort of minute man for all kinds of calls," though this time there was no return of the earlier mental afflictions. In the meantime, support for Ten Brook continued to deteriorate and Grant, now a regent, continued to press the cause of his friend. In June 1877, the Board fired Ten Brook and offered the post to Davis, now age 41. After some understandable vacillation, he accepted.

Although Davis never again, until the last years of his life, returned to the helpless condition in which he had found himself following his breakdown in 1857, there is scarcely a year for which the record does not show some reference to an ailing condition of some sort. Pushing his energies to the limit of endurance, he relied upon long summer vacations for recuperation. Until his marriage in 1880 (to Ellen Regal, no children), he spent these summers at his old home in Cushing, thereafter at other ocean resorts in New England. Without the chance thus provided to read and study, it is doubtful that he could have been so well read as he was or that he could have prepared for and conducted his instruction in bibliography.

Without question, Davis's chief claim to the attention of later generations of librarians rests upon his pioneering credit course in bibliography, first offered in 1883. However, credit for this innovation must be shared with the Michigan Board of Regents, which eighteen years earlier, in 1865, adopted a remarkable resolution, introduced by Henry C. Knight, by which the librarian was "authorized and requested to deliver a series of lectures upon the subject of books and bibliography." Though this resolution probably descends from Emerson's well-known call (first made in 1847) for furnishing colleges with "professors of books," it went much further than Emerson, or apparently anyone else in this country, had contemplated. The lectures were to be a function of the librarian who, besides talking about "best books," as contemplated by Emerson, was also expected to talk on bibliography, presumably in its several aspects.

Although librarian Ten Brook, in 1870, responded to the regents' resolution by delivering a series of four or five informal lectures, he apparently did not offer them again after 1871. But for Davis the commitment was an integral part of his job. As assistant librarian, he was familiar with the regents' resolution and with his chief's short-lived efforts to comply. During the fall and winter of 1872-1873, while he was librarian-elect, he spent much time studying the literature of bibliography and German, a language of much importance to the student of that subject. Then in the fall of 1878, in his second year as librarian, he delivered a series of six lectures, in later years expanded to eight. In these lectures, he attempted to cover historical bibliography, practical aspects of using the library, and subjects such as "Fiction—Its Place in a Course of Reading" and "Historical Novels." He continued to give these lectures for many years, though on a reduced basis after 1883.

Although the informal lectures seem to have been unique among American academic institutions of the time, both in number and scope, Davis was prepared to go further. In the spring of 1883, he introduced an elective credit course in bibliography, offered one hour a week. Nineteen lectures presented bibliography in three aspects: 1) "historical," 2) "material" or "practical" (chiefly devoted to descriptive aspects of the book), and 3) "intellectual" (classification systems and a discussion of the best books in seven main fields of knowledge). Davis's command of the first division, historical bibliography, is impressively revealed in his unpublished book, "From the Papyrus Roll to the Modern Book; Chapters in Historical Bibliography." The fruit of over a quarter-century of study, this text, if it had achieved publication, would doubtless have had a long and useful career.

In 1886, at the Milwaukee Conference of the American Library Association, Davis described his bibliography course at some length in a paper which was later published in *Library Journal* as "Teaching Bibliography in Colleges." Davis's influence is directly traceable to the introduction of similar courses at Cornell (1886), Colorado (1893), and the Michigan Law School (1892), and by 1892, there were at least five or six institutions offering formal instruction in bibliography. Beyond that point, the continuing impact of Davis's pioneering efforts becomes obscure. On becoming librarian emeritus in 1905, Davis was appointed lecturer on bibliography. From then until his full retirement in 1914 he gave the course in expanded form, extended over two semesters.

Though Davis attended only two ALA conferences, those of 1879 and 1886, they led to friendship with Melvil Dewey (q.v.). When Dewey's Columbia College School of Library Economy opened in 1887, Davis was among those invited to give a series of special lectures, an office he continued to fill until the School's removal to Albany three years later.

The 28 years of Davis's tenure (1877-1905) at Michigan were within the 38 years of James B. Angell's great presidency (1871-1909), during which time the University developed quantitatively and qualitatively as a major institution of instruction and research. Yet there were never sufficient funds for the University to keep pace with material requirements, and this lack of funds extended to the Library, despite Angell's strong support. Davis often characterized his administration as a "struggle for books," appropriations for which had to be directly coaxed from the legislature. As a bookman-librarian, Davis labored to provide a basic scholarly and instructional apparatus. But an eight-fold increase in the collections between 1877 and 1905 was not sufficient for the Michigan Library to keep pace with its principal competitors for numerical strength. As Francis Goodrich (q.v.) described it, the Library was of the "traditional type, administered by a scholar for scholars. . . . The book collection was exceptional but not in the least popular." That it was not more "popular" was not due so much to lack of sympathy on the part of Davis, who was widely read in current literature, but to the priority given to research and to meeting known instructional needs.

The "struggle for books" was also generally a "struggle with books." Even the landmark event of the Davis years, the 1883 Library building, with its multi-tier stack, "seminary," and special reading areas, was soon outgrown. After unsuccessfully attempting a fixed location classification, the Library reclassified to a modified Dewey in the late 1890s, with the catalogs of the Ten Brook era being redone according to the Cutter rules. Additionally, heavy service demands had to be met by a small staff. Davis was well aware of the deficiencies of his regime, and during the last year of his tenure the library was actually run by his successor-designate, Theodore Wesley Koch (q.v.), who, with Davis's enthusiastic support, introduced a number of modernizing innovations.

Although Davis's college work had been interrupted before the end of his second year, Michigan awarded him an honorary M.A. in 1881, by which time he had been adopted as a member of the class of 1859. Upon his complete retirement in 1914, he became the first recipient of the Professor George P. Williams Emeritus Professorship. He died in Ann Arbor on June 10, 1919.

The general esteem for Davis is well represented by a statement made by William Warner Bishop (q.v.):

I recall gratefully and vividly his many kindnesses to me in my student days—his patience and tolerant listening to my youthful projects—his warm and friendly encouragement to study in the field of the book arts—his constant touch with my own professional advancement and progress. It is a great thing for a university to have had such a man as librarian. It is a greater thing to have so lived that service and friendliness are the chief impressions left on one's colleagues.

Biographical listings and obituaries—*Dictionary of American Biography* 5 (Byron A. Finney); *Who Was Who in America* I (1897-1942). **Books and articles about the biographee**—Abbot, John C. *Raymond Cazallis Davis and the University of Michigan General Library, 1877-1905.* Doctoral dissertation, School of Library Science, University of Michigan, 1957; Bishop, William Warner. "Raymond C. Davis, 1836-1919." *Library Journal* 44:541 (Aug. 1919); Grant, Claudius B. "Raymond C. Davis." *The Michigan Alumnus* 26:129-31 (Dec. 1919); Severance, Henry O. "Raymond C. Davis, 1836-1919." *College and Research Libraries* 2:344-47 (Sept. 1941). **Primary sources and archival materials**—Davis, Raymond C. "An Autobiography; or the Reminiscences of One More Distinguished for Length of Days Than for Greatness of Achievement." (Unpublished manuscript). Ann Arbor: Michigan Historical Collections, University of Michigan.

—JOHN C. ABBOTT

DELANEY, SADIE PETERSON (1889-1959)

Sadie Johnson was born on February 26, 1889, in Rochester, New York. She was the daughter of James and Julia Frances Hawkins Johnson. In 1906, she married Edward Louis Peterson, and they had one daughter, Grace. She divorced Peterson in 1921 and was remarried, in 1928, to Rudicel A. Delaney. She had attended high school in Poughkeepsie, New York, and had received her college education at the College of the City of New York, and her training in librarianship in the New York Public Library.

In 1920, Sadie Delaney went to work at the 135th Street Branch of the New York Public Library, located in the heart of Harlem. In 1924, she went to Tuskegee, Alabama, to organize the library in the Veterans Administration Hospital, where she remained throughout the rest of her career.

During the four years she worked in the 135th Street Branch of the New York Public Library, she demonstrated her profound interest in people by using library materials, services, and innovative activities to help improve the quality of life. She worked with young Negroes, Chinese, Jews, Italians, and people of other ethnic backgrounds by having regular story hours and discussion groups for them in the Library, and the Library became a community and cultural center for people with a wide range of interests. For delinquent boys and girls, she had special group sessions designed to inspire them to develop cultural and vocational interests through reading and participating in library activities, which would in turn give them both guidance and self-confidence. She had special programs for foreign-born young people to help them to understand and adjust to the culture of this country. She became interested in the blind, learned Braille and Moon Point, and taught blind people to read.

She affiliated with parent-teacher groups, Boy Scout leaders, and YMCA officials and brought these groups to the Library, where she worked with them in planning and implementing their programs. Too, for five years, she served on the Advisory Board of the National Association for the Advancement of Colored People. She organized a Book Lovers' Club and brought authors and readers together to discuss their works. Her great interest in Negro life and literature led her to help develop a Negro collection in the 135th Street Branch of the New York Public Library. Through the Book Lovers' Club, she came in contact with young Negro writers such as Countee Cullen, Claude McKay, and Langston Hughes. With her encouragement and help, they met potential publishers and contacted established writers in the New York area. Too, she organized the first Negro art exhibit in the New York Public Library, giving the same type of encouragement and initial push to the artists that she did to Negro writers. During this period, she also came to know Arthur A. Schomburg (q.v.), the Puerto Rican-American historian and collector of books by and about Negroes, who later gave his valuable collection on the Negro to the New York Public Library.

In 1923, she was asked to take the position of librarian at the Veterans Administration Hospital in Tuskegee, Alabama. Reluctant to accept the position because she was not sure that she could adjust to living in the Deep South, she agreed to work at Tuskegee for six months to organize the Library. She got a six-month leave of absence from the New York Public Library and began her work at Tuskegee on January 1, 1924. At the end of the six-month period, she was deeply engrossed in her work and was enthusiastically dedicated to developing library services to meet the needs of Negro war veterans who were physically handicapped and/or suffering from mental and emotional problems.

When she began her duties as librarian on January 1, 1924, she had a small room with one chair, one table and 200 volumes. In 1954, when she was honored for thirty years of library service in the Veterans Administration Hospital at Tuskegee, the patients' library had more than 13,000 volumes, the medical library had over 3,000 volumes, there were modern library quarters and equipment and a staff of six librarians to assist the chief librarian.

Delaney's greatest accomplishment was not in the improvement of facilities, however, but in the techniques she created and experimented with in using library materials and library activities to rehabilitate the hospital patients, especially mental patients. She pioneered in bibliotherapy, which she defined as "the treatment of patients through selected reading."

Sadie Delaney conferred with doctors and psychiatrists to learn the backgrounds and problems of patients. Then on the basis of this information, she visited patients on wards with the book cart to interest them in reading and to tell them of the special groups and clubs that met in the library. Often she would tell stories, read poetry, or sing songs—popular songs, hymns, and Negro spirituals—and one or more patients would join with her in the songs. In this way, the patients gained confidence in her and would talk freely about their problems. Too, records of patients' reading and library-sponsored activities were kept and made available to the doctors.

Delaney's major thrust was to get the disabled veterans involved in the various club activities in the library and to work with them in groups. The Press Club, the Philately Club, the Numismatics Club, art groups, and the Nature Study Club were among the most popular. Additionally, many patients worked as aides in the library. They were taught to mend books and to make bindings for old books and for scrapbooks. Blind patients, many of whom were mentally disturbed, had access to talking books. There were also classes in Braille reading and writing, and patients who learned Braille taught other blind patients to read and write.

In 1927, the library began making announcements of library activities and book talks by radio. Patients and library staff participated in these programs, and each year the library sponsored a book fair and art exhibit. Each library club had elaborate displays of its scrapbooks, art work and other materials related to its special subject area. Patients gave book reviews as well and spoke on subjects of interest to them. These activities, vital in the rehabilitation of patients, relieved the tedium of hospitalization and provided an outlet for self-expression, the development of self-confidence, initiative, and patience.

Delaney did volunteer work with blind people through Alabama, serving on the Library of Congress Committee for Work with the Blind. An active member of the Hospital Library Division of the American Library Association, she also served on the ALA Council from 1946 to 1951.

Librarians in other Veterans Administration Hospitals throughout the United States, as well as hospital librarians from European countries and from South Africa, went to Tuskegee to observe and learn Sadie Delaney's methods of bibliotherapy. Library schools at the University of North Carolina, the University of Illinois, and Atlanta University sent students there for internships to learn her methods. She also wrote about them, publishing such articles as: "The Library—A Factor in Veterans Bureau Hospitals," *U.S. Veterans Bureau Medical Bulletin* 6:331-33 (1930); "Plan of Bibliotherapy in a Hospital," *Library Journal* 63:305-308 (April 15, 1938); and "Library Activities at Tuskegee," *Medical Bulletin of the Veterans Administration* (October 1940).

She received many awards and honors in recognition of her work. In 1956, the U.S. Veterans Administration conferred upon her its top award for the excellence of her work. In 1950, Atlanta University awarded her the honorary degree of Doctor of Humanities. The citation read as follows:

> Librarian of distinction in the New York Public Library System and the Veterans Administration Hospital at Tuskegee, Alabama, who has been a pioneer in utilizing reading materials in the rehabilitation of delinquent boys and girls, in the rehabilitation and cure of mental patients, and in the development of techniques for teaching the blind to read; one whose methods are being used throughout the world in hospitals as a means of relieving suffering humanity, particularly those who have served their country in war; member of the League of Nations Committee on Hospital Library Service, of the International Library Association, and of the Hospital Library Division of the American Library Association; contributor to the literature on hospital library service and bibliotherapy and teacher of hospital librarianship; cited for meritorious service to veterans by the American Legion and honored by the National Urban League; recognized leader among librarians who has unselfishly devoted her life to helping mentally and physically handicapped members of society; great humanitarian, who has labored tirelessly with courage, fearlessness, patience and love.

Sadie Delaney was a small, gracious lady who carried herself with great dignity and had boundless physical energy. Every evening, her dining room table was set with fresh flowers, candles, and silver or crystal finger bowls. She collected fine china, historic ceramics, beautiful glass, and rare porcelains. Her home was like a museum furnished with carefully selected antiques. She had an excellent collection of photographs of prominent Negro authors, artists, and leaders, with whom she corresponded regularly, and thus she had files of historically significant letters. Her stamp and coin collections were most extensive, and many people from far and near visited her home to see her collections. Many items in her various collections have been placed in the George Washington Carver Museum at Tuskegee Institute. An active member of the Episcopalian Church in Tuskegee, she also took a great interest in helping students at Tuskegee Institute.

Articles about Delaney's work appear in some 51 publications, and she contributed to library,

educational and medical journals. Her death occurred on May 4, 1958.

Biographical listings and obituaries—[Obituary]. *Medical Library Association Bulletin* 46:495 (July 1958); [Obituary]. *Wilson Library Bulletin* 33:14 (Sept. 1958); *Who Was Who in America* III (1951-1960); *Who's Who in Library Service*, 3rd ed.; *Who's Who in the South and the South West* (1956-1960). **Books and articles about the biographee**—"American Hospital Librarian Honoured." *Book Trolley* 7:38-39 (Summer 1950); [Biographical sketch and portrait]. *Library Journal* 72:1175 (Sept. 1, 1947); Cantrell, Clyde H. "Sadie P. Delaney: Bibliotherapist and Librarian." *Southeastern Libraries* 6:105-109 (Fall 1956).

—VIRGINIA LACY JONES

DEWEY, MELVIL (1851-1931)

Melvil Dewey was and remains a charismatic and inevitably controversial figure in American librarianship. Many of his achievements, however, have been overshadowed by the success of his well-known classification and are yet to be evaluated in perspective. He was a man of action and of vision, confident and supremely skilled in rationalizing his goals and methods of attaining them. He frequently implemented ideas viewed by others more conservative as being impossible; yet in many of these ideas can be found the germinal concepts of activities in the twentieth century. His rare persuasive skill in inspiring others to pursue causes and courses which he championed either endeared him to or antagonized his contemporaries. Because of his complex personality and his accomplishments, Dewey continues to challenge inquiry; efforts to describe and appraise him have led to his being the subject of more biographic sketches, fragmentary or detailed, and more tributes than any other American librarian.

Melvil (originally Melville Louis Kossuth) Dewey (for a brief time spelled by him Dui) was born on December 10, 1851, in Adams Center, near Watertown, New York. The youngest of five children of Joel and Eliza Green Dewey, he was a descendant of Thomas Dewey, who sailed with the Winthrop fleet from England to the Massachusetts Bay Colony, arriving there in 1630. The young Dewey's parents, displaying their admiration for Louis Kossuth (the Hungarian patriot then being honored in the United States), named their son for him. Dewey later abandoned use of that part of his name and, as of 1875, he omitted the final *le* from the spelling of his first name.

Dewey married Annie Roberts Godfrey, librarian of Wellesley College, on October 19, 1878; they had one son, Godfrey, born September 3, 1887. Following the death of his wife in 1922, he married on May 28, 1924, Emily McKay Beal, long associated with the Dewey family at the Lake Placid Club. He was graduated from Amherst College in 1874 and in 1877 was granted a master's degree. In 1902 he was awarded honorary degrees (LL.D.) from both Syracuse University and Alfred University.

Despite some justifiable concern over his health as a child, he had an enviable physique and bearing. Because of his height of nearly six feet and his firm, prominent jaw line, he grew increasingly striking in appearance as he matured. His blue-gray eyes, alert and observing, seemed to reflect his inner compulsive energy. His hair (and beard or mustache, when worn) was in his youth a rich chestnut in color, so dark that to some it was more black than brown. He was quick in thought and movement and he spoke generally in "terse, vigorous, staccato phrases."

Dewey's adult life may be divided into two major phases, one being his early and active years in the library profession (1872-1905), the other, his Lake Placid Club years in the Adirondacks and later in Florida (1895-1931). This brief sketch relates primarily to his formative years and to his contributions to the library profession. In no way does this diminish the importance of the Lake Placid Club years, but these years merit separate study because the milieus and challenges of Dewey's two worlds were distinctly different.

FORMATIVE YEARS

These include the years that Dewey's family lived in the village of Adams Center. Through the two biographies, written by Fremont Rider (q.v.) and Grosvenor Dawe, and through the early pages of his "Journal," Dewey emerges as a dutiful son, a serious and occasionally emotional youth, often brooding, self-appraising, opinionated, and dedicated to causes. Frequent references appear in his "Journal" to attendance at school, to working in his father's Boot and Shoe Store, and to reading.

His education was typical of that available in district schools of the time: terms of varying length, different instructors, and home study. At an early age, Dewey taught briefly at Toad Hollow, near his home, and was awarded a teaching certificate in 1867. He later attended the Oneida Seminary, where his "standing was given as the best in the school," and in 1869, he received a New York State Regents Certificate.

While there was a religious atmosphere in his home, there was not "influence & intimacy," as Dewey recalled, because of the reputation of his parents as the "hardest workers in town." He emulated his parents in fulfilling religious duties, however, by being active in several churches in the community. His "Journal" contains expressions of faith, of anxiety, of inner turmoil, until at the age of eighteen he decided that the ministry was not to be his calling.

However, Dewey's boyhood years were not Spartan within the context of the times. He had friends of all ages, he was intensely involved in the local lodge and other village societies, and he made money selling books and managing a circulating library which he created. Yet, even with this industry, Dewey reproached himself for idleness, feeling happiest only when "engaged in earnest labor of some kind."

Among the characteristics foreshadowing his adult life was his commitment to causes; he was an activist who determinedly supported views that he considered right, such as those held by the Good Templars, a group dedicated to temperance reform. So strong were his convictions that he engaged in a debate on the duty "to discountenance in all honerable [sic] ways, the manufacture, sale and use of tobacco." Another was his ready recognition of the value of the metric system on which, typifying his support of current and often unpopular issues, he wrote as early as 1867.

Dewey's acquisitive and enumerative instincts, manifested in various ways throughout his life, were reflected in his annual appraisal, undertaken on each birthday, of himself and of his personal possessions. For example, at the age of eighteen he carefully noted the titles of 85 books which he owned, and he also planned to arrange and classify systematically everything in his personal collection.

After Dewey's father relinquished his business in 1868, the family moved to Oneida. While there, Dewey explored places of interest such as the Oneida Community and its library, where he "found quite a number of books" he wanted to see. He visited also the libraries of Cornell University in Ithaca and of the University of Rochester. It was, then, in Oneida that Dewey identified the educational world as his "destined place." His wish, "to inaugurate a higher education for the masses," while tenuous when it was stated, was to find fulfillment in his support of public libraries. A brief teaching experience at Barnhard's Bay (November 1869-March 1870) strengthened his feeling that it was his destiny to be an educator and a reformer. Recognizing the need to continue his own education, Dewey attended Alfred University for fourteen weeks. Though he felt that they had been some of the happiest weeks of his life, Dewey chose to enter Amherst College, an older institution with a much larger library than that in Alfred University.

AMHERST

It seems to have been Dewey's concern over his health and over his lack of exercise that contributed to his choice in 1870 of Amherst College. Since Amherst had a reputation for its inclusion of physical education in its curriculum, Dewey was attracted to the College because of the requirement of regular gymnasium exercise and his need for it. Whatever the other reasons, Dewey's Amherst days were full and rewarding.

Though he had determined originally, as of July 13, 1870, to "mingle in society very little during the next 4 years," he soon freed himself from his self-imposed isolation. His "Journal" records a variety of activities which would have exhausted a less vigorous person, and his circle of friends was ever expanding, particularly among the young ladies whom he visited and with whom he rode, studied, and shared many social pleasures. Dewey summarized one of his later Amherst years by saying "I have behaved pretty wel this year—haven't girld it at all, only a little necessary gallantry." It was at Amherst also that he developed a life-long friendship with Walter Stanley Biscoe (q.v.), who seemed content to live in Dewey's shadow.

By 1873, Dewey was employed in the Amherst Library as an assistant. Here he found an outlet for his organizational skill, for soon after being on the Library staff, he identified as a major problem the system used in shelving books. In his search for an alternate approach, he began to reject the plan of shelving by absolute or fixed location, a plan wherein the shelves were numbered and books were placed in numeric sequence after row and shelf numbers were assigned. With his conviction that "management is e [the] watchword," and recognizing the need to know more about libraries and their functioning, Dewey planned site visits to several distinguished libraries of the day. He visited the New York State Library in 1873, noting that the books were "arranged alphabetically paying no attention to subjects." Earlier in that same year, he had made a memorable visit to Boston, where he visited the Harvard Library and later introduced himself to Charles A. Cutter (q.v.) of the Boston Athenaeum, whom he regarded as a "gentlemanly librarian," and to Justin Winsor (q.v.) of the Boston Public Library. He shared with Winsor his views on centralized cataloging, saying that "of necessity e bk [a book] must be catalgd [catalogued] by some central tribunal."

While at the Boston Public Library, Dewey observed its absolute location system, which used numerals with letters as subdivision devices instead of fractions. Reflecting his own search for a satisfactory notation, he recorded in his "Journal" that subdivisions of numerals should not be letters but rather that "the decimal—applied with some flexibility seems to be e [the] best possible notation." His knowledge of other systems, among them "the plan of the St. Louis Public School Library, and that of the Apprentices' Library of New York," did not lessen his interest in a decimal notation. He studied in detail the St. Louis plan, however, for on May 13, 1873, in response to an inquiry from Dewey, William Torrey Harris, superintendent of public schools in St. Louis, mailed to him "some sheets containing an essay on classification & the scheme actually in use in our library."

Though Dewey acknowledged his indebtedness to "the inverted Baconian arrangement" of the St. Louis system, the letter from Harris arrived after he had submitted to the Library Committee of Amherst College, on May 8, 1873, his own proposal for a "Library Classification System." That he was thinking originally of nine rather than ten main classes is evident from his proposal; his notational pattern was based, however, on the decimal principle, as the first sentence of his proposal suggests:

> Select the main classes, not to exceed nine and represent each class by one of the (ten digits) nine significant figures. Subdivide each of these main heads into not more than nine subordinate classes, and represent each sub class by a digit in the first, or ten's, decimal place.

While Dewey noted in the proposal that "books on the same subject are found all together (as far as is possible to make close classification of books)," he did not suggest the order of the classes. With his decimal structure, however, he sought advice and guidance from the faculty members of Amherst and from friends such as Charles A. Cutter and John Fiske, the latter of Harvard College Library.

Dewey continued to experiment with his classification following his appointment as the Amherst Library's assistant librarian after his graduation in 1874. Not only did he receive valuable assistance from Biscoe, he also welcomed faculty analyses, noting once that Professor Seelye "came in and worked on his heads giving me quite a lift." Dewey assumed final responsibility for preparing the classification for publication, obtaining copyright in response to his requests dated March 22 and April 2, 1876.

In his later Amherst years Dewey moved toward the adoption of simplified spelling and the use of abbreviations in his personal writings. He finally adopted and used throughout his life Lindsley's Takigrafy (a system of shorthand) in which he became proficient in a remarkably short time.

1876

The *annus mirabilis* of the library world, 1876, was also the year which catapulted Dewey into prominence. His involvement with the three major events of the year confirmed irrefutably the prediction made by *Publishers' Weekly* in 1874 that he would "become a valuable addition to the ranks of librarians." The three events were: 1) the beginnings of the *Library Journal*, 2) the founding of the American Library Association, and 3) the publication of his classification system.

Library Journal

While it is to "The Library Corner" of *Publishers' Weekly* that the *American Library Journal* (later *Library Journal*) traces in large part its antecedents, Dewey on his own had initiated discussion in Boston concerning a library publication with Cutter, Winsor, and the Ginn brothers. His inquiries finally led to an association with Frederick Leypoldt (q.v.) and Richard R. Bowker (q.v.) in their plans for a similar publication. He was appointed managing editor of the new *Journal* in 1876 and through its pages expressed his views on practical matters and issues of the day. In it, Dewey first proclaimed that "the time has at last come when a librarian may, without assumption, speak of his occupation as a profession" and that "our leading educators have come to recognize the library as sharing with the school the education of the people."

American Library Association

Simultaneously with the planning of the first *Journal* for librarians, the idea of a conference of librarians emerged. Among those who insured the success of such an undertaking were Frederick Leypoldt and Richard R. Bowker of *Publishers' Weekly*, Charles A. Cutter, Justin Winsor, and the youthful Dewey.

The impression that Dewey made on William E. Foster (q.v.), one of those present at the Conference, indicates that Dewey emerged quickly as a dominant figure:

> We have before us a young man ... the youngest, so far as can be learned, of the 103 persons present.... He is an extremely lithe, wiry, and "lively" person. His mental activity is plainly as pronounced as his physical activity.... He appears almost smooth-shaven, having a moustache only, in contrast to most of the others present.... Despite his youth, he is accustomed to wear spectacles to help his vision. His voice is rather high-pitched than otherwise. His rapid method of delivery sometimes reminds one of Horace's description of Pindar.

The Conference, held in Philadelphia, proved to be the founding meeting of the American Library Association. While each of the original conveners contributed to its success, it was Dewey's organizational instinct and perseverance that insured continuity of the Association. He served willingly and effectively as secretary and treasurer during the 1876 Conference and continued as secretary, by subsequent re-elections, for fourteen years.

Dewey's Classification

The classification which Dewey had been refining for three years was published anonymously, though Dewey's name appears as copyright holder. It was entitled: *A Classification and Subject Index for Cataloguing and Arranging Books and Pamphlets of a Library* (Amherst, 1876). Wider publicity was given to the classification when, through Cutter's request to John Eaton (q.v.), U.S. Commissioner of Education, Dewey's explanation was included in the report on *Public Libraries in the United States of America*, published also in 1876. Despite Dewey's prominence at the Conference, he refrained from commenting on his classification except upon request.

BOSTON

Dewey moved to Boston from Amherst in April 1876. While there, he spent several frustrating and occasionally chaotic years furthering his business career. He was originally concerned with metric measurement matters and publishing relations with the Ginn brothers; however, he involved himself more and more with *Library Journal* and the American Library Association.

In his capacity as secretary of the Association, he devoted his energy to its development and, in 1879, succeeded in having it incorporated under Massachusetts state law on a date coinciding with the day of his birth: December 10. It was during his Boston days that Dewey formulated what became the motto of the Association: "The best reading for the largest number at the least expense [later changed to cost]."

In 1877, Dewey was one of the American librarians who participated in the Conference of Librarians held in London. In a pattern he was quickly crystallizing, Dewey assumed managerial responsibility for planning the American visitation. With the formal establishment of the Library Association of the United Kingdom, Dewey, like the other delegates, was elected to honorary membership. Among the others was Annie R. Godfrey, to whom Dewey was later married. Through their long years of marriage, her understanding and her compassionate and serene nature counterbalanced Dewey's impulsive over-extension of his activities and his often abrasive pursuit of his goals.

The importance of the *American Library Journal* was recognized at the London Conference when, following Dewey's suggestion, the newly formed Association voted that the publication be adopted as its official organ, with the understanding that it would be known as the *Library Journal.* Despite this tribute, Dewey's relations with Frederick Leypoldt and R. R. Bowker were less than cordial because of their differing views on patterns of publication and solutions to the critical financial difficulties besetting the *Journal.*

Dewey withdrew from his editorial association with the *Library Journal* as of January 1, 1881, and, in announcing his resignation, the publisher praised him for his "genuine enthusiasm and indefatigable labors." It was a well-deserved tribute for, throughout the initial five years, Dewey had contributed generously to the content of the *Journal*, a special contribution being his column, "Notes and Queries." In that column, Dewey's responses to questions from librarians concerning specific, technical, and routine details demonstrated the emerging profession's need for practical information. [Editor's note: In 1881 Cutter succeeded Dewey as the editor of the *Library Journal*. The struggle for leadership within the ALA and the fact that Dewey "lost esteem" among some library readers are mentioned in the biography on Cutter.]

In attempting to minimize some of the problems, Dewey sought other ways to assist in library development, one being standardization of library supplies, forms, and equipment. His first effort, The Readers and Writers Economy Company, was a financial failure, but undaunted, he formed another company, Library Bureau, an outgrowth of the Supplies Committee of the American Library Association. This venture, more successful than the first, not only introduced numerous form cards, accession records, shelf list records, and vertical files, it fostered acceptance of the size of the catalog card (7.5x12.5 cm.) currently being used. The Library Bureau, active also in publishing activities, later became a division of Remington Rand, Inc.

In addition to his library-oriented activities, Dewey's interest in simpler spelling involved him in the founding (1876) of the Spelling Reform Association, which he served as secretary, except for a brief period, until his death. He served also on an advisory committee for spelling and pronunciation for Funk and Wagnalls' *Standard Dictionary* and later became a member of the Executive Board of the Simplified Spelling Board, organized in 1906 with funds contributed by Andrew Carnegie (q.v.). Similarly, he had sustained his early enthusiasm for metric measurement and, in 1876, he became secretary of the newly organized American Metric Bureau, of which Frederick A. P. Barnard, president of Columbia College, was president.

NEW YORK

Dewey's opportunity to leave Boston came with his appointment as librarian of the libraries of Columbia College, New York, on May 7, 1883. Not only did President Barnard, who had known Dewey through their metric association, envision him as dynamic and successful in the position, but also the Library Committee of the Board of Trustees was impressed by his reputation and by his knowledgeable presentation of library problems. This reputation accrued to Dewey curiously enough not through actual library experience, for not since his Amherst days had he been attached officially to a library, but through other channels, notably his professional activities, his classification system, and his writings.

Dewey, with the financial support of and unusually high degree of independence granted to him by the trustees, quickly designed a program for reorganizing library services. He selected his staff, among them Walter Biscoe, who assumed responsibility for classifying the collections according to Dewey's classification, at the same time refining it further. Of Dewey's staff of twenty, thirteen were men; the seven women all were assigned to technical, not public, service. Six of the women were Wellesley College graduates who were to become known as the "Wellesley Half-Dozen." Among the factors contributing to their accepting the appointments was Dewey's reputation at Wellesley. He was highly regarded and well known there because of the use of his classification, because of the work being done by the Library Bureau staff and, in addition, because of Mrs. Dewey's earlier association with the Library. By selecting these Wellesley graduates, Dewey became inextricably involved in meeting the training needs of inexperienced persons entering the profession. This involvement, however, gave him a chance to experiment while he was formulating plans to establish a formal training program.

Dewey did not confine his organizational zeal to Columbia College alone, for in 1885 he succeeded in forming the New York Library Club, the first of many similar local clubs. Also in 1885, he published the greatly enlarged second edition of his classification, entitled *Decimal Classification and Relativ Index*, which contained not only many expansions but numerous subject and notational changes and relocations. Its publication provoked an attack by Frederick B. Perkins (q.v.) and Jacob Schwartz (q.v.), both creators of classification systems, who impugned Dewey's integrity. Dewey responded in an equally disparaging manner.

Not only through the exchange of such impassioned views but through other writings, Dewey became increasingly well known during his Columbia College days. In addition to his contributions to *Library Journal*, he began his editing of *Library Notes* (v.1-4, 1886-1898). Containing both inspirational and practical articles, such as "Attractions and Opportunities of Librarianship" and "Simplified Library School Rules," his new journal served as a text for librarians in need of self-teaching aids and later for those in formal training programs.

In 1887, Dewey made what was for him an irreversible decision: he opened his School of Library Economy on January 5, despite overwhelming obstacles both within the profession and at Columbia College. In admitting women, seventeen out of an enrollment of twenty, Dewey exceeded the directives of the trustees. Prior to that date, Dewey, espousing the cause of women in the profession, had made an address in 1886 before the Association of Collegiate Alumnae on "Librarianship as a Profession for College-Bred Women." While Dewey knew that his unconventional and defiant act would magnify opposition to his person and to his methods, he knew also of President Barnard's concern over the education of women and had found in him an ally. As early as 1879 the subject of the admission of women had been pondered by the trustees and compromises were in the making. Dewey merely expedited an inevitable action.

Following the opening of the School of Library Economy, Dewey was never able to gain official approval of his action and, in addition, his relations with the faculty of the College were deteriorating. Though he had the vigorous support of President Barnard, who felt that Dewey "had been a constant stimulus to intellectual efforts at the College," Dewey's position was in jeopardy, his resignation and termination of the School inevitable. (For a full account of Dewey's activities, see Winifred B. Linderman's "History of the Columbia University Libraries," Ph.D. dissertation, Columbia University, 1959, Chapter 3.)

ALBANY

Consequently, when Albany beckoned, Dewey removed himself from the internal strife at Columbia College, for which he bore large responsibility. He was known to the regents in Albany not only through his long acquaintance with Henry A. Homes (q.v.), state librarian (who had died in 1887), but also through his stirring speech at the Twenty-Sixth Convocation of the University of the State of New York, 1888, on "Libraries as Related to the Educational Work of the State." He had been appointed consulting librarian by the regents and, later, on December 12, 1888, at the age of 37, he was elected unanimously secretary and treasurer of the Board of Regents and director of the State Library. Following his immediate acceptance of the appointment, Dewey presented to the regents on January 10, 1889, the consent of Columbia College to the transfer of the Library School to Albany. The regents quickly approved the plan submitted by Dewey "for training librarians and cataloguers in connection with the work of the library, giving them instruction and supervision instead of salary for services rendered to the library." At the close of the winter term on March 30, therefore, Columbia College authorities formally transferred the School and its resources to Albany, where it became known as the New York State Library School.

At the meeting on January 10, 1889, Dewey also reviewed his ideas on the anticipated accomplishments of the University and included the resolution of the Regents' Convocation of 1888, which had endorsed the view that "public libraries should be recognized as an essential part of the State system of higher education." The regents voted unanimously that "such libraries as may be found worthy of the distinction shall be officially recognized as a part of the University of the State of New York." Thus, with his characteristic urge for instant action, Dewey furthered two of his major concerns: 1) continuity of his training school for librarians and 2) recognition of the public library as an educational agency.

Dewey continued his professional activities, assuming more responsibility when elected president of the American Library Association in 1890. He served again as president in 1892-1893. From 1889 to 1892, he was also the first elected president of the Association of State Librarians, which became known as the State Library Association in 1893. In 1890, he fostered the creation of the New York Library Association, of which he became first president. Like other organizations bearing Dewey's imprint, the New York Library Association set a precedent for the founding of similar organizations throughout the country. Later, during 1896-1897, Dewey was president of the newly created Library Department of the National Education Association.

As secretary of the Board of Regents, Dewey became embroiled in matters affecting the educational structure of the state, significantly the division of responsibilities between the Board of Regents and the Department of Public Instruction. Through a revision of the law pertaining to higher education, written in large part by Dewey and enacted in 1892, the regents became more powerful than they were previously. According to Dewey, the law "recognized the connection of the library with education and the state with a breadth and liberality unequalled by any other state or country." The superintendent of public instruction, Andrew Sloan Draper, not always in sympathy with new directions, accepted the presidency of the University of Illinois upon the expiration of his official term in 1892.

Meanwhile, as director of the State Library, Dewey seized the opportunity to mold it for "educating the masses," serving as a "people's college." He extended loans to institutions belonging to the University and encouraged use of the State Library as a reference inquiry center for the state. However, his fertile and inventive mind was at its best in designing service programs. Among his creations were a Medical Division (1891), a Sociology Division (1891), a lending library (Capitol Library, 1892) for the use of state employees in Albany, a Woman's Library (1893), and a Library for the Blind (1896). He also encouraged use of the Library by children, emphasizing that use was not a matter of age but of proper behavior. In 1893, Dewey initiated a program of travelling libraries to tour the state, and, from this innovative program, extension or statewide library services later developed.

Dewey broadened the scope of the State Library's collection by including resources other than books, which he considered "a means to an end, not a fetish." Thus, it contained pictures, photographs, slides, and lantern slides as well as books, and all were available for loan. Dewey anticipated including other media also, such as "rolls of the world's best music for the mechanical piano and organ players" and rooms wherein these could be played. He sought also to "bring the general efficiency of . . . [the] staff to the highest practicable point." He experimented in management techniques and with new equipment, encouraging the use of the typewriter and the telephone as time-savers.

Aware that small libraries would need assistance in organizing their collections, Dewey issued the first abridged edition of his classification in 1894; in the same year, Edition 5 of his *Decimal Classification and Relativ Index* appeared. The printing of two thousand copies, the largest number printed of an edition as of that date, promised continuing use of the classification in libraries new and old; the printing of 7,600 copies of Edition 6, in 1899, confirmed its usefulness.

Dewey inevitably encountered suspicion and hostility because of the ever-increasing extension of his activities. Not only his involvement with the educational program of the state but some of his personal actions prompted allegations against him as early as 1895. A subcommittee appointed to investigate the matter concluded, however, that "not a single charge involving . . . [his] integrity and official conduct" had been sustained.

Dewey did not heed the warning inherent in such an attack, and feeling vindicated, he proceeded with his plan to develop a retreat in the Adirondacks, an area in which he and his wife, Annie Godfrey, had found relief from the discomforts of the ragweed season and its pollen. The spot finally chosen was Lake Placid, New York, where, in 1894, the Deweys remodeled a small boarding house, the Bonnie Blink, into a clubhouse for those invited to its opening in 1895. From a modest estate, the Deweys, with their charm, ingenuity, and zeal, created the Lake Placid Club, a center for summer recreation. The Club from the beginning had a policy of selective membership as well as customs reflecting "simplicity, wholesomeness, and exceptional standards, authoritatively maintained." Thus, from the beginning, the Club was in no way similar to hotels then existing in the Adirondacks; and it was, according to Dewey, fulfillment of an "iridesent [sic] dream" of 1878.

Further professional recognition came to Dewey when he was among those invited to meet with the U.S. Congress Joint Committee on the Library "for the purpose of inquiring into the condition of the

Library of Congress." Dewey expressed his hope that "with the new order will come a new name . . . the National Library," which he defined as "a center to which the libraries of the whole country can turn for inspiration, guidance, and practical help." Commenting in 1951 on the impact made by those testifying at the hearings, Verner Clapp (q.v.) concluded that "there is no doubt that Melvil Dewey's name led all the rest."

Dewey was honored signally in 1898 when Governor Theodore Roosevelt, in his inaugural address, praised the accomplishments of the New York State Library during what could have been called the "Dewey Decade." The governor, who served as chairman of the Library Committee in 1899, appointed Dewey a member of a special commission to recommend a plan of unification of the state's educational activities. Dewey then found himself entangled politically, for it was suggested that he had fomented unification in order to encompass the elementary schools of the state under his jurisdiction as secretary of the Board of Regents. Though Dewey signed the report of the Commission, he wrote to Governor Roosevelt criticizing the plan as "needlessly extravagant" and suggesting amendments that would have broadened the regents' elective powers. Recognizing, however, that the official recommendations were in conflict with the interest of the Board, Dewey offered his resignation as secretary, to be effective on January 1, 1900. The Board, while accepting his resignation at his insistence, applauded Dewey as being "an organizer of genius, an executive of great skill, [and] an educational leader of marked originality and energy." Having thus attempted to remove himself from political pressure, Dewey planned to devote his time to his professional interests: the Library School, the State Library, and the Home Education [Adult Education] Department.

His international reputation was enhanced during his Albany years not only by the use of his classification scheme in other countries but also by his permitting its use, in 1895, by the Office International de Bibliographie (Bruxelles), associated with the Institut International de Bibliographie. It was adopted after study as the basis of the Universal Decimal Classification. Dewey was an official delegate of the U.S. government to the 1897 International Library Conference held in London, where the Bodleian librarian of Oxford University praised him for having "done more than all the other librarians combined in making librarianship a recognized profession." Later, in 1900, as a result of the participation of the New York State Library in the Paris Exposition, Dewey received three out of nine Grand Prix awarded to the United States: one for his library exhibit, one for his home education exhibit, and one as a personal tribute.

The esteem in which Dewey was held, however, had no effect on the Albany scene after 1900. With the Unification Act of 1904, the State Department of Education was created through consolidation of the Department of Public Instruction with the University of the State of New York. As a result of the change, Dewey was named director of libraries and home education (and of the Library School), whereas Andrew Sloan Draper returned to New York as the first commissioner of education, to whom the director of libraries would be responsible.

Draper quickly let it be known that he had "differed much in years gone by" with Dewey and that he was "tentatively opposed to many of the projects" being undertaken by him. He objected further to Dewey's "unfortunate predisposition . . . to set up something different only because it is different." Despite the evident animosity, Dewey endured the indignities with outward equanimity, continuing his recently designated duties as well as his Lake Placid Club and Company activities.

The year 1904 was an active one for Dewey both professionally and personally. Among the events was the appearance of the *A.L.A. Catalog: 8,000 Volumes for a Popular Library, with Notes*, which, jointly edited by the New York State Library and the Library of Congress, identified New York again as a leader in the profession. The *New International Encyclopedia* (New York: Dodd, Mead, 1904, c.1903) included Dewey's concise survey of libraries, with both historical and practical data, under the heading "Libraries" (pp. 193-214). More honor came to him when he was awarded a gold medal at the Louisiana Purchase Exposition, held in St. Louis, for his activities in New York State.

On a personal basis, in the winter of 1904/1905, the Deweys daringly experimented with a winter season for Lake Placid Club members, although Godfrey Dewey was the only member of the family in residence at the time. As a result of the successful season, the Club continued to develop its potential and became known as the pioneer in recreational winter sports in America. Thus, at the age of 53, Dewey seemed to be at the peak of his career.

Suddenly, in 1905, a challenge to Dewey's incumbency as state librarian created a furor. A petition, dated December 20, 1904, addressed to the regents and signed by eleven prominent Jewish citizens of New York State, requested his removal because, while serving as a "high public official," he had endorsed the anti-Semitic admission policy of the Lake Placid Club. Among the nationally known librarians who defended Dewey's professional reputation were Mary Eileen Ahern (q.v.), editor of *Public Libraries*; James H. Canfield, librarian, Columbia University; and Herbert Putnam (q.v.), Librarian of

Congress. The Board of Regents viewed his notable attainments and reputation as inconsequential, however, when compared to the political import of the discriminatory taint widely publicized through the press, primarily *The Sun* of New York City. Consequently, within a month, the Board, of which Draper was a member, issued a "formal and severe public rebuke" to Dewey. While claiming that the charges were based on "misapprehension of facts," Dewey offered, on September 20, 1905, his resignation as director of the State Library, of the Home Education Department and of the Library School. His resignation, to be effective January 1, 1906, was accepted. At the meeting on September 20, Draper's recommendation that "supervision of school libraries no longer be allied with the State Library but be made a separate division of the [Education] Department" was adopted by the Board. Draper recommended also that the State Library and Home Education each become divisions of the Department. In adopting these recommendations, then, the regents abrogated the concept of unity in library services as proposed by the Unification Act.

During the critical days of 1905, Dewey attended the Portland Conference, where divisive views were being expressed concerning the value of and need for library training. Dewey later expanded his comments into an appraisal of "The Future of Library Schools," wherein he surveyed the whole field of training. He also sponsored the creation of the American Library Institute, whose membership would include ex-presidents of the American Library Association.

Upon his resignation, a feeling of "universal deep regret" permeated the profession. The New York Library Association recognized his services, stating that "his personality has been central and stimulating in the great library movement which in this and other lands has so significantly characterized the last 25 years."

LAKE PLACID CLUB YEARS

Dewey immediately transferred to Lake Placid the total of his organizational genius and dynamic energy. Under his leadership the Club, continuing both as a summer and a winter resort, had a high house count of 1,500, an estate of 10,000 acres, and an annual business of two million dollars in 1930, a year before his death. It was known not just for recreation, however; it was identified also as "a university club in the wilderness." The widely publicized III World Olympics, held in Lake Placid in 1932 largely because of the untiring efforts of Godfrey Dewey, further enhanced the prestige of the Club both at home and abroad.

In 1927, Dewey fulfilled his wish of having a subtropical resort, establishing, in association with his second wife, Emily Beal, the short-lived "Lake Placid

Club South," located in Florida in the village of Lake Stearns, later re-named Lake Placid.

Earlier, in 1922, Dewey had applied for and obtained from the regents of the University of the State of New York a provisional charter creating the Lake Placid Club Education Foundation (now the Lake Placid Education Foundation); an absolute charter was granted in 1926. The Foundation's objectives may be summarized under three headings: restoration, schools, and seedsowing. Through such objectives, Dewey continued his commitment to his special interests, among which were simpler spelling, the metric system, and calendar reform. Dewey considered simpler spelling the most important and requested that "this chief purpose shal not be neglected." In 1925, the Foundation took over Lake Placid Florida School, established in 1905 by John M. Hopkins, as the basis of Northwood School for Boys in Lake Placid.

Dewey's Lake Placid Club years, during which a unique institution and a foundation of worldwide fame emerged, are yet to be studied. Though Grosvenor Dawe attempted "to weave a life story . . . show the man and his way . . . and his major achievements," Godfrey Dewey found Dawe's appraisal "wholly inadequate." He felt that Dawe had failed to give an "authentic or vital picture either of the man or of his work . . . [a man] forever spending next year's income year before last and some how getting away with it . . . [a man] wholly selfish in the pursuit of unselfish ideals," yet accomplishing what "no lesser genius, perhaps no other human being" could have done (letter from Godfrey Dewey to Dawe, December 6, 1932).

While he had accomplished what "no lesser genius" could have done, Dewey's personal involvement in the library world lessened during his Club years. He continued editing his column, "Library Notes," in *Public Libraries* for several years and encouraged the New York Library Association to hold their meetings at Lake Placid. Among the librarians with whom he continued to share ideas and close friendships were May Seymour (q.v.) and Katharine L. Sharp (q.v.), who, with the three Deweys, formed the "Cedars Five," the real policy makers in the formative years of the Club.

Dewey continued his interest in his Decimal Classification, though he assigned editorial responsibility for it to May Seymour, whom Godfrey Dewey identified as a "specialist in omniscience." She devoted her time while at the Club chiefly to the classification and was involved with Edition 11 at the time of her death in 1921. Throughout the years, however, Biscoe was the chief, most authoritative consultant on the structure and development of the classification. Dewey's final introduction, written for Edition 12 and dated December 10, 1926, is a classic and has been included in subsequent editions (other than Edition 15) because of its historical importance.

When printed Library of Congress cards were made available in 1901, librarians, individually and through the American Library Association, began to request that Decimal Classification numbers be added to the cards. While the decision to do so was thirty years in the making, Dewey supported the idea, seeing the addition of the numbers as "extending stil further . . . [the National Library's] alredy great servises to the libraries of the cuntry at larj." In 1927, Dewey approved the transfer of the editorial office of the classification, by invitation, to the Library of Congress, where it has remained since that date. In 1930, a year before Dewey's death, an office supported by the American Library Association was established in the Library of Congress for the purpose of adding Decimal Classification numbers to printed cards. In 1933, the Library of Congress assumed the responsibility and continues to offer the service both through its printed cards and through its book catalogs.

To insure continuity of the classification, Dewey had conveyed earlier through a deed of gift to the Foundation in 1924 all copyrights of his *Decimal Classification and Relativ Index* with the stipulation that monies/profits derived from the sale of each edition be devoted to the editing, publishing, and dissemination of future editions. As the classification moves into its own second century, the stipulation still holds.

Although Dewey had withdrawn from active participation in the American Library Association, he was invited to the Fiftieth Anniversary Conference in 1926. In his address, "Our Next Half-Century," it is reported that the "clear, far-seeing vision of the dreamer was in full cry" and that he was received with great applause. At the Seventy-Fifth Anniversary in 1951, the hundredth anniversary of his birth, Dewey was among the distinguished personalities honored by inclusion in "A Library Hall of Fame."

Despite any personal shortcomings, Dewey's imprint on librarianship endures. His influence on librarianship has extended far into the twentieth century through the use of his classification, his innovative ideas of library services, his formalizing library training/education, the work of the graduates of Columbia College and the New York State Library School, and his involvement in associational activities at the international, national, state, and local levels.

He lived long enough to see his Albany School returned, in 1926, to Columbia University, where it was merged with the Library School of the New York Public Library and became known as the School of Library Service. It was an act belatedly acknowledging the wisdom of his youth. In 1938, a Melvil Dewey Professorship of Library Service, endowed by the Carnegie Corporation of New York, was established at Columbia University as an enduring tribute to him.

Though he wrote in his "80th birthday letr 10 Dec 31" somewhat optimistically that "Melvil Dewey is not a watch that wears out to be discarded but lyk a sun dial wher no wheels get rusti or slip a cog or get tired & long for rest," he died a short time later, on December 26, of a cerebral hemorrhage at "Lake Placid Club South." His ashes now lie in a family vault in the North Elba Cemetery near his beloved Lake Placid Club in the Adirondacks.

Biographical listings and obituaries—Dewey, Adelbert M. *Life of George Dewey . . . and Dewey Family History. Being an Authentic Historical and Genealogical Record* . . . Westfield, Mass.: Dewey Publishing Co., 1898; "Dewey Family History," Compiled by Louis Marinus Dewey . . . Assisted by William T. Dewey . . . and Orville C. Dewey. Entry 4775: "Melvil Dewey"; *Dictionary of American Biography*, Suppl. 1 (H. M. Lydenberg); Linderman, Winifred B. "Dewey, Melvil." In *Encyclopedia of Library and Information Science*. New York: Marcel Dekker [c1972], v. 7, pp. 142-160; *National Cyclopaedia of American Biography* 23; [Obituary]. *Lake Placid News*, Lake Placid, Florida, December 26, 1931, p. 1; [Obituary]. *Lake Placid News*, Lake Placid, New York, January 1, 1932, p. 1; [Obituary]. *Malone Evening Telegram*, Malone, New York, December 29, 1931, p. 2; [Obituary]. *Post-Standard*, Lake Placid, New York, December 27, 1931, p. 1; ["Tributes to Melvil Dewey"]. *Library Journal* 57:145-58 (Feb. 1, 1932); *Who Was Who in America* I (1897-1942). **Books and articles about the biographee—**Biscoe, Walter S. "As It Was in the Beginning." *Public Libraries* 30:72-80 (Jan. 1925); Biscoe, Walter S. "Melvil Dewey, 1851-1931." *New York Libraries* 13:38-40 (Feb. 1932); Columbia University. School of Library Service. *School of Library Economy of Columbia College, 1887-1889: Documents for a History.* [New York]: Columbia University School of Library Service, 1937; Columbia University. School of Library Service. "First Founder's Day Exercises." *Library Service News* 4:17-24 (Jan. 1933); Columbia University. School of Library Service. ["Melvil Dewey Number"]. *Library Service News* 3:17-28 (Dec. 1931); Dawe, George Grosvenor. *Melvil Dewey, Seer: Inspirer: Doer, 1851-1931.* Biografic Compilation. Club ed. Lake Placid Club, N.Y.: Melvil Dewey Biografy, 1932; Dewey, Godfrey. "Dewey, 1851-1931." *Library Journal* 76:1964-65 (Dec. 1, 1951); Dewey, Godfrey. "Sixty Years of Lake Placid Club." [Lake Placid Club, N.Y.: 1955?]. "Reprint of a talk given by Godfrey Dewey, Agora Auditorium, August 4, 1955"; Forbes, Jesse F. *The Chronicles of '74 Since Graduation from Amherst College.* Warren, Mass.: H. M. Converse, 1885. At head of title: 1874-1884. "Printed—Not Published"; Foster, William E. "Five Men of '76." *ALA Bulletin* 20:312-23 (Sept. 1926); Gambee, Budd L. "The Great Junket: American Participation in the Conference of Librarians, London, 1877." *Journal of Library History* 2:9-44 (Jan. 1967); Gunther, Emma H. "Annie Godfrey Dewey, February 11, 1850-August 3, 1922." *Journal of Home Economics* 15:357-67 (July 1923); Holley, Edward G. *Raking the Historic Coals: The A.L.A. Scrapbook of 1876.* [Urbana, Ill.]: Beta Phi Mu, 1967. (Chapbook no. 8); "A Library Hall of Fame [for the 75th Anniversary of the American Library Association]." *Library Journal* 76:466-72 (March 15, 1951); *Library Notes: Improved Methods and Labor-Savers for Librarians, Readers and Writers.* Edited by Melvil Dewey. v. 1-4; June 1886-Sept. 1898. Boston: Library Bureau, 1887-1898; Linderman, Winifred B. "History of the Columbia University Libraries." Unpublished Ph.D. dissertation, Columbia University, 1959. Chapter 3:"Dewey the Organizer," pp. 87-183; New York (State) State Library, Albany. [*Annual Reports*] . . . Reports for

1889-1905 used for this study. At head of titles: 1889-1903: University of the State of New York; 1903-1905: New York State Education Department; New York (State) State Library School, Albany. [*Annual Reports*] . . . Reports for 1889-1905 used for this study. Reports before 1900 appear in the annual reports of the New York State Library within the text or as an appendix. From 1900 to 1905 the reports were published separately as Bulletins; New York (State) State Library School, Albany. *The First Quarter Century [of the] New York State Library School, 1887-1912.* [Albany]: New York State Library School, State of New York, Education Department, 1912; New York State Library School Association. ["Letters Honoring Melvil Dewey on His 80th Birthday"]. *Library School News Letter* 1 (Dec. 1931). [6 p.]; New York (State) University. *Official Minutes of the Regents of the University During the Secretaryship of Melvil Dewey, 1889-99.* Albany: 1900; New York (State) University. *Official Minutes of the Regents of the University During the Secretaryship of James Russell Parsons, Jr., 1900-1903.* Albany: 1904; New York (State) University. *Journal of Meetings of the Board of Regents* . . . Held at the Education Department in the Capitol, April 26, 1904-March 12, 1908. Albany: 1908; Perkins, F. B., and J. Schwartz. "The Dui-Decimal Classification and the 'Relativ' Index. A Duet." *Library Journal* 11:37-43 (Feb. 1886), 11:68-74 (March 1886); Rider, Fremont. *Melvil Dewey.* Chicago: American Library Association, 1944. (American Library Pioneers, no. 6); Roseberry, Cecil R. *A History of the New York State Library.* Albany, N.Y.: New York State Library, State Education Department, University of the State of New York, 1970; Takeuchi, Satoru. "Dewey in Florida." (Vignettes of Library History, no. 2). *Journal of Library History* 1:127-32 (April 1966); Townsend, Reginald T. "A University Club in the Wilderness." *Country Life* 38:50-53 (June 1920); For recent (1975) publicity on the Lake Placid Club, see Kathryn Livingston. "Timeless Lake Placid." *Town & Country* 120:180-89, 218-20, 232 (Dec. 1975); U.S. Bureau of Education. *Public Libraries in the United States of America: Their History, Condition, and Management.* Special Report. Part I. Washington: GPO, 1876; U.S. Congress. Joint Committee on the Library. *Condition of the Library of Congress.* [Washington: GPO, 1897]. (54th Congress, 2d session. Senate Report no. 1573); Vann, Sarah K. *Training for Librarianship Before 1923; Education for Librarianship Prior to the Publication of Williamson's Report on Training for Library Service.* Chicago: American Library Association, 1961; Vann, Sarah K. *Melvil Dewey: His Enduring Presence in Librarianship.* Littleton, Colo.: Libraries Unlimited, 1977. Includes a comprehensive bibliography of Dewey's writings as well as writings about him; Williamson, W. L. *William Frederick Poole and the Modern Library Movement.* New York: Columbia University Press, 1963. Chapter 7 contains a critical view of Dewey. **Primary sources and archival materials—**Interviews, 1960-1977; Deo B. Colburn, Lake Placid Club, New York; Godfrey Dewey, Lake Placid Club, New York. *Manuscript Sources (including typed and mimeographed sources):* Colburn, Deo B. Correspondence and Papers. (His personal files, Lake Placid Club); Dewey, Godfrey. Correspondence and Papers. (His personal files, Lake Placid Club); Dewey, Melvil. Melvil Dewey Papers. Columbia University Libraries, Division of Special Collections, Rare Book and Manuscript Library. (Box numbers 1-104 plus 6; Pamphlets P-1–P-73). *Documents of special value:* "Credo: What 80 Years Experience Has Taut Me to Believ." [1931]; "Journal," December 10, 1886-August 27, 1877. Referred to as "Diary" by some; "3/4 of a Century." (Text typed; date handwritten: February 1926). Incomplete. *Letters from Dewey to:* "Dear Classmates of '74," Lake Placid Club in Florida. [1928?]; "A Fu Personal Frends from Our Florida Branch, 7 Lakes, Lake Placid, Hylands Co, Fla: 80th

Birthday Letr 10 Dec 31"; Herbert Putnam, 5 Jan 25; Governor Theodore Roosevelt, 2 Ja '00; Porter Sargent, 18 N 29; James I. Wyer, 18 Dec 16; Lake Placid Club Education Foundation. "*Official Documents* for Reference by All Foundation Trustees." [1921-1928]. Among the eight documents are: 1. Preliminary Letter of Melvil Dewey, Founder (17 Dec. 1921); 2. Provisional Charter by the Regents (26 Jan. 1922); 5. Founder's Letter of Transmittal (31 Oct. 1924); 7. Absolute Charter by the Regents (28 Oct. 1926); 8. Founder's Supplementary Letter of Transmittal (3 Sept. 1928); Letter from Melvil Dewey to "My Dear Fellows." Amherst, Mass.: May 1, 1875. (University of Illinois Archives); Melvil Dewey Centennial, Lake Placid Club, N.Y., 1951. [Transcript of Speeches/Remarks Made During the 100th Anniversary of the Birth of Melvil Dewey, December 10, 1851]. Includes tributes from Library Bureau, Remington Rand, Inc., Verner Clapp, and Carl M. White.

—SARAH K. VANN

DICKINSON, ASA DON (1876-1960)

Asa Don Dickinson was born May 15, 1876, in Detroit, Michigan, the son of Asa DeZeng and Harriet Hyde Dickinson. His 35-year career as librarian included positions at the University of Pennsylvania, Brooklyn College, and the University of the Punjab, in Lahore, India. Well known as compiler of *The World's Best Books*, he was also editor or compiler of a large number of popular books and bibliographies. He died in retirement at Swarthmore, Pennsylvania, in November 1960.

The Dickinson family traced its American descent from one Gideon Dickinson, who came to Stonington, Connecticut, from Nottinghamshire, England, presumably in the Colonial period. Asa Don received his secondary education at the Brooklyn Latin School and, in 1894, began studies at Columbia Law School, terminated after two years by a prolonged illness. Two recuperative years of travel and residence in Europe followed, and by the turn of the century, he was enjoying the quiet but unprofitable life of a chicken farmer in Westwood, New Jersey.

Reading that Andrew Carnegie (q.v.) proposed to give the city of New York a large number of new libraries, it occurred to Dickinson that, as a lover of books, he might qualify as librarian of one of these. Attempting to enroll in the New York State Library School at Albany, he learned that he was too late to take the entrance examination for the coming year. As this examination sought in part to ascertain the applicant's knowledge of the best in literature, Dickinson used the intervening year to study lists of "best books," seeking those titles most frequently repeated, to the end of compiling a new list which would contain the *best* of the "best books." This study had two results. First, it provided a lifelong bibliographic hobby, resulting in five "best books" lists, for which Dickinson is probably best remembered. The second result must surely have been to present the New York State Library School with its best-prepared candidate for the 1902-1903 class.

From 1903 to 1906, Dickinson was assistant librarian, involved with branch libraries, at the Brooklyn Public Library. Here he wrote the first of many articles for *Library Journal*; a satire of reference services in the June 1905 issue showed his humorous bent this early. At Brooklyn, he organized a library for the blind and made a plea for a national library for the blind at the American Library Association meeting of 1906, which led to his chairmanship of the Committee on Service to the Blind. From 1906 to 1907, he was librarian at Union College, Schenectady, New York; from 1907 to 1909, at the Leavenworth (Kansas) Public Library; and from 1909 to 1912, at Washington State College in Pullman.

In 1912, Dickinson was invited by his friend Russell Doubleday to join Doubleday, Page and Company, as editor. He was on the staff until 1918, preparing a dozen or more popular histories, biographies, and anthologies, mostly for young people. One of his publishing schemes was the "College Presidents' Library," a middle-brow version of President Eliot's *Harvard Classics*. Although this anthology never materialized, it resulted in the production of a list of classics by Dickinson which the company published as *One Thousand Best Books* in 1924. Dickinson continued to do occasional editorial chores for Doubleday after 1918, particularly on their encyclopedia, for which he served as managing editor beginning in 1928.

For the year 1915-1916, Dickinson obtained leave to serve as librarian of the University of the Punjab for the Indian government. To train librarians there, he wrote a textbook, *The Punjab Library Primer*, published by the University in 1916. This "souvenir of a great adventure" was written in three weeks at Gulmarg, a remote spot in the Himalayas. The *Primer* is a practical handbook of "library economy," apparently based on notes from his Albany library school classes, updated and adapted for the Indian situation, with bibliographical references. Reflecting the missionary zeal and ideal of service expounded by Melvil Dewey (q.v.), Dickinson expressed the philosophy that a library should have one purpose—"the development and enrichment of human life, by supplying to each reader the book best suited to his needs"—and that the most important rule of library management was "that the whole premises be permeated with a cheerful and accommodating atmosphere." The chapter entitled "The Librarian" is a paraphrase of Dewey's introductory lecture at Albany on "The Qualifications of a Librarian."

In 1917, Dickinson was rejected for military service because of impaired eyesight, but he was destined to aid the war effort in another way. The year 1918 saw him working as "dispatch agent" for the ALA War Service Program, supervising the shipping of 6,000 books a day to Paris from Hoboken waterfront saloons emptied of their usual content by

Prohibition. Herbert Putnam (q.v.), director of this program, sent him to Paris in December 1918 to supervise a similar warehouse for forwarding the books to soldiers. Dickinson amusingly described both experiences in papers at ALA conferences.

Returning to librarianship in 1919, Dickinson became the first trained librarian of the University of Pennsylvania Library, which witnessed improved management and greater student use during his twelve-year administration. While there, he published the second of his "best books" compilations.

His last professional assignment started in 1931 as Brooklyn College librarian. Dickinson overcame a difficult administrative problem in unifying the collections, scattered in various downtown loft buildings, within a spacious new library which he designed for the new campus in Flatbush and which opened in 1937. His administration has been described as "democratic," with resulting popularity among staff, faculty, and students. Always the bookman, he required new books to pass over his desk for examination and application of Dewey numbers. This must have spurred the compilation of *Best Books of the Decade, 1926-1935*, published in 1937. He built the Library up to a collection of 90,000, with an annual circulation of 600,000 a year, before he retired. In these years, he was well known for lectures and radio talks on bibliographical subjects. The "Dickinson Room" was established in his honor to house the Library's archives and special collections.

On September 1, 1944, Dickinson retired to Swarthmore, Pennsylvania, where he published the last two compilations of "best books" in 1948 and 1953. The final volume, *The World's Best Books*, with an apt subtitle, "Homer to Hemingway, 3,000 Books of 3,000 Years, 1050 B.C. to 1950 A.D., Selected on the Basis of a Consensus of Expert Opinion," is an annotated bibliography, with four indexes by date, nationality, subject, and title. A review in *Library Quarterly* in October 1953 found it "richly inclusive" but "unabashedly middlebrow," too contemporary, filled with transient titles, and with a Western—indeed, Anglo-American—emphasis belying its title.

Dickinson had married Helen Winslow in Brooklyn on June 6, 1908, and they had three children, Asa, Elizabeth, and Helen. Family, home, books, hiking, and gardening were his favorite recreations. Of distinguished appearance, he was a political independent, an Episcopalian, a member of the American Library Association and other library organizations, as well as patriotic and social clubs. He died November 14, 1960, at Swarthmore, at the age of 84.

Biographical listings and obituaries—[Obituary]. *New York Times*, Nov. 15, 1960, p. 39, col. 3; "Obituary Notes. Asa Don Dickinson." *Publishers Weekly* 178:24 (Dec. 5, 1960); *National Cyclopaedia of American Biography* B; *Who Was Who in America* IV (1961-1968); *Who's Who among North American Authors, 1935-1940*. Los Angeles: Golden Syndicate Pub. Co., 1939; *Who's Who in Library Service*, 1st ed., 2nd ed., 3rd ed. Books and articles about the biographee—"Asa Don Dickinson." *Library Herald* 3:195 (Jan. 1961); Gosnell, Charles F. "Asa Don Dickinson." *College and Research Libraries* 5:357-58, 367 (Sept. 1944); "Librarian Authors." *Library Journal* 56:703 (Sept. 1, 1931); Millett, Fred B. "Reviews, *The World's Best Books*." *Library Quarterly* 23:301-303 (Oct. 1953). Primary sources and archival materials—The libraries of Brooklyn College and the University of Pennsylvania each report limited collections of manuscripts and printed materials relative to Mr. Dickinson.

—BUDD L. GAMBEE

DICKINSON, GEORGE SHERMAN (1888-1964)

George Sherman Dickinson was born in St. Paul, Minnesota, on February 9, 1888, the son of George Richardson and Annette Thomas Dickinson. He was educated in the public schools of Zanesville, Ohio, and at Oberlin College, from which he was graduated Phi Beta Kappa in 1909. Dickinson received his Mus. B. from the Oberlin Conservatory of Music in 1910 and his A.M. from Harvard University in 1912. During the academic year 1910-1911, he was instructor of music theory and organ at Oberlin, and after his return from Harvard he served as assistant professor of music theory, 1912-1913.

On September 9, 1913, Dickinson married Bessie May McClure in Newark, Ohio. The Dickinsons left immediately for a projected two-year study period in Europe, and during the winter of 1913-1914, Dickinson studied theory, composition, and orchestration in Berlin under Hugo Kaun and Paul Juon. The beginning of World War I cut short the planned stay, and the Dickinsons returned to the United States in September 1914. By the second semester of that academic year, he was reappointed to the Oberlin faculty as assistant professor of organ; the following year, he taught history of music.

In the fall of 1916, Dickinson began his long tenure at Vassar College—as assistant (1916-1919), then associate (1919-1922), and finally full professor of music appreciation and history (1922-1953); as acting chairman of the Music Department, 1922-1923, 1930-1931; as chairman, 1932-1944; and first music librarian, 1927-1953. His responsibilities were great, his accomplishments many, and in three specifics his contributions unique. As professor of music, he directed the gradual shift of emphasis away from "appreciation" and factual history to the historical study of music literature in aesthetic and critical terms. He developed an introductory course, "Music as a Literature," which first appeared in the Vassar College catalog for 1923-1924; in 1927-1928, as part of the new curriculum for the class of 1931, it became a two-semester course and in 1934-1935, a prerequisite for all other literature courses in the Music Department.

As acting chairman of the Music Department, Dickinson planned and executed the construction and furnishing of the Belle Skinner Hall of Music. Completed in 1931, Skinner Hall is one of the most beautiful and most appropriately equipped college music buildings in the United States. In its central portion is the library—the reading room two stories high, with three tiers of open stacks on the inside wall. Adjacent to the reading room are listening rooms, each equipped with piano, record playback equipment, and records, scores, and books for class reserve. At the formal opening of Skinner Hall (1931), Dickinson wrote *The Belle Skinner Hall of Music* and described his Library as

> a collection of music and books about music totaling about 7500 bound volumes. The concentration of all of the library facilities of the department in one suite of rooms is invaluable. These quarters are deserved by what has grown to be one of the best diversified and most closely classified college libraries of music in the country.

Above the reading room is the museum where various musical instruments, autographs, valuable editions, and special exhibits are displayed.

As music librarian, Dickinson developed a *Classification of Musical Compositions*, which is the only viable alternative to the Library of Congress *Class M*. The Dickinson Classification provides various combinations of factors with which it is possible to construct schedules appropriate to each of the different types of music libraries: loan and performance, reference and musicological, general or small. The collection at Vassar is classified by original medium, the option most appropriate to reference and musicological libraries. Before Dickinson published the final version of his *Classification*, Richard S. Angell, then of the Columbia University Music Library, adapted the manuscript classification for Columbia's use. That adaptation, subsequently known as the "Vassar-Columbia" scheme, has been used since 1934 at Columbia [Columbia University Music Library. *Manual for the classification and cataloging of music scores (1955 version): The "Vassar-Columbia" classification scheme integrated with the cataloging procedure manual of the Columbia University Music Library*. And the whole expanded and revised by Virginia G. Haft. (New York: Columbia University, 1955)]; other versions of the Dickinson Classification are in use at several locations of the City University of New York. In 1967, the State University of New York at Buffalo adopted both Dickinson's original classification tables and Vassar's card catalog for its new music library.

At Vassar, Dickinson originally intended to provide a class catalog only—in actuality, a public shelf list. Gradually, however, an alphabetical catalog was developed, the initial emphasis being on those collections whose titles did not readily reveal their contents and on the analysis of *Denkmäler*. Before consenting to the construction of an alphabetical dictionary catalog to be used in conjunction with the classified catalog, Dickinson and his professional associate, Natalie Mestechin, consulted authorities on the use of two catalogs at the same time, especially Harriet MacPherson (q.v.) of the Columbia University School of Library Service. Dickinson was concerned about whether an alphabetical catalog would be a luxury or a necessity. As a well-trained scholar with comprehensive knowledge of the literature, he considered his historically worked out classification adequate, and an alphabetical approach an unnecessary concession to the library's users. The alphabetical catalog does not, however, include subject headings; rather, library users consult the class catalog under appropriate class numbers.

Dickinson articulated his concept of the library vis-à-vis the study of music on the occasion of the formal dedication of Skinner Hall in 1931. He found the main factor in his development of suitable music courses along theoretical, historical, or applied lines to have been

> the constantly expressed viewpoint that music is to be regarded as literature to be known and loved; that first-hand judgments are the true ones; that familiarity with the past is the basis for creation or analysis in the present, and gives security to the act of recreation of music by performance. Accordingly the facilities for examination of music as literature have been constantly enlarged, until there is now at the disposal of the student an exceptionally complete library touching on essentially every field which a college student can profitably investigate, either along the lines of theory or of history, even offering materials for training in the elements of musicology.

Dickinson's emphasis on the study of music as a literature produced at Vassar the first American undergraduate courses in musicology. In December of 1929, he reported four courses at Vassar which dealt "in as advanced a way as seems possible to undergraduates, with the historical and critical aspects of music." Oliver Strunk's survey of United States musicology found Vassar's courses almost unique:

> Insofar as it is possible to judge from printed catalogues and announcements, the fundamental problem of method is stressed only at Cornell and Vassar. Only Vassar and Yale appear to recognize the importance of introductory bibliographic studies.

Dickinson demonstrated his concept of the library as the heart of the music department by 1) his location of the library in the "central portion of the building," 2) his classic article, "The Living Library," in *Notes* (June 1946), in which he described his "ideal" music library, and 3) his classification scheme for the systematic organization of music. "Dickie," as he was affectionately called by the Vassar girls, made the library the center of his teaching; in "The Living Library" he described a library as

> not only a place where *things* are kept; it is still more a place where *ideas* are kept. The things which you draw out of the library must be returned or you will be fined. The ideas, on the contrary, may be retained. Without realization that the library is a boundless source, we and the library are both the poorer. The only significant conception of the music library is, in truth, one which acknowledges it as a fundamental, comprehensive center of materials of all sorts for the teaching and learning of music.

His philosophy of effective library administration required fully trained professional librarians working in conjunction with subject scholars who participated in the organization of the materials in the library. The librarians were also familiar with the subject and adequately trained in languages.

Dickinson regularly used his sabbatical leaves for research and study: 1921-1922 in London and Paris; 1928 in Vienna and Paris; 1935 in Munich and Paris; and 1949 in New York City. After his retirement in 1953, he spent fourteen months engaged in research in Munich, Vienna, and Rome. During the summer of 1930, the Dickinsons conducted a group of Vassar students on a tour of the musical centers of Europe. He taught musicology in summer sessions at the University of California, 1938; Harvard, 1940; the University of North Carolina, 1947; and Columbia University, 1949. He was active in the Music Library Association (president, 1939-1941); the Music Teachers' National Association (vice-president, 1938); the College Music Association; and the Society for Music in the Liberal Arts College. In the American Musicological Society, he was chairman of the organizing committee in 1934, and president in 1947 and 1948. Glen Haydon states that Dickinson was, "as chairman of the Publication Committee during those [same] years ... directly responsible for the founding of the [Society's] *Journal*."

In 1910, Dickinson was elected an associate of the American Guild of Organists. Oberlin College awarded him an honorary Mus. D. in 1935, and in 1961, the Vassar College Music Library was renamed The George Sherman Dickinson Music Library "in honor of his distinguished service as Professor of Music, 1916-1953 and Music Librarian, 1927-1953" (dedicatory plaque).

Dickinson published seven books in addition to the *Classification* and numerous articles in the *Proceedings* of the MTNA, the *Journal of Aesthetics and Art Criticism*, *Notes*, *Musical Quarterly*, etc. The books are studies of musical style—*Foretokens of the*

Tonal Principle (1923, in the Vassar Mediaeval Studies); *The Growth and Use of Harmony* (1927, volume 4 of the *Fundamentals of Musical Art*), *The Pattern of Music* (1939); *Music as a Literature: An Outline* (1953); *A Handbook of Style in Music* (1965)—and the role of music in the liberal arts college: *The Study of Music as a Liberal Art* (1953) and *The Study of the History of Music in the Liberal Arts College* (1953).

George Sherman Dickinson died at his home in Chapel Hill, North Carolina, on November 6, 1964. He was survived by his wife; they had no children. In his memorial tribute, Professor Glen Haydon wrote of Dickinson's

> many fine qualities. One of his characteristics, much appreciated by all who knew him well was—along with his often sharp criticism of shoddy work in teaching and his intolerance of mediocrity in high places—his very fine sense of humor. He had a wonderful knack of rounding off some of his drastic criticisms with a sly turn that only served to make his observations all the more telling. He had an unusual passion for music and never missed an opportunity to hear a good concert. He loved books and was interested not only in their contents, but also in their external appearance, for typography was one of his hobbies.

An intensely private individual, Dickinson left no papers; the Vassar-related documents were destroyed at the time of his retirement, the remainder after his death by his widow—at his request.

Biographical listings and obituaries—Haydon, Glen. "George Sherman Dickinson, 1888-1964." *Journal* of the American Musicological Society 18:219-21 (Summer 1965); *National Cyclopaedia of American Biography* 51; [Obituary]. *Music Library Association Notes* 21:522 (Fall 1964); [Obituary]. *New York Times*, Nov. 8, 1964, p. 88; *Who Was Who in America* IV (1961-1968); *Who's Who in Library Service*, 2nd ed. **Books and articles about the biographee**—Bradley, Carol J. "The Dickinson Classification for Music: An Introduction." *Fontes Artis Musicae* 19:13-22 (1972/1-2). **Primary sources and archival materials**—Interview by this author with Mrs. G. S. Dickinson (May 13-15, 1971) and Natalie Mestechin (June 29-30, 1973).

                                        —CAROL JUNE BRADLEY

DITZION, SIDNEY HERBERT (1908-1975)

Sidney Ditzion was one of a limited number of librarians whose scholarly reputation and achievements far transcended the boundaries of librarianship. A trained historian and sociologist, he was in every sense a disciple of Merle Curti. In his later years particularly, he turned to sociological research in American social mores and morals. For the librarian, however, he is best known for his landmark work on

American library history, *Arsenals of a Democratic Culture*, published, after its acceptance as a doctoral dissertation at Columbia, by the American Library Association in 1947.

Ditzion was born in Philadelphia, November 23, 1908. He received his bachelor's degree from the College of the City of New York in 1929; the B.L.S. from Columbia University in 1934; the M.S. in education from CCNY in 1938; and the Ph.D. in history from Columbia in 1945. On January 24, 1931, he married Grace Finke of New York, who was herself a teacher and an artist. They had two children, Lynne Shaw and Bruce.

Though he had many offers to go elsewhere and did some teaching in ancient and modern history at CCNY and some summer teaching at Columbia, he was devoted to the library at City College, where he practiced his profession his entire life. From 1928 to 1939, he served as the assistant to the librarian there, and from 1940 to 1959, held the post of assistant librarian. In 1960, he moved across to the History Department at CCNY, and in 1971, was promoted to full professor.

Sidney Ditzion made a major contribution to the intellectual history of American, and library, history with the publication of his brilliant and scholarly *Arsenals of a Democratic Culture: A Social History of the American Public Library Movement in New England and the Middle States from 1850 to 1900* (1947). In this work, Professor Ditzion pioneered in the assessment of library development within the context of American social, political, and intellectual history. As he wrote in 1973, the new library history must recognize that "the real roots of institutional impetus must be pulled up out of the soil of social circumstances and operational ideas. The sources of movement must be sought in the ways of thinking that pervade communities and permeate the civic and social actions of both leaders and the led." This view of the need to study library development within the context of the "coeval culture," so persuasively applied in Ditzion's book and many articles, inspired and directed a whole generation of library historians. And while he moved, later in life, to a series of broader studies of American social history, he retained his interest in libraries and provided important support and advice to many younger scholars.

Throughout his professional life, Ditzion was one of those productive scholars who never permitted his typewriter to grow cold. An unusually large volume of material, in a wide variety of subjects, and all of it in the highest scholarly tradition, poured from his study. To historians, educators, and social scientists, his best known work was his *Marriage, Morals, and Sex in America: A History of Ideas* (1953). Shortly after his death on June 30, 1975, Ditzion's friends and associates formed the Sidney H. Ditzion

Foundation, the purposes of which are to provide for annual visiting lectureships in American social history, research grants to deserving students in intellectual and social history, and sponsorship of academic convocations.

I first came to know Sidney through his writings, two essays which appeared in the *Library Quarterly*, when I was beginning work on my own doctoral program at the University of Chicago: "Social Reform, Education and the Library, 1850-1906" [9:156-84 (1939)] and the following year, "Mechanics and Mercantile Libraries" [10:192-219 (1940)]. It was this common interest in American library history at a time when we were both engaged in doctoral research that brought us together and laid the foundation for a lasting friendship.

"Sidney Ditzion," Merle Curti wrote in the preface to *The First Three Hundred Years*, "was an original and distinguished scholar who belongs to history. His place is secure." To those librarians who, like the present writer, were privileged to know him and who profited from his work, he will always be the scholar's librarian and the librarian as scholar.

Biographical listings and obituaries—*Contemporary Authors* (1941); *Directory of American Scholars: Volume I, History* (1963); *Who's Who in Library Service*, 2nd ed., 3rd ed. Primary sources and archival materials—Materials on Sidney Ditzion are not readily available, since he was not given to recording his biographical data in the standard bibliographic compilations. The writer is heavily indebted for his information to Mrs. Grace Ditzion. Ditzion's article, "The Research and Writing of Library History," in Conrad Rawski, ed., *Toward a Theory of Librarianship* (Metuchen, N.J.: Scarecrow Press, 1973), pp. 55-69, provides many insights into his view of the library in society.

—JESSE H. SHERA

DOREN, ELECTRA COLLINS (1861-1927)

Electra Collins Doren was born December 4, 1861, at Georgetown, Ohio, the daughter of John Gates and Elizabeth Bragdon Doren. She graduated from the Cooper Female Seminary, Dayton, Ohio, in June 1879. Her education then continued under private tutors, through visits to libraries of the Eastern United States in 1892, in the library school in Albany, New York, 1894-1895, and by study in France, England, and Italy, 1899-1900. She never married.

In September 1879, at the age of eighteen, she was appointed assistant librarian of the Dayton Public Library. In 1880, she began work on a dictionary card catalog, which resulted in 1884 in an analytical dictionary catalog (of 20,000 volumes) in book form. She became head librarian of that Library in September 1896. In February 1905, she resigned to assist William Howard Brett (q.v.) in planning and developing the library school at Western Reserve University. Under Brett as dean, she served as director and head instructor until June 1906, when ill health forced her return to Dayton. She again headed the Dayton Library from April to September 1910, while the librarian, Linda M. Clatworthy, was on leave for study and travel in Europe.

Upon Clatworthy's resignation over the Library Board's decision to close the four school branch libraries to restock the flood-ravished main library, Electra C. Doren was reappointed head librarian beginning September 1, 1913, a position she held until her death in March 1927. Her successor was Paul North Rice (q.v.).

Electra C. Doren's awareness of and contribution to the development of public library development in the United States are shown in what she identified as "milestones" in Dayton: dictionary card catalog introduced (1880), public access to shelves, children's room established (1899), special work with factory workers instituted (1908), regional branches established (1914), service to community agencies and groups emphasized (1916), outreach service offered to the military (1917), school branches, classroom libraries and substations opened (1919), bookmobile service extended to city areas not located near branches (1923), summer reading contest for children sponsored (1924).

While Electra C. Doren's obvious contribution to librarianship was in and through the development over almost half a century of the Dayton Public Library, her early recognition of the need for education in librarianship beyond casual on-the-job training is also of lasting importance. She established a two-year library apprentice training course in Dayton in 1896. Doren was an adjunct lecturer during 1903-1904 at the Training School for Children's Librarians, Carnegie Library of Pittsburgh. She also served on the American Library Association's Committee on Cooperation with the Library Department of the National Education Association.

Doren was active professionally as vice-president of the American Library Association 1900-1901, American Library Association Councillor 1903-1904, president of the Ohio Library Association 1905, member of the American Library Association Publishing Board 1905-1906, member of the American Library Association War Service Committee and Executive Board 1917-1920, and member of the American Library Institute.

Electra Collins Doren was mentor and lifelong friend to Harry Miller Lydenberg (q.v.), who was a messenger and assistant in the Dayton Library from 1890 to 1892. At the time of her death, he said: "What she was, what love and respect for self and her character; what a happy memory she leaves in a small band of people who knew her so many years, these are things that are perhaps not so obvious but none the less important and none the less permanent."

Linda Anne Eastman (q.v.), in her book on William Howard Brett, reports that when he saw the 1884 printed dictionary catalog of the Dayton Library, largely Doren's work, he was "impressed at once by its practicality for public library use, [and] sought acquaintance with this remarkable woman, who became one of his lifelong friends." Brett decided on the dictionary form for recataloging of the Cleveland Public Library, which resulted in the 1889 book catalog of that Library.

In Electra C. Doren's last several years, she was concerned with the planning and construction of a branch library in North Dayton. After her death, the Library Board decided to name the branch after her. At the dedication on January 3, 1928, her close friend Linda Anne Eastman said: "She felt very strongly that books are one of the greatest blessings in life, that they help to form character, that they help us to know how to live, and that they help us to face death bravely and without fear."

Her longtime Dayton associate Virginia Hollingsworth has given us the most intimate personal recollections of Electra C. Doren as a disciplinarian—insistent on decorum (no cosmetics, no bobbed hair until June 1924), yet democratic in her attitude toward all the staff and all library users. She is remembered as devoutly religious and full of love for and kindness to her fellow humans. Later, her staff would recall her as "our fearless, little Napoleon"—recall her in love and not in derision.

Biographical listings and obituaries—[Obituary]. *Libraries* 32:177-79 (1927); *Who Was Who in America* I (1897-1942); *Women of Ohio*. Ed. by Ruth Neely. Springfield, Ill.: S. J. Clarke (sponsored by the Ohio Newspaper Women's Association), 1937. Vol. 2. Books and articles about the biographee—Hollingsworth, Virginia. "A Dedicated Life: Memories of a Great Librarian." *Wilson Library Bulletin* 28:782-87 (May 1954); Eastman, Linda Anne. *Portrait of a Librarian: William Howard Brett*. Chicago: American Library Association, 1940; Faries, Elizabeth. *A Century of Service; History of the Dayton Public Library*. Dayton, Ohio: Dayton Public Library, 1948; Kingery, Robert E. *The Dayton and Montgomery County Public Library and Its Precursors*. (Work in progress, 1977); Marshall, J. D., ed. In his *American Library History Reader*. Hamden, Conn.: Shoe String Press, 1961. pp. 270-78. Primary sources and archival materials—Electra Collins Doren's papers are in the local history collection of the Dayton and Montgomery County Public Library, Dayton, Ohio. Public Library and Museum. Dayton, Ohio. *Annual Reports* 1896/7-1904/5, 1911/14-1926/27.

—ROBERT E. KINGERY

DOUGLAS, MARY TERESA PEACOCK (1903-1970)

Mary Teresa Peacock was born February 8, 1903, in Salisbury, North Carolina, the daughter of Philip N. and Mary E. Trotter Peacock. She earned the A.B. degree from The Woman's College of the University of North Carolina (now the

University of North Carolina at Greensboro) in 1923, and began her career as, successively, an elementary teacher, high school teacher of English, and school librarian in her home town.

As noted in a biographical sketch in the records of the North Carolina Department of Public Instruction:

From the time she began to teach in 1923, in an elementary school in Salisbury, North Carolina, Mary Peacock Douglas ... believed that every school should have a library. With no thought of being a librarian herself, she set about to find books and space to make a library in that first school. Two years later she was teaching in high school, and again she felt the need for a library. A six weeks' summer session in library science, which she took to prepare herself for the work, convinced her there was more to learn and launched her career in school library service.

She received the B.S. in L.S. degree from the School of Library Service, Columbia University, in 1931, and did additional study at Teachers College, Columbia University, and the University of North Carolina at Chapel Hill. On August 25, 1931, she married Clarence DeWitt Douglas, who was for many years comptroller of the North Carolina State Board of Education. They had no children.

On July 1, 1930, Mary Peacock began work as the first state school library adviser in the North Carolina Department of Public Instruction, a position newly created with funds from the General Education Board of the Rockefeller Foundation. She served in this position through June 30, 1947, making notable contributions to school library development in North Carolina, the South, and the nation. To her, carrying the message of school libraries meant writing, visiting, talking, and demonstrating. She prepared for publication by the North Carolina Department of Public Instruction several widely used handbooks, including the *North Carolina School Library Handbook* (1st through 4th editions, 1937, 1938, 1942, 1952), *Book Displays—January to December* (1947), and *Planning and Equipping the School Library* (1946 and 1949 editions). She travelled extensively—usually by bus in those days—participated heavily in programs and meetings of education, library, and civic groups, and worked closely with other state school library supervisors in the Southern states on such projects as school library standards and a basic course of study in library education for school librarians.

Mary Peacock Douglas was soon recognized as a professional leader, serving as chairman of the School and Children's Section of the North Carolina Library Association, and the School Libraries Section of Southeastern Library Association (1937-1938). She was president of the North Carolina Library Association (1939-1941), chairman of the American Library

Association's School Libraries Section (1943-1944), president of ALA's Division of Libraries for Children and Young People (1944-1945), and chairman of the national organization of State School Library Supervisors (1946-1947).

She left state supervision in June 1947 to become the first supervisor of libraries in the Raleigh, North Carolina, City Schools, and continued in this position until her retirement on June 30, 1968. Here she led the development of an outstanding program of library service growing out of the cooperative efforts of teachers, librarians, and administrators. Special program emphases included teamwork by teachers and librarians in selecting and utilizing materials for curriculum purposes and the development and improvement of reading guidance techniques, including a planned, on-going, read-aloud program for children in all elementary schools.

Douglas's influence was felt through her publications, which offered practical guidance, geared to the needs of the time, in establishing and improving school libraries; through her work on state, regional, and national efforts to develop school libraries, particularly in the area of standards; and perhaps most notably through the force of her presence and leadership in conferences, workshops, and programs of professional and civic groups. For it was the professional and personal example she set as a pioneering state school library supervisor, her effectiveness in interpreting the role and contributions of school libraries to educators, librarians, and the general public, and her influence on the thousands of people with whom she worked that made her, as Sarah Jones has said, "a legend in her own time."

Her *Teacher-Librarian's Handbook*, published by the American Library Association in 1941 (revised edition, 1949), sold more than 50,000 copies and was translated into Korean, Japanese, Spanish, and Turkish. *The Pupil Assistant in the School Library* (ALA, 1957) and *The Primary School Library and Its Services* (UNESCO, 1961), as noted by Mary Virginia Gaver, each filled "a serious gap at the time of publication." She contributed over the years to many library and education periodicals.

Douglas's work on school library standards was highlighted by two of her fellow state school library supervisors in the Winter 1969, issue of *North Carolina Libraries*, for which Sarah Jones wrote: "School librarians in the South will be forever grateful to her for [her] work with Dr. J. Henry Highsmith in their successful efforts to establish and improve the school library standards of the Southern Association of Colleges and Schools." Mae Graham of Maryland recognized her contribution as editor of *School Libraries for Today and Tomorrow*, the 1945 standards of the American Library Association, as follows:

My most satisfactory pictures are those in my mind; I have several such pictures of Mary Peacock Douglas. The first one is dated October 13, 1944. She is standing before a fiery session of the ALA Council, asking approval of the new standards for school library programs. Objections raised ranged from frivolous to ignorant. She incisively disposed of each, approval was voted, and *School Libraries for Today and Tomorrow* became a reality. It is reasonable to believe that the 1969 *Standards for School Library Programs* would not have been possible if Mary had been a less vigorous advocate twenty-five years ago.

Mae Graham's tribute continues with a recollection of Douglas as workshop leader, teacher, and speaker:

Another picture is a kaleidoscope made up of teachers, librarians, school administrators, students; group size varies from one to a thousand, but Mary is teaching them what they need to know about school libraries, and teaching with the enthusiasm and expertise that promote understanding and acceptance.

Douglas taught summer courses and workshops in library science in colleges and universities ranging from the East Coast to Hawaii, and served as speaker at education and library association meetings in still more places. A résumé she prepared in March 1968 lists 33 states, plus "others," in which she had worked. Eleanor E. Ahlers wrote: "Above all she will be remembered by thousands of librarians as a workshop leader who was easily able to combine practicality with inspiration and good fun." Florrinell F. Morton, among others, saw as Douglas's special contribution "her ability to communicate with the leadership of the educational community with which she has served as liaison for the library profession."

Mary Peacock Douglas received the Grolier Society Award in 1958, in recognition of her contribution to stimulating and guiding reading by children and young people. She was featured as "Tar Heel of the Week" by the Raleigh, North Carolina, *News and Observer* on November 26, 1961, and was selected as a state honorary member of Eta State, the Delta Kappa Gamma Society, in 1962. Among the honors of which she was proudest were her election in 1960 as an alumna member of Phi Beta Kappa by the Woman's College, which had no chapter during her undergraduate days, and the naming of a new elementary school in Raleigh the Mary P. Douglas School. A contemporary report (March 1968) states that it was "believed to be the first school in the nation named for a living school librarian," and Douglas found great joy in working with "her" school. On her retirement, the North Carolina Association of School Librarians established the Mary Peacock Douglas Award to honor outstanding

contributions to school libraries in the state, and she was its first recipient in fall 1968. *North Carolina Libraries* (Winter 1969) featured tributes to her from colleagues in many states.

In the first year of her retirement, Douglas stayed as busy as everyone had predicted: reading aloud to children in elementary schools throughout Raleigh, working on special projects for "her" school, planning and preparing for summer workshops she would teach. But time was running out for her. In the late summer of 1969, she was found to have an inoperable malignancy, which caused her death on January 29, 1970.

It is very hard to describe Mary Peacock Douglas to those who did not know her, for the impact of her personality is the lasting impression. As I wrote of her in 1969:

Webster has the word for Mrs. Douglas: charisma. . . . Mary Peacock Douglas' personal magic of leadership has been a guiding force in school library development, extending in space from North Carolina throughout the South, the nation, and the world, and in time from the 1920's on. No terminal date can be fixed, for she has made her mark on all of us who follow her. Her warm concern, her practical judgment, her positive approach, her total commitment are indelible impressions. We are indeed blessed to have had such a leader when we needed her most.

Biographical listings and obituaries—*A Biographical Directory of Librarians in the United States and Canada*, 5th ed.; [Obituary]. *American Libraries* 1:518 (June 1970); [Obituary]. *North Carolina Libraries* 28:7 (Winter 1970); *Who's Who in Library Service*, 1st ed., 2nd ed., 4th ed. **Books and articles about the biographee**—"Tar Heel of the Week." Raleigh, North Carolina, *News and Observer*, Nov. 26, 1961; "Tributes to Mrs. Mary Peacock Douglas." *North Carolina Libraries* 27:4-16 (Winter 1969). **Primary sources and archival materials**—The files of the North Carolina Department of Public Instruction contain: biographical sketch of Mrs. Douglas; résumé prepared by Mrs. Douglas, March 1968; news clipping (source of publication unidentified) on the Mary P. Douglas School; nomination of Mrs. Douglas for the Grolier Society Award.

—MARY FRANCES K. JOHNSON

DRAPER, LYMAN COPELAND (1815-1891)

Draper was born September 4, 1815, in western New York, the grandson of a Revolutionary War soldier. He studied at Granville College and at the Hudson River Seminary, but left without a degree in 1837. The University of Wisconsin honored him with a doctorate in 1872.

Although Draper held a variety of jobs, his principal interest was in collecting historical manuscripts and in interviewing people with knowledge of the trans-Allegheny pioneers and the Revolutionary War era. His activities required extensive travelling, which was supported by Peter A. Remsen, the husband of his cousin Lydia. In 1853, a year and a half after his patron died, Draper married Lydia and adopted her daughter Helen. By this time he had already established a sizable collection of carefully recorded interviews, original documents or copies he transcribed, and a massive file of correspondence with everyone he thought could provide information in his broad areas of interest. He was an untiring and innovative pursuer of historical truth throughout his life, travelling whenever his means permitted. When he could not travel, he encouraged others to collect information on his behalf. For example, when he was unable to secure the commission he sought during the Civil War, he urged members of Wisconsin regiments to keep diaries of their wartime experiences. At other times he wrote out elaborate interview schedules which his correspondents used to question illiterate farmers about their families' settlement in the Ohio River basin. He also frequently arranged to borrow manuscripts so that he could have copies made for his collections.

In 1852 he moved to Madison, Wisconsin, with the hope of securing the position of state librarian based upon his reputation as a historian and through the influence of a former college classmate, Charles H. Larrabee, a Wisconsin Supreme Court Judge. Because of the highly partisan nature of the position, it was not available to him. Instead, he was instrumental in the re-establishment of the State Historical Society of Wisconsin, and in 1854 he was elected corresponding secretary. With his usual vigor, he began to build the Society's library, largely through a very wide exchange program of state documents and the solicitation of donations from carefully cultivated honorary members. From an original collection of 50 volumes, he built a library numbering 120,000 volumes by the time of his retirement in 1886. His will stipulated that his personal collection, rich in manuscripts and the result of his fifty-odd years of interviewing and writing, was to be donated to the Society upon his death. He also edited the first ten volumes of the *Wisconsin Historical Collections*, which were ranked among the best of their type. Although Draper is highly regarded as an editor and a collector of material, he has little reputation as a historian because he could not organize and interpret his findings. Throughout his life he tried to write his projected major works, but a psychological quirk made it impossible for him to commit himself to publishing history. As Reuben Thwaites (q.v.) has recorded in his memoirs of Draper, so long as it was possible that some new fact might be discovered, he preferred to continue collecting evidence.

In 1857, Draper was elected superintendent of public instruction. It was in this position that he undertook to improve education and libraries in Wisconsin. He made an exhaustive survey of the condition of

libraries, which he found to be deplorable. The next year he published his conclusions in *The Tenth Annual Report on the Condition and Improvement of the Common Schools and Educational Interests of the State of Wisconsin*. The larger part of the report was an extensive collection of quotations gathered from the works of notable educators and literary men on the value of reading and the importance of libraries as the means by which individuals and communities could improve their circumstances. Horace Mann declared that it "presented the most persuasive and effective argument for education that has ever been offered to the world." During 1858-1859, Draper proposed and successfully lobbied for a law that would establish a School Library Commission to produce a list of approved books and would provide for township library boards and for librarians; this law also generated a large pool of funds earmarked for book acquisition from the state school and property tax revenues. Unfortunately, before the plan was brought to fruition, the Civil War began, and the $88,000 which had been set aside for library use under the new law was returned to the general school and revenue funds. As a result, library development in Wisconsin suffered a significant setback.

Draper was a man of small stature; and, except for the time he was in the field collecting, he typically complained of a variety of illnesses, particularly when faced with deadlines for his histories. His financial condition was always precarious until his retirement years, primarily because of his continual expenses in collecting and the failure of several abortive publishing schemes. In his later years, after a series of family misfortunes, he became actively involved in spiritualism, often testing his contacts by asking historical details which were not likely to be very widely known. He was frequently surprised by their knowledgeable responses, but he was careful not to let any of the information revealed to him by this method become interpolated into his histories.

Lyman Copeland Draper died August 26, 1891.

Biographical listings and obituaries—*Dictionary of American Biography* 5 (Joseph Schafer); *National Cyclopaedia of American Biography* 9; *Who Was Who in America*, Historical Volume (1607-1896); Wisconsin. State Historical Society. *Dictionary of Wisconsin Biography*. Madison, 1960. **Books and articles about the biographee**—Conaway, Charles William. "Lyman Copeland Draper: 'Father of American Oral History'." *Journal of Library History* 1:234-41 (Oct. 1966); Hesseltine, William B. *Pioneer's Mission: The Story of Lyman Copeland Draper*. Madison: State Historical Society of Wisconsin, 1954; Kellogg, Louise Phelps. "The Services and Collections of Lyman Copeland Draper." *Wisconsin Magazine of History* 5:244-63 (1922); Thwaites, Reuben Gold. "The Draper Manuscripts." In his *How George Rogers Clark Won the Northwest and Other Essays in Western History*. New York: McClurg, 1903. pp. 335-59; Wisconsin. State Historical Society. *The American Collector*. Donald R. McNeil, editor. Madison: State Historical Society of Wisconsin, 1955. **Primary sources and archival materials**—The extensive collection of letters, diaries, scrapbooks, and unpublished manuscripts are in the State Historical Society of Wisconsin, Madison.

—CHARLES WILLIAM CONAWAY

DRURY, FRANCIS KEESE WYNKOOP (1878-1954)

Francis Keese Wynkoop Drury was born February 9, 1878, in Ghent, New York, the son of John Benjamin and Henrietta Wynkoop Keese Drury. The elder Drury was a clergyman in the Dutch Reformed Church—"minister, editor, and reviewer who inspired many with a love of books," according to his son in the dedication of one of his own books. After attending Rutgers Preparatory School, New Brunswick, New Jersey, F. K. W. Drury attended Rutgers University, from which he received his A.B. in Greek and German in 1898 and his A.M. in publishing in 1905. In the latter year, he also received his B.L.S. from the University of Illinois, having completed two years of study.

Drury's first library position was that of assistant in the Gardner A. Sage Library of the New Brunswick Theological Seminary (Reformed Church of America), 1899-1903. From there, he went to the University of Illinois, where he remained until 1919, serving as order librarian from 1903 to 1907, as acting librarian from 1907 to 1909, and as assistant librarian for the next ten years. He also served as lecturer in the Library School of the University of Illinois from 1905 to 1919, teaching order work and book selection. He became assistant librarian, John Hay Library, Brown University, in 1919, where he remained until 1929. His next move was to Chicago, where he was executive assistant for adult education with the American Library Association until 1931. In that year, he became city librarian of Nashville, Tennessee, where he remained until 1946, retiring at the age of 68. During the years 1932-1952, Drury served as a visiting lecturer, Peabody Library School, where he taught book selection, public library administration, and a course in library and adult education. At one time he also served as lecturer in library science at the University of Buffalo.

On August 28, 1907, Drury was married to Martha Blanche Walker of Evanston, Illinois, who died in December of 1930. They had one son, John Benjamin. F. K. W. Drury died in Nashville on September 3, 1954.

Drury made the transition well from university to public librarianship, and although his writings are general enough to apply to nearly all types of libraries, he is probably best remembered as a public librarian. While city librarian of the Nashville Public Library, Drury developed the book collection significantly, increasing holdings by 28 percent—from 106,000 to 136,000. His budget during that same time period increased from $35,000 to $50,000. In 1936, Drury opened the Parent-Teacher's Room in the main library building for the meetings of such groups. With an aim toward county-wide service, Drury directed the establishment of branches in west Nashville and south Nashville, a business branch in the Chamber of Commerce, a book lending station in the northeast sector of the city, and other special stations to serve minority groups and the city parks. During his administration, the county saw the first use of bookmobile service. (Drury did not live to see the establishment of Metropolitan Nashville-Davidson County Government, which has made full county-wide service a reality.)

During the mid-1930s, Drury was active in the Nashville Library Club Committee on Delimitation of Fields of Interest. This committee, which involved representatives from all the major libraries of the city, was an early example of effective local cooperation which sought to define areas of responsibility in collection-building in various fields, to eliminate unnecessary duplication, and to establish channels for exchanging duplicate materials.

Drury's administrative duties seem not to have hampered his writing, for he was a prolific author of works on reading, drama, book selection, and order work in libraries. Perhaps his best known books comprise part of the Library Curriculum Studies series of ALA: *Book Selection* (1930) and *Order Work for Libraries* (1930). *What Book Shall I Read?* (1933), a rather lengthy adaptation and revision of *Books and Reading* by W. E. Simnett, highlighted a very productive period in Drury's life.

Drama, a lifelong interest of Francis K. W. Drury, provided an opening for his writing career when he served as editor of *Some of the Best Dramas* (1917); *The Power of a God and Other One-Act Plays*, by Thatcher Howland Guild (1919); and *Plays of Today: 100 of the Best Modern Dramas* (1921). In 1925, he published *Viewpoints in Modern Drama*, and his last book was the well-known *Drury's Guide to Best Plays* (1953). Drury's other publications include: *College Life and College Sports* (1925), *Novels Too Good To Miss* (1926), *The Broadcaster and the Librarian* (1931), *The Library and the Fraternity House* (Peabody Contributions to Librarianship, no. 5, 1935), and *Specimens of Reading Lists* (1936). He contributed numerous articles to *ALA Bulletin*, *Booklist*, *Illinois Libraries*, *Library Journal*, and other periodicals.

Drury's library texts reflect both an unshakable foundation of library experience (*Order Work*) and a genuine love of books and learning (*Book Selection* and *What Book Shall I Read?*)—as well as a range of book knowledge certainly comparable to that of Helen Haines (q.v.). However, *Book Selection* brought criticism from Professor Douglas Waples of the newly established Graduate Library School at the

University of Chicago. After conceding that Drury's work "meets every reasonable requirement that a book should meet in order to acquaint prospective librarians with the best current library practice in selecting books of most value to a given community," Waples went on to deplore what seemed to him to be a serious deficiency in the prevailing methods of book selection in libraries. According to Waples, this deficiency consisted in the methods used to diagnose community needs—namely, the community survey, personal contacts, and library records. Waples expressed the hope that future textbooks would contain a suggestion that

> book selection should be guided by a continuous, resourceful, and systematic search for facts concerning the community's needs; that such facts demand appropriate methods of investigation and a large amount of hard work; and that hard work is needed both to apply methods developed in other fields and to develop new methods that may prove more effective in diagnosing the needs of library patrons as such.

Waples voiced a new point of view, which was to be heard increasingly in the library profession and which was to be adopted by Drury's successor, Robert S. Alvarez, who had studied under Waples at Chicago.

Beyond the pleasures of reading, Drury knew the rewards of the spoken word—drama—and, in addition to his writings, he was active until his death in the Community Playhouse in Nashville, acting in many of its productions and serving as treasurer and member of the Board of Directors. He also was active in the Shakespeare Club of Nashville, and members of both organizations served as his pallbearers. Drury was a member of the Westminster Foundation in Nashville and the Hillsboro Presbyterian Church, where he taught Sunday school for over fifteen years. Thus, the obituary which read "Francis Keese Wynkoop Drury, ... retired City Librarian, author, teacher and community leader" captured very well the last twenty-odd years of his life in Nashville.

Given his dedication to librarianship and his standing in the library profession, it is not surprising that Drury was a member of library associations at every level—local, state, regional, national—wherever he happened to reside. He had the distinction of serving as president of the state library associations of Illinois, Rhode Island, and Tennessee, as well as vice-president of the Southeastern Library Association. In turn, he encouraged his staff in Nashville to affiliate with professional organizations and took them to meetings and introduced them to leaders in the profession. Scholastically, he was a member of Phi Beta Kappa, and socially, a member of Zeta Psi fraternity.

F. K. W. Drury served his country during both World Wars in special ways. During the First World War, he was librarian in the American Library Association War Service in Camp Wadsworth, South Carolina, and later he was put in charge of book selection at its headquarters in Washington, D.C. True to his calling, he developed various book lists for hospitals and war libraries and filled massive orders of books for overseas military libraries. World War II affected him in a different way, for he had planned to retire as head of the Nashville Public Library at the age of 65, which fell in the year 1943. But because of the wartime shortage of librarians, he stayed on until 1945, when his successor, Robert S. Alvarez, was named.

Beyond his involvement in community and religious affairs, Drury's life was not without its surprising aspects. While at Rutgers he was captain of the football team and a member of the track team. And although hardly a ray of humor penetrates the soberness of his writings, Drury's keen and gentle sense of humor is attested to by those who knew him personally. This side of his nature was most clearly manifested by his membership in The Bibliosmiles: A Rally of Librarians Who Are Nevertheless Human, founded by a group of restless librarians on May 28, 1907, at Asheville, North Carolina. Complete with its own constitution and by-laws, the group voted to "take everything seriously except himself or herself." Its motto was "Homo sum and then some." John Cotton Dana (q.v.) (Grand Ha Ha of the Bibliosmiles) was elected chairman pro-tem at the first meeting, and Charles F. Lummis (q.v.) (Grim Reality) read to the assembled group the purpose of the meeting: "Probably no other profession, except perhaps the ministry, tends so much to crystallize and fossilize as that of the librarians. ... It is high time to formulate a permanent protest against undue solemnity in the profession. It is time to engender an organization whose chief and specific function shall be to see what a joke we all are—especially when we assemble." Among those assembled at that time were Samuel Swett Green (q.v.) (Superintendent of Edification), F. K. W. Drury (Subdued Snicker) and other luminaries of early twentieth century American librarianship. Drury's association with the Bibliosmiles apparently lasted for several years, though the group's activities were sporadic.

Throughout most of his lifetime, Drury kept meticulous records on nearly everything that touched his life—daily events, gifts, purchases, taxes, relatives, meals, genealogy, greeting cards, church activities, etc. Espousing the philosophy of "Why wonder about a thing when you can know?" Drury kept an extensive 3-by-5 card file, cross-referenced and arranged in Dewey Decimal order. His penchant for order could also be seen in the notes he made for his books, all of which he kept, and he tried earnestly, though not always successfully, in those pre-credit-card days, to make his important numerals match, such as his telephone and automobile license. When asked by a reporter if he became a librarian because he liked to keep records or liked to keep records because he was a librarian, he simply replied: "I never gave it a thought. I suppose it just ran in my nature to keep records."

Fortunately for librarianship, it was in his nature to write from many of those records and to share the fruits of his methodical harvest. His publications stand as a solid contribution to the literature of library practice and to the librarian's inextinguishable love of books. His scholarship and his practice joined in the concept that books belong to the people and that the public library is a vehicle to that end. As his good friend Charles Lummis said to the Bibliosmiles: "We are given a little brief authority, and the most authoritative of all tools; and we tend to forget that we are, after all, mere retailers of Tinned Humanity. We are apt to forget that the books we pass out belong, after all, to the public and not to us." Surely Drury must have applauded that address heartily.

As a practicing librarian, Drury's impact was more localized than were his writings, but he did have the dedication to see a job through and to do it well. On a Peabody College faculty personnel data form, filled out by Drury in May of 1952, he listed only three libraries with which he had held positions since 1903: "Univ. of Illinois, Brown Univ., Nashville Public." And that, in fact, was his career in brief.

Biographical listings and obituaries—"F. K. W. Drury, Former City Librarian Dies." *Nashville Banner*, Sept. 3, 1954, pp. 1, 8; *National Cyclopaedia of American Biography* 43; [Obituary]. *Library Journal* 79:1877 (Oct. 15, 1954); [Obituary]. *Tennessee Librarian* 7:7 (Oct. 1954); *Who Was Who in America* III (1951-1960); *Who's Who in Library Service*, 1st ed., 2nd ed. Books and articles about the biographee—Davis, Louise. "Pigeon Holed." *Nashville Tennessean Magazine*, Nov. 30, 1952, pp. 42-43; "F. K. W. Drury to Retire." *Library Journal* 71:766 (May 15, 1946); Waples, Douglas. "Review of Francis K. W. Drury, *Book Selection*." *Library Quarterly* 1:95-97 (1931). Primary sources and archival materials—Fisk University Library. *Report of the Librarian*, 1936-37. Personal papers and files in the Peabody School of Library Science, Nashville, Tennessee; other papers now in the possession of John (Jack) Drury of Nashville.
                                            —EDWIN S. GLEAVES

DUDGEON, MATTHEW SIMPSON (1871-1949)

Born in Madison, Wisconsin, on June 18, 1871, Matthew Dudgeon grew up in Baldwin, Kansas. His father had served as a minister of churches in the Madison area, but he retired to a farm near Baldwin. In Baldwin, Dudgeon attended Baker University, where he majored in Greek and Latin and played intercollegiate tennis and baseball. After graduation in 1892, Dudgeon returned to Madison and earned a law degree in 1895. Following service in the Spanish-American War, he was elected district attorney for

Dane County, Wisconsin, for the period 1899 to 1903. In 1900, Dudgeon married Mabel Cunningham, daughter of a Kansas Supreme Court justice; the couple had two daughters, Lucile and Edith, both of whom became librarians.

In 1903, Dudgeon won election to the Wisconsin State Assembly, where he served for one term. At the same time, he established a legal practice in Madison (the firm of Lewis, Briggs and Dudgeon), specializing in the law of public utility regulation. Concurrently he lectured at the University of Wisconsin on the regulation of public utilities.

Upon completion of his term in the legislature, Dudgeon was employed for several years by the Wisconsin Legislative Reference Library in Madison to draft legislative proposals. Henry E. Legler (q.v.), secretary of the Wisconsin Free Library Commission (which administered the Legislative Reference Library), was so impressed with Dudgeon's abilities that when Legler resigned as secretary to become librarian of the Chicago Public Library, he nominated Dudgeon to be his successor.

When Dudgeon became secretary of the Wisconsin Free Library Commission in 1909, he assumed a number of major responsibilities. He directed the Library School of the University of Wisconsin, administered travelling libraries for over 1,500 rural communities, and advised all of the state's public libraries.

World War I presented an unparalleled opportunity for the American Library Association to enhance its organizational prestige by providing library materials to military personnel in America and in Europe. Dudgeon became the director of domestic camp libraries in August 1919, the first salaried employee of the Library War Service. Embracing the opportunity to elevate the profession's status, Dudgeon told camp librarians in November 1917 that the Library War Service marked "the beginning of a new era in the development of libraries." Further, to Dudgeon the war represented an "opportunity to demonstrate to the MEN of America—that library work is a profession," for he clearly wanted to erase the notion that librarians were passive and effeminate. For Dudgeon and others, then, combining the corporate ideal of efficient management with the bibliographical expertise of librarianship was the best way to win public esteem. After his service as director of the camp libraries, Dudgeon served as a domestic field representative for the War Service in the Midwest, and during 1919 and 1920, served in various capacities in Europe. It was during this period that Dudgeon perceived the great possibilities of libraries as agents for adult education.

In 1920, Dudgeon was appointed director of the Milwaukee Public Library, a post which he held for 21 years. Under his stewardship, the Library responded innovatively and pragmatically to changing community needs. During the expansionist 1920s, the Library's holdings more than doubled, increasing from 386,175 volumes at the beginning of the decade to 858,315 volumes in 1930. Many new services were introduced during his tenure: departmentalized reference services and a readers' bureau facilitated research, telephone and parcel post delivery provided service for shut-ins, and extension collections in more than 2,500 locations improved the public's access to information. Dudgeon was particularly committed to expanding and upgrading the Library's system of branches.

A pioneer in the library adult education movement, Dudgeon served as vice-chairman of the ALA Commission on Adult Education in 1924 and published a brief monograph entitled *The Worker and the Library* in 1929. In an address before the Wisconsin Library Association [quoted in *ALA Bulletin* 24:68-69 (1930)], Dudgeon had some brisk things to say about education:

> adult education was directly opposed to the camel theory of education which holds that men are mentally camels who can, by a cramming process imposed upon them in early youth in the schools, be educated once and for all so that as they go forward on life's journey they need never again indulge in additional education.

> This scheme might be termed the "K.K.K." [sic] process, if you excuse the spelling. They Kaught the child, Konfined him in the school room, Kept him quiet, and Krowded and Krammed what they termed an education down his more or less unwilling throat. When they had done this, the individual was "educated"—he had reached the highest point of his mental effectiveness.

Dudgeon worked hard on behalf of ALA and related professional organizations. Among his many positions were ALA treasurer, 1927-1941; chairman of the Adult Education Board, 1926-1933; fellow of the American Library Institute; member of the ALA Executive Board, 1915-1918, and president of the League of Library Commissions, 1914-1915.

Although the mandatory retirement age was 70, Dudgeon chose to leave the directorship of the Milwaukee Public Library a year early. His comment in the *Milwaukee Journal* (July 27, 1949) was: "I decided to go while everyone was willing that I stay, rather than stay until everyone was willing that I go." He died on July 26, 1949, nine years after that decision.

Biographical listings and obituaries—[Obituary]. *Milwaukee Journal*, July 27, 1949; [Obituary]. *Wisconsin Library Bulletin* 45:112 (Sept. 1949); *Who Was Who in America* III (1951-1960); *Who's Who in Library Service*, 1st ed., 2nd ed. Books and articles about the biographee—Still, Bayrd. *Milwaukee: The History of a City*. Madison: State Historical

Society of Wisconsin, 1948; "Who's Who in the A.L.A.: Matthew S. Dudgeon." *ALA Bulletin* 24:68-69 (1934); Young, Arthur P. "The American Library Association and World War I." Ph.D. dissertation, University of Illinois, 1976. **Primary sources and archival materials**—Dudgeon's papers (1906-1920) are held by the Wisconsin State Historical Society (8 boxes—4 feet). The records of the ALA War Service Committee (1917-1920) in the ALA Archives at the University of Illinois Library (Urbana) also contain some material on Dudgeon.

—TED SAMORE

DUNBAR, RALPH McNEAL (1890-1970)

In 1968 the Legislative Committee of the American Library Association presented a special citation to Ralph McNeal Dunbar. This well-merited award recognized his persistent and dedicated efforts to expand and improve library services throughout the United States, and it particularly noted his administration at the federal level during the initial period of the Library Services Act of 1956.

Dunbar, who headed the first unit of the U.S. Office of Education to assist libraries and library development for twenty critical years after its establishment, had a varied background. He was born in Elkton, Maryland, on July 7, 1890. He graduated from George Washington University in 1912, earned his M.A. from Columbia in 1914, and studied at the University of Chicago from 1935 to 1937 after receiving an ALA fellowship award. While at Chicago, Dunbar began a dissertation on university library administration under the personal guidance of Dean Louis Round Wilson, who expected that this would open up the field to further study. Unfortunately, Dunbar was never able to complete his dissertation, due to his heavy responsibilities at the U.S. Office of Education.

He began his library career as an assistant with the District of Columbia Public Library from 1907 to 1912. Then, after a year as an instructor at the 23rd St. Preparatory School in New York City, he held various positions with the Brooklyn Public Library from 1913 through 1918. In 1918 Dunbar was an officer candidate with the Field Artillery, Officers School, Camp Zachary Taylor. In the same year he married Grace J. Sleeper, the beginning of a long and happy union. From 1919 through 1924, he was a field librarian with the Morale Division of the Bureau of Navigation, U.S. Navy.

Then, as his library career took a new direction, Ralph Dunbar became assistant librarian and associate professor at Iowa State College in Ames, Iowa, a position he held until 1937. In the following year he was appointed chief of the newly established Library Services Division of the U.S. Office of Education, the duties of which included "the development of public, school, and other library services throughout the country." The establishment of the Division was the result of years of efforts by librarians, and particularly by the American Library Association. One of Dunbar's teachers at Chicago, Carleton B. Joeckel (q.v.), was especially active in promoting a library division at Washington, and Dunbar was undoubtedly influenced by Joeckel's views on the services to be offered by the new agency. The creation of the Division signified, then, Congress's long-delayed recognition of the vital part that libraries play in the educational structure of the nation. Behind the success of every organization, however, is a person, and the success of the first "library office" was due to Ralph Dunbar and the capable staff he recruited to assist him.

The Library Services Division of the Office of Education had its share of problems. Until the passage of the Library Services Act in 1956, the Division was understaffed, while the range of questions and problems to be handled was extremely wide. Realizing that, with few exceptions, the state library agencies were poorly staffed and inadequately funded, and that they lacked the needed official status, Dunbar worked constantly to strengthen these agencies. Under his sensitive leadership, the groundwork was laid for the passage and success of the Library Services Act, legislation to promote the further development of public library services in rural areas.

Dunbar was able to assemble basic and essential national library statistics, to analyze and disseminate them, and to explain their significance; he had a keen understanding of the great variety of needs in library services; and lastly, he was sufficiently loyal and dedicated to work long and hard when it was necessary. His background was useful to the federal government in attracting top librarians into the new library unit, and he was also called upon to suggest appropriate persons to serve on the new and critically important library advisory committees. He was either author or joint author of a variety of government publications. Yet, with his outlook, humor, and perception of what was really important, Dunbar surmounted the wave of paperwork and regulations that threatened to engulf his new staff.

In 1958, Ralph Dunbar officially retired from federal service, but he remained in Washington and continued his valuable contributions to librarianship as a special consultant to the Washington Office of the American Library Association and to the Brookings Institution. His abilities were generously made available to his profession until his death on June 8, 1970. John G. Lorenz, who worked closely with him and who succeeded him as director, had this comment on Ralph Dunbar: "It was his understanding of the importance of library service to people and the nation and his willingness to work cooperatively with

all those who wanted to extend and develop library service that resulted in the successful programs which his selfless leadership achieved."

Biographical listings and obituaries–[Obituary]. *Library of Congress Information Bulletin* 29, No. 25:322-23 (June 25, 1970); [Obituary]. *Library Journal* 95:2868 (Sept. 15, 1970); [Obituary]. *Wilson Library Bulletin* 45:105 (Sept. 1970); *Who's Who in America* 31 (1960-1961); *Who's Who in Library Service*, 1st, 2nd, 3rd eds. **Books and articles about the biographee**–[Article concerning citation by ALA Legislative Committee to Dunbar] *ALA Bulletin* 62:1042-43 (Oct. 1968).

–HERBERT A. CARL

DUNKIN, PAUL SHANER (1905-1975)

Paul Shaner Dunkin served his chosen profession of librarianship as a noted practitioner, teacher, and writer. Dunkin was born on September 28, 1905, in Flora, Indiana, to E. W. and Daisy Shaner Dunkin, and his early interests were in English literature and the classics. As a Phi Beta Kappa graduate of DePauw University (A.B., 1929), Dunkin continued his work in classics, earning his master's degree from the University of Illinois (1931) and later the Ph.D. in classics, also from Illinois (1937). Between earning the master's and doctoral degrees there, he obtained the B.S. in library science as well. He married Gladys Hammond.

His library career began with his appointment in 1935 as cataloger in the University of Illinois Library, prior to which time he had been a graduate assistant in classics there. Dunkin remained on the staff until 1937. From Urbana, he moved to the Folger Shakespeare Library in Washington, D.C., first as senior cataloger (1937-1950) and later becoming chief of technical services (1950-1959).

In a somewhat dramatic change of focus, Dunkin left the Folger Library in 1959 to assume the duties of professor in the then-new Graduate School of Library Service at Rutgers University. His distinguished service there was recognized in 1971 by his designation, upon retirement, as professor emeritus.

During his term at the Folger Library, Dunkin wrote the first edition of his well-known monograph, *How to Catalog a Rare Book* (Chicago: American Library Association, 1951). This publication, now in its second edition, is recognized as a source for clear and uncomplicated instructions on rare book cataloging.

Dunkin was particularly active nationally in the field of descriptive cataloging during the 1950s and 1960s, serving as a critical proponent of the general approach developed by Seymour Lubetzky in his editing of the *Anglo-American Cataloging Rules*. Beginning with a paper in 1956, "Criticisms of Current Cataloging Practice" (prepared for the 21st Annual Conference of the University of Chicago

Graduate Library School), Dunkin became a regular contributor to the discussions that accompanied the code revision process from 1956 to the publication of the *Anglo-American Cataloging Rules* (Chicago: American Library Association, 1967). He provided the commentary for Lubetzky's *Code of Cataloging Rules: Author and Title Entry: An Unfinished Draft* in 1960 and, through his "Year's Work" reviews of cataloging and classification activities (in *Library Resources and Technical Services*) and his many other papers, he noted the progress of the *Rules* as the drafts were studied both in the United States and abroad.

Dunkin's service to the library profession included not only his contributions to the revised cataloging code but also numerous committee activities on behalf of the American Library Association and its divisions. In 1963, he was elected vice president (president elect) of ALA's Resources and Technical Services Division. His 1964-1965 term as president, however, was marred by an accident that prevented his full activity.

An avid bibliographer and rare book enthusiast, Dunkin maintained memberships in several bibliographic societies. His dissertation, *Post-Aristophanic Comedy*, was of sufficient value to be published by the University of Illinois (1948), and the scholarly allusions regularly appearing in much of his library writing can probably be attributed to his early training in the classics. Many of his publications included references to literature, ranging from the classics to Walt Kelly's satirical comic strip "Pogo." Certainly his major work, *Cataloging U.S.A.* (Chicago: American Library Association, 1969), as well as the collection of some of his shorter essays in *Tales of Melvil's Mouser; or Much Ado about Librarians* (New York: R. R. Bowker, 1970), reveal the piquant sense of humor, originality in expression, and educated literary perspective characteristic of all his writings. His last book, *Bibliography: Tiger or Fat Cat?* (Hamden, Conn.: Archon Books, Shoe String Press, 1975), returns to the theme of bibliography, analyzing that field and asking if there has really been an advance.

After some years in Washington, Dunkin undertook the editing of *D.C. Libraries* from 1953 to 1955. Soon thereafter, beginning in 1957, he served as assistant editor for cataloging and classification of *Library Resources and Technical Services*, and in this capacity, he prepared the annual reviews of the year's work in cataloging and classification: pithy, perceptive, sometimes satirical reviews that drew both praise and criticism for their outspokenness. In 1967, upon the untimely death of Esther Piercy (q.v.), he became editor of the journal.

As editor, Dunkin gently demanded hard thought, clarity, simplicity in writing, and good organization from his assistant editors. In their dealings with authors, he admonished them to avoid jargon, and always to keep in mind "the lone cataloger in West Podunk" who expected to learn from articles in the journal. His whimsical skepticism of all writing where complexity and obscurity were substituted for clear thought, logic, and expression resulted in a journal that was both readable and informative.

While editor of *LRTS*, Dunkin also wrote a column called "Viewpoint" for *Library Journal*. In recognition of these and his many other contributions, both to the profession and to its literature, the Cataloging and Classification Section of ALA's Resources and Technical Services Division chose him for its highest award, the Margaret Mann Citation, in 1968. The text of the citation is a fitting summary of his work:

> In recognition of his contribution to the development of the philosophy and techniques of organizing recorded human knowledge. An innovative practitioner, stimulating teacher, chronicler and critic, author and editor, indefatigable committeeman and elder statesman with a refreshingly young perspective, Dr. Dunkin has earned the respect of the entire library profession for his modestly-worn erudition, grace and wit.

Paul Dunkin occupied a unique niche in the field of cataloging and classification. He was noted for his bibliographic talents, which extended beyond the sometimes narrowly conceived limits of pragmatic library technical services. Reflecting both quiet reason and outrageous humor, his words will continue to inspire and annoy the serious students of cataloging for years to come.

Dunkin died on August 25, 1975.

Biographical listings and obituaries—*A Biographical Directory of Librarians in the United States and Canada*, 5th ed.; *Contemporary Authors* 33; "Paul S. Dunkin, 1905-1975." *American Libraries* 6:537 (Oct. 1975); *Who's Who in Library Service*, 2nd ed., 3rd ed. **Books and articles about the biographee**—Carnovsky, Ruth French. "Paul S. Dunkin." *Library Resources & Technical Services* 12:447-49 (Fall 1968); Hickey, Doralyn J. "In Recognition of the Retiring Editor of *LRTS*: Paul S. Dunkin." *Library Resources & Technical Services* 15:277-78 (Summer 1971); Hickey, Doralyn J. "Paul Shaner Dunkin, 28 September 1905—25 August 1975: An Appreciation." *Library Resources & Technical Services* 19:293 (Fall 1975).

—DORALYN J. HICKEY

EAMES, WILBERFORCE (1855-1937)

"Day by day all in touch with him came to see the knowledge he had of books in an amazing, almost bewildering spread of languages, knowledge of books in both their physical makeup and in the character and importance of the message they gave." Thus did Harry M. Lydenberg (q.v.), director of the New York Public Library, describe (in "Two Bookmen") his colleague, Wilberforce Eames, who was known in his latter years as the dean of American bibliographers. Lydenberg continued:

> I remember so well in his last years turning to him to ask his advice and judgment about a seventeenth century book with, what I thought, a title page cleverly "doctored" to show it had been printed at Boston instead of London. My own impression was clear, but a "feeling" rather than result of careful analysis. His approach to the problem was logical, careful, thorough, step by step; checking of impressions on the page in question, study of the paper itself, comparison with other impressions on several other pages and in other books of the same time and place and kind. This was a penetrating, final analysis of what the material before us told as to its treatment. Next came a study of books printed in the same period by this and other printers, what one might fairly deduce from their generally accepted imprints and other related data. Then and there, as so often before, I stood before him as pupil before master.

Wilberforce Eames was born October 12, 1855, in Newark, New Jersey, the son of Nelson and Phoebe Harriet Crane Eames. His father, of Yankee New England stock, was a country schoolmaster and farmer until 1861, when he moved to Brooklyn to open a stationery shop. Wilberforce's self-education began at home with the mastery of a series of primers and readers before he began attending private school at the age of nine. His only brother died in 1867; after that, young Wilberforce went to public school for a brief period. At the age of twelve, he suffered a dog-bite, and while lying in bed, he read Gibbon's *Decline and Fall of the Roman Empire*. From Gibbon, he made a list of all the references to other works, with an eye toward future reading. In 1868 or 1869, he convinced his mother to take him to Manhattan to buy a copy of Herodotus from the bookstore of William Gowans. From that moment on, he knew that his vocation, too, would be in the book world.

However, young Eames first faced the problems of the moment. By the age of thirteen, he was out of school, never to go back. After a time as an errand boy, he went to work for the neighborhood *East New York Sentinel*, a short-lived venture that lasted only six months during 1870. Still, it was by performing the tasks of printer's devil that the boy gained the groundwork for a knowledge of printing. Later in the year, Eames went to work for the post office,

carrying the mailbag from East New York to the post office in Brooklyn and waiting for the return pouch. It was natural for Eames to discover the pleasure of browsing in a neighboring bookstore while waiting for the mail, and during this time, his knowledge of books grew. His acquaintance with the store owner flourished to such an extent that, three years later, Eames left the postal service to work in the bookstore.

For the next six years, he stayed at the bookstore of Edward R. Gillespie, learning the ins and outs of the antiquarian book trade. One of his first accomplishments was to purchase from his employer the 65-volume set of the *Universal History* for 35 dollars, a great sum for his modest means. In several years at Gillespie's, Eames came to know quite a few bibliophiles, including Thomas W. Field, author of the *Essay towards an Indian Bibliography* (1873). This sparked his study of American Indians and Americana. From another collector, Daniel G. Treadwell, came an interest in Oriental books.

Moving on to the firm of N. Tibbals and Sons in 1879, Eames gained experience in the current book trade: purchasing new books, attending auctions, and even selling at camp-meetings. This company specialized in theological works, so it is not unusual to find that Eames contributed to the editing of the Tibbals version of the British *New Testament* revision (1882). His interest in American Indians was heightened when he met James Constantine Pilling about 1880. Pilling was compiling a list of works on Indian linguistics for the Bureau of Ethnology, a work subsequently printed in 1885 as *Proof-Sheets of a Bibliography of the Languages of the North American Indians*. Eames, having become a close friend of Pilling, was also his co-worker on the bibliography. He contributed sections on John Eliot, Cotton Mather, Experience Mayhew, and others. The work on Eliot was published in monograph form in 1890 under the title *Bibliographic Notes on Eliot's Indian Bible and His Other Translations and Works in the Indian Language of Massachusetts.*

From Tibbals', the emerging bibliographer moved to the stores of Henry Miller for a year or so, and then on to the second-hand bookstore of Charles L. Woodward, where he became a friend of such notable bookmen as Garcia Icazbalceta, John Russell Bartlett, Paul Leicester Ford, and John Nicholas Brown. Thus launched on the bibliographer's course, Eames entered a personal subscription to the *British Museum Catalogue of Printed Books*, which he described as "the one set of books to which I owe the greatest help of all." In 1882, he made an important move by acquiring, at the auction of the library of Dr. Edmund Bailey O'Callaghan, a 1685 edition of the *Eliot Bible* in the Natick dialect and also the first complete set ever offered for sale of the *John Carter*

Brown Catalogue, compiled by Bartlett. This catalog deepened his interest in Americana and resulted in his purchase of a set of Joseph Sabin's (q.v.) *Dictionary of Books Relating to America*. Eames's bibliographical education proceeded at a brisk pace and led to his editorship of subsequent "Sabin" volumes. His colleague at the NYPL, Victor Hugo Paltsits (q.v.), has described well (in his "Wilberforce Eames: A Bio-bibliographical Narrative") the series of events which followed:

> At Woodward's shop he had met Joseph F. Sabin. The father—Joseph Sabin—had died, and the publication of the "Dictionary" had been suspended. Mr. Eames soon developed in his mind an idea for the continuation of the work, which he broached to the younger Sabin. He proposed to continue Sabin's "Dictionary" as a labor of love and for the experience it would afford him. This arrangement was made and continued for all time. . . . His only tangible reward for his hours of labor and sacrifices, always intentional and acceptable on his part, was the receipt of a set of the page-proofs of the parts he edited, which he added to the rest of his set, formerly purchased by him.

Eames began his task of continuing this work—a bibliography of all that had been written about America—where Joseph Sabin had left off, with the heading "Pennsylvania." In a relatively short period of eight years, Eames produced six volumes of "Sabin." His first volume, Volume XIV, was published in 1884, and he continued, with the aid of Paul Leicester Ford, through part of Volume XX, "Smith, Henry E.," published in 1892. By that time, Eames's other responsibilities were such that he no longer could devote the necessary amounts of time to the bibliography. Set aside as a formal project, except for a brief period in 1906, the *Dictionary* had to wait until 1927 to resume publication.

Several of the parts of "Sabin" had been reprinted as separates. Paltsits (again in the "Narrative") has quoted letters to Eames from John Russell Bartlett on their quality:

> Dr. Bartlett gave high praise to Mr. Eames's monographic studies. . . . The Ptolemy was "all that is to be said, and will prove very useful to students of geography." . . . He characterized the monograph on the "Bay Psalm Book" as "excellent and thorough," adding: "Your work is well done and leaves nothing more to be said regarding the work."

The thoroughness and diligence of Eames's work prompted R. W. G. Vail (q.v.), who finally completed "Sabin," to write: "Thus he carried the 'Dictionary' along with him while he grew in bibliographical stature until he became . . . the greatest American bibliographer who ever lived."

During the time when Eames was working on "Sabin," he was employed by George Henry Moore, head of the Lenox Library, who had met Eames at Woodward's and hired him as his personal assistant in 1885. The Lenox Library, when Eames joined the staff, had been in existence for fifteen years as a "public library" housing James Lenox's collection of rare books and manuscripts. Lenox and his sister, Henrietta, had also provided endowment funds to maintain the Library, and others subsequently added to both the collections and the endowment, prior to its becoming part of the New York Public Library in 1895. Because of its rare books and manuscripts, the Lenox Library was never a general or popular lending library but more of a museum, since preserving the materials and making them available to scholars was a major objective. Nonetheless, after 1887, access to the collection was easier, and under Eames's administration, scholars were always welcome.

Eames became a full member of the Lenox staff in 1888. After a trial period as assistant librarian following Moore's death in 1892, Eames was elected librarian of the Lenox Library on June 2, 1893. His response to greater responsibility was increased activity. He organized the 1892 Columbus commemorative exhibition, its highpoint being the oldest folio edition of the Columbus letter of discovery written in Spanish in 1493. Also, he published, on behalf of the Library, *The Letter of Columbus on the Discovery of America*, which was a facsimile of the only illustrated copy of the Latin letter and which also contained reprints of the oldest four editions in Latin, all held by the Lenox Library. Eames's contributions to the Library included liberalizing the atmosphere of restraint (the legacy of Lenox), which he did by promoting service to the user: creating one of the first printed short-title lists, instituting a card catalog, and lengthening the opening hours. The Lenox Library was becoming a more modern research library, and under Eames's supervision, it gained many important additions, including the George Bancroft library, the Robert L. Stuart collection, and Wendell Prime's Don Quixote collection.

On May 23, 1895, the Lenox Library merged with the Astor Library and the Tilden Trust to form the New York Public Library. Eames continued in charge of the Lenox section under the unique title "Lenox Librarian," similar to "Bodley's Librarian." For the rest of his life, he was a distinct part of the NYPL. When the sections were brought together in the new building at 5th Avenue and 42nd Street in May 1911, he was appointed chief of the American History Division. He was also in charge of the Reserve, the Manuscript, and the Map rooms. In this capacity as a reference librarian, Eames devoted much of his time at the NYPL to tracking down the bibliographical queries of other scholars. On January 1, 1916, the sixty-year-old Eames relinquished his administrative duties and was named bibliographer of the Library, free to pursue his desires and to work as he pleased.

Outside of the Library, he also won many honors and worked on publications. In 1893, he was elected to the American Antiquarian Society and, three years later, was awarded his first degree from any school, an honorary M.A. from Harvard University. It was significant, coming after his work at the Lenox Library, that he was cited as being "studious of the subject-division of all knowledge, and of the means of keeping accessible multiplying stores of knowledge." Fittingly, Eames was one of the founders of the Bibliographical Society of America and served as its first librarian (1905-1909). He was the original editor of the NYPL *Bulletin*, begun in 1897. The following year, he published a bibliography of *Early New England Catechisms*, and he continued his work on John Eliot with *The Logic Primer* (1904) and *John Eliot and the Indians, 1652-1657* (1915). He compiled a "List of the Catalogues, &c., published for the English Booktrade from 1595-1902," which formed a major part of Adolf Growoll's *Three Centuries of English Booktrade Bibliography*, published in 1903.

Another facet of the man was Eames the book collector. From the *Universal History* days until 1905, he gathered a collection of some twenty thousand volumes, housed in his modest frame home in Brooklyn. Being single, he was able to pile up the books from wall to wall, until it even reached the point that the floors had to be reinforced. The story has been told, perhaps apocryphally, that he solved the problem of sitting space by stretching a hammock across the room and swinging back and forth to pick up the desired book. These books were not collected, however, just to gather dust. Vail observed: "He liked to own the books he read and so his library grew, but only after he had finished a volume did he write his name on the upper corner of its fly leaf, for he felt that he could not really claim it as his own until he knew its contents." Additionally, as a quick judge of books, Eames was unsurpassed. Lydenberg described his method (in "Wilberforce Eames As I Recall Him"):

> First came a swift glance at the cover, next at the end papers, then checking the first and last leaves, a careful fluttering of the whole to find any loose sheets, careful page-by-page collation, checking of maps and other inserts. By that time the physical book had been accepted or rejected or noted for further attention. It was no mere superficial scanning; more of the contents having been digested and absorbed by that time and under those circumstances than any other mortal could hope for.

However, after suffering an appendicitis attack in 1904, Eames decided that his collection was getting out of hand, and the auction sale of his personal library began in May 1905. In general, the books dealt directly or indirectly with communication, through the printed word or linguistics. Eames had long made it his habit to pursue knowledge of a topic into whatever language it led him. Consequently, as Lawrence C. Wroth (q.v.) of the John Carter Brown Library has explained in "Wilberforce Eames," he learned

> enough of the ancient Oriental tongues to decipher cuneiform tablets, enough Chinese to be able to collect intelligently in the fields of Chinese history and literature, enough Latin to enable him to handle problems of fifteenth century books with ease and authority, and enough of native American languages to make his contribution to Pilling's linguistic bibliographies of the first importance.

Between 1905 and 1916, he sold or gave away most of his collected volumes. They included groups of Americana, European history and literature, Asian and Egyptian history and literature, and bibliography and the book arts. Most of his American Indian collection went to the NYPL, as did part of his African linguistics library (the rest went to the Library of Congress). The Newberry Library bought the works on India; his Japanese collection and part of his Chinese and Korean collection were sold to the Case Memorial Library, Hartford, Connecticut; and the rest of his Oriental collection was sold to the NYPL. The Oriental books had been part of the personal library of the distinguished Sinologist James Legge and had occasioned Eames's meeting in 1904 with the French scholar Henri Cordier, who saw to it that the American bibliographer was named an honorary member of the Académie d'Instruction Publique des Beaux Arts et des Cults (1905).

Once Eames had depleted his library, he started collecting again. In 1916, he began compiling works of American imprints to trace the development of printing in the United States, and he published *The First Year of Printing in New York* in 1928. His interest along these lines had evolved earlier through the utilization of photostatic copies. First using a camera which he bought in 1911, he reproduced title-pages and pamphlets, and then he worked with a photostat machine purchased by the NYPL in 1912. In addition to this pioneering work, his use of photostatic copies to build up histories of American printers led the British librarian A. W. Pollard to state, "Mr. Eames has played a greater part than any one else in showing how it may be done." His collection of American imprints became a major part of the Henry E. Huntington Library in 1924. With the proceeds, Eames moved from using a tool as modern as the photostat to collecting ancient Sumerian and Assyrian seals and cuneiform tablets.

As Eames's bibliographic skills and helpfulness became well known in scholarly circles, the honors awarded to him mounted. In 1924, the University of Michigan conferred upon him the degree of LL.D. on June 16, and two days later, Brown University presented him with the Litt.D. On December 19, 1924, his co-workers in the book world surprised him with *Bibliographical Essays: A Tribute to Wilberforce Eames*, a *Festschrift* that featured a biography by Paltsits. The fact that one of the essays was contributed by the famous Chilean scholar, José Toribio Medina, speaks well of Eames's position in international circles, though he personally never left the boundaries of the United States. The Bibliographical Society (London), awarded him its gold medal in 1929, a dual compliment in that Eames was the first American to receive it, and in the presentation he was cited as the "doyen of American bibliography." In 1931, the New York Historical Society, of which he had long been a member, added its gold medal to his honors.

The societies and associations to which he belonged reflect his various scholarly interests. He was vice-president of the New York Library Club from 1897 to 1899, and president the following year, was an honorary member of the American Library Association, and a fellow of the American Academy of Arts and Sciences. His historical interests included membership in the American Historical Association, the Colonial Society of Massachusetts, and the Massachusetts Historical Society. He also belonged to the Hakluyt Society, the American Oriental Society, and the Society of Biblical Archaeology. In addition, Eames held corresponding membership in the American Jewish Historical Society and honorary membership in the Grolier Club.

In his later years, Eames continued his intellectual endeavors. Work on "Sabin," having been interrupted in 1892 by the new responsibilities of directing the Lenox Library, resumed in 1927. Ever since the brief effort of 1906, the main problems had been financial, but funds from the Carnegie Corporation and others, and the backing of the Bibliographical Society of America, made publication possible. Eames saw sporadic printing of the later parts through the press, but by 1930, he decided that a full-time editor was needed to complete the bibliography. So his former NYPL colleague, R. W. G. Vail, librarian of the American Antiquarian Society, assumed the task, and Eames was able to witness the completion at long last in 1936, the year before his death. His meticulous scholarship was as well represented in the continuance as it had been when he first worked on "Sabin." The section on Captain John Smith was published separately in 1927, and the intricate work on Vespucci prompted Paltsits to exclaim that it "exceeded the work of all other scholars who had

endeavored to unravel the typographical problems involved therein."

One of his last tasks was to catalog the collection of Herschel V. Jones, which was the greatest private library of Americana of the day. He also contributed annotations to the catalog of the John Carter Brown Library at Providence, which he visited once a year in his capacity as a member of the Visiting Committee. Despite being struck by cancer in mid-1937 and hospitalized in September, Eames worked on one last article concerning a "lost" John Eliot imprint, which he traced to King's College, London. His death came on December 6, 1937. By his will, the major part of his estate went to the New York Public Library for the establishment of a "Wilberforce Eames Americana Fund" for collecting materials relating to the Americas printed before 1801.

Eames's life may rightly be said to have revolved around books. As for his other affairs, in "Wilberforce Eames As I Recall Him," Lydenberg wrote:

He had little interest in music or other forms of art—except as art is shown in the making of books. Companionable and attractive, respect-compelling, even endearing, he was scarcely the typical good mixer. An indoors man for most of his life, he did come in later years to enjoy the out-of-doors, his love of nature being more as the general picture than as particular scenes or specimens.

He did go hiking and fishing, and on the trips to the out-of-doors he loved to take photographs, which he carefully mounted in albums. "He ate little, slept little, drank and smoked not at all, and for most of his life, lacked kith or kin," noted Wroth. He was a lifelong bachelor. Wroth has explained that he "was a venerated and greatly loved figure long before his death. He was the shyest and most modest of men. He would have been inconspicuous in any gathering if he had ever allowed himself to be present at a gathering."

On the trips to the mountains, Eames never escaped books, as conversation invariably turned their way. As Wroth (again in "Wilberforce Eames") described this facet of the man,

Lean, gray, quick and active, he never rode anywhere if it was possible to walk, and he was still able in his eightieth year to make his younger friends puff breathlessly behind him on the hills. His talk about books was the most wonderful thing his associates have ever known, full of exact facts, reminiscence and curious lore, a rich spontaneous giving in response to a simple question about a name or a date. It had a peculiar quality because, despite his gentleness and deep humanity, books were more important in his life than men.

Yet the modest scholar had the ability to work with people, necessary for a librarian. "He was as calm and composed when faced by crises as when meeting daily routine tasks," observed Lydenberg, continuing in "Wilberforce Eames As I Recall Him,"

> I never heard him raise his voice, in protest or in applause, though each might be equally vigorous and unmistakable. I wished many a time I might hear him break loose, stamp his foot, pound the table, glare, blurt out one hearty oath—just to show that he could. Never once was that wish gratified. . . . Reproofs and corrections were made with disarming firmness, clearness, finality. His protest against unfairness to others was stronger than against himself.

The respect which other bibliographers have for Eames is due as much to his personality as to his few published efforts. While the accuracy and completeness of works like "Sabin" are remarkable, the debt that scholars owe Eames is based just as much on his service-oriented approach. As Wroth stated in an obituary, "He was without ambition except to know and to serve. Hardly an American bibliographical work of his time but owes him, directly or indirectly, for generous aid, direction, or encouragement." His idea of service was to produce exact lists for organizing and controlling written information, and moreover, to share his knowledge with others. It is only natural to use Lydenberg's words (in "Wilberforce Eames") to summarize his contributions to the book world:

> Others may have been more prolific in output, others more constant in devotion to one particular quest, but no one combined as he did the striking qualities of accuracy, patience, penetration, wideness of scope, persistence—above all, the kindly, unfailing, generous, unstinted offering of himself and all he knew to anyone that desired and needed the help he could give in so unique a fashion.

Wilberforce Eames, the self-educated man, had become the model bibliographer.

Biographical listings and obituaries—*Dictionary of American Biography*, Supp. 2 (Harry M. Lydenberg); *National Cyclopaedia of American Biography* 9; *Who Was Who in America* I (1897-1942). **Books and articles about the biographee**—Cannon, Carl L. *American Book Collectors and Collecting*. New York: H. W. Wilson, 1941. pp. 348-58; Lydenberg, Harry Miller. "Wilberforce Eames." *Library Journal* 63:22-23 (Jan. 1, 1938); Lydenberg, Harry Miller. "Wilberforce Eames As I Recall Him." *Proceedings of the American Antiquarian Society* 65:213-33 (Oct. 1955). (Additional remarks by Lawrence C. Wroth, pp. 233-36); Lydenberg, Harry Miller. "Two Bookmen." In *The Joshua Bloch Memorial Volume*, ed. by A. Berger, L. Marwick, and I. S. Meyer. New York: New York Public Library, 1960. pp. 1-9; Paltsits, Victor Hugo. "Wilberforce Eames, a Bio-Bibliographical Narrative." In *Bibliographical Essays: A Tribute to Wilberforce Eames*. First published 1924; reprint ed., Freeport, N.Y.: Books for Libraries Press, 1967. pp. 1-26; Paltsits, Victor Hugo. "Wilberforce Eames, American Bibliographer." *Inter-American Review of Bibliography* 3:252-63 (Sept.-Dec. 1953); *Proceedings and Addresses at the Presentation of the New York Historical Society's Gold Medal to Dr. Wilberforce Eames . . . Friday, November 20, 1931*. New York: New York Historical Society, 1932; Stark, Lewis M. "The Writings of Wilberforce Eames." *Bulletin of the New York Public Library* 59:515-19 (Oct. 1955). (Contains complete list); Strakosch, Avery. "Wilberforce Eames." *Avocations* 1:437-42 (Feb. 1938); Vail, R. W. G. "Wilberforce Eames." *Proceedings of the American Antiquarian Society* 48:16-23 (April 1938); Winship, George Parker. "Wilberforce Eames: Bookman." *Bulletin of the New York Public Library* 42:2-9 (Jan. 1938); Wroth, Lawrence. "Wilberforce Eames." *New York Herald Tribune Books*, Dec. 19, 1937, p. 17. **Primary sources and archival materials**—Eames's papers are held at the New York Public Library.

—W. DAVENPORT ROBERTSON
—EDWARD G. HOLLEY

EASTMAN, LINDA ANNE (1867-1963)

Linda Anne Eastman served the Cleveland Public Library for almost half a century: 3 years in relatively minor capacities, 22 years as vice-librarian under William Howard Brett (q.v.), and 20 years as head librarian. She began her service in 1892 at 12½ cents an hour and was receiving an annual salary of $9,000 when she retired in 1938, toward the end of a Depression-ridden decade. In her first year, the Library had all of 18 employees, if one counted the pages, and a few less than 58,000 books. When she left the institution—the only woman librarian to have assumed so much responsibility in a city as large as Cleveland—there were twelve hundred employees and more than two million volumes in the Library. She continued in Brett's illustrious footsteps and blazed new trails of her own.

The Eastman family came to New England in 1636 and appeared in Ohio in 1828; on the paternal side, it was descended from Miles Standish. Linda Eastman was born in Oberlin in 1867, two years after the close of the Civil War, to William Harvey and Sarah Redrup Eastman. When she was seven, the family moved to Cleveland, where she resided during most of the 95 years of her life. She attended the public schools of Cleveland, graduating from West High with honors, and after completing a course at the Cleveland Normal School, she taught for six years. Her first job was in a small frame school in west Cleveland where she began to borrow books from the public library. As she found the books more influential than the oral lessons, she came to feel that the library was the real center of the educative process. She wrote:

> I love books, and the part of teaching which is so uncongenial to me is the forcing of knowledge into those pupils who have no taste at all for books or reading—and they, in our public schools, are legion. The library worker is constantly helping people to the books they want, and also bringing to their notice those of which they knew nothing, and it seems to me the field is as broad, in an educational way, as that of the schools.

By 1892, she had made up her mind; she wrote that she was "willing to begin at the bottom and run my risk in working up, for the sake of engaging in an occupation toward which I have long felt an inclination."

She began library work as an apprentice at one dollar per eight-hour day and soon received appointment as assistant in the West Side Branch at $900 a year. It was the first branch established by the Cleveland Public Library and was situated near the market in a barren room over a store. While working there, she took an extension course from the New York State Library School at Albany. Then, in 1894, the Library opened its second branch and Eastman was made librarian. In the same year, she edited the first issue of the *Open Shelf*, a selective, annotated list of new books; the publication is now (1977) in its eighty-third year. Two years later (in 1896), she became vice-librarian, second in command in the entire Cleveland system. When Brett was killed in 1918, the Library Board did not hesitate; there were numerous male applicants for the top post, but Eastman was elected unanimously. Charles E. Kennedy, prominent journalist and veteran member of the Board, was convinced that in the choice of Eastman "the trustees paid a debt to one whose creative, intelligent work along library lines has never been surpassed." Actually, she had neither applied for the position nor indicated in any way that she wanted consideration. John Quincy Adams once said that the job should seek the person, not vice versa. Eastman was in complete agreement with the New England Puritan.

During Eastman's two decades as head librarian, all divisions and departments of the Library expanded their services. Beyond this achievement, there were three new operations that were innovative or unique —and sometimes both: services to hospitals, the blind, and municipal welfare institutions; a Travel Section; and a Business Information Bureau. The Cleveland Library had long been in the front rank of those providing special services to potential readers who were handicapped or restricted for one reason or another. In the early years, the moving force behind this progressive program was Eastman, who with her enthusiasm and untiring support kept it going in the face of bitter disappointments and annoying delays. From its beginning, she regarded the Library for the Blind (in Braille and talking books) as her own special project, and by the time she retired in 1938, it was serving all of northern Ohio and some thirty thousand registered readers. In connection with service to hospitals and welfare institutions, she liked to quote the author and humorist John Kendrick Bangs, who once asserted that if he were a doctor, he would make books a part of the *materia medica* and would prescribe them for his patients.

The Travel Section was unique when it first appeared in 1926, and it remains so. From the Eastman era to the present, the Cleveland Public Library has offered basic travel information that probably cannot be duplicated in any library in the world. Although Cleveland was not the first to have a Business Information Bureau, in due course its service in this area was among the best—very possibly the best offered by public libraries in the United States. The major reason for this enviable reputation was the librarian selected by Eastman to head it, Rose Vormelker, who held the position for more than a quarter of a century.

On the negative side, Eastman inherited the Depression of the 1930s, which was both a boon and a bane to the Library. It was a boon because of the increased potential for service; in that decade, libraries constituted a major welfare agency during dark days—providing a "relief line of the spirit" by supplying the populace with good books, a great source of comfort to discouraged, unemployed men and women. Business was in a tailspin elsewhere but was escalating in the Cleveland Public Library; the number of book users and total circulation increased by 20 percent, to the highest figure in its long history—before or since. But as borrowers were in economic distress, so was the Library. Its tax base was eroding, and the institution was faced with serious reductions in financial support. Eastman had to cut salaries, staff, and book purchases, close some branches and put others on reduced schedules. In spite of these handicaps, particularly exasperating when there were so many extra demands on the Library, Eastman maintained a high level of institutional morale. It was her greatest triumph.

In 1938, when she was 71, she retired—full of years and honors. She lived on for another quarter century before her death on April 3, 1963, when she was nearing the age of 96. During her active career the honors had come in profusion. In her own profession, she had been president of the Ohio Library Association (1903-1904) and of the American Library Association (1928-1929). She had received honorary degrees from Oberlin, Western Reserve University, and Mount Holyoke College, and special citations came from the Cleveland Chamber of Commerce, the Citizens League of Cleveland, and the Carnegie Corporation of New York. She was a full professor in the Library School of Western Reserve University, achieving that rank in spite of the fact that she had no college degree. She enjoyed this academic distinction and observed that if William Howard Brett was the "father" of the school, she had long considered herself the "grandmother . . . a sort of doting grandmother."

She was intensely proud of her profession and of her colleagues. Although they were still far from perfect, she believed "library folk . . . to quote from the Psalms, 'just a little lower than the angels.' " But her outstanding characteristics were humility and modesty. Alfred Benesch, who was a member of the Cleveland Board of Education for many years, would say:

> The test of her greatness is her deep humility—not the humility that doubts its own power, but the humility characterized by a curious feeling that greatness is not in the individual, but rather through the individual who sees something divine in all the children of men.

Biographical listings and obituaries—[Obituary]. *ALA Bulletin* 57:783-85 (Sept. 1963); [Obituary]. *Library Journal* 88:1974 (May 15, 1963); [Obituary]. *Wilson Library Bulletin* 37:736 (May 1963); *Who Was Who in America* IV (1961-1968); *Who's Who in Library Service*, 2nd ed. **Books and articles about the biographee**—Cramer, C. H. *Open Shelves and Open Minds: A History of the Cleveland Public Library.* Cleveland: The Press of Case Western Reserve University, 1972; Phillips, Cecil Olen. "Linda Anne Eastman: Librarian." Master's thesis, School of Library Science, Western Reserve University, 1953; Wright, A. E. "Linda Anne Eastman: Pioneer in Librarianship." Master's thesis, Kent State University, 1952.

—C. H. CRAMER

EATON, ANNE THAXTER (1881-1971)

Anne Thaxter Eaton, one of the great children's librarians, was born on May 8, 1881, in Beverly Farms, Massachusetts, to Charles Henry and Jane M. Eaton. Before she was a year old, however, the family moved to New York City, where she was educated at Brearly School. She received a B.A. from Smith College (probably in 1905, though *Who's Who in Library Service* gives the year as 1903). Then in 1906, she received her B.L.S. from the New York State Library School at Albany. Twenty years later, she would complete the requirements for her M.S. at the same school.

Her first job was as librarian of the Pruyn Library in Albany (1906-1910). She left that position to become assistant librarian of the University of Tennessee Library in Knoxville (1910-1917). From Tennessee, she returned to New York when, upon the advice of Mary E. Hall (q.v.), Otis William Caldwell appointed her librarian of his newly founded progressive school, Lincoln School of the Teachers College, Columbia University. She served there from 1917 until her retirement in 1946.

Anne T. Eaton began an association with libraries early in her life. Andrew Carnegie (q.v.) was a member of her father's parish; more importantly, however, her father gave her complete freedom of his personal library. This background, coupled with her later education, her professional library training and experience, and her empathy with children, prepared her to meet the challenge of setting up a library for a school that was operated under the principles espoused by John Dewey, who was teaching at Columbia at the time.

Otis Caldwell, the principal, organized Lincoln School partly in response to a highly influential article by Abraham Flexner, a respected member of the Board of Education, on "The Modern School" (*Review of Reviews*, April 1916). Saturated with progressive ideals and methods, Flexner described a school whose goal was to make education real and vital, and to discipline the mind by "energizing it through doing real tasks." Instead of compelling students to study, the "modern school" would take advantage of their spontaneous interests. To accomplish this, Caldwell realized that students would need a broad range of books and an exceptional librarian to direct their spontaneous interests in fruitful directions.

In 1917, Eaton organized the school library in what Frances Clarke Sayers has called

> the vanguard of a great educational movement. She was responsible in large measure for the successful working of its principles, but she never lost her own inner wisdom and integrity in all the rush and whirl of concept, theory, and method. She never used the jargon of the theorists, but always spoke straight forwardly of books and children together. She was by way of being a paradox; the most highly effective disciple of a cult which she followed in her own way.

Anne Eaton was a primary resource for ideas, information, and imagination; and students and teachers repeatedly acknowledged her influence on courses, describing her ability to bring children to books. She had a special talent for reaching children and developing what she called an "elasticity of mind." She believed that imaginative literature and especially poetry "stretch the mind as well as science and mathematics do" (*Reading with Children*, 29). She used the wonder and magic she found in books like an enchantress; under her influence many children learned to love reading. As Ellen Buell Cash said, "She got to them, whether or not they were literary."

One student, quoted by Sayers, describes the effect she had on him.

> It was the most natural thing in the world for a Lincoln School student to bring to Miss Eaton the ideas and the things that seemed most important to him. In my time only white mice were barred, and they were excluded regretfully and with apologies. . . . It is my firm conviction that Miss Eaton made a far greater contribution to the mental health and spiritual happiness of the students than any or all the psychologists and psychiatrists employed for the school. . . . Hers was the happy faculty of seeing the best side of each of us, without drawing comparisons. . . . I

trace the acquirement and deepening of dozens of interests and tastes to her example and encouragement.

In 1932, Anne Eaton began reviewing children's books for the *New York Times*, and from 1935 to 1946, she was co-editor of the children's department with Ellen Buell Cash. The hundreds of reviews she wrote reveal a deep knowledge of children's literature, and her criticisms convey the great zest she had for books as well as her uncommon perceptions into children's sensitivities and experiences. Before reviewing a new book, she often would try it out on her students if she or Ellen Buell Cash felt uncertain about it. When a new editor wanted her to do capsule reviews to save space, she left the *Times* rather than compromise. Besides the *Times*, she wrote as well for *Parents' Magazine*, *The Horn Book Magazine* and *Commonweal*.

She also wrote articles and textbooks and compiled reading lists and anthologies in addition to her review work. Among her articles were "On Reading Aloud" (*Horn Book*, June 1925), "An Appreciation of Laura E. Richards" (*Horn Book*, July 1941), "Widening Horizons: 1840-1890" (in *A Critical History of Children's Literature*, edited by Cornelia L. Meigs; Macmillan, 1953), "Reading without Boundaries" (in *Essays Presented to Anne Carroll Moore* [q.v.], edited by Frances L. Spain; New York Public Library, 1956), and "Reviewing and Criticism of Children's Books" (*Bulletin of the New York Public Library*, 1956). Her most widely acclaimed book was *Reading with Children* (Viking, 1956), which sought to advise adults as to what children should read. Anne Eaton received the James Terry White Medal in 1941 for notable published professional writing in the library field for that book. A companion volume, *Treasure for the Taking* (Viking, 1957) critically appraises 1,580 children's books in 64 categories, and it remains a standard work. With Lucy Fay, Anne Eaton co-authored a textbook, *Instruction in the Use of Books and Libraries* (3rd ed., Faxon, 1928). She had previously written *School Library Service* for ALA publication (1923). Eaton's major anthology was *Animals' Christmas; Poems, Carols, Stories* (Viking, 1944). Her *Standard Catalog for High School Libraries; a Selected Catalog of 4555 Books* went into a fifth edition (with Dorothy E. Cook and Dorothy Herbert West; Wilson, 1947).

Through her writing and reviewing, Anne Eaton influenced the tastes of children, parents, educators, and certainly children's librarians for many years. Her fresh, direct style is as classic as the books she described. Her reviews and essays often glowed from the "intrinsic joy-giving quality" she found in the best children's books. This quality she used as a standard for criticism: "This joy in the writing, which in turn makes for joy in the reading, is the touch

stone to distinguish real literature in books for boys and girls" (*Reading with Children*).

Even after she retired in 1946, Anne Eaton continued to be active. From 1952 until 1971, she was a volunteer in St. Luke's School Library. Every Tuesday, she read to classes and gave special programs at Christmas. She also taught children's literature at St. John's University in Brooklyn and was a member of the Books Across the Sea Committee for the English Speaking Union.

Over a period of fifty years, she was one of the most influential children's librarians, and she helped shape the literary tastes of a generation through her reviews and bibliographies. A New Englander by temperament in spite of her New York City childhood, she possessed a lively sense of humor and a fair and open mind. She died on May 5, 1971, in New York, a few days short of her ninetieth birthday.

Biographical listings and obituaries—*New York Times Biographical Edition* 2; [Obituary]. *New York Times*, May 9, 1971; *Who's Who in Library Service*, 1st ed. **Books and articles about the biographee**—Sayers, Frances Clark. "Anne Eaton of Lincoln School." In *Summoned by Books*. New York: Viking, 1965; also appeared as an article in *Horn Book* 23:322 (Sept.-Oct. 1947).

—MARGO SASSE

EATON, JOHN (1829-1906)

John Eaton was born near Sutton, New Hampshire, on December 5, 1829, the oldest of nine children of John and Janet Andrew Eaton. His early education was scanty because his father deemed it appropriate that the oldest son should help with the large family farm. Later, however, John, Jr., was able to work his way through the Thetford [Vermont] Academy and afterwards, Dartmouth College, from which he received his A.B. in 1854. He served as a superintendent of an elementary school in Cleveland (1854-1856) and then as the superintendent of schools in Toledo (1856-1859). In the latter position, he began what became a lifelong interest in the sociological problems of education and in the collection and analysis of statistical data. Finding himself somewhat unsatisfied, however, he enrolled in the Andover Seminary in 1859. When he graduated in 1861, the Civil War had already begun and he joined the 27th Ohio Volunteer Infantry as chaplain. In 1862, General Grant placed him in charge of the thousands of ex-slaves who were flocking to the Union army. In the course of his work, which ultimately brought him the rank of brigadier general, Eaton worked assiduously at providing for the freedmen not only the necessities of life but also an elementary system of instruction.

After the War, Eaton edited the reconstructionist Memphis *Post* (1865-1867), served as the Tennessee state superintendent of instruction (1867-1869), and in 1870 was appointed by President Grant as U.S. commissioner of education. Under Eaton, the Bureau of Education became a strong force in shaping the American public education system. Eaton's office published a wide variety of educational statistics and gave tacit support to the growing idea of public supported education, although Eaton himself remained neutral with regard to formal educational philosophies. His particular concern was that the ameliorative and uplifting effects of education might lead ultimately to the goal of an enlightened democracy. He was active, too, in promoting nursing education, in encouraging international educational opportunities, and in providing an educational program for the territory of Alaska.

Eaton's contribution to the library movement was distinctive. From 1874 to 1876, he worked with library leaders to produce the monumental Bureau of Education report, *Public Libraries in the United States of America: Their History, Condition and Management, Special Report.* Through the activity required to publish that report, his office became an information clearinghouse that helped in the establishment of the American Library Association at the Centennial Exhibition in 1876. Between 1876 and 1886, when he retired from the Bureau, Eaton continued to publish for the Association various pamphlets and articles on library management. He helped to produce another statistical count of libraries for the 1884-1885 Bureau report, and labored to arouse librarians' interest in presenting the library movement at the New Orleans Cotton Exhibition in 1885.

From 1886 until the end of his life, Eaton continued his educational endeavors. He served as president of Marietta College, Ohio (1886-1891), and Sheldon Jackson College, Salt Lake City (1895-1899), and he organized the public education system in Puerto Rico (1899-1900). He devoted the remaining years of his life to preparing his memoirs of the war years (*Grant, Lincoln and the Freedmen*) and died on February 9, 1906.

Biographical listings and obituaries—*Dictionary of American Biography* 5 (Donald M. McMurry); *Who Was Who in America* I (1897-1942). **Books and articles about the biographee**—Corbett, Elizabeth M. "ALA Centennial Vignette No. 8." *American Libraries* 7:21 (Jan. 1976); Mason, Ethel Osgood. [Biographical sketch of John Eaton]. In John Eaton, *Grant, Lincoln and the Freedmen.* New York: Longman, Green, and Co., 1907; Miksa, Francis. "The Making of the 1876 Special Report on Public Libraries." *Journal of Library History* 8:30-40 (Jan. 1973); Smith, Glenn. "John Eaton, Educator, 1829-1906." *School and Society* 97:108-112 (Feb. 1969); Williams, Mary S. "The Library Work of the Bureau of Education." *Library Journal* 12:64-66 (Jan./Feb. 1887).

—FRANCIS L. MIKSA

EDMANDS, JOHN (1820-1915)

Fifty-six years of library service secured little fame for the practical-minded librarian of the Philadelphia Mercantile Library. Born in Framingham, Massachusetts, on February 1, 1820, to Jonathan and Lucy Nourse Edmands, descendants of a seventeenth-century colonist, John Edmands grew up on a farm, attending a district school some six months of the year until 1836. After a five-year apprenticeship to a carpenter, he entered Phillips Academy, Andover, graduating in 1843. He then entered Yale College, where he gained his early library experience in 1846 by serving as assistant librarian to the Brothers in Unity—a college literary society. During his tenure, he and Samuel Richards compiled a dictionary catalog of the Brothers' library under the tutelage of Yale's librarian, Edward C. Herrick. Elected librarian of Brothers in Unity the following year, Edmands put together an eight-page pamphlet entitled *Subjects for Debate with References to Authorities* (1847). This brief subject index, intended as a general reference tool for debaters, was the seed from which sprang the more ambitious *Index* of Edmands' successor at the Brothers in Unity library, William Frederick Poole (q.v.).

After graduating from Yale in 1847, Edmands taught school in Rocky Mount, North Carolina, for one year, returning to Yale to attend Divinity School from 1848 to 1851. Though licensed as a Congregational preacher by the New Haven West Association of Ministers, he did not follow the ministry as a career, but remained at Yale as assistant librarian until 1856. He then accepted a temporary position at the Mercantile Library of Philadelphia, preparing a supplement to that Library's 1850 printed catalog. Upon the resignation of Seth C. Brace as librarian in June 1856, Edmands was chosen as librarian for the Mercantile Library, a position he held until his retirement in 1901. He continued to maintain connections with the Library as librarian emeritus until his death in 1915, at age 95.

Edmands' tenure at the Philadelphia Mercantile Library was characterized by practical professionalism and attention to detail. In 1878, during the heyday of individual classification schemes, he devised a system for the Philadelphia Mercantile based on an alphanumeric author arrangement within a relatively simple subject breakdown (*Explanation of the New System of Classification Devised for the Mercantile Library of Philadelphia*, 1883). This grouping of similar subjects and of works of a given author allowed the shelves to serve as their own catalog. Though never widespread, the system was found useful in a number of libraries and was retained at the Philadelphia Mercantile until 1944.

For seventeen years, beginning in 1882, Edmands served as editor of the *Mercantile Library Bulletin.* Issued quarterly, the *Bulletin* brought together annotated accession lists, selective reading lists on Wycliffe, Luther, Goethe, and others, lists of works on current topics of interest, and the most extensive list of historical novels published to that time. It was also noted for the painstaking bibliographic studies, those on the Latin hymn *Dies Irae* and *The Letters of Junius* being especially noted by contemporaries.

Edmands was an active ALA member from its founding to 1903, serving on many committees and attending conferences diligently. He also served as the first president of the Pennsylvania Library Club (1890). A frequent contributor to *Library Journal*, he delivered a paper on alphabetizing at the 1887 ALA Conference, which was included as an appendix to the second and third editions of Charles A. Cutter's (q.v.) *Rules for a Dictionary Catalogue.*

Modest and self-effacing before his superiors and fellow professionals, Edmands was energetic in his bibliographic work and constantly available for consultation with patrons. Behind his spare frame and bushy white beard was a vitality that kept him busy and still publishing at age 95. Throughout his life, he remained active in the church. A founder of the Congregational Church in Philadelphia in 1864, he continued as deacon and clerk until 1911, leaving for posthumous publication *The Evolution of Congregationalism* (1916).

Edmands lost his first wife, Abigail Lloyd Edmands, in January 1883, after a marriage of 29 years. His second marriage, to Ellen Elizabeth Metcalf in 1889, ended with her death three years later. In 1893, he married Clarinda Roberts, who survived him. He had no children. Edmands died on October 17, 1915.

Biographical listings and obituaries–*Dictionary of American Biography* 6 (Thomas L. Montgomery); *National Cyclopaedia of American Biography* 12; *Who Was Who in America* I (1897-1942); [Obituary]. *Library Journal* 40:824 (1915). Books and articles about the biographee–Clapp, Verner W. "A.L.A. Member No. 13: A First Glance at John Edmands." *Library Quarterly* 26:1-22 (Jan. 1956).

–MICHAEL BUTLER WESSELLS

EGAN, MARGARET ELIZABETH (1905-1959)

Margaret E. Egan was born at Indianapolis, Indiana, on March 14, 1905, the only daughter of Frank L. and Mary Elizabeth Treat Egan. For most of her early years, she was a resident of Pittsburgh, Pennsylvania, where she graduated from Scheneley High School. She attended Barnard College from 1926 to 1928. During the summers, she was employed in the editorial department of the Oxford University Press. For two years, she taught in the English-speaking school in the Dominican Republic.

Upon returning to the United States, she enrolled in the library training course of the Cincinnati Public Library, and also completed her work for the baccalaureate degree at the University of Cincinnati in 1930. From 1933 to 1940, she was readers' advisor in the Cincinnati Public Library. During that period, she conducted a pioneer study in individual reading guidance without personal contact. The data were gathered from individual reading records of men in the Civilian Conservation Corps at camp Fort Thomas, Kentucky, and results were published in the *Library Quarterly* for October 1937.

In 1940, Margaret Egan enrolled for a year of graduate study at Yale University, her major interests being government and political science, with particular emphasis on the Far East. The following year, 1941, she enrolled in the doctoral program of the Graduate Library School of the University of Chicago, where she completed all the requirements for the degree except the writing of the dissertation, which she never finished.

From 1943 to 1946, she was librarian of the Industrial Relations Center at the University of Chicago, and she taught part-time in the Graduate Library School. She was subsequently appointed a full-time member of the faculty of the Graduate Library School, at the rank of assistant professor, a position that she held until 1955, when she accepted a position as associate professor at the School of Library Science of Western Reserve University (now Case Western Reserve University) in Cleveland, Ohio, where she remained until her death. At Western Reserve, she taught in the library school and also conducted research in the School's Center for Documentation and Communication Research. She was particularly effective in forging bonds of understanding between what might be called conventional librarianship and the innovations brought to the field through documentation and information science. She was a master teacher, especially in the use of the Socratic method, as well as a highly competent research investigator.

Active in professional library associations, in 1949-1950 she was president of the Illinois chapter of the Special Libraries Association. Because of a protracted struggle with an increasingly serious heart condition, her life was cut short at the very height of her productive years.

Her bibliography is not large; however, with the present writer she prepared the report on U.S. National Bibliography for the UNESCO Conference on International Bibliographic Services, held in Paris in November 1950, and with him she also edited the 1950 Chicago Conference on Bibliographic Organization, subsequently published by the University of Chicago Press. She also conducted and edited the papers presented at a 1952 Chicago conference on

Communication and Specialized Information, again published by the University of Chicago Press (1955). Also, with the present writer, she wrote *The Classified Catalog*, published by the American Library Association (1956). This study was done under a grant from the John Crerar Library of Chicago, and was designed primarily to help the administrators of that library develop its own classified catalog, one of the few such bibliographic instruments in the United States.

While on the faculty of the University of Chicago, and subsequently at Western Reserve University, she was the chief architect of the sequential courses in the literature of specific subject fields, her contribution being mainly concerned with the literature of the social sciences. She also pioneered a course in "bibliographic organization," which, together with the present writer's "theory of classification," represented the first introduction of documentation and information science into library school curricula. Throughout her professional life, she was dedicated to the philosophy of the unity of librarianship as a discipline, and bibliography as central to its practice. She published a number of articles pertaining to this subject, including "Bibliographic Control in the Social Sciences" (*American Documentation* 2:11-12, January 1951); "Foundations of a Theory of Bibliography" (*Library Quarterly* 22:125-37, April 1952); and "Library and Social Structure" (*Library Quarterly* 25:15-22, January 1956).

Margaret Egan died of an aneurysm on January 26, 1959, shortly before her fifty-fourth birthday, leaving an all-too-meager record of her productive career, so her influence must live on through the students and others who profited so richly by association with her.

It is impossible to write objectively and dispassionately of a person who gave so generously and unsparingly of herself for the benefit of others, a person with whom one has been privileged to work over a period of more than ten years, as did this writer with Margaret Egan. Even today, on those rare occasions of contemplating what I have published, I am amazed to find how much of it is her speaking through my own halting prose. "Social epistemology," both the term and the concept, were hers, but because I have given it wide currency, despite frequent disclaimers, it has generally been attributed to me. At her memorial service, John Schoff Millis, then president of Western Reserve University, took as his text the words of Saint Paul to the Romans, "The glory that is revealed in us," as the apotheosis of her spirit. As for myself, perhaps the best that can be done is to quote from a letter received from Ralph R. Shaw (q.v.) at the time of her passing. "Hers was one of the truly great minds of American librarianship."

Biographical listings and obituaries–[Obituary]. *Ohio Library Association Bulletin* 29:27 (April 1959); Thornton,

Eileen. [Obituary]. *College and Research Libraries* 20:151-52 (March 1959); *Who's Who in America* 29 (1956-1957); *Who's Who in Library Service*, 2nd ed., 3rd ed. **Books and articles about the biographee**–"Have You Heard: In Memoriam–Margaret E. Egan." *Special Libraries* 50:180 (April 1959); Shera, Jesse H. "In Memoriam." *Ohio Library Association Bulletin* 29:27 (April 1959).

–JESSE H. SHERA

ELMENDORF, THERESA HUBBELL WEST (1855-1932)

Since Theresa Elmendorf's achievements seem to have taken place about half a century earlier than comparable developments elsewhere, it is important to place them in their proper time setting. She was born in Pardeeville, Wisconsin, November 1, 1855, the daughter of Hubbell and Helen Maria Roberts West. While she was still young, her family moved to Milwaukee, where she was educated in the public schools and finished her formal education at Miss Wheelock's Seminary in 1874.

Her career as a librarian began in 1877, when she joined the staff of the library of the Young Men's Association of Milwaukee. Soon after, when this library was transferred to the city, she became an assistant librarian in the Milwaukee Public Library. In 1880, when Milwaukee had a population of 115,587, she was made deputy librarian.

While she was deputy librarian of the Milwaukee Public Library, Theresa West compiled the *Systematic Catalogue of the Public Library of the City of Milwaukee* (Milwaukee, 1885-1886), a work of more than 1,700 pages. In the light of the career she followed later, the note on page 1673 becomes most interesting: "The system of classification in use in [the Milwaukee Public] library is mainly the one, devised by Mr. Melvil Dewey [q.v.] ... and subsequently introduced, with slight modifications and amplifications, in the library of the Young Men's Association of Buffalo in 1878."

In 1892, she succeeded Klas Linderfelt (q.v.) as librarian, following his arrest for embezzlement of library funds. She held this distinguished position (by now Milwaukee's population had passed 200,000) until October 3, 1896, when she married Henry Livingston Elmendorf, the librarian of the public library in St. Joseph, Missouri, and a vice-president of the American Library Association.

The newlyweds travelled to London, where Mr. Elmendorf served as the manager of the London office of the Library Bureau. In July 1897, they returned to the United States, settling in Buffalo, New York, where he assumed the position of librarian of the Buffalo Public Library. It had been established in that year as a publicly supported library to succeed a private subscription library, the Buffalo Library, itself the successor of the Young Men's Association of

Buffalo. It would appear that a woman who had achieved remarkable success as a public librarian had married at 41 and abandoned her career. Not so!

While Theresa Elmendorf seems to have held no library job for the ten years of her marriage, she had certainly not abandoned her career. During these years between her marriage in 1896 and her husband's death on July 8, 1906, she was very busy in library affairs. She compiled the *Descriptive Catalogue of the Gluck Collection of Manuscripts and Autographs in the Buffalo Public Library* (Buffalo, 1899). This work, more than 150 pages long, is a catalog of a distinguished collection of manuscripts, unusual in a public library, the most notable item being Samuel L. Clemens's manuscript of *Huckleberry Finn*. As in the case of Milwaukee's *Systematic Catalogue*, Elmendorf's editorship is disclosed in the preface but is not recognized on the title page.

While still "unemployed," she was selection editor for the American Library Association's *Catalogue of Books for Small Libraries* (1904). She was also, during this time, the president of the New York Library Association for the 1904-1905 term.

Since she had much more experience as an administrator of a large public library than her husband (Milwaukee in 1890 was four times the size of St. Joseph, Missouri), it is easy to believe that she had some role in the innovations that her husband introduced in the Buffalo Public Library. One of these was the creation of the Open Shelf Room, in which books were made more accessible and more attractive to patrons. Another was the "Buffalo Plan" of public library service to the schools. In any case, Elmendorf, when she resumed her formal library employment, devoted much time to promoting and publicizing this plan of service to schools.

She is identified as the author of *Classroom Libraries for Public Schools* (4th ed., 1923). Perhaps she was the editor of the earliest, anonymously edited, version of 1899. In 1911, she wrote an address for the New York State Teachers Association, and it was later revised and published as *Buffalo's System of Public School and Public Library Cooperation*.

When Henry L. Elmendorf died in July 1906, the Board of Trustees of the Buffalo Public Library appointed Walter L. Brown (q.v.), the vice-librarian, as his successor and appointed Theresa Elmendorf vice-librarian. According to the Buffalo newspapers of the time, the Board considered the possibility of appointing her to succeed her husband, but she held the post of vice-librarian until her retirement in 1926.

She was most active in the American Library Association, which she joined in 1882. She was a member of the ALA Council and was elected vice-president of the Association at the 1895 Denver conference. She was a regular attendant at ALA

meetings, being present for at least seventeen conferences. In 1911, Theresa Elmendorf was elected president of the ALA, the first woman to be chosen for this post, and she presided over the Ottawa conference of 1912.

She was a great believer in reading lists as tools for public betterment. During her lifetime, she edited and published many of them on various subjects. In 1917, she edited *Poetry: The Complementary Life*, a selection from the Open Shelf Room of the Buffalo Public Library. In 1921, she compiled a short reading list entitled *United States*, which was reprinted by the American Library Association after having been published by the Buffalo Public Library. Even after she retired in 1926, she continued her work. In 1928, she prepared the bibliography of poetry and poets which was issued as part of *Winged Horse*, by Joseph Auslander and F. E. Hill. In 1931, this bibliography was expanded and annotated by including appreciative notes gathered from many sources and separately published by the American Library Association as *Poetry and Poets: A Reading List*.

Theresa Elmendorf died at her home in Buffalo on September 4, 1932.

In a note published in the *Bulletin of Bibliography* a year before she died, F. W. Faxon (q.v.), himself a leader in the library field, reminisces about her executive ability in Milwaukee and the esprit de corps of her staff. He concludes by saying, "Whenever we think back to the days of these old time A.L.A. leaders, we feel sorry for the present generation of young librarians who missed the inspiration of such co-workers."

Biographical listings and obituaries—*National Cyclopaedia of American Biography* 23; [Obituary]. *Buffalo Courier Express*, Sept. 5, 1932, p. 13; *Who Was Who in America* I (1897-1942). **Books and articles about the biographee**—[Biographical sketch]. *Library Journal* 76:468 (March 15, 1951); *Buffalo Courier Express*, Sept. 17, 1926, p. 15; Faxon, Frederick W. "Our Frontispiece: Theresa West Elmendorf." *Bulletin of Bibliography* 14:93-94 (May-Aug. 1931).
                                        —PAUL M. ROONEY

ESTERQUEST, RALPH THEODORE (1912-1968)

The son of Frank A. and Julia Sanberg Esterquest, Ralph Theodore Esterquest was born in Chicago, Illinois, on May 6, 1912. He married Dorothy E. Watson on August 15, 1936, and they had two children, Shelley and Peter. Ralph Esterquest died on August 10, 1968, in Wellesley Hills, Massachusetts.

Ralph Esterquest received his A.B. at Northwestern University in 1933, with majors in sociology and anthropology, and he spent 1933-1934 at Columbia University doing graduate work in anthropology. For part of this time, he held a Field Fellowship at the Laboratory of Anthropology in

Santa Fe, New Mexico. He earned his B.S.L.S. at the University of Illinois in 1936, and received his M.A. in 1940 at the same institution.

Esterquest's professional career started at Northwestern University, where he served as reference assistant and cataloger in 1936-1937, after which he moved to the University of Illinois as an acquisitions assistant in 1938-1940. After completing his education, Esterquest accepted the position of assistant librarian for the Institute for Advanced Study at Princeton University, 1940-1942. From there, he moved to the national scene by becoming manager of the Publishing Department, American Library Association, 1942-1943. His interest in interlibrary cooperation took him to the position of director of the Pacific Northwest Bibliographic Center, Seattle, for the years 1944-1946. From there, he moved to the University of Denver to serve as assistant director of libraries and professor for the years 1946-1949. He left Denver to become director of the Midwest Inter-Library Center (now the Center for Research Libraries), Chicago, Illinois, for the years 1949-1958. Esterquest left the Chicago position to become, on January 1, 1954, librarian and a member of the faculties of the Harvard Medical School, School of Dental Medicine, and School of Public Health. He was responsible for planning the Francis A. Countway Library of Medicine at Harvard University and for combining the collections and services of the medical and dental libraries in this new building, which is considered an exemplary model of a medical library building. He served as librarian of this Library from 1965, when it opened, until his death.

While working at the Midwest Inter-Library Center, Esterquest received a Fulbright Senior Research Fellowship to study interlibrary cooperation in the British Isles during the academic year 1953-1954. Also, while serving as librarian of the Countway Library of Medicine, he was on leave from Harvard for the academic year 1967-1968 to serve as director of the International Relations Office of the American Library Association.

Although Esterquest was interested in all facets of librarianship, two primary interests seem to dominate his professional activities. His concern for interlibrary cooperation is demonstrated by his service to the Pacific Northwest Bibliographic Center (Seattle), his membership on the Board of Directors of the Bibliographical Center for Research, Rocky Mountain Region, Inc. (Denver), and his directorship of the Midwest Inter-Library Center (Chicago). His year of study as a Fulbright senior research fellow resulted in the publication of the ACRL Monograph *Library Cooperation in the British Isles* (ALA, 1955).

Esterquest's second major concern was his interest in medical librarianship. The Countway Library

Building Program, brilliantly conceived and exceedingly functional and efficient, still stands as a model for medical libraries. His participation in the Medical Library Association included the chairmanship of the Federal Relations Committee, membership on the Board of Directors (1963-1964), and many other assignments. This strong interest in medical librarianship allowed him to contribute to the studies of the Senate Committee on Governmental Operations on Biomedical Information and to marshall support for the passage of the Medical Library Assistance Act of 1965. He also served as a member of the National Library of Medicine's Advisory Committee on Research and Training. A major contribution was his work on the Joint Committee of the Association of American Medical Colleges and the Medical Library Association in developing guidelines for medical school libraries.

His interest in interlibrary cooperation and medical librarianship merged when he issued the 1963 report *Strengthening Medical Library Resources in New York State* for the commissioner of education of the state of New York.

But this dynamic, independent man went beyond the two primary concerns of his life. He was the motivating force for the establishment of the Mountain-Plains Library Association and served as its first president (1948). He served as president of the Chicago Library Club and as a member of the Executive Board of the Illinois Library Association. He was repeatedly elected to the ALA Council at different periods of his career. As a consultant, he assisted library development at the Atlanta University Center, the California State Library, the Mississippi State Library, the University of Wisconsin, the University of Michigan, and as a Ford Foundation consultant to the Southern California Libraries. Overseas, he served as a building consultant in Ulfe, Nigeria, and Trinity College (Dublin, Ireland).

Ralph T. Esterquest was a man of warmth, humor, and energy. Through his critical judgment and his insight into the many problems of organization, he contributed much to interlibrary cooperation and medical librarianship.

Biographical listings and obituaries—[Obituary]. *AB Bookman's Weekly* 42:734 (Sept. 2, 1968); [Obituary]. *Library of Congress Information Bulletin* 27:504-505 (Aug. 15, 1968); [Obituary]. *Library Journal* 93:3089 (Sept. 15, 1968); *Who Was Who in America* V (1969-1973); *Who's Who in Library Service*, 2nd ed., 3rd ed., 4th ed. **Books and articles about the biographee**—*College and Research Libraries* 19:42 (Jan. 1958); *Harvard Library Bulletin* 17:103 (Jan. 1969); *Medical Library Association Bulletin* 46:295 (April 1958); *Medical Library Association Bulletin* 56:550 (Oct. 1968).

—JOHN T. EASTLICK

EVANS, CHARLES (1850-1935)

Toward the end of Charles Evans's long life, shortly after the publication of volume twelve of his *American Bibliography*, Lawrence C. Wroth (q.v.), librarian of the John Carter Brown Library, wrote a letter of appreciation for the bibliographer's work:

I want to congratulate you most sincerely on the addition of another volume to the great series. It must be a very great satisfaction to you to look back upon the progress of this piece of work and to realize that you have accomplished, single handed, something that most men would have undertaken only with the support of a staff of trained workers. All of us who are working in Americana have cause to thank you every day of our lives.

Wroth recognized and paid tribute to a fact that subsequent scholars have also noted: the *American Bibliography* was uniquely the product of the devotion of one man. With a faithfulness that has few parallels, Charles Evans in the first three decades of the twentieth century published twelve massive volumes recording American printing from its beginning in 1639 almost to the end of the eighteenth century. He worked in a day before large foundation grants, university-based research institutes, and the other support now regarded as so essential to extensive bibliographical enterprises. Although it is upon the *American Bibliography* that his fame chiefly rests, Evans was also a librarian and he served a number of libraries for roughly a quarter of a century before he committed himself wholly to his bibliographical work.

Charles Evans was born in Boston on November 13, 1850, the second son of Charles Peter and Mary Ewing Evans. His father, a mariner of either Danish or Welsh descent, came to America by way of Ireland, where he had married Mary Ewing. Family life was not stable for the Evanses, for within eight years, they had lived in five different locations, and within nine years, both parents died. Fortunately, Charles was placed in the Boston Asylum and Farm School for Indigent Boys on July 13, 1859, where he was joined by his brother, Thomas John Evans, the following year. At the time of their admission, the Boston Farm School on Thompson's Island was one of the city's distinguished charitable institutions. About 100 boys from the ages of eight to sixteen were enrolled regularly, and they maintained a regimen of spartan living conditions, strict academic work, and manual labor on the farm, combined with strong religious training. Both of the Evans boys testified that they thrived on this program, and later, John Evans would be the first alumnus to serve on the Board of Managers. Charles Evans expressed his own gratitude in a nostalgic address on the school's one hundredth anniversary in 1914 and in another memorial address in 1918.

After seven years on Thompson's Island, Evans was again given an unusual opportunity. Samuel Eliot, a trustee of both the School and the Boston Athenaeum, selected him as an assistant in the library of the latter institution, an apprenticeship which Evans took on June 12, 1866. In later years, Evans was to call the Boston Athenaeum "the alma mater of my bibliographical life." No phrase could have been more appropriate, for the Boston Athenaeum became his liberal arts college and professional training school as well. As one of the country's distinguished cultural institutions, the Athenaeum drew to its library and art gallery some of the most prominent scholars, statesmen, and literary figures of the nineteenth century. With superb collections, and with one of the country's great librarians, William Frederick Poole (q.v.), the Athenaeum provided a firm foundation for Evans's later bibliographical as well as practical library work. Poole took a personal interest in his young assistants, and many of the library apprentices later became prominent librarians themselves.

Charles Evans not only idolized William Frederick Poole, he depended upon him for most of the library jobs he ever held. After thirteen years as librarian, Poole left the Boston Athenaeum in 1869 to do independent consulting, including a stint as half-time librarian-consultant at the Cincinnati Public Library. One of Poole's consultantships involved selection of 8,000 volumes for the new Indianapolis Public Library. Recognizing the need for a librarian who would organize the collections and make a catalog, Poole urged the Indianapolis Library Committee to invite Charles Evans to become their first librarian. The Committee moved cautiously on the matter but eventually offered Evans the post in mid-November 1872. Encouraged by his former Boston mentor, Evans accepted the post. Prior to his departure for Indianapolis, the proprietors of the Athenaeum arranged a farewell party and gave him a gold watch as a token of their esteem.

Despite an initial unfavorable reaction from the city's newspapers, who demonstrated a Midwestern prejudice toward the "Boston import," Evans went to work with all the zeal of his 23 years and soon made the Indianapolis Public Library one of the leading such institutions in the country. Within three years of its opening, the Library ranked sixth in circulation of books among tax-supported public libraries in the country. More importantly, the Library was engaged in a multiplicity of activities of benefit to the local citizens: preserving local history, acquiring good books, publicizing its services through the local press, serving the youngsters, and providing materials for the professional man. Testimonials to its value came from all kinds of citizens, who rose to the defense of the staff when they were attacked by the inveterate newspaper letter writers, especially those who thought it was unwise to depend upon citizens to make their own best judgments about what should be acquired and read. A number of leading citizens formed the Indianapolis Library Club in 1877 with Evans's encouragement, and he became its first secretary.

Toward the midpoint in Evans's librarianship at Indianapolis, the library profession took steps to organize itself as an association. Poole played a major role in this effort, and he encouraged his protégé to be similarly involved. On October 4-6, 1876, 103 librarians met in the rooms of the Historical Society of Pennsylvania, and, on the last day, formed the American Library Association. When the roll book was passed around to secure names of members, Melvil Dewey (q.v.) became number one and Charles Evans number two. Evans had also read a paper at the conference on "The Sizes of Printed Books," and, along with Dewey and Reuben A. Guild (q.v.), had served as one of the conference secretaries. During the following year, he wrote reviews for the fledgling *American Library Journal* and was elected ALA's first treasurer. Although he did not continue an active role with ALA after 1878, he was elected an honorary member of the Association at the fiftieth anniversary conference in 1926. In October 1877, Evans was one of the 21 Americans attending the first international conference of librarians in London.

The rapid progress of the library in Indianapolis, the esteem given it by the citizens, and the aggressiveness with which Evans promoted the library cause had all contributed to his growing reputation as a librarian. However, storm clouds were gathering in the city, and political factions vying for power sought the removal of Evans as librarian, ostensibly because of his rigid enforcement of library rules. Despite strong support for Evans in the press and among a number of citizens, the School Board by a tie vote of 5 to 5 refused to re-elect him as city librarian for the coming year, and his services were terminated on August 3, 1878.

Despondency over his dismissal at Indianapolis led Evans (who lacked both medical ability and training) to a foolhardy trip to Memphis, Tennessee, in mid-September to nurse one of his friends, Dr. J. G. E. Renner, a victim of the yellow fever epidemic. Hoping to help him get his job back, friends urged him to return after Renner's death, and Evans continued to live in Indianapolis for another year. Despite searching, no library jobs opened for him and, in mid-1879, he went to Fort Worth, Texas, where he worked variously as a salesman for a stationery firm, as a newspaper man, and as a bookkeeper. One major event occurred during these years: on April 8, 1884, he married Lena Young, daughter of a local cattleman and hardware dealer.

Late in 1884, Evans had an opportunity to return to library work. Enoch Pratt, a wealthy Baltimore merchant, had given the city funds for a central library and four branches. In the process of visiting other public libraries to observe their methods, one of the trustees had been very impressed with Poole's administration in Chicago. He asked Poole for a recommendation for the post of assistant librarian and Poole recommended Evans. Negotiations moved quickly, and Evans became the assistant librarian of the Enoch Pratt Free Library effective January 1, 1885.

In the next two years, Evans's prodigious energy and professional competence were devoted to acquiring and processing books for the new library. Within a year, the main library contained 20,000 fully cataloged volumes, and there were an additional 12,000 volumes in the branches. However, relationships between the chief librarian, Lewis H. Steiner, and Charles Evans deteriorated to such an extent during the second year that Enoch Pratt asked for Evans's resignation, which was accepted on December 1, 1886.

Again Evans turned to Poole and asked for help, for now he had two children (Gertrude and Eliot Howland) as well as a wife to support. He had tried to secure a position in the East but none materialized. Poole put him in touch with the Omaha Public Library, which wanted its book collection reclassified and a finding list produced. Using the Poole classification scheme with the alphabetical numbering scheme of John Edmands (q.v.) as he had done at Baltimore, Evans began work on April 18, 1887, and completed his work the following April. He not only had classified and cataloged the collection but had helped move the library to its new quarters and plan some of the arrangements. Nonetheless, he again ran into trouble with the Board. As Enoch Pratt, fully appreciative of Evans's talents, said of his one fault, "his temperament don't [sic] brook serving under a master."

Evans returned to Baltimore and was out of work for a year while he searched for other jobs. In the late fall 1888, a movement began among his friends in Indianapolis to have him return to the librarianship of the Indianapolis Public Library. This was not the first time Evans had been asked back; a somewhat repentant Board had approached him in 1883, but he had declined. This time the chairman of the Board had written Poole, and Evans's mentor had given him some sound advice about not passing up this position and not making conditions, advice which Evans was determined to follow. The Board elected Evans librarian and he resumed his duties in Indianapolis on March 19, 1889. Again his internal administration of the Library was superb. Since his predecessor was reported to be deficient in this area, Charles Evans's accomplishments seemed impressive. He formulated a personnel classification plan, reorganized the work force, tightened up the regulations for patrons, and began reclassification of the collections. Unfortunately, in his relations with the Board, he was to be no more successful this second time than he was the first. In 1891, he became embroiled in an argument with the Board on the matter of a new library building. Following Poole's lead in believing that a library building should be functional and not an ornament, Evans forced the school commissioners to listen to Poole's advice about buildings and became intemperate concerning the architect's plans. The results were predictable: he failed to win re-election in May 1892, despite strong support in the press and among some staunch friends.

Evans again turned to Poole asking assistance. He had never been a prosperous man, and his family had grown with the addition of Charles Sumner Evans. This youngster, later to become famous as golfer "Chick" Evans, provided additional incentive for Evans to find a post quickly. Several leads were unpromising, despite what Poole noted as deep respect for Evans in the profession, and, in July 1892, he took a temporary post as head of classification and reference at the Newberry Library in Chicago under Poole. This temporary post turned out to be the best that Evans could find, and he remained there until January 1895, a year after Poole's death, when he was forced out by the new assistant librarian, Alexander J. Rudolph (q.v.).

Evans was out of work this time until August 1895, when he was employed to classify the collections of the McCormick Theological Seminary. In March 1896, he was approached by Edward G. Mason about the possibility of organizing the collections of the Chicago Historical Society. Though unwilling to leave McCormick at the time, Evans did become a part-time consultant to the Society during the spring and early summer. However, the prospect of a permanent post led him to reconsider his decision and he accepted the position of secretary and librarian of the Society on July 1, 1896. His next six months were spent putting the library collections in order in time for the December dedication ceremonies for the new building. For five years, Evans worked diligently to obtain additional members and resources for the Society. Early in 1897, he began reclassification of the collections, but the project proceeded slowly since the officers refused his request for additional assistance. For most of his period with the Society, Evans was the only full-time employee. In January 1901, there began to be increasing friction between Evans and the Executive Committee of the Board of Trustees, which finally led to Evans's dismissal at the end of the year.

Thus ended Evans's career as a librarian, a career that had certain elements of success but which had been marred by far too many evidences of failure.

President John N. Jewett, in a letter to a member of the Chicago Historical Society, noted that "Mr. Evans apparently wanted the absolute management, and his obstinacy of disposition led him to disregard in many things the specific directions of the Committee and to offensively insist upon his own judgment and methods." This had been the record of Evans's previous dealing with administrators and boards. That he was right in many instances cannot mitigate his intemperate behavior in working with men who had policy-making power. Charles Evans was capable of rare kindliness and geniality, as many of his friends testified, but he rarely applied these charms to board members. Unfortunately, this was a serious oversight, and it made his career as a library administrator a failure.

Immediately after his dismissal as librarian of the Chicago Historical Society, Evans decided not to seek another position but to concentrate on the completion of a bibliographical project he had had under way for some time. To a startled bibliothecal world, he sent out an eight-page circular in January 1902, announcing that he was preparing a privately printed, signed, and numbered edition of *The American Bibliography*, which he described as "a chronological dictionary of all books, pamphlets and periodical publications printed in the United States of America from the genesis of printing in 1639 down to and including the year 1820 with bibliographical and biographical notes." He estimated that his bibliography would contain about 70,000 titles when completed, and he set the price of each volume at $15. As soon as he received assurance of 300 subscribers, he planned to undertake publication.

Since Evans had never produced a bibliography before and since previous bibliographers had faltered in so mammoth a task, other librarians tended to be skeptical. However, skepticism of his ability had never deterred Evans and it did not now. Indeed, his previous failures as a librarian seemed destined to be overshadowed by a work which would prove to the world that there was a Charles Evans with whom to contend. Over the next three decades, he would produce a twelve-volume work which Clarence S. Brigham (q.v.), librarian of the American Antiquarian Society after 1907 and a strong Evans supporter, would call "one of the greatest bibliographical compilations of all time."

Just when Evans decided to undertake this bibliography is uncertain. Some have indicated that he had the idea as early as his Boston Athenaeum days. In his 1902 circular, Evans mentioned having begun the work "more than sixteen years ago," or about 1886. However, there is little evidence to suggest that Evans did any substantive work on such a compilation before he joined the Newberry Library staff in 1892. The idea may have been there, and he may have done some minor work, but he was not living where this was a realistic possibility. The Newberry Library was another matter. Strong in bibliographies, printed catalogs, and early Americana, the Newberry would have provided not only collections to support such efforts but also William Frederick Poole, who had earlier done some bibliographical analysis himself at the Boston Athenaeum, and who was there to provide encouragement. Moreover, a letter from Samuel Eliot, his Boston guardian, gives some indication that this was the period when he began serious planning for the bibliography. Doubtless there was also opportunity to continue some work later at the Chicago Historical Society. So the idea probably came to fruition some time during the 1890s.

When Charles Evans began active work on the *American Bibliography* in 1902, that book became the core of his existence, the single consideration worthy of attention. All the ordinary social and familial obligations and pleasures that make life enjoyable for most people were ruthlessly subordinated to the main task. The bibliography took the place of association meetings, of profession, of children, and of wife in his affections. Not that this began immediately, but as the burden of doing all the work by himself increased, Evans's ordinary social contacts fell by the wayside as he devoted his days and nights to his self-appointed task. Fortunately he was a strong man, vigorous and virile, and he had not the slightest doubt that, at the age of 51, he could successfully complete his project. Humility had never been one of his strong virtues, and his initial assurance of his ability irritated more than one bibliographer who had been working in the field for some time.

As Evans's critics, and even his friends, suggested, to produce a first-rate bibliography would require intensive examination of the major collections of early American printed books. That meant trips to the American Antiquarian Society, the various libraries in Boston, the John Carter Brown Library in Providence, the Library of Congress, and various libraries in New York and Philadelphia. How much personal research would he do? No one believed he could compile such a record solely from bibliographies and catalogs in Chicago.

Charles Evans was well aware of the necessity for such trips, and he had tried to find the money for such a trip so he could check his work before the publication of his first volume. However, he was unable to find anyone who would finance such a venture. Turned down again and again in his attempts to raise money for even the printing of the first volume, he finally turned to his Indianapolis friends, John H. Holliday, Addison C. Harris, and George T. Porter, who guaranteed his note at the Union Trust Company using subscriptions to the bibliography as collateral. The bank agreed to advance the money for printing and distribution, charge $100 for collecting the funds, and charge Evans six percent interest on any overage. As each volume was printed, the same arrangement continued and ultimately eight volumes, containing 25,074 entries, and published over eleven years, were financed this way.

In order to publish at all, Evans had to become his own business manager, errand boy, distributor, etc. He bought his own paper, secured bids from different companies to obtain the best prices for specific items, supervised all the work directly, and made arrangements with the express company and post office for mailing the completed books, all carefully hand wrapped at his home, which became the warehouse for the books.

The first volume of the *American Bibliography* appeared in November 1903, almost two years after Evans's first announcement. The volume received a mixed reaction. Covering the period from 1639 to 1729, it included 3,244 titles, or over 1,000 more titles than any previous work for this period. Evans had written a six-page preface to the work and included the list of 218 subscribers to date, of whom 53 were foreign libraries. In his preface, he stated firmly his bibliographical creed:

> The chronological arrangement has proved its perfect adaptability and superiority for reference, to an alphabetical arrangement of authors as the work proceeded. Its advantages are many.... The grouping of historical events and subjects which evoke publication are to the student of literary history of first importance. To the bibliographical student, and all book lovers are such, the date of publication is the most important fact in the identification of books and editions; it is the key to all investigation.... For remembrance, we repeat, the fact of first importance in bibliographical research is the date—always the date!

Upon this basis, Evans proceeded to his task of gleaning information for his titles in the *American Bibliography*. First he worked from bibliographies and printed catalogs in the Newberry and Chicago Public Libraries. On three-by-five-inch slips of paper cut in half, Evans wrote his notes for the imprint. At the top of the slips was always the date, then the name of the author, followed by a full description of the work itself, with locations, where known, and any other bibliographical facts which Evans believed important. He then stored these slips in corset boxes, tied them together with leather shawl straps, and, as he subsequently visited other libraries to collect additional bibliographic data, he built up his file of American imprints year by year. As Lawrence Wroth later remarked, "Shawl straps and corset boxes! Truly those were the horse and buggy days, and yet out of them came the shining monuments of scholarship that we call 'Evans.'"

With the publication of his first volume, Evans justified the faith of his friends and began a pattern of research activity that was to continue for the rest of his life. First he would make the basic file in Chicago, then visit libraries in the East which contained American imprints. Invariably he underestimated the time to work through a library's collection of imprints. Frequently he unearthed stacks of pamphlets, broadsides, college theses, and government publications that had never been organized before. Even working twelve- and eighteen-hour days he could not accomplish all that he wished. On his trips, he would often indicate to his wife in Chicago, "I arrived at the Library of Congress this morning at 9. I did not rise from my seat until 9:45 this evening, except to call for more books." Without lunch or dinner, and oblivious to all except the daily newspapers, Evans steadfastly pursued his task. As recreation, when libraries were closed, he went to amusement parks and zoos, explaining that his rule was "to see the Books and the animals." As time progressed, he received more help from fellow bibliographers and librarians, who sent him lists and, in the case of the American Antiquarian Society and the John Carter Brown Library, checked items for him.

As the table below indicates, the first eight volumes proceeded at a fairly brisk pace until 1915:

The *American Bibliography* of Charles Evans

Vol.	Period Covered	Printer	Date Published	No. of Pages
I	1639-1729	Blakely Press	November, 1903	446
II	1730-50	Blakely Press	March, 1905	448
III	1751-64	Blakely Press	May, 1906	446
IV	1765-73	Hollister Press	October, 1907	440
V	1774-78	Columbia Press	May, 1909	455
VI	1779-85	Columbia Press	May, 1910	445
VII	1786-89	Columbia Press	December, 1912	424
VIII	1790-92	Columbia Press	April, 1915	432
IX	1793-94	Columbia Press	January, 1926	491
X	1795-96, *M*	Columbia Press	February, 1929	451
XI	1796, *N*-97	Columbia Press	February, 1931	399
XII	1798-99, *M*	Columbia Press	February, 1934	419

Evans had built up a subscription list of about 375 and had managed to keep going with an amazing amount of self-sacrifice. How he survived financially is a mystery, for he rarely made a profit from the bibliography. Yet he could look back upon his work with genuine satisfaction. His reputation and his bibliographical skills had steadily improved. He regarded his election to membership in the American Antiquarian Society in 1910 as one of the two great honors of his life. With the publication of volume eight, just before the beginning of World War I, Charles Evans was one of America's leading bibliographers.

The following decade was to be a period of despair and despondency for Charles Evans. World War I, which cut off his foreign subscribers and increased printing and other costs substantially, resulted in a halt of his publication program. Evans continued to work on the next two volumes, but he saw little prospect for their publication. His earlier financial backers died, and he could not procure other funds to advance his work. However, in 1924, at the instigation of Theodore Wesley Koch (q.v.), Northwestern University librarian, the American Library Association appointed a committee to help Evans revive his bibliographic effort through the sale of 25 of the sets remaining in his possession. Enough new subscriptions were obtained so that the 74-year-old Evans could resume his work. The price for volume nine, which appeared in 1926, was raised from $15 to $25. Volume ten, covering 1795 and part of 1796, appeared in January 1929, just before the stock market crash. Evans had already given up his original goal of describing all imprints up to 1820 and was now willing to settle for 1800, which he expected to reach with three more volumes. However, the financial problems occasioned by the Depression seemed insurmountable.

At this point, Clarence S. Brigham and the American Antiquarian Society again came to his aid and requested a grant of $1,000 from the American Council of Learned Societies for help in publishing volume eleven. Although Evans was reluctant to accept such assistance, he was at the end of his resources, and Brigham's diplomacy eased the pain. ACLS provided another $3,000 for volume twelve, but, in the midst of that effort, Lena Evans died (October 6, 1933), and this combined with the publication and distribution of volume twelve was to sap Evans's strength. Another 21 years would elapse before Clifford K. Shipton (q.v.) and the American Antiquarian Society brought out volume thirteen, thus completing Evans's revised plan.

The last year of Evans's life brought him the recognition for which he had long wished. Again through the efforts of Brigham, Brown University conferred upon him the honorary degree of Doctor of Letters at the June 1934 commencement. This was the other great honor of which he was particularly proud. As he had labored over the years without recognition from any institution, Evans thought that he might have to wait for posterity to evaluate his contributions to scholarship. The trip to Brown and the ceremonies were a deeply moving experience for Charles Evans, and to more than one person, he confided that it was "the happiest day of my life."

Despite Brigham's urgings that he complete volume thirteen, Evans had lost the will to continue. His strength deteriorated in the next few months, and he died the following year, on February 8, 1935. Evans was cremated and his ashes were buried in Memorial Park Cemetery, Evanston, beside those of his wife and an infant daughter, Constance.

How valuable was Evans's bibliography? No bibliographical compilation is ever complete, or even, as Evans asserted his would be, "nearly complete." Over the years, newer bibliographic techniques, additional bibliographers concentrating on geographic areas, improvement in cataloging in some libraries, and the discovery of new materials have all added significantly to Evans's basic work. Yet the *American Bibliography*, instead of being relegated to the museum of outgrown reference works, remains one of the fundamental sources for early American imprints. As one individual has noted, "Evans numbers are to American printed books of the seventeenth and eighteenth centuries what Child numbers are to ballads or Köchel numbers to Mozart."

In 1955, Clifford K. Shipton, librarian of the American Antiquarian Society, published the thirteenth volume of Evans, thus completing Evans's revised plan of listing imprints through 1800. In 1959, Roger P. Bristol published volume fourteen, a cumulative index to all the volumes, which he followed in 1961 with an index to printers, publishers, and booksellers indicated in Evans.

Under Shipton's direction, the Readex Microprint Corporation reproduced the text of all the non-serial titles in Evans, and Shipton used this opportunity to correct some of Evans's errors. Shipton has estimated that about one in ten of the original Evans entries is a "ghost" or contains a serious bibliographical error. As an index to the microprint edition, Shipton and James K. Mooney issued a two-volume *National Index of American Imprints* through 1800, which they called the "short-title Evans," in 1969. Finally, as a result of the bibliographic work of many people, Bristol published a *Supplement to Charles Evans' American Bibliography* in 1970, which added about 11,000 titles to the original 39,000.

Doubtless there will continue to be additions to Evans's basic work, but Frederick Goff, writing in the preface to Bristol's *Supplement*, expressed the view that the basic work is done: "Inevitably new entries will of course continue to turn up from time to time, but it is fair to state that Evans' great work is now virtually finished nearly 70 years after it was begun. A splendid bibliographical tool in its final form is now available to the world of scholarship which is devoted to America's earliest printed books." One is reminded of Lawrence C. Wroth's letter to Charles Evans's son, Eliot, in 1952: "It must be a great satisfaction to you to feel that your father's work was one of enduring usefulness to historical and literary scholarship. All of us who knew him are proud of his achievement."

Biographical listings and obituaries—*Dictionary of American Biography*, Suppl. 1 (Clarence S. Brigham); [Obituary]. *ALA Bulletin* 29:163-64 (March 1935); *Who Was Who in America* I (1897-1942). **Books and articles about the biographee**—Brigham, Clarence S. *Charles Evans, 1850-1935, a Biographical Sketch*. Reprinted from the *Proceedings of the*

American Antiquarian Society, April 1935; Bristol, Roger P. Introductory material in *Supplement to Charles Evans' American Bibliography*. Worcester, Mass.: American Antiquarian Society, 1970; Holley, Edward G. *Charles Evans, American Bibliographer*. Urbana, Ill.: University of Illinois Press, 1963. (A complete list of Evans's works and other Evans material can be found on pp. 323-30); Shipton, Clifford K., and James E. Mooney. Introductory material in *National Index of American Imprints through 1800*. Worcester, Mass.: American Antiquarian Society, 1969; Williamson, William L. *William Frederick Poole and the Modern Library Movement*. New York: Columbia University Press, 1963.

—EDWARD G. HOLLEY

FAIRCHILD, MARY SALOME CUTLER (1855-1921)

Mary Salome Cutler was born June 21, 1855, in Dalton, Massachusetts, the daughter of Artemas (Artemus?) Hubbard and Lydia Wakefield Cutler. As vice-director of the New York State Library School from its founding in 1889 until 1905, she was not only a competent executive and inspiring teacher but also an influential pioneer in library education. She died on December 20, 1921, in Washington, D.C., at the age of 66.

Artemas Cutler was a papermaker from Hinsdale, New Hampshire, and Lydia was his second wife. He became blind when Mary was an infant, and her memory of reading aloud to him in later childhood was one of the influences that directed her to the world of books. Mary attended Dalton High School where she seems to have enjoyed her English classes in particular, for she carefully saved her compositions written between 1866 and 1870, and they may now be found among her husband's papers at Duke University. Upon completion of high school work, she was offered a position in the Reverend Mr. Edson L. Clarke's community library, but she was unable to accept it as she was leaving for Mt. Holyoke Seminary. Later, as a believer in professional training for librarians, she was thankful to have turned down a job she would have been so poorly prepared to fill.

In 1875, Salome Cutler was graduated from Mt. Holyoke and remained there as a teacher of Latin until poor health forced her to resign in 1878. During the following recuperative period, she was once more attracted to library work, apparently in part by the activities of the newly formed American Library Association. In 1884, after experience in cataloging a small rural library, she applied to Melvil Dewey (q.v.) for assistance in locating a position in a public library. Dewey, in his second year as librarian of Columbia College, lost no time in recruiting her as cataloger in his own library. When, in 1887, Columbia College reluctantly gave Dewey permission to open a School of Library Economy, Cutler became in addition an instructor of cataloging.

After a stormy career at Columbia, Dewey, in 1889, became secretary of the Board of Regents of the University of the State of New York, and director of the State Library. One of his first acts was to transfer his library school to Albany, and with it came Salome Cutler, who was made vice-director in 1890. She received the degree of Bachelor of Library Science from the school in 1891.

While Dewey was the titular head of the school and gave frequent and dynamic lectures, it was Cutler who was responsible for its day-to-day operation and for a heavy teaching load as well. Being the first of its kind, and a great success, the school exerted a tremendous influence on early library education. Naturally, the colorful and controversial Dewey has received most of the credit for this, and certainly he was the prime mover; but Cutler seems to have given form and substance to the Dewey dream. Her administration, which exactly paralleled the Dewey years, echoed and reinforced his philosophies. Many writers attest to her remarkable executive abilities and credit her with a major role in the establishment of high standards of admission to and achievement within the school; the emphasis on detail, thoroughness, and accuracy; the carefully planned curriculum; and the placement of outstanding students in influential positions. In addition to administrative duties in the school, she was also in charge of the New York State Library for the Blind. The memory of her father's plight is said to have prompted her to undertake this added responsibility, and she is remembered as a pioneer in library service to the blind.

The inspirational quality of her teaching was highly praised by her contemporaries. Her enthusiasm and her faith in the perfectibility of mankind sustained her missionary zeal for the library movement. Her specialties were cataloging, book selection, and a seminar that combined library history with a study of contemporary libraries.

Salome Cutler wrote extensively, publishing at least seventeen articles in the period from 1887 to 1908. The majority are in *Library Journal*, but others appeared in *The Library*, the *Library Association Record*, *Public Libraries*, the *New York State Library Bulletin*, and the *American Journal of Sociology*. The articles are on a wide variety of subjects, including Sunday opening, philanthropy, library service to children, and women in librarianship. She also edited many publications for the library school, such as its manual of cataloging rules.

Her article, "The Function of the Public Library," published in *Public Libraries* (November 1901), was widely admired and contains the famous sentence frequently quoted in connection with her philosophy of public library service: "The function of the library as an institution of society is the development and enrichment of human life in the entire community,

by bringing to all the people the books that belong to them."

A major interest in both her teaching and her writing was book selection. While she never was able to write the book she intended on the subject, her creed is probably best expressed in her article, "Principles of the Selection of Books" (*Library Journal*, October 1895; summarized in *Public Libraries*, June 1903). As indicated in the quotation above, she firmly believed that books should be carefully selected to enrich and uplift the community. Her principles of book selection, which became dogma for many years after in library schools, included the importance of positive, not negative, criteria; of knowing the community served; of selecting for all groups within it, non-users as well as users; and of the well-rounded, unbiased collection.

Cutler was a very active member of the American Library Association, attending meetings, reading papers, and serving as vice-president (1894-1895 and 1900-1901) and as member of the Council (1892-1898 and 1909-1914). In 1903, she went as ALA representative to an international meeting in Leeds, England, where she read a paper on work with children and young people in American public libraries. The paper was subsequently published in the *Library Association Record* (December 15, 1903).

Her greatest work for ALA, however, was as chairman of the committee to arrange an ALA exhibit at the World's Columbian Exposition in Chicago in 1893. There were those in the Association who felt that such responsibility should be reserved for a man, but Salome Cutler and her committee of fifteen, after three years of arduous work, produced an impressive display. Included were a "comparative exhibit" of library equipment and practice; a "model library" for the average American small town; and a catalog of the same library, edited by Cutler and published by the U.S. Bureau of Education. This was the first of a series of annotated book selection lists for small public libraries that came to be known as the *A.L.A. Catalogs.*

In her forty-second year, Salome Cutler married a man ten years her junior, the Reverend Mr. Edwin Milton Fairchild (1865-1939), a Unitarian minister, lecturer, and author connected with the Educational Church Board in Albany. The engagement was announced in the spring of 1897, and they were married on July 1, in Troy, New York. She is said to have aided him greatly in his work, and he is described by a student of the period as "hovering in the background" of his wife's busy career, for she decided to continue with her work at the library school. The wisdom of this move was questioned by none other than Katharine L. Sharp (q.v.), who directed the library school of the Armour Institute in Chicago, which was soon to become the library school of the University of Illinois with Sharp continuing as its head. One of the New York State Library School's most brilliant graduates and a close friend of Cutler, Katharine Sharp wrote to the bride-to-be on May 18, 1897:

I wish you all happiness in the new life, but I wish for your sake that you were going to rest, while I rejoice for our sakes that you are to continue the work.

I hope the fortunate man is worthy of you—but I never shall believe it.

There are many glowing tributes to this remarkable woman, Salome Cutler Fairchild. To choose one from among them: Isabel Ely Lord of the class of 1895-1897, writing in *The First Quarter Century of the New York State Library School* (published by the School in 1912), says that Miss Cutler's quarters were "very literally the center for the life of the school" (p. 46). After describing the rest of the faculty, including Dewey, she adds (p. 50):

It was Miss Cutler's ideal of life and work that we saw clearest, her patient consideration of every point, her insistence on a philosophic, an ethical, and an economic basis for our work, her never-failing sense of justice ... her generous giving of the very best she had—it was all these that made the largest influence of the New York State Library School for many ... who still bless her name.

While Salome Fairchild's influence over the women students was widely recognized, it was not limited to them. Edwin H. Anderson (q.v.) of the class of 1892, who followed Dewey as director of the School and later became director of the New York Public Library, said of her, "I am personally and professionally more indebted to Mrs. Salome Cutler Fairchild than to any other librarian or teacher. That is the literal fact and I gladly testify to it" (*Public Libraries*, July 1924, p. 350).

The verdict was not unanimous, however. Sydney B. Mitchell (q.v.), a prominent librarian who was a student at Albany in 1903-1904, saw Salome Fairchild in a somewhat less adulatory light. In a rather critical evaluation of his year at the School (published in *Library Quarterly* in October 1950), he pays tribute to her idealism and to her "on the whole ... very good" influence on the students, but adds: "She seemed somewhat confined to the library dogma of her day, to be little receptive to new ideas or criticisms of those then accepted, and to have kept herself so 'unspotted from the world' that her relation to it seemed somewhat tenuous" (p. 275).

Pictures and contemporary descriptions show Fairchild as a tall, gaunt woman, with a long, plain

face, and the air of a person whose frail constitution was sustained by an indomitable spirit. She was never in robust health, and the burden of years of administration, teaching, speaking, and writing exacted a severe toll on her mental and physical resources, until on September 22, 1905, after eighteen years in Dewey's two library schools, she resigned. At this same time, Dewey was having difficulties with the regents, resulting in his resignation on January 1, 1906. However, Fairchild insisted that her departure had nothing to do with this event; indeed the reason for her retirement was what was termed in those days a "nervous breakdown."

During her retirement, when health permitted, she became a professional lecturer on book selection and the history of the public library movement in America. For the latter subject, she had organized slide lectures, a teaching method described in her article in *Library Journal* (February 1908). She may be said to have been, therefore, a pioneer in audiovisual methods in library education. Her work was similar to that of her husband who, during those same years, worked to found an institute to sell sets of printed lectures with accompanying slides to school systems on the subject of moral education. When Alice B. Kroeger (q.v.), director of the Drexel Library School in Philadelphia, died on October 31, 1909, Salome Fairchild took over as acting director for four months while a successor was being chosen.

In her later years, Fairchild lived in Maryland and suffered from deteriorating health, until on December 20, 1921, she died of a cerebral hemorrhage in a sanatorium in Washington, D.C. Her estate was left by way of her husband to the National Institution for Moral Instruction, Washington, D.C., of which he was a founder and guiding spirit. The Alumni Association of the New York State Library School established the Salome Cutler Fairchild Memorial Fund to aid the library school. In 1951, she was honored by being selected as one of forty leaders of the library movement in "A Library Hall of Fame," published in *Library Journal* (March 15, 1951). A greater, if less tangible, memorial, was provided by the nearly 350 women and 100 men who were graduated from the School during her years as administrator and teacher, and who, in very high proportion, became leaders of the profession as librarians and library educators.

Biographical listings and obituaries—*Cyclopaedia of American Biographies* 3; *Dictionary of American Biography* 6 (James I. Wyer); *National Cyclopaedia of American Biography* 20; *Notable American Women* 1 (Joseph A. Boromé); *Who Was Who in America* I (1897-1942). **Books and articles about the biographee**—"As It Was in the Beginning." *Public Libraries* 29:349-52 (July 1924); "Librarians: Cutler, Miss Mary S." *Library Journal* 22:275 (May 1897); "A Library Hall of Fame." *Library Journal* 76:468 (March 1951); Mitchell, Sydney B. "The Pioneer Library School in Middle

Age." *Library Quarterly* 20:272-88 (Oct. 1950); New York State Library School. *The First Quarter Century of the New York State Library School, 1887-1912.* Albany, N.Y., 1912. **Primary sources and archival materials**—In the Edwin Milton Fairchild Papers held in the Duke University Library (Durham, North Carolina) are approximately 120 items concerning Mrs. Fairchild, including her high school themes, letters relative to her marriage, and a few other pertinent items.

—BUDD L. GAMBEE

FARGO, LUCILE FOSTER (1880-1962)

Lucile Foster Fargo ranks as one of the real pioneers in the school library field. She belongs in the company of such key figures as Mary E. Hall (q.v.), long-time librarian at Girls' High School in Brooklyn, the two Marthas—Wilson and Pritchard (q.v.)—Marion Louis, and others who gave impetus to the development of school libraries in the early years of the twentieth century. However, she did not confine her career solely to the school library field but contributed significantly to other areas of librarianship, including library education and professional writing.

Fargo was born in Lake Mills, Wisconsin, on October 18, 1880. Her education seems to have been unusually extensive for a woman of her era. An A.B. in 1903 was followed in 1904 by an M.A.—both from Whitman College in Walla Walla, Washington. In 1907-1908, after teaching high school in Baker City, Oregon, she was enrolled in and received a certificate from the New York State Library School at Albany. Here she was in excellent company, for among her classmates were such library leaders as Essae M. Culver (q.v.), Carl H. Milam (q.v.), Isabella Rhodes, and Joseph Wheeler (q.v.).

After completing her year at Albany, she returned to the West Coast to do library work. In the Library Association of Portland (later the Portland Public Library), she held positions in both the cataloging and reference departments during the year following library school. From there she went to Spokane, Washington, to become librarian at the North Central High School, a post she was to hold from 1909 to 1926 and in which she was to establish her reputation as one of the prime figures in the development of high school library service. During that time, there is evidence that she was constantly seeking to broaden her own background of experience, and she engaged in various types of library work for short periods; one summer in the California State Library, another in the Seattle Public Library, and in 1920, two months of war service for the American Library Association in Honolulu. This contact with her professional organization was to prove important later in her career.

That her influence was being felt in the field of education at an early date is evidenced by the fact that R. T. Hargreaves, her principal at North Central High School, gave a paper in 1915 to the Department of Secondary Education at the National Education Association Convention in Oakland, California, entitled "The Possibilities of the High School Library." This paper, printed in the NEA 53rd Annual *Proceedings*, reflects Lucile Fargo's rich and far-seeing philosophy. It was at this same convention that the California Association of School Librarians was established. Several leaders in library service to young people, such as Martha Wilson, Effie Power (q.v.), and C. C. Certain (q.v.) of school library standards fame, were there to give the new organization their blessing. No mention, however, is made of Lucile Fargo's presence; but then, in those days, school librarians did not usually travel as far as from Spokane to Oakland to attend educational meetings unless they were participating in the program.

In 1926, Fargo became general assistant for the ALA Board of Education for one year, and this forecast the new directions that her career would take. In 1927, she was selected to write the definitive textbook on school librarianship as part of the ALA's Curriculum Study Series. *The Library in the School*, published first in preliminary form in 1928, was to continue through four editions until 1947 under her authorship. Although the book is now dated, its impact on school libraries should not be minimized.

With the completion of *The Library in the School*, her career in library education had begun. From 1930 to 1933, she was connected with the new George Peabody College Library School, serving as both associate director and director. In commenting on her relations with Peabody, Fargo said, in a letter (February 9, 1932) to Herbert Hirshberg (q.v.), director of the School of Library Science at Western Reserve University:

> I have felt that I should stay with the school until accreditation was assured; and presumably, until my three-year contract had expired. The first has been accomplished. . . . As for the second point, it may be wise either to go or stay, depending on the outcome of a frantic administrative situation in the college itself. Ever since I have been here that administration has reminded me of Juno and the Paycock—"Always in a state of chassis."

Apparently she decided to complete her contract despite the administrative "state of chassis," because she remained until 1933. Then she left to become a research associate at the Columbia University School of Library Service and continued there until 1935, while devoting part of her time to professional writing.

In 1937, she became associate professor at the Western Reserve School of Library Science. This, her last major position, terminated in 1945, when she reached the age of 65. Writing had now become her primary interest, and she viewed any position from the point of view of its providing her an opportunity to write. In another letter (July 31, 1936) to Hirshberg, discussing the possibility of the post at Western Reserve, she states her feeling in this matter:

> As you know, I am interested in professional writing and have become fairly successful at it. But it cannot be carried on successfully on a free lance basis—a professional connection is essential, both from the point of view of prestige and because writing alone will not pay one's board and keep.

Following her departure from Western Reserve, she retired to Berkeley, California, where she continued her professional and literary writing while serving as the librarian of the First Congregational Church. Finally, after a decade, failing health forced her to discontinue all of her professional activities and to seek care in a nursing home, and she died July 5, 1962, at 82 years of age. Considering her long years of service and her impact on one very important facet of librarianship, it is amazing and sad that her death went practically unnoticed.

Her list of writings over the years is impressive. *The Library in the School* is still considered an important work in this field: every phase or problem of school librarianship has its share of extensive discussion, and routine procedures are described in detail *ad infinitum*. If the minutiae of the work could have been somewhat refined, it might have proved less tedious reading for future school librarians.

Fargo also wrote four teen-age novels, the best known being *Marian-Martha*, a library career book. Other titles useful to school librarians could be cited, but it is in her papers and articles, written for public presentation, that her insight and rich personality come through. Several of her articles were selected from various professional journals for inclusion in Martha Wilson's *School Library Experience*, First Series. Although they appeared in the twenties, their modern philosophy and sparkling style are noteworthy, as are key ideas that were to be accepted as "new" at a much later date. She always made her points in a very vivid and personal way, which impressed them on the listener or reader for some time to come. "Seventeen and the Reference Librarian" is a good example, as the opening paragraph will show:

> There is five feet, 11 inches of him—or six feet two if you judge by what protrudes beyond coat-sleeve and trouser-leg. He drapes himself over the high desk. "Say, *She* says sumpthin' about Holly Rod or whatever it was. I don't know, but mebbe it's Holy Rod, and anyway, it's history and—what period in history? . . . Why—er—the first period, an' I forgot it last night an'—oh, I get-cha. You mean what time in history. Why—I dunno. She didn't tell us, but I gotta have it next period, an'

say (ingratiatingly), cant-cha get me sumpthin' real short? Gee, I gotta have it this morning 'cause if I get another goose-egg, I get kicked off the team, an' the bell rings in ten minutes, an' say, cant-cha give it to me quick?"

You, and that means you or me or any other red-blooded reference librarian, ditch all your theories of method and "give it to him quick! . . ."

School librarians over the years have reason to salute Lucile Fargo and to express deep gratitude to her for the rich and stimulating image of service that she created in the early stages of school library development.

Biographical listings and obituaries—New York State Library School Association. *Register of the New York State Library School, 1887-1926*. Albany, N.Y., 1959; *Who Was Who in America* VI (1974-1976); *Who's Who in Library Service*, 1st ed., 2nd ed., 3rd ed. **Books and articles about the biographee**—[Biographical sketch]. *Library Journal* 70:1029 (Nov. 1, 1945). **Primary sources and archival materials**—On file at the Case Western Reserve University School of Library Science (Cleveland, Ohio) is correspondence between Fargo and Herbert Hirshberg. The author also corresponded with friends of Fargo in preparing the sketch.

—ALICE BROOKS McGUIRE

FAXON, FREDERICK WINTHROP (1866-1936)

Frederick Winthrop Faxon was born August 24, 1866, at West Roxbury, now part of Boston, Massachusetts, the son of Marcus and Augusta Chalmers Fernald Faxon. He was educated at the Boston Latin School, where he was graduated in 1885 and, later, at Harvard, where he obtained his baccalaureate degree in 1889. That same year, he joined the company of Soule and Bugbee, a firm that published and sold law books, to work in the newly formed Library Department. He married Adeleine True Thompson on May 16, 1900.

Faxon immediately showed an unusual combination of an inherent interest in bibliography and good business instincts and training. In 1902, he was made manager of the Library Department, he became a director of the firm in 1911, and he was made president and treasurer in 1913. He bought the Boston Book Company (previously Soule and Bugbee) in 1918 and changed the name to the F. W. Faxon Company. He continued as proprietor until his death in 1936, at which time ownership was transferred to Albert H. Davis, Sr., Faxon's cousin-in-law, who had joined the Company in 1929. The firm remains under the same family.

Frederick Winthrop Faxon was not a librarian, but for almost forty years, he devoted himself to serving librarians and promoting the library idea. He was the first to realize the tremendous wealth of biographical and historical data, as well as some of the New World's finest literary information, to be found in magazines, and in magazines alone. Devoting his life to a study of the American magazine, he left behind him an institution unique in the nation's literary field. Before his death he had accumulated the greatest possible fund of information on the history of American magazines, their publishers, the dates of their beginnings and endings, and the authors and artists who contributed to them. In writing to his college class secretary, he said: "I consider I have been the means of helping many library searchers for information."

His interest in libraries and magazines greatly influenced the nature and the scope of the Faxon Company's publishing programs. In 1897, he established the *Bulletin of Bibliography*, the Company's oldest continuing publication, as a medium for the publication of articles, bibliographies, reading lists, and other material helpful to libraries. In addition to editing the *Bulletin*, Faxon contributed editorial comments and articles, compiled bibliographies, and wrote the regular feature, "Births, Deaths and Magazine Notes," distinguishing himself as an historian of American magazines. In 1897, he also published his *Bibliography of Ephemeral Bibelots*. In 1907, the first volume of the *Useful Reference Series of Books* was published. This series, which lists over one hundred publications to date, began as an outgrowth of the *Bulletin of Bibliography*. In 1908, he established the *Annual Magazine Subject Index* (reprinted by G. K. Hall as *Cumulated Magazine Subject Index, 1907-1949* in 1964), and in the following year, the *Dramatic Index* (still in print in a cumulative edition: *Cumulated Dramatic Index, 1909-1949: A Cumulation of the F. W. Faxon Company's Dramatic Index*, G. K. Hall, 1965), both of which were published annually from 1909 to 1949. Faxon continued editorial supervision of both until his death. The *Magazine Subject Index* was conceived as a complement to the major indexes of the day, William F. Poole's (q.v.) and H. W. Wilson's (q.v.), including as it did state historical magazines and other periodicals not listed elsewhere. His other publications included *Modern Chap Books and Their Imitators* (1903), *Checklist of Popular English and American Periodicals* (1908), and *A Bibliography of Literary Annuals and Gift Books, American and English* (1912).

Faxon was secretary of the American Library Association from 1900 to 1903, travel secretary from 1896 to 1900, chairman of the Travel Committee from 1902 to 1934, and an official ALA delegate to the meeting of the Library Association of Great Britain at Liverpool in 1912. During his lifetime, Faxon attended 43 ALA conferences. He was a member and served as treasurer of the Bibliographical Society of America, was president of the Massachusetts Library Club in 1931-1932, and held various offices and committee memberships in numerous

library organizations (Special Libraries Association and state library associations in Rhode Island, New York, New Jersey, Michigan, Pennsylvania, and Wisconsin). All these activities brought him in contact with, and endeared him to, many people in the library world. Following his death on August 31, 1936, it was noted in the *Wilson Bulletin for Librarians* that "few men had more friends among librarians." It was also said, in the *Iowa Library Quarterly* (September 1936) that "to those who have travelled on a special train to the ALA conferences, news of the passing of Frederick W. Faxon, of Boston, will come with a sense of loss. He was genial, accommodating and to meet him was to always meet an old friend."

Faxon's usefulness, as described by Mary E. Bates in her memorial to Faxon in the *Bulletin of Bibliography*, was not confined to the library world. He had been permanent secretary of the Boston Latin School class since 1888 and held membership in the Harvard Club in Boston and the Appalachian Mountain Club. He was a Swedenborgian and an active member of his church, and in many ways a very useful citizen. He spoke before library audiences in many parts of the country, always in his quiet, modest manner and with no thought of praise or financial remuneration. An enthusiastic traveller, Faxon visited all states of the United States; he also lived in London for seven months and spent four months visiting France, Belgium, Germany, Holland, Switzerland, Ireland, Scotland, and Wales. His extensive collection of photographs from numerous ALA conventions, which he left to the American Library Association, bears witness to his interest in photography.

Faxon has been described as a man who exemplified service without officiousness, who radiated good will, who brought to every activity poise and stability, to every enterprise a wise intelligence. He was highly respected and honored by his staff. He has also been described as a "man who possessed a rare sense of humor and sharp wit, which he could use with telling effect to enliven long or tedious business sessions, yet never so as to cause hurt."

Biographical listings and obituaries—[Obituary]. "Frederick Winthrop Faxon." *Wilson Bulletin for Librarians* 11:144 (Oct. 1936); *Who Was Who in America* I (1897-1942). Books and articles about the biographee—Alcott, William. "Frederick Winthrop Faxon." *Library Journal* 61:680-81 (Sept. 15, 1936); Alcott, William. "Frederick Winthrop Faxon." *American Library Association Bulletin* 30:934 (Oct. 1936); Bates, Mary E. "In Memoriam: Frederick Winthrop Faxon (August 24, 1866-August 31, 1936)." *Bulletin of Bibliography* 16:41 (May-Aug. 1937); "Frederick Winthrop Faxon." *Bulletin of Bibliography* 14:180-86 (Sept.-Dec. 1932); "Frederick Winthrop Faxon." *Harvard Alumni Bulletin* 39:105-106 (Oct. 1936); Redstone, Edward H. "Frederick Winthrop Faxon." *Bulletin of Bibliography* 15:181 (May-Aug. 1936); "Tribute to F. W. Faxon." *Library Journal* 61:860 (Nov. 15, 1936).

—KATHERINE CVELJO

FELLOWS, JENNIE DORCAS (1873-1938)

Jennie Dorcas Fellows was born April 4, 1873, in Griswold, Connecticut, the daughter of Franklin Ebenezer and Jane Eliza Stiles Fellows. For three years after her graduation from the Norwich (Connecticut) Free Academy in 1892, she assisted librarian Henry Watson Kent at the Academy's library. Kent, one of Melvil Dewey's (q.v.) students and previously a cataloger at Columbia College, persuaded her to go to the New York State Library School, from which she received a diploma. In 1897, Fellows became a cataloger at the Worcester (Massachusetts) Free Public Library, then under the direction of Samuel Swett Green (q.v.). Two years later, she took a step that was to make possible her major contribution to American librarianship, as she left Worcester for a position with Dewey at the New York State Library.

During her first years at the Library, she successfully performed a multiplicity of duties, including cataloging, classification, editing, and teaching. For teaching a course in basic cataloging, Fellows prepared as a text her *Cataloging Rules* (Library School Bulletin No. 36, 1914). After a process that had the perfectionist, melancholic Fellows ready to destroy and be done with both the original and the revision, as she wrote to May Seymour (q.v.), a revised *Cataloging Rules* was published by H. W. Wilson (q.v.) in 1922. Widely used in libraries and library schools, it was called by Harriet E. Howe (q.v.) an "exceedingly valuable book which should be in the possession of all interested in cataloging problems" (*Library Journal*, May 1, 1922, p. 408).

However, Fellows is remembered today not as a cataloging teacher but as a classifier. In 1911, she became assistant to May Seymour, who served Dewey as editor of the Decimal Classification from 1891 until her death thirty years later. As one of her responsibilities, Fellows acted as intermediary between Seymour (at the Lake Placid Club editorial office) and Walter S. Biscoe (q.v.), Dewey's protégé and the actual long-term theoretician (in Albany). This was necessary because Biscoe was intolerably slow in writing responses to queries and could be forced to pronounce on a subject only when confronted face to face. Thus, Fellows, through repeated interviews with Biscoe, achieved a thorough understanding of the system which enabled her, upon Seymour's death in 1921, to become the new editor of the DDC immediately.

Seymour had done most of the work on the eleventh edition of the DDC, but it became Fellows's responsibility actually to get it through publication (1922). She then had the primary responsibility for editions twelve (1927), thirteen (1932), and much of fourteen (1942), three of the best in the DDC series. The fourteenth has been judged a landmark in the literature of library classification.

Fellows was totally dedicated both to Dewey and to the work she did. Indeed, she was so concerned that when the bill for printing the twelfth edition was settled at $13,000 rather than her original estimate of $10,000, she tried to help financially. She offered her stock in Lake Placid to the Foundation (the DDC copyright holder) to help make up the difference, this in the belief that the work was more important than her own financial well-being.

The thirteenth edition, however, also brought to the fore a different side of Dorcas—her desire to champion yet another of Dewey's manifold causes, that of simplified spelling. In a brief comment on the edition, entitled "Spelling Reform and D.C. Classification [sic]" (*Library Journal*, February 15, 1933, p. 166), Robert K. Shaw questioned whether a work such as the DDC was the "proper vehicle for the advance of spelling reform propaganda." Fellows (by now Dorkas Fellows) wrote a long defense ("Spelling Reform and Decimal Classification," *Library Journal*, July 1, 1933, pp. 610-11); she felt that "An earnest believer in any doctrine or policy must as a matter of conscience work for its advancement through whatever means he has at his disposal." She never relented on the point.

At about this time, the fundamental structure of the DDC was being questioned, as well. Henry E. Bliss (q.v.), writing in his book *The Organization of Knowledge in Libraries* (1933), attacked Dewey's scheme under such headings as "Important Sciences Mangled," and "Confusion Confounded." Bliss was also hostile to the new Library of Congress Classification but since the use of Dewey's scheme was more widespread, it was the obvious target. Of course, Bliss's objections could not have been answered to his satisfaction without totally restructuring the DDC. Too, Bliss had his own scheme to promote. Yet this was clear indication that Dewey's work was still subject to serious challenge even at this relatively late date.

The major challenge, of course, came from the LC system. In her article "Library of Congress Classification vs. Decimal Classification" (*Library Journal*, April 1, 1925, pp. 291-95), Fellows sought to outline the differences and advantages of the two methods. Naturally, the DDC emerged as clearly superior, although she did admit that the LC scheme had some good points. Yet, she was not blindly opposed to anything to do with LC, as she might have been expected to be. Indeed, she cooperated greatly in helping to solve the problems involved in printing Dewey numbers on LC cards, which began under the direction of David Haykin (q.v.) in 1930, after the DDC editorial offices were moved to the Library of Congress in 1923.

For Dorkas Fellows, the editorship of the Dewey Decimal Classification was a position that entailed continuous struggle, and its demands required all of her strength. Melvil Dewey did, of course, retain a degree of control over the work until his death in 1931. He also encouraged Fellows constantly, even though they sometimes disagreed as to the proper direction for the development of the classification. In a letter to her dated December 20, 1931 (six days prior to his death), Dewey told her: *"Do n wori. Takes ur strength and hurts n helps"* and *"dont feel hurrid. i[t] cripls eficiensi"* [Dewey's emphasis].

During the 1920s, Fellows gradually became convinced that it was impossible to coordinate her work with that of the group that was developing the *Classification Décimale* in Europe. Her opinion may have developed during a visit to a bibliographic conference in Geneva in 1924 and a visit in Brussels with the leaders of the Institut International de Bibliographie. However, both Melvil Dewey and his son Godfrey continued to cherish the hope for a truly international classification. Fellows's active opposition also resulted from conflicts with Godfrey, who, both before and after his father's death, had a varying degree of responsibility for the DDC. This combination of professional and personal factors apparently served to convince Fellows that international efforts were futile, and she never ceased to resist them.

Other conflicts arose with committees of librarians appointed from time to time to advise on the development of the DDC. The classification was very important to most American libraries, and American librarians naturally wished to influence the direction of its growth. But Fellows was a highly skilled classifier, a true expert, by the time that the first committee began to function, and it was in her nature to rely on her own experience rather than on the opinions of others she held to be less knowledgeable than herself about the details of the work.

In later life, Dorkas Fellows was plagued by ill health as well as by those persons opposed to her views. In 1931 her illness was diagnosed as cancer of the spine. By 1935, it was becoming clear that she could not continue with the DDC indefinitely; however, she managed to hold the editorship until August 1, 1937. Even after her resignation as editor, Fellows continued, despite great physical discomfort, to help prepare the fourteenth edition of the classification. She died on October 10, 1938, at her home in Norwich, Connecticut.

Dorkas Fellows was a short woman who wore glasses for astigmatism complicated by diabetes; a photograph appears in the ALA *Catalogers' and Classifiers' Yearbook* No. 8 (1940) and in the February 1933 issue of *Library Service News*.

In addition to a rather somber view of life (which seemed to her "a thing not greatly to be desired," as she wrote to Emily Dewey on October 31, 1936), Fellows held strong opinions. She also would express them bluntly, yet she was easily hurt if anyone except Melvil Dewey criticized her work. In the above-mentioned *Yearbook*, Myron Getchell, one of her assistants, wrote of her:

> ... uncompromisingly accurate and thorough, self-sacrificingly and self-effacingly devoted, sincere and steadfast in her adherence to principle, forthright and unfaltering in the defense of her convictions, to which she brought a direct and penetrating pungency of style which left her meaning unmistakable, she gave her all to the work that lay before her.

These attributes made it possible for Dorkas Fellows to expand the usefulness and influence of the Dewey Decimal Classification, a work that has constituted one of America's chief contributions to the world of librarianship.

Biographical listings and obituaries—*Who Was Who in America* I (1897-1942). **Books and articles about the biographee**—Comaromi, John P. *The Eighteen Editions of the Dewey Decimal Classification*. Albany, N.Y.: Forest Press, 1976; Getchell, Myron Warren. "Dorkas Fellows." *Library Journal* 63:272 (Dec. 1, 1938). This article appeared with the same title but in a slightly shortened form and signed by David J. Haykin as well in *Wilson Library Bulletin* 13:272 (Dec. 1938); Getchell, Myron Warren. "Dorkas Fellows, Cataloger and D.C. Editor." In *Catalogers' and Classifiers' Yearbook*, No. 8. Chicago: American Library Association, 1940, pp. 14-19. **Primary sources and archival materials**—Fellows's papers can be found at the Decimal Classification Division of the Library of Congress, at Forest Press in Albany, New York, and in the Melvil Dewey Collection at Columbia University.

—HAYNES McMULLEN

FERGUSON, MILTON JAMES (1879-1954)

Milton James Ferguson was born on April 11, 1879, in Hubbardstown, West Virginia, the son of William H. and Nancy Anne Strother Ferguson. While he was a small boy, his family moved to Kansas and then took part in the historic homestead run into Oklahoma, becoming settlers of what is now Norman. Working his way through school, he helped construct the first building of the University of Oklahoma by driving a mule that hauled and hoisted bricks. Ferguson received his A.B. with Phi Beta Kappa honors from the University in 1901, and in 1906, his A.M. degree. In 1902, he received a certificate in librarianship from New York State University in Albany, after which he returned to the University of Oklahoma to serve as librarian from 1902 to 1907. In 1933, he was awarded an honorary Doctor of Letters from New York University. He married Rose M. Barnett, and their daughter, Ruth B., was librarian at the Prospect Branch of Brooklyn Public Library at the time of his death.

While serving as assistant librarian for the State of California from 1908 to 1917, he was in charge of the law collection. Finally weary of being asked, in challenging tones, "Are you an attorney?," he decided to become one; and shortly after being admitted to the California Bar Association (1917), he was appointed state librarian, a post he held until 1930.

When the Brooklyn Public Library Board of Trustees called Ferguson to the post of chief librarian, they were quoted in the press as saying they had sought the best librarian in the United States and had found "one of the best known and most advanced librarians in the country with a distinguished record." This record, besides his activities in Oklahoma and California, included library surveys for the Carnegie Corporation in the Union of South Africa, Rhodesia, and Kenya Colony in 1928-1929. (Later on, he was to conduct similar studies in Concord, New Hampshire, the state of Louisiana, and Prince Edward Island.) Ferguson came to Brooklyn in the heart of the Depression, and his 1931 annual report is more than apropos to the situation facing public libraries in the 1970s:

> Some people may hold the view that the Public Library is a sort of luxury to be indulged when money is easy but to be put aside when the economic shoe pinches. The period of the depression has proved quite the contrary. People have flocked to libraries finding recreation and means to study for the old job or the new one. Libraries are the main reliance of the majority of people for continuance and effective progress in education.

Another problem facing Brooklyn Public Library in 1930 was the "architectural monstrosity" that had long been under construction as the new Central Library. Under Ferguson, the building was not only completed but was refashioned in accordance with twentieth century design. Francis R. St. John (q.v.), upon replacing Ferguson at BPL, said that Ferguson would long be remembered for his many achievements—the most outstanding of which were the opening of the central building and bringing national distinction to the Library.

A resolution made by the BPL Staff Association upon Ferguson's retirement in 1949 read: "RESOLVED, that both the Brooklyn Public Library holdings and we, its librarians, have benefited greatly by his unceasing emphasis on literary matters; by his scholarly knowledge and joyful appreciation of books and bookmaking." In the resolution, the Association

listed his accomplishments in Brooklyn Public Library between 1930 and 1949 as: the opening of the Central Library (Ingersoll Memorial), the creation of new administrative positions, the introduction of a regional branch system, the organization of a business reference branch, the modernization of procedures, the inauguration of a pension system, the extension of sabbatical leaves, the inauguration of a scholarship fund for staff members, and the liberalization of vacations for professional study.

The praise from his professional colleagues was matched by that from the public. In the *Brooklyn Eagle*, columnist Joe Early wrote, "There is no more effective cultural leader or more earnest administrator in Brooklyn affairs today than Milton J. Ferguson."

A member of many professional and civic organizations, his presidencies included those of the American Library Association (1938-1939), the California and New York Library Associations, the National Association of State Libraries, the League of Library Commissions, the New York (City) Library Club, and the Brooklyn Council for Adult Education. He was also an active Rotarian and Boy Scout worker.

He was a frequent contributor to library literature, and his major writings include: *Memorandum: Libraries in the Union of South Africa, Rhodesia and Kenya Colony* (1929), *American Library Laws* (ALA, 1930), *A Look at the Concord, New Hampshire, Public Library* (ALA, 1938), and *Brooklyn Public Library, Ingersoll Memorial: A Description of the New Building* (R. R. Donnelley and Sons, 1942).

Beginning in 1937, Ferguson was chairman of the Forest Press's Decimal Classification Committee, which carried on Melvil Dewey's (q.v.) work. On March 1, 1949, Ferguson assumed complete leadership of the project, taking over from Esther Potter, who had served as project director, but not editor, since December 1944. (Leota Johns had been editor briefly in the 1940s, but she left because of family concerns. After her departure, and prior to Ferguson's appointment, there had been no actual editor, and all work had been done by the Committee and a leaderless staff.) The widely anticipated *Decimal Classification*, Standard (15th) edition, was issued by Forest Press in 1951. It immediately attracted much unfavorable comment because of the substantial changes introduced, many of them apparently on Ferguson's sole editorial authority (he evidently did not consult with the Committee, among whose members were Godfrey Dewey, the son of Melvil Dewey, and Fremont Rider [q.v.]). (For a complete review of the edition, see Thelma Eaton's "Dewey Reexamined," in the May 1, 1952, *Library Journal*, pp. 745-51.)

Following the generally poor reception of the fifteenth edition, the directors of Forest Press, led by

Godfrey Dewey, decided that Ferguson's term as editor would end on October 31, 1951. Then, with Dewey as editor (although only on a part-time basis), a revision of the fifteenth edition appeared, with a new index designed to meet complaints about the index to the original fifteenth edition. This edition was the last to be issued separately by Forest Press, but it was the first to incorporate Melvil Dewey's name into the title: *Dewey Decimal Classification and Relative Index*, Standard (15th) edition revised (Forest Press, 1952). (Subsequent editions were produced under the editorial supervision of the Library of Congress, under a contractual arrangement with the Forest Press.) Ferguson stayed on as an editorial consultant and chairman of the Decimal Classification Editorial Policy Committee (the name had changed by then) until his resignation on September 7, 1953.

Ferguson had a lifelong interest in fine printing and book collecting, and he devoted great care to the BPL Treasure Room. Too, he was an honorary member of the Print Makers Society of California and the California Society of Etchers. He was an alert, warm person with pleasant manners, a rare combination of scholar and businessman, and a joiner who seemed to have a knack of naturally rising to the top of the organizations he joined. People were charmed by his stories of the early days in Oklahoma and his dry humor. His humor, in fact, had a way of frequently bursting through customarily solemn occasions, such as, for example, the annual report in which he referred to the long unfinished Central Library building as having "more long-distance records than all the marathon runners since the time of Pheidippides." Milton J. Ferguson died on October 23, 1954.

Biographical listings and obituaries—[Obituary]. *College and Research Libraries* 16:216-17 (April 1955); [Obituary]. *Library Journal* 79:2106 (Dec. 1, 1954); [Obituary]. *Library Review* 113:52 (Spring 1955); [Obituary]. *Publishers Weekly* 166:1889 (Nov. 6, 1954); *Who's Who in the East*, 14th ed.; *Who Was Who in America* III (1941-1960); *Who's Who in Library Service*, 1st ed., 2nd ed. Books and articles about the biographee—"A.L.A. President Honored." *Library Journal* 64:30 (Jan. 1939); Comaromi, John Phillip. *The Eighteen Editions of the Dewey Decimal Classification.* Albany, N.Y.: Forest Press, 1976; Freeman, Margaret B. "The Brooklyn Public Library: A History." Unpublished manuscript, 1970, Vol. 1; "Librarian Authors." *Library Journal* 58:208 (March 1, 1933). Primary sources and archival materials—The clipping file of the Brooklyn Public Library contains some pertinent material.

—PATRICIA SENN BREIVIK

FLETCHER, WILLIAM ISAAC (1844-1917)

William Isaac Fletcher was an outstanding librarian, a pioneer library educator, a prolific writer, editor, and indexer, and a leader in the American Library Association and in the profession. Fletcher was born on April 23, 1844, in Burlington, Vermont, but his parents soon moved to Massachusetts and settled in Winchester, a suburb of Boston, where his father was a printer. As a boy, he was sickly and did not finish high school.

His introduction to the world of libraries occurred at the age of seven, when he was awed by a visit to the Boston Athenaeum with his father. Later, he revisited it with his father and, once, visited it alone, only to be rudely thrown out by an attendant. The latter incident made him a lifelong advocate of a friendly and inviting attitude among librarians, especially for small boys.

Fletcher made his formal entry into librarianship at the small Winchester town library, as assistant librarian and then librarian for two years. He admitted, however, that he learned just as much about books from frequent haunts of Boston's secondhand bookstores. In the fall of 1861, he joined the staff of the Boston Athenaeum, taking the place of his brother, who had entered army service. His brother had been appointed as a library apprentice in 1860, with the help of the family pastor, who was a friend of William F. Poole (q.v.), the director of the Boston Athenaeum.

At the Athenaeum, Fletcher was placed in charge of the circulation desk where, when not serving library patrons, he collated all new volumes and prepared them for cataloging. In accomplishing this, he was able to do much browsing and reading. He worked at the Athenaeum from 1861 to 1866, except for three months in the summer of 1864, when he volunteered for a brief tour of army service, spent in general duty around Washington.

Fletcher left the Athenaeum in 1866 to serve as librarian in Lawrence and Taunton, Massachusetts, and Waterbury, Connecticut, all newly established libraries in urban industrial centers. This was followed by service as assistant librarian in the Watkinson Library at Hartford, Connecticut, the Watkinson being an endowed library of some 26,000 volumes, open to the public and, in Connecticut, second in size only to Yale.

In September of 1883, Fletcher was invited to Amherst College for an interview, was immediately offered an appointment, and began his duties in November. There seems to be no record of how Fletcher was thought of or contacted by Amherst, but one source believes it may have been through Melvil Dewey (q.v.), with whom Fletcher was already on friendly, though often argumentative, terms. William Fletcher seems to have made an immediately favorable impact on the college community. Within one month of his arrival, the student newspaper wrote of his "kindness and obliging disposition." Within one year, the college president expressed his satisfaction with Fletcher in the annual commencement report.

It is significant that beginning with the 1884-1885 issue, the *Catalogue of Amherst College* begins to include descriptive information about the library's sources and services. Before this time, there had been very little library information in this annual publication. In 1884, Fletcher received the honorary degree of Master of Arts from Amherst.

Fletcher soon became an accepted and important member of the town community as well. He came to Amherst with his wife, whom he had married in 1869, and with a daughter and two sons. Still another son was born in Amherst in 1884. Fletcher became a member of the local school board, a charter member of the local historical society, and for 25 years was the clerk of the college church, where he also conducted Bible classes.

Amherst College was, at the time of Fletcher's appointment as librarian, going through a period of change from the classical and religious education of the past to one with more emphasis on secular studies. More electives were being offered as well as courses of a pre-professional nature. There was also an increase in extracurricular life, particularly through the growth of fraternities and organized athletics.

There is evidence that upon Fletcher's arrival the college library was unbalanced in content, poorly arranged, and little used. When he left 28 years later, the library was playing a very important role in the everyday operation of Amherst. First, Fletcher more than doubled the size of the collection, from 42,906 volumes in 1884 to 102,485 volumes in 1911. Furthermore, its subject coverage was in better balance than it had been. Second, as a result of constant pleading and justification, Fletcher more than tripled the annual amount being spent for books, from $2,175 in 1884 (the first year that the college library even had a formal book budget) to almost $7,000 in 1911.

Third, Fletcher also improved the services of the Amherst library. One of his first acts was to provide students with free access to the stacks. The hours of service were doubled, the card catalog was improved and expanded, and the collection was constantly reclassified to reflect changes in knowledge and the addition of new subjects. Believing in personal assistance to faculty and students, Fletcher began a series of eight lectures on the use of the library; he soon changed his mind about formal lectures, however, and favored more informal instruction within the library. He collected the most important bibliographical reference works in the main circulation area, with instructions for their use so that students could be self-reliant and independent in their studies. Finally, in his last year he attained still another goal—that of a bigger and better staff to meet the needs of a growing collection as well as those of library service.

William Fletcher retired, was appointed librarian emeritus in 1911, and was succeeded by his son. Born in 1874, Robert Fletcher was a graduate of Amherst (class of 1897); he followed in his father's footsteps by entering librarianship as a profession, serving as librarian from 1911 to 1935. Thus, the father and son team of librarians at Amherst provided a total of 52 years of service.

William Fletcher's career as a library educator began, as we have seen, with his instruction on library use at Amherst College. More formally, it began when he was a guest lecturer in Dewey's new library school at Columbia. In 1891, he began his "Summer School for Librarians" as a private venture using Amherst College facilities and as part of the long-successful summer school for instruction in foreign languages which had been conducted at Amherst since 1877.

Fletcher organized this school to provide a brief, practical course for beginners in library work or for librarians of small libraries who had no training. The course consisted of his lectures on classification, cataloging, buying books, etc.—along with work experience in the Amherst College Library. This combination of lectures and supervised practice work lasted for four hours a day, for five (later six) days per week, for six weeks, during which the students familiarized themselves with library procedures they would use. Also, through critical, comparative study, they developed the judgment as to why these procedures were the best to use. However, it was not all study and work. There were social gatherings at the Fletcher home as well as excursions and picnics, for William Fletcher had a genuine interest in each of his students and kept in close touch with them in later years.

The Amherst Summer School for Librarians grew with each year and attracted students from as far away as Indiana to the west and Washington, D.C., to the south. Beginning with about 30 students in 1891, the enrollment increased to 54 by 1902. The size was then cut in half in an effort to raise admission standards. In 1905, Fletcher discontinued the School as he was nearing retirement and probably wanted to rest and recuperate during the summer months. Even though it closed in 1905, Fletcher's School served as a model for other institutions, which provided their own modifications. As an example, the University of Wisconsin started a comparable six-week summer course in 1895, through the urging of the State Library Commission.

William Fletcher joined the American Library Association in 1878 (as member number 184) and remained active almost until the time of his retirement. He attended the ALA conferences of 1877,

1879, 1883, 1885-1894, 1896-1904, and 1906 (23 in all), and was designated secretary pro-tem of ALA for the 1891 conference at San Francisco, when Secretary Frank P. Hill (q.v.) was forced to give up the journey because of illness. Fletcher was subsequently elected president of ALA and served during 1891-1892. When the new constitution of the American Library Association was adopted in 1892, he was chosen as one of the ten original councillors.

Fletcher served on many ALA boards and committees, two particularly important ones being the Publishing Board, which directed the early indexing projects of ALA, and the Cooperative Cataloging Committee, which played a key role in the provision of printed catalog cards by the Library of Congress. In 1896, Fletcher (along with other prominent librarians, including William Howard Brett [q.v.], Melvil Dewey, and Herbert Putnam [q.v.]) represented ALA before a joint congressional committee on the reorganization of the administration of the Library of Congress.

Still another role Fletcher performed was that of advisor and counsellor to friends and professional colleagues. As an example, he suggested to Charles Evans (q.v.), his friend from Athenaeum days, that he should get two or three outstanding librarians to examine and endorse his projected *American Bibliography* and to include such backing in a circular. Fletcher felt that such an advertising circular, if widely distributed, would bring the subscribers that Evans so badly needed for financing his monumental, multi-volume work.

He was also active in local library affairs, serving as a trustee of the Amherst town library from 1886 to his death and as president of the Board of Trustees for 26 years, and being personally involved in book selection for the library. In addition, he was a trustee of the public library at Conway, Massachusetts (a gift of Marshall Field of Chicago), and he worked toward the development of better library service throughout Massachusetts.

As an author Fletcher was fairly prolific. He was also a frequent speaker at ALA and other library meetings, and many of his speeches appeared in the *Library Journal* (which acted as the official publication of the American Library Association until the ALA *Bulletin* began in 1907). He contributed articles on a wide variety of topics to the *Library Journal*, *Public Libraries* and other leading library periodicals. He contributed also to non-library periodicals, like *Cosmopolitan*, *Critic*, and *Nation*, on topics ranging from the public library movement to descriptions of the Boston Public Library and the Library of Congress and a report on the ALA Conference of 1899 in Atlanta. His earliest published contributions were to the now-famed *Public Libraries in the United States of America*, published by the U.S. Bureau of

Education in 1876. Two of the three sections he wrote in this work reflected his then-current public library work experience, these being "Public Libraries in Manufacturing Communities" and "Public Libraries and the Young." The third was an article entitled "General Considerations Respecting Historical Research."

William Fletcher was perhaps best known as an author because of his book *Public Libraries in America*, published in 1894, which contains not only many of Fletcher's ideas and thoughts about libraries, but also an attempt to interpret the role of the library in its social setting. Even though the public library movement was just finding acceptance, Fletcher was seeking to explain the origins of the public library as an historical phenomenon. But the history and role of the public library are not the only topics covered in this work. There are chapters on library laws, library buildings, the roles of the librarian and library within the community, and schools and academic institutions. Other chapters cover book selection, classification and cataloging, reference work, various aspects of library management, library training, and the ALA, with descriptions of representative libraries. An appendix gives examples of library regulations, opinions on Sunday openings of libraries, and statistical and tabulated data on libraries, library gifts, and special collections in libraries.

Also included in the appendix is Fletcher's Scheme of Classification. In 1894, this was reprinted (with alterations, additions, and an index) as a separate publication. His is a simple and elastic system of classification based on thirteen main classes:

(J)	Juvenile	
A	Fiction	
B	History	Sections 15 to 75
C	English and American Literature	Sections 1 to 13
D	Biography	Sections 81 to 82
E	Travels	Sections 85 to 120
F	Science	Sections 125 to 172
G	Useful Arts	Sections 179 to 240
H	Fine and Recreative Arts	Sections 245 to 277
I	Political and Social Science	Sections 279 to 350
K	Philosophy and Religion	Sections 352 to 416
L	Works on Language and in Foreign Languages	Sections 421 to 456
R	Reference Works	Sections 461 to 468

As can be seen, Fletcher further divided his main classes into numerical subdivisions. For example, under Class C, History, 15 would be Philosophy and Study of History, 16 would be History of Civilization, and 17, Historical Essays and Miscellaneous, while 33 is Ireland, 40 is Italy, and 71 is India. A few numbers were left out at the end of each general division to provide for inserting new classes. However, Fletcher advised that additional classes could be inserted at any point by giving them the number of the preceding class with a letter added. The books in each class were supposed to be numbered consecutively. Subdivisions could be made as needed in any class by assigning blocks of numbers to a particular subject. The main point of all of this was that the librarian could feel free to change the numbers or the order of the classes as he or she saw fit.

Fletcher was also known as an indexer, primarily through his association with *Poole's Index to Periodical Literature*. William Poole (q.v.) edited and published the first two editions in 1848 and 1853, but in 1876 he asked the ALA for assistance in making the third edition a cooperative venture of many librarians. Fletcher became associate editor of this third edition (1882). Five-year supplements were published in 1888 and 1893, with Fletcher playing an increasingly important role in editing and indexing, and the 1893 supplement was under his sole editorship. After Poole's death in 1894, three more supplements were published (in 1897, 1903, and 1908) covering the years 1892-1906, and each having Fletcher as editor. In 1901, an abridged edition was published covering 37 periodicals and aimed at small libraries, and a supplement to this was published in 1905. Fletcher continued as the main editor for both of these publications. Beginning about 1901, there was competition from the H. W. Wilson Company, when it began to publish the *Readers' Guide to Periodical Literature*. Because this index came out much more frequently, it survived, while *Poole's Index* was phased out.

Fletcher also edited the *ALA Index to General Literature* (1893) and its second edition (1901). This was similar to *Poole's Index to Periodical Literature*, but instead of indexing periodical articles, it indexed the contents of books of essays, biographical collections, travel, history, and the publications of literary and historical societies. It was often referred to as the "ALA Essay Index." Previously Fletcher had edited the *Cooperative Index to Periodicals*, which came out annually from 1883 to 1892 and formed the basis for the supplements to *Poole's Index*. This was succeeded by the *Annual Literary Index*, which Fletcher edited with R. R. Bowker, and which was published by the *Publishers' Weekly* from 1893 to 1904. In 1906, this became the *Annual Library Index*, with Fletcher continuing to edit it (along with Helen E. Haines [q.v.]) until 1910. This was then superseded by the *American Library Annual*. Still another example of Fletcher's indexing activity was his index of *The Catalogue of the American Library of the Late Mr. George Brinley of Hartford, Connecticut*. This catalog was compiled by J. H. Trumbull and published in five volumes by the Press of Case, Lockwood and

Brainard Company, in Hartford between 1878 and 1893. Fletcher's *Index* was published separately in 1893.

Contemporary observers characterized Fletcher as genial and kindly, with a sympathetic and gracious manner, a keen and eager mind, and a capacity for hard intellectual work. He was small and wiry in appearance. Fletcher died on June 15, 1917, in South Amherst, Massachusetts. In 1951, during the 75th anniversary of ALA, William Isaac Fletcher was one of forty outstanding librarians selected to the Library Hall of Fame.

Biographical listings and obituaries—*National Cyclopaedia of American Biography* 12; *Who Was Who in America* I (1897-1942). Books and articles about the biographee—Bobinski, George S. "William Isaac Fletcher, an Early American Library Pioneer Leader." *Journal of Library History* 5:101-118 (April 1970). This contains an extensive biobibliography of writings by and about Fletcher; Engley, Donald B. "The Emergence of the Amherst College Library, 1821-1911." Master's thesis, Graduate Library School, University of Chicago, 1947; "Fletcher Memorial Tablet." *Library Journal* 63:746 (Oct. 1938); Jones, E. L. "As It Was in the Beginning." *Public Libraries* 29:522-26 (1924).

—GEORGE S. BOBINSKI

FLEXNER, JENNIE MAAS (1882-1944)

Jennie Maas Flexner, born in Louisville, Kentucky, on November 6, 1882, was the first child of Jacob Aaron and Rosa Maas Flexner, of Bohemian and German Jewish ancestry. Her paternal grandfather, a hatter, had seven sons and two daughters, among them Abraham Flexner, noted for his landmark analyses of medical education and higher education, and Simon Flexner, an eminent bacteriologist who contributed to the control of meningitis and served as director of laboratories for the Rockefeller Institute of Medical Research. Jacob Flexner (1853-1934), first a druggist and later a physician of prominence in Louisville, was one of the founders of the Anti-Tuberculosis Association, and he and Rosa Flexner reared five children. Morris Flexner, Jennie's only brother, was a physician in Louisville for many years; her sister Hortense Flexner King, a poet, taught at Bryn Mawr, while a second sister, Alice Flexner Rothblatt, was a social worker. It was a family distinguished for two generations by their intellectual achievements and their dedication to human service.

Educated first in the public schools of Louisville and then by private study while she worked, Jennie M. Flexner attained a scholarship that was largely the product of effective independent study. She worked as a secretary for two years in the law offices of her uncle, Bernard Flexner, and then as secretary for the editor of the *Louisville Herald* before she accepted a position at the Louisville Public Library in February 1905. Her keen mind, love of reading, and intellectual curiosity led William F. Yust, librarian of the Louisville Free Public Library, to endorse her unqualifiedly for professional study at the Western Reserve University (later Case Western Reserve University) Library School, despite her lack of a college education. She entered Western Reserve's class of 1908-1909 as one of its eighteen full-time students.

Blue-eyed and vivacious, with golden brown hair, Jennie Flexner was instantly recognized for her strength and leadership ability. She was elected president of her class, made only the highest grades, and had contact with library leaders who served on the faculty, among whom were William Howard Brett (q.v.), Linda Eastman (q.v.), and Effie Power (q.v.). Her practice work was conducted at the East Branch of the Cleveland Public Library. Jennie Flexner felt close enough to Western Reserve's Library School, its faculty and its students, that in 1923 she accepted the office of president of its Alumni Association. She completed her year's program in 1909 and received the certificate that represented her satisfactory qualification as a librarian.

Returning to the staff of the Louisville Public Library, Flexner found her burgeoning ideas and enthusiasm for reader services a handicap in working with some of the older staff, and she soon transferred to technical services, where she was less challenging to her supervisors. Yust did not let her talents go unused, however, and in 1910, he placed her in charge of the Library's training class, a responsibility which she carried throughout her period of service in Louisville. In 1912, Yust named her to the just-vacated post of head of the Circulation Department, and in this position, Flexner developed her concepts of service to readers and evolved her effective model for circulation work based on the new open-shelf concept.

Flexner's professional activity and charismatic leadership skills made themselves felt beyond the Louisville Public Library. In 1923, she was elected president of the Kentucky Library Association, a position she held for two years. In this period, she became active in recruiting Negroes to library education, and in 1926, she served as a member of the Council of the American Association for Adult Education.

While the fields of library education and adult education were always tied closely to Flexner's work, services to readers remained the core of her concern, and she was an obvious choice to write the first textbook on circulation work in public libraries. During the late spring and summer of 1926, she went on leave to serve as a staff member working on the American Library Association's curriculum study. Based on analysis of the duties and traits of circulation librarians at a time when the professional services of reading guidance and community contacts were an inherent part of this work, the study took Flexner to some fifty public libraries with reputations for substantial circulation activities. These field visits, as well as the intellectual stimulus of work under the guidance of W. W. Charters and Sarah C. N. Bogle (q.v.), provided Jennie Flexner with a broad perspective that was reflected in the textbook as well as in Flexner's maturing professional philosophy.

The first draft of the text, *Circulation of Books in Public Libraries*, was distributed in 1926 by the American Library Association for experimental use and comment, and the revised text appeared the next year as *Circulation Work in Public Libraries*. Reviewers of the text were laudatory and saw it as significant for both the novice and the practitioner, identifying the principles of service behind circulation and service procedures, and replacing a rule of thumb with philosophically based service concepts and guidelines to practice. No volume covering this area of work has since had the scope of Flexner's text.

Having built the circulation services of the Louisville Public Library to an active open-shelf service over sixteen years, and having studied the advisory services in Chicago, Milwaukee, and elsewhere, Jennie Flexner was ready to move to a new professional challenge. In 1928, she accepted an invitation to establish a readers' advisory service for the New York Public Library. The position in New York required organizing an advisory service for the users of both the great research collections of the Reference Department and the large branch library system of the Circulation Department. Flexner brought to the task her scholarly knowledge of books, ability to organize, skill in working with two well-differentiated departments, and enthusiasm. The modest, accessible Readers' Adviser's Office opened March 4, 1929.

The public events of the next fifteen years, the Depression and then World War II, dictated the emphases of the readers' advisory service from that office. Experience confirmed that guidance of the individual reader was the basic and first aspect of the service, since the personal needs of the unemployed, the displaced, and the distraught who sought help from books required the personalized attention that such service was designed to provide. Beyond this emphasis on the individual reader, however, the readers' advisory service also offered help to groups, with two focal points: 1) providing lists and materials to study groups on a local basis or nationally through radio or national study programs, and 2) using other local agencies as channels to potential individual users of the advisory service.

The Depression led Flexner to an intensive search for "readable books" and to active conferences with publishers to produce "simple, well-written" introductions to new fields of knowledge. From 1931 to 1938, unemployed persons comprised close to half of the users of the Readers' Adviser's Office, many of them building background in vocational and cultural areas to increase their individual employability. In reflection after her death, Morse Cartwright commented: "Miss Flexner undoubtedly saved the lives of a few and the reason of many during the economic depression."

World War II and its preliminary European unrest were the stimulus to Flexner's intensive work with foreign-born refugees. Nazism had sent thousands of well-educated professionals to this country through New York City in the 1930s, and the Public Library response was hospitable and widespread. Jennie Flexner was one of those who provided information, referral, and guidance to those seeking to live and work in this country. She chaired ALA Committees on Work with the Foreign-Born and on Refugee Librarians and provided a sustained resource of reading lists to the National Refugee Service. As World War II developed and thousands of young Americans became involved, Flexner served as adviser to the Council on Books in Wartime and as chairman of an Armed Forces Editions Advisory Committee, enabling a fine selection of readable books to reach young men and women in the services throughout the world. As readers' adviser in the New York Public Library, Jennie Flexner provided professional leadership toward meeting some of the basic social problems of her time.

Flexner's organizational work with the New York Public Library was developed with skill. On her arrival, she spent close to a year working in the various departments and branches related to the task of her new office, and the work of the office was always effective in the coordination role it was established to achieve. By 1936, the first two branch system readers' advisers were appointed; by 1938, there were seventeen, and by 1943, there were twenty-nine. The branch system of advisory service was thoroughly integrated into branch adult services.

Her two formal reports on readers' advisory service carried out the responsibility of the Readers' Adviser's Office to provide guidance to public libraries in this area of service. With Sigrid A. Edge, Flexner authored *A Readers' Advisory Service* (1934). This manual described succinctly the goals, procedures, and record of readers and services provided by the New York Public Library Readers' Adviser's Office in 1932 and 1933. The service was presented in the context of adult education, and the manual pointed up the significance of the Office's contact with continuation school students, with the probation department, and with the occupational adjustment service.

The second report, *Readers' Advisers at Work* (1941), was jointly authored by Jennie Flexner and Byron C. Hopkins; it provided a quantitative analysis of readers, their backgrounds, the topics that interested them, and the books they read. It included both the basic model of planned reading programs and less formal adaptations evolved in the branch system. A preliminary basis for norms was offered in this report, and if the tide against formal advisory service had not been well under way at this time, the report might well have encouraged other public libraries to prepare comparable analyses. These two reports remain the classic statements of the formal readers' advisory service of the 1930s and offer useful background to the development of public library service to the independent adult student.

Flexner's final published monograph, *Making Books Work* (1943), was designed for the independent adult student. It shows her fine perception of the need to make the user of the service increasingly independent of library resources. In 1938, the first year of the American Library Association's Joseph W. Lippincott Award, Jennie Flexner was one of five eminent librarians who did not receive the Award but who were nevertheless cited by the Lippincott Award Committee for their notable contributions. She was cited for her "judgment and discrimination" in development of readers' advisory services and her publications in the field.

Having moved into the New York Public Library position at the onset of the Depression, Flexner closed her career at the height of World War II. She died at the age of 62 on November 17, 1944, at her home in New York City. With each new social demand, Jennie Flexner had found a creative response through her work as a readers' adviser.

Jennie Flexner's enormous vitality, enthusiasm, spontaneity, and love of books and people made their impact on numerous librarians as she worked on ALA's Board of Education for Librarianship (1927-1932), as a member of the ALA Council (1928-1933), and as second vice-president (1929-1930). She spoke to numerous groups of library school students and represented librarianship to endless national and local organizations, who turned to her because of their need for reading lists and skilled library selection of reading materials. She had the respect of all who worked with her.

Because Jennie Maas Flexner was as much an educator as a librarian, it was fitting that three of the six persons invited to present brief appreciative comments at her memorial services in New York City were adult educators with whom she had worked intensively in the New York Adult Education Council and the American Association for Adult Education. Morse Cartwright's warm appreciation of Jennie Flexner as "a person of distinction" and as educator and counselor saw her capacity to use books for the benefit of people as a high art. Franklin F. Hopper (q.v.) stressed Jennie Flexner's active mind, her "genius for personal relationships," and her "ready and effective sympathy for all efforts to bring books and people together."

Biographical listings and obituaries—*Current Biography* (1945); *Dictionary of American Biography* 3 (Sidney Ditzion); Hopper, Franklin F. "Jennie M. Flexner [Obituary]." *Library Journal* 70:37 (Jan. 1, 1945); *Notable American Women* 1 (Sigrid A. Edge); [Obituary]. *New York Times*, Nov. 18, 1944; [Obituary]. *Publishers Weekly* 146:2087 (Nov. 25, 1944); *Universal Jewish Encyclopedia*, 1939-1943, Vol. 4; *Who's Who in Library Service*, 1st ed., 2nd ed. Books and articles about the biographee—Cartwright, Morse A. "Remarks . . . at Memorial for Miss Jennie M. Flexner, December 14, 1944, New York City." Louisville, Ky.: Louisville Public Library. (Typescript); Edge, Sigrid A. "Jennie M. Flexner." *Bulletin of Bibliography* 17:1-2 (Jan.-April 1940); Johnston, Esther. "Jennie Maas Flexner, 1882-1944." In Emily Miller Danton, ed., *Pioneering Leaders in Librarianship*. Chicago: ALA, 1953, pp. 61-73; "Lippincott and White Awards." *ALA Bulletin* 32:764-66 (Oct. 15, 1938); Monroe, Margaret E. *Library Adult Education*. New York: Scarecrow Press, 1963, pp. 294-307. Primary sources and archival materials—Edge, Sigrid A. Correspondence with Margaret E. Monroe, March 16, 1974; New York Public Library. *Annual Report of the Readers' Adviser*. (1929-1943); Reece, Ernest J. Letter to Thirza E. Grant, December 15, 1944. (Available in files of Case Western Reserve University, School of Library Science); Yust, William F. Letter to Julia M. Whittlesey, September 4, 1907. (In files of Case Western Reserve University, School of Library Science.)

                                    —MARGARET E. MONROE

FOGARTY, JOHN E. (1913-1967)

John E. Fogarty (Dem., R.I.) earned a place among the influential figures of librarianship by contributing in a crucial way to the federal library legislation of the 1950s and 1960s. The forms of his legislation and the amounts of the funds, the first federal monies made available, were chiefly made possible because Fogarty served as chairman of the House Appropriations Committee's Sub-Committee on Health, Education, and Welfare for a number of years.

Fogarty's early life hardly predicted the powerful place he eventually would hold in affecting libraries and librarianship. Born in Providence, Rhode Island, on March 23, 1913, raised by his Irish immigrant parents in rural Rhode Island, he moved up in economic and social status in ways that would have delighted Horatio Alger. One of six children, he finished high school but went to work immediately as a bricklayer's helper, eventually becoming a master bricklayer. Election to the presidency of Rhode Island Union Local No. 1 proved him an able politician, and, in 1940, he was elected to the Congress where, except for a brief stint in the Navy in 1944, he remained for the rest of his life.

Fogarty's leadership in regard to libraries was paralleled by a similar involvement with other cultural areas and by his particularly notable contribution to health legislation. The pattern of his work took similar forms in connection with the various fields. Evidently open to advice from others, he became a close associate of leading health figures such as Paul Dudley White, the heart specialist, Dr. Sidney Farber, the cancer expert, and Mary Lasker of the important Lasker Foundation. Working with these leaders, Fogarty vigorously supported both the necessary legislation and the appropriations required to make the new laws effective. The budget for the National Institutes of Health rose from three million to over one billion dollars. His funding efforts provided the support for much of the research on cancer, heart, and other major diseases. Funds came along for building medical schools and hospitals and for training medical personnel. Legislation that bore his mark undergirded rehabilitation of the handicapped, housing for the elderly, and research on gerontology.

Fogarty's support for library programs seems to have been similarly and powerfully affected by the close advice of several leading figures, most notably Elizabeth G. Myer, director of the Department of State Libraries of Rhode Island, John A. Humphry, then associate commissioner of education of New York, and Germaine Krettek, then head of the American Library Association's Washington Office. Fogarty first came into direct contact with the library world after the Library Services Act was passed in 1956. Despite President Eisenhower's refusal to include an appropriation for LSA in his Executive Budget, Fogarty took the leadership in inserting the money into the congressional budget. His efforts and activities to that end served not only to get the money but also to convince Fogarty himself of the importance of the library cause.

Later, he pushed through an extension of the Library Services Act at its expiration in 1961. In 1964, he directed the debate and passage of the Library Services and Construction Act, and in 1966, he amended LSCA with Title III, Library Cooperation, and Title IV, for services to the physically handicapped and institutionalized. This public library legislation was supplemented by such acts as the Elementary and Secondary Education Act and the Higher Education Act, both of 1965. Other library-related outcomes of Fogarty's support were the Medical Library Assistance Act of 1965 and the Interstate Compact Act of 1960, a bill that set the legal framework underlying much of the library profession's effort to establish national library networks and cooperation.

The financial and professional results of Fogarty's legislation were long-term and fruitful. The Library Services Act provided in excess of forty million dollars to small communities and state agencies. The Library Services and Construction Act, in its turn, contributed several hundreds of millions of dollars to public and state library agencies. Unquestionably, many of the cooperative ventures of the sixties and seventies have been funded by Title III of LSCA. The massive development of library services to physically handicapped and institutionalized persons stems from Title IV of the same legislation.

A sum relatively equal to LSCA monies was made available for the development of academic libraries through the Higher Education Act. One of the major provisions of this legislative effort was a substantial amount of money for the training of librarians at the master's and doctoral levels. One of the longest-lived benefits of Fogarty's work is the number of library educators whose training was paid for by the HEA. The Medical Library Assistance Act, responsible for the provision of at least 75 million dollars since its inception, can be seen as a major force behind the rapid improvement of medical libraries. The National Library of Medicine and the development of the computerized data bases emanating from the NLM were also funded by the MLAA.

It is likely that Fogarty's legislation on behalf of libraries has been responsible for at least a billion dollars coming to libraries of all types. Since so much of that money was provided on a matching basis, matching 50-50 or more, it can be reasonably estimated that John Fogarty's efforts were responsible for three to four billion dollars being spent on behalf of libraries in the past twenty years.

Fogarty's legislative activities, he often related, grew from his wish to make available for new generations the sorts of health and educational facilities that had been so sorely lacking in his own early years. He succeeded so notably that, just as the medical profession began to call him Congress's "Mr. Health," so the librarians named him "Mr. Library." The American Library Association further recognized his contributions by electing him an honorary life member in 1966.

On January 10, 1967, Fogarty died suddenly in his Washington office, leaving a legislative legacy that continues to benefit millions of Americans who are served by the nation's hospitals, schools, and libraries.

Biographical listings and obituaries—*Current Biography* (1964); [Obituary]. *Library Journal* 92:517 (Feb. 1, 1967); [Obituary]. *Wilson Library Bulletin* 41:547 (Feb. 1967); *Who Was Who in America* II (1961-1968). **Books and articles about the biographee**—"ALA Tribute to Representative Fogarty." *Library of Congress Information Bulletin* 26:53 (Jan. 1967); "Awarded an Honorary Life Membership in ALA." *Library of Congress Information Bulletin* 25:417 (Sept. 1966); Healey, James S. *John E. Fogarty: Political Leadership for Library Development.* Metuchen, N.J.: Scarecrow Press, 1974. **Primary sources and archival materials**—The Fogarty papers are housed in the John E. Fogarty Collection, in the Library of Providence College, Providence, Rhode Island.

—JAMES S. HEALEY

FOIK, PAUL JOSEPH (1879-1941)

Born in Stratford, Ontario, Canada, on August 14, 1879 (1880?), Paul J. Foik immigrated to the United States at an early age to pursue religious and academic studies at Notre Dame University, where he entered the Seminary of the Congregation of the Holy Cross. He received the Ph.B. degree from Notre Dame in 1907, completed his theological studies at Holy Cross College in Washington, D.C., and was ordained in 1911. In 1912, he completed a Ph.D. degree in history at Catholic University of America. That same year, Foik was assigned by his order, the Congregation of the Holy Cross, to return to Notre Dame to serve as librarian of that institution. He held this position until 1924, when he was transferred to Austin, Texas, to become the librarian of St. Edward's College, where he served until his death seventeen years later.

Paul J. Foik made many unique contributions to librarianship in the United States. As librarian at Notre Dame, he planned the Lemonnier Library, which, when dedicated in 1917, was the "first separate library building in any Catholic college in the United States." Father Foik also established a program of library courses at Notre Dame, which marked the beginning of formal library training under Catholic auspices in the United States.

One of the founders of the Catholic Library Association, Foik served as its chairman from the time it was begun as a section of the Catholic Education Association in 1921 until the year 1929. During its formative years, the Association's most consuming priority was the initiation of a Catholic periodical index. Foik was chairman (1925-1928) of the committee that worked to secure funds for the project, which became a reality in 1930 with the publication of the first issue of the *Catholic Periodical Index* (H. W. Wilson Company).

A prolific writer, Foik contributed many library articles to Catholic educational periodicals. These were most notable for furnishing information to people, like himself, who were assigned library responsibilities but had not had the opportunity for formal training in the field. His dissertation, *Pioneer Catholic Journalism*, was published as a monograph of the United States Catholic Historical Society (New York, 1930). He was also the author of many articles on historical topics, but his most outstanding literary contribution was concerned with the seven-volume work, *Our Catholic Heritage in Texas, 1519-1936* (Austin, Texas, 1936-1959, sponsored by the Texas Knights of Columbus Historical Commission and written by Carlos E. Castañeda). Father Foik labored to bring together and organize the archival sources necessary for the writing of this definitive source, and he served as editor of the work until his death. The documents collected (many were microfilmed in Mexican archives) now comprise a portion of the Catholic Archives of Texas, located at diocesan headquarters in Austin.

Father Foik was elected a fellow of the Texas Historical Association (1931), and he was also a charter member of the Texas Geographical Society (1933), a corresponding member of the Sociedad Mexicana de Geografía (1940), and a member of the Philosophical Society of Texas (1940). In 1954, he was one of one hundred people selected for inclusion in the Texas Hall of Remembrance for the Heroes and Heroines of Education, featured at the 1954 Texas School Centennial of the State Fair of Texas.

A man of medium height, with brown eyes, Foik was described as plump or portly, with an infectious laugh and an ever-present cigar. According to a contemporary, "He had the ability to pass on to others some of his own enthusiasms. . . ." Countless students, and his fellow librarians and historians, were influenced by his zeal for books, libraries, and the lessons of history. Certainly, his ability to develop commitment in those with whom he came in contact must be accounted as an accomplishment at least as important as the professional accomplishments of his own life. His death came on March 1, 1941.

Biographical listings and obituaries–*The Canadian Who's Who*. Sir Charles G. D. Roberts and Arthur Leonard Tunnell, eds. Toronto, Canada, 1938. Vol. II; *Who Was Who in America* I (1897-1942). **Books and articles about the biographee**–Bresie, Mayellen. "Paul J. Foik, C.S.C., Librarian and Historian." Master's thesis, The University of Texas, 1964; Byrne, Paul R. "Paul Joseph Foik, C.S.C." *Catholic Library World* 12:183 (March 1941).

                                      —MAYELLEN BRESIE

FOSTER, WILLIAM EATON (1851-1930)

In the Trustees' Room of the Providence (Rhode Island) Public Library, there hangs a picture of a rather dour-faced Yankee. The face is spare, framed by a wing collar, and looks quizzically at the viewer, and nothing in the picture suggests the importance of the man represented. For William E. Foster, first librarian of the Providence Public Library, played a major role in the origin of many public library services, in the direction of the public library movement in the United States, and in the inauguration of the American Library Association.

Born in Brattleboro, Vermont, June 2, 1851, to Joseph Coggin and Abigail Ann Eaton Foster, William Foster grew up in Beverly, Massachusetts. In the fall of 1869, he entered Brown University, where he displayed a great interest in books and libraries, as Clarence Sherman (q.v.) notes:

His was a quiet, retiring, and studious nature that found satisfaction and pleasure in the college

library where he spent much of his free time. Indeed, it has been said of him that in one of his courses which had proved to be disappointing, he "cut" all the classes he could in order to read books in which he was deeply interested in the college library.

The "cut" classes did not appear to hinder his academic development, for he graduated with his class in 1873. After graduation, he took the position of librarian of the Hyde Park, Massachusetts, Public Library. He did so chiefly at the urging of Reuben A. Guild (q.v.), then librarian at Brown. The year 1876 was important to Foster for three reasons. First, he received his M.A. from Brown (he would be awarded an honorary Litt.D. in 1901). He attended the meeting of a small group of librarians that resulted in the founding of the American Library Association. Finally, he left Hyde Park to become a cataloger at the Turner Free Library in Randolph, Massachusetts. Sherman points out:

he was not content to confine his efforts to the somewhat limited requirements of his office. He wanted to grow professionally and without delay. There was no library school to enter in those days, so he did the next best thing. For about two years he worked on a part-time schedule in the Boston Public Library, where he came under the direct influence of perhaps the greatest librarian of his time, Justin Winsor [q.v.].

He remained at Turner only a year, for early in 1877, a group of citizens in Providence offered Foster the opportunity to come to Rhode Island to assist in the opening of the Providence Public Library. He accepted the appointment, and in June 1877, Foster took up the work of selecting, classifying, and cataloging the Library's initial collection of ten thousand volumes. On February 4, 1878, the Providence Public Library was opened in quarters on a second floor of a downtown office building.

Because there was so little to work with in the area of cataloging (this immediately followed Melvil Dewey's [q.v.] first published schedule in 1876, of which Foster was unaware), Foster designed his own system. He was later to say that, had he known that Dewey was at work on a similar program, he would never have gone to such lengths. (The Foster system numbers are still on some of the volumes in the Providence Public Library.) When Dewey's scheme came to his attention, Foster immediately employed it; however, he was not completely satisfied with Dewey's work. He exchanged the 800s (Language and Literature) with the 300s (Social Sciences), since he thought that language and literature more rationally followed religion and preceded philology than did the social sciences.

Foster's work in Providence covered the period 1877 to 1930. When the Library's quarters became too small, he directed the move to larger rooms. But even they were soon outgrown, and on March 15, 1900, he moved the collection into the large new building in the center of downtown Providence. That edifice provided library services for many people both within and outside of the city, until a new addition was constructed in the early 1950s. But the building program was not the most outstanding of Foster's accomplishments.

As the Library's services grew and became multi-faceted, he decided that some segregation of activities would help the staff perform those services. So it was that the Library was one of the first to introduce a section for children, and the new Monthly Reference Texts on important topics, first issued at that time by the Library, attracted considerable attention both at home and abroad, as Sherman notes:

> In the new building ... the Providence Public Library was one of the first libraries to have an Information Desk in addition to a Reference Room; an Art Department with printed matter not only for the occasional reader but especially for the professional artist and the commercial designer; a Music Division with scores and librettos for use at home or in the studio; an Industrial Department to aid the engineers and mechanics of a great industrial city; and a Foreign Department to serve, not only the foreign language needs of the cultured readers, but those of the foreign-born who have so densely populated New England.

Obviously, Foster was an innovator. Some might say that those were times when few of the services many of us now take for granted were offered; nonetheless, Foster recognized the needs of his constituency and moved to provide for those needs. He was responsible for the development of school library services through the use of the public library by grammar school children. (He is reputed to have been a very liberal individual for his time.) He encouraged the selection of library materials with a variety of points of view, and he even encouraged the Library's patrons to make suggestions concerning books to be purchased in the future, another of his firsts and an indication of his deep faith in his constituents.

Despite his administrative labors, Foster retained his scholarly bent. In addition to a large correspondence, he found time to prepare journal articles and books, the most important of which, according to his contemporaries, were: *The Civil Service Movement* (1881), *Libraries and Readers* (1883), *Stephen Hopkins: A Rhode Island Statesman* (1884), *Town Government in Rhode Island* (1886), *The Point of View in History* (1906), and *How to Choose Editions* (1912). He also wrote *The First Fifty Years of the Providence Public Library* (1928).

Being a leading librarian, he lectured at several classes in the New York State Library School.

Foster's philosophy of library education embodied concepts once again being recognized in educational circles in the 1970s. Margaret Stillwell, former rare book librarian of Brown University, who also comments on Foster's sense of humor, describes Foster's pedagogical method. In the Providence training classes,

> each student was on an independent schedule. Instruction was given by the head of each department. There were no examinations, and there was no specified time for the termination of the course. A student remained in a given department until in the opinion of the department head he had mastered its work so thoroughly that he could be called in as a substitute for any length of time, with the assurance that the department would be run efficiently. That grade achieved, the student automatically moved on.

And finally, again from Stillwell, there is a brief, but more human description of Foster, by one of his contemporaries, George Parker Winship (q.v.), librarian of Brown University:

> Mr. Foster was one of the leading librarians of the last century. Mr. Winship spoke of him in that way, he said, because his innovations had been made during that time. Mr. Foster had developed his own classification and cataloging system as detailed as Dewey's. In fact it was rumored that Dewey got some of his ideas from Foster. And he had developed his own student-training methods. A very unusual man.

At the end of his career at Providence, William Foster was honored by the Library's trustees with the title "librarian emeritus for life." By giving him that title, they formally recognized his achievements there, for he had built a collection of ten thousand books housed in a part of a building into a system comprising a central library, twelve branches, and over one hundred miscellaneous agencies. The number of volumes had risen to 400,000, with circulation figures of 1,300,000 books reaching almost 90,000 registered patrons.

Yet, his achievements notwithstanding, Foster remained an essentially modest man. At his Library's fiftieth anniversary, he had to be persuaded by the trustees to sit for a picture, since he wanted attention to focus on the Library and not himself. Also, when ALA celebrated its fiftieth anniversary, Foster contributed a paper, but he did not read it himself. Rather, he stayed away from the conference, fearing that he, as one of the few surviving charter members, would receive disproportionate attention. Someone else read his paper to the group.

Foster married Julia Appleton in 1886, and she survived him at his death at the age of eighty on September 10, 1930. There were no children. What Foster did leave was a record of distinct achievements. His Providence dircectorship of 53 years had contributed approaches and concepts that would provide the basis for many of the services, activities, and departmental divisions that are taken for granted today.

Biographical listings and obituaries–*Who Was Who in America* I (1897-1942). **Books and articles about the biographee**–Koopman, H. L. "William Eaton Foster–An Appreciation." *Library Journal* 55:282-83 (1930); "Mr. Foster's Anniversary at Providence." *Library Journal* 53:175-76 (1928); Sherman, Clarence. "Our Frontispiece: William E. Foster." *Bulletin of Bibliography* 14, No. 3 (Sept.-Dec. 1930); Stillwell, Margaret Bingham. *Librarians Are Human.* Boston: Colonial Society of Massachusetts, 1973.

–JAMES S. HEALEY

FRANKLIN, BENJAMIN (1706-1790)

Benjamin Franklin was born on January 17, 1706 (January 6, 1705, Old Style), the tenth son and fifteenth offspring of Josiah and Abiah Franklin of Boston. His father was a soap- and candlemaker, but a man of considerable education and status in the community, and he resolved to make Benjamin the "Tithe of his Sons" to the church. For this reason, he sent his precocious young son to school in Boston, but he was forced to cut Benjamin's education short when the expense became too great. Thus, the elder Franklin discarded plans for his son's career in the church and began a search for a trade that would suit the lad.

Because of his intense interest in reading, which Franklin recalled must have occurred very early "as I do not remember when I could not read," Benjamin was apprenticed to his brother James, a printer and soon-to-be newspaper publisher, in Boston in 1718. From this apprenticeship, which ended with Franklin running away to Philadelphia and then London in 1723, he gained the necessary experience to later establish the printing, publishing, and bookselling business in Philadelphia that was to make his fortune and his fame. In 1728, he formed a printing partnership with Hugh Meredith; in 1729, he became publisher of the *Pennsylvania Gazette*; in 1732, he published the first of his famous and very profitable almanacs–*Poor Richard's Almanack*; in 1741, he published the first, but short-lived, magazine to be printed in the Colonies; and in 1748, he retired from his publishing business, leaving affairs in the hands of his partner, David Hall.

Franklin has been defined as many-sided, and his life reflects this complexity. In addition to his career as printer, he became one of the best-known scientists of his day, especially prominent for his experiments with electricity. He was as well an active and successful humanitarian who organized many of Philadelphia's most significant civic projects, including the Library Company of Philadelphia (1731), the American Philosophical Society (1743), the Philadelphia Academy (later to be the University of Pennsylvania–1749), and the Pennsylvania Hospital (1751). He was a prominent diplomat, representing Pennsylvania in London from 1757 to 1762, and from 1764 to 1775, and the Continental Congress in Paris from 1776 to 1785. He was on the committees that drafted both the Declaration of Independence and the Articles of Confederation and he attended the Constitutional Convention in Philadelphia in 1787.

Franklin, "America's first Citizen of the World," has been frequently described as a child of the Enlightenment, and along with Thomas Jefferson (q.v.), he became known as one of its most illustrious representatives. While the Enlightenment influenced him decidedly, however, it is perhaps wiser to see his personality and drive as a product of the Enlightenment's influence in the unique American environment. Fully in the European tradition in his love for books and reading, though, Franklin always retained this particular passion despite the fullness of his life, the pressures of frequent travel and his heavy responsibilities. Certainly he was a leading figure in the establishment of a multitude of libraries in this country.

Franklin recalls that as a boy he read widely in his father's many religious works (a practice he later regretted), and the works of John Bunyan and Cotton Mather had a particular influence on him. Indeed, Franklin wrote to Samuel Mather in 1784, and noted that "When I was a boy, I met with a book entitled [*Bonifacius* or] *Essays to Do Good*, which I think was written by your father," and he recalled that reading this little book had a marked influence on his behavior "through life; for I have always set a greater value on the character of a *doer of good*, than on any other kind of reputation." Mather's ideas on the "doers of good" appealed to Franklin's sense of duty and moralism and squared nicely with the humanism of the Enlightenment. Franklin found the other basic tenets of the Enlightenment appealing as well: the belief in order grounded upon Newtonian premises, the belief in intellectual freedom, and the belief in reason as a guide to correct action. One can see the particularly American mix of these basic themes in Franklin's long and fruitful life. Few men in American history can be credited with such consistent humanism and benevolence, for throughout his life, he worked to help his fellow men in any way he could. Also, few men pursued truth with such vigor and openmindedness as Franklin.

His voracious appetite for knowledge and his desire to improve himself and others led him to organize his now-famous Junto in Philadelphia in 1728. The group's purpose was to nurture honest and decorous debate and thought and to contribute in any way possible to the betterment of mankind. The club, made up of twelve young Philadelphians of primarily humble origins, was dedicated to the ideal of the search for truth. Franklin expressed this basic belief in intellectual freedom when he wrote that "when Truth and Error have fair Play, the former is always an overmatch for the latter." Four years later, he noted that "In the present real State of Human Nature, surrounded as we are on all sides with Ignorance and Error, it little becomes poor, fallible Man to be positive and dogmatical in his Opinions."

In their search for knowledge and understanding, his friends in the Junto were constantly frustrated by their lack of books. In an attempt to solve this problem, Franklin suggested in 1730 that the members of the Junto all bring their books to the little room where the group was then meeting, and by thus "clubbing our Books to a common Library, we should . . . have each of us the Advantage of using the Books of all the other Members, which would be nearly as beneficial as if we owned the whole." However, the experiment was short-lived since some of the members felt that their books were not being properly cared for and the arrangement was inconvenient.

But the intelligence of "clubbing" as a means of providing increased access to books was readily obvious to Franklin, who "set on foot my first Project of a public Nature, that for a Subscription Library." This library, founded in 1731 and chartered in 1742 as the Library Company of Philadelphia, was the first established in this country and in Franklin's words "Mother of all N. American Subscription Libraries now so numerous." Especially proud of these libraries, he was confident that his Library was imitated by other communities and that "these Libraries have improved the general conversation of the Americans," and have made the "Common Tradesmen and Farmers as Intelligent as Most Gentlemen from other countries." Scholars have been skeptical of Franklin's claim that the Library Company spawned all the other subscription libraries of the period, but Margaret Korty has demonstrated convincingly that Franklin's creation was indeed very influential in the establishment of other subscription libraries throughout the Colonies.

Franklin retained interest in the Library Company throughout his life, served as its librarian for a short time (December 1733-March 1734), and, from 1746 to 1757, served as secretary to the Company. When he died he was very specific about the disposition of his share of stock in the Company; "My share in the library company of Philadelphia, I give to my grandson, *Benjamin Franklin Bache*, confiding [sic] that he will permit his brothers and sister to share in the use of it."

Franklin's humanitarian spirit, his love of books, and his faith in the average man's ability to learn if given the opportunity led him to encourage the establishment and development of libraries in a variety of different institutions over the years. The list is extensive and includes the libraries at Harvard and Yale, the library at the American Philosophical Society, and the library at the Pennsylvania Hospital, now considered the first medical library in the country. He also donated a parish library to the town of Franklin, Massachusetts.

Perhaps because of his involvement in the establishment of subscription libraries and other libraries which could be described in their own day as "public," Franklin's book-collecting interests have gained far less attention than those of other eighteenth century bookmen like Thomas Jefferson. However, a reading of his *Autobiography* and his *Letters* will reveal Franklin's lifelong obsession with books and reading. Throughout his life, he determinedly studied in every spare moment. Whenever the books were available and he had the funds, Franklin preferred to purchase works for his private library, but if this was impossible, he would go to great lengths to borrow books. His constant difficulty in getting books was a principal motivation for the Philadelphia Library Company, and he wrote in his *Autobiography* that, once established, "This Library afforded me the means of Improvement by constant Study, for which I set apart an Hour or two each Day; and thus repair'd in some Degree the Loss of the Learned Education my Father once intended for me. Reading was the only Amusement I allow'd my self. . . ."

As his fortune increased, Franklin purchased more and more books. Margaret Korty has made a careful study of Franklin's "world of books" and concluded that he purchased most of them while he was abroad after 1757. In 1772, when he was forced to move when his landlady gave up her house, he noted that:

I am amaz'd to see how Books have grown upon me since my return to England. I brought none with me, and have now a Roomfull; many collected in Germany, Holland and France; and consisting chiefly of such as contain Knowledge that may hereafter be useful to America.

During the Revolution, while Franklin was in France, his library was in the hands of his daughter and son-in-law. When Philadelphia was occupied by the British, the library was moved to a house "near Bethlehem" for safekeeping, and the bill of lading referred to "14 Boxes and 4 Truncks" requiring "three Waggon-loads" to remove. While the majority of the library thus escaped damage, legend has it that Major André, who occupied Franklin's home during the Revolution, confiscated several of the volumes overlooked in the hasty removal of the library from the city.

After his return to the country in 1785, Franklin was forced to enlarge his home to accommodate his library, which was described by Manasseh Cutler in

1787 as the "largest and by far the best private library in America." When Franklin died in 1790, the library contained some 4,276 volumes. He gave the largest number of these to his daughter Sarah, his grandson William Temple Franklin, and several libraries. That part of the collection in the hands of William Temple Franklin eventually was placed in the hands of N. G. Dufief, a London bookseller. Ironically, among the many buyers, Thomas Jefferson purchased a 24-volume set for his private library—a library that has generally been considered the finest of his day—and many of the remaining books were purchased by American libraries, where they are highly prized possessions today.

With his wife Deborah dead (December 19, 1774), Franklin spent his last years with his daughter Sarah, the wife of Richard Bache, a Philadelphia merchant. Franklin had been estranged from his son William, who supported the British cause during the Revolution, and his second son, Francis Folger (1732-1736), died young. Troubled with kidney and bladder stones, Franklin turned frequently to his books for distraction from the pain. As the pain grew greater, Franklin, with characteristic inventiveness, designed a tub where he could take hot water baths to ease the pain. One visitor remembered that the tub was shaped like a shoe, "He sits in the Heel, and his legs go under the Vamp; on the Instep he has a place to fix his book, and there he sits and enjoys himself."

As a young man, this most cosmopolitan of Americans, this *philosophe* who cherished freedom of thought so highly, had composed a mock epitaph for himself. Although not used when he died, it conveys perfectly the spirit of a man possessing a life-long interest in books:

The Body of
B. Franklin,
Printer
Like the Cover of an old Book,
its Contents torn out,
And Stript of its Lettering and Gilding,
Lies here, Food for Worms,
But the Work shall not be wholly lost:
For it will, as he believ'd, appear once more,
In a new & more perfect Edition,
Corrected and Amended
By the Author.
He was born Jan 6. 1706
Died [17 April 1790].

Biographical listings and obituaries—*Dictionary of American Biography* 6 (Carl L. Becker); *National Cyclopaedia of American Biography* I; *Who Was Who in America*, Historical Volume (1607-1896). **Books and articles about the biographee**—Conner, Paul W. *Poor Richard's Politicks; Benjamin Franklin and His New World Order*. New York, 1965; Crane, Verner. *Benjamin and the Rising People*. Boston, 1954; Harris, Michael H. "Pennsylvania Library History: A Bibliography." *PLA Bulletin* 25:19-28 (1970). (Also concerns Franklin's libraries); Korty, Margaret. "Benjamin

Franklin and Eighteenth Century American Libraries." *Transactions of the American Philosophical Society* New Series, 55:1-83 (1965); Korty, Margaret. "Franklin's World of Books." *Journal of Library History* 2:271-328 (1967); Stourzh, Gerald. *Benjamin Franklin and American Foreign Policy*. Chicago, 1954; Tourtellot, Arthur B. *Benjamin Franklin: The Shaping of Genius—The Boston Years*. New York: Doubleday, 1976; Van Doren, Carl. *Benjamin Franklin*. New York, 1938. **Primary sources and archival materials**—Franklin, Benjamin. *Autobiography*. Ed. by Leonard Labaree *et al.* New Haven, 1964; Franklin, Benjamin. *Papers*. Ed. by Leonard Labaree *et al.* New Haven, 1959– .

—MICHAEL H. HARRIS

FREEMAN, MARILLA WAITE (1871-1961)

Marilla Waite Freeman was born on February 21, 1871, at Honeoye Falls, New York, the daughter of the Reverend Mr. Samuel Alden Freeman (descended from John Alden) and Sarah Jane Allen Freeman (descended from Miles Standish). She grew up in what has been referred to as "the aristocracy of the parsonage, where riches were of the mind and spirit." Early in life she had decided on librarianship as the career she wanted to follow, and she had classified and cataloged her father's scholarly library before completing her training.

Her initial entrance into library work, in 1892, was as an apprentice in the Newberry Library, Chicago, under its distinguished director and historian William Frederick Poole (q.v.). She followed this experience by entering the University of Chicago, working part time in its library, and earned her Bachelor of Philosophy degree there in 1897. Years later, on the occasion of the University's fiftieth anniversary (October 31, 1941), she was awarded the Distinguished Service Medal of the University of Chicago, "For outstanding achievement in the field of librarianship and as head, until her retirement last year, of the Main Library of Cleveland Public Library." Only sixteen men and three women out of forty thousand graduates were so honored.

Her professional library career began immediately after her graduation, first as organizer and administrator of a small new public library in Michigan City, Indiana (1897-1902), then as administrator of the Davenport (Iowa) Public Library (1902-1905); as reference librarian in the Louisville (Kentucky) Public Library (1905-1910) and at a similar post in the Newark, New Jersey, Public Library (1910-1911). From 1911 to 1921, she was librarian of Goodwyn Institute, Memphis, Tennessee (now the Cossitt-Goodwyn Business, Science and Technology Department of the Memphis Public Library), where her term of office included a year as hospital librarian (1918) at Camp Dix, New Jersey, during World War I. Upon return from her war service, she enrolled in the University of Tennessee (night) Law School (1919-1921) and was admitted to practice before the

Tennessee Bar in 1921. Although she never practiced, the training qualified her to accept a position in the Foreign Law Department at the Harvard Law Library (1921-1922).

How she approached and performed in each of these tasks is perhaps best revealed in her papers and addresses published in the library press of the time, several of which were selected for inclusion in *Classics of American Librarianship*, edited by Arthur E. Bostwick (q.v.), and for *Readings in Library Methods*, edited by L. D. Arnett and E. T. Arnott (1931). These writings, which spanned a period of sixty years (1899-1959), are as pertinent today as when they were written. They show her innate liberalizing force and her conviction that public libraries should and can be flexible institutions, tuned to the needs of the times and not "cemeteries for dead facts." She was a much-sought-after lecturer on the library, poetry, and related subjects. One talk, entitled "The Psychological Moment" (in a series she gave at the New York State Library School), was reprinted several times and was required reading at a number of other library schools.

There was nothing about her of the "hush" traditionally associated with librarians. In her presence, one was aware of her tremendous vitality, vivid and dramatic personality, keen interest in people, wide knowledge of books, contagious enthusiasm, and deep desire to make the library of genuine use for everyone. She rebelled vigorously at "red tape," usually to the disgust of those who revered it. She did not speak in whispers, sometimes explaining, "I do not have a library voice."

She was a leader in the pioneer group of librarians working at the turn of the century who emphasized the potential practical use of libraries as well as their educational significance for all. Accordingly, new applications of library services were developed and brought to the attention of workers as well as entrepreneurs, scholars, students, educators, the sick, lonely, handicapped, children, young people, the aged, and the blind. Yet she never forgot that providing facilities and materials needed in browsing for recreation and inspiration were also important functions of libraries. Audiovisual services were anticipated through a creative use of pictures and art exhibits.

While at Goodwyn Institute, Marilla Freeman enlisted the cooperation of her representatives in Congress to supply multiple copies of government publications, especially those of the United States Food Administration and Farmer's Bulletins, for free distribution to library visitors. She encouraged other librarians to do likewise, always making sure the local press was notified of their availability free for the asking. It was her policy to build resources, explain and encourage their use, make them readily available,

and publicize the fact. "Show and tell" was her philosophy.

She realized, too, the need for established standards and more facilities for library training to make librarianship a recognized profession, and she practiced what she preached. One of her papers included a suggested examination for library assistant candidates, which she no doubt used in her own staff training procedure.

She enlarged the scope of her lectures by adding her great love, poetry. She became a dedicated member of the Poetry Society of America and of the Academy of American Poets. Though not a poet herself, she felt poetry had a tremendous potential for providing enjoyment and understanding of life among all peoples. She was able to share her enthusiasm in introducing and interpreting poets, old and new, to various audiences. One newspaper editor said, "Her talks on poetry were highlights of anyone's literary experience." John Masefield, when poet laureate of England and invited to speak in Memphis, responded to his introduction with

"How jolly for an able seaman
To be met by the charming and
gracious Miss Freeman."

Years later, May 12, 1937, he was speaking in London on Coronation Day honoring King George VI, and in concluding his speech (broadcast over shortwave radio), Masefield said, "I shall never forget going to a city library in Memphis, Tennessee, and seeing a big and beautiful room for the use of the youth of the city which had been arranged by Marilla Freeman, who now directs your great library at Cleveland, Ohio." Miss Freeman did not hear this herself, but news reporters did and pointed out that her name was the only one mentioned other than that of the King in this address beamed to listeners all over the world.

Frederick Winslow Taylor's work in developing scientific management for increased industrial production interested her greatly, and she saw ways to apply his basic principles (the scientific management of time, labor, methods, and resources) to reference work in libraries that had the potential of making even a small public library a clearing house of information. She presented this idea in a paper before the American Library Association in 1913. The paper was reprinted several times and selected for inclusion in L. D. Arnett and E. T. Arnott's *Readings in Library Methods* in 1931.

Her varied experience was the prelude to her longest library commitment, which began when she accepted Linda Anne Eastman's (q.v.) invitation to become librarian of the Main Library in the Cleveland Public Library (1922-1940), with the specific responsibility to strengthen its scholarly research collections. The materials there today bear evidence of the ability and foresight with which she fulfilled that assignment. But she did much more. She was instrumental in creating a more tolerant book selection policy. Abhorring library censorship, she campaigned vigorously against it; on controversial subjects, she insisted all sides be represented, asking only that the author be sincere in his writing and that he be permitted a hearing, so to speak, in the public library. A superficial book was "grist for her mill" if there was the slightest evidence that it lifted a reader from boredom, sorrow, or despair.

In addition to intensive work on developing the resources in the collections, several specific accomplishments stand to Freeman's credit during her administration of the Main Library. She was responsible, jointly with Ina Roberts (publicity director of the Library), for a unique experiment in library cooperation with motion picture management executives. After much correspondence and hours of conferences discussing the possibility of preparing and distributing book marks listing books pertinent to the film being shown, this became a *fait accompli.* These book marks, financed by theaters, became known as the "Cleveland Book Marks," and were widely distributed at theaters, clubs, restaurants and elsewhere. Books in history and biography, many of which had "rested" on the shelves for some time, saw active circulation. Used throughout the country, the idea spread to cover art exhibits, concerts, and other fields.

The Readers' Advisor service and active cooperation with the many community organizations in the adult education movement (which eventually became the Adult Education Department) stand as other specific accomplishments. Finally, the creation and development of the Business Information Bureau (now Department) claimed much of her time and enthusiasm. It was the first effort of a public library to establish a business service within the framework of a large main library. Other libraries had emphasized business information within their collections or had established branches in city business centers, but no attempt had been made to acquire the growing resources needed by the business community, and to segregate under one department the obvious business materials already in collections. That it grew from an empty desk to the largest service of its kind in the country must be laid largely to Freeman's understanding and interest, accompanied by the very vocal acceptance and concern of the business community itself.

Such are the "words" of her specific contributions to the Cleveland Public Library, but in no way do they convey the "music." Her tremendous interest in people led one newspaper feature writer to say, "Her personality and generosity were not only attributes— they were a deep vital, living, and moving spirit among us." She stated her philosophy thus:

A public library should be the most democratic institution in the community. It must have no prejudices of race, religion, politics or literature. It cannot take sides on any question but must give out impartial information to all. A library is at least as essential to a city's development as its schools, its churches, and its courts of law. It is the working laboratory of all men and women who are making and doing and thinking things.

This was her conviction and she knew it could happen only with a staff equally motivated. Consequently, on numerous occasions, she would exhort them "to always wear the approachable look," "never be so busy with desk work that you fail to volunteer assistance to readers," "find what is needed—or provide knowledge of where it may be obtained." She showed great personal concern too for staff development and professionalism, and she kept an eye open for readers who might become significant practitioners of their dreams.

In 1921, Floyd Dell portrayed a librarian, Miss Raymond, in his novel, *Mooncalf.* Readers were eager to know whether she represented someone he knew, and he readily admitted it was indeed Marilla Freeman, who was the librarian in Davenport, Iowa, where he resided in 1902. In a later volume, *Homecoming: An Autobiography*, he described his memory of her as follows:

Marilla Freeman was an extraordinarily beautiful young woman, tall and slender, wide-browed, with soft dark hair, grey-blue eyes, a tender, whimsical mouth, and a lovely voice—an idealist, and also a practical person, who immediately took charge of my destinies. I fell in love with her deeply, and became from the first moment of our friendship involved in a battle of wills with her—a battle not mitigated by the great affection we had for one another. From her point of view the situation was a simple one: here was a young poet, who, besides encouragement, needed to learn conscious control of his art; and who needed friends among those who were interested in writing and writers. This very wise program was rebelled against by me, violently protested at every point, but on every point yielded to and carried out. The fact was that for the first time I had met a person capable of bossing me; and though the bossing was done with angelic sweetness and patience, it was implacable. I resented it bitterly that a goddess should stoop to these practical matters. I wished to remain in the enchanted circle of her affection; I wanted her to be a kind of mother-goddess. And she, with all the powers thus given her, was very gently and very firmly and very wisely pushing me out into the world of reality.

Freeman was active in professional library, civic, educational, and cultural organizations all her life. She served as a member of the American Library

Association Council (1917-1922) and as its vice president (1923); as president of the Library Club of Cleveland and Vicinity (1928-1929); on the Board of Directors of the Women's City Club and on several of its committees (1934-1938); as member of the University of Chicago Club, and its president (1933-1934); the Novel Club and its president (1930-1931); and the National Adult Education Association, to name but a few!

She left the Cleveland Public Library in July 1940, at retirement age but not to retirement. The note on her resignation form gives as the reason for leaving, "To fill deferred lecture engagements before library schools, colleges, and other organizations." And the next twenty years saw her headquartered in New York City, as librarian of St. Joseph's Hospital under the auspices of the New York Tuberculosis and Health Association. She also represented the Cleveland Public Library in acquiring underground and clandestine documents pertaining to World War II for the special World War II collection in the Cleveland Public Library's History Department. While in New York, she filled numerous speaking engagements, wrote and presented many papers on library and community affairs, chaired the American Library Association's Motion Picture Preview Committee and edited the *Library Journal* column "New Films from Books" until 1959.

In announcing Freeman's resignation from the Cleveland Public Library, Charles E. Rush (q.v.) said,

Indeed it is as an interpreter of the Library to the public, the originator of many new methods of library cooperation in the field of public relations, the stimulating adviser to countless library patrons, and as a lecturer, that her vivid personality and friendly presence will be missed from the Main Library, as well as the cultural life of this city.

Of the many efforts made to portray Marilla Waite Freeman adequately, Dr. C. H. Cramer's comment seems to have been most successful. He said,

It was a long and remarkable professional record; she was a stimulating contributor to the *Library Journal* for sixty years, an active member of the American Library Association for almost seven decades. She had a vision of what libraries should become, and through these professional channels was able to inspire many younger librarians with a desire to bring these ideals into being. She also had the rare gift of breathing life into everything that interested her. When she left one of her early posts a disappointed trustee of the library thrust a remarkable tribute into her hand as she boarded the train. "Oh yes," he had written, "someone else can be found to do the work—but who will breathe upon the clay?"

She died on October 29, 1961.

Biographical listings and obituaries–[Obituary]. *The [Cleveland] Plain Dealer*, Oct. 31, 1961; [Obituary]. *Library Journal* 86:4157 (Dec. 1, 1961); [Obituary]. *New York Times* (Oct. 31, 1961); [Obituary]. *Open Shelf* (Cleveland Public Library). No. 11-12:32 (Nov. 1961); *Representative Clevelanders*. Cleveland: Cleveland Topics Co., 1927; *Who's Who in Education* (1937-1938); *Who's Who in Library Service*, 1st ed., 2nd ed., 3rd ed.; *Who's Who of American Women*, Vol. 1. Books and articles about the biographee– Cramer, C. H. *Open Shelves and Open Minds: A History of the Cleveland Public Library*. Cleveland: The Press of Case Western Reserve University, 1972; Dell, Floyd. *Homecoming: An Autobiography by Floyd Dell*. New York: Farrar, 1933 (reprinted by Holt, Rinehart, Winston, 1961); Kurlander, R. In *The [Cleveland] Plain Dealer*, June 23, 1940; McDonald, Gerald D. [Biographical note]. *Bulletin of Bibliography* 19:29 (Jan.-April 1947). Primary sources and archival materials–Freeman, Marilla Waite. "The Psychological Moment." *Library Journal* 16:55-62 (Feb. 1911); Freeman, Marilla Waite. "Scientific Management, and the Reference Department as a Bureau of Information." American Library Association *Bulletin* 7:330-36 (1937); Personnel records in the Cleveland Public Library.

—ROSE L. VORMELKER

FRICK, BERTHA MARGARET (1894-1975)

Bertha Margaret Frick was born January 4, 1894, in Rockwell City, Iowa. After graduating from Rockwell City High School, she attended Grinnell College for three years, then graduated from Iowa State University at Ames with a major in mathematics. She did further study at the University of Colorado in 1923. For ten years, she was a mathematics teacher in secondary schools in Iowa, Colorado, and Virginia.

In 1928, she was awarded the Lydia Roberts Fellowship to attend the Columbia University School of Library Service, from which she received both her bachelor's (1929) and master's degrees (1933). While studying at Columbia, she was also a cataloger in the Queensborough Public Library from 1929 to 1931. Then, in 1931, Bertha Frick joined the staff of Columbia University, where she stayed until her retirement in 1960. At Columbia she was able to combine her interests in mathematics and cataloging and to begin a specialized interest in manuscripts. For seven years, she cataloged some of Columbia's Special Collections, including the David E. Smith Collection of mathematics books. From 1938 to 1945, she held the title of curator of the Smith Collection, the Plimpton Collection (in humanities and education), and the Dale Collection (books about weights, measures, and the metric system).

During this same period, she began to teach in the School of Library Service and became one of its internationally known scholars. She taught cataloging and classification, and the history of books and printing. In addition, she taught a course in the study of illuminated manuscripts, an avocation that developed into an intense and lifelong study. As a lecturer about illuminated manuscripts, Bertha Frick had no equal, and many of her students felt that this was the finest course of their professional education. Her appreciation and enthusiasm for manuscripts were combined with an encyclopedic knowledge, which she continued to expand throughout her life. She was an internationally recognized expert, and her extensive travelling included visits to many specialized collections, some of which were rarely shown to visitors.

Her interest in cataloging and classification resulted in two major professional activities. From 1953 to 1960, she was a member of the Decimal Classification Editorial Policy Committee. Earlier, in 1950, she had assumed the editorship of *Sears List of Subject Headings*, sixth edition, and also edited the seventh and eighth editions. (The *List* was begun by Minnie E. Sears [q.v.].)

In 1951-1952, Frick was a member of the ALA-U.S. Army group of librarians who established the Japan Library School at Keio University in Tokyo and who were its first faculty. During this period, she developed another lifelong enthusiasm, this for Japanese art and manuscripts. At the conclusion of this assignment, the Japanese Ministry of Education honored her for her contribution to library education in Japan by presenting her with a rare and unusual Japanese scroll. Made in the seventeenth century, the scroll tells the Tale of Urashima Tarō. It is more than 36 feet long, and contains seven large illustrations hand-painted in color. This gift was a signal honor since the scroll is one of Japan's national treasures, which are rarely if ever allowed to leave the country. Eventually, Bertha Frick loaned the scroll, and then gave it, to Columbia's East Asian Library, "so others could enjoy it."

As a teacher, Frick insisted on high standards of performance from her students and was intolerant of careless work. Many students who were willing to accept these requirements became personal friends, and in her later years, she visited former students all over the world. Although she officially retired from Columbia as associate professor in 1960, she continued to teach in summer sessions for several years, at Columbia and other library schools. In 1963, she made a survey of college libraries in Indonesia, the Philippines, Hong Kong, Taiwan, and Korea for the United Board for Christian Higher Education in Asia. As on other trips, she found many former students working in these libraries.

In 1965 the American Library Association awarded her the Melvil Dewey [q.v.] Medal, one of its highest professional honors, "for creative professional achievement of a high order."

As a traveller, Bertha Frick allowed no difficulties to keep her from visiting places of interest to her. She was one of the few in those days to visit the ancient Asian city of Petra as soon as travel there was

possible, and on her first visit, she slept on the ground, since a hotel was not yet built. Too, she was one of the early American visitors to the ancient Japanese Buddhist monastery, Koya San. Her genuine scholarly interest and her personal warmth gained her a welcome in many remote places.

She spent the last years of her life at the Meadow Lakes retirement community in Hightstown, New Jersey. She continued some research at the Princeton University Library and travelled frequently until 1973. She died at Meadow Lakes on October 21, 1975.

Biographical listings and obituaries—*A Biographical Directory of Librarians in the United States and Canada*, 5th ed.; [Obituary]. *Library Association Record* 78:185 (April 1976); [Obituary]. *School Library Journal* 22:15 (Jan. 1976); [Obituary]. *Wilson Library Bulletin* 50:301 (Dec. 1975); *Who's Who in Library Service*, 1st ed., 2nd ed., 3rd ed., 4th ed. Books and articles about the biographee— "ALA Awards Winners." *ALA Bulletin* 59:659 (July 1965); "Bertha Frick to Study East Asian Libraries." *Wilson Library Bulletin* 37:714 (April 1963); "Miss Frick Retires." *Wilson Library Bulletin* 35:265 (Nov. 1960).

—JANE E. STEVENS

GEROULD, JAMES THAYER (1872-1951)

James Thayer Gerould was a university librarian and a compiler of historical and literary reference volumes who rose to prominence in the first forty years of the twentieth century. Born in Goffstown, New Hampshire, on October 3, 1872, Gerould was the son of Samuel Lankton and Laura Etta Thayer Gerould. Gerould's father was a Congregational clergyman. After preparatory education at Cushing Academy (Ashburnham, Massachusetts), Gerould earned his way through Dartmouth College and received an A.B. degree in 1895. This was the only earned academic degree Gerould ever received; he did not attend a library school. In June 1932, however, on the day that his son Albert Chamberlain Gerould received a bachelor's degree there, Dartmouth awarded the elder Gerould an honorary Litt.D. degree for his many accomplishments.

James Gerould married twice: first, in 1900, to Mary Aims Chamberlain, and secondly, in 1940, after Mary Chamberlain's death, to Winifred Gregory [Winifred Gregory Gerould, q.v.], a leading bibliographer and librarian, whose name became as well known to reference librarians as his.

Gerould's first full-time position was in 1896, when he became assistant librarian at the General Theological Seminary and lived at the University Settlement, New York City. After only a year there, Gerould moved to the Columbia University Library to become supervisor of the Serials Department (1897-1900). In 1900, Gerould moved to the Midwest, where he spent the next two decades. From 1900 until 1906, he headed the University of

Missouri Library, and from 1906 to 1920, he headed the University of Minnesota Library. Both state institutions were full of youthful vigor and free of tradition, and neither library had been headed previously by a full-time, experienced librarian. On each campus, when graduate work expanded rapidly, Gerould was able to reorganize and push the libraries ahead vigorously. Re-cataloging and re-classification projects were launched, book collections were enlarged notably, and new library buildings were planned. At Minnesota, many small independent libraries were integrated into one, the Minnesota book collection grew from 50,000 to 250,000 volumes, and its English history section was improved to the extent that it reached a level of national importance.

In 1920, Gerould left the Midwest to head the Princeton University Library, where he instituted a policy of open stack access that resulted in very few book losses. Recorded circulation increased 175 percent while student enrollment increased only by 40 percent. He reorganized the Princeton Library, gave much attention to collection development (enlarging the Library from 450,000 to 900,000 volumes), and planned a new library building as well. Curiously, at Missouri and Minnesota as well as Princeton, Gerould designed new university library buildings that were not completed until after he had left the campus.

In 1938, when 66 years of age, Gerould became Princeton's librarian emeritus and moved to Washington, D.C., where he was a bibliographic consultant to the Library of Congress for a year before settling finally in Williamsburg, Virginia.

James Thayer Gerould's contributions to the work of national and local library associations were significant and extensive. A member of the American Library Association Council, he was chairman or a member of several committees dealing with significant bibliographic projects. His membership in the Bibliographical Society of America led him to assist in preparing several major bibliographies. Too, Gerould was one of the few persons ever to be president of three state library associations: Missouri (1901-1902), Minnesota (1913-1914), and New Jersey (1922-1923). In addition, he was a fellow of the American Library Institute, a member of Phi Beta Kappa, Delta Kappa Epsilon, the Nassau Club of Princeton, and the Princeton and Century Clubs of New York.

Gerould was mainly responsible for organizing the Association of Research Libraries in 1932. He sought to provide a medium through which research library problems could be considered effectively without involving a large and heterogeneous membership. The Association's members have been able to give sustained consideration and effective implementation to many useful research projects in the intervening years.

Gerould's publications are perhaps the most significant and lasting contributions of a busy, varied, and useful career. In 1894, when a college junior, Gerould published his first compilation, a bibliography of Dartmouth College. Long before they were married, he and Winifred Gregory collaborated on a *Bibliography of Minnesota Mining and Geology* (1915). Gerould was also literary editor of *The Bellman* (1916-1918) and contributed articles to *Current History* (1926-1933). He collaborated with Wallace Notestein in publishing *The Sources of English History of the 17th Century in the University of Minnesota Library* (1921). In 1928 and 1929, the H. W. Wilson Company published *Selected Articles on Inter-Allied Debts and Revision of Debt Settlements* and *Selected Articles on the Pact of Paris.* Compiled with Winifred Gregory Gerould, *A Guide to Trollope* was published by Princeton (1948).

Such essential reference publications as the *Union List of Serials in Libraries of the U.S. and Canada* (1927), *List of the Serial Publications of Foreign Governments* (1932), *Union List of Newspaper Files in the Libraries of the U.S. and Canada* (1937), *The Census of Medieval and Renaissance Manuscripts in the U.S. and Canada* (1937), and *List of International Congresses and Conferences, 1840-1937* (1938) were published with Gerould as either coordinating committee chairman, committee member, or one of the compilers. The importance of these indexes to scholars cannot be overemphasized. Their preparation involved the cooperation of hundreds of libraries, the assistance of numerous learned societies, and the wide support of several educational foundations. Through his contacts with individuals and organizations engaged in research and publication, and his practical publishing knowledge, Gerould greatly increased the usefulness of these resources to American scholars.

Gerould's best-known report, *The College Library Building: Its Planning and Equipment*, resulted from a Carnegie Corporation commission and appeared in 1932. This report has been listed in hundreds of bibliographies since that time and is still being used and listed. (A second edition was published, as well as a Chinese translation.) While still at Minnesota, Gerould had distributed an annual sheet giving certain statistics for a group of university libraries. He then continued the practice at Princeton, and the so-called "Princeton Statistics" appeared for many years, to be superseded only by the Association of Research Libraries statistics. He also published papers in leading library journals.

Gerould was, for a time, a leader in social welfare work as well as in library work. In Minneapolis, he served at various times as president and director of the Minneapolis Public Health Association, director and secretary of the Board of Associated Charities, and president of the Central Council of Social

Agencies and of the Public Health Federation. During World War I, he was American Red Cross director for Minnesota and assistant manager of the Northern Division.

Gerould's portraits show a spare and determined Yankee administrator with a friendly twinkle in his eye. He was said to be practical, a warm advocate of worthy causes, and a keen supporter of any movement he entered. He read voraciously in many fields, visited bookshops, and loved music and the theater. Gerould was an enthusiastic sportsman, familiar with canoe travel on many of the waterways of this country and Canada, and he was as well a golfer and a camper. His political affiliation was Democratic. He died in Williamsburg on June 8, 1951.

Biographical listings and obituaries—*National Cyclopaedia of American Biography* 41; [Obituary]. *College and Research Libraries* 12:379 (Oct. 1951); [Obituary]. *Libri* 1:383-5 (1951); *Who Was Who in America* III (1951-1960); *Who's Who in Library Service*, 1st ed., 2nd ed.   **Books and articles about the biographee**—Gilchrist, D. B. "James Thayer Gerould." *Bulletin of Bibliography* 15:101 (Jan.-April 1935); Heyl, Lawrence. "James Thayer Gerould: Some Recollections of an Associate." *Princeton University Library Chronicle* 14:91-93 (Winter 1953); "Librarian Authors." *Library Journal* 59:309 (April 1, 1934); Lydenberg, Harry M. "Dr. James T. Gerould." *Library Journal* 64:26-27 (Jan. 1, 1939); Wilson, Louis R., and Maurice F. Tauber. *The University Library*. New York: Columbia University Press, 1956, pp. 535-37.

—JOHN F. HARVEY

GEROULD, WINIFRED GREGORY (1885-1955)

Born in 1885 in Independence, Iowa, to Alonzo Goodrich and Almira Webster Gregory, Winifred Gregory graduated from East Waterloo, Iowa, High School in 1905. She attended Iowa Summer School for Library Training in 1907 and worked as an assistant in the Waterloo, Iowa, Public Library from 1907 to 1909. After receiving her diploma from the Wisconsin Library School in 1910, she was a branch librarian for the Minneapolis Public Library in 1910 and held a position in the library of the University of Minnesota School of Mines from 1911 to 1916. She worked in the Technology Division of the St. Paul Public Library from 1917 to 1919 (except for a time in 1918, when she was a hospital librarian in Asheville, North Carolina). It was during this time that she compiled *Bibliography of Minnesota Mining and Geology* (University of Minnesota, 1915) and *Improvement of the Upper Mississippi River: A Bibliography* (in *Bulletin* of the Affiliated Engineering Societies of Minnesota, 1918).

From 1920 to 1923, she was in the Technology Department of the Carnegie Library in Pittsburgh and, in 1924, she began her editorial work for the American Library Association. Her first project was the *Union List of Serials* (Wilson, 1927), which had

been "in process" since 1913, when the American Library Association appointed a committee on a union list of serials. Gregory brought to completion in three years a volume of 1,580 pages with entries for 75,000 serial titles in 225 libraries in the United States and Canada. "It was rightly hailed as the most notable bibliography ever sponsored by American libraries, as an amazing accomplishment, and as a forward step comparable in importance to the decision to distribute Library of Congress printed cards" (Preface, *Union List of Serials*, 3rd ed., 1965). Following this came *List of the Serial Publications of Foreign Governments* (Wilson, 1932), which listed the holdings of 85 libraries in the United States and Canada and was a pioneering effort, since in no single country was there a list on which she could build.

During this time, she was honored to be the representative of the American Library Association at the Rome meeting of the International Congress of Bibliography in 1930. From 1932 to 1933, she was executive assistant to the American Library Association Committee on Cooperative Cataloging. In 1934, she edited *American Newspapers, 1821-1936* (Wilson, 1937) and described the process in the *ALA Bulletin* (September 1935). This listed the holdings of some 5,700 newspaper offices, court houses, associations, private collectors and libraries, including, as Gregory noted, everything from the Hickville *Times* to the London *Times*. It is a monumental work that has never been superseded. After the newspaper list came *International Congresses and Conferences, 1840-1937* (Wilson, 1938), a bibliographical landmark listing the holdings of 110 libraries and standardizing the titles of those "publications without a country" usually ignored by trade bibliographies. Then came six years of work on the second edition of the *Union List of Serials* (Wilson, 1943), a massive volume of 3,065 pages listing between 115,000 and 120,000 titles in more than 600 libraries.

In December 1940, Winifred Gregory married James Thayer Gerould (q.v.), the librarian emeritus of Princeton University. With her husband, she wrote *A Guide to Trollope* (Princeton University Press, 1948).

Winifred Gregory Gerould was a woman of perseverance and tact. While preparing *Foreign Governments*, she obtained permission to work in the New York City Bar Association library although, at that time, women lawyers in New York City were allowed only one day a year in that library. While working on the same list, she was denied entrance to the basement of the Bibliothèque Nationale, where the government documents were shelved. Not one to be deterred, she spoke to the American ambassador, who succeeded in getting permission for her to enter the stacks. There she worked for several days—accompanied by a guard who held a candle, since there was no electricity.

Winifred Gregory Gerould's gift was the ability to organize masses of detail into an orderly arrangement and to coordinate the records of numerous institutions into a coherent whole. Her contribution to librarianship lies in the pattern she established, and the standard she set, as the editor of the union lists which bear her name—lists which remain as enduring and indispensable tools for the librarian and researcher. She died in Williamsburg, Virginia, on December 10, 1955.

Biographical listings and obituaries—[Obituary]. *College and Research Libraries* 17:262-63 (May 1956); [Obituary]. *Wilson Library Bulletin* 30:500 (March 1956); *Who's Who in Library Service*, 1st ed. Books and articles about the biographee—Gottschalk, Paul. *Memoirs of an Antiquarian Bookseller.* 1967, p. 17.

—MARILYN L. HAAS

GILCHRIST, DONALD BEAN (1892-1939)

Donald Bean Gilchrist was born in Franklin, New Hampshire, on January 11, 1892, the son of Harry W. and Martha Bean Gilchrist. He began his library career as a student assistant in the Library of Dartmouth College. After receiving his A.B. degree from Dartmouth in 1913, he entered the New York State Library School at Albany, from which he received the B.L.S. degree in 1915.

Gilchrist then took his first professional position as head of the Interlibrary Loan Department at the University of Minnesota, serving one year. However, with the approach of World War I, he entered the U.S. Army in 1916, and after service on the Mexican border during 1916-1917, Gilchrist was sent to France. Here he had duty as an artillery captain from August 1917 to December 1918. Meanwhile, on June 26, 1918, he was married to Ella Trowbridge of Des Moines, Iowa. They had one son, David Trowbridge Gilchrist.

While in France, Gilchrist was librarian of the American Commission to Negotiate Peace (1918-1919). In 1919, he returned to civilian life, and in October of that year, he went to the University of Rochester at Rochester, New York, as librarian. Despite the leadership of able presidents during the last half of the nineteenth century, the privately endowed University of Rochester was a relatively unknown, impecunious liberal arts college before 1900. Then, under the far-sighted leadership of President Rush Rhees (1900-1935) and with the financial backing of George Eastman, Rochester's leading industrialist, the University underwent a rapid expansion to become a genuine university. The University library was to benefit from this expansion. Even though the library had had the guidance of one of the foremost academic librarians of the nineteenth century, Otis Hall Robinson (q.v.), in 1919, it had only 81,000 volumes and a budget amounting to no

more than $20,000. Gilchrist foresaw the changes and growth that lay ahead for the school, and argued persuasively with President Rhees for a library which could anticipate and respond to future developments in curriculum and research. During the 1920s and in 1930, the University added the Eastman School of Music, the School of Medicine and Dentistry, and built a completely new campus for the Men's College. Under Gilchrist's guidance, three new libraries were established and developed: the Sibley Music Library, the Edward G. Miner Library, and the Rush Rhees Library, which became the principal University library. With a tower for the bookstacks and a projection of nineteen floors, the Rush Rhees Library was considered an outstanding example of a building with a multi-tier stack. Also, the building was planned carefully to provide for future expansion.

An effective spokesman for change, Gilchrist followed the example of Otis Robinson in developing the university librarian's role from the passive one of custodian of books, to the more active one of trying to bring book and reader together. One of the features of the Rush Rhees Library was an attractive browsing room. It was said of Gilchrist that,

being a librarian of the new school rather than the old, his prime concern was not the possession but the use of books. To keep them safe was not enough; we must keep them moving. Hence his constant quest for convenience and system and dispatch. They were not ends in themselves but means to the multiplication of readers. Whether for the use of scholars in research or of students in routine assignments, he held that the best books should be accessible at the right place and the right time.

A stocky man with dark brown hair and a small moustache, Gilchrist was said to have resembled Douglas Fairbanks, Sr., the actor. A good storyteller who loved to talk about books and fishing, he was friendly and vital, outgoing, with a hearty laugh that accented his lively sense of humor. Both human and humane, he felt a genuine accomplishment in helping even one individual. His enthusiasm for outdoor activities such as camping, fishing, and tennis was balanced by his talent for architectural design, which produced plans for several libraries, including those for the interior detail (printers' marks, seals, etc.) of the Rush Rhees Library. His eye for detail was seen in his hobbies of building ship models and collecting bookplates.

Gilchrist contributed a number of articles to professional journals; edited a news sheet called the *Fortnightly Bulletin*, which carried notes on books and on aspects of library service; and contributed a series of informal columns on books and literary figures to the University's student newspaper under the pen name of Henry Pyecroft.

Gilchrist's activities were not confined to Rochester, however, as he was active in many professional library associations. He was a fellow of the American Library Institute, chairman of the College Library Advisory Board of the American College Association, and a member of the New York State Library Association. However, the two organizations with which he was most closely identified were the Association of Research Libraries and the American Library Association.

Gilchrist was one of the organizers and the first executive secretary of the Association of Research Libraries, serving from 1932 to 1937. In the latter year, he became a member of the Association's Advisory Committee. This organization sponsored and published *Doctoral Dissertations Accepted by American Universities*, which differed from earlier lists in that it included dissertations in all fields of study. Gilchrist became the first editor. According to his successor as editor, Edward A. Henry, Gilchrist worked out the original plan and helped secure subsidies from the American Council of Learned Societies and from the National Research Council. Finally, he edited the first six numbers (1933-1939) until his unexpected death in the summer of 1939.

In the late 1930s, Gilchrist became increasingly active in the American Library Association. At the time of his death, he was a member of the ALA Council. He had served as chairman of the Joint Committee to Investigate Problems of Indexing and Abstracting Services. Also, he was chairman of the ALA Advisory Committee on the second edition of the *Union List of Serials*, which was published after his death. As in the case of *Doctoral Dissertations*, the work Gilchrist started was finished by someone else, but the final product was largely the result of his inspiration.

Gilchrist died suddenly on August 4, 1939, while on a vacation in his beloved New Hampshire. His death brought expressions of shock and grief, as well as tributes from his fellow librarians, who looked upon his untimely demise as a serious loss to the library profession.

Biographical listings and obituaries–*New York State Library School Register, 1887-1926.* New York: New York State Library School Association, Inc., 1959; [Obituary]. *ALA Bulletin* 33:696 (Oct. 1, 1939); [Obituary]. *Library Journal* 64:604 (Aug. 1939); [Obituary]. *New York Libraries* 10:242 (Aug. 1939); [Obituary]. *Wilson Library Bulletin* 14:81 (Sept. 1939); *Who Was Who in America* I (1897-1942); *Who's Who in Library Service*, 1st ed. **Books and articles about the biographee**–Hayes, Catherine D. "The Gilchrist Years." In "The History of the University of Rochester Libraries–120 Years." *The University of Rochester Library Bulletin* 25 (Spring 1970); Henry, Edward A. [Introductory material]. In *Doctoral Dissertations Accepted by American Universities*, no. 7, 1939-1940 (Association of Research Libraries, 1940), p. iii; de Kiewiet, C. W. "Rhees, Rush." *Dictionary of American Biography* 2. **Primary sources and**

archival materials–The papers of Donald Bean Gilchrist covering his tenure as librarian of the University of Rochester are in the Department of Rare Books, Manuscripts, and Archives, Rush Rhees Library, University of Rochester.
                                                –CATHERINE D. HAYES

GILLETT, CHARLES RIPLEY (1855-1948)

Charles Ripley Gillett's life revolved around Union Theological Seminary in the city of New York. Born in New York on November 27, 1855, he was the son of Ezra Hall and Mary J. Kendall Gillett. His father had been a pastor in New York, a part-time librarian at Union, and a professor of political science at New York University. Charles studied civil engineering at the University (B.S., 1876; A.M., 1877), and upon graduation, he entered Union and also became an assistant in the library. He was chosen as his class's fellow for 1880-1881, and at the end of that term, the school granted him the funds to study at the University of Berlin (1881-1883). In 1886, he was ordained a Presbyterian minister. He would later receive his D.D. from New York University (1898), and Beloit College would honor him with an L.H.D. (1899).

Gillett married Kate Van Kirk of Yonkers, New York, on April 26, 1881. They had five children.

Returning to New York City from Berlin in 1883, Gillett was made librarian at Union Theological Seminary, a post he would hold until 1908. He said at this time that the aggregate titles and volumes of the school amounted to 115,000, which made it the largest library of a theological seminary in the United States and tenth in size in the list of collections in U.S. educational institutions. The McAlpin Collection of British History and Theology was said by this time to include the work of nearly all of the most famous British divines of the eighteenth and nineteenth centuries. The materials on the Deistic, Trinitarian, and Non-Conformist controversies was said to be almost complete.

In 1905, Willis James contributed $1,030,000 for the construction of new facilities for the Seminary, and the present site on Morningside Heights near Columbia was selected. A committee of the faculty was appointed immediately to consider the needs of the institution in connection with the new buildings, and it reported to the meeting of the professors on April 12. The library was to be the chief academic building, with a reference room twice the size of the old one. Stack space for 200,000 volumes and room for expansion were requested.

Gillett's twenty-fifth and final annual library report was submitted to the Board of Directors on May 12, 1908. During the year, he had spent a great deal of time in the development of a scheme of classification based on the subject index that he had prepared for the Library. The system was the foundation, along with the work of Hugo Münsterberg, on which the Union Theological Classification Scheme was developed later under the guidance of Julia Pettee (q.v.), who joined the Library as a cataloger in 1909. Up to this time, no specific classification scheme had proven useful in so specialized a collection.

Gillett, who, according to Union's directors, had devoted the best 25 years of his life to the Library, retired as librarian on August 1, 1908. He had also been an instructor (1893-1908). He then served the institution in succeeding years not only by continuing as secretary to the faculty (1898-1929), but as registrar (1908-1925), dean of students (1913-1929), and alumni secretary, retaining the latter office until 1948. He was named librarian emeritus in 1929.

Gillett's activities, however, were not entirely at the Seminary. He was assistant curator in the department of antiquities at the Metropolitan Museum of Art from 1900 to 1910, and his writings concern these activities as well as his library-related and ecclesiastical interests. In conjunction with the Metropolitan he published the *Catalogue of Egyptian Antiquities in the Metropolitan Museum in New York* (three editions), the third volume of the *Descriptive Atlas of Cypriote Antiquities in the Metropolitan Museum* (1904), the *Catalogue of Cypriote Stone Sculptures in the Cesnola Collection in the Metropolitan Museum* (1904) the *Catalogue of Pottery and Terracottas in the Cesnola Collection in the Metropolitan Museum* (1905). For the Seminary Library, Gillett prepared the five-volume *Catalogue of the McAlpin Collection of British History and Theology, 1501-1700.* He translated Krü's *History of Early Christian Literature* (1897) and Harnack's *Monasticism* (1895). In addition to preparing Union's general catalogs (1886, 1898, 1908, 1918, 1926, 1936), Gillett also contributed to the critical departments of theological and literary journals. His final book was *Burned Books, Neglected Chapters in British History and Literature* (1932).

Gillett died at the age of 92 in 1948. His full-time service to the institution stretched from his appointment as librarian in 1883 until his retirement 46 years later. His part-time appointments, beginning in 1877 as a student assistant in the Library and continuing for 19 years after his retirement, make a total of 23 years. These 69 years are one of the longest periods of professional service to one institution in the annals of American education.

Biographical listings and obituaries—*Who Was Who in America* IV (1961-1968). **Books and articles about the biographee**—Coffin, Henry Sloane. *A Half Century of Union Theological Seminary.* New York: Charles Scribner's Sons, 1954; "Librarian Authors." *Library Journal* 57:1043 (1932); Prentiss, George Lewis. *The Union Theological Seminary in*

the City of New York. New York: Anson D. F. Randolph and Co.; and Asbury Park, N.J.: M. & C. Pennypacker, 1899.

—THOMAS P. SLAVENS

GILLIS, JAMES LOUIS (1857-1917)

James Louis Gillis, California state librarian and promoter of county libraries, was born on October 3, 1857, in Richmond, Iowa, the son of Charles and Emily Gelatt Gillis. He was not yet four years old when his family moved overland by ox-train, settling first in Nevada. Six years later, they pushed on to California, eventually making Sacramento their permanent home.

James's formal education was limited. Schooling ended before he was fifteen, when, in 1872, he began work as a messenger for the Sacramento Valley Railroad. He remained in the employ of the railroad (part of the politically powerful Southern Pacific system) until 1894, rising to the position of assistant superintendent.

On Christmas Day, 1881, he married Kate Petree. The Gillises had three daughters, the eldest of whom, Mabel Ray Gillis (q.v.), became, like her father before her, a state librarian of California.

After leaving the railroad, Gillis deepened his involvement in Republican politics, and, for three sessions of the legislature—in 1895, 1897, and 1899—he served as clerk of the Committee on Ways and Means of the General Assembly. Between sessions he was keeper of the archives, but his second period in that post was interrupted by a stint as deputy in the State Library and an unsuccessful attempt to secure appointment as librarian.

Among the possible appointments in the state government, that of librarian had become particularly attractive to Gillis. (The Board of Trustees, who at that time were elected by the legislature, chose the librarian.) When the position again became vacant, Gillis secured the appointment, beginning his tenure as state librarian on April 1, 1899. At that time, there was no reason to fear for the Library, which had survived and grown for half a century under political control. Neither was there reason to suspect that a new era in its history was opening. Gillis's motivation in seeking the position cannot be precisely explained. He was not an extremely bookish man, in either the literary or bibliophilic sense. He was an administrator who observed that the State Library was not operating at full capacity and that it offered a congenial opportunity to practice sound management while rendering a real public service.

His first concern was to improve the internal operations of the Library. He revised the book-order records, began a bulletin of accessions, extended dictionary cataloging to include the entire collection, launched the indexing of California newspapers, and created a new general reading room. At the next session of the legislature, the State Library was awarded a fixed appropriation, to replace the uncertain income previously available from specified fees collected in the secretary of state's office.

None of these changes altered the fundamental character of the Library, which was open to the general public only for reference. Circulation was restricted to state officers and the judiciary. An enlargement in the functions of the Library, which in half a century had grown to more than 100,000 volumes in size, was no doubt inevitable; and Gillis, in his first report, reiterated a suggestion made by his predecessors that the Library seek permission to lend books beyond its walls. The immediate pressure for extending the Library's service arose, however, from the efforts of the Library Association of California to create a state commission that could promote libraries and serve areas of the state not covered by existing agencies.

Gillis was naturally not pleased at the prospect of a rival library agency competing for funds. A conference was arranged between the State Library trustees and representatives of the Association, and the latter were reminded of the difficulties of securing a completely new agency with a separate appropriation. In contrast, enlargement of the State Library's role could be achieved simply by altering a few words in the Political Code, and the change was accomplished at the legislative session of 1903.

With its powers thus enlarged, the Board of Trustees authorized a tour by their librarian to observe state agencies in the Midwest and East. The experience was a turning-point in Gillis's career as librarian. Mary Eileen Ahern (q.v.), editor of *Public Libraries*, noted the change. She first met Gillis in Chicago near the beginning of his tour, and then spoke with him again as he was returning. She recalled that Gillis's "reserve power" had been transformed by his observations into a "dynamic force" (*Public Libraries*, vol. 22, 1903, pp. 308-309).

Gillis increasingly assumed the role of California's library leader, beginning with implementation of the State Library's new lending powers. Before the close of 1903, he organized travelling libraries, small rotating collections dispatched to rural communities in the care of local custodial groups. Collections were also prepared for study clubs, and books were lent to local libraries and, in some cases, even to individuals. In 1904, the circulation of books for the blind began.

In addition to offering direct library services, Gillis planned for the State Library to act as a clearinghouse of information and as a promotional agency. He began by making a survey of the California library scene, published in 1904 as *Descriptive List of the Libraries of California*. Thereafter he attempted to keep abreast of the state's library developments by

enforcing the legal provision requiring each public library to send to the State Library a copy of its annual report, and by subscribing to an extensive newspaper clipping service. On the basis of these sources, he initiated a newsletter that became the substantial periodical *News Notes of California Libraries* in 1906. He also sent into the field two organizers to work with local interests in promoting new public libraries. All these "commission" activities—library promotion, travelling and study club libraries, and lending to local institutions (as well as books for the blind)—were combined in 1905, into an Extension Department, which in the following year was complemented by a new Reference and Loan Department to handle the actual bibliographical and circulation work entailed in the extension services.

Gillis also introduced a new legislative reference service. It was first called a Sociological Department, since Gillis regarded it not only as a service to the legislature but also as a reference aid for local governments and for others interested in public affairs. Gillis also inaugurated documents exchanges, and began, with trained catalogers, the recataloging of the Library. This burst of activity was soon followed by a period of curtailment, when remodeling of the Capitol between 1906 and 1908 forced a suspension of some general services. Although much of the collection was temporarily in storage, Gillis saw that the most essential services, including the extension activities, were maintained.

In the meantime, he became deeply involved in organized professional activities in California. In 1906, he was elected president of the state organization which, at his suggestion, changed its name from Library Association of California to California Library Association. Gillis, who served as president for eight terms (from 1906 to 1910 and 1911 to 1915) made particular use of district Association meetings to involve more of the rank and file of the profession in discussions and activities. For Gillis, the Association thus became the complement of his Extension Department, another tool in improving the library system. Gillis was never as active at the national level as he was in state affairs, although he attended four ALA conferences and was elected to the Council in 1911. He was a member of the National Association of State Libraries, of which he was twice elected president (1906 and 1914), and a member of the American Association of Law Libraries.

The last half of Gillis's eighteen-year service as librarian was devoted particularly to the promotion of county libraries—his best-known accomplishment. His field agents had been remarkably successful in organizing free city libraries. Rural areas, however, were still not served except by the scattered travelling collections, and Gillis saw county libraries as the answer to California's problem.

By 1908, Gillis was publicizing the idea, and a county-wide service was started by contract between the Sacramento city library and Sacramento County, utilizing an obscure provision of the municipal free public library law. Then, in 1909, a new state law specifically authorizing county libraries was enacted. Under the law of 1909 and its revision in 1911, an extensive system of county libraries arose, at first consisting of stations maintained under contract by a city library, but later comprised primarily of separate and distinct county library systems. Before his death in 1917, Gillis saw all but 22 of California's 58 counties provided with geographically complete library service.

The county library system was headed by the State Library, which not only continued to promote and publicize developments but also served as the bibliographical and interlibrary loan center, utilizing a new union catalog as a major tool. As chief of the "system," Gillis presided at annual conferences of the county librarians and was one of three members of a board of certification for the librarians of the new agencies. He had always been concerned over lack of properly trained personnel and had tried unsuccessfully in 1909 to obtain authorization and funds for a library school. In 1914, without special funds, he inaugurated at the State Library the California State Library School, which functioned until after his death.

Ultimately Gillis hoped to augment the State Library system with regional branches, standing between the local agencies and the State Library. The gift to the state of the private Sutro Library, on condition that it remain in San Francisco, seemed to fit into the scheme perfectly. Although the state government failed to make a special appropriation, Gillis persuaded the State Library trustees to accept the Sutro collection, and it was opened as a San Francisco branch early in 1917. Gillis saw it as much more than the specialized collection that it then was. He regarded it as the beginning of a true regional branch, a dream never realized.

Another achievement that eluded Gillis was new quarters for the State Library. Like many other librarians, Gillis found himself repeatedly calling for more adequate physical space for his Library, which was scattered over all floors of the Capitol building. Progress was made in 1914, when a state bond issue was passed that would eventually make possible the construction of a library-courts building. Gillis was actively engaged in planning for the new quarters, which were long in being realized. He was, in fact, on July 23, 1917, returning from lunch in anticipation of a meeting with the architect when the heart attack occurred that very shortly ended his life.

The American library pioneers of the turn-of-the-century generation came from diverse backgrounds. In Gillis's case, the background was business and politics, and he applied the expertise acquired in the first 42 years of his life to a new career in the library field, where he became an outstanding example of a state leader. Although nationally admired because of the success of his program, he was essentially a state leader because of the geographical remoteness of his region from the other main areas of library progress.

As a leader, his strength lay not in swaying large groups but in individual relationships. Those who worked with him recalled fondly his personal warmth, the magnetism of his glance, the firmness of his handshake, the reliability of his word, his understanding and patience as a listener, and the inspiration of his ideas. He had the ability to identify promising people and to secure their involvement in his growing library program. In particular, he found and developed the young women—the "Gillis girls" (of whom Harriet G. Eddy became one of the best known)—who brought their abilities and enthusiasms to the staff of the State Library and to the direction of the new county libraries.

His ideas were not original. He was an observer, a listener, an adapter, and a coordinator. He developed ideals, but he was not a perfectionist. He was ever the practical business man. In fact, while librarian, he maintained personal interests in Sacramento business concerns and in local fraternal and civic organizations. Politically he moved into the dominant Progressive wing of the Republican Party. It was because he was regarded as a safe and reliable man that he enjoyed the confidence of his trustees and his other political colleagues.

Physically he would not have stood out among his peers. Always well dressed, rather stocky in build, blue-eyed, gray-haired at the last (and by then without the moustache of earlier years), Jim Gillis was in appearance a typical prosperous business man and politician of the Theodore Roosevelt-Hiram Johnson era.

Gillis spoke and wrote tersely. He did not leave a substantial body of written material. A bibliography of his published writings shows a modest number of articles in professional journals and in various California publications, mainly on the themes of county libraries and the state library's functions. His monument was not what he wrote, but what he did—or more accurately, what he succeeded in getting others to do.

He was memorialized in 1931 when the main reading room in the California State Library was designated James L. Gillis Hall. But for librarians, he stands as the great promoter of the California county library plan, the most successful arrangement—to that date—for bringing free library service to all.

Biographical listings and obituaries—*A Volume of Memoirs and Genealogy of Representative Citizens of Northern California*. Chicago: Standard Genealogical Publishing Co., 1901, pp. 257-60; *Who Was Who in America* I (1897-1942). **Books and articles about the biographee**—Brewitt, Theodora. "James L. Gillis." In *Pioneering Leaders in Librarianship*, ed. by Emily Miller Danton. Chicago: American Library Association, 1953, pp. 74-84; *The California Librarian* 18:220-38 (Oct. 1957). Issue devoted primarily to Gillis; Conmy, Peter. "James Louis Gillis, Westerner and Librarian." In *An American Library History Reader*, ed. by John David Marshall. Hamden, Conn.: Shoe String Press, 1961, pp. 215-41; Haverland, Della. "James L. Gillis." *Pacific Bindery Talk* 7:83-86 (Jan. 1935); Irvine, Leigh. *A History of the New California*. New York: Lewis Publishing Co., 1905, vol. 1, pp. 526-28; Kunkle, Josephine Hannah. *A Historical Study of the Extension Activities of the California State Library*. Ph.D. dissertation, Florida State University, 1969; *News Notes of California Libraries* 52:633-714 (Oct. 1957). Anniversary issue, devoted to Gillis; Smith, Susan T. "James L. Gillis and the State Library." *California Library Bulletin* 11:155-56 (June 1950). **Primary sources and archival materials**—Material on James Louis Gillis can be found in the biennial reports of the California State Library, the proceedings of the American Library Association, and the handbook and proceedings of the California Library Association.

—RAY E. HELD

GILLIS, MABEL RAY (1882-1961)

Mabel Ray Gillis was born in Sacramento, California, September 24, 1882, and lived there until her death on September 6, 1961. She received her bachelor's degree from the University of California and later was awarded honorary doctorates from California College in Peking, China, from the University of California, and from Mills College. She belonged to numerous professional organizations: the American Library Association, the California Library Association (president 1928-1929), the National Association of State Libraries (president 1934-1935), the American Foundation for the Blind, and the California Congress of Parents and Teachers.

Mabel Gillis came from a family devoted to libraries. Her father, James Louis Gillis (q.v.), was the state librarian of California from 1899 to 1917. Mabel went to the State Library soon after her graduation from the University of California and worked in the department serving the blind. After her father's death in 1917, she was made assistant to his successor, Milton J. Ferguson (q.v.). When Ferguson went east thirteen years later, Mabel Gillis was appointed as the eleventh state librarian of California, the first woman to fill this position.

Gillis was especially interested in the welfare of her staff, and a staff organization was formed with her as the first president. Along with staff development, she also worked to increase and improve the collections and services of the Library. She gave particular attention to a union catalog whose ultimate objective was to include a record of every book in all the libraries of California.

During Gillis's period of service, the State Library was moved from the capitol into the spacious Library and Courts Building; because of her careful planning, library service was not discontinued for a single day during the move. During the Second World War, she was the California director of the Victory Book Campaign, collecting half a million gift books for servicemen in camps overseas. She received international recognition when, in 1933, she was elected a trustee of the California College in Peking, China.

Mabel Gillis, having been on the California State Library staff for 47 years, retired in 1951. She served with concern, efficiency, and capability; a person of dignity and distinction, she helped the California State Library to become one of the foremost in the nation.

Biographical listings and obituaries—[Obituary]. *College and Research Libraries* 23:72 (Jan. 1962); [Obituary]. *Library Journal* 86:4262 (Dec. 15, 1961); *Who's Who in Library Service*, 1st ed., 2nd ed., 3rd ed. **Books and articles about the biographee**—"Miss Gillis Retires." *News Notes of California Libraries* 46:349 (April 1951); Warren, Althea. "Mabel Ray Gillis." *The California Librarian* 12:197-98 (June 1951).

—MARTHA BOAZ

GILMAN, DANIEL COIT (1831-1908)

Fifth of nine children of William Charles and Eliza Coit Gilman, Daniel Coit Gilman was born July 6, 1831, at Norwich, Connecticut. Gilman attended Norwich Academy, and the family later moved to New York City, when the boy was fourteen. Gilman received his baccalaureate degree from Yale in 1852. From his marriage to Mary Ketchum in 1861, there were two daughters, Alice and Elisabeth. Mary Ketchum Gilman died in 1869, and Gilman married Elizabeth Dwight Woolsey in 1877. During an enormously productive career, which spanned six decades, Gilman held many prestigious positions: Yale College librarian (1856-1865); professor of physical and political geography at Yale's Sheffield Scientific School (1863-1872); and the presidencies of the University of California (1872-1875), Johns Hopkins University (1875-1901), and the Carnegie Institution of Washington (1902-1904).

Librarianship beckoned early. In the summer of 1848, Gilman assisted Seth Hastings Grant at the New York Mercantile Library and prepared a catalog of volumes from George Washington's library for bookseller Henry Stevens. Library work as a serious pursuit was undoubtedly nurtured by Gilman's uncle, James L. Kingsley, with whom Gilman boarded during his college years. Kingsley, prominent classicist and senior author of the Yale Report of 1828, had been Yale's librarian from 1805 to 1824. As an undergraduate, Gilman was commended by fellow students for "extraordinary service" to the Linonian Society Library.

Gilman's contribution to the historic Librarians' Conference of 1853 was unobtrusive but significant. He personally secured several names for the convention "call" and represented Yale in the absence of librarian Edward C. Herrick. *Norton's Literary Gazette*, of which Gilman was an editor, carried several editorials urging librarians to attend the conference. Of the 82 convention delegates, Gilman perhaps surpassed them all in terms of subsequent national stature.

Late in 1853, Gilman and his close friend Andrew Dickson White departed for a tour as attachés to the American legation at St. Petersburg, Russia, and Gilman found ample time to visit England, France, and Germany. The extended European sojourn was a germinal period for Gilman's views on the goals, structure, and curriculum of higher education. While in Europe, he wrote a number of pieces on libraries, museums, and learned societies for *Norton's* and subsequently published his observations on higher education in Henry Barnard's *American Journal of Education* (1856).

When Gilman accepted the post of assistant librarian at Yale in 1856 (librarian after 1858), he entered a position of promise and frustration. At one time, Yale could claim the nation's largest academic library, but institutional support for the library had declined during the presidency of Theodore Dwight Woolsey. Despite such problems as insufficient acquisition funds, inadequate heat in the winter months, and the need to pay an assistant from his own salary, Gilman struggled courageously to improve library conditions. He maintained a close rapport with faculty and students, publicized library collections through the campus literary magazine, and vainly attempted to complete catalog reforms initiated by his predecessor. Although Gilman seemed to enjoy the job, he confided to Andrew White in 1859 his disappointment that "I have so little intercourse with students, so few opportunities to reach or in any way influence them."

Since informal complaints about library shortcomings had failed to achieve results, Gilman initiated a series of memoranda to President Woolsey and the Yale Corporation. Gilman's litany of library and personal needs was extensive: heated building, longer hours, quiet place for study, catalog accessible to the public, permanent assistants, increased acquisitions, and salary increases for the librarian commensurate with the teaching faculty. Sensing that the impasse would not be resolved, Gilman resigned on June 1, 1865. His successor was Addison Van Name (q.v.). President Woolsey, in a cool letter of acceptance,

suggested to Gilman that "you can in all probability secure for yourself, while yet young and enterprising, a more lucrative, a more prominent and more varied, as well as stirring employment."

From 1866 to 1872, Gilman served as full-time professor of geography, librarian, and secretary of the governing board of Yale's Sheffield Scientific School. His contributions to geography included 110 "Geographical Notices," written for Benjamin Silliman's *American Journal of Science and Arts* between 1858 and 1869, covering geographical explorations and research throughout the world. Although Gilman was not a theoretician, he was a seminal figure in the professionalization of geographical scholarship. Fund raising, public relations, and contact with government agencies were challenges presented by Sheffield that Gilman met with distinction. His later university presidencies would profit from this early exposure to promotional activities and the dynamics of scholarly research.

Invited to the presidency of the University of California in 1872, Gilman guided the young school for three stormy years. Political machinations, spearheaded by leaders of the Grange movement, whipsawed the University throughout Gilman's tenure, for the Grangers were embittered over the alleged lack of support for agricultural studies. Library requirements of the University of California were mentioned in Gilman's first inaugural, and he boldly called for the expenditure of one million dollars for a comprehensive collection and competent staff. Expansion of the library's meager holdings was Gilman's special concern. He secured several substantial gifts, persuaded the state legislature to vote a supplemental appropriation, and donated six hundred volumes from his personal collection. In a special report to the Board of Regents in 1875, Gilman reaffirmed the need for a university library to collect substantive material and pointed with considerable pride to the doubling of holdings to twelve thousand volumes during his presidency.

When the trustees of Johns Hopkins solicited nominations for their first president, Gilman was the unanimous choice of four university leaders. Gilman's presidency coincided with a period of unparalleled change in higher education. At Johns Hopkins, often a pacesetter, the Ph.D. degree was fully established, student fellowships were instituted, departments became major sources of faculty power and prestige, and the results of scholarly investigations were disseminated through university-sponsored journals.

There is considerable evidence that Gilman influenced the direction and operations of the Johns Hopkins Library. Although committed to doctoral education and research excellence, Gilman and the trustees did not plan for a large library in the early years. Instead, the University would exploit the resources of Baltimore libraries, especially the rich collection of the Peabody Institute, while the University Library would acquire a core collection of reference titles and disperse class-related titles to various seminar locations. Gilman pursued library cooperation by courting the Peabody, encouraging interlibrary loan for the Hopkins faculty, and promoting the use of Baltimore libraries by publishing the nation's first regional union list of current periodicals. Although decentralization and regional cooperation were emphasized in the school's first two decades, the Johns Hopkins Library had become the nation's tenth largest academic library by the turn of the century. And Johns Hopkins, with one-sixth of Harvard's resources, produced nearly twice as many doctorates as did Harvard between 1876 and 1902.

Gilman's influence on library affairs extended beyond Johns Hopkins. He served as vice president (1882-1883) and councillor (1883-1886) of the American Library Association. The Mercantile Library of Baltimore was saved largely through Gilman's efforts and was reopened in 1888. In 1898, Gilman drafted the section on the Baltimore City Library for the new charter commission. Unhappy over lack of a library at his vacation retreat in Northeast Harbor, Maine, Gilman and several friends founded a reading room in 1891. He also served as a trustee on the Peabody and Enoch Pratt Library Boards. Also, librarians and bookmen communicated with Gilman about everything from job recommendations to library architecture. Among his correspondents may be counted William E. Foster (q.v.), William F. Poole (q.v.), Justin Winsor (q.v.), Andrew Carnegie (q.v.), John S. Billings (q.v.), Melvil Dewey (q.v.), and Charles Evans (q.v.). Dewey, for example, asked Gilman whether he should move from Columbia's School of Library Economy to the directorship of New York's State Library.

An inveterate writer, Gilman wrote scores of educational articles and published several books. His major books include two biographies, *James Monroe* (1883) and *The Life of James Dwight Dana* (1899), and two collections of speeches and essays, *University Problems in the United States* (1898) and *The Launching of a University and Other Papers* (1906).

Gilman's library writings, neither extensive nor especially analytical, deserve notice because of their content, stylistic elegance, and cultured audience. His two 1865 works (*Hours at Home* and *Papers of the New Haven Colony Historical Society*) on Bishop George Berkeley's library benefactions, especially to Yale, were the first extended accounts of Berkeley's philanthropy published in America. Speaking at the dedication of Cornell's Sage Library in 1891 (in *University Problems*), Gilman deftly traced the history of libraries, discussed the role and qualifications

of academic librarians, and forecast changes in collection development. He urged that academic librarians possess competence in a scholarly field and be accorded professorial status, and that bibliography be recognized as the professional specialty of librarianship. No other nineteenth century university leader matched Gilman's high estimate of academic librarians' value to the scholarly community. On collection development, Gilman noted the futility of acquiring comprehensive collections, supported the principle of subject differentiation, and proposed the adoption of systematic weeding and storage programs.

Gilman related the theme of books and libraries to politics and diplomacy in an 1898 Princeton University address (in *Launching of a University*). As examples of the library's impact on national affairs, Gilman cited the Venezuelan boundary dispute and the Spanish American War. Gilman, a member of President Cleveland's boundary commission, attested to the importance of cartographic resources in resolving the controversy. Ambivalent over the nation's new territorial responsibilities, Gilman nevertheless believed that the library should be a partner in the new mission of spreading Christian civilization and democratic values: "Let the libraries be our armouries where we may be equipped." For Gilman, libraries were sources of civic enlightenment and historical perspective, but above all they served as sentinels of the American political system.

A tall man, full of energy, extroverted on public matters but reserved about his family, and blessed with good health, Gilman was a commanding presence in higher education for over fifty years. R. H. Chittenden, historian of the Sheffield School, described Gilman as possessing a "sanguine temperament, rich in expedients, undaunted by real or fancied obstacles, ready to devise a hundred ways of surmounting a difficulty, and with schemes innumerable for improving conditions." Many other qualities help to explain Gilman's achievements: managerial competence, practical idealism, articulate communication, social conscience, and genuine concern for the welfare of friends and colleagues. He died on October 13, 1908.

Biographical listings and obituaries—*Dictionary of American Biography* 7 (Samuel Chiles Mitchell); *National Cyclopaedia of American Biography* 5; *Who Was Who in America* I (1897-1942). Books and articles about the biographee—Chittenden, Russell H. *History of the Sheffield Scientific School of Yale University, 1846-1922.* New Haven: Yale University Press, 1928. Volume 1; Cordasco, Francesco. *Daniel Coit Gilman and the Protean Ph.D.* Leiden: E. J. Brill, 1960; Flexner, Abraham. *Daniel Coit Gilman, Creator of the American Type of University.* New York: Harcourt, Brace and Co., 1946; Franklin, Fabian. *The Life of Daniel Coit Gilman.* New York: Dodd, Mead and Co., 1910; French, John C. *History of the University Founded by Johns Hopkins.* Baltimore: Johns Hopkins Press, 1946; Hawkins, Hugh. *Pioneer: A History of the Johns Hopkins University, 1874-1899.* Ithaca: Cornell University Press, 1960.

(Expanded typescript version available in the Johns Hopkins University Library); Madsen, David. "Daniel Coit Gilman at the Carnegie Institution of Washington." *History of Education Quarterly* 9:154-86 (Summer 1969); Stadtman, Verne A. *The University of California, 1868-1968.* New York: McGraw-Hill, 1970; Wright, John K. "Daniel Coit Gilman: Geographer and Historian." *Geographical Review* 51:381-89 (July 1961); Young, Arthur P. "Daniel Coit Gilman in the Formative Period of American Librarianship." *Library Quarterly* 45:117-40 (April 1975). **Primary sources and archival materials**—The major collection of Gilman correspondence is in the Johns Hopkins University Library, with additional holdings in the libraries of Cornell, Enoch Pratt, Harvard, and Yale, and in the New York Public Library.

—ARTHUR P. YOUNG

GITHENS, ALFRED MORTON (1876-1973)

Alfred Morton Githens, the son of William Henry and Frances Githens, was born August 25, 1876, at Philadelphia, Pennsylvania. He received his baccalaureate degree from the University of Pennsylvania in 1896. After graduation, he studied at the Pennsylvania Academy of Fine Arts, the American Academy in Rome, and the École des Beaux-Arts in Paris. In 1906, he married Charlotte Sands; they had three children, Alfred, Charlotte, and Frances.

During the early part of his architectural career, Githens worked in the offices of Cass Gilbert and Charles McKim (whose work was influenced by Henry H. Richardson [q.v.]) and for the commission responsible for the restoration of the L'Enfant plan for Washington, D.C. In 1906 he became a partner of Charles Haight, a prominent New York architect. This partnership continued until Haight's death in 1917. During World War I, Githens formed an architectural firm with Edward Lippincott Tilton (q.v.), a New York architect who had become a specialist in library design. Tilton and Githens continued their practice until Tilton's death in 1933.

During the 1920s, Githens served as a part-time faculty member in the architectural departments at Columbia and Princeton Universities. From 1937 to 1942, he was in partnership with Francis Keally. Githens remained active in library architecture until the mid-1950s when, at nearly eighty years of age, he retired to California.

During the 1920s and early 1930s, the Tilton and Githens firm designed or consulted on public library buildings in Wilmington, Delaware; Morristown, New Jersey; Durham and Asheville, North Carolina; Washington, D.C.; Brooklyn and Queens, New York; Providence, Rhode Island; Highland Park, Michigan; Richmond, Virginia; and Baltimore, Maryland. The firm was responsible for library buildings at George Peabody College, the Welch Medical College of Johns Hopkins University, Emory University, and Randolph-Macon College. Tilton and Githens also designed art galleries in Manchester, New Hampshire,

and Springfield, Massachusetts; a natural history museum in Springfield; and the Bergen County (New Jersey) Building. After Tilton's death, Githens designed or advised on library buildings in Mount Vernon and Brooklyn, New York; Concord, New Hampshire; Cincinnati, Ohio; Lancaster, Pennsylvania; and at the University of Iowa and the University of Georgia. Githens retired from active practice after the completion of the Lancaster and Georgia buildings.

For their design of the Wilmington library building, Tilton and Githens in 1925 received a gold medal from the American Institute of Architects for excellence in the architecture of public buildings. Githens was elected as fellow of the American Institute of Architects in 1944.

Githens' major writings on library architecture include his work with Joseph L. Wheeler (q.v.), *The American Public Library Building* (1941); a report with Ralph Munn (q.v.) for the city of New York on the design of branch library buildings (1945); an article on "The Theory of Branch Library Design," in *Library Journal* (July 1945); the chapter on "The Architect and the Library Building," in *Library Buildings for Library Service* (1947), edited by Herman H. Fussler; and the chapter on "Libraries" in *Forms and Functions of Twentieth-Century Architecture* (1952), edited by Talcot Hamlin. The Wheeler and Githens book was one of the major contributions to the literature of American library architecture in the twentieth century.

Through his long associations with Tilton, Wheeler, Angus Snead Macdonald (q.v.), and Ralph Ellsworth, Githens was part of two major developments in library architecture during the first half of the century—the open plan and the modular building. The open plan in libraries was designed to keep the main service floor free of permanent walls and partitions. Before 1919, the major examples of this style were Tilton's designs for the Springfield and Somerville, Massachusetts, buildings. After the First World War, the open plan reached its fullest development in the Wilmington and Enoch Pratt buildings, with which Githens and Tilton were associated; in these, the bookstacks were removed to the floor below the main reading rooms.

The modular plan for constructing library buildings was a natural development of the open plan. Equally-spaced supporting columns permitted openness much like a department store or warehouse not only on the main service floor but on every floor. Further, the modular building was planned so that books could be stored on free-standing shelving in all parts of the structure. Githens was responsible for the plans that Macdonald used in his promotion of the modular library during the 1930s and 1940s.

Githens maintained a correspondence with both Macdonald and Wheeler throughout the 1940s and 1950s. Joseph Wheeler acknowledged that even though Tilton and Githens were only consulting architects for the Enoch Pratt building, it was Githens who actually planned the library. He was, Wheeler said, "a wonderful man and a genius at beautiful design—gracious is the word."

Alfred Githens died in August 1973.

Biographical listings and obituaries—*American Architects Directory*, 3rd ed.; *Who Was Who in America* V (1969-1973). Primary sources and archival materials—Correspondence between Githens and Angus Snead Macdonald is included in the Macdonald papers at the University of Virginia. Correspondence between Githens and Joseph L. Wheeler is included in the Wheeler papers at Florida State University.

—DONALD E. OEHLERTS

GJELSNESS, RUDOLPH H. (1894-1968)

Rudolph H. Gjelsness was born in Reynolds, North Dakota, on October 18, 1894, the son of Marius and Caroline Lee Olsen Gjelsness. His Norwegian heritage, enriched by the bilingual culture of his boyhood, was to play an important role in his career as librarian and educator.

Following his graduation from high school in Reynolds, young Gjelsness entered the University of North Dakota in 1912, taking his bachelor's degree from that institution in 1916. A year later, he resigned as high school principal in Adams, North Dakota, to join the American Expeditionary Force shortly after the entry of the United States in World War I. Following the Armistice in 1918, he was detached from Army service to serve as reference librarian with the A.E.F. in Beaune, France, and with this introduction to librarianship, he returned to the United States determined to enter upon a library career. He then became an order assistant at the University of Illinois, where he completed his B.L.S. degree in 1920.

Gjelsness's first professional post as a librarian was at the University of Oregon, where he became order librarian in 1920. Two years later, he accepted the position of senior bibliographer at the University of California, and he spent the year 1924-1925 at the University of Oslo with a fellowship from the American Scandinavian Foundation. In the land of his ancestors, his boyhood love of the old Norse stories told him by his parents fostered a new enthusiasm for Norwegian literature. Thus, during the years immediately following his return to the United States, Gjelsness translated into English a number of short stories and novels by Norwegian authors, including Johan Falkberget's *Lisbeth of Jarnfjeld* (New York, 1930).

Gjelsness's first contribution to library literature appeared in the July 1925 issue of *Public Libraries*, "A Librarian's Year in Norway." There was little in the article about libraries, however, for he confessed that "it seemed a more fruitful field to devote myself to Norwegian literature." As would be true in all of his writings, as well as his conversation and correspondence even with close friends, Gjelsness revealed little of himself, although he noted at the end of the article: "When I return, I shall be interested in a position where I could develop or organize something."

Rudolph Gjelsness's long association with the University of Michigan began in 1925, following his return from Norway. He was appointed assistant librarian and chief classifier by William Warner Bishop (q.v.). The following year, Bishop founded Michigan's library school and almost immediately involved Gjelsness in part-time teaching. His first course, offered in the summer session 1927, was "National and Regional Bibliography."

In 1929, Gjelsness left Michigan to become chief of the Preparation Division of the New York Public Library and a lecturer in library science at Columbia University. Bishop prevailed upon him to return to Ann Arbor in the summer of 1932 as a visiting professor, and it was during that same summer that he was married to Ruth Elizabeth Weaver. Then, from 1932 until 1937, Gjelsness was head librarian at the University of Arizona, where he built up collections and gave new prestige to the library.

In 1937, Bishop succeeded in obtaining an endowment gift of $150,000 from the Carnegie Corporation of New York for the support of Michigan's library school, this with the understanding that the income would be used to add a full-time professor to the teaching staff. Rudolph Gjelsness was Bishop's choice for the post. With his own approaching retirement in mind, and with his expectation that the combined directorship of the University Library and chairmanship of the Department of Library Science then would be divided, Bishop deliberately chose the man to succeed him in the chairmanship. The courses for which Gjelsness would be responsible were: "Periodicals and Serials," "Foreign Government Documents," and "History of Modern Publishing and Book Distribution."

Gjelsness succeeded William W. Bishop as chairman of the Department of Library Science in 1940. "The Department is most fortunate in this new appointment," Bishop informed alumni, "which brings to its direction a man fully acquainted with its problems and a leader both among librarians and among teachers of librarianship." Bishop continued: "In his hands the ideals of high scholarship and of rigid entrance requirements, insuring a carefully selected group of students, are not only safe but certain to develop." Gjelsness spent the next quarter of a century, until his retirement with professor emeritus status in 1965, as chairman of the Department of Library Science. During his tenure, the University of Michigan conferred 2,269 degrees in library science, including 47 doctorates. The full-time faculty increased from four to seven, augmented with a number of part-time lecturers.

Although family responsibilities limited his work in professional organizations during the later years of his career, during the 1930s and 1940s, Gjelsness was active in the work of the American Library Association. He chaired the Committee on Cataloging and Classification from 1930 to 1933, and from 1935 to 1941, he headed the Catalog Code Revision Committee. He was editor-in-chief of *A.L.A. Catalog Rules: Author and Title Entries* (1941). From 1941 until 1947, he was treasurer of ALA.

Gjelsness had a strong commitment to international librarianship and took a special interest in bringing foreign students to the University of Michigan. He co-directed the summer school at Bogota, Colombia, in 1942, and he spent 1943-1944 (on leave from Michigan) as director of the Benjamin Franklin Library in Mexico City, during which time he also headed the Union Catalog Project. A sabbatical year (1962-1963) was spent as library consultant to the president of the University of Baghdad, Iraq, under sponsorship of the Ford Foundation.

Upon his retirement, still vigorous in health and intellect, Professor Gjelsness kept a promise that he had made many years earlier—to return to the University of Arizona. He thereupon began a new career as chief of the Special Collections Division of that library. His services as a library educator continued to be sought, and, after returning to the University of Michigan to teach during the 1968 summer session, he left for the University of Puerto Rico to assist in the founding of the Graduate School of Librarianship. He was struck and killed by an automobile on his second day in Rio Piedras, on August 16, 1968. His wife, Ruth, and two children, Elizabeth and Barent, survived him.

Many honors came to Professor Gjelsness during his lifetime, ranging from his election to Phi Beta Kappa and Phi Kappa Phi during his collegiate days to the awarding of honorary doctorates by Luther College (Litt.D., 1953) and the University of North Dakota (LL.D., 1958). In 1954, he was the recipient of the first Beta Phi Mu award for distinguished service to education for librarianship. In 1966, a *Festschrift* was published in his honor by the University of Virginia (*Books in America's Past*), containing essays written by a number of those who had written their doctoral dissertations under his direction.

Rudolph Gjelsness once described a Norwegian novelist whom he admired (Johan Falkberget) as a "lean and gentle man." These words also describe Professor Gjelsness, but one must add the words "scholarly and unpretentious." Few of his colleagues called him Rudolph and fewer still, Rudy. He avoided using the first person in his conversation, and he seldom referred to his youth or his family. An authority on many aspects of librarianship, including publishing and printing history, and an avid book collector, he rarely displayed his expert knowledge. Only his closest friends knew of his talents as a painter and a pianist. A very private human being, he shared neither his sorrows nor his triumphs, although he was a patient and sympathetic listener to other people's problems. Nothing gave him greater pleasure than the success of his students, for whom he had a phenomenal memory, and he was tireless in his efforts to assist them in their advancement in the library profession.

Wallace J. Bonk, who succeeded Professor Gjelsness in 1964 as chairman of the Department of Library Science at Michigan, observed in a letter to alumni in 1965: "To many of us, Mr. Gjelsness *was* the Department." No better tribute can be paid to the memory of this "lean and gentle man."

Biographical listings and obituaries—[Obituary]. *Library of Congress Information Bulletin* 27:542 (Sept. 5, 1968); [Obituary]. *Library Journal* 93:3511 (Oct. 1, 1968); [Obituary]. *Michigan Librarian* 34:22-3 (Oct. 1968); *Who Was Who in America* V (1969-1973); *Who's Who in Library Service*, 1st ed., 2nd ed., 3rd ed., 4th ed. Books and articles about the biographee—*Books in America's Past.* Charlottesville, Va.: University of Virginia, 1966. (*Festschrift* in honor of Gjelsness.)

—RUSSELL E. BIDLACK

GOODRICH, FRANCIS LEE DEWEY (1877-1962)

In a long career as a university library administrator, association officer, and contributor to library literature, Francis Goodrich was recognized as an unusually successful librarian. Goodrich was born at Manchester, Michigan, near Ann Arbor, on January 17, 1877, the son of Edward Payson and Mary Isabella Howell Goodrich and a descendant of William Goodrich of Suffolk, England, a Connecticut settler in 1635.

Goodrich's formal education, which was considerable for a librarian of his period, started in the Manchester public schools. He then attended Michigan State Normal College, Ypsilanti (now Eastern Michigan University), 1893-1897, where he completed the four-year education curriculum and was certified to teach. In 1936, that institution awarded him an honorary Master of Education degree. Goodrich took a Bachelor of Arts degree in 1903 at the

University of Michigan, Ann Arbor. Then, after two years at the New York State Library School in Albany, Goodrich was awarded a B.L.S. degree in 1906. He returned to Michigan to work, and was also awarded an M.A. in medieval history by the University in 1916.

Early in his career, Goodrich worked as assistant librarian of the college in Ypsilanti, 1900-1904, where he came under the influence of Genevieve Walton, one of the leading figures in state library circles. He held a part-time position as assistant cataloger while a library school student in Albany (1904-1906). After graduation from Albany, he went to the John Crerar Library in Chicago as assistant reference librarian but resigned only seven months later to begin his Michigan career. Following these initial short-term positions, Goodrich spent almost his entire career in three libraries: the University of Michigan General Library, the library of the City College of New York, and the University of Michigan William L. Clements Library. These positions covered the years 1907-1962.

Goodrich started his University of Michigan career as the accessions assistant. From 1907 to 1920, he held a variety of positions including that of assistant librarian. In 1916, he was made reference librarian. Then in 1917, he was granted a two-year leave of absence to organize three camp libraries in the South, in cooperation with the American Library Association. After the armistice, he also went briefly to Paris and Beaune, France, to carry out the same kind of work. Following his return to Michigan, he became associate librarian in charge of public service in 1920. While he was there, the Library increased in size from 300,000 to 800,000 volumes, and he received training from two well-known library directors, Theodore W. Koch (q.v.) and W. W. Bishop (q.v.). Then, in 1930, he accepted a new position.

From 1930 to 1945, Goodrich headed the library of the City College of New York. While he was at CCNY, the book collection doubled in size, circulation tripled, and the professional staff grew from 17 to 30 members. He was able to bring several departmental libraries into the main library with faculty acceptance. When he retired in 1945, the CCNY staff presented Goodrich with a volume containing nearly 200 letters from friends and library associates, and *Library Journal* published an issue featuring tributes from persons who had worked closely with him.

Finally, Goodrich returned to the University of Michigan at age 68, but this time to the William L. Clements Library. He became curator of printed books there (1945-1946) on a full-time basis, then remained on a part-time or occasional and unpaid basis as consultant in bibliography from 1946 to 1962. In the later years, he dropped in twice a week

to work on complex cataloging and bibliographic problems until his death at age 85.

Goodrich taught part-time in library schools during a major part of his career, primarily at the University of Michigan. Briefly in 1908, he was an instructor for the Indiana Public Library Commission's Summer School Institute for Librarians. He taught in the University of Michigan Summer School for Library Methods (1909-1919, and in 1922), and also was a special lecturer in the Department of Library Science at Michigan (1927-1930 and several summers), teaching well past retirement. Goodrich taught in the University of Chicago Graduate Library School Summer Session of 1932 and in the Columbia University School of Library Service spring semester of 1933. A skilled teacher, he taught courses on such topics as library administration, library architecture, and special collections. He became quite well known as an authority on American library architecture and served as a consultant in that field.

Goodrich was very active as well in local and national library associations. In 1901, he delivered a paper to the Michigan Library Association on public documents for a small library, the forerunner of numerous services which he was to render to that organization, including being its president in the trying years of 1917 and 1918. He was president of the New York City Library Club, and the Ann Arbor Library Club. In the American Library Association he held many offices, including the chairmanship of the Committee on Fellowships and Scholarships.

Goodrich was a member of the Sons of the American Revolution, the American Library Institute, New York Library Association, Archons of Colophon, Bibliographical Society of America, Psi Gamma Delta, and the Grolier Club. In addition, he was a member of the Michigan Historical Society, Washtenaw Historical Society, Ann Arbor Dunwarkin Club, Signature Club, Golden Rule Masonic Lodge, and the alumni associations of the University of Michigan and Eastern Michigan University.

From 1910 to 1914, he was the first editor of *Michigan Libraries*, and for many years, he was a frequent book reviewer for *The Library Quarterly*. He was also the editor of *Education for Librarianship, Final Report of the Committee on Fellowships and Scholarships of the ALA* in 1943 and contributed numerous articles to library periodicals on building, reference, and administrative problems. With William Randall, he was co-author of *Principles of College Library Administration* (1936, with a second edition in 1941). For more than a decade, this was the best-known American textbook of academic library administration, and it brought the two authors national reputations.

Francis Lee Dewey Goodrich's last years were spent while living with a sister in Ann Arbor, Michigan, where he died July 27, 1962. Goodrich's finest qualities were those of sincerity, integrity, modesty, and unselfishness. His ability to maintain friendly relations with academic student bodies as well as with faculty members, in spite of severe library problems, were well known throughout his career. These characteristics, combined with his obvious knowledge of the field, made Goodrich a well-known leader.

Biographical listings and obituaries—*National Cyclopaedia of American Biography* E; [Obituary]. *Ann Arbor News*, July 28, 1962, p. 14; *Who Was Who in America* V (1969-1973); *Who's Who in Library Service*, 1st ed., 2nd ed., 3rd ed. Books and articles about the biographee—Rockwell, W. W. "The Record of F. L. D. Goodrich." *College and Research Libraries* 6:356 (Sept. 1945); Wright, H. N., S. W. McAllister, and C. F. McCombs. "Tributes to Francis L. D. Goodrich," *Library Journal* 70:715-17, 741 (Sept. 1, 1945).
—JOHN F. HARVEY

GOODWIN, JOHN EDWARD (1876-1948)

Although I knew John E. Goodwin only during the last ten years of his life and was a member of his staff for half that time, it was never obvious to me why he had become a librarian. He was not bookish, articulate, nor an inspiring leader. Yet his motivation and character were strong. Born on October 1, 1876, on a farm near East Middleton, Wisconsin, to Henry and Mary Hope Goodwin, he came to maturity virtuous, honest, and dependable, as well as meticulous and thorough in all that he undertook. He would have been successful in almost any field that called for those qualities.

The quiet nature of librarianship as it was practiced around the turn of the century probably drew Goodwin to it. At the University of Wisconsin (1897-1901), as a student under Frederick Jackson Turner, he seemed headed toward a teaching career in history. Then a summer job with the Wisconsin State Library Commission changed his course. After two years' work in the Legislative Reference Division, Goodwin went on to the New York State Library School at Albany, and in 1905, he received the B.L.S. There he formed a lifelong friendship with Sydney B. Mitchell (q.v.), a student in the class ahead. Upon graduation, Goodwin went to Stanford University as assistant librarian, under George T. Clark, in charge of stacks and circulation. He also was catcher on the faculty baseball team, whose first baseman was President David Starr Jordan. When the earthquake of 1906 that destroyed San Francisco also wrecked most of Stanford's buildings, Goodwin aided in the massive clean-up, thereby gaining a life-long distaste for plaster dust.

In 1912, Goodwin went to Austin as librarian of the University of Texas. He remained there until 1923 and, among other valuable lessons (including planning a new building and chairing a library science department), he learned what politics can do to cripple a university.

Goodwin's next move was back to California, as librarian of the University of California's Los Angeles campus. Under the directorship of Ernest Carroll Moore, UCLA was on the threshold of becoming a major institution. All that Goodwin had learned at Albany, Stanford, and Austin, as well as his quiet strength, admirably fitted him to lay the foundations for what was destined to be one of the country's leading research libraries.

He came to a library without distinction in collections, staff, or building. "I have found the library," he wrote to Moore in his characteristic style, "conspicuous for its lack of much of the essential literature in the various fields of knowledge." The UCLA Library then numbered 39,000 mostly pedagogical volumes inherited from the former Normal School. Included were hundreds of multiple copies of texts used (and often written) by the faculty. Worse, Goodwin found Moore without any vision for the Library, reconciled to its remaining a kind of branch of the Berkeley Library, never to exceed 200,000 volumes. In a memorandum to himself, Goodwin declared, "I am unable to adjust myself to the vision of a restricted future for this institution."

Adjust himself he did not. When he retired twenty years later (having in 1927 declined the prestigious librarianship of Stanford University in order to finish the job at UCLA), Goodwin left a basic reference, bibliographical, and periodicals collection of half a million volumes, a monumental library building on the new campus at Westwood, and an able female staff in cataloging and reference.

Goodwin worked quietly, steadily, and wisely. He also proved ingenious in adapting physical facilities to unforeseen needs, and he used to say jokingly that he was probably a better carpenter than librarian. When a shipment of Library of Congress proof slips arrived and there were neither trays in which to file them nor money to buy any, Goodwin made several hundred trays from the heavy cardboard of empty towel cartons. Once, when shown a warped vellum binding, he promptly bore it off to the basement and made a press case for the volume. He was a very practical man. He was also kindly. On my first day at work, I managed to overturn a loaded truck just as Goodwin was passing through the department. He stopped and, with a faint smile, showed me how to steer a heavy book truck.

If it had not been for two major social cataclysms, Goodwin would have achieved even more than he did. These were the Depression and World War II, both of which curtailed the growth of the collection and staff and the expansion of the building. They also came close to breaking his spirit and his will.

Goodwin's failure to retain a balanced staff was due to his unaggressive character. When he filled key positions with strong women, they made sure that no men were advanced over them. Although the growth of UCLA called for more administrative leadership than he could give, Goodwin refused to appoint an assistant librarian of either sex. As a result, a number of promising male librarians came there but left to take more rewarding careers elsewhere. They included John J. Lund, Mortimer Taube (q.v.), Frank A. Lundy, Jens P. Nyholm, Benjamin A. Custer, and Seymour Lubetzky.

As he aged, Goodwin's energy waned. Among his meager papers preserved at UCLA is a clutch of scrap P-slips on which he was given to jotting his reflections. Illness and the deepening Depression led him to write, "I contemplate my vision for the Library and compare it to reality as measured by accomplishment, and I cannot but confess the heartache of disappointment." And in 1934, "Fifty-eight years old, but there are devilishly annoying reminders that the bottom of the incline may be just around a turn or two. A few years will not be enough! Could I have had support in a larger measure! We should have accomplished much, much more. Would that I might live and be reasonably well for ten more years!"

Live he did for those ten years and then, after retirement, for another four years. The Depression was followed by war and, even more troubling, by faculty discontent, particularly with Goodwin's opposition to decentralizing the library system and his failure to provide facilities for special collections, including rare books and manuscripts.

Left a widower in 1944 by the death of Jeannette Boynton Storms Goodwin, in 1946, John Goodwin married his former reference librarian, Fanny Alice Coldren, who survived him. He had no children. Upon Goodwin's retirement in 1944, Sydney Mitchell appraised his old colleague and friend as follows:

His ideal seems to be that of a fine, well-balanced team under one leader with opportunity for all within it but little encouragement for anyone considered too keen on individualism, even if that may mean overlooking exceptional qualities. Like some rather quiet and not particularly articulate men, he is more observant than is often supposed and has shown shrewdness and insight in dealing with people. He has a quiet but pungent sense of humor. When someone told him that I had injured my wrist in a fall over a church step in Chicago, he remarked that I had better go to church more often or stay away altogether.

Goodwin died in Los Angeles on November 18, 1948.

Biographical listings and obituaries—*Who Was Who in America* II (1943-1950); *Who's Who in Library Service*, 1st ed., 2nd ed. **Books and articles about the biographee**—Mitchell, Sydney B. *Mitchell of California.* Berkeley, Calif., 1960; Mitchell, Sydney B. "John Edward Goodwin." *College and Research Libraries* (June 1944); Powell, Lawrence C. *Fortune and Friendship, an Autobiography.* New York: R. R. Bowker, 1968; Powell, Lawrence C. "John E. Goodwin, Founder of the UCLA Library, an Essay toward a Biography." *Journal of Library History* (July 1971); Vosper, Robert. *Books at UCLA.* Los Angeles, Calif.: Friends of the UCLA Library, 1961.

—LAWRENCE CLARK POWELL

GOULD, CHARLES HENRY (1855-1919)

Charles Henry Gould was born on December 6, 1855, in Groveton, New Hampshire, the son of Joseph G. and Abigail Gould and grandson of Ira Gould, one of the pioneers of the Montreal milling industry. Gould completed his education by taking a B.A. degree from McGill University in 1877, winning the Hiram Mills Gold Medal for proficiency in classics.

Following graduation, he was associated with his grandfather's firm for the greater part of the next fifteen years. Then in 1892, Gould was selected by the Board of Governors of McGill University as university librarian, the appointment to take effect on September 1, 1893. Having had no library training, he spent the year prior to taking office preparing himself for his new position, and during this year, he first met such prominent American librarians as Charles Ammi Cutter (q.v.) and Melvil Dewey (q.v.).

Gould, the first full-time librarian of McGill's new Redpath Library, devoted himself to the formative tasks of library organization, individualistic in nature and characteristic of nineteenth century librarianship. These, as he put it in his 1909 presidential address to the American Library Association, "had to do with the single book as the first term in a series that culminated in the working library—the final one. That was co-ordination—of the forces *within* the library." To this end he applied his business experience to the problem of bringing book acquisition procedures under library control. Part of his difficulties arose from the existence of the autonomous law and medical libraries on the campus, over which he failed to establish centralized control. Yet it was established that he was to be consulted on such basic matters as cataloging and arrangement in the interests of uniformity within the University's collections. For the purpose of organizing the Redpath Library collections, he selected the Cutter Expansive Classification Scheme, one which he saw as "more elastic and, so far as it is finished, more scientific." He also steadily enlarged the collection, from some 34,000 volumes to over 170,000 during his career.

In a day when bibliographic tools as we know them were conspicuous by their rarity, Gould sought in 1900 to arrange Canada's participation in the *International Catalogue of Scientific Literature*. By 1906, he was directing the Canadian efforts, but not until 1913 could he secure a grant from the Dominion government to start the work, which was always threatened by insecure financial provisions.

Gould saw the library's responsibility as extended beyond the immediate university community to readers at a distance from established libraries. His concerns led him to make the McGill library's resources available to Montreal area libraries in the form of a contract cataloging service. He also established, with endowment support, the Travelling Libraries, a book box service like those being developed in other jurisdictions under the direction of provincial or state library services. As early as 1901, Gould saw nothing untoward in augmenting books with lectures and non-print media such as stereoscopes, lantern slides, and wall pictures.

As an administrator, Gould also saw the necessity for developing specialized training for library staff. His in-training program, started in 1899, proved sufficiently successful to justify the establishment of a more formal program, the McGill University Library Summer Schools, launched in 1904 after consultation with Dewey and continuing annually with but one interruption until World War I. His goal was to expand the program to an eight-month course, but this did not happen in his lifetime.

For all his accomplishments in developing the services of the McGill library, he was always conscious of the effects of the limitation of bibliographic resources on the library's efforts. Already in the nineties, Gould had been corresponding with the libraries of Harvard, the University of Toronto, and Parliament in Ottawa to establish bilateral arrangements for interlibrary loans. Thus, his concern for the internal development and organization of the collections was paralleled by a corresponding one for improved and extended service to readers. He and others developed the idea that libraries among themselves might form an interconnected system, thus increasing the quantity and the variety of books available to readers. His ALA presidential address gave lucid expression to this new dimension in his thinking:

> ... the problems which now confront us are different from the earlier ones. They no longer have to do with libraries as final terms in a series, but as the *first* terms in a new series of larger proportions. The twentieth century has the task of evoking method and order *among* rather than *within* libraries ... welding them into a complete system. ... Such an organization, such a system of libraries, is the final term in the new series. In it

the libraries of the country would stand not as independent units, but as *inter*-dependent partners. And its ultimate attainment should, I believe, be the aim *par excellence* of this generation of librarians.

He saw the entire continent as divided into large regions, each with its "reservoir" library to coordinate activity among the libraries of the region, with regional libraries developing policies to coordinate work among themselves. As Gould saw it, "Their work would be not to displace what already exists, but to correlate it and increase its effectiveness."

Yet he was no misty-eyed idealist. He drew attention to the differing responsibilities of college and research libraries, of state library agencies, and of public libraries large and small. Thus, he saw the need for coordination as being not just national, but at least continental in scope, and ultimately international. Writing after his death, Mary E. Ahern (q.v.) used these words to describe the ALA conference whose theme was coordination: "In 1908-09, a period of unusual activity and change, he served as president of the A.L.A., and the Bretton Woods Conference ... stands out ... as one of the most valuable and delightful in the history of the A.L.A."

Gould had already chaired the ALA Committee on Foreign Documents, and following his presidential year, he headed the Committee on Co-ordination until his death. From this vantage point, he helped work out the techniques that would be required to develop the network he had described, the first problem being that of interlibrary loan. By 1917, the Committee presented for adoption by the membership a "Code of Practice for Inter-Library Loans." It was accepted, and represented a recognition of the need for a minimal agreed policy and procedure to govern interlibrary loan practice, as a part of the slowly growing structure of a system of "interdependent partners."

Though Gould's orientation was toward service through books, he was neither blind to nor opposed to the newer concept of information service animating the new Special Libraries Association. In 1912, he joined with Arthur Bostwick (q.v.) and Clement Andrews (q.v.) in urging that the ALA accept the application of the SLA for affiliation, as this would attract a number of desirable members to the annual conference. This, they believed, would bring "a point of view new to most members of the American Library Association, could hardly fail to impart fresh interest to the discussion of familiar topics, and suggest fresh topics worthy of investigation."

Gould took part in the affairs of a variety of associations, though there was no provincial library association in Quebec with which to work. As for the ALA, he joined in 1893 and remained a member throughout his life. He attended the Second

International Conference of Librarians in London (1897), as well as regular meetings of the Ontario Library Association. He was a member of the Ex Libris Society, the Champlain Society, and a member and president (1912-1913) of the Bibliographical Society of America. Gould was also elected a charter fellow of the American Library Institute in 1906, took part in its meetings regularly, and in 1917 was elected to its governing board.

In Gould's case, this participation appears to indicate a genuine spirit of helpfulness to colleagues, and a sense of inter-dependence. His reputation grew and his advice was increasingly sought on questions as diverse as building plans, equipment, classification systems, cataloging, departmental libraries, collection development, and library education. A sampling of his correspondence indicates the extensive range of his contacts throughout the book and library world, a surprising number of which represented warm personal as well as professional and business relationships.

His death on July 30, 1919, in Montreal, prompted real and deep regret, and memorial notices unanimously praised his warm and kindly character together with his very real ability. As one writer put it, "He was never a voluminous contributor to library literature, but his investigations and the conclusions which he reached were always presented with well balanced judgment and definite suggestions, so that his reports form valuable commentaries on the development of real progress."

Biographical listings and obituaries—"Death of the University Librarian." [Obituary]. *The McGill News* 1:26 (1919); *Macmillan Dictionary of Canadian Biography* (1963); **Books and articles about the biographee**—Ahern, Mary Eileen. "Mr. Charles Henry Gould, a Fellow of the American Library Institute, 1906-1919." American Library Institute. *Papers and Proceedings*, 1920, pp. 52-54; "An Appreciation of C. H. Gould." *Library Journal* 44:562 (Sept. 1919); "Charles Henry Gould." American Library Association *Bulletin* 14:318 (1920); Lomer, Gerhard R. "Charles Henry Gould." *Bulletin of Bibliography* 13:22 (1927). There is a photograph of Gould facing page 21 of this issue of the bulletin; Makela, Ritva. *McGill University Library During the Tenure of Charles H. Gould as University Librarian, 1893-1919.* Occasional Papers, no. 5. Montreal: McGill University, Graduate School of Library Science, 1974; *People We Meet.* Montreal: McGill Outlook, 1903. Apparently a student publication with caricatures of prominent members of the faculty and administration, including Gould, with a verse about each; Stuart-Stubbs, Basil. *A Survey and Interpretation of the Literature of Interlibrary Loan.* Vancouver: University of British Columbia Library, 1975. The first two chapters contain much material on Gould's role in promoting and developing the ideas of interlibrary cooperation and establishing the first interlibrary loan code. **Primary sources and archival materials**—Dyck, Jacqueline. *Preliminary List of Incoming Letters of McGill Librarian C. H. Gould,* 1899. Record Group 40, Accession 654. Montreal: McGill University, University Archives, Jan. 1974; McLeod, Norman C. *A Preliminary List of the Incoming Letters of McGill Librarian Charles Henry Gould,* 1896. Record Group 40, Accession 654. Montreal: McGill University, University Archives, April 1974; Rooney, Thomas. *A Preliminary List of the Incoming Letters of the McGill Librarian, Charles H. Gould.* Record Group 40, Accession 654/1898, A-C, Items 1-162. Montreal: McGill University, University Archives, Jan. 1974; Tallman, Julie I. *A Preliminary List of the Official Papers of Charles Henry Gould.* Record Group 40, Accession 654, Items no. 1-146, 1895. Montreal: McGill University, University Archives, Dec. 1973.

—KEITH CROUCH

GRAHAM, BESSIE (1881-1966)

Bessie Graham, the eldest daughter of Dr. John and Emily Richter Graham, was born in 1881, in Philadelphia, Pennsylvania. Educated in private schools in Philadelphia, she entered nearby Bryn Mawr College in the fall of 1898. Although the records indicate that she was a good student, she left after her freshman year. Thereafter, her dislike of regimentation and her strong, independent spirit led her to use the world and its books as her college. Her independent reading, which was more scholarly, diverse, and copious than that offered in most college curricula, gave her knowledge that would be invaluable later. In 1910, she entered the Department of Library Science at Drexel Institute, where she received an excellent foundation in reference and bibliographic work from Alice Kroeger (q.v.), predecessor to Isadore Mudge (q.v.) as the compiler of *Guide to Reference Books.*

In 1914, the Philadelphia Booksellers' Association asked her to organize the Philadelphia Booksellers' School at the William Penn Evening High School. The School, the only one of its kind in the United States at that time, was open to anyone who passed the entrance examination and who had at least two years of high school or the equivalent in actual book-trade work. The curriculum included methods of indexing, library classification, and cataloging; instruction in current book news; and an introduction to outstanding books in all areas of literature.

Graham's textbook for the course was the *Publishers' Weekly.* To keep the course from becoming too "theory" oriented, she kept in touch with the practicalities of bookselling by working as a clerk in a bookstore during the summer of 1917. The School's reputation spread quickly, and several schools in New York and Boston soon offered similar courses. Graham commuted from Philadelphia to New York to teach classes at the New York Public Library. The demand for the bibliographies and assignments that she compiled for the courses was so great that *Publishers' Weekly* printed the entire course weekly from 1918 to 1919.

An outgrowth of the School was to become one of the standard works in bookselling and librarianship. In 1921, Graham published the first edition of *The*

Bookman's Manual, a guide to literature that discussed the comparative merits of different categories of books. The book was so popular that two printings were required. It was revised in 1924 and updated at three- to six-year intervals for the next seventeen years. (R. R. Bowker recently published the twelfth edition under the title *The Reader's Adviser.*)

From 1921 to 1924, Bessie Graham served as the librarian in "the oldest free circulating library in the United States," the Apprentices' Library in Philadelphia.

The Booksellers' School was transferred to the University of Pennsylvania in 1923. Then, a year later, it became the Department of Library Science, at Temple University, and the curriculum was expanded to meet the demand for teacher/librarians who could pass the Pennsylvania certification requirements. Graham headed the faculty and taught reference, bibliography, and book selection. In order to keep current with the practical world, she also worked as a substitute in several school libraries in Philadelphia. Yet, although she agreed that knowledge of library techniques was necessary, she believed very strongly that knowledge of the contents of books was much more important to a librarian.

Between 1917 and 1930 she contributed several articles to various periodicals. These articles, which ranged from a discussion of utopias to book reviews, revealed her broad interests, her concern with world affairs, her inherent idealism, and her keen sense of humor.

She resigned as director of Temple University's Department of Library Science in 1940 and a year later terminated her work on *The Bookman's Manual.* However, she remained extremely active in the book world—compiling the annual list of literary prizes winners for the *Britannica Book of the Year* for the next seven years. During World War II, former students who had become army librarians besieged her with requests for reading lists for draftees.

Bessie Graham remained active professionally in the American Library Association, and she received the highest honor of her life when she was elected to honorary membership in the American Booksellers' Association (one of only two people ever to be so honored). Having officially retired, she was able to devote more time to her hobby of collecting facsimiles of rare books, and to an interest which rapidly became a hobby—helping women learn to invest their savings safely and profitably. She also continued reading avidly and serving as consultant to booksellers and librarians alike until her death on September 2, 1966. Her objective was always to improve the professions of both bookselling and librarianship through well-trained personnel, and her teaching and her bibliographic work were directed toward that goal.

Biographical listings and obituaries—[Obituary]. *Library Journal* 91:4620 (Oct. 1, 1966); [Obituary]. *Philadelphia Inquirer*, Sept. 3, 1966; [Obituary]. *Publishers Weekly* 190:48 (Sept. 19, 1966). **Books and Articles about the biographee**—Campbell, Mildred W. "Bessie Graham, Bibliophile." Master's thesis, Texas State College for Women, 1953; "Librarian Authors." *Library Journal* 50:691 (Sept. 1, 1930); McKee, Rose. "No. 1 Trouble Shooter." *Philadelphia Inquirer*, Nov. 16, 1941.

—MARY JANE PLATOU

GREEN, BERNARD RICHARDSON (1843-1914)

During the last half of the nineteenth century, librarians and architects struggled for solutions to the problems the world's major libraries were facing in storing and servicing their rapidly growing collections. These problems were not effectively met until 1888, when Bernard Richardson Green, a civil engineer and specialist in the construction of harbor fortifications, was appointed as superintendent of construction for the Congressional Library Building.

Bernard Green, the son of Ezra and Elmina Minerva Richardson Green, was born at Malden, Massachusetts, on December 28, 1843. His direct descendants reach back to one of the early settlers of New England, James Green, who arrived in Malden shortly after 1634. Bernard Green attended the Malden public schools, then was graduated with a S.B. degree in civil engineering from the Lawrence Scientific School of Harvard University in 1864.

Upon graduation, he began immediately in the service of the government, devoting fourteen years to the construction of seacoast fortifications of Maine; Portsmouth, New Hampshire; Boston Harbor; and Newport, Rhode Island. In the spring of 1877, Green moved to Washington, D.C., and was given charge, under Colonel (later General) Thomas L. Casey, of a number of important construction projects: the Washington Aqueduct, completion of the State, War, and Navy Building, the Army Medical Museum, the principal buildings of the U.S. Soldiers Home, and completion of the Washington Monument.

Bernard Green owes much of his professional reputation to his work on the State, War, and Navy Building, where he contributed to a savings of $2,225,000 in construction costs, and his work on the Washington Monument, where his correction of his predecessor's errors permitted completion of the project, which was hailed as an engineering marvel. Green's considerable reputation as a civil engineer was recognized by the commission for the construction of the Congressional Library Building, which employed him on March 19, 1888, to be superintendent of construction.

While Green was in immediate charge of all phases of the Library's construction, his most important contribution was the design of the bookstacks and conveyor system. His problem was to develop a book storage system with a capacity for 4,500,000 volumes, a collection larger by far than any existing in the United States. In addition to storage capacity, other requirements Green considered were light, ventilation, flexibility, communication, fire protection, rapid transmission of books, cleanliness, durability, and simplicity. Green was the first library designer to consider these problems as an integrated system.

The stack design, patented by Green in 1890, consisted of an all-steel framework with cast iron shelf supports and white marble slab floors. The conveyor system developed by Green was capable of carrying materials from the farthest point in the stacks to the main reading room in three minutes. He was also responsible for the design of much of the other mechanical apparatus in the building, including the pneumatic tube system and the specially constructed newspaper and map shelves.

Authorities such as Keyes Metcalf recognized Bernard Green's stack design for the Library of Congress as the beginning of the modern bookstack. By 1930, over two hundred libraries in the United States and abroad, including such major institutions as the New York Public Library and Harvard University's Widener Library, employed his design. Even though the principal manufacturer of the Green bookstack, Snead and Company, began to make design modifications as early as 1915, Green's technological contributions have continued to have a strong influence on library planning.

Following its completion in 1897, Green stayed with the Library of Congress as superintendent of the building and disbursing officer until his retirement from government service in 1913. During this period, he also served as consulting engineer for the Corcoran Gallery of Art, the Washington, D.C., Public Library, and the Pennsylvania State Capitol. In his capacity as chairman of the President's consultative board on the location and design of public buildings, he advised on many other projects. Green also was a consultant for the construction of the New York Public Library and served on the jury in the first architectural competition. Green lectured and wrote on library design and was recognized by his contemporaries as one of the leading authorities in the field.

Bernard Green did not permit the heavy burden of his work to interfere with his keen sense of responsibility to his community and profession. He served as a director of the Union Trust Company and a trustee of the Corcoran Gallery of Art. He was a trustee and Sunday School superintendent of All Soul's Church, president of the Cosmos Club, vice president of the American Society of Civil Engineers and treasurer of the Philosophical Society of Washington and the Washington Academy of Sciences. Green was an active member of the American Unitarian Association, the Unitarian Club, National Society of Fine Arts, American Association for the Advancement of Science, National Geographic Society, Potomac Canoe Club, and the American Library Association.

Much is revealed about the man in his detailed journal of the construction of the Congressional Library Building and his scrapbook of newspaper and other public accounts of his work, his professional activities, his private life, and items of special interest to him. Though the entries in Green's journal are brief, they provide a comprehensive daily record of the Library's construction. Personal references to Green are scarce, but mention of his subordinates, their achievements and mishaps, are frequent. Direct quotations in newspaper accounts show Green to be concise in speech, decisive, well informed, modest, and quick to accept responsibility.

Green's scrapbook also shows his strong attachment to his native New England and a deep devotion to his family. He was married at Malden, Massachusetts, on January 1, 1868, to Julia E. Lincoln. They had four children—Bernard Lincoln, Julia Minerva, William Ezra, and Arthur Brooks. Bernard Richardson Green died in Washington, October 22, 1914.

Biographical listings and obituaries—*National Cyclopaedia of American Biography* 20; *Who Was Who in America* I (1897-1942). Books and articles about the biographee—Baumann, Charles H. *The Influence of Angus Snead Macdonald and the Snead Bookstack on Library Architecture.* Metuchen, N.J.: Scarecrow Press, 1972; Hilker, Helen-Anne. "Monument to Civilization." *Quarterly Journal of the Library of Congress* 29:234-66 (Oct. 1972). Primary sources and archival materials—Green, Bernard Richardson. "The Building of the Library of Congress." In Smithsonian Institution, *Annual Report, 1897.* Washington, 1898; Green, Bernard Richardson. Scrapbooks. [Library of Congress microfilm edition.]

—KIMBERLY W. DOBBS

GREEN, SAMUEL SWETT (1837-1918)

Samuel Swett Green was born in Worcester, Massachusetts, February 20, 1837, the son of James and Elizabeth Swett Green. Librarian of the Free Public Library of Worcester from 1871 to 1909, and a founder of the American Library Association, he was internationally recognized through his writings, most of which describe his innovations at the Worcester Library in such areas as public service, work with schools and factory workers, and interlibrary loan.

The Greens were an old and prominent Worcester family, as was his mother's family, and this enabled Samuel to boast of four progenitors who had come over on the "Mayflower." Samuel's father was an apothecary whose business was lucrative enough to give each of his three sons a Harvard education followed by professional training (law, medicine, and theology).

Elizabeth guarded her sons carefully, encouraged them to stay at home, and taught them such skills as embroidery. The father, on the other hand, bought his sons ponies and tried to interest them in outdoor activities. Samuel was a frail child, shy and quiet, and he suffered from long periods of semi-invalidism until he was in his thirties. While he blamed his mother's overprotectiveness for his poor health and weak eyes (from too great an application to books and embroidery), he never married and cared for her until her death, in 1901, at the age of 93.

He attended a private school run by Mrs. Sarah B. Wood, where he probably received his first introduction to libraries, as it housed the Worcester Lyceum library and the "Bangs Library" of the Unitarian Church, both open on Saturdays with Mrs. Wood in charge. Public grammar school followed, and then, from 1849 to 1854, the Worcester High School. In 1854, Samuel went to Harvard where, in spite of "bad health and worse eyesight," he completed his Bachelor of Arts degree in 1858. His yearbook portrait shows him to have had refined features in a face dominated by large dark eyes, but it cannot indicate his diminutive five-foot-two stature. Later he was also to receive an M.A. from Harvard in 1870, and in 1877, he was elected to Phi Beta Kappa.

Although he is said to have had few friends and to have lived very quietly at Harvard, he reported feeling "languid" for two or three years thereafter. As a diversion, he travelled in the summer of 1859 on the sailing ship "Racehorse" to Smyrna, which gave him a love of the sea. Then, in later life, he enjoyed repeated trips to England.

In 1860, the languorous invalid enrolled at Harvard's Divinity School. He soon had to leave because of his health, but by 1861, he was ready for a second try and successfully completed the course in 1864. He had been troubled by religious and philosophical questions, but his studies provided him with satisfactory answers. As Unitarians, the Greens were considered theological liberals, but Green seems to have out-liberaled the liberals. After his first sermon shocked his congregation, he decided that his theology was "unsaleable," and because of this and poor health, he gave up all further thought of continuing in the ministry.

Green's stay in divinity school coincided with the years of the Civil War, but he was called up for the draft anyway. He reported to the provost marshal armed with certificates from doctors explaining that if he were drafted, he would become "incapacitated at once." To his chagrin, the officer in charge took one look at him, said, "You are too short," and rejected him without ever glancing at his papers. Following divinity school, he became a bookkeeper briefly in the Mechanics National Bank of Worcester and then teller in the Worcester National Bank from 1864 to 1870. However, in 1870, he resigned because of an attack of rheumatic fever and travelled to "the West" to recover.

In January 1867, he had become a member of the Board of Directors of the Free Public Library of Worcester. This Library had resulted from the 1859 gift by Dr. John Green (Samuel's uncle) of his library of some 7,500 volumes to the city, followed later by a legacy of $30,000 for the Library's support. The Green library was merged with the collection of the Worcester Lyceum and Library Association to form the Free Public Library of Worcester, with about 12,000 volumes. The new Library had opened in 1860 under the charge of the Reverend Zephaniah Baker, a Universalist minister who had lost his voice some years before and who used his position as librarian largely to facilitate his historical researches; he badly neglected the "public" aspects of the Library.

The young banker enthusiastically entered into his duties as a director. Made secretary of the Board, he at once investigated methods of organizing and circulating books, and produced a 25-page printed octavo report on the subject. He was concerned that the Library was uncared for and little used, particularly his uncle's books. The "Green library" was a non-circulating reference collection, and Green explained to the Board that the 60,000 inhabitants of Worcester must have thousands of questions that could be answered by referring to the Library through the intermediacy of a sympathetic librarian. When the invigorated Green returned from his Western trip in 1870, he found the Board equally agitated over the state of the Library, and the president asked him to become librarian.

It would be hard to imagine a better choice. Samuel Swett Green was 33, of scholarly bent, with a demonstrated enthusiasm for libraries and library management, and his interest in this particular library was reinforced by family associations. He also had a modest knowledge of practical finance through his banking career and was at the moment unemployed. January 15, 1871, the day on which Green took over as librarian of the Free Public Library of Worcester, was the turning point in his career and an important date in the history of the American library movement as well.

To begin with, Green's assumption of his new position coincided with an abrupt improvement in his health. He writes that, in 1870, he had his last sickness; after the invigorating experience of his Western journey, the adoption of an abstemious diet, and taking over his duties as librarian, he never again was ill until near the end of his 81 years. In his case, librarianship seems to have had a therapeutic effect.

Only his eyesight remained weak, and to spare it, he had to depend upon secretaries to read to him throughout his long career. But he never mentioned his affliction or allowed it to interfere with his work.

Green wasted no time in putting the Free Public Library of Worcester on the "library map" and keeping it there for the 38 years he served as librarian. Though new to the field, he attended the famous 1876 conference of librarians held in Philadelphia in connection with the Centennial Exposition. Moreover, he had a part of his Library's sixteenth annual report, describing his accomplishments at Worcester, printed as a pamphlet and distributed to the delegates. Still more importantly, he presented a paper, subsequently published in *American Library Journal* (November 1876), entitled "Personal Relations between Librarians and Readers." It was his first professional paper, and it established his fame as a librarian on a solid basis. It is still quoted and looked upon as a landmark of library literature.

In a narrow sense, this paper described the desirable management of the reference and, to a lesser extent, the circulation departments of the Library; however, its main accomplishment was to define his doctrine of public service. This thesis, first stated here and reiterated throughout his career, is generally conceded to be his principal contribution to librarianship. He began this paper by saying,

> When scholars and persons of high social position come to a library they have confidence enough, in regard to the cordiality of their reception, to make known their wishes without timidity or reserve.

> Modest men in the humbler walks of life, and well-trained boys and girls, need encouragement before they become ready to say freely what they want.

> A hearty reception by a sympathizing friend, and the recognition of some one at hand who will listen to inquiries ... make it easy for such persons to ask questions, and put them at once on a home footing.

He then gave examples of typical reference questions and in describing techniques of answering them, he presented a remarkable explanation of the subtleties of the "reference interview." He described the ideal reference librarian, one who welcomed the public with warmth and answered their questions with efficiency, as a paragon of many virtues, all meticulously specified. His philosophy of service was summed up with perhaps his most famous statement, one well calculated to appeal to the businessmen who presumably dominated most library boards: "A librarian should be as unwilling to allow an inquirer to leave the library with his question unanswered as a shopkeeper is to have a customer go out of his store without making a purchase."

This portrayal of the service-oriented librarian struck a responsive chord in reporters, who had apparently met too many of the opposite kind, and Green was proud that his idea attracted favorable comment in newspapers in Boston, New York, London, and eventually even France and Germany. In librarianship, this paper provided one of the best expressions of a major tenet of the faith of the "modern library movement."

In 1877, British librarians decided to hold a library conference in London similar to the American conference of the previous year. They invited the newly founded American Library Association to send a delegation, and Samuel Swett Green was selected as one of the official representatives. While the sixteen American librarians who attended were not asked to read papers, they did contribute in a lively manner to the discussions, and of course Green was prominent among them. In fact, it was in defense of "sensational" fiction in libraries that he made his famous remark that any girl who was led astray by reading novels lacked the sense to avoid this fate even if she did not read them. While this conference is covered in great detail in its own *Transactions* and in several other places, the most engaging description is Green's own in his *The Public Library Movement* (Chapter VI), published in 1913 after his retirement.

A second area in which Green was considered a pioneer was in public library service to schools, although the idea was first prominently advocated in 1876 by Charles Francis Adams, Jr., of Quincy, Massachusetts, in a speech later widely reprinted. In 1879, Green called a meeting with school authorities and proposed a five-point program of ways in which the Worcester Free Public Library might help teachers and students. Never one to hide his light under a bushel, Green described his plan in a paper read at a meeting of the American Social Science Association in 1880 (reprinted in the October 1880 *Library Journal*). In 1883, he published an anthology of papers on the subject entitled *Libraries and Schools* (New York: F. Leypoldt, 1883). He continued writing on this topic more than on any other for many years and was widely recognized for leadership in the area.

Green wrote copiously on most of the topics of interest to the library world of his day, and his writings were generally based on the practices of the Worcester Library. *Library Journal* alone, from 1876 to 1913, contains well over forty of his articles, reports, and substantive contributions to discussions. His devotion to the philosophy of service was responsible for articles on adapting the library to "constituencies," and on aids and guides for readers, although in later years, he accepted open access to shelves less wholeheartedly than did some of his contemporaries. He was proud that Worcester was the first sizable library in New England to open on Sundays (December 8, 1872), and that the Boston Public Library soon followed suit. In book selection, he was concerned about providing books for various groups in the community and was scornful of those who would outlaw fiction. He discussed his special efforts to attract both factory workers and business-men to the library. Reference service was a particular emphasis at Worcester, and he was an early proponent of interlibrary loan and cooperation among libraries. A member of the local art society, he opened the Library's doors to art exhibits and in the 1870s organized in the Library a picture file of thousands of photographs and lithographs of great paintings, sculpture, and architecture. As early as 1877, Green was advocating academic courses for librarians and supported Melvil Dewey (q.v.) against some of the more conservative librarians in his efforts to establish a library school in the early 1880s.

Samuel Swett Green was described as an eloquent speaker, with a fine voice, and a homely humor much admired at that time. The American Library Association was his favorite forum, and indeed, many of his publications originated as papers read before this organization. He was one of the original incorporators of ALA in 1879, and attended the eighteen national meetings from 1876 through 1884, and eleven there-after, his last being in 1911. He was active on committees, a member and president of the Council, vice-president in 1887, president in 1891, and a fellow of the American Library Institute.

By 1884, Green had made available a monumental 1,300-page book catalog of the Worcester Library, and supplements appeared in 1889 and 1896. Beginning in 1887, he delivered annual lectures on public libraries as educational institutions at the Columbia School of Library Economy, and when that institution moved with Dewey to Albany, Green's lectures continued at the new location. The first state public library commission was founded in 1890 in Massachusetts with Green as a member, a position he held until he retired from library work in 1909. When Dewey was unable to go to California for the ALA meeting in 1891, he resigned as president and his term was filled out by Green, who presided at the sessions in San Francisco and delivered a presidential address reiterating the theme of public service. On April 1 of the same year, the Worcester Library opened its new building on Elm Street, adjacent to and supplementing its old quarters, after a long campaign by Green and his trustees for funds. The building also served as art museum until 1898, when the museum moved to its own location.

For the World's Columbian Exposition in Chicago in 1893, ALA prepared an extensive exhibit on the progress of the library movement since 1876 and held its annual meeting, an attempt at a world congress of librarians, at the fair. Of course Green took a promin-ent part, reading a paper, "The Adaptation of Librar-ies to Constituencies," and chairing a part of one session. After this conference, he retired to a con-siderable extent from active participation in national library affairs, although he attended more meetings, continued to write papers, and devoted his remaining years more particularly to the Worcester Library. In 1895, "catalogers from Albany" completed the classification of the Library according to the Dewey system, and in the same year the first of eight delivery stations was established, most of which were to develop into branches. In 1900, the Library opened a children's room, with gratifying results.

Outside of librarianship, Green was a joiner of many organizations, a founder of others, and typi-cally an officeholder in most of them. Together with his life-long bachelor friend Stephen Salisbury (1835-1905), he thoroughly enjoyed the cultural and social groups of Worcester. However, his particular interest was in history, and he belonged to at least a dozen historical and patriotic societies in America and Britain. His historical writings appeared regularly in the *Proceedings* of the American Antiquarian Society, and he bolstered a lively interest in Roman archaeology in Britain by frequent trips there in the early years of this century.

Despite the fact that Samuel Swett Green had become by the turn of the century a famous librarian, and the Worcester Library had shared his prominence, the last six or seven years of his administration were clouded by controversy. A small but vocal minority of the Board were highly critical of his work and sought to have him replaced. In 1904, Melvil Dewey was hired as an unbiased expert to survey the Library and make a report. Not surprisingly, Dewey praised Green's accomplishments and the generally splendid state of the Library, making only a few minor suggestions including the need for an assistant librar-ian. It was later disclosed that Green had offered to resign at that time, but he stayed on at the request of the president of the Board, although there was con-tinued hostility. Robert K. Shaw, in his adulatory biography, admits that "it should in fairness be stated that, in spite of Mr. Green's devoted zeal in popu-larizing his library, a number of honest patrons . . . who did not establish personal contact with librar-ians, found the library atmosphere sometimes a little chilly."

It was not until January 12, 1909, that Green retired, at the age of 72 and after 42 years of service to the Library, 38 of them as its librarian. He left the Library in the hands of a man of his own choice, Robert K. Shaw (1871-1956), who had been made assistant librarian in 1905 as a result of the Dewey survey. Green was made librarian emeritus and was given an office in the building and the services of his favorite secretary for up to one hour a day. In March, Mayor James Logan sponsored a testimonial dinner to Green attended by 46 of the city's "best-known residents," one of whom, Justice Arthur P. Rugg, made the following remarkably perceptive statement: "The people of Worcester don't appreciate the distinction that Librarian Green has given us. The history of libraries will never be written without the name of Samuel S. Green written large."

In his retirement years Green remained active, appearing daily at his office. He wrote, but never published, a manuscript explaining his personal theology, entitled "Peace in Doubt." He published *The Public Library Movement in the United States, 1853-1893: From 1876, Reminiscences of the Writer* (Boston: Boston Book Co., 1913). The bulk of this book constituted a year-by-year account of the public library movement, compiled from his memories and records, but also depending heavily on *Library Journal*. The book includes biographical sketches of Justin Winsor (q.v.), William Frederick Poole (q.v.), Lloyd Pearsall Smith (q.v.), and Charles Ammi Cutter (q.v.), but with lesser emphasis, it gives as well his impressions of virtually every prominent librarian of the period. The last chapter discusses the writer's contributions to this history, but inevitably he played an important role throughout the book, and he frequently supplies the reader with personal and often amusing anecdotes that add a great deal of humanity to the story. Green also wrote an autobiographical sketch in the December 1913 issue of *Library Journal.*

In his later years, Green was described as dark-complexioned and very agile, often surprising younger companions, and pictures show him with a neatly trimmed beard and large deep-set eyes. His remarkable health failed slowly over the years, but he continued his daily visits to the office until November 27, 1918. He died December 8 of that year at the Maple Hall Sanitarium in Worcester, at the age of 81. A small private funeral ceremony was held at the Forest Hills Crematory Chapel on Long Island.

In 1926, Robert K. Shaw's biography of Green was published by ALA, and printed by D. B. Updike at the Merrymount Press. In 1951, Green was among the forty librarians chosen for *Library Journal's* "Library Hall of Fame" on the occasion of ALA's seventy-fifth anniversary. Actually, Samuel Swett Green might well have been put in a more exclusive group, possibly one of a dozen outstanding librarians of 1876 who pioneered a new profession, for he was a true professional. He saw that the major excuse for a profession was service; he took an active role in the professional organization; he supported education for librarianship; he wrote extensively and well on professional problems; and he practiced what he preached in a long, devoted, and distinguished career.

Biographical listings and obituaries—*Dictionary of American Biography* 7 (Frederick W. Ashley); *National Cyclopaedia of American Biography* 6; [Obituary]. *Library Journal* 44:58 (Jan. 1919); [Obituary]. *Public Libraries* 24:33 (Jan. 1919); *Who Was Who in America* I (1897-1942). Books and articles about the biographee—"Editorial: S. S. Green Retires." *Public Libraries* 14:55 (Feb. 1909); Garver, Austin S. "Samuel Swett Green—An Appreciation." *Library Journal* 34:269-71 (June 1909); Green, Frances. "He Wanted Everyone to Read, Read, Read." *Worcester Sunday Telegram,* May 23, 1965. Feature "Parade" section, pp. 6-8; "A Library Hall of Fame, Compiled for the 75th Anniversary of the American Library Association, 1876-1951." *Library Journal* 76:466-72 (March 15, 1951); Nelius, Albert A. "Bibliography of S. S. Green." 1968. (Unpublished list in the possession of Budd L. Gambee); "The New President of the American Library Association." *Library Journal* 16:233 (Aug. 1891); "One of the Pioneers—Samuel Swett Green." *Library Journal* 51:843 (Oct. 1926); Shaw, Robert K. *Samuel Swett Green.* American Library Pioneers, No. 2. Chicago: American Library Association, 1926.

—BUDD L. GAMBEE

GREENE, BELLE da COSTA (1883-1950)

Belle da Costa Greene was born on December 13, 1883, in Alexandria, Virginia, to Richard and Genevieve Van Vliet Greene. (Her middle name came from her maternal grandmother, Genevieve da Costa Van Vliet.) Upon the separation of her parents, Belle removed with her mother to Princeton, New Jersey, where Mrs. Greene supported the family by giving music lessons. When Belle finished school, no money was to be had for her further education, so she went to work in the Princeton University Library for Ernest C. Richardson (q.v.), her first inspiration in librarianship.

In 1905, after her brief apprenticeship at the Princeton Library, Belle da Costa Greene began a liaison with a family and collection that has immeasurably enriched the scholarly materials available in a broad range of fields. On the recommendation of his nephew, who knew Greene at Princeton, Pierpont Morgan hired the 21-year-old woman as librarian in charge of his private collection. In this capacity, she was responsible for organizing the diverse collection of autographed manuscripts, medieval illuminated manuscripts, incunabula, first editions, and early bindings that Morgan had acquired in twenty years, preparing it for the move into the new library on 36th Street in New York City. She was assisted by Ada Thurston. Subsequently, as Morgan himself devoted more attention to collecting, she assumed greater responsibility for acquiring his desiderata. She had no college education but adopted very early a procedure of learning as much as she could from the scholars with whom she was in contact. She was a familiar figure at auction sales and with dealers, where she often spent large sums, but she viewed her role more as a scout for Morgan, ferreting out quality accessions, researching them, but relegating to him the actual determination to acquire. In 1926, Morgan told the Earl of Leicester after an expensive purchase, "My librarian told me she wouldn't dare spend so much money but just the same I wouldn't be able to face her if I went home without the manuscripts."

Morgan died in 1913. In his will, he stipulated that Belle da Costa Greene was to remain in charge of the library, which he willed to his son, J. P. Morgan. Collection development slowed somewhat during this period, due as much to settling the estate and to the war in Europe as to J. P. Morgan's initial disinterest. In 1924, after Morgan's interest in the collection was kindled, the Pierpont Morgan Library was incorporated as a public institution, amply endowed by Morgan in honor of his father, and Belle Greene was appointed director. During her 24-year tenure, she presided over the Library's transition to a public institution, maintaining always a perspective on the unique needs generated by both the collection itself and its users. The comprehensive dictionary catalog, with about ten entries per item, included analytic and subject cards for important bindings, provenances, iconographic representations, and heraldic paintings. A special iconography file of over 10,000 entries further increased access to illuminated manuscripts. By 1948, the year of her retirement, the Library had acquired an additional 17,000 items of a secondary nature to supplement the primary research collection and had devised a special classification scheme for their arrangement. These activities, along with facsimile publication, increased the collection's availability for scholarly use.

For interested non-specialists, Belle Greene developed an annual lecture series that brought noted scholars to lecture on topics related to the Library's interest. Many of these lectures were subsequently published. Following an addition to the Morgan Library in 1928, she also introduced the policy of having at least two annual exhibitions, whose catalogs were often reference works in themselves. Her own writings, all published by Pierpont Morgan Library, detail the activities of the Library during her tenure: *A Review of the Growth, Development and Activities of the Library, 1924-29* (1930); *Review of the Activities and Acquisitions of the Pierpont Morgan Library from 1930 through 1935* (1937); *Review of the Activities and Acquisitions of the Pierpont Morgan Library from 1936 through 1940* (1941); *Review of the Activities and Major Acquisitions of the Pierpont Morgan Library, 1941-1948* (1949).

The primary research collection did not stagnate during her directorship, and its quality and representativeness are an even greater reflection of her achievement. Lawrence Wroth (q.v.), who was associated with her as a consultant, states:

To the happy task of acquisition, Miss Greene has brought two highly individual characteristics, a sense of cultural values which disregards with certitude the unimportant in art or letters and an instinct for the authentic, a feeling for realness, a recognition of quality which can be likened to the possession of "absolute pitch" in a musician.

Books and manuscripts were selected only after careful consideration of their relationship to the collection as a whole, and she was in a unique position to assess this, since she had actively participated in the collection's development for all but two decades of its existence. Belle Green's successor commented in wonder about picking up book after book in the collection only to discover on their leaves annotations in her handwriting—bibliographical references, verbal comments by the scholars she often consulted, and questions about writings on the subject, notations often accumulated over a period of years.

Morgan funds placed Greene in the enviable position of usually being able to outbid other institutional buyers. In practice, however, she liberally interpreted the Morgans' willingness to yield precedence to the national institutions of Europe and America. Sir Frederick Kenyon, director of the British Museum, recalls that she had once instructed the British Museum's agent to bid beyond what the Museum was able to pay to acquire a twelfth century manuscript, with the additional amount to be considered a gift from the Morgan Library. Her willingness to aid European libraries extended even further. She was a member of the Committee for Restoration of the Louvain Library after World War I, and was awarded the Palmes d'Officier de l'Instruction Publique from France in 1921, and later the gold medal of a Grand Officier from the same order, as well as similar honors from Italy and Belgium.

She was a witty, charming, sometimes imperious woman who early in her career affected Renaissance gowns and jewelry in keeping with the opulence of the library in which she reigned. She later grew more businesslike in her attire. Yet, she endeared herself to the scholars she served by her generous attention to and interest in their work, and to library students and others sincerely curious about the collections by her interesting, kind answers to their questions. Among her scholar-admirers was Bernard Berenson, the noted art historian. As noted in several biographies, his admiration was both personal and professional. Her loyalty to her staff can be seen in the fact that, during the Depression, she refused to cut their salaries, saying that their having no raises was bad enough.

She never married but adopted her younger sister's son, Robert Leveridge. He had been born in her home after his father's death in World War I. The boy remained with his aunt after his mother's remarriage but was later killed in World War II.

Belle Greene was the first woman designated a fellow of the Medieval Academy of America and she was a fellow in perpetuity of the Metropolitan Museum of New York. She also served as a charter member of the Advisory Committee to the Board of Trustees, Walters Art Gallery; a member of the Visiting Committee, Fogg Art Museum, Harvard University; and a member of the Librarian's Advisory Council at the Library of Congress. She was on the editorial boards for the *Gazette des Beaux Arts* and *Art News*, and was a Board member for the College Art Association and the Index Society as well. At the time of her death on May 10, 1950, friends and colleagues had been preparing a testimonial volume, later published as *Studies in Art and Literature for Belle da Costa Greene* (Princeton, 1954). Her ashes are in Kenisco Cemetery, Valhalla, New York.

Biographical listings and obituaries–*Dictionary of American Biography*, 4th Suppl.; *Notable American Women* 2 (Dorothy Miner and Anne Lyon Haight); [Obituary]. *New York Times*, May 12, 1950; [Obituary]. *Publishers Weekly* 157:2560 (June 10, 1950). **Books and articles about the biographee**–*Art News* 47:13 (Nov. 1948); "Belle of the Books." *Time*, April 11, 1949; Buhler, Curt F. "Belle da Costa Greene." *Speculum*, July 1957. (Reprinted in his *Early Books and Manuscripts: Forty Years of Research*, 1973); *First Quarter Century of the Pierpont Morgan Library: A Retrospective Exhibition in Honor of Belle da Costa Greene*, 1954; Louchheim, Aline B. "The Morgan Library and Miss Greene." *New York Times*, April 17, 1949; Miner, Dorothy, ed. *Studies in Art and Literature for Belle da Costa Greene*. Princeton, N.J.: Princeton University Press, 1954.

—MARILYN DOMAS WHITE

GRIFFIN, APPLETON PRENTISS CLARK (1852-1926)

Appleton Prentiss Clark Griffin was born in Wilton, New Hampshire, the son of Moses Porter and Charlotte Helen Clark Griffin, on July 24, 1852. A descendant of Roger Conant and Samuel Appleton, prominent figures in seventeenth century Massachusetts, Griffin was educated in the schools of Medford, Massachusetts, and with private tutors. On October 23, 1878, he married Emily Call Osgood of Cambridge, Massachusetts. Their children were Mary Florence, George Appleton, Thomas Sergeant, Perry, and Grace Gardner. Grace, who died in 1950, was a prominent bibliographer in her own right, having edited *Writings on American History* from 1906 to 1940.

At age thirteen, Griffin joined the staff of the Boston Public Library as a "runner" on December 1, 1865. As of May 1, 1868, his salary was $260 per year, and as of 1869, he was an "assistant" in the Shelf Department. In 1872, he became assistant custodian in that department and three years later

was appointed custodian of the shelves, which title he held until 1889. In this position, he reported annually to the librarian as to the number of volumes added, withdrawn, and missing. While this was generally a routine matter, he reported to Mellen Chamberlain in 1882 that: "Some embarrassment has been felt in locating the books in their classifications, owing to the limited shelf room in many sections of the library."

On April 13, 1889, he was given a second title, that of custodian of the building. In December of that year, when the Library was experimenting with evening service, Griffin was assigned to work two evenings per week, for which he was paid four dollars per evening. The following month he was assigned to Sunday service, for which he was paid $9.33 per day. The following year, he was put in charge of the combined book and ordering department. While in charge of the ordering department, he selected most of the thousands of volumes which the Library purchased.

By 1891, he was evidently a high-ranking member of the Library's administration, for, during June and July of that year, he served as clerk pro tem at four meetings of the trustees. On April 22, 1892, he was appointed keeper of books. Less than a month later, on May 10, he presented to the trustees a request for a salary increase. On June 28, he received a $500 raise to $2,750. This was slightly more than ten times his compensation of 24 years earlier.

He remained at the Boston Public Library until October 1, 1894, when he left under what appear to be strained circumstances, for, on September 5, the following entry appears in the trustees' minutes:

> Voted that owing to the re-organization of the Library Service, the position of Assistant Keeper of Bates Hall for evening service be discontinued on the first of October, 1894. Ordered that Mr. A. P. C. Griffin, the incumbent of said office, be notified that his services will not be required after that date.

This action appears to have created somewhat of a stir, as evidenced by 44 copies of an undated petition to the trustees on Griffin's behalf, which today repose in the archives of the Library. The petition, signed by such prominent Bostonians as Edward Everett Hale, D. C. Heath, and John F. Fitzgerald, began:

> We respectfully request your honorable body to reinstate Mr. A. P. C. Griffin in the Staff of the Boston Public Library, believing that his special qualifications fit him to be a great help to enquirers in Bates Hall,—a fact to which many of us can testify from our own experience,—and that his presence in the Library would be of real service to the public.

It goes on to note that when Griffin left the Library he "had a more intimate acquaintance with the library books, their nature, number, and special value, and of the whereabouts of historical treasures than any man now living," and refers to his "meritorious work during twenty-nine years of continuous service." It appears from the trustees' minutes that this petition was never acted upon.

It was during these years in Boston that he began compiling the bibliographies for which he is best known. Frederick W. Ashley said of his Boston days, "In the course of fifteen years, he stood among the best bibliographers in the country." His publications, which occupy some four pages of the *National Union Catalogue, Pre-1956 Imprints*, pertain to a wide variety of subjects. John Addington Symonds praised his elaborate list on the Renaissance, which appeared in the *Bulletin of the Boston Public Library* between July 1879 and January 1882. His bibliographical account of the discovery of the Mississippi was published in the *Magazine of American History* in March and April of 1883.

Griffin spent the period 1895-1896 at the Boston Athenaeum, where he compiled the *Catalogue of the Washington Collection in the Boston Athenaeum*, published in 1897. For a few months late in 1896, he was keeper of manuscripts of the New York Public Library, during which time he began to organize and calendar the collections. He resigned early in 1897.

On August 27 of that year, he was appointed assistant librarian of the Library of Congress by John Russell Young (q.v.). On that very day, the Library was in the process of moving to its own building from its overcrowded quarters in the Capitol. David C. Mearns, who joined the staff in 1918 and was a contemporary of Griffin, notes that Griffin's first duties were that of principal assistant in the main reading room and that, when he came to Washington, he was "one of the most experienced and most proficient technicians in the country."

In 1900, upon the creation of the Division of Bibliography, Griffin was appointed chief bibliographer. Here he was in his glory. During the eight years in which he occupied this position, he published over fifty bibliographies. Broad subject fields in which he compiled several lists were labor relations, banking, elections, Negroes, and islands throughout the world. He is best remembered for his *Bibliography of American Historical Societies*. The revised and enlarged second edition of this monumental work was published as the second volume of the 1905 annual report of the American Historical Association.

On August 14, 1908, upon the death of Ainsworth Rand Spofford (q.v.), Griffin became chief assistant librarian. In this position, he was both head of reference services and chief selection officer of the Library.

In addition to his daily duties, he also found time to participate in scholarly societies and activities. He was elected to the Colonial Society of Massachusetts on February 3, 1896, and to honorary membership in Phi Beta Kappa at Brown University in 1909. He was also a member of the Columbia Historical Society (Washington) and the Bunker Hill Monument Association. The sketches of Philip Freneau, Robert Fulton, Thomas Gage, and Nathanael Greene which appeared in *Appleton's Cyclopedia of American Biography* were from his pen. He also served as a member of the Honorary Fiftieth Anniversary Committee of the American Library Association in 1926.

In 1922, when Griffin reached retirement age, Herbert Putnam (q.v.), then Librarian of Congress, appealed to the Classification Board to permit Griffin to continue in his position, as allowed under the law in exceptional cases. Citing Griffin's lifetime of service to libraries, Putnam wrote: "He has acquired a knowledge of the literature required in research, such as could not be duplicated except in a like period by a man of like ability and persistence." Putnam also noted that "he is indeed the foremost expert in that regard in any library in the United States." The Classification Board subsequently agreed, and Griffin's term was extended for a two-year period on two occasions.

Griffin was still actively serving as chief assistant librarian when on Friday afternoon, April 16, 1926, he died at his home in Washington at the age of 74, after a brief illness. Following services at the Church of the Epiphany in that city, he was buried in Mount Auburn Cemetery in Cambridge, Massachusetts.

Herbert Putnam, in a statement released to the press on that occasion, recalled Griffin's "absorption of the four great research libraries with which he had been associated, his industry, and unusual 'flair' for the 'submerged' in source material." Thus ended the 61-year career of the man of whom David C. Mearns would later remark: "He was said to be a wonder, and he was."

Biographical listings and obituaries—*Dictionary of American Biography* 7 (Frederick W. Ashley); [Obituary]. *Library Journal* 51:435 (May 1, 1926); [Obituary]. Washington, D.C. *Evening Star*, April 17, 1926, p. 7; *Who Was Who in America* I (1897-1942). **Books and articles about the biographee**—Colonial Society of Massachusetts. *Publications* 26:450 (1924-1926); Lydenberg, Harry Miller. *History of the New York Public Library*. New York: New York Public Library, 1923; Mearns, David Chambers. *The Story Up to Now: The Library of Congress, 1800-1946*. Washington, D.C.: GPO, 1947. **Primary sources and archival materials**—Boston Athenaeum. *Annual Report of the Librarian*. (appropriate years); Boston Public Library. *Annual Report* and unpublished minutes of the Trustees' Meetings; U.S. Library of Congress. *Annual Report of the Librarian of Congress* (1897-1926). Clippings and drafts relative to his bibliographic endeavors, memos to the Librarian of Congress while chief bibliographer, and a volume of copies of his outgoing correspondence for the years 1908-1917 are in the Central Services Division of the Library of Congress.

—JOHN D. HASKELL, JR.

GRIGGS, LILLIAN BAKER (1876-1955)

Lillian Baker was born in Anderson, South Carolina, on January 8, 1876, the daughter of William F. and Cora Wilhite Baker. She attended Agnes Scott College (1892-1895), and on April 21, 1897, married Dr. Alfred Flournoy Griggs by whom she had one child, Alfred, Jr., in 1899. After the death of her husband in 1908, Griggs entered the Carnegie Library School, Atlanta (now Emory), and received her certificate in the spring of 1911. Her career was to encompass both academic and public librarianship, but she would be chiefly concerned with advancing the cause of libraries in North Carolina and the Southeast.

Upon receiving her certificate, Griggs became librarian of the Durham (North Carolina) Public Library, where she served for the next thirteen years (1911-1924). She was North Carolina's first professionally trained public librarian, although academic librarians such as Louis Round Wilson were already having a decided impact upon the state. During her time in Durham, she was very successful in enlisting the citizens in the library cause. Believing that every city library should also be open to all residents of the county, Griggs began such loans from the library even before she persuaded county officials to provide the funding to make that service official. She organized and classified the collections, established a branch library in the mill district, circulated small collections to the county school, developed a high school library, and helped start a library for the Negroes of Durham. Rural library service, which was important to her, was the theme of her first article in the *North Carolina Library Bulletin* (March 1915). She would return to this theme subsequently, but her stress was always upon the human contact. As she indicated at the ALA Seattle Conference (1925), "a successful applicant to me for a position in a public library is one who loves people first and books second."

The vigor with which this "small lady with delicate features and a bubbling sense of humor" made an impact upon library services in Durham led to her election as treasurer (1913-1917) and then twice as president of the North Carolina Library Association (1918-1919 and 1931-1933). In 1918, she joined the Library War Service of the American Library Association, where she served as supervisor of library service to Naval and Coast Guard Stations on the Gulf Coast, and the following year, she was in charge of mail lending and hospital library service for the army of occupation in Coblentz, Germany.

Returning to Durham late in 1919, Griggs entered into the final planning for a new library building, for which she had secured Carnegie funds prior to her leave of absence for war service. After its completion in 1921, she persuaded the Kiwanis Club to provide money for a bookmobile to extend library service to rural citizens. This was reportedly the first bookmobile in North Carolina and one of the first in the South.

From 1924 to 1930 Griggs served as director of the North Carolina Library Commission, where she guided the establishment of public libraries in counties throughout the state. In recognition of her leadership in developing public libraries in North Carolina, she was elected president of the National League of Library Commissions in 1929. When North Carolina librarians at their 1927 conference formed a Citizen's Library Movement to help local people develop and improve public libraries, Griggs prepared the groundwork for the movement. Through her work on the Julius Rosenwald Fund's Advisory Committee, Griggs had a wide influence on the planning for library development in the South. During the summer of 1930, she lectured at a library institute for Negro librarians supported by the Rosenwald Fund at Spelman College.

At the peak of her public library career, when she was at the helm of North Carolina public library service, Griggs turned her professional expertise to academic librarianship, giving a new direction to her career. In 1930, she accepted an offer to become librarian of the new Woman's College of Duke University, a challenge to build a college library from "book one" into an undergraduate collection. Although public librarians continued to seek her advice, Griggs began to refer to undergraduate student service as her "theme-song."

Griggs's innovative drive immediately prompted her to establish the Booklover's Room—a type of browsing room—where "poetry, drama and music evenings" were held for the students. She summed up the philosophy behind her Booklover's Room and her insistence on open stacks in a reply to Louis Round Wilson's request for her suggestions on how a college library serves the college: "[it should] infuse the love of books and libraries into the heart of the average student to such an extent that a library will be necessary to his contented life." Open stacks and special library service programs for undergraduates that Griggs developed at the Woman's College Library had a direct impact on Duke University's director of libraries, B. Harvie Branscomb, in the development of his study of college libraries, *Teaching with Books* (1940). In addition to her contributions in developing students' extracurricular reading, giving them easy access to the collection, and promoting their interest in the arts, Griggs used her own extensive knowledge of books to build an excellent undergraduate collection.

In 1931, when she was elected a second time to be president of the North Carolina Library Association, a public librarian wrote to Griggs that it was a real source of gratification to have her once more "a sort of supreme court for the state in library affairs." In 1933, she became president of the Southeastern Library Association. For many years she served on the Council of the American Library Association. She worked with the University of North Carolina librarian, Robert Downs, on a state planning committee for libraries, and she served on a committee with Susan Grey Akers, dean of the UNC library school, to plan a library science program for the consolidated University of North Carolina in 1933. She also took active part in numerous other groups, such as the North Carolina Literary and Historical Society, North Carolina Folklore Society, League of Women Voters, Durham Women's Club, and book clubs. She retired in 1949 at the age of 73, and she died six years later on April 11, 1955.

Throughout her varied career, first in public and then in academic librarianship, Griggs held to the central theme of taking books and the love of books to everyone, and she inspired those around her to develop similar goals. College library browsing rooms and the need for rural public library service were topics for speeches at library meetings, some of which were published. Evelyn Harrison said that Griggs had "a talent for friendship which knew neither race, creed, or rank . . . her keen sense of humor made her a delightful companion and a friend to be treasured, a rare personality."

Biographical listings and obituaries—[Obituary]. *Library Journal* 80:2218 (Oct. 15, 1955); *Who's Who in Library Service*, 1st ed., 2nd ed. **Books and articles about the biographee**—[Biographical sketch]. *North Carolina Library Bulletin* 8:2 (Dec. 1930); [Biographical sketch]. *North Carolina Libraries* 13:29 (Nov. 1954); Harrison, Evelyn. "Lillian Baker Griggs." *Library Notes* (Duke University) 31:9-10 (Nov. 1955). **Primary sources and archival materials**—Correspondence and other unpublished manuscripts are in the Duke University Archives and the Southern Historical Collections of the University of North Carolina at Chapel Hill.

—BETTY YOUNG

GUILD, REUBEN ALDRIDGE (1822-1899)

Reuben Aldridge Guild was born May 4, 1822, in West Dedham (now Westwood), Massachusetts, the son of Reuben Aldridge and Olive Morse Guild. Reuben was the second of eleven children and his childhood homelife appears to have been happy, secure, and, as he himself said, wholesome. His father, a blacksmith by trade, was also an officer in the militia, frequently a committee-man for the district school, a deacon of the Unitarian Church for forty years, and, for many years, the superintendent of the Sunday School. His mother was reportedly intelligent, cheerful, and loving. For several summers before

her marriage, she had been a teacher at the district school and, undoubtedly, Reuben got much of his dedication to learning from his mother.

The younger Guild was educated in Dedham and West Roxbury as preparation for entering a business career. Before the age of 17, he worked in a country store near home and, at 17, he went to Boston, where he worked two years for Charles Warren & Co., dry and domestic goods dealers. Brought up as a Unitarian, in 1840, Reuben became a Baptist and decided to dedicate himself to the ministry, whereupon he left business for further education.

Guild's education included Day's Academy (1840-1841) and Worcester Academy (1841-1843). Undoubtedly influenced by a number of instructors who were Brown University graduates (including Charles Coffin Jewett [q.v.]), Guild entered Brown in 1843 and was graduated in 1847 with the sixth honor and as a member of Phi Beta Kappa. In 1850, he was awarded his master's degree from Brown and, in 1874, he received an honorary LL.D. from Shurtleff College, Upper Alton, Illinois.

Upon graduation in 1847, Guild was offered a position as assistant librarian at Brown under Charles Coffin Jewett, who had been librarian since 1841. Foregoing his intention to enter the ministry, he accepted and began work in September 1847. In March 1848, Jewett left Brown to become librarian of the Smithsonian Institution and Guild was offered Jewett's position. In an era when men became ship captains at ages a good deal less than 26, Guild's appointment was not unusual and, as Guild himself pointed out much later, "having had a business experience of five years in a large dry goods store in Boston and in a variety store in my native town, having had charge of a book store at the Worcester Academy and been for two years Librarian of the United Brothers Society while a student in college," he was prepared to undertake the job.

The library at that time consisted of fewer than 20,000 volumes, half of which were cataloged. For part of the time up to 1860, Guild had an assistant but, from 1860 to 1877, he ran the library single-handedly. Along with the regular library business, this included helping to plan the new library, which opened in the spring of 1878. From 1878 until his retirement in 1893, Guild had the services of one assistant who, for the most part, handled circulation. On the other hand, Guild, because of the move to the new library and the growing collection, felt it necessary to establish a new cataloging system and, from 1878 to 1893, cataloged about 48,000 volumes. While doing this, as Guild notes in his final report to the Library Committee, he also had to handle all ordering, audit and, except at the end, pay all bills, record all accessions, acknowledge all gifts, conduct a large correspondence, see to the binding of books and periodicals, examine the library, and make monthly reports.

Guild's energy must have been boundless, for his activities went beyond his work as librarian. He was instrumental, with publisher Charles B. Norton (q.v.), in convoking the first librarians' convention in September 1853. As a member of the Business Committee, along with the Reverend Mr. Osgood of New York, he was charged with the production of a "popular library manual which shall embody the most important information upon the chief points in question." The result of this (and unfortunately one of the few practical results of that convention) was Guild's *Librarian's Manual*, published in 1858. Whether this met the librarians' need for a manual is debatable, as the work is not a manual of library practice. Rather, it is an annotated bibliography of bibliographies concerning both books and libraries, with a lengthy section of sketches of important libraries of the day. Guild was also appointed to a three-man committee on permanent organization, but this idea was to bear no fruit until 1876.

In 1876, Guild was again on hand for the convention of librarians held in Philadelphia that did produce concrete results, among them the founding of the American Library Association. Guild was elected one of three secretaries of the convention and he took active part in various debates. Continuing his interest in fostering cooperation among librarians, he attended the first International Conference of Librarians in London in 1877, serving on the Council. In recognition of this, he was elected honorary member of the Library Association of the United Kingdom.

During his long years of residence in Providence, Guild was active with numerous civic, religious, and cultural organizations. His activities included: member of the Common Council of Providence, seven years; member of the school committee, usually as secretary, fifteen years; secretary of the Brown University Alumni Association, fifteen years; president and essayist of the Rhode Island Baptist Sunday School Convention, seventeen years; secretary of the Rhode Island Baptist Education Society, five years; member of the Rhode Island Historical Society; member of the American Antiquarian Society; and secretary for the preliminary meetings for the establishment of a free public library in Providence (1871-1872).

In addition to these activities, Guild edited several volumes of letters and sermons and produced many brief biographies and historical sketches. His most important works were *Librarian's Manual* (1858), *Life, Times and Correspondence of James Manning* (1864), *History of Brown University* (1867), and *Early History of Brown University* (1897).

While Guild was a very busy man, he managed, with personal warmth and concern, to influence

many generations of Brown students. In his fairly extensive correspondence with former students, one can sense a genuine feeling of appreciation toward him. Upon Guild's death, William Carey Poland, a Brown professor, reminisced that in his four years as a Brown student (1864-1868), he remembered Guild as "cheery and helpful. He was generous and unselfish to us all. He seemed to enter easily into our ways of looking at things. He gave us aid in our reading. He could understand us, and always treated our immaturity with consideration." Poland remembered another student at graduation remarking, "Well, after all, there is no man to whom I feel more indebted for uniform courtesy, kindness and helpfulness, than to Reuben A. Guild." While these comments came in a eulogy, they were undoubtedly genuine. George W. Dow, a former Brown student, wrote in a letter (January 22, 1895) to Guild's successor, "If that good natured, genial librarian is still living (R. A. Guild) tell him I would be glad to give him a good hearty shake of the hand were he within reach."

Guild married Jane Clifford Hunt on December 17, 1849, and they had six children, two of whom died during childhood; however, very little can be discovered of Guild's home and family life. The fact that one daughter wrote glowingly of her father shortly after his death suggests that his qualities were recognized at home as well as on campus. Reuben Aldridge Guild died May 13, 1899.

Reuben A. Guild's accomplishments were many and substantial, although no single thing he did constitutes a monumental achievement. He was instrumental in early library cooperative efforts, he was active and influential in community affairs, he wrote and edited many useful works, and he helped to build and organize the Library of one of America's leading universities during a critical time in its growth.

Biographical listings and obituaries—*Dictionary of American Biography* 8 (George H. Genzmer); *National Cyclopaedia of American Biography* 3; *Who Was Who in America*, Historical Volume (1607-1896). **Books and articles about the biographee**—American Historical Society, New York. *Colonial Families*. New York: The Society, 1925; Bronson, Walter C. *The History of Brown University, 1764-1914*. Providence, R.I.: Brown University, 1914; King, Henry M. *Memorial Discourse on Reuben Aldridge Guild*. Providence, R.I.: Press of F. H. Townsend, 1899(?); Poland, William C. *Reuben Aldridge Guild, LL.D., Librarian of Brown University*. Providence, R.I., 1900. **Primary sources and archival materials**—Guild's papers are in the John Hay Library, Brown University.

—JONATHAN S. TRYON

HADLEY, CHALMERS (1872-1958)

Chalmers Hadley was born on September 3, 1872, the son of Evan and Ella Quinn Hadley in Indianapolis. Of Quaker stock, Evan Hadley was a physician and educator who paid close attention to his son's education. As a result, Chalmers attended public schools in Indianapolis and then earned his B.L. degree from Earlham College (Richmond, Indiana) in 1896. Chalmers Hadley had developed a love for books and reading during his youth, and he spent a number of years after graduation from Earlham working with several different Philadelphia newspapers. In 1905, he made the fateful decision to enter library work and attended Melvil Dewey's (q.v.) New York State Library School in Albany. It was clear that Hadley was destined for a successful career, as was testified to by his younger (and soon to be famous) roommates, Charles H. Compton (q.v.) and Louis F. Bailey. Compton noted that Hadley was a stimulating and cultured speaker who always conducted himself as a gentleman.

Upon graduation in 1906, Hadley was appointed secretary and state organizer of the Indiana Library Commission. After serving for three years with considerable distinction in that post, he was appointed executive secretary of the American Library Association, a position which he held until 1911.

It was in 1911, when Hadley accepted the post as director of the Denver Public Library, that he began his most significant period of service to the profession. At Denver (1911-1924), and as director of the Cincinnati Public Library (1924-1946), Hadley aggressively fought to extend public library services to the general population. His achievements were extraordinary. In Denver, he guided the construction of nine branch libraries and placed dozens of smaller collections in community centers, fire stations, the schools, and even department stores. In Cincinnati, he successfully gained support for the establishment of some thirteen new branches, pioneered in the development of bookmobile services, and substantially upgraded the staff. In the words of Thomas Jones, the president of Earlham College, "with high integrity, attention to detail, and a devotion to the arts, he became an educator, not only of individuals, but whole communities." Upon his retirement in 1946, he was considered one of the most accomplished public librarians in the nation.

From the outset of his career in librarianship, Hadley was very active in professional affairs. He served as the president of the League of Library Commissioners (1907-1908); president of the Colorado Library Association (1914); president of the American Library Association (1919-1920); president of the Ohio Library Association (1925); and president of the Ohio Historical and Philosophical Society (1945). During World War I, he served actively with various War Library Programs and was a volunteer in the Library War Service during 1918-1919.

Hadley was an extremely literate and avid book collector who counted among his intimate friends many of the best-known authors of his day, including Christopher Morley, James Whitcomb Riley, and the illustrator George Ade. An informed and avid patron of the arts, he gave generously of his time and money to cultural affairs in Colorado, Indiana, New York, and Ohio. His great knowledge of literature, especially poetry, and his widespread cultural activities were acknowledged when he was awarded honorary Litt.D. degrees by the University of Denver in 1914 and Earlham in 1952.

Chalmers Hadley rounded out his professional involvement by contributing frequently to the literature of librarianship. Among his many writings, a book on public library buildings (ALA, 1926), and his biography of John Cotton Dana (q.v.) (ALA, 1943) are considered the most significant. Hadley was also interested in library education; his article entitled "What Library Schools Can Do for the Profession" was published in the *ALA Bulletin* (July 1912).

In 1917, Chalmers Hadley married Edna Florence Hendrie, the daughter of a Denver manufacturer, and they lived happily together until his death on May 11, 1958. Hadley's life in librarianship was characterized, in the words of Charles H. Compton, by "a love of books, discriminating taste, appreciation of the arts, music and theatre, and delight in the beauty of nature." His total involvement in these matters reflected his belief that libraries represented an essential part of the cultural life of the community.

Biographical listings and obituaries—*National Cyclopaedia of American Biography* 33; [Obituary]. *Library Journal* 83:1895 (June 15, 1958); [Obituary]. *Ohio Library Association Bulletin* 28:13 (July 1958); [Obituary]. *Wilson Library Bulletin* 33:14 (Sept. 1958); *Who Was Who in America* III (1951-1960); *Who's Who in Library Service*, 1st ed., 2nd ed. **Books and articles about the biographee**—"In Memory of Chalmers Hadley." *Guide Post* (Cincinnati Public Library) 33:1-30 (Nov. 1958). **Primary sources and archival materials**—The records of the Denver Public Library (1911-1924), the Cincinnati Public Library (1924-1946), and the American Library Association (especially 1919-1920) contain documents pertaining to Hadley's administration.

—MICHAEL H. HARRIS
—TRINA E. KING
—EDWARD D. STARKEY

HAINES, HELEN ELIZABETH (1872-1961)

Helen Elizabeth Haines was born in New York City on February 9, 1872, the eldest child of Benjamin Reeve and Mary Hodges Haines. Educated entirely by her mother and private tutors, she was fond later of quoting George Bernard Shaw's quip that his education was not interrupted by schooling. She was awarded the honorary Master of Arts degree from the University of Southern California in 1945.

To assist her mother in the support of a household that included four younger sisters, she accepted commissions as an indexer and author while she was still in her teens. Her first major publication was *The History of New Mexico from the Spanish Conquest to the Present Time, 1530-1890* (1891), which she described as a pot-boiler paid for by a short-lived publishing house. She also worked briefly as a secretary in an engineering firm. But a family friend, Mary Wright Plummer (q.v.), later director of the Pratt Institute Library School, put Haines's career back on the bibliographical track. Plummer, whom Helen Haines described as her "library godmother," secured a position for the young lady with R. R. Bowker (q.v.) in February 1892. Appreciating in a short time his new employee's unusual competence, Bowker quickly increased her responsibilities. In addition to assisting with the production of *Library Journal* and *Publishers' Weekly*, she was also assistant editor-in-charge of the *American Catalogue* for 1890-1895, associate indexer for the *Library Journal* index for 1876-1897, and assistant editor and compiler of *State Publications* and the *Annual Literary Index*. In 1896, she was appointed managing editor of *Library Journal*. A description of her Bowker years is provided in her article " 'Tis Fifty Years Since: Publishers' Weekly Office in an Earlier Day" (*Publishers' Weekly* 151:278-83, January 18, 1947.

One of her duties as editor of *Library Journal* was to act as recorder for the American Library Association and to compile, edit, and index its annual *Proceedings*, which were published as a special number of that periodical. She also served on ALA's Executive Board. Her charm and competence won for her many friends and admirers among both the "establishment" and the rank and file of her profession. In 1906, she was elected second vice-president of ALA. She also held offices in the New York State Library Association and was active in the New York City Library Club.

Haines's frail constitution was not equal to these demands. In 1906, she contracted tuberculosis. The usual curatives of the time were applied, as well as the more radical treatment of a sub-zero winter spent mostly outside in upstate New York. For a while her condition seemed improved, but, in April 1907, an abortive attempt to resume work convinced her that her career was ended. She resigned all her positions in March 1908, and, in the company of her mother and two of her sisters, she migrated west in search of a better climate and, with it, the possible recovery of her health. At this time, she was granted a lifetime pension by Andrew Carnegie (q.v.).

The family settled first in Ft. Collins, Colorado, but if its climate was salutary, the elevation was uncomfortable. And after New York City, Ft. Collins was perhaps too restful. At that time, Pasadena,

California, enjoyed the reputation as a haven for persons suffering from pulmonary diseases. It also offered the additional advantages of cultural activities and proximity to a large metropolis. Haines lived in Pasadena for over half a century in a modest but attractive cottage which she named "Pepper-Tree Nook."

Her recovery was tenuous at best. One of the hardest aspects of her strict regimen was the absolute necessity to do always less than she wanted. "How hellish it is," she wrote to a friend, "for a lively and ambitious person to be constantly tied up to damaged machinery." As her strength allowed, she renewed her former library interests and slowly began to participate in California library affairs. In 1909, her article "Library Legislation in California" appeared in *Library Journal* (34:167-8, April 1909) and the first of two articles on library periodicals in *Bulletin of Bibliography* (6:2-5, October 1909). In 1910, "Present Day Book Reviewing" was published in *The Independent* (69:1104-1106, November 7, 1910). That same year, her book review column "The Library Table" was begun, inaugurating an association with the Pasadena *News* and its successors that was to last for over forty years.

By 1914, she was well enough to give lectures on book selection, modern fiction, and the history of libraries and books to the training class of the Los Angeles Public Library. She became a full-time member of the faculty at about the same time that the training class was transformed into a library school. Her extensive bibliographical and professional experience, her impressive knowledge of literature, and her enthusiasm all fused in her teaching. Her contribution to the program was significant.

Haines also presented a series of public book talks for the Long Beach, Los Angeles, and Pasadena public libraries. She reviewed books in several newspapers and periodicals, including *Dial, Independent, Nation, New York Herald Tribune*, and *Saturday Review of Literature*, and she published articles about libraries, the book trade, and contemporary literature. These and still other activities shared a common theme: the promotion of the literary tradition of librarianship. Helen Haines was both sensitive and receptive to change, but she believed that librarianship should be book-centered, and for this reason, she was a vigorous critic of what she called the "mechanistic non-literary attitude" of the "new" library science which began its ascendancy in the 1920s.

But if she distrusted library scientists, she was no less dissatisfied with many of her more traditionally minded colleagues whose literary tastes she regarded as narrow and bigoted. This flaw was perhaps most clearly seen in their restrictive attitude toward contemporary fiction. Never one to avoid the controversial in a good cause, Miss Haines had made this genre her particular specialization, and she unceasingly urged librarians to be tolerant of and receptive to new types and tendencies in fiction. In 1923, Sydney B. Mitchell (q.v.) invited her to lecture on contemporary fiction to his book selection class at the University of California at Berkeley. The series was repeated in 1924 and 1926. In 1925, she prepared the course on book selection for the American Correspondence School of Librarianship offered by Gaylord Brothers of Syracuse, New York, and for several years, she revised the work of the students enrolled in this course. She also devised and directed the book selection course given by Columbia University's Home Study Department from 1928 to 1934.

As early as 1916, she had considered writing a book selection text modelled upon Josephus N. Larned's (q.v.) A Talk about Books (1897). The home study course provided a first step in that direction. Finally, in the early 1930s, she began composing Living with Books: The Art of Book Selection. At the urging of Dean Charles C. Williamson (q.v.) of Columbia University's School of Library Service, Columbia University Press awarded Haines a grant to support the writing of this work. Haines was a meticulous writer, and it was not until 1935 that Living with Books was published in the series "Studies in Library Service." The work received favorable reviews and quickly became a standard textbook and reference source in library schools and libraries throughout the United States. Its popularity rested in part upon its generally engaging style, a style that is indeed animated compared to the wooden prose of its nearest competitor—Francis K. W. Drury's (q.v.) Book Selection (1930). But reviews also mentioned favorably such features as the ripe judgment exhibited in her book lists and her modern and liberal attitude. The book's popularity called for several impressions.

Haines returned to teaching in the summer of 1936, presenting an extension course on "Current and Contemporary Literature" at UCLA. That same year and for several years thereafter, she taught book selection at the University of Southern California during the academic term and at Columbia University in the summer. However, she did not teach in 1938-1939, having been granted funds by Columbia University Press to write an analysis and appreciation of contemporary fiction. This study, What's in a Novel? (1942), was less successful than Living with Books, much to Haines's disappointment, for it was her favorite of the two. Had she elected to treat more fully the "great books" or the more sensational material of the period covered by her survey, instead of focusing on the less turbulent mainstream of contemporary fiction, sales would perhaps have been better. Reviews, while generally favorable, did refer to the middle-brow tastes of this work.

The continued popularity of Living with Books, on the other hand, encouraged Columbia University Press to provide Helen Haines with a royalty advance toward the preparation of a second edition. This task took three years. The new edition, which appeared in Haines's seventy-eighth year (1950), was extensively revised to reflect the profound changes in popular reading interests (or what she may have thought ought to be reading interests) brought about by world events of the war years. Most reviewers appreciated her attitude. However, it was probably inevitable in the early 1950s that her representation of divergent points of view, particularly political ones, should provoke some harsh criticism. Oliver Carlson's "A Slanted Guide to Library Selections" in The Freeman (2:239-242, January 14, 1952) charged that Living with Books in its second edition exhibited a strong pro-Soviet bias. Elinor S. Earle's "Reply to Carlson" in the ALA Bulletin (25:105-110, April 1952) provides an effective rebuttal, noting in particular Carlson's quoting and interpreting of passages from Living with Books out of context. Other than this defense, Haines received little support from her colleagues. She was probably not entirely surprised. Her disappointment in her colleagues' lack of what she regarded as appropriate advocacy of intellectual freedom was of long duration.

It is preferable to select as the finale to Haines's distinguished career her election to the 1951 Joseph W. Lippincott Award for outstanding achievement in librarianship. At the award ceremony in Chicago, Haines made a brief and moving speech, later published in Library Journal (76:1494-95, October 1, 1951). Her last years were marred by ill health, and she died in Altadena, California, on August 26, 1961.

Although burdened with a frail body, Haines was a lively and dynamic person, an effective public speaker, and by all accounts a master teacher. Her writing reflects her sharp intellect and wide-ranging interests. She possessed a delightful wit which emerges from some of her less formal publications. For several decades she was a leading exponent in this country of the school which held that librarians serving the general public should have broad, discriminating literary judgment and a personal knowledge of books. One effect of this philosophy was her criticism of censorship from within libraries. She was even more vigorously opposed to censorship from external sources. Through her writing and her work with such organizations as the California Library Association's Committee on Intellectual Freedom, which she helped found in 1940 and which she chaired for several years, she must be ranked as an influential advocate of intellectual freedom in this country during a difficult period.

Biographical listings and obituaries—[Obituary]. *College and Research Libraries* 23:72 (Jan. 1962); [Obituary]. *Library Journal* 86:3459 (Oct. 15, 1961); [Obituary]. *Publishers Weekly* 180:42 (Sept. 25, 1961); *Who's Who in Library Service*, 1st ed., 2nd ed. **Books and articles about the biographee**—Brewitt, Theodora R. "Helen E. Haines, a Sketch and Appreciation." *Bulletin of the California Library Association* 5:87-90 (March 1944); Harlan, Robert D. "Helen E. Haines." *Encyclopedia of Library and Information Science.* Allen Kent, Harold Lancour, Jay E. Daily, eds. New York: Marcel Dekker, 1973, Vol. 10, pp. 278-84; Hyers, Faith H. "Helen E. Haines." *Bulletin of Bibliography* 20:129-31 (Sept.-Dec. 1951); Moore, Everett T. "Innocent Librarians." *ALA Bulletin* 55:861-62 (Nov. 1961); Moore, Everett T. "The Intellectual Freedom Saga in California: The Experience of Four Decades." *California Librarian* 35:48-53, 55-57 (Oct. 1974); Sive, Mary R. "Helen E. Haines, 1872-1961, an Annotated Bibliography." *Journal of Library History* 5:146-64 (April 1970).

—ROBERT D. HARLAN

HALL, MARY EVELYN (1874-1956)

Born in Brooklyn on March 1, 1874, as one of five children of Charles C. and Rachel Willis Smith Hall, Mary E. Hall left Brooklyn for one year to attend Oberlin College in 1893-1894, then returned to attend Pratt Institute Library School. After her graduation in 1895, she accepted a position as reference assistant at Pratt Institute Free Library. At Pratt, she came into close professional contact with two persons she acknowledged as helping to shape her ideas about high school library service: Anne Carroll Moore (q.v.), an 1896 Pratt graduate who served as children's librarian at the Free Library before building a national reputation as chief of children's services for the New York Public Library, and Mary Wright Plummer (q.v.), director of the Institute's Library School and Free Library. (Plummer was probably as instrumental in the selection of Hall as librarian at Girls' High School, Brooklyn, in 1903 as she had been in the selection in 1900 of another Pratt graduate, Mary Kingsbury, as the first trained librarian to serve a public high school in the United States—Erasmus Hall, also in Brooklyn.) Hall remained as librarian of Girls' High School until her retirement in 1944.

The innovative library program at Girls' High School and Hall's creativity, drive, and organizational ability gradually became known through her activities in New York librarians' and teachers' associations; her speeches at state and national library and education association conferences; articles she published in library periodicals; and her extensive personal correspondence with school and public librarians, initiated as part of annual reports on high school library development that she prepared, first as chairman of a Committee on High School Libraries of the New York Library Association (1908-1912), and later as chairman of an identically named committee of the National Education Association Library Department (1911-1918).

In New York state, Hall expanded her promotion of school libraries from the New York Library Association to the New York State Teachers' Association, where she established a Library Section and became the Section's first president (1910-1911). Meanwhile, she had attended her first NEA conference in 1910. The next year, she was appointed chairman of the NEA Library Department Committee on High School Libraries, and the following year she was elected president of the Department. Her most significant NEA contributions to school library development occurred not through the Library Department, however, but through two important publications sponsored by other NEA groups. Hall's report, as chairman of a Committee on the Library and Its Equipment (of the English subcommittee of the influential NEA Commission on the Reorganization of Secondary Education), was published in *The Reorganization of English in the Secondary Schools* (U.S. Bureau of Education, Bulletin 1917, no. 2). Much of the content of Hall's report was later incorporated in the first national standards for school libraries, *Standard Library Organization and Equipment for Secondary Schools of Different Sizes*, called the Certain Report after its chairman, C. C. Certain (q.v.). Hall served as a member of the joint National Education Association-North Central Association Committee that prepared the standards published by NEA in 1918 and ALA in 1920.

While busy with NEA activities, Hall helped form a Library Section in the National Council of Teachers of English, but its existence was short-lived (1913-1918). Much more significant was her role in helping to establish a School Library Section in the American Library Association, still in existence as the American Association of School Librarians. Hall served as the section's first president (1915-1916). Being concerned with the quality of library services, she wrote several articles, among them "A Day in a Modern School Library" (*Bulletin of High Points in the Work of the High Schools in New York City*, May 1919) and "The Development of the Modern High School Library" (*Library Journal*, September 1915).

Short, plainly dressed, and nondescript, Hall hardly looked like a leader, but leader she was. Those who knew her mentioned her vivid, colorful personality, her energy, and her driving force in work and play. Martha Wilson dedicated her compilation of *Selected Articles on School Library Experience* (H. W. Wilson, 1925), one of the first comprehensive books on school library methods, to Mary E. Hall, "Dean of High School Librarians, the guide and inspiration of us all, whose enthusiasm has been a flame to kindle many lesser torches, whose creative genius and organizing ability have ever been most generously devoted to the cause of school libraries." Lucile F. Fargo (q.v.), like Wilson a leader in school library development, claimed in her basic text, *The Library in the School* (4th ed., ALA, 1947), that "the name of Mary E. Hall stands out as the number one pioneer in the school library field." Hall, with Martha Wilson, Lucile Fargo, and five others, was awarded honorary membership in the American Association of School Librarians in 1947 for pioneering work in school librarianship. The citation noted that she had made the library of Girls' High School a demonstration library to which administrators and librarians from all parts of the country turned when establishing other school libraries, and that through her correspondence, lectures, and work in NEA and ALA she had been a constant inspiration to others (ALA *Proceedings*, 1947 conference). Not mentioned was her role in establishing the very association that honored her, the American Association of School Librarians, and her contribution to the first national standards for school libraries. She died on November 7, 1956.

Biographical listings and obituaries—*Who's Who in Library Service*, 1st ed., 2nd ed. **Primary sources and archival materials**—Letters of Mary E. Hall to Mildred C. Batchelder (Nov. 18, 1944-May 9, 1947) are located in the ALA Archives at the University of Illinois (Urbana-Champaign).

—PATRICIA B. POND

HANSON, JAMES CHRISTIAN MEINICH (1864-1943)

In an obituary of J. C. M. Hanson in *Library Journal*, Pierce Butler (q.v.) wrote,

it is probably safe to say that in our time no other single individual has exerted a stronger and more immediate influence on the daily routines of so many working librarians and library users. . . . Every person who uses a Library of Congress card or one prepared according to the A.L.A. *Cataloging Rules* is a direct beneficiary of Mr. Hanson's bibliographical and administrative genius.

Jens Christian Meinich Hansen was born on March 13, 1864, in Sørheim, Norway, 158 miles northwest of Oslo. He was the second son of eight children of Gunnerius and Eleonore Röberg Hansen, and his father was a government official and landowner of middle-class means. Hanson's mother's half-brother, Hans Röberg, who was living in Decorah, Iowa, at the time, had offered to educate one of the Hansen male children in the preparatory course at Luther College in Decorah. In 1873, Jens Hansen (age nine) was sent to Decorah with a Norwegian Lutheran minister who was returning to Iowa from Norway. His forename Jens was transformed by his young American friends to the nickname Jim and later formalized as James; also, his surname was Americanized from Hansen to Hanson. In later years, he consistently initialized his forenames, and was known formally as J. C. M. Hanson.

In 1874, Hanson enrolled in the Preparatory Department of Luther College. Hanson's parents had originally planned for him to return to Norway after he completed the three-year preparatory course; but in 1877, Hanson failed to complete the final examinations. Through the recommendations of the college authorities, Hanson's parents allowed him to complete the course the following year and to remain for the four-year college course. He received his A.B. degree in 1882.

Upon completion of this degree, Hanson had originally planned to follow some of his friends and former countrymen by going to the Dakotas, but a chance meeting with the Reverend U. V. Koren, president of the Norwegian Lutheran Church, caused him to go to Concordia Theological Seminary in St. Louis to pursue a degree in divinity. After two years, however, he decided that he felt no personal call to the ministry, though he remained deeply religious throughout his life.

Although Hanson did not complete his final year at the Seminary, his first employment was nonetheless church-related. In the fall of 1884, he was appointed principal and teacher at the parochial school of Our Saviour's Church in Chicago, a Norwegian Lutheran institution. He also served as *klokker* and superintendent of the Sunday School for Our Saviour's during the four years he was to spend in Chicago on this assignment. He supplemented his income during this period by teaching English to adult Scandinavians at the Montefiore Evening School, which was operated by the Chicago Board of Education, and during the summer months, by pitching for baseball teams in the Chicago area.

In the fall of 1888, Hanson enrolled for graduate study for one year at Cornell University. In 1889, he was awarded the Andrew D. White Fellowship in history and political science, which allowed him to continue for a second year. During his two years at Cornell, he studied under Charles Kendall Adams and Moses Coit Tyler. He also met and was influenced by George William Harris, the librarian at Cornell, who is said to have determined Hanson's choice of librarianship as a career. Hanson was as well a pitcher for the Cornell baseball team and an active member of the Kappa Sigma fraternity. After his second year of graduate study, Hanson again had to seek employment because of a lack of funds. Pierce Butler says that Hanson had a choice between an instructorship at a college in Arkansas—teaching history and coaching the baseball team—and an appointment to the Newberry Library (*Library Quarterly*, April 1934).

Hanson returned to Chicago in 1890 to accept the appointment as a cataloger at the Newberry Library, which had been newly organized under William Frederick Poole (q.v.), former librarian of the Chicago Public Library. Hanson was exposed to a variety of library operations under Poole's direction, with his primary responsibilities being those of a cataloger. In this capacity, he used Charles A. Cutter's (q.v.) *Rules for a Dictionary Catalogue.* Charles Martel (q.v.), who was later to work under Hanson at the Library of Congress, joined the staff of the Newberry Library in 1892. Hanson also had the opportunity to work with George Watson Cole (q.v.), E. H. Anderson (q.v.), George E. Wire (q.v.), and William S. Merrill (q.v.) during his four years at the Newberry. Also during this period, he married one of his former parochial school students, Sarah Nelson, on November 26, 1892. Five children were to result from their marriage.

In 1893, one of Hanson's former Cornell teachers, Charles Kendall Adams, who had since become president of the University of Wisconsin, offered Hanson the position of chief cataloger for the University of Wisconsin libraries. Hanson accepted the position and was to remain in Madison for five years. In choosing a classification system for the Library, Hanson assisted the librarian, Walter McMynn Smith, in selecting Charles A. Cutter's *Expansive Classification.* As the final expansion of Cutter's system was not completed at this point, the Sixth Expansion or Classification had to be used and expanded locally. At this point, Hanson developed a modified outline and different notation for Cutter's system; however, he did not employ either of these changes in the application and expansion of EC at the University of Wisconsin. These possible modifications were to be of significance in his next professional position.

In 1897, the Library of Congress was involved in several major changes: the new main building was finally completed and ready for occupation; Ainsworth Rand Spofford (q.v.), the Librarian of Congress since 1864, retired (to become assistant librarian); and the administrative staff was being greatly expanded and reorganized. The new Librarian of Congress, John Russell Young (q.v.), was seeking a head for the Catalog Department. As previous appointments to the administrative staff had come from the East and the South, it was politically necessary to choose someone from the West or Midwest. President Andrew D. White of Cornell University recommended Hanson to Young, and on September 1, 1897, Hanson became chief of LC's Catalog Department. Hanson describes his early years at the Library of Congress in an article entitled "The Library of Congress and Its New Catalogue" in *Essays Offered to Herbert Putnam* [q.v.], (Yale University Press, 1929):

> The situation found by the writer on taking charge September 1, 1897, was not particularly encouraging. There were between 750,000 and 800,000 volumes in sore need of recataloguing and reclassification, great quantities of new books

pouring in, no shelf list or official catalogue, no furniture or equipment, and a force consisting of three holdovers from the old *regime,* respectively fifty, sixty-eight, and seventy-six years old, wedded to the old system and wholly out of touch with recent library development.

During his first year at the Library, Hanson had his former colleague at the Newberry Library, Charles Martel, appointed as chief classifier.

Hanson was directly involved in or responsible for at least five significant developments during his thirteen years at the Library of Congress (1897-1910): the Library of Congress Classification, the Library of Congress subject headings, the new catalog of the Library of Congress, the form and system of distribution of printed catalog cards, and the formulation of new cataloging rules.

Young charged Hanson and Martel with developing a new classification system for the Library of Congress, which was still using a modified version of the system devised by Thomas Jefferson (q.v.). Hanson and Martel investigated the major published schemes, especially Melvil Dewey's (q.v.) *Decimal Classification* (then in its fifth edition) and Cutter's *Expansive Classification.* The *Decimal Classification* was rejected because both Martel and Spofford disliked its notation and because Dewey refused to allow any major changes in his system.

However, Cutter's *Expansive Classification* influenced the new LC classification in two ways: first, the outline to the Sixth Expansion of the *Expansive Classification* was used by Hanson in developing the outline for LC Classification; second, the Seventh Expansion of Class Z, Book Arts, was used by Martel as the basis for Class Z, Bibliography and Library Science. The only major change in the order of the *Expansive Classification* in Hanson's revision was his placing the arts—fine arts, music, and literature—between the social sciences and the physical sciences. This change appeared in Hanson's notes developed at the University of Wisconsin Library. The more significant change was in the notation. Cutter's outline of classes consisted basically of subject classes using a single letter. The single letters were then to be expanded by adding one or two additional letters. Hanson's revision used the single letters but expanded them numerically to form the notation. This resulted in the mixed notation of letters and numbers that was to be used for LC Classification. By 1901, the notation was further expanded by using double instead of single letters. (A full discussion of Hanson's other accomplishments at the Library of Congress may be found in Edith Scott's University of Chicago dissertation, "J. C. M. Hanson and His Contributions to Twentieth Century Cataloging.")

Hanson's other major contribution of this period was his work with the 1908 Anglo-American cataloging rules. In 1900, he was appointed chairman of the ALA Publishing Board's Advisory Catalog Committee with the charge to revise and expand the ALA *Condensed Rules for Author and Title-Catalog of 1883*. Under Hanson's direction, it became the Committee on Cataloging Rules and attempted to reach some form of international consistency and agreement. The Committee was also expanded to be a joint committee of the American Library Association and the Library Association of the United Kingdom. William Warner Bishop (q.v.) describes Hanson's involvement (in the April 1934 *Library Quarterly*): "As chairman, Mr. Hanson had a difficult task in reconciling diverse points of view and really different interests. After several years of study he took the American draft to England, where in long and sometimes painful sessions the various principles were studied and differences reconciled." When *Catalog Rules: Author and Title Entries* (commonly referred to as the Anglo-American rules of 1908) was published, there were only eight differences of rules between the American and British versions.

In 1910, Hanson left the Library of Congress to return to Chicago to become the associate director of the University of Chicago Libraries. In this position, he was the highest ranking librarian at the University of Chicago, which was then following the academic tradition of appointing a scholar (not a professional librarian) as the director of libraries. Dr. Ernest D. Burton, head of the Department of New Testament Theology, was appointed director. At Chicago, Hanson attempted to convert a departmentalized system of decentralized collections into a functioning centralized system. His mixed successes in this regard are discussed in A. Th. Dorf's article (April 1934 *Library Quarterly*) entitled "The University of Chicago Libraries," which closes with the following statement:

> Within the power delegated to him, and with the possibilities for development which had to be adhered to during his tenure of office, Mr. Hanson accomplished something that in the history of the University of Chicago should never be forgotten. His work revealed not only a high order of skill, but a profound grasp of the problems of library administration and of the proper relation of the library to the university and to the world of scholarship. A pioneer in the field of library administration, Mr. Hanson's achievements were of significance not only in the development of American libraries, but in library science in general. His work justly commands the admiration of those who appreciate not only technical accomplishments, but who value rich scholarship, catholic spirit, and integrity of character.

Hanson continued with the University of Chicago Libraries until 1928. From 1926 to 1928 he served as acting director.

With the organization of the Graduate Library School at the University of Chicago in 1928, Hanson joined the faculty as a professor of bibliography, classification, and cataloging. Also that year, the Crown of Norway named him Commander of the Order of St. Olav of the Second Class. Besides teaching at the Graduate Library School, he chaired the Editorial Board that established *Library Quarterly* in 1931 and served as associate editor of *Library Quarterly* until his retirement in 1934.

During his first year with the Graduate Library School, Hanson was selected as one of a group of American cataloging experts to assist in the reorganization of the Vatican Library under a Carnegie Corporation grant. William Warner Bishop, who served as leader of the group, wrote also of Hanson's contribution to this assignment: "he was—again with Mr. Martel—greatly influential in drawing up the Vatican *Norme*, perhaps the best of modern cataloging codes, and one which goes far to reconcile European and American practice."

In 1931, Hanson was awarded an LL.D. degree by Luther College and also served for five months of that year as a consultant to the Library of Congress. Also during this period, he lectured at the library schools of Columbia University and the University of Michigan.

At the age of 70, Hanson retired from the University of Chicago Graduate Library School. The April 1934 issue of *Library Quarterly* was dedicated to him as a *Festschrift*. He retired to his rural home in Sister Bay, Wisconsin, where he completed his one major monographic work, *A Comparative Study of Cataloging Rules Based on the Anglo-American Code of 1908, with Comments on the Rules and on the Prospects for a Further Extension of International Agreement and Co-operation* (University of Chicago Press, 1939). He also continued to write articles and reviews, including his autobiographical article "Organization and Reorganization of Libraries" (*Library Quarterly*, July 1942). On November 8, 1943, J. C. M. Hanson died at Green Bay, Wisconsin.

Hanson's personality and his effect on his fellow workers were summed up by J. Christian Bay (q.v.) in an obituary in the January 1944 *Library Quarterly*:

> We saw Hanson daily coming and going with a little handbag filled with catalog cards to which he gave a final revision. The very hands of the blond giant gradually seemed more and more fitted to hold a bunch of cards and turn them over, while a single glance would mark a flaw or pick out a triumph of skill. To hear him say, "That's first rate," was a reward long remembered and cherished.

Biographical listings and obituaries—Butler, Pierce. "James Christian Meinich Hanson, 1864-1943 [obituary]." *Library Journal* 68:988 (Dec. 1, 1943); *Dictionary of American Biography* 3rd Suppl. (Edith Scott); *National*

Cyclopaedia of American Biography 34; *Who Was Who in America* II (1943-1950); *Who's Who in Library Service*, 1st ed., 2nd ed. **Books and articles about the biographee—** Immroth, John Phillip. *A Guide to the Library of Congress Classification.* 2nd ed. Littleton, Colo.: Libraries Unlimited, 1971; LaMontagne, Leo E. *American Library Classification with Special Reference to the Library of Congress.* Hamden, Conn.: Shoe String Press, 1961; *Library Quarterly* 4 (April 1934). Entire issue devoted to Hanson; McMullen, Charles Haynes. "The Administration of the University of Chicago Libraries, 1892-1928." Ph.D. dissertation, University of Chicago, 1949; Scott, Edith. "Hanson, J. C. M." In *Encyclopedia of Library and Information Science.* Allen Kent, Harold Lancour, and Jay E. Daily, eds. New York: Marcel Dekker, Inc., 1973, Vol. 10; Scott, Edith. "J. C. M. Hanson and His Contribution to Twentieth Century Cataloging." Ph.D. dissertation, University of Chicago, 1970. **Primary sources and archival materials—**Hanson, J. C. M. "The Library of Congress and Its New Catalogue: Some Unwritten History." In William Warner Bishop and Andrew Keogh, eds. *Essays Offered to Herbert Putnam.* New Haven, Conn.: Yale University Press, 1929.

—JOHN PHILLIP IMMROTH

HARRIS, WILLIAM TORREY (1835-1909)

William Torrey Harris was born September 10, 1835, to William and Zilpah Torrey Harris, at North Killingly, Connecticut. He grew up in North Killingly and Providence, Rhode Island, and attended Yale, which he left in 1857 during his junior year to move to St. Louis, Missouri. In 1858, he married Sarah Tully Bugbee of Putnam, Connecticut. They had four children, Theodore, Ethan, Charlotte, and Edith.

Harris was primarily known for his work in public education and philosophy. He began his formal teaching career in St. Louis in 1858 and rose through various ranks to become superintendent in 1868. By the time he resigned his position in 1880, his leadership and administrative foresight engendered national acclaim for the St. Louis school system and worldwide interest in its activities. During the same period, Harris received an honorary degree from his alma mater, the beginning of academic awards and honors which by the end of his life included four honorary LL.D. degrees and two honorary Ph.D.s (Brown University, 1893, and the University of Jena, 1899).

After a brief period devoted to teaching and lecturing, his reputation as an educator had so increased that Col. Francis W. Parker, in urging his appointment by President Benjamin Harrison as the fourth commissioner of education, could speak of Harris as the "acknowledged head of educational affairs in the United States." Harris assumed the post of commissioner on September 12, 1889, and continued in it until June 19, 1906. Under his guidance, the Bureau of Education took the powerful role of influencing the general character of public education that it retains today. Perhaps more than any other person, Harris was responsible for the organizational

structure and public support that has been fundamental to American public education since his time.

Harris's influence was due in part to his own broad intellectual interests and to his outstanding abilities as a writer and speaker. A broad-shouldered man of medium height, pale and thin, with auburn hair and beard, Harris was never seen without his glasses, which he wore only to conceal a glass eye, the result of a boyhood accident with firecrackers on the Fourth of July. He loved classical music and was a student of languages and Indian philosophy, but the greatest influence in his life was the study of the philosophy of the German idealists. Together with Henry C. Brokmeyer and Denton J. Snider, he founded the St. Louis Philosophical Movement. Throughout his life, he delivered hundreds of addresses and wrote countless articles and books. Among his notable publications were his editions of *Appleton's School Readers*, his contributions to Johnson's *Universal Encyclopedia*, and his *Psychologic Foundations of Education* (1898). From 1867 to 1893, Harris published the *Journal of Speculative Philosophy*, which presented the first systematic study by Americans of German idealist thought, as well as some of the earliest writings of such modern American philosophers as Charles S. Peirce, Josiah Royce, John Dewey, and William James.

Harris's publication of the *Journal*, as well as his own extensive contributions to its pages, epitomized his own well-developed philosophical orientation. He had been deeply affected by his study of George W. F. Hegel and of idealist thinking in general, which formed the basis of his comprehensive philosophy of life and his enthusiasm for public education. He forcefully promoted the public school as an instrument to bring about the culture of the individual student and thereby ensure the highest form of democracy.

Because of that educational ideal, Harris had considerable enthusiasm for and influence on library development. In 1890, he delineated his idea of the connection between education and libraries in an address to the American Library Association entitled "The Function of the Library and the School in Education": "Next after the school and daily newspaper comes the library in educative power. These three institutions are the great secular means which our people have to prepare themselves for their singular destiny" (*Library Journal* 15:C28; 1890). He went on to explain that, while the school provided the skills and the first occasion for individuals to truly educate themselves, the library and the newspaper provided the materials to read. Of the two, the library was in the unique position not only of providing the best record of mankind's thoughts and experiences, but of providing guidance in approaching that total record. For Harris, this division of responsibilities towards mankind's self-education was obvious. Most people finished their formal education with grammar school, and newspapers continued to expand people's intellectual horizons beyond their own limited worlds. But it was only through the public library that true, intensive self-education could be continued indefinitely.

Harris's specific contributions to library development followed naturally from his philosophy. From his earliest days in St. Louis, he had been a member of the St. Louis Mercantile Library and a strong supporter of the St. Louis Public School Library. In 1870, he published his scheme for a book classification for the Public School Library in the *Journal of Speculative Philosophy*. A book classification scheme was, in his view, fundamental to the orderly acquisition of knowledge because it in itself provided guidance for the reader. Although he ostensibly based his scheme on the thinking of Francis Bacon, he was convinced that Bacon's pure approach to knowledge was not adequate for classifying books. With some insight gained from Edward Johnston's adaptation of Bacon's ideas in a classification scheme for the College of South Carolina in 1836, and from Hegel's three-fold division of all reality, Harris constructed what he felt to be a logical, viable division of knowledge into categories suitable for books. Three major divisions of forms of knowing (Science, Art, History) as opposed to Bacon's divisions (Historical, Poetical, Philosophical) provided a structure in which to arrange the various subject categories of books. He then subdivided these classes by the ordering principle of general before specific, and well-established before less-established.

Harris's classification might have remained only one among many devised during the nineteenth century except that it was discovered by Melvil Dewey (q.v.) when the latter was developing his own Decimal Classification. In a letter to Harris dated May 9, 1873, Dewey spoke of having read Harris's *Journal* explanation of the St. Louis scheme and requested a copy of the catalog in which it was contained. Dewey's subsequent debt to Harris's order of subjects, though never acknowledged, is evident in a comparison of the two schemes:

Dewey		Harris
		SCIENCE
Philosophy	100-199	Philosophy
Theology	200-299	Theology
Sociology	300-399	Social & Political Sciences
		Jurisprudence
		Politics
		Social Science
Philology	400-499	Philology
Natural Science	500-599	Natural Sciences & Useful Arts
		Mathematics
		Physics

Dewey		Harris
		Natural history
		Medicine
Useful Arts	600-699	Useful Arts and Trades
		ART
Fine Arts	700-799	Fine Arts
Literature	800-899	Poetry
		Prose Fiction
		Literary Miscellany
History	900-999	HISTORY
		Geography and Travels
		Civil History
		Biography
General Works	000-099	APPENDIX—Miscellany

Harris's and Dewey's correspondence on the matter of classification provided a second point through which Harris exercised his influence on library development. From that early date, the two men formed a strong and enduring friendship that provided a contact between Harris and professional librarians. Dewey, as first editor, named Harris among the original contributing editors of the first issues of the *Library Journal* in 1876.

Their interests also converged in the spelling reform movement. When Dewey spoke at the 1878 meeting of the Spelling Reform Association in St. Louis, he became the secretary of the Association and Harris became a vice-president. Later, after Harris had become the commissioner of education, he authorized the Bureau of Education to underwrite Dewey's promotion of the American Library Association's exhibit at the 1893 Columbian Exposition. The Bureau also published the papers of the 1893 ALA meetings in a volume that Dewey hoped would replace the by then famous *1876 Special Report* on public libraries issued by Harris's predecessor at the Bureau, General John Eaton (q.v.), and a multitude of library-oriented reports, notably the second, third, and fourth editions of Charles A. Cutter's (q.v.) *Rules for a Printed Dictionary Catalogue.*

Harris retired from the Bureau of Education in 1906, having earned the gratitude of a generation of teachers and librarians. He remained a strong advocate of his educational and personal philosophy throughout the remaining years of his life in Providence, Rhode Island, where he died on November 5, 1909.

Biographical listings and obituaries—*Dictionary of American Biography* 8 (Ernest Sutherland Bates); *National Cyclopaedia of American Biography* 15. **Books and articles about the biographee**—American Philosophical Association. *William Torrey Harris, 1835-1935.* Chicago: Open Court Publishing Company, 1936; Comaromi, John Phillip. *The Eighteen Editions of the Dewey Decimal Classification.* Albany, N.Y.: Forest Press Division of the Lake Placid Education Foundation, 1976; Graziano, Eugene E. "Hegel's Philosophy as Basis for the Dewey Classification Schedule." *Libri* 9, no. 1:45-52 (1959); Leidecker, Kurt F. "The Debt of Melvil Dewey to William Torrey Harris." *Library Quarterly* 15:139-43 (April 1945); Leidecker, Kurt F. *Yankee Teacher: The Life of William Torrey Harris.* New York: The Philosophical Library, 1946; Perry, Charles M. *The St. Louis Movement in Philosophy.* Norman: University of Oklahoma Press, 1930;

Roberts, John S. *William Torrey Harris*. Washington: National Education Association, 1924.

—LISA deGRUYTER DILLON
—FRANCIS L. MIKSA

HARRISON, ALICE SINCLAIR (1882-1967)

Alice S. Harrison was born February 21, 1882, in the family home in Austin, Texas, and died there January 26, 1967. She attended the Austin Public Schools and earned a Bachelor of Literature degree from the University of Texas in 1904. Her professional education was at the University of Illinois summer sessions in 1914 and 1920 and at Columbia University summer sessions in 1915 and 1929, the latter under Mary E. Hall (q.v.). Harrison taught at the University of Texas Preparatory School, 1904-1912. Small in stature, reserved, and "very much a lady," she maintained an almost complete separation between her professional and personal lives.

Alice Harrison became librarian at Austin High School in 1912. She also functioned as the school district's voluntary supervisor of libraries beginning in 1912, but was officially named coordinator of libraries in 1938, a position she held simultaneously with that of Austin High School librarian until her retirement in 1947. She accepted teaching assignments in library science with the University of Texas during the summers of 1924, 1925, 1929, and 1931. In 1922, with Elva Bascom, she wrote "High School Libraries" in a study titled *The Problems of Educational Administration in Texas*.

In 1912, when Alice Harrison was hired as librarian for Austin High School, neither she nor Superintendent A. N. McCallum knew what a school librarian was to do, but they decided that her status should be that of a teacher. She was given little direction and no guidelines for the position, so she found it necessary to discover for herself what a high school librarian should do. From extensive reading and from visiting schools throughout the country that had exemplary libraries, she determined that her task was to bring students and books together, to select new materials, to know the materials well enough so that she could recommend them to her patrons, and to make materials easily accessible and available to students. She also felt keenly responsible for supplying materials that would help students in all their courses, not just literature, and for helping to meet some of the personal needs of individual students. For example, she provided a rotating loan collection of textbooks to help students who could not afford to purchase their own; she provided library space to display students' creative work, and she gave shy students opportunities to contribute to the school through working in the library. She also attempted to work with teachers in curriculum planning, but she found that the concept was too new to be widely accepted before 1930. Before there was a public library, Alice Harrison donated her time to provide summer library service to the entire community, using the Austin High collection.

Very skillfully did she educate her superintendent and principals to the potential of the library in the curriculum and to library needs. By 1914, she set goals for library service in elementary schools in the district and worked with parents and principals to implement such service. By 1921, there were libraries in all schools and each was staffed by at least a half-time teacher/librarian. She conducted extensive programs of in-service education for librarians and with them developed a *Course of Study* for school libraries in 1934, one of the first in Texas. She visited all of the libraries in the district regularly and counseled with the librarians about their programs.

Alice Harrison was a member of the American Library Association, one of the early members of the Texas Library Association, a founder of the librarians' section of the Texas State Teachers' Association, and a founder and first president of the Austin Library Club.

While none of her achievements appears particularly unusual, nevertheless they have an historical significance. She was the first school librarian in Texas with the rank of teacher, and by example, she contributed greatly to the development of school libraries throughout the state. In the Southwest, she was a pacesetter, an innovator, and a pioneer. While she may not have generated a great many new ideas, she was creative in putting the ideas of others into effective practice long before most schools even entertained the ideas. Her colleagues expressed deep affection and respect for her; they admired her resourcefulness, imagination, initiative, and straightforward manner.

To the present day, Austin schools boast of professionally staffed libraries in each school, a goal fought for and won by Alice Harrison through demonstration of effective library service and through dedicated, patient effort. The growth of school libraries in other schools in Texas and the prominence given instructional resources in the state education agency may, in part, also be traced to the competent demonstration of superior school library service that she provided.

Books and articles about the biographee—Herring, Billie Grace Ungerer. "Alice S. Harrison, Pioneer School Librarian, 1882-1967." Master's thesis, The University of Texas, 1967; Holden, Opal. "The History of Library Service in the Austin Public Schools." Master's thesis, The University of Texas, 1962; Junkin, Ruth Martindale. "Study of Library Service in the Elementary Schools of Austin." Master's thesis, The University of Texas, 1953. **Primary sources and archival materials**—The minutes of the Austin Independent School

District Board of Education, the Brooks-Harrison Family Papers (Austin-Travis County Collection, Austin Public Library), Harrison's letters, papers, and reports (held by the Library Supervisor, Austin Independent School District), and the Archives of the Texas Library Association (Texas State Library, Austin) all contain material concerning Harrison.

—BILLIE GRACE HERRING

HARRISSE, HENRY (1829-1910)

Born in Paris on March 24 (?), 1829, to Abraham and Annette Marcus Prague Herisse, Henry Harrisse immigrated in the 1840s to the United States, where he was to become a bibliographic pioneer in the field of early Americana. A lawyer by trade, Harrisse (when he changed the spelling of his surname is uncertain) is remembered for his historical bibliographies, which not only are so complete as to be considered standards even now, but which also are so arranged as to have changed the whole concept of the term "bibliography." American bibliographic work before Harrisse ventured into the field had been limited to compiling lists; Harrisse made the contribution of placing citations in bibliographic and historical relationship to each other.

Harrisse entered the book world inauspiciously as a teacher in Winnsboro, South Carolina, in 1847. In 1853, he was awarded an honorary Master of Arts from South Carolina College, which he had attended. From 1853 to 1856, the outspoken Harrisse caused disturbances among both students and faculty at the University of North Carolina at Chapel Hill, where he served as instructor of French while at the same time earning his law degree there. After teaching at Georgetown University for a short time, Harrisse moved west to practice law in Chicago. He met with no luck there, but in 1861, on the payroll of a Spanish client, Harrisse moved to New York, where his bibliographic adventures began.

Having written some minor philosophical articles in the South and some for the *North American Review*, Harrisse began to take an interest in historical subjects, and in 1863, he made a most fortunate acquaintance with the famous New York book collector and lawyer, Samuel L. M. Barlow. Harrisse became a frequent visitor to Barlow's library, and in 1864 he published, in a printing of four copies, his first bibliographic achievement, the *Biblioteca Barlowiana*, a catalog of the 8,000-volume Barlow collection. By 1866, Harrisse had gleaned enough knowledge from Barlow's library to publish, with his friend's backing, *Notes on Columbus* and, more importantly, the *Bibliotheca Americana Vetustissima: A Description of Works Relating to America, Published between the Years 1492 and 1551.* The work represents a turning point in the history of American bibliography, not only in its coverage but also in its

arrangement. Up until this time, barely one hundred titles dealing with the discovery period of American history were known. Harrisse located about three hundred titles published between 1493 and 1551 by imposing himself upon the often parsimonious collectors of the great private libraries. Under what to him were humiliating circumstances, these librarians limited Harrisse's use of the collections to one or two books at a time, for which he generally had to be able to provide a title in advance. The hot-tempered bibliographer always resented the way he was treated during this period; he once observed, "It was like feeding an elephant with a tea spoon." Whatever the circumstances of his studies, Harrisse did accomplish in his *Bibliotheca Americana Vetustissima* an awakening of the possibilities of bibliography by placing the works together in a historical context, citing their relationships to each other and to events surrounding their publication. Furthermore, he always made it a practice to be skeptical of secondhand information and to attempt to examine the original documents themselves.

The publication of the *Bibliotheca Americana Vetustissima* attained more fame in Europe than in America, so Harrisse sailed back to France, where he became acquainted with the greatest savants of the time. Then, in 1869, the Americana pioneer returned to settle permanently in France. In Paris, he had set up his law practice to serve Americans, and for the first time he began to make more than just a subsistence salary. He travelled to Spain to do firsthand research on Columbus, but he roused the anger of the Spanish for revealing that the contents of the Biblioteca Colombina were disappearing to wind up in the hands of collectors. In 1872, he published a volume of "Additions" to the *Bibliotheca Americana Vetustissima* of more than one hundred titles, and in the same year, he wrote a bibliographical history of the French discoverers, *Notes pour servir à l'histoire, à la bibliographie et à la cartographie de la Nouvelle-France et des pays adjacents, 1545-1700.* During the next thirty years, Harrisse wrote more than forty works dealing with Columbus or his son, Ferdinand. He also published bibliographic and cartographic histories of the Portuguese Corte-Reals (1883) and of John and Sebastian Cabot (1896). *The Discovery of North America*, published in 1892, is considered to be Harrisse's principal history.

With bushy side-whiskers and a long face, the pudgy Harrisse had a rather sad appearance. Although highly critical of others, he could hardly bear criticism himself. He was a friend of George Sand, Ernest Renan, and the historian Henry Vignaud, but in his later years Harrisse became withdrawn, probably because of his tremendous vanity and his failing eyesight and other physical ailments. Offered an honorary Doctor of Laws degree from Yale

University in 1892, he was too ill to travel to America to accept it. Awarded the Cross of the Legion of Honor the same year, he complained that he had not been made an "officier." A lifelong bachelor, Harrisse, upon his death on May 13, 1910, willed most of his fine personal collection to the Library of Congress. Harrisse's critical sharpness in the field of rare books was never fully appreciated; he made next to nothing from the sale of his books, a fact of which he was painfully aware. The value of his work lies in the bibliographical tradition which he began and in the untold numbers of American histories which scholars have been able to produce as a result of Harrisse's basic research.

Biographical listings and obituaries–*Dictionary of American Biography* 1st Suppl. (Randolph G. Adams); *National Cyclopaedia of American Biography* 18. **Books and articles about the biographee**–Adams, Randolph G. *Three Americanists: Henry Harrisse, Bibliographer; George Brinley, Book Collector; Thomas Jefferson, Librarian.* Philadelphia: University of Pennsylvania Press, 1939; Goff, Frederick R. "Henry Harrisse: Americanist." *Inter-American Review of Bibliography* 3:3-10 (Jan.-April 1953); Growoll, Adolf. *Henry Harrisse, Biographical and Bibliographical Sketch.* New York: The Dibdin Club, 1899; Knight, Edgar W., ed. *Henry Harrisse on Collegiate Education.* Chapel Hill: University of North Carolina Press, 1947.   **Primary sources and archival materials**–Harrisse's papers are divided among the New York Public Library, the William L. Clements Library (Ann Arbor, Michigan), and the Southern Historical Collection of the University of North Carolina (Chapel Hill). See especially his "Epistolae," an unpublished autobiography (1883). His personal copy of *Bibliotheca Americana Vetustissima*, with his extensive corrections, additions, and marginalia, is in the Library of Congress, as are his own copies of his other works.

–W. DAVENPORT ROBERTSON

HASSE, ADELAIDE ROSALIE (1868-1953)

Adelaide R. Hasse was born September 13, 1868, in Milwaukee, Wisconsin, the oldest of five children of Hermann Edward and Adelaide Trentlage Hasse. Her father, a well-known surgeon, practiced in Milwaukee and Missouri until, in 1885, he moved his surgery and family first to Arkansas and then to Los Angeles. Due to several changes in her environment during her school years, Adelaide apparently never completed any degree work, but she did study in several public schools and with private tutors. Dr. Hasse's enthusiasm for reading, travelling, and writing was inherited by his daughter, who also inherited his penetrating analytical skills and keen critical eye. This talent first became evident in 1889, when Adelaide was employed as Tessa L. Kelso's assistant at the Los Angeles Public Library. Kelso was a knowledgeable and occasionally controversial librarian who focused Hasse on her lifelong specialization in government documents. As Hasse later wrote, "She [Kelso] was so sympathetic in her efforts that, almost without being aware of having done so, somehow I had organized the collection of documents, not

inconsiderable, in the Los Angeles Public Library, devised a classification for them, and had begun a checklist of them." This checklist became her first monograph publication, one of nearly three dozen published during the sixty years of her career, which helped to identify and organize state, federal, and foreign documents.

Not surprisingly, in the then small world of librarians who demonstrated unique bibliographical skills, Hasse was singled out for quick advancement. During the six years she remained at the Los Angeles Public Library, she also helped to reorganize the Santa Barbara Public Library and the Pasadena Public Library. In addition, when Kelso pioneered in establishing the first public library training class, Hasse was a key proponent of the course of study and outlined the work in a series of seminal articles published in volume 20 (1895) of *Library Journal.*

In 1895, Congress created the office of the superintendent of documents, and Hasse's work brought her an offer to serve as librarian of the new organization. She arrived in Washington in late May of 1895 and began her work under the leadership of F. A. Crandall, superintendent of documents. Her duties included care of the documents and, more importantly, she was asked to pull together the numerous collections of documents stored around the Capitol. Within six weeks of her arrival, the office had, according to her account, "reclaimed and classified nearly 300,000 documents."

After two years in Washington, the next stage of Hasse's life began. In her privately printed pamphlet, *The Compensations of Librarianship* (1919, p. 2), she described the key event as a visit from John Shaw Billings (q.v.):

I had fairly well developed the classification for the documents when, one day, Dr. Billings, Director of the New York Public Library, paid us a visit. Dr. Billings examined the library, but especially the classification, which he went over quite carefully. This is the same classification adopted from the checklist and now in use, in an expanded form by the Superintendent of Documents.... A very short time after Dr. Billings' visit to us, I received an offer from him to come to the New York Public Library, there to build up what Dr. Billings wished to be a great document collection.

Hasse moved to New York in 1897 and spent the following 21 years, until 1918, within the assorted walls which made up the New York Public Library. She considered Billings to be a superlative librarian in all respects, and his vision was wide enough to perceive and support her unique bibliographical expertise and potential. Within a few years, as Phyllis Dain wrote in her history, *The New York Public Library* (1972, p. 115), "under the supervision of Miss Adelaide R. Hasse, an expert documents bibliographer and cataloger, [the collection] became, the *Library Journal* observed, 'so completely equipped and so well organized as to form a model of its kind. ...' Miss Hasse and her staff produced valuable bibliographies and checklists [and] in 1911 ... they provide[d] service directly to the public."

In connection with her work, Hasse travelled widely, including, in 1902, a trip to London, during which she located a copy of the presumedly lost *Bradford Journal*, the first book printed in New York. She later edited the 1693 journal, as well as the *New York House Journal* of 1695. Her early years in the New York Public Library were extremely productive and well regarded in many circles; the documents collection grew to 300,000 volumes and the list of her published indices now included the multivolume *Index of Economic Material in Documents of the States of the United States*, authorized by the Carnegie Institution of Washington. In 1913, John Shaw Billings died, and for the next few years, Hasse and the administration of the New York Public Library moved on a collision course. She believed that Billings's successor, Edwin H. Anderson (q.v.), was an inferior administrator and an individual opposed to her own work and interests. In 1916, her much-treasured documents catalog was transferred to the Cataloging Division, where she conceived her work of sixteen years to be lost. After two more years of serious disagreements, on October 7, 1918, the Executive Committee of the Board of Trustees asked for her resignation and, despite her attempts to gain a hearing before the Committee, she was "terminated" later in the month after she refused to resign. Those who supported the Executive Committee's decision noted her sharp personality conflicts with members of the staff; she, in turn, associated her firing with both ill-founded rumors regarding her pro-German sentiments and manipulations on the part of the Library administration.

Despite the shocking blow to her pride and professional standing, Hasse's career did not end in 1918. Indeed, her work during the next two dozen years continued unabated. She returned to Washington and, from 1919 until 1921, organized the War Industries Board records and those of the Council of National Defense; in 1921, she was assistant in the Statistics Bureau in the Department of War. From 1923 until 1932, she was bibliographer to the Brookings Institution and, from 1929 until 1939, was chief of the Index Division of the *U.S. Daily*, while also serving (1934-1939) as a research consultant for the Works Progress Administration. From 1939 to 1941, she served as an editorial analyst for the Temporary National Economics Committee, while also lecturing during the 1930s at George Washington University and at Catholic University in the early 1940s. After several years of retirement, she returned in 1948 to

assist William S. Jenkins in the editing of state records for microfilm publication. Finally, in 1952, at the age of 83, she officially retired and, one year later, on July 29, 1953, she died at the Washington Sanitarium, after an extended illness.

Adelaide Hasse's long career was notable in many respects. Her indices, checklists, and bibliographies cover such diverse subjects as urban real estate appraisal, foreign government documents on finance, demolition-blighted areas, the "unemployed employables," the trade paper press, old-age security, public archives of the thirteen original states, public documents published as serials, publications of the Department of Agriculture, U.S. documents related to foreign affairs, and explorations printed in U.S. documents. The key index, mentioned earlier, which identifies economic material in documents of the various states of the United States, was reprinted in the 1960s by Kraus and is still found in all major reference collections.

In addition, Adelaide Hasse was a volatile and controversial commentator on the library scene, publishing over fifty articles from 1894 through 1939 in both the library and the popular press. Her work in the organization and classification of government documents produced discussions useful to collections of every size, and she was easily identified as one of three or four outstanding specialists in the field. She wrote perceptively about the role of libraries and, at the turn of the century, described the library as having the potential to be an indispensable service plant, which could, if it would, function as an agent of industry and the government. In 1919, *The American Magazine* profiled Hasse and quoted her as saying, "I had something to sell and I sold it. A public library is essentially a place of service and what holds good for the entire library holds good for each department."

She was critical of the quality of library schools and their products, suggesting in "The Teaching of Reference Work in Library Schools" (*Library Journal* 14:583; September 1919) that the library should "function primarily as an information center [with] the school's curriculum composed almost wholly of instruction in sources of information and in the art or science of the organization of information." She was an incisive analyst, quick to point out error, little forgiving of sloppy thinking or romantic impracticalities, but always able to provide clearcut suggestions for improvement and change.

Hasse also had a lifelong involvement with professional associations—local, regional, and national. Life member number 779 of the American Library Association, she served on numerous ALA committees, including the early Committee on Library Schools and, for many years, as either member or chairman of the Public Documents Committee. She was a member of the Council from 1908 through 1913 and presented nearly a dozen papers at various conferences. During the 1920s and 1930s, she became active in the Special Libraries Association, was editor of *Special Libraries* in the early twenties, and was instrumental in the organization of the Washington, D.C., chapter, serving as its first president. In 1953, she was awarded an honorary SLA membership, and when she died, her obituary in *Special Libraries* (44:344; October 1953) reflected her colleagues' approbation: "Tireless in her work, her entire career was devoted to the teaching and practice of her chosen profession and countless librarians are indebted to her for the counsel and advice she was willing to give, and for the reference tools, bibliographies and indexes to government documents, that she bequeathed to the world."

It is nearly impossible to summarize in a few words a life so dedicated, so involved, and so complex. Adelaide Hasse was not an easy individual to know or to like; she did not tolerate fools easily nor did she pretend an undue modesty about her own accomplishments. Perhaps the best way to epitomize her sixty years is to quote from *Compensations of Librarianship* (p. 24), which she published to explain her dismissal from the New York Public Library and to reaffirm her belief in her profession. She concludes:

I trust that no one who has read thus far will have gotten the impression that I am at all sceptical about our work.... Most sincerely do I believe that it is work of immense and of, as yet, quite unrealized possibilities.... The time is not long to wait, and there is much eager young life awaiting the new situation. By no means let us lose faith in the future of our work.... Never forget that it is the spirit with which you endow your work that makes it useful or futile. Let us always work towards the end that the compensations of librarianship may at least be honorable, and that the true spirit of workmanship may be kept alive among us.

Adelaide Hasse kept that true spirit for sixty years; she was, indeed, a workman who realized both her own possibilities and the compensations of librarianship.

Biographical listings and obituaries—[Obituary]. *Library of Congress Information Bulletin* 12:13 (Aug. 3, 1953); [Obituary]. *Library Journal* 78:1497 (Sept. 15, 1953); [Obituary]. *New York Times*, July 30, 1953, p. 23; [Obituary]. *Special Libraries* 44:344 (Oct. 1953); [Obituary]. *Wilson Library Bulletin* 28:30 (Sept. 1953); *Who Was Who in America* III (1951-1960). **Books and articles about the biographee**—"Author Gives Credit." *DC Libraries* 10:34 (April 1939). Reprint of an excerpt from Ida Tarbell's *All in a Day's Work*; Bowker, R. R. "Women in the Library Profession." *Library Journal* 45:639-40 (Aug. 1920); Childs, James Bennett. "Hasse, Adelaide Rosalie." In *Encyclopedia of Library and Information Science*. Allen Kent, Harold

Lancour, and Jay E. Daily, eds. New York: Marcel Dekker, 1973, Vol. 10; "Hasse, Hermann Edward." *National Cyclopaedia of American Biography*. New York: White, 1937, Vol. 16, pp. 167-68. **Primary sources and archival materials**—The bulk of material related to Hasse is found in her own prolific writings, published from 1894 through the late 1930s. Her privately printed pamphlet, *The Compensations of Librarianship* (1919), defines her personal experiences in libraries and gives her view of the controversy at the New York Public Library.

—LAUREL A. GROTZINGER

HAVEN, SAMUEL FOSTER (1806-1881)

Samuel Foster Haven was born in Dedham, Massachusetts, on May 7, 1806, the son of Samuel and Betsey Foster Haven. He began college at Harvard but took his first degree at Amherst in 1828. Afterward, he was admitted to the bar in Middlesex County and began the practice of law in Lowell, Massachusetts.

Haven's law practice gave him the opportunity to express his exacting aptitude for research and for weighing evidence related to local cases. It led him as well into the serious study of early New England history, especially that of Colonial charters and records. He published his first work in 1836 on the occasion of the bicentennial of Dedham and afterward, besides a variety of shorter articles, was responsible for the publication of several volumes of documents related to Colonial history. Perhaps his best known work was *Archaeology of the United States*, published by the Smithsonian Institution in 1856 and consisting of historical and bibliographical essays on the subject. His only son, Samuel Foster Haven, Jr., was born in 1831 and lost his life serving the Union cause as a physician during the Civil War. He too shared his father's interest in American history and compiled a catalog of American publications prior to the American Revolution. Samuel Haven, Sr., included his son's accomplishment in Isaiah Thomas's *History of Printing in America* when he edited and published a second edition of that work in 1874.

In April 1838 Samuel Haven became the librarian of the American Antiquarian Society in Worcester, Massachusetts, a post that he held until his death. His duties extended far beyond that of librarian, however, and approached more nearly that of an executive secretary. His career at the Society had several focuses. He was an antiquarian and an archaeologist who served well the Society's original interest in collecting the documents and artifacts of American civilization. Toward this end, he was instrumental in the Society's effort to make available to the scholarly world historical records, the most important of which were those of the Massachusetts Bay Colony. He was not content simply to collect the data of history, however. In his view, the material of history needed to be carefully weighed and used to reconstruct the real relations in the past by means of a sound literary style. In this respect, he participated directly in the first efforts to develop a native and scholarly historical profession. He did not himself, however, write major works of this sort. Rather, he was content to collaborate in the production of such works by giving extensive help to other scholars, the most notable, perhaps, being John Gorham Palfrey.

Still another focus of his career, his work as a librarian, complemented his historical interests. As a developer of the Society's collections, his work was broad in scope and thorough. His penchant for details and his encompassing memory not only aided his collecting but made it possible for him to provide scholars with access to the library's holdings beyond anything that the catalogs could accomplish.

His library work transcended these abilities, however. In the words of one of his contemporaries, Charles Deane, his work was notable as well for its warm and generous spirit.

> He had also the higher gift for a librarian, which is as rare. This is a moral gift, and not merely an intellectual faculty. He loved to see his treasures used. He did not hide them in a napkin. He was sincerely glad when a new investigator appeared, and it did not seem to matter that the man was crude in method, rough in manner or ignorant as a hound. Mr. Haven was there to help him in all such things.

It was this professional outlook, scholarliness, and a strong sense of service that in his later years he was able to contribute to the emergence of goals in the library profession. He worked as well through his many contacts with other leading scholarly librarians of his day.

Although never of great strength, Samuel Haven travelled widely on behalf of the Society. During his later years he often battled sickness, but he carried on his work despite a growing weakness and died while still active as a librarian on October 5, 1881.

A portrait of Haven by E. L. Custer was presented to the Society in 1879. Additionally, Haven left his books and a small endowment for a Haven Alcove in the Library of the Society he had served for over forty years.

Primary sources and archival materials—Haven is not listed in any of the standard biographical tools, and other works on him are not easily found. The American Antiquarian Society is listed as having six boxes of Haven's papers. The *Proceedings* of the American Antiquarian Society contain a wealth of material by and about him from 1838 to 1881. As librarian, his detailed reports appeared twice a year; as a member of the Publications Committee and as a Councilor, he also made frequent reports. In addition, he found time to read and publish papers on historical and archaeological subjects. Tributes on the dedication of his portrait (1879), his

retirement (1881), and his death provide many insights as to his character and accomplishments. Thus, the AAS *Proceedings* constitute the primary source for material on him.

—FRANCIS L. MIKSA

HAYKIN, DAVID JUDSON (1896-1958)

David Judson Haykin was born at Novozybkov, in what is now the Bryansk oblast of the Russian SFSR, on January 18, 1896, the oldest son of Joseph L. and Grace R. Haykin. His father taught soapmaking, his grandfather was a forester.

The family arrived at Ellis Island on August 7, 1909, and eventually settled in Omaha, Nebraska, where the father and mother ran a corner grocery store and David attended the public schools. He entered the University of Nebraska at Lincoln but soon afterward enlisted in the U.S. Army Medical Corps. On May 18, 1918, before being shipped overseas, he married his high school sweetheart, Irene Atwood Wilson. After two years of service in army hospitals in France and Germany, he returned to the University of Nebraska, where he was graduated with a B.A. in June 1921, with a major in chemistry. He had taught that subject the previous winter in the Teachers College High School attached to the University.

Haykin's introduction to library work had begun several years earlier. During his undergraduate years, he worked as a student assistant in the University library, and after basic training at Fort Riley, he was put in charge of the medical officers' reading room. From 1921 to 1924, he was a senior library assistant at the University of Nebraska, while taking graduate courses in Indo-European and Semitic philology. At this point, Malcolm G. Wyer (q.v.), librarian of the University, persuaded Haykin that his best career potential lay in library work and guided him to the New York State Library School in Albany, New York. He received his Bachelor of Library Science from that school in 1925.

That summer, Haykin worked as a reference assistant in the New York Public Library's Division of Economics and Public Documents. In the fall, he went back to Albany for a two-year period as head cataloger in the New York State Library. From 1927 to 1930, he was head of the Catalog Department and an instructor in the library school at the Queens Borough Public Library, New York City.

In April 1930, Haykin moved to Washington, D.C., where he set up the American Library Association Office for Decimal Classification Numbers on Library of Congress Cards. Joining the staff of the Library of Congress in 1932, he was first chief of its Division of Documents; then from 1934 to 1940, he was chief of the Cooperative Cataloging and Classification Service. During 1939 and 1940, he was acting chief of the

Catalog Division. Throughout the 1930s, he continued his graduate study in Semitic philology at the Catholic University of America, where he taught courses in library science as well. During the years that George Washington University had a library school, he also lectured there.

With the reorganization of the Library of Congress and establishment of the new Processing Department in 1940, Haykin entered upon what was to be the capstone of his life's work. He was appointed chief of the new Subject Cataloging Division on January 2, 1941. Here, for the first time in library history, the subject control of literature was concentrated in a group of specialists who both classified and assigned subject headings to books in their own areas of expertise. The transformation this made toward greater specificity in subject headings soon became apparent in the considerable increase of headings printed in subsequent editions of *Subject Headings Used in the Dictionary Catalogs of the Library of Congress.*

From the start, Haykin held weekly meetings of his subject catalogers to discuss new proposals. Here he gradually hammered out a basic philosophy and theory, which culminated in his monograph, *Subject Headings, a Practical Guide* (Washington, D.C.: GPO, 1951). On September 1, 1952, he relinquished his administrative duties to become the Library's consultant-specialist in subject cataloging and classification. He was at work on a *Subject Heading Code* at the time of his death.

Haykin's interest in Decimal Classification continued throughout his career, as evidenced by his many articles in library journals and other publications. From 1941 to 1956, that work was done by a section in the Subject Cataloging Division under his care.

He served as chairman of the ALA Committee on Resources of American Libraries (1933-1935); he was president of the District of Columbia Library Association (1945-1947); was a member of the U.S. Board of Geographical Names (1951-1953); and was president of the ALA Division of Cataloging and Classification (1952-1953). In June 1957, the American Library Association awarded David Haykin the Margaret Mann Citation "for nationally distinguished leadership in the systematic development of subject cataloging and classification."

For many years, Haykin was a trustee of All Souls' Unitarian Church in Washington and a member of its choir. He was also a member of the Bibliographical Society of America, the American Name Society, and the Inter-American Bibliographical and Library Association. He loved to carve miniatures in wood and stone, and he left a distinguished collection of miniature books.

David Haykin was a small, eager person. In his years as chief of the Subject Cataloging Division at the Library of Congress, he was always happiest when a cataloger came to him with a serious problem and he could dart around from reference books to catalog and book decks helping to solve it.

He was stricken in his office at the Library of Congress on April 22, 1958, and taken to George Washington University Hospital suffering from a heart attack. He died there on May 4 from a dissecting aortic aneurysm. He was survived by his father, wife, son David Judson Haykin, Jr., and daughter Joan Irene.

Biographical listings and obituaries—[Obituary]. *College and Research Libraries* 19:336 (July 1958); [Obituary]. *Library of Congress Information Bulletin* 17:233-35 (May 5, 1958); [Obituary]. *Library Resources and Technical Services* 2:196-97 (Summer 1958); [Obituary]. *Wilson Library Bulletin* 33:14 (Sept. 1958); New York State Library School. *Register, 1887-1926.* Albany, N.Y., 1959; *Who Was Who in America* III (1951-1960); *Who's Who in Library Service,* 1st ed., 2nd ed., 3rd ed. **Books and articles about the biographee**—Clapp, V. W. "David Judson Haykin." *Library Resources and Technical Services* 1:147-48 (Fall 1957). **Primary sources and archival materials**—Records of Haykin are in the personnel and information files of the Library of Congress. The author also interviewed Irene Haykin and David J. Haykin, Jr.

—LEONARD ELLINWOOD

HAZELTINE, MARY EMOGENE (1868-1949)

Mary Emogene Hazeltine, the oldest child and only daughter of Abner and Olivia A. Brown Hazeltine, was born on May 5, 1868. Following an early education in Jamestown, New York, public schools, Mary Emogene entered Wellesley College, graduating with a B.S. degree in 1891. For two years following her graduation, Mary Emogene Hazeltine was assistant principal of Danielson High School, Connecticut, but in 1893, she returned to Jamestown to become librarian of the James Prendergast Free Library. It was here that she was converted by the missionary spirit prevalent among library workers at this time and became a firm believer in the gospel of the public library.

She became active in the New York State Library Association, serving as president in 1902. During the 1890s, having joined the American Library Association, she attended many conferences and wrote the 1896 official account of the post-conference excursion in the Rocky Mountains following the Denver Conference. At the Philadelphia Conference in 1897, she delivered a paper on ways to achieve library publicity, giving examples of what she herself had done to extend the services at Jamestown. In 1898, she was assigned responsibility for local arrangements connected with the ALA Lakewood-on-Chautauqua Conference. In this manner, despite her lack of formal training, she was accepted into the profession and began to make her own contributions, thus becoming widely known in library circles.

As a result of these activities, she could not long escape the notice of Melvil Dewey (q.v.), who, in 1901, invited her to be the resident director of a Summer School for Library Training at Chautauqua, New York, which was inaugurated in connection with the work of the Chautauqua Assembly. For the next four summers, she ran this six-week school for librarians and assistant librarians of small public libraries who were unable to attend the extended courses of the regular library schools.

Her capacity for administrative and educational leadership thus demonstrated, Mary Emogene Hazeltine was called in 1906 by the Wisconsin Free Library Commission to head its Instructional Department and to lead a new library school in Madison. At this time, although there were 142 free public libraries in Wisconsin, only thirty professional librarians were available to serve in them. Consequently, a full-time library school was recognized to be essential if thoroughly prepared librarians were to be provided for Wisconsin's small public libraries.

Though broadly similar to other schools, the curriculum of the Wisconsin Library School contained an unusually well planned field work program, which took place after the students had completed study of cataloging, classification, reference, and book selection. During February and March, students worked in two different Wisconsin libraries, where they were visited and advised by faculty. Because this was a Commission school, all public libraries of the state could be claimed as the legitimate laboratory for this experience, and at the same time, untold benefit in organizational accomplishments accrued to the libraries from this reciprocal arrangement.

By 1909, the program initiated by Mary Emogene Hazeltine was so well thought of that a joint course with the University of Wisconsin was established, whereby students in their senior year might enter the School, receiving twenty credits toward their B.A. as well as the certificate of the School. The profession also recognized the excellence of the program. In the first year of its founding, this ninth library school in the nation was one of five which met the educational standards established by the ALA Committee on Library Training. In 1915, it was one of six charter members of the Association of American Library Schools. Graduates of the program soon began to be in demand in other states, many of them achieving national and international prominence.

The Wisconsin Library School was unique among schools for the broad scope of the educational program of the Commission's Instructional Department. In addition to the daily program of the regular school, the faculty paid visits to libraries, held summer

sessions for assistants who were unable to attend the regular program, organized institutes, and provided booklists and articles for the *Wisconsin Library Bulletin*. In 1917, under Hazeltine's supervision, the faculty prepared an *Apprentice Course for Small Libraries* (published by the American Library Association).

Hazeltine's own scholarly contribution was mainly in the field of bibliography, which she regarded as a sideline to her educational work. *Anniversaries and Holidays*, first published in 1928, was most recently revised in 1975. *One Hundred Years of Wisconsin Authorship* appeared in 1937. In the course of her Commission work, many articles of practical advice appeared in *Wisconsin Library Bulletin*.

Always interested in drama, she met regularly with a Madison troupe to perform for enjoyment. She also advanced dramatic readings as a means of promoting interest in the best books. In her busy life, she found time to be a member of several groups at the University of Wisconsin—the College Club, Fortnightly Club, and the Mozart Club. She also worked for the Wisconsin Library Association and was a member of the Congregational Church.

Mary Emogene Hazeltine could not be called an innovator, for she brought neither new techniques nor a unique philosophy to bear upon librarianship. She was, however, an educator of energy and administrative ability as well as a ready adapter of ideas that she had observed to be successful elsewhere. Highly individual and strong in her convictions, she insisted on the rights of others to their own opinions, admiring intellectual independence and honesty in students who disagreed with her. Blessed with a prodigious memory and a keen sense of humor, she thrived on contests of wit. In her 32 years as preceptor of the Wisconsin Library School, from which she retired in 1938, she trained over a thousand librarians, starting at a time when librarianship was only beginning to be an aggressive movement. She at all times believed in the power of the book to influence a reader's life, and her philosophy was that librarianship stood between the social vocations and teaching. The fact that it partook of the nature of both, and was at once both social and educational, constituted its broad appeal. Althea Warren (q.v.), one of her students, spoke of Hazeltine's wisdom and indomitable enthusiasm, and the latter quality led her upon retirement to volunteer her reference services to the Jamestown library.

She was personally honored for her contributions to librarianship by election to the American Library Institute, and on the seventy-fifth anniversary of the American Library Association, Mary Emogene Hazeltine was placed in the American "Library Hall of Fame" (as chosen by *Library Journal* 76:466-72; March 15, 1951). She died on June 17, 1949, and is buried in Lakeview Cemetery, Jamestown, New York.

Biographical listings and obituaries—*Dictionary of Wisconsin Biography*, 1960; *Notable American Women* 2 (William

Converse Haygood); [Obituary]. *Library Journal* 74:1303 (Sept. 15, 1949); [Obituary]. *New York Times* (June 18, 1949); *Who Was Who in America* II (1943-1950); *Who's Who in Library Service*, 1st ed., 2nd ed. **Books and articles about the biographee**—Condon, Mary Marjorie. "Mary Emogene Hazeltine: A Bibliography." Madison, Wisc., 1960; Fenster, Valmai R. "The University of Wisconsin Library School, a History, 1895-1921." Ph.D. dissertation, University of Wisconsin, 1977; *Library Journal* 76:468-69 (March 15, 1951); Potter, Virginia. "Mary Emogene Hazeltine, 1868-1949." Madison, Wisc., 1960; *Wisconsin Library Bulletin* 33:90-95 (May 1937). **Primary sources and archival materials**—Hazeltine's letters and papers are in the archives of the University of Wisconsin and the Wisconsin State Historical Society.

—VALMAI R. FENSTER

HEWINS, CAROLINE MARIA (1846-1926)

Caroline Maria Hewins was born October 10, 1846, in Roxbury, Massachusetts, the daughter of Charles Amasa and Caroline Chapin Hewins. Librarian of the Hartford, Connecticut, Public Library for fifty years, she became nationally famous as a pioneer in library work with children. She died in Hartford on November 4, 1926, at the age of eighty.

The Hewins family proudly traced its lineage to Jacob and Mary Hewins who had come from England to Sharon, Massachusetts, in 1656. Her father was the co-founder of a highly successful firm of haberdashers in Boston, Hewins and Hollis, later merged with Filene's. In Caroline's infancy, the family moved to Jamaica Plains, and when she was seven, to West Roxbury, where they lived in a fine home surrounded by five acres of gardens, meadows, and woods. It was a large household; Caroline was the oldest of nine children and at one time a great-grandmother, grandmother, two aunts, and an uncle were members of the *ménage*.

A precocious child, Caroline was reading by the age of four. Her early education at home and at private schools was followed by Eliot High School at Jamaica Plains. In 1862, she entered the Girls' High and Normal School of Boston to prepare for teaching. Her greatest preoccupation in these early years was books. She loved to read, to be read to, and to read to others, particularly her brother and sisters. This period of her life is described in an autobiographical memoir, *A Mid-Century Child and Her Books* (1926). Throughout her adult life, Hewins collected the books she remembered from her childhood, reconstituting in her office at the Hartford Public Library the children's library of her youth.

While studying at the Normal School, Caroline Hewins had occasion to do some research at the Boston Athenaeum. She was so impressed with this scholarly institution that, upon completion of her studies, she arranged to work there in 1866-1867 under the guidance of its famous librarian, William Frederick Poole (q.v.). During the years that followed, she taught in private schools in the Boston area and took courses at Boston University, but it was the library profession, not teaching, that she chose for her life's work.

The Hewins family apparently was uneasy about Caroline's career-woman tendencies. Her father built an ell for her on the house in West Roxbury to induce her to remain with them, but Caroline could not be dissuaded from venturing into the foreign territory of Connecticut. In 1875, the Young Men's Institute of Hartford, Connecticut, needed a librarian; Caroline applied and was accepted. She left, however, with parental blessing and in later years, she returned when she could, especially at Christmas.

The Institute was an old private subscription library, at this time having a membership of about six hundred men and women who paid from $3 to $5 a year to use a collection of some 20,000 books. Although there were few members with children, and consequently few children who used the library, Hewins at once turned her attention to the children's collection. She found what few books there were shelved alphabetically with adult fiction, an unwholesome proximity in her eyes. For a local paper, she wrote articles about young girls asking for the novels of Ouida and little boys asking for the *Police Gazette*. A wholesale weeding and burning of objectionable books from the children's collection resulted, as she sought to raise reading standards above what she called the "immortal four": Optic, Alger, Castlemon, and Martha Finley.

Hewins's approach was by no means totally censorious; in fact, over the years, she introduced innumerable projects designed to interest children in books and libraries, all based on her own wide knowledge and the quality collection she gradually amassed. She encouraged children to report their reading preferences, information she put to good use in selection and guidance. A chapter of the Agassiz Association (for nature study) was formed, with Miss Hewins leading her charges on Saturday nature walks in good weather and nature book talks in bad. She opened Library membership to the schools, with fees paid in some cases by the administration, in others by the students themselves, penny by penny. Collateral reading lists were provided for teachers, and in time classroom libraries were sent out, making the Hartford Public Library a leader in the movement for cooperation between public and school libraries.

On frequent trips abroad, Hewins wrote letters to her young friends which often appeared in the *Hartford Courant*. In 1923, a selection was published as *A Traveller's Letters to Boys and Girls*. Also, with her young patrons in mind, she collected dolls on her trips and exhibited them at the Library. Every New Year's Day, a "doll's reception" was held, with little girls bringing their Christmas dolls to the Library to meet those of Caroline Hewins.

Hewins delighted in giving book talks and telling stories, and beginning in about 1898, she started summer book talks, an early version of the summer reading clubs subsequently so popular. She also had a lively interest in drama, writing and directing plays, pageants, and Maypole festivals based on children's literature, with young library users as performers. Her concern for disadvantaged children was so great that she lived among them at the North Street Settlement House for twelve years, founding there a long-lived drama club and establishing a small branch library which she personally kept open for one hour each evening.

In 1878, when the Young Men's Institute was absorbed by the older Hartford Library Association, Hewins started the *Bulletin of the Hartford Library Association*, which continued throughout her career under various titles. A quarterly designed primarily to list new acquisitions, it also contained, from the first, selected lists of books for children. In 1882 Frederick Leypoldt (q.v.), owner of *Publishers' Weekly*, asked her to compile a list of recommended children's books, which he then published that same year in pamphlet form as *Books for the Young: A Guide for Parents and Children* (reprinted in 1884). This in turn led to a similar list by her for the American Library Association Publishing Board, *Books for Boys and Girls: A Selected List* (1897, with revised editions in 1904 and 1915).

The prefaces to these ALA lists give some insight into Hewins's philosophy of book selection for children. Her emphasis was heavily on the classics, which she felt enriched the lives of children and enabled them to appreciate literature and art as adults. She disliked the books in series then so popular, and considered them "cheap and slovenly in style, melodramatic in incident. . . . After several years reading of this kind, a boy or girl has of course no power of enjoying a story of higher type" [1915 ed.]. Although modern realistic stories did not appeal to her, she admitted that "a few stories of modern life that have become general favorites, even though they have faults of style like 'Little Women,' or a sensational plot like 'Little Lord Fauntleroy' are in the list for the sake of the happy, useful home-life of the one and the sunshiny friendliness of the other" [1897 ed.].

Hewins was not a romantic sentimentalist, however, in her view of children and their response to books. She realized that the home environment often affected children's reading ability and that the child who has been brought up with books "will be reading from grown-up books when others the same age are stumbling through children's easy stories" [1915 ed.]. She was not sanguine about the ability of the school or the library to uplift the average child to the world's best books:

Ninety children out of one hundred in the public schools below the high school read nothing for pleasure beyond stories written in a simple style with no involved sentences. Nine out of the other ten enjoy novels and sometimes poetry and history written for older readers, and can be taught to appreciate other books, but not more than one in the hundred has a natural love of the best literature [1897 ed.].

Above all she deplored the fact that contemporary education tended to denigrate the bookish child.

Although children's rooms were becoming recognized as legitimate parts of public libraries in the 1890s, Hewins had great difficulty in convincing her trustees of the need for one. She credited her final success to a picture published in a local paper of the Hartford Library reading room on a Sunday afternoon showing fifty-one children and two adults. Rooms in an old home next to the Library were converted into a children's department in 1904. A fireplace and deep windows provided a homey setting for books, dolls, stuffed birds, pictures, and child-sized furniture. In 1907, a full-time children's librarian, Sarah S. Eddy, was hired, although Hewins continued her stories, clubs, theatricals, and many other activities for which she was by now famous.

While Caroline Hewins is characterized as a children's librarian, it must be remembered that she capably ran a growing city library. The Hartford Library Association became a free library in 1892, and in 1893 formally adopted the name "Hartford Public Library." By 1925, the last year of her service, it had a collection of 150,000 volumes, which greatly strained the Library's facilities in the venerable Wadsworth Athenaeum where it was located throughout Hewins's tenure. The Library's influence had been greatly increased by the establishment of branches and deposit stations in schools, factories, and settlement houses. In the children's library, circulation had risen from about 35,000 when it opened in 1904 to over 98,000 volumes in 1925.

On the local level, Hewins was prominent in the Hartford Librarians' Club, and in 1891, was a founder of the Connecticut Library Association, of which she was president in 1912-1913. In 1893, she was largely instrumental in persuading the Connecticut legislature to create the Public Library Committee, a prototype of the state library commission, and she served as executive secretary without pay for some years. As Connecticut had no "library visitors" or state extension workers, Caroline Hewins travelled widely by horse and buggy advocating public libraries in towns and villages, always with a special plea for good books for children.

In addition to the many clubs she created in connection with the Hartford Public Library, Hewins was an enthusiastic member of civic and cultural organizations, including the Business and Art Society, and the Daughters of the American Revolution. It often seemed that where no club existed, she was determined to found one, as in the case in 1897 of the Education Association, a forerunner of the Parent Teachers Association. She lectured at library schools and educational workshops, and taught a children's literature class in Hartford for librarians and teachers. Never one to limit her duties to the Library, she visited children in classrooms and even their homes to discuss their reading.

Nationally Caroline Hewins was very active in the American Library Association. R. R. Bowker (q.v.) stated that, judging from her ALA number 263, she must have joined the Association in 1879, at the time of the third conference in Boston. Whatever the reluctance of lady librarians may have been to speak at early ALA conferences, it was soon banished by Hewins's example, as she frequently read papers at these meetings. She is recorded as the first woman to speak from the floor of an ALA conference, her question referring to the use of the dog tax to buy library books. An informal meeting of eight children's librarians which she called at the Montreal meeting in 1900 resulted ultimately in the establishment of the Children's Section of ALA. She was an ALA councilor from 1885 to 1888, and again from 1893 to 1902, and was vice-president in 1891. In 1897, she was one of two women in the delegation of American librarians who read papers at the Second International Conference of Librarians in London, where she spoke at length on children's literature as seen by children themselves.

Her papers and many other articles appeared regularly over a span of many years in *Library Journal*, but they are particularly numerous in the 1890s. Well over half were on children's book selection and other aspects of children's work, but she also wrote on what was then termed general library economy, discussing the many areas of library work in which she was involved. Articles by her also appeared in *Public Libraries* and other library and educational periodicals. Through her speeches, writings, and the example she set at the Hartford Public Library, she became a major figure of the public library movement of her day, particularly in the area of children's work, of which she is regarded as the most influential founder.

In 1911, Trinity College of Hartford awarded Caroline M. Hewins an honorary master's degree in recognition of her distinguished services to Hartford and as an educator. She was the first woman to be so honored by this men's college, and at the conclusion of the presentation, President Luther doffed his cap and exclaimed, "Hail, first daughter of Trinity," to prolonged applause.

On February 15, 1926, the Hartford Librarians' Club celebrated Hewins's fifty years of service to the

Hartford Public Library by presenting her with a sum of money which was used to establish the Caroline M. Hewins Scholarship Fund for Children's Librarians. The fund has since annually assisted a young woman, preferably from Hartford or New England, to train for children's work in public libraries.

By the fall of 1926, Hewins was still active in the library, despite her advanced age. Although an attack of bronchitis near her eightieth birthday on October 10 caused her to miss the ALA conference at Atlantic City, she was determined to participate in the Halloween festivities of the Children's Department of the New York Public Library and to view the books in the fall exhibit. Anne Carroll Moore (q.v.), children's librarian of the New York Public Library, was a special friend, and the fall visit to New York was a tradition of long standing. On this visit, Hewins approved the final proofs of *A Mid-Century Child and Her Books*, to be published in November by Macmillan with an introduction by Moore dated "Hallowe'en, 1926."

Hewins returned to Hartford on Saturday, October 30, and on Sunday, enthusiastically regaled her friends with an account of her trip. But that night, she was stricken with pneumonia from which she died on Thursday, November 4, 1926. The *Quarterly Bulletin*, which she started in 1878, in its January 1927 issue contained the resolutions on her death by the president of the Board of Directors, Wilbur F. Gordy. Coincidentally, the same page of that issue listed *A Mid-Century Child* among the new accessions to the Library.

Pictures show Caroline Hewins to have been erect of posture and plain of face, and she has been described as a typical New England school teacher. A small woman, she was endowed with an abundance of energy, a cheerful and gregarious disposition, superior intelligence, and a great love and understanding of children. She was one of the most eloquent supporters of the public library movement, particularly as it educated the young in preparation for a fuller life.

Caroline Hewins has not been forgotten in library circles. Her collection of children's books is now the property of the Connecticut Historical Association. In 1946, Frederic G. Melcher (q.v.) of the R. R. Bowker Company established the Caroline M. Hewins Lectureship to provide an annual lecture on children's books at New England Library Association meetings. Hewins was also one of forty leaders included in the "Library Hall of Fame," compiled on the occasion of the 75th anniversary of ALA, and published in *Library Journal* (76:466-72; March 15, 1951). The present building of the Hartford Public Library contains the Caroline M. Hewins Story Hour Room in her memory.

Biographical listings and obituaries—*Cyclopaedia of American Biographies* 4; *National Cyclopaedia of American Biography* 21; *Notable American Women* 2 (Jennie D. Lindquist); *Who Was Who in America* 1 (1897-1942). **Books and articles about the biographee**—Bowker, Richard R. "Women in the Library Profession." *Library Journal* 45:545-49 (June 15, 1920); "A Library Hall of Fame, Compiled for the 75th Anniversary of the American Library Association, 1876-1951." *Library Journal* 76:466-72 (March 15, 1951); Lindquist, Jennie D. "Caroline M. Hewins and Books for Children." In Caroline M. Hewins, *Caroline M. Hewins, Her Book*. Boston: Horn Book, 1954, pp. 79-107; Miller, Bertha Mahony, ed. "Caroline M. Hewins." *Horn Book* 24:1 (Feb. 1953). [Contains articles about Hewins by Jennie D. Lindquist, Frederic G. Melcher, Alice M. Jordan, and Anne Carroll Moore]; Root, Mary E. "Caroline Maria Hewins." In Emily M. Danton, ed., *Pioneering Leaders in Librarianship*. Chicago: American Library Association, 1953, 1st series, pp. 97-107; Root, Mary E. "As It Was in the Beginning; Caroline M. Hewins, Lover of Children." *Public Libraries* 30:246-50 (May 1925); Root, Mary E. "A Valiant Life—a Triumphant Death." *Library Journal* 51:1027-28 (Nov. 15, 1926); Wright, Harriet S. "Miss Hewins and Her Class in Children's Reading." *Library Journal* 38:210-11 (April 1915). **Primary sources and archival materials**—The Hartford, Connecticut, Public Library's *Annual Report* and its *Quarterly Bulletin* for the years of Hewins's tenure contain information about her.

—BUDD L. GAMBEE

HILL, FRANK PIERCE (1855-1941)

Frank Pierce Hill was born on August 22, 1855, in Concord, New Hampshire, the son of Cyrus and Nancy Walker Hill. He received his undergraduate degree in 1876 from Dartmouth College and was awarded an honorary degree of Doctor of Letters from that institution in 1906. In 1880, he married Annie M. Wood, and they had six children.

Above all else, Frank Pierce Hill is to be remembered as an organizer of free public libraries. While known best for his work in Newark and Brooklyn, prior to these efforts, and within the first nine years of his professional work, Hill had organized three libraries: Lowell, Massachusetts (1879-1884), Paterson, New Jersey (1885-1887), and Salem, Massachusetts (1888).

Hill was elected the first librarian of Newark, New Jersey, in 1889. In the fiftieth anniversary issue of *The Library* (published by The Public Library of Newark, New Jersey), he was extolled for having provided a setting for the Library both in program and building through his unusual organizing ability and remarkable foresight. The Newark Library was originally housed in the building erected by the oldest library in the city, the Newark Library Association, and Hill quickly saw the need for a new facility, and he spearheaded the efforts to procure the building which to this day is a lasting memorial to him.

Upon Hill's resignation as librarian, the Board of Trustees of the Newark Free Public Library passed a resolution on June 6, 1901, in appreciation of Hill "not only in respect of his personal qualities, but chiefly on account of the great work that he has done for this Library . . . ," and recommended him to the Brooklyn Public Library as one they considered to "stand at the head of his profession." The Resolution spoke the following of Hill:

He came to the position at the time the Library was instituted; when there was no building, no books and no organization. He formulated the work from the beginning, organized the Library staff, and created relations between the Library and the people which have continued, and will continue, to bear the mark of his personality. His work here has rendered popular a public institution second only in importance to the public schools, and his services thus rendered to the public of our city have been of a character and quality which is beyond present estimation.

Hill accepted the post of librarian at Brooklyn Public Library because he believed that the Library was destined to hold a leading position among the public libraries of the future. Coming to Brooklyn as its second executive director, the first of whom had served for a brief two years, Hill saw the Library's future in the establishment of "branches in every section of the city, stored with all that is good, helpful and entertaining in literature; a library conducted with liberality toward the people, with equity toward the employees and with satisfaction to the Directors."

In his thirty years as chief librarian, the services and resources of Brooklyn Public Library grew significantly, and perhaps Hill's outstanding ability as an organizer can best be demonstrated by the fact that the Library growth that took place between 1903 and 1930 occurred with an administrative staff increase of only four (from eight to twelve):

	1903	1930
Branches	20	35
Staff	173	438
Books	360,502	1,035,142
Circulation	1,614,437	7,438,364

Hill understood the importance of interaction between libraries, and he encouraged staff participation in professional associations and meetings. He was elected in 1890 as the second secretary of the American Library Association, succeeding Melvil Dewey (q.v.), and he served for five years. In 1904, he was elected vice-president of the Association and he became president in 1905. At his initiative, ALA sponsored a system of uniform annual statistics for large public libraries in 1913 and planned special ALA meetings for large public libraries beginning in 1922. During World War I, Hill again evidenced his organizational ability by chairing the ALA Committee for the United War Work Campaign, which raised $1,700,000 to build libraries at camps and recreational centers and to provide other reading materials for the armed forces. In addition to these ALA activities, Hill also visited numerous libraries and attended library related conferences both in the United States and abroad. In 1914 he attended the International Exhibit of Book Industries at Leipzig and the Pan-Anglican meeting in Oxford.

When Hill retired from Brooklyn Public Library at the age of 75, the Board of Trustees expressed its appreciation for his service by awarding him a $4,000 annual lifetime allowance, hoping to draw upon his experience during his retirement.

Frank Pierce Hill's publications reflect both his work in the American Library Association and his concern for the areas his libraries served. The fact that his publications do not include major writing efforts so much as efforts as compiler and editor again reflects his outstanding abilities as an initiator and organizer. His major publications include: "Address of the President: One Phase of Library Development" (*Library Journal* 31:3-9; August 1906); *American Plays, Printed 1714-1830; a Bibliographic Record* (Stanford, Calif.: Stanford University Press, 1934 [Compiler]); *Library Service for Soldiers and Sailors, the Story of the Million Dollar Campaign of the American Library Association* (Chicago: American Library Association War Finance Committee, 1918); *Library Service* (Prepared by Emma V. Baldwin. Chicago: American Library Association, 1914 [Editor]); *Committee on the Deterioration of Newsprint Paper* [Report] (Chicago: American Library Association, January 1913); *James Bertram: An Appreciation* (New York: Carnegie Corp., 1936); *Lowell Illustrated: A Chronological Record of Events and Historical Sketches of the Large Manufacturing Corporations* (Boston: Forbes Company, 1884 [Compiler and Editor]); *Books, Pamphlets and Newspapers Printed at Newark, New Jersey, 1776-1900* (Newark: Private Press of Courier-Citizen Company, 1902).

Frank Pierce Hill died on August 24, 1941.

Biographical listings and obituaries—*Current Biography* (1941); *National Cyclopaedia of American Biography* 2; [Obituary]. *Library Journal* 66:738 (Sept. 1, 1941); *Who Was Who in America* IV (1961-1968); *Who's Who in Library Service*, 1st ed. Books and articles about the biographee—Baldwin, E. V. "Frank P. Hill." *Library Journal* 66:780-81 (Sept. 15, 1941); "Fifty Years, 1889-1939." Newark, N.J.: The Newark Public Library, n.d.; Freeman, Margaret B. "The Brooklyn Public Library: A History." Vol. 1. Unpublished manuscript, 1970; *The Library* 4 (Oct. 1939); Locke, G. H. "Dr. Frank P. Hill—An Appreciation." *Library Journal* 55:282 (1930); Winser, B. "Frank Pierce Hill, 1885-1941." *ALA Bulletin* 35:511-12 (Oct. 1, 1941). Primary sources and archival materials—A sizeable collection of Hill's correspondence is in the ALA archives, University of Illinois.

—PATRICIA SENN BREIVIK

HIRSHBERG, HERBERT SIMON (1879-1955)

Herbert S. Hirshberg was born to Simon and Eva Warschauer Hirshberg in Boston, July 7, 1879. He studied cello throughout his youth, and he attended Brookline High School and Harvard College, where he was active in musical circles. Upon his graduation, magna cum laude, in 1900, he went to work for his father, a wholesale shoe merchant, but illness forced him to work for a time as a private tutor. In 1902, he attended a "summer school of library economy" at Amherst under William I. Fletcher (q.v.) and, after passing the required examinations, accepted a job as cataloger of foreign books and incunabula at the Boston Public Library, serving at the same time as reviser of cataloging at Simmons College Library School. From 1903 to 1905, he attended the New York State Library School at Albany, earning the B.L.S. and working as a cataloger at the New York State Library. During the summer of 1904, he worked at the Morse Institute Library at Natick.

Upon graduating from library school, Hirshberg was appointed music cataloger at the Library of Congress. His next position was at the Carnegie Library of Pittsburgh, and in 1908, he was appointed reference librarian at the Cleveland Public Library by William H. Brett (q.v.). This was the beginning of a long and distinguished service in Ohio libraries. He found time in 1910 to return to Pennsylvania to marry Blanche Lowe of Meadville, the children's librarian of the branch of which he had been in charge in Pittsburgh.

One job never seemed sufficient to absorb Hirshberg's energy and initiative. While serving as reference librarian at Cleveland Public, he was instructor in reference and bibliography at the Western Reserve Library School, 1909-1914, directed the development of a municipal reference branch in City Hall, and managed a series of free public lectures in Cleveland branch libraries.

In late 1914, he left Cleveland to become chief librarian at Toledo, Ohio, where the library trustees were eager to establish a widespread branch library system. Hirshberg immediately negotiated the renewal of a gift offer of $125,000 by the Carnegie Foundation for the erection of five branch libraries, and he managed the incredible feat of having these constructed and opened simultaneously: South, Locke, Mott, Kent, Jermain. He also opened several branches in school libraries and organized the annual Toledo Library Week, in cooperation with the Toledo Advertising Club.

Hirshberg left Toledo in 1922 to become the state librarian of Ohio. In the 104 years of its existence, the State Library had never had a professional librarian at its head, and a new state librarian was appointed nearly every time a new governor was elected. In a 1921 study of the Library, Dr. William H. Allen reported, "At present the library service is not only at a standstill but has for sometime been losing ground.... It is surprising that in a great state like Ohio it should be necessary to urge that state library service be taken out of politics ... no part of Ohio's public work is more in politics than the State Library." For obvious reasons, Hirshberg was reluctant to accept this position, but he was finally persuaded by friends and colleagues that he could make a much-needed contribution to library service in Ohio.

In his term as state librarian, Hirshberg did indeed justify their confidence. He carried out a program that strengthened existing libraries, developed county libraries, and, through mail services and travelling libraries, expanded service to areas without local libraries. He initiated work with school libraries and expanded and improved legislative reference service. He also worked for the improvement and simplification of library laws, achieving better tax support for public libraries through legislation that both put an end to direct Board of Education control of public libraries and permitted the establishment of school district libraries, which increased from 33 to 81 in number. He visited virtually all the public libraries of the state during his first two years in office; there is no record that previous librarians had visited any. But in spite of these accomplishments, all did not go smoothly for Hirshberg. On January 27, 1927, Governor Victor A. Donahey vetoed the library appropriation bill, forcing the closing of the State Library, and the Legislature did not override this veto in spite of pressure from the profession and the public.

Another challenge, however, appeared for Hirshberg in the directorship of the Akron Public Library, which he assumed in August 1927. The Library's facilities were adequate for a city of 60,000, but Akron had reached a population of 225,000. The city was faced with a five percent reduction in total revenues, with certainly no prospect of any increase in the $56,000 allotted the Library. To meet this crisis, the Library transferred, under Hirshberg's guidance, from a municipal to a school district form of support, which permitted a special tax levy for public library purposes. By the following spring, the new Board approved a budget of about $115,000, permitting the expansion of services and the planning of new branches. In September 1929, Hirshberg left Akron to assume the dual role of dean of the School of Library Science and director of libraries at Western Reserve University.

In his annual report for 1928-1929, President Vinson of Western Reserve wrote,

perhaps by the time this report is formally presented to the Trustees ... the successor of Miss

Tyler as Dean of the Library School will have been nominated.... There is a large and increasing number of libraries in and around the University, the coordination of which would, it is thought, work to the great advantage of all.... It has not seemed to the Administrative Officers of the University impossible to find a Dean for the Library School who might at least make a beginning of such coordination.

Hirshberg did this. He not only expanded and strengthened the School of Library Science, he also established a University Library and laid the groundwork for its future growth.

On October 29, 1929, Dean Hirshberg wrote to Sarah C. N. Bogle (q.v.), at ALA Headquarters, asking her reaction to certain "proposals which the faculty of the School is considering in relation to the future policies of the School." These were essentially an upgrading of the combined course to a strictly graduate program, a specialization in school and children's libraries and in public library administration, plus a "curriculum for teacher-librarians in elementary and platoon schools." This last objective was apparently never addressed again as such, although preparation for elementary school librarianship was later incorporated in the program in Library Service to Children. Although the School maintained a strong program in public library service, the specialization in administration was never completely realized, but the programs in school and children's library service continued to flourish. Other projects were initiated but did not become permanent.

Hirshberg was appointed at Western Reserve to serve as dean of the School of Library Science and director of the University Libraries. The latter appointment was not made final, however, until December 4, 1929, when the University trustees created the office of director of libraries of Western Reserve University, Adelbert College, Cleveland College, and the Cleveland School of Architecture, and elected Hirshberg to this office. He was also named director of Case Library. The Leonard Case Library, an independent subscription library with a fine collection of about 100,000 volumes and a considerable endowment, was moved from downtown Cleveland to the campus in 1926 to provide a research library for graduate studies. When Hirshberg came to Reserve, there were thirteen independent college and professional school libraries, and sixteen departmental libraries in the University. The first step he took was to merge the two largest libraries, Case and Adelbert College. Five years later, in July 1934, the Case Library trustees voted the use of $25,000 for renovating, remodeling, and equipping a building to house both the Library and the library school. Since Hirshberg had fully prepared plans anticipating such a move, however, a concentrated effort made possible its accomplishment in record time. The Library opened for service early in November, the School of Library Science having moved in in August. The building, named Thwing Hall in honor of former WRU President Charles F. Thwing, was dedicated on his eighty-first birthday, November 9, 1934.

Even with the move to Thwing Hall, the merging of the various libraries proceeded slowly. In his report for 1934-1935 as director of libraries, Hirshberg wrote, "It seems evident that revolutionary change is neither desirable nor feasible and that through cooperation and reasonable planning results can be reached which will eliminate many of our present difficulties without resorting to radical measures...." He made the following recommendations:

Formation of a union catalog for all libraries of the University,

Outlining of fields of purchase and book collection,

Designation of the University Library as a central reservoir,

Study of the means of financial support,

Designation of a University Library Council.

"A combined medical, dental, pharmacy, and nursing library built adjacent to and coordinated with the Cleveland Medical Library" was another project for the future.

A regional union catalog, separate from the University Library catalog and including the holdings of some 47 libraries, also became a reality. Hirshberg, with the assistance of Professor Robert C. Binkley, worked out the cataloging procedures, which involved filming the catalogs of such libraries as Oberlin, Ohio State, University of Cincinnati, Xavier, Ohio Wesleyan, The Hayes Memorial Library, the University of Michigan, and the major libraries of greater Cleveland. The work of copying the film onto cards was done at Thwing by a force of federally-funded Works Progress Administration typists under the supervision of the University Library. The project was begun in April 1936 and completed by 1939.

Meanwhile the Library collections continued to grow through the addition of other WRU collections, such as the collection of the School of Education, and through substantial gifts, such as the libraries of Dr. Thwing and of prominent Cleveland families, all of which necessitated changes in space allotment in Thwing Hall. A policy of assigning budget contributions from the various schools was eventually established. Hirshberg repeated in his annual reports the need to formulate a definite program of cooperative book purchases and "division of field" as essential in the development of resources.

Throughout his career, Hirshberg was active in professional organizations, held offices and served on committees in such associations as the American Library Association, the Ohio Library Association, the American Library Institute, the National Association of State Libraries, etc. He was particularly concerned with legislation, finance, library education, and certification. The latter he believed essential for raising the standards of library service but, in spite of his efforts, certification was not achieved in Ohio. He also served as adviser and consultant to libraries and library schools and he brought many library leaders to the School as visiting lecturers. Another offshoot of his wide knowledge of librarians and libraries was his keen interest in the placement of the School's graduates and his effectiveness in matching them to appropriate positions.

Dean Hirshberg was also instrumental in the creation of a film, "New Books for Old," released in 1938 with the cooperation of the Library Binding Institute. Additionally, he wrote for professional journals and published several books: *Elements of the Library Plan*, *Subject Guide to Reference Books*, and (with Carl Melinat) *Subject Guide to Government Publications*. His specialties in teaching were reference and administration.

During the Great Depression, the University had to cut salaries to ease its own financial problems, sometimes cutting them by 25 to 50 percent. Too, Hirshberg had three bouts of severe illness in the winters of 1935-1936, 1937-1938, and 1942-1943, so he wasn't always able to carry out his heavy responsibilities. Thus his faculty, especially Thirza Grant, Bertha Barden, and Harriet Long, maintained the School under most difficult circumstances, when he was unable to do so.

Hirshberg retired as dean in 1943 and as director of libraries in 1945. At this time, the Hirshbergs left Cleveland and established their residence in Winter Park, Florida, where Hirshberg remained active in professional affairs through his work as editorial consultant for the Americana Corporation and his very lively interest in the Winter Park Public Library. He served as president of its Board of Trustees and was working on plans for a proposed addition to the Library on the day of his death, September 15, 1955.

Hirshberg's interests and abilities were wide-ranging. In addition to libraries, scholarship, books, and music, he had an ingenious practical bent, as witnessed by a gadget called a "fine computer" which he devised and which, for years, hundreds of libraries used to their advantage. He was a devoted family man, justifiably proud of his charming wife and their four sons, and was a warm and gracious host. Often the Hirshbergs were "at home" to students and colleagues, and he was a great promoter of class picnics. He liked young people, and though he may at first have seemed somewhat formidable to them (a tall, rather gaunt man), they soon discovered that he had interest, understanding, a ready wit, and, as one of his colleagues has said, "a gentle heart (somewhat hidden but still there)."

Hirshberg truly lived for many years on "borrowed" time. The critical illnesses he sustained would have defeated a person of less courage and determination. Due to his own indomitable spirit, the devotion of his wife, and the support of his colleagues, he was able to carry on. As John Boynton Kaiser (q.v.) said of him, "Herbert Hirshberg repaid the loan a hundred-fold in service to his profession and his community and in gracious and considerate affection for friends and family."

Biographical listings and obituaries—[Obituary]. *Cleveland Plain Dealer*, Sept. 17, 1955, p. 11; [Obituary]. *College and Research Libraries* 17:94 (Jan. 1956); [Obituary]. *Library Journal* 80:2218 (Oct. 15, 1955); [Obituary]. *New York Times*, Sept. 16, 1955, p. 23; [Obituary]. *Toledo Blade*, Sept. 17, 1955; *Who Was Who in America* III (1951-1960); *Who's Who in American Education* 9 (1939-1940); *Who's Who in Library Service*, 1st ed., 2nd ed., 3rd ed. **Books and articles about the Biographee**—Kaiser, John B., et al. "Herbert S. Hirshberg, 1879-1955; Four Tributes to a Library Educator...." *Library Journal* 80:2819-21 (Dec. 15, 1955); Pardee, Helen L. *Story of the Akron Public Library*. Akron, Ohio, 1943; Richardson, Lyon N., and Harriet G. Long. "Herbert S. Hirshberg—July 7, 1879-September 15, 1955." *WRU SLS Alumni Association News Bulletin* no. 54 (Dec. 1955); Strong, George F. "Herbert S. Hirshberg." *Bulletin of Bibliography* 17:105-107 (Dec. 1941). **Primary sources and archival materials**—Cohen, Sidney. "Biographical Data on State Librarians of the Ohio State Library." Master's thesis, Kent State University, 1961; Archival material, which can be found at Case Western Reserve University, includes *Annual Reports* of the president, the dean of the School of Library Science, and the director of libraries (1929-1945), as well as Hirshberg's correspondence.

—MARGARET KALTENBACH

HODGES, NATHANIEL DANA CARLILE (1852-1927)

N. D. Carlile Hodges was born April 19, 1852, in Salem, Massachusetts, the youngest son of John and Mary Osgood Deland Hodges. He was graduated from Harvard in 1874 with an A.B. degree and continued his studies at the University of Heidelberg for a year and a half. During 1876 and 1877, he was a private tutor in mathematics at Cambridge, Massachusetts, and for the next four years (1877-1881), he was an assistant in the physics laboratory of Harvard. In 1879, as a result of his work in molecular physics, he was elected a fellow of the American Academy of Arts and Sciences and in 1882, he was elected to the American Association for the Advancement of Science. In 1883, he was appointed assistant editor of *Science* magazine, which was then in the process of resuming publication (with a subsidy from Alexander Graham Bell and Gardiner G. Hubbard) after a lapse of several years since its founding (by Thomas A. Edison). In 1885, Hodges was appointed editor of *Science*, and he remained with the periodical until 1894. While editor of *Science*, he was married to Adele Louise Goepper of Cincinnati on May 13, 1886; they had no children.

In 1895, Hodges became an assistant at the Astor Library, New York, and this seems to have been the beginning of his career in library science. He resigned in 1897 to accept a position in the Harvard Library, where he reclassified the scientific books. On April 20, 1900, Hodges was appointed librarian by the Board of Trustees of the Cincinnati Public Library. He remained librarian there until he retired September 1, 1924.

Active in national library circles, Hodges was a strong contributor to the work of the American Library Association; he opened its Chicago headquarters during his term as twenty-fourth president of ALA (1909-1910). He also served as a member of the Chicago Public Library Advisory Commission in 1909, and the Ohio Library Association elected him as its president (1904-1905). However many national and state positions and honors he held, Hodges is remembered chiefly as the man who, building on the work of such illustrious predecessors in Cincinnati as William Frederick Poole (q.v.), developed the Cincinnati Public Library into one of the finest public libraries in the country.

Although the Cincinnati Public Library was a county library making some effort to extend services outside the central library when Hodges arrived, the Board of Trustees was opposed to branches in the city or county. James Albert Green, then a member of the Board, explained to the press at the time of Hodges' death:

> At the time of his coming we had but one branch, and to tell the truth the trustees of the library were a bit dubious about even one branch. We had an idea then that there were only so many books that would be read and we took it for granted that for every 100 books circulated by the branch there would be 100 books less circulated by the Main library. It seemed to us quite possible that branch libraries would merely duplicate the work of the Main library and that to its disadvantage. On the contrary the more call there was for books at the branch and the more reference work that was done there—the more call for books and the more reference work at the Main library. We found out to our surprise that library work could be made intensive and that the greater and more widespread the facilities, the greater would be the number of readers. We were entirely cured of that strange and erroneous idea of duplication—though with our limited experience it was natural.

Having thus convinced the Board of the desirability of extending library service to as many people as possible, Hodges, at the time of his retirement, had created, in addition to one central library, 26 branches, 56 deposit stations, 116 school stations, and 60 miscellaneous stations in firehouses, playgrounds, etc.

Another of Hodges' innovations in Cincinnati was the introduction of open shelves to the Library, and here again Green describes the situation: "The one time we ever had any serious differences of opinion was when he proposed open shelves. Some of us thought half the library would be stolen over night. But Mr. Hodges insisted on trying it out and I am glad to say the open shelves are still here."

In February 1901, Hodges introduced to the Library the story hour for children. In an effort to help children's work and adult lecturers in the community, he also developed for loan a large "magic lantern slide" collection, many of them made from his own negatives of photographs of his extensive travels abroad.

His original interest in science was reflected in the building of a strong scientific collection, and he often appealed to business for funds to buy a particular collection that was for sale. Hodges also encouraged work with the blind, begun soon after his arrival and developed very rapidly until a complete department was created. This department not only served the local area, but loaned materials all over the United States and grew to be one of the largest libraries for the blind in this country.

Hodges was described during his tenure as librarian in Cincinnati as being tolerant, affable, courteous, and unassuming. Portraits of him show a mild-faced, scholarly-looking man wearing spectacles and a short beard. All personal descriptions of him mention his discriminating love for books, his unexpected sense of humor, and his great respect for knowledge.

His writing consisted of articles in journals; he left no major written work. On November 25, 1927, he died at his home in Mt. Healthy (a Cincinnati suburb) after a long illness. Hodges was a Unitarian and was buried from that church in Cincinnati's Spring Grove Cemetery.

Biographical listings and obituaries—*National Cyclopaedia of American Biography* 12; [Obituary]. *Cincinnati Enquirer*, Nov. 26, 1927, p. 22; [Obituary]. *Library Journal* 52:1176 (Dec. 15, 1927); *Who Was Who in America* I (1897-1942). **Books and articles about the biographee**— Goss, The Rev. Charles Frederick. *Cincinnati: The Queen City, 1788-1912.* Cincinnati: S. J. Clarke Publishing Co., 1912. Vol. III, pp. 645-46; Greve, Charles Theodore. *Centennial History of Cincinnati and Representative Citizens.* Chicago: Biographical Publishing Co., 1904. Vol. II, pp. 375-76.

—J. RICHARD ABELL

HOMES, HENRY AUGUSTUS (1812-1887)

Henry Augustus Homes was born March 10, 1812, in Boston to Henry and Dorcas Freeman Homes. His parents provided him with great wealth but also with the Puritan virtues of piety and dedication to work. He attended Phillips Academy (Andover, Massachusetts) from 1822 to 1826 and entered Amherst College at fourteen, graduating in 1830. He then studied theology at Andover (1830-1832), and medicine and theology at Yale (1832-1834), receiving his M.A. from Amherst in 1834. He next studied in Paris for a year, specializing in Arabic. In June 1835, he was ordained by the French Reformed Church and went to Turkey as a missionary. Besides preaching, teaching English, practicing medicine, and serving as the mission's business manager, Homes wrote and translated religious works and contributed articles on Eastern history, geography, and social customs to the *Missionary Herald*. He explored the Levant in 1837, Mesopotamia and Kurdistan in 1839. On April 15, 1841, he was married to Anna Whiting Heath of Brookline, Massachusetts. In 1851, Homes left his mission to serve the American legation at Constantinople as interpreter and *chargé d'affaires*, and for several months as acting consul. He returned to Boston with his wife, a son, and a daughter in 1853.

In September 1854, Homes accepted a temporary appointment to organize the 43,000-volume collection of the New York State Library, and in the following year, he was appointed an assistant librarian. In 1862, he became supervisor of the Miscellaneous Department (renamed the General Library in 1863), responsible for all collections except the Law Library. For a clientele of government officials, scientists, and historians, Homes built major collections in political science, American history, biography, genealogy, and scientific patents. Handicapped by a minuscule budget, he sought donations of collections and used an exchange program among domestic and foreign libraries to build a renowned collection of 134,000 volumes. During his tenure, the Library acquired the state's Colonial archives and the draft copies of Washington's Farewell Address and Lincoln's Emancipation Proclamation. Homes indexed and calendared many major collections, including the papers of the Colonial administrator Sir William Johnson and Governor George Clinton. His varied interests also led him to write pamphlets on history, heraldry and medals, religion, and philosophy. In recognition of his work, Columbia College conferred the degree of Doctor of Laws upon him in 1873. Additionally, following the 1876 American Library Association organizational meeting, Homes emerged as one of three original ALA vice-presidents.

Chief among Homes' professional publications are the three-volume catalog to the State Library collections (1855) with frequent supplements, and a report, *The Future Development of the New York State Library* (1879). Many of the ideas in the latter work, which were based upon procedures developing at libraries throughout the world, seemed novel at the time but are now an integral part of modern librarianship. Homes's influence can be seen at the State Library in particular, many of the current practices and functions having been instituted by him. Among his recommendations were that book selection and the establishment of regulations should be handled by the administrator rather than the trustees or funding agency, that books should circulate through an inter-library loan system, that towns should be authorized to establish free libraries supported by local taxes, and that schools and colleges should establish pro-fessorships of books and reading. He encouraged research libraries to define their role as distinct from that of public libraries. In architecture, he opposed ornamentation that attracted non-readers, encouraged compact storage and small rooms with uniform heat, and favored keeping book stacks separate from and cooler than reading rooms, thereby reducing both heating expenses and damage to books.

He also published many articles in the *Transactions of the Albany Institute* and wrote for other publications as well. His *The Correct Arms of the State of New York* (1880) convinced the state legislature to adopt his model as the standard form for official use in 1892.

Stricken with Bright's disease in June 1886, Homes took a leave of absence that continued until his death on November 3, 1887. One eulogist admired his incessant labors, lack of avocations, and content-ment with the duties of his office. He tended to be introverted and moody, economical in his speech, and, despite a lack of pretension, fixed in his views. A newspaper artist portrayed him with strong features set in the dour expression of a New England dooms-day preacher. Yet he had a dry wit, and his few close friends were devoted to him.

Henry Homes, like all the leading librarians of his time, was a well-read man with a natural aptitude but no special training in librarianship. A new era began with his successor at the State Library, Melvil Dewey (q.v.).

Biographical listings and obituaries—*Amherst College Biographical Record.* Amherst, Mass., 1963; *Dictionary of American Biography* 9 (A. Everett Peterson); *National Cyclopaedia of American Biography* 13; [Obituary]. *Albany Evening Journal,* Nov. 3, 1887; *Who's Who in America* 4 (1906-1907). **Books and articles about the biographee—** Albany Institute. *Transactions.* Vol. XII (1893); Grant, Asahel. *The Nestorians.* 1845; New-England Historic Genealogical Society. *Proceedings.* (Jan. 1888); Roseberry, Cecil R. *A History of the New York State Library.* Albany: New York State Library, State Education Department, University of the State of New York, 1970.

—PETER R. CHRISTOPH

HOPPER, FRANKLIN FERGUSON (1878-1950)

Franklin F. Hopper, library administrator, adult educator, and leader of library associations, was born September 17, 1878, at Eatontown, New Jersey, to Rulif and Elizabeth Croxson Wikoff Hopper. He received an A.B. from Princeton in 1900 and an

honorary Litt.D. in 1947. Immediately after graduating from Pratt Institute Library School in 1901, he went to the Library of Congress as a cataloger. In 1903, he was branch librarian at the Carnegie Library in Pittsburgh, where he became the order librarian from 1904 until he left in 1908 to head the public library in Tacoma, Washington.

In 1914, Hopper was called to the New York Public Library by the director, Edwin H. Anderson (q.v.), who had known him at Pittsburgh. Hopper came to New York as an expert in the book field, with a wide knowledge of publishing and close personal relationships with publishers and book dealers throughout the world. Among his many accomplishments as chief of the Order Division, he helped to organize the Staff Association at the New York Public Library, becoming its first president in 1917. At the time, this organization was considered a daring attempt for librarians to express their opinions on a large library's policies.

When he became chief of the Library's Circulation Department in 1919, Hopper skillfully brought together into one organization all the various private circulating libraries which had consolidated with the New York Public Library but which were still separate because a largely untrained staff clung to diverse technical practices. He also faced the problem of a public that had a tremendous mixture of cultural backgrounds, a situation augmented by the huge immigration during the early part of the century. Under Hopper's guidance, though, the Library became famous for its work with the foreign-born. He hired librarians who could speak the native languages of the readers, and he developed notable collections of books from foreign countries. He was also concerned about the needs of Negroes, and for them he found an especially capable librarian, Ernestine Rose (q.v.), who was supported by a complex program involving a new library building, a grant from the [Andrew] Carnegie [q.v.] Corporation and another Carnegie grant for the purchase of the remarkable Arthur A. Schomburg [q.v.] Collection of books on Negro literature and history.

When he became the fourth director of the New York Public Library in 1941, Hopper guided its policies through the difficult years of World War II, and he was responsible for removing the Library's treasures to vaults elsewhere in the country for safekeeping. He also had to find ways to meet the greatly increased demands on the Library's research facilities, including the pressures of military and industrial users, at a time when acquiring foreign books, one of the Library's distinctive features, was arduous and often impossible. In spite of ill health, Hopper continued in this position until the Library reluctantly allowed him to retire in 1946.

Hopper was a leader in adult education and in the 1930s introduced the readers' advisory and adult education services to the NYPL. Also intensely interested in the development of services for young people, he furthered the Library's work with children. Under his administration, a picture collection and a music library were begun as well. All of these services were later copied in various forms throughout the world, but at the time, they were considered radical innovations.

In all of these developments, Franklin Hopper insisted that the quality of the staff was most important. According to Harry Miller Lydenberg (q.v., his predecessor as director), Hopper was convinced that "it is the spirit behind the books that makes a library." He also insisted that readers must have superior books, going so far as to encourage authors to write them and publishers to produce them. Throughout the Depression of the 1930s, he struggled for money to buy books to aid the desperately poor, who could often afford no education except the Library.

Extremely active in library associations, Hopper became noted for his urbanity, charm, and inexhaustible wit. He was one of the committee of six that founded the Pacific Northwest Library Association, and in 1909-1910, was its first secretary; in 1913-1914, he was its president. He also was president of the New York Library Association, 1925-1926, and of the New York Library Club, 1923-1924. He was a member of the Executive Board of the American Library Association, 1925-1929, and vice-president, 1935-1936. His efforts to serve ethnic groups in New York City were recognized when Hopper was awarded the Order of the White Lion by the government of Czechoslovakia. He was a trustee and vice-president of the American Foundation for the Blind, and trustee of Fisk University, Skidmore College, Pratt Institute, the American Merchant Marine Association, and the Council on Adult Education for the Foreign-Born. He was also president of the Chappaqua Public Library and a member of the Executive Board of the American Association for Adult Education. During World War I, Hopper was manager for New York City of the American Library Association War Service campaign to provide books for soldiers and sailors; during World War II, he was a member of the Executive Board of the Council on Books in Wartime and also served on the national Executive Committee of the Victory Book Campaign.

Of Hopper's writings, two are considered to be his major works: *Order and Accession Department* (American Library Association, 1911; revised 1916 and 1926); and *Three Men—Their Intellectual Contribution to America* (Princeton University Press, 1944).

Franklin Hopper married Marion Stephens of New York City, January 6, 1917. They had three children: Elizabeth, Stephen, and Ann.

A leader in libraries and library associations, and a close friend of librarians, publishers, authors, and booksellers, Franklin Hopper was a national influence in the book world for over forty years. At his death, in San Francisco on November 29, 1950, the Library of Congress *Information Bulletin* (December 4, 1950) printed this statement: "As a colleague Dr. Hopper was an honor to his profession, as a person he was generous in wisdom, warm in friendship and great in heart."

Biographical listings and obituaries—[Obituary]. *New York Public Library Bulletin* 54:613 (Dec. 1950); [Obituary]. *New York Public Library Bulletin* 55:159-61 (April 1951); [Obituary]. *Pacific Northwest Library Association Quarterly* 15:115-16 (April 1951); *Who Was Who in America* III (1951-1960); *Who's Who in Library Service*, 1st ed., 2nd ed. Books and articles about the biographee—Collison, R. L. W. "Portrait of a Librarian." *Library World* 44:125-26 (March 1942); "Progressive Librarian." *New Yorker* 17:12 (Nov. 8, 1941); "Retirement Announced." *Library Journal* 71:468-69 (April 1, 1946); St. John, F. R. "Franklin Ferguson Hopper." *College and Research Libraries* 7:347 (Oct. 1946).

—JOHN MACKENZIE CORY
—LAWRENCE P. MURPHY

HOSMER, JAMES KENDALL (1834-1927)

James K. Hosmer was born in Northfield, Massachusetts, on January 29, 1834, the son of George Washington and Hannah Poor Kendall Hosmer, and descended from James Hosmer who settled in Concord, Massachusetts, in 1635. Young Hosmer entered Harvard at age seventeen, graduating in 1855 as class poet. He studied theology at Harvard for the next four years, and, in 1860, was ordained as clergyman of the Unitarian Church in Deerfield, Massachusetts. He was married twice: in 1863, to Eliza A. Cutler who died in 1877, and in 1878, to Jennie P. Garland. He had four sons and three daughters, five of whom survived their father.

In 1862, Hosmer enlisted as a private in the 52nd Massachusetts Volunteer Infantry, serving as corporal until the regiment was dismissed at the end of 1863. His journal of military service was published in 1864, under the title *The Color-Guard*; the book was widely acclaimed and led to many important contacts and friendships.

Hosmer returned to the Deerfield church but felt that his theological views were unorthodox, and in 1866, he accepted a professorship at Antioch College. He studied in Germany in 1870 and two years later, became professor of history at the University of Missouri. In 1874 he began an eighteen-year tenure as professor of English and German literature at

Washington University in St. Louis. Then in 1892, Hosmer was appointed head librarian of the Minneapolis Public Library, established only three years earlier. He retired from that position in 1904, at the age of seventy, to devote the remainder of a long life to writing and scholarship. In 1902-1903 he served as president of the American Library Association. Honorary doctorates were awarded him by the University of Missouri, Washington University, and Harvard University.

Throughout his long life, Hosmer wrote widely and published prolifically—novels, stories, and articles on widely ranging topics for magazines and newspapers; textbooks, such as *A Short History of German Literature* (1878); works of popular history: *A Short History of Anglo-Saxon Freedom* (1890), *A Short History of the Mississippi Valley* (1901), *The History of the Louisiana Purchase* (1902); narrative history including two volumes in the original *American Nation* series edited by A. B. Hart: *The Appeal to Arms, 1861-1863*, and *The Outcome of the Civil War, 1863-1865*, both published in 1907.

Three of Hosmer's biographies were characterized by objectivity and conciseness at a time when such qualities in biographical writing were rare: *Samuel Adams* (1885), *The Life of Young Sir Henry Vane* (1888), and *The Life of Thomas Hutchinson* (1896). Eight years after his retirement he published a volume of essays and reminiscences, *The Last Leaf*. He also wrote a detailed and lengthy autobiography which has never been published and is now in the possession of the Minnesota Historical Society.

Hosmer's annual reports and other writings done while he headed the Minneapolis Public Library delineate the goals and ideals that shaped the nature of his librarianship. "The Public Library should be regarded as a great cooperative scheme for supplying the community with literature. Books and magazines are scarcely less necessary than bread," he wrote in 1903.

He also believed that a library must aggressively seek to expand its appeal, to increase its service. Books that merely sat on shelves were unimportant; they must be circulated and read. He rejoiced that his Library not only had many branches but that it supplied books to 35 different public schools within the city. He was acutely conscious of the need to secure and retain superior and dedicated staff members, and he felt it was important that 41 percent of the Library's budget went for salaries. As he left the librarianship, he pointed out that the Minneapolis Public Library had the largest per capita circulation of any library in any city of over 200,000 population in the United States.

Hosmer asserted, in his last annual report to the Library Board of the Minneapolis Public Library (December 31, 1903), that

It is in accordance with the best traditions of such institutions as ours that Librarians shall not be entirely absorbed in administrative details, but shall be fruitful of works, of benefit first to the communities which they serve, and second to the world at large. They have at hand, as do no other men, the treasures of the past. What better than that, as do no other men, so far as time and strength allow, they shall express the essence of those treasures, and impart it in a form convenient for their generation.

Certainly throughout a long life—as clergyman, as professor, as librarian, and even in retirement, Hosmer lived up to the ideal of being "fruitful of works."

Perhaps the finest tribute to Hosmer as a librarian is found in two actions taken by the Library Board of the Minneapolis Public Library in 1925 and 1926. In the former year, they named Hosmer librarian emeritus. In 1926, they renamed the 36th Street Branch the "James K. Hosmer Branch." Earlier, on his ninetieth birthday, the Minneapolis Six O'Clock Club had recognized Hosmer's thirty-year membership with a special dinner. Among the many speakers to pay tribute to Hosmer was Gratia A. Countryman (q.v.), who had succeeded him as head librarian of the Minneapolis Public Library and who spoke at length of the leadership furnished the Library between 1892 and 1904 by the guest of honor.

James K. Hosmer died on May 11, 1927.

Biographical listings and obituaries—*Dictionary of American Biography* 9 (Solon J. Buck); Hosmer, G. I. *Hosmer Genealogy* (1928); *National Cyclopaedia of American Biography* 6; [Obituary]. *Library Journal* 52:607 (June 1, 1927); [Obituary]. *Minneapolis Morning Tribune*, May 12 and 13, 1927; *Who Was Who in America* I (1897-1942). **Books and articles about the biographee**—*Apocrypha Concerning the Class of 1855 at Harvard College* (1880); [Article]. *Minneapolis Morning Tribune*, Nov. 26, 1902; "As It Was in the Beginning." *Public Libraries* 29:130-32 (1924); Countryman, Gratia A. "James Kendall Hosmer, 1834-1927." *Bulletin of Bibliography* 13:193-94 (Sept.-Dec. 1929); *Proceedings* of the American Antiquarian Society, n.s. 37 (1928); *Report of the Secretary of the Class of 1855 of Harvard College* (1865). **Primary sources and archival materials**—Hosmer's unpublished autobiography is in the Minnesota Historical Society Library. Letters, reports and memorabilia in the possession of the Minneapolis Public Library concern his years there.

—RALPH ADAMS BROWN

HOSTETTER, ANITA MILLER (1889-1963)

Anita Miller Hostetter provided national leadership in the development and monitoring of library education programs in the United States over the thirty-year period from 1925 to 1955.

She was born in Ladoga, Indiana, on October 18, 1889, to William Robert and Emma Adell Miller Hostetter. Her forebears were among the early colonists in America, and her grandparents were part of the migration to the West, bringing the heritage of the East and Virginia to the frontier. Family lore indicates that her grandmother, when entertaining in their log cabin first home, would dress as for a formal dinner. As the farm prospered, her grandparents moved to the town when her mother was a young girl. Her father, a partner in the major department store for the area, travelled frequently to such business centers as Chicago and St. Louis, giving the family, including the two daughters Anita and Marie, a continuing sense of what the outside world was like.

The family moved to Denver in 1907, where both Anita and Marie attended a private high school for girls. Anita attended the University of Denver for two years and then the University of Kansas, where she received the A.B. degree in 1917. Later, she earned the B.L.S. from Illinois (1920). She also took courses at the University of Chicago in 1925-1926.

Her first library experience was as a substitute at the Denver Public Library during 1914-1915. She next served as a student assistant in the chemistry library, during 1915 and 1916, while an undergraduate at Kansas. Her first professional position was as assistant librarian at the Kansas State Teachers College at Emporia from 1920 to 1924. The next year, she was in Omaha in the library of the technical high school, thus broadening her experience to include this large segment of librarianship.

Hostetter's formal involvement with American Library Association activities began in 1925. Along with Harold F. Brigham, she was appointed research assistant to W. W. Charters in the Library Curriculum Study; both of the assistants had been trained in Charters' methods. The next few years were to be rich indeed, with the newly created office committed to making "a scientific analysis of library work" as a prerequisite to designing an appropriate curriculum and preparing suitable textbooks. Some six titles were to appear in the series, each the work of a specialist, and each involving extensive field studies and collaboration with specialists other than the author. Final editing became the staff's responsibility. Credit for the extensive work of the research assistants is typified in the preface to James I. Wyer's (q.v.) *Reference Work*: "Sincere and grateful acknowledgments are due ... particularly to Harold F. Brigham and Anita M. Hostetter, two exceptionally competent and clearheaded young librarians."

But the activities outlined above are only a prelude to those that followed, as Hostetter served first as executive assistant to the newly created Board of Education for Librarianship (1928-1932), and as its chief executive officer from 1933 until her retirement in 1955. During this period, she became recognized within ALA as a staff person of unusual competence and, externally, as an expert on library education and personnel. She was the key person working with the Board in the development and implementation of the 1933 standards, and the guiding hand that assisted both the Board and the profession in the transition to the 1951 standards (until her retirement in 1955). She deserves recognition not only for the direct benefits of her personal work but also for many of the achievements of individuals and groups with whom she worked.

Colleagues who have carried Board responsibilities in other years testify to the high quality of Anita Hostetter's work and personal influence. Keyes Metcalf, chairman in 1937, tells of his month on the road with her, visiting colleges in California and Texas that were planning new library education programs at a time when jobs for graduates were non-existent. "Anita proved to be good company, with a good sense of humor, and ready to speak her mind frankly and persuasively not only to librarians, but to college and university presidents and trustees. Anita was personally responsible for stopping a half dozen schools on this trip and, indirectly, many more."

After assisting Hostetter in her study of the training programs for teacher-librarians in 1936, Margaret Rufsvold commented that Hostetter's "farsighted recommendations" were the basis of all later developments in the training of U.S. school librarians. Later, during the early 1950s, when the American Association of Universities and the National Commission on Accrediting were determined to restrict accreditation to regional associations, many schools were being visited and evaluated under the 1951 standards. Jack Dalton, chairman of the Board of Education for Librarianship from 1953 to 1955, reports that Board members consulted Hostetter concerning numerous questions that beset them during this fast-paced and confusing era, and she had the answers. Sarah Rebecca Reed, who later held Hostetter's position at ALA, saw Hostetter's "remarkable insights, wisdom and knowledge" readily apparent in her reports.

Anita Hostetter wrote not only for the Board, however, but for professional journals (primarily the *ALA Bulletin*) as well, her principal subject being, of course, the education of librarians. She also contributed papers to numerous conferences, participating in one such meeting at Atlanta University's School of Library Science soon after it was founded in 1941 to replace the then-defunct Hampton Institute Library School ("Questions for a New Library School," Library Conference, Atlanta University, pp. 1-7). Her "Administrative Problems in Library Education: A Discussion" appeared in Bernard Berelson's *Education for Librarianship* (1949, pp. 268-71).

A paper that Hostetter delivered to a Richmond conference (and that appeared in *ALA Bulletin* 30:770-74, August 1936) depicts the ideal role that she sought for the library in education. Explaining her belief that instruction in the use of the library should be as completely integrated into a school's curriculum as possible, she said

the librarian can through tact, patience, and intelligent service so demonstrate the values of integrated library instruction that ultimately the teachers will be ready and qualified to guide in the use of the library. The librarian must, however, always retain general oversight of the program for integrated library instruction in the school. Library instruction can thus assume an integral position in the curriculum; its distinct offerings are of content and of method. Strange to say when content and method of library instruction are apparently submerged in the classroom project, library instruction has become a rich aspect of the curriculum and gives its highest service.

In 1959, Anita Hostetter received the Beta Phi Mu award. The citation reads in part: "To Anita Hostetter whose loyalty, dedication, high intelligence, and competence ... has been a constructive and wholesome force in advancing the profession of librarianship and improving the education of its practitioners." To her belongs much of the credit for the evolution of library education from vocational education to an academic discipline. Bringing to the task her analytical mind and her intellectual strength, she synthesized the contributions of library leaders from various areas of librarianship into solid national library education standards and guidelines. Anita M. Hostetter died on May 2, 1963.

Biographical listings and obituaries–[Obituary]. *ALA Bulletin* 57:854-55 (Oct. 1963); [Obituary]. *Library Journal* 88:2485 (June 15, 1963); *Who's Who in Library Service*, 1st ed., 2nd ed., 3rd ed. Books and articles about the biographee–"ALA Awards." *Wilson Library Bulletin* 34:4 (Sept. 1959); "Beta Phi Mu Award." *Library Journal* 84:2148 (July 1959); Morton, Florinell F. "Anita Hostetter." *ALA Bulletin* 57:884-85 (Oct. 1963); Parker, W. W. "1959 ALA Awards, Citations and Scholarships." *ALA Bulletin* 53:700 (Sept. 1959). Primary sources and archival materials–The most complete record of Hostetter's correspondence, reports, and working papers are held by ALA (either at headquarters in Chicago or at the archives at the University of Illinois, Urbana). There are also two archival collections in the Columbia University Libraries: 1) the combined personal and official files of Francis St. John (q.v.) and Richard H. Logsdon (concerning BEL and the Library Education Division) and 2) Jack Dalton's official and personal papers (concerning BEL and related ALA activities). See also BEL documents, of which she was frequently author.

–RICHARD H. LOGSDON

HOWE, HARRIET EMMA (1881-1965)

Harriet E. Howe was born December 10, 1881, in Urbana, Illinois, the daughter of William Renfrew and Althea G. Pocock Howe. She earned the Bachelor of Library Science degree from the University of Illinois

in 1902, the Ed.M. degree from Harvard in 1928, and was awarded an honorary Doctor of Library Science degree by Colorado Women's College, Denver, in 1945. Her professional life was completely dedicated to the service of librarianship, and she was eminently effective both as a librarian and as a professor and administrator of library education programs.

Little is known about Harriet Howe's background prior to her entry into the then unique Illinois State Library School in the late 1890s. However, she immediately came under the influence of Katharine Lucinda Sharp (q.v.), who did much to encourage and develop the characteristics that mark Harriet Howe's personality and leadership qualities. Her biographical sketch of Katharine Sharp, published in Emily Danton's *Pioneering Leaders in Librarianship*, cites Sharp's professional knowledge, forcefulness, critical facilities, and management aptitude–these are also key facets of Harriet Howe's successful career.

Howe's professional life was long and varied, a mixture of teaching and practical library work. From 1904 to 1906, she was instructor at the University of Illinois and directed the University of Washington School of Librarianship program during the summers of 1905 and 1906. She gained key professional experience as head cataloger at the University of Iowa from 1906 to 1910, serving also as an instructor in Iowa's Summer School for Library Training, from 1907 to 1909, and as its director in the summers of 1914, 1915, and 1917. Leaving Iowa in 1910, she became chief cataloger of the Minneapolis Public Library, where she remained until 1913, when she accepted a position as assistant professor at Western Reserve University, Cleveland. In 1917, Harriet Howe moved further east, to Boston and Simmons College where, until 1924, she was an assistant professor in its library school. During the summers from 1920 to 1923, she gained additional experience teaching at Columbia University, New York City.

Howe's several years of involvement in library education, as well as her active professional life, brought her an offer, in 1924, to serve as executive assistant of the American Library Association Board of Education for Librarianship, where she worked closely with another key woman leader, Sarah C. N. Bogle (q.v.). Then, in 1927, she was selected to teach at the prestigious new library school at the University of Chicago where she held an associate professorship until 1931, when she was named director of the newly formed School of Librarianship at the University of Denver. As professor and director of the School until her retirement in 1950, she enhanced her national reputation as an educator and helped Malcolm G. Wyer (q.v.), Denver's dean, to establish a unique program of library education. After her retirement in 1950, she moved to Colorado Springs to live, but was asked, in 1953, to serve as acting director of the University of Southern California Library School, a position which she held for two years. In the early years of her retirement she also accepted an appointment as cataloging professor at Florida State University. She returned to Colorado Springs in 1955, and prior to her death spent over fifteen years travelling, writing, and continuing some of her professional interests. In November of 1965, she moved to Sun City, Arizona, to be near her nephew, Richard Heitsmith, but a few weeks later, on December 5, 1965, five days before her eighty-fourth birthday, she died.

Throughout her life, Harriet Howe was active in professional organizations. She was a member of the American Library Association, the Special Libraries Association, the National Educational Association, the American Association of University Women, Administrative Women in Education, the Chicago Library Club, and Altrusa International. She was elected to numerous offices and appointed to several committees in these organizations including the Council and Executive Board of ALA.

In addition to her many contributions to professional organizations, she also published a number of key articles and prepared reviews of professional books. Among her papers are a 1948 study, "Administrative Problems in Library Education" (in B. R. Berelson, ed., *Education for Librarianship*, Chicago: ALA, 1949); an article on the "Future of Librarianship" (*Library Journal*, February 1, 1947); and "Two Decades in Education for Librarianship" (*Library Quarterly*, July 1942). These are strong examples of her articulate and forthright style. In her writings, as in her work, she expertly combined a pragmatic philosophy with her commitment to education for librarianship and the profession as a whole.

A career such as Harriet Emma Howe's, which encompasses several positions and a special kind of personal enthusiasm and willingness to experiment in a variety of situations, is difficult to summarize. There is little doubt that she was an imaginative leader who generated many ideas. Her ideas became realities of the classroom through her teaching, and components of the Denver School of Librarianship through her forceful administration. Like her early mentor, Katharine Sharp, she was a strong advocate of delegating authority. Referring to the assignment of decision-making, she wrote,

> A load of responsibility fell on the teacher's shoulders in making that decision, but she found out that there were many ways to accomplish the end desired, and she had courage to try out different ones with differing groups of students. Also the lesson in administration, the great one of delegating authority, remained as a guide to that instructor throughout her professional life.

Although Howe was referring to Katharine Sharp, this was clearly her own precept as well. In addition, Harriet Howe was described by her colleague Isabel Nichol as an individual who was especially known for *her* "feeling of *responsibility*, of her *thoroughness* and *exactitude* in all that she undertook."

These facets of her personality brought her recognition as an innovative and courageous educator. In 1931, when the University of Denver's School of Librarianship was founded, she and Dean Wyer introduced into the curriculum a program that represented a break with the traditional arrangement of library school courses. The assorted individual courses were restructured into three key units: Book Arts, Library Administration, and Cataloging and Classification. Along with the faculty, Howe and Wyer believed that the students could develop individual interests as to type of library within these broad areas of competency, and, as a result, could more effectively interrelate principles of library management.

Another major innovation was the introduction, in 1947, of the "Denver Plan." A basic core curriculum became part of the undergraduate program as a prerequisite to graduate study in librarianship. Completion of the core curriculum was followed by a single year of graduate study—replacing the more typical two years leading to a second bachelor's degree—which brought the student a Master of Arts degree. The University of Denver thereby pioneered in what became a major change in the degree structure of library programs. The B.S. in L.S. was abandoned as the first professional degree and a materials-centered, graduate degree became accepted throughout the United States.

Although completely committed to education for librarianship and the goals of the profession, Harriet Howe was also a splendid human being—a woman noted for her compassion, her interest, and her concern for others: friends, family, colleagues. Among the first to be considered were the students, who were so close to her work. Their future as contributing members of society, as professionals, and as individuals was always uppermost in her mind. She worked closely with them and helped to identify their special aptitudes and to counsel them in appropriate career paths. Outside of her library work, she was involved in community development and larger educational circles. This was noted when, in 1940, the Colorado Library Association gave her an award for "outstanding contributions to the cultural growth of Colorado." Harriet Howe never asked for special recognition, but her continuing role in the profession, even after retirement, was a mark of the value that her colleagues placed on her work. The ultimate tribute came to her in 1960, when, at the age of 79, she was awarded the Dewey Medal by the American Library Association "for her pioneering spirit and leadership in professional training and her creative administration." In presenting the award, Paul Kebabian said, "Few have had the courage and the will to proceed with such dedication; few have had the opportunity to create substance out of an idea as did Harriet Howe in her twenty year career at the Denver University library school." Perhaps, however, the final assessment is best found in Harriet Howe's own words, for as she said of Katharine Sharp, so might it be said of her: "Maybe ... the highest tribute that can be paid to the pioneers is that they possessed qualities worthy of emulation and that these qualities can be passed on to successive generations. . . ."

Biographical listings and obituaries–[Obituary]. *Library Journal* 91:225 (Jan. 15, 1966); *Who's Who in Library Service*, 1st ed., 2nd ed., 3rd ed. **Books and articles about the biographee**–"Awards and Citations for 1960." *Library Journal* 85:2740 (Aug. 1960); Nichol, Isabel. "Harriet E. Howe." *The Colorado Library Association Bulletin* 29:3-4 (Jan. 1952); Slocum, G. F. "1960 ALA Awards, Citations, and Scholarships." *ALA Bulletin* 54:688-89 (Sept. 1960).

–MARTHA BOAZ
–JOHN T. EASTLICK
–LAUREL A. GROTZINGER

HUNT, CLARA WHITEHILL (1871-1958)

Clara Whitehill Hunt was an active participant in what has often been called America's significant contribution to the library world–service to children. She was one of a small group of pioneers, active in the first part of the twentieth century, who established children's rooms, trained children's librarians, fought for recognition of quality children's literature, and began formulating the objectives, standards, and goals that molded modern public library service to children. Born in 1871 to Edwin and Mary M. Brown Hunt in Utica, New York, Clara Hunt was awarded a teaching certificate from the Utica Free Academy in 1889. She became interested in children's reading while serving as a principal at a small primary and kindergarten school. Excited by the contribution the public library could make to education, her enthusiasm was enhanced by Louise Cutter, a "trained" librarian at the local public library. In 1896, she decided to become a librarian herself.

After graduation from the New York State Library School at Albany in 1898, Hunt organized and opened the new children's room at the Apprentice's Library in Philadelphia. Dr. Frank P. Hill (q.v.), then director of the Newark Public Library, met her at that year's American Library Association conference and offered her a position. In October 1898, she went to Newark as an assistant in the Reference Department, but also in charge of planning a children's room for the building that was to open in 1901.

In 1903, Dr. Hill, now chief librarian of the Brooklyn Public Library, offered Clara Hunt the position of superintendent of work with children, one of the few such positions in the country that was filled with a trained professional. Under her direction, the small Children's Services Department at Brooklyn Public grew along with the library system to become one of the most extensive children's divisions in the country. Andrew Carnegie (q.v.) Foundation grants ensured the building of several libraries every year, and Hunt prepared over thirty new children's rooms, including extensive physical plans. She also faced the problem of finding trained children's librarians, a rarity at that time. Ever resourceful and dedicated, she decided to pick "the right kind of people," and to train them. In her own words, "it goes without saying that she must be a person of brains and force of character, else, with the best-heart in the world, her attitude toward the children may be sentimental and her juvenile book collection a menace rather than an asset to her community." In 1914, she began a Training Course for Children's Librarians, which continued until 1930.

Hunt's second requirement for good children's services was "the right kind of book," and she believed strongly in children's books as a moral force. Her first book, *What Shall We Read to the Children* (1915), grew out of her strong convictions that "when librarians know enough to tolerate only the positively good books, many noble forests will be saved which are now being slaughtered to furnish paper for books that waste young minds." She frequently attacked in print the "cheap trash" she felt was being produced, while defending vigorously the artistic quality of "good" children's books.

The third essential of which she spoke frequently was the training of children in "good library manners." This, she explained, was the library's role in citizen training, not only toward better decorum in the library, but mainly to foster respect for law and government. Her strict training dictums were partially tempered by her pleas for "a friendly welcome" and "unvarying courtesy" to children.

Hunt, a frequent contributor to library literature, served as chairman of the Children's Literature Section of the American Library Association in both 1904 and 1921. Her *Library Work with Children* (1929) was a part of the "Manual of Library Economy" series of the American Library Association, and was an outgrowth of Hunt's dedication to properly training children's librarians. In addition, she wrote four children's books: *About Harriet* (1916), *The Little House in the Woods* (1918), *Peggy's Playhouses* (1924), *The Little House in the Green Valley* (1932). "I hope you notice," she said in her autobiographical sketch for the *Junior Book of*

Authors, "some things I cannot leave out of any story I write for children: good fathers and mothers, delightful books, and the country!"

Hunt retired in 1939 and moved to Sudbury, Massachusetts, where both her parents were born. She died on January 11, 1958, in the countryside she loved so dearly.

Biographical listings and obituaries–[Obituary]. *Antiquarian Bookman* 21:244 (Jan. 27, 1958); [Obituary]. *Horn Book* 34:93 (April 1958); [Obituary]. *Publishers Weekly* 173:203 (Jan. 27, 1958); *Who Was Who in America* III (1951-1960); *Who's Who in Library Service*, 1st ed. **Books and articles about the biographee**–Bowker, R. R. "Some Children's Librarians." *Library Journal* 46:787-90 (Oct. 1, 1921); "Clara Whitehill Hunt." In Stanley J. Kunitz and Howard Haycraft, *Junior Book of Authors.* New York: H. W. Wilson Co., 1954; Holbrook, Barbara. "Clara Whitehill Hunt." *Wilson Bulletin for Libraries*, April 1929, pp. 539, 553.

–PATRICIA GLASS SCHUMAN

HUNT, HANNAH (1903-1973)

Hannah Hunt was born February 27, 1903, in Chicago, to Melville M. and Carrie Kerlin Hunt. She completed her secondary education in Chicago in 1920, at which time her family moved to Lakewood, Ohio. She entered Earlham College in 1921, spending only one year in residence. Upon her mother's death, and against her father's wishes, she insisted on staying home for the next two years to look after her younger sister and brother, instead of returning to college. She worked in the Lakewood Public Library during these two years and continued to work there during the summers after her return to Earlham in 1924. She earned her baccalaureate degree in 1927.

In 1928, Hannah Hunt accepted a field assignment with the American Friends Service Committee in a babies' and children's hospital at Chalon, France. The next two years were spent with the Cleveland and Lakewood public libraries. In 1931, she earned a B.S. in L.S. degree at Western Reserve University. After more than twenty years in the field, she returned to Reserve in 1954 to earn the M.S.L.S. and to become a full-time member of the faculty. These years were spent chiefly in library service to children and young adults in public and school libraries in such dissimilar places as Evanston, Illinois; Lakewood, Ohio; Honolulu; Los Angeles; and Rockford, Illinois. She also taught at Western Michigan during several summer sessions and spent a year and a half (February 1951–June 1952) as a member of the American faculty appointed by the American Library Association to teach at the Japan Library School, Keio University in Tokyo. On the completion of her term there, she became Young Adult Specialist for ALA's American Heritage Project, an assignment that took her to many parts of the United States.

When Hannah Hunt first came to Reserve in the fall of 1930, she intended to specialize in public library children's work and take "sufficient general training in case opportunity should arise in another department," adding the hope that the "present course will serve as a basis for further study." Apparently her training enabled her to serve not only as a public library children's librarian, but also as an elementary and a junior high school librarian, and a young adult librarian in public libraries. Her teaching assignments at Western Michigan University and Keio reflected these interests. However, her desire for "further study" was not realized until 1954, when she returned to Western Reserve.

Her teaching responsibilities at Western Reserve University included courses in young adult literature and in school library administration. Hunt also found herself in charge of a school library program—not quite what she had anticipated, but a situation that she nevertheless met in her usual conscientious and responsible fashion. Her fear that she was shortchanging both areas of her responsibility (that is, young adult work in public libraries and in school libraries) led her, with the encouragement of a member of the school's Visiting Committee, to seek support for the funding of a true school media program. Her efforts were rewarded with grants in 1966 from two foundations in Cleveland, which made possible not only the appointment of a specialist, but also the purchase of adequate resources to support the program.

Throughout her career, Hannah Hunt was active professionally, as a member of ALA, serving on Council and various committees, and as chairman of the Young Adult Services Division. She was also active in the Ohio Library Association and the Ohio Association of School Libraries. For several years, she sponsored a Student Library Assistants' Workshop at Reserve, and she organized other workshops and institutes.

She loved to travel—witness her year in France as a young woman, her years in Honolulu and in Tokyo, and her peripatetic job with ALA. Her colleagues at Reserve said that she so loved to travel that when she returned to Reserve (located on Cleveland's east side) she "made daily travel mandatory by building a charming home of California redwood, with a Japanese garden—but in Lakewood!" (located west of Cleveland). Her love affair with Hawaii and Japan extended not only to students from these areas, but also to students from other overseas countries and to displaced persons. In addition, during her years of teaching, she served as foreign student counsellor, a responsibility that she carried out with deep concern and care for each individual. At a banquet honoring her on her retirement in May 1967, the alumni presented her with a "passport" and funds for travel, and she was able to enjoy a return visit to Hawaii and several other trips before she was stricken with a fatal illness. She died on December 27, 1973.

Those who knew her will remember Hannah Hunt's thoughtfulness, her loyalty, and the time she gave so generously without sparing herself. Her painstaking and meticulous attention to detail, her emphasis on basics and a solid foundation will always come to mind. All of this seriousness of purpose was tempered by a delightful sense of humor. One experience she relates in a little pamphlet (written shortly before her death) called, "Christmases Remembered": in speaking of going to Keio University, she wrote, "My delight in the opportunity was somewhat deflated by the Army Medico who processed me in Chicago. Jabbing needles in both of my arms, his irritation erupted with, 'Of all the things MacArthur needs over there I'll never understand why I get orders to process a half-pint librarian on the double.'"

Her contribution to the profession was high idealism, a belief in the worth of each individual, and a commitment to service based on order and method, all of which were transmitted to her colleagues and her students. And there was an eagerness to take American librarianship to foreign lands, which in the early 1950s was rare. She was a gentle, tough lady who never did care that she did not know the difference between her personal and professional lives.

Biographical listings and obituaries—A Biographical Dictionary of Librarians in the U.S. and Canada, 5th ed.; [Obituary]. American Libraries 5:127 (March 1974); [Obituary]. Library Journal 99:528 (Feb. 15, 1974) and 99:615 (March 1, 1974); [Obituary]. Wilson Library Bulletin 48:538 (March 1974); Who's Who in Library Service, 4th ed. Books and articles about the biographee—[Biographical sketch]. ALA Bulletin 46:332 (Nov. 1952). Primary sources and archival materials—Material about Hannah Hunt is contained in the Archives of Case Western Reserve University.

—MARGARET KALTENBACH
—JOHN A. ROWELL

HUTCHINS, FRANK AVERY (1851-1914)

Frank Hutchins, a brilliant man of rare vision and modesty, a pioneer librarian and active leader in the library world of Wisconsin, was born on March 8, 1851, in Norfolk, Ohio. During his lifetime he was teacher, bookseller, newspaper man, library trustee, and librarian. Again and again his friends described him as a humanitarian, public servant, scholar, and practical idealist. He helped to gain legislative, financial, and professional support for both the educational work of school and public libraries and the extension of library services throughout the state of Wisconsin. An initiator who would take no credit

for the events he helped to set in motion, he recognized the abilities of others and encouraged them to carry out new ideas.

His father, Allen Sabin Hutchins, a school principal and classics teacher, had emigrated from New York and, in 1853, joined his brother Charles A. Hutchins at a farm they had purchased in Walworth County, Wisconsin. In 1858, they moved to Beaver Dam, where Allen Hutchins became president of Wayland University (later Wayland Academy) and Charles became an instructor. Both his father and uncle were classical scholars and leading Wisconsin educators, so Frank Hutchins was born among books. His early education was gained at home and in his father's school. In 1866, Frank's sister, Dorothea, was born, and in later years, she devoted her life to his care.

His father's illnesses and difficulties at the University forced his retirements and the family's moves back and forth from Beaver Dam to Baraboo, and to Beloit. From 1871 to 1873, Frank was a student at Beloit College, but he left college before graduation due to illness. In 1874, he taught school briefly at Fond du Lac, where his uncle Charles was city superintendent and principal of high schools. For a time Frank travelled for a book company; then followed a period of illness.

In 1884, he purchased an interest in a Democratic weekly, the Beaver Dam Argus, for which he was editor. He also served as city clerk of Beaver Dam, and it was at this time he became involved in library affairs. He was an organizer of the Beaver Dam Free Library Association, which was formed August 30, 1884. He served as secretary from 1884 to 1895, when a bequest of $30,000 by a local banker, J. J. Williams, provided a large library building. From the beginning of his library work, Hutchins believed in open shelves that enabled "persons to choose books from the shelf without the help of librarians"; he also felt "that the value of a public library is not measured by the number of books it contains, but by the number and kind of people who use the books, the kind of books they use, and the kind of use they make of them, and that these factors are largely determined by the intelligence, tact, tireless energy of the librarian."

During the period 1891 to 1895, when his uncle Charles was assistant state superintendent of schools, Hutchins served as library clerk in the office of the state superintendent of schools. In this position, he promoted and organized public school libraries and saw the need to bring public library services to rural areas. It was said in 1913 that his persistence in "driving home the truth of the importance of school and public libraries in education" was a message sometimes "unwillingly" heard and even avoided by busy educators. He subsequently devoted his life to advancing the education of all the people of Wisconsin, particularly that of people who lived in rural areas and small villages and hamlets, by delivering to them good reading and current information on the issues of the day.

He was constantly active in library development, along with two other Wisconsin leaders and friends, Lutie E. Stearns (q.v.), teacher and librarian, and Senator James Stout, legislator and philanthropist. These three provided leadership in those areas which John Colson has identified as influential in the change from association libraries to free public libraries: the example of philanthropy, the establishment of the profession of librarianship and its leadership in Wisconsin, the establishment of a state agency, and the thrust of the public library movement into political operations. Hutchins was actively involved in all aspects of development: he drafted legislation; he promoted the organization of the Wisconsin Free Library Association, the Traveling Library Service, the Legislative Reference Library, and municipal and county public libraries; and he helped to develop educational programs for librarians. Hutchins advocated support of the free library by public taxation in the same way as the common school, and among his colleagues at the American Library Association, he angrily denounced the idea of libraries as charitable institutions that must be dependent on gifts and almsgiving.

In 1895, the Legislature established the Wisconsin Free Library Commission. Hutchins served as a member without remuneration. When, in 1897, further legislation permitted reorganization, Hutchins became secretary, and Senator Stout (whose support had achieved legislation and who had personally financed travelling libraries) became chairman. Under this guidance, state services were developed, based on a strong belief in the value of learning and continuing education for everyone.

Books, periodicals, and reading lists for students were taken to farming areas and backwoods districts, to soldiers' camps and women's study clubs, and to villages of less than 1,500 inhabitants. The annotated, user-oriented lists of "Books for Small Libraries" and "Buying List of Recent Books" were taken over by ALA and became the well-known *Booklist*. Special subject collections with study outlines, German book collections, and Scandinavian collections were sent out as well as the hundreds of travelling libraries. Hutchins reported, "They supply an urgent need that has not been supplied by any other agency, they are carrying into hundreds of homes new thoughts and information, higher aspiration and ideals, new forces that are making for better individuals, family, and social life." On the management side, selection of potentially appealing books was made by trained experts, and savings in purchases, care of collections,

and more efficient and practicable methods of management were also instituted. He pointed out that schools teach children to read and that libraries broaden the educational system for neglected adults and "enable them to pursue a life-long system of learning."

In 1901, the documents department, which became the Legislative Reference Library, was organized. Also, the Summer Library School, initiated in 1895 and headed from 1899 by Cornelia Marvin Pierce (q.v.), had demonstrated its success by 1902. Hence, Hutchins was able to state in his *Fourth Biennial Report, 1901-1902* for the Commission that "It has come to be a recognized fact that trained service is essential to the proper conduct of a library, and that the librarian must be a woman who combines with professional training a broad culture and excellent education."

By 1903, Hutchins was seriously ill and, in 1904, he was forced to resign from the Commission. With the recovery of his health, Hutchins returned to Madison in 1906 and became active in the initiation of the University of Wisconsin's Extension Division. A new pattern of formal and informal education was developed within four departments: formal education through correspondence study instruction; platform teaching comprised of lectures, lyceums, and entertainment programs; forum teaching through debate and discussion based on study of primary sources; and community institutes to promote general information and welfare. Hutchins was secretary of the Department of Debating and Public Information from 1907 to 1914, and he brought to it his contacts, his experience, and his wide associations of earlier years. There he developed the "package library," in which parcel-post mail packages made up of newspaper clippings, magazine articles, and government and other reports were fitted to the requirements of individual users. Leaflets set forth specific questions, analyses, and references, and the Department suggested topics and sources of information on public questions that were proposed for general reading and study as well as debate.

Hutchins has also been credited (as have other more famous men—Charles McCarthy [q.v.] among them) with the concept described as "The Wisconsin Idea." His university extension work helped to carry out the idea that the boundaries of the campus are the boundaries of the state. When he was a member of the Madison Public Library Board, he worked to have Sunday lectures for older people and Saturday afternoon talks for children. He was a member of the American Library Association, the American Library Institute, and Wisconsin Library Association.

Although this quiet, gentle, self-effacing man devoted his life to bringing books, information, and pleasure to people, he received little financial reward or recognition during his active working days. However, both he and his accomplishments were recognized a year before the end of his life. He was the guest of honor at a testimonial dinner on January 13, 1913, at which time he was given a volume of 117 letters of tribute that bore testimony to his "worth and work." His ill health continued, and on January 25, 1914, he died from cerebral thrombosis (developed as a result of an accident). Interment was at Baraboo, Wisconsin. On May 20, 1914, a memorial service was held in the University Music Hall to honor Frank Avery Hutchins and his work. Jane Addams of Hull House, Chicago, was the speaker, "in recognition of Mr. Hutchins' spirit so akin to settlement work."

Of Frank A. Hutchins it was said, "the increasing enlightenment of the people constituted his entire interest." He belongs to that small group of men and women who formed and developed the modern library movement and made the library profession what it has become. Hutchins may be best understood through his own statements, which document his interest in lifelong learning and his sensitivity to the value of books for the reader.

Biographical listings and obituaries—*Dictionary of Wisconsin Biography* (1960); [Obituary]. "Frank Avery Hutchins." *Wisconsin Library Bulletin* 10:1:1-16 (Jan.-Feb. 1914); *Who Was Who in America* III (1951-1960). **Books and articles about the biographee**—Birge, E. A. "The Background of the Library School." *Wisconsin Library Bulletin* 27:121-23 (May 1931); Colson, John. "The Public Library Movement in Wisconsin." Doctoral dissertation, Graduate Library School, University of Chicago, 1973; Curti, Merle, and Vernon Cartensen. *The University of Wisconsin, 1848-1925.* Madison: The University of Wisconsin Press, 1949, 2 vols.; "Frank A. Hutchins' Worth and Work: A Volume of Letters from His Many Friends, 1912." Manuscript, State Historical Society of Wisconsin, Manuscripts Section; Kent, Alan E. "Frank Avery Hutchins: Promoter of 'the Wisconsin Idea.' " *Wilson Library Bulletin* 30:73-77 (Sept. 1955); Marvin, Cornelia. "The Spirit of the Wisconsin Pioneer." *Public Libraries* 30:182-90 (April 1925); Rosentreter, F. M. *The Boundaries of the Campus.* Madison: University of Wisconsin Press, 1957; Titus, W. A. "The Hutchins Family in Wisconsin." *Wisconsin Magazine of History* 16:244-51 (March 1933). **Primary sources and archival materials**—Hutchins, Frank A. *Two Years of Progress of the Libraries in Wisconsin.* (Reprinted from the *Second Biennial Report of the Wisconsin Free Library Commission,* issued Oct. 1898); Lighty, William Henry. Letters, Carbon Copy Archives, State Historical Society of Wisconsin.

—HELEN HUGUENOR LYMAN

HUTCHINS, MARGARET (1884-1961)

Born September 21, 1884, in Lancaster, New Hampshire, to Frank Dorr and Anne C. Carleton Hutchins, Margaret Hutchins attended Lancaster High School and Academy (1898-1902), entered Smith College in 1902, and was graduated in June 1906, having majored in Greek and philosophy. She was a member of Phi Beta Kappa, the Philosophical Club, and the Literary Society. She read French, German,

Latin, and Greek, considered at the time to be evidence of her being a well-educated woman. At the University of Illinois, she was graduated from the Library School in 1908 with a B.L.S. degree with honors, receiving an M.L.S. degree from Columbia University School of Library Service in 1931.

Her experience eventually embraced both university and public library service, but first she was employed at the University of Illinois in 1908 as a reference librarian by Phineas Windsor (q.v.), who, in a letter to Joseph L. Wheeler (q.v.), said, "Miss Margaret Hutchins is about as good a reference librarian as I have ever known, and I have seen some good ones. She has an unusually keen mind, broad interests, a splendid knowledge of what we call reference material, is quick at catching new points of view, has good common sense, good judgment, and is herself a hard worker."

She was active in the American Library Association, reviewed professional literature, and, while an assistant professor at Columbia, wrote her still useful classic book, *Introduction to Reference Work* (Chicago: ALA, 1944), which reflected her 35 years of experience and her careful verification of facts. While a member of ALA, she served as secretary of the Reference Librarians Section, Association of College and Research Libraries, and as a member of a number of other committees. Her writings also included a guide to the use of libraries, and articles on interlibrary loans, teaching reference, and teaching bibliography. *Guide to the Use of Libraries* resulted from collaboration with A. S. Johnson (q.v.) and M. S. Williams and went through five editions, the last in 1936.

When asked to list her chief community or leisure-time activities, she replied, "Never had any leisure time!" However, she did find time to serve as treasurer of the University of Illinois Woman's Club and on committees of the Columbia University Woman's Faculty Club.

She remained at University of Illinois in reference work from 1908 to 1927, teaching during the summers of 1926 and 1927 at Chautauqua Summer Library School; from 1927 to 1930, she was a reference specialist at Queens Borough Public Library. In July 1931, she went to Columbia University School of Library Service as an assistant professor (with a salary of $4,000), where her major interest was in bibliography and reference administration. She wrote that she was not interested in changing her position, although she might sometime consider a summer school teaching appointment elsewhere.

In an article in the June 1923 *Illinois Alumni News,* "The Reference Librarian," she wrote, "One of the hardest things we have to do is to find out what a person wants." She still held this view twenty years later when she wrote her *Introduction to Reference Work*, devoting a chapter to the reference interview, in which she said that

> the first requirement made of the reference librarian is approachability, not only easy access physically, but . . . intellectual and spiritual access as well. This is to be accomplished not by the librarian's composing his face in a fixed Mona Lisa smile, but by letting it show his inner feelings of interest and welcome.

She stressed the need for treating the inquirer with respect, for "frankness on the part of the librarian in admitting ignorance or uncertainty as to the meaning of a topic," and for talking the language of the reader, all of this sound advice for the beginner. In addition, the chapters on bibliographical, biographical, historical, geographical, and statistical questions reflected her long years of careful, informed use of pertinent sources for such questions. Her journal reading consisted of the *Atlantic Monthly*, *Literary Digest*, *Libraries*, *Library Journal*, and *Wilson Library Bulletin.*

Margaret Hutchins was a fine, thorough teacher, and although she intimidated her students with difficult examinations, she was fair in her assignments, and her lectures were clearly organized. Without the flair of Isadore Gilbert Mudge (q.v.), whose classes she took over when Miss Mudge gave them up, she nevertheless inspired her students with a desire to do careful reference work. She was withall quiet, modest, and pleasant in manner.

Her later years, after her retirement from Columbia, were spent in her summer home (May to November), and she wintered at the House of the Holy Nativity, an Episcopal convent with which she had been associated for over 25 years. Death occurred in a Bay Shore, Long Island, hospital, January 4, 1961 at the age of 76. Maurice F. Tauber recalls that she called him and his wife one day and asked if they would take her to a place on Long Island. When they arrived, she casually said, as they were moving her bags, that she expected to stay there for the rest of her life. It was the House of the Holy Nativity.

Margaret Hutchins's reputation rests firmly on her contributions to reference service and to teaching. With a solid education, an ability to work hard, and a real desire to serve mankind, she remained all her life a credit to her profession.

Biographical listings and obituaries—[Obituary]. *College and Research Libraries* 22:156 (March 1961); [Obituary]. *Illinois Libraries* 43:313 (April 1961); [Obituary]. *Library Journal* 86:1759 (May 1, 1961); *Who's Who in Library Service*, 1st ed., 2nd ed., 3rd ed. **Books and articles about the biographee**—Patterson, Charles D. "Hutchins, Margaret." In *Encyclopedia of Library and Information Science.* Allen Kent, Harold Lancour, and Jay E. Daily, eds. New York: Marcel Dekker, 1974. Vol. 11; Tompkins, Miriam D. "Professor Hutchins Retires." *Library Service News* (Columbia University School of Library Service) 15:1 (Jan. 1953).

—FRANCES NEEL CHENEY

IDESON, JULIA BEDFORD (1880-1945)

Julia Bedford Ideson, a pioneer Texas librarian and leader in state, regional and national library associations, was born July 15, 1880, in Hastings, Nebraska, to John Castree and Rosalie Baesman Ideson. While still a child, she moved to Houston, Texas, where her 42-year career as city librarian was ended by death July 15, 1945.

Her father and mother, both descendants of early Maryland families, were booklovers. This, and the fact that her father for some time operated a book store, gave Julia Ideson an inclination toward librarianship. She attended the University of Texas at a time when a course in library training was set up by librarian Benjamin Wyche (the only professionally trained librarian in the state at that time). She was one of four who received a certificate for taking the course from November 1901 to June 1902, after which she worked as a cataloger for the University of Texas Library during the year 1902-1903.

In 1903, the Houston Lyceum and Carnegie Library was established as a free public library on the foundation of a 55-year-old subscription library. Julia Ideson became librarian in October of that year. Through four decades, she developed a thriving municipal system (known after 1921 simply as the Houston Public Library), which kept pace with the rapidly growing city. From a staff of two and a half in 1904 (with holdings of 13,228 volumes and circulation of about 60,000), by 1945 it had grown to have a staff of 47, with 265,707 volumes and circulation of some 600,000, with six branches and a bookmobile in addition to the Central Library. During her tenure as librarian, Ideson saw the dedication of two main library buildings—the first, a Carnegie building dedicated March 2, 1904, and the second, the new Central Library dedicated October 18, 1926. The three-story Central Library, in Spanish Renaissance style, exemplified her tenet that it was not enough for a library to be functional; it must offer delight to the eye.

A tall, stately blonde with commanding good looks, boundless energy, leadership and executive abilities, and interest in people, Julia Ideson expressed her talents through community and professional service more than through scholarship. Though her writings are principally reports and addresses to various associations, she did edit *Handbook of Texas Libraries*, no. 2 (1908) and *Handbook of Texas Libraries*, no. 4 (1935), which constitute a rich source for Texas library history. In Houston, she was active in a great variety of organizations, from the YWCA to the Foreign Policy Association, the Downtown Club, and the League of Women Voters, and she served on several committees of the City Council and the Chamber of Commerce. In 1929, she was chosen for her civic and professional achievements as Torchbearer of the Year, and she was the first Houston woman to be listed in *Who's Who in America* (1932).

Julia Ideson was a member of the Houston Interracial Commission and also the Texas Interracial Commission. The Colored Carnegie Branch Library was established in Houston in 1909, and she was considered a leader in providing library service for blacks in the South.

A charter member of the Texas Library Association, organized in 1902, she served as secretary (1907-1909); as president (1910-1911); and on many committees. Her work on the Legislative Committee (1916-1917) led to the enactment of the County Library Law of 1917. Appointed to the first Examining Board set up under that law, she continued to serve for twenty years. Again, as chairman of the Legislative Committee (1929-1933) she successfully opposed a proposal to abolish the Texas State Library. In 1935, the Texas Library Association honored her as its outstanding pioneer. She provided the Texas Library Association with a discussion of penal libraries as early as 1922; served on the Association's committee on penal and eleemosynary libraries; and from 1935 to 1938 served as a consultant to the Huntsville Penitentiary Library. Her list of books for the Library, based to some extent on a Minnesota list, was one of the early compilations of vocational books designed to be of use to prisoners in their future life.

A charter member of the Southwestern Library Association (October 22, 1922), she served on various committees, was president for a two-year term (1932-1934), and actively planned and participated in the Association's meetings.

In 1905, she joined the American Library Association and in 1907, as one of the four representatives from Texas, attended her first ALA Annual Conference in Asheville, North Carolina. In 1919, she volunteered her services to the ALA War Service Committee, and for eight months she was stationed at a regional library for the armed forces near Brest, France. She was a Council member of the American Library Association (1920-1925, 1932-1933, 1936, and 1938); Executive Board member (1922-1923, 1932-1933); and first vice-president (1932-1933). Besides chairing the Membership Committee (1922-1923), she was also, as chairman of the Subscription Books Committee (1926-1929), instrumental in leading ALA to assume publication of *Subscription Books Bulletin*, as it did in 1930.

Her interest in library personnel and their training and needs was continuous, but it was epitomized in her will, which left the residue of her estate for the establishment of a library staff benefit fund for the Houston Public Library staff.

At the time of her death in 1945, the Houston Public Library was referred to as the lengthened shadow of Julia Ideson; it was developed through her force of character, her perseverance, her intelligent planning, and her unswerving devotion. She also left her constructive mark on the library movement in Texas, the Southwest, and the country as a whole.

Biographical listings and obituaries—*News Notes* 21:3 (Oct. 1945); West, Elizabeth Howard. "Julia Ideson." *Library Journal* 70:829 (Sept. 15, 1945); *Who Was Who in America* II (1943-1950); *Who's Who in Library Service*, 1st ed., 2nd ed. **Books and articles about the biographee**—Franklin, Louise. "Ideson, Julia Bedford." In *The Handbook of Texas, a Supplement, Volume III*. Austin: Texas State Historical Association, 1976; McSwain, Mary Brown. "Julia Bedford Ideson, Houston Librarian, 1880-1945." Unpublished master's report, University of Texas, 1966; Philosophical Society of Texas. *Proceedings, 1945*. Dallas, Texas: The Society, 1946. **Primary sources and archival materials**—Houston Public Library. *Annual Report*, 1904-1953. Houston, Texas (typewritten); Julia Ideson's letters and papers are held in the Julia Ideson Case, Houston Public Library, Houston; Southwestern Library Association Archives, Texas State Library, Austin; Texas Library Association Archives, Texas State Library, Austin; and University of Texas Archives, Austin.

—MARY BROWN McSWAIN

ISOM, MARY FRANCES (1865-1920)

Mary Frances Isom was born in Nashville, Tennessee, on February 27, 1865, the only child of John Franklin and Frances A. Walter Isom. Her father was an army surgeon stationed in Nashville. Although she remained single, she later adopted a ten-year-old child, Berenice Langton, the daughter of a Cleveland friend. After the Civil War, the family returned to Cleveland, where Mrs. Isom died a few years before Mary Frances entered Wellesley in 1883. Poor health interrupted her education after one year, and she stayed in Cleveland, serving as hostess and companion for her father until his death in 1899.

Encouraged by her girlhood friend Josephine Adams Rathbone (q.v.), who had been urging her to take a library course, Mary Frances Isom, at the age of 34, entered the Pratt Institute Library School, where Rathbone served on the faculty. Mary Frances studied there from 1899 to 1901 taking, in addition to the regular library program, an advanced historical course. According to Josephine Rathbone, "No graduate ever took away ... a more thorough equipment for the work." She also took away a vision of service that she always acknowledged she had gained from Josephine Rathbone.

In May 1901, she went to Portland, Oregon, to catalog a collection of books that had been given to the Library Association of Portland, a subscription library, with the stipulation that the collection be open to all the people of the city. In the midst of the transition from a private to a public library, the head librarian left; a month later, the Library Board appointed Isom to take his place. A year later, the library became a county library serving not only Portland but all of Multnomah County.

In 1905, her inspiration led the Oregon Legislature to establish the State Library Commission. As a member of the Commission (a role she filled until her death), she was instrumental in bringing another great librarian to Oregon. Her enthusiastic descriptions of the progress taking place in Oregon library work lured Cornelia Marvin Pierce (q.v.) to Oregon to assume the post of state librarian. "The possibilities ahead of us seem unlimited ... nothing has been done—everything to do."

The entire Pacific Northwest profited from Isom's interest in promoting libraries. Calling a meeting in 1904 for all Oregonians concerned about library service, she organized the Oregon Library Association. In an effort to foster local pride in library affairs, the state group invited the American Library Association to meet in Portland for the 1905 convention. In 1909, Mary Frances Isom helped found the Pacific Northwest Library Association, serving as its second president in 1910-1911. Although her colleagues on the national level elected her to the ALA Council and voted her second vice-president for 1912-1913, her first allegiance belonged to the regional association, as she acknowledged in a letter to Cornelia Pierce:

> You know I am still a Philistine as regards the ALA.... I think that a small association that is alive is more important for our people than the larger one. I firmly believe that every library mortal in Oregon must belong to PNLA. I burn with missionary zeal.

A similar enthusiasm sustained her during the construction of the Central Library Building in 1912. Her creative collaboration with the architect resulted in a handsome public building that still serves a large metropolitan population. She stated her vision of the library's role in society at the opening of the new building in September 1913:

> Many years ago the public library was called the "University of the people" ... these shelves point the way to self-education.... The public library is the people's library, it is maintained by the people for the people, it is the most democratic of our democratic institutions; therefore to be of service to all the people of the community, to meet their needs and to contribute to their pleasure is its simple duty.

Mary Frances Isom never forgot that she was librarian of a public library that belonged, in her words, "to the many and not to the few," and an eagerness to anticipate the community's needs marked her library policy. A contemporary recalled her efforts to use the library to help Portland's immigrants. She persuaded members of the city's foreign population to share aspects of their culture in performances and exhibits presented in the branch libraries "with little parties arranged after each show in order to make all mingle and get acquainted."

Disappointed that many children were not taking advantage of the opportunities afforded by the Library, Isom sought closer cooperation with the public schools, warning that "thousands of the children of Portland ... have no books except the textbooks which they will soon give up ... having been taught to read, not what to read, a knowledge which may well be a curse instead of a blessing." Thus began a system of classroom collections, selected and organized by the public librarians but paid for with funds appropriated by the School Board.

Her success with the School Board was only one demonstration of her remarkable gift for generating support for library activities. The county commissioners never failed to respond to her requests for more funds to meet increased demands for service. Certainly, the Multnomah County Library showed exceptional growth under her leadership. By 1920, instead of the Central Library and the three county stations opened in 1903, service was provided in 211 agencies including 146 schools. The number of books increased from 40,000 to 294,000, operating expenses from slightly more than $20,000 to nearly $189,000. The Library numbered more than one-third of the county's population among its registered borrowers.

With the advent of World War I, Mary Frances Isom became the ALA's director of war work in Oregon and southern Washington, with responsibility for organizing hospital and camp libraries. She also devoted her energies to other war work and to Liberty Bond drives. At this time, the refusal of her assistant librarian to buy bonds (because of pacifist convictions) became a public issue, and superpatriots among the county commissioners called for the woman's resignation. Throughout the unfortunate episode, Isom rejected demands that she dismiss her assistant even when it was suggested that, by defending the staff member, she had proved her own disloyalty.

In the last months of the war, Isom volunteered for service in France, where librarians were needed to organize materials for men faced with weeks of demoralizing idleness before being brought home. The 53-year-old woman who arrived in France in November 1918, must have appeared an unlikely volunteer. Gray-haired, small of stature—about five feet three inches tall, with a plump but trim figure—she was distinguished-looking rather than pretty. Her eyes gave evidence of a will, as one admirer expressed it, "which was nothing if not direct and bent on results."

"I shall never forget," wrote Burton Stevenson (q.v.), director of the ALA's French War Service, "the first time she came into my office in Paris . . . no one could have failed to be impressed by her sincerity, her earnestness, her vigor. . . . Her only anxiety was to be of service. 'Put me wherever you need me,' she said—and meant it." Later she reported to Stevenson that organizing the camp libraries gave her the most interesting work of her life and in some ways "the most difficult." The psychological strain of seeing seriously wounded men compounded the exhaustion resulting from her work. In a letter to her library staff in Portland, she wrote, "I can stand anything now. I can even look on the most horrible wounds without flinching. You remember Tom Sawyer and his sore toe, that is always the spirit in which they are exhibited."

These memories must have strengthened her as she returned to Portland in April 1919, knowing that she was dying of cancer. In the words of a contemporary, "the end was like the life itself." During the last months of her life, she worked at the Library several hours each day, carrying out her duties "as if she expected to continue at her post another twenty years." She died April 15, 1920. Among her bequests was one for $5,000 to start a pension fund for "my beloved staff."

Her staff respected and admired her; it cannot be claimed that they felt real affection for her. Possibly her expectations were too high. She was, according to Cornelia Pierce, rigid in her discipline and organization. Like a surgeon making rounds, she would progress through the Library, pausing in the doorway of each of the five reading rooms before entering to correct an unlucky assistant. Countering that picture, however, is the story of her arrival at the Library on Christmas Eve. Relieving the trainee at the desk, she said, "You have a family. I have none. Go home and enjoy the holiday."

She achieved with her friends an informality lacking in her staff relations. A witty, gay, and relaxed hostess, she entertained Portland friends and visiting librarians at her Sunday "at-homes," occasions noted for their conversation and food. Because of the income from her father's estate, her life could have been a continual round of "at-homes," of days spent at her beach cottage (this cottage, through the generosity of her daughter, now belongs to the Library), of travel, and of leisure. She chose, instead, the life of a librarian dedicated to the concept of service and to building a system of libraries that would enrich the lives and leisure of others.

Her friend and colleague Cornelia Pierce, writing in her capacity as Oregon state librarian, summarized her achievements: "To relate the story of Miss Isom's connection with the libraries of Oregon, is to give the whole history of library development within the state, as she was the founder of all our library institutions and associations."

Announcing Mary Frances Isom's death, Josephine Rathbone, her former mentor, recalled: "One of her favorite poems from childhood was Tennyson's 'Ulysses.' I remember her reading it aloud years ago, her eyes glowing with the words, 'How dull it is to pause, to make an end, to rest unburnished, not to shine in use.' " These lines interpret the life of service of Portland's pioneer librarian, Mary Frances Isom.

Biographical listings and obituaries—*Dictionary of American Biography* 9 (Nellie B. Pipes); *Notable American Women* 2; [Obituary]. *ALA Bulletin* 14:318-19, 493 (July 1920); [Obituary]. "Mary Frances Isom." *Public Libraries* 25:256 (May 1920); *Who Was Who in America* I (1897-1942). **Books and articles about the biographee**—Bowker, R. R. "Women in the Library Profession, II." *Library Journal* 45:587-92 (July 1, 1920); Johansen, D. "Library and the Liberal Tradition." Oregon State College, 1959. 23p.; Kingsbury, Mary E. "To Shine in Use: The Library and War Service of Oregon's Pioneer Librarian, Mary Frances Isom." *Journal of Library History* 10:22-34 (Jan. 1975); Library Association of Portland. "Memorial Number—Mary Frances Isom, Librarian 1902-1920." *Monthly Bulletin* (May 1920); "The Passing of Mary Frances Isom." *Public Libraries* 25:261-62 (May 1920); Van Horne, Bernard. "Mary Frances Isom: Creative Pioneer in Library Work in the Northwest." *Wilson Library Bulletin* 33:409-416 (Feb. 1959).

—MARY E. KINGSBURY

JACOBS, JOHN HALL (1905-1967)

John Hall Jacobs was born in Bolivar, Tennessee, on November 27, 1905, to Henry Lee and Lou Donnie Hammons Jacobs. He received his B.S. from West Tennessee State Teachers College (now Memphis State College) in 1928. He then did graduate work at Peabody College, the University of Akron, and the University of Tennessee (summers of 1929, 1930, and 1932, respectively). In 1932, Jacobs received a Rosenwald Scholarship to attend the Emory University Library School, from which he received an A.B. in library science (1933).

Between receiving his undergraduate degree and his library degree, Jacobs had been teacher/librarian in the Collierville (Tennessee) High School, capitalizing on his training as a library assistant while attending West Tennessee State. Then, in 1934, Jacobs became supervisor of the Shelby County (Tennessee) libraries, thus beginning a long association with public libraries. In June 1936, John Hall Jacobs married Frances Stamps; they were to have a daughter, Nina Frances.

In 1938, Jacobs was called to direct the New Orleans Public Library, succeeding Edmund McGiveran. His term at New Orleans was briefly interrupted during World War II, when he was on active duty with the U.S. Naval Reserve (1943-1945), first as assistant commander of Louisiana Polytechnic Institute's V-12 unit (1943-1944), and then, until his release from duty, as commanding officer at Dubuque, Iowa. During the 22 years of his tenure at New Orleans, Jacobs supervised the improvement of branch service, but his most outstanding contribution to the New Orleans Public Library was to oversee the planning and development of the new central library building, dedicated on November 22, 1959.

Jacobs's activities were not confined to New Orleans, however. Upon leaving New Orleans in 1960, he went to Atlanta, Georgia, to become director of the Atlanta and Fulton County Public Library System. Faced with the problems of working in an outdated building originally donated by Andrew Carnegie (q.v.), Jacobs supervised a major renovation and modernization of the central building. He reorganized and expanded services and was able to have five additional branch libraries constructed as well.

His expertise in problems of both library management and building construction was widely recognized. He taught library administration in the library schools of Florida State University, the University of Illinois, and Syracuse and Emory Universities. (His versatility was demonstrated in his teaching courses on modern drama and the novel, as he did when teaching night classes at Emory.) Over the years, Salt Lake City (Utah), Madison (Wisconsin), Dallas (Texas), Jacksonville (Florida), and Tampa (Florida), as well as numerous smaller community libraries, called upon him as a consultant on buildings and services.

Yet Jacobs also found time to work for the profession as a whole on the local, state, regional, and national levels. He served as president of the Tennessee Library Association, the Louisiana Library Association (1947-1948), and the Southwestern Library Association (1946-1948). At the time of his death, he was president of both the Southeastern Library Association and the City of Atlanta Department Heads Association. For the American Library Association, he was a member of the Executive Board (1958-1962) and also a member of the Headquarters Building Committee when the new headquarters was constructed at 50 East Huron Street in Chicago to replace the old McCormick Mansion. Too, he chaired the ALA Personnel Administration Committee and the Library Binding Committee.

As a writer, John Hall Jacobs contributed to professional journals on a variety of topics. Moreover, he edited the *Louisiana Library Association Bulletin*,

and he was assistant editor of the *Southeastern Librarian*, the official journal of the Southeastern Library Association.

Yet in the midst of all of these activities on behalf of his libraries and his profession, Jacobs found time to indulge in his own pastimes, particularly his fondness for sporting events. He had at one time taken up coaching (the girls' basketball team at Collierville) but had to quit because of his health. A devout member of the Second Ponce de Leon Baptist Church in Atlanta, he taught a young men's Bible class for a number of years. Widely read, he collected first and autographed editions.

John Hall Jacobs died, following a long illness, on July 27, 1967. When the Southeastern Library Association met in Atlanta in 1970, Dean Robert Downs of the University of Illinois delivered the John Hall Jacobs Lecture as a memorial. Tributes by friends and colleagues appeared in the *Southeastern Librarian*, and in one of them (17:136; Fall 1967), his longtime friend Rees M. Andrews, Jr., summarized the attitudes of librarians and non-librarians alike:

> John Hall was a man of integrity. He was a strong leader, yet he was tolerant and understanding. He was interested in every man's opinion. He was a very rational man, and he didn't allow his emotions or prejudices to interfere with his principles. This is one of the many reasons his library associates loved and honored him. His policy of open and honest dealings with his personnel resulted in a high level of staff morale. His fellow workers recognized him as being a forward looking and forward planning person.... Truly the libraries of both Atlanta and New Orleans will be forever grateful to this respected figure.

The multitude and variety of his services make the last statement true for the profession as a whole.

Biographical listings and obituaries–[Obituary]. *Southeastern Librarian* 17:132+, 205 (Fall-Winter 1967); *Who Was Who in America* IV (1961-1968); *Who's Who in Library Service*, 2nd ed., 3rd ed., 4th ed. **Books and articles about the biographee**–Andrews, Rees M. "Tribute to John Hall Jacobs." *Southeastern Librarian* 17:136 (Fall 1967); [Biographical sketch]. *Southeastern Librarian* 14:56 (Spring 1964); McNeal, A. L. "John Hall Jacobs: In Memoriam." *Southeastern Librarian* 17:135 (Fall 1967); Rheay, Mary Louise. "Jacobs, John Hall." In *Encyclopedia of Library and Information Science*. Allen Kent, Harold Lancour, and Jay E. Daily, eds. New York: Marcel Dekker, 1975, Vol. 13.

                                            –BOHDAN S. WYNAR
                                            –KOERT C. LOOMIS, JR.

JAMES, HANNAH PACKARD (1835-1903)

Hannah Packard James was born in South Scituate, Massachusetts, on September 5, 1835. Her father, William James, was a Massachusetts legislator and prominent local citizen. On her mother's side, she was reported to be a direct descendant of John Alden. James was educated in the district school at South Scituate and at a private school. She showed an early fondness for books and would later remark that she couldn't remember the time when she compiled her first catalog. During the Civil War, she worked with the Sanitary Commission.

In 1870, when the Newton, Massachusetts, Free Library opened, Hannah James, who had been trained at the Boston Athenaeum, became the librarian. She remained in Newton for seventeen years, where she established the public library on a sound footing. By the time of the U.S. Bureau of Education's *Public Libraries in the United States of America: Their History, Condition and Management, Special Report* (1876), the Newton Free Library reported a collection of 10,088 volumes and an annual circulation of 42,000. James's interest in architecture, especially ecclesiastical architecture, led her to spend the summer of 1882 studying in England. She also used this period to purchase photographs for the Library from $1,000 in funds appropriated by the Library trustees. She was interested in all areas of library administration and became embroiled in a minor controversy over the purchase of fiction for the Library in 1884.

In 1887, upon the recommendation of Melvil Dewey (q.v.), the trustees of the Osterhout Free Library in Wilkes-Barre, Pennsylvania, employed Hannah James to be the first librarian. The trustees had $400,000 from the estate of Isaac Osterhout as an endowment and they remodelled a Presbyterian church for the Free Library. James convinced the trustees that the Osterhout Free Library should be a free circulating library from the beginning. She set to work on a finding list that would be published when the Library opened on January 29, 1889, with a dedicatory address by Melvil Dewey.

James's activities in the community were numerous. She was a member of St. Stephen's Episcopal Church and held positions in the Free Kindergarten Association, United Charities, and the Society of Colonial Dames. She had a strong interest in Dante and was active in the local society. James also was a member of the local Wyoming (Pennsylvania) Historical and Geological Society, which she served as member of the Publishing Committee from 1899 to 1903. Her own publication, *The Library News-Letter* (1891-1902), which carried ads and cost the citizens fifty cents per year, was a means by which she informed the community and encouraged their involvement with the Library.

James was one of the early leaders in the movement to establish strong relations between the public library and the schools. She worked with teachers and educational leaders in both Newton and Wilkes-Barre. In 1892-1893 she contributed an article, "Libraries in Relation to Schools," to the *Papers Prepared for the World's Library Congress Held at the Columbian Exposition.* She was active in promoting a Library Department in the National Education Association and was named to the ALA Committee on Cooperation with this new department in 1896.

Although she did not attend the 1876 conference, Hannah James became ALA member number 210 and attended her first conference in Boston in 1879. After that she was a very active member of ALA, serving on various committees and on the ALA Council (1882-1887 and 1892-1903). She served as a vice-president, 1896-1898. Along with John Edmands (q.v.) and Thomas L. Montgomery (q.v.), she promoted the establishment of the Pennsylvania Library Association in 1891.

James was one of the American members to attend the Second International Library Conference (1897) in London, where she and Caroline M. Hewins (q.v.) were the only two women to deliver prepared addresses. James's paper traced the history of special training for library work in this country. She noted that "character, intelligence, executive ability, and a thorough training are the factors that count, and these are the qualities which the training schools are striving by their methods of education and elimination to furnish." Earlier she had been one of the visiting lecturers for Melvil Dewey's first class at Columbia and had written a paper on the need for apprentice training after graduation from library school. She subsequently lectured to other library schools and developed an interest in library training.

James's trip to England made a decided impression upon one correspondent, who noted, "I remember with special pleasure how proud all of us had reason to be of an American woman who could talk to English men and women on formal as well as personal occasions, and make so strong and delightful an impression upon our kinsfolk across the sea." Upon her return from England, James gave a full account of her trip abroad in the Osterhout newsletter, and the following year she wrote an article on "Women in American and British Libraries" for the *Library World* (London). She took obvious pride in the fact that American women were not bound by precedent and had been able to become directors not only of small, but also of some large libraries, "commanding the same salary as men in similar positions." James encouraged her English sisters to go and do likewise.

Among James's notable achievements were good public relations with her community, the development of library service for school children and young people, high standards of reference work, and the enunciation of a policy on book selection that emphasized the development of quality book and periodical collections.

Hannah James was a handsome woman. Her colleagues reported that she had a forceful personality but a good sense of humor. She had a keen interest not only in her own work but also in that of younger librarians, who received encouragement from her.

She had to give up library work because of illness in November 1902, but she continued to do some book selection and took an active interest in library activities. She died on April 20, 1903, and was buried in South Scituate (now Norwell), Massachusetts. According to *Library Journal*, "Within the circle of her chosen life work she had been a leader in newer methods and the broader work that have wrought so great a change in public library ideals, and at the same time she was always an influence for sanity, for common sense and for conservatism."

Biographical listings and obituaries–[Editorial]. *Library Journal* 28:216 (May 1903); "Necrology: Hannah P. James." *Library Journal* 28:130 ["Conference of Librarians" Report paging] (June 1903); [Obituary]. In Rev. Horace Edwin Hayden, ed. *Proceedings and Collections of the Wyoming Historical and Geological Society*, 1904. Vol. 8, pp. 300-304; [Obituary]. In F. C. Johnson, ed. *The Historical Record of Wyoming Valley*. Vols. 12-14, p. 58. **Books and articles about the biographee**–"As It Was in the Beginning." *Public Libraries* 29:176-78 (April 1924); "In Memoriam–Hannah Packard James, September 5, 1835-April 20, 1903." *Library Journal* 28:240-41 (May 1903); Poland, Myra. "Hannah Packard James." *Bulletin of Bibliography* 8:91-92 (Oct. 1914).

–JOAN M. COSTELLO
–EDWARD G. HOLLEY

JEFFERSON, THOMAS (1743-1826)

Thomas Jefferson, the third President of the United States, was born a British subject at Shadwell, Virginia, on April 13, 1743, the eldest son of Peter and Jane Randolph Jefferson. Peter Jefferson died when Thomas was fourteen years old, leaving his young son as the administrator of his valuable lands and property and as head of a large household, consisting of his mother, younger brother, six sisters, and about thirty slaves. Thomas was also responsible for the education of the younger children and the payment of his sisters' dowries.

For his own education, Jefferson entered the College of William and Mary in 1760, where he came under the influence of William Small, professor of natural philosophy and mathematics, and George Wythe, professor of law and the foremost jurist in colonial Virginia. These two men exerted a great influence on Jefferson's intellectual development, and he spent five years studying law under George Wythe before seeking admission to the bar.

Jefferson began the practice of law in 1767. Between law cases and overseeing the plantation at Shadwell, he read voluminously and led an active social life in Williamsburg. On New Year's Day 1772, Jefferson married a young widow, Martha Skelton. He was regularly re-elected to the Virginia House of Burgesses from 1771 to 1773. In June of 1775, the Virginia Assembly appointed him to the Virginia delegation at the Second Continental Congress in Philadelphia. Because of what John Adams called "his peculiar felicity of expression," Jefferson was placed on the committee to draw up "A Declaration of the Causes of Taking Up Arms." In May of 1776, the Virginia Assembly passed a resolution instructing its delegates in Congress to support a motion declaring "the United Colonies free and independent states...." Jefferson's pen gave expression to the ideas of Congress in the resulting Declaration of Independence.

From 1776 to 1781, Jefferson was occupied with the political development of the Commonwealth of Virginia. In June 1777, he was elected governor by the Assembly and served two terms as war governor. In September 1782, his wife died, and thoroughly shaken by her death, he retired from public life for a period of time.

From 1784 to 1789, Jefferson served as the American minister to France; then in 1790, George Washington asked him to accept the position of secretary of state. He next served as John Adams's vice president from 1797 to 1801. In 1801, he was elected President, and during his two terms of office, he more than doubled the size of American territory through the Louisiana Purchase. In 1809, he retired to his home at Monticello.

During his lifetime, Jefferson gathered three libraries for himself and one for the University of Virginia. In 1770, the first was destroyed by a fire that leveled his ancestral home. Jefferson's attitude toward books is clearly expressed in a letter to John Page:

> My late loss may have perhaps reac[hed y]ou by this time, I mean the loss of my mother's house by fire, and in it, of every pa[per I] had in the world, and almost every book. On a reasonable estimate I calculate th[e cost o]f books burned to have been £200 sterling. Would to God it had been the money[; then] had it never cost me a sigh!

He immediately began collecting his second and most famous library, which numbered some 6,500 volumes when he sold it to the Congress in 1815. After the purchase of his second library, Jefferson began acquiring a third, concluding that he could not live without books regardless of his financial condition. By the time of his death on July 4, 1826, this collection had grown to nearly 1,000 volumes.

Jefferson loved books as material objects, but his libraries were first and foremost for use. He bought carefully, always mindful of the edition, binding, and condition of his books. Yet his ultimate purpose was not bookish ostentation, but rather utility–his library was extensively used by its owner and by many scholars who requested access, always graciously granted, to its treasures.

Jefferson recognized that careful organization of libraries was necessary for ready use. As a result, he developed a classification system for his library. This system, based on the divisions of learning devised by Sir Francis Bacon and revised by d'Alembert, was widely adopted by catalogers for nearly a century. Its foundation was a threefold division of knowledge—history, philosophy, and the fine arts. As Judge Woodward, Jefferson's friend, noted:

> Books, it was observed by Mr. Jefferson, may be classed according to the faculties of the mind employed on them. These are first, the memory, secondly, the reason, and thirdly, the imagination; which are applied, respectively, first, to history, secondly, to philosophy, and thirdly, to the fine arts.

The Library of Congress catalogs, issued after the acquisition of Jefferson's library, were all essentially structured on Jefferson's plan, but with frequent modification.

While Jefferson viewed books as having immediate and practical benefits for the scholar, he was also committed to the idea that the free flow of information among the people was essential for the preservation of the Republic. This principle, which has since become central to librarianship, was perhaps best articulated when he noted that the people "may safely be trusted to hear everything true and false and to form a correct judgement between them." He had great faith in the citizen's ability to be "governed by reason," and argued that every effort must be made to "leave open to him all the avenues of truth."

Jefferson led efforts to enable citizens to acquire the information necessary for intelligent decision making. As early as 1770, he drafted legislation designed to provide for the establishment of a public library wherein "the learned and curious" might study "without reward or fee."

As President, Jefferson also had a direct hand in planning and selecting the books for the earliest library established by Congress in the new Capitol. In 1802, he wrote to Abraham Baldwin, under whose direction the balance of funds appropriated for the Library was expended:

> I have prepared a catalogue for the Library of Congress in conformity with your ideas that books of entertainment are not within the scope of it, and that books in other languages, where there are not translations of them, are to be admitted freely. I have confined the catalogue to those branches of science which belong to the deliberations of the members as statesmen, and in these have omitted those classical books, ancient and modern, which gentlemen generally have in their private libraries, but which cannot properly claim a place in a collection made merely for the purpose of reference.

Jefferson's bibliographical program and the accompanying list of *desiderata* formed the basis of the purchases for the Library until 1806.

His interest in books and higher education in his native Virginia gave a Jeffersonian thrust to the development of the University of Virginia Library. He personally planned the Library building, chose much of the initial collection, classified the materials acquired, and was consulted in the selection of the first two librarians. His involvement in the development of the University of Virginia Library is a proud page in that institution's history.

Perhaps Jefferson's greatest legacy to libraries, and his major importance to library history, lies in the sale of his magnificent library to the country in 1815. Plagued by desperate financial difficulties and stimulated by the British destruction of the Library of Congress in the War of 1812, Jefferson offered his library, judged the best in America, to the Congress for approximately 25,000 dollars. As he pointed out to his friend Samuel H. Smith, "I have been fifty years making it, and have spared no pains, opportunity or expense, to make it what it is." Jefferson's offer stirred a great controversy in Congress—a controversy ostensibly fueled by the "atheistical, irreligious and immoral" nature of the collection, but in reality generated by long-standing and deep enmities between Jefferson and many members of Congress. Nevertheless, by the margin of ten votes, Congress consented to the purchase of Jefferson's library and the nation acquired one of its greatest literary treasures.

Biographical listings and obituaries—*Dictionary of American Biography* 10 (Dumas Malone); *National Cyclopaedia of American Biography* 3; *Who Was Who in America*, Historical Volume (1607-1896). **Books and articles about the biographee**—Adams, Randolph G. "Thomas Jefferson, Librarian." In his *Three Americanists*. Philadelphia: University of Pennsylvania Press, 1939, pp. 69-96; Bestor, Arthur. "Thomas Jefferson and the Freedom of Books." In his *Three Presidents and Their Books*. Urbana: University of Illinois Press, 1963, pp. 1-44; Davis, Richard B. *Intellectual Life in Jefferson's Virginia, 1790-1830*. Chapel Hill: University of North Carolina, 1964; Gillespie, David, and Michael H. Harris. "A Bibliography of Virginian Library History." *Journal of Library History* 6:72-90 (1971); Johnston, William D. "The Destruction of the Old Library and the Purchase of the Jeffersonian Library." In his *History of the Library of Congress*. Washington, D.C.: Government Printing Office, 1904, pp. 65-104; LaMontagne, Leo E. "Jefferson as Classifier," and "Jefferson and the Library of Congress." In his *American Library Classification: With Special Reference to the Library of Congress*. Hamden, Conn.: Shoestring Press, 1961, pp. 27-62; Peden, William H. "Some Notes Concerning Thomas Jefferson's Libraries." *William and Mary Quarterly* 1:265-72 (1944); Servies, James A. "Thomas Jefferson and His Bibliographic Classification." Master's thesis, University of Chicago, 1950; Sowerby, Millicent, comp. *Catalogue of the Library of Thomas Jefferson*. Washington, D.C.: Library of Congress, 1952-59. 5 vols. **Primary sources and archival materials**—Cometti, Elizabeth, ed. *Jefferson's Ideas on a University Library: Letters from the Founder of the*

University of Virginia to a Boston Bookseller. Charlottesville: Tracy W. McGregor Library, University of Virginia, 1950.

—SISTER DEBORAH HARMELING
—MICHAEL H. HARRIS

JENNINGS, JUDSON TOLL (1872-1948)

Judson Toll Jennings was born September 24, 1872, at Schenectady, New York, the son of Charles Edward and Elizabeth Ann Henry Jennings. He attended Union College, Schenectady, in 1894-1895, following which he entered the New York State Library School as a member of the class of 1897. Money was none too plentiful and he worked as a page in the New York State Library while going to school. He married Eleanor McKelvey of La Crosse, Wisconsin, on April 12, 1898. They had three daughters, Elizabeth, Frances, and Eleanor.

In 1903, Jennings left the New York State Library to become librarian of the Carnegie Free Library, Duquesne, Pennsylvania, which post he held till 1906, when he was recalled to the State Library in Albany to serve as director's assistant. Then, on October 1, 1907, he succeeded Charles Wesley Smith as librarian of the Seattle Public Library where, except for a six months' leave of absence in 1918-1919, he served as Seattle's city librarian continuously until his retirement in the summer of 1942 at the age of seventy.

During World War I, Jennings organized the Camp Lewis library at American Lake, Washington, and was supervisor of the Fort Lawton naval training camp libraries in Seattle (see his article "Camp Lewis Library," *Public Libraries*, March 4, 1918). With the signing of the Armistice in 1918, arrangements were made by the American Library Association to send Jennings to its Paris headquarters, where he was assigned to organize and administer library service for the Army of Occupation, 3d Army, at Coblentz, Germany. The Army of Occupation numbered between two hundred fifty and three hundred thousand men, and the forces were stationed in about three hundred permanent stations. At least as many more villages had detachments of American soldiers in them. The need and opportunity for library service was great, and books in the tens of thousands were distributed through the cooperation of accredited welfare organizations like the Red Cross, YMCA, and Knights of Columbus, in addition to the army units themselves. (See his article in the 1919 *Proceedings* of the Pacific Northwest Library Association.)

Jennings had definite ideas as to the theory, function, and scope of public library work, and his application of these ideas to local problems resulted in large accomplishments. When Jennings accepted the Seattle post, the Seattle Public Library was sixteen years of age and had occupied the building

financed by Andrew Carnegie (q.v.) for only ten months. Its borrowers then numbered slightly over 28,000, which number had grown to 123,000 at the time Jennings retired 35 years later. Under Jennings's inspiration, Seattle increased the Library's income per capita, added branch libraries and neighborhood stations, extended service to the county by contract, further developed school libraries, secured retirement pension benefits, stimulated gifts for both special library services and purchase of books for special collections, and initiated the important work of the Library's Adult Education Department.

As head of the largest library in the Pacific Northwest, and with a special aptitude for quiet leadership, Jennings's influence was vital and widespread. It was natural that others should look to him to take the lead in movements to improve state and regional library services. The Pacific Northwest Library Association was organized in 1909, and Jennings became its first president; he was elected again to that office in 1921.

In December 1931, Jennings called a meeting of the Washington State Executive Committee of the Pacific Northwest Library Association for the purpose of considering the organization of a state library association. At this meeting, held in Jennings's office at the Seattle Public Library, it was voted to organize such a state association, and a previously prepared constitution was adopted. Six months later, although Jennings was unable to attend, the first meeting of the present Washington Library Association was held at Paradise Lodge at Mount Rainier. In the absence of Jennings, Charles W. Smith (q.v.), librarian of the University of Washington Library, presided over the meeting that unanimously elected Judson T. Jennings the first president.

Jennings worked indefatigably for many years for legislation in the state of Washington that would permit and assist in library service to all. Under his chairmanship, the Washington Library Association brought out, in 1935, its "Program for Library Development in the State of Washington." The principal objectives listed in the report were free library service for every person in the state and adequate financial support for this service; trained personnel (certification); library service in every school building; and cooperation in book collecting and in providing materials for research.

His election as president of the American Library Association in 1923 afforded Jennings the opportunity to promote his conviction of the importance of the public library as an instrument for adult education. In his ALA presidential address in Saratoga Springs, New York, July 4, 1924 (printed in the January-November 1924 *ALA Bulletin*), he stated,

the library is logically ordained as the direct and primary agency for adult education. The fundamental tool of education is the book. The chief thing our children learn in school is the ability to read. The formal education in our schools and colleges is at best largely guidance in reading and this is becoming more true every day. If we can persuade students when they leave school that their education has but just begun and that it is something that lasts thru life, then we must also tell them that it must be acquired largely thru reading. For the great majority the books required for this reading must be obtained at the public library. Then why should not the librarian, a specialist in books, guide the reading and become the chief factor and agent in adult education?

Jennings's connection with adult education was of national significance, and as chairman of the American Library Association's Adult Education Commission from 1924 to 1926, he imparted to the work a vitality that has grown and borne fruit up to the present time. During his chairmanship, the Commission devoted two years to a study and analysis of the library aspects of adult education and reported its findings in "Voluntary Education through the Public Library," published by ALA in 1926 and also appearing in *Libraries and Adult Education* (4, no. 2:35-60; April 1929). The Commission was of the opinion that the library's contribution to adult education resolved into three major activities. First of all, and on its own responsibility, the library owes consulting and advisory service, supplemented by suitable books, to those who wish to pursue their studies alone, rather than in organized groups or classes. In the second place, there is an obligation to furnish complete and reliable information concerning local opportunities for adult education available outside the library. Third, the library should recognize as a fundamental duty the supplying of books and other printed material for adult education activities maintained by other organizations.

Jennings died in Seattle in his seventy-fifth year on February 8, 1948. Gertrude Andrus, long-time associate and friend who served as his superintendent of children's work from 1908 to 1919 and from 1940 to 1946, characterized Jennings in the following terms:

> He was a very modest man and his shyness made many people feel that he was aloof and unapproachable. In spite of the honors conferred upon him by local and national associations, he refused to think of himself as important. It was the work that counted and not the personal acclaim. In making decisions he was slow. Each problem was considered and pondered and when a conclusion was reached, his staff felt a sense of great security in his judgment and confidence in his ability to meet the situation.

A bronze memorial to Judson Toll Jennings was unveiled at the Seattle Public Library on February 7, 1950, bearing the following tribute: "He built the tradition of progressive library service so firmly that the Pacific Northwest will forever be indebted to him."

Adam Strohm (q.v.), retired librarian of the Detroit Public Library, wrote the following to the staff of the Seattle Public Library: "The arrival yesterday of the Judson Jennings plaque evoked thoughts of rare warmth. . . . The friends of Judson Jennings cherish his memory as a leader of rare skill. . . . The recognition given to him is a tribute to a personality of innate winsomeness, integrity and refreshing cheerfulness."

Biographical listings and obituaries–Andrus, Gertrude. "Judson Toll Jennings [Obituary]." *News Flash, Supplement* (Seattle Public Library Staff Association), Feb. 12, 1948; *National Cyclopaedia of American Biography* D; [Obituary]. *Library Journal* 73:729 (May 1, 1948); [Obituary]. *Library News Bulletin* 16:393-94 (Feb.-March 1948); [Obituary]. *Pacific Northwest Library Association Quarterly* 12:94 (Jan. 1948); Richards, John Stewart. "Judson Toll Jennings, 1872-1948." [Obituary]. *Washington State Library Bulletin* (Feb.-March 1948), pp. 353-54; *Who Was Who in America* II (1943-1950); *Who's Who in Library Service*, 1st ed.; *Who's Who in the State of Washington*, 1939-1940. **Books and articles about the biographee**–[Biographical sketch]. *Library Journal* 76:469-70 (March 15, 1951); Johns, Helen. *Twenty-Five Years of the Washington Library Association*. Palo Alto, Calif.: Pacific Books, 1956; "Our Frontispiece: Judson Toll Jennings." *Bulletin of Bibliography and Dramatic Index* 12, No. 9:165 (Jan.-April 1926); Ruby, Edward E. "Library Work in the Army of Occupation." *Proceedings of the Tenth Annual Conference*, Pacific Northwest Library Association, 1919.

–WILLARD O. YOUNGS

JESSE, WILLIAM HERMAN (1908-1970)

William Herman Jesse was born September 16, 1908, at Versailles, Kentucky, the son of Watson McIlvain and Helen Wolf Jesse. The family later moved to Nicholasville, Kentucky, where his enthusiasm and ability in football earned young Jesse a scholarship to Transylvania College in 1929. After two years, he transferred to the University of Kentucky and was graduated in 1933 with an A.B. in English.

The Johnson County, Kentucky, public school system then offered him a combined position as basketball coach, English teacher, and librarian. The library assignment became the major influence in Jesse's career. In order to provide students with a variety of books on a limited budget, he initiated a program of interlibrary cooperation among the county schools and personally arranged for the rotation of packages of books centered on teaching units. By 1935, he was library director of the Johnson County School System.

Realizing that his future lay in librarianship, Jesse worked for a year as an insurance salesman in order to afford tuition at Columbia University. When he arrived at Columbia in 1937, one of the assigned readings was his own first published article describing the Johnson County cooperative plan. He received the B.S. in L.S. in 1938 and went to Providence, Rhode Island, to serve Brown University as Readers' Division chief, under the tutelage of librarian Henry B. Van Hoesen (q.v.). On September 12 of that year, following a ten-year courtship begun in Nicholasville, Jesse married Edith Miller. Two daughters were born to them, Nan and Alice. Also while in Providence, he commenced the studies in bibliography which were to earn him an A.M. in bibliography from Brown in 1945.

By 1942, he had left Brown to become Stephen A. McCarthy's assistant library director at the University of Nebraska. In January of 1943, he accepted a war service appointment in Washington at the U.S. Department of Agriculture Library as head of the Readers' and Reference Division. Within the same year, a pool of some forty applicants had been narrowed to three candidates for the position of librarian at Tennessee. Just before a decision was reached, a fourth and final candidate entered, and on September 1, 1943, William H. Jesse became librarian and professor of bibliography at the University of Tennessee. (The title was later changed to director of libraries.)

Throughout the next quarter century, Jesse's vision of service, first exhibited in Johnson County, developed fully and left its imprint on libraries and librarians alike. Coupled with a concern for the users of libraries was a keen aesthetic sense that enabled him to develop a national reputation as a library building consultant. During Jesse's most active consulting period, involving more than 45 libraries, Keyes Metcalf observed that the two busiest consultants around were Ralph Ellsworth and William Jesse. On Tennessee's Knoxville campus, two additions to the James D. Hoskins Library and a versatile, separate undergraduate library attest to his skill as a consultant. Perhaps because of its close relationship to his work as a consultant, his favorite academic committee assignment was on the committee for long-range planning. His visualizing of future campus needs, often in advance of others, proved to be an invaluable asset to the University.

Jesse's faculty for manipulating alternative solutions to a problem, and thereby perceiving overriding trends or needs, extended beyond buildings and space. Although hints of this characteristic are revealed in his contributions to professional literature, it was most sharply shown in his relations with people around him. Conversation for Jesse was never

contrived. He was able to learn and to contribute in talking with people of diverse education and backgrounds, and he never demeaned anyone. He was quick to recognize excellence and to encourage self-confidence so that an individual's potential could be realized. He believed that administrative decisions affecting staff should be made in favor of the individual's career, for, in the long run, this benefitted the institution. Certainly these qualities assisted him as a visiting lecturer for nearly a decade during summer sessions in the library schools at Columbia, Illinois, and Florida State.

In a real sense of staff development, the continuing annual event of the University of Tennessee Library Lecture Series, commencing in 1949 with Maurice Tauber's "Book Classification in University Libraries," was to "demonstrate the stature" of librarians to librarians and their colleagues. A concrete support of his belief in the place of librarians within the academic scene was his success in gaining faculty rank for them in 1950. The same year, the establishment of the Mary E. Baker Scholarship Fund, which has provided unobligated financial assistance to over twenty people, stimulated the non-academic staff to expand its own horizons.

Among the highlights affecting the stature of the University of Tennessee Library as a whole, its admission to the Association of Research Libraries in 1962, following a long, hard-fought effort, must be one of the brightest. On the heels of the Tauber lecture, the collection was reclassified from Dewey Decimal Classification to that of the Library of Congress. The eight-year project was completed in 1957, with no disruption of service and at an imperceptible cost. In 1959, completion of a wing to the main library building introduced two new services: a collection specially planned to serve undergraduates and the Special Collections Library to house and preserve historical documents, source materials, rare books, and manuscripts. During the same year, the Library Development Program was inaugurated. The Estes Kefauver papers and a wing in which to house them were obtained in 1966. Three years later, a separately housed undergraduate library was opened. By 1970 the Knoxville campus collection, which had had fewer than 200,000 volumes in 1943, reached the million mark.

However, one of Jesse's greatest contributions to his profession was a modest book of 68 pages with the title *Shelf Work in Libraries*, published by the American Library Association in 1952. Unlike many professionals, who tended to look on shelving library books as a housekeeping chore, Jesse recognized the need not only for orderly shelves, but also for continual shelving of books and periodicals. Only in this way could the library avoid having a backlog of unshelved and therefore inaccessible books. Because he succeeded so well in imparting this view, Jesse's book became a source of both information and inspiration to other librarians.

An active participation in associations was concomitant with Jesse's natural response to people. He was a life member of the American Library Association and a member of its Council from 1941 to 1945. From 1943 to 1947, he was on the Committee on College and University Buildings of the Association of College and Reference Libraries, serving as the Committee's chairman in 1946-1947. He was president of the Southeastern Library Association during 1946-1948. Active in the Southern Association of Colleges and Secondary Schools, he served on its Library Committee on Standards. He was a member of the Tennessee Library Association, the American Association of University Professors, and the Bibliographical Society of America. He was a member of Pi Kappa Alpha and was a co-founder of Beta Phi Mu. He was a lifelong member of the Presbyterian church.

Whenever time permitted in his active professional life, he thoroughly enjoyed the hunting and fishing that abound in east Tennessee, and his early years as a football player and referee made him much more than an ordinary observer of the Volunteers' games. At home, he listened to his wide-ranging collection of recorded music nearly every day.

On July 1, 1965, as he was delivering a paper at the ALA Pre-Conference Institute on Buildings held in Detroit, he suffered a stroke. Although he never fully regained his physical health, he actively guided the Library with his thinking and his example until his death in Knoxville on July 1, 1970. He is buried in Nicholasville, Kentucky.

Biographical listings and obituaries—*A Biographical Directory of Librarians in the United States and Canada*, 5th ed.; *Directory of Library Consultants* (1969); Townsend, Daphne H. "William H. Jesse." [Obituary]. *Tennessee Librarian* 23:5-6 (Fall 1970); *Who Was Who in America* V (1969-1973); *Who's Who in Library Service*, 1st ed., 3rd ed., 4th ed. Books and articles about the biographee—Holt, A. D. "William H. Jesse—A Tribute." *Southeastern Librarian* 21:24 (Spring 1971); McNeal, Archie L. "William H. Jesse—A Memorial." *Southeastern Librarian* 21:23 (Spring 1971); Townsend, Daphne H. "William H. Jesse: A Tribute." *The University of Tennessee Record* 73:3-4 (Dec. 1970); William H. Jesse [Memorial Resolution by the Tennessee Library Association]. *Tennessee Librarian* 27:52-53 (Spring 1975). Primary sources and archival materials—Information was obtained through an interview with Edith Miller Jesse, August 24, 1975. The Jesse papers are preserved in the Library of the University of Tennessee, Knoxville.

—ROBERT JULIAN BASSETT

JEWETT, CHARLES COFFIN (1816-1868)

From the publication of his much-heralded catalog of the Brown University Library in 1843, to the fatal attack of apoplexy that struck while he was at his desk in the Boston Public Library in 1868, Charles Coffin Jewett was the pivotal figure in American librarianship. He was the first man to hold a full-time post as an academic librarian, the first librarian of what very nearly became the national library of the United States, the president of the first formal conference of librarians, and the first superintendent of the country's premier nineteenth century public library.

He was born on August 12, 1816, the son of Paul and Mary Punchard Jewett. Paul Jewett, of the sixth generation of Jewetts to call themselves Americans, was a young minister in Lebanon, Maine. Among his three brothers, Charles Coffin could count John Punchard Jewett, who was later to gain considerable fame as the publisher of *Uncle Tom's Cabin*. Charles married Rebecca Green Haskins on April 5, 1848. There were no children.

As a youngster, Charles attended the Salem Latin School and, like his father before him, enrolled at Dartmouth (Rhode Island) College and then quickly transferred to Brown. Jewett appears to have developed a keen interest in books early in life and this love of books, coupled with his lack of personal fortune, made him a ready user of libraries. However, upon his arrival at Brown he found a library that, like those of the other Colonial colleges, was poorly suited for the needs of a reader with voracious and wide-ranging interests.

Fortunately, Jewett had recourse to several fine literary society libraries at Brown. These societies, like their counterparts in most of the colleges in America, were primarily debating societies, and their interests served all areas of academic and public concern. Since their debates were expected to be learned, as well as rhetorically correct, students immediately recognized the need for substantial libraries from which to mine their material. It was in the library of the Philermenian Society, the oldest at Brown, that Jewett gained his first actual "professional" experience, when he and a classmate cataloged and arranged the several thousand books belonging to the Society.

After being graduated (the youngest member of his class) in 1835, Jewett taught briefly before deciding to continue his studies and prepare for a career in the ministry at Andover Seminary. It was a school of great prestige, and its three-year program provided the opportunity for young scholars of superior ability to develop their talents under the most stimulating conditions. Andover was also a conservative institution, one bound by basic tenets of patience, piety, stability, and temperance. A dedicated student, Jewett excelled at Andover and continued to cultivate his interest in languages, especially "Oriental Languages and Eastern Antiquities." While a student at Andover, he was offered a second opportunity to catalog a library. Professor Oliver A. Taylor invited him to assist in the preparation of the Andover Library catalog of 1838, which provided a model for many other catalogs—especially those prepared later by Taylor's famous pupil.

Jewett's library experience at Brown and Andover, coupled with his increasing familiarity with bibliographical affairs and his obvious scholarly attributes, admirably qualified him for the profession he was soon to enter and serve with distinction. That profession opened to him in the autumn of 1841, when he accepted the position as librarian at Brown University. In 1841, the Brown University Library numbered some 10,000 volumes and ranked as one of the better collections in the country. Moreover, President Francis Wayland's consistent and enlightened support of the Library, united with the generosity of the friends of Brown, made the position one of the most sought-after in America.

During his years as librarian at Brown, he achieved many small successes, but his day-to-day activities are overshadowed by two major accomplishments: the appearance of his landmark *Catalogue of the Brown University Library* in 1843, and his astounding book-buying tour of Europe in 1844-1845. Jewett noted, in his preface to the 1843 *Catalogue*, that his first and foremost task was to catalog the collection. This was not easy, for little standardization in cataloging practice had been achieved by that time, and questions relating to selection and format of entries, and the arrangement of entries once established, were proving both perplexing and controversial problems.

Taylor's influence on Jewett's catalog is obvious and is readily acknowledged in the preface. As Jewett noted, his catalog was made up of two parts: an alphabetically arranged "descriptive catalog" of all books in the Library and an alphabetically arranged "index of subjects." This approach constituted a conclusive break with the tradition of preparing catalogs arranged by some logical classification, and the addition of the alphabetical subject index was instrumental in the evolution of a catalog made up of one alphabetical sequence containing author, title, and subject entries—that is, the modern dictionary catalog. Once published, the catalog was widely hailed as a major advance in cataloging practice, and its success catapulted Jewett into a position of great prominence among the librarians of his day.

Having completed the pressing task of cataloging the Library collection, Jewett accepted the position of professor of modern languages and literature while agreeing to continue as librarian. Accompanying the offer was the promise of a European tour designed to allow the scholar-librarian to study modern languages and literature, while at the same time buying books for the Library and making contacts with European librarians in order to study their methods. Jewett

achieved unprecedented success in all aspects of his endeavor. But most significant was the fact that, when he returned to America in December of 1845, he was able to report the acquisition of some 7,000 books purchased at an average cost of $1.20 a volume.

After returning home, he entered into his dual role with vigor, but he grew more and more aware of his responsibility as a library leader. In 1846, he wrote a pamphlet entitled *Facts and Considerations Relative to Duties on Books*, in which he objected to the proposed tariff on imported books and articulated a view that has since become the librarians' creed. However, in his own time, his stance was viewed as a progressive and forceful argument in favor of removing all artificial obstacles to the free flow of information in a democratic society.

In 1846, Joseph Henry, secretary of the newly established Smithsonian Institution, "an establishment for the increase and diffusion of knowledge among men," was authorized to appoint "an assistant who shall be librarian." Joseph Henry was one of the country's most prominent scientists, and he wanted the Smithsonian Institution to be an agency that sponsored and published research. His conception of the Smithsonian's role was opposed, though, by an influential group of literary and political leaders, who advocated making the Smithsonian "a grand and noble library" designed to serve as a national resource for scholars and literary figures. The champion of the "big library" advocates was Charles Coffin Jewett, and in 1847 he was appointed librarian at the Smithsonian.

While the years from 1847 to 1854 were to prove extremely fruitful for Jewett, they were also the most frustrating of his life, as Henry consistently thwarted the plans of the "big library" advocates to make the Smithsonian the national library of the United States. However, between his appointment and his dismissal he achieved several influential and highly noteworthy objectives. The compilation and publication of his *Notices of Public Libraries*, hailed as the "pioneer attempt to give a description to our libraries," was completed in 1851 and did much to focus attention on the Smithsonian Library as a center of bibliographical knowledge.

A second major development of his tenure at the Smithsonian was his now-famous plan to prepare a national union catalog that would be printed by a unique system of stereotyping entries (making clay molds from which actual printing plates could be derived). This decision set the stage for an unfolding drama that would prove both frustrating and rewarding for Jewett. On the one hand, his plan to prepare stereotype plates made of Indiana clay—a plan William Frederick Poole (q.v.) dubbed Jewett's "*Mud Catalogue*"—was a dismal failure, one of the most devastating of Jewett's life. But, almost inadvertently, his plan for a stereotyped catalog forced him to prepare rules that would insure that "catalogues should all be prepared on a uniform plan." That is, each entry prepared in the cooperating libraries would meet the Smithsonian requirements and would mesh nicely with the cards from other libraries, all of which would eventually constitute Jewett's national union catalog.

This desire for uniformity, expressed by every great cataloger since, led Jewett to begin a work that was eventually to appear as the second part of his *On the Construction of Catalogues of Libraries, and of a General Catalogue, and Their Publication by Means of Separate, Stereotyped Titles, with Rules and Examples* (1852). The *Rules* immediately became the basic guide to cataloging practice and were not supplanted until the publication of Charles Ammi Cutter's (q.v.) *Rules for a Printed Dictionary Catalogue* (1876). Indeed, they became so influential that cataloging historian Jim Ranz labeled the third quarter of the century the "Age of Jewett."

Jewett's third major contribution came in the form of his active and central involvement in the first conference of librarians held in this country in 1853. Jewett, the foremost librarian in the land by mid-century, was fully supportive of the conference idea first proposed by Charles B. Norton (q.v.), the publisher and library book agent. With his aid, the conference was held, 82 men met in New York on September 15, 1853, and Jewett was elected president of the group. At the meeting, he twice addressed the conferees: first, in his presidential address, he urged them to commit themselves to service to their countrymen, to break down barriers to free communication of information, and to recognize the significance of books and libraries in the life of a democratic nation; second, he described at length his stereotype catalog scheme.

Upon his return from the welcome respite provided by his attendance at the Librarians' Conference, Jewett found himself quickly enmeshed in a battle to preserve his dream of a great national library at the Smithsonian. Increasingly, the battle was being billed as a war between science and literature, between scientific research and libraries, between the dynamo and man. For Jewett the situation proved disastrous. In his efforts to preserve the "big library" concept of the Smithsonian's role, he took extreme measures to defeat Henry, and, in doing so, committed abuses of his authority that placed him in obvious insubordination to his superior. Once Jewett had advanced far beyond his defenses, Henry struck decisively, finally removing Jewett on January 13, 1855. For Jewett, much was lost: his vision for a national library, his stereotyped catalog scheme, and his ideas on a national union catalog. But his reputation remained

intact among the men of literature, who viewed him as a "literary martyr to science," and it was to them that he turned, "thoroughly disheartened," for shelter and support.

Jewett was shaken and embittered by the Smithsonian experience. However, he did not turn his back on librarianship, as did Melvil Dewey (q.v.) after his forced retirement from the New York State Library. In June 1855, Jewett left for Boston, where he was employed first as a cataloger, then as the equivalent of an "acquisitions librarian," and finally, as the first superintendent (1858) of the new Boston Public Library. In the latter capacity, he earned $2,000 a year and enjoyed the respect due the nation's most prominent librarian.

Once in Boston, Jewett found himself in close contact with the country's foremost scholars and bookmen—George Ticknor (q.v.), Edward Everett, and others—and he was allowed the leisure to further cultivate his already well-developed talent for organizing libraries. He was involved in a number of imaginative programs: 1) he continued to lead in the area of catalog production, 2) he pioneered in circulation-system design, and 3) he remained unrivaled among the nation's scholar-librarians, building a magnificent collection at Boston. Jewett certainly retained his supremacy in the eyes of his colleagues, although the lack of any sort of library literature to analyze, and the paucity of Jewett manuscripts, make such matters difficult to assess. During his later years he fell back, as do so many who were at the cutting edge of progress in their youth, and frequently found himself being identified with the conservative position in questions relating to cataloging, Sunday opening, and circulation policies.

Jewett was struck by a serious attack of apoplexy while working at his desk in the Boston Public Library on the afternoon of January 8, 1868. Realizing that the end was near, he pleaded to be carried home to Braintree and his wife and children. There, attended by his family and several friends, he passed away early the next morning. He was 52 years old.

In his own day, he was at the zenith of his profession despite his defeat at the Smithsonian—he was the man to whom most people looked for leadership in library affairs; he was the first thoroughly professional American librarian. After his death, his name was mentioned with respect at nearly every meeting of the American Library Association before 1900, and in 1886, William Frederick Poole made Jewett the topic of his presidential address, noting that:

Our profession is a debtor to Prof. Jewett for his early and scholarly services in bibliography and in library economy.... Indeed, he may justly be ranked as the ablest and most zealous of the early American reformers in the methods of library management.

A year later, Reuben Aldridge Guild (q.v.) recalled the "elegance of his person, the refinement of his manners, his pleasant voice, his kindly smile, his cordial affection for his friends, and his urbanity towards all," concluding that Jewett was acknowledged by all as an "honor to our profession, a model librarian . . ."

Perhaps Charles Coffin Jewett's greatest contribution was his professionalism. He deplored the fact that so few had "devoted themselves professionally to bibliography," and he constantly worked to increase the numbers of those "who feel a professional interest in the office of librarian."

Biographical listings and obituaries—*Dictionary of American Biography* 10 (William Coolidge Lane); *National Cyclopaedia of American Biography* 5; *Who Was Who in America*, Historical Volume (1607-1896). **Books and articles about the biographee**—Adler, Cyrus. "The Smithsonian Library." In George Brown Goode, ed., *The Smithsonian Institution, 1846-1896*. Washington, 1897, pp. 265-302; Boromé, Joseph. *Charles Coffin Jewett*. Chicago: American Library Association, 1951; Cole, John Y. "Of Copyright, Men, and a National Library." *Quarterly Journal of the Library of Congress* 28:114-36 (1971); Guild, Reuben Aldridge. "Memorial Sketch of Prof. Charles Coffin Jewett." *Library Journal* 12:507-511(1887); Harris, Michael H., ed. *The Age of Jewett; Charles Coffin Jewett and American Librarianship, 1841-1868*. Littleton, Colo.: Libraries Unlimited, 1975. Contains a comprehensive bibliography of Jewett's works; Johnston, William Dawson. "The Smithsonian Institution and the Plans for a National Library." In his *History of the Library of Congress, Volume 1, 1800-1864*. Washington: Government Printing Office, 1904, Chapter 10; Ranz, Jim. "The Age of Jewett, 1850-1875 . . ." In his *The Printed Book Catalogue in American Libraries, 1723-1900*. Chicago: American Library Association, 1964, Chapters 3 and 4; Utley, George Burwell. *The Librarians' Conference of 1853*. Chicago: American Library Association, 1951; Whitehill, Walter Muir. *The Boston Public Library: A Centennial History*. Cambridge: Harvard University Press, 1956. **Primary sources and archival materials**—Few of Jewett's manuscript letters have survived to this day. Some will be found in the archives of Brown University; some in the Boston Public Library.

—MICHAEL H. HARRIS

JOECKEL, CARLETON BRUNS (1886-1960)

Carleton Bruns Joeckel, librarian, educator, author, was born at Lake Mills, Wisconsin, on January 2, 1886, the only child of John and Emma Wilhelmina Joeckel. In 1904, he entered the University of Wisconsin, where he came under the influence of teachers supporting the humanitarian and reform legislation proposed by the state's governor (and later senator) Robert M. LaFollette. Here he developed the philosophy of service and progress that guided many decisions in his later life.

After graduation from the University in 1908, Joeckel enrolled at the New York State Library School at Albany, with the goal of becoming a professional librarian. He completed the two-year program required for the B.L.S. degree in 1910 and accepted a position as secretary to the librarian of the St. Louis Public Library. A year later, he moved to the University of California at Berkeley as assistant reference librarian and superintendent of circulation in the University Library. He held this post three years.

Although Joeckel was destined to be both a long-time critic and an ardent supporter of public libraries, his only employment in this area was in the Berkeley Public Library. He was appointed librarian there in 1914, and except for a two-year leave of absence, during which he served in the United States Army in World War I, he directed the library's growth and development until 1927. His army career began in 1917, when he enlisted and received a commission as a second lieutenant. He served in France with the 363d Infantry, 91st Division, and, at the time of his discharge in 1919, held the rank of captain. While this meant an interruption in the career of the young librarian, his experience in the army brought Joeckel in contact with organization and management on a large scale. Therefore, his two years in uniform were by no means wasted.

His first venture into teaching came while he was in Berkeley, where he was offered an opportunity to teach part-time in the School of Librarianship at the University of California. In 1927, Joeckel elected to leave library administration and become a full-time educator. He joined the faculty at the University of Michigan as associate professor of library science and three years later was advanced to the rank of professor. While at Michigan, he completed work for the degree of Master of Arts in political science.

In 1933, on leave from the University of Michigan to pursue study for an advanced degree at the University of Chicago, Joeckel established a record at the Graduate Library School by completing in three quarters all the requirements for the Ph.D. The degree was conferred in 1934. Then he returned to Michigan to teach one more year, during which time he was a vigorous critic of the autocratic policies and frequent absences of the director of the Department of Librarianship, William Warner Bishop (q.v.). In 1935, Joeckel left Michigan and accepted an appointment as professor of library science at the University of Chicago.

The ten years Joeckel spent at the University of Chicago were among the most productive of his life. He found that teaching and guiding research were congenial tasks, and he took a warm personal interest in his students. His standards of scholarship were high, and he insisted that students adhere to them. If he seemed overly critical of work he suspected did not reflect the maximum potential of the individual, he was just as quick to commend excellence. More than one student who continued graduate study beyond the master's level attributed the relative ease with which he completed a doctoral dissertation to the high standards of research and writing learned earlier under Joeckel's tutelage. Although Joeckel's major interest was in public libraries, a sizeable number of those who worked under his guidance moved into colleges and universities, where excellence of research was valued highly.

Joeckel found time also for extensive research and writing of his own. His doctoral dissertation (published as the *Government of the American Public Library* in 1935) was written from a sound background in political science and library experience. It was hailed by Norwegian librarian Wilhelm Munthe as the most important contribution by a graduate library school student up to that time (1939), since it lifted American library research to a high plane. In both his dissertation and later publications, Joeckel emphasized his belief that larger units of service were needed to provide adequate library service to the people of America. The ideas developed in the *Government of the American Public Library*, as well as in later publications such as *Library Service* (prepared for the President's Advisory Committee on Education–1938), and *A National Plan for Public Library Service* (in collaboration with Amy Winslow, 1948) gained for Joeckel the appellation "chief architect of the modern public library system in America" from his fellow librarians.

In 1937, in cooperation with a faculty colleague, Leon Carnovsky (q.v.), Joeckel undertook a survey of the Chicago Public Library, which was released in 1940 as *A Metropolitan Library in Action*. Publications which he edited included *Current Issues in Library Administration* (based on the 1938 summer institute at the Graduate Library School); *Post-War Standards for Public Libraries* (1943); and *Library Extension: Problems and Solutions* (1946). His last published work was *Reaching Readers: Techniques of Extending Library Services* in 1949. The first James Terry White Award made by the American Library Association was given to Joeckel in 1938 in recognition of his notable published professional writing.

Joeckel's contributions to professional organizations were considerable. At various times, he held office as president of the California Library Association (1919-1920), president of the Michigan Library Association (1930-1931), and second vice president of the American Library Association (1936-1937).

In April 1940, the newly appointed Librarian of Congress, Archibald MacLeish, appointed Joeckel chairman of the Librarian's Committee to survey the processing departments of the Library of Congress. The Committee's recommendations called for a

sweeping reorganization of the processing operations and provided guidelines for future growth.

During the 1930s, Joeckel was a strong advocate of federal aid to libraries. The creation of the Library Services Division in the Office of Education in the 1930s, and the passage of the Federal Library Services Act in the 1950s, as well as the adoption of National Public Library Standards, are monuments to Joeckel's efforts.

With the retirement of Louis Round Wilson in the summer of 1942, Joeckel was named dean of the Graduate Library School at the University of Chicago, the first alumnus to be so honored. Shortly before his leaving, Wilson had obtained a grant from the [Andrew] Carnegie [q.v.] Corporation to establish a one-year library program for undergraduates. To Joeckel fell the tasks of recruiting teachers and establishing a basic curriculum, at a time when the United States was involved in World War II and both students and faculty were being siphoned into war industry and military service. That the School was able to build under such adverse circumstances is a tribute to Joeckel's leadership. Despite wartime restrictions on travel, the Graduate Library School was able to sponsor three summer institutes for librarians in service: the Library in the Community (1943), Library Extension: Problems and Solutions (1944), and Personnel Administration in Libraries (1945).

In his administration of the School, Joeckel was ably assisted by two who were already colleagues—Leon Carnovsky, who was made assistant dean, and Pierce Butler (q.v.)—and by Lowell A. Martin, who joined the faculty. Martin appraised Joeckel as the ideal administrator, providing goals and direction, helping colleagues if they needed assistance, yet giving great freedom. Joeckel's colleagues found him never autocratic or authoritarian, ready to listen to other points of view, and fair in judgments and decisions.

In accordance with a long-standing personal plan to retire from active administrative duties when he neared the age of sixty, Joeckel resigned as dean in the summer of 1945 and returned to Berkeley, where he became associated with the University of California as a professor in the School of Librarianship. Here he planned to devote part of his time to teaching and some to research and writing. Joeckel remained on the faculty until his final retirement in 1950, working after 1946 under Dean J. Periam Danton, one of his fellow students at Chicago in 1933-1934. A severe attack of shingles forced Joeckel to revise his plans, to take a sick leave in 1949, and to retire in 1950.

The final decade of Joeckel's life was spent in retirement and declining health at Berkeley, but his last years were brightened by two events. On the occasion of his seventieth year, in 1956, former colleagues and students at Michigan, Chicago, and California presented him with a volume of testimonial letters. Two years later, in 1958, Joeckel received the ALA's Joseph W. Lippincott Award for distinguished service to the profession. He died on April 15, 1960.

Joeckel married Emma H. Kelly in 1911; the marriage ended in divorce. In 1929, he married Gladys E. Hatch, who survived him. He had no children.

Joeckel is a significant figure in American librarianship not only for his own contributions, but also for the impact he made on his colleagues and students. For forty years, his professional career reflected the main currents in the library world.

Biographical listings and obituaries—[Obituary]. *College and Research Libraries* 21 (Sept. 1960); [Obituary]. *Library Journal* 85 (July 1960); [Obituary]. *Library Quarterly* 30 (July 1960); [Obituary]. *Wilson Library Bulletin* 34 (June 1960); *Who's Who in America* 28 (1954-1955); *Who's Who in Library Service*, 1st ed., 2nd ed., 3rd ed. Books and articles about the biographee—[Biographical sketch]. *College and Research Libraries* 6:255 (June 1945); Mitchell, S. B. "Carleton B. Joeckel." *Library Service News* 5:53-54 (April 1936).

—THOMAS S. HARDING

JOHNSON, ALVIN S. (1874-1971)

During the period 1886 to 1917, and particularly during 1898 to 1917, Andrew Carnegie (q.v.) donated $41,033,850 to 1,412 communities in the United States for the construction of 1,679 public library buildings. This library philanthropy had a great impact upon American public library development, but although most people know generally about Carnegie's library benefactions, few are aware of the important role that Alvin Johnson played in Carnegie Corporation library philanthropy.

By 1915, the trustees of the Carnegie Corporation began to show concern over the status of Carnegie building grants. There was also some question in their minds about the value of continuing these grants. As a result, on November 18, 1915, the trustees authorized Alvin S. Johnson, an economics professor at Cornell University, to make a study of Carnegie libraries and particularly to see if the building grants to communities were worthy philanthropic investments.

Johnson was born near Homer, Nebraska, on December 18, 1874, and died in Upper Nyack, New York, on June 7, 1971. He earned B.A. and M.A. degrees from the University of Nebraska and a Ph.D. in economics from Cornell University. He also served as an economics professor at the University of Nebraska, the University of Chicago, and Stanford University. Johnson was later to become editor of the *New Republic* (1917-1923), director of the New

School for Social Research (1923-1943), and associate editor of the *Encyclopaedia of the Social Sciences* (1927-1933). Johnson's interest in libraries continued, however, as evidenced in his *The Public Library: A People's University*, a study of adult education in U.S. libraries, published in New York by the American Association for Adult Education in 1938.

For the Carnegie study of 1916, Johnson made a ten-week tour of the entire country, visiting some one hundred Carnegie libraries, and presented his incisive and far-sighted report to the Carnegie Corporation. A copy of the report was printed in 1919, but it has, unfortunately, never been widely disseminated. It stands as a landmark in library literature, since it not only dealt with the status of Carnegie libraries but also reviewed Carnegie public library philanthropy and analyzed the conditions and needs of the public library in the United States. Because Johnson's report was influential in changing the whole emphasis of future Carnegie library benefactions, it deserves wider recognition; consequently, its main points are summarized below.

Johnson first of all recognized the importance of the free library as a social institution providing both cultural and practical service of great value to each community. He predicted a great future for the public library, saying that it would play a significant role in advancing popular intellectual progress. However, he also described the free library as a service to the public, who, while recognizing its benefits in a general way, did not appreciate them sufficiently to compel civil authorities to make adequate provision for library service or to control the quality of such service as was provided—a worthy field, indeed, for philanthropy to provide an impetus.

He suggested, however, the desirability of adapting to local conditions any philanthropic initiative in establishing library service. Such philanthropy should not be uniform. In states that were already progressive in library development, grants might only be given for extending library service, while in those states that were still lacking in library growth, library donations might include not only new buildings but also books and subsidies to pay librarians to cultivate the library habit. Even different cities within the same state might well receive varied treatment. As an example, Johnson said that more resources should be given to a city with a large, unskilled, foreign-born population than to one with a native-born, skilled element in preponderance.

In Johnson's opinion, contrary to the past Carnegie Corporation viewpoint, a small library could justifiably share its building with, or allow its occasional use by, other organizations in the community, such as the Chamber of Commerce or a local women's club. Not only would this help the library's finances, since heating and lighting expenses could be shared, but it would also bring in people who might not otherwise use the library.

Johnson felt that a library that merely provided reading matter in answer to requests of the community was not properly employing its opportunities. An efficient and successful public library engaged itself actively in creating a demand for reading and in directing existing reading interests. A good public library stimulated library use through lectures, book lists, and contacts and cooperation with schools, churches, and other groups. At the time, many public library trustees and librarians considered this a novel idea.

To do all of this, the library staff first needed to have a systematic knowledge of the community. It then needed to win the friendship and support of increasing proportions of both people and organizations to establish the library as an important agency of the community, an agency able to compete successfully with other forms of town improvement in its financial claims. He found little evidence of this kind of activity during his survey.

In the final analysis, the efficiency and success of the library was largely dependent on the character and training of the librarian and his or her ability to understand the community and cultivate the reading habit. Johnson emphasized the great need for a much larger number of trained librarians in both Carnegie and non-Carnegie public libraries. He also felt that library education had to be improved so that librarians would have a good knowledge of books, of their selection and reference use, and of the social and economic conditions of the community. A librarian had to have the kind of education that commanded respect and standing in the community, would lead to success in reader guidance, and would elicit cooperation from schools, clubs, and other cultural and social agencies. Johnson recognized that salaries of librarians were very low, but he felt that improvement of library training and service would have to come before an increase in salaries could be justified.

He found that Carnegie libraries were generally poorly supported. The 10 percent annual maintenance fee was certainly not enough, but again, rather than have the Carnegie Corporation demand high annual support, it would be far better for the community to become convinced of the library's importance and to be willing to provide for it generously—even before any Carnegie grant for a building.

Johnson also made some specific recommendations regarding Carnegie building grants. The provision of library buildings for over fifteen years had been generally beneficial, since it had helped public libraries spread to many new areas and people. The architectural standards set forth by Carnegie officials were lauded as valuable for all public libraries, but the fruitfulness of donating money for buildings varied widely. Indeed, Johnson questioned whether the Corporation might not turn to other areas of library philanthropy.

If Carnegie officials were to continue investing philanthropic funds in the provision of library buildings, Johnson saw the prospect of efficient library service as their only justification. To do this, he argued that the Corporation should augment its regular investigation of a grant application (through questionnaires and mail inquiries) with the employment of expert field agents to visit a community requesting a grant and to investigate the possible success of an investment in a building. They would examine the proposed site of the building (most Carnegie buildings were poorly located), discover possibilities of library cooperation, and in general, spread ideas that the Corporation viewed as correct concerning libraries, their operation, and their financial support. Employing four or five such agents would amount to an additional cost of 2-4 percent of the average of the 1.5 million dollars per year then being donated for buildings, but it might prevent bad investment.

Johnson also felt strongly that the Corporation should have definite assurance that Carnegie buildings would be staffed by trained librarians. In the cases of small communities that could not afford professional librarians, the Corporation should, he said, provide such a staff member for a period of from three months to one year in order to get the library in the new building organized and started correctly. This would save the community some money during the first year, money that could be spent for books, and would also provide for the on-the-job training of a local person who could take over after the "Carnegie" librarian left. Again, this would be an expensive undertaking. From 50 to 75 librarians would be needed per year, but Johnson felt that the investment of an additional 10 percent of the total spent for buildings each year would be worthwhile, since the result would be efficient library service. In any case, whatever course the Corporation decided upon, Johnson emphasized the need for scholarships for library school students (at least one hundred per year) as well as the need for other funds to expand current library-training institutions and to organize new library schools.

In addition, Johnson made a strong plea for the establishment of model libraries in certain parts of the country to demonstrate to a more or less indifferent public the value of library service. Finally, he urged the Corporation to assist the American Library Association financially in its program and activities toward the improvement of libraries.

In his autobiography, *Pioneer's Progress* (1952), Johnson recalls that he faced the wrath of James Bertram (q.v.), the secretary of the Carnegie Corporation, at the formal presentation of his report to the Corporation trustees. Bertram declared that Johnson's proposals flew straight into the face of Andrew Carnegie's intention that there should be no centralized control and that no money should be spent on the administration of gifts. However, on November 7, 1917, the Carnegie Corporation terminated building grants. No new applications for the erection of library buildings were to be considered since wartime demands were being made on money, labor, and materials. After World War I ended, grants were never resumed, although the Corporation did honor requests still in progress.

The Carnegie Corporation then reassessed its entire library philanthropy program and followed many of Alvin Johnson's recommendations. It first sponsored the C. C. Williamson (q.v.) study of 1918, which revolutionized library education. A Carnegie-supported study in 1924 by W. S. Learned (q.v.) emphasized the public library as a medium for spreading information, called for expanded services to be provided by the American Library Association, and urged local and regional experiments and demonstrations leading to better ways of getting books to the people. Throughout the 1920s and into the 1930s, the Corporation provided funds for ALA, library-training fellowships, demonstration libraries, and both old and newly established library schools. These activities of the Corporation to improve public library service have continued. Two more recent examples were the Public Library Inquiry of 1949-1950 and the Public Library Standards of 1956, both studies financed by Carnegie grants and both paving the way for two very important developments—the growth of public library systems and the beginning of federal grants for the extension and improvement of public library service and the construction of public library buildings.

Although Alvin Johnson was not a librarian or even a person directly associated with libraries, he made many keen and penetrating observations about them. His landmark report changed the library philanthropy policies of the Carnegie Corporation and, as a result, played an important role in American library development.

Biographical listings and obituaries—*Current Biography* (Aug. 1942); *Who Was Who in America* V (1969-1973). Books and articles about the biographee—Bobinski, George S. *Carnegie Libraries: Their History and Impact on American Public Library Development.* Chicago: American Library Association, 1969. Primary sources and archival materials—Johnson, Alvin S. *Pioneer's Progress: An Autobiography.* New York: Viking, 1952; Johnson, Alvin S. *A Report to Carnegie Corporation of New York on the*

Policy of Donations to Free Public Libraries. New York: Carnegie Corporation, 1919.

—GEORGE S. BOBINSKI

JOSEPHSON, AKSEL GUSTAV SALOMON (1860-1944)

Aksel G. S. Josephson, chief cataloger of Chicago's John Crerar Library from 1896 to 1923, was born October 2, 1860, in Upsala, Sweden, the son of Jacob Axel and Hilda Augusta Josephson. During the 1880s, Josephson worked as a bookseller at Quaritch's in London, but after a few years, he returned to Upsala and established an antiquarium. Following this unsuccessful venture, he served from 1892 to 1893 as librarian of Upsala's Verlandis Arbetarbibliotek. In 1893, he migrated to the United States, entered the New York State Library School in Albany, and studied under Melvil Dewey (q.v.) from October 1893 through March 1894. After leaving library school, Josephson performed bibliographic work with *Publishers' Weekly* and, from 1894 to 1896, served as a cataloger with the Lenox Library in New York City. He was naturalized a U.S. citizen in 1898, and he married Lucia Engberg of Chicago in 1899.

For 27 years, Josephson devoted his energy to the construction of Crerar's tripartite catalog. J. Christian Bay (q.v.) stated that "to him belongs the merit of developing that tripartite catalogue which has stood many tests of accuracy and practical usage." He took an active part in the organization and development of cataloging codes and mastered these types of endeavors and the many associated bibliographic problems.

Josephson's professional activities included writing and compiling, and his *Bibliographies of Bibliographies* (1901) attracted nationwide attention. He compiled "Avhandlinger och program ut givna vid Svenska och Finska Akademir och Skolor, 1892-97" and from 1904 to 1914 contributed articles on bibliographies and book reviews to *The Nation*. Papers and critical book reviews by Josephson appeared regularly in the old *Chicago Dial*, and he contributed material on Swedish and English books to New York City's weekly *Nordstjernan*. Also included in his writings are *A List of Books on the History of Science* (1911) and *A List of Books on the History of Industry* (1915).

Playing a leading role in the organization of the Bibliographical Society of Chicago, Josephson served as president of this Society from 1903 to 1904. He assisted in founding the Bibliographical Society of America, and was secretary (1909-1912), chairman of the Publication Committee (1914-1916), and editor of the Society's *Papers* and *Bulletin* (1901-1911 and 1914-1918). Josephson also served as the president of the Chicago Library Club, 1901-1902, and was secretary of the Swedish Historical Society of America from 1907 to 1909. In 1919, he was elected a fellow of the American Library Institute.

During the 1890s, a number of American librarians and scholars were discussing the problems of national and international bibliography. Josephson was most persistent in the development of a bibliographic standard of perfection and, in 1894, recommended the establishment of international bibliographical bureaus founded and supported by the various national governments. In 1899, he proposed the founding of a national bibliographical society that would compile a complete bibliography of American literature.

Aksel Josephson was recognized as a librarian and distinguished bibliographic scholar. His dedication to bibliography and bibliographic control cannot be questioned, but his little-known efforts toward the establishment of higher standards for library education were generally ignored by the profession. Sarah Vann, in her *Training for Librarianship before 1923*, was the first to identify Josephson and give him credit for his work toward better schools of library service.

In 1896, Josephson asked if "librarianship was a learned profession." Even though he felt that cataloging and the minor arts of library economy were instructionally well presented, he did not feel that the library schools and training classes of the 1890s, as they were conducted, could supply the needs of a learned profession. He noted that the comparative study of different systems of classification was significantly neglected, and that little was done to familiarize students with the principles of classification of knowledge as the foundation for the classification of books. He objected to John Cotton Dana's (q.v.) efforts to make library work delightful for young women, and he felt that too much significance was given to the concept that the library was not a business office, but a center of public happiness first, and then a center of public education. Josephson presented his own plan for training for librarianship: a school of bibliography and library science, affiliated with a major university under the guidance of leaders of both scholarship and practical ability, where bibliography could be studied "in its nobler sense, and in its useful application."

After proposing his school of bibliography and library science, Josephson concluded that the library schools of 1896 could offer little to librarianship in its search for recognition among the learned professions. Historically, his search for scholarly curriculum content was the first constructive effort in the struggle to have library schools identified as professional and not technical schools. His first major proposal, that library schools be affiliated with

universities, was a concept declared much later as fundamental by C. C. Williamson (q.v.) in his study *Training for Library Service* (1923).

During the period from 1900 to 1902, when the New York State Library School Association was conducting an extensive study of the School's curriculum, Josephson was serving as second vice-president. Among the recommended changes adopted was a 1902 announcement by Melvil Dewey that admission to the School's regular two-year course was limited to graduates of registered colleges, thus elevating the program to graduate status.

Josephson formulated a two-year library school curriculum that would have redirected the current trend of having the second-year program an extension of the first. He was concerned that the high entrance requirements might exclude those who could serve in lower grades of library work, and he proposed that a definite distinction be made whereby the junior course, or first year, provided preparation for minor positions, and the second, or senior year, be an independent post-graduate program in connection with some university with a large staff of instructors and "rich" libraries. He presented his proposal to the American Library Association's Committee on Library Schools in 1896, and later in 1901, reiterated his proposal before the ALA's Round Table on Professional Instruction in Bibliography. The Round Table expressed little interest in his proposal; and neither at that time nor later did they indicate approval or disapproval. Josephson's dream did become a reality in his lifetime, however, with the opening of the Graduate Library School at the University of Chicago in 1928, five years after his retirement at Crerar. Many of the courses offered by Pierce Butler (q.v.) were along the lines Josephson had envisaged.

Twenty-one years after his earliest proposal, Josephson urged the establishment by some university of a course in bibliography and library administration for library school graduates and for graduate students in general. His projected plan of 1917 called for the award of a master's degree after six years of study. Josephson suggested the adoption of the seminar method as a mode of study, with emphasis on the theoretical and historical aspects, and with adequate, but minimal, practice work. Williamson appears to have ignored the plan, and there is no evidence that he ever consulted with Josephson or considered the merits of this 1917 plan.

Little recognition, if any, was given to Josephson for his efforts in upgrading library science education, and after fighting the long battle, he seemed to resign himself and concentrate his efforts on bibliographic control and on the construction of the tripartite Crerar catalog. After serving as chief cataloger for 27 years, Josephson was forced to retire due to ensuing blindness, and his resignation was accepted with regrets by the Board of Directors on April 19, 1923. From 1923 through 1938, however, he served as consulting cataloger with the Crerar Library.

In 1934, Josephson moved to Fairhope, Alabama, and devoted his last years to writing, by dictation, aesthetic and historical material. After the death of his wife, he moved across the bay to Mobile, Alabama. Due to his blindness, he fell and fractured his pelvis, which resulted in his death. He died in Mobile's City Hospital on December 12, 1944, at the age of 84, and is buried in Fairhope, Alabama.

Probably the greatest tribute rendered to Josephson was by J. Christian Bay, when he said: "He took great interest in recording books on the history of science, but the Crerar catalogues are his greatest contribution, and his work in connection with them was stupendous."

Biographical listings and obituaries—"Famed Librarian Dies in Mobile" [Obituary]. *Mobile Register* (Dec. 13, 1944); [Obituary]. *Library Journal* 70:78 (Jan. 15, 1945); [Obituary]. *Library Journal* 70:223 (March 1, 1945); [Obituary]. *College and Research Libraries* 6:258 (June 1945); *Who Was Who in America* II (1943-1950); *Who's Who in Library Service*, 1st ed. **Books and articles about the biographee**—Bay, J. Christian. *The John Crerar Library, 1895-1944*. Chicago: The John Crerar Library, 1945; Foos, Donald D. "Aksel G. S. Josephson, 1860-1944, Precursor." *Proceedings of the 4th Library History Seminar, February 26, 1971*. Tallahassee: School of Library Science, 1971. [microcard]; Vann, Sarah K. *Training for Librarianship before 1923*. Chicago: American Library Association, 1961. **Primary sources and archival materials**—Limited personal files on Josephson are available at the John Crerar Library in Chicago, Illinois. The New York Public Library Personnel System has no record of his employment, nor does the University of the State of New York (N.Y. State Library) have any record of his school enrollment. A Mr. R. Childs (now retired) from the Library of Congress indicated that possibly Mr. Josephson's archival records are in Mobile, Alabama, where Mr. Josephson's step-daughter (name unknown) now resides.

—DONALD D. FOOS

KAISER, JOHN BOYNTON (1887-1973)

John Boynton Kaiser was born in Cleveland, Ohio, on January 1, 1887, the son of Peter Henry and Beza N. Kaiser. He was graduated from Western Reserve University in 1908 with a B.A., and he received the B.L.S. from the New York State Library School in Albany in 1910 and the M.L.S. from that institution in 1917. While at Albany, he was employed in the New York State Law Library, and after receiving his degree, as assistant state librarian in charge of legislative reference work at the Texas State Library in Austin (1910-1911). These two positions were to give him a strong interest in both public administration and the legal aspects of public library organization and operation, in which he became well known as his career as a library administrator developed.

On May 14, 1910, Kaiser married Gertrude I. Swift, who died April 2, 1940. They had one son, Boynton Swift Kaiser. Kaiser's marriage to Mary K. Cooper took place on December 31, 1942, and was terminated by divorce on June 15, 1961; he then married Margaret M. Whaley on September 30, 1961; she died on September 6, 1964. Kaiser was again married on May 1, 1972, to Gladys S. Henderson, who survived him.

During the period 1911-1914 he was departmental librarian in economics and sociology at the University of Illinois, and also served as lecturer in the library school at that University. The Tacoma Public Library invited Kaiser to become its chief librarian in March 1914, his first position of major responsibility in the public library field, and he remained there for about ten years. During his tenure at Tacoma, the first general notice of his courage to face political situations came to public attention when he sued the mayor of Tacoma to compel him to sign a warrant issued by the city controller for travel expenses authorized by the Board of Library Trustees. He won a favorable ruling from the Superior Court of the state of Washington in 1917.

Kaiser was elected president of the Pacific Northwest Library Association for the 1917-1918 term. During World War I, he served as librarian at Camp Knox, Kentucky, from November 1918 to January 1919, and at Camp Upton, New York, from January to May 1919, after which he returned to the Tacoma Public Library.

After almost ten years in public library work at Tacoma, John Kaiser decided to move into the academic library field when he accepted appointment at Iowa State University, Ames, as the director of libraries and of the Library School. There he remained until 1927, when he was chosen to become librarian of the Oakland Public Free Library, Oakland, California, and secretary of the Oakland Public Museum, the Snow Museum, and the Oakland Art Gallery, dual positions requiring a broad range of responsibilities in various fields of informal education. It was at Oakland that Kaiser developed his great interest in and involvement with Civil Service and with personnel administration—two areas of public service to which he gave considerable study and attention. They were subjects in which he believed and on which he wrote.

When Oakland celebrated Kaiser's tenth anniversary as librarian, it was noted that the number of volumes in the library, the circulation of books, and the circulation per capita had all increased at least 100 percent. Also, the level of library financial support had been almost doubled. Josephine DeWitt, in an article in *Library Journal* (62:286-87; April 1, 1937) relating to his tenth anniversary dinner, reported, "One of Mr. Kaiser's fundamental conceptions regarding library administration is that it is about the most highly cooperative enterprise, certainly among publicly supported activities, in which communities engage." Under Kaiser's administration, the libraries in Oakland and later in Newark were actively represented in community organizations, and staff members were encouraged to participate in community enterprises.

In 1942, Kaiser was selected by the Board of Trustees of the Newark, New Jersey, Public Library to be its director, succeeding Beatrice Winser (q.v.) who had just retired as director following a difference of opinion with the Board over administrative principles. As director of the Newark Public Library, Kaiser maintained an impersonal and objective approach to problems of Board and city relationships and operation. He instituted modern management policies and procedures, and developed, in cooperation with the Library Board, what became recognized as a model of by-laws for a library board, setting forth the powers and responsibilities of the Board and the library director under New Jersey library law.

During his administration in Newark, Kaiser also sponsored and secured approval of a "Personnel Classification and Pay Plan" and a "Work Simplification Survey," using outside professional assistance to undertake a complete job analysis of all library positions. This resulted in the adoption of completely new position and pay plans, including on-going self-survey techniques and personnel rating plans. Long a close observer and student of library organization, Kaiser was one of the first library executives to assign to assistant directors, in an organizational chart, responsibilities that included specific areas of supervision and advisory and research functions as well.

His general philosophy regarding the public library was expressed by him in stating the general objectives of the Newark Public Library:

The Public Library's major objective is to provide a high quality informational, educational, cultural, and recreational service through published experience, and the power of print for every man, woman, and child in the city, on an unbiased, non-partisan, and trustworthy basis. The library's program is a composite. It is the sum total of its activities carried on, and coordinated to achieve the major objective.

To his associates in the Newark Public Library, he had both an "official" and an "unofficial" side. Officially, he was formal and studiously objective, and he required that all recommendations be made in writing. Unofficially, he could be quite informal, with a considerable capacity for kindness and thoughtfulness in his personal relationships.

During his service at the Newark Public Library, the Board of Trustees and the city inaugurated bookmobile service, erected one branch library,

institued bedside library service in seven hospitals, established two school-community libraries in new public school buildings, administered one of the first large-scale modernizations of a monumental public library building following World War II, and reorganized the departmental structure of the Library at that time. Also under Kaiser's administration, the Newark Public Library scored a "first" in the field of professionally written, designed, and printed reports using modern public relations techniques, the first and best known of which was "The Power of Print" (1946). He felt that yearly reports were repetitious and there was not enough that was new and different to justify their wide distribution. Instead, he issued brief mimeographed annual reports, chiefly statistical in nature to meet legal requirements, and well-prepared, general reports by professional writers that were issued approximately every five years and recorded library progress, problems, and needs.

In addition to his interest in public library organization and management, Kaiser wrote and lectured on such subjects as municipal and legislative reference service, Civil Service, library publicity, personnel, staff rating plans, budget presentation, professional library salaries, and legal aspects of library service. Among his best known contributions to library literature are *The National Bibliographies of the South American Republics* (Boston Book Company, 1913), which was reprinted from the *Bulletin of Bibliography* 7:138-41 (July 1913); *Law, Legislative and Municipal Reference Libraries: An Introductory Manual and Bibliographical Guide* (Boston Book Company, 1914—Useful Reference Series, No. 9); "Winning Support," a chapter in *Current Problems in Public Library Finance*, edited by C. P. P. Vitz (American Library Association, 1933); and two chapters in *Current Issues in Library Administration*, edited by C. B. Joeckel (q.v.) (University of Chicago Press, 1939), namely, "Personnel: The Key to Administration," and "Problems of Library Finance." In addition to contributing a chapter on personnel administration, Kaiser was also editor of "Legal Aspects of Library Administration," the April 1958 issue of *Library Trends*.

Kaiser was elected president of the New Jersey Library Association (1948-1949) and was an active member of the American Library Association—member and chairman of several of its committees, a Council member (1940-1945, 1949-1950), and second vice-president (1949-1950). He served on the Trustees' Advisory Committee to the School of Library Service at Columbia, and for a number of years was an active liaison between the New York State Library School Association, of which he was president, and the library school at Columbia (which succeeded the New York State Library School). In 1958, he was awarded the Edna M. Sanderson Award for Distinguished Service in Library Work by the Alumni Association of the Columbia University School of Library Service. Rutgers conferred the L.H.D. degree on Kaiser in 1960 for his professional contributions. From 1960 to 1963, he served as executive secretary of the American Documentation Institute (now the American Society for Information Science).

Among his outside-the-library interests were the Public Personnel Association, of whose New Jersey chapter he was president (1957-1958), and Phi Beta Kappa (president of its New Jersey Alumni Association, 1951-1953). He was also a member of Beta Theta Phi, Phi Delta Phi, Rotary, and the California Writers Club.

Kaiser's favorite avocation was philately, and he not only was an avid collector in areas of specialization, but also a thorough and continuing student in philatelic matters as well. He took an active role in related organizations and contributed to journals in that field. The Walter McCoy Award for Excellence in Philatelic Writing was presented to Kaiser by the American Philatelic Congress in 1953.

On the occasion of his retirement from the directorship of the Newark Public Library in 1958, there was issued "An Annotated Bibliography of the Writings of John Boynton Kaiser Published 1911 to 1958" (The Newark Public Library, June 1958), which was updated and revised by Kaiser in 1967. This bibliography includes a list of periodicals and serials to which Kaiser contributed, is indexed by subject and is quite complete.

John Boynton Kaiser died in Winter Park, Florida, September 30, 1973.

Biographical listings and obituaries—*Current Biography* (1943); *New York State Library School Register, 1887-1926.* New York, 1928; [Obituary]. *American Libraries* 4:663 (Dec. 1973); *Who Knows—and What, Among Authorities—Experts—and the Specially Informed.* Chicago: Marquis, 1949 and 1954; *Who Was Who in America* VI (1974-1976); *Who's Who in Library Service,* 1st ed., 2nd ed., 3rd ed., 4th ed. **Books and articles about the biographee**—DeWitt, Josephine. "John B. Kaiser Honored." *Library Journal* 62:286-87 (April 1, 1937). Abridged from *Pacific Binding Talk* 9:145 (1937); Gilmore, Jean Elizabeth. "John Boynton Kaiser: Summary of Sixteen Years of Service." *California Library Association Bulletin* 4:143-45 (June 1943); "Newark's New Librarian." *Library Journal* 68:255 (March 15, 1943); Schein, Bernard. "John Boynton Kaiser." *Bulletin of Bibliography* 21:1-3 (May-Aug. 1953). **Primary sources and archival materials**—The Newark Public Library *Scrapbooks* (1944-1958) and the Library's clipping files contain material concerning Kaiser.

—JAMES E. BRYAN

KAISER, WALTER HERBERT (1910-1971)

Walter Herbert Kaiser was born at Cape Girardeau, Missouri, on February 27, 1910. During his early years, he established his lifelong attachment to the St. Louis Public Library where, because of his intense interest in books, he was allowed free run of the adult areas of the main library. After graduating from Southeast Missouri State College in 1930, he taught one year in Birch Tree High School. He then returned to St. Louis Public to take a certificate in that Library's training program and to work as a library assistant until 1934, when he went on to the Tennessee Valley Authority as a reference librarian. When the American Library Association-[Andrew] Carnegie [q.v.] Fellowship Grants were made in 1939, Walter Kaiser joined the distinguished group that attended the Chicago Graduate Library School, where he received his master's degree in 1940.

Two public library jobs occupied the rest of his career, except for one brief trip to Washington, where he found governmental libraries not to his liking. He was city librarian at Muncie, Indiana, from 1940 to 1945 and librarian of the Wayne County (Michigan) Library System from 1945 until his death on May 10, 1971. He was survived by his wife, Virginia Conover Kaiser, and two daughters. His contributions to professional thought are reflected in the more than thirty articles to various journals and collections from 1938 to 1970, but it was as a public library administrator that the library profession knew and admired him.

Walter Kaiser earned an international reputation as an administrator with an unusual talent for simplifying and improving methodology in library operations. The Kaiser Charging System, a self-charge transaction system also known as the Wayne County Charging System, was characterized by the George Fry & Associates' "Study of Circulation Control Systems" as "the system which combines the greatest number of time reducing factors, and which is the most economical system in the greatest number of situations. . . ." Kaiser was the first librarian to put a fully synchronized book processing system into daily operation. He introduced basic concepts which have been copied extensively, such as "no cards, no registration," in 1952, and the use of a catalog card as a book pocket (1957), as well as ideas less well known, such as self-shelving by children (1964), an external plastic book pocket for use on the outside of books (1969), and a simplified and complete system of classification and bibliographic control of paperback books (1970). About this last, Joseph Wheeler (q.v.) wrote, "let me thank you enthusiastically for that remarkable treatise on paperback handling in latest *L.J.* [95:2875-83; September 15, 1970]. I'm glad they had the horse sense to give it the space it took, for nothing has or will provide such an encouragement to libraries to do justice to paperbacks."

These "inventions" were only the recognized minority of the creative contributions that characterized Walter Kaiser, who profoundly influenced those who worked with him or observed his work. He was especially proud of former employees who excelled because of his influence, and at the time of his death, these included administrators of large public libraries, of systems like Wayne County itself, and a state librarian, all of whom kept in touch with their mentor.

Those who worked with Kaiser in more recent years were not fully aware of how much he achieved before coming to Wayne County. Carleton B. Joeckel (q.v.), dean of the Graduate Library School of the University of Chicago, wrote to Adam Strohm (q.v.), who was screening candidates for Wayne County in 1944, "We think of Walter Kaiser as one of the best public librarians we have among the alumni of the school.... He is a public librarian by instinct and interests...."

His influence and creativity came from within, from a dedication rarely seen. He read much but was not an ivory tower scholar, preferring to bring more to his reading than he took from it. He had a broad-ranging interest in how others thought, invented, and managed, but always with an eye to using their ideas with his own in the service of librarianship. His long-time friend Ernest Miller, later to be librarian at the Cincinnati Public Library, wrote Strohm in 1944 that "Kaiser is one of those rare librarians who is an enthusiastic reader himself...." It might almost be said that his dedication to library service, however, was so complete that even his dreams were harnessed to contribute to that end. James Hunt, now at Cincinnati, tells of a call from Kaiser on New Year's Eve to discuss an idea that had just occurred to him.

From scientific management, Kaiser derived the conviction that discovering the most efficient way to do the routine and supportive things of librarianship would free the energies and skills of librarians for truly professional tasks. He sought out and hired the best personnel available. He changed the image of library service in Wayne County from extension work alone to a professionalized and stable system of semi-autonomous libraries. He worked with governmental officials and library boards to secure the financial base for a regional library system which, at the time of his death, served three counties and was a model for similar efforts elsewhere.

The extent of his professional commitment is illustrated by the fact that articles by him are listed in each bound volume of *Library Literature* from 1938 until his death, and that six of these articles detailed his pioneering approaches to the practice of librarianship. Because of interest created by these articles and by word of mouth, scores of librarians representing about forty nations came to see what Walter Kaiser was doing, and almost all went home with some exportable technique to improve library practice. C. H. Vermuelen, city librarian of Cape Town, South

Africa, wrote after visiting in 1966, "In looking back to my study tour of the United States, I undoubtedly consider my visit to your library the most significant one concerning simplification and elimination of routines ... and am now working on the elimination of much 'dead wood' in my own organization."

Though not all who read his articles could visit the United States, from all over the world came inquiries such as the following: Mr. Barbarasi of the Hungarian National Library wrote in 1964 expressing great interest in the articles, "Synchronized Book Processing" (*Library Journal* 86:752-54), and " ... New Face and Place for the Catalog Card" (*Library Journal* 88:186-88; January 15, 1963) and asking, "If we could get a report on your library for our readers ... the size of the article rests with you." S. Möhlenbrock, director of public libraries in Gothenburg, Sweden, writing on "Efficient Library Administration" in the *Unesco Bulletin for Libraries* (January-February 1962), reported adopting photo charging for the main library and larger branches, "and the Wayne County charging system for all other units within the system." These, and similar requests and reports, testify to the fact that Walter Kaiser had, through his writings, a significant impact on many librarians he never saw.

Kaiser believed that public libraries should provide information and recreation to the ordinary library user, and he was intolerant of waste and inefficiency that interfered with that purpose. He knew from his own youth in St. Louis how vitally important libraries could be. He knew also, from his early professional years during the Great Depression, that it was the public's money that was being spent, and that many librarians were careless and inefficient in using the money taken from the public. Those who thought of him only as innovator, inventor, or tough administrator missed the total picture. He was a librarian first of all.

Formal recognition was not absent. In 1966, the Michigan Library Association inaugurated a Librarian of the Year award to go to the librarian who had "evidenced personal professional achievements plus initiative and creativity...." The award went to Walter Kaiser "as a recognized leader among librarians." The next year, the Melvil Dewey (q.v.) Medal was awarded him for his "eminent contributions particularly in those fields in which Melvil Dewey was so actively interested...." In many ways this was precisely true, for, with the possible exception of formal library training, Walter Kaiser made substantial contributions in all the areas for which Dewey is noted.

There is very little biographical material on Walter Kaiser in the literature. His works and his articles are so potent that few have thought to search behind them for their creator. It remains for someone to explore more fully the life and work of Walter Herbert Kaiser, who, throughout his career, produced ideas and methods to improve library service, especially in public libraries.

Biographical listings and obituaries—*A Biographical Directory of Librarians in the United States and Canada*, 5th ed.; [Obituary]. *American Libraries* 2:673 (July 1971); [Obituary]. *Library Journal* 92:2039 (June 15, 1971); [Obituary]. *Michigan Librarian* 37:23 (Summer 1971); *Who's Who in Library Service*, 2nd ed., 3rd ed., 4th ed. **Books and articles about the biographee**—*ALA Bulletin* 61:872 (July 1967); *Library of Congress Information Bulletin* 25:509 (July 27, 1967); "Awards, Citations, and Scholarships." *Library Journal* 92:2729 (Aug. 1967); "ALA Awards." *Wilson Library Bulletin* 42:25 (Sept. 1967). **Primary sources and archival materials**—Personal and professional correspondence of Walter H. Kaiser is in the possession of the Wayne County Federated Library System and Virginia Conover Kaiser.

—LEO T. DINNAN

KEOGH, ANDREW (1869-1953)

The librarian of Yale University, Addison Van Name (q.v.), was to write auspiciously for a new appointee in his report of 1899:

The Library has also secured a valuable addition to its staff in Mr. Andrew Keogh, late sub-librarian of the Newcastle-upon-Tyne Public Library, who at the opening of the College Year took charge of the Linonian and Brothers Library. During the coming year, while retaining some of the more important duties of that position, he will act also as reference librarian of the University Library [quoted in James T. Babb, "Andrew Keogh: His Contributions to Yale," *Yale University Library Gazette* 29:49 (October 1954)].

Born November 14, 1869, at Newcastle-upon-Tyne, England, Andrew Keogh was to secure his education and his first professional experience there before his departure to America. He attended the elementary school and Rutherford Institute before continuing his education at Durham College of Science, all the while making extensive use of the Newcastle-upon-Tyne Public Library. When a vacancy occurred there, he was asked to join the staff even though it meant discontinuing his studies.

Keogh's careful preparation for the reception of foreign librarians on a tour following the International Library Conference in London in 1897 brought him to the favorable notice of the American visitors, and particularly of Jessica Sherman Van Vliet, later to become his wife. Having decided to seek further professional advancement in America, he renewed these contacts upon his arrival in January 1899. He received numerous offers from public librarians, but, committed to academic library work, he finally accepted the position of librarian of the Linonian and Brothers Library at Yale in August,

only to begin work a month early to help out in cataloging. In the following year, he received a coveted appointment as reference librarian.

With the appointment of John C. Schwab as University librarian in 1901, Keogh helped to reorganize the Library, making it a real research center for students as well as faculty through his work of recataloging and his bibliographical activities, especially a course in bibliography. This interest was to find reflection in activities of many organizations, including the Bibliographical Society of America, of which he was a founder and president (1913-1914), and the Bibliographical Society [of England]. Keogh also contributed to numerous bibliographical projects, including one for the U.S. government to organize a bibliographical office of inquiry in anticipation of the Paris Peace Conference.

In 1904, he had received the degree of Master of Arts at Yale; in 1912, he was appointed assistant librarian. On the sudden death of John Schwab in early 1916, Keogh was named acting librarian. President Hadley, after wide consultation among prominent librarians, named Andrew Keogh librarian of Yale on July 1, 1916.

Due to Keogh's insistence, the Yale University Council voted in 1919 that the Sterling Memorial Library be the principal building to be erected from the John W. Sterling bequest. Planning the building was to be his major concern until its dedication in 1931, involved as he was in preparing exceedingly detailed specifications for the architect. Meanwhile the collections were augmented by outstanding gifts and acquisitions, due in large part to his effective relations with alumni and outstanding book collectors.

Keogh received the highest honor of his profession when he was elected president of the American Library Association for 1929-1930. His presidential address, "Scholarship in Library Work," was a statement of his lifelong objectives for the profession. In this, he looked forward to the great expansion of higher education and the need for greatly enlarged libraries and services in academic institutions. He also asked for higher academic training for librarians as well as greater opportunity for scholarly study and writing (see his article "Scholarship in Library Work," *ALA Bulletin* 24:307-309; September 1930).

Keogh's retirement in 1938 closed an active career which had seen outstanding contributions to his University's Library and to the profession at large: the planning of the Sterling Memorial Library; the development and amalgamation of the collections, during their greatest growth in the history of that Library, which he had made a service institution for the entire Yale community; and the development of a devoted staff who were given wide latitude in conducting the work of their departments. He had, moreover, shown himself particularly effective in public relations by securing enthusiastic support of alumni and book collectors in the building of the Library collections.

Reflecting his personal as well as his professional associations, Keogh was co-editor of two collections of essays, the first being *Essays Offered to Herbert Putnam by His Colleagues and Friends on His Thirtieth Anniversary as Librarian of Congress* (with William Warner Bishop [q.v.]; Yale University Press, 1929). Later, he joined with Harry M. Lydenberg (q.v.) in editing *William Warner Bishop, a Tribute* (Yale University Press, 1941).

His death on February 14, 1953, removed a notable figure from the Yale scene. A man of tremendous memory, he had developed an extraordinary store of knowledge. While his was a temperament of reserve, he expressed a "gentle position of leadership" which arose from his instinctive shyness. This was made effective, however, by his clarity of purpose. Modest and quiet, he nevertheless revealed a "keen edge of humor" which somewhat belied his calmness and placidity.

Biographical listings and obituaries—[Obituary]. *Library Journal* 78:571 (April 1, 1953); [Obituary]. *Libri* 2, No. 4:349 (1953); *Who Was Who in America* III (1951-1960); *Who's Who in Library Service*, 1st ed., 2nd ed. **Books and articles about the biographee**—*Papers in Honor of Andrew Keogh, Librarian of Yale University*. By the Staff of the Library, 30 June 1938. New Haven: Privately printed, 1938; Rollins, Carl Purington. "Andrew Keogh (November 14, 1869-February 13, 1953)." *Yale University Library Gazette* 28:139-43 (April 1954). **Primary sources and archival materials**—Interview with Harry Harrison, Head, Circulation Department, Yale University Library, 25 Feb. 1975; Interview with J. Gordon Kenefick, Associate Librarian for School and Departmental Libraries Emeritus, Yale University Library, 4 March 1975; Yale University. Library. *Report[s] of the Librarian of Yale University 1898/1899-1937/1938*. New Haven, 1899-1938; *Yale University Library Gazette* (various articles, especially James T. Babb, "Andrew Keogh: His Contribution to Yale," Oct. 1954).

—DAVID C. LIBBEY

KEPPEL, FREDERICK PAUL (1875-1943)

Frederick Paul Keppel, the son of Frederick and Frances Vickery Keppel, was born July 2, 1875, in Staten Island, New York. He received a Bachelor of Arts degree from Columbia University in 1898, and, after two years' work at Harper and Brothers publishers, returned to Columbia as assistant secretary in 1900. He was secretary there from 1902 to 1910, and dean of the college from 1910 to 1918. He left to serve, first as assistant to the secretary of war, Newton Baker, and then as third assistant secretary of war, a post which he resigned in 1919. The next year, he became director of foreign operations for the American Red Cross, and from 1920 to 1922, he was the U.S. administrative commissioner at Paris for the

International Chamber of Commerce. In 1922, he served as secretary of the committee on the plan of New York City and environs, and from 1923 to 1941, he was president of the [Andrew] Carnegie [q.v.] Corporation of New York. Following his retirement, he served on the War Relief Control Board and, later, on the State Department Board of Appeals on Visa Cases.

Keppel married Helen Tracy Brown on January 31, 1906, in Flushing, New York, and they had five sons, Frederick Paul, Charles Tracy, David, Gordon, and Francis. Their long-time residence was in Montrose, New York. Chiefly associated with his work in philanthropy, the honorary degrees that Keppel received included ones from Columbia, the University of Pittsburgh, the University of Michigan, Hamilton University, Union College, the University of Toronto, the University of Melbourne (Australia), and St. Andrews (Scotland).

One can practically chart Keppel's career from educator to public official to foundation officer by noting his publications. Several are collections of essays, of which most were prepared as speeches. They include: *Columbia* (Oxford University Press, 1914), *The Undergraduate and His College* (Houghton, 1917), *Some War-Time Lessons*... (Columbia University Press, 1920), *The International Chamber of Commerce* (American Association for International Conciliation, 1922), *Education for Adults and Other Essays* (Columbia University Press, 1926), *The Foundation: Its Place in American Life* (Macmillan, 1930), *The Arts in American Life* (McGraw-Hill, 1933), *Philanthropy and Learning* (Columbia University Press, 1936), and "Looking Forward: A Fantasy." This last-mentioned essay appeared in a collection edited by Emily Miller Danton, *The Library of Tomorrow* (American Library Association, 1939).

Though he was not a librarian and was not exclusively committed to the development of libraries, Keppel, as president of the Carnegie Corporation during a critical period, was significant not only because of the financial support he helped to provide, but also because of his intense interest in and influence on the development of certain aspects of librarianship. His work in the War Department during World War I gave him a close-up view of the work of the American Library Association's Library War Service; and early in his long tenure as a foundation president, he sought out American Library Association leaders and senior staff members. He believed that philanthropic funds had their best effect when they went to groups or individuals who had good long-range plans based on such funds, but who were not totally dependent on them for the future.

C. C. Williamson's (q.v.) 1923 landmark study of library education was funded by the Corporation, and a series of library education grants followed. These were made to institutions, to ALA for both the development of standards and accreditation procedures and channelling to institutions and individuals seeking fellowship assistance. The Corporation provided $830,000 annually, or about one-sixth of ALA's income, from 1926 to 1941, for two major activities. These were grants totalling five million dollars for various ALA activities and for its endowment and another series of grants for the development of college and university libraries. Other grants provided for demonstrations of library service, publications, and emergency services before and during World War II.

Keppel worked closely with librarians in selecting projects to be funded and sought their advice in the implementation of those projects. His interest extended to encouraging Ralph Beals (q.v.) to enter the library profession and to a firm expression of his respect for the profession and his concern that librarians would themselves show initiative and leadership. Major advisers to the Corporation in his time included Milton Ferguson (q.v.), Charles Rush (q.v.), Franklin F. Hopper (q.v.), and Miriam Tompkins (q.v.). Harry M. Lydenberg (q.v.) and William Warner Bishop (q.v.) provided special advisory services. Following Keppel's death on September 9, 1943, a junior colleague, John M. Russell, wrote: "FPK never approached a problem in a conventional way. His way was original, and hence interesting and creative. For this reason, it was sometimes difficult for the legal or academic person to appreciate him fully. He had too much of the artist in his makeup."

The kindly intelligence which still shows in photographs of Keppel, a white-haired man with military moustache, suggests a willingness to be unconventional, to take some risks. He did that with librarianship, and the rewards are still being reaped.

Biographical listings and obituaries—*National Cyclopaedia of American Biography* E and 32; [Obituary]. *Library Association Record* 46:17-18 (Jan. 1944); [Obituary]. *Library Journal* 68:735 (Sept. 15, 1943); [Obituary]. *New Zealand Libraries* 6:209 (Sept. 1943); *Who Was Who in America* II (1943-1950). **Books and articles about the biographee**—Anderson, Florence. *Library Program, 1911-1961.* New York: Carnegie Corporation of New York, 1963; *Appreciations of Frederick Paul Keppel, by Some of His Friends.* New York: Columbia University Press, 1951. **Primary sources and archival materials**—The files of the Carnegie Corporation contain material by and about Keppel.

—PEGGY A. SULLIVAN

KINKELDEY, OTTO (1878-1966)

Otto Kinkeldey was born on November 27, 1878, in New York City, the son of Carl Ferdinand and Clara Koestler Kinkeldey. He received his baccalaureate degree from the College of the City of New York in 1898, with Phi Beta Kappa honors. In 1900, he was graduated from New York University with an M.A. in English literature and philosophy. During the next two years, he studied music under Edward MacDowell at Columbia University.

In 1902 Kinkeldey went to Germany to continue his musical education—first at the Königliches akademisches Institut für Kirchenmusik in Berlin, later at the University of Berlin, from which he received the Ph.D., *summa cum laude,* in 1909. His dissertation, *Orgel und Klavier in der Musik des 16. Jahrhunderts; ein Beitrag zur Geschichte der Instrumentalmusik.* Mit Notenbeilagen (Leipzig: Breitkopf & Härtel, 1910) was reprinted in 1968 (Hildesheim: G. Olms) in the original German. (The typescript of an unpublished English translation by Dr. Sirvart Poladian, with corrections by Kinkeldey, is in the New York Public Library.) The German dissertation is the only book Kinkeldey published, although he wrote many articles for scholarly journals.

From 1909 to 1914, Kinkeldey taught organ, theory, and music history at the University of Breslau and served as librarian of the Königliches Institut für Kirchenmusik connected with the University. Kinkeldey recorded 1906-1907 as his first library experience; Carleton Smith records (p. 27) that Kinkeldey "was sent by the Prussian government on a musical research trip through the ducal, church, and town libraries of the central German states for the purpose of cataloguing and describing the printed and manuscript music and the books on music stored up in these libraries." A long vacation in America, planned for the summer of 1914, was so complicated by World War I that Kinkeldey resigned his positions as teacher and librarian in Breslau to remain in America. On March 15, 1915, he became chief of the Music Division at the New York Public Library.

On August 14, 1915, Otto Kinkeldey was married to Herminie Frances Trost; the Kinkeldeys had no children.

After the war, Kinkeldey's major concern was building up the New York Public Library's Music Division. The first step was a buying trip through Europe (1921-1922), where he bought for several other American libraries in addition to the NYPL. The second was his extremely successful bidding at the Wolffheim auction in Berlin, 1928, where Richard Angell states (p. 262) that "he was acknowledged by Europeans to be the most careful and discriminating buyer." Again, he bought for several American libraries. Speaking of Kinkeldey's success in collection building, Philip Lieson Miller (member of the Music Division staff, NYPL, 1927-1959; chief, 1959-1966) says that from 1930 on, subsequent chiefs "inherited a going concern, the building from there on out was simply building on the foundation Kinkeldey laid. And I think that this really can't be stressed too firmly."

In 1923, Kinkeldey left the NYPL to serve as head of the Music Department of Cornell University. He returned to the NYPL in 1927. George Sherman Dickinson (q.v.) of Vassar College, Kinkeldey's confidant and colleague, wrote of his friend's accomplishments at the New York Public Library:

> Since the scholar and the library are inseparable, it is not peculiar that Dr. Kinkeldey should have applied his gifts to library administration. In this capacity he has had a fundamental influence. Through his wide knowledge of the literature, the music collection of the New York Public Library was built up during his tenure as Chief of the Music Division to the place of second in the country, both in quantity and in quality of content, and in certain respects the collection is unique. Although he was not conventionally trained in library science, Dr. Kinkeldey's grasp of the technical aspects of library organization is comprehensive, with that added specialization called for in the field of music by its uncommonly intricate and particular problems.

Dickinson continued that Kinkeldey's primary interest lay

> in the service which the library can render to the scholar as an individual. Here Dr. Kinkeldey never fails. He is invariably ready with information and suggestion, and no musical subject lies far afield from his phenomenal range of interest and knowledge. His generous assistance, especially to younger scholars, has left a clear mark upon American musical research.

From his stunning success at the New York Public Library, Kinkeldey returned to Cornell University in 1930 with a dual assignment: first professor of musicology in the United States and University librarian. That he was eminently successful in the first role cannot be questioned; but despite the skill he brought to its problems, Kinkeldey presided over the nadir of the Cornell Library's existence. In his first annual report, 1930-1931, one word stands out: "Inadequate."

> The library building is wholly inadequate. . . . The sum available for staff salaries is inadequate. . . . The sum available for the purchase of new books falls far below the figure which would keep the number and quality of new acquisitions on a par with the foundation stock of former years. . . .

The year 1931-1932 found "no changes except for the worse." In 1932-1933, he was capable of some humor at the hopeless situation.

> We may console ourselves with the thought that the Library has proved itself entirely modern in its failure to conform to the accepted laws of physics. . . . The relativity theorists will have to find a place in their system for the concept of complete fulness. We are demonstrating the theorem that two bodies, when they take the form of books or of library workers, can occupy the same space.

Although there were a few bright rays, Kinkeldey's annual reports continually lamented "the dangerous congestion" of the shelves and the lack of "adequate working quarters and facilities . . . for a loyal staff." Kinkeldey's frustration at the University's neglect of its library finally vented itself in the last report he wrote, that for 1944-1945: "It matters not how many young men and library maidens are sacrificed annually to propitiate the monster, the Minotaur will eventually crush us all, or drive us into the madhouse." Six months after that report, Kinkeldey went on leave—January 1 to June 30, 1946—ending his sixteen-year tenure at Cornell with a somewhat unusual terminal leave.

It may have been during his first stint at Cornell that Kinkeldey accomplished most for the libraries. In 1924, he purchased an entire library of important musical sets—*Denkmäler*, *Gesamtausgaben*, and music periodicals—from Leo Liepmannssohn, Antiquariat, in Berlin. As shrewd with library monies as with his own, he persuaded Liepmannssohn to accept a large reduction in price if Cornell bought the lot. Liepmannssohn agreed, both because of the lot sale and "in view to further purchases, which as I trust may result in the future." That purchase became the foundation of the Cornell music library.

Although he remained active in the Music Library Association, addressing its annual meeting as late as February 5, 1960, Kinkeldey spent his post-Cornell years as a teacher. From 1946 to 1958, he was a guest lecturer at major universities from coast to coast. In 1958, when he actually "retired" at age 79, he resumed his collection building for the New York Public Library. Miller says that Kinkeldey travelled daily from his home in South Orange, New Jersey, to the NYPL—to work. He would ask Miller if certain items in current dealers' catalogs had been ordered; if not—usually because of lack of funds—he would have his European agent acquire them for the Library. The bulk of the day, he worked at his little table in the closed music stacks.

As plans for Lincoln Center matured, Kinkeldey expressed his unalterable opposition to removing the Music Division from the 42nd Street building. When the move was accomplished, he refused to set foot inside the new quarters in Lincoln Center. Miller has said that "because his feelings about Lincoln Center were so strong it is the more remarkable that he left a generous bequest to the Music Division." Kinkeldey died on September 19, 1966, a few weeks short of his eighty-eighth birthday.

At an informal meeting of American music librarians in June 1931, Kinkeldey was elected first president of their new organization, the Music Library

Association. From the very beginnings of his service at the NYPL, one of his major concerns had been the musical education of the public and its conconcomitant, the qualifications for effective music librarianship. In a 1916 speech before the New York Library Club (typescript at NYPL; abstract in the New York Library Club *Bulletin*, March 1916), he identified those qualifications as knowledge of the archaeologist's methods; sufficient paleographic skill to permit correct reading of ancient manuscripts; knowledge of graphic and plastic arts, acoustics, the economics of music, the teaching of music and—of primary concern—literature, "the literatures of all peoples and of all times." Kinkeldey concluded:

> It is evident, from all of this, how much the music librarian is dependent upon his colleagues. There is probably no field of special work in the library which requires the sympathetic aid of so many specialists of other kinds in order to be cultivated successfully.

No wonder, fifty years later, that he so adamantly opposed the separation of the Music Division from the other divisions of the Reference Department. Kinkeldey later outlined the educational requirements for music librarianship in a statement read before the joint ALA/MLA in June 1937: "Training for Music Librarianship: Aims and Opportunities" (*ALA Bulletin* 31:459-63; August 1937). His statement remains the profession's standard.

The 1916 speech also enumerated the "technical problems connected with the use of music in a library." These included the absence of musical bibliographical aids; the peculiarities of music printing, publishing, and binding; the lack of cataloging codes capable of accommodating music; and the shelving and circulation problems. Even as he labored to create an actual music collection, he devoted long hours to the technical problems of cataloging and public service. So concerned was he with those aspects that Miller refers to the Preparation Division's concern that the Music Division was "spoonfeeding" the public.

By the time the Music Library Association was formed in 1931, Kinkeldey could identify four problems in music librarianship that might be solved by cooperative effort:

> The development of a uniform system of definitions and abbreviations for descriptive purposes in cataloguing, the adoption of a uniform order for the catalogue details and for descriptive notes on catalogue cards.... [Establishing] a reliable series of plate numbers for dating purposes, and the co-operative contribution to a series of dated addresses for countries where plate numbers were not so common.... [and] the cultivation of certain special fields by individual libraries so that

there would not be so much competition in the purchase of musical books and compositions....

Kinkeldey was awarded an honorary Doctor of Letters (Litt.D.) by Princeton University in 1947, elected a fellow of the American Academy of Arts and Sciences in 1942 and a member of the Bibliographical Society of America in 1931—in whose *Papers* one of his most important articles was printed: "Music and Music Printing in Incunabula" (v. 26:89-118 [1932]). He served as first president of the American Musicological Society, 1934-1936, and again from 1940-1942; he was active in the Music Teachers National Association as well as in various library organizations other than the Music Library Association. On the occasion of his seventieth birthday, he was honored with a *Festschrift* by the Music Library Association (*Notes* 6 [December 1948]) and for his eightieth birthday by the American Musicological Society (*Journal* of the American Musicological Society, 13:1-269 [1960]—also printed separately).

Dickinson described Kinkeldey as "reserved and modest," an individual who was most spontaneous "in the presence of the comparatively small and sympathetic group of the classroom. He [was] fully drawn out before others only in the warmth of scientific controversy or in the pursuit of a line of reasoning." Paul Henry Lang reported a "quiet, friendly, and slightly reticent man, contemplative and observant rather than dynamic," but

> stern when a principle is involved or when some charlatan is holding forth on the rostrum. Poking the stem of his pipe in the direction of the unfortunate offender, he would mark every downbeat in the closely cropped sentences with which he set the fellow aright, point by point.

Otto Kinkeldey stands unique in American musical experience; on the one hand he is the father of American musicology, and on the other, the builder of a music library second only to the national library. Perhaps H. Earle Johnson, a former student, said it best: "To Kinkeldey, teaching and librarianship were an inseparable mission."

Biographical listings and obituaries—*Baker's Biographical Dictionary of Musicians*, 5th ed., 1965 and *Supplement*, 1971 (Nicolas Slonimsky); Grout, Donald Jay. "Otto Kinkeldey, 27 November 1878–19 September 1966." *Acta Musicologica* 39:1-2 (1967); *Grove's Dictionary of Music and Musicians*, 5th ed., 1954 (Gustave Reese); Lang, Paul Henry. "Editorial [Obituary, Otto Kinkeldey]." *Musical Quarterly* 53:77-79 (Jan. 1967); LaRue, Jan. "Otto Kinkeldey (1878-1966)." *Die Musikforschung* 20:121-22 (1967); Reese, Gustave. "Otto Kinkeldey (1878-1966)." American Musicological Society *Journal* 19:433-34 (1966); *Who Was Who in America* IV (1961-1968); *Who's Who in Library Service*, 1st ed., 2nd ed. **Books and articles about the biographee**—Angell, Richard S. "Otto Kinkeldey." *College & Research Libraries* 7:262-63 (July 1946); Dickinson, George Sherman. "Otto Kinkeldey, an Appreciation." *Musical Quarterly* 24:412-18 (1938); Downes, Olin. "Musicologist at

60." *The New York Times*, Nov. 27, 1938; Hill, Richard S. "Kinkeldey, Otto." *Die Musik in Geschichte und Gegenwart*. Friedrich Blume, ed. Volume 7, columns 924-926. Kassel: Bärenreiter, 1958. [Includes the best published bibliography of his writings]; Johnson, H. Earle. "Gladly wolde he lerne, and gladly teche: A Remembrance of Otto Kinkeldey." *Notes* 30:242-49 (Dec. 1973); Lang, Paul Henry. "Editorial." *Musical Quarterly* 45:85-87 (Jan. 1959); Smith, Carleton Sprague. "Otto Kinkeldey." *Notes* 6:27-37 (Dec. 1948). [Copious quotes from Kinkeldey's letters and a portrait.] **Primary sources and archival materials**—Kinkeldey's papers are deposited in Special Collections of the Music Division, The New York Public Library and the Olin Library, Cornell University; Oral history interview with Kinkeldey conducted by Donald J. Grout, July 22, 1965; transcripts at NYPL and Olin Library; the import of the interview is somewhat diminished by Kinkeldey's advanced age and frailty at the time; Oral history interview with Philip Lieson Miller conducted by CJB, New York City, June 8, 1974.

—CAROL JUNE BRADLEY

KNAPP, PATRICIA L. BRYAN (1914-1972)

Patricia L. Bryan, only child of Raymond and Florence Poggio Bryan, was born December 31, 1914, in Youngstown, Ohio. She grew up in Chicago, attending Hyde Park High School and the University of Chicago, from which she held all her academic degrees (B.A., 1935; M.A., 1943; Ph.D., 1957). She moved into academic librarianship directly from college, first at St. Xavier College (1935) and then at Chicago Teachers College (1936), at which time she began her graduate study in librarianship. Following her marriage to Robert Segrist Knapp on December 28, 1938, Patricia B. Knapp moved as his career and wartime service dictated. First they went to Memphis briefly (1939), then back to Chicago to continue her work at Chicago Teachers College, then (in 1942) to Florida, where she became an Army librarian, first at Sarasota Army Air Force Base, then at the Personnel Redistribution Command in Miami Beach. She resigned her Army library position in 1945 to return to Chicago, where she became librarian of George Williams College.

The ten years from 1945 to 1955 were rich developing years for Patricia Knapp, with her work as college librarian and assistant professor of English supplemented by doctoral study at the University of Chicago. Additionally, she engaged in intensive volunteer activity with the Independent Voters of Illinois, serving as a neighborhood chairman, as congressional district political action chairman, and as a member of the Board of Directors.

During these years, she published articles on academic librarianship, among them "Selecting Books for Reluctant Readers—in College" (in *Proceedings* of the Annual Reading Conference, University of Chicago, 1953) and "Suggested Program of College Instruction in the Use of the Library" (*Library Quarterly* 26:224-31; July 1956—reprinted in *The Library-College*, Louis Shores, ed.; Drexel, 1966). She also started a career-long investigation of the sociology of librarianship with an article on "The College Librarian: Sociology of a Professional Specialization" (*College & Research Libraries* 16:66-72; January 1955). Her doctoral dissertation focused on the fusion of academic librarianship with academic instruction, a concern for Knapp not only in her work as an academic librarian but in her consistent preference as a librarian to be also a faculty member. The excellence of her doctoral research was recognized when it was published as an ACRL Monograph; *College Teaching and the College Library* (ALA, 1959) became a classic in its area of research.

In September 1955, Knapp joined the faculty of the department of library science of Rosary College as an associate professor. With her husband's move to Detroit in 1958, she resigned from Rosary College and joined the faculty and library staff of the Monteith Project of Wayne State University. Here she was given the utmost freedom to develop library service to the largely independent study program that Monteith College represented within Wayne State University's structure. This initiated the period of Knapp's highest scholarly productivity, and the concepts that flowed from the experimental library service established for Monteith have enriched reference and bibliographic services as well as library education. Her book, *Monteith College Library Experiment* (Scarecrow, 1966), describes both her goals and her experiences in the project.

Following the two-year experimental Monteith library program (1960-1962), Patricia Knapp moved from the University library staff to an appointment as professor in the library science department at Wayne State University. Here, for the next eight years, she gave strength to the teaching faculty in the areas of cataloging, research methods, and academic librarianship, and leadership in the development of the library education program. A highly effective teacher, Knapp became deeply committed to library education and its well being, and served as president of the Association of American Library Schools in 1970. Flexible and responsive to the demands of the increasingly talented young faculty membership of the Association, she gave leadership in developing informal structures that allowed membership activity and creativity. (For her views on the Association, see her article "Reflections on A.A.L.S.," *Journal of Education for Librarianship* 10:251-56; Winter 1970.) Serious illness led to her resignation from the faculty of the library school a few months before her death in November 1972.

Knapp's years as a faculty member at Wayne State University were rich in professional friendships and consultantships. She became one of the major resources to the "Library College Idea," a movement of creative young academic librarians spurred by Patricia Knapp, Louis Shores, and their own enterprise to make libraries truly effective learning agents in the academic setting. Knapp's presence at their meetings was greatly sought and provided an occasion for fruitful exchange. (See her articles "Guidelines for Bucking the System," *Drexel Library Quarterly* 7:217-21; July 1971 and "The Academic Library Response to New Directions in Undergraduate Education," U.S. Office of Education, 1970.)

Library-centered learning, whether in undergraduate education or in the library school, was an important concept in Knapp's professional thinking. She was sensitive to the significance of independent study and other library-dependent modes of learning, to the impact of newer media in the learning resources center structure. She saw these aspects of higher education as affecting librarian-faculty relations and student-materials interactions, and all this controlled with an organizational function and academic sociological milieu that needed penetrating analysis if librarians were to exercise truly effective professional control of materials use and library services.

Knapp's continuing research and publication related to the college library as a teaching instrument, the academic librarian within the academic structure, and directions for change in library education. In the productive twenty years of her scholarship, Knapp contributed an impressive record of sound, seminal publication.

Her concern for the understanding of the differences of knowledge and its related literature among disciplines not only guided her instruction of bibliographic assistants in the classic Monteith Project, but structured her analysis of faculty-library relationships. During the campus revolutions of the late 1960s, Knapp analyzed the student subcultures and their effect on libraries and library use. Always alert to the implications of change and ready to revise her conceptual framework to include the new event and the new phenomenon, Knapp's thinking appealed not only to the knowledgeable but also to the eager novices.

Robert T. Jordan, in assessing her report on the Monteith College library experiment in a *Library Journal* review (February 15, 1967, pp. 752-53), commented:

> The education-library philosophy in this book may be summarized as the idea that a college education should be a series of exercises in independent discoveries of the systems of ways and patterns in which knowledge is organized in preparation for life-long discovery, rather than the normal accumulation of facts through lecture-textbook-test. The college library should play a central role in the process of questing (inquiry

contrasted to acquiry), and the typical college librarian should operate both as a teacher and as a librarian. . . .

The book in hand is evidence of Pat Knapp's high level of sophistication and competence in social science research. She was a highly influential person at Monteith, and her work is still infused in the curriculum.

Stanley E. Gwynn, in his review of the publication for *Library Quarterly* (July 1967, pp. 299-302), pointed out that

> this book reports not a neat experiment in the latter sense and a neat conclusion but a somewhat untidy exploration of unknowns combined with a somewhat fumbling struggle to develop a methodology where none has existed and a means to appraise the effectiveness of that methodology. But, while the book does not reach many firm conclusions, it is invaluable because of the new ground it breaks, because it has identified some significant problems, and because it offers some promising approaches to the solution of those problems. Much of its value derives from the fact that it is, with one possible exception, an objective account of the failures as well as the triumphs of the researchers and of how the growth of their knowledge led to the abandonment of some strongly held hypotheses and to the construction of a new program based on revised conceptions.

Patricia B. Knapp's professional career evolved in the context of a rich personal life up to her final illness and death on November 19, 1972, in Detroit. She had shared a close companionship with her husband, whose hobbies of swimming, golf, and music matched her own. She was indeed a liberated woman to whom it had probably never occurred that there was an alternative style for herself.

Biographical listings and obituaries—*A Biographical Directory of Librarians in the United States and Canada*, 5th ed.; [Obituary]. *Wilson Library Bulletin* 47:7 (Jan. 1973); *Who's Who in Library Service*, 3rd ed., 4th ed. **Books and articles about the biographee**—[Contributor's note]. *Library Quarterly* 26:233 (July 1956); [Biographical sketch]. *Illinois Libraries* 35:347 (Oct. 1953); [Biographical sketch]. *Library Quarterly* 13:342 (Oct. 1943).

—MARGARET E. MONROE

KOCH, THEODORE WESLEY (1871-1941)

Librarian, author, translator, bibliophile, civic leader, Theodore Wesley Koch possessed an appealing personality coupled with an impressive intellect that earned him many friends and wide recognition throughout a distinguished career. At the time of his death, he was well known as Northwestern University's outstanding librarian.

Koch was born in Philadelphia, Pennsylvania, August 4, 1871, the son of William Jefferson and

Wilhelmina Bock Koch. His father was a grain broker; both parents came from Pennsylvania Dutch backgrounds. He had a sister, Mabel, and his two brothers, Harry and Charles, continued in the family business. Theodore grew up in Philadelphia, where he studied both Latin and Greek at Central High School. After graduating in 1888, he enrolled in the University of Pennsylvania, receiving his A.B. in 1892. He enjoyed studying languages—not only Romance languages, his major field, but Greek and Sanskrit as well. He also enjoyed using languages; one of the high points of his college days was a vacation trip he and his cousin Oliver Lenz took to Europe, working on a cattle boat to pay their passage across the Atlantic, so as to spend three months hiking through Germany, France, and the British Isles.

At Pennsylvania, Koch's academic record was such that, when a chapter of Phi Beta Kappa was formed there sixteen years after his graduation, he was among those elected. After leaving Pennsylvania, he resisted pressures to join the other men of his family in the brokerage business, "The Bourse," and went to Harvard, where, in 1893, he earned a second A.B., followed by an M.A. in Romance languages (1894).

On the recommendation of Harvard's well-known Dante scholar Charles Eliot Norton, Koch next moved to Cornell University in Ithaca, New York, where he spent the next five years as bibliographer of the library's Dante collection. In compiling the *Catalogue of the Dante Collection Presented by Willard Fiske* (Cornell University Library, 1898-1900. 2 vols.), Koch began his apprenticeship as a librarian. The catalog, with 15,000 entries, remains the most comprehensive bibliography of works by and on Dante. This, the first of Koch's many publications, established his reputation as a bibliographer.

For two years, 1900 and 1901, Koch studied at the Collège de France at the University of Paris. The time spent there strengthened his language abilities and firmly established his interests in French culture. On July 7, 1902, after his return from France, Koch was appointed assistant in the Catalog Division of the Library of Congress.

On April 14, 1904, he was appointed assistant librarian at the University of Michigan, Ann Arbor, and, upon the retirement of Raymond C. Davis (q.v.) in 1905, Koch was named University librarian.

For the next ten years, Koch showed that he possessed impressive administrative and bibliographic skills, as the University of Michigan Library was transformed by his energy. The reading room was made comfortable and attractive, a reference collection of several thousand volumes was built up, and for the first time, circulation was instituted and the periodical room opened to the public. Staff operations were reorganized and library procedures modernized with innovations such as Library of Congress cards.

It was at Ann Arbor in 1907 that Koch met and married Gertrude Priscilla Humphrey, for seven years the librarian of Lansing Public Library. They had one child, Dorothy Alden.

Partly due to Koch's enthusiasm, library methods courses were offered, on an experimental basis, for the first time in the summer of 1909. Koch acted as director of the School of Library Science, giving lectures on library administration, library buildings, book selection, and the physical composition of the book. Koch was also active in the Michigan Library Association, serving both as vice-president and president. From May to August of 1914, Koch was in charge of the American Library Association exhibit at the Leipzig Exposition.

In 1915, in campaigning for a new library building, Koch found himself caught in the middle of a dispute between the Michigan legislature and members of the Board of Regents. One member of the Board of Regents, William Clements, had from the first strongly disagreed with Koch's library policies. The impasse was resolved with a request for Koch's resignation. A large majority of the faculty, feeling that their librarian had been wronged, signed a statement in his support. After a year's leave of absence from Michigan, he returned on October 13, 1916, to the Library of Congress as chief of the Order Division.

While Koch was at Ann Arbor, he had undertaken a history of the libraries built by Andrew Carnegie (q.v.). The substantial work, *A Book of Carnegie Libraries* (H. W. Wilson, 1917), grew out of Koch's studies of library architecture.

In 1917, Koch was sent to England for the Library of Congress to attempt to end government censorship of scholarly and scientific publications. In London, observing what the British War Library Service was doing, he urged the American Library Association to establish a similar service for American servicemen. His *Books in the War: The Romance of Library War Service* (Houghton Mifflin, 1919) describes the efforts of the ALA program.

After destruction, during the War, of the 300,000-volume library of the University of Louvain in Belgium, with its many unique treasures, Koch became active in the reconstruction of the Library's collections. He wrote a pamphlet, *The University of Louvain and Its Library* (J. M. Durant, 1917) in connection with his efforts to gain broad support for the Library's restoration. Ironically, the restored collection and library were again burned in 1940.

On September 1, 1919, Koch assumed the position of librarian of Northwestern University in Evanston, Illinois, and it was here that his career especially flourished. In his tenure from 1919 to 1941, Koch effected great changes in the Library's collections, staff operations, and building facilities.

When Koch arrived, the Orrington Lunt Library, hailed when built in 1894 as "the finest library of the West," had become totally inadequate. It had been built to house a collection of 29,000 volumes and 19,000 government publications, for a student body of 500. By 1919, the collection had grown to 120,000 volumes and 90,000 government publications; the Evanston student population was 2,500. Parts of the collection were in storage, in departmental offices, or in seminars; a staff of nine, reduced from fifteen in 1918, had been demoralized by the summary dismissal of Koch's predecessor, Walter Lichtenstein. Book funds were inadequate for the growing university, and the collections, weak in many areas, were incapable of supporting faculty research.

Koch gave attention first to his staff, reorganizing and filling positions with key people, many of whom stayed for long periods, thus providing stability and continuity. With his quick wit and keen sense of humor, he endeared himself to his staff.

In order to relieve the congestion of the Lunt Library, Koch secured more space in the building for library use. Every possible niche was filled with books, and additional storage space was requisitioned. In 1924, 10,000 volumes of the School of Commerce Library were moved out of Lunt to the Commerce Building. Nonetheless, Lunt's floors sagged, the walls cracked with the weight of the books, and outdated wiring constantly threatened fire. Rallying faculty and student support, Koch relentlessly petitioned the administration for a new building.

In 1929, when a bequest from Charles Deering, supplemented with gifts from other members of his family, made a new building a certainty, Koch devoted himself to all aspects of the planning. The project captured all his imagination and enthusiasm as he consulted constantly for two years with the architect James Gamble Rogers. As a tribute to Koch for his role in planning the building, his bust in stone was placed in the third floor decoration, in the same way medieval stone carvers and builders added their faces to cathedrals as signatures. Charles Deering Library, overlooking the broad meadow fronting Sheridan Road on the Evanston campus, was dedicated on December 29, 1932.

The building reflected Koch's ideas and philosophies in many features: a separate government publications department, a rare book room, a browsing room, research carrels, a book exhibit area, seminar rooms, and efficient book stacks. Although Koch realized the need for a larger building, budget restrictions made that impossible. Annual accessions in 1919 had been 8,500 volumes, increasing to 16,000 in 1931-1932. At the time of the move into Deering, the collection totalled 230,000 volumes and

190,000 government publications. Because the building promised to be adequate for only a decade, plans for future expansion were made but never implemented. Jens Nyholm (Northwestern librarian following the tenure of Effie Keith as acting librarian, 1941-1944) reported at the end of his first year that, in 1945, the building was ninety percent filled with a collection of 438,040 cataloged volumes and 548,386 government publications.

Like many librarians, Koch always felt himself hampered by a lack of sufficient book funds. Not only did the Great Depression force the University twice to reduce salaries by ten percent, but it also cut back the book budget from $42,500 to $24,500. To offset such reductions, Koch turned to friends of the Library and to book lovers outside the University, and it was not uncommon during his administration to find that the number of gift volumes often equalled that of volumes purchased. In other ways, too, Koch used book funds with careful stewardship. On a trip to London at his own expense in 1934, for example, Koch bought many books at Depression prices. Through his efforts, the Biblioteca Femina collection of 3,000 volumes, assembled for the International Conclave of Women Writers of the International Congress of Women held in Chicago in 1933, was deposited at Northwestern. The Schwitkis collection of 9,500 volumes of German literature was a gift in 1938. In 21 years, while the Evanston campus student population increased from 3,000 to 5,000 and the faculty from 220 to 330, Koch built the collection from 120,000 to 377,000 volumes.

Koch was always deeply involved in both University activities and those of the library profession. A member of several standing University committees, he particularly relished his duties as chairman of the Harris Lecture Committee of Northwestern. Under his leadership in the 1920s and 1930s, Evanston audiences enjoyed hearing and meeting men of letters such as John Livingston Lowes and J. Middleton Murry, biologists such as Julian Huxley, archaeologists such as Sir Rennell Rodd, as well as spokesmen for currents of European thought ranging from Bernard Faÿ to Count Carlo Sforza and historians such as Sir Arnold Toynbee.

Yet, despite the attention he gave to affairs of the University and the community, Koch's greatest involvement was with the library profession. From 1922 to 1937, he was a member of the Board of the Evanston Public Library. In 1927, he was president of the Chicago Library Club. Invited in 1908 to join the American Library Institute because of his contributions to library scholarship, he served as its secretary-treasurer from 1922 to 1924, and as its president from 1931 to 1933. A life member of the ALA in 1927, he was a delegate to the [British] Library Association's fiftieth anniversary meeting, he served on several committees, and, in 1926, became vice-president. His interest in libraries and librarians resulted in numerous articles, including "Some Old-time Old-world Librarians" (*North American Review*, August 1914) and "New Light on Old Libraries" (*Library Quarterly*, April 1934). Visits abroad resulted in articles (most of them in *Library Journal*) on the British Museum Library, the Imperial Public Library in St. Petersburg, the Vatican Library, the Bibliothèque Nationale, and the Bodleian Library at Oxford.

His interest in books was further evidenced in his enthusiastic interest in book fairs. On visits to Europe, he attended the Leipzig Book Fairs in 1922 and 1926. In 1925, he was chairman of the Committee of Patrons for the Chicago German Book Exhibit, an enterprise intended to reestablish intellectual contacts and cooperation between Germany and America. On several trips abroad he took part in annual meetings of the Library Association of the United Kingdom (1901 at Plymouth, 1908 at Brighton, 1909 at Sheffield, 1911 at Perth, and 1913 at Bournemouth). His clearly written reports of these meetings were published in *Library Journal*.

In 1928, accompanied by his wife and daughter, Koch conducted a bibliographical tour of European libraries, bookshops, and publishing houses for nineteen American librarians. In 1929, he was one of two American librarians invited to preside at sections of the International Library and Bibliographical Congress in Rome and Venice. Koch's topic at his section was "Book Trends and Book Collecting."

Koch's interests in fine printing, book production, typography, and bookplates were manifest in his publications, some of which, like *Reading, a Vice or a Virtue?* (Northwestern University, 1926), were intended as fund-raising endeavors as well.

Koch, who spoke several languages, was also a skillful translator. Among his more notable translations are *Tales for Bibliophiles* (Caxton Club, 1928), *Bibliomania, a Tale*, by Gustave Flaubert (Northwestern University Library, 1929), *Francesco Colonna, a Fanciful Tale of the Writing of the Hypnerotomachia*, by Charles Nodier (1929), *Eden Anto*, by Antonio Fogazzaro (Roxburghe Club, 1930), *The Mirror of the Parisian Bibliophile, a Satirical Tale*, by Alfred Bonnardot (1931), *The Assembly of Books*, by Julius Haarhaus (Charles Deering Library, 1932), *'My Republic'*, by Paul Lacroix (Caxton Club, 1936), and *The Old Book Peddler and Other Tales for Bibliophiles* (Charles Deering Library, 1937). He also translated some of his own articles into French, among them, "Les livres à la guerre" (1920), "Bibliothécaires d'antan" (1923), and "La bibliothèque publique de Petrograd" (1923).

Koch's interest in fostering French culture was evident in his long-continued memberships in the French Club of Evanston and the Alliance Française of Chicago, and he was for many years a member of the Alliance's Board of Directors. In 1940, on the recommendation of the French ambassador, Koch was decorated by the French government with the Cross of the Knight of the Legion of Honor at the June commencement exercises.

From his early days in Ithaca, Koch had maintained the strong interest in Dante indicated by his *Catalogue*. Accordingly, from the first, the Dante collections in Deering received his attention, and Koch saw to it that carvings and busts of Dante look down on readers in Deering. He was a life member of the Dante Society of Cambridge, Massachusetts, and an honorary member of the Dante Society of London.

Koch also maintained memberships in the Grolier Club, the Bibliographical Society of America, and the First Editions Club of London. He was made an honorary member of the Roxburghe Club of San Francisco, which published his translation of *Eden Anto*. Membership in the Caxton Club, the society of bibliophiles in Chicago, brought him great satisfaction, and for many years he served as president. Here he met many who shared his interests in printing and book collecting, and the Caxton Club printed three Koch titles as well. From this membership he drew many library donors, and the Caxton Club itself made contributions to both the collections and the gardens of the Charles Deering Library.

A popular speaker, he often illustrated his talks with lantern slides, and he was often asked to repeat his lecture on literary forgeries. He was a member of the University Club in Evanston and for many years its president, a member of the Cliff Dwellers of Chicago and the Evanston musical society, the MacDowell Club. His home in Evanston was frequently filled with friends from the Library, the University, and from libraries all over the world.

Koch died on March 23, 1941, at the age of 69. He was to have retired on August 31; however, Koch had no intention of retiring to a life of inactivity and had announced his candidacy for the position of treasurer of ALA. Northwestern University President Franklyn Snyder led the memorial service and gave the address at the First Congregational Church of Evanston. Koch's ashes were buried in the Forest Hill Cemetery, Ann Arbor, Michigan.

Following Koch's death, his family received a great number of tributes, according to Koch's friend Francis L. D. Goodrich (q.v.). Goodrich, in a tribute in *College and Research Libraries* (3:67-70 [Dec. 1941]), delves into Koch's personality as well as his professional accomplishments. Assessing Koch in terms of "the spontaneous expression of an inner force which is the individual himself," Goodrich notes that

> Theodore Wesley Koch was endowed with an unusual personality.... His was a nature censorious only of inartistic and shoddy work and base motives. He had a gift for friendship. He did not live to know how wide was his circle of influence. It extended far beyond the localities in which he was a resident. Each lecture which he delivered added to it, and each visitor to the university who was privileged to meet him immediately came under the spell of his charm. He was known and loved throughout the United States and in many European countries.

So great was the response from Koch's friends that a substantial memorial book fund was established for rare and finely printed books for the Charles Deering Library. The gardens of the Library, carefully planned by him, were renamed the Koch Memorial Gardens. His contributions to the literature of the profession, his translations, and his legacy on the Northwestern campus will not easily be forgotten.

Biographical listings and obituaries—*Current Biography* (1941); Koch, Richard Henry. *Thirty Ancestors of Richard Henry Koch.* Pottsville, Pa.: J. F. Seiders, 1939; Snyder, Franklyn B. "Theodore Wesley Koch." *Address of Franklyn B. Snyder of Northwestern University at the Funeral Services Held in Evanston, Illinois, March 26, 1941.* Chicago: Northwestern University and the Caxton Club, 1941; University of Pennsylvania. *Biographical Catalogue of the Matriculates of the College.* Philadelphia, 1894; *Who Was Who in America* I (1897-1942); *Who's Who in Library Service*, 1st ed. Books and articles about the biographee—Goodrich, Francis L. D. "Theodore Wesley Koch, 1871-1941." *College & Research Libraries* 3:67-70 (Dec. 1941); Greenfield, Harlan G. "Theodore Wesley Koch, Northwestern's Great Librarian, 1919-1941." *The John Evans Club Newsletter* (Summer 1972); Keith, Effie. "Report of the University Librarian." *President's Report.* Evanston, Ill.: Northwestern University, 1940-1941; Koch, Theodore Wesley. "Selected Bibliography." Evanston, Ill.: Unpublished manuscript, Special Collections Department, Northwestern University Library; Lewis, Eleanor F., and Muriel Murray. "New Deering Library to Be Ready for Use by First of Year." *N.U. Alumni News*, Dec. 1932, pp. 13-14; Maxwell, Margaret. *Shaping a Library: William L. Clements as Collector.* Amsterdam: Nico Israel, 1973. Primary sources and archival materials—American Library Institute. *Handbook.* Chicago, 1938; Bestor, Dorothy Koch. Letters. [dated] Dec. 11, 1974; Feb. 3, 1976; Chicago Library Club. *Directory of Libraries of the Chicago Area.* Chicago, Ill., 1933; *Harvard College Class of 1893 Fortieth Anniversary.* Norwood, Mass., 1933, pp. 155-56; Koch, Theodore Wesley, ed. *Charles Deering Library Bulletin* No. 1 (March 1932), No. 2 (June 1932). Evanston, Ill.: Northwestern University; Koch, Theodore Wesley. "Report of the University Librarian." *President's Report.* Evanston, Ill.: Northwestern University, 1919-1939; Koch's papers are held by the Northwestern University Archives, Evanston, Illinois, and in the Michigan Historical Collection, the University of Michigan, Ann Arbor.

—ROLF ERICKSON

KOOPMAN, HARRY LYMAN (1860-1937)

Harry Lyman Koopman was born at Freeport, Maine, on July 1, 1860, son of Charles Frederick, a cabinet-maker who had emigrated from Sweden in 1848, and Mary Brewer Mitchell Koopman. Young Koopman received the A.B. degree from Colby College in 1880 and the *pro forma* A.M. in 1883. He served briefly as principal of a grammar school in Claremont, New Hampshire, then moved in 1881 to New York City, where he became a clerk in the Astor Library. After experience at the Astor, he was employed as a cataloger at Cornell University in 1883-1884, at Columbia College in 1884-1885, at Rutgers College in 1885-1886, and then at the University of Vermont in Burlington from 1886 to 1892.

The years in Burlington permitted Koopman to establish himself. There he could easily pursue his interests in mountain climbing, gardening, and astronomy. His life became settled in another way with his marriage, on June 27, 1889, to Helen Luise Mayser, who had come to Burlington from Württemberg, where her father was a teacher in Heilbronn. When the University received as a gift the notable collection of George Perkins Marsh, the diplomat and philologist, Koopman undertook the preparation of a catalog, which, when published in 1892, brought him favorable attention. In that same year, he left Vermont to undertake a year of study at Harvard University, receiving the A.M. degree in 1893. He was then appointed librarian of Brown University, receiving the added title of professor of bibliography in 1908, the year that Colby College awarded him the honorary Litt.D. degree. (The degree was not awarded by Harvard, as reported in the *National Cyclopaedia of American Biography* article on Koopman.)

At Brown, Koopman dealt with the full range of library problems, the most prominent of them at first being the crowded building. He began immediately to plan for construction of a new library, meanwhile reclassifying the collection from the existing fixed-location scheme to Charles A. Cutter's (q.v.) Expansive Classification, thus allowing flexible use of the space. A substantial gift from Andrew Carnegie (q.v.) permitted construction of the new John Hay Library, opened in 1910 and named, at Carnegie's suggestion, in memory of the American statesman. The new building included Koopman's innovative "Students' Library," which contained on open shelves the best and newest books in the fields covered by the curriculum along with recent volumes of the most-used periodicals, a pioneering predecessor of the undergraduate library. The Library's eight-stack floors, reading and conference rooms, and space for special collections became filled during Koopman's tenure as librarian with volumes that grew in number from 80,000 to 400,000. The special collections included such notable gifts as the collection of rare books, classics of fine printing and binding, manuscripts, and incunabula given by Professor P. D. Sherman of Oberlin College.

During Koopman's 37 years as librarian at Brown, he carried on a wide range of activities. He became known as the advocate of the idea that every large library should make accessible to its patrons, as he had done at Brown, a carefully selected standard collection of books in addition to its total collection especially adapted to its needs. He strongly opposed unrestricted censorship of literature, most notably in 1929, when he publicly condemned the U.S. customs restrictions against importation of a number of classics, among them Voltaire's *Candide*. His activities on the national library stage were largely as an individual librarian rather than as an active officeholder, though he participated in the American Library Association's conferences and in the meetings of the American Library Institute, serving as its president from 1928 to 1930. He joined more prominently in state library organizations, being president of the Massachusetts Library Club from 1900 to 1901 and president of the Rhode Island Library Association from 1904 to 1907.

Koopman belonged also to a number of other organizations that reflected his interests, including the Simplified Spelling Board, The Skyscrapers (an amateur astronomical society), the Authors' Club of New York and of London, the Boston Society of Printers, and the Rhode Island Historical Society. His writings similarly represented his responsibilities and interests. For Brown University, he published in 1895 its *Historical Catalogue*, jointly edited *Memories of Brown*, a series of college recollections of Brown students (1898), and served from 1906 to 1917 as associate editor of the *Brown Alumni Monthly*. In 1931, after his retirement, he edited Hawthorne's "Mr. Higginbotham's Catastrophe."

In addition to his editorial work, Koopman wrote poetry, literary and historical works, and addresses on professional and literary topics, many of them later published in learned journals. His published writings included: "The Great Admiral" (1883); "Orestes and Other Poems" (1888); "Woman's Will" (1888); "The Mastery of Books" (1896); "Morrow-Songs" (1898); "At the Gates of the Century" (1905); "The Librarian of the Desert" (1908); "The Booklover and His Books" (1917); "Hesperia, an American National Poem," I-VI (1919-1924); "The Guerdon" (1921); "The Narragansett Country" (1927); "The Eternal Pilgrim" (1928); and "Materna" (1930). In his late years a frequent contributor to the *Providence Journal* and, after his retirement from Brown, a member

of the editorial staff of that newspaper, he published poetry as well as articles on themes reflecting his literary and historical interests and a monthly astronomical feature, "Planets and Stars." Over the years, his yeoman work of scholarship enriched his bibliography with scores of short notes on bibliographical, printing, and literary subjects.

Koopman's quietly sound and responsible contributions reflected his temperament and convictions. In religion he adopted the considered intellectual principles of Unitarianism. A philosopher as well as a scholar, his sympathies were broad and based on careful reflection, fully weighing the opinions of others though he remained always faithful to his own convictions. He was a kindly critic and generous-minded friend who made himself beloved by those who knew him. Upon his retirement in 1930, he was appointed both librarian emeritus and professor emeritus, continuing his active scholarly work in Providence until his death on December 28, 1937. His two children were Mary Fredrika and Karl Henry Koopman.

Biographical listings and obituaries—*National Cyclopaedia of American Biography* 29; [Obituary]. *Library Journal* 63:75 (Jan. 15, 1938); *Who Was Who in America* I (1897-1942); *Who's Who in Library Service*, 1st ed. **Books and articles about the biographee**—Blanchard, E. R. "In Memory of Dr. Koopman." *Library Journal* 63:109 (Feb. 1, 1938); Bronson, W. C. *The History of Brown University*. Providence: Brown University, 1914; Faxon, W. "Harry Lyman Koopman." *Bulletin of Bibliography* 13:169 (1929); *Historical Catalogue of Brown University*, 1895-1960; "Librarian Authors." *Library Journal* 55:64 (1930). **Primary sources and archival materials**—The contributor also utilized the files in the John Hay Library, Brown University, his personal knowledge, and the suggestions of Mrs. Clarence Horace Philbrick, daughter of Koopman.

—DAVID A. JONAH

KROEGER, ALICE BERTHA (1864-1909)

Alice Bertha Kroeger was born May 2, 1864, at St. Louis, Missouri, one of four children of Adolph Ernst and Eliza Bertha Curren Kroeger. She attended the St. Louis public schools and was graduated from high school in 1881. Although her father was a distinguished journalist and translator and a frequent writer on philosophical topics, his involvement as a municipal treasurer led to a series of misunderstandings over the transfer of city funds and brought his conviction for forgery in the third degree. He spent two years in prison before he was exonerated and the governor gave a full pardon. The effect of this tragic episode on his family was devastating. The embarrassment, loss of financial security, and accompanying illness that Adolph Kroeger experienced appeared particularly inhibiting on his daughter's development, and Alice remained shy and seemingly aloof all of her life. Upon her graduation from high school, her father's failing health and the resultant financial needs forced her to seek immediate employment, and it was logical for a child from a literary family to find a position as a clerk at the St. Louis Public Library.

She served as an assistant in the St. Louis issue department from 1882 until 1889, learning, like almost all apprentice librarians of that time, through experience rather than any formal course of instruction. Fortunately, the St. Louis Public Library was administered by the wise and scholarly Frederick M. Crunden (q.v.), who was extremely supportive of his staff and who apparently singled out Alice Kroeger as an individual of considerable literary background and library potential. In 1889, the American Library Association held its annual conference in St. Louis, and Alice Kroeger's name first appeared in the professional journals—even if mispelled Kraeger (probably due to her pronouncing it as "Kray-ger" rather than "Krow-ger"). At a special session over which Charles A. Cutter (q.v.) presided, he called upon Kroeger to express her concerns about library management. She was too shy to speak out, but Cutter summarized her comments and noted that she emphasized that catalogers should meet and work with the public so that they might do a better job of cataloging.

Alice Kroeger had apparently found a home in the library world and was perceptive enough to recognize that special schooling could help her in her work. In October of 1889, she enrolled in the New York State Library School, Melvil Dewey's (q.v.) famous school, which had transferred from Columbia College only a few months before and which attracted the cream of the crop of emerging key figures in librarianship—especially those destined to play major roles in library education. Among Alice B. Kroeger's classmates were Mary E. Robbins, Katharine L. Sharp (q.v.), and Edwin Hatfield Anderson (q.v.). Kroeger studied at Albany from October until April 1890, when she dropped her program to take a position as cataloger at the St. Louis Public Library—undoubtedly because the position was a promotion and she needed funds to continue her studies. She remained for less than a year, until February of 1891, when she returned to Albany to complete the two-year program after slightly more than a year's actual study. Since she had not earned a prior college degree nor had credit for any formal college courses, she did not receive the B.L.S. upon graduation; this was reserved for those who had such credentials. However, in July 1891, she received the School's diploma *with honor*, which indicated that three quarters of all the required work had been completed with examination standings of ninety percent or over.

The year before Alice Kroeger's Albany graduation, the second library school in the United States

had opened at Pratt Institute in Brooklyn. Dewey's pioneer program had high aims and was based on a two-year course of study, but it was quickly evident that trained library assistants could logically be prepared at the vocational schools, such as Pratt, Drexel, and Armour, which were opening across the country. In 1891, the Drexel Institute of Art, Science, and Industry (in Philadelphia) initially provided for eleven areas of study ranging from artistic courses through the practical arts. By 1892, the number of subjects had expanded considerably, and librarianship was one of them. Dr. James MacAlister, president of the Institute, had asked Melvil Dewey to recommend a librarian for the Institute when it opened in the fall of 1891, and Kroeger was Dewey's first choice. The plans for the training class were also under discussion, and the charter description of the Institute's Department of the Library and Reading Room concluded: "A school for the training of librarians will be organized at an early day in connection with the library." On October 20, 1892, Alice B. Kroeger issued a leaflet announcing that the first class in library work would be organized "in accordance with the standards which have been established in schools already in existence. The instruction ... embraces two courses: Library Economy and Cataloguing; with lectures on English literature, bibliography, and the history of books and printing."

The Drexel Institute Library School helped to seal the pattern of early training programs by utilizing many of the Albany program precedents. Rigorous entrance examinations, covering a variety of literary, historical, and contemporary topics, were used to select knowledgeable young women, and their course of study was clearly modeled on Dewey's curriculum. From the first, Drexel classes were limited in size because of the restricted physical quarters and number of available instructors. Kroeger served as the main instructor and, for the first few years, Bessie R. Macky, also assistant librarian, taught certain classes. President MacAlister lectured on the history of books and printing, and a variety of guest speakers provided expertise on bibliography and other specializations. An early report by Kroeger to *Library Journal* noted that "instruction is in the form of talks or lectures, with practical work under supervision, and includes the two sides of library work—the technical and the literary, or bibliographical."

By 1903, the entrance requirements had been modified to include knowledge of French and German, and an enrollment maximum of twenty students per term had been set. The entire course of study for students actually lasted only eight months, since the "extreme heat of Philadelphia" precluded a longer academic year for the young women and their instructors. Nine of the first entrance class of ten students received certificates of completion, and they and the majority of each graduating class in the next few years found "assistant" positions in the immediate Pennsylvania area. In later years, though, it was noted that some students took the course for personal gratification rather than as a basis for employment.

Alice Bertha Kroeger spent the remaining years of her short life as librarian and director of the Library School at Drexel. In 1908, the year before her death, she reported to the Minnetonka Conference of the American Library Association that the Library School curriculum had not undergone major changes during its history. Technical changes in library procedures and rules were incorporated in the curriculum, but the kinds of courses and the practice work remained largely the same. As Kroeger described it,

> The curriculum has not been materially altered in the 16 years which have elapsed since the opening, but many minor modifications have been introduced to keep abreast with the progress of the library movement which has been so rapid in recent years. A one year course of study cannot be subject to much change.... The evolution of the course of study in the school has therefore been a working towards a proper adjustment of the elements which make up the library of today—the people, the books and the methods by which the right books and the right people are brought together.

Clearly, her philosophy and administration of the Drexel Institute Library School during its first seventeen years succeeded admirably in meeting the solid, practical goals which motivated its establishment and continuation during these pioneer years of library education.

Alice Bertha Kroeger was an active member of ALA and of the Pennsylvania Library Club, where she served on the Executive Committee several times as well as being elected vice-president for 1895-1896. She was also elected a fellow of the American Library Institute in 1907. Her role in ALA began in 1889, when she became member number 728. Her professional experience as a cataloger made the Catalog Section her special interest; thus, she presented several papers on cataloging at the annual conferences, and was elected chairman of the Section just before her death. In addition, she served on the Council, as recorder in 1908, and on several committees, including one dealing with the preparation of catalog rules for small libraries. She and several other directors of library schools also served on the Committee on Library Training during the first years of its existence.

Along with her establishment and administration of the Drexel Institute Library School, Kroeger contributed greatly to the library literature of the era. Most of her work emphasized the strong, practical

nature that characterized her life and her teaching. Of particular note is her introductory text, *Guide to the Study and Use of Reference Books: A Manual for Librarians, Teachers and Students* (ALA, 1902; revised edition, 1908). The text became an immediate "bestseller" with librarians since it provided the first authoritative guide to the reference literature. In fact, the Kroeger text established a tradition that has continued to date. The third edition (1917), almost a decade after Kroeger's death, retained her name as author but was revised and enlarged by Isadore Mudge (q.v.). Today, of course, the Mudge series has been replaced by Winchell and by Sheehy, but each of the succeeding volumes has built upon the Kroeger objective of producing a systematic listing of reference books.

In addition to the manual on reference, Kroeger compiled a publication entitled *Aids in Book Selection* (1908), intended for use in small libraries as a guide to buying books and using sources; it updated several lists that were out of date at that time. She also wrote articles on a variety of practical library concerns, including such diverse topics as treatment and care of books in terms of their physical preservation, a survey of means by which to encourage "serious" reading, the role of women librarians, the value of the ALA cataloging rules, library nomenclature, cooperative cataloging, the responsibilities and duties of the "desk assistant," the arrangement of entries in catalogs, library school curricula, and the public library and the child. Invariably, the approach was found to be direct, pragmatic, and immediately useful by practitioners in the field. At a time when little effective codification had been accomplished in terms of library practices, Alice Kroeger was highly respected for her intellectual skills and meaningful application of rules and procedures to library concerns. Like so many others of that period, she combined her work as an instructor of library science with her actual administration of the Drexel Institute Library. Her profession clearly dominated her life and her interests.

Although she was physically attractive, with long, dark auburn hair and a lovely complexion, she made few close friends who shared anything other than interests in the field of librarianship. She spoke at assorted library meetings, gave papers, visited and spoke at libraries and library schools, but underlying all her activities was a consuming desire to be of service. To many of her students and some colleagues, she appeared stern and overly concerned with following the rules. The Library School and Library at Drexel, under her administration, were known for their thoroughly sober and conservative atmosphere; the rule of order was the thing to be understood, and some of the students considered her direction to be "chilly and formal." However, Kroeger set no standard for the students to which she herself did not adhere. She was circumspect in all of her actions, and she placed the obligations of the Institute and her work above her own well-being—a fact that apparently brought grave physical problems. She came to Drexel at the age of 27 and stayed until her death at the age of 45. The death certificate attributed her final heart failure to neurasthenia or pernicious anaemia, but those who knew her felt that it was brought about by self-neglect and malnutrition due to overwork and an inability to judge her own stamina. Kroeger had vacationed in Europe during the summer of 1909 and returned to open the fall term at Drexel in October, despite the fact that she was not well. She lectured to her class on Wednesday, fell ill, and died four days later on Sunday evening, October 31, 1909, at the Homeopathic Hospital in Philadelphia. One of her students later noted that

> the public tribute paid her was substantial. . . . The [memorial] service was held at noon in the Administration Building Auditorium which was packed with Drexel students, faculty and administration. After a moving eulogy by President MacAlister, all sat in silence. . . . At precisely one o'clock all could hear the train pulling away from the station heading for St. Louis carrying the body of Alice B. Kroeger. The great organ then played the "Dead March" from Handel's oratorio, "Saul."

She was buried at Bellefontaine Cemetery, St. Louis.

Her tragic and early death took the library world by surprise; every major journal noted that it was an unexpected shock that could not be fully comprehended at that time. The Pennsylvania Library Club passed a resolution noting in part, "her happy influence in the interest of everything which furthers the welfare of library administration, and the well-directed energy with which she aided others to equip themselves for the fulfillment of those ideas which shall give to the library profession a greater significance and greater fields for achievement in time to come." Friends and co-workers felt keenly the loss of one who had offered so much to the field and had so much left to offer. Ultimately, however, the finest tribute was paid by an anonymous student who sent a brief tribute to Alice Bertha Kroeger to be published in the *Library Journal*. The eulogy noted the "splendid, systematic training" received at Drexel, but more importantly, it cited the "enthusiasm awakened in us by her whose heart and soul were in the work, who saw and made us see its opportunities and its many phases of interest and benefit to us. . . . To Miss Kroeger's influence, justice and cheerfulness we owe one of the most helpful and inspiring memories of our lives."

Clearly, her life was a dedicated one, perhaps singleminded to a point of being driven beyond human capabilities; but clearly, also, she made the years of her life significant ones, and that can never be faulted.

Biographical listings and obituaries—*Notable American Women* 2 (Harriet D. McPherson); [Obituary]. *Library Journal* 34:518 (Nov. 1909); [Obituary]. *Public Libraries* 14:383 (Dec. 1909). **Books and articles about the biographee**—[Biographical sketch]. *Library Journal* 76:470 (March 15, 1951); Mariani, Doris. "Some Reminiscences of Alice B. Kroeger." *Graduate School of Library Science Newsletter*, No. 6 (Spring 1974); Nehlig, M. E. "The History and Development of the Drexel Institute Library School." Master's thesis, Drexel Institute School of Library Science, 1952; "Tribute to Alice Bertha Kroeger." *Library Journal* 34:551 (Dec. 1909). **Primary sources and archival materials**—Files of *Library Journal* (1892-1909) and *Public Libraries* (1896-1909).

—LAUREL A. GROTZINGER

LANE, WILLIAM COOLIDGE (1859-1931)

To be able to number Anne Hutchinson, John Alden, Priscilla Mullins, and John Coolidge among one's ancestors augured well for an enterprising young New Englander aspiring to a career in Massachusetts during the latter half of the nineteenth century.

For William Coolidge Lane, born to William Homer and Caroline Matilda Coolidge Lane on June 29, 1859, in Newtonville, Massachusetts, it was a definite asset. After attending the district and grammar schools of Newton and completing his secondary education at Newton High School, Lane was admitted to Harvard in 1877. By the end of his sophomore year, he had received highest honors in classics and had earned his reputation as a "dig," as the more serious students of his day were called. During graduation exercises in 1881, he delivered an address entitled "The Relation between Greek and Modern Life," received an honorable mention in natural history, and was one of 25 members of his class elected to Phi Beta Kappa.

For Lane, choosing a vocation was not difficult; even before graduation, he had decided to become a librarian. Though he spent that summer unemployed, in September, Justin Winsor (q.v.), librarian at Harvard, offered him a temporary position in the Ordering Department at the College Library. Eight months later, Winsor promoted him to superintendent of the Cataloging Department, with a specific charge to revise the catalog's subject headings by devising a numerical system that would simplify references from one subject heading to another. Lane's subsequent efforts led to the publication of a list of 15,000 subject headings with numbered references.

As Lane's achievements in the Library gained recognition, his circle of activities broadened. In 1882, he helped edit the University catalog, and two years later, the Harvard Corporation asked him to coordinate the entire effort. In 1888, Winsor appointed him assistant librarian. Though Lane was still expected to develop the public catalog for the University, his administrative responsibilities increased substantially. In 1889, the Harvard chapter of Phi Beta Kappa elected him secretary (a post he retained for the next thirty years), and from 1891 to 1892, Lane served as president of the Massachusetts Library Club.

By 1885, Lane's interests began to extend beyond Massachusetts. That year, he joined the American Library Association, and in 1886, he helped organize the ALA's Publishing Section. Lane served as the Section's secretary for the following decade, then became its chairman until 1911. Under his guidance, the ALA printed many of its early bibliographical aids. Lane also served as part-time lecturer at Columbia College's School of Library Economy from 1887 to 1889, and he retained the position when the School of Library Economy became the New York State Library School, serving as part-time lecturer there until 1891.

In April 1893, at age 34, Lane left Harvard to become head librarian at the Boston Athenaeum. As successor to Charles A. Cutter (q.v.), he inherited a staff of 22, who were regularly engaged in issuing catalog cards for current publications to subscribing libraries across the nation. Indeed, Lane's extensive professional experiences and reputation in cataloging circles probably led to his selection for the post.

But the Athenaeum years were only a temporary interruption in a life devoted to serving Harvard. On October 22, 1897, the position of Harvard College librarian fell vacant with the death of Justin Winsor. Because of Lane's previous twelve-year tenure at Harvard, his brief but successful term as director of the Boston Athenaeum, and his service to the ALA, many believed he was Winsor's logical successor. Thus, it came as no surprise to his academic colleagues when, on January 22, 1898, the Harvard Board of Overseers selected the 39-year-old Lane (the *Boston Evening Transcript* called him "an unusually young man for the position") as Harvard College librarian.

Upon assuming the new position, Lane inherited several problems. The main library was housed in Gore Hall which, despite its several expansions, was not adequate to house new acquisitions. In 1898, the collection had numbered 269,000 volumes and 222,000 pamphlets. Yet the annual rate of acquisitions was climbing by 50 percent. Lane devised temporary solutions to house this surge of new materials, but at the same time, he worked to satisfy the students' need for more study space. Convinced that a college library must combine stacks with sufficient study facilities to meet the needs of

research scholars, Lane concluded that Harvard needed a bigger library, and probably a new one. But in 1898, prospects for a new library were dim. Lane had to trust that the power of persuasion would bring eventual changes.

The year 1898 proved to be important for Lane. Not only did he return to his alma mater as librarian, he was also elected president of the American Library Association. While many of the duties related to his year-long term were mere formalities, one of them had a profound impact on the library world. When Librarian of Congress John Russell Young (q.v.) died unexpectedly in January 1899, his vacant post became a political football. As president of the ALA, Lane felt compelled to recommend a potential successor to President William McKinley. The President asked Lane to come to the White House to suggest a candidate. R. R. Bowker (q.v.), who accompanied Lane into the Oval Office, described the conference as a diplomatic triumph for the ALA president:

> The best service for the library profession in which I have participated since the organization of the American Library Association was when associated with Librarian Lane of Harvard in the conference with President McKinley which resulted in Herbert Putnam's [q.v.] appointment as Librarian of Congress in 1899. To the energy, firmness, and tact of William Coolidge Lane, President of the American Library Association for the year 1898-99, is largely due the benefit of that selection.

Although Bowker probably overestimated Lane's influence on McKinley, there is little doubt that Lane played a significant part in Putnam's selection.

After successfully completing his term as ALA president, Lane once again returned his full attention to Harvard. By 1899, the Library was falling further behind in its efforts to meet demands placed upon it by an accelerated acquisitions rate and increased student use. In his 1902 annual report, Lane included figures showing that the Library's holdings had doubled since 1881, quadrupled since 1861. With even larger enrollments expected at Harvard in the future, Gore Hall would not suffice much longer. In response to Lane's pleas, the Harvard Corporation appointed a special committee "to study the future needs of the College Library." As a participating member of that group, Lane was instrumental in forcing the committee to confront three fundamental questions: 1) Should Harvard have one central library, or a number of separate special libraries? 2) How much storage space could be saved by separating "live" (high circulation) volumes from "dead" (low circulation) volumes? 3) Would it be better to enlarge Gore Hall, or erect a new library building? After considerable internal deliberation, the Committee invited the Corporation, the College faculty, and the Library staff to discuss the questions openly. Group consensus favored not only a centralized library operation, but also a new building; and most people felt that discriminating between "live" and "dead" books offered no economy consistent with the needs of scholars. Lane's arguments concerning library expansion had finally won public and official support. But buildings cost money, and in Harvard's long history, no one had ever donated funds specifically for the construction of a library. In 1902, none seemed forthcoming.

On May 12, 1903, at Andover, Massachusetts, Lane married Bertha Palmer, daughter of Jacob Peabody and Annie Kimball Palmer of New York. Within four years, the Lane family had doubled with the addition of two daughters, Margaret and Rosamond. The Lanes quickly established a seasonal pattern of living. Fall, winter, and spring found them at the original Lane home, but the Cambridge summer heat drove them to Mrs. Lane's family summer house in Boxford, where Lane spent his leisure time gardening.

During this time, the crowded conditions in Gore Hall had become intolerable, and even the construction of a two-story concrete addition in 1907 provided only temporary relief. Then, in 1909, a Visiting Committee of the Board of Overseers requested that the Corporation appoint a committee of architects to determine whether the future needs of the Library could best be served by enlarging and/or renovating Gore Hall, or by constructing a new library building. The architects rejected the alternative of renovating Gore. They suggested that successive sections of a new library building could be erected on the south side as needed, ultimately to be completed with a facade on the north when Gore was razed. This plan incorporated solutions to the major problems Lane had encountered since 1898, and now all Harvard lacked was a benefactor to transform the plan into reality.

In 1912, Mrs. George D. Widener approached the president of Harvard, A. Lawrence Lowell, with an offer to fund the construction of a library if the College would agree to house the rare books and manuscripts collected by her recently deceased son, Harry Elkins Widener (Harvard A.B., 1907), in the new building. Lowell promptly showed Mrs. Widener the planning reports of 1902 and 1909, and the two tentatively agreed to build the Harry Elkins Widener Memorial Library.

Though Lane was pleased with Mrs. Widener's gift, he also recognized that the physical and operational transition to a new library would be difficult. Because the new edifice was to be built on the site of the old, temporary quarters had to be readied to maintain library service. Lane worked quickly. He first secured

use of the upper floor of Massachusetts Hall as a temporary reading room; next he furnished the lower floor of the same building as a supplementary reading room for American history, with special shelving for congressional and parliamentary documents. Randall Hall, originally constructed as a dining facility but vacant since 1911, provided enough space for stacks sufficient to house 400,000 volumes. Lane also located the Library's delivery room and card catalog on Randall Hall's first floor, and established the Library staff offices in the former serving rooms and kitchens. He housed other sections of the Library at Andover Theological Seminary, Emerson Hall, Robinson Hall, and ten other buildings on campus. After the Library was successfully "relocated," Gore Hall was demolished. Harvard officials turned the first shovel of dirt for the new building on February 11, 1913, and laid the cornerstone on June 16, 1913.

The changes in the physical structure of the Library were accompanied by simultaneous changes in the Library's administrative structure. Since Justin Winsor's day, the Harvard University Library had been governed by a Library Council consisting of the president, the librarian, and six other persons appointed by the Corporation. The Council was designated to "make rules for the administration of the Library; to direct the purchases of books to the extent of funds applicable for that purpose, and to visit and inspect" departmental and special libraries. The librarian, on the other hand, was responsible for "the care and custody of the Library" and was obligated "to supervise its internal administration, enforce the rules, and conduct the correspondence; and to make annually a written report on [its] condition." This organizational system worked smoothly in all but one area: no provision existed for any meaningful cooperation between the Library and its departmental satellites. This caused few problems in 1880, since the total holdings of outside libraries numbered only 60,000 volumes and all acquisitions were processed through the College Library and cataloged by its staff. However, by the time Lane became librarian, the increasing number of acquisitions by satellite libraries placed a heavy burden on the central cataloging processes. As a result, Lane advocated that departmental libraries hire assistants capable of cataloging their own acquisitions, in order to relieve the burden at the College Library. He also asked that catalogers in these libraries send a record of all titles received to be filed in the central College Library public catalog. But as the librarian became less occupied in the affairs of the departmental libraries, it became more evident that an official link was necessary. In 1910, the Board of Overseers created the office of director of the University Library, with that person to serve as chairman of the Library Council as well. While the librarian was to continue administering the College Library, the Board required that the director regulate the operations of all campus libraries and receive their annual reports, that he visit and inspect each departmental library, and that he be an *ex officio* member of the departmental administrative committees. In November 1910, the Board curiously bypassed Lane for the new position and instead named professor A. C. Coolidge as Harvard's first director of the University Library. Although Lane reconciled himself to the new situation, the Board's decision was a grave disappointment he never forgot.

While the University Library instituted a new administrative structure, and while the Widener building was being constructed, Lane was also supervising a final revision of the public catalog. Several years earlier, he had determined that the official catalog, used primarily by the staff, had to be transferred to standard card size. He also mandated that the public official catalogs had to be made complete by interfiling the same titles in each and that a union catalog had to be compiled from the reorganized official catalog by combining it with the complete file of the Library of Congress holdings. By the time the complete revision was accomplished, Harvard had added over a million new cards to its public catalog, and in the process had filed and handled over two million more. Lane then directed his Catalog Department to recast the whole subject catalog in dictionary form, and to merge it with the author catalog. The staff finished this task on June 1, 1915, just in time to move from the kitchens of Randall Hall into the new quarters at the Harry Elkins Widener Memorial Library.

On the morning of Commencement Day 1915, Mrs. George Widener presented President Lowell with the key to the building named in honor of her son. That afternoon, the Library staff began to shift its entire operation into Widener Library. By mid-August, 645,000 volumes had been removed from Randall Hall and the thirteen other temporary depositories and placed on Widener's shelves. On opening day of fall term, the new Harvard Library was ready to serve its patrons.

In 1923, after eight years of what he labelled "adjustment" in Widener, Lane celebrated his twenty-fifth anniversary as the Harvard librarian. Since accepting the position, he had guided library expansion from 600,000 to 2,187,000 volumes, which were distributed among Widener (housing 1,175,000) and its 44 satellite libraries. He directed the rise of the annual budget of $19,000 to more than $60,000 and staff growth from 25 to 152. On Commencement Day 1928, President Lowell cited Lane as the "Librarian of Harvard for thirty years, to whom scholars are grateful for the accessibility of its vast collection." He then conferred upon Lane an

honorary Master of Arts degree. On September 1, 1928, the 69-year-old Lane retired as Harvard's librarian emeritus. Less than three years later, after a brief illness, Lane died at his Cambridge home on March 18, 1931.

Biographical listings and obituaries–*Boston Evening Globe*, March 19, 1931; *Boston Evening Transcript*, March 18 and 19, 1931; Briggs, W. B. "William Coolidge Lane." *Massachusetts Library Club Bulletin* 21:31 (1931); *Harvard Crimson*, March 19, 1931; Merrill, W. S. "William Coolidge Lane, 1859-1931." *Libraries* 36:155-57 (1931); *National Cyclopaedia of American Biography* 12; *The Twentieth Century Biographical Dictionary of Notable Americans* 6; *Who Was Who in America* I (1897-1942); "William Coolidge Lane." *Harvard College Class of 1881: Fiftieth Anniversary Report* (1931), pp. 231-36. **Books and articles about the biographee**–Blake, Robert P. "William Coolidge Lane." *Proceedings of the American Academy of Arts and Sciences* 70 (1936). **Primary sources and archival materials**–Letters to and from Lane in his capacity as Harvard College librarian are in the Harvard University Archives.

                                        –WAYNE A. WIEGAND

LARNED, JOSEPHUS NELSON (1836-1913)

Josephus Nelson Larned was born May 11, 1836, in Chatham, Ontario, the son of Henry Sherwood and Mary Ann Nelson Larned. Henry Larned was a contractor from the United States whose business required the family to move from place to place, and when Josephus was twelve years old the family moved from Canada to Buffalo, New York. There he attended public school until he was sixteen years old, at which time he left school. For the rest of his life, however, he continued a program of self-education. In 1895, he was awarded an honorary A.M. degree from Dartmouth College.

On April 29, 1861, Larned married Frances Anne Kemble McCrea. The marriage lasted until his death 52 years later. Their three children were Sherwood J., Mary, and Anne M.

At age seventeen, Larned took a job as bookkeeper for a ship supply store, and later became a clerk for two transportation companies in Buffalo. In an attempt to improve his fortunes, he moved to Iowa in the spring of 1857, but, because he did not like the "West," he returned to Buffalo in the fall of 1857. Newspaper work had always appealed to him, so he obtained a position with the *Buffalo Republic*. Two years later, he joined the editorial staff of the *Buffalo Express*. For thirteen years, Larned worked for the *Express* (1859-1872), and he also maintained a financial interest in the paper for eleven years (1866-1877). Mark Twain worked for the *Express* for two years toward the end of Larned's tenure, though they worked together on the editorial staff for only nine months. Larned's editorials were wide-ranging in their topics but were predominantly on political themes. He wrote editorials for the Union cause during the Civil War, though he later became a strong advocate of international peace.

In the fall of 1871, Larned was elected superintendent of education for the city of Buffalo, the only public office he ever held. He served as superintendent for two years (1871-1873), and, while in that office, he wrote two annual reports. In one of these, he proposed an elected Board of Education, in order to avoid a change of educational policies each time a new Common Council (the governing body of the city) was elected. He said that Buffalo was the only major city in the United States that was so directly exposed to, and so poorly protected from, the political make-up of the city council.

Larned wanted well-prepared teachers, especially those teaching in the first few grades. He wanted history stressed in the curriculum, and he wanted technical and vocational education provided for those students who were qualified for it and desired it. Larned suggested that German should be taught in the public schools in Buffalo, since it was reasonable to expect the city's residents to know something of the native language of a large percentage of its population. In addition, he thought that such an action would encourage the city's German-speaking families to send their children to public schools; it was only natural that they would want their children to learn to read and write German as well as English. His attempts were futile, and his extreme dislike of the political control of the public schools caused him to leave the position of superintendent of education in 1873.

In 1836, a group called the Young Men's Association of the City of Buffalo had been formed as a literary society, and one of its first acts was to establish a subscription library. In 1877, the Association, recognizing the need for a person to administer the Library, amended its charter "to cure the evil influence upon the library of an annual change in administrative committees" and, in April 1877, Josephus Nelson Larned, "a gentleman competent to fill the evident vacancy in the Library," was appointed superintendent of the Association's Library.

Larned's chief duty was to select and purchase books; however, upon taking office, he found that the very first task confronting him was the preparation of a library catalog. Previous catalogs had been made, starting in 1847 and with the most recent one having been made in 1870. By 1877, though, the catalog was in dire need of revision because the collection had grown so much in the past seven years.

To acquaint himself with library administration and library practices before beginning his work, Larned visited several of the outstanding libraries in New York state and New England to investigate their systems of management and their classification systems. While in Boston, he met Melvil Dewey (q.v.)

and learned about the classification system that Dewey had devised for the Amherst College Library. Larned thought that the Dewey classification system would solve many of his "most troublesome problems," and between May 1877 and January 1878, he had thirty thousand books classified in that manner. As a result, the Young Men's Association's Library in Buffalo was the first large, general library to have its complete holdings classified by the Dewey system. For the new catalog, Larned chose to follow the kind of catalog that Charles A. Cutter (q.v.) had devised for the Boston Athenaeum. The Buffalo Library flourished under Larned's leadership, and in 1886, the Young Men's Association changed the name of the Library, in order to avoid confusion with the Young Men's Christian Association, to the Buffalo Library.

Throughout his entire career as superintendent of the Buffalo Library, Larned was very much interested in the quality of the Library's collection. In 1880, he was exchanging accession lists with other libraries in order to compare acquisitions and noted that "the comparison has appeared to be very favorable to us." Most English language publications of importance had been ordered, and the Library's collection of books in French and German was improving. Larned also cooperated with the Worcester (Massachusetts) Public Library and the Boston Athenaeum in preparing printed lists of new acquisitions. Cutter, of the Athenaeum, had originated the plan, which called for the lists to include quotations from the best reviews of each book listed. The three libraries prepared the lists, according to Cutter's plan, for acquisitions common to the three libraries, and the Athenaeum published the lists.

The quality of books in the Buffalo Library had been a matter of utmost importance since the Library's founding in 1836. Larned brought to his position as superintendent of the Library a strong philosophy of maintaining quality in the Library's collection. In his 1882 annual report, he included a long statement on "The Novel Question," saying that there was no question but that the Library must set some standards of quality, both literary and moral, in the field of romance literature, below which "it will not go in furnishing books to its patrons, young and old." In his *Library Journal* article, "Selection of Books for a Public Library" (August 1895), he recommended that librarians consult "people specially competent to appraise" the books in question when selecting books.

In another article published in the *Library Journal*, "The Freedom of Books" (July 1896), and again in his address to the American Library Association's 1896 Cleveland Conference, Larned discussed the value of good books for developing the mind. He spoke out strongly against the danger that the common mind of the age might be "trivialized and vulgarized by its newspapers and its commerce" and placed his faith "in a future of finer culture for mankind upon the energy of free public libraries in distributing good books far more than any other agency that is working in the world." He thought that the libraries had only just begun to win readers over "from unwholesome newspapers to wholesome books." These ideas on book selection and quality of collections were later summarized in a collection of his articles and speeches entitled *Books, Culture and Character* (1906).

Larned was concerned as well with selecting books and other materials about Buffalo and the Niagara Frontier. He built a collection of books, pamphlets, and other materials relating to Buffalo and the Niagara Frontier, as well as books that were published in Buffalo. The literature of the Niagara Frontier was "far richer than that of most other points in the United States as far West" as Buffalo, in his opinion, and he thought it only logical that the Library should contain the most complete collection of records on regional history. His interest in the history of the city was shown also by the fact that he wrote a two-volume *History of Buffalo* (1911).

Larned had always had a deep interest in the education of young people, and, as early as 1871, the teachers in the city had been given free membership in the Buffalo Library. In 1883, he issued free library tickets to fifty school children in the city. The practice proved to be so popular, and the children used the Library so much, that by 1895 one thousand free tickets were distributed to the city's children. His 1896 annual report stated that the most important event of the year in the Library was the opening of the Children's Room. The Children's Room was so heavily used that, within four months after it opened, it had to be moved to a larger room. Larned also compiled "Books for Young Readers," one of the first bibliographies of children's literature; and, in 1897, he published *A Talk about Books* (originally an address he gave to the students of a local high school in Buffalo and later included in his *Books, Culture and Character*).

In 1887, the Buffalo Library moved to a new building, which was considered a "model library" and had been designed with Larned's help. He had included in the new building a lecture-room and a classroom. It was his purpose to experiment with opening the Library to a wider audience and to extend the services of the Library as an institution of education. He opened the reading rooms on Sunday afternoons to non-members of the Library. The experiment was a great success, and he commented in his annual report on how quiet and well-behaved the Sunday afternoon users were. In the same year, an experimental course of lectures, including discussions

and reading guidance, was given in the Library, with a similar course the following year. These experiments in "university extension courses" were reported in Larned's article in the *Library Journal*, "An Experiment in University Extension" (January 1888). The courses, paid for partly by the people attending the courses and partly by the Library, were well attended and had paid teachers and carefully planned lectures, discussions, and reading lists; however, they were discontinued after the second year because the Library suffered a financial loss through them.

Another of Larned's innovations was the establishment of a browsing-reading section of the Library called "The Nook," a comfortable room where all of the newest books were kept for a period of time before they were moved to the stacks. In 1894, he reported that the "Nook" was heavily used and that, as a result of getting additional funds that year, he had been able to make several new acquisitions for it. Then, in 1896, Larned made the Buffalo Library an open stack library, something extremely rare in libraries at that time.

Shortly after he became superintendent of the Buffalo Library, Larned began a spindle for questions and answers called the "Query Hook," an idea borrowed from Justin Winsor (q.v.) at Harvard. He received so many questions on historical subjects that he began to keep the questions and their answers on the spindle for ready reference. These questions and answers, carefully written, classified and arranged by Larned, grew so large in number that, when the need for further compilation was seen, he redid the entire collection in a form that resulted in his book *History for Ready Reference* (1895). He also assisted William F. Poole (q.v.) with the new edition of Poole's *Index*, as well as helping with the American Library Association's index to general literature project. Starting in 1885, Larned compiled what he called "Finding Lists," indexes of periodicals, books and pamphlets in the Library. The second one was published in 1886, the third in 1896.

Larned was actively involved in the American Library Association from 1882 until 1903; on its Finance Committee (1881-1887), on its Executive Board (1884-1887, 1894), and as its vice-president (1896-1898). He hosted the American Library Association conference at Buffalo in 1883, and prepared the ALA model library at the World's Columbian Exposition in 1892. He served as president of the American Library Association in 1893-1894.

From 1882 to 1903, Larned wrote continuously for the *Library Journal* on a variety of subjects. He was influential, through ALA, on the subject of classification systems, having used Dewey's system for a large general library collection first, and having proposed alternatives, including one of his own.

Additionally, fellow ALA members considered him an expert on library architecture after his building program at Buffalo in 1887, the same year that he served on the ALA's Library School Committee and taught at Dewey's School of Library Economy at Columbia College (later University). Moreover, he was president of the New York (State) Library Association (1896) and prepared a paper on international library cooperation for the Second International Library Conference in London in 1897.

There seemed to be no aspect of librarianship in which Larned was not interested. His writings in the *Library Journal* from 1882 to 1903 concern such topics as the quality and selection of books for the library; library buildings; the organization of library materials, including pamphlets; book binding and book braces; circulation systems, including charging systems and borrowing regulations; controlling book loss; and indexing library materials. In addition, Larned was particularly interested in public libraries.

From the time the Buffalo Library opened its reading rooms on Sunday afternoons to the general public in 1887, Larned became a leader in the drive to create a free public library for the citizens of Buffalo, and he mentioned in several of his annual reports (particularly between 1892 and 1896) the increasing use of the Library by the general public. He pointed out, too, the serious lack of funds to support the needs of a collection that would serve the public in general.

On December 12, 1896, the Board of Managers of the Buffalo Library announced in a newspaper article "the critical circumstances of the Library" and asked for the city's cooperation in joint arrangements to make the Library a free library, with the financial support that was so desperately needed. The announcement was greeted with enthusiasm, and in February 1897, arrangements were completed to make the Buffalo Library a free, public, circulating, and reference library for the residents of the city of Buffalo.

Two months later, in April 1897, Josephus Larned resigned as superintendent of the Library, although reports vary as to why he did so. Augustus Shearer states that "he was not in sympathy with the new Board of Directors," and Sidney Ditzion (q.v.), says in *Pioneering Leaders in Librarianship* (pp. 118-19) that "he lacked both a sense of humor and the tact necessary for handling social and political leaders. The truth was that he did not like the backslapping insincerity, that *sine qua non* of the successful politician."

During his twenty years as superintendent of the Buffalo Library, Larned made many changes in the Library as well as many contributions to the profession of librarianship. His enrichment of the Buffalo Library's collection is evident from the number of

truly rare and valuable works that he bought, though he always had to work with a shortage of funds.

Following his retirement, Larned devoted his years to writing, lecturing, travelling, and participating in social and civic activities. From 1898 to 1902, he worked on the massive project of editing a bibliographical guide to American history entitled *The Literature of American History*, an eight-volume work published for ALA by Houghton, Mifflin (1902).

Larned renewed his interest in the Civil Service Reform Association of Buffalo, an association that he had formed with fourteen other citizens of the city. He had devoted much time to the cause of international peace, and, prior to retirement, he was the first president of the Buffalo Peace and Arbitration Society. He was a member of the Thursday Club, the Buffalo School Association, the Buffalo Historical Society, the Executive Committee of the Municipal League, and was, as well, an honorary member of the Saturn Club. Nationally, he was a member of the American Library Association and the American Historical Association.

Josephus Nelson Larned's major interests were study, scholarship, history, civic affairs; he wrote for *Library Journal* and for other journals on many subjects, in addition to the books he wrote. He continued to write after his retirement from the Library, his most famous work being his *Seventy Centuries of the Life of Mankind* (1907, 2v.). He did not actively seek the company of others except where his strong sense of public duty required him to take part in community affairs. He received much praise for his work, his lectures and his writings, but he always accepted it with an "unaffected modesty." He had a strong sense of fairness in his dealings with people, and in addition, he possessed a good sense of humor and was quite witty.

Larned, who came to the profession of librarianship from another profession, journalism, educated himself in all areas of librarianship. His contributions to the field range from administration, library buildings, classification and organization (plus selection) of materials, to the most minute details of the work. Yet his one constant aim was that libraries become free, public libraries that would serve their true purpose, institutions for the education of all people. He believed in the selection of materials that would serve the needs of the public, the ease of accessibility of those materials, and an open atmosphere in the library to attract people to use it for educational purposes. He was one of the first librarians to develop the university extension program in a library in an attempt to further his goal of making the library a public educational institution. Among all of his outstanding accomplishments in librarianship, his role in the development of the public library system in the United States was perhaps his most outstanding contribution to librarianship.

Portraits show that Larned was a rather handsome man with a high forehead. He wore his hair slightly long, just below the tips of his ear lobes, and wore a moustache with a modest beard. The most common portrait shows him wearing pince-nez, wire-framed glasses.

Sixteen years after his retirement as superintendent of the Buffalo Library, on August 15, 1913, Mr. Larned died at his home in Orchard Park, New York. He was buried in the Forest Lawn Cemetery in Buffalo.

Biographical listings and obituaries—*Dictionary of American Biography* 11 (Augustus H. Shearer); *National Cyclopaedia of American Biography* 16; [Obituary]. *Buffalo Express* (August 24, 1913); *Who Was Who in America* I (1897-1942). **Books and articles about the biographee—** Brown, W. L. "J. N. Larned." *Bulletin of Bibliography* 13:125-26 (1928); Ditzion, Sidney. "Josephus Nelson Larned." In Emily Miller Danton, ed., *Pioneering Leaders in Librarianship*. Chicago: American Library Association, 1953, pp. 108-119; Ditzion, Sidney. "Social Ideas of a Library Pioneer, J. N. Larned." *Library Quarterly* 13:113-31 (April 1943); Goldberg, Arthur. *The Buffalo Public Library*. Buffalo, N.Y.: Privately printed, 1937; Olmsted, John B. "Josephus Nelson Larned." Buffalo Historical Society. *Publications* 19:3-33 (1915); Young, Betty. "Josephus Nelson Larned and the Public Library Movement." *The Journal of Library History* 10:323-40 (Oct. 1975). **Primary sources and archival materials—**"Chronological List of the Writings of J. N. Larned." Buffalo Historical Society. *Publications* 19:133-36 (1915); Buffalo & Erie County Public Library. "J. N. Larned, Superintendent of the Buffalo Library, 1877-1913." Bound scrapbook of newspaper clippings about Mr. Larned, 1877-1913; Buffalo Library. *Annual Reports*. 1877-1898; *Library Journal* 1-39 (1876-1914).

—ELIZABETH W. SMITH

LEARNED, WILLIAM SETCHEL (1876-1950)

Born in Alpena, Michigan, on June 5, 1876, to William Chandler and Adda Setchel Learned, William S. Learned earned two degrees at Brown University (A.B. in 1897, and A.M. in 1908). He studied in Berlin and Leipzig (1909-1911) and received the Ph.D. degree from Harvard in 1912. He was awarded three honorary degrees, the Litt.D. by his alma mater, Brown (1939), the LL.D. by Lawrence College, Wisconsin (1933), and the LL.D. by the University of Saskatchewan (1936). He married Evelyn Blanche Williams in 1903; she died in 1934. He had one child from this marriage, Annabel Frampton. He was married again in 1936 to Charlotte McMahon Smith.

Learned's career as an educator began in Montour Falls, New York, where he was a teacher in Cook Academy from 1897 to 1901. From there, he went on to be principal (1901-1904) at the University School in Providence, Rhode Island, and then he was

a senior master at the Moses Brown School in Providence, Rhode Island (1904-1909). He went to Berlin as an exchange teacher (1909-1910) and was also a student in Berlin and Leipzig (1909-1911). He returned to Harvard as a student (1911-1912) and later was a research fellow there (1912-1913). Learned's honors included membership in Phi Beta Kappa, Phi Delta Kappa, Delta Upsilon, and the Century Association.

William Learned rose to prominence as a staff officer of the Carnegie Foundation for the Advancement of Teaching, where he worked from 1913 until his retirement in 1946. He did considerable exploratory research as a member of the Carnegie Foundation's Division of Educational Enquiry. Although the obituary notice that appeared after his sudden death on January 3, 1950, noted that Learned was best known as founder and director of the Graduate Record Examination, his own major objective was to invigorate the functioning pattern of education. Paul Douglas, in his biography of Learned, *Teaching for Self-Education*, noted that Learned's fundamental purpose was "to encourage a habit of self-education which would continue as an on-going intellectual activity throughout life. Learned's research was based on one dominating purpose: the improvement of *teaching for self-education* as a life goal."

Learned's major contribution to librarianship was in a book that brought a new philosophy to librarianship: *The American Public Library and the Diffusion of Knowledge* (1924). In this volume, Learned developed his theory of a professionally staffed, functionally organized, community-centered public library that should serve as an intelligence center for all people. He thought that librarians as well as teachers should be professionally trained scholars who could "fit books to individual human needs." Consequently, he stressed the need for professional education of librarians in a permanent career plan. He also thought of the free public library as the chief instrument of our common intellectual and cultural progress. He felt strongly that one of the primary factors in a sound education was "a professionally administered collection of books adapted to individual concern, displayed to excite personal interest, and recommended to encourage growth" (*Teaching for Self-Education*, p. 24). Learned felt that the 1,804 library buildings provided by Andrew Carnegie (q.v.) to communities in the United States and Canada were a great boon to education, and he was in complete agreement with Carnegie's concept of the library as a "true community center for a comprehensive, popular education suited to all ages."

Biographical listings and obituaries—*Who Was Who in America* II (1943-1950). **Books and articles about the biographee—**Douglas, Paul. *Teaching for Self-Education: As a Life Goal*. New York: Harper & Brothers, 1960.

—MARTHA BOAZ

LeFEVRE, ALICE LOUISE (1898-1963)

Alice Louise LeFevre (known as Louise) was born April 20, 1898, in Muskegon, Michigan, the daughter of George and Alice Ducey LeFevre. She was graduated from Wellesley College in 1920, later studied at the Library School of New York Public Library (earning her certificate in 1923), and received her M.S. degree from Columbia University in 1933. Following her graduation from Wellesley, she returned to Muskegon and worked as an assistant librarian in the children's room from 1921 to 1922 and as librarian of Bunker Junior High School from 1923 to 1926. At this point, she served for one year as an assistant at the American Library Association Board of Education for Librarianship office. She then moved to Cleveland, where she was high school librarian at John Hay High School from 1926 to 1930.

LeFevre then turned her attention to library education, where she built a distinguished career. In 1933-1934, she was an instructor at the New York State College for Teachers in Albany. This was followed by two years as assistant professor at the Louisiana State University Library School, Baton Rouge (1934-1935), and at the University of North Carolina School of Library Science as a visiting professor (1938 and 1939). During the summers of 1936-1943, she taught at the New York University Library School in Chautauqua, New York. In 1939, she became a member of the faculty at St. John's University in Brooklyn, remaining there until 1945, when she came to Kalamazoo, Michigan, to organize the program in librarianship at Western Michigan College of Education.

While teaching at St. John's University, LeFevre organized the new young adult program in the Public Library in New Rochelle, New York (1935-1937). In 1940, she served as a consultant for the school library survey in the White Plains, New York, school system. The entire gamut of library service was of interest to LeFevre, the theoretical aspects as well as the practical.

Always one who believed in contributing to the profession through association activities, LeFevre was a member of the Michigan Library Association, the Adult Education Association, and the Michigan Education Association. In 1948, she served as president of the Michigan Library Association. In 1954, she served simultaneously as president of the ALA Division of Libraries for Children and Young People and as president of the Association of American Library Schools. In 1960, she was named president of the Teachers' Section, Library Education Division, ALA, and in 1961, she was elected to the ALA Council. Meanwhile, she was appointed editor of *Top of the News* (1944-1946). She also chaired the Children's Section of the Michigan Library Association and served for three years on the ALA Editorial Committee. Always eager to expand her own professional horizons, LeFevre was involved continually as both a learner and a contributor.

LeFevre's most intimate professional friends included Margaret Scoggin (q.v.) and Jean Roos, and the three of them were leaders in pioneering library service for young adults. They organized centers for young people in public libraries, collaborated in publications, and worked closely together to promote the young people's round table in ALA (which ultimately became part of the Division of Libraries for Children and Young People, and then YASD). LeFevre was particularly interested in international library developments, giving strong support (with Margaret Scoggin and Mildred Batchelder) to Jella Lepman's plan for an international youth library in Munich. Another friend with whom she worked closely was Constance Rourke. Together they wrote the book *Audubon*, and LeFevre was constantly on the lookout for material to assist Rourke in all her writings.

Louise LeFevre's greatest contribution to the library profession came in 1945, when she was selected by President Paul Sangren of the then Western Michigan College of Education in Kalamazoo to assume the position of director of the Department of Librarianship. A grant from the Kellogg Foundation that was matched by the College had made the Department's creation possible the same year. A need existed for librarians trained to cope with the new books being poured into schools, as well as county and community libraries, in southwestern Michigan, as part of a "five for me" drive. Nora Beust, Leon Carnovsky (q.v.), and Ralph Ulveling, along with Zoe Wright from the Kellogg Foundation library, had proposed an educational program to meet this need. The choice of Louise LeFevre to implement this program proved to be a wise one.

A woman of wit, intelligence, and charm, LeFevre could cajole, scold, argue, and persuade almost anyone to her way of thinking when it came to promoting library science. An indomitable person, she was generous to a fault. Although she suffered from a severe physical handicap resulting from a childhood accident, she never used this as an excuse. Whether she was hiking, swimming, trudging to meetings, working in school libraries, or presiding at professional conferences, she was fully and enthusiastically involved. She inspired her students and fellow teachers even when there were only three full-time and one half-time faculty members teaching 29 courses. While her knowledge of and commitment to books was paramount, she was always eager to try new audiovisual materials and technology in library service and in library education.

The first classes in the new Department of Librarianship were introduced in the spring semester of 1946 with two students and three courses. The primary objectives were to develop skills in selection, organization, and use of books and teaching materials, and to stimulate an interest in books and reading at the elementary and secondary levels. The program itself was designed to serve the needs of schools K-12, to provide service in small communities and rural areas, and to help teachers and prospective teachers to broaden their knowledge of books and other library materials.

In 1946, a second faculty member was added, Mate Graye Hunt, and the program was associated with the Division of Teacher Education. Together, LeFevre and Hunt developed courses, recruited students, educated counselors, and served as consultants to libraries in southwestern Michigan. Meanwhile, LeFevre was working toward ALA accreditation, which was achieved in 1948 when the Department was designated as a Type III library school.

Always one to experiment, LeFevre designed internship experiences for all of the undergraduate students, not only in schools but also in the Department's new county library program. Students spent three weeks off-campus working in county libraries in southern Michigan as well as going on field trips. In her first five-year report, LeFevre noted not only the integration of the Department in the Division of Teacher Education, but also the separation of the faculty from the college library staff, as well as the faculty's freedom to promote programs, the development of criteria for field work, and the publication of a separate bulletin describing the program.

Keeping abreast with societal and educational changes, LeFevre used her administrative strength toward both the expansion of courses to meet all types of library needs and the development of a graduate program that would change the undergraduate major to a minor, promoting it primarily as a recruitment device. The years 1955-1958 were hectic and traumatic in LeFevre's career. She supervised the academic changes from a department in teacher education to an academic unit in the new graduate studies program, later the Graduate College. With the University librarian, Katharine Stokes, LeFevre planned the new quarters in Waldo Library, which was then under construction. She developed a graduate program to meet the 1951 ALA accreditation standards and saw this accomplished in 1958-1959. The faculty was expanded to three and then four persons, and LeFevre laid groundwork for a colloquium program that would bring national leaders in the field as guest lecturers. Enrollment was increasing; national and international visibility was developing; a graduate residence center was planned in Lansing.

Unfortunately, as the whole program was burgeoning in 1962, LeFevre became ill, and in 1963, she was forced to take sick leave that became a permanent farewell to her career. In recognition of her contribution to the profession, the Michigan Library Association made her an honorary member; the University named one of its new residence halls for her; and tributes and resolutions came from the many professional groups in which she had been so vitally involved. Following her death on June 18, 1963, the alumni and faculty created the Alice Louise LeFevre Memorial Scholarship Fund, and the seminar room in the expanded School of Librarianship quarters was dedicated to her in 1970, on the School's twenty-fifth anniversary.

Active in Altrusa and Delta Kappa Gamma, LeFevre also chaired the Borgess Hospital Fund Drive in 1954. Her friends remember her for her love of life, her love of cats, and her love of miniature books. This latter hobby began when she was living in New York, and the actual "Tom Thumb" cataloging of the collection was carried on at the Hobby Club meetings. The collection is still in existence; among its two hundred volumes are many valuable titles in English and other languages, including volumes bound in silver and fine leather, several Bibles, and works of Kate Greenaway and other early children's authors.

Alice Louise LeFevre was a charming woman, an indefatigable worker, and an intelligent conversationalist. The highest accolade that can be given to her is to be found on the dedication plaque in the residence hall named in her honor—

"With the faith to attain the Vision
With the laughter to light the way."

Biographical listings and obituaries—[Obituary]. *College and Research Libraries* 24:332 (July 1963); [Obituary]. *Journal of Education for Librarianship* 3:293 (Spring 1963); [Obituary]. *Library Journal* 88:2668 (July 1963); [Obituary]. *Wilson Library Bulletin* 38:27 (Sept. 1963); *Who's Who in Library Service*, 1st ed., 2nd ed., 3rd ed. **Books and articles about the biographee**—[Biographical sketch]. *Michigan Librarian* 13:6 (June 1947); "Honorary Member: Alice Louise LeFevre." *Michigan Librarian* 29:17 (June 1963); *Perspectives: A Library School's First Quarter Century, 1945-1970*. Valerie Noble, ed., Kalamazoo: School of Librarianship, The Graduate College, Western Michigan University, 1970.

—JEAN E. LOWRIE

LEGLER, HENRY EDUARD (1861-1917)

Henry E. Legler was born in Palermo, Sicily, on February 22, 1861. His parents were Henry, a German-Swiss, and Raffaela Messina Legler, of Sicily. Young Legler's mother died while he was still an infant, and he was raised by a devoted sister. The family lived in Switzerland until soon after the American Civil War, when they emigrated to the United States and settled in La Crosse, Wisconsin, in 1873. Henry finished his formal education in the public schools there. On September 4, 1890, he married Nettie M. Clark of Beloit, Wisconsin, and they had three sons, Frederic, Henry M., and John.

After leaving school at age seventeen, Henry became a typesetter in a La Crosse printing shop, and then a reporter for the *La Crosse Republican-Leader*. Some time later, he joined the *Milwaukee Sentinel*, first as a reporter and then as city editor. In 1888, he was elected a Republican member of the Wisconsin Assembly, representing Milwaukee's 7th district. He served one term, and did not stand for re-election, as in 1890, he was appointed secretary (and executive officer) of the Milwaukee Board of Education. In this position, he led the Board to develop a close working association between the Milwaukee public schools and the Milwaukee Public Library, a program that gained wide attention among librarians and educators. It was during this period that his interest in librarianship matured, and in 1904, he accepted the position of secretary (and executive officer) of the Free Library Commission of Wisconsin.

Frank A. Hutchins (q.v.) had been the Commission's secretary during its first decade, and it was an active, prominent agency in the promotion and development of public library service. Legler did not permit the Commission to slacken. In 1905, the *Wisconsin Library Bulletin* was established. In 1906, the Wisconsin Summer School of Library Science (the predecessor of the University of Wisconsin Library School) was founded; in 1909, still operated by the Commission, it became the Wisconsin Library School, with a full-time program. The Commission's Travelling Library program was substantially extended, and a central loan collection was established (Wisconsin did not, and does not, have a state library). The Legislative Reference Library, established in 1901 as the Commission's Document Department under the supervision of Charles A. McCarthy (q.v.), continued its aggressive development as the nation's foremost legislative reference and research agency.

In addition to his work as secretary of the Free Library Commission, Legler also found the time to serve, in 1906-1907, as the first secretary (without salary) of the University of Wisconsin Extension Division. Legler believed strongly that the University should play a greater role in adult education than it did, and he saw the Extension Division as the best instrument for engaging the University in that endeavor.

In 1909, the directorship of the Chicago Public Library became vacant. The CPL, once one of the nation's distinguished public libraries, had stagnated for several years, and its Board was determined to reverse this condition. It was also determined that the appointment of a new chief librarian should be made without the patronage influence long attendant to even the most minor positions in the city government. Accordingly, under a new city civil service

law, a panel of distinguished librarians was appointed to review applications and recommend one candidate. The panel members were Herbert Putnam (q.v.), Clement W. Andrews (q.v.), Frank P. Hill (q.v.), and Howard O. Sprogle. They interviewed nineteen candidates and finally recommended the appointment of Henry E. Legler. It should be noted that the panel did not regard any of the nineteen as "clearly pre-eminent," and one member strongly dissented from the Legler recommendation. Even so, within the profession there was general approval of the decision. It was the first time that appointment to the directorship of a major public library had been made under civil service procedures. *Library Journal* saw the real significance of the appointment in the fact that it was controlled by "a board of trained professionals who knew the men, their character, and their work."

When Legler came to the Chicago Public Library, he found it "a mansion which many people were afraid to enter." For a generation, its operations had been conducted in a spirit of conservatism remote from the people. In 1909, it had only one branch, and in a city of two million people there were fewer than 97,000 card-holders. Thus, the annual circulation of books was far less than one per capita. Additionally, the 210 employees of the Library were not organized for effective service to the public. Their morale was low, reflecting disorganization, low salaries, the inadequacy of codified appointment and promotion procedures, and the lack of a retirement system, which compelled many staff members to hang on long past the point of superannuation. Finally, the Library's operations were severely handicapped by the works of the "Juul Law" (named for State Senator Niels Juul), which provided that as the tax revenues increased, the Library's mill levy rate would decrease proportionally. Although the 1891 statute was repealed in 1917, it was a financial "iron maiden" for both the Library and Legler during his tenure there.

Legler's attitude toward the task confronting him was announced soon after his arrival as chief librarian:

Our problem is to reach all the people of the city. How can we do it? Certainly not through this palace. It is too remote from most of the people. Besides, it is repellent to many. It is too grand. The Library must reach out, and expand. It must interweave with the business and home life the pleasant and educative things which the Library has to offer.

Legler served only six and a half years as chief librarian at Chicago (he was on leave during the last four months of his life), but it was the most remarkable period of development in the Library's record. Circulation increased to 5,602,806 volumes during 1917, the number of library card holders increased to

289,504, the number of branches went from one to forty, and the staff jumped from 210 to 489. In 1915, Legler won an increase in the tax rate for the Library, from six-tenths of a mill to one mill, which meant a $200,000 annual increase in the Library's income. Too, a breathtaking number of new programs and activities was established in the Library during 1910-1917. In 1910, the Board established a classification system and graduated pay schedules for librarians and other employees. The same year saw a training class established in the Library. The years 1911-1912 saw the establishment of deposit collections at various places around the city and of a Civics Department in the Main Library. In 1913-1914, nineteen Industrial Deposit Libraries were installed in those firms whose employees numbered from 1,000 to 10,000. Each firm furnished quarters, a librarian for the deposit library, and transportation of books to and from the Main Library. The Chicago Public Library selected and provided the books, and also provided reference service to the deposit libraries. In 1914-1915, a music department and a foreign book room were established in the Main Library, and a parcel post delivery service for books was inaugurated. In 1915-1916, branches were established in three high schools. The increase in library staff also necessitated a reorganization of personnel operations, with establishment of a new classification and grade structure. The training class's curriculum also was reorganized, and the new curriculum involved 165 hours of instruction, plus reading courses.

In addition to all this, at the end of November 1916, the Board made public a plan (in development since 1912) for reorganizing the Library. It called for elimination of the main-library-and-branches concept, to be replaced by five regional branches, seventy auxiliary branches, sixty deposit stations, one hundred industrial and commercial branches, twenty-two high school branches, three thousand classroom libraries, and one hundred (or more) special deposits (special collections for various groups and institutions in the city). In the plan, the most ambitious yet attempted by any American public library, could be seen the full development of Legler's earlier statement about interweaving the library into the life of the entire city.

Legler's last year with the Chicago Public Library was, in planning terms, the most ambitious of his career. The following extensions of service were planned for 1917-1918: continued development of the plan published in 1916; reorganization of the delivery stations; the establishment of a Business and Information Bureau in the Loop; reorganization of the Municipal Reference Library; establishment of an Educational Division to work with the schools and in adult education; improvement of the publications program; reclassification of the 800,000-volume general collection; the establishment of agencies maintained by the Board of Education; the establishment of an Illinois History Collection; a city-wide advertising campaign; and the provision of library staff for five hospital and corrections institutions in the city. The *Chicago Daily News* was not wide of the mark in its comment that Henry E. Legler "revolutionized" the Chicago Public Library.

Legler's administration of the Library was marked as well by his concern for the staff's welfare. On his arrival, he found it excessively burdened by superannuation, and the establishment of a retirement system was one of the achievements in which he took the most pride. He was also concerned for the on-the-job welfare and comfort of the staff, and he worked diligently to develop rest, recreation, and dining facilities for them. In many respects, his plans for staff welfare were significantly in advance of conventional thinking about the matter.

The major defect in Legler's direction of the Library was the institution, in 1911, of a program for the censorship of fiction considered for addition to the collections. "So large is the proportion of . . . novels . . . with sex complications, that, during the past year the Chicago Public Library had admitted . . . no fiction until passed upon by members of the staff after personal examination." In his defense, it may be said that Legler's ideas about fiction did not vary significantly from those of most of his American colleagues, nor from those of society in general, and his views, at least, were candidly stated.

Legler joined the American Library Association upon his appointment to the Wisconsin Free Library Commission, and he immediately became active in its affairs. He founded the ALA *Booklist* in 1904 and served as its editor until 1916. In 1905, he was elected chairman of the League of Library Commissioners, an ALA auxiliary. He was a member of the ALA Publishing Board, and its chairman in 1908-1909. He was a member of the Council, 1909-1913, and president of the Association, 1912-1913.

Legler's interests extended into a number of fields related to librarianship, and he was a member of the Bibliographical Society of America, a fellow of the American Library Institute, a member of the Caxton Club of Chicago, the American Historical Association, the State Historical Society of Wisconsin (he served one term on the Society's Board of Curators), the Milwaukee Press Club, and the Chicago City Club.

Throughout his adult life, Legler demonstrated an interest in history and literature. He wrote several books, including a biography of Henry de Tonty, a seventeenth century explorer of the Mississippi Valley region (Milwaukee, 1896); *Leading Events of Wisconsin History* (Milwaukee, 1898); *A Moses of the Mormons*, a biography of James Strang (Milwaukee,

1897); *Of Much Love and Some Knowledge of Books* (Chicago, 1912); and *Walt Whitman, Yesterday and Today* (Chicago, 1916). Indifferently regarded today, they were accepted in his lifetime as tangible evidence of his scholarly merit and humanistic principles, and they still demonstrate a man strongly invested with the ideals and virtues of classical scholarship.

It is not apparent from his writings on the subject that Legler ever developed a coherent philosophy of librarianship. (His most significant writings about the profession are in *Library Ideals*, compiled and edited by his son, Henry M. Legler, and published in 1918.) Although, according to Jens Christian Bay (q.v.; director of the John Crerar Library), Legler's "radical idealism" led him to consider the public library as the institution best suited to foster the development of an enlightened and humane society, Legler's own writings about that institution reflect a fundamentally conservative attitude toward society, tempered by nostalgia for the qualities of the pastoral democracy he supposed America to have been. In the midst of his tenure at the Chicago Public Library, he wrote (in "The Problem of the Cities") of the dangers to the republic that urbanization brought with it, and of the need to improve the qualities of rural life, since "upon the people who are near to the soil will devolve the task of holding in balance the restless and turbulent . . ." population of the cities. In his ALA presidential address, he warned his colleagues not to allow their increasing specialization to divert them from their mission of uplifting the urban working classes, who were an increasing threat to the safety and good order of the nation: "There is grave danger that the race will develop a ragtime disposition, a moving picture habit, and a comic supplement mind." In 1915, he viewed World War I as a sign of the disintegration of civilization—and charged public librarians to intrude themselves into the schools to rekindle the American mission to work "the miracle of human evolution" from which a better civilization would be built ("Next Steps," an address to the New York State Library Association, 1915). All in all, he placed an impossible social burden upon the institution and its servants. It would be better to his memory to forget his writings on librarianship, and to remember his plan for the development of the Chicago Public Library.

It is difficult to peer beyond the words about Henry Legler and perceive the person. The works about him are short and uncritical, written by people seeing him through a veil of remembered friendship. But it can be said he served Chicago well. He died in Chicago on September 13, 1917.

Biographical listings and obituaries—*Dictionary of American Biography* 11 (Louise Phelps Kellogg); *National Cyclopaedia of American Biography* 24; [Obituary]. *Chicago Daily News*, Sept. 13, 1917; [Obituary]. *Chicago Tribune*, Sept. 13, 1917; [Obituary]. *Milwaukee Sentinel*, Sept. 14, 1917; *Who Was Who in America* I (1897-1942). **Books and articles about the biographee**—"Henry Eduard Legler. In Memoriam." *Library Journal* 42:951-54 (Dec. 1917); Warren, Althea, and Pearl Field. "Henry Eduard Legler, 1869-1917." In Emily Miller Danton, ed., *Pioneering Leaders in Librarianship*. Chicago: ALA, 1953. **Primary sources and archival materials**—Chicago. Public Library. *Annual Report*, 1910-1917.

—JOHN C. COLSON

LEIGH, ROBERT DEVORE (1890-1961)

On September 13, 1890, Robert Devore Leigh was born to Charles Pascal and Olivia Belle Thompson Leigh in Nelson, Nebraska, but he grew up and attended school in Seattle, Washington, where his father owned and operated the Leigh Lumber Company. Endowed with a strong constitution, keen mind and sanguine temperament, young Robert found ample scope and fulfillment for his varied abilities and interests. He was graduated from high school and, motivated perhaps by family pride in his English forebears (seventeenth century settlers of New England who had produced ministers, teachers, and two college presidents), he then chose to cross the continent to enter Bowdoin College in Maine.

As an undergraduate, Robert continued to exercise his marked administrative talents by participating in a variety of extracurricular activities. That his studies were pursued with equal vigor is attested by his election as a junior to Phi Beta Kappa and to two other honor societies. In 1914, he was graduated *summa cum laude* as class valedictorian, with the highest academic grades of the preceding decade.

On a graduate fellowship, one of two awarded by Bowdoin College, Robert Leigh then entered Columbia University, where he was awarded a Master of Arts degree in political science in 1915. Back in Oregon to undertake his first teaching assignment, he served for a year at Reed College as an instructor in government, then as assistant professor from 1917 to 1919. Meanwhile, on June 23, 1916, he had married Mildred Adelaide Boardman, starting a family of his own that in due course included two daughters, Helen Devore and Virginia B. He also had accepted his first governmental appointment, serving from 1917 to 1919 as assistant educational director for the United States Public Health Service, which he began to study in detail.

An offer from Columbia University to serve as lecturer in government from 1919 to 1922 made it possible for him to return there and begin work on his doctorate. He spent the years 1922 to 1928 at Williams College as the first appointee to the A. Barton Hepburn Professorship of Government. In 1927, Columbia University conferred on him the Ph.D. degree in political science after completion of his dissertation, "Federal Health Administration in the United States," one of the studies leading to organization of the Department of Health, Education and Welfare. Later, he received honorary LL.D. degrees from Colgate University (1933) and from Bowdoin College (1935).

At the age of 38, Leigh was called to Vermont to become the first and organizing president of Bennington College, a post he held from 1928 to 1941. During his earliest years there, he devoted his energies in large part to raising funds, planning for, and building this new, experimental college for young women; but, in addition, he carried responsibility for designing the program of studies, formulating the progressive method of instruction, selecting a suitable faculty, and recruiting the student body. Then began the long-term task of guiding this democratically organized community of scholars and students toward fulfillment of individual and group aspirations. Yet he found time to prepare a book entitled *Group Leadership* (Norton, 1936), and time, also, to serve as acting dean in 1939 for Bard College, then affiliated with Columbia University.

Leigh implemented his plan for effecting regular changes in the presidency of Bennington College as incumbents reached their maximum usefulness by announcing his own retirement from that position in 1941 at the age of fifty. For the rest of his life, nevertheless, he maintained cordial relations with the college and close ties with friends on the faculty. Some ten years later, he and Mildred Leigh realized their dream of building a large, attractive house on land they owned nearby, where summer months were spent entertaining friends, visiting with their children and grandchildren, gardening, and playing golf in the beautiful Vermont countryside that they loved.

Under a grant from the Rockefeller Foundation to conduct field studies in social science instruction, Leigh served through 1941 as a staff member at the Institute for Advanced Study at Princeton, New Jersey; he also accepted appointment as special adviser to the National Resources Planning Board for 1941-1942. After the attack on Pearl Harbor and the U.S. entrance into World War II, Leigh moved to Washington, D.C. There he served with distinction as liaison officer of the Public Health Service with other wartime agencies; as acting assistant director of the National Resources Planning Board in the Executive Office of the President. From 1942 to 1944, he was director of the Foreign Broadcast Intelligence Service of the Federal Communications Commission, in charge of monitoring and analyzing enemy broadcasts for the major war agencies. He served from 1943 to 1944 as chairman of the United Nations Monitoring Committee.

Convinced that maintenance of peace in the postwar years would depend upon the power of a worldwide, informed public opinion, Leigh returned to the academic world in 1944 as visiting professor of political science at the University of Chicago and as director of the Commission on Freedom of the Press (1944 to 1946) under the chairmanship of Robert M. Hutchins, then chancellor of the University. With Llewellyn White, the assistant director, he conducted a study of international mass communication that was published as the first report of the Commission under the title *Peoples Speaking to Peoples* (University of Chicago Press, 1946). Their specific proposals (addressed to the United States Congress, the Department of State, and the Federal Communications Commission) were aimed at effecting cooperation among the information agencies in this country while safeguarding both the needs of private industry and the requirements of governmental responsibility.

In the full maturity of his exceptional powers of mind and spirit, and with a broad, varied experience in teaching, administration, and research, Robert Leigh entered the library world as director from 1947 to 1950 of the Public Library Inquiry of the Social Science Research Council. As noted on page three of his final, general report, this project (financed by Andrew Carnegie's [q.v.] Carnegie Corporation) was undertaken in response to a request from the American Library Association for a study that would provide "an appraisal in sociological, cultural, and human terms of the extent to which the librarians are achieving their objectives," and "an assessment of the public library's actual and potential contribution to American society."

That American public libraries be examined and evaluated by a team of non-librarians was a proposal almost without precedent. To insure the sought-for objectivity and detachment from any official or unofficial library controls, all members of the Inquiry staff were chosen by the director from social science disciplines or from one of the communications fields. Although two librarians, along with five social scientists, served on an advisory committee appointed by the Council to provide guidance and criticism, each investigator was left free to report his own findings and judgments. The director's report was based on the 19 special studies, including several conducted by him, that were produced with the aid of 24 research associates and assistants.

Also without precedent was the large amount of time spent at meetings of librarians in discussion, criticism, and evaluation of the Inquiry reports prior to their publication. Thus, at the August 1949 annual conference of the University of Chicago Graduate Library School, the entire week of meetings was devoted to a systematic review both of seven of the special studies and of the director's general report (then available in first draft form). Critiques of each report were presented by a professional librarian and a non-library expert, respectively, in the field related to each study; the author then was given an opportunity to respond. During the following three months, at seven regional library conventions held in various parts of the country, special or general aspects of the Inquiry reports were presented and discussed at more than seventy sessions.

The Chicago conference papers were published in 1950 by Columbia University Press, with Lester Asheim as editor, in a volume entitled *A Forum on the Public Library Inquiry*. In a summary chapter, Ralph Munn (q.v.), director of the Carnegie Library of Pittsburgh, concludes that the Inquiry

> has made clear our status in relation to the other media of mass communication. It has defined for us our potential groups of users. It has suggested methods by which we can integrate ourselves in the body politic. It has recommended new and improved methods of operation. It has outlined aims and objectives which are attainable. But above all it has given us facts. May we have the courage to use them boldly in revising our course.

Leigh's general report of the Public Library Inquiry, *The Public Library in the United States*, also was published in 1950 by Columbia University Press, in a series that made available in separate volumes six reports of special studies by individual staff members. In his review of the Leigh report in *Library Quarterly* (April 1951), Carl B. Roden (q.v.) stated that "the Public Library Inquiry was an impressive undertaking, well planned and exceedingly well carried out." He called it "the most exhaustive and comprehensive survey of the public library from the external viewpoint of the intelligent observer thus far available." More than a quarter century later, this characterization still holds. Meanwhile, the general report has been immensely influential in the reformulation of public library standards, in the development and implementation of the concept of larger units of service, and in the provision of new perspectives for the education of librarians.

In undertaking this project, Leigh had returned once again to Columbia University, where the officers of the School of Library Service had provided office space and library services for the Inquiry's research staff and director. By 1950, when the work was nearing completion, he had become deeply immersed in national library concerns and especially interested in the problems of graduate library schools as they moved through a period of transition in degree structure, curriculum revision, and accreditation standards. When invited to become a visiting professor at the Columbia School of Library Service, he found many reasons for accepting. Not least was the School's location in New York City, in close proximity to the center of the communications industry.

In collaboration with Alice Bryan, a psychologist on the School's faculty and author of the personnel

study for the Inquiry, Leigh developed and taught a section of a new, required course in public communication and the library. From 1950 to 1952, he served as director of a communications study for the Russell Sage Foundation, assisted by Alice Bryan. Together they were instrumental in founding the Columbia University Seminar in Public Communication, with Leigh serving as the first chairman. Drawing on his Inquiry studies in education for librarianship (published by Columbia University Press in 1952 as a section in Bryan's book *The Public Librarian*), he conducted a seminar for advanced students on that subject and edited a volume of their reports published by Columbia University Press in 1954 under the title *Major Problems in the Education of Librarians*. He found time as well to conduct a survey of librarian education in California.

During these post-war years, the Columbia library school had moved toward establishment of a new degree structure and had instituted a program of advanced studies leading toward a doctoral degree. Its status and independence as a graduate professional school were strengthened by separation of the position of dean from that of director of the University libraries and by making each a full-time assignment. When Carl M. White, who prior to this change had held the dual position and thereafter the deanship, resigned in 1954, Leigh was requested and agreed to serve as acting dean. So effective was his leadership and so evident was the high regard in which he was held by faculty, students, and alumni that, in 1956, he was appointed dean of the Columbia University School of Library Service. He held this position until reaching the age of mandatory retirement in 1959, when he was appointed dean emeritus.

Leigh's contributions during his five-year administration, a period of great activity and significance in the history of the School, were described in considerable detail in the November 1959 issue of its *School of Library Service News*. He organized and directed a comprehensive faculty study of the first-year curriculum, which culminated in a basic revision of the master's degree program; he facilitated development and administration of the new D.L.S. program by establishing a standing committee on the doctorate that met regularly under the chairmanship of a faculty member; he revitalized the work of the other standing committees and encouraged a vigorous program of research and publication.

Leigh kept the faculty in touch with the field by drawing to the School visiting library administrators and specialists from the metropolitan area and beyond; he involved the alumni, many of whom held positions of leadership in the profession, in planning with faculty and students for the welfare of the School. Continually in demand for services to the library profession, he served as chairman, member, or consultant of official commissions and committees to study and report on public library service in New York state, on librarian education in New Jersey, and on formulation of standards for public libraries in New York, California, and the country at large.

Shortly before Leigh's retirement as dean of the Columbia school, Mildred Leigh, his wife and companion for 43 years, died unexpectedly on May 19, 1959. In September, he attended a reception at the School at which he was the guest of honor, and the faculty and staff presented him with a hand-somely bound volume of letters from colleagues and former associates. He expressed pleasure at the presence of his successor, Jack Dalton, who had been his first choice for the deanship, and his own satisfaction that he was leaving the School in good hands.

Soon thereafter, he left New York to begin a comprehensive survey of public and school libraries commissioned by the governor of Hawaii, in which he was aided by Professor Carolyn Crawford, a specialist in school library work on the faculty of the University of Hawaii. The first volume of Leigh's report, dealing with organization and government and entitled *Governor's Study of Public and School Libraries in the State of Hawaii*, was published in Honolulu by the Department of Public Instruction in 1960. He did not live to see publication of his proposed second volume. In a very favorable review of the first volume in *Library Quarterly* (January 1962), Harold Hamill begins by noting that "any publication which bears the name of Robert D. Leigh as author is of more than passing interest to a profession lastingly enriched by his many contributions."

On October 22, 1960, Robert D. Leigh married Carma Zimmerman, librarian of the California State Library, and became a resident of that state. Three months later, at the age of seventy, he suffered a heart attack while arriving by plane at Chicago's O'Hare Airport to attend the ALA Midwinter Conference. He died several days later, on January 31, 1961, at the American Hospital in Chicago. At this conference he was to have been formally named director of the ALA's State Library Standards Project, a fifty-state survey financed by the Carnegie Corporation.

Robert Leigh's career was unique in that he was equally gifted and successful in teaching, administration, and research; equally at home in the academic world, in government service, among fellow social scientists, and in library circles where, in his later years, his activities were centered. He was an articulate, urbane, and stimulating teacher; a forceful, democratic, and humane administrator. The reports of his research investigations were widely praised as models of painstaking, judicial, and significant institutional analysis. Most characteristic of his personal qualities were his civility in discourse, unfailing kindness to colleagues and students, and boundless enthusiasm for work.

To Lucy M. Crissey, one of his most valued staff assistants at the Columbia School, he was above all else a very interesting human being. In the May 1961 issue of its *School of Library Service News*, she wrote:

> The range of his interests was wide, embracing . . . such diverse subjects as art, baseball and tennis, the opera, theatre, and the movies. In any group he could find common ground for stimulating conversation, to which he brought humor and the flavor of his own personality. . . . Adept in the art of communication, he shared his enjoyment with others, adding much to their pleasure and profit. Among his friends and colleagues perhaps the recollection of Dr. Leigh's zest is as good a memorial as anyone could want.

Biographical listings and obituaries—Crissey, Lucy M. "Robert D. Leigh" [Obituary]. *School of Library Service News* 22:3 (May 1961); *Current Biography* (1961); *Leaders in Education*, 2nd ed.; [Obituary]. *College and Research Libraries* 22:221 (May 1961); [Obituary]. *Library Journal* 86:775 (Feb. 15, 1961); [Obituary]. *New York Times*, Feb. 1, 1961, p. 35; [Obituary]. *Wilson Library Bulletin* 35:662 (March-April 1961); *Who Was Who in America* IV (1961-1968); *Who's Who in Library Service*, 3rd ed. **Books and articles about the biographee**—Asheim, Lester, ed. *A Forum on the Public Library Inquiry*. New York: Columbia University Press, 1950, pp. 170-71; Bryan, Alice I. *The Public Librarian*. New York: Columbia University Press, 1952, pp. 299-425; Bryan, Alice. "Robert Devore Leigh." *School of Library Service News* 20:1-4 (Nov. 1959); Gesheidle, Gertrude E. Review of *A Forum on the Public Library Inquiry*. *Library Quarterly* 21:219-23 (July 1951); Roden, C. B. Review of *The Public Library Inquiry*. *Library Quarterly* 21:129-33 (April 1951); "Tall House and Robert D. Leigh." *Hawaii Library Association Journal* 17:1-2 (May 1961).

—ALICE I. BRYAN

LESTER, ROBERT MacDONALD (1889-1969)

Robert MacDonald Lester was born in Center, Alabama, on November 7, 1889, to the Reverend Samuel Robert and Ann Virginia Watson Lester. He received one A.B. degree from Birmingham-Southern College in 1908 and another from Vanderbilt University three years later. He was a Buhl fellow in the classics at the University of Michigan (1911-1912) and received an M.A. from Columbia University in 1917. Besides Birmingham-Southern (1931), he was later honored with degrees from the University of New Mexico (1936), Tulane University (1940), Duke University (1941), St. Francis Xavier, Canada (1953), University of North Carolina (1958), University of Chattanooga (1960), University of the South (1943), and Acadia University, Canada (1933).

Lester's early career was in colleges and secondary schools, concluding with the superintendency of the Covington, Tennessee, schools from 1919 to 1921. For the next five years, he was at Columbia University in the Department of English, instructing in the college, serving as administrative officer for undergraduate men, and as assistant to the director of university extension. He also served as a private in World War I, and prior to that, on January 30, 1915, he had married Memory Aldridge. Their one son was Lester's namesake.

A self-styled "philanthropoid," Lester became assistant to the president of the [Andrew] Carnegie [q.v.] Corporation of New York in 1923, and was secretary from 1934 until 1954. He served as associate secretary (1947) and secretary (1949-1954) of the Carnegie Foundation for the Advancement of Teaching. From 1954 until his death in 1969, he was executive director of the Southern Fellowships Fund.

Lester's work at the Carnegie Corporation included the writing of numerous progress reports and summaries, and his rapport with librarians and other educators led to his being invited to speak at their conferences and write for their publications. Among these varied items are *A Thirty Year Catalog of Grants...* (Carnegie Corporation, 1942); *Getting and Forgetting an Education*, the 1936 commencement address at the University of New Mexico (Volume 9, Number 4, of the University *Bulletin*); notes for an informal talk to the American Library History Round Table in Miami, Florida, on June 19, 1956, entitled "The Carnegie Corporation and the Library Renaissance in the South"; and "What about the Library?" (*Library Journal* 71:843-47, 908-909 [June 15, 1946]).

As secretary to the Foundation during the presidency of Frederick Paul Keppel (q.v.), Lester maintained a close rapport with the library field, attending conferences of the American Library Association and other library groups, making note of potential leaders, and commenting on library developments with a critical but avuncular air in his memoranda for the Corporation. Keppel maintained a demanding office schedule of short interviews with scarcely a break between them, and Lester customarily dealt with the details of grants and projects. He worked closely with Carl H. Milam (q.v.), who was ALA secretary and later executive secretary in that period, and with William Warner Bishop (q.v.) of the University of Michigan, who was for a long time associated with the Corporation's program of support for college libraries and who also regularly sought aid for international library programs. Lester was a preliminary sounding-board for those seeking Keppel's support, a tart critic of some of their proposals, and a sharp observer and evaluator of programs that received funds. His role as critic became even more important

after Keppel's retirement, because he was the Foundation's best-informed staff member in the area of librarianship. As the Foundation offered its support to other kinds of programs as well, Lester also became more critical of library programs. He was always skeptical of those who thought too readily about seeking Foundation funds, and commented once to the New Jersey Library Association: "The glamour of having received a foundation grant has more than once caused a recipient and his work to be regarded as far more important than the results of his project justified."

He was especially aware of ALA's contribution to library development. In that same New Jersey talk in 1946, he described the ALA's role as he saw it: "A great central professional association . . . representing the combined efforts and ambitions of its scores of allied groups and its thousands of individual members, has given an incredible strength, dignity and force to the library movement."

Lester left the Corporation to direct the Southern Fellowships Fund, a program established by the Council of Southern Universities to administer grants to encourage recruitment and training of young persons of high caliber for possible faculty appointments at educational institutions in the region. In this position, he also had some influence on library developments. He died February 21, 1969. However, in his own review of the decade 1926-1936, he refers to the Carnegie Corporation's "notable ten-year library service grant, for financing the [American Library] Association, for transferring library schools to university auspices, and for many strategic library demonstrations," which suggests that he considered that to be the time of his major activity and contribution to librarianship.

Biographical listings and obituaries—*Who Was Who in America* V (1969-1973). **Primary sources and archival materials**—*Appreciations of Frederick Paul Keppel, by Some of His Friends.* New York: Columbia University Press, 1951; Archives of the American Library Association. Chicago, Ill.; Archives of the Carnegie Corporation of New York; papers of Carl H. Milam, Jamaica, Iowa (home of Mrs. Wm. A. Seidler, Milam's daughter).

—PEGGY A. SULLIVAN

LEYPOLDT, FREDERICK (1835-1884)

Frederick Leypoldt was born November 17, 1835, in Stuttgart, Germany; his name was originally Jakob Friedrich Ferdinand Leupold. He was the son of a prosperous butcher who hoped that young Friedrich would help in the shop and carry on the business. However, the boy was romantic by nature, fond of literature and the stage, and quite unwilling to live in his father's way. Finally, at the age of nineteen, he was permitted to seek his fortune in the United States. Arriving in New York, he found work in the foreign bookstore of F. W. Christern, also a German. For the rest of his life, Leypoldt was to be part of the book world, always involved in bookselling and in the publishing of books and periodicals; his bibliographic publications constituted the primary record of American book production of his time.

In 1867, Leypoldt married Augusta Harriet Garrigue, fourteen years younger than he, Mrs. Christern's niece. His young bride helped him improve his English, and in later life, she was a great help to him in his bibliographic work. The couple had five children; Mrs. Leypoldt and three of the children survived the father of the family. Leypoldt's death at the age of 49 was widely attributed to overwork and worry; he had certainly worked night and day for many years and his almost continuous financial difficulties were sufficient to justify despondency. The immediate cause, however, was "brain fever," which would now be diagnosed as meningitis or encephalitis.

Although Leypoldt is mainly remembered for his bibliographic publications and the founding, with R. R. Bowker (q.v.), of what is now the R. R. Bowker Company, he was at first a bookseller and then a general publisher before concentrating on the work that made him famous.

After two years in Christern's employment, young Leypoldt returned to Germany with the thought of pursuing a career in the book industry there. However, he found Europe less congenial than the United States, and, on his return to this country, Christern re-employed him. Yet, the two men disagreed fundamentally about bookstore management, and in 1859, Christern helped Leypoldt open his own bookstore in Philadelphia, with books in several languages. The business prospered until the Civil War made importing difficult and expensive.

Leypoldt then turned to publishing as a sideline and became noted for the artistic format of his volumes. He began to publish foreign-language grammars and readers, editing some of them himself under the semi-transparent pseudonym of F. Pylodet. Leypoldt established a branch in New York City in 1864, and soon he moved his entire operation there. In the next year, a young graduate of Yale University, Henry Holt, offered him a manuscript that he had to refuse. However, the young man was interested in becoming a publisher and had some ready cash, so Leypoldt took him into partnership. The firm of Leypoldt and Holt, dating from January 1866, was not as deeply in debt as Leypoldt had been before.

Leypoldt and Holt continued to issue translations and texts for language study, but Leypoldt soon found that he most enjoyed the preparation of the firm's *Literary Bulletin*, a monthly record of current foreign and American books. This publication, after some changes of name and a merger, became *The Publishers' Weekly* in 1873. Meanwhile, Leypoldt had sold his interest in the publishing house; the firm was one of the ancestors of the present Holt, Rinehart and Winston. Around 1868 or 1869, Leypoldt seems to have begun to give full time to his bibliographic enterprises, and his withdrawal from the connection with Holt seems to have been complete by 1871.

Several bibliographic projects grew out of *Publishers' Weekly* and its predecessors. The first to be of general usefulness was *The Publishers' Trade List Annual*, essentially a binding together of the current catalogs of American publishers; it first appeared in 1873 as *The Uniform Trade List Annual*. Leypoldt's was not the first such compilation in the United States, but it was the first to approach completeness, and the only one to continue for any length of time. A far more ambitious and useful publication was *The American Catalogue*, an attempt to list, alphabetically, all of the books currently available from American publishers. After years of work and great expense, it appeared in final form in 1880 and 1881. Leypoldt was the first publisher of *Index Medicus*, in 1879; it was to be, for many years, the standard bibliography of current medical literature.

The undertaking of most interest to librarians was *The Library Journal*, first published by Leypoldt as *The American Library Journal* in 1876, with Melvil Dewey (q.v.) as managing editor. Dewey had planned such a publication in Boston, but Leypoldt and his young associate R. R. Bowker had also considered a separate journal for librarians. The idea may have been mainly Dewey's, but Leypoldt took all financial responsibility and lost money from the start, partly because of a financial arrangement almost unbelievably favorable to Dewey. Even though Dewey agreed, later, to a reduction in his income as editor, the *Journal* had lost about $2,400 by 1880, and Leypoldt was persuaded by business associates to discontinue it. However, the outcry from librarians was so loud that Leypoldt quickly started it up again, and it has continued to this day.

Another of Leypoldt's efforts on behalf of librarians is less well remembered and perhaps less significant: the publication of several books and pamphlets, in the years just before his death, most of them selected lists of good reading. The first of these was a *Reading Diary of Modern Fiction* (1881), which he personally compiled; among the others were *Books for the Young*, compiled by Caroline M. Hewins (q.v.), then the librarian of the Hartford, Connecticut, Library Association, and *Library Aids*, by Samuel S. Green (q.v.), the librarian of the Worcester, Massachusetts, Free Library. Green's *Library Aids* was a revision of an article published elsewhere; Leypoldt added other reprinted material and expressed the hope that this would be the first of a series of library annuals; he was not to have the opportunity to carry on the idea because he died within a year of the book's publication.

Clearly Leypoldt was interested in libraries, but it is difficult to determine with any exactitude what he thought about them. His *Publishers' and Stationers' Weekly Trade Circular*, beginning with the issue for January 18, 1871, carried occasional factual notes and articles about libraries. Three years later, in the January 10, 1874, issue of its successor, *The Publishers' Weekly*, news items began to be gathered in a "Library Corner." Thirteen such columns were printed through January 1875, averaging eight or nine items apiece. A few months later, a similar department, "Library and Bibliographical Notes," was started. After Leypoldt's death, Melvil Dewey claimed to have suggested the last-named column, probably unaware of the existence of Leypoldt's earlier articles about libraries.

It is difficult to separate the ideas and the published work of Leypoldt and Bowker; they were closely associated from 1873 on, and Bowker had done some writing for Leypoldt earlier than that. A few letters indicate that Bowker and Dewey were mainly responsible for the management of *Library Journal.* A printed notice was sent to *Library Journal* subscribers, at the time of its financial crisis in 1880, over the names of both Leypoldt and Bowker, wherein the writer described himself as a "friend of the library movement." Both men were certainly that.

Leypoldt was, of course, a friend of booksellers and publishers as well; he was widely respected for his unselfish contribution to the advancement of the book trade. However, his almost complete lack of business ability was often exasperating to those who held his interests most dear, his wife and close associates at *Publishers' Weekly*. He was a very affectionate person and his feelings were easily hurt; years after his death, a story was still being circulated about a string which he kept stretched behind his desk for drying handkerchiefs after emotional incidents. In appearance he was short, with a large moustache; in manner he was courtly and graceful. At least one friend thought he must surely have had some French blood. He died on March 31, 1884.

Biographical listings and obituaries—*Dictionary of American Biography* 6 (Anne S. Pratt); [Obituary]. *Publishers' Weekly* 25:435-40 (April 5, 1884); *Who Was Who in America*, Historical Volume (1607-1896). **Books and articles about the biographee**—Beswick, Jay W. *The Work of Frederick Leypoldt, Bibliographer and Publisher.* New York: R. R. Bowker, 1942; Bowker, R. R. "The Library Journal and Library Organization: A Twenty Years' Retrospect." *The Library Journal* 21:5-9 (Jan. 1896); Growoll, Adolf. "Frederick Leypoldt." In his *Book-Trade Bibliography in the United States in the XIXth Century.* New York: The Dibdin Club, 1898. (Also printed separately for the Dibdin Club in 1899 as *Frederick Leypoldt: Biographical and Bibliographical Sketch*, 15p.); Rider, Fremont. "The Origin and Early

History of the *Weekly.*" *Publishers' Weekly* 151:272-78 (Jan. 18, 1947). **Primary sources and archival materials**—The Bowker collection of papers at the New York Public Library includes some letters to and from Leypoldt; other letters mention him.

—HAYNES McMULLEN

LINDERFELT, KLAS AUGUST (1847-1900)

On May 22, 1892, the Executive Committee of the American Library Association voted to accept Klas August Linderfelt's resignation as ALA's president "to take effect from the time of [his] election" in 1891. The Committee then directed Secretary Frank P. Hill (q.v.) "to record William I. Fletcher [q.v.] as President for the entire term," thereby forever erasing the Linderfelt name from the official list of ALA presidents. How this curious set of circumstances came about was the result of a bizarre series of events that began with Linderfelt's April 28, 1892, arrest for embezzling funds from the Milwaukee Public Library.

Born in Sweden in 1847, Linderfelt lost his mother at the age of five, his father at the age of eleven. Despite these destitute beginnings, he earned a doctorate at Sweden's Upsala University, and by the time he immigrated to Milwaukee in 1870, he carried with him an impressive set of educational credentials. He quickly obtained his first job teaching classics at Milwaukee College, but shortly thereafter began to exhibit an active interest in libraries for the first time. When Milwaukee opened its new public library in 1880, Linderfelt applied for and was granted the job of chief administrator.

For the next twelve years, Linderfelt distinguished himself in both the library and the library profession. He wrote several articles on library economy, and in 1890, Charles Ammi Cutter (q.v.) published his *Eclectic Card Catalog Rules.* That same year, the trustees of the Milwaukee Public Library and Museum printed his report on a proposed new library/museum complex. It appeared that his years of personal research, his extensive correspondence with prominent librarians, and his tour of the major libraries of the East and Midwest would finally bear fruit. The building that Milwaukee finished in 1897 was largely the result of Linderfelt's efforts.

Linderfelt joined the American Library Association shortly after his appointment as Milwaukee's public librarian in 1880. He was an active and frequent participant at conferences, often exhibiting a willingness to speak on a wide range of library topics. He served as a councillor from 1883 to 1891, as vice-president from 1890 to 1891, and at the ALA's San Francisco meeting of that year, he was elected to succeed Samuel Swett Green (q.v.) as the Association's president.

On April 28, 1892, however, Linderfelt was arrested for embezzling funds from the public treasury. Initial investigations indicated that the librarian had absconded with approximately $4,000, but the manner in which he had obtained the money led Milwaukee's city accountant to pursue the investigation further. Several members of the Library's Board of Trustees began a campaign to restore the funds to the public treasury and reinstate Linderfelt as librarian. They were probably perplexed about losing the man who had been the driving force behind efforts to get Milwaukee a new library/museum building, especially since the efforts were far beyond the planning stages in 1892. The local press objected vehemently, and on May 3, one newspaper reminded its readers that, four years earlier, Linderfelt had been the subject of an investigation into the Library fines collection. But the investigation had been dropped in 1888, when two trustees reportedly contributed from their own pockets to cover the $2,000 shortage Linderfelt had accumulated over a three-year period.

In the meantime, the ALA Executive Committee had met informally and unofficially on May 2 at Frank Hill's house in Newark to discuss the effect of Linderfelt's plight on the Association's mid-May conference at Lakewood, New Jersey. Melvil Dewey (q.v.) had already suggested to William Frederick Poole (q.v.) that "the best way is to avoid any mention and apparent knowledge of the dreadful episode at our [Lakewood] meeting." Justin Winsor (q.v.) lamented that "it would be a pity to have notices respecting the coming conference go out with his name attached." The Executive Committee decided to follow Dewey's advice, and except for its own action of May 22, the official record of the conference bears no mention of Linderfelt's name.

Back in Milwaukee, Linderfelt's woes were multiplying. On June 24, the city accountant completed his investigations and found that Linderfelt had actually embezzled $9,095.06 since 1883, a total more than twice the sum for which he was initially suspected. (He had done so by a system of billing the Library twice for foreign purchases and pocketing the difference.) In addition, the investigation revealed that the librarian had used an unsuspecting Board chairman to cover another $500 theft in 1888. The disclosures quickly halted further efforts to have Linderfelt reinstated.

When Linderfelt's case was called on July 12, he entered a plea of *nolo contendere*. (Speculation was that he used the money to support an expansive style of living that his salary was inadequate to support.) His lawyer quoted freely from the numerous letters submitted in Linderfelt's behalf by prominent librarians, and remarked that Boston's Library Bureau promised Linderfelt a job, provided he was cleared of all charges and free from threat of further

prosecution. He then left his client at the mercy of the court. To everyone's surprise, the presiding judge rendered his decision immediately. He declared the plea was "virtually one of guilt," and announced that "sentence will be suspended." Linderfelt left for Boston that same afternoon.

The judge's decision shocked Milwaukee's citizens, many of whom immediately began agitating for Linderfelt's rearrest and return to Milwaukee. The city's newspapers were universal in condemning the decision, and on one occasion, two thousand Milwaukee citizens gathered at a local meeting hall to show their indignation. On July 18, the mayor ordered the district attorney to rearrest Linderfelt on any charge for which he had not yet been tried, but by this time the defaulting librarian was one step ahead of the authorities. He had already fled the country, thereby escaping further prosecution. Poole, who had watched the Linderfelt case from the start, remarked sardonically: "They let him off without punishment, and are now chasing him around the world to arrest him for another trial."

After a brief stay in Sweden, Linderfelt went to Paris to obtain a medical degree. Thereafter he was associated with *La Semaine Médicale* until his death on March 18, 1900. His legacy to librarianship—the building that houses the Milwaukee Public Library—still stands as a monument to his efforts, but the trail of his financial misdeeds has been largely forgotten by both the citizens of Milwaukee and the library profession.

Biographical listings and obituaries—[Obituary]. *Library Journal* 25:194 (April 1900). **Books and articles about the biographee**—[Article]. *Library Journal* 17:155, 184a-184b (May 1892); Gregory, John G. *History of Milwaukee, Wisconsin*, II. Chicago: The S. J. Clarke Publishing Company, 1935, p. 1186; "Librarians." *Library Journal* 17:250 (July 1892); Thomison, Dennis. "The ALA and Its Missing Presidents." *Journal of Library History* 9:362-64 (1974); Wiegand, Wayne. "The Wayward Bookman: The Decline, Fall, and Historical Obliteration of an ALA President." *American Libraries* 8:134-37 (March 1977) and 8:197-200 (April 1977); West, Theresa. *History of the Milwaukee Public Library*. Prepared for the Columbian History of Education in Wisconsin. Milwaukee: City Printer, 1890-95. **Primary sources and archival materials**—William Frederick Poole Papers, Newberry Library; George Watson Cole Papers, ALA Archives, University of Illinois; William S. Merrill Papers, Newberry Library; Historical Record Collection, Box 1, Local History Room, Milwaukee Public Library.

—WAYNE A. WIEGAND

LOCKE, GEORGE HERBERT (1870-1937)

George Herbert Locke was born in Beamsville, Ontario, March 29, 1870, the son of Joseph and Elizabeth Mackay Locke. Educated in the local schools, he then attended Victoria College, University of Toronto, where he took an honour B.A. in classics in 1893. He lectured in classics at Victoria College while working on his M.A., and after receiving this degree (1895), was awarded a fellowship in the College of Education, University of Chicago. His first term at Chicago lasted until 1897, when he left to spend two years teaching history and theory of education at Harvard. He returned to Chicago in 1899 as an associate professor at the College of Education. During his term at Harvard, he married Grace Isabel Moore, the eldest daughter of John Moore of Moore Park, Toronto. They had one son, Macalastair.

Locke remained at Chicago until 1905, having been appointed dean of the College of Education in 1903. For most of his years there, he also served as editor of the *School Review* (1900-1906), the leading journal of American secondary education of the time. He left Chicago the second time to become an assistant editor in the educational division of the Boston publishing firm of Ginn & Co., with whom he stayed until 1907.

From Boston he returned to Canada, to be dean of the School of Education, Macdonald College, McGill University. This was his last position in a "formal educational institution," although it was his contention that the profession he found himself entering in 1908 (librarianship) was equally an education profession, albeit of a co-ordinate status with the formalized, structured, curriculum-centered education of the schools.

In 1908, the Toronto Public Library needed a new director, and Locke was the final choice for the post. He spent nearly 30 years as director of the Toronto Public Library, taking over a small system with a staff of 26, an inadequate central building with 4 small branches, and an exceedingly small budget. By the time of his death on January 28, 1937, there was a staff of 232, a new central building, and 16 sizeable branches. There were also several children's reading rooms in the local settlement houses. This expansion was due, in no small measure, to Locke's own ability to attract funds and personnel from both Canadian and American sources.

George Locke came to librarianship with no formal training for the profession, and perhaps with no previous commitment to it, but he came with his own concept of what the public library stood for and what he felt it should try to achieve. Locke viewed the public library's chief function as the introduction of the pleasures of literature to the public at large. Again and again, in speeches made to librarians and trustees throughout Canada, the United States, and Britain, he argued for the public library's having a role in the process of continuing education, since it provides the means to allow an individual to realize his full potential in his own time, at his own speed.

In a speech given in Tennessee (April 1926), he said that librarians must first believe in their jobs and understand why their profession exists and has existed over time. One must, he declared, ask not only, "*What* is a librarian?" but also "*Why* is a librarian?" The librarian's background, he told his audience, is the entire field of knowledge, and the profession is as educational as the teaching profession, with the difference that librarians are not concerned with instruction, and no fixed boundaries of age or condition exist in the library's clientele. He felt that the public library had to be viewed as a social and educational institution, not only to give librarians a sense of professional direction, but also to give them a sound basis for argument with local boards when budgets needed increasing. When the Great Depression arrived, Locke argued even more forcefully that libraries had to demonstrate that they gave value for the monies they received, and during the 1930s, he was suggesting to both Canadian and American audiences that public libraries might establish "registers" of the unemployed who were actually reading in preparation for future work in a particular trade. Then, libraries might note on job applications that an individual had been trying to stay abreast of developments in his trade.

Elected to the presidency of the American Library Association for the 1926-1927 term, Locke spoke around the United States and elsewhere (for he was invited to be one of the principal speakers at the Jubilee Conference of the [British] Library Association in Edinburgh, 1927). He reiterated his conviction that the public library was a great, intellectual public utility, of immense importance to the continued well-being of the democratic state. As a part of his presidential address to the ALA, he said:

> The great task of this generation is to save democracy, to preserve it and to inspire it. We represent a great democratic institution which can furnish not only the material resources by which this may be greatly aided, but we are reaching out to furnish interpreters of these resources so that individuals may equip themselves for intelligent service ... and also that they may acquire the knowledge that will enable them to exercise a right judgment in all things.

Libraries could serve this purpose properly only if the resources that they were furnishing to their users were of "good" quality, Locke noted, and when he spoke to the New York meeting of the National Association of Book Publishers in 1927, he urged them to concentrate on the publication and sale only of "good" literature. He was disturbed by being offered an annual list of novels all priced identically, regardless of their individual worth, and memoirs and biographies that were so heavily padded by their authors as to leave them deadening. Such books, when purchased for libraries, usually died on the shelves, making the library little better than a cemetery for the publishers' output. So anxious was he to have people read not only good books, but books they liked, that he wrote two works of popular Canadian history himself: *When Canada Was New France* (1919) and *Builders of the Canadian Commonwealth* (1923).

During his year as ALA president, he grew concerned both about its size and about the steady removal of power from the office of the president. He felt that the then substantial membership of some 10,000 persons was too large to allow the holding of worthwhile annual meetings, and he therefore proposed the idea of having biennial meetings of the entire membership, with regional meetings in the alternate years. He further urged the extension of the president's term in office to two years, to keep the power of the office from being usurped by the permanent general staff. Since the library is a social institution, personal leadership was seen as necessary to the professional organization, and holding office for two years would give the president a better grasp of the problems of the ALA.

The director of the Toronto Public Library was as busy at home as he was abroad. He was instrumental in developing services to children in the Toronto system, and it was he who persuaded Lillian Smith to leave the New York Public Library and return to Canada to handle children's services in Toronto. Eventually, their efforts combined with others' in the development of the separate facility known as Boys and Girls House. Between them, they developed a system of training courses to prepare librarians for children's work, at a time when no professional library training was available in Ontario.

Besides the two books he wrote for his library clientele, Locke wrote for several of the major professional journals, such as *Libraries*, *Library Journal*, and *Illinois Libraries*, as well as the major Canadian library journal of his time, the *Ontario Library Review*. His work also appeared in the British publication *Nineteenth Century*, and he was supervising editor of many of the publications in the field of Canadian bibliography prepared and published by the Toronto Public Library while he was director. He found time to contribute to various educational journals in both Britain and the United States, and wrote the study of English history for the ALA's "Reading with a Purpose" series.

Styled as "Genial George" by some of his staff and colleagues, Locke was interested in and reached out into the Toronto community he served. He was their chief librarian, and as quick to fill in at "story-hour" as anyone on his staff, but he took his place in the community as well—especially in the university community in Toronto. He was a member of the American Association for the Advancement of Science, the Dominion Education Association, and

the Arts and Letters Club in Toronto. He also served on the Board of Regents for his alma mater, Victoria College. For his services to both the University and the community, the University of Toronto conferred an honorary LL.D. on him in 1927.

He came to librarianship as an educator, and remained an educator while being a librarian, but he did not view the two professions as separate suits of clothing; they were one, woven of the strong Irish tweed of his ancestors. His untimely death in Toronto on January 28, 1937, was marked in three countries, by three library associations, and by many non-librarians who appreciated his work. His close friend, Principal Wallace of University College, University of Toronto, wrote of him,

> his interest was in education in the broadest sense of the word, and specialized training in cataloguing or general administration would have seemed to him merely incidental. The result was that he knew very definitely what he believed a great city library should seek to accomplish. It must be a living educational force in the community, and his broad experience and scholarly acquaintance with educational problems had fitted him admirably to be the leader in what he regarded as one of the greatest of educational enterprises. He is an outstanding example of the truth that preparation for one's life work, especially if it is to be in the field of administration, should not be too narrowly specialized.

Biographical listings and obituaries—*Macmillan Dictionary of Canadian Biography*, 3rd ed. (1963); [Obituary]. *Bibliotekarz* 9:119 (Aug.-Sept. 1937); [Obituary]. *Library World* 39:193 (March 1937); *Who Was Who in America* I (1897-1942); *Who's Who in Library Service*, 1st ed. **Books and articles about the biographee**—Hill, Frank Pierce. "George Herbert Locke." *Bulletin of Bibliography* 15, No. 3:41-42 (April 1934); Morgan, Henry James, ed. *The Canadian Men and Women of the Time*, 2nd ed. Toronto: Briggs, 1912, p. 661; Wallace, Malcolm W. "Dr. George Herbert Locke." *Ontario Library Review* 21, No. 2:59-60 (May 1937).

—MARGARET ANDERSON

LOGASA, HANNAH (1879-1967)

Hannah Logasa was a major contributor to librarianship in the United States; as a pioneering school librarian, she brought books to teachers and students, and she compiled several unique and classic bibliographies, still widely used throughout American libraries. Her work as a school librarian began when she became the first librarian at the University of Chicago High School, a laboratory school where interest in experimentation was high. She demonstrated how the library could fit into the secondary school program, maintaining that the school library was "not an ornament in the educational process, but a necessity."

Many details of Logasa's early life are unknown. Her father, Seth, was a Russian immigrant who settled in Rock Island, Illinois, where she was born February 22, 1879, and where her two younger brothers and a sister were also born. Their mother, Ida Waterman, died when the children were young and, after their move to Omaha, Hannah helped in the small family grocery. She did not go to high school, but educated herself by reading. (She eventually won a Bachelor of Philosophy degree and a Phi Beta Kappa key from the University of Chicago in 1921.) She had an early scholarly interest in German literature, medieval history, the French language, Russian history, and Russian literature.

Logasa began her library career at the Omaha Public Library and Museum, entering service in May 1904 as a general worker at a salary of $25.00 per month. The following year, she asked for a leave of absence to attend the summer session of the University of Chicago. In 1906, she attended a summer school session in library training at the State University of Iowa. On November 1, 1910, she was named an alternate in the Circulation Department of the Omaha Public Library. Put in charge of statistical records and accounts, she earned a salary of $55.00 per month.

On March 10, 1914, librarian Edith Tobitt requested that the Library Board grant Logasa a leave of absence from May 16 to September 30 to attend the American Library Association Conference in Washington in May, to go to Europe for the intervening period, and to attend the British Library Association meeting in September. At the Washington conference, Logasa found a new job, and on May 21, 1914, she wrote to Mr. Stephens, secretary of the Omaha Public Library Board, saying she had accepted the position of high school librarian at the University of Chicago at a salary of $1,500 a year. She was sorry to sever her connection with Omaha Public Library and hoped she would not regret it.

Logasa began as librarian of the University High School of the University of Chicago on September 1, 1914, working under Charles Judd, head of the University of Chicago's School of Education. He was quoted as saying that when Logasa was hired in April 1914, he felt that she was a "growing woman," and she impressed him immediately. So, for the next 25 years, until her retirement in 1939, her efforts were turned toward the development of one of the pioneer laboratory school libraries. She was the first librarian there and highly successful, notably for her attitudes toward school library administration and public relations, as well as for publications on these topics.

At this time, there were no books on school libraries. Thus, Logasa had to proceed by intuition, although she knew of the work of a famous school librarian, Mary E. Hall (q.v.) of Brooklyn. Years later,

Logasa would publish *The High School Library: Its Function in Education* and other books to fill this gap.

She worked toward a library-oriented classroom. She tried to get students and teachers to the library, and she tried to help the poor reader and those with study problems by conducting reading guidance sessions. She published the widely used, innovative *Study Helps* for students, and the unique *Chicago Sustained Application Profile Sheet* to measure length of concentration. The latter was used in her conferences with students on their study habits, used by teachers in the laboratory school, and later published in *The Study Hall in Junior and Senior High Schools*, a book that showed her keen interest in the relationship between the school library and the study hall. The University of Chicago also published another experimental work, her *Tests for the Appreciation of Poetry*.

Logasa believed in publicity for the school library, and students in the library edited *The Daily Exhaust*, a bulletin-board "newspaper" intended to stimulate reading and interest in current events. To the first book fair ever presented in a school library, she invited speakers such as Thornton Wilder, as well as the librarian of the Chicago Public Library and the librarian of the University of Chicago. Students also gave book talks.

She organized a series of sessions on high school libraries at the annual conference of accredited schools at the University of Chicago on April 16, 1915, where the high school library was discussed at the general meeting, and fourteen section meetings were devoted to the importance of the library in relation to various subject areas, with illustrative exhibits. Mary E. Hall wrote that this was "one of the most notable meetings of teachers and librarians ever held."

She was a member of the National Education Association, the National Council of Teachers of English, and the American Association of School Librarians. She was on the National Education Association's Department of Secondary Education Committee on High School Libraries in 1915, and on the NEA's Library Department Committee on High School Libraries in 1917.

When Evangeline Colburn, a teacher, came to the University of Chicago in 1921 to establish the Elementary School Library there, she became a good friend of Hannah Logasa's, who was her "kindly supporter." Colburn writes: "All I find [in my records] is *more* evidence of her kindness and *selflessness*—a fine character. She did no advertising, but was recognized for her quiet efficiency." In 1940, at the University of Colorado in Boulder, when Logasa conducted her regular summer session in library work, Colburn gave a course in reading under Logasa's aegis.

In 1928, Hannah Logasa became an instructor at the University of Chicago, giving courses in education (library science) at the University's downtown campus. In 1929, she started conducting courses in library science for the University of Chicago Home Study Department, another pioneering effort. She started with one course, eventually had three, and carried on this work for over thirty years.

Logasa was highly professional in the best sense. In addition to her library and school duties, she produced several publications: *Biography in Collections* appeared in three editions; *Historical Fiction* in two, followed by six more editions in retirement (a seventh appeared posthumously); and *An Index to One-Act Plays* and its *Supplement 1924-1931* were followed by four more supplements. Along with these came her books on administration and many articles. All of her periodical articles are very objective, practical, and formal in tone. They reveal little of Logasa's personality, except for her passionate belief in the value of the school library to both teachers and students.

She was asked to be guest instructor at many schools, and apparently she enjoyed doing this. She began her peripatetic teaching with work at DePaul University (1927), went to the Riverside Library Service School (summers, 1929, 1931), the University of Washington (summers, 1936, 1937, 1939); the George Peabody Teachers College (summer, 1938; spring, 1941). In the summers of 1940 and 1941, she taught for the Department of Education, University of Colorado at Boulder, as noted.

Logasa retired from the laboratory school in 1939, at the age of sixty. That year's *Correlator*, the school's yearbook, contains a picture of her and mentions she is one of the senior class sponsors. Retirement, which to Logasa was only a technicality, hardly slowed her energetic pace. She went to live in Lincoln, Nebraska, and soon was engaged in work with the Teachers College Faculty of the University of Nebraska.

Hannah Logasa maintained her interest in the Omaha Public Library throughout her life. In March 1943, she wrote to the librarian of the Omaha Public Library, Bertha Baumer, asking about temporary employment there at a salary of 60 cents an hour. Both Baumer and Logasa agreed that it would be worthwhile for Logasa to spend some time getting ready for work as a substitute in the various library departments. Baumer wrote: "I do hope you will like Omaha well enough to make it your home and that there will be enough work to encourage you to continue to remain in our City. This fill-in-job will prove interesting, I am sure, if you can adjust yourself to the odd hours, etc."

Her bibliographies continued to appear. The third edition of *Biography in Collections* came in 1940; *Book Selection Handbook for Elementary and Secondary School* was published in 1953. (This eventually became *Book Selection in Education for Children and Young Adults* in 1965.) *World Culture* appeared in 1963, and her last bibliography, *Science for Youth*, in 1967. In addition, several articles appeared in *Social Studies*, *Phi Delta Kappan*, *Wilson Library Bulletin*, and *Library Journal*.

She also continued to accept guest teaching assignments, including positions at the University of Southern California in 1947, Florida State University in 1950, and Texas State College for Women in 1953.

Her friend Hazel Pulling, who knew her at Florida State University and Texas State College for Women, writes, "She was a good friend of mine—though no one ever got beyond the 'Miss.' Actually, she did not retire, which was part of her nature."

In 1953, when she was 74 and leaving teaching at Texas State College for Women, as well as giving up her extension work in Dallas and Fort Worth, she wrote to the Omaha Public Library for a part-time appointment as readers' advisor at the Omaha Public Library. Arthur Parsons replied on February 19, 1953: "We are quite proud of you as a former staff member who has made such a good name for herself in the Library profession," and said he wished to discuss the matter of a job with her but mentioned strict civil service rules about age. This unconcern about advancing years seems to have been typical of Hannah Logasa. She spent no time "counting herself to death." A. E. McKinley, Jr., one of her long-time publishers, mentions that he "did not have the pleasure of meeting her until 1963. I found her even at that time (in her eighties) a person with ideas and the drive to develop them."

She maintained a strong sense of humor, and among her hobbies were sports and writing poetry. She taught her two younger brothers and sister to play baseball, made speeches at University High School pep rallies, rooted for the Chicago White Sox, and acted as occasional coach of the University High School track team. She represented both the Library and the Athletic Department on the laboratory school's student council. Her lifelong charitable projects, quietly and modestly done, are cited by several of her friends and family. She was a long-time member of Hadassah.

In 1963, Hannah Logasa had a serious illness and was frail from that time on. Robert McMorris, a newspaper interviewer from the *Omaha World*, in a personal interview published after her death in 1967, described her as shy and retiring, and said that she tried to avoid publicity. She wore drab, mostly grey, clothing. McMorris describes her as frail and tiny—five feet tall and weighing only about eighty pounds.

She was very proud of her association with the University of Chicago, was kept on their faculty list until her death, and stipulated in her will that proceeds from her books were to go to the University. In her will, she also left $500 to the Omaha Public Library for the purchase of books, a final testimony to her lifelong loyalty to the institution where she had begun her career.

Hannah Logasa died in Omaha on December 11, 1967, just two months before her eighty-eighth birthday.

Biographical listings and obituaries—*Who's Who in Library Service*, 1st ed., 2nd ed. **Books and articles about the biographee**—[Biographical sketch]. *Library Journal* 72:999 (July 1947); McMorris, Robert. "Hannah Logasa: A Name to Remember." *Omaha World-Herald*, December 16, 1967; Pulling, Hazel A. "Hannah Logasa." *Bulletin of Bibliography* 22:1-3 (Sept.-Dec. 1956). **Primary sources and archival materials**—The following people, many of whom knew Miss Logasa personally, assisted the author: A. E. McKinley, Jr.; Hazel A. Pulling; Patricia Clatanoff; Evangeline Colburn; Mrs. J. R. DePencier; Ruth Logasa Wasserman; Mrs. Abraham Goldhammer; Elizabeth Hoffman, librarian of the University of Chicago High School Library; Patricia Bleick; Patricia Pond; Mrs. Lu Ouida Phillips; John Jamieson; and Beverly Heinle.

—IRENE P. NORELL

LUDINGTON, FLORA BELLE (1898-1967)

Flora Belle Ludington was born November 12, 1898, at Harbor Beach, Michigan, the daughter of Bertram Winslow and Ella Elizabeth Winterbottom Ludington. She started as a freshman in 1916 at Whitman College in Walla Walla, Washington, and completed her undergraduate work at the University of Washington, receiving an A.B. in library science in 1920. She attended the New York State Library School during 1921-1922 and was granted the B.L.S. from there in 1925, the same year in which her M.A. in history was conferred by Mills College. For many years she taught summer sessions in the library schools of the University of Texas (1930), San Jose [California] State Teachers College (1931), and Columbia University (1936, 1938, 1939, 1941, 1942, and 1943). Mills College awarded her the honorary Doctor of Laws in 1953, and she received the American Library Association's Joseph W. Lippincott Award in 1957. At the time of her retirement as librarian of Mount Holyoke College in 1964, the Alumnae Association of the University of Washington School of Librarianship selected her as Distinguished Alumna of 1964.

The citation from Mills College, honoring one of its graduates who had also been a member of its library staff for fourteen years, read: "Alumna of this college, and held in its affections; librarian who is a lover of learning as well as a custodian of books; leader in her profession at home and its honored representative abroad." This recognition by Mills

College, coming in the year of her presidency of ALA, marked the climax of a distinguished career. In a period of service spanning four decades as a college librarian, she was also a part of the library world's stand for intellectual freedom and the leadership taken by American librarians in developing library service in other countries.

But this was the later "F.B.L." Involved as she was to become in the professional library movement in the United States and in international librarianship, her consuming passions in life were always books and reading. Books, both as physical objects and as communicators of ideas, played a part in her life from the very beginning. The family moved west from Michigan, with a brief stay in Bonner's Ferry, Idaho, settling finally in Wenatchee, Washington, when Flora Belle Ludington was fourteen. As a high school student, she became a volunteer worker in the newly established library donated by Andrew Carnegie (q.v.) and had available to her more books than she had ever seen before.

Though she began her college studies at Whitman, she transferred to the University of Washington because of its undergraduate library science major. Two men there significantly influenced her intellectual and professional development—Vernon L. Parrington in the Department of English and William E. Henry, founder and dean of the School of Librarianship. After graduation, she spent a year on the staff of the University Library and was then encouraged to go east for further professional training. At the New York State Library School in Albany she studied under James I. Wyer (q.v.) and Jennie D. Fellows (q.v.). She did practice work at Michigan with William Warner Bishop (q.v.).

In 1922, she was appointed reference librarian at Mills College, California. By the time she left, fourteen years later, she was associate librarian and assistant professor of bibliography. At Mills, her personal and professional interests in reading, in books, and in rigorous intellectual inquiry coalesced and strengthened her professed role as librarian: to convey such interests to others. As a reference librarian, she encouraged students to read beyond class assignments. As a resident of one of the dormitories for seven years, she read aloud to students and taught them to delight in books.

She continued her own intellectual growth and discipline by embarking on an M.A. in history at Mills College, which she was granted in 1925. Her thesis title was *The Newspapers of Oregon: 1846-1870*. Here, she branched away from her literary interests to pursue the history and politics of a pioneer and frontier region.

Ludington was in the right place at the right time to become a part of the San Francisco Bay area group of book lovers, printers, and collectors: John Henry

Nash, the brothers Grabhorn, Albert Bender, Rosalind Keep, Aurelia Henry Reinhardt, Helen Gentry, and others.

Within the Mills library, Ludington developed special collections, mounted exhibits, and prepared catalogs for them. *Qvintvs Horativs Flaccvs: Editions in the United States and Canada, as They Appear in the Union Catalog of the Library of Congress*, edited by Anna C. Brinton and Flora B. Ludington (while not published until 1938, when she was at Mount Holyoke), was the product of the Horace Bimillenium Exhibit at Mills College. Mills also had its own press, the Eucalyptus Press, in which she was involved. Her own personal library contained modern first editions and copies of Grabhorn, Doves, and Kelmscott Press books.

In 1936, Flora Belle Ludington was appointed librarian of Mount Holyoke College, in South Hadley, Massachusetts. On the surface, it seemed a radical departure for this Eastern "establishment" women's college to turn to the West Coast, and a non-alumna, for this position. Mary Olivia Nutting and Bertha Blakely, the two previous librarians, had been both alumnae and New Englanders. However, Mills College was a daughter college of Mount Holyoke, and the Ludingtons came from New England stock.

Ludington quickly sensed the tradition in which the college was rooted and showed her own consciousness of the value of that tradition by rapidly immersing herself in Mount Holyoke's history. She responded to the fact that 1937 was Mount Holyoke's centennial year by indulging her own personal interests and talents in preparing an exhibit and catalog of *An Exhibition of One Hundred First Editions Paralleling the History of Mount Holyoke College*. Although Ludington's career was to become more and more absorbed by local, national, and international library matters, she maintained her membership in the Bibliographical Society of America and in 1955 wrote the foreword to the Parke-Bernet auction catalog of the Henry S. Borneman collection.

The late 1930s brought great changes to Mount Holyoke. The retirement of President Mary Emma Woolley and the controversial appointment of a man, Roswell Gray Ham, to replace her, coinciding with the retirement from the faculty of distinguished women scholars, signalled the end of an era. Flora Belle Ludington, energetic, dignified, confident, and a thorough professional, stood out among the new appointments to the faculty.

Her predecessor, Bertha E. Blakely, had recently completed a building program for the Library, so Ludington's own interests in collection building ideally suited the College's needs at that time. During her second year at Mount Holyoke, she undertook an extensive survey of the Library's collections and

involved the faculty in this process, which increased her awareness of the fact that a small college library simply could not afford to be self-sufficient.

Interlibrary cooperation and the sharing of resources, while not new ideas, were given new impetus by the financial stringencies of the times. Throughout the late 1930s, discussions, led by Fremont Rider (q.v.) of Wesleyan College with the librarians of Smith, Amherst, Mount Holyoke, and Trinity, explored the idea of the creation of a "regional library." The reports of the so-called "Connecticut Valley Plan," prepared under the direction of Newton McKeon of Amherst and Ludington, were lent by Wesleyan to libraries interested in cooperative enterprises. Though the wider regional plan was never implemented, the informal cooperative relationship that already existed among the libraries of Amherst, Mount Holyoke, and Smith was formalized in 1951 with the incorporation of the Hampshire Inter-library Center, Inc.: a research collection of highly specialized, little-used, serial publications. Ludington regarded the establishment of this cooperative venture as one of the most exciting and interesting library enterprises in which she had been engaged. Her estimate of its importance gains significance in the context of her participation in important national and international library affairs.

She joined the American Library Association in 1922 and was always an active member. Also a member of library organizations on the West Coast, Ludington expanded her professional involvement after her arrival at Mount Holyoke. She served for many years on the governing Council of ALA, with committee assignments as diverse as the Committee of a Code of Ethics for Librarians and the International Relations Board.

The latter assignment led to her chairmanship, during World War II, of the Special Committee on International Cultural Relations and to her personal participation in the overseas program of the United States Office of War Information. While on war leave from Mount Holyoke, she was the first director of the OWI's United States Information Library in Bombay during the years 1944-1946. Then, in 1948, she was in Japan as a Visiting Expert and Adviser to the Education Section of the Supreme Commander, Allied Powers (SCAP). She was a member of the ALA Committee on the Japan Library School, which was established at Keio University in 1951. The year 1957 saw her in Ankara, Turkey, on an inspection trip for the Ford Foundation of the Institute of Librarianship, and the Rockefeller Foundation gave her a travel grant in 1959 to observe library development in Africa.

During 1952-1953 and 1953-1954, Ludington was first president-elect and then president of the American Library Association. These were years of threats to intellectual freedom at home from the witch-hunting of McCarthyism and abroad from the propaganda of the Cold War. Ten years earlier, in a pamphlet entitled *Books and the Sword: Symbols of Our Time* (1943), she had spoken for the Association in condemning Nazi subversion of German libraries and librarianship for use as propaganda tools. During the year of her presidency, censorship and the right to free access to books were still concerns of the Association. Thus, in 1954, Ludington was in Munich and Berlin observing the work of Radio Free Europe and its "balloon offensive," and in America that same year, she participated in the Westchester Conference, which produced the "Freedom to Read" document.

During her tenure as president of the American Library Association, the position of Librarian of Congress became vacant with the retirement of Luther Evans. Ludington chaired the ALA Special Committee to Offer Its Services to the President on the Appointment of the New Librarian of Congress. The committee urged that the position be filled by a professional librarian rather than a political appointee and submitted a list of names to President Eisenhower; L. Quincy Mumford, one of the names on that list, became Librarian of Congress.

Integrating her Mount Holyoke responsibilities with her national and international roles was exacting and demanding. For Flora Belle Ludington, it took physical effort, courage, and an iron will. She was seriously ill following her return from India, and she was told she would never walk again. She did, but with a distinctive gait, the approach of which was easily recognized by all members of her staff. She never fully recovered her health during the rest of her life, though it was not until after her retirement in 1964 that her illness was diagnosed as multiple sclerosis. The three years after her retirement were spent in several hospitals and nursing homes. She died at the Chapel Hill Nursing Home in Holyoke, Massachusetts, on March 23, 1967.

Flora Belle Ludington was a formal person. Imperious at times, she demanded attention. Although of only average stature, her manner and bearing were such that her entrance into a room did not go unnoticed. She was an avid gardener who delighted in the natural beauty of the Connecticut Valley and never felt that spring had come until the trailing arbutus was in bloom. It is perhaps apocryphal, but it is said that she refused to be considered for a position as the head of a major urban library because she would not leave "the most beautiful copper beech in the country," which was outside her office window.

Arthur Ryan, retired editor of the *Holyoke Transcript and Telegram* and contributor to its "Oracle" column, wrote of Flora Belle Ludington as follows:

She had high social qualities. It was a delightful hour spent in her company as she told the story of

her latest venture in some distant part of the world, or closer to home. She was a vivid story teller and some of her ventures provided plenty of material for listeners to bear in mind for the rest of their days.

The text of the Joseph W. Lippincott Award sums up her achievements: "Miss Ludington has demonstrated a level of public and private statesmanship which should be both a deep source of satisfaction to her and a continuing challenge to all members of her profession."

Biographical listings and obituaries—*Current Biography* (1953); [Obituary]. *Library Journal* 92:250 (July 1967); [Obituary]. *Wilson Library Bulletin* 41:876 (May 1967); *Who's Who in America* 33 (1964-1965); *Who's Who in Library Service*, 1st ed., 2nd ed., 3rd ed., 4th ed. **Books and articles about the biographee**—Bevis, D. "Notable Alumna—Flora Belle Ludington." *Pacific Northwest Library Association Quarterly* 21:84-87 (Jan. 1957); Bevis, Dorothy. "Our Frontispiece: Flora B. Ludington." *Bulletin of Bibliography* 21:193-95 (Jan.-April 1956); [Biographical sketch]. *ALA Bulletin* 47:325 (July-Aug. 1953); [Biographical sketch]. *Publishers Weekly* 162:133 (July 12, 1952); "Flora Belle Ludington Will Retire in June." *Wilson Library Bulletin* 38:598 (April 1964); Johnson, Margaret L. "Flora Belle Ludington: A Biography and Bibliography." *College and Research Libraries* 25:375-79 (Sept. 1964). **Primary sources and archival materials**—Material by and about Flora Belle Ludington is held in the College History and Archives Collection of the Mount Holyoke College Library, South Hadley, Massachusetts. A complete listing of the published works of Ludington forms part of the Johnson article.

—ANNE C. EDMONDS

LUHN, HANS PETER (1896-1964)

Hans Peter Luhn was a pioneering engineer and consultant in information science whose ideas and innovations will be used in libraries for many years to come. Luhn was a pioneer in the development and application of automatic measuring and controlling devices, binary arithmetic systems, switching devices, serial binary computers, electronic information scanning, and storage and retrieval devices. He originated statistical methods for automatic indexing and for abstracting and matching literary information, and he has been referred to as the father of information retrieval.

Luhn was born in Barmen, Germany, on July 1, 1896, the son of Johann Peter and Emma Maria Kahle Luhn. His father was a leading printer, and Luhn was apprenticed early to a printer. He attended elementary and high school in Barmen, then studied briefly at the Schweizerische Handels Hochschule, St. Gallen, Switzerland (1914), returning later to take course work in technology, physics, and accounting (1918-1920). (He had served as a communications officer in the German Army from 1915 to 1917, with assignments in France, Rumania, Bulgaria, and Turkey.) In 1920, he began his long association with the textile industry, as assistant manager of a textile mill in Italy; then in 1923-1924, he was a freelance textile designer. Luhn arrived in the United States in 1924 and became a naturalized citizen nineteen years later. From 1924 to 1927, he was a financial secretary at the International Acceptance Bank on Wall Street in New York. He next became an assistant to the president of the Textile Machine Works in Reading, Pennsylvania (1926-1929), and from 1930 to 1933, he worked as an executive in Shamokin, Pennsylvania, for the Cellulose Products Corporation. In 1933, Luhn founded H. P. Luhn and Associates, New York, and worked as an engineering consultant through the firm until 1941.

In 1941, Hans Peter Luhn joined the International Business Machines Company, where he was a senior research engineer and then manager of information retrieval research in the Research Center and in the Advanced Systems Development Division. Luhn's introduction to the information science or documentation world came in 1947-1948, as a result of approaches by James Perry and Malcolm Dyson to IBM. They requested that an IBM machine be designed to search chemical structures coded according to the Dyson notation system, and Luhn was asked to work on the project. By 1953, Luhn was spending an increasing amount of time in information science. He pioneered in the application of data processing equipment to the bibliographical and information retrieval problems of libraries and documentation centers, and he was widely recognized for his contributions to the programs of professional organizations. After retiring from IBM in 1961, Luhn served as a consultant in business intelligence systems and information science. By this time, he had become an international lecturer, inventor, and traveller, well known throughout the information world.

After his death in 1964, the New York Chapter of the American Documentation Institute held an H. P. Luhn Memorial Meeting. In October 1965, the Delaware Valley Chapter of the American Documentation Institute gave its award for the best contribution of the year to H. P. Luhn, posthumously. Still later, ADI established an information science scholarship fund in his name.

Peter Luhn was a member of several professional associations: the American Association for the Advancement of Science, the Association of Computing Machinery, Association of Symbolic Logic, Deutsche Gesellschaft für Dokumentation, International Federation of Documentation, the Institute for Electrical and Electronics Engineers, Special Libraries Association, and the American Documentation Institute (now the American Society of Information Science). He was president of the latter organization for the last year of his life. In addition, he was a member of the advisory board of the School of Library Science at the University of Southern California (1959-1964).

Luhn preferred to communicate orally rather than in writing. However, his few writings were important in the field, though most of them were published originally as IBM technical reports discussing his current research and findings. Later, they were given wider distribution in other publications. Luhn was far more interested in contributions to the field than to its literature, and he wanted more to excite experimentation and action than to report formally. He also contributed to the field's terminology by more precise definitions of the terms used. When Carlos Cuadra studied key information science contributions, Luhn's name led all the rest on three of four listings of major contributions. He ranked fifth among the 25 highest scoring authors in terms of publication densities, and he ranked in the top ten of the most frequently cited authors in the field.

As program chairman for the 1963 annual American Documentation Institute Conference, Luhn edited the papers published in advance of the conference and made the resulting volume one of his most significant contributions. The papers were typeset automatically with the aid of electronic information processing equipment. This volume of technical articles, *Automation and Scientific Communications*, was probably the first to be produced in this manner.

Luhn had a wide range of engineering interests, from components to complete systems, from logical design to manufacturing processes. IBM gave him a great deal of freedom to follow up leads, whether or not they were related to current product development, and his work was characterized by the wide variety of his interests and the number of inventions he carried through to successful engineering models. Among his associates at IBM was Steve Furth, who helped sell Luhn's ideas both within and outside the company. Luhn always tried things out to learn how they worked and kept user needs constantly in mind. Means were economically balanced to ends, ends were regarded in the cold light of the law of diminishing returns, and common to all of his projects was his economy of effort other than his own. A recurrent theme in his work was that the problems of indexing language and meaning are at the crux of all information systems. At one point, Luhn had accumulated the largest number of IBM-assigned patents ever issued to an IBM employee.

Luhn was the first, or among the first, to work out many of the basic techniques now commonplace in information science: full text processing (essentially, using concordances as indexes); catch-word title indexing (now known as KWIC or key word in context, a name he invented); the use of statistical methods to produce mechanized indexes (auto indexing); automatic abstracting; the application of random superimposed coding (actually originated by others) for screening indexes; SDI, or selective dissemination of information (another Luhn coinage), where the profile (probably another Luhn term) of a person's interests is matched against the text or its index key words (as Luhn called them).

In many ways, Luhn was ahead of his time. Some of his ideas anticipated later developments in computer technology but were not considered practical at the time. Later, of course, advances in unforeseen directions made some of his specific inventions obsolete. Nevertheless, although not many of his numerous inventions were incorporated into IBM product lines, his constant flow of new ideas and fresh approaches to engineering problems challenged his associates to develop solutions that did reach production. His engineering contribution was primarily that of a catalyst stimulating others to higher creative effort.

Hans Peter Luhn was a sensitive, gentle, elegant man, well dressed, intelligent, articulate, and polite, with a great sense of fun. He had a happy, generous nature, and his concern for the welfare of other persons was well known. He was a member of local clubs in the Armonk, New York, area where he lived, and tennis, skiing, mountain climbing, and painting were his hobbies, as well as gourmet cooking and dining and stamp collecting. He was also always an enthusiastic promoter of information retrieval. He died on August 19, 1964.

Biographical listings and obituaries—[Obituary]. *Library Journal* 89:3718 (Oct. 1, 1964); [Obituary]. *Library of Congress Information Bulletin* 23:476-77 (Aug. 24, 1964); [Obituary]. *Special Libraries* 55:517 (Sept. 1964); *Who Was Who in America* IV (1961-1968). **Books and articles about the biographee**—Cuadra, Carlos A. "Identifying Key Contributions to Information Science." *American Documentation* 15:289-95 (Oct. 1964); Elias, A. W. "Peter Luhn." *American Documentation* 16:249 (Oct. 1964); Grosch, H. R. J. "Who's Yellow." *Datamation* 8 (Feb. 1962); Schultz, Claire K. *H. P. Luhn: Pioneer of Information Science, Selected Works.* New York: Spartan Books, 1968; Schultz, Claire K. "Luhn, Hans Peter." In *Encyclopedia of Library and Information Science.* Allen Kent, Harold Lancour, and Jay E. Daily, eds. New York: Marcel Dekker, 1975, Vol. 16.

—JOHN F. HARVEY

LUMMIS, CHARLES FLETCHER (1859-1928)

In addition to being "the most creative librarian in California history," Charles F. Lummis (Lum-mis) was poet, athlete, author, editor, columnist, publisher, recorder of folksongs, archaeologist, ethnologist, photographer, Casanova, pioneer conservationist, philanthropist, and founder of the Southwest Museum of Art, Science and History. And, without benefit of library training school, he made library history. Lummis was an aggressive, almost pugnacious extrovert. He was below average height, but, since he needed only four hours sleep daily, he customarily accomplished two days' work each 24 hours. An individualist in thought, action, and dress, he usually wore Indian jewelry, corduroy, and a cowboy sombrero, and he carried a flask. He lamented the fact that American men spend the major portion of their lives in the pursuit of wealth, as he believed that the making of friends was more worthwhile. A few of his friends included John Muir, Theodore Roosevelt, David Starr Jordan, Frederic Remington, Charlie Russell, and Charles Eliot Norton.

Lummis was born in Lynn, Massachusetts, on March 1, 1859, the son of Professor Henry W. and Harriet Waterman Fowler Lummis. As a boy, he overcame a distorted spine by means of a rigorous regimen of athletic exercises, and while in college, he participated actively in boxing, wrestling, long distance running, and canoeing.

Professor Lummis prepared young Charlie for Harvard (class of 1881) by starting him at Latin at seven, Greek at eight, and Hebrew at nine, along with history, literature, philosophy, etc. Upon his arrival at Cambridge, in 1877, he discovered that he had already read most of the books required during the freshman year. Thus he seemed to major in poker, poetry, and athletics, all of which he found useful on the frontier. Meanwhile, he earned part of his expenses by tutoring students in Latin and Greek and by selling more than 12,000 copies of his *Birch Bark Poems*. This unique book, printed on real birch bark, brought him letters of commendation from Longfellow, Holmes, Lowell, Whittier, Whitman, and others.

The miniature volume *Birch Bark Poems* came into being while Lummis was the printer at a resort hotel in the White Mountains of New Hampshire during the summer of 1878. Another outcome of this summer was his fathering of a child of whose existence he was unaware until she was a mature woman; when he toured New England, she read a story about him in a Boston paper and identified herself in a letter. When they met, he persuaded her to join his family in Los Angeles.

In 1880, Lummis was the first member of his class to marry when Dorothea Rhodes, of Chillicothe, Ohio, whom he had known over a year, became his wife. She was a handsome, talented woman with a strong personality, which made it possible for her to obtain her M.D. degree at Boston Medical College. She was also an accomplished poet and musician. After leaving Cambridge, the Lummises lived in Chillicothe, where he became the editor of the *Scioto Gazette*. Here he became fascinated with Indian artifacts, which abounded in the area.

While recovering from a bout with malaria, Lummis decided to visit the frontier so vividly described in books he read by Captain Mayne Reid, pioneer author of the Great American Desert. To do this he wrote Colonel Harrison Gray Otis, publisher of the fledgling *Los Angeles Times*, proposing that he would walk across the country, meanwhile forwarding a weekly letter reporting his observations and adventures, if a job on the paper awaited him on his arrival. After receiving a favorable reply, in the fall of 1884, he set out on his trek from Cincinnati to frontier Los Angeles. Paralleling the Santa Fe railroad, which was then under construction, he crossed eight states and arrived at Los Angeles on February 1, 1885. When he reached San Gabriel Mission on the last leg of his 3,500-mile journey, he found Colonel Otis waiting for him with a hamper of food and drink. Thus began a friendship of two strong personalities that extended over 30 years. The new friends walked the last ten miles of the journey to Los Angeles, and the next edition of the *Times* carried the story of Lum's arrival and his joining the staff of the paper, written by Colonel Otis. Shortly thereafter Lummis became the first city editor.

The new editor was amused to discover that before he was on the payroll, he had already increased the circulation of the *Times*. He also discovered that the once-drowsy cowtown had become a bustling city of 12,000 people (U.S. rank number 75), most of whom were newly arrived land speculators anticipating the completion of the Santa Fe railroad. The "Boom of the '80s" had already started. Culturally, the town was above Dodge City, but only slightly. A dozen years earlier, the last lynching was held, and later came the massacre of nineteen Chinese. The well-dressed man of that day carried a pair of six-guns and a knife in each boot. The town was run largely from the backrooms of saloons, and heavy drinking, unlimited gambling, and prostitution were rampant.

After two years of the hustle-bustle in the news room of a boomtown newspaper, Lummis suffered a massive paralytic stroke brought on by his puritanic habit of working 18 to 20 hours per day. To recuperate, he went to the San Mateo, New Mexico, sheep rancho of Amado Chaves, a friend he had met while hiking across the country.

Soon after his arrival at the Chaves rancho, Lummis followed his own prescription to combat paralysis: daily doses of hunting, fishing, and breaking wild horses. His recovery is recorded in his little book *My Friend Will* (1911). While at the rancho, he was the first person to photograph the Easter crucifixion re-enactment rites performed by the Penitentes religious cult. Although the cultists were intimidated by Lummis's revolver atop his camera, they engaged a gunman who trailed him to the Isleta Pueblo. A bullet fired from ambush by the assassin struck Lummis in the right cheek. The Pueblo school teacher, Eva Douglas, sent for Dr. Dorothea, and together they nursed him back to health, meanwhile becoming such good friends that Dorothea, who had been unable to bear children in ten years, agreed to divorce Lummis so that he might marry Eva. In time, she bore four children. Lummis dedicated *The Land of Poco*

Tiempo (1893), "To Eva and Dorothea." Among his books influenced by his stay in New Mexico were *A New Mexico David* (1891), *Some Strange Corners of Our Country* (1892), *A Tramp across the Continent* (1892), *The Spanish Pioneers* (1893), *The Man Who Married the Moon* (1894), *The Enchanted Burro and the King of the Broncos* (1897), and *Mesa, Canyon and Pueblo* (1897). He also wrote for the *Britannica* and *Americana* encyclopedias.

Upon returning to Los Angeles, Lummis accepted the editorship of *The Land of Sunshine* magazine in November 1894. He immediately converted this Chamber of Commerce publication into a first-rate, illustrated regional magazine whose staff of nationally known writers won him the respect of Eastern editors; and for 160 monthly issues, he was the magazine. Among his contributors were David Starr Jordan, Charles Warren Stoddard, Ina Coolbrith (q.v.), Edwin Markham, Joaquin Miller, George Parker Winship (q.v.), and Mrs. Jessie Benton Fremont.

Having decided to make a photographic study of the historic San Fernando Mission, he was shocked upon discovering the dilapidated condition of the abandoned relic. From this experience he evolved the California Landmarks Club to preserve historic buildings, chartered by the state in 1895. The Club preserved half a dozen missions.

Upon his election as librarian of the Los Angeles Public Library in 1905, a furor developed among the staff of sixty women, as he had not attended a library school and he was replacing a woman. His rejoinder was, "Isn't there a place for an author and a businessman in a library?"

In time the "Library War" subsided and Lummis swept through the undeveloped Library in its cramped quarters in the antiquated City Hall. Because little thought and money had been applied to the facility prior to his election, there was much to be done by the new librarian, who had imagination, energy, and the backing of the Board. He accepted the post on condition that each member of the staff should receive an increase in salary of $5.00 or more per month. Since they had been existing on peasant wages of $35.00 up, the monetary expenditure would not be monumental.

As a "new broom," Lummis made several major changes: creating a Department of Western History, which sought "to obtain the biographical data and a photograph of every man and woman of importance in the history of California up to date, gathered from them alive"; placing emphasis on the Reference Department as the "brain and marrow of the Library"; modifying the Dewey system; establishing a roof-garden reading room where smoking was permitted; strengthening the training school; establishing a *real* inventory; creating a label to be pasted on the spines of books by unqualified authors (it read: For later and more scientific treatment of this subject see so-and-so, with author and call number); advocating sabbaticals for the staff to visit other libraries; and acquiring considerable Spanish Americana, especially documents pertaining to the American Southwest.

Other improvements included: joining the American and California Library Associations; making banned publications such as the *Christian Science Monitor*, Mormon journals, and the writings of H. Rider Haggard available to readers; inserting expert reviews in new books; providing a public drinking fountain; utilizing display cases for the Library's new treasures (previously, it had had no treasures); introducing a mimeograph and a typist's chair; obtaining competitive bids for the purchase of library supplies; offering library cards to people in the city telephone directory; engaging pages, and insisting that they do the ladder climbing; branding valuable books L A P L on the fore-edge; providing guides to assist newcomers; and setting aside a room where the staff could prepare and enjoy warm meals. He made the Los Angeles Public Library first in circulation throughout the country. On March 10, 1909, the *Boston Transcript* stated, "There is no library publication today so interesting as the annual report of the Los Angeles Public Library." Lummis was librarian from 1905 to 1910, when he resigned after a tenure longer than any of his predecessors.

Among the many honors that Lummis attained, most prominent were: being knighted by King Alphonso XIII of Spain for having written *The Spanish Pioneers*; receiving the blessing of a Pope for his work in preserving California missions and espousing the sanctification of Padre Junípero Serra, who brought civilization to California; and receiving the Doctor of Literature from Santa Clara University. Also, he was life member of the American Institute of Archaeology, of the Hidalgos of America, and of the Hispanic Society of California. He was a member of the literary Sunset Club, the musical Gamut Club, the California Writers Club, and the Authors' League of America. At the Panama-Pacific Exposition in San Francisco in 1915, Lummis's paper "What's the Matter with California Literature?" was read. The Lummis Home is now a City and State Historical Cultural Monument.

One of Lummis's major contributions to librarianship has not survived. It was a "Rally of Librarians Who Are Nevertheless Human," which he founded and named The Bibliosmiles. This group of unbound librarians came into being at the 1906 ALA conference and convened during four later conferences. Those admitted included W. P. Cutter, John Cotton Dana (q.v.), Joseph F. Daniels, Margaret C. Dyer, Samuel S. Green (q.v.), Frederick H. Hild, Charles R. Dudley, F. K. W. Drury (q.v.), Harold L. Leupp,

Edward J. Nolan, E. L. Pearson (q.v.), G. W. Peckham, Purd B. Wright, James L. Gillis (q.v.), Adelaide R. Hasse (q.v.), Tessa Kelso, George Parker Winship (q.v.), and "Don Carlos" Lummis. The Bibliosmiles had all the paraphernalia of a well-organized society—a seal, a badge, a grip, a password, and a high sign. They had a national anthem, an official dew and a national flower. The password was "Cheer up, ALA," the official dew was California apricot brandy, the seal was an open book with the legend "Homo Sum—and then Sum." At their annual dinner, they joyously sang "My Dewey, 'Tis of Thee, Sweet Ex- of Albany," "On the Road to Carnegie, Where the Six Best Smellers Be," and other songs provided by Lummis. The motto for the Bibliosmiles was "To Keep the Bookdust Off Our Own Topshelves."

Lawrence Clark Powell wrote in his *California Classics Reread* on Lummis's philosophy of librarianship:

His concern was with every aspect of the library—its housing and technical equipment, its collections, its reference services, staff organization and welfare. Many of his progressive ideas are fully applicable today. To understand his library, he visited other libraries throughout the country, attended library conferences and was recognized as a worthy colleague by leaders of the profession. His exciting, sensible annual reports can be profitably read today by library students, as well as by practicing librarians. There is no memorial to him in the library he led, and yet the record shows that in those few years he proved to be the most creative librarian California has ever known.

Following his resignation from the Library in 1910, he continued his editing and writing, but he never completed his autobiography or the history of California upon which he was working when he accepted the post of librarian. He died November 25, 1928.

Biographical listings and obituaries—*Dictionary of American Biography* 11 (John C. Parish); *Who Was Who in America* I (1897-1942). **Books and articles about the biographee**—Bingham, Edwin R. *Charles F. Lummis: Editor of the Southwest.* Huntington Library (1955); "Charles Fletcher Lummis." In John D. Bruckman, *The City Librarians of Los Angeles.* Los Angeles: Los Angeles Library Association, 1973, pp. 32-37; Gordon, Dudley. *Charles F. Lummis: Crusader in Corduroy.* Los Angeles: Cultural Assets Press, 1972; Gordon, Dudley. "Lummis: Aggressive Librarian." *Wilson Library Bulletin* 45:399-405 (Dec. 1970); Gordon, Dudley. "Lummis: Founder of the Bibliosmiles." *California Librarian* 22:17-22 (Jan. 1961); Gordon, Dudley. "The West's Incomparable Don Carlos." *Harvard Alumni Bulletin* (Oct. 14, 1967). **Primary sources and archival materials**—The bulk of Lummis's papers are at the Southwest Museum. Other collections are at the Huntington Library, University of California (Irvine), Occidental College, and the Los Angeles Public Library.

—DUDLEY GORDON

LYDENBERG, HARRY MILLER (1874-1960)

An intense commitment to the world of books and scholarship, a prodigious and catholic knowledge of and memory for books in all their aspects, together with sharp intelligence, uncommon energy, a flair for detail yet a keen sense of the important, and the drive and persistence born of early struggles as a fatherless boy who had to make his own way, combined to form in Harry Miller Lydenberg one of the best and most respected librarians of his day. There was hardly a facet of scholarly librarianship that Lydenberg was not interested in and did not contribute to in an important way, and he was a leader, along with John Shaw Billings (q.v.) and Edwin Hatfield Anderson (q.v.), in the creation of one of the world's great research libraries.

Lydenberg was born in Dayton, Ohio, on November 18, 1874, the first child of Wesley Braxton and Marianna Miller Lydenberg. Wesley Lydenberg died in 1879 at the age of 38, leaving his wife and small children—Harry, Walter, and baby Miriam (who died a few months afterwards)—with little more than his Civil War rifle and saber (which Harry Lydenberg gave to the Ohio Historical Society Museum in 1956). The jobs that Harry Lydenberg took as a boy to help his mother keep the family in genteel poverty were in a sense apprenticeships for his life work. His newspaper route drew him into the paper's press room and gave him an early familiarity with printing, and while attending Central High School (from which his father had graduated first in his class), he worked as a page in the Dayton Public Library. At Harvard, which he attended on a Bowditch Scholarship from 1893 to 1896, he worked in the University Library during the three years he took to complete the four-year course. Besides an A.B. *magna cum laude*, which he received with the class of 1897, he earned highest honors in history and government and election to Phi Beta Kappa and managed to find time to row on the Charles River.

As of July 1896, he was taken on at the Lenox Library in New York City as a probationary cataloger, which was changed to a permanent appointment the following fall. The Lenox Library was a privately endowed collection of rarities and Americana that had the year before merged with the Tilden Trust and the Astor Library, an endowed general reference library, to form the New York Public Library, which was eventually to become a unique, mammoth dual system, one part dedicated to reference and research, the other to circulation and community services. The new director, John Shaw Billings, was on the lookout for promising young librarians to help him transform the Astor and Lenox Libraries into a unified research library of first rank. At a time when other libraries were also on the verge of expansion and capable young men and women

with library experience were at a premium, Harry Lydenberg's potentialities were quickly recognized, both at the New York Public Library and elsewhere. He soon had responsibility at the Lenox for classifying and arranging books and compiling bibliographies and, in 1897, took charge of the manuscript collections. To prevent him from being enticed to another library, Billings raised his salary and then, in 1899, promoted him to the new position of assistant to the director. When Edwin H. Anderson came in 1908 to be assistant director, Lydenberg was appointed reference librarian (chief of the research collections). Upon Billings's death in 1913, Anderson, thirteen years Lydenberg's senior, succeeded to the directorship; in 1928, Lydenberg was named assistant director, and in 1934, upon Anderson's retirement, director, a position he held until his own retirement in 1941. He met his wife at the New York Public Library: on January 23, 1912, the small, quiet, spare bachelor of 37, who lived with his mother and spent his evenings working at the Library, married Madeliene Rogers Day, whom he had known for fourteen years. From 1914 to 1941, they lived in Scarsdale, New York, where they raised their two children, John and Mary.

Lydenberg performed various duties at the New York Public Library, including organizing the move in 1911 to the monumental new central building on 42nd Street and Fifth Avenue. Later, as assistant director and then director, he had many administrative responsibilities. He is most remembered, however, for his many-sided and passionate concern for the research collections. In this he was carrying on and enhancing a heritage passed to him by such great collectors as Wilberforce Eames (q.v.) and Billings, especially the latter, whom he virtually worshipped. For over thirty years, Lydenberg was the dominant influence in the Reference Department (the original name of the Research Libraries), presiding over its development during what may be called the golden age of the New York Public Library, when it had few competitors in prestige and size.

Lydenberg's consistent attention to acquisitions resulted in a three-fold increase in the holdings of the Reference Department, from nearly a million books and pamphlets at the end of 1907, just before he was named reference librarian, to nearly three million (including uncataloged materials and films) at the time of his retirement in 1941. This quantitative accomplishment constituted, in a research library, an impressive qualitative achievement as well: a balanced, comprehensive, broad-ranging assemblage of research materials, including unusual collections and materials on subjects that academic research libraries did not at the time commonly acquire. The scope and extent of these resources are described in Karl Brown's detailed *Guide to the Reference*

Collections of The New York Public Library (NYPL, 1941). Evaluations by nationally known authorities of local and national library resources during the 1930s and 1940s also testify to the strength and excellence of the research collections of the New York Public Library, both in an absolute sense and in relation to other research libraries, many of which had more money to spend as well as faculty members on hand to help select books.

In amassing such myriad resources, Lydenberg conceived that he was creating a cumulative record of human endeavor for use by future as well as present generations. He saw each acquisition, however small or seemingly trivial in itself, in its historical context and in connection with other documents, as part of a grand and ever growing structure of potentially useful information. The universality of his collecting was a conscious expression of his sense of responsibility to posterity. This approach was implemented in a program of prompt, systematic identification and acquisition of out-of-print books, pamphlets, documents, serials, and continuations through purchases, gifts, and exchanges on a global scale. In this process Lydenberg drew upon the competencies of the chiefs of the divisions of the Reference Department and indeed infused the whole establishment with his concern for completeness. At the same time he kept a constant, close watch over all the collections to insure that everything of significance was acquired.

After the First World War, when the book trade had been disrupted and revolutionary political and economic changes created a need for documentation that Lydenberg was keenly aware of, he himself went abroad on behalf of the Library. His mission was to buy materials, study the book market, and establish and re-establish contacts with governments, institutions, and booksellers. Nearly three out of the five months in the fall and winter of 1923-1924 that he was in Europe he spent in Eastern Europe and post-revolutionary Soviet Russia; in Riga, Moscow, and Petrograd he was joined by Dr. Avrahm Yarmolinsky, chief of the Slavonic Division of the New York Public Library (with his wife, the poet Babette Deutsch). Their considerable efforts enabled the Library to build its Slavonic Division into a leading resource in its field. Besides conducting his library business (often under difficult, time-consuming conditions), Lydenberg looked up people for friends and staff members, noted conditions meriting action by American Library Association committees and other groups at home, and made speeches to librarians anxious for information about American libraries. Though not able to speak any of the Slavic languages, he managed everywhere with French or German, and for a conservative, middle-class, middle-aged American on his first trip abroad, was remarkably sympathetic to the problems and the cultures of the struggling peoples that he observed with his curious eye. He appreciated French cooking, Dutch painting, Russian expansiveness, and German desperation.

Lydenberg's zeal for collecting went beyond systematic acquisition of materials to the pursuit of special collections and potential donors. Among the many collections acquired during his administration, perhaps the most distinguished were the Berg Collection of English and American Literature, the additions to it of the Howe and Young Collections, and the Phelps Stokes Collection of American Historical Prints. He also encouraged Karl Küp, adviser (or curator) of the Spencer Collection, in his worldwide travels to find beautifully illustrated and bound books for that rare assortment of treasures. Holdings in ephemera and nonbook materials, including the new Theater Collection and Picture Collection, were also greatly developed in Lydenberg's time.

His liberal, expansive acquisition policies (belying the conservatism of his nature and his politics—he always voted Republican), together with his reverence for learning and his personal research interests, helped to set a style for the Reference Department of the New York Public Library. It was almost like a learned academy, a community of scholars and bibliographers committed to research and learning—for themselves, for their profession, and in behalf of their readers. The staff was encouraged to do scholarly work in the form of bibliographies and substantive research, much of which was published in the *Bulletin of The New York Public Library*. This journal, started by Billings in 1897 and guided by Lydenberg for some forty years, has been characterized as one of the great bibliographical enterprises of Lydenberg's day, furnishing as it did access to the collections not only of the New York Public Library but of other libraries as well. Lydenberg also either personally answered or supervised answers to numerous letters of inquiry that came to the Library, replies that demonstrate the man's conscientiousness, scrupulous scholarship, and high ideals of service. Also, in the interest of accessibility to collections in a library whose books stood mainly in stacks closed to the public and were rarely loaned outside the building, he worked through the years on revising and extending Billings's shelf classification and the subject headings in the great public card catalog, for which, following Billings's practice, he for years would select periodical articles to be indexed. In 1912, again to improve convenience of use, Lydenberg had installed in the Reference Department a Photostat machine, one of the first in any library, for readers wishing to make copies of materials.

Lydenberg was as interested in the form as in the content of books. He cultivated warm relations between the New York Public Library and the publishing community and fostered high esthetic, editorial, and technical standards for the substantial printing and publishing programs of the Library. At his invitation, the American Institute of Graphic Arts each year opened its annual Fifty Books show at the Fifth Avenue building, and in 1935, the Library inaugurated the Richard Rogers Bowker [q.v.] Memorial Lectures in concert with the R. R. Bowker Company to serve as a forum for discussions of problems common to authors, publishers, librarians, and readers. Lydenberg's early comprehension of the gravity of the problem of preserving library materials put the New York Public Library in the forefront of efforts to deal with it systematically. With John Archer, superintendent of the Printing Office, he devised a laboratory to carry out experiments in the preservation of paper and books. The fruit of their thinking and experience was presented in *The Care and Repair of Books*, which was published by Bowker in 1931 and went into four editions. Lydenberg was also instrumental in convincing newspaper publishers to contribute to his program of treating newsprint with Japanese tissue, then to issue rag editions for libraries, and finally to microfilm their files; he also experimented with microfilm and then adopted it as a means of preserving materials and saving space.

In his concentration on collections in all their aspects, Lydenberg complemented his close associate and chief, Edwin Anderson, who focused on administration, especially staff development. From the time he was appointed assistant director in 1928 to help the aging Anderson until his retirement in 1941 after seven years as director, however, Lydenberg had to occupy himself with library-wide administration, including the branch system (the Circulation Department), where he had never worked, and during a difficult period of economic depression and then the onset of the Second World War. Though his inclinations and interests were scholarly, his belief in the value of libraries to aid and stimulate the creation and communication of knowledge extended to the popular library, which he conceived as crucial for the cultural and intellectual growth of the community. Collections and services expanded under his administration, including a number of innovations; a pension system was finally adopted for the staff; and the Circulation Department managed to hold its own and even to open three new branches, including the Nathan Straus Branch for children and young people.

Lydenberg's administrative style was informal and practical. He operated on a personal basis, before the time of job descriptions and rigorous budgeting procedures and when a staff's devotion, like his own, might be counted on regardless of low salaries. While not particularly interested in the details of management and leaving much of the day-to-day administration to the excellent and experienced chiefs of the Reference and Circulation Departments, he usually knew what was going on and saw to it that his subordinates carried out their responsibilities effectively.

The Board of Trustees considered him irreplaceable and his loss (from time to time seemingly threatened by offers of important directorships elsewhere) irreparable, a prospect they tried to prevent through a salary increase and promotions. With the death in 1932 of Lewis Cass Ledyard, Board president and longtime trustee, came unusual acknowledgement of Lydenberg's value. In addition to two million dollars for the Library, Ledyard bequeathed to Lydenberg (as well as Anderson) $40,000 in "grateful appreciation" for "devoted and efficient service" and "loyal and faithful co-operation" in the Library's interest (Lewis Cass Ledyard, Jr., to H. M. Lydenberg, August 2, 1932, Lydenberg Papers, NYPL). When Lydenberg wanted to retire at the age of 65, the trustees persuaded him to stay on for a year and a half more, but for no longer. He thought he should make way for younger leaders and fresher viewpoints, and he was determined to leave while still healthy and vigorous. Besides the numerous letters sent to him on the occasion, his retirement, effective October 1, 1941, was marked by a *Festschrift*, *Bookmen's Holiday*, published by the New York Public Library in 1943 as a surprise to him. After his departure, he deliberately kept out of the Library's affairs, but he remained interested in and always felt close to his "beloved NYPL" (HML to Anderson Friends, January 14, 1947, Lydenberg Papers, NYPL), his "first love . . . and life work" (quoted in DCM, *Library of Congress Information Bulletin* 19:196-97; April 18, 1960).

His New York years had encompassed much more than service to that institution. He had been involved in almost every significant effort in the United States to improve and expand access to library resources for scholars, including, for example, the first *Union List of Serials in the United States and Canada* (1924-1926), of whose Advisory Committee he was chairman; the first *Census of Fifteenth Century Books Owned in America*, printed in 1918 and 1919 by the New York Public Library for the Bibliographical Society of America; and the completion of Joseph Sabin's (q.v.) *Bibliotheca Americana*. In the American Library Association, of which he was elected president for 1932-1933, he was active on committees concerned with foreign acquisitions and the promotion of union lists and bibliographies, was involved in national planning for libraries, and served, in 1938, on a special committee chosen to suggest, in vain, a candidate for Librarian of Congress. At his initiative, the National Bureau of Standards undertook research in the early 1930s on environmental effects on books and other records. Other organizations in which he took a leading part were the Bibliographical Society of America (of which he was president for 1929-1931), the American Council of Learned Societies (which he served as secretary-treasurer for 1937-1941), the Typophiles, American Antiquarian Society, American Philosophical Society, American Institute of Graphic Arts, and the New York Library Club (of which he was president for 1917-1918). He was a founder of the Association of Research Libraries and of the Joint Committee on Materials for Research (of the Social Science Research Council and American Council of Learned Societies) and a charter member of the Committee on Conservation of the United States National Resources Planning Board. He participated in surveys of the libraries of the University of Pennsylvania and the American Academy of Arts and Sciences and, from 1929 to 1933, taught library history at the School of Library Service of Columbia University.

Throughout the years, Lydenberg was also usually working on some piece of research or writing. Besides numerous articles, reviews, reports, and anonymous contributions to the *Bulletin of The New York Public Library*, he translated from the French two books by André Blum, *On the Origins of Paper* (Bowker, 1934) and *The Origins of Printing and Engraving* (Scribner, 1940), and wrote and edited several books himself. Among these were: *History of The New York Public Library, Astor, Lenox and Tilden Foundations* (NYPL, 1923); *John Shaw Billings . . .* ("American Library Pioneers, I"; ALA, 1924); *The Care and Repair of Books*, with John Archer (Bowker, 1931); *Paper or Sawdust: A Plea for Good Paper for Good Books* (New York, 1924); *Archibald Robertson, Lieutenant-General, Royal Engineers; His Diaries and Sketches in America, 1762-1780* (NYPL, 1930); and *Crossing the Line: Tales of the Ceremony during Four Centuries* (NYPL, 1957).

Lydenberg retired from the New York Public Library just before the United States entered World War II; always interested in the international aspects of librarianship and ready to serve his country, he spent the next five years in international work. On October 22, 1941, he sailed for Mexico City to take up the position of director-librarian of the new Biblioteca Benjamin Franklin. A forerunner of the United States Information Service libraries, it was sponsored by the Coordinator of Inter-American Affairs (an agency of the United States government) and the American Library Association and was governed by an American-Mexican Board of Directors. The goals of the library, which had also the cooperation of the Mexican government, were to disseminate information about the United States and about American library techniques, to improve United States-Latin American relations, and to ease interchange of publications between Mexico and the United States.

In August 1943, Lydenberg left Mexico for Washington to direct the new International Relations Office of the American Library Association. Stationed at the Library of Congress, he planned and organized the work of the Office, which in various ways laid the basis for the library and bibliographical programs later sponsored by Unesco. In the course of developing programs to aid foreign libraries and to spread information about American research and scholarship, he travelled extensively in Latin America and worked with governmental and international organizations and scholarly associations. He also at times served at conferences and otherwise as the Washington representative of the American Library Association, and Archibald MacLeish, Librarian of Congress, would consult him about problems at the Library of Congress, where, from 1940 to 1946, he held the position of honorary consultant for planning the collections. Then, for the first six months of 1946, he went to Europe (mainly Germany) as a member of the Library of Congress Purchasing Mission. At the age of 72, he moved tirelessly around war-ravaged Germany—just as he had after the First World War when he had perceived signs of the second war that was to come—reopening contacts, assessing the publishing and library situations, acquiring books and journals, and wearing out his younger colleagues with his energy.

At the end of October 1946, Lydenberg gave up active library work (though not service on various committees). After travelling some and then living in Gatlinsburg, Tennessee, he and his wife settled, in June 1947, in Greensboro, North Carolina, where he continued his researches, served on the public library board, and tended his garden. In 1956, the Lydenbergs went to live in Westerville, Ohio, near their daughter and her family, where, after suffering for several years the effects of a serious stroke, Harry Lydenberg died on April 16, 1960, in his eighty-sixth year.

In his later years, Lydenberg had received a number of honors. In 1949, the American Library Association, in which he held honorary membership, presented him with the Joseph W. Lippincott Award for notable achievement in librarianship; he was made a Cabellero del Orden del Sol de Peru in 1947; the Sociedad Cientifica Antonio Alzate of Mexico elected him an honorary member; and he was awarded honorary degrees by five educational institutions, including Yale and Columbia Universities. He also enjoyed active membership in several elite clubs in New York and Washington and had participated in the civic life of Scarsdale, serving from 1922 to 1933 as town assessor, from 1928 to 1940 as secretary of the Board of Trustees of the public library, and for many years as a Westchester County grand juror.

His personal life was simple, frugal, home-centered, and, like his temperament, quiet. His wife and mother (who lived with his family and died at age 95) were deeply involved in Methodist church and mission activities, an interest he did not particularly share, though he did go to church regularly. He was well known for walking whenever he could. Besides his pleasure in it, walking saved money, something he, the self-made man who had to support his family on a librarian's salary, never could forget. Other pastimes were gardening (including vegetables stored in a root cellar for the winter months) and mountain climbing. For years, he and several librarian friends (including Keyes Metcalf, Charles C. Williamson [q.v.], and Paul North Rice [q.v.]) would hike regularly in the Catskill Mountains, talking libraries all the time. Most of Lydenberg's book collecting propensities were satisfied at the New York Public Library, but he did buy for himself accounts of New World and Old West explorations and first editions of Mark Twain, whom he much admired—perhaps an indication of the ironic strain in the man upon whom honors rested, if not lightly, then casually.

Though Lydenberg remained modest and self-effacing, impressions reinforced by his small stature and unprepossessing appearance, it was through unpretentiousness rather than humility. He was not above offering to wash the dinner dishes for his Russian hostess in Kiev just as he did at home, and he did not stand on ceremony or rank. But he had a sense of his own worth and competence; he knew who he was and where he was going. His energy, dynamism, and ability to follow projects through to completion, calmly and quietly, were extraordinary, as were his lucid mind and unfailing memory. He had the knack of doing several things at once: talking on the telephone, signing letters, checking periodicals, and carrying on a face-to-face conversation, all in an unflustered, deliberate, but expeditious manner. He was a good committee man, skilled in collaborative enterprises and tolerant of different ideas and personalities. Yet, in his understated way, he was very much his own man. Albeit sympathetic and considerate, he was not overtly warm or outgoing; he was reserved, or as some have put it, austere. He demanded much of himself, and by example, of others, and he could be tough and hardheaded when necessary. But his brown eyes under bushy brows and behind metal rimmed glasses could be twinkling as well as piercing; he had a sly sense of humor and a kind heart. He influenced and inspired many men and women at the New York Public Library and elsewhere, some of whom became leading librarians themselves. Friends, colleagues, and staff members not only respected him enormously, they liked him immensely. He was, they felt, a great man, a rare combination, as the Bibliographical Society of America [*Papers* 54:129 (April-June 1960)] noted at his death, of "ability and humanity."

Biographical listings and obituaries—*Dictionary of American Biography*, Suppl. 6 (forthcoming) (Phyllis Dain); *National Cyclopaedia of American Biography* 49; [Obituary]. *College & Research Libraries* 37:308-310 (July 1960) (Keyes D. Metcalf); [Obituary]. *New York Times*, April 17, 1960; [Obituary]. *New York Tribune*, April 17, 1960; *Who Was Who in America* IV (with incorrect death date); *Who's Who in Library Service*, 1st ed., 2nd ed., 3rd ed. **Books and articles about the biographee**—*Bookmen's Holiday: Notes and Studies Written and Gathered in Tribute to Harry Miller Lydenberg.* New York: The New York Public Library, 1943. [Includes George L. McKay, "A Bibliography of the Published Writings of Harry Miller Lydenberg" (pp. 5-26, which has omissions]; Brown, Karl. "H. M. Lydenberg." *Library Journal* 85:1870-72 (May 15, 1960); Dain, Phyllis. "Harry M. Lydenberg and American Library Resources: A Study in Modern Library Leadership." *Library Quarterly* (Oct. 1977); Evans, Luther. "The Little Man Who Isn't Here: *or* The Caboose That Pushed the Streamliner." *Library Journal* 72:152-54 (Jan. 15, 1947); Freehafer, Edward G. "Harry Miller Lydenberg, 1874-1960: A Tribute." *Bulletin of The New York Public Library* 64:295-97 (June 1960); Fulton, Deoch. "Harry Miller Lydenberg, 'A Man Joyous and Stimulating to Know.'" *ALA Bulletin* 47:145-47 (April 1953); Fulton, Deoch. "Harry Miller Lydenberg, 1874-1960." *ALA Bulletin* 54:668-70 (Summer 1960); Mearns, David C. "H.M.L." *Library of Congress Information Bulletin* 19:196-97 (April 18, 1960); Stam, David H. "A Bibliography of the Published Writings of Harry Miller Lydenberg, 1942-1960." *Bulletin of The New York Public Library* 64:298-302 (June 1960), which supplements McKay, above, in *Bookmen's Holiday*; Dain, Phyllis. *The New York Public Library: A History of Its Founding and Early Years.* [New York]: The New York Public Library, Astor, Lenox and Tilden Foundations, 1972; Lydenberg, Harry Miller. *History of the New York Public Library.* New York: The New York Public Library, 1923. [The last two works have information on the development of the New York Public Library during Lydenberg's first fifteen to twenty years there.] **Primary sources and archival materials**—The Lydenberg Papers in the New York Public Library Manuscript Division, 1919-1960, consist of correspondence and other documents relating to his non-New York Public Library activities and personal life. The Library's archives contain much Lydenberg material, as do the minutes of the Board of Trustees and its committees, the *Bulletin of The New York Public Library*, the *Annual Reports*, and various Library publications. Material relating to Lydenberg's Washington days may be found in the American Library Association's archives. Lydenberg himself supplied many details of his life in Harvard College. Class of Ninety-Seven. *Fiftieth Anniversary Report.* Cambridge (Mass.): Printed for the Class, 1947. Many former colleagues of Lydenberg supplied information about him in interviews, as did his son, John Lydenberg, who also kindly allowed some private papers to be perused. Information about Harry Lydenberg's Harvard years was verified in *Secretary's First Report, Harvard University Class of 1897.* Cambridge, Mass.: [1900?].

—PHYLLIS DAIN

MACDONALD, ANGUS SNEAD (1883-1961)

Trained as an architect, but destined to devote most of his career to the manufacture of bookstacks, Angus Snead Macdonald has had a more profound effect on the way libraries look and function than most librarians. Ralph Ellsworth, in the dedication of his book *Planning the College and University Library* (Boulder, Colo., 1960), wrote, "To Angus Snead Macdonald, originator of most of the new ideas in library planning."

Macdonald was born in Louisville, Kentucky, on November 7, 1883, one of five children of Allan Lane and Fannie Burnley Snead McDonald [sic]. His father moved to San Francisco when Macdonald was about twelve years old. His mother was the daughter of Charles Scott Snead, the founder of Snead & Company, manufacturers of iron products. In his late childhood, Macdonald and his family lived with his uncle, Udolpho Snead, president of Snead & Company at the time. Macdonald was educated at the Louisville Male High School (later the University of Louisville) and the Columbia University School of Architecture. Shortly after his graduation from Columbia in 1905, he joined the family business, serving in various capacities before becoming president in 1916. He was president until the company was dissolved in 1952.

Snead & Company had specialized in architectural and ornamental iron since its founding in 1849. It supplied the iron work for a number of government buildings constructed in Washington, D.C., in the latter part of the nineteenth century. It was the successful bidder on the large multi-tier bookstack contract for the new Library of Congress in 1891. Employing the patents of Bernard Richardson Green (q.v.), engineer and later superintendent of the Library, Snead & Company quickly became a leader in the new specialty—manufacturing and erecting bookstacks and related equipment. Under Macdonald's leadership, the company gradually moved away from Green's relatively heavy, fixed, and ornate designs to a product that was lighter, simpler, and much more flexible. Too, Macdonald is generally credited with improving lighting and ventilation for bookstacks. He introduced the first continuous concrete floor in bookstacks, and developed the "convertible stack," which permitted the substitution of small office and reader spaces for book shelves and supports. He also was responsible for a complete redesign of Green's book conveyor. Joseph Wheeler (q.v.) has said of Macdonald, "No one has ever done so much for the important matter of housing books effectively.... He was always ready to help others without profit for himself."

From the latter part of the nineteenth century to 1952, Snead & Company supplied bookstacks for hundreds of libraries in the United States and abroad (franchises were authorized in England, France, and Australia). Its major contracts included several installations for the Library of Congress (1891-1937), the New York Public Library (1905), and Harvard University's Widener Library (1915). In the 1920s,

Snead furnished stacks for the libraries of the universities of Illinois and North Carolina, and for the Vatican; and in the 1930s, for Columbia, Northwestern, and Yale University libraries. The firm also erected the tower stacks at the universities of Rochester (1931) and Texas (1932) and supplied the compact storage facility in the Midwest Interlibrary Center (1952, later the Center for Research Libraries). During the latter half of the nineteenth century, Snead's plant was located in Louisville, Kentucky, but shortly after the turn of the century, it was moved to Jersey City, New Jersey. In 1937, the company opened a branch in Orange, Virginia, and closed the Jersey City facility at the conclusion of World War II.

Macdonald was genuinely concerned that libraries were failing to serve as popular educational centers, so he believed they must be made more attractive and easier to use in order to achieve their full potential. Prior to World War II, large libraries in the United States generally separated readers and books. The books were housed in efficient multi-tier bookstacks (many of which were built by Snead & Company), and the library users sat in grand, high-ceilinged reading rooms. The card catalog and the library staff served to bring books and readers together. In his pioneering article "A Library of the Future" (written in 1933 as a contribution to a *Festschrift* for Wilhelm Munthe and reprinted in *Library Journal*, December 1 and 15, 1933), Macdonald pictured an entirely different library, one in which readers and books mingled freely. The imaginary library was, above all, comfortable, attractive, and highly flexible. It featured relatively low (eight-foot) ceilings, and artificial illumination and ventilation to provide year-round comfort in its large interior areas. Stack, office, and reader spaces were completely interchangeable.

During the 1930s and early 1940s, Macdonald continued to talk, both publicly and privately, about what he later called the modular library. In the closing years of World War II, he worked closely with Ralph Ellsworth in planning a new library building for the University of Iowa. In 1945, he published "New Possibilities in Library Planning" (*Library Journal*, December 15, 1945). Again, he argued for a flexible building that was well lighted and fully air-conditioned. Such a building was to be based on a cluster of regular prisms of space, or "modules," which, as he said some years later, "involves more than rows of regularly spaced columns.... The term is not purely physical, it should be directed by a philosophy which aims toward removal of constrictions on library functions and provides for future expansion." Macdonald's article was well timed to stimulate a new approach in the post-World War II building boom for libraries.

To demonstrate the feasibility of modular library construction, and in spite of war-time steel shortages, he built a two-story model on the grounds of Snead & Company, near Orange, Virginia, in the spring of 1945. The model was inspected by many librarians and architects who were planning to build as soon as conditions permitted. Julian Boyd, then librarian of Princeton University, described the model as "an exciting landmark in library architecture." During the months immediately following World War II, Macdonald and other members of the staff of Snead & Company crisscrossed the country hoping to attract new business for the firm and, at the same time, promoting the modular concept of library construction.

It is ironic that at the time Macdonald was most successful in presenting his ideas for a new type of library, he lost control of the company. Conversion to a peace-time economy was difficult for many American firms, but in the case of Snead & Company, it proved fatal and left Macdonald somewhat embittered. He believed that the company was the victim of an unusual combination of circumstances, intrigues, and tardy payments on government contracts. Whatever the cause, the manufacturing facilities of Snead were acquired by the Winfield Corporation in 1946, and the plant soon became the property of Virginia Metal Products. The sales and engineering departments of the company were reorganized and continued until 1952, relying on the manufacturing facilities of Globe, Wernicke and other metal fabricators. Financial and legal difficulties arising out of the Midwest Interlibrary Center contract provided the final blow. The small remaining assets and good will were sold to Globe, Wernicke in 1952. From 1952 to 1955, Macdonald served as an independent consultant to librarians and architects. In 1956, at the age of 73, he formed Everdure, Inc., a continuation of his ASM Corporation. This company has specialized in the treatment and manufacture of wood fencing and related products.

In the years between the end of World War II and Macdonald's death in 1961, the vast majority of larger libraries built in the United States (and many of those built abroad) incorporated his ideas. Gone were the enormous staircases, the monumental reading rooms, and the separate, multi-tier bookstacks. The new buildings featured regularly spaced columns, free-standing bookstacks, and much greater flexibility than hitherto had been possible. (Some recent critics see a return to the monumental, but in a different context.) Although many forces for change were at work during the 1930s and 1940s—changes in public taste, technological advances, curriculum modifications, to name a few—Macdonald's ability to anticipate these changes and synthesize them into a meaningful plan for library design is indeed remarkable. While not all of Macdonald's ideas were adopted (his blending of structural and ventilation systems was largely rejected by architects, for instance) he was, nonetheless, very effective both in developing these ideas and in persuading the library community to adopt them. These latter endeavors were abetted by an often charming personality, an admirable reputation as a builder of high-quality bookstacks, and the opportunity and energy to travel widely. Alfred Morton Githens (q.v.), noted library architect, has written, "Most types of [building] plans gradually evolve, but the principles underlying this were thought out by one person [Macdonald]."

His published writings include almost two dozen articles and pamphlets that have appeared both at home and abroad. He wrote almost exclusively for library and architectural periodicals. Two of his most important articles are referred to above, but other significant contributions include "Library Lighting" (*Library Journal*, March 1, 1931); "Some Engineering Developments Affecting Large Libraries" (*ALA Bulletin*, September 1934); "The Library Bookstack," in Joseph L. Wheeler (q.v.) and Alfred Morton Githens, *The American Public Library* (Chicago: American Library Association, 1941); *Morrow's Library* (Orange, Va.: Privately printed, 1948); "Libraries Unchained" (*Library Journal*, January 15, 1953); and "Building Design for Library Management" (*Library Trends*, January 1954).

In 1911, Macdonald married Elizabeth Prentiss Avery, who bore a daughter, Frances Avery, in 1914, and a son, Angus Avery, in 1918. The son was killed in an airplane crash in 1970. Macdonald's marriage to Elizabeth ended in divorce in 1934. In 1935, he married Amy Barker, who survives him and manages the affairs of Everdure at their farm home near Orange, Virginia. Macdonald had lettered in track at Columbia and had enjoyed good health most of his life; however, his health began to fail in 1960 and he died on February 21, 1961, following surgery.

Biographical listings and obituaries–"A. S. Macdonald, Authority on Library Architecture, Dies." *Library Journal* 86:1433 (April 1, 1961); "Angus Macdonald, Library Architect." *New York Times*, Feb. 22, 1961, p. 25; "Angus Snead Macdonald, 1883-1961." *Virginia Librarian* 8:22 (Summer 1961). **Books and articles about the biographee**–Baumann, Charles Henry. *The Influence of Angus Snead Macdonald and the Snead Bookstack on Library Architecture.* Metuchen, N.J.: Scarecrow Press, 1972; "Angus Snead Macdonald to Be Consultant." *Library Journal* 87:1790 (Oct. 15, 1952). **Primary sources and archival materials**–Macdonald left four pages of unpublished biographical notes. In addition, there are sixteen file drawers of the records of Snead & Company in the University of Virginia Library in Charlottesville, which include much of Macdonald's business and personal correspondence.

—CHARLES H. BAUMANN

MacPHERSON, HARRIET DOROTHEA
(1892-1967)

Harriet D. MacPherson was born on June 11, 1892, in College Point, New York, the daughter of John Donald and Esther Ella Nora Smith MacPherson.

Her formal education prepared her well for a professional career. She received a bachelor's degree from Wellesley College in 1914, a master's degree from Columbia University a decade later in 1924, and a Ph.D. from Columbia University in 1929, all with concentration on modern language and literature. Her modern language instruction was supplemented by attendance at the University of Nancy, France, in the summer of 1923, where she obtained a *Diplôme Supérieur*, and at the Sorbonne, in the summer of 1925, where she obtained a *Certificat*.

MacPherson's early career was that of a person who anticipated making French and Spanish language and literature her specialties and who expected to teach and research these subjects on a university level. She spent a year (1915-1916) as a high school teacher in Netcong, New Jersey. Several of her publications represented this field: *Editions of Beaumarchais Available for Study in New York City* (New York Public Library, 1925), *Censorship under Louis XIV, 1661-1715* (Institute of French Studies, 1929), and *R. L. Stevenson: A Study in French Influence* (Institute of French Studies, 1930).

Harriet MacPherson's initial period of activity in modern language and literature overlapped her early library cataloging period and eventually gave way to it. Her library education was received at the New York Public Library, from which she was awarded a certificate in 1917. Throughout her fifty-year library career, from 1917 to 1967, MacPherson worked as a cataloger, taught cataloging, or maintained a close interest in the field. She had considerable influence in cataloging and contributed to the field until a few months before her death. From 1917 to 1924, she was a cataloger and reviser at the Columbia University Library, and from 1924 to 1928, she was head cataloger at the City College of New York Library. These eleven years of practical cataloging experience, including cataloging administration, prepared her well for a career as a Columbia University cataloging teacher—a career that began in 1927 and lasted until 1943.

As a cataloger, MacPherson made numerous contributions. She wrote a short book, *Some Practical Problems in Cataloging* (American Library Association, 1936). The book reviews and papers that she contributed to professional library periodicals each year are listed in the cumulated volumes of *Library Literature*. With the exception of a five-year period, she served on advisory committees for the Dewey Decimal Classification from 1937—when she became a member of the original Dewey Decimal Classification Committee—until 1962, four years after her formal retirement, when her term as a member of the Decimal Classification Editorial Policy Committee (formed in 1956) expired. She served as vice-chairman of the latter in 1957 and in 1962. She was chairman of the American Library Association Cataloging Section during 1932 and 1933, and a co-editor of the *ALA Cataloging Rules for Author and Title Entries* in 1941. She was a member of the Advisory Board for both the preliminary 1941 and the final 1949 editions of these cataloging rules. Her final contribution to cataloging was the preparation of an index to the second edition of the *Anglo-American Cataloging Rules* (1967).

Harriet MacPherson made her mark in college librarianship as well. In 1943, she left her post as assistant professor of library service at Columbia University to enter college library administration. For five years, she was librarian at Smith College in Northampton, Massachusetts, one of the largest women's college libraries in the country. From 1943 to 1949, she was a member of the ALA Board of Education for Librarianship, and she chaired the Board in 1945-1947. From 1946 to 1950, she was a member of the ALA Council representing the Association of College and Research Libraries (ACRL).

In 1948 MacPherson joined the faculty of the Drexel Institute of Technology Library School (now Drexel University) in Philadelphia, where she spent the last decade of her active professional career. She went there as professor of library science and dean-designate and, upon the retirement of Marie Hamilton Law, became dean of the Library School and director of libraries, holding these positions until her retirement in 1958.

Harriet MacPherson's career in library education was an outstanding one, also. Well prepared by her years of teaching and library administration for the post as dean of the third oldest library school in the country, she was able in her decade of service at Drexel to extend and improve the curriculum and to convert the old B.L.S. degree program to the M.S. in L.S. degree program. In her years at Drexel, the traditional strength in special librarianship was maintained while enriched offerings made specialization possible in other fields as well. Along with other similar schools, Drexel began to emphasize research as part of the new program and to require a research paper for the degree. In addition to her work at Drexel, she was president of the Library Education Division of the American Library Association in 1950-1951.

During her active career, she was a member of many professional groups: the American Library Association, the Special Libraries Association, the

Bibliographical Society of America, the Modern Language Association, the New York Library Club, the New York Regional Cataloging Group, the American Association of University Women, the League of American Penwomen, Phi Delta Gamma, and Phi Kappa Phi. She was a Republican and Presbyterian, after having earlier belonged to the Reform Church in America.

Numerous additional honors came to Harriet D. MacPherson. She was editor of the Spanish and French section of the ALA *Booklist* (1929-1932) and an ALA delegate to the [British] Library Association Conference in 1935. She was vice-president of the Columbia University Woman's Faculty Club in 1936-1938. In 1950-1951, she was second vice president of the American Library Association, and in 1951, she was chairman of the Committee for the 75th Anniversary of ALA's Founding, in Philadelphia. In 1959, she was awarded the honorary Doctor of Literature degree by Drexel Institute of Technology and the Distinguished Achievement Award by the Drexel Library School Alumni Association.

After her retirement in 1958, MacPherson moved to Arlington, Virginia, to be closer to friends and to be near her long-time summer residence in Scientists' Cliffs, Maryland. There, she continued professional activities with several years of work for the Science Service, the League of American Penwomen, the American Association of University Women, and the District of Columbia Library Association.

Harriet Dorothea MacPherson was a vital, enthusiastic and serious woman whose name was respected throughout the library profession. Tall and thin, she was a warm and sincere person, with a genuine interest in both faculty and students. In addition, she is remembered as something of a task master who maintained high standards and complete dedication in all of her work, expecting the same high standards and complete dedication of all who worked with her.

The *Library of Congress Information Bulletin* said that her death on March 26, 1967, was a great loss to the library profession, for she had contributed generously to the teaching and practice of librarianship, and she left a legacy of enthusiasm and wisdom to her former friends and pupils, many of whom were among the leaders in librarianship.

Biographical listings and obituaries—[Obituary]. *U.S. Library of Congress Information Bulletin* 26:232-33 (April 6, 1967); *Who's Who in America* 29 (1956-1957); *Who's Who in Library Service*, 1st ed., 3rd ed., 4th ed. **Books and articles about the biographee**—*College and Research Libraries* 13:184 (April 1952).

—JOHN F. HARVEY

MAGRUDER, PATRICK (1768-1819)

Patrick Magruder was born in 1768 (the day and month are unknown), one of the seven sons and four daughters born to Revolutionary War Major and Mrs. Samuel Wade Magruder at their family estate, "Locust Grove," in Montgomery County, Maryland. Patrick attended Princeton College and returned home to become a lawyer. Even at this early age he suffered from the ill health that was to plague him throughout his life and was to force him to be out of Washington at the time when he was most needed there in 1814.

In the 1790s, the young attorney married Sallie Turner of Georgetown, then a part of Maryland. They had one daughter, Louisa, and three sons, Edmund, Theophilus, and Patrick Henry. He was married again, on May 30, 1811, to Martha Goodwyn, the eldest daughter of Congressman Peterson Goodwyn of Virginia. Adelina Virginia and Napoleon Bonaparte Magruder were born of this marriage. Patrick outlived both his wives.

Becoming active in politics, he served in 1797 as a member of the Maryland House of Delegates from Montgomery County for one term. He next became a justice of the peace and in 1802 an associate judge of the county circuit court. In his races for the United States House of Representatives as a Republican, he lost in 1801 and 1803, and won in 1804. Magruder's service in the Ninth Congress was rather ordinary. After a very bitter campaign, his was the only Maryland House of Representatives seat lost by the Republicans in 1806.

His term as a member of the Ninth Congress ended March 3, 1807. A month later, John J. Beckley (q.v.), clerk of the House of Representatives and first Librarian of Congress, died (April 8, 1807). When the Tenth Congress convened on October 26, 1807, it found itself confronted with eight applicants for the vacant clerkship of the House. That same day, the representatives proceeded to elect a new clerk as soon as they had organized and chosen a speaker. The first ballot was declared invalid. In this race for the clerkship, Magruder came in second on the next two tallies to Nicholas Van Zandt, Beckley's chief assistant.

Before the next vote, Joseph Randolph of Roanoke interrupted the procedure. He attacked Van Zandt as one of the assistant clerks who in the previous Congress had not properly maintained the secrecy of a closed session of the House of Representatives. Denied a chance to speak on his own behalf, Van Zandt fell in the polling, and Magruder jumped to first place in what had once been a field of four serious contenders. Winning the office of clerk of the House on the fifth ballot, Magruder held the post concurrently with that of Librarian of Congress for the next three Congresses.

Also on October 26, the day of Magruder's victory in the House, three congressmen suggested his name to President Thomas Jefferson (q.v.) as a likely choice for the position of Librarian of Congress. In the only known application of Magruder for this position, they wrote simply, "Mr. Magruder having been appointed Clerk of the H. R. U. S. we recommend him to your notice as a proper person to be appointed librarian."

His selection as Librarian of Congress because of his clerkship was not as automatic as his predecessor's had been. President Jefferson was not convinced he wanted to give that post to the clerk of the House, whoever he might be. This doubt arose because of his friendship for one of the many competitors for the post, William Mayne Duncanson. At least eight persons, several of whom had worked in the Library of Congress under Beckley, applied for that job. Duncanson was perhaps tainted with Aaron Burr's conspiracies, and Magruder had both precedence and politics on his side. Thus, Jefferson decided not to risk Duncanson's appointment, and Magruder as clerk was also appointed Librarian of Congress.

Jefferson did not act until after Congress convened that October and elected its officials. On November 6, less than two weeks after Magruder's application for the position and about six months after the bulk of the other applications were submitted, he tersely told Magruder that he had the job and that he could take over responsibility for the Library from Van Zandt, who had acted as interim Librarian.

Beckley had largely delegated the day-to-day operations of the Library to one of his assistants at any given time. Continuing this tradition, Magruder was not much involved in the routine of the Library of Congress. This, of course, was the normal practice of librarians in that time period. Librarians were regarded as custodial employees, while the selection and procurement of books were left to a committee of the governing board of the institution involved. This same committee, as a rule, also handled the financial affairs of the Library. So when Magruder delegated his Librarian's chores to one of his assistants, he was not neglecting his major responsibilities.

For example, during two of Magruder's years as Librarian, the Joint Congressional Committee on the Library of Congress published reports on the Library (1808 and 1809). These reports were signed by the Committee's chairman, Samuel L. Mitchell, and emphasized gifts, book selection, and finances, none of which were the concern of the Librarian.

The extent to which Magruder involved himself in the production of the 1808 and 1812 book catalogs of the Library of Congress is questionable. John Quincy Adams recorded a Library Committee meeting of November 20, 1807, which decided that one of its members would superintend "the making and printing of a new list of the books." The rules of the Library required the Librarian to "preserve due lists and catalogues" of the books under his care, but given the customs of the time and Magruder's

sporadic ill health as well as his delegation of operational control of the Library, it is impossible to state what his role might have been in the production of these catalogs, other than his routine obligation as clerk of the House to oversee their printing.

The new rules for the governance of the Library that were promulgated in the 1808 catalog were revised in the 1812 catalog, but again, no records exist to indicate Magruder's involvement with this congressional procedure. He did stay active in Republican politics, however, occasionally recommending someone to Jefferson for an appointment to office because of his sound politics. He was also active in Washington Masonic organizations.

In December 1813, Magruder's ill health returned, and the House of Representatives voted approval of George Magruder, his brother and his chief clerk in the Office of the Clerk, to serve as acting clerk of the House.

On August 24, 1814, Patrick Magruder was again on sick leave in Virginia, having left Washington in the latter part of July. On that August evening, the British Army captured the city of Washington and burned the United States Capitol and with it the Library of Congress. Soon after the withdrawal of the British, President Madison called a special session of Congress, for which Magruder returned. Magruder then wrote the speaker of the House reporting the destruction not only of the Library but also of the vouchers that proved that he had properly spent the government funds entrusted to his office. He asked for a congressional investigation into the conduct of his office before the fire and into his accounts and the handling of the funds for which he was responsible. The speaker promptly appointed a Select Committee to investigate the circumstances discussed in Magruder's letter.

Two of his clerks, one overage and one sent back from the Bladensburg battlefield for that purpose, had attempted to save Magruder's office records, though there was neither time nor available transportation to save the books of the Library itself. Magruder claimed that his clerks had done all they could and that he would not have left the city had he thought a British invasion imminent. Unfortunately for Magruder, as he was forced to admit in his exchange of letters and reports with the Select Committee, the clerks had neglected to save his fiscal records while saving almost all other papers. The concern was not for the funds for the Library, which had always been under control of the Joint Committee on the Library, but rather for his contingency fund as clerk of the House. He had been keeping a large part of it in his brother's personal checking account and not submitting the proper vouchers to prove its correct expenditure to the Treasury Department auditors. The Select Committee computed that Magruder had received $50,863.16 from the Treasury without properly accounting for its expenditure. They credited him with $30,988.57½ as the amount he had probably spent properly. It was the remaining $19,874.58½ for which the House wanted him to account.

The ensuing Committee investigation into Magruder's finances brought to light several other irregularities. His expenses had not always been approved by the appropriate congressional authorities as he had claimed. He sometimes drew advances without spending his previous withdrawals from the Treasury. His staff was not properly paid. Patrick and his brother were even unable to tell Congress in which bank they had deposited $6,000 in government funds.

In January 1815, the House of Representatives debated the removal of Magruder from his clerkship because of the discrepancies in his records and because of his neglect of his duties while his staff handled his contingency fund without supervision. While the House was between debates on his character, Magruder resigned as clerk of the House and by inference also the office of Librarian of Congress. He felt that at his age he should not have to defend his conduct and additionally, that many congressmen had already prejudged him.

Thus, it was not the destruction of the Library of Congress and Congress's resultant anger that caused Magruder, second Librarian of Congress, to lose his position. Rather, it was the question of impropriety in the use of his contingency fund that forced his indignant resignation. This issue was raised after the discovery that these records had accidentally been left behind for the British to destroy.

Magruder left Washington to settle on "Sweden," his wife's plantation near Petersburg, Virginia, with a federal claim still hanging over his head. The outcome of this government suit against him is not known, however. Less than four years later, December 24, 1819, Patrick Magruder died and was buried at "Sweden."

Biographical listings and obituaries—*Biographical Directory of the American Congress*; *Who Was Who in America*, Historical Volume (1607-1896). **Books and articles about the biographee**—Gordon, Martin K. "Patrick Magruder: Citizen, Congressman, Librarian of Congress." *Quarterly Journal of the Library of Congress* 32:154-71 (July 1975). **Primary sources and archival materials**—The Maryland Historical Society holds two collections of Magruder and related families' papers. The National Archives holds materials on Patrick Magruder in: Letters of Application and Recommendation during the Administration of Thomas Jefferson; the same series for the James Madison years; the Records of the Joint Committee on the Library of Congress; the Miscellaneous Treasury Accounts of the First Auditor of the Treasury Department, 1790-1840; and, Circuit Court Records, District of Columbia. The Library of Congress holds Magruder-related items in the Thomas Jefferson, Josias William King, and James Madison Papers. Published primary

sources are: *American State Papers: Miscellaneous Series* (Volume II): 245-68; and *Annals of Congress*, in which the elections of Magruder are at the beginning of the 10th, 11th, 12th, and 13th Congresses.

—MARTIN K. GORDON

MANN, MARGARET (1873-1960)

Margaret Mann was born in Cedar Rapids, Iowa, on April 9, 1873, the third child of Amasa and Emily Devendorf Mann. Margaret Mann's first eighteen years were spent in that Iowa community; her father was a respected dry goods merchant who later became an insurance accountant. In 1890, the Mann family moved to Chicago. Margaret's formal general education ended in 1893 with the attainment of a high school diploma from Englewood High School, Chicago, Illinois. Although she was renowned throughout her life for her scholarly interests and wealth of knowledge, the only college course work that she completed was a few hours in history taken at the University of Illinois. Additional library training was gained at the Armour Institute in Chicago between 1893 and 1895, but the Institute did not award a degree and her two-year course of study in the Department of Library Economy qualified her only for a certificate and advanced "diploma" from the Institute.

Margaret Mann's family was not wealthy, and the opening of the Armour vocational institute in Chicago, in 1893, presumably suggested a practical and reasonable career for 20-year-old "Maggie." She enrolled in September 1893 in the first library class at Armour, which was directed by Katharine Sharp (q.v.). Margaret's work was superior and after a year's study, she was hired to catalog in the Armour Institute Library. While employed there, she enrolled in a second year of library study and added teaching to her responsibilities, both at Armour and in the Wisconsin summer school, thus beginning a career that was to be marked by her unique cataloging and teaching abilities. When the Armour Institute library class was transferred to the University of Illinois in 1897, Mann accompanied Sharp, who had become both mentor and close friend. For six years at Illinois, she polished her cataloging as well as her teaching skills. The profession was in the midst of a number of unique changes that were reflected in Mann's interests as well as her future. Much of this was later summarized by William W. Bishop (q.v.), who wrote:

Up to the time of the World's Fair at Chicago in 1893 ... attention had been—I think we may safely say—largely centered in the internal management of ... libraries, on such matters as bookstacks and binding, cataloging and classifying, charging and registration systems. Of course I do not mean that other matters did not occupy thought and receive attention, but we may truly say that the emphasis was on the internal side. In the next few years two other matters began to forge ahead—buildings and library extension. And then followed with almost alarming rapidity a sudden expansion of the activities of the library in every external relation. First the story hour and children's work was the great discovery, then traveling libraries and commission work, then branch libraries spring up almost like the dragon's teeth of the fable, work with schools, with clubs, with every form of social organization which could use books. [W. W. Bishop, "Cataloging as an Asset; An Address to the New York State Library School, May 1, 1915." Baltimore, The Waverly Press, Williams & Wilkins, 1916, p. 6.]

At the University of Illinois, under the direction of Katharine Sharp and with colleagues such as Isadore Mudge (q.v.) and Minnie E. Sears (q.v.), Margaret Mann played a significant role. The Library itself needed heavy "reordering." There had been no consistent policy of cataloging and classification since the Library had opened in the 1860s. However, by the end of the first year, and with the assistance only of students from the library school, all of the books had been accessioned, shelf-listed, and prepared for the shelves. By 1899, Mann was serving both as assistant librarian and senior instructor. There were numerous problems, including execrable working conditions, but Margaret Mann continued to develop and hone her cataloging skills while gaining teaching expertise. For a time, she personally handled all government documents, college catalogs, and miscellaneous library school material. As instructor, her interests went beyond cataloging and classification into life-long concerns with government publications and children's work—the latter probably directly influenced by her sister Alma, who was trained as one of the first "kindergarten" teachers in this country. Of course, both Armour and the Illinois State Library School were active in preparing students for all phases of library extension; special emphasis was given to service to the underprivileged, to schools, and to the immigrant communities as well as to the more typical library patron. Mann's entire career gives indication of her concern for that extension of library service—at Pittsburgh, in New York and Paris, and later at Michigan, where Bishop would recognize its impact on the library school curriculum.

Regardless of her other interests, cataloging and classification continued to be one of Mann's key concerns, and her knowledge of that evolving field brought her to the attention of Edwin H. Anderson (q.v.), then librarian of the [Andrew] Carnegie [q.v.] Library at Pittsburgh. In 1902, despite her close friendship and loyalty to Katharine Sharp, Margaret Mann found it impossible to turn down an offer to move to Pittsburgh as head of the Cataloging Department and, of course, as instructor in the library school associated with the Library. During this period, she was also involved with library programs at Western Reserve and in the public library at Riverside, California, as well as lecturing and writing. The Carnegie Library in Pittsburgh was the pinnacle of the philanthropist Andrew Carnegie's library efforts, and the collection was both large and of considerable breadth. When Mann arrived on the scene in 1903, she had to cope with the agonies of a building under construction as well as a collection that had outgrown the staff that serviced it. From 1903 to 1919, she gained immense experience and earned a nationwide reputation based on her ability to supervise and direct the entire cataloging process. In particular, her major accomplishment was supervising the preparation and publishing of the great classed catalog of the collections of the Carnegie Library. Earl C. Kubicek, assessing her career in 1947 ("One of Ours, a Scholar and the World of Books," p. 46) described her monumental task:

The work was on a large scale, and was carried on in the face of almost insurmountable practical difficulties. The impressive array of volumes, the visual result of Miss Mann's supervisory effort, is still used for review by other libraries. Dr. Bishop wrote of this undertaking by Miss Mann, "She supervised the publication of the classified catalogue of the Carnegie Library of Pittsburgh, which was and remains, one of the finest of its kind."

In addition, during those same years when she was administering the cataloging department so efficiently, she was also engaged in teaching in the library school. Some of her first work related to the cataloging of materials for children and young adults came out of her contact with her teaching colleagues at Carnegie who specialized in this area at the turn of the century.

As the years passed, Mann gave every indication that Pittsburgh would be her permanent home. However, in 1918, she became active in the camp libraries sponsored by the American Library Association, and there is some evidence to suggest that the War and its impact on her brought a degree of dissatisfaction with what she was doing. She was only in her mid-forties, and felt the need to be at a new task—things were too well organized in Pittsburgh. When in 1919, a former director of the Carnegie Library, Harrison Craver (q.v.), approached her to come to New York City to recatalog and organize the assorted collections of the united Engineering Societies Library, she did not refuse. For five years, from 1919 through 1924, she focused her attention on the task of pulling together the varied materials that made up the Engineering Societies Library. It was indeed a challenge—to provide expert advice and a well-ordered catalog to a totally new kind of patron—the professional engineer who had little patience with rules and regulations. Margaret Mann arrived in May of 1919, and on July 1, began a complete recataloging of the multiple collections. Among her other accomplishments was the development of a classification for scientific management, and one of her more interesting professional statements is found in an article entitled "Teaching Cataloging" (*Library Journal* 46:929-33; November 15, 1921). Not surprisingly, she was also employed part time by the library school at the New York Public Library; her years of exceptional work plus her concise and coherent teaching style had marked her in terms of her instructional ability.

Given Mann's reputation and widespread activity in the American Library Association, plus a close friendship with Sarah C. N. Bogle (q.v.), few individuals were surprised when, in 1924, it was announced that Margaret Mann would travel to the ALA-sponsored Paris Library School to conduct classes in cataloging and classification. Although she was not fluent in French, she easily impressed the students in Paris with her thorough knowledge. During her two years there, she gained an international reputation and made numerous friendships lasting long after her retirement from the profession in 1938. Family obligations, as well as a number of exciting job offers, necessitated her return to the United States in 1926. The most persuasive offer was that of William Warner Bishop, who did everything possible to employ her in his newly formed library school at the University of Michigan.

Bishop's assessment of Margaret Mann (in "Report to the President," May 5, 1926; University of Michigan School of Library Science Archives) could hardly have been stronger:

> Without exception every one in the country says that Miss Margaret Mann, now teaching cataloging and classification in the Ecole de Bibliothécaires in Paris, . . . is the best teacher of these subjects to be found anywhere. . . . Despite her lack of academic study, she is one of the best-read people I have ever met in my life, and a teacher recognized universally as one of the best authorities on cataloging.

Margaret Mann came to Ann Arbor as an assistant professor; she also had been selected to write the cataloging text sponsored by ALA as part of their curriculum study series—the first basic texts prepared in and for the field of librarianship. Her introduction to cataloging and classification was published in 1930 and rapidly became the librarians' bible for those subjects.

The years at Michigan, from 1926 until her retirement in 1938, were grand and good years. She was quickly promoted from assistant to associate professor and was honored, almost without exception, as a

scientific cataloger and exceptional teacher. Her writings, in this period as well as earlier, were prolific, ranging from articles on the techniques and components of cataloging to such diverse topics as research and reference in the special library, the future of cataloging, the teaching of cataloging and classification, and personal interests in government publications, subject analysis, and children's literature. Her text, *Introduction to Cataloging and Classification of Books* (Chicago: ALA, 1930; 2nd ed., 1943), was recognized as the primary teaching text almost before it was published and remains, even today, a major guide to the principles of cataloging and classification. She was active in several professional organizations including, of course, the American Library Association, where she was elected first vice president in 1924 and served several times on the Executive Board, the Council, and numerous committees. In addition, she was involved in various state associations throughout her career and held membership in the Bibliographical Society of America, the Association des Bibliothécaires Français and the American Library Institute.

At the age of 65, in 1938, Margaret Mann retired from active teaching at the University of Michigan. She continued to live in Ann Arbor for several years, working on the 1943 revision of her famous textbook. In 1945, she moved to California to live with her niece and died there August 22, 1960. She is buried beside her parents in Cedar Rapids, Iowa.

Margaret Mann's long and splendid life is one that almost defies synopsis into a few summary statements. From 1894 through 1938, she amazed her colleagues and students with her ability to focus on the essentials of cataloging and classification in such a way as to demonstrate its absorbing interest and never-ending variety. Her personality and general presence were impressive; individuals may not have liked her, but they could not help but admire her articulate and brilliant style. In a field that lacked so much definition, Margaret Mann brought preciseness, clarity, and method to thousands of students. Much of the respect and admiration in which she was and is held was summed up in a letter from Laura Colvin to Dorothy R. Shaw (February 15, 1950):

> I think Miss Mann was the most enthusiastic and dynamic professor under whom I have ever had the privilege to study. Along with her intense interest in cataloging, its opportunities, and its discipline, she brought a rare quality of human understanding and a quick sense of humor to her teaching. The inspiration she instilled in her students has been a powerful influence in their professional work. . . .

All of us would like to claim as much.

Biographical listings and obituaries—*Australian Library Journal* 10:2 (Jan. 1961); *Chula Vista Star-News*, Aug. 25,

1960; *College and Research Libraries* 22:75 (Jan. 1961); *Library Journal* 86:3634 (March 15, 1961); *Wilson Library Bulletin* 35:198 (Nov. 1960); *Who Was Who in America* V (1969-1973); *Who's Who in Library Service*, 1st ed., 2nd ed. **Books and articles about the biographee**—Bishop, William Warner. "Margaret Mann." *Catalogers' and Classifiers' Yearbook* 7:11-14 (1938); Grotzinger, Laurel. "Margaret Mann: The Preparatory Years." *Journal of Education for Librarianship* 10:302-315 (Spring 1970); Grotzinger, Laurel. "The Proto-Feminist Librarian at the Turn of the Century: Two Studies." *Journal of Library History* 10:195-213 (July 1975); Hickey, Doralyn J. "Margaret Mann Citation in Cataloging and Classification." In *Encyclopedia of Library and Information Science.* Allen Kent, Harold Lancour, and Jay E. Daily, eds. New York: Marcel Dekker, 1976, Vol. 17; Kubicek, Earl E. "One of Ours; a Scholar and the World of Books." *Illinois Tech Engineer and Alumnus* 12:23, 46, 48 (1947); Michigan. University. Department of Library Science. *Alumni Notes* 11:3-20 (July 1962); Shaw, Dorothy R. "The Life and Work of Margaret Mann." Unpublished master's thesis, Drexel Institute of Technology, 1950. **Primary sources and archival materials**—The Mann papers are primarily located at the University of Illinois and the University of Michigan. The American Library Association Archives at Illinois as well as their student and faculty archives contain material. Both the University Library and the School of Library Science at Michigan have primary documents. Additional papers and documents are held by Laurel A. Grotzinger, Western Michigan University, Kalamazoo, Michigan.

—LAUREL A. GROTZINGER

MARTEL, CHARLES (1860-1945)

Charles Martel, the architect of the Library of Congress classification system, was a member of a small but influential group of men who developed—in the first decade of the twentieth century—the national bibliographical services of the Library of Congress. This group was led by Herbert Putnam (q.v.), Librarian of Congress from 1899 to 1939, and included, in addition to Martel, J. C. M. Hanson (q.v.), Thorvald Solberg (q.v.), Charles H. Hastings, and S. T. Stefansson. Martel's primary contribution was the development of the new classification system, one that today has achieved worldwide importance. But he also contributed to other fundamental innovations, such as the creation of the new card catalogs, the cataloging of copyright entries, the distribution and sale of printed catalog cards, and the eventual creation of uniform cataloging rules.

Martel came to the Library of Congress in 1897 to work as the assistant to J. C. M. Hanson in the new Catalog Division. Hanson left the Library in 1910, and two years later, Martel became chief of the Division. He served as chief until 1929, when he stepped aside to become a consultant in cataloging, classification, and bibliography.

William Warner Bishop (q.v.), who served as superintendent of the Reading Room at the Library of Congress from 1907 to 1915, described Martel as "indefatigable, spending most of his evenings in the library, and putting in such long hours of work as to

seem unbelievable." According to Bishop, Martel was "short, quick in his movements, but slow of speech," and therefore "far from impressive to a chance acquaintance." Nonetheless, "when one got to know him, his attainments and his knowledge were simply overwhelming." Bishop concluded that the Library of Congress "was most fortunate in having Hanson and Martel, a team which has never been equalled anywhere." The three pioneers, Bishop, Hanson, and Martel, would be reunited in 1928 as a special commission to develop a printed card catalog for the Vatican Library.

Martel, whose original name was Karl David Hanke, was born in Zurich, Switzerland, on March 5, 1860. He was the son of Franz Hanke, a well-known antiquarian bookseller, and Gertrude Maria Strässle Hanke. As Martel himself explained, as a youth he was "in daily touch with a stock of books of the nature of a general reference library of circa 250,000 volumes, absorbing in growing the details of the business of bookselling, methods of cataloguing and classification, etc. with no inconsiderable knowledge of books and literature." He completed the *Gymnasium* course in Zurich in 1876 and attended the University in 1876-1877. Accompanied by an older brother, Martel spent from May to September 1876 in the United States, visiting in New York, Philadelphia, and Chicago. In Zurich and realizing that there was little likelihood of his inheriting substantial portions of his father's estate, he emigrated to the United States in late 1879 or early 1880, first settling in North Carolina but also spending time in Louisville, Kentucky; Salem, Missouri; and David City, Nebraska. His occupations included farmer, waterfront worker, and school teacher. In 1887, he had apparently gone down the Ohio River with a group of migrants to Dent County, Missouri, where he became an American citizen under the name of Charles Martel. Other details about his name change are unclear. In 1900, Martel had married and had a son Rennie (Renaud). His wife died in 1906, and thereafter, Martel lived not far from the Library of Congress and concentrated his interests there.

From 1888 to 1892, Martel worked as an assistant to a lawyer in Council Bluffs, Iowa, and became an estate manager. For over a decade, he had worked in various public libraries as a volunteer, and in early 1892, he took a positive step toward making librarianship his full-time career by applying for a position at Chicago's Newberry Library, headed at that time by William Frederick Poole (q.v.). He joined the Newberry staff in February 1892, going to work in the Order Department under the supervision of William Stetson Merrill (q.v.). It was at the Newberry that Martel met J. C. M. Hanson. The two men stayed in touch even after Hanson left the Newberry·the next year to become head cataloger at the University of Wisconsin Library in Madison.

Between 1893 and 1897, Martel held several positions at the Newberry, including cataloger, head of the Department of Arts and Letters, and curator of early books and manuscripts. According to the personnel form that Martel filled out at the Library of Congress in 1897, he also "engaged in classification, and in revision of the official catalogue" while at the Newberry.

In September 1897, John Russell Young (q.v.), the new Librarian of Congress, appointed Hanson to head the Library's new Catalog Division. Hanson convinced Young to hire Martel, who began work as Hanson's assistant on December 1, 1897. The new Library of Congress building had recently opened and the collection of approximately 800,000 volumes classified by the Baconian system (with modifications) was being moved from the Capitol into the new structure. It had been clear for several years that the entire collection needed reclassification, and Martel's first task was to analyze the old classification system to see if any of it might be salvaged. His conclusion, stated in a report to Librarian Young, was negative; Martel was convinced "that everything must be worked over anew."

Martel rejected the use of any classification systems then in existence and, according to Leo E. LaMontagne, "a final decision on what classification or classifications were to form the basis for the new system was not rendered." But the Catalog Division was authorized by Librarian Young to proceed with the reclassification of the old chapter 38, Literature and Bibliography, in accordance with an eclectic system that, as devised by Martel, would "profit by the experience of other large reference libraries and utilize the best features of all existing classifications." Chapter 38 was chosen for practical reasons, since the Library desperately needed to acquire the bibliographic volumes that would be classed in that section and because, according to LaMontagne, "the new classification devised for it would not preclude the choice of an existing system for the rest of the Library." Charles Martel prepared the new classification schedule, leaning in part on the Expansive Classification of Charles A. Cutter (q.v.). He worked quickly, for *Class Z, Bibliography and Library Science*, was completed by mid-1898. Over 6,000 volumes were added to the new Class Z shelflist.

After Class Z was completed, Young apparently decided that additional staff was needed before full-scale reclassification could continue. It appears that Martel himself never stopped classification work, but Hanson and others were soon busy with other developments of an equally fundamental nature. On May 14, 1898, in a cooperative undertaking with the Copyright Office, the Catalog Division began preparing book entries for copyright deposits for the *Catalog of Title Entries*. Two months later, the Government Printing Office began printing, on cards, fifty copies of each entry from the *Catalog*. The printed cards enabled the Library to establish three new dictionary catalogs, one for the public and two for the cataloging staff. Hanson, Solberg, Martel, and others worked long hours in creating nothing less than the basis for the national bibliographic services of the Library of Congress, particularly the printing, sale, and distribution of catalog cards that would be started by Herbert Putnam in October 1901.

John Russell Young died in office in early 1899 and all reclassification efforts were officially suspended in April 1899 when Herbert Putnam, formerly head of the Boston Public Library, became Librarian of Congress. Putnam was an experienced library administrator who fully recognized the need for reclassification but also was acutely aware of the national role that the Library of Congress might play for the benefit of other American libraries. He therefore asked Hanson and Martel to once again reassess the possibility of using a classification scheme already in existence, recognizing the potential advantages of uniformity if a standard system could be adopted.

In October 1899, Putnam asked Congress for new positions to be used in part for reclassification and the creation of a new shelflist. A few months later, he wrote Melvil Dewey (q.v.) and asked if the Decimal Classification were being revised; if so, he thought the Library of Congress might possibly be able to use it. Dewey's answer was negative, however, and by October of 1899, Putnam was convinced that a new classification system had to be devised. During this period Martel, with Hanson's support, continued his opposition to adopting the Dewey Decimal system or any other classification scheme currently in use. At Putnam's request, however, the two men solicited opinions from many librarians and prepared a detailed report reasserting their view that a new system was needed.

In January 1901, Martel and five assistants began reclassifying the old chapter 4, America, into the new Classes E and F. The basis was the eclectic scheme prepared by Martel during the years 1898-1900, although Putnam still had not fully accepted the scheme. In May 1901, the Librarian arranged for Martel and William P. Cutter, chief of the Order Division, to visit William I. Fletcher (q.v.) at Amherst, Charles A. Cutter at the Forbes Library, and Melvil Dewey at the New York State Library in Albany. The potential benefits of using a revised Cutter or Dewey system were again reviewed. According to William P. Cutter, his uncle "expressed himself as perfectly willing to make any changes which after careful consideration seem necessary," but Dewey "absolutely refused to make any, basing his argument on the inconvenience which would result to the large number of libraries already using the Decimal Classification."

Martel's report to Putnam conveyed the same information, and Putnam soon agreed to the full development of Martel's eclectic scheme, which borrowed certain features of Cutter's Expansive Classification but was based primarily on the special characteristics of the Library's own collection. In 1905, addressing the American Library Association, Putnam expressed his disappointment, not with Martel's scheme, but with the Library's failure to find an existing system that it could use:

> How excellent a service if the national library could adopt a classification which would become universally current! We have had visions of one. They have passed. We considered long, but felt obliged to conclude that no existing system likely to be considered generally current would serve our purpose without modifications which would defeat the very purpose of uniformity—that is, identical call numbers. We have proceeded to construct a system of our own, and have thus added one more crime to the calendar, and further confusion.

Charles Martel was responsible for the philosophic base of the new Library of Congress classification scheme. Furthermore, it was Martel and Hanson who convinced Putnam that an entirely new system was needed. In 1940, on the occasion of Martel's eightieth birthday, his friends presented him with a volume of letters. In his letter, Hanson looked back to the Library of Congress years, informing Martel:

> There is no librarian, living or dead, to whose assistance and counsel I owe more than I do to you, especially during those years from 1897 to 1910 when we worked together in the Library of Congress. Not only did you assume the chief burdens in connection with the planning, development, and application of the new and minute classification, but your help and advice on the many difficult questions that arose in regard to the new catalog and cooperative work assumed by the Library in 1901, never failed.

In his 1911 annual report to Librarian Putnam, Martel summarized both his ideal and his achievement:

> It has been the endeavor from the beginning to incorporate in the classification scheme the results of the experience gained both in the first application of the schedules in reclassification and in later continued use in classifying new books. A certain ideal was kept in view but it was a practical one. The ambition was to make the best of an unrivaled opportunity to produce a classification in which the theory and the history of subjects as represented in a great collection of books should

constitute the principal basis for the construction of the scheme, compared and combined of course with their presentation as derived from other classifications and treatises.

In one of his very few papers, "Cataloging, 1876-1926," presented at the American Library Association conference of 1926, Martel mentioned two great steps taken in connection with ALA Rules towards universality. He pointed out that

> one great step in that direction has been accomplished: the quite general adoption of the American standard size card 7.5 x 12.5 cm. Another move to be hoped for in foreign cataloging practice is more extended and uniform application of the rule for corporate entry, especially with reference to government publications and the official publications of institutions, societies and other bodies or organizations, in preference to the quite widespread practice of anonymous title entry customary in continental European catalogs and bibliographies.

In the mid-1920s, William Warner Bishop, who was then heading the University of Michigan Library (Ann Arbor), had become seriously interested in a plan to make the vast resources of the Vatican Library more available to the scholarly world by the adaptation of modern catalog rules in the preparation and printing of catalog cards so widely used by American libraries as well as to some extent elsewhere. With the support of the [Andrew] Carnegie [q.v.] Endowment for International Peace, arrangement was made for a highly technical mission from the United States to advise the Vatican Library on drafting suitable catalog rules, on beginning increased cataloging of Vatican Library resources, and on the printing of catalog cards. An American mission, consisting of Bishop, Hanson and Martel (despite the latter's somewhat frail health), went to the Vatican Library early in 1928. During the few months of the mission, Martel, on the basis of his experience in drafting and applying the ALA Rules, his vast linguistic knowledge, and his personality, was unusually helpful with the drafting and application of the Vatican cataloging code.

After his return to the Library of Congress as chief of the Catalog Division, Martel continued active service until the fall of 1929, when he became an active consultant in cataloging, classification, bibliography, and reference work. Annita Melville Ker Johnson, then a cataloger of specialized material, commented in a private letter about going to "consult him on thorny bibliographical problems in two Portuguese collections. He was always so simple in his explanations and so kind in manner." On his eightieth birthday, in 1940, Martel received a *Liber amicorum*, a manuscript volume of tributes from his many friends far and wide, but he did not retire until

May 1, 1945. On May 15, 1945, Charles Martel succumbed to a heartstroke.

Biographical listings and obituaries—*Annual Report of the Librarian of Congress for the Fiscal Year Ended June 30, 1945.* Washington, 1946, pp. 149-50; *Who Was Who in America* II (1943-1950); *Who's Who in Library Service*, 1st ed., 2nd ed. **Books and articles about the biographee**—Bishop, William Warner. "The Library of Congress, 1907-1915: Fragments of Autobiography." *Library Quarterly* 18:1-23 (1948); Childs, James Bennett. "Charles Martel." In *Encyclopedia of Library and Information Science.* Allen Kent, Harold Lancour, and Jay E. Daily, eds. New York: Marcel Dekker, 1976, Vol. 17; Cutter, William Parker. *Charles Ammi Cutter.* Chicago: American Library Association, 1931. (American Library Pioneers, III); LaMontagne, Leo E. *American Library Classification, with Special Reference to the Library of Congress.* Hamden, Conn.: Shoe String Press, 1961; Scott, Edith. "J. C. M. Hanson and His Contribution to Twentieth-Century Cataloging." Ph.D. dissertation, University of Chicago, 1970. **Primary sources and archival materials**—*Annual Reports of the Librarian of Congress for the Fiscal Years 1897-1945.* Washington, 1897-1946; Dent County, Missouri. Circuit Court Records; *The Liber Amicorum, Dedicated to Charles Martel on His Eightieth Birthday, March the Fifth, 1940.* Library of Congress; Washington, D.C. Library of Congress. Archives; Zurich, Switzerland. Stadtarchiv. Records.

—JAMES BENNETT CHILDS
—JOHN Y. COLE

MARTIN, ALLIE BETH DENT (1914-1976)

Allie Beth Martin was president of the American Library Association at the time of her death on April 11, 1976. A lifetime of leadership in the library world and in library association activities was thus brought to an untimely close.

Allie Beth Dent was born in the small town of Annieville, Arkansas, on June 28, 1914, the eldest daughter of Carleton G. and Ethel McCaleb Dent. She had two sisters, Jean and Mary. Much of her early life was spent in Batesville, Arkansas, where she was graduated from high school in 1932. She received a bachelor's degree in English from Arkansas College in 1935, and her years as a student assistant in the college library launched her career as a librarian.

Following her college years, she was named librarian of Batesville's first public library, established largely through her efforts and funded by the Works Progress Administration. In 1936, she moved to Little Rock to become librarian of Little Rock Junior College, and in July of 1937, she was appointed assistant to the secretary of the Arkansas Library Commission, then a new state agency. Her unbounded enthusiasm for public librarianship, which characterized a career of over four decades, was nurtured during these early years of library expansion in her native state. In the fall of 1937, Allie Beth Dent married a young journalist, Ralph F. Martin.

Allie Beth Martin left the Commission in 1938, and in 1939, earned her Bachelor of Science degree

from George Peabody School of Library Science. Her husband's penchant for newspaper work ended shortly after the birth of their only child, Elizabeth Erhard, and he entered the University of Arkansas Medical School. During these years, she returned to librarianship as director of the Mississippi County Library in Osceola, Arkansas, and later, from 1942 to 1947, she served again on the staff of the Arkansas Library Commission. Her leadership qualities were recognized by her associates, and she was elected president of the Arkansas Library Association in 1945 and was editor of *Arkansas Libraries* from 1945 to 1947.

During her husband's internship and residency in New York, Martin attended Columbia University School of Library Service, receiving her master's degree in 1949. Her thesis title was "State Aid and the Establishment of Large Unit Libraries." Her legislative activities in later years were focused on both subjects as means of achieving higher quality and more efficient library service.

Dr. and Mrs. Martin, with daughter Betsy, took up residence in Tulsa, Oklahoma, in 1949. Dr. Martin practiced medicine in Tulsa and Sand Springs, and for some time wrote a column on medicine for a Tulsa newspaper. Allie Beth Martin applied for a position in the outdated, overcrowded, and financially starved [Andrew] Carnegie [q.v.] Library in Tulsa. Although no single position was open, the director employed her, and for the first year she worked in many capacities and departments. Her interest in young people led to her appointment as children's librarian in the Tulsa system in 1950. This interest remained with her, and one of the highlights of each **ALA** conference for her was the Newbery-Caldecott Awards banquet, which she regularly attended. She also served as Tulsa's extension librarian from 1951 to 1961.

During these years, Martin was an active member of the Oklahoma Library Association. She edited the official journal, *Oklahoma Librarian*, from 1953 to 1954, and was elected president for the term 1955-1956. Her committee work included legislation and planning, and she became politically astute but always realistic. In 1961, in recognition of her numerous contributions, the Oklahoma Library Association honored her with its Distinguished Service Award, given "to the individual professional librarian who has effectively demonstrated for a period of ten or more years a valid, thorough, and imaginative concept of librarianship and library service, and has expressed that concept in actual practice." In the presentation speech, Martin was characterized as having "this rare faculty of transferring to others enthusiasm for, and a belief in all phases of library activities, and the ability to create in others this zest for difficult and discouraging jobs."

In November 1961, citizens of Tulsa approved a bond issue of $3.8 million to construct a new central library building, build much-needed branch libraries, and strengthen a totally inadequate book collection. State legislation, for which Martin had worked vigorously, provided a 1.9 mill levy for continuing support, and the Tulsa City-County Library (TCCL) was born.

Martin was named acting director of the system in 1962, and director in 1963. Construction work on the new main library began in 1963, and it was dedicated on June 30, 1965. The building reflects Martin's philosophy that libraries should be both functional and beautiful and should be planned to support the public library's role as the center for community information, education, recreation, and culture. Martin's ability to transform an outdated library into what is recognized as a model system was described by the editor of a local newspaper: "To a demanding administrative job Mrs. Martin brought a rare blend of hard work, inspiration, persuasion, and—when necessary—toughness."

As a result of the extensive study and travel that preceded the building program, Martin and the architect, Charles F. Ward, formed a consultant firm in 1965 (Library Design Associates, Inc.), and libraries in Oklahoma, Kansas, Texas, Arkansas, and New Mexico profited from the expertise of this team.

The nineteenth branch of TCCL was nearing completion when Martin died, and for the first time in Tulsa's history, a library building was named for an individual: the Allie Beth Martin Regional Branch Library. An editorial in the *Tulsa Tribune* commented: "They named a new regional library for Allie Beth Martin a while back (in February 1976). . . . But it really wasn't necessary to put her name on a building for most Tulsans to know that this one woman was—as much as any one person could be—the heart and soul and mind of Tulsa's library system."

Martin was committed to staff development. She was an ardent advocate of participatory management. In-service training, workshops, scholarships, attendance at professional meetings, and other activities to promote staff competency and enthusiasm for librarianship were always in her thinking.

Her boundless energy enabled her to administer a large and successful library system and to participate in other activities. She was a visiting associate professor of the University of Oklahoma School of Library Science, lecturing and teaching on the campus and conducting extension courses in the Tulsa area. She was a regular book reviewer for *Library Journal*. She contributed widely to other professional journals. Her philosophy and comments on activities and problems were voiced in a series of editorials ("Viewpoint," appearing in *Library Journal* during 1971) on a wide spectrum of topics:

continuing education, the role of the library as a community intelligence center, multi-media services, and the relationship of members and chapters to the American Library Association.

Many honors and awards were hers. One of which she was especially proud was her appointment by U.S. Speaker of the House of Representatives Carl Albert as one of his congressional appointees to the National Advisory Committee of the White House Conference on Library and Information Service, scheduled for the late 1970s. Her undergraduate college named her a distinguished alumna. In 1975, the University of Tulsa conferred upon her the honorary degree of Doctor of Humanities. In 1963, she was given the Newsmaker Award by Women in Communications, and in 1964, the Oklahoma chapter of American Women in Radio and Television presented her with the Woman of the Year Award. She was given a Certificate of Merit by Oklahoma State University. In December 1975, *Ladies Home Journal* nominated her for the Woman of the Year Award in the field of the humanities and community service.

In what Martin called her "sample case," a briefcase of gigantic proportions always crammed with projects under way or still in the germinating stage, it was only to be expected that part of the contents would relate to library associations. In Arkansas and later in Oklahoma, she had achieved stature. The next step was in the Southwestern Library Association, which she served as president in 1969-1970. What has been called the rebirth or revitalization of this regional association occurred under her leadership. In 1969, SWLA received the J. Morris Jones-ALA Goals Award, which resulted in the study "ALA Chapter Relationships—National, Regional, and State" (American Library Association, 1970). Grace Thomas Stevenson was the project director.

Also during Martin's term as president of SWLA, and as a result of her conviction that cooperation was the key to many solutions, SLICE (Southwestern Library Interstate Cooperative Endeavor) was born, partially funded with grants from the Council on Library Resources, and with support as well from the six state libraries represented. In February 1973, Martin was appointed project director of CELS (Continuing Education of Library Staffs), another concept to which she gave enthusiastic support. SWLA was made a vital force in the region, and the 1976 biennial conference in Albuquerque, New Mexico, was dedicated to Martin's memory.

Allie Beth Martin became a member of the American Library Association in 1935. She served on the executive boards of the Children's Services Division and the Public Library Association. She was a member of the ALA Membership Committee for many years, and its chairman from 1968 to 1973. She also chaired the Committee for a Greater ALA until 1967.

Martin wrote the study "A Strategy for Public Library Change," a project of the Public Library Association financed by a grant from the Council of Library Resources and the National Endowment for the Humanities. When it was published in 1972, it was heralded in a *Library Journal* editorial with the statement, "You have to hand it to Allie Beth Martin. With her leadership the study was published slightly more than a year after the grant was announced. . . . The report is a masterpiece of its kind: concise, straightforward, and readable. . . . A fine document."

Martin was elected to the ALA Council for the term 1972-1976, and to the Executive Board in 1973. In 1974, she became president-elect, and on July 4, 1975, at the ALA San Francisco conference, she became president of the American Library Association. Only a few months later, in October, she underwent surgery for cancer. Her indomitable spirit carried her through the 1976 Midwinter meeting of the Association and led to an unprecedented expression of appreciation by the ALA Council for her courageous leadership:

> Her competent performance and dedication to ALA's interests beyond thought of personal discomfort have given us an example of professional commitment rarely seen. She has touched the lives and careers of many among us, and brings to the profession a rich contribution of ideas, performance and encouragement. . . . We express our admiration of a great woman, a colleague, and a human being who understands the satisfaction of devoted service.

In spite of the increasing severity of her illness, she went frequently to her office until the final two weeks before her death on April 11, 1976. Her survivors include her daughter Betsy Piper, also a librarian; a grandson, David; and her two sisters. Her husband had died in 1968.

At ALA's centennial conference in Chicago, on July 20, 1976, Allie Beth Martin was named a Centennial Honorary Member, the Association's highest honor. The citation quotes from her inaugural address, "In Touch with Tomorrow," in which she challenged the Association to assure the delivery of user-oriented library and information service to all as its mission for its second century.

The June 1976 centennial issue of *American Libraries* was dedicated to Martin. CLENE (Continuing Library Education Network and Exchange) established an Allie Beth Martin Lecture for its assembly meetings. The Tulsa City-County Library established a scholarship fund for the continuing education of its staff members. The Arkansas Library Association funded a scholarship in her honor. State library journals across the nation expressed sorrow at her death and carried tributes to this dynamic woman.

As a person, Allie Beth Martin was a tapestry of many interests, many talents, many tastes. She was a worldwide traveller with appreciation for cultures other than her own. She enjoyed good food and was a gourmet cook. Her binoculars often focused on the birds in her garden. She appreciated the fine arts in all areas. She was indefatigable in the goals she set for herself, and expected others to be as tenacious. Her sense of humor was keen, and her hearty laughter lightened many a professional gathering. At her request, she was cremated following a memorial service at All Souls Unitarian Church in Tulsa on April 14, 1976.

· **Biographical listings and obituaries**—*A Biographical Directory of Librarians in the United States and Canada*, 5th ed.; *Current Biography* (1975); [Obituary]. *American Libraries* 7:238 (May 1976); [Obituary]. *Library Journal* 101:1175 (May 15, 1976); [Obituary]. *New York Times*, April 14, 1976, p. 42; [Obituary]. *Oklahoma Librarian* 26:3 (April 1976); *Who's Who in America* 39 (1976-1977); *Who's Who of American Women* 9 (1975-1976). **Books and articles about the biographee**—"ALA President Elect—Allie Beth Martin." *American Libraries* 6:22 (Jan. 1975); "The Centennial Issue of *American Libraries* Is Dedicated to Allie Beth Martin." *American Libraries* 7:332 (June 1976); Cooke, Eileen D. "Allie Beth's Spirit Carries on in Work for White House Conference." *American Libraries* 7:441 (July 1976); Fontaine, Sue. "Allie Beth Martin—A Tribute." *Library Journal* 101:1161 (May 15, 1976); Kennedy, Frances. "Allie Beth Martin: A Profile." *Oklahoma Librarian* 26:9-10 (July 1976); Stratton, John B. "Allie Beth Martin Honored for Distinguished Service." *Oklahoma Librarian* 11:45 (July 1961); Swartz, R. G. "Remembering Allie Beth Martin." *Wilson Library Bulletin* 50:773-74 (June 1976).

—FRANCES KENNEDY

McANALLY, ARTHUR MONROE (1911-1972)

Arthur Monroe McAnally was born on January 11, 1911, in Delaware, Arkansas, the son of Perry A. and Anne Humphreys McAnally. His elementary and secondary education was received in the public schools of western Arkansas. McAnally's higher education began at the University of Arkansas, where he was a student in 1928-1929. After transferring to the University of Oklahoma, he completed a B.A. in English in 1933, a B.A. in library science in 1935, and an M.A. in English in 1936. His library education was continued at the University of Chicago Graduate Library School, where he received a master's degree in 1941 and a Ph.D. in 1951. His doctoral dissertation was entitled "Characteristics of Materials Used in Research in United States History."

While still a student at the University of Oklahoma, McAnally was married to Lucille McGeorge, on February 6, 1935. They had three children, Marilyn Anne, Elizabeth Ann, and Perry Arthur.

McAnally's professional career was unusually varied. It began as a student assistant in the University of Oklahoma Library. His first professional position was in Edinburg, Texas, where he was supervisor of libraries for the junior college and public schools (1935-1938). There followed appointments as assistant librarian, University College, Northwestern University (1938-1939); assistant librarian, Knox College, Galesburg, Illinois (1939-1941); librarian, Bradley University, Peoria, Illinois (1941-1944); librarian, Wisconsin State Teachers College, Milwaukee (1944-1945); librarian, University of New Mexico (1945-1949); assistant director for public services, University of Illinois (1949-1951); and director of libraries, University of Oklahoma (1951-1972). He also served as director of the University of Oklahoma Library School from 1951 to 1960 and taught library administration in the School as well.

McAnally's professional experience included two periods of foreign assignments. In 1948, he was selected by the Library of Congress and the U.S. State Department to spend seven months as director of libraries at the oldest university in the Americas, the Universidad Nacional Mayor de San Marcos, Lima, Peru (see his "Reorganizing a South American University Library," *College & Research Libraries*, October 1949). A second appointment took him to the Mideast, where he served under Ford Foundation auspices and had a Fulbright appointment as visiting professor in the Ankara University School of Librarianship during the academic year 1963-1964. (His detailed report on this experience was condensed for publication in the *Oklahoma Librarian*, April 1965, in an article entitled "Teaching in a Foreign Library School.")

Virtually all of McAnally's numerous contributions to professional literature were in the form of periodical articles. *Library Literature* records at least sixty titles from 1937 to 1972. The topics dealt with demonstrate his wide range of interests: cataloging and book processing, book selection for junior college libraries, school libraries, adult education, library education, library service to undergraduates, organization of college and university libraries, departmental library systems, interlibrary loan standards, college and university library architecture, library cooperation, and the status of college and university librarians. His studies of interlibrary loan practices and efforts to develop national standards for such loans, undertaken for the Association of Research Libraries, had a significant influence. (See, for example, his "Interlibrary Loan, Library Cooperation," University of Tennessee Library Lecture, 1972; and "Recent Developments in Cooperation," *College & Research Libraries*, April 1951.)

In his last years, McAnally was concerned particularly with the place of professional librarians in academic institutions. Among his noteworthy contributions on this subject are: "The Dynamics of Securing Academic Status" (*College & Research Libraries*, September 1957); "Privileges and Obligations of Academic Status" (*College & Research Libraries*, March 1963); and "Status of the University Librarian in the Academic Community" (in *Research Librarianship*, ed. by Jerrold Orne [New York: Bowker, 1971]). McAnally's deep concern for this problem culminated in a landmark article (co-authored with Robert B. Downs and published posthumously), "The Changing Role of Directors of University Libraries" (*College & Research Libraries*, March 1973), a work that inspired widespread discussion and a reconsideration of the role of the library administrator in the structure of a modern university.

As director of the University of Oklahoma Library, McAnally's achievements were of substantial importance. Under his administration, a major addition to the central library building was completed in 1958 (discussed in a *Library Journal* article, "Building Ideas for Academe," December 1, 1956). With the addition, the available library space was more than doubled, and he was able to pioneer in what were, for that time, controversial innovations—faculty studies, open stacks, and subject reference areas. Collection development was of central concern, and the Oklahoma collection grew from approximately 450,000 to 1,300,000 volumes in the course of his administration. He was instrumental in forming the notable DeGolyer History of Science Collection and the Bass Collection of Business History at Oklahoma. He also obtained faculty status for the University Library staff and instituted a system of full staff participation in administration of the Library.

McAnally was an active participant in the work of various library organizations. He served as president of the New Mexico Library Association in 1947, of the Southwestern Library Association, 1960-1962, and of the Oklahoma Library Association in 1967.

Among many committee memberships, his most constructive work was carried on as chairman of the ACRL Committee on Academic Status for Librarians, the ARL Interlibrary Loan Study Committee, and chairman of the ACRL University Libraries Section. He was a member of the American Library Association Council from 1958 to 1962.

McAnally's intellectual vigor and ever insistent professional demands on himself and his colleagues for quality were softened by his sense of humor and his keen concern for the profession and the people in it. His interests ranged from numismatics to Western history to classic sport cars, and he was a vigorous and enthusiastic outdoor sportsman. He maintained a cabin at an altitude of 10,000 feet in Wyoming's Snowy Range Mountains, was a member of the Centennial Rod and Gun Club and the Indian Territory Posse of Oklahoma Westerners, and was an ardent fisherman and hunter. He dropped dead of a heart attack while on a hunting expedition on November 30, 1972.

Biographical listings and obituaries—*A Biographical Directory of Librarians in the United States and Canada*, 5th ed.; *Directory of Library Consultants*, 1969; *Who Was Who in America* V (1969-1973); *Who's Who in Consulting*, 2nd ed.; *Who's Who in Library Service*, 2nd ed., 4th ed.; Zink, James K. "Arthur M. McAnally [Obituary]." *Oklahoma Librarian* 23:29-30 (Jan. 1973). **Books and articles about the biographee**—Gibson, Arrell M. "Arthur M. McAnally: Portrait of a University Librarian." *Oklahoma Librarian* 23:6-7, 31-33 (April 1973). **Primary sources and archival materials**—The records of McAnally's tenure at the University of Oklahoma are in that University's Library.
—ROBERT B. DOWNS

McCARTHY, CHARLES (1873-1921)

Charles McCarthy was born in Brockton, Massachusetts, of poverty-striken Irish immigrant parents, John and Katherine O'Shea McCarthy, on June 29, 1873. Although he attended public schools, he was largely self-educated until attending Brown University, Providence, Rhode Island, where he was granted a Ph.B. in history in 1897. (In 1913, an honorary Doctor of Letters was also awarded.) Talent for playing football enabled him to become coach at the University of Georgia, where he earned enough money to begin graduate work at the University of Wisconsin in Madison. In 1901, he completed his Ph.D. in history under the direction of the famous historian Frederick Jackson Turner. McCarthy's dissertation on the Anti-Masonic Party won the Justin Winsor [q.v.] Prize, the highest award of the American Historical Association. In that same year, he married Lucile Schreiber; one daughter was born to them in 1905.

The year McCarthy graduated, the Wisconsin State Historical Society library collection, which had been housed in the Madison State Capitol, was moved from the Capitol to its own newly constructed building on the University of Wisconsin campus a mile away. Someone was needed to take charge of the documents remaining at the Capitol so that legislators could have them available at call. Professors who had taught McCarthy, such as J. Franklin Jameson at Brown and Turner at Wisconsin, thought the new position ideal for him because they knew how sensitive he was to the changing contemporary milieu, and how much he perceived the need to revamp laws and actively support change. Turner saw in the library position McCarthy's "opportunity to get in touch with legislation and help shape it," and that is precisely what McCarthy did for the remaining twenty years of his life. In preparation for the new position, McCarthy took a few technical courses in librarianship, but what he mastered in classification and cataloging courses was not what made him the famous librarian he became. It was rather what he

brought to the profession—the dimensions of an alert mind, rich experience, and a scholarly approach—that eventually made him successful.

McCarthy envisioned in the empty shell of the documents room a place to develop a non-partisan service for individual legislators so that the library would ultimately benefit both state and nation. The need for this type of legislative research center came from two late nineteenth century phenomena. First, the growth of direct democracy meant that persons elected to office were usually inexperienced in legislative procedures. An analysis of the membership of the Wisconsin legislature from 1901 to 1921, the period of McCarthy's activity, shows that a preponderant percentage of the lawmakers were farmers, lumbermen, and small businessmen, all unfamiliar with statute making. Second, the sudden impact of industrialization meant that well-researched and innovative laws had to deal with unprecedented situations. Understandably, the complexity of the times had not been foreseen by Wisconsin constitution drafters in 1848. Thus, McCarthy sought to collect information from all over the country and from other industrializing areas of the world so that its availability might help legislators to revise existing laws and to devise new ones to meet the new situation. Dependence on lobbyists and special interest groups would be eliminated, and law could be based on scientific research done in a special reference library.

The Legislative Reference Library, as this division of the Wisconsin Free Library Commission came to be called, bifurcated into two subdivisions, research and bill-drafting. The first of these was masterminded by McCarthy himself, who assumed its personal direction at all times. He would stay in his Library office as late as needed, sometimes overnight when the legislature was in session. He wrote or telegraphed every possible source of information for materials supporting both sides of an argument. Some regular correspondents were William Allen White, Gifford and Amos Pinchot, Ireland's Horace Plunkett, and England's Lord James Bryce. Not content with merely sending for descriptions of what was happening, however, McCarthy often went to observe firsthand. In pursuit of material for the workmen's compensation bill, he spent three months in Europe, going through hospitals and factories and observing in courts where cases of laboring persons were judged.

Once the material had been gathered into one place, McCarthy had a unique way of organizing it. He would indicate bills and articles to be saved, and a clerk would clip and mount each article, then give each the classification number that a book on the topic would receive. Notebooks held materials that were assigned the same classification. In short, a "book" evolved from all the current clippings on a particular topic. The "book" expanded each week as new material was added, thus remaining current.

The second Legislative Reference Library division, that of bill-drafting, had scarcely any personality of its own to compare with the dynamic research division personally directed by McCarthy, though it was equally publicized and likewise imitated. So successful was this technical division that over ninety percent of the bills drawn up in the 1901-1921 period were drafted in the "bill factory." Before this, lobbyists were often the chief writers of bills. Such innovative measures as minimum wage, water power regulation, workmen's compensation, continuation schools, and direct primary elections went through the bill-drafting division before they were voted into law in the Assembly.

To many staunch conservatives, "stalwart" Wisconsin residents, the Library was the source of seemingly reckless legislation. Others in the state (and Wisconsin was considered the leading progressive state) encouraged the innovative institution. Support came from other states and finally from legislators in Washington. Different types of people supported the Library—intellectuals of all varieties, ordinary citizens (the Library was often called the "people's lobby"), the American Bar Association, professional librarians, Republicans, Democrats, Socialists, Progressives of 1912, and "progressives" of all varieties. Robert M. LaFollette, both as governor and as U.S. senator, was an ardent backer of the Library, referring to McCarthy as a "man of marked originality and power" when urging support for a similar institution in Washington. Political officials from other states agreed with LaFollette's appraisal, and quickly the LRL was imitated in many states. Frequently, the first person hired was a protégé of McCarthy who had been trained in Wisconsin. Cities, too, called for McCarthy's expertise. In 1912, Philadelphia's mayor brought a group of one hundred city officials to observe Madison's experiment. Variations of the Library also sprang up at university centers such as Harvard, Columbia, and the University of Cincinnati. A unique variation was the permanent bureau set up by the Socialist Party and modeled on the Madison blueprint, with one of McCarthy's staff as assistant director. Duplicate institutions were founded in Dublin, Manila, Ceylon, and elsewhere overseas.

McCarthy's other accomplishments should be noted, though none was as significant as the Library. In 1912, he published *The Wisconsin Idea*, describing Wisconsin's progressive movement. Theodore Roosevelt wrote the preface. So impressed was the presidential candidate with the LRL librarian's ideas that he invited McCarthy to be one of his chief platform advisors at the Progressive Party convention that year. McCarthy was also research director for the Federal Commission on Industrial Relations in 1914-1915. He

served as first assistant to Food Administrator Herbert Hoover in 1917-1918 and went on a fact-finding trip to Europe for the War Labor Policies Board in 1918. After a short career of twenty years of service, McCarthy died, following a long illness, on March 26, 1921, at the age of 47.

Biographical listings and obituaries—*Dictionary of American Biography* 11 (Louis B. Wehle); Cooke, Morris Llewellyn. "In Death of 'Father of the Wisconsin Idea' Republic Has Lost One of Its Master Builders." *Public Ledger*, April 11, 1921; Littell, Robert. "McCarthy of Wisconsin." *New Republic*, April 27, 1921; Wehle, Louis B. "Charles McCarthy, 1873-1921." *Survey*, April 9, 1921. Books and articles about the biographee—Casey, Marion. "Charles McCarthy: Policy Maker for an Era." Ph.D. dissertation, University of Wisconsin, 1971; Casey, Marion. "Charles McCarthy's 'Idea': A Library to Change Government." *The Library Quarterly* 44 (Jan. 1974); Fitzpatrick, Edward A. *McCarthy of Wisconsin*. New York: Columbia University Press, 1944; Hochstein, Irma. "Work of Charles McCarthy in Fields of Minimum Wage, Child Labor and Apprenticeship Legislation in Wisconsin." Master's thesis, University of Wisconsin, 1929; Plunkett, Horace. "McCarthy of Wisconsin." *Nineteenth Century*, June 1915; Woerdehoff, Frank J. "Dr. Charles McCarthy: Planner of the Wisconsin System of Vocational and Adult Education." *Wisconsin Magazine of History*, Summer 1958; Woerdehoff, Frank J. "Dr. Charles McCarthy's Role in Revitalizing the University Extension Division." *Wisconsin Magazine of History*, Autumn 1956. Primary sources and archival materials—The State Historical Society of Wisconsin has 51 boxes of McCarthy papers plus many other collections that shed light on his career. Because of his wide contacts, McCarthy letters are also found in the collections of many leading out-of-state progressive leaders.

—MARION CASEY

McGUIRE, ALICE REBECCA BROOKS (1902-1975)

As an educator, as a practitioner in an experimental school library, as a consultant and speaker, as a leader in professional organizations, and as an author, Alice Brooks McGuire was influential in the field of school librarianship for more than four decades.

Alice Rebecca Brooks was born in Philadelphia, Pennsylvania, on August 9, 1902, the daughter of John and Anna Brooks. After graduation from high school in Amherst, Massachusetts, in 1919, she earned the A.B. degree from Smith College (1923). Two years of work as a teacher of Spanish and an assistant in the library of Slippery Rock State Teachers College (1923-1925) convinced her that she should choose librarianship as a career. Subsequent education at Drexel Institute of Technology (now Drexel University) (B.S. in L.S., 1926), Columbia University (M.S. in L.S., 1932), and the University of Chicago (Ph.D., 1958) gave her the educational background for distinguished service. At Columbia, she was an [Andrew] Carnegie [q.v.] fellow in 1931-1932; at Chicago, she held a university fellowship in 1944-1945.

After receiving her first professional degree in 1926, Alice Brooks, known to family and friends as "Sally," returned to Slippery Rock State Teachers College as a library assistant for two years. Then she accepted the invitation of the library school at Drexel to teach in the area of library services to children. She remained at Drexel as professor until 1944, meantime filling summer teaching appointments at the University of Southern California (1936), Albany (1939-1942), and Geneseo (1943).

In 1944, Sally Brooks went to the Graduate Library School, University of Chicago, as an instructor in library work with children and as a doctoral student. Her students at Chicago remembered her as a creative teacher who alerted them to the opportunities for developing children's motivation for reading and learning. During her stay in Chicago, she also served as director of the Center for Instructional Materials (later known as the Center for Children's Books) at the University, 1944-1949.

It was at Chicago, too, that she married John Carson McGuire, a professor of educational psychology, who joined the faculty of the University of Texas at Austin in 1949. In Texas, Sally planned to teach and finish her doctoral dissertation; but University nepotism rules thwarted efforts of the Graduate School of Library Science at Texas to employ her while her husband was employed there. Correspondence on file at Texas indicates that she was sorely disappointed at the turn of events, but she did not choose to be inactive professionally; instead, she agreed in 1951 to become the librarian of a new public elementary school (Casis) designed to serve as the laboratory school for the University. Characteristically, she did an outstanding, enthusiastic job—so much so that her library philosophy of service, communication, and participation came to be widely admired and emulated by librarians and school administrators during the 1950s and 1960s. Through supervising the internship of future school administrators and librarians with school library specializations, she continued to teach university students on an individual basis. Also, she taught formally during two summers (Arizona, 1958; Columbia, 1965).

In 1967, practitioner Alice Brooks McGuire, still youthful in spirit, reached the retirement age of 65. In the intervening years since 1949, the University of Texas nepotism rules had been changed, so she was employed as a teacher by the Graduate School of Library Science until 1972. While on the University faculty, she taught one summer at the University of Washington (1971) and, after her second retirement, one semester at the University of South Florida (Spring 1975).

As a practitioner in an elementary school library, she was beloved by several generations of children, who called her "Mrs. Library McGuire." But perhaps her main contribution as a practitioner came through her frequent service as a speaker, consultant, and workshop director throughout the country from 1951 until her death in 1975. In these latter capacities, she campaigned to educate school administrators, as well as librarians, to the contributions that a library can make to the educational program of a school. In 1964, Casis was chosen by the American Association of School Librarians to be one of three elementary schools in the United States to serve as centers for the demonstration of exemplary library services. Funds were provided by the Knapp Foundation to support the demonstration and to make it possible for school administrators, librarians, and teachers to travel from all over the United States during the years 1964-1967 to observe McGuire's library program in action. Although the Knapp grant enabled Casis School to add some new activities and materials, it had already been recognized as a well-established, quality program.

In professional organizations at the national level, Sally McGuire made her mark in the American Library Association as a member of the Board of Education for Librarianship, the Awards Committee, the Committee on the Code of Ethics for Librarians, and as a two-time member of Council (1954-1958, 1967-1970). In the Children's Services Division, she was three times a member of the Newbery-Caldecott Committee, Chairman of the Research Committee, and member of the Jane Addams Book Award Committee. In 1962, she received the Grolier Award in recognition of her activities in the fields of children's literature and reading.

As president of the American Association of School Librarians in 1953-1954, and as a member of its Board of Directors, she brought breadth of vision to this organization early in its emergence as a full-fledged division of ALA. Her leadership helped to keep alive the cooperative relationship that bound children's librarians and school librarians together in their common concern for the quality of children's books and reading. She participated in the AASL School Library Development Project and the work of its 1960 Standards Committee. Also, she was a member of library committees in the International Reading Association and the National Council of Teachers of English. The librarians of Texas named her "Librarian of the Year" in 1968.

The bibliography of her writings published between 1932 and 1975 contains more than eighty items, all dealing in some way with library services to children and young people. She was a pioneer in the area of analyzing children's books in terms of developmental themes and values. As director of the Center for Instructional Materials (University of Chicago, 1944-1949), she was the founding editor of the *Service Bulletin*, forerunner of the *Bulletin of the*

Center for Children's Books. Her reviews gave particular attention to a book's value for a child's personal development. Through contacts with writers, she sought to identify the beliefs reflected in their writings and the values they hoped to communicate to children. In the process, she formed lasting friendships with many authors and illustrators.

Also in publishing, she was editor of *Top of the News* (1949-1950), school and children's library editor for the *Wilson Library Bulletin* (1950-1960), on the Advisory Board of *Compton's Encyclopedia* (1969-1972), and contributing editor in children's literature for *The Reading Teacher* (1969-1972).

When she died suddenly in 1975, Alice Brooks McGuire left a rich professional legacy built on her intellectual acumen and her uncompromising sense of values. She also left a host of friends who remembered her zest for life, her animation and enthusiasm, her contagious laughter, her wit, and her lively interest in new scenes and new activities, and above all, her integrity and great respect for all people. One close colleague, Sara Fenwick, said in *In Celebration of Alice Brooks McGuire* (p. 22), "To all of us she exemplified an approach to the continuity of living and learning and giving that we would cherish." Alice Brooks McGuire died on July 8, 1975.

Biographical listings and obituaries—*Biographical Directory of Librarians in the United States and Canada,* 5th ed.; *Foremost Women in Communications,* 1970; [Obituary]. *American Libraries* 6:509 (Sept. 1975); *Who Was Who in America* VI (1974-1976); *Who's Who in Library Service,* 3rd ed., 4th ed. Books and articles about the biographee— "ALA Awards and Citations for 1962." *Library Journal* 87:2692 (Aug. 1962) (portrait); "Alice Brooks McGuire." *Top of the News* 6:26 (May 1950) (portrait); *In Celebration of Alice Brooks McGuire.* Privately published by Annabelle Quigley, 1976. Primary sources and archival materials— Files of the Graduate School of Library Science, The University of Texas at Austin contain material concerning Alice Brooks McGuire.

—CLAUD GLENN SPARKS
—MATTIE RUTH MOORE

McKIM, CHARLES FOLLEN (1847-1909)
See RICHARDSON, HENRY HOBSON

McMURTRIE, DOUGLAS CRAWFORD (1888-1944)

Douglas Crawford McMurtrie, bibliographer and recognized authority in the field of graphic arts, was born July 20, 1888, at Belmar, New Jersey, one of the two children of William McMurtrie, a well-to-do industrial chemist, and Helen M. Douglass McMurtrie. His first years of schooling began at Hamilton Institute Military Day School in New York City. At Horace Mann School, at the young age of thirteen, he gained his first printing and publishing experience. In partnership with three schoolmates, under the influence of the writing of "that competent essayist,

Joseph Addison," he established "The Junior Spectator," which undertaking marked the beginning of the careers of three noted men: Douglas C. McMurtrie, a typographer, noted bibliographer, and a foremost authority on American imprints; Edward Goodman, a name famous in theatrical history; and Morris Ernst, the famous American lawyer and defender of "freedom of speech" in print. The Hill School of Pottstown, Pennsylvania, was young McMurtrie's next educational destination. Here he had an opportunity to work out some of his early theories of typographical arrangement while he served as the business manager of the School's yearbook.

In 1906, he was sent to the Massachusetts Institute of Technology to study electrical engineering. While there, he was typographical designer of the Institute's yearbook and served as managing editor of the college newspaper. He also acted as campus correspondent for three Boston daily newspapers—an activity that was, however, soon to be curbed because of the intriguing items he wrote about the School. Interest in typography soon won out over training as an engineer, and after three years, he left school without graduating. He subsequently moved into the field of printing, which remained both his vocation and his avocation until his unexpected death on September 29, 1944, at the age of 56. He participated fully in all aspects of the printing industry: designing typefaces and quality publications; owning his own press and producing his own materials; studying printing as both a technical skill and an art form; establishing bibliographic control over American imprints, particularly early printing within each state; and studying the historical development of his craft.

McMurtrie joined the Pittsburgh Typhoid Fever Commission in 1909 to work as a statistician, but he soon handled the printing production of that organization. From Pittsburgh, he went back to New York as a freelance designer and printer. His former classmate Edward Goodman commissioned him to print the theatrical weekly program for the *Band Box Theatre.* McMurtrie responded with a program that reflected his artistic flair: cream laid paper, wide margins, quarto size, set throughout in original Caslon and adorned with a cover design and lettering by Frederic W. Goudy! Ingalls Kimball, co-designer of the famous Cheltenham typeface, saw one of the programs, and McMurtrie forthwith became general manager of the Cheltenham Press and typographical advisor to the Cheltenham Advertising Agency. His duties there were primarily managerial, however. Not until 1917 did McMurtrie become involved again in the production end of the printing business, when he was appointed director of the Columbia University Printing Office.

While manager of the Columbia University Printing Office, McMurtrie produced many outstanding volumes. When Columbia's plant equipment was sold in 1919, he became president of the Arbor Press plant. With all his "artistic flair," McMurtrie was continuously guided by an instinct for the practical. His strong feeling that high-quality printing could best be produced in the country, free from metropolitan distractions, "yet close enough to a large city to provide easy access to customers and materials," led him to build a modern printing plant at Greenwich, Connecticut, in 1921. The work produced at the new plant was praised for its exceptional quality, especially since it was done in "a period when facilities for the production of fine printing were relatively scarce." Lack of a greater working capital, however, forced him that same year to sell the plant to Condé Nast Publications which, in turn, became Condé Nast Press. McMurtrie was engaged as general manager. During his employment with the Condé Nast Press (1921-1923), he designed two typefaces, McMurtrie Title and Vanity Fair Capitals, and helped design the format for the *New Yorker* magazine.

In 1923, McMurtrie turned again to freelancing in New York for two years, during which time he served as editor of *Ars Typographica*, a "little magazine" of the printing world (1925-1926). In 1925, he became typographic director of the Cuneo Press in Chicago and, in 1926, he accepted the position of director of typography at the Ludlow Typograph Company. McMurtrie remained with the Ludlow firm until his untimely death.

McMurtrie's responsibilities at the Ludlow firm were primarily in advertising and public relations, for which he was excellently suited, "being gregarious, sociable, fluent, and an excellent copywriter." The Ludlow firm provided him with substantial support for his writing and research. However, even before he became associated with the Ludlow Typograph Company, he conceived the design—later named Ultra-Modern—which was accepted and cut by Ludlow and became recognized as the first modern design offered by any American typefounding company in a full range of upper and lower case. This face became instantly popular and led the list of best-sellers in Ludlow's typographic repertory. McMurtrie also designed deluxe publications and catalogs for the Metropolitan Museum of Art and pioneered in the design and production of fine trade books for the Macmillan Company and for other organizations. A number of his works have been included among the "Fifty Books of the Year," a selection made by the American Institute of Graphic Arts on the basis of the physical excellence of the books—typographic design, binding, paper, etc.

McMurtrie was an ardent proponent of the adoption of printing innovations and was largely responsible for a closer study of and heightened American interest in modern European typography.

He was a co-founder of the Continental Type Founders Association, which brought many European typefaces to the United States. He himself imported the original Didot typeface, and the Cochin, Narciss, Le Mercure, and Astree typefaces. His 1929 book *Modern Typography and Layout* presented his ideas at this time.

McMurtrie's activities as bibliographer and historian of printing alone provide sufficient claim to his remembrance. He prepared English translations of documents related to Gutenberg, *The Gutenberg Documents* (1940), and published a notable history of printing, *The Golden Book* (1927). Subsequently retitled simply *The Book* (1938), it has served as a textbook for numerous courses in printing history. Shortly before his death, he displayed an intense interest in the underground press of Europe during World War II, and published several periodical articles while preparing to write a major book on the subject.

He also devoted a great deal of time and effort to uncovering the much-neglected records of the beginnings of printing in America and observed that, for many states, there was no record of first printings and, for others, the records were contradictory. He projected a multi-volume history of printing in the United States as the first comprehensive survey since Isaiah Thomas's *History of Printing in the United States* (1810), and he initiated a painstaking research effort to document the history of printing within each state. His numerous pamphlets and journal articles on local printing document his progress, but only Volume 2 (1936) of his project, covering the Middle-Atlantic states, was completed before his death. He revised previously accepted records of the beginnings of printing in at least fourteen states.

In 1936, McMurtrie was appointed project director for the American Imprints Inventory that was carried out under the auspices of the Works Progress Administration. He was criticized for recruiting people without bibliographic experience and training to do the local inventorying, but he trained them well and established a central office where editorial control was maintained through the assistance of his associate, Albert H. Allen. When the war interrupted the WPA-supported work, the Bibliographical Society, through its president, Thomas W. Streeter, arranged for foundation support; thus, the project was continued for a time at the Newberry Library in Chicago. The slips gathered by his workers, and estimated at over fifteen million, remained in manuscript form at the Library of Congress and were used infrequently for student papers and scholarly research. Eventually Ralph Shaw (q.v.) and Richard Shoemaker (q.v.) relied heavily on them in preparation of their *American Bibliography*. McMurtrie directed another WPA project—an unpublished index to printing periodicals;

its thousands of cards were later transferred to Michigan State University.

Douglas McMurtrie did not receive the accolades of scholarly bibliographers while he was alive, a factor that affected him more than would be expected. Questions are still raised about who was intellectually responsible for his publications. In a comprehensive bibliography of his separately published works in 1942, he commented:

My associate, Albert H. Allen, has contributed in a large degree to the value of my bibliographical and historical writings published during the past fifteen years, and I desire to make this general, yet grateful acknowledgement of his cooperation. While I have done almost all the exploration and field work, Mr. Allen, by his able and painstaking work, has contributed immeasurably to the comprehensiveness, consistency, and accuracy of the material published.

An appraisal of McMurtrie's work is found in Charles F. Heartman's *McMurtrie Imprints* (1942). Although McMurtrie's contributions encompass a variety of subjects—including a children's story about Gutenberg, *Wings for Words* (in collaboration with Don Farran, 1940)—his chief importance lies in the bibliographical works that number over five hundred titles.

A somewhat flamboyant man in both size and demeanor, McMurtrie was not always accepted by professional bibliographers, whose judgment about the quality of his work may have been affected by their astonishment at the tremendous range of his interests and the sheer volume of his production. He was generous in allocating time to his interests in printing associations and library activities and was a frequent and invariably interesting guest speaker at conferences. He maintained extensive correspondence with bookmen and "his seemingly boundless physical energy when in pursuit of an elusive imprint" amazed his friends.

His early interest in crippled people, especially children, eventually led him to edit and publish the *American Journal of Care for Cripples.* In 1915, he became president of the Federation of Associations for Cripples. The extensive personal library he amassed on the subject was subsequently given to the Society for Crippled Children. As a recognized authority on the rehabilitation of disabled persons, he was also appointed director of the Red Cross Institute for Crippled and Disabled Men, which was responsible for the physical and emotional rehabilitation and vocational training of disabled veterans of World War I. He described the work with disabled soldiers in his works: *Vocational Re-education of Disabled Soldiers and Sailors* (1918) and *The Disabled Soldier* (1919). McMurtrie is credited with setting up the first modern shop for the manufacture of prosthetic devices (artificial limbs) and setting up the first training school in this country for adult cripples. Another valuable feature of his work with the Red Cross was his contribution in connection with the blind.

McMurtrie was active in many organizations and was an officer in several. He was vice-president, Continental Type Founders Association (1925-1926); president, John Calhoun Club, Chicago (1929); editor, *Bulletin of the Chicago Historical Society* (1934); and chairman of both the Invention of Printing Anniversary Committee (1939-1940) and the Educational Commission (1940), both committees of the International Associations of Printing House Craftsmen, Inc. He was elected to membership in many distinguished literary, bibliographical and scholarly organizations: Bibliographical Societies of London and America, American Institute of Graphic Arts, Society of Typographic Arts, American Historical Association, Southern Historical Association, Mississippi Valley Historical Association, Gutenberg Gesellschaft and Deutscher Buchgewerbeverein. Living in Chicago as he did, McMurtrie was a well-known figure to the members of the American Library Association headquarters staff. He attended numerous ALA conferences and often spoke at them.

No appraisal of Douglas Crawford McMurtrie, writes Herbert A. Kellar in his articles on McMurtrie, is adequate without reference to his appearance, physical energy, personality and intellectual traits, all of which in combination contributed to produce a unique, dynamic figure. Kellar described him as "immense in size, a veritable giant, standing well over six feet tall and weighing, in his prime, approximately four hundred pounds. Possessed of great physical strength and endurance, directed by a versatile mind, he evidenced phenomenal energy in whatsoever he undertook to do." His interests were so varied that Kellar further wrote:

Engaged in research; writing articles and books; dictating; making speeches; holding conferences; listening to music at concerts, the opera or elsewhere; attending the theatre; traveling; participating in conventions; dining and dancing; his varied activities consumed all the working hours of the day and reached far into the night. Sleep meant little to him and a few hours of rest invariably were sufficient to renew his energies.

McMurtrie was known to be generous with his time and vast knowledge, supplementing the information sought from him personally through an extensive correspondence, both in this country and abroad. He was a fluent lecturer and engaging conversationalist. His wit and generosity won him many friends, though some were put off by his flamboyance. He found great pleasure in dancing, at which he was excellent, and "people often stopped dancing themselves to watch him." He was an excellent cook and connoisseur of food, and was well known among chefs and restaurant proprietors in this country and abroad for both his culinary knowledge and his appreciation for good food.

He had married Adele Koehler on February 20, 1915; they had three children, Havelock Heydon, Helen Josephine, and Thomas Baskerville.

Librarians, bibliographers, and scholars in all fields and all over the world for a number of generations will remain indebted to McMurtrie for his achievements. Randolph G. Adams wrote in an obituary of McMurtrie that

> for many years to come there will be those who remember Douglas McMurtrie for many other things besides his bibliographical contributions and his seemingly boundless physical energy when in pursuit of an elusive imprint. His personality, his geniality, his stimulating conversation and above all his hearty laugh will never be forgotten by those who knew him.

McMurtrie's contribution to the world of learning and humanity has been acclaimed by many, but the most eloquent praise has been made by Herbert A. Kellar, who wrote:

> The variety and quality of Douglas Crawford McMurtrie's contributions to the knowledge of advertising, fine printing, bibliography, and the history of printing, and his services as a humanitarian, are distinguished and lasting. His accomplishments and fabulous personality early set him off as a man apart from his contemporaries. For many years, tales and stories accumulated about his activities, and these were often related with gusto and admiration at gatherings of those who knew him. As I have said and written at other times, Douglas McMurtrie became a legend within his own time.

Biographical listings and obituaries–Adams, Randolph G. "Douglas Crawford McMurtrie, 1888-1944 [Obituary]." *Bibliographical Society of America News Sheet*, no. 65:3-4 (Jan. 1, 1945); *Current Biography* (Biography: June 1944; Obituary: Nov. 1944); "D. C. M'Murtrie, 56, Designer of Type [Obituary]." *New York Times* (Sept. 30, 1944); *Dictionary of American Biography*, 3rd Supplement (James M. Wells); "Douglas Crawford McMurtrie: 1888-1944 [Obituary]." *College and Research Libraries* 6:82-83 (Dec. 1944); "Obituary: Douglas C. McMurtrie." *Publishers' Weekly*, Oct. 7, 1944, p. 1505; [Obituary]. *Wilson Library Bulletin* 19, no. 3:155 (Nov. 1944); *Who Was Who in America* I (1943-1950). **Books and articles about the biographee**– Bond, John C. "Rewrite American History." *The Christian Science Monitor*, March 23, 1940, p. 7; "Douglas C. McMurtrie." *New York Herald Tribune Weekly Book Review*, Oct. 29, 1944, p. 28; Heartman, Charles F. *McMurtrie Imprints; A Bibliography of Separately Printed Writings by Douglas C. McMurtrie on Printing and Its History in the United States... With an Appraisal of McMurtrie's Work*. (Privately printed for The Book Farm.) Hattiesburg, Miss., 1942. *Supplement*. Biloxi, Miss.: (Privately printed for The Book Farm), 1946; Kellar, Herbert A. "The Historian and

Life." *Mississippi Valley Historical Review* 34:3-36 (June 1947); Kellar, Herbert A. *Douglas Crawford McMurtrie: Historian of Printing and Bibliographer*. Washington, D.C., 1955; McCoffrey, Frank. *An Informal Biography of D. C. M.* [Privately printed], 1939; Towne, Jackson E. "Douglas C. McMurtrie, 1888-1944." *Stechert-Hafner Book News* 16:17-19 (Oct. 1961).

–KATHERINE CVELJO
–MARILYN DOMAS WHITE

MEEHAN, JOHN SILVA (1790-1863)

John Silva Meehan, printer, publisher, and Librarian of Congress, was born in New York City on February 6, 1790, and was educated there. He went to Burlington, New Jersey, in 1811 or 1812, to take part in the printing of Richard S. Coxe's *New Critical Pronouncing Dictionary of the English Language*, but in January 1815 was back in New York City, where he was warranted as a midshipman in the United States Navy. Assigned to serve aboard the Brig *Firefly*, he remained with that vessel until April, the restoration of peace with Great Britain having thwarted plans to cruise in the West Indies in pursuit of enemy commerce. He was offered a commission in the Marine Corps but chose to take up printing again and moved to Philadelphia. There, with Robert Anderson, Meehan began publishing a Baptist journal in 1818. After moving to Washington in 1822, the two began publishing a weekly newspaper, *The Columbian Star*, also under Baptist auspices.

In 1826, Meehan turned to the publication of a political journal and acquired the *Washington Gazette*. Renamed *The United States' Telegraph*, the newspaper was friendly to Andrew Jackson and John C. Calhoun. However, it soon became apparent that Meehan was not mounting the desired type of attack against the Adams administration, and the *Telegraph* was taken over by the dynamic and forceful Duff Green. After leaving the *Telegraph*, Meehan served for a time as secretary of the Board of Trustees of Columbian College. He is also said to have continued his support during this period for the election of Jackson in 1828.

On May 28, 1829, Meehan was appointed by Jackson as the fourth Librarian of Congress. Eminently acceptable on the score of his past political loyalty, he was nevertheless careful throughout his long incumbency to avoid partisan activity. George Watterston (q.v.), whom he replaced, had been less so, and resorted unsuccessfully to a press campaign to set aside Meehan's appointment. For years thereafter, Watterston used threats, cajolery, and flattery in vain attempts to regain his former position.

Meehan was 39 years old when he became Librarian. He was 5 feet, 7 inches tall, had brown hair, brown eyes, and a complexion tending toward the florid. By most accounts he was amiable, gentlemanly, precise, anxious to be of service, and a good businessman. The Library that he took over occupied the greater part of the central portion of the western front of the United States Capitol. Some 16,000 volumes reposed there, carefully arranged on shelves in the Library's alcoves according to the classification scheme inherited from Thomas Jefferson (q.v.). Meehan began his career in the Library with one assistant and gradually increased his staff to five, including his son, Charles Henry Wharton Meehan, who later was placed in charge of the Library's law department. The Librarian's salary was $1,500 in 1829 and eventually rose to $2,160. During Meehan's last year in the Library (1861), the total appropriation was $17,000.

Two opportunities were presented, in 1836 and 1844, which, if acted upon, would have set the Library of Congress upon a course toward becoming the first library in the land. The first of these involved an offer to purchase the library, famed throughout Europe, of Count Dimitrii Petrovich Buturlin. The price for this unique collection, consisting of 25,000 volumes and a number of valuable manuscripts, was in the range of $50,000 to $60,000, well below its true value. Although the support of the Joint Committee on the Library was given, a resolution favorable to the purchase of the Buturlin Library was rejected on the floor of the Senate. The loss of the Buturlin Library also had the effect of serving as a precedent for the rejection in 1844 of an offer to purchase the 10,000-volume library of the Durazzo family in Italy, considered one of the choicest private libraries in Europe. For all practical purposes, notice had been given that the Library of Congress was to remain a legislative library and that proponents of a national library would have to look elsewhere.

Meehan appears to have played no role in the attempt to acquire these two collections. This passivity was in keeping with his view of the Librarian as a creature of Congress, whose bidding he was always careful to do. Meehan's most significant encounters, understandably, were with the members of the Joint Committee and particularly with its chairman. In 1845, at a time when the Library was described in a guide book as consisting of "about forty thousand volumes, in a large and elegant room, and disposed in order by an excellent librarian," Senator James Alfred Pearce of Maryland came to the Committee. An era of extraordinarily close collaboration between Pearce and Meehan was thereby inaugurated, although there was never any question of the deferential nature of this relationship. Pearce, in fact, must thenceforth be considered as the dominant figure in Library affairs.

The legislation establishing the Smithsonian Institution in 1846 contained an interesting provision relating to federal copyright law that had the potential of greatly enriching the Library's collections.

According to this provision, one copy of each book, map, chart, musical composition, print, cut, or engraving produced in the United States was to be placed in the Library of Congress. However, the implementation of this grand scheme for building national library resources was hindered by practical difficulties and impeded by differences of opinion. The legislation itself was faulty because it failed to provide Meehan with any means of compelling copyright deposits to be made, and, furthermore, the actual validity of a copyright did not appear to depend on a deposit. Meehan, who had many routine duties to perform and who found the processing of copyright deposits burdensome, did what was expected of him but was otherwise unenterprising. In 1859, the copyright provision, insofar as it involved the Library of Congress, was repealed.

The most dramatic event of Librarian Meehan's long incumbency occurred on December 24, 1851. Sometime before 8 o'clock on that morning, the Library Room was reported to be on fire, and in a few hours' time it was almost totally destroyed. An estimated 35,000 volumes were lost, including two-thirds of Jefferson's library; some 20,000 volumes, many of which were housed in adjoining rooms, were saved. A few buckets of water would have been enough to extinguish the flames at the outset, but the rapid and extensive spread of the fire soon carried the situation beyond all control. No blame was ever attached to Meehan for the catastrophe, and plans were made almost immediately for the reconstruction of the Library Room and the acquisition of the books to stock it. Congress responded in both instances, voting special appropriations that eventually amounted to $85,000 for the purchase of books and $93,000 for the restoration of the Library Room. On July 6, 1853, Meehan took formal possession of the restored Library, thought by some to be one of the most beautiful rooms in the world. Meehan was preoccupied over the next few years with replacing the lost books, but for the most part, he moved cautiously, relying upon the Library's earlier catalogs in preparing his want lists, and dealing almost exclusively with the firm of Rich Brothers in London. Some opportunities were presented for enlarging the Librarian's powers at this time, but Meehan preferred to follow the more modest tradition of working closely within the framework of the Library Committee. As a result of the special appropriations of 1852 and annual appropriations of $5,000 thereafter, the Library grew rapidly in the years after the fire, and in April 1856, Meehan was able to announce to Senator Pearce that 36,000 volumes from those catalog-based want lists had been purchased and that the losses had been entirely made good.

The international exchange of duplicate library materials as a means of enlarging and enhancing the collections of the Library of Congress was first promoted before Congress in 1840. The idea originated with Alexandre Vattemare (q.v.), a French citizen who had already achieved some success with this form of cooperation in Europe. He found favor with Congress, and Meehan was authorized to participate. However, the Librarian, who held a low opinion of Vattemare and believed in more traditional channels of acquisition, did not actively prosecute the international exchange program. Vattemare returned to the United States in 1848 and broached more ambitious plans, for which he again received congressional approval. The program now began to show some results, but growing distrust of Vattemare (not only by Meehan but by other American librarians and by French officials as well) and the poor quality of some of the materials received through Vattemare's agency led in 1853 to the abandonment of the exchange program.

Four printed catalogs of the contents of the Library were prepared by Meehan and his staff—in 1830 (258p.), 1839 (747p.), 1849 (1022p.), and 1861 (1398p.). A number of supplementary catalogs issued in intervening years tended to add to the cumbersomeness of a system based on the increasingly outmoded Jeffersonian classifications. Although Meehan never undertook it himself, one attempt was made at the Library of Congress in 1853 to carry out a wholesale reformation of cataloging through the preparation of stereotype plates for titles of the volumes in the Library. The brainchild of Charles C. Jewett (q.v.), librarian of the Smithsonian Institution, this system, by eventually taking account of the catalogs of other libraries, was promoted as a means toward central, uniform cataloging. Appropriations failed, however, and Jewett, who had continued to guide the stereotyping program, was dismissed from the Smithsonian in 1854. Lacking such essential support, the program soon faltered and came to a close.

Meehan experienced few serious threats of removal during his many years as Librarian. It had been his practice to remain cautiously non-political throughout his public life, and he had his record of survival to show how successful he had been. With the election of Lincoln in 1860, however, Meehan found himself in a difficult position. Senator Pearce, with whom he was so closely identified, had left the Whig party in 1856 to become a National Democrat. Although Pearce was a Unionist, he was also a Marylander, representing a state that was generally pro-Southern, and he found himself unable to declare boldly and clearly for the Union. As far as the Library of Congress was concerned, this meant a diminution of the chairman's influence. As far as John Silva Meehan was concerned, it meant the end of his long career. Although there were rumors of pro-Southern

sympathies on the part of Meehan, no evidence exists to this effect. Ainsworth Rand Spofford (q.v.) later was to say that Meehan had been removed only because he was "a very ancient fossil." Senator Pearce tried to intervene with Lincoln in Meehan's behalf, but to no avail, and John G. Stephenson (q.v.), an Indiana physician, replaced him on May 24, 1861. Meehan took his dismissal calmly and without rancor.

His retirement was not entirely untroubled, for his successor prepared an elaborate report for the Joint Committee detailing the shortcomings of the Library. Beyond the criticism leveled at him at the conclusion of his almost 32-year administration, some has followed him throughout the years, based on the broad grounds that Meehan and those others who had influence and authority in Library matters were willing to settle for too little. The history of the Library over the period 1829-1861 appears to be a chronicle of lost opportunities, opportunities for the enhancement of the Library through international and domestic exchanges, through the vigorous observance of copyright provisions, through timely special purchases, and by other means as well. Vision, imagination, and vigor seemed to be lacking, particularly concerning matters that by their very nature would have placed the Library on the road to becoming a true national library. Yet, given the reality of the situation, which involved the general apathy of Congress where Library affairs were concerned and which must take account of the measured manner in which the powerful Senator Pearce controlled the Library, it is not so surprising that it was, and remained, a legislative library, the kind of library that Congress wanted.

Meehan survived in retirement for approximately two years, dying of apoplexy at his home on Capitol Hill on April 24, 1863. An obituary noted that "he was remarkably punctual and assiduous in his duties, unobtrusive, moral, and domestic in his habits, and of sterling integrity as a man." He had been married twice, first in 1814 to Margaret Jones Monington, who died in 1826, shortly after the birth of their seventh child; and then to his wife's sister, Rachel T. Monington, in October 1827. Rachel bore him two children. Only three of Meehan's children are known to have survived him.

Biographical listings and obituaries—National Cyclopaedia of American Biography 13. Books and articles about the biographee—Cole, John Y., Jr. "Ainsworth Spofford and the 'National Library'." Unpublished dissertation, George Washington University, 1971; Johnston, William Dawson. History of the Library of Congress, 1800-1864. Washington, 1904; McDonough, John. "John Silva Meehan." Quarterly Journal 33, No. 1:3-28 (Jan. 1976); Mearns, David C. The Story up to Now: The Library of Congress, 1800-1946. Washington, 1947. Primary sources and archival materials—John Silva Meehan Papers, Manuscript Division, Library of Congress; Librarian's Letterbooks, Library of Congress Archives, Manuscript Division, Library of Congress.

—JOHN McDONOUGH

MELCHER, FREDERIC GERSHOM (1879-1963)

Frederic Gershom Melcher was managing editor, editor, and co-editor of the *Publishers' Weekly* for over forty years, head of its parent publishing house, the R. R. Bowker [q.v.] Company (New York), and a leader in key areas of the book industry during a period of major expansion. As an active participant in the organizations of booksellers, publishers, librarians, typographers, and authors, he exerted wide influence. In an era when colorful personalities were prominent in the industry and corporate structure was secondary to individual management, Melcher held a recognized place because of his enthusiasm for books and his warmth in personal relations, and he was credited with encouraging many young persons to enter the book industry and the library profession.

Melcher was born April 12, 1879, in Malden, Massachusetts, to Edwin Forrest and Alice Jane Bartlett Melcher. Four years later, the family moved to Newton Center, then a relatively isolated country village, where he took a college preparatory course at Newton High School, hoping to enter Massachusetts Institute of Technology. At the time of his graduation, however, a combination of family illness and poor economic conditions led him instead to look for a job. His maternal grandfather, having a family interest in the Boston building that housed the then-famous Estes & Lauriat Bookstore, inquired about an opening for him there, and in June 1895, at $4 a week, Fred Melcher went to work in Lauriat's mail room.

Within a few years, he became a salesman on the main floor of Lauriat's and became known to the store's clientele for his knack of matching books to customers and his personal charm and enthusiasm. His instinct as a bookseller was proved when, in effect, he launched Arnold Bennett's *Old Wives' Tale* in the United States by placing an order for five hundred copies. This prompted the American publisher, George H. Doran, to give the book a major promotion so that it became a best seller.

Melcher also took charge of the sale of children's books at Lauriat's. With the help of review lists prepared by Caroline M. Hewins (q.v.), he attracted to Lauriat's a sizeable clientele seeking advice about children's reading. Thereafter, he encouraged in many ways the new trends toward specialized publishing and library work for children: through his friendships with pioneering editors and librarians, through editorials and articles in *Publishers' Weekly* and *Library Journal*, and through publicity and promotion campaigns for children's reading. In 1947, he set up in Caroline Hewins's honor an annual lectureship on New England children's books, to be given at the meetings of the New England Library Association.

In 1910, he was married to Marguerite Fellows, later an author of children's books, plays, and Americana. In 1913, the family moved to Indianapolis, where he had been named manager of the W. K. Stewart Bookstore. During his five years at Stewart's, the Indiana literary movement—the "Hoosier school" of writing—was at its height. Melcher became acquainted with Booth Tarkington, George Ade, James Whitcomb Riley, and Meredith Nicholson and promoted their work. He also met Vachel Lindsay and helped circulate his poems. Later, he became known among librarians and others for his own readings of Lindsay and other poets who had become friends, especially Carl Sandburg and Robert Frost.

It was in Indianapolis also that Melcher became a friend of Edwin and Robert Grabhorn, fine printers whose later work in San Francisco was to achieve acclaim. Fred Melcher had already learned at Lauriat's to appreciate excellence in design and book production. For the rest of his life, he encouraged and extolled the fine printers and designers of his era and counted many as close friends and associates, notably Bruce Rogers, W. A. Dwiggins, Paul A. Bennett, and Joseph Blumenthal.

Melcher's interest in library work also flowered in Indiana, and, though he was a commercial bookseller, not a librarian, he was named vice-president of the Indiana Library Association (1917-1918). His range of activities clearly expressed a growing sense of the book world as a diverse but essentially common enterprise.

It was natural, therefore, that, in 1918, when he read in *Publishers' Weekly* that the editorship was vacant, he applied to Richard Rogers Bowker for the job and was accepted. At about the same time, two persons who were to be Melcher's associates until his retirement joined the firm: Louis C. Greene (*PW* advertising manager, later company president and chairman) and Mildred C. Smith (co-editor of *PW*, company secretary, later editor-in-chief). During his first years in New York, Melcher divided his time among three activities—serving not only *PW* but also the American Booksellers Association as secretary (1918-1920) and the National Association of Book Publishers as executive secretary (1920-1924). For a short while, the latter two jobs overlapped. Melcher was also president of the Booksellers' League of New York (1924-1925), and active in the New York Library Association (president in 1936).

As a speaker and writer on library matters, Melcher stressed several themes: improving library service for children so as to make them feel at home with books and libraries; professional education in library service; enhancement of the status of librarians; understanding of the author's—and therefore the librarian's—essential stake in copyright; the book as the library's central concern; the role of books in the community; and book industry cooperation in promoting books and reading.

R. R. Bowker died in 1933, and in January 1934, Melcher was named president of the company. He served until 1959, when he resigned to become chairman, and was succeeded by Greene.

Melcher was a founder, with Franklin K. Mathiews (librarian of the Boy Scouts), of Children's Book Week. He was the originator and donor, starting in 1922, of the annual Newbery Medal for "the most distinguished book for children" and, beginning in 1937, of the annual Caldecott Medal for "the most distinguished picture book for children," awards administered by the ALA Children's Services Division. Melcher was also a founder and strong promoter of the American Booksellers Association's quadrennial book presentation program for the White House Home Library, first given in the Hoover administration.

In 1943, Melcher established an annual citation for the creative performance of a publisher; the honor was (and is) named for two pioneers of the American book trade, Matthew Carey and Isaiah Thomas. Melcher's interest in excellence in book production was expressed in numerous other ways as well. In 1927-1928, he was president of the American Institute of Graphic Arts. He was awarded the AIGA Medal in 1945. He established the book design section of *PW* in the 1920s. In the 1940s, he published privately a series of five facsimiles of children's miniature books, reproduced from rare specimens surviving from the late eighteenth and early nineteenth centuries.

In 1954 Melcher, who had long advocated an American effort analagous to the National Book League in Great Britain, became a founding member of the National Book Committee. Among his additional interests, Melcher was vice-president of the Copyright Society of the U.S.A., vice-president of the P.E.N. American Center, active in the American Civil Liberties Union, a member of the council of the Authors League, and a member of the book selection committee for the English-Speaking Union's Books-Across-the-Sea program in World War II.

He frequently represented U.S. publishers in overseas relations. He addressed the Associated Booksellers of Great Britain and Ireland at Oxford in 1924, and he was a U.S. delegate to six congresses in Europe of the International Publishers Association (1931, 1936, 1954, 1956, 1959, 1962) and served on its steering committee. He was consultant to the Office of War Information, London (1946) and consultant to the occupation forces in Japan on copyright and the reestablishment of Japanese publishing (1947).

In 1958, he received an honorary Litt.D. degree from Rutgers University and, in 1959, a similar degree from Syracuse. He was named honorary chairman of the Children's Book Council, honorary fellow of the American Booksellers Association, emeritus

member of the National Association of College Stores, and a life member of the ALA's Children's Services Division, which, in 1955, established a scholarship in his honor. In 1962, he received the Regina Medal of the Catholic Library Association for his support of children's literature. His fiftieth anniversary in the book industry was marked at a dinner at the Waldorf-Astoria in New York, May 21, 1945, with about seven hundred persons attending and Christopher Morley presiding.

For 45 years, Melcher was active in civic and church affairs in his home town of Montclair, New Jersey. He was a member of the town's Board of Education for thirteen years, president of the trustees of the Montclair Unitarian Church, and a trustee of the Montclair Art Museum.

At the time of his death, on March 9, 1963, he was survived by his widow; his son, Daniel, later a president of the Bowker Company; and his daughters, Nancy and Charity.

Biographical listings and obituaries—*Current Biography* (1963); "Frederic G. Melcher—1879-1963" [by Roger H. Smith and Chandler B. Grannis]. *Publishers' Weekly*, 183:17-19, 36 (March 18, 1963); *Who Was Who in America* IV (1961-1968); *Who's Who in Library Service*, 1st ed., 2nd ed., 3rd ed. Books and articles about the biographee—Grannis, Chandler B. "Frederic G. Melcher." *The Calendar* (Children's Book Council) 31:2 (May-Aug. 1972); Masten, Helen Adams, ed. Frederic G. Melcher Memorial Issue. *Top of the News* 20:3, 177-207 (March 1964) (articles by Storer B. Lunt, Helen Adams Masten, Frederic G. Melcher ["On Becoming Acquainted with Books, Education for Whatever"], Irene Smith Greene, Ruth Gagliardo, Mildred C. Smith, Anne J. Richter, Ruth Hill Viguers); Melcher, Daniel. "Frederic G. Melcher As I Knew Him." *ALA Bulletin* 61:1, 56-62; Quigley, Margery. "The Beginnings of a Legend: Fred Melcher." *The Horn Book* 16, No. 4 (July-Aug. 1940). Primary sources and archival materials—Melcher, Frederic G. "Vachel Lindsay: An Account of a Friendship." *Indiana University Bookman* 1:5 (Dec. 1960); [Smith, Mildred C., ed.] *Frederic G. Melcher: Friendly Reminiscences of a Half Century among Books and Bookmen.* New York: Book Publishers Bureau, 1945.

—CHANDLER B. GRANNIS

MERRILL, JULIA WRIGHT (1881-1961)

Julia Wright Merrill was born in Chillicothe, Ohio, on September 11, 1881, one of two daughters of Chester Wright and Mary Franklin Merrill. Her father was head librarian of the Cincinnati Public Library from about 1880 until his retirement in 1887. Julia was only five years old when she was introduced to the library field. In 1886, her father took her to the conference of the American Library Association in Milwaukee, and their names are among those who took the post-Conference excursion. This experience and subsequent contacts with the profession must have appealed to Julia, since she entered the training class at Cincinnati Public Library in 1898 and served there as an assistant until 1902. At this time, she enrolled in the library school at the University of Illinois, earning her B.L.S. degree in 1903.

Julia Merrill is best known for her long career at ALA headquarters, but before joining that staff in 1925, she held several important professional positions. From 1903 to 1906, she worked with the Wisconsin Library Commission, teaching during summers at their library school and serving during the rest of the year as a field agent. She was acting librarian of the Cedar Rapids, Iowa, Public Library during 1906. For the next ten years (1907-1917), she was the head of city and county extension at the Cincinnati Public Library. At the end of this service, she went back to the Wisconsin Library Commission, again serving as field agent and instructing part-time at the young library school at the University of Wisconsin, Madison. This service was followed by three years (1922-1925) as chief of the Organization Division in the Ohio State Library.

After 1925, until her retirement in 1946, Merrill was associated with the ALA headquarters staff. Her main interest in library work, shown at least as early as her Wisconsin days, was extension of library service to readers beyond the normal area served to the outlying suburbs and rural areas. Her first position at ALA was that of executive assistant in the Library Extension Division, which she held from 1925 to 1933. In this work, she travelled widely throughout the United States, encouraging projects in rural library services and cooperating with non-library projects in rural extension. She was always urging the inclusion of library services, counseling and reporting on governance and on means of financing such projects, and continually furthering library extensions in various ways. Her reports to ALA headquarters on these trips show her to be energetic, exceptionally dedicated to this mission, and capable of much attention to details, but she did not lose perspective, and she always had a good sense of humor (as when she reported that a rural social services project director awarded her, with much ceremony, a medal left over from a conference several months earlier). In 1933, the Library Extension Division was reorganized under the Information and Advisory Services. Merrill became the head of this department and also of the Public Library Division, of which the department was a part. In this position, which she held until her retirement, she gained the widest recognition. In 1944, she served as acting executive secretary of the Association, while Carl Milam (q.v.) served on a mission to Latin America for the U.S. State Department.

In addition to her early teaching in Wisconsin, she also taught summers in the Ohio library school and at Columbia. She wrote numerous articles, reports, and surveys. Her principal books were *Regional and District Library Laws* (1942) and *The State Library*

Agency (1945). In her writing, she was clear, direct, and original. Her enthusiasm for promoting library services shows through everything she did and wrote.

Julia Merrill had many friends and was much admired for her work in the American Library Association. When she retired in 1946, Carl Vitz, at that time librarian of the Cincinnati Public Library, paid this tribute:

> We realize as not before how indefatigable she has been and how self-effacing in her relationship to the Association and to the many boards and committees which she has served. She has devoted a life-time of service to library extension. The public library and rural areas have been her chief concern, and in their interest she has worked day and night—in the field and in the office; with librarians, trustees, and lay groups; writing, advising, conferring, and planning; behind the scenes; and in behalf of others, who all too often have received the credit, while she, satisfied if only the cause of libraries could be furthered, turned to new problems.

After retirement she moved to Cincinnati, where she continued to live until her death on February 5, 1961.

Biographical listings and obituaries—Clift, David. "Memo to Members." *ALA Bulletin* 55:221 (March 1961); *Who Was Who in America* VI (1974-1976); *Who's Who in Library Service*, 1st ed., 2nd ed., 3rd ed. Books and articles about the biographee— Vitz, Carl. "Julia Wright Merrill." *ALA Bulletin* 40:96-97 (March 1946). Primary sources and archival materials—American Library Association, Committee on Library Extension, Field Notes, 1931-1936, typewritten; University Archives, University of Illinois, Urbana, Illinois (file no. RS 29/2/16).

—ROLLAND E. STEVENS

MERRILL, WILLIAM STETSON (1866-1969)

William Stetson Merrill was born in Newton, Massachusetts on January 16, 1866, the elder son of Richard Eastman and Emma Frances Stetson Merrill. After attending the public schools of Newton, he entered Harvard College, where he worked in the library as a student assistant under the supervision of William Coolidge Lane (q.v.), a close family friend. After Merrill was graduated in 1888, Lane recommended him to William F. Poole (q.v.), who was then recruiting staff members for the recently established Newberry Library. Merrill moved to Chicago with some trepidation, for he expected to miss his native region and particularly the opportunity to hike and climb in the White Mountains of New Hampshire. Although he never lost his taste for the mountains, he soon settled himself contentedly in the Midwest, and in 1896 he was married to Mary Hancock Allen of Chicago. He found the work at the Newberry satisfying and agreeable.

At first, the Newberry staff worked together informally to prepare the way for opening a great scholarly library. Merrill worked closely with Poole, essentially as his office assistant. In January 1891, when formal titles were assigned, he was named superintendent of the Accessions Department. In 1895, after Poole's death, he was named head of the Classification Department. Classifying at the Newberry Library differed from that task in most libraries of the time, in part because of the scholarly character of the collection and in part because of Poole's views on classification. In contrast to the detailed subdivision of subjects in the popular Decimal Classification of Melvil Dewey (q.v.), Poole's policies called only for broad subject divisions, with the arrangement of topics under those subjects to be determined by the classifier. This responsibility, along with the subject-divisional plan of service to readers, accounted for the recruitment of staff members with substantial subject preparation. These circumstances laid a considerable burden of interpretation upon the Newberry's classifiers. Even after Poole's death, when the Expansive Classification of Charles A. Cutter (q.v.) replaced Poole's own, this responsibility led to efforts to formulate general policies to guide the application of the classification system to particular cases. Finally, in 1912, Merrill prepared a course of lectures on the topic. This work, later published under the title *Code for Classifiers*, was circulated in a limited edition in 1914 and finally issued by the American Library Association in 1928, with a second edition in 1939 and a third in 1954. A translation into Japanese is projected for publication in 1977. It was for this book that Merrill was most widely known.

Classification continued to interest Merrill even after 1918, when he was named head of the Public Services Department, a position in which he served until 1928. For his last two years at the Newberry, he was supervisor of the Technical Procedure Department. In his 41 years at the Newberry Library, Merrill served under four librarians: William Frederick Poole, John Vance Cheney, W. N. C. Carlton, and George B. Utley (q.v.). After his retirement, he worked for several years as a classifier at the John Crerar Library of Chicago before moving finally to Oconomowoc, Wisconsin, the lakefront community that had attracted him from his earliest days in the Midwest.

Merrill lived a long life in retirement. After the death of his first wife in 1922, he had been married in 1924 to Ethel Elliott Owen. Having three sons surviving from his first marriage, he now had a daughter by his second. In the years in Oconomowoc, he continued to be active, both with physical exercise (in his walks, swimming, and boating), and with his involvements with the Catholic church. Even late in life, he regularly visited the public library, where it is

remembered that he spoke to Great Books discussion groups about his recollections of William James as his teacher at Harvard. On his hundredth birthday, Oconomowoc celebrated William Stetson Merrill Day, an occasion for birthday cards from such diverse people as children in the parish grade school and President Lyndon B. Johnson, as well as a gala party attended by his children and grandchildren. He lived to celebrate three more birthdays and to become Harvard's oldest living graduate before he died on April 4, 1969.

Throughout his career, Merrill was active in professional library projects. As early as 1891, he compiled the *Index to Publications* of the Archaeological Institute of America. He was in charge of the American Library Association's indexing program from its inception in 1913, continuing from 1916, when the H. W. Wilson Company took over the actual publishing, until 1931, when Wilson finally assumed complete responsibility for the work. He developed his own systems of book numbers, guide-card classification, and music entries. He contributed to numerous projects and publications that related to Catholic library affairs, and he wrote articles for library periodicals. Merrill's work was characterized by a quiet, cheerful, and logical competence that enabled him to make sound contributions to American librarianship in the tradition of the leaders whom he venerated such as Poole, Lane, and George Watson Cole (q.v.). These contributions earned him the accolade, "the great American classifier."

Biographical listings and obituaries—[Obituary]. *Chicago Tribune*, April 5, 1969; *Who's Who in Library Service*, 1st ed., 3rd ed., 4th ed. Books and articles about the biographee—"Librarian Authors." *Library Journal* 57:657 (1932); "Merrill at 100." *Library Journal* 91:205 (1966). Primary sources and archival materials—In addition to the typescript memoirs (Case fZ 584.61885), the Newberry Library has Merrill's personal papers and other documentation of his career. The Oconomowoc Public Library has substantial files of biographical material. The Merrill family has deposited papers in the William Stetson Merrill Collection of the University of Wyoming in Laramie.

—D. W. KRUMMEL
—W. L. WILLIAMSON

MERRITT, LeROY CHARLES (1912-1970)

LeRoy Charles Merritt was born to Arthur F. and Amanda Polze Schimmelpfennig in Milwaukee, September 10, 1912. He changed his surname to Merritt before 1937. His higher education was at the University of Wisconsin (B.A. and Library School Certificate, 1935) and the Graduate Library School, University of Chicago, where he received the Ph.D. in 1942. He married Mary A. Liebenberg on September 14, 1935, and they had three children, James LeRoy, Lauren Vail, and Jeanette Averill.

Merritt began his professional career as assistant librarian in Documents and Serials at the University of Colorado (1937-1938). He was then, successively, documents librarian, Colorado State College of Education, Greeley (1938); research assistant, Graduate Library School, University of Chicago (1938-1940); editorial associate, Union Catalog Survey, American Library Association (1940-1941); librarian and associate professor of librarianship, Longwood College, Virginia (1942-1946); in charge of library materials, Special Services Headquarters, U.S. Army, Paris (1944-1945); associate professor (1946-1950), professor (1950-1966), acting dean (1960-1962), and associate dean (1964-1966), School of Librarianship, University of California; and dean, School of Librarianship, University of Oregon (1966-1970).

Merritt overcame two substantial handicaps to become a nationally known figure in library education: he came from the humblest of backgrounds and his physical appearance was unprepossessing. He was barely five feet tall, dumpy in stature, and had a speech defect that, in times of stress, excitement, or fatigue, was pronounced. That he won not only professional success but also the affection of almost everyone who knew him and the respect of those who knew his work was the result of an alert, quick mind; genuine kindliness and interest in people; great drive and industry; loyalty; and, perhaps above all, absolute intellectual honesty and courage. Without being at all a Pollyanna, he was, moreover, a man of unusually cheerful and even disposition. He and his family were devoutly religious and highly principled. His life revolved around his profession, his family and home, and his church; he had no other important interests.

Merritt had spent the academic year 1936-1937 in residence at the Graduate Library School, University of Chicago, where he came to the attention of Professor Carleton B. Joeckel (q.v.). He left for Colorado in the summer of 1937, but one year later, he returned to Chicago to become Joeckel's research assistant. In 1945, Joeckel left Chicago to join the faculty of the School of Librarianship at the University of California. Here he was probably instrumental in the invitation to Merritt to come to California as associate professor in 1946. Merritt owed much to Joeckel's friendship and counsel, and their pleasant association continued until Joeckel's death in 1960.

Merritt's call in 1946 from a little-known Virginia college to the School of Librarianship of the University of California brought him to a major institution at a time of tremendous post-War development. The School soon recognized the qualities mentioned above, particularly his diligence and his willingness to undertake and to do well almost any job that needed to be done. He was appointed vice-chairman and also served for a dozen years as an unofficial associate dean. In 1964, when funds for the associate deanship

finally became available, Merritt was the first person appointed to the position, one that he held until his departure for the University of Oregon in 1966.

Merritt's twenty years in California were years of great development in the quality and scope of the Berkeley School. In all these developments, he played a significant, and sometimes a determining role, not only through his labors but also, often, as friendly critic and devil's advocate, and always as strong right arm of the administration. He served on a large number of University as well as local, state, and national professional committees, was a trustee of the Freedom to Read Foundation, was president of the Association of American Library Schools (1966), and at the time of his death was president-elect of the ALA Library Education Division.

Merritt's principal publications included: *The United States Government as Publisher* (1943); *Use of the Subject Catalog of the University of California Library* (1951); "Municipal and State Document Collecting in the Rocky Mountain Region," in *Public Documents* ... (1938); "National Associations of State Officers and Their Publications: A Directory," in *Manual on the Use of State Publications* (1940); "Administrative, Physical and Quantitative Aspects of the Regional Union Catalog," in *Union Catalogs in the United States* (1942); "Bookstock," in *Library Buildings for Library Service* (1947); "Research in Librarianship," in *Year's Work in Librarianship, 1948* (1952); *Book Selection and Intellectual Freedom* (1970); and (with M. Boaz and K. S. Tisdel) *Reviews in Library Book Selection* (1958). He also was editor of the ALA *Newsletter on Intellectual Freedom* from 1962 to 1970.

As his publications demonstrate, Merritt was chiefly interested and active in book selection, education, research, and administration. He directed, or participated in, numerous surveys of public libraries in California, among them those of Arcadia, Hayward, La Jolla, Oakland, Pacific Grove, and Vallejo; and he wrote nearly a score of articles on book selection and book collections. But perhaps his greatest devotion, at least in the last decade of his life, was to intellectual freedom. His appointment in 1962 as editor of the *Newsletter on Intellectual Freedom* gave him a national sounding board that he utilized to the fullest. Under his editorship the publication became a bright, highly readable journal of advocacy. Merritt's editorials, news comments, and book reviews were forthright, uncompromising, and never dull. In 1969, he won the Robert B. Downs Award for his contributions to the cause of intellectual freedom.

In 1966 he became the first dean of the new library school at the University of Oregon, which he developed with his usual diligence and professional acumen to accreditation by the ALA a year later. At Oregon, he demonstrated his ability to achieve much on very little money. He recruited a small but able faculty and embarked on such pioneering ventures as a year-long Institute on Archival Librarianship, under the Higher Education Act.

Merritt died by his own hand on May 22, 1970, at the age of 57. After his death, the LeRoy C. Merritt Humanitarian Fund was established as a memorial, a measure of his national reputation.

Biographical listings and obituaries—*Contemporary Authors*, v. 33; Nicholson, Wesley G. "He Will Be Greatly Missed: LeRoy Charles Merritt" [obituary]. *Pacific Northwest Library Association Quarterly* 34:25-26 (July 1970); [Obituary]. *California Librarian* 31:211-12 (July 1970); [Obituary]. *Library News Bulletin* 37:223-24 (July 1970); [Obituary]. *Newsletter on Intellectual Freedom* 19:49-51 (July 1970); *Who Was Who in America* VI (1974-1976); *Who's Who in Library Service*, 2nd ed., 3rd ed., 4th ed. Books and articles about the biographee—"LeRoy Charles Merritt Is the First Recipient of the Robert B. Downs Award." *Library Journal* 94:2873 (Sept. 1, 1969); Swank, Raynard C. "LeRoy C. Merritt Appointed First Dean of the New Library School at the University of Oregon." *California Librarian* 27:266-68 (Oct. 1966). Primary sources and archival materials—Records pertaining to Merritt's administration at the University of Oregon are held at that institution.

—J. PERIAM DANTON

MEYER, HERMAN H. B. (1864-1937)

The thirty-year (1905-1935) career of Herman H. B. Meyer at the Library of Congress was remarkable for its contributions to the Library and to the profession as a whole. Writing in 1935, William Warner Bishop (q.v.) asserted: "Probably no one man in the ranks of American librarians has rendered so many services to such a variety of people, and always with a fresh, personal zest and with distinguished success." The broad range of Meyer's activities was a reflection of his many personal interests—he was a gaslight engineer, a professional librarian, a book collector and friend of young authors, a bibliographer, and a careful student of administration and administrative technique.

Herman Henry Bernard Meyer was born in New York City on October 17, 1864, to Charles Henry and Freuda Margaret Henrietta von Kroog Meyer. In 1885, he was graduated from the Columbia University School of Mines with a degree in mechanical engineering. Meyer subsequently spent sixteen years as a gaslight engineer, first with the Oregon Iron Works in New York City and then with the Union Gas Light Company in Brooklyn. In the autumn of 1901, his career took a new direction: he enrolled in the Pratt Institute Library School (but evidently did not earn a degree). He then worked for two years in the New York Public Library. On January 3, 1905, he came to the Library of Congress as chief of the Periodical Division, the first in a series of important posts he held at the Library. A year and a half later, on July 1, 1906, Librarian of Congress Herbert

Putnam (q.v.) named Meyer as the new chief of the Order Division. His career in the Order Division also was short-lived. In late 1908, Putnam appointed chief bibliographer Appleton P. C. Griffin (q.v.) as the new chief assistant librarian, filling the vacancy created by the death of Ainsworth R. Spofford (q.v.). On November 1, 1908, Meyer became the new chief bibliographer and head of the Bibliography Division.

As the Library's head bibliographer, Meyer personally produced a wide range of bibliographies, all published by the Library. The subjects ranged from capital punishment (1910) to the income tax (1921). During the next two decades, he also devoted himself to professional and scholarly activities. In 1922, Howard University conferred a Litt.D. on Meyer. His active concern with "professional questions and . . . the advancement of librarianship in its service to practical affairs" led him to the presidency of the American Library Association in 1924-1925. In this capacity, he strongly urged support for the construction of an ALA headquarters building. His official duties in the Bibliography Division and his personal interest in book collecting made him an active member of the Bibliographical Society of America, while he served as president from 1926 to 1929. He was one of the Society's two representatives on the American Council of Learned Societies and served as secretary-treasurer of the Council. Meyer also was a fellow of the American Library Institute and a founder of the Shakespeare Society of Washington (president, 1919-1920).

In December 1921, Meyer was made acting director of the Library's Legislative Reference Service (LRS), a duty he carried out in conjunction with his responsibilities as head bibliographer until some time in 1923, when William Adams Slade took over the duties of bibliographer. Meyer exerted great influence in the shaping of the Legislative Reference Service, which, since its establishment in 1915, had received comparatively little administrative attention. For reasons not entirely clear, Meyer was not given the unqualified title of "director" until 1928, but the energy and quality of his leadership was never doubted. In 1929, the *State Law Index* was inaugurated. In 1933, a revision of the *Index to the Federal Statutes, 1874-1931* was published; the volume was highly praised. Between 1921 and 1935, when Meyer retired from the Legislative Reference Service and the Library, the LRS staff increased in size from 5 to 48, the number of questions submitted by Congress for response increased annually from approximately 1,000 to 25,000, and the annual LRS appropriation rose from $25,000 to approximately $92,000.

In 1931, in the Pratt-Smoot Act, Congress appropriated funds to provide books for the adult blind of the United States, these monies to be spent under the direction of the Librarian of Congress. The Library had operated a reading room for the blind since 1897, but the acquisition of books for the blind on such an extensive scale was a new function. Not surprisingly, Librarian Putnam turned to Meyer to administer the new project, Books for the Adult Blind; Meyer continued to direct the LRS as well. The new task was performed as effectively as Putnam had expected, and in this sense, Meyer may be considered the "founding father" of what today are undeniably two of the most important and unique services of the Library of Congress: the Congressional Research Service and the Division for the Blind and Physically Handicapped. The range of Meyer's administrative experience in the Library led William Warner Bishop (q.v.) to claim in 1935 that "probably no one living knows the Library of Congress in its entirety as he does." That statement is an enormous tribute to H. H. B. Meyer.

In addition to his bibliographic work, Meyer wrote about a dozen articles for professional journals on a variety of topics, including library extension, the metric system, the professional librarian and adult education, and business libraries. One subject that concerned him was the definition of librarianship and library work. Meyer held that librarianship was a profession that had behind it a body of knowledge "just as the profession of medicine has back of it medical chemistry and botany, pathology, therapeutics and so on." In a 1925 address before the Virginia State Library Association, Meyer defined library science as "that branch of human knowledge which treats of the production, care, and use of the records of human knowledge," and then carefully outlined each component of his definition. He concluded by asserting: "Librarians accepting such a definition and living up to it need have no fear of being excluded from the learned professions."

H. H. B. Meyer retired from the Library of Congress on October 1, 1935, and devoted himself to book collecting and bibliography. On January 16, 1937, Meyer died of pneumonia. He was survived by his widow, Helen Harris Spalding Meyer, to whom he had been married on September 3, 1894. She donated many of her husband's books to the institution to which he had devoted himself for thirty years.

Biographical listings and obituaries—*National Cyclopaedia of American Biography* 27; *Who Was Who in America* I (1897-1942); *Who's Who in Library Service*, 1st ed. Books and articles about the biographee—Ashley, Frederick W. "H. H. B. Meyer." *Library Journal* 61:880-81 (Nov. 15, 1936); Bishop, William Warner. "H. H. B. Meyer." *Bulletin of Bibliography* 15:143 (Sept.-Dec. 1935). Primary sources and archival materials—Meyer's official correspondence is in the Library of Congress Archives.

—JOHN Y. COLE

MILAM, CARL HASTINGS (1884-1963)

Carl Hastings Milam was born October 22, 1884, in Harper County, Kansas, the son of George L. and Florence Burch Milam. The family lived in Kansas, Missouri, and Oklahoma during his youth, and Milam was graduated from the University of Oklahoma in 1907. After receiving a certificate from the New York State Library School in 1908, he worked as a cataloger in the Purdue University Library from 1908 to 1909, and as organizer for the Public Library Commission of Indiana from 1909 to 1913.

In 1910, Milam married Nell Robinson, whom he had met when they were both students at Oklahoma. Their two daughters were Margery, whom they adopted while living in Birmingham, Alabama, and Mary Virginia.

Milam was influenced to choose librarianship as his career by Milton James Ferguson (q.v.), who was librarian at the University of Oklahoma while Milam was a student there. He enjoyed his work at Purdue, but the larger salary of the state organizer allowed him to plan to marry. Furthermore, his work with the Commission included travel, preparation of reports, consultation in library planning and development, presentation of speeches, and workshops. Not only were these activities enjoyable, but they also provided valuable experience for the major work of his career. He left Indiana in 1913 to become director of the Birmingham, Alabama, Public Library, and stayed there until 1919 (including time on leave to work in the American Library Association Library War Service). He considered the opening of a branch library for service to Negroes his major accomplishment in that position. Throughout these years, he also regularly attended the annual ALA conferences and participated in its programs. He was president of the League of Library Commissions from 1912 to 1913 and was elected a member of the ALA Council in 1915 and a member of the Executive Board in 1919.

The Library War Service, an ALA endeavor supported by funds from the [Andrew] Carnegie [q.v.] Corporation and other sources, attracted Milam's interest from the time it was tentatively planned. He took leave from Birmingham in 1917 to become assistant to the Service's director, Herbert Putnam (q.v.), then Librarian of Congress. He stayed on as acting general director while Putnam was overseas and finally became general director in 1919. The enthusiastic response to this ALA activity, and the recognition of the need for more service directed to people who had not had experience with adequate library service before, led to the development of an "Enlarged Program," conceived by Milam and other

ALA leaders as a way for the Association to stimulate more and better library service for all, including such previously neglected groups as the hospitalized and the blind.

In the Library War Service, Milam's responsibilities included those for the selection of personnel for the Washington headquarters; communication and supervision of dispatch center, camp libraries, and overseas libraries; negotiations with the U.S. Army and other parts of the federal government; policy preparation; general planning; and public relations work for the Service. This experience strengthened his sense of the value of good public relations programs for libraries and sharpened his administrative skills. The visibility and respect he earned from his colleagues while in this position led to his being named director of the ALA's Enlarged Program. Even though that Program failed to win popular support, Milam saw in the ALA and its plans for the post-World War I years the possibility of carrying out some of the activities associated with the Enlarged Program. In March 1920, upon the resignation of George B. Utley (q.v.) as ALA secretary, Milam assumed that post, where he spent the next 28 years, the major portion of his professional career.

"Mr. ALA" was the appellation Milam received because of his close identification with the Association for such a long period of time. His good rapport with Frederick P. Keppel (q.v.) and Robert Lester (q.v.) (president and secretary, respectively, of the Carnegie Corporation) was a major factor in the Carnegie Corporation's contributions toward various ALA programs and toward ALA's own endowment fund. Library education and international library development were two of Milam's main interests that received major emphasis from within the Association throughout the era of his leadership. Other foundations were also active in library development in that period; however, Milam was convinced that there was a need for federal government support as well, although that did not come on a major scale until his years of retirement. Within the Association, many people resisted the prospect of federal funding, which they were sure would lead to federal control. Then, in the Roosevelt administration, when the U.S. government began to concern itself with social and educational programs to a greater extent than in the past, the needs related to the Great Depression of the 1930s were so critical that libraries had low priority for support.

Although Milam was a widely recognized spokesman for the Association and for librarianship in general, his position was somewhat anomalous. As secretary and, later, executive secretary, of the ALA, he was not free to speak on library issues when his personal views might be counter to policies of the Association, although, as in his determined support of the idea of federal support for libraries, he might present his own arguments forcefully to regional library associations or other audiences of librarians in the hope of encouraging them to consider his point of view. He was acknowledged to be an effective, if not elegant, writer, but many of his statements grew out of group or committee discussions and were not directly attributed to him. He worked most effectively with small groups of people, and, indeed, his close association with the ALA Executive Board led members of the larger ALA Council to consider him to be not only out of touch with their needs and interests but high-handed in his treatment of them. These criticisms and others concerning his priorities in handling ALA's funds increased greatly in the years following World War II, as a new, younger leadership, rather like that with which Milam had been identified after World War I, came forward.

After 28 years of work at ALA headquarters in Chicago, Milam left two years before his anticipated retirement to become, in 1948, the director of the United Nations Library. When he went there, decisions had to be made about personnel policies and about systems of cataloging and classification, and numerous other administrative tasks had to be performed and codified for the future. Doris Dale has described his two years there as the ones that "set the library on a firm course." His zest for international library development, which had been evident in his enthusiastic attendance at several conferences of the International Federation of Library Associations and other international organizations, added to his enjoyment of those developing years at the U.N. headquarters. He might have remained longer, but his wife's poor health prompted him to retire at age 65 and to return to Barrington, Illinois. There, Mrs. Milam died in 1956 after a long illness during which he served as her nurse.

The controversial ALA presidential election of 1949 is an event that many persons associate with Milam. He was invited to run for ALA president in late 1948, and, overcoming his own misgivings, he agreed. The presidency was an honor, and Chalmers Hadley (q.v.) and George Utley, his two predecessors as ALA secretary, had served terms as president after their tenures in the ALA executive post. Milam's friends encouraged him to accept the honor of nomination as the only candidate, but at the 1949 Midwinter ALA meeting, strong resistance came from a variety of dissidents. Clarence Graham, the youthful director of the Louisville, Kentucky, Public Library, became a petition candidate and defeated Milam in the election. The rejection by the ALA membership in a mail vote hurt and puzzled both Milam and his associates. The most likely explanation appears to be that ALA members were tired of the leadership that he had exerted so strongly for so long.

Partly because of the strong feeling directed toward him, Milam was not named an honorary member of ALA until 1954. Twenty years earlier, he had received his first honorary doctoral degree from Southwestern College in Memphis, Tennessee. His second was granted a year later by Lawrence College in Appleton, Wisconsin.

An assessment of Milam's career must emphasize five notable achievements: his success as a fund-raiser for the American Library Association; his personal leadership in both ALA and general library plans and development; his image as a national and international leader in librarianship; his interest and leadership especially in public library development and adult education programs in libraries; and his contributions to development of the United Nations Library.

Milam lived in Evanston, Illinois, during the years when he worked at ALA headquarters in Chicago, and he and his wife were active in civic affairs there, although his loyalty to the Democratic Party somewhat limited his political activities in Republican Evanston. He enjoyed gardening at his home and, in retirement, he raised evergreen trees for sale, but this venture gave only a modest return because of the demands his wife's illness made on his time and energies. Fishing was a favorite form of relaxation for him throughout his life, and a typical vacation found him fishing in the West with one or two other men, happily roughing it.

The picture of Milam that appeared on the *ALA Bulletin* for October 1963 (the issue in which his death was announced) shows him as most librarians remember him in his last active years: a stocky, vigorous-looking man whose white hair had thinned and disappeared on top. His pipe was in his hands, and his dark eyes were alert behind his glasses. That year, although he wrote to David Clift (q.v.), his successor at ALA, that he had hoped to see the new ALA headquarters building, he was afflicted with arthritis. At the age of 78, he was too tired to go to Chicago from his little home in Barrington for the ALA conference in June. He was planning to move to his daughter's home in Jamaica, Iowa, when he died in his sleep in Barrington on August 26.

Biographical listings and obituaries—*Who Was Who in America* IV (1961-1968); *Who's Who in Library Service*, 1st ed., 2nd ed., 3rd ed. **Books and articles about the biographee**—Dale, Doris Cruger. *The United Nations Library: Its Origin and Development.* Chicago: American Library Association, 1970; Danton, Emily Miller. "Mr. ALA: Carl Hastings Milam." In J. D. Marshall, ed., *American Library History Reader.* Hamden, Connecticut: Shoe String Press, 1961; Fontaine, Everett O. "People and Places of the Milam Era." *ALA Bulletin* 58:363-71 (May 1964); Sullivan, Peggy. *Carl H. Milam and the American Library Association.* New York: H. W. Wilson, 1976. **Primary sources and archival materials**—Dale, Doris Cruger, ed. *Carl H. Milam and the United Nations Library.* Metuchen, N.J.: Scarecrow Press, 1976. [A brief diary kept by Milam during his two years as director of the UN Library comprises the bulk of the volume. Also includes a bibliography of his published works]; Milam's papers are held by his daughter Mary (Mrs. William A. Seidler), in Jamaica, Iowa.

—PEGGY A. SULLIVAN

MITCHELL, SYDNEY BANCROFT (1878-1951)

Sydney Bancroft Mitchell was born in Montreal on June 24, 1878, of Scotch-Irish parents, James and Sarah Cooper Mitchell. French remained his fluent second language. Born with a congenital hip dislocation, he rolled like a sailor; and yet so strong was his reconciliation with his misshapen body that in his initially disconcerting presence one became aware only of the man's serenity and wisdom. While obtaining the B.A. (1901) and M.A. (1904) at McGill University in the great days of Stephen Leacock, Mitchell worked in the library. When they were reluctant to hire a cripple, he set a record for climbing the stack staircase from bottom to top and back again. Thenceforth, no one questioned his ability to get around fast on his own legs. He went on to the New York State Library at Albany for the B.L.S. in 1904, and then returned to McGill for four years as a cataloger.

In 1908 he married Rose Frances Michaels, a Canadian-English Jewess, and they followed his friend John E. Goodwin (q.v.) to California, where, until 1911, Mitchell headed the Order Department in the Stanford University Library.

His next move was to Berkeley. Except for a year (1926-1927) of teaching library science at the University of Michigan, Mitchell remained there, in the University of California, for the rest of his life. As head of the Library's Accessions Department (1911-1919), associate university librarian (1919-1926), and as the founding director, then dean of the School of Librarianship (1927-1946), Mitchell became respected as a man who could be trusted with people and libraries.

His research was horticultural rather than bibliographical. He became one of the West's best gardeners and writers on gardening and plant breeding. His prize iris, La Purisima, was as lovely as its name. Flower shows drew him as well as library conferences. He was president of both the California Library Association (1938-1939) and the California Horticultural Society (1933-1943), and for many years he edited the Society's *Journal.* He became internationally famous and received numerous awards and medals as an iris breeder. In springtime, the Mitchell garden in the Berkeley hills was a fairyland that drew visitors from afar.

Mitchell was a nearly unerring judge of people. His graduates went far and high to positions of achievement and influence. Many returned for counsel, though, and the Mitchell tea kettle was always on the boil. He was a tireless talker, and so wide were his connections that his conversation became a kind of far-ranging humanistic travelogue. Politics, education, psychology—all the social forms of human intercourse interested him. His classroom style was outspoken and sometimes salty. In his hierarchy of values, people were more important than books, and when the chips were down, he would probably have chosen flowers over people.

Mitchell and his wife, Rose, had no children, other than his graduates. His life was shaped by her. Originally a fellow cataloger, a gardener, good cook and warm hostess, an attentive listener and discreet interrupter, Rose Mitchell (whom he called Buddy) was the ideal helpmate—spirited, humorous, and darkly beautiful. She survived him by four years.

Before his death, Mitchell had begun to write his memoirs, installments of which appeared in *The Library Quarterly*, but he was too busy to finish them. Together with other writings, a bibliography by Betty Rosenberg, and an essay by Cora Brandt on Mitchell as a horticulturist, they were published posthumously as *Mitchell of California; the Memoirs of Sydney B. Mitchell: Librarian, Teacher, Gardener*, with a preface by Lawrence Clark Powell (Berkeley, 1960). The Rosenberg bibliography is particularly valuable because it contains the pith of each contribution.

It is unfortunate that Mitchell never wrote his planned books on university librarianship and library education, although he did contribute frequently to library periodicals. Librarianship's loss was horticulture's gain. He wrote prolifically on gardening as the editor of *Sunset* magazine. His horticultural books are *Gardening in California* (1928), *From a Sunset Garden* (1932), *Your California Garden and Mine* (1947), and *Iris for Every Garden* (1960).

Sydney Mitchell died in Berkeley on September 22, 1951. He lives in his books and in his graduates and their graduates as an inspiring example of what a man can achieve.

Biographical listings and obituaries—[Obituary]. *California Librarian*, December 1951); [Obituary]. *New York Times*, Sept. 23, 1951; *Who Was Who in America* II (1943-1950) [This entry has the wrong death date; the error is corrected in *Who Was Who in America* III (1951-1960)]; *Who's Who in Library Service*, 1st ed., 2nd ed. Books and articles about the biographee—Goodwin, John E. "Sydney B. Mitchell." *College and Research Libraries* 5:278-81 (June 1944); Powell, Lawrence Clark. "Mitchell of California." *Wilson Library Bulletin* 28:778-81, 790 (May 1954), reprinted in his *A Passion for Books*. World Publishing, 1959;

Sayers, Frances Clarke. "Sydney B. Mitchell." *Library Journal* 72:906-907 (June 1, 1947). Primary sources and archival materials—*Mitchell of California; the Memoirs of Sydney B. Mitchell: Librarian, Teacher, Gardener*. Berkeley, Calif., 1960. Mitchell's papers are at the University of California, Berkeley, archives and the School of Librarianship. The author also utilized his personal knowledge of Mitchell.

—LAWRENCE CLARK POWELL

MONTGOMERY, THOMAS LYNCH (1862-1929)

Thomas Lynch Montgomery was born in Germantown, Pennsylvania, on March 4, 1862, the son of Oswald C. and Catherine Gertrude Lynch Montgomery. He received his early education at Ury House in Fox Chase, the Hill School in Pottstown, Andalusia Hall in Cornwells, and finally the Episcopal Academy in Philadelphia, where he was graduated in 1879. He took his A.B. degree in liberal arts from the University of Pennsylvania in 1884, after an undergraduate career which included such varied extracurricular activities as cricket and baseball, memberships in the Philomathean Society, Phi Kappa Sigma fraternity, and the University Chess Club, and a brief but enjoyable experience as librarian of a local Sunday school.

In 1886, Montgomery became actuary and librarian of the Wagner Free Institute of Science in Philadelphia, a position he held for seventeen years. During that time, he helped to found the Pennsylvania Library Club in 1890 and to organize the first branch of the Philadelphia Free Library in 1892. In 1894, he was appointed trustee of the Free Library, and he was elected chairman of the Board in 1924. He married Brinca Gilpin of Philadelphia on October 16, 1889, and the young couple had one daughter who died in early childhood. Brinca died in 1921, and on April 14, 1925, he married Mrs. Susan Keim Savage, widow of William L. Savage.

In 1903, Montgomery was appointed state librarian of Pennsylvania. He was a successful and imaginative administrator who laid the foundations for the State Library through collection development, preservation, and public services. During an eighteen-year tenure that spanned the administrations of five Pennsylvania governors, he was responsible for the collection and preservation of thousands of volumes reflecting the life and history of Pennsylvania. At the outset of his administration of the State Library, he was instrumental in developing a Legislative Reference Service designed to upgrade the quality and accuracy of bills written by Pennsylvania legislators. In his work with the Public Records Office, he directed the organization and preservation of numerous collections of Pennsylvania archival material. Under his leadership, the State Museum expanded its collections and public service activities.

Montgomery also advocated the development of rotating book collections for small communities "for the use of those who would otherwise have little opportunity to see good books." He foresaw the modern concept of extended reference services through photocopying, which he believed could link rare and unique sources to a wider community of researchers. He sought to extend State Library hours to seven days a week and to keep it open longer in the evening for "all to benefit from the knowledge contained within these walls." He pioneered in the development of visual aids by acquiring thousands of lantern slides for use by the state's educational, fraternal, and religious institutions. While many other state libraries were perceived as mere agents for the development of state governments, Montgomery worked to establish the Pennsylvania State Library's role as a resource for the development of all of the state's people and institutions.

During his tenure as state librarian, Montgomery edited thirty volumes of the *Pennsylvania Archives* and a second edition of *Frontier Forts of Pennsylvania.* He also served as vice president of the Swedish Colonial Society, registrar of the Pennsylvania Society of the Sons of the Revolution, president of the Philobiblon Club, and secretary of the Pennsylvania Library Commission. He held memberships and was active in the American Historical Association and the American Library Association. In the latter, he served as president from 1917 to 1918, a year crucial to a profession attempting to enlarge its service activities during World War I.

On October 31, 1921, Montgomery left the State Library to become librarian of the Historical Society of Pennsylvania, in which he had held membership since 1906. He also became the Society's corresponding secretary in 1928. While librarian of the Historical Society, Montgomery continued his contributions to Pennsylvania history by editing the official publication of the Society, *The Pennsylvania Magazine of History and Biography.* In honor of his historical work, Muhlenberg College granted him an honorary Litt.D. in 1913.

Montgomery died in Philadelphia of a heart attack on October 1, 1929.

Biographical listings and obituaries—*National Cyclopaedia of American Biography* 24; [Obituary]. *Library Journal* 54:913 (1929); *Who Was Who in America* I (1897-1942). Books and articles about the biographee—[Biographical sketch]. *The Pennsylvania Magazine of History and Biography* 54:89-92 (1930); Goodcharles, Frederick A. "Memorial Address on Dr. Thomas Lynch Montgomery." *Bulletin of the American Library Association* 24:546-48 (1930); "Our Frontispiece: Thomas Lynch Montgomery, Litt.D., 1862-1929." *Bulletin of Bibliography* 14:141-42 (1932).

—RONALD D. KRASH

MOORE, ANNE CARROLL (1871-1961)

Anne Carroll Moore was born in Limerick, Maine, on July 12, 1871, the daughter of Luther Sanborn and Sarah Hidden Barker Moore. She was graduated from the Bradford (Massachusetts) Academy in 1891 and began reading law with her father at home, but the sudden deaths of both her father and mother early in 1892 changed her life abruptly. After living with her brother and his family for several years, she left Maine in 1895 and entered the Pratt Institute Library School in Brooklyn, New York, to begin training as a librarian.

Shortly after her graduation from Pratt in 1896, she was offered a position as head of the children's department at the new Pratt Institute Free Library. This was the first library built with a special room designed for children's work, and the challenge of setting up a pioneer children's program was irresistible. With characteristic thoroughness, Moore set out to learn not only about children's books, but about the children themselves and the institutions that served them. It was at this time that kindergartens were being introduced in America and settlement houses were being started in large cities. Anne Carroll Moore investigated the services of these new agencies and defined for herself and for librarians who came after her the distinctive role that the public library could play in the life of a child.

In the first annual report of the Pratt Library, for the year ending June 30, 1897, Moore wrote:

the library should not forget that its true function in the work of education is to provide the means found in books and instruction in their use. Let us use kindergarten methods as far as they help us to this end, and by all means let us have the kindergarten spirit; but let us not turn the Children's Library into a kindergarten, a creche, or a club. Clubs may easily grow out of the Children's Library, and it is most desirable that they should; but the Library itself should be sought as a mental resource, it seems to us, and if we can educate one generation of children to regard it in this way, the problem of self-education is not far from being solved....

This emphasis on the library as an educational environment, however, did not preclude the use of devices to make the library attractive. The children's room at the Pratt Institute Free Library became a colorful place, decorated with art works and enlivened by exhibits to mark holidays, special interests, or national events. Many of the practices that Moore was to bring to the New York Public Library, and which were later copied by libraries across the country, were first instituted at Pratt.

It was at Pratt that Moore became convinced of the value of story telling as a part of children's library services. Marie Shedlock (q.v.), an English story teller, had been invited to Pratt to tell stories to the trustees and to teachers. In her book *New Roads to Childhood*, Moore described what followed:

> Story telling for the grown people soon led to a memorable story hour for children. The circulation of books was stopped one Saturday morning and the children came to their room to listen to stories while the books stood listening also. . . .

> There was never any doubt in my mind after that morning that a children's library should have a regular story hour, but finding a story teller of the right sort was not an easy matter. Poor story-telling is more disastrous than poor story-writing which can be skipped or left entirely alone without affecting anyone else.

During her ten years at Pratt, Anne Carroll Moore established herself as one of the leading authorities on library work with children. Her articles in library journals were widely quoted; and when, at the Montreal Conference of the American Library Association in 1900, the Club of Children's Librarians was formed, she became its first chairman. This organization later became the Children's Services Division of the American Library Association.

When the directors of the New York Public Library decided to inaugurate services for children, Moore was asked to head these services. The 65 branch libraries promised by Andrew Carnegie (q.v.) would soon make the New York Public Library the largest library system in the country. Planning and coordinating children's work in such a system offered a real challenge to a woman of Moore's energy and vision, and she decided to try it.

In September 1906, she became supervisor of work with children at the New York Public Library, a position she was to hold for 35 years. Her first task was to visit all of the 36 branch libraries of the newly consolidated circulation department to meet the children's librarians and to inspect the book collection. The collections were disappointing; many of them were either the remnants of Sunday school libraries, gifts, or books collected haphazardly by people with little or no training in evaluating children's books.

One of Moore's first official actions was to abolish the age limit that barred children from some of the branches. She then set to work to improve the collections and the services. She tried to eliminate out-of-date and undesirable books, to increase the number of non-fiction titles, and to duplicate more extensively the recognized standard books for children. To improve services to children, Moore arranged for monthly meetings of the children's librarians so that, through discussion and the exchange of ideas, they could develop a feeling for the work that was being done. In 1908, the new grade of children's librarian was created. An assistant could qualify for this title by earning the recommendations of her branch librarian and the supervisor of work with children, completing at least six months of service in three different children's rooms, and writing a paper on her observations and conclusions about the work.

In each of the branch libraries, Moore established a children's reading room—a collection of non-circulating children's books that were put on the shelves as they came from the publishers rather than being bound in drab library bindings. Children's librarians found these collections valuable as an ever-present source of story reading materials, and generations of children discovered through them that the library was a comfortable place to spend a few hours reading rather than just a place to select a book to take home. During the low-budget days of the 1930s, these reading collections made it possible for many children to use the library even though the book stock was low. Five or six children could read one copy of a book, each child leaving a slip of paper to mark his place between visits.

With the opening of the New York Public Library's new building at Fifth Avenue and 42nd Street in 1911, the Children's Services Division was able to expand. The building became a focus of interest for visitors to the city, and Anne Carroll Moore was alert to the need of introducing writers, publishers, artists, and public figures to the world of children's books. In 1918, Frederic G. Melcher (q.v.), editor of *Publishers' Weekly*, and Franklin K. Mathiews of the Boy Scouts of America came to Moore and proposed that a Children's Book Week be established. The three of them drew up plans, and in 1919, the first celebration of Children's Book Week was held in the Central Children's Room with Kate Douglas Wiggin (educator and author of *Rebecca of Sunnybrook Farm*) as the main speaker.

During the years immediately following World War I, children's books were increasingly recognized as an important area of publishing. In 1918, George H. Doran announced the inauguration of a new monthly magazine, *The Bookman*, for which Anne Carroll Moore was asked to write a regular column on books for children. From November of 1918, when her first review appeared, until 1926, when the journal ceased publication, she wrote a series of memorable columns, many of which were collected in *Roads to Childhood: Views and Reviews of Children's Books* (1920), *New Roads to Childhood* (1923), and *Cross Roads to Childhood* (1926). In her columns, Moore not only reviewed contemporary children's books but also reintroduced older books, always extolling the importance of literature for children and warring against low standards:

We are tired of substitutes for realities in writing for children. The trail of the serpent has been growing more and more clearly defined in the flow of children's books from publishers to bookshop, library, home, and school—a trail strewn with patronage and propaganda, moralizing self-sufficiency and sham efficiency, mock heroics and cheap optimism—above all, with the commonplace in theme, treatment and language—the proverbial stone in place of bread in the name of education.

In 1924, she found another outlet for her critical talents, this time in the *New York Herald Tribune*'s weekly review, *Books*. Using the heading "The Three Owls," Moore edited the children's section of this review from 1924 until 1930. Here, as in her *Bookman* column, she campaigned for a recognition of the importance of children's books:

First impressions of pictures, rhymes and stories are both enduring and elusive. They are, I believe, of greater importance than is commonly recognized because they are unforgettable. . . .

Fine picture books exert a far more subtle influence in the formation of reading tastes and habits than it is possible to estimate, for their integrity is unshakable.

For many years, Anne Carroll Moore was the acknowledged leader of children's book critics in the United States. Josiah Titzell called her page in the *Herald Tribune* the "yea or nay of all children's literature" (*Horn Book* 18:218; July 1942). When the newspaper cut back the space allotted to children's books, Moore gave up her page but kept the title, and she eventually offered "The Three Owls" as a column to the newly founded *Horn Book* magazine. Besides her own contributions, Miss Moore was often consulted for editorial advice about *Horn Book* articles and she sometimes helped make decisions about which books should be reviewed. She was also largely responsible for special issues of the journal, among them tributes to Marie Shedlock, L. Leslie Brooke, and Helen Sewell. Through her writings and editorial work, Moore helped to introduce and to build up a following for writers and illustrators like Wanda Gág, Rachel Field, Leslie Brooke, Hendrik Willem Van Loon, and Maud and Miska Petersham. Her enthusiasm for fairy and folk tales from many countries, her delight in fantasy, and her dislike of "didacticism, condescension, and propaganda" influenced a generation of librarians and publishers. Although not all of her judgments have stood the test of time, her insistence on taking children's books seriously and evaluating them as works of literary art rather than as moral tracts or therapeutic tools helped to make possible the development of a rich, distinguished body of American children's literature.

Even while she was writing these critical pieces regularly and carrying on her work at the Library,

Moore found time to write two children's books. The first of these, *Nicholas: A Manhattan Christmas Story*, was published in 1924, and its sequel, *Nicholas and the Golden Goose*, appeared in 1932. The main character in both of these books was a small wooden doll named Nicholas. Moore actually had such a doll, given to her one Christmas by the staff at the Library. She carried the doll with her everywhere and often used it in her talks with children at the libraries she visited. In her books, she brought the doll to life and took him through a series of adventures based on her own activities and interests. She herself appeared in both books as a character called "Ann Caraway." In the first book, she and Nicholas enjoy the wonders of New York City at Christmas—wonders ranging from the new traffic light tower at Fifth Avenue and 42nd Street to a fanciful party at the Library where Sinbad, Washington Irving, and Palmer Cox's Brownies are among the guests. *Nicholas and the Golden Goose* takes the pair on a trip to England and France, where they visit Beatrix Potter and the new children's libraries in France.

As her career at the New York Public Library drew to a close, honors came to Moore from varied sources. In 1940, the first Constance Lindsay Skinner Gold Medal was awarded to her by the Women's National Book Association and the Booksellers' League of New York. In the same year, the University of Maine awarded her the honorary degree of Doctor of Letters.

After her retirement in 1941, Moore taught at the Graduate School of Librarianship at the University of California, Berkeley, for a semester; continued "The Three Owls" column; gave lectures at Pratt Institute Library School and at library conferences; and kept in touch with the children's work at the New York Public Library. Her last long piece of writing was an appreciation of Beatrix Potter that appeared in *The Art of Beatrix Potter* (1954).

In 1955, Pratt Institute awarded Anne Carroll Moore the degree of Doctor of Letters, and in 1960, the Catholic Library Association's Regina Medal was given her. Although nearly ninety years old, Moore kept her lively interest in books and in life until her death on January 20, 1961.

In her biography of Anne Carroll Moore, Frances Clarke Sayers sums up the impact that this woman had on librarianship for children:

One person more than any other gave shape and content to the new profession, to the greatest degree and in the fullest measure: Anne Carroll Moore. . . . To be sure, confluence of period and place set the stage for her achievement, but the color and character of her accomplishment derived from the quality of her imagination; her courage and stubborn determination; her shrewd, New England practicality; her logical, analytical mind, which, like a pyrotechnical display, could turn and light up the sky with its rocketing commitment to joy.

Biographical listings and obituaries—[Obituary]. *Library Journal* 86:845-47 (Feb. 15, 1961); *Who Was Who in America* IV (1961-1968); *Who's Who in Library Service*, 1st ed. Books and articles about the biographee—Akers, N. M. "Anne Carroll Moore: A Study of Her Work with Children's Libraries and Literature." Master's thesis, Pratt Institute Library School, 1951; Brotherton, Nina C. "Anne Carroll Moore." *Library Journal* 66:710 (Sept. 1, 1941); Miller, B. M. "Anne Carroll Moore—Doctor of Humane Letters." *Horn Book* 37:183-92 (April 1961); Sawyer, Ruth. "Anne Carroll Moore: An Award and an Appreciation." *Horn Book* 36:191-99 (June 1960); Sawyer, Ruth. "Anne Moore of Limerick, Maine, Minister without Portfolio." *Horn Book* 26:245-51 (July-Aug. 1950); Sayers, Frances Clarke. *Anne Carroll Moore*. New York: Atheneum, 1972; Sayers, Frances Clarke. "Postscript: The Later Years." *Horn Book* 37:193-97 (April 1961); Sayers, Frances Clarke, and C. Horovitz. "Remembrance and Re-creation: Some Talk about the Writing of a Biography." *Horn Book* 48:444-51 (Oct. 1972); Spain, Frances Lander, ed. *Reading without Boundaries*. New York: The New York Public Library, 1956. (This volume includes an excellent bibliography of works by Anne Carroll Moore and those written about her before 1955); Spain, Frances Lander. "Tribute to Miss Moore." *Library Journal* 86:846-47 (Feb. 15, 1961); "Tribute to Anne Carroll Moore." *Top of the News* 18:31-41 (Dec. 1961); Wessel, M. A. "Anne Carroll Moore." *Catholic Library World* 31:211-14 (Jan. 1960).

—ADELE M. FASICK

MORIARTY, JOHN HELENBECK (1903-1971)

John H. Moriarty was born November 9, 1903, in Waterbury, Connecticut, the son of Joseph C. and Pearl Helenbeck Moriarty. In Waterbury, he served as a page in the public library while attending elementary school and high school. His adult professional career, except for seven years (1926-1933) as office manager for the New York Telephone Company in Buffalo, was entirely devoted to libraries. He married Helen Jean Merritt in 1933, and they had three children: Paula, Stephen, and Mark.

In 1926, he received a B.A. degree from Columbia College and was elected to Phi Beta Kappa. During his college years, he was employed in the Engineering Societies Library. He then entered the business world, but evidently Moriarty did not look forward to the prospect of devoting his working life to the Telephone Company. In 1933, he consulted Augustus H. Shearer, librarian of the Grosvenor Library in Buffalo, on opportunities in the library profession. Encouraged by Shearer's advice, Moriarty resigned from the Telephone Company to enter Columbia University's School of Library Service. This decision, made in the depth of the Depression of the 1930s, reflected his confidence in his future in the library profession. He secured a B.S. (1934) and an M.S. (1938) in library service from Columbia University. From 1935 to 1939, he was librarian at the Cooper

Union Institute of Technology and at the same time taught in the social philosophy department there and in Columbia's School of Library Service. In 1939, he became assistant to the director of libraries at Columbia, concerned with establishing centralized responsibility for acquiring materials, improving accounting methods, and codifying cataloging practices. He also continued his teaching at Columbia, giving courses in government publications and in reference and bibliographical method.

Moving to the Library of Congress in 1941, Moriarty served first as chief of the Accessions Division, and following the reorganization, as assistant director of the Acquisition Department. He was responsible for improving and expediting the acquisition and recording procedures, centralizing the receipt of all materials, and establishing a new serials record division. In this war period, too, he was a member of an interdepartmental committee charged with acquiring foreign (including enemy) publications at their source and expediting their transmittal to the United States. The technical publications acquired were of particular value in wartime.

Moriarty's opportunity to manage his own library came in 1944, when he was appointed to the directorship at Purdue University. Following the end of World War II, a period of expansion in higher education offered ample scope for his organizational talents and vigorous personal management style. Increasing enrollments were matched by library growth, and the libraries at Purdue, which reported holdings of 200,000 volumes in 1944, held more than a million in 1970, when he retired. Moriarty's policy of service was to put the books where the users were, and the result was a strong system of departmental and school libraries located in the academic buildings where instruction and research were carried on. This policy necessarily meant duplication, which was accepted as the means of providing access, and less emphasis was placed on the traditional concept of completeness sought by acquisition of primarily unique titles. Although the various libraries specialized in particular subject areas, the concept of a system cooperating in service to the entire university was stressed.

Expansion on Purdue's West Lafayette campus was paralleled by the establishment of Regional Campus Libraries around the state of Indiana. Beginning in makeshift quarters and supporting two-year programs, these were brought up to a level adequate for four-year undergraduate programs and graduate courses as well.

Moriarty's appointment in 1950 as director of Purdue's Audio Visual Center, in addition to his heading the library system, produced a relationship between the established service functions of libraries and the newer methods and materials of audiovisual service that has had growing benefits for the teaching faculty and their students. The concept that the student could use media and audiovisual equipment as readily as he could books and periodicals was an innovation. The practical applications of audiovisual service were also the subject of original research carried on within the Center. In addition, Moriarty served as a consultant in the planning of several library buildings, and this work provided further opportunities for realizing his belief in the interrelationship between audiovisual materials (and associated services) and traditional library holdings (and their associated services).

He continued his involvement in library education by teaching in the University of Illinois Graduate School of Library Science during the summers of 1950, 1953, and 1956.

Moriarty's writings reflected his approach to problems—direct, practical, positive. His article "The Special Librarian—How Special" (*Special Libraries* 36:39-46; February 1945) showed a clear awareness of the information needs that would have to be met following the end of World War II, and the role that special librarians would be expected to fill. His very practical concerns about academic status for librarians were summed up in the article "Academic in Deed" (*College and Research Libraries* 31:14-17; January 1970). Achievement of faculty status by Purdue librarians had been a lengthy and sometimes uncertain struggle, and in the article, Moriarty made it clear that library professional staffs and library directors had new obligations to meet and that failure to do so could have drastic effect.

His leadership in the development of a system of resources and services was accompanied by his equally active roles in professional organizations, in the University, in the state, and in the local community. These activities represented his commitment to all aspects of his profession and to his responsibilities as a citizen. As a member of the American Library Association, Indiana Library Association, Special Libraries Association, American Society for Engineering Education, and the University Film Producers Association, Moriarty served on numerous committees and as an officer. In ALA, besides chairing committees, he was on the Council in 1947-1949 and 1964-1967. In Indiana, he participated in groups advising the Department of Public Instruction and the legislature. In West Lafayette, where he lived, he was a member and president of the School Board in a period of rapid expansion of the system. His membership in Rotary International involved him in community affairs beyond university concerns.

In his relations with others, Moriarty looked for the imagination and energy that he believed would further the library profession; in return, he provided encouragement and opportunity to those who

worked with him. Participating in small groups or appearing before large audiences, he demonstrated a well-developed ability to present his position effectively. His classical training, an active style, a keen sense of humor, and evidence of physical vitality made a forceful combination in influencing others. Characteristically, in retirement, he continued to work for library development. Circulating a petition for the establishment of bookmobile service out in the county, John H. Moriarty suffered a fatal heart attack while trying to free his car from the snow on February 13, 1971.

Biographical listings and obituaries—*Biographical Directory of Librarians in the United States and Canada*, 5th ed.; *Directory of Library Consultants*. New York: R. R. Bowker, 1969; *Who's Who in America* (1950-1951–1970-1971); *Who's Who in Library Service*, 2nd ed., 3rd ed., 4th ed.; *Who's Who in the Midwest* (1970-1971). **Books and articles about the biographee**—[Biographical sketch]. *College and Research Libraries* 5:363-64 (Sept. 1944); [Biographical sketch]. *Library Occurrent* 14:291-92 (July-Sept. 1944).

—KEITH DOWDEN

MORLEY, LINDA HUCKEL (1881-1972)

Linda H. Morley was born on June 8, 1881, in Philadelphia, Pennsylvania, the daughter of John Barry and Anita Linda Huckel Morley. She spent her early working years in the Newark (New Jersey) Public Library, first as chief of its Branch and Station Department (1907-1910), then as its reference assistant (1910-1912); she followed this with an assignment as head of its Foreign Branch (1913-1916). In 1917, she succeeded Sarah B. Ball as librarian of its Business Branch, a post she held until 1926. It was here that she gained her reputation as a trail-blazer in developing the practical use of documented business information as well as some not yet in final print.

During these years, two significant national developments led to the recognition of the information needs of the business community. One was the growing number of university and collegiate schools of business, and the other was the broadening statistical research programs conducted by business, industry, and government. Such increased interest in published facts and figures created the market for more books, periodicals, and government documents.

Realizing that no bibliographical and other tools were available to facilitate the use of this tremendous accumulation of materials, Morley (in collaboration with A. C. Kight) began to compile guides, lists, indexes, extensive annotated bibliographies, and other aids to serve this purpose. Among the first of these was *2400 Business Books*, published in 1920, and its supplement, *Business Books, 1920-26*, published in 1927. These two volumes were the basic bibliographical search tools for business publications for many years. In 1924, another collaboration with A. C. Kight produced the *Mailing List Directory: A Classified Index to Trade Directories*. The business world welcomed these guides just as enthusiastically as librarians, and they were introduced and reviewed in professional business publications as well as in library literature.

Morley also played a significant role in the Special Libraries Association, organized in 1909 to meet a need felt by librarians working primarily in the fields of business and technical information in private corporations, municipal research bureaus, engineering firms, public utilities, and in business and technical departments in public and academic libraries. She served as its vice president (1924-1925), as editor of its publications (1928-1935, including also chairmanship of its Publications Committee during 1928-1932), as chairman of both its Professional Standards and its Training and Professional Activities Committees, and in other capacities. She was a frequent speaker before special library and business groups. Some of her many papers are indexed in *Library Literature* from 1927 through 1951. On the occasion of the SLA's fiftieth anniversary in 1959, she was named to its Hall of Fame.

From 1926 to 1941, Linda Morley was research librarian for Industrial Relations Counselors, Inc., in New York, an organization concerned with various phases of industrial relations: unemployment compensation, unemployment insurance, job analysis, employer-employee relations, and related data to provide management with necessary facts on which to base decisions relating to industrial relations problems. She shared her expertise as a special lecturer at the New York Public Library's library training class (1923-1927), which merged with Columbia University School of Library Service to become the first professional library school offering a course in special libraries. Morley organized and taught this course from 1927 to 1950. For a short time in 1950, she taught the same course at the Pratt Institute Library School.

In 1941, she established her own business as a corporation library consultant and library research service in New York; this continued in operation until 1952 and was used by many people both in the business community and in corporation libraries. One of her contracts was as research assistant for an author on local history in New York over the period from 1950 to 1963.

Among the tools she devised, in cooperation with other special librarians, was *Contributions toward a Special Library Glossary*. Like most of her publications, this was planned as a piece of "convenience goods" to help answer the many requests for a definition of a special library and other terms new to the special library field. Comprised of some 84 terms

from the more comprehensive *A.L.A. Glossary of Library Terms*, it was widely reviewed, not only in English-language journals but also in foreign-language ones, such as *Bibliotheekgids* (27:123-24; Nov.-Dec. 1951).

Linda Morley was elected to the Council of the American Women's Association in New York in 1937, and was a member of the American Library Association, the New York Library Association, and the Association of American Library Schools, as well as the Special Libraries Association. It was her role as an interpreter of how business facts and figures could be put to practical use that established Morley as a pioneer in this phase of library service.

She moved from New York to St. Joseph's Manor in Trumbull, Connecticut, in 1965 and, with A. C. Kight, soon began work on another book about "information departments" in business organizations. Her co-author, associate, and long-time friend, A. C. Kight, preceded Linda Morley in death at St. Joseph's Manor on March 17, 1972, before the book was completed. She died at the Manor on August 5, 1972.

Biographical listings and obituaries—[Obituary]. *Special Libraries* 64:54 (Jan. 1973); *Who's Who in Library Service*, 1st ed., 2nd ed., 3rd ed., 4th ed. Books and articles about the biographee—"Hall of Fame: Linda H. Morley." *Special Libraries* 50:292 (Sept. 1959). Primary sources and archival materials—The Newark Public Library has materials relevant to Morley's tenure there.

—ROSE L. VORMELKER

MORSCH, LUCILE M. (1906-1972)

Lucile M. Morsch was born on January 21, 1906, in Sioux City, Iowa, the second daughter of Jacob and Lydia Meyer Morsch. She received her A.B. (in English) from the State University of Iowa in 1927, working also as a part-time student assistant in the Library from 1924 to 1927 under the direction of Amelia Krieg. After graduation, she continued for a year as a catalog librarian in the Library. Then, for two years, she received the Lydia C. Roberts Fellowship (for an Iowa citizen), which enabled her to attend the School of Library Service at Columbia University; she received a B.S. in library science in 1929 and the M.S. degree in 1930. During the school year 1928-1929, she organized cataloging and classification procedures in the Tarrytown, New York, Public Library—an undertaking that foreshadowed her later accomplishments in library management. For the summer of 1929, she was an assistant in the Preparations Division, New York Public Library, and in the summer of 1930, she taught at the Library School of Louisiana State University.

The autumn of 1930 saw her back at the University of Iowa Library, where she was cataloger for one year and first assistant for four years in the Catalog Department. During this time, the acting director of the Library, Grace Wormer, described her as "blessed with good health ... unusual energy, initiative, industry, vision, open-mindedness, and a friendly, likable personality." Her accomplishments during this period bear out this description. As an undergraduate, she had been chosen for Mortar Board (a women's honorary society), and later, at Columbia, was elected to Beta Phi Mu, the library honor society. She joined the American Library Association in 1929, and attended all but two of its annual conferences from then until the late 1960s.

An intense person of great driving ambition and energy, Morsch made her mark early. At the 1931 New Haven ALA meeting, she was elected secretary of the newly formed Junior Members Round Table. A committee was appointed at this time to consider the feasibility of compiling a supplement to H. G. T. Cannons' *Bibliography of Library Economy, 1876-1920.* By the time of the second Junior Members meeting in April 1932, this committee had presented to the ALA Editorial Committee preliminary plans and a proposal for such a supplement, to cover the period 1921-1932. The plans and proposal were speedily accepted and ALA Headquarters, on behalf of the Junior Members Round Table, selected Lucile Morsch, who by now was a member of the JMRT Executive Board, to act as editor. The new publication, renamed *Library Literature*, was compiled in record time. What began in April 1932 was already in the hands of the publishers by October 1933—a manuscript of 1,728 pages! It appeared in 1934, the first volume in a series which continues to the present day. In speaking of Morsch's leadership, Joseph L. Wheeler (q.v.), then librarian of the Enoch Pratt Free Library in Baltimore, wrote:

> Most of her work as Editor was carried on at Iowa State University. ... Miss Morsch had to organize the project, make the editorial decisions, and coordinate the efforts and the indexing of the group of forty volunteer Junior Members, scattered nationwide, who contributed most of the entries; their names ... now read like a *Who's Who.* ... The resulting volume was a model of indexing under far from easy conditions. It illustrates Lucile Morsch's capacity to plan, organize, guide, and work with others, and get results.

Wheeler, who met her at ALA Headquarters while she was finishing this work, persuaded her to come to the Enoch Pratt Library as associate head (title: head classifier) of the Catalog Department in 1935. Here, as he puts it, "she was called upon for the actual reorganization of the routines and assignment of work, and, most of all, a daily supervision of such high quality that the rise in morale was more than notable in a department where time and therefore salary waste had been a nightmare for years." The results of this reorganization are apparent in her

Catalog Department Manual (Enoch Pratt Library, 1940). The *Manual* is a detailed description of physical layout, work flow pattern, what to do in each job, how to handle each of the special classifications and collections in the Library, and even details of what authorities to use in establishing entry. Among other things, there was an established routine of cooperation with other local libraries, including non-competitive purchasing for library collection resources, something that was to be revived thirty years later for the identical reason: need for economy. A part of the Morsch innovation was omitted from the *Manual*: the idea of devoting full attention to one item at a time with the desk clear of all extraneous or distracting material.

During the period at Enoch Pratt, Lucile Morsch taught at Columbia for three summers (1937-1939), and reorganized the Catalog Department of the New Orleans Public Library (1938). She continued to serve on the Publication Committee of the ALA Catalog Section (from 1934-1935 to 1937-1938; chairman 1935-1936). She was on the Editorial Board of this Section's *Catalogers' and Classifiers' Yearbook* from 1936 to 1938, being chairman for *Yearbook* No. 5 (1936). This *Yearbook* was notable for being the first devoted to papers on a single subject. She also served as secretary of the Catalog Section (1936-1937), member of the third ALA Activities Committee (1939-1940), the ALA Cooperative Cataloging Committee (1936-1941, chairman 1940-1941), the ALA Committee on Cataloging and Classification (1939-1941), and was elected to the ALA Council for four years, beginning in 1940. In her spare time, she compiled a *Check List of New Jersey Imprints, 1784-1800* (Baltimore, 1939).

On November 18, 1940, two months after becoming head of the Catalog Department at Enoch Pratt, and as a result of a major reorganization, she was appointed the first chief of the Descriptive Cataloging Division at the Library of Congress. Again quoting Wheeler, the appointment was

> a new position of great responsibility, involving new viewpoints and procedures and much new personnel. Her first task was to consolidate a diffuse organization of 29 units into 12 sections and clarify somewhat obscure practices, modify them according to a new set of principles, and codify them. These included the initiation in May, 1941 of a series of fellowships in cooperative cataloging to improve the entire relationships in this field, resulting in the welcome *Cooperative Cataloging Manual* in 1944.

As can well be imagined, a reorganization of a division in the Library of Congress was a quantum jump above similar activity at Enoch Pratt. It called for practical goal-setting, strong leadership, firm control, and sound decision-making; in fact, it took all of

Morsch's abilities—planning, executive, and persuasive—to inspire, cajole, or otherwise move a division employing about one hundred individuals into action. She was action-oriented, moving fast, making decisions fast, learning fast, and above all keeping her eye on the ultimate goals of the Division. She knew all of her people well enough to say something specific about each one when introducing them to visitors. In problem-solving situations, especially those involving invited participants from outside the Library, her good memory, initiative, and remarkable self-control were used to advantage.

Not all was work, however. On May 20, 1944, she married Dr. Werner Bruno Ellinger, who was legal specialist in the LC Subject Cataloging Division and later had much to do with the development of the LC classification for Law, Class K. (She retained her maiden name professionally, however.) At this time, she was president of the ALA Division of Cataloging and Classification (1943-1945) and thereafter began to exhibit the interest in Latin American libraries which, in 1949, was to take her on a State Department-sponsored whirlwind tour encompassing no fewer than 99 libraries in 70 days. Her main concern, even in Latin America, was cataloging.

For some time, there had been a strong movement afoot to modify, simplify, and update the Anglo-American Code (*Catalog Rules; Author and Title Entries*; ALA, 1908). No small factor in motivating action was the cost of cataloging. Then, as now, libraries wanted the results of fine cataloging without the cost. Then, as now, there was pressure to simplify the complex without losing any detail in the process. Then, as now, there was inadequate research upon which to base sound decisions. By 1940, a Catalog Code Revision Committee had been appointed and the profession was invited to provide information and suggestions for improving the Code. In 1941, the Committee's *ALA Catalog Rules; Author and Title Entries. Preliminary American Second Edition* appeared.

This publication was severely criticized. The critics, of course, did not agree as to what was wrong, and, while some of their ideas, such as omitting title entries, now seem amusing, there was no consensus for objective research studies that might have given direction to the work of revision. For the next eight years, the matter of Code revision generated much heat but very little light. Even after publication of the *ALA Cataloging Rules for Author and Title Entries* in 1949, criticism continued to such a degree that within six years another Catalog Code Revision Committee had been appointed. Its work was completed in 1967 with the *Anglo-American Cataloging Rules.* This, in turn, was revised practically from the day of issuance, and by 1974, a third Code Revision Committee had been appointed. The continuous concern

with the Code—two codes and three committees within 25 years—suggests that basic questions have never been properly answered; possibly they have not even been properly identified, and certainly they have not yet been adequately investigated.

Code revision could not fail to interest Lucile Morsch. Even before moving to the Library of Congress in late 1940, she had been writing articles on cataloging. These had included suggestions about improving Library of Congress work. She had maintained that uniformity of entry was both the major problem and the major objective in cataloging. At the same time, she thought that differences in descriptive cataloging were the province of the individual library and decried the practice of slavishly following the Library of Congress in this respect. The first important production in her new position, aside from reorganization, was standardization of cooperative cataloging procedures, and the second, ironically, was the preliminary edition of the *Rules for Descriptive Cataloging*, which, in its final version, was accepted in 1949 as the second part of the new catalog Code.

In the name of cost cutting, these *Rules*, which she earlier had considered unnecessary in codified form, were to become embalmed through the functioning of the cooperative cataloging system and later entombed by automation efforts. The Morsch view was that cataloging is an art, part and parcel of the larger field of bibliography, and she emphasized that the cataloger must be aware of "relationships between books." Somehow, such views became distorted in the drive for uniformity in entry—"entry" being used in the sense of the total bibliographic description rather than (her preference) the citation-derived definition of "entry" as the most effective single entrance point to the catalog as a finding list.

It is interesting to note that by 1974, the idea of standardization of *descriptive* bibliographic elements (other than the main entry) had come to be an internationally agreed-upon factor, due in no small measure to the distribution of cataloging copy from such centralized points as the Library of Congress and the British National Bibliography. The Morsch view of strict uniformity in entry and freedom in description had been turned around completely, although it was followed in the giant pre-1956 *National Union Catalog* published for the Library of Congress by Mansell, and also, since the late 1960s, by the Shared Cataloging Program for those items taken from non-American national bibliographies.

Although she wrote over twenty articles of more than passing interest between 1939 and 1967, those Morsch efforts that remain outstanding are on simplified cataloging (1940-1941), the challenge of cataloging (1942), and a review of the Code-necessitated relationship between the Library of Congress and the American Library Association (1967). The first two are still very timely, while the latter might be considered a blueprint for action in the 1970s.

After the publication of the 1949 Code, Lucile Morsch became the first recipient of the ALA Margaret Mann [q.v.] Citation in 1951. Next, she was elected to a second term on the Council, and progressively became second vice-president (1952-1953), first vice-president (1956-1957), and president (1957-1958) of the American Library Association. At the Library of Congress in May 1953, not long after returning from temporary rotation as chief of the General Reference and Bibliography Division (1951-1952), she was appointed deputy chief assistant librarian of Congress, the highest library position to which a woman had been appointed in this country. In this office, she served as deputy first to Verner Clapp (q.v.) (1953-1957) and then to Rutherford Rogers (1958-1962).

The position of deputy chief assistant librarian brought wider horizons as well as more administrative duties. In addition to being president of ALA, Lucile Morsch became a member of the United States National Commission for UNESCO (1957-1962). She undertook a second tour for the State Department in 1960, this time through Yugoslavia, Greece, Cyprus, Turkey, Lebanon, the United Arab Republic, Israel, India, and Pakistan. Two of her lectures from the tour have been preserved in Carl M. White's *Bases of Modern Librarianship* (1964). Not long after the tour, another reorganization at the Library of Congress and the grant of extended leave to the chief of descriptive cataloging brought her back as chief of her old Division for a period of three years, beginning in late 1962. Shortly after receiving a Federal Service Award in 1965, she took an early retirement—the tremendous drive and energy had reached its end. One final honor—ALA's Melvil Dewey [q.v.] Medal—was hers in 1966. After a few quiet years, she died suddenly on July 3, 1972, very shortly after the death of her husband.

Lucile Morsch was an alert, youthful-looking person of average size and very erect posture. In conversation, one received the impression of dynamic energy tightly controlled. Her portrait in the *Journal of Cataloging and Classification* (Summer 1951) is closest to this biographer's memory of her appearance. In addition to her competence, co-workers remember details such as her beautiful handwriting, her practice of wearing a corsage to work each day, her interest in colleagues who took extra pains with their work, and her grace in putting them at ease. She did not tolerate ineptitude and she also tended to antagonize those who preferred a more static existence than she. Her common sense as well as humor slip through at times in her writing: "Unfortunately too many of us have assumed that the

catalog is perfect and the people are nitwits." She was almost legendary in her own time, as well as a representative of it.

It has been noted here that Lucile Morsch was highly motivated to be a success in the library profession. The manifestation of success is apparent in the reward system upon which the social stratification of any profession is based. Recognition via awards, appointment to prestigious jobs, and enhanced visibility result in prerogatives such as the exercise of power, "gatekeeping" (control of access to information and power), and the right to be consulted on major courses of action. Lucile Morsch's career demonstrates the reward system very well. Her part in the revival of a major tool for current bibliography, *Library Literature*, resulted in the Enoch Pratt job, which in turn produced the management innovations described in the *Manual*. This brought the Library of Congress descriptive cataloging position and with it production and oversight of the *Cooperative Cataloging Manual* and the *Rules for Descriptive Cataloging*, for which the immediate awards were the Department of State tour of Latin American libraries and the Margaret Mann Citation. The long-term rewards were the deputy chief assistant librarian job, the Near Eastern tour for the State Department, the Federal Service Award, and the Melvil Dewey Medal. All this was enhanced and promoted by an increase in visibility through ALA ranks from junior member to president. "Gatekeeping" was exercised as the "voice" of the Library of Congress in Code-making and application, as well as in the selection and promotion of personnel. In conclusion, one may say that, had she been born 25 years later, with equivalent accomplishments at equivalent ages, Lucile Morsch might well have become Librarian of Congress.

Biographical listings and obituaries—*Current Biography* (1972); "Directory." *Catalogers' and Classifiers' Yearbook* No. 6 (1937), p. 169; [Obituary]. *Library Journal* 97:2519 (Aug. 1972); [Obituary]. *Library of Congress Information Bulletin* 31:314-15 (July 14, 1972); [Obituary]. *Wilson Library Bulletin* 47:16 (Sept. 1972); *Who's Who in America* 28-34 (1954/1955-1966/1967); *Who's Who in Library Service*, 1st ed., 2nd ed., 3rd ed., 4th ed.; *Who's Who of American Women*, 1st ed. (1958-1959), 3rd-6th eds. (1964/1965-1970/1971). Books and articles about the biographee—[Biographical sketch and portrait]. *ALA Bulletin* 50:466 (July/Aug. 1956); [Biographical sketch and portrait]. *Journal of Cataloging & Classification* 7:73-75 (Summer 1951); "Chief of the Descriptive Cataloging Division at Library of Congress Retires." *Library Journal* 91:80 (Jan. 1, 1966); Cole, John Y. "Morsch, Lucile M." *Encyclopedia of Library and Information Science.* Allen Kent, Harold Lancour, Jay E. Daily, eds. New York: Marcel Dekker, 1976, Vol. 18; "Lucile Morsch Retires." *Library of Congress Information Bulletin* 24:619-20 (Nov. 22, 1965); "1966 ALA Award Winners." *Library Journal* 91:3637 (Aug. 1966); "Personnel: Lucile M. Morsch." *College & Research Libraries* 14:444 (Oct. 1953); "Retired from Library of Congress on December 30." *Wilson Library Bulletin* 40:397

(Jan. 1966). **Primary sources and archival materials**—The Library of Congress has the records concerned with Morsch's tenure with that institution, and additional material is to be found in the American Library Association Archives at the University of Illinois.

—PHYLLIS A. RICHMOND

MUDGE, ISADORE GILBERT (1875-1957)

Isadore G. Mudge was born March 14, 1875, in Brooklyn, New York, one of four children of Alfred Eugene and Mary Gilbert Ten Brook Mudge. Both her parents and grandparents were unusually well educated, and every opportunity for scholarly preparation was provided for the Mudge children. Isadore attended the Adelphi Academy in Brooklyn and, after her graduation in 1893, was admitted to Cornell University, where she earned her Bachelor of Philosophy degree in 1897. While at Cornell, Mudge gained early recognition as a scholar and historian; she was elected to Phi Beta Kappa during her junior year. She was also strongly influenced by the teaching of George Lincoln Burr, historian, archivist, and librarian, who was primarily responsible for Isadore's choice of librarianship as a career. One year later (1898), she enrolled in the New York State Library School at Albany and, under the inspired directorship of Melvil Dewey (q.v.), earned the Bachelor of Library Science degree, with distinction, in 1900.

Although Isadore Mudge was, throughout her life, a devout "Easterner," she was persuaded to join Katharine Lucinda Sharp's (q.v.) staff at the University of Illinois. Sharp, within the few short years between 1893 and the turn of the century, had firmly established a university tradition for library education in the Midwest. Her school at Urbana, Illinois, was a strong competitor to Dewey's own in New York, and she demanded the best of Dewey's graduates for her own faculty. Mudge became head of the reference department at Illinois (1900) and, during her three years in this position, did much to develop both its services and its collections. In Mudge's annual report of 1901-1902, she stressed the need for a balanced, easily accessible, useful reference collection through which the student would be led to "independent" use of library resources. These principles were basic to her entire life's work.

Katharine Sharp was a hard taskmaster and was known for her unsparing expectations of her staff. Each member was involved in developing a phase of the University Library, and each was expected to teach within the library school. Although Isadore Mudge was both intelligent and hardworking, she could also recognize the limitations of the Illinois situation. This, coupled with an offer for advancement, brought her resignation from Illinois to become head librarian at Bryn Mawr College in 1903. There, until 1908, Mudge had an opportunity to develop her

own professional skills and to determine her ultimate career interests. In 1908, she left her position at Bryn Mawr for a number of reasons and, for the next three years, lived a varied and peripatetic existence. She taught part-time in the Simmons Library School in Boston (1910-1911); she began work on a revision of Alice Bertha Kroeger's (q.v.) *Guide to the Study and Use of Reference Works* ...; she and a former colleague from Illinois—Minnie E. Sears (q.v.)—wrote *A Thackeray Dictionary*; she assisted in the compilation of W. D. Johnston's *Special Collections in Libraries in the U.S.*; and, in 1911, she prepared the first of nearly thirty annual reviews of reference books that would be published under her name in *Library Journal* from 1911 to 1929.

Isadore Mudge returned to the New York area in 1911 to accept a position as gifts and exchanges librarian at Columbia University. A few months later, she was appointed as reference librarian and, until her retirement in 1941, she served the University in some capacity as a reference specialist. These years at Columbia became the basis for the widely held assessment that Mudge is "the best known and most influential reference librarian in the history of American librarianship." Prior to her arrival at the institution, the reference department had been given minimal attention by the professional staff. Mudge's philosophy—i.e., that the library staff was both obligated and equipped to provide bibliographic service to professors and graduate students, as well as beginning students—was not an idea that had been asserted at Columbia. In fact, the scholarly users of the University Library, as was true of users of the majority of libraries of that period, presumed that they should find their own answers—reference service was not yet a traditional library responsibility.

Mudge began at once to develop a reference collection and staff that were capable of providing sophisticated help to any reader—regardless of his background and previous experience. Her task was not an easy one to accomplish, for a number of reasons. As indicated, she began her work at a low level; this concept of service was supported neither by the existing collection nor by the talents of her assistants. A change of the magnitude that she anticipated would, necessarily, take several years, since resources could not be reallocated in order to channel substantial funds into a special "reference" budget. In addition, few of the specialized users were aware of the fact that there were librarians, especially female librarians, who had the requisite scholarly background, as well as the library skills, to help them in their respective studies. Fortunately, the remarkable Nicholas Murray Butler was then president of Columbia, and he became one of Isadore Mudge's early supporters—he found her "incredibly resourceful in meeting his varied reference and bibliographic needs." Mudge's ability to answer questions, to provide relevant bibliographical data, to assess the level of the patron's need, and to instruct her assistants in some of the same areas did not long remain a secret. As her own experience grew, so did her ability, and in her teaching, she eventually developed a succinct phrase that she believed encapsulated the components of effective reference: material, mind, and method. The "method" was of special import and suggests the precursor to today's concern for effective search strategies. The reference librarian's approach to the question, the analysis of the question and its background and, of course, the identification of alternative approaches were basic to success in the encounter.

During her early years at Columbia, Isadore Mudge's concerns were largely focused on the development of the reference area and its services. Her teaching, as a result, was reserved to training her own staff. However, in 1926, the New York State Library School at Albany and the library school that operated within the structure of the New York Public Library merged to form the School of Library Service at Columbia. Mudge became an associate professor of bibliography in the School and, beginning in 1927, taught the course entitled "Bibliography and Bibliographical Methods." For the next fifteen years, she was to continue to teach the course and, in the teaching, to become nationally known for her methodology of reference. Her by then excellent experience at the reference desks of several institutions provided the basis for the practical component, while her keen intellect and personal scholarship established a unique theoretical base. Undoubtedly, the example set in this course influenced the nature of similar courses in numerous other library schools in this country. This came about for two reasons. First, students from the School at Columbia became teachers in other programs and, as disciples of Mudge, carried her message and methods to their students. More important, without question, was her long association with the *Guide to Reference Books*, then the undisputed leader among reference guides. After the 1909 death of the original compiler, Alice Bertha Kroeger, Mudge worked on supplements to the Kroeger editions and, in 1917, produced her own first full edition (the third) of the work. She eventually compiled three more editions (1923, 1929, and 1936) before passing on the responsibility. One of Mudge's protégées at Columbia and a talented successor, Constance M. Winchell, notes in her preface to the seventh edition:

Miss Mudge became the outstanding authority on reference books, and her *Guide* has been known and consulted in libraries throughout the world. She was particularly well-fitted for the work by her long experience both as a teacher and as a

reference librarian.... Her thorough familiarity with reference books and reference techniques, her clear thinking, her wide knowledge and remarkable memory, and her deep interest in the subject and in the student or research worker, all combined to impress her influence on succeeding generations of students, colleagues—all who used her book.

Isadore Mudge's writing, as already suggested, was not limited to the preparation of her famous guide. Her early literary enthusiasms were lifelong characteristics, as evidenced by her Thackeray dictionary and a George Eliot dictionary. She compiled several specialized bibliographies and also contributed to the literature of librarianship through a series of seminal articles on reference and its relationship to other library systems. Not surprisingly, she was a member and officer of several library associations, including the New York Library Club, the New York State Library Association and the American Library Association. As an active participant in these organizations, she was an articulate spokeswoman for such projects as depository sets of Library of Congress cards, the *Union List of Serials*, the expansion and refinement of Wilson services, standardized interlibrary loan policies, and almost any form of cooperation that would enhance a library's capability to provide information. Her emphasis, in whatever she undertook, was the encouragement of procedures that would give librarians a higher degree of bibliographical control over the available resources.

Mudge's work, in the 1920s and 1930s, increasingly became the model by which reference librarians and their competence were judged. Her reputation was accurately evaluated when Winchell commented that "probably no other one person has contributed so much to raising the standards of reference collections and reference service in the libraries of this and other countries." On rare occasions, the members of a profession publicly acknowledge that quality of pioneer spirit and devotion. In 1958, the American Library Association established the Isadore Gilbert Mudge Citation in her honor; it was to be given to those individuals who, in the image of Mudge, had made a "distinguished contribution to reference librarianship."

Separate from her professional life was Isadore Gilbert Mudge, the individual. "She was a delightful and warm human being . . . loving of and loved by her family and a wide group of friends." Part of Isadore's great success as a reference librarian was based on her ability to be, as so often described, "approachable," and this pleasing and open facet of her personality was amplified in all of her relationships with her friends. Despite her dedication to and satisfaction in her work, Mudge had the capacity to set it aside, to relax, and give her attention to her travel or her gardening or her entertaining. She enjoyed various recreational experiences—the theatre, music, and all of the special attractions of a busy metropolitan community. After she retired in 1941 from the Columbia University reference department and, in 1942, from teaching in the School of Library Service, she lived fifteen pleasant years, most of them in her cottage in the countryside of northern Westchester. Eventually, her physical infirmities forced her to the status of a semi-invalid, and she died in the College Manor Nursing Home, Lutherville, Maryland, on May 16, 1957.

Isadore Mudge was a librarian's librarian. In addition to her intellectual stature, her excellent education, and her breadth of library experience, she brought a peculiar sensitivity, a unique perception, to a field in the throes of defining its own goals and aspirations. Where there had been little that was precise or even logical, Mudge brought rational conceptualization and articulated a reference function. She fit the mold of the scholar-librarian of whom James I. Wyer (q.v.), in his classic textbook on reference work, wrote, "because of his library training and experience [he] will be a broader man than any that he serves. He will be able to suggest untouched sources, an unexplored path, a promising field. . . ." Not he, but *she* did all of that.

Biographical listings and obituaries—*Who Was Who in America* III (1951-1960); *Who's Who in Library Service*, 1st ed.; Winchell, C. B. "[Obituary of] Isadore Gilbert Mudge." *College and Research Libraries* 18:329-30 (July 1957). **Books and articles about the biographee**—Evans, A. P. "God Almighty Hates a Quitter." *Columbia Library Columns* 2:13-18 (Nov. 1952); "Spot of Brightness." *Columbia Library Columns* 9:14-20 (May 1960); Waddell, J. N. "Career of Isadore Gilbert Mudge: A Chapter in the History of Reference Librarianship." Unpublished doctoral thesis, Columbia University, 1973; Waddell, J. N. "Mudge, Isadore Gilbert." *Encyclopedia of Library and Information Science.* Allen Kent, Harold Lancour, Jay E. Daily, eds. New York: Marcel Dekker, 1976, Vol. 18, pp. 287-90. **Primary sources and archival materials**—Columbia University. Libraries. *Report of the Librarian*, 1911-1942; Columbia University. "Library Correspondence," 1910-1941, Mudge file. (Columbia University. Libraries, Special Collections); Columbia University. Libraries. Reference Department. Annual Report. 1904-1906; 1911/12-1940/41. (Columbia University. Libraries. Special Collections); Mudge, Isadore G. *Thirty-Year Report, 1911-1941.* (Columbia University, Libraries. Special Collections and Columbia University, Libraries. Reference Department).

—JOHN N. WADDELL
—LAUREL A. GROTZINGER

MUNN, RALPH (1894-1975)

Ralph Munn was born in Aurora, Illinois, on September 19, 1894, to Walter Ferguson and Jennie Wood Munn. His educational pursuits led him to the University of Denver, where he earned the B.A. in 1916 and went on to receive the LL.B. in 1917. After serving with the U.S. Army in France from 1917 to

1919, Munn entered the New York State Library School at Albany, where he received the B.L.S. in 1921. On June 6, 1922, he married Anne Shepard; they were to have two children, Robert Ferguson and Margaret Jean.

Reference librarian in the Seattle Public Library was Ralph Munn's first professional position (1921-1926), and he then moved to Flint, Michigan, in 1926, to become librarian of the Public Library. From 1928 to 1964, he served as director of the [Andrew] Carnegie [q.v.] Library of Pittsburgh, becoming "director emeritus" upon retirement. Simultaneously with the directorial responsibilities, he served as dean of the Carnegie Institute of Technology from 1928 to 1962.

Ralph Munn's professional life was devoted to fostering young people's careers, upgrading professional services to the public, and general involvement with the problems of the profession. This led to his appointment to the Pennsylvania "Governor's Commission on Public Library Development, 1930-1931." Then, in 1934, he undertook a four-month tour to study the library situation in Australia and New Zealand, and the publication of his survey results was the basis for reorganization in those countries, where he became known as the "father of the modern library movement." In 1950, he was one of three delegates to a UN Conference at Malmo, Sweden, to determine the needs of libraries throughout the world.

In this country and abroad he was frequently called upon to appear before governmental bodies to support appeals for the expansion of library services and facilities. One of his undertakings was a survey for the New York Planning Commission in 1943.

Ralph Munn was very much aware of the needs of young people—and one of his concerns was to make libraries more attractive to them. He was instrumental as well in realizing the importance of services to outlying areas, including bookmobile service as well as branch libraries. Munn believed in developing the library into a "real community center," even to including duplicate bridge and dancing if the appropriate facilities were available. While he was director, city-wide library service was consolidated and county residents gained use of Pittsburgh's library facilities. The growth of public library service that Ralph Munn fostered did much for the state of Pennsylvania as a whole—forming a system under which Pennsylvania was divided into 29 districts and turning the Carnegie Library in Oakland into a resource center in technology for the entire state. His plan for the Federation of Libraries in Allegheny County, Pennsylvania, ultimately led to his being awarded the Pennsylvania Library Association's first "Distinguished Service Award" in 1959.

In 1947 he toured libraries in Central and South America to apply his expertise in those countries and was selected by the U.S. Department of State to speak in Lima, Peru, at a presentation of books to their National Library, which had been rebuilt following a fire. For his work in behalf of this reconstruction, he was awarded a citation from the Peruvian government.

One of Ralph Munn's attributes was that he did not lose interest once he had completed a survey of a particular area. Even a decade after his tour of Australia, he graciously received a stream of young Australian librarians anxious to gain experience in America but unable to find jobs. The lack of job opportunities for these young people was due partly to immigration restrictions and partly to differences in U.S. requirements. Ralph Munn was generous to these people. He not only created space on his staff, but he also took a personal interest in each individual, ensuring that at all times they were treated in the same manner as their American colleagues, especially in such matters as salary and participation in staff activities.

After World War II, he was able to foresee the new demands that would be placed on public library service and the "need for consolidation or federation of the existing small independent libraries of the county or region." He was an early advocate of mechanizing for searching and repetitive tasks. His interest in modern management theory was combined with his belief that young people should be given as many growth opportunities as possible. He practiced this himself, by permitting his young staff to become involved in decision-making. He gave them opportunities to participate in business meetings, which gave them practice in book selection and policy-making decisions. He considered his "professional hobby" to be "boosting young people." His pet peeve was "tradition-bound librarians," and he strove to avoid this in his own situation. His message to young people was always "prepare yourself to exert the leadership which is so greatly needed to bring library service to its full usefulness as an agency of popular education."

In 1949, when the profession was recruiting men into library schools (and the GI's were flocking to school), he issued a warning about the overzealous recruitment of males who were "seeking a shabby security" in positions to which able women should normally advance. He noted that even then, in a predominantly "women's profession," the large percentage of positions in top administration were filled by men—that men might secure more and more of the attractive positions not because they were abler but because governing authorities preferred to hire men. He feared that, as a result of this practice, superior women might cease to enter a profession in which too many of the rewards were reserved for men.

Ralph Munn was a warm and sincere person, respected for his professional as well as personal integrity. Elizabeth Nesbitt, long associated with him, identified his distinguishing traits in an article in *Library Journal* (88:2424-25; June 15, 1963):"his forcefulness and forthrightness, his sound integrity, his sense of humor and of the ridiculous, his dislike of sham, his ability to communicate with such clarity and vigor as to leave his listener no doubt as to what he means." These qualities were in evidence even while he was a student. His very first job in a library was in a situation where there had been difficulty with student aides. Nesbitt described his appearance on the scene as follows:

A solution . . . appeared one day in the person of a young law student whose distinguishing characteristics at that time were a red head, square jaw, quiet mien, and a ready vocabulary which was both forceful and picturesque. He was placed in charge of the coltish attendants whom he soon handled with the entire success which he has since shown.

In addition to his great success as a librarian and consultant, Ralph Munn was active in ALA and other organizations. In ALA, he held committee positions and performed many other duties and assignments, and was elected to the presidency (1939-1940), having had as his opponent the famous C. C. Williamson (q.v.). In 1963, he was selected to present the dedicatory address for the new ALA Headquarters building.

Among the honors bestowed upon Ralph Munn were an Honorary Litt.D. from the University of Pittsburgh (1940) and an Honorary LL.D. from Waynesburgh College in Pennsylvania (1960).

Ralph Munn's retirement became effective October 1, 1964, at which time he was named director emeritus of the Carnegie Library of Pittsburgh. During his retirement, he continued to be advisor and consultant to the many librarians he had launched on their careers. The fund to support the Ralph Munn Lecture Series, begun at his retirement, subsequently became the Ralph Munn Creative Scholarship Program, through which young librarians are still receiving encouragement and assistance.

Following Ralph Munn's death on January 2, 1975, the American Library Association passed a resolution expressing its sense of loss and its appreciation for his contributions to the profession of librarianship. In the resolution he was characterized as exemplifying the highest ideals, as both a professional and a private citizen.

Biographical listings and obituaries—*ALA Yearbook: A Review of Library Events, 1975.* Chicago: ALA, 1976, p. 253; *Biographical Directory of Librarians in the United States and Canada,* 5th ed.; "Memorial Resolution for Ralph Munn (1894-1975)." *Australian Library Journal* 24:89 (April 1975); [Obituary]. *American Libraries* 6:252 (April 1975);

[Obituary]. *Pennsylvania Library Association Bulletin* 30:38 (March 1975); *Who Was Who in America* VI (1974-1976). **Books and articles about the biographee**—[Biographical sketch]. *Library Journal* 74:1640 (Nov. 1, 1949); "Changes at the Carnegie Library of Pittsburgh." *Pennsylvania Library Association Bulletin* 20:41 (Nov. 1964); Nesbit, Elizabeth. "Ralph Munn [Profile]." *Library Journal* 88:2424-25 (June 15, 1963); "Ralph Munn and Australia." *Australian Library Journal* 24:138-43 (May 1975).

—REGINA F. BERNEIS

MURRAY, DANIEL ALEXANDER PAYNE (1852-1925)

Daniel A. P. Murray, an employee of the Library of Congress from 1871 until his retirement in 1922, was one of the most prominent Negro librarians in the United States during the late nineteenth and early twentieth centuries. Murray held a series of responsible positions at the Library, but his most significant achievement was his work as a bibliographer of Afro-American literature. Encouraged by two prominent Librarians of Congress, Ainsworth Rand Spofford (q.v.) and Herbert Putnam (q.v.), Murray systematically gathered data about "the progress of the Colored Race" for two major projects. The first was an exhibit at the Paris Exposition of 1900, which resulted in his compilation *Preliminary List of Books and Pamphlets by Negro Authors for the Paris Exposition and the Library of Congress*, published by the Library of Congress in 1900. Murray's second endeavor, an encyclopedia about Negroes and their achievements, was never completed, even though a descriptive prospectus with sample entries was issued by the World's Cyclopedia Company of Chicago and Washington in 1912. The projected six-volume *Murray's Historical and Biographical Encyclopedia of the Colored Race throughout the World* was to include "25,000 biographical sketches of men and women of the colored race in every age." In addition to the biographical entries, this ambitious work was to include:

A bibliography of over 6,000 titles of books and pamphlets which represent the colored race's contribution to the world's literature, a synoptical list of all books of fiction by Caucasian authors that deal with the race question as a feature, and a list of nearly 5,000 musical compositions by colored composers in every part of the world.

Daniel A. P. Murray was born on March 3, 1852, in Baltimore, Maryland. A free Negro, his father was George Murray, a timber inspector, and his mother was Eliza Wilson Murray. Daniel was named after a friend of his father's, Daniel Alexander Payne (1811-1893), a bishop in the African Methodist Episcopal Church and the first Negro president of Wilberforce University. Young Murray graduated

from the Unitarian Seminary in Baltimore in 1869, an education "supplemented by private instruction in the languages." Many of his vacations were spent in Washington, D.C., where his older brother was in charge of the U.S. Senate restaurant in the Capitol, and it was here that Murray met Ainsworth Rand Spofford, Librarian of Congress. According to Murray, Spofford was "a man of strong anti-slavery convictions and singularly free from the blight of color prejudice." On January 1, 1871, Spofford hired Murray and made him a personal assistant; at the time, the Library of Congress had a total of 12 employees. In the prospectus for his encyclopedia, Murray states that in his work of "seeking answers for Congressional inquirers," he "came across a vast deal of material of transcendant importance to the colored race, and I determined to make the effort to gather it together."

On April 2, 1879, Spofford's industrious assistant married Anne Jane Evans of Oberlin, Ohio. They eventually had seven children.

Under Spofford, Murray served in various professional capacities, but on July 1, 1897, Spofford was replaced as Librarian of Congress by John Russell Young (q.v.). The new Librarian implemented an administrative reorganization and Murray became an assistant in the Catalog Department at an annual salary of $1,200—a sum $300 less than he had made before the reorganization. Between 1897 and 1899, Murray also served in the Periodical and Smithsonian Divisions. His fortunes at the Library improved during the administration of Herbert Putnam, who took office as the new Librarian of Congress in April 1899 and soon assigned Murray to work on the Negro bibliography for the Paris Exposition.

In addition to his activities at the Library, Daniel Murray also achieved prominence in Washington, D.C., civic affairs. Active in real estate and the construction trade, he was the first Negro elected to the city's major business association, the Board of Trade. In this capacity, he helped draft taxation laws and successfully advocated the introduction of industrial training in the District public schools. In October 1899, Murray was named to a "national commission" that escorted Admiral George Dewey from New York to Washington to receive a $10,000 sword awarded him by Congress. Murray also served on the committee that arranged the ceremonies for President McKinley's 1901 inauguration; a contemporary, Edwin A. Lee, wrote that Murray's success in this capacity was a significant step toward overcoming racial prejudice in Washington, efforts "for which Mr. Murray has acquired lasting fame."

The Paris Exposition opened in May 1900. The U.S. special agent in charge, Thomas J. Calloway, wrote that "the most creditable showing in the exhibit is by Negro authors, collected by Mr. Daniel Murray of the Library of Congress." The same collection was exhibited at the Buffalo Pan-American Exposition (1901) and the Charleston, South Carolina, American and West Indian Exposition, which opened in December 1901. After they were returned to the Library of Congress, the approximately 500 volumes selected by Murray were kept together and formed the nucleus of a "Colored Author Collection" under Murray's supervision. This collection, plus his personal library, formed the basic working tools for his encyclopedia project. The biographical information he was gathering also led to Murray's collaboration with Will W. Allen in the preparation of *Banneker, the Afro-American Astronomer* (1921).

Daniel Murray retired from the Library of Congress on December 31, 1922. Librarian Putnam made special mention of Murray's 52-year term of service in the 1923 Library of Congress annual report: "Mr. Murray's extraordinary record, exceeded probably in but a single instance, was also remarkable in the almost unbroken continuity and regularity of his attendance." Murray continued to work on his encyclopedia, and in a June 1925 letter apparently addressed to a potential publisher, he explained why he had undertaken the gigantic project:

> I am actuated by a desire to preserve to coming generations the excellent traits the Negro has shown in the past, and upon the showing urge the world at large to accord to him and his kin justice and the station he may honestly claim upon an examination of the evidence found in the record.

> To the Afro-American youth of the Nation, the many evidences of what may be accomplished by patriotic exertion will, I am sure, act as a direct incentive to virtuous emulation.

Murray died on December 31, 1925. He bequeathed his private library of nearly 1,500 books and pamphlets to the Library of Congress; today, the Daniel Murray Pamphlet Collection is housed in the Rare Book Division of the Library. After his death, his widow continued to work on the encyclopedia for nearly two more decades. In 1966, the Murray family donated the notes, clippings, and biographical sketches prepared by Mr. and Mrs. Daniel Murray for their projected *Historical and Biographical Encyclopedia* to the State Historical Society of Wisconsin.

Books and articles about the biographee—Caldwell, A. B., ed. *History of the American Negro*. Atlanta, Ga.: A. B. Caldwell Publishing Co., 1922. Vol. 6, pp. 25-27; Harris, Robert L., Jr. "Daniel Murray and His Encyclopedia of the Colored Race." *Phylon* 37:270-82 (Sept. 1976); Lee, Edwin. "Daniel Murray." *The Colored American Magazine* 5:432-40 (Oct. 1902); U.S. Library of Congress. *The Negro in the United States: A Selected Bibliography*. Comp. by Dorothy B. Porter. Washington: Library of Congress, 1970. (Preface). **Primary sources and archival materials**—Correspondence and records pertaining to Murray's career at the Library of Congress are in the Library of Congress Archives. The prospectus for the projected encyclopedia, along with other materials relating to Murray's career, are housed in his Pamphlet Collection in the Rare Book Division. Other material is in the State Historical Society of Wisconsin.

—JOHN Y. COLE

NELSON, CHARLES ALEXANDER (1839-1933)

Charles Alexander Nelson was born on April 14, 1839, in Calais, Maine, the son of Israel Potter and Jane Capen Nelson, both descended from old New England families. He attended private schools in Maine, of which the most significant was the Male Academy at Gorham (1854-1855), where he experienced his first library work. After his family moved to Cambridge, Massachusetts, in 1855, Charles enrolled in Harvard College, receiving his A.B. in 1860. While at Harvard, he served for three years as an assistant in the library under Ezra Abbot (q.v.) and John Langdon Sibley (q.v.).

After a year of tutoring Greek and Latin in Albany, New York, Nelson studied civil engineering at the Lawrence Scientific Institute of Harvard and received his A.M. in 1863. He taught mathematics for a year in Boston and, from 1864 to 1865, served as a civil engineer with the Union Army at New Bern, North Carolina. He remained in New Bern until 1873, in work related to the Reconstruction Act, occupying at the same time several prominent public posts. In 1872, he married Emma Norris of Slaterville, New York, and they had two daughters, Gertrude Jane and Ruth Augusta. From 1873 to 1877, he engaged in literary work and in the book business in Boston. After one year as the librarian and as a teacher of Greek at Drury College, Springfield, Missouri, Nelson returned to Boston as the manager of the Old South Bookstore and as editor of its publications.

From 1881, Nelson was the chief catalog librarian at the Astor Library in New York and produced (1886-1888) a notable four-volume supplement to Joseph G. Cogswell's (q.v.) 1857 Astor catalog. He also lectured at Melvil Dewey's (q.v.) Columbia College School of Library Economy in 1887. He moved to New Orleans to become the first librarian of the Howard Memorial Library (1888-1891), and thence to the Newberry Library (1891-1893) as a cataloger. From 1893 until he retired in 1909, Nelson was the deputy librarian of Columbia University. He also lectured at the New York State Library School and the Pratt Institute Library School from 1894 to 1898. Following his first retirement, he joined the Merchants' Association of New York in November 1913. From then until his final retirement in 1926, he compiled an index-digest of the Association's activities.

Most notable among Nelson's library and bibliographical achievements was the Astor catalog, for which he received diplomas of honorable mention at the Buffalo Pan-American Exposition and the Charleston, South Carolina, Exposition, both in 1901. In addition to reviews and articles, his other notable works were the *Catalogue of the Avery Architectural Library* (1895) and the *Index to the Minutes of the Common Council of the City of New York, 1675-1776* (8 vols., 1905-1906). He was also active in professional library activities, serving as secretary of the American Library Association, as an assistant editor of the *Library Journal* (1886-1888) and twice as the president of the New York Library Club. The ALA made him an honorary life member in 1927. He was active as well in a variety of other scholarly organizations, among them the American Historical Association and the Bibliographical Society of America (secretary).

Emma Nelson died on April 6, 1926. Charles A. Nelson died at Swarthmore, Pennsylvania, on January 12, 1933.

Biographical listings and obituaries—*Dictionary of American Biography* (C. C. Williamson); *National Cyclopaedia of American Biography* 24; [Obituary]. *Library Journal* 58 (Feb. 1, 1933); [Obituary]. *New York Times*, Jan. 14, 1933; *Who's Who in America* 17 (1932-1933). **Books and articles about the biographee**—"Charles A. Nelson." *Library Journal* 34:386 (Aug. 1909); Duncan, W. H. "Charles A. Nelson." *Library Journal* 30:178-79 (March 1905); Lydenberg, Harry M. *History of the New York Public Library, Astor, Lenox, and Tilden Foundations.* New York: NYPL, 1923.

—FRANCIS L. MIKSA

NORTON, CHARLES BENJAMIN (1825-1891)

Charles Benjamin Norton was born July 1, 1825, in Hartford, Connecticut. Since his career was a many-faceted one, and since he worked so much behind the scenes, we lack many of the basic facts of his life. In his early years, he is said to have worked in bookstores, first in Boston and later at Appleton's in New York. The year 1851 saw him at the Crystal Palace Exhibition as a commissioner. The remainder of this decade was the period of his brief but forceful impact on American librarianship. Working out of New York, Norton served as a bookseller, library agent, publisher, and general promoter of bibliographical efforts. By the end of the decade, Reuben A. Guild (q.v.) tells us, Norton "had met with reverses and was unable to go on . . . acting as an agent of librarians." He was in service during the Civil War, from which he emerged as a brigadier general. His diverse efforts in later years were concerned with mining investments and the promotion of world's fairs, among other matters. After the Paris fair of 1867, he remained in Paris with his family as publisher of the *Centennial Gazette*, and, in 1886, he was

the first editor of the *Civil Service Chronicle.* He was in Chicago, helping to plan the Columbian Exposition, at the time of his death on January 29, 1891. Little is known of his family, and the gaps in his career are large.

Norton's publishing career was distinguished by the monthly *Literary Gazette* (1851-1855, known at first as the *Literary Advertiser* and also for a time appearing semi-monthly), and the annual issues of *Norton's Literary Register* (1852-1861, also with various titles, at first *Norton's Literary Almanac*). The annual drew its features mostly from the *Literary Gazette*, but also usually included a valuable book-trade bibliography, the second continuing booktrade bibliography for this country. (Orville Roorbach's [q.v.] *Bibliotheca Americana* was first published in 1849, and supplements followed.) It is the *Literary Gazette*, this country's first library periodical, that provides a particularly useful touchstone of library thought during what was probably the most active period in our nation's library history before 1876.

We know that Norton's contributors included such illustrious figures in the library and book worlds as Samuel Austin Allibone, Daniel Coit Gilman (q.v.), and Seth Hastings Grant. Norton and his contributors (they can not always be identified) ranged adventuresomely through a variety of intellectual topics, writing with erudition, honesty, and enthusiasm. They reviewed new books of all kinds with candor and interesting insight, kept a keen ear to the ground for reports on the activities of scholars and scholarly groups of all kinds (including the nascent American Association for the Advancement of Science), and convincingly expressed opinions on people and events of the time.

The great love and particular concern of the *Literary Gazette* contributors always remained the printed book. Among the important articles are Allibone's survey of the principles of bibliography, early discussions of the landmarks of Americana, and reports on commerce in books. Norton, who served as an agent at book auctions, reported on the major sales in America and in Europe and also kept his readers informed of the acquisition of major collections by particular libraries. He discussed library buildings, collections, and needs, both in occasional articles on particular topics and in a series devoted to specific American and European institutions. Although he clearly did whatever he could to further the cause of American library development, he withdrew his support for Charles Coffin Jewett (q.v.) at (or perhaps just after) the height of the battle with Joseph Henry over the library program at the Smithsonian Institution. As one would expect of a man of Norton's scholarly and bibliophilic sympathies, Norton's attitude was less supportive of general public library service than of service to research and advanced study.

Norton's great contribution to the Librarian's Conference of 1853 has long been accepted. "The inception of that gathering," Seth Grant reminded Norton in later years, "was due wholly to yourself." It was the *Literary Gazette* for July 15, 1852—and probably Norton himself, George B. Utley (q.v.) has argued—that first proposed a meeting for the benefit of the nation's libraries. "The importance of having these various institutions well managed, demands more careful consideration than it usually receives. Anyone who, in traveling from city to city, has visited the Libraries, will be struck with the differences which they exhibit where external conditions appear to be nearly the same." The participants registered in New York at 71 Chambers Street, which was Norton's bookstore; the official registration list was published, first in the *Literary Gazette*, and later (in revised form) in the 1854 *Register*. The minutes of the meeting appeared regularly in the *Literary Gazette*, and in December 1853, the final draft memorial from the convention to the United States Congress was publicized. Although he was never active in library matters in later years, Norton arranged for a reunion of the 1853 participants at the 1887 American Library Association convention at the Thousand Islands.

As publisher of Reuben Guild's *Librarian's Manual* (1858), Norton nurtured this country's first important treatise on library management. Norton had announced the book as early as January 15, 1852, but on February 1, 1854, he was forced to acknowledge a delay. The work had been "hastily sketched and outlined," and besides, Edward Edwards was working in England on a similar text. But above all, one suspects, Guild, like so many other American librarians, had discovered an immense world of common problems in need of common solutions. Much of this discovery can be attributed to the 1853 convention and the *Literary Gazette*. Thus, while Norton himself was never a librarian, his contribution to the library profession was none the less noteworthy, and in many respects, his efforts in promoting the Conference of 1853 foreshadowed the later work of another publisher, Richard Rogers Bowker (q.v.), in helping to bring about the first meeting of the American Library Association in 1876. Adolf Growoll, the American booktrade bibliographer, described Norton as a man "of fine military appearance, courteous and of a cheerful disposition."

Biographical listings and obituaries—*Lamb's Biographical Dictionary of the United States*, edited by John Howard Brown. Boston: Lamb, 1903, Vol. 6, pp. 29-30. **Books and articles about the biographee**—Krummel, Donald W. "The Library World of *Norton's Literary Gazette*." In *Books in America's Past: Essays Honoring Rudolph H. Gjelsness*, edited by David Kaser. Charlottesville: The University Press of Virginia, 1966, pp. 238-65. [This contains further bibliographical references]; Linder, LeRoy H. "*Norton's Literary Register*: A View of American Publishing in 1855." *Library*

Chronicle of the University of Texas 6:22-28 (Spring 1958); Utley, George B. *The Librarians' Conference of 1853*. Chicago: American Library Association, 1951. **Primary sources and archival materials**—There is no known collection of Norton's personal papers, but letters may be found in the papers of several of his correspondents; an exchange of letters with Seth H. Grant is preserved in the ALA archives.

—D. W. KRUMMEL

NOYES, STEPHEN BUTTRICK (1833-1885)

Stephen Buttrick Noyes was born on August 28, 1833, in Brookfield, Massachusetts, the son of the Reverend George Rapall and Eliza Wheeler Buttrick Noyes. Both the Noyes and Buttrick families were descendants of early New England settlers and included among their numbers distinguished ministers and civic leaders. George R. Noyes himself led a distinguished career in the Harvard Divinity School (1840-1868) as a professor of Hebrew and other Oriental languages and published noteworthy translations of the Old Testament books of the Psalms, Job, and the Prophets.

Stephen Noyes attended the Hopkins Classical School in Cambridge, Massachusetts, during the 1840s (most likely as a classmate of Charles Ammi Cutter [q.v.]) and enrolled at Harvard College in 1849. He received his A.B. degree in 1853, counting among his classmates both Charles W. Elliot and Justin Winsor (q.v.). He worked at the Boston Athenaeum under the direction of Ezra Abbot (q.v.) from August 1854 to July 1855, after which he was employed until the fall of 1857 as a clerk in the Brooklyn firm of Noyes & Whittlesey. After another period in Cambridge, he returned to Brooklyn on February 20, 1858, to apply for the position of librarian in the recently formed Mercantile Library Association of that city. He was appointed to that position on March 1, 1858, the Library itself first opening to the public in May 1858 with nearly 7,000 volumes on its shelves. The Library had increased in size to more than 19,000 volumes when, on October 3, 1865, Ainsworth Rand Spofford (q.v.) offered Noyes a position at the Library of Congress. He resigned his Brooklyn post on October 10 and moved to Washington, D.C., where he planned and to a great extent carried out (with Frederic Vinton [q.v.]) the two-volume *Catalogue of the Library of Congress: Index of Subjects* (1869). On June 15, 1868, however, he was informed of his unanimous re-election to his previous post at the Brooklyn Library and, on August 31, 1868, arrived again in Brooklyn to resume the librarianship of that institution.

Noyes married Sophia O. Anthony of Brooklyn on October 20, 1870, and they had two children, Annie Anthony and George Holland. But Sophia died while the children were still infants, and her death was followed by that of their son when he was nine years old. Noyes remarried on June 14, 1882, to Susan Wilson Wylie. Their one child, Sidney B. Noyes, was born on March 24, 1883. Late in 1884, Stephen Noyes became acutely ill of gastritis and, on December 20, travelled with his wife to Deland, Florida, to rest and recuperate. His sudden death there on March 8, 1885, at so relatively young an age, shocked both the library profession at large and his local Brooklyn community and was met with an outpouring of warm praise for his library work. Subsequently, the Brooklyn Library (it had discontinued referring to itself as a "mercantile" library prior to his death), which he had guided through its formative years and for which he had built a solid foundation of service, became the Brooklyn Public Library.

Stephen Noyes's professional career was marked by several notable themes. In 1876, he joined other professional librarians in forming the American Library Association and in contributing articles to the Bureau of Education's *Public Libraries in the United States of America . . . Special Report*, including his "Plan of [the] New Catalogue of the Brooklyn Mercantile Library." He served as an associate editor of the *Library Journal* during its early years, occasionally contributing papers and notes to its pages. And he participated regularly in annual ALA discussions, especially on the topic of subject cataloging. Noyes also eminently fulfilled in his library work the then-current notion that a librarian was first and foremost to be a cultural missionary dedicated to uplifting popular culture. Toward this end he bent every means, and his administration of the Brooklyn Library for 25 of its first 28 years was remarkable for his serious pursuit of this goal.

Noyes was also an accomplished bibliographer and through his efforts, the book collection of the Library grew to over 80,000 volumes. Moreover, his contemporaries testified more than once during his life that the collection was exceptionally well selected and that it was far more valuable than the collections of many libraries that were much larger and better funded. Furthermore, Noyes was praised for his knowledge of the specific books in the Library and for his ability to use that knowledge in what he considered to be the librarian's highest calling— advising readers. For the scholar, his aid was scholarly and rigorous. In this connection, he was an active member of several historical societies and an astute bibliographical detective. The latter is particularly demonstrated by the many notes in the *Library Journal* in which he identified anonymous and pseudonymous authors.

To the less than scholarly, however, his aid was no less enthusiastic and was marked by sensitivity and understanding. In this respect, he did not hesitate to promote the reading of fiction during a time when it was not always reputable for scholarly librarians to do so. On the other hand, he never ceased his efforts to lead persons from fiction to solid works of non-fiction. It was in the latter vein that he praised the Boston Public Library's publication of its *Class List for English Prose Fiction, including Translations and Juvenile Books, with Notes for Readers, Intended to Point Out for Parallel Reading the Historical Sources of Works of Fiction* (6th ed., 1877). He strongly agreed with the evaluative and descriptive notes in this work, paraphrasing Justin Winsor's opinion that "the best chance for success in inducing more careful habits of reading lies in the gradual awakening of a deeper interest by connecting, in one course of instruction, the imaginative and historical renderings of the same thing." (See his review in the *Library Journal* 1:292; April 1877.) In the same review, he went on to give his own approach to the role of fiction in a library in the statement:

> That the public taste for fiction predominates in an excessive ratio is undoubtedly true, and it would be quixotic for a popular library to attempt to ignore it. Most libraries help to regulate and educate this appetite by exerting a discreet liberty of exclusion in the purchase of fiction, and by bringing to the notice of their subscribers attractive books in other departments of literature. The present edition of this catalogue is the first one in which the combination of historical references with the *ground-work* of fiction has been attempted, and is a distinct and valuable addition to the accumulating helps to popular culture provided for its readers by the Boston Public Library.

Noyes had already sought to bring the same sort of "helps" to the Brooklyn community through the publication of the Brooklyn Mercantile Library's own *Class List of English Prose Fiction*. The first two editions (1869, 1873) of this useful readers' advisory aid were issued as separate publications. The last two editions (1877, 1884) were, however, simply offprints of the fiction section of his far more influential *Catalogue of the Mercantile Library of Brooklyn: Authors, Titles, Subjects, and Classes* (3 vols., 1877-1880).

Noyes's catalog, described in advance of its publication in the Bureau of Education's 1876 *Special Report*, is important because it was the most polished representative of the alphabetico-classed subject catalog tradition available and because it provided the chief ideological opponent of Charles Cutter's alphabetical-specific dictionary catalog system. Noyes, like Cutter, had been deeply influenced by the work of Ezra Abbot and by the latter's alphabetico-classed card catalog of the Harvard College Library. Both men were likewise aware of the usefulness of the dictionary catalog tradition represented by the work of William F. Poole (q.v.) and Charles C. Jewett (q.v.). Whereas Cutter went on to perfect the latter tradition, Noyes went on to perfect the alphabetico-classed tradition, first in the 1869 Library of Congress subject index to its 1865 author catalog, and ultimately in his Brooklyn catalog. The latter work differed from Abbot's original plan in that it merged authors, titles, and subjects in a single alphabet, rather than keeping the subject section separate as Abbot had done. But it nevertheless remained true to Abbot's idea that most specific subjects should be gathered alphabetically under their including classes, the latter to be placed in the main alphabetical sequence of authors and titles. Thus, like Abbot, Noyes, for example, not only placed all particular flowers under "Botany" and all particular insects under "Insects," but he also placed all biographical works under the heading "Biography" and all geographical entries under the broader heading "Countries." Finally, cross references from specific subjects to their proper class locations were also placed in the main alphabetical sequence.

The Brooklyn catalog engendered much praise both for its comprehensiveness and for its practicality. Its comprehensiveness was due in no small part to its extensive use of analytical entries. For example, of about 11,000 entries in the "Biography" class, more than 8,000 of these were from periodicals and collections of essays. Its special practicality lay in the ease with which sections of the catalog could be printed separately (as in the Fiction list) for special advisory use or for updating.

Cutter, representing the direct alphabetical-specific entry viewpoint, criticized this arrangement for not representing the thought patterns of what he considered the great majority of library patrons who sought direct access to individual subjects, especially persons and places. Cutter claimed that experience had taught him that requiring such patrons to search under broad classes for specific subjects (e.g., under "Biography" for persons; under "Countries" for individual places; under "Botany" for individual flowers; under "Insects" for individual insects) was too much to expect of them. Noyes countered by claiming that in his own experience, although a patron might be familiar with the names of some individual subjects, he would not know them all; and that

the best way to teach him what books your library has [for example] on all sorts of flowers and insects is to place them under the respective headings BOTANY and INSECTS, the individual flowers or insects constituting an alphabetical series; so that the average reader can readily see all that the library has, and not waste time in searching indefinitely in the general alphabet for headings which perhaps do not exist. (See his

"Cataloguing: Yearly Report," *Library Journal* 8:168; September/October 1883).

Furthermore, he felt that the tendency "to accumulate a vast array of incongruous subdivisions of all the varied departments of science and literature under the name of such country or place as happens to figure in the title" (a marked tendency in Cutter's pure alphabetical-specific system) gave rise to "great practical inconveniences." (See his contribution to "The Plan of the New 'Poole's Index'; a Library Symposium," *Library Journal* 3:141; June 1878.) Because subarrangement was in his opinion only a practical matter, he felt that the average reader would be more adequately helped by bringing specific subjects together under comprehensive headings rather than by isolating them as particulars. Furthermore, any subarrangement under a comprehensive heading should be limited to a simple structure.

Both Noyes's and Cutter's respective ideas about patrons' thinking patterns were aired publicly between 1876 and 1884. Cutter went so far as to admit, however, that Noyes's approach might well be ultimately successful because it was contrived to correspond "to the public's unsystematic association of ideas." (See Cutter's "Library Catalogues," p. 545.) Both men had imitators of their work, but these imitations are notable for their blending of the two traditions. Noyes's sudden death silenced the most able proponent of the alphabetico-classed tradition. Nevertheless, his views have persisted in the form of a constant tendency toward alphabetico-classed practices in dictionary catalog subject heading work. This tendency, in fact, represents an important compromise of Cutter's alphabetical-specific system now in wide use.

Biographical listings and obituaries—*Lamb's Biographical Dictionary of the United States* 6:39; *National Cyclopaedia of American Biography* 18; [Obituary]. *New York Times*, March 12, 1885; "Stephen B. Noyes [Obituary]." *Brooklyn Daily Eagle*, as reprinted in *Library Journal* 10:52-53 (March 1885). **Books and articles about the biographee**—Cutter, Charles A. "Library Catalogues." U.S. Bureau of Education. *Public Libraries in the United States of America: Their History, Condition, and Management. Special Report. Part I.* Washington, D.C.: Government Printing Office, 1876; Cutter, Charles A. [*Catalogue of the Mercantile Library of Brooklyn ... Part I:A-C*]. *Nation* 24:365-66 (June 21, 1877); Cutter, Charles A. [Notice of *Catalogue of the Mercantile Library of Brooklyn ... Part II:D-M*]. *Library Journal* 3:346 (Nov. 1878); Cutter, Charles A. Notice of *Analytical and Classed Catalogue of the Brooklyn Library* [Parts I-III]. *Library Journal* 5:325-26 (Nov./Dec. 1880); Cutter, Charles A. [Mr. Noyes' Catalogue of the Brooklyn Library]. *Nation* 32:73-74 (Feb. 3, 1881); [Cutter, Charles A.] Editorial. *Library Journal* 10:47 (March 1885); Evans, Charles. Review of *Catalogue of the Mercantile Library of Brooklyn ... Part I:A-C. Library Journal* 1:330-31 (May 1877); Jones, Lynds E. Review notice of *Class List of English Prose Fiction, including Juveniles and Translations, Mercantile Library of Brooklyn*, 3rd ed. *Library Journal* 3:70 (April

1878); Miksa, Francis L. "Charles Ammi Cutter: Nineteenth Century Systematizer of Libraries." Ph.D. dissertation, University of Chicago, 1974; Noyes, J. B. "Stephen B. Noyes: A Biographical Sketch." *Library Journal* 10:103-104 (March 1885); Ranz, Jim. *The Printed Book Catalogue in American Libraries: 1723-1900*. Chicago: American Library Association, 1964 (ACRL Monograph No. 26).

—FRANCIS L. MIKSA

OLCOTT, FRANCES JENKINS (1872-1963)

Frances Jenkins Olcott was born, according to most records, in 1872, in Paris, France, the daughter of Franklin and Julie Emily Fish Olcott. An exhaustive search of published records has failed to reveal her exact birthdate. She was graduated from Melvil Dewey's (q.v.) New York State Library School in Albany in 1896. From 1897-1898, she was assistant librarian at the Brooklyn Public Library. She left this position to create and later become head of the children's department of the [Andrew] Carnegie [q.v.] Library of Pittsburgh, a position she held until 1911. From 1900 to 1911, she was also organizer and director of the Library's Training School for Children's Librarians. When she left Pittsburgh in 1911, she moved to New York, where she wrote, edited, and compiled more than 24 books for children. She died in New York on March 29, 1963, at the age of 90.

From her early days, Olcott wished to become a librarian. After spending her childhood in France (her father was vice-consul-general for the United States in Paris when she was born), her family returned to Albany, New York. Her proximity to the library school at Albany may have influenced her decision to study there.

In the beginning stages of public library work with children, the only provisions made were for separate book collections and separate children's rooms. Olcott pioneered in the organization of children's work with the development of the children's department in the Carnegie Library of Pittsburgh. Ralph Munn (q.v.) stated:

> Carnegie Library has excelled in its services to boys and girls ever since the day, early in 1898, when Frances J. Olcott was given the task of establishing the children's department. It was pioneer work. Since rather few children could come to the library or its branches, Miss Olcott took the library to them. Small collections of books were installed in homes, and the children of the neighborhood swarmed in to meet the visiting librarian, listen to a story, and borrow a book. Storytelling became an art, and each children's librarian had a repertoire of folklore and legends.

The children's department provided cooperation with schools and playgrounds, home libraries and clubs, and storytelling. Through "mother's afternoon and teachers' evenings," an attempt was made to bring the home, the school, and the public library together.

In the second stage of public library work with children—the training of young women specifically for children's work—the field became one of organization, expansion, and specialization. Elva S. Smith (q.v.) wrote, "Among the librarians who were instrumental in determining the trend of children's work during this second period, Frances Jenkins Olcott must be accounted one of the most influential." Olcott was founder of a training class "to provide children's librarians for the Carnegie Library of Pittsburgh." She was appointed by the librarian, Edwin H. Anderson (q.v.), as principal of the Training School for Children's Librarians. The training class was named the Training School because the demand for trained children's librarians outside Pittsburgh grew and students from many parts of the country came to Pittsburgh to attend the school. Olcott spoke of this project:

> An important part of the work is the preparation for library work with the children. In the beginning of the work we made decidedly unsatisfactory experiments in employing untrained help.... So we found it imperative to establish a training class to supply the children's librarians for our own library. This training class developed into a training school, and since the time of its organization in 1900, we have not been able to supply the demand for trained children's librarians.... This spring we had more than 30 positions to fill and no more than six women to send out into the field.

A reporter for the *Pittsburgh Press* described Olcott as a small woman who moved quickly and spoke rapidly. She had bright eyes and a confident decisive way, always able to locate the information she sought.

The Carnegie Library of Pittsburgh provided Olcott with an "experimental laboratory" to test her new ideas. By reporting the results of her experiences to the rest of the United States through periodical articles, library reports, and library association activities, she brought attention to the children's library movement. *Rational Library Work with Children* was published by ALA in 1907 and her *Library Work with Children* was reprinted by ALA in 1914. In addition to this, graduates of her training program carried her basic principles of children's librarianship throughout the country. Reading lists, bibliographies such as *Selected Class Room Libraries: A List of 200 Good Books for Children* (New York State Teacher's Association, 1912), and catalogs prepared for her department were circulated widely. During her tenure at Carnegie, she "collected, edited and indexed fairy tales, stories, biographies, poems for her classes and circulating department staffs." The training program that she organized was eventually a part of the Carnegie Institute of Technology and finally moved to the University of Pittsburgh, where it exists today as the Graduate School of Library and Information Sciences.

Frances Olcott left Pittsburgh to spend her time "devoting myself to writing." Her bibliography contains over 24 works for children, many of which have been revised and reprinted. Among these are *Good Stories for Great Birthdays* (Houghton, 1922), *Good Stories for Great Holidays* (Houghton, 1914), *Children's Reading* (Houghton, 1912), *Wonder Tales from China Seas* (Longmans, 1925), *Arabian Nights Entertainments* (Holt, 1923), *Wonder Tales from Goblin Hills* (Longmans, 1930), *Bible Stories to Read and Tell* (Harper, 1932), and *Good Stories for Anniversaries* (Houghton, 1937).

Elva Smith commented that "the underlying principles [of library work with children] constantly stressed by Miss Olcott have borne the test of time." One of these, as restated, was that "library work with children is of educational value; its function is as important as that of the schools and it should be a vital force in the life of a community."

Biographical listings and obituaries—"Frances Jenkins Olcott, 90; Founded Children's Library [Obituary]." *The New York Times*, April 4, 1963, p. L-17; Kunitz, Stanley J., and Howard Haycraft, eds. *Junior Book of Authors*. 2nd ed., rev. New York: H. W. Wilson, 1951. [The autobiographical sketch of Frances Jenkins Olcott, pp. 230-31]; [Obituary]. *Antiquarian Bookman* 31:1526 (April 15, 1963); *Who's Who in America* 19 (1936-1937). **Books and articles about the biographee**—Gordon, Gertrude. "Greater Pittsburgs [sic] Successful Women No. 20–Miss Frances Jenkins Olcott." *The Pittsburgh Press* [an undated clipping from the Pennsylvania Room, Carnegie Library of Pittsburgh]; Meigs, Cornelia, and others. *Critical History of Children's Literature: A Survey of Children's Books in English, Prepared in Four Parts under the Editorship of Cornelia Meigs*. Rev. ed. New York: Macmillan, 1969; Munn, Ralph. "Books Alive since '95: The Carnegie Library of Pittsburgh 1895-1945." Reprinted from *The Carnegie Magazine* (Oct. 1945); Showers, Victor C. "Forty Years of Library School Education." *The Carnegie Magazine* 4:99-102; Smith, Elva S. "As It Was in the Beginning: Frances Jenkins Olcott." *Public Libraries* 30:417-20 (Oct. 1925).

—BLANCHE WOOLLS

PALTSITS, VICTOR HUGO (1867-1952)

Victor Hugo Paltsits, librarian, bibliographer, historian, was born in New York City on July 12, 1867, the son of William Thomas and Sidonia Ida Loose Paltsits. His formal education ended with the completion of the eighth grade at the age of fifteen. For the next four years, he worked days and studied mathematics and science at the Cooper Union during evenings. From 1884 to 1885, he worked with Thomas A. Edison in the latter's first machine shop. In later years, he continued his part-time study,

primarily in languages. On July 21, 1891, he married Anne Mueller, and they were the parents of two children: Florence and Victor John. Mrs. Paltsits died on June 29, 1944.

In 1888, Paltsits joined the staff of the Lenox Library. He earned several promotions and, in 1895, when the Lenox Library was consolidated with the Astor Library and the Tilden Trust to form the New York Public Library, he became assistant librarian to John Shaw Billings (q.v.), the librarian. The late Clifford K. Shipton (q.v.) wrote that Paltsits "firmly believed that 'the most enjoyable part of life is work,' and he bemoaned the fact that life did not contain hours enough to permit him to do all of his historical research and editing which were waiting for his hand." In 1907, Governor Hughes appointed him New York state historian, a position he filled with distinction for four years. In 1911, he became research assistant to I. N. Phelps Stokes, then preparing his six-volume *Iconography of Manhattan Island*. He continued to be associated with Stokes, as part-time consultant, until 1928.

In 1914, Paltsits returned to the New York Public Library as its first keeper of manuscripts. In 1916, he also assumed the post of chief of the American History Division, and he held both positions until his retirement, in 1941, at the age of 74. Thus, all but 7 of Paltsits's 53 years of library and historical work were devoted to the New York Public Library. Between 1915 and 1926, he was also in charge of all of the Library's public exhibitions and, during the same general period, he was curator of the Spencer Collection of Fine Books. His service in all of the above areas was characterized by minute attention to detail as well as by an imaginative expansion of both holdings and services. Judged solely by his administrative leadership, Victor Paltsits was a superb librarian. Yet Shipton wrote, "He was an antiquarian rather than a librarian; he never realized that space, bulk, usefulness, and cost of accession must be taken into consideration in accepting materials, but he did not try to force his ideas upon others."

Robert W. Hill, who succeeded Paltsits in the Manuscript Division of the New York Public Library, has written that in spite of his "multiplicity of supervisory posts, Dr. Paltsits' pen poured forth a steady stream of published works. As new rarities or collections of historical documents came in, often upon his recommendation, he publicized their significance through the scholarly journals." More than forty such articles are listed in the index to the *Bulletin* of the New York Public Library, and he probably published at least as many articles in other journals. In the very month of his death, the NYPL *Bulletin* carried his "The First Printed Bible and Its Arrival in America in 1847." He contributed a vast number of biographical sketches to both the

Dictionary of American Biography and *Appleton's Cyclopedia of American Biography* (88 sketches to the latter alone).

Paltsits's first book was his edition of *The Journal of Captain William Pote, Jr., during His Captivity in the French and Indian War* (New York Public Library, 1896), and his last book, 55 years later, was a revised edition of Henry Stevens's *Recollections of James Lenox and the Formation of His Library* (New York Public Library, 1951). Various volumes of *Who's Who in America* list a stream of volumes edited or authored by Victor Hugo Paltsits.

Paltsits was, however, no cloistered scholar. As a young man, he had been active in the organizational work of his political party, and he always retained a deep interest in civic affairs and a sense of responsibility for political participation. He was an active member of several churches during his lifetime, and in his later years was an elder in the First Presbyterian Church of Jamaica. He served loyally and effectively in many local undertakings, and also found time to be interested in gardening and to enjoy an occasional fishing trip on Long Island Sound.

One of Paltsits's most significant contributions to American scholarship was his leadership in the establishment of archival procedures and policies. As early as 1909, while he was New York state historian, Paltsits read a paper titled "Tragedies in New York's Public Records" before the first open meeting of the Public Archives Commission of the American Historical Association. He was a member of this Commission from 1908 to 1924 and was its chairman from 1911 to 1922. In 1912, at a meeting of the American Historical Association, he read a paper titled "Plan and Scope for a Manual of Archival Economy for the Use of American Archivists." This paper has been termed "the first systematic presentation of the science of archives in America." Margaret Norton has written that, at the time of his death, Paltsits had "long been acknowledged as the foremost American bibliographer of his generation," and that "he had a profound influence upon the development of archival techniques in this country." Long a member of the Society of American Archivists, which he had helped to found, he was continued as an honorary member after his retirement.

A founding member of the Bibliographical Society of America, Paltsits served as its president in 1938-1939. A man with broad interests, he had also helped to found the American Military History Foundation and the History of Science Society, as well as the Society of American Archivists. In 1904, he was elected to the American Antiquarian Society and was an active member for the rest of his life, contributing numerous papers to its *Proceedings*. The Doctor of Literature degree was conferred on him by both Brown University (1936) and Rutgers University

(1938), and a large number of learned societies accorded him recognition as honorary fellow or life member. It has been written that his two most dominant personal characteristics were generosity and loyalty. He died on October 3, 1952, and was buried in Woodlawn Cemetery, New York City.

Biographical listings and obituaries–*National Cyclopaedia of American Biography* 17; [Obituary]. *Library Journal* 77:1968 (Nov. 15, 1952); [Obituary]. *New York Times*, Oct. 5, 1952; [Obituary]. *Wilson Library Bulletin* 27:278 (Dec. 1952); *Who Was Who in America* III (1951-1960); *Who's Who in Library Service*, 1st ed. **Books and articles about the biographee**–Hill, Robert W. "Victor Hugo Paltsits." *Bulletin* of the New York Public Library 56:554-56 (Nov. 1952). [Consult the files of this publication as well]; Norton, M. C. "Victor Hugo Paltsits, 1867-1952." *American Archivist* 16:137-40 (April 1953); Shipton, Clifford K. "Victor Hugo Paltsits." AAS *Proceedings* 62:110-13. **Primary sources and archival materials**–Manuscript material is held by the New York State Library (Albany) and at the New York Public Library.

—RALPH ADAMS BROWN

PARGELLIS, STANLEY (1898-1968)

Stanley Pargellis, fifth librarian of the Newberry Library, was born to Mortimer and Bertha McCrory Pargellis on June 25, 1898, in Toledo, Ohio. His father was a YMCA administrator who moved throughout the Midwest and West. Stanley Pargellis took his B.A. from the University of Nevada in 1918 and for brief periods served in the Coast Artillery Corps, worked in business, and attended Harvard Law School. In 1921, he became a Rhodes Scholar at Exeter College, Oxford, where he received a B.A. (1922) and M.A. (1929). In 1923, he returned to become instructor in English and history at the California Institute of Technology. This same year saw his marriage to Elizabeth S. Allen, to which union were born three children, Margaret, Allen McCrory, and Katherine. In 1925, Pargellis moved to Yale University, where he was an instructor in history (1926-1929), later assistant professor (1930-1942), and where he received his Ph.D. (1929). During these years, his scholarly reputation was established, first through *Lord Loudoun in North America* (Yale University Press, 1933), based on his dissertation, and later through *Military Affairs in North America, 1748-1765* (Appleton, Century, 1936), based on the Cumberland Papers at Windsor Castle; *Complaint and Reform in England, 1436-1714* (Oxford University Press, 1938), an anthology that he edited with William Huse Dunham; and some two dozen contributions to the *Dictionary of American Biography*.

In 1942, Pargellis began his two decades in Chicago as librarian of the Newberry. The distinguished American historian Ray Allen Billington has summarized his achievement: "He inherited from his predecessors a good library in the humanities, too little known outside Chicago; he bequeathed to his successor an internationally famous institution which attracts scholars from all the western world." To phrase it differently, what was recognized as a great "librarian's library," in the spirit of his predecessor, George B. Utley (q.v.), became under Stanley Pargellis a "scholar's library," something eminently in keeping with the flourishing academic involvement in humanistic research that began after the war. The transition was achieved most conspicuously through Pargellis's various special programs, and most effectively through his sympathetic personal style. Fellowships were established for visiting scholars. Conferences were also held in the Library—both of established organizations and on special topics related to the Newberry's programs—usually followed by a reception graced by the finest of what (at the University of Chicago and elsewhere) was known as "Northwestern punch." The publications program of the Library was expanded and visually enhanced, and the *Newberry Library Bulletin* was instituted in order to call attention to promising new research material that had been added to or discovered in the Library. The Library was then no longer merely a reservoir of useful books; it was a marketplace, haven, battleground, working headquarters—whatever environment the scholar needed to work best with his documents.

Above all, the close personal concern of Stanley Pargellis for the individual scholar, particularly the fledgling researcher, contributed much to the change in the Library's role. Many a doctoral candidate will remember sessions at the feet of "Mr. P.," engaging in an informal two-man seminar and pursuing a dialogue filled with the most provocative and productive of leading questions. (The atmosphere could be called somewhat patronizing: one was usually called "My boy"; but one often received an invaluable grant for a month or two in residency the next summer, with living accommodations in the Library's nearby Irving Apartments, perhaps a gourmet dinner at the Tavern Club, a study in the Library, and the most genuine and serious of encouragement.) Apart from the many younger scholars who enjoyed such a happy scholarly relationship, such peers as Stanley Morison and Archer Taylor were among his respected friends. He could also take pride in the scholarly projects that he promoted, such as Wright Howes's *US-iana*, as well as in the persons he brought to the staff of the Library, such as Hans Baron and James M. Wells.

Pargellis was a joiner: his list of memberships was a long one, and, in an awesomely high percentage of them, he served as both a leader and a worker. He nursed *Poetry* magazine through its dark hours, working with editors and trustees and providing special quarters in the Irving Apartments. He served on the directorates of such prestigious organizations as the American Council of Learned Societies, the American

Historical Association, the Association of Research Libraries, the Institute of Early American History and Culture, and the commissions for both Fulbright awards and Rhodes scholarships. His interests also extended to the immediate community of St. Chrysostom's Church, Francis Parker School, and various groups in the Lincoln Park area. While his own background, and the opinion of his powerful trustees, tended strongly to conservatism, he spoke out tellingly against Senator Joseph McCarthy around 1950, and later for Adlai Stevenson's presidential aspirations.

Among the opportunities that came his way, two were to lead to particular benefits to the Newberry's collections. Addressing the Newcomen Society and other business groups, Pargellis spoke out on behalf of the preservation of the records of American business (see, for example, *The Judgment of History on American Business* [Newcomen Society, 1943] or *The Corporation and the Historian* [Newcomen Society, 1944]). Even today, his articles are among the most respected and frequently recalled in this area. Through such efforts, in turn, the Newberry was to acquire the massive and valuable collections of papers of the Illinois Central and Burlington railroads. Similarly, the Newberry-Rockefeller program for creative writers was to yield some of the best known Midwestern literature of the 1940s, as it was to lead eventually to the Newberry's Midwest Manuscript Program, under the initial guidance of Lloyd Lewis.

His other acquisitions for Newberry were many, but special mention should be made of the bequest of Alfred Hamill, his close friend and his first president of the Newberry Trustees, with whom he was to work so pleasantly in his early years at the Library; the William B. Greenlee collection of Portuguese materials; and, eventually, the Everett D. Graff collection of Western Americana. French political pamphlets of the sixteenth century and the Revolution, eighteenth century British pamphlets, "Wright fiction," and early bibliographies were among his proudest achievements.

One of Pargellis's favorite efforts was that of defining the Library's collection development policies. At Newberry, he inherited a very wide mandate for acquisitions: the ancient Chicago Public-John Crerar compact had been inconsistently interpreted as the institutions had grown, and the Newberry commitment to "the humanities" was at once too broad, too inhibiting, and too problematical. Pargellis set out to identify the strengths of the collection and to "build to" them. In several papers, Pargellis took the unpopular position of advocating selectivity in an age of the blanket order. His practice of waiting for reviews of current books might have been dangerous in many institutions; in a library like the Newberry, it reflected a profoundly naive faith in the justice of scholarship. Indeed, the true way to build a library, as he saw it, was the "buy-a-good-book-when-you-see-it method" (see his "Building a Research Library," *College and Research Libraries* 5:113 [1944]). His working relationship with the antiquarian booksellers, and particularly those with conspicuous scholarly interests, was understandably stimulating, generally affable, and always intense.

The basis for his method, as he described it in "Building a Research Library," clearly reflected a humanistic philosophy firmly grounded in nineteenth century liberalism: "The librarian who deliberately and indiscriminately gathers in everything he can is traitor to our civilization.... He is preserver of mediocrity, slave to the fiction of size, and servant to the specious gospel of relativity in human affairs." But, in that same article, Pargellis willingly conceded that "one of the skills we lack is intelligent bibliography-making." Addressing the Bibliographical Society of America, he acclaimed "Gesner, Petzholdt, et al." as heroes in the cause of bibliography that was rigorously selective and thoughtfully annotative. He wrote in the Society's *Papers* (53:20 [1959]) that "if a bibliographer fails equally to use his discrimination and his imagination, he is not living up to his responsibility."

As a librarian, Pargellis remained somewhat aloof from the technical side of librarianship. His friendships among research library administrators, to be sure, were notably close, intense, and devoted. Like his books, these had been carefully and individually selected, the criteria being personal style and scholarly substance. His home, on into the wee hours during ALA Midwinter Conferences, graced by fine music, fine discourse, and fine port, was the scene of a mixture of conviviality, gossip, and searching ideas. At the same time, he viewed himself mainly as one who worked *in* more than *with* books. Such an involvement, as he saw it, reflected nothing more, or less, than the responsibility suggested in John Stuart Mill's maxim that men must be men before they are professionals. His case is stated nowhere more boldly than in his challenge to the American Library History Round Table in 1948 (printed as "Long Life to the Library History Round Table," *Wilson Library Bulletin* 22:601 [1948]):

> Librarians ... tend to be systematizers, blueprint-makers, counters, planners, worshippers of the mimeograph, discoverers of laws governing the actions of men in groups, standardizers, fillers-out of forms, fomenters of vast projects, disregarders of men and women as individuals, and interested only in mankind—and books—in the mass. Since I believe in none of those things by themselves, but only when thoroughly leavened with large doses of history and philosophy and poetry, I stand before

you as something of a heretic in this year and age, who nevertheless considers these librarians of the [abovementioned] variety to be the real heretics in the long time-span of human affairs.

His associations with librarians were thus based on a high level of moral discourse. In the article "On Being a Librarian" (*American Oxonian* 40:4 [1953]), he wrote, "A librarian's job is to get the right books into a library and to make them available under right conditions to the right sort of readers." The key word, he naturally conceded, was "right." Furthermore, he agreed that American libraries were doing a splendid job in providing the right conditions; and the right readers, he was willing to accept, were determined within the mandate of the institution. The right books were scarcely a problem for the enormous research library, with its vast funds and efficient operations. Like the enlightened liberal that he was, however, he preferred to determine in his own conscience, and to defend courageously and on the most rigorous intellectual grounds the "right" books from the "trash."

Among the honors conferred on him were the degrees of LL.D. from Lawrence College (1945) and Northwestern University (1956). His scholarly production flourished through his first decade at the Newberry, and culminated in the massive *Bibliography of British History: The Eighteenth Century, 1714-1789* (Oxford: The Clarendon Press, 1951), a completion of a project begun by D. J. Medley. His scholarly interests ranged widely during his Newberry years, to include other areas of American exploration, business history, bibliography, and bibliophily. His last studies were the unpublished Rosenbach Lectures in Bibliography for 1962, devoted to "Americana Collectors in Europe and England, 1600-1800." Pargellis spent his first retirement year in Canberra, Australia, on a Fulbright Award to advise the Commonwealth National Library. He returned to his summer home in Cape Porpoise, Maine, visiting frequently in Chicago. After the death of his wife, he married Mabel J. Erler, who had assisted him long and well at the Newberry in his work with antiquarian booksellers. Stanley Pargellis died in Chicago on January 6, 1968.

Biographical listings and obituaries—*Who Was Who in America* IV (1961-1968); *Who's Who in Library Service*, 3rd ed. **Books and articles about the biographee**—Heinz Bluhm, editor. *Essays in History and Literature, Presented by Fellows of The Newberry Library to Stanley Pargellis* (Chicago: The Newberry Library, 1965). [Includes an excellent biographical appreciation by Ray Allen Billington, "Stanley Pargellis: Newberry Librarian, 1942-1962," pp. 3-18, as well as a complete list of "The Writings of Stanley Pargellis" by the present contributor, pp. 221-31.] **Primary sources and archival materials**—The personal papers of Stanley Pargellis are at the Newberry Library.

—D. W. KRUMMEL

PEARSON, EDMUND LESTER (1880-1937)

Edmund Lester Pearson was born in Newburyport, Massachusetts, on February 11, 1880, the son of Edmund Carlton and Tamzen Maria Richardson Pearson. Pearson was a Yankee in the true sense of the word and, although he was to live a good part of his life outside of New England, he always maintained strong ties with that area and kept many of his New England characteristics, including his sense of humor. When he died on August 8, 1937 (of bronchial pneumonia after a long illness), his body was quite naturally returned to Newburyport for burial.

After growing up and attending public schools in Newburyport, Pearson went to the Hopkinson School in Boston for a year prior to entering Harvard, where he received his B.A. in 1902. A chance remark by a family visitor led him to enroll in Melvil Dewey's (q.v.) New York State Library School at Albany, where he received his B.L.S. in 1904, after having spent the summer of 1903 as an assistant in the Montague Street Branch of the Brooklyn Public Library.

In the fall of 1904, he went to the District of Columbia as a reference librarian in the public library. He served briefly there as assistant librarian before moving, in 1906, to the Library of Congress as an assistant in the Copyright Division. In 1908, he became a cataloger and acting librarian of the Military Information Division of the War Department. In October 1908, Pearson moved to Asheville, North Carolina, to work as a cataloger for Philip S. Henry, a noted art and book collector, in his private library at Zealandia Lodge.

While in Washington, Pearson met Mary Jane (Sally) Sellers, who was working at the public library. They were married on October 15, 1908; they were to have no children.

In order to concentrate on writing, Pearson returned to Newburyport in 1909. While there, he served on the Board of Trustees of the Newburyport Public Library (1912-1914) and wrote two books. In 1914, he moved to New York City and, in mid-April of that year, became editor of publications for the New York Public Library. He served in that capacity until he resigned at the end of June 1927, except for a brief period in 1917-1918, when he served as an officer in the U.S. Army in a camp near Moriches, New York. As editor of publications, his contact with other library staff was limited and he was not in any sense a practicing librarian.

Pearson's interests, as shown by his literary output, were initially quite varied and included astronomy, Lord Timothy Dexter, Theodore Roosevelt, and all aspects of books and reading. He wrote three books on books: *Books in Black or Red* (1923), *Queer Books* (1928), and *Dime Novels* (1929). Above all, he had an abiding interest in murder and by the

mid-1920s had begun to concentrate on that subject. He left the New York Public Library in order to concentrate, as a freelance writer, on that subject. He wrote numerous articles on true-life murder cases, and they formed the basis for five books.

Despite that interest and his sternly moralistic views on capital punishment, Pearson himself was a gentle, mild-mannered person who could not even bring himself to kill a mouse. He was of medium height, had a round, smooth poker face and twinkling blue eyes. He was fond of tennis, Americana, and long walks. He was justly celebrated as a raconteur, and his conversations, especially those with Sally, sparkled with wit. He was friendly with many of the literary figures of New York, including Christopher Morley, who described Pearson as "a waggish creature, a soul of eminent wit and worth, a twinkling sage, a bibliocubicularist, a bibliophag, a lover of bouillabaisse, a former second loot in Uncle Sam his army, a droll commentator on the human farce."

In 1905, Asa Wynkoop, a library school classmate of Pearson's and then assistant inspector of public libraries in New York, initiated a column of library news called "The Librarian" in the *New York Evening Post*. That column gave Pearson both the idea and the title for his own column, which was to appear in the *Boston Evening Transcript*, a conservative New England paper that was one of the most learned and widely read newspapers of the time.

Pearson's first column appeared on Wednesday, March 28, 1906. The next fourteen years saw 734 columns produced (each averaging between 1,500 and 2,000 words); they appeared in almost every Wednesday edition of the *Transcript*. Pearson's purpose was well stated in his column of January 28, 1914, when he said, "Even at the penalty of being considered unscholarly and flippant in some quarters, it is perhaps as well to try to show that librarianship is a bookish profession at its best; always a human calling which does not forever dwell on the inaccessible heights of learning; and that it may be made and frequently is made a very interesting pursuit indeed. It has also, much as some people regret to admit it in public, its light and amusing incidents." His column often contained reprints from, or comments on, the publications of various libraries. It also contained his comments upon the literary and library events and topics of the day, most especially upon his pet peeves, which included the American Library Institute, bibliographers, catalogers, censorship, children's reading, efficiency experts, the location of ALA meetings, simplified spelling, and universal languages. Throughout World War I, the column was strongly colored by Pearson's anti-German and anti-pacifist views. It was always highly original and frequently consisted of fictional accounts, generally satirical and with a sharply implied moral, of libraries and

librarianship. The Ezra Beesly Free Public Library of
Baxter (and its staff and readers) were most often the
"source" for those accounts. Pearson's last column
appeared on May 26, 1920. The column was continued by others in the *Transcript* until March 25,
1936, but without the same quality.

The column served as the main source for *The
Library and the Librarian* (1910), *The Librarian at
Play* (1911), and *The Secret Book* (1914), as well as
for some of *Books in Black or Red*. More recently, an
edited collection of the columns, *The Librarian*
(Scarecrow Press, 1976) has been published.

A series of correspondence on the oldfashioned
librarian and his attributes in *The Dial* led Pearson to
produce a page of a librarian's almanac in his column
for July 24, 1907, which subsequently was enlarged
into *The Old Librarian's Almanack* (1909). That was,
according to the title page, "a very rare pamphlet first
published in New Haven Connecticut in 1773 and
now reprinted for the first time" but was, in fact,
entirely of Pearson's making. Many people initially
accepted it as genuine, and it was the center of much
attention and controversy.

There were widely conflicting views about the
column and its value. Always able to poke fun at
himself, Pearson once described himself as "that
flippant person . . . who scandalously jeers and japes
at Our Profession." Others were equally but more
seriously unkind. *Public Libraries* remarked editorially, "One has only to read what is said in print of
library service by ill-informed persons, say, The
Librarian . . . to see how one can pronounce wrong
judgement on things with which he is not familiar."
Others thought more highly of his work and he was
said, by one reviewer, to be entitled to "a first place
among the literary interpreters of his profession." His
friend John Cotton Dana (q.v.) said in a letter, "I
don't know if you are of the opinion of Henry W.
Kent and myself, that Pearson has the literary touch,
and his stuff is to our thinking thoroughly good talk
on library matters."

Pearson's column was one that created considerable interest and reaction and presented both to
librarians and to the general readership of the *Transcript* his lively and provocative comments upon
libraries and librarianship. It seems unlikely that it
had the pernicious influence on his non-library
readers that some of his librarian critics felt it would,
and it seems equally unlikely that it had any major
influence on the policies and procedures of
librarianship. It is of value because it contains some
of the most analytical and perceptive contemporary
comments that are available upon the library scene in
the United States in the first part of the twentieth
century.

Biographical listings and obituaries—*Dictionary of American Biography*, 2nd Supplement (Earle F. Walbridge);
National Cyclopaedia of American Biography 28; *Twentieth

Century Authors; *Who Was Who in America* I
(1897-1942). Books and articles about the biographee—
Smith, James W. "Edmund Pearson—Librarian and Analyst of
Crime." *Boston Evening Transcript*, Feb. 29, 1929, Book
section, p. 1. Primary sources and archival materials—
Durnell, Jane B., and Norman D. Stevens, eds. *The Librarian*.
Metuchen, N.J.: Scarecrow Press, 1976; What are left of
Pearson's personal papers are now in the possession of Mr.
and Mrs. Emile Burn of Alexandria, Virginia.

—NORMAN D. STEVENS

PERKINS, FREDERICK BEECHER (1828-1899)

Frederick Perkins became notable in the late nineteenth century as an author and editor as well as a
librarian. He was born in Hartford, Connecticut, on
September 28, 1828, the son of Thomas Clap and
Mary Foote Beecher Perkins. After preliminary
schooling, Perkins entered Yale in 1846, but left
without a degree two years later to study law in the
office of his father. He taught school in New York
City and Newark, New Jersey, before returning to
Hartford in 1851 to be admitted to the bar, although
he evidently never practiced law. He completed his
education by graduating from Connecticut Normal
School (1852). In 1860, Yale conferred on him an
honorary Master of Arts degree.

Rather than practice law, Perkins taught school
and began an editorial career in Hartford. In 1854, he
joined the staff of the *New York Tribune*, but, three
years later, he returned to Hartford to become
assistant editor of *Barnard's American Journal of
Education*. At the same time, he began his library
career as librarian of the Connecticut Historical
Society. Perkins spent the next dozen years writing
and editing. He edited the first volumes of the
Galaxy, worked on the staff of the *Independent*,
aided his uncle Henry Ward Beecher in editing the
Christian Union, and assisted his brother-in-law
Edward Everett Hale in editing *Old and New*.

In 1874, Perkins joined the Boston Public Library
as bibliographer, special cataloger, and secretary to
the librarian, Justin Winsor (q.v.). He also contributed
editorial advice and five articles to General John
Eaton's (q.v.) Bureau of Education special report,
Public Libraries in the United States of America
(1876), was a member of the American Library
Association's Cooperation Committee (1877-1880),
compiled a *Checklist of American Local History*
(1876), was associate editor of *Library Journal*
(1877-1880), edited the ALA *Catalog* (1879-1880),
and served as the first editor of Boston's *Saturday
Magazine* (1877-1880). In January 1880, however, he
resigned his positions to become consulting librarian
and aide to Melvil Dewey (q.v.) at the Readers and
Writers Economy Company. Six months later, he
accepted the librarian's post at the newly founded
San Francisco Free Public Library. During his tenure
at San Francisco, Perkins continued to work for the

ALA as vice-president (1881), councillor (1882), and special reporter on fiction (1883-1884). He exhibited great interest in classification, contributing articles on the subject and publishing his own classification scheme in 1881.

In 1887, Perkins found himself under attack by San Francisco newspapers, which characterized his library management as checking library growth and repelling the public. Perkins's stern ways, culminating in a $20 fine for roughing a noisy child patron, brought about widespread indignation. Perkins retaliated by blaming the Board of Trustees and the city government for lack of financial support. In August 1887, Perkins submitted his resignation. Faced by continuing charges of mismanagement brought by his successor, John Vance Cheney, Perkins called for a full investigation by the Board of Trustees in 1888, a call that was tabled by the Board. A figure of controversy in the library world, Perkins held various editorial and bibliographic consulting positions until 1894, when he returned to the Eastern seaboard. He died in Morristown, New Jersey, on January 27, 1899.

Perkins was endowed with a brilliant and retentive mind but a restless disposition. He diffused his skills over many fields and locales, denying to any one the full concentration of his talents. Also, the greater part of his work, being editorial in nature, was thus anonymous and is found in the periodicals that he took part in editing. Tall and straight, he was a man of outspoken convictions, with a facility for expression and a penchant for confrontation. His zeal, courage, and erudition were praised by contemporaries. Perkins's notable works include a biography, *Charles Dickens* (1870); a novel, *Scrope; or the Lost Library* (1874); short stories, *The Devil-Puzzlers and Other Stories* (1877); and a classified bibliography, *The Best Reading* (1872). The latter ran to four editions and served as a basic reference tool for many libraries. For his views on librarianship, his article "Public Libraries and the Public, with Special Reference to the San Francisco Free Public Library" (*Library Journal* 10:223-29 [Conference issue, 1885]) is enlightening.

Perkins was married to Mary Ann Westcott of Providence, Rhode Island, in 1857. They had two sons and two daughters before her death in 1893. In 1894, he was married to Frances Johnson Beecher (his uncle James's widow) of Guilford, Connecticut, who survived him.

Biographical listings and obituaries—*Dictionary of American Biography* 14 (George B. Utley); "Frederick Beecher Perkins [Obituary]." *Library Journal* 24:82-83 (Feb. 1899); [Obituary]. *New York Tribune*, Feb. 4, 1899; *Obituary Record of the Graduates of Yale University*, 1899; *Who Was Who in America*, Historical Volume (1607-1896). **Books and articles about the biographee**—Haverland, Della B.

"Frederick Beecher Perkins." *Pacific Bindery Talk* 8:19-22 (Oct. 1935).

—MICHAEL B. WESSELLS

PETTEE, JULIA (1872-1967)

Julia Pettee was born on August 23, 1872, in Lakeville, Connecticut, the daughter of William Everett and Julia Ensign Pettee. She attended Mount Holyoke Seminary and College in 1889-1890 and again in 1891-1892, finishing the Seminary program and taking the first year of college work. In 1894, she entered the Pratt Institute Library School in Brooklyn, from which she was graduated in 1895. Against the wishes of relatives, who felt that she would ruin her life by too much learning, she then went to Vassar College, where she worked half-time as a cataloger in the library while continuing her education. She remained at Vassar as a cataloger until 1909, but during that period, spent two summers and a half-year leave of absence reorganizing and cataloging the collection of the Rochester Theological Seminary Library.

In 1909, she became head cataloger at Union Theological Seminary in New York, where she remained until her retirement in 1939. There she established her reputation as a cataloger, especially in the area of religion. Pettee is best known for the classification system that she developed for the Union Theological Seminary over a period of years, during which she attempted "the recasting of the whole field of knowledge according to the point of view of the theologian." In general, the framework chosen by her for that scheme followed that worked out by Hugo Münsterberg for the arrangement of exhibits at the St. Louis Congress of Arts and Sciences in 1904; it was described by him in an article in the May 1903 issue of the *Atlantic Monthly*. Münsterberg stressed the interrelationship of the various aspects of human knowledge, an approach that greatly appealed to Pettee. Her summary of the main divisions of her classification was as follows:

(1) Historical sciences, which set forth the genetic relationships of human activities and intellectual life: (a) Literature, and (b) History.

(2) Sciences presenting knowledge in its logical and systematic relationships: (a) experimental sciences of the physical universe and of mental life, which systematize the first hand facts of observation; and, (b) normative sciences, which coordinate the results of all special knowledge into consistent philosophical or theological systems.

(3) Practical sciences, which are chiefly concerned with the means and methods of directing human activities.

The Union Classification followed that of Charles A. Cutter (q.v.) in using both letters and numbers in its notation, which was designed to be easily expanded. While the arrangement of the sections on theology was original with Pettee, she borrowed from parts of the developing Library of Congress classification system for the arrangement of non-religious material. The *Classification of the Library of Union Theological Seminary* was first published in 1924 and a revised edition was issued in 1939. A second revised edition, edited by Ruth C. Eisenhart, was published in 1967. Of that classification system, which is still used by many theological libraries, Jannette Newhall says in *A Theological Library Manual* (1970):

> The strongest point in favor of the Union Classification for seminary libraries is the amazing breadth of its application of theological knowledge to the needs of a theological library. The information it provides about the names of Church fathers, periods of Church history, titles of Christian classics, and many more items, make it a reference book of first quality for any library.

Pettee also developed a *List of Theological Subject Headings and Corporate Church Names* for use at Union and a specialized list of subject headings for theological libraries. It was first published in 1924 and a second edition, which contained a valuable list of religious bodies, was published in 1947. That list, which contained information on the origin, organization, etc., of religious groups, was published separately as *List of Churches; Official Forms of the Names for Denominational Bodies with Brief Descriptive and Historical Notes* (1948) and is still a useful reference tool. Although many theological libraries, even those using the Union Classification, now prefer to use the Library of Congress *List of Subject Headings* because of its continuous revision, Pettee's work in this area, as in classification, stands as a major contribution to theological librarianship. Pettee remains unexcelled as a contributor to the development of cataloging and classification theory and practice in the field of theology.

Pettee's expertise in this field was recognized, and she served from 1932 to 1941 on the ALA Catalog Code Revision Advisory Committee, which revised the Anglo-American *Catalog Rules* of 1908. She chaired the Subcommittee on Religious Headings for that Committee.

Following her retirement from Union Theological Seminary in 1939, Pettee worked half-time at Yale University supervising the reclassification of the religious books in the Sterling Library. During her seven years at Yale, she also published *Subject Headings: The History and Theory of the Alphabetical Subject Approach to Books* (1946). After presenting a useful and much-needed summary of the

development of alphabetical arrangement as a basis for library catalogs, Pettee proposed solutions to problems arising in the use of subject headings, especially in large libraries. Her conservative stand, which did not waver throughout her long career, was that "logical analysis of subject matter and consistency of entry are our tools . . . but tools are not an end in themselves. There is no infallible substitute for the good judgement of the cataloger, who knows the literature and sees clearly both the service he wishes to render, and the best means of meeting this service."

Julia Pettee's first contribution to library literature was published in 1904, her last in 1962. In addition to some 36 articles in various professional journals, mainly about theological cataloging and classification, she had given many talks and produced innumerable working papers and drafts of classification schedules, lists of subjects, proposed rules of entry, etc.

In many other ways, she was a remarkable person. Although hard of hearing for much of her life, she managed a full and active career. She adopted a daughter, Mary Ellen, at a time when that was unusual for a single person, and successfully raised her in an atmosphere of warmth and friendship. At the time of her retirement from Yale in 1946, she moved to Mayflower Farm in Salisbury, Connecticut, near her native Lakeville, where she continued to lead an active life. There, in addition to entertaining visitors and gardening, she pursued her active interest in local history and genealogy. A biography of one of her ancestors, *The Reverend Jonathan Lee and His Eighteenth Century Salisbury Parish*, was published in 1957, when Pettee was 85, and she was working on a history of Salisbury up until the time of her death, at the age of 95, on May 30, 1967.

Biographical listings and obituaries—[Obituary]. *Library Journal* 92:3371 (Oct. 1, 1967); *Who's Who in Library Service*, 1st ed., 2nd ed., 4th ed. **Books and articles about the biographee**—Pearson, Lennart. "The Life and Work of Julia Pettee, 1872-1967." American Theological Library Association *Newsletter* 18, No. 2, Supplement:25-92 (Nov. 14, 1970); Raeppel, Josephine. "Julia Pettee." *ALA Bulletin* 47:417-19 (1970). **Primary sources and archival materials**—Julia Pettee's papers and correspondence are in the collection of the Union Theological Seminary Library, New York.

—CONSTANCE RINEHART

PIERCE, CORNELIA MARVIN (1873-1957)

Cornelia Marvin was born in Monticello, Iowa, on December 26, 1873, to Charles Elwell and Cornelia Moody Marvin. She attended secondary schools in St. Paul, Minnesota, and Tacoma, Washington (1887-1891). In 1894-1895, she was a student at the Armour Institute Library School in Chicago (which later became the University of Illinois Graduate School of Library Science). She joined the faculty at

Armour in 1895 as an "assistant," and, in 1896-1897, taught courses in reference and bibliography. She also organized school libraries in Princeton, Illinois, and St. Cloud, Minnesota, and the Davenport, Iowa, Public Library during 1896. When the School moved to Urbana in 1897, Marvin became librarian of the Scoville Institute of Oak Park, Illinois. In the summers of 1897 and 1898, she served as head of the Wisconsin Library Commission Summer School of Library Training.

In July 1899, she left the Scoville Institute to become a full-time employee of the Wisconsin Library Commission as library instructor and director of the Summer School of Library Training. In 1905, she resigned her position at Wisconsin to become the first secretary of the newly created Oregon Library Commission. The Library Commission became the State Library in 1913, with Marvin as state librarian from 1913 to 1928.

In December of 1928, she resigned from the State Library and married former Oregon governor Walter M. Pierce. From 1931 to 1935, she was a member of the Oregon State Board of Higher Education. When Walter Pierce was elected to the U.S. Congress in 1932, she became his secretary, chief assistant, speechwriter, and advisor. Together, the Pierces spent ten years in Washington, fighting the legislative battles of the New Deal era. In 1942, following his defeat in the election, the Pierces retired to their Oregon farm near Salem, where they devoted their time to urging others to become active in the causes that they had so long supported. Walter Pierce died in 1954, and Cornelia Marvin Pierce in 1957.

Cornelia Marvin Pierce was a woman of strong convictions and great energy. Her appearance—"small in stature, blond, pink and white, and blue-eyed"—concealed a character described as "a human dynamo with a mind that works like harnessed lightening." She spent nearly half of her long and productive life as a librarian, but in a larger sense, she was throughout her career a public servant. She had a grasp of public affairs that was frequently characterized as "brilliant" and directed her abundant energy into a wide variety of educational and political activities. As a librarian, she was a creator and innovator, with a gift for inspiring others with some of her enormous enthusiasm for the public service aspects of librarianship. Mary Eileen Ahern (q.v.), in an editorial note in *Public Libraries*, described Marvin as having perhaps "the widest knowledge of library administration in all its bearings of anyone in America."

Throughout her career, she was motivated by a definite plan of political and social reform. In this sense she was typical of the reformers of the "Progressive Era." As a young woman, she went with the library students from Armour into the infamous Chicago stockyards slums to set up "home libraries."

In these efforts, she worked with Mary McDowell, head of the stockyards settlement house, and met Jane Addams and Florence Kelley. From the urban problems of Chicago, she moved to Wisconsin, the famous "laboratory of democracy," where statewide reform efforts were presided over by Governor Robert M. La Follette. The Wisconsin Library Commission, under the leadership of Frank Avery Hutchins (q.v.), its founder and secretary, labored to achieve for all Wisconsin citizens the free and convenient access to information that would prepare them to make the intelligent political decisions of which their leaders believed them capable. One of the most admired features of the "Wisconsin idea," the Legislative Reference Library, was designed by Hutchins, but was guided through the legislature by Cornelia Marvin when Hutchins fell ill.

Although she often functioned as Hutchins's assistant, Marvin's chief task in Wisconsin was to travel throughout the state, visiting small public libraries, advising on establishment, reorganization, and extension of their services, and conducting training "institutes." The summer school that she conducted each summer was an immense success, so much so that the Commission determined to establish a permanent library school. The one-year program offered by the Commission in 1906 eventually developed into the Library School of the University of Wisconsin—the only one of the many library summer schools to make such a transition.

After Frank Avery Hutchins retired because of ill health in 1904, Cornelia Marvin decided to accept the position of secretary to the recently created Oregon Library Commission. Although she felt some reluctance to leave Wisconsin, apparently the challenge of Oregon, with its great distance, sparse population, and growing political awareness was irresistible. When she began her work as secretary of the Oregon Library Commission on August 1, 1905, she was given a room in the State House, a desk, some stationery, and an appropriation of $2,000. There were no books and no employees. Outside of Portland, Oregon had no tax-supported free libraries, no trained librarians, no travelling libraries, no school libraries, no organized or cataloged library, and it was impossible to secure in the state any of the supplies necessary for library work. In order to survey the state, Marvin travelled with speakers from the school superintendent's office, frequently into areas that were accessible only by horse-drawn stages. She spoke before farm groups, teachers' meetings, granges, women's clubs—to any one who would listen—about the importance of libraries and library service.

Cornelia Marvin quickly realized that many of the small towns should not attempt to establish public libraries. With this in mind, she developed services that were centered on the Library Commission (later the State Library) in Salem. Small towns and rural communities were supplied with "travelling libraries" (collections of fifty volumes, approximately half non-fiction, including some "serious" reading and materials on current public questions). In order to supply up-to-date material on stimulating issues for debating societies and club meetings, she developed "package libraries" of public documents, speeches, clippings from periodicals and newspapers, and even pages chopped from books or encyclopedias. (Such cavalier treatment of books shocked many librarians, and visitors to the Commission always asked to see the "clipped cyclopedias.")

After the State Library was created in 1913, the increased book fund made possible the purchase of books to answer the requests of the small public libraries and individual rural users. The State Library's mail-order service thrived, especially after the passage of the parcel post law and the later special library post (for which Oregon legislators, encouraged by Cornelia Marvin, were largely responsible). The volume of mail-order service that was provided by the State Library in spite of its severely limited staff and space is difficult to grasp. During the month of January 1916, there were 646 mail-order requests and 555 shipments—accomplished by the full-time service of four people. Letters were always answered promptly, often on the same day. Marvin boasted in 1917, with some justification, that "the Oregon Library system offers a much freer use of books and more nearly approaches the idea of full library privileges for all, than does any other state system." Oregon was one of the first states to provide for county support of library service, and in later years, Cornelia Marvin Pierce became an advocate of multi-county regional service.

As state librarian, Cornelia Marvin felt a personal responsibility for the welfare of the people of Oregon. The library compiled endless lists of the "best" books on all subjects, encouraged parents to purchase better books for their children to read, and crusaded against unscrupulous subscription book dealers. Legislative reference service in Oregon did far more than simply respond to direct requests for assistance. Frequently, Marvin notified legislators of materials she thought they should consult or sent them unsolicited information that pertained to their work. She wrote to agencies and institutions all over the nation for advice so that she could recommend the best legislative measures when she was asked for material. She even advised the sponsors of legislative measures on political strategy.

During her years as state librarian, Cornelia Marvin was actively involved in national and regional library organizations, although her attendance at meetings was restricted by the remoteness of her location. The Pacific Northwest Library Association, which she and

Mary Frances Isom (q.v.) helped establish in 1909, absorbed much of her attention. She was second vice-president of the American Library Association in 1919-1920, served three terms on the Council, and was a member of several committees, including those on library training, library cooperation with other countries, and national certification and training. In 1911-1912, she was president of the League of Library Commissions and in 1917, she became the second woman president of the PNLA. During World War I, she served for several months as director of the ALA Library War Service for troops on the Mexican border.

At the time of Marvin's resignation from the State Library in 1928, Oregon had 82 free public libraries, 706 travelling library stations, and 29,816 mail-order patrons. In the last biennial period for which she was librarian, the Library reported 48,782 shipments of library material containing some 276,855 volumes. All this had been accomplished with library quarters cramped beyond belief and appropriations smaller than the libraries of some small cities. Venting the frustrations of many years, Cornelia Marvin deliberately created a state-wide furor when she resigned—citing the inadequacy of her appropriations and blasting the legislature for its shortsightedness.

After her marriage to Walter Pierce, the real reason for her resignation, she continued to play a leading role in Oregon educational and political affairs. As a member of the newly created Board of Higher Education, she helped design a plan for the unification of Oregon's institutions of higher education, particularly the libraries. When Walter Pierce was elected to Congress in 1932, she became his secretary and, virtually, a second representative—Walter liked to point out to his constituents that they had two representatives for the price of one. They served in Washington until Walter's defeat in the congressional election of 1942.

Cornelia Marvin Pierce, with her incisive intellect and ready wit, spoke and wrote incessantly but produced relatively few formal contributions to the literature of librarianship. Her characteristic method of communicating her many views on public and professional issues was by personal letter. The files of the Oregon State Library and the Cornelia Marvin Pierce Papers contain countless copies of her letters to librarians, public officials, and persons in various positions of authority all over the nation encouraging, exhorting, or informing them of situations that demanded their attention. The biennial reports of the Oregon State Library during her tenure provide a lively, and sometimes humorous, view of the Library's activities and accomplishments. She was also the author of *Small Library Buildings: A Collection of Plans Contributed by the League of Library*

Commissions (American Library Association Publishing Board, 1908), and several journal articles.

During the last few years of her life, Pierce became increasingly disillusioned with the state of society. At her death on February 13, 1957, following a long illness, the woman who had attempted to create a great Oregon system of higher education and who had believed in the political ability of the common people, left the bulk of her estate to Reed College, a small private liberal arts school—in the hope that it would assist in creating the well-informed and critical minority of citizens whose leadership in public affairs she had come to consider the only hope of American democracy.

Biographical listings and obituaries—[Obituary]. Oregon. Forty-ninth Legislative Assembly. Regular Session. Senate Concurrent Resolution No. 9 [honoring Cornelia Marvin Pierce]. **Books and articles about the biographee**—Brisley, Melissa Ann. "Cornelia Marvin Pierce, a Political Biography." Bachelor's thesis, Committee of American Studies, Reed College, 1966; Brisley, Melissa Ann. "Cornelia Marvin Pierce: Pioneer in Library Extension." *The Library Quarterly* 38:125-53 (April 1968); Johansen, Dorothy O. *The Library and the Liberal Tradition.* Corvallis: Friends of the Library, Oregon State College, 1959; Johansen, Dorothy O. "Cornelia Marvin Pierce." *Oregon Democrat*, Feb. 1957. **Primary sources and archival materials**—The Cornelia Marvin Pierce Papers. Oregon State Library, Salem, Oregon; The Files of the State Library, 1905-25. Oregon State Library, Salem, Oregon; Oregon State Library. *Biennial Reports*, 1907-1927. Oregon State Library, Salem, Oregon.

—MELISSA BRISLEY MICKEY

PIERCY, ESTHER JUNE (1905-1967)

Esther Piercy was born in Los Angeles on June 15, 1905, to Watt B. and Magdalen Henderson Piercy. A graduate of the Boise Senior High School and the University of Idaho (B.A., 1930), she received her professional degree (B.S. in library science) from the University of Illinois in 1932. She later attended some summer sessions at the University of Chicago (1938, 1939, and 1944). After ten years as cataloger and head of the Cataloging Department at the University of New Mexico (1934-1944), and a summer as a cataloger at the University of Chicago, Piercy became head of the Processing Department and assistant librarian at the Worcester, Massachusetts, Free Public Library. From 1948 until her death, she was chief of processing at the Enoch Pratt Free Library in Baltimore, where she was responsible, among other things, for planning a complete recataloging and reclassifying project.

Esther Piercy was active in professional organizations, particularly the American Library Association, which she served in many ways, including membership on both its Council and its Executive Board. She was also a member of the Decimal Classification Editorial Policy Committee (1961-1967). Chief of all

was her service as editor of the *Journal of Cataloging and Classification* [*JCC*] (1950-1956) and as editor of *Library Resources and Technical Services* [*LRTS*] (1957-1967), a journal formed by the merger of *JCC* and *Serial Slants.* She built a modest pamphlet into a substantial, scholarly quarterly. For her work as an editor, she received the Margaret Mann [q.v.] Citation in Cataloging and Classification in 1958. Following her death in Baltimore on January 10, 1967, the Summer and Fall 1967 issues of *LRTS* were prepared as "Studies in Memory of Esther J. Piercy," Parts I and II.

In 1959-1960, Piercy was director of the Consumer Reaction Survey of the Cataloging-in-Source experiment conducted by the Library of Congress, and her detailed report of that survey was published in LC's *Cataloging-in-Source Experiment* (1960). She wrote the chapter on "Organization and Control of Materials" in *Local Public Library Administration* (International City Managers' Association, 1964), and her *Commonsense Cataloging* (Wilson, 1965) was a widely used manual for the organization of books and other materials in school and small public libraries. At the time of her death, she had planned and was beginning to edit "Cooperative and Centralized Cataloging" (*Library Trends*, July 1967). It was completed by Robert L. Talmadge.

Esther Piercy rarely talked publicly about herself, but on one occasion ("Reading Critically," *Maryland Libraries*, pp. 4-7 [Spring 1967]), she told her colleagues at Pratt:

I grew up in a reading family. . . . No adult could sit down and thus produce a lap without being prepared to have that lap shortly occupied by a child and book with the demand that he be read to. . . . I was frustrated over having to be so dependent and believed ardently that learning to read was the greatest thing that could happen to me—and I've never changed my mind. . . . I'm a slow reader . . . I have had a life-long love-affair with words. I am fascinated by them and take almost a sensuous pleasure from finding them used wisely, skillfully, freshly. . . . I was an English major. . . . However, I don't regret my wasted education.

Esther Piercy was first of all a humanist. But this humanist could begin a book properly named *Commonsense Cataloging* with the words, "This book is designed to be practical." Not the least product of her kind of humanism was her editing of *JCC-LRTS*.

In the Piercy memorial issue of *LRTS*, Edwin Castagna praised her vision, courage, and superb organizing ability in the technical services at Pratt; but he also remarked that "Esther helped destroy the stereotype" of the dull, plodding cataloger. She was a "passionate partisan of the Baltimore Orioles," a "discriminating critic" in her reviews for the

Baltimore Sun. "She wrote, as she dressed, with style." She was a "gracious hostess in her pleasant apartment, which had been one of Baltimore's old carriage houses," "an admirer of Adlai Stevenson," and "a charming lady who liked to be where the action was."

Also in this memorial issue, John Cronin told of Esther Piercy's patient and formidable Consumer Survey for Cataloging-in-Source. Her staff visited 200 libraries, and she herself drew up elaborate plans, met with ALA committees, journeyed to 64 libraries, publishers, and bookstores in 14 states. It was an exhausting "transcontinental journey" with its "close connections, long hours, hit-or-miss meals ... living out of a suit-case," but she enjoyed it and returned with delighted tales of adventures on the road.

Elizabeth Rodell wrote of Piercy and ALA-RTSD (*LRTS* 12:103-105 [1968]):

> Hardly a week went by that we did not ask her something.... The folders are full of her replies, often dashed off on scraps of paper in moments of her busy days, but tireless, sparkling, full of vision and good sense.... About RTSD she cared enough to criticize us sharply; it was best to avoid her after a dull inconclusive board meeting; and yet underneath there was the steady assurance that what we were about was worth doing.

Esther Piercy died in Baltimore on January 10, 1967.

Biographical listings and obituaries—[Obituary]. *Library Journal* 92:729 (Feb. 15, 1967); [Obituary]. *Library Resources and Technical Services* 11:166 (Spring 1967); *Who's Who in Library Service*, 2nd ed., 3rd ed., 4th ed. **Books and articles about the biographee**—Colburn, E. B. "Esther June Piercy." *Library Resources and Technical Services* 2:223-24 (Fall 1958); Rodell, Elizabeth. Article in *Library Resources and Technical Services* 12:103-105 (1968); Shera, Jesse H. "In Memoriam: Esther Piercy" [letter]. *Wilson Library Bulletin* 41:671 (March 1967); [Studies in memory of Esther June Piercy, editor of *Library Resources and Technical Services*, 1957-1967]. *Library Resources and Technical Services* (Summer and Fall 1967 issues). **Primary sources and archival materials**—Piercy, Esther J. "Reading Critically." *Maryland Libraries*, Spring 1967, pp. 4-7.

—PAUL S. DUNKIN

PLUMMER, MARY WRIGHT (1856-1916)

Mary Wright Plummer was born March 8, 1856, in Richmond, Indiana, to Jonathan W. and Hannah A. Plummer. Her parents were of a long line of Quakers successful in business and education, and no biography of Mary Wright Plummer should fail to appreciate the influence of the Society of Friends on her thinking and way of life. She attended the Friends Academy in Richmond and, when seventeen, moved with her family to Chicago, where her father was a wholesale druggist. In 1881-1882, she attended

Wellesley College as a special student and, except for this year, she remained in Chicago with her family until 1886, where she taught for four years, read, and wrote poetry, some of which was published in literary magazines of the time. The extent of her "special" studies at Wellesley is unknown, but her ability to read and speak Spanish, German, Italian, and French has been commented on in the literature.

Her library career began in January 1887, when she joined Melvil Dewey's (q.v.) first class in the School of Library Economy at Columbia College, and from that date, she plunged into an active life as one of the American pioneers in the field of library education, children's librarianship, and even international librarianship. In her first year at Columbia, she was already poised, self-confident, intelligent, and capable of hard work. A clear and forceful writer, she was singled out from the first class in the library school to present her impressions of the curriculum at a meeting of the American Library Association in September 1887 ("The Columbia College School of Library Economy from a Student's Standpoint," *Library Journal* [September-December 1887]). The following October, as she began the senior year of library school, she was retained as an instructor for the beginning junior class. She finished the program in 1888 and went to the St. Louis Public Library as a cataloger for two years under Frederick M. Crunden (q.v.). In 1890, she resigned and spent the summer in Europe (the first of three trips she was to make abroad); then, in the fall, she came to the Pratt Institute Free Library to assist in administration and to help run a training class for beginning librarians. The training class soon expanded into a library school, and, in 1895, Plummer became both head of the school and director of the Library at Pratt as well. She retained both positions until 1904, when the two were separated at her request so that she could devote her full time to the needs of the Pratt Institute Library School. She remained at Pratt until 1911, when she left to become the first principal of the library school of the New York Public Library, which opened in September of that year. She served there until her death in 1916.

Mary Plummer was active in library organizations, as president of the New York Library Club (1896-1897 and 1913-1914), as president of the New York State Library Association (1906), and as chairman of the Committee on Library Training of ALA (1903-1910, guiding it through the difficult task of establishing standards for library training). In 1900, she was a United States delegate to the International Library Congress in Paris and in July and August was in charge of the ALA exhibit at the Paris Exposition. She was also vice-president of ALA, and later served as its second woman president in 1915-1916.

Her publications include a collection of poetry called *Verses* (privately printed in 1896 and 1916); *Roy and Ray in Mexico* (1907), *Roy and Ray in Canada* (1908), and *Stories from the Chronicle of the Cid* (1910), all written for children; and *Hints to Small Libraries* (1894 and subsequent editions), a work that represents her continued interest in the problems of libraries not able to afford professional help. In her youth, she was described as a "book hungry girl"; indeed, reading counted as more than one joy in her life, and she spoke about them all in a short work entitled *The Seven Joys of Reading*, which she read before the New York State Library Association in 1909; in October 1910, it appeared in the *Sewanee Review* and was reprinted on several occasions. She also published numerous articles on librarianship in the *Library Journal*, *Pratt Institute Monthly*, *ALA Bulletin*, and other journals. Her expertise as an educator was noted when she was selected as author of the section on training for librarianship published in the *Manual of Library Economy* (ALA, 1913).

When Plummer came to Pratt Institute in 1890, the library training class was limited to those who wanted a shorter, less expensive program of instruction than that offered by the New York State Library School in Albany. Unlike the New York School's more intense training, Pratt provided at that time a knowledge of its own system of cataloging and technical processes; no degree or certificate was awarded, but students received a letter of reference at the end of the period of instruction. By 1893, competitive examinations were given, but Plummer always kept the entrance requirements flexible without lowering standards. She herself had never received a college degree, and she never wanted to turn away a student who might show a talent for librarianship but not have the proper, formal credentials.

In 1894, Miss Plummer took a year's leave of absence to visit libraries in Europe. After her return in 1895, she was appointed head of the Pratt Institute Free Library and director of its Library School, and she reorganized the School by broadening the scope of the curriculum and appointing a regular faculty from among those members of the Pratt Library staff who showed an ability to teach. This date and Plummer's reorganization mark the end of the library training classes and the real beginning of the Library School. The curriculum continued to change after 1895, and, over the years, Plummer designed it to become more library-oriented, with deepened content and more time allocated for practice work. In 1895, a student at Pratt faced a one-year curriculum of 500 hours of classroom work in 28 subjects and 274 hours of practical work; by 1907, there had been 21 new subjects introduced, all of them concerned with librarianship in the form of book selection, history of

the book, history of libraries, library buildings, and indexing. By the latter date, the only non-library course was the study of contemporary English, American, and European literature, which Plummer insisted upon because entrance examinations had shown the "average student fresh from college" to be weakest in this subject.

In 1896, the Library School at Pratt added a second, separate year to its curriculum. Called the "Historical Course" and fashioned along the lines of European education for librarianship, it was set up to train students for "libraries of a more scholarly type or to catalog private libraries containing old and rare books." Courses were taught on bibliography, advanced cataloging, ancient and modern continental literatures, history of books and printing, history of binding, engraving, Italian (because Plummer believed that the Italians were then publishing the best works in library science), stenography and "a general survey of larger matters of library administration." The course was not limited to library students but was open to all who could pass the entrance examinations which were given in literature, history, French, German, Latin, and library economy. By 1908, the course had been offered four times and, considering the strong public library orientation of most library school training in the United States at that time, this can be considered a good record. Plummer tells us, however, that most of the students who finished this second year went into public libraries and, although they did not apply their specialized knowledge often, they claimed that a certain confidence from their training exerted itself upon their work.

In 1895, a new building was planned on campus for the Pratt Institute Free Library. At Plummer's suggestion, it included a children's room, the first of its kind to be incorporated in any new library building, with furniture to fit its patrons. It reflected her lifelong interest in the proper education and training of children, in which the library occupied an important position. As a demonstration of this interest, another second-year program, this for training children's librarians, was begun in 1899. It included the history of children's books, a study of the child and "of that routine called the social side," and a study of the work in the children's room at both the Pratt Library and other libraries as well. The work was supplemented by visits to children's libraries, practical work, and study of the classes in the Department of Kindergartens at Pratt Institute.

However, Miss Plummer did not look upon the program as the "final equipment for the children's librarian." She expected students to learn to think, to become permanently interested in the subject, and to pursue independent study throughout their lives. After 1900, the course was withdrawn because a training school for children's librarians had been established at Andrew Carnegie's (q.v.) Carnegie Library in Pittsburgh. In 1907, evidently by popular demand, a three- to four-month apprenticeship course was offered after the usual year's work in the Library School at Pratt. This was partly connected with the children's library at the New York Public Library, and no graduate of the Pratt Institute Library School would be recommended as a children's librarian without this added practicum. It is significant and reflective of Mary Wright Plummer that, while she kept her library school up to date and provided needed education, she was careful not to duplicate special programs offered in other schools.

Plummer's work at the Library School of the New York Public Library, beginning in 1911, exhibited the same energy and enthusiasm that she had shown at Pratt, and the trials of opening a new school on short notice were set forth by her with good humor in *Library Journal* (January 1912). The program was not innovative but rather reflected the demands of the institution that had sponsored it. Entrance requirements remained essentially the same as at Pratt, and a second year was added, consisting mainly of practice work. She had hardly begun to organize the school, however, when she became ill. She took a year's leave of absence, beginning in 1915, but she never recovered and died of cancer in 1916 at her brother's home in Dixon, Illinois.

In 1901, Plummer predicted greater specialization in library education and greater cooperation between schools in order to take advantage of one another's specialties. She wanted to produce a well-trained graduate, but at the same time she did not want to abandon scholarship in the library. She beseeched an awareness of the damage of concentrating too much on technique and executive ability, and hoped for the day when the leading universities of the United States would have chairs of librarianship and offer courses similar to those given by Dr. Karl Dziatzko at Göttingen. Mary Wright Plummer built a strong curriculum in her library schools, always keeping it related to the needs of the working world. She had said that if a library school did not train a student for work in libraries "as they now exist" then that school was failing not only the student but the profession as well. Thus, while she may have wished for a more scholarly approach to libraries and librarianship in the United States, she never let her personal desire interfere with the realities of her responsibility.

During her year in Europe in 1894-1895, Plummer visited a number of libraries in Italy, Germany, and France. She was always received courteously and her obvious interest in and enthusiasm for learning about all aspects of service and control in each place seems to have elicited sympathetic responses. In her articles in *The Nation*, Plummer treats us to an analysis of the library systems in Bayreuth, Nürnberg, Venice,

Rome, Florence, and Paris, among other places. Many things impressed her, not the least of which was the education and training of the librarians. What especially interested her, though, was the educational requirement expected of librarians in the Italian system, and she analyzed it with undisguised respect, for the Italian government had united all the country's libraries into a well-functioning system of service and had kept the high traditions of scholarship by requiring the applicants for library positions to pass a rigid examination. Plummer wondered in her reports whether there was anything of value for American libraries in "this admirably ordered system." She did not, however, attempt the impossible. She had no desire to create the counterpart of the Italian scholar in American libraries, but she did want qualified professionals in the field, and for her that meant persons well educated, able to read foreign languages, well versed in the literature of the ages, and enthusiastic about reading.

Her concern for the role of women in librarianship also distinguished Plummer. Melvil Dewey's insistence on having women attend the classes in the School of Library Economy had been a decided factor in the rapid demise of the school at Columbia College. The "feminine" question arose again in the first decades of the twentieth century when statements were made concerning the appropriateness of library education for men, the implication being that the sexes were biologically doomed to lead and follow, at least in librarianship. Mary Wright Plummer never paid much attention to these expressions; but there can be no doubt that she was aware of their existence and sensitive to them, for there are several passages in her writings where she makes reference to the role of women in librarianship, as the record of her visits to European libraries in 1894-1895 shows. She never failed to record the presence of women in the libraries she visited, or to indicate any separate treatment of them. On a visit to Bayreuth, she writes (*The Nation*, October 25, 1894) that the librarian offered her a printed catalog of the library there, and, when she wanted to pay for it, he refused, "saying with a humorous twinkle in his eye, 'Bitte—mit Collegen!' and I enjoyed the joke of a woman's presuming to be a librarian quite as much as he." It was a two-edged statement, and Plummer was confident enough in her ability to know who was wielding the blade. Plummer also noted (*The Nation*, January 3, 1895) that the archives held by the Biblioteca Leonina were closed to women and mused on the fact, wondering if it was "because women can't keep a secret? There must be some important ones in all such collections, and there is no telling to what deprivation Eve's unfortunate curiosity may have condemned all her daughters."

In 1898, Plummer published short biographies of five "Eminent Librarians" (only one of whom was an American) and Signora Sacconi-Ricci, assistant librarian of Florence's Biblioteca Marucelliana, was included among them. Signora Sacconi-Ricci's father had been the prefect of the National Library in Florence. Plummer related that, in the Signora's struggle to follow in his footsteps, she broke a tradition in Italy against the admission of females into the Gymnasia and later passed all competitors in the entrance examination for an apprenticeship in the National Library; a year later she committed the same success in the examination for the post of assistant librarian (*Pratt Institute Monthly*, January 1898). Plummer ends the sketch of Signora Sacconi-Ricci by noting that she had become actively engaged in loosening Italian women's bondage to tradition and custom, though Plummer seemed to draw no parallel to the situation in America. Mary Wright Plummer was not a militant; she was evidently content to make her progress through accepted channels, a step at a time. Perhaps it is here that her Quaker heritage is most visible, as it taught her tolerance in the midst of intolerance, patience, understanding and the "gift to be simple," though not ineffectual.

In various articles, Plummer stated that "good breeding" or "good manners" were a prerequisite for the good librarian. No student in her library school could be recommended without them. Something formal is implied here, and more than a taint of class consciousness. Yet, such a judgment cannot be pushed too far, for any criticism of her attitude must take into account the then-current view of the role of the public or free library in American society. It was generally considered to be an institution for elevating public taste, a place, as Plummer has expressed it, where the unlearned "should be guarded from their own ignorance." In order to achieve this objective, she believed the librarian should be possessed not only of a good education but also of the necessary discrimination that could merge with the goals of the institution and help keep out "imposters in book form." She sought, then, not a formal "front" for the library, but a cultured person who knew books, who loved them, and who could judge their worth. Much of her insistence on "good breeding" should be understood in this light.

Where book selection itself was concerned, she tended in the beginning to be a trifle strident in her declarations. In 1897, she said that the ability to read was a mixed blessing for children, that it could be considered a curse unless they were provided with worthwhile books (*Library Journal*, November 1897). At the end of her life, she changed her attitude, and in her presidential address to ALA (read for her in Asbury Park on June 26, 1916), she presented a stunning justification for the freedom to read and the

right of the library, indeed its necessity, to uphold that freedom. It was a remarkable address, still worth reading, and a fitting capstone to the career of a remarkable woman. She died of cancer on September 21, 1916, yet her influence and example were such that we can agree with the person who said (*Library Journal*, December 1916), "it will be a long time before we realize that she is not still with us."

Biographical listings and obituaries—*Dictionary of American Biography* 15 (Harry Miller Lydenberg); "Mary Wright Plummer [Obituary]." *Library Journal* 41:727, 756-57 (Oct. 1916); *National Cyclopaedia of American Biography* 21; *Notable American Women 1607-1950* (Ruth Hewitt Hamilton); [Obituary]. *New York Times*, Sept. 22, 1916; *Who Was Who in America* I (1897-1942). **Books and articles about the biographee**—[Biographical sketch]. *Library Journal* 76:470-71 (March 15, 1951); Holbrook, B. E. "Mary Wright Plummer." *Wilson Library Bulletin* 13:409 (Feb. 1939); "A Library Life. . . ." *Library Journal* 41:865-81 (Dec. 1916); "Memorial Meeting for Mary Wright Plummer [at NYPL]." *Library Journal* 41:889-91 (Dec. 1916); Moore, Anne Carroll. "Mary Wright Plummer, 1856-1916." *Bulletin of Bibliography* 14:1-3 (1930); "Tributes to Miss Plummer." *Library Journal* 41:817-18 (Nov. 1916). **Primary sources and archival materials**—Material relevant to Plummer and her work is held at both Pratt Institute and the New York Public Library.

—ROBERT A. KARLOWICH
—NASSER SHARIFY

POLLACK, ERVIN HAROLD (1913-1972)

Ervin H. Pollack was born in St. Louis, Missouri, on April 19, 1913, to Jacob Morris and Tillie Padratzik Pollack. He died suddenly, at the age of 59, on June 9, 1972, and was survived by his wife, Lydia Weiss Pollack, two children, Jay R. and Joan, and his brother, Rabbi Herman Pollack, of Massachusetts. Ervin Pollack did his undergraduate work at St. Louis University (1932-1935), took the Juris Doctor degree from Washington University (1939), and studied library science at Columbia University from 1939 to 1941, while serving as assistant to the librarian in the Columbia Law Library. He did not take a library degree. During 1942, Pollack was librarian of the New York law firm of Hays, Podell and Shulman, and from that year to 1947, he held the position of secretary of the Office of Price Administration. In 1947, he was appointed law librarian and assistant professor at the Ohio State University. He later advanced to full professorship and director of research services at Ohio State while continuing his duties as librarian.

Three years before his death, Pollack addressed the question of an ethics code for law librarians ("An Ethical Code for Law Librarianship?," *Law Library Journal* 62:415-16 [November 1969]), expressing his fundamental thought on the relationship between his profession and society:

We must view law as a multi-faceted instrument of human relationship. Its vitality and force, which we help create and direct, give it the broadest meaning and the deepest significance. Its growth and stability find security in the resources of our libraries. We should be aware of the roles of precedent and circumstance that make for change, so that our resourcefulness is put to its fullest test and use. For us, the law library must be measured by more than court reports, statutes, and citators; it is the harbinger of ideas through which others create and structure institutions and meet and fulfill individual requisites.

As a member of this combined group, the law librarian should seek, above all, to be an effective instrument for the dissemination of legal information. He should hold for himself the best standards of librarianship. Through his conduct he should foster a general appreciation of the value of library service. He should respect and defend free inquiry, and should strive to be objective in rendering his professional services.

Pollack was correct in assessing the heavy responsibilities of his profession; and by his own career, he was justified in requiring of his colleagues the highest standards of performance.

As a teacher, as a writer, as a library administrator, and as an organizer for his profession, Pollack was at the same time both pragmatic and visionary. He taught courses in jurisprudence, legal process, and legal research and writing, but his teaching extended, through his writing, far beyond the sound of his voice. For nearly two decades now, many law students have won entrance to legal literature through Pollack's *Fundamentals of Legal Research* (which went through four editions). He was also author of *Legal Research and Materials* and edited *Ohio Court Rules Annotated*, *Ohio Unreported Judicial Decisions prior to 1823*, the *Brandeis Reader*, and *Human Rights* (Amintaphil). His books and articles, which span thirty years, show scholarly work not only on law librarianship but also on trade practices and the philosophy of law. At the time of his death, he had completed a manuscript titled *Jurisprudence: Principles and Applications* (now planned for publication in 1977).

As head of the Law Library at Ohio State, he made it the sixth largest academic law library in the nation, increasing its holdings from 70,000 to 305,000 volumes. Mathew F. Dee wrote ("In Memory of Ervin H. Pollack," *Law Library Journal* 65:469 [1972]) that Pollack "detested mediocrity and rarely tolerated for long an unsatisfactory situation without planning its improvement." Combining his innovative tendencies with his tirelessness, he earned that most sincere of compliments, the call to consultantship. Among organizations that benefited from his advice were the Library of Congress and the

Department of State. As consultant to the former, he participated in drafting the KF (American Law) classification. The Organization of Central American States awarded him its Certificate of Merit and dedicated to him its publication *Central American Economic Integration Law*. Occasionally, he was even asked to arbitrate in labor disputes. The distinguished rare book collection he developed at Ohio State was named for him and dedicated to his memory.

Pollack was an unceasing organizer, a founder and later president of the Ohio Association of Law Libraries, a president of the American Association of Law Libraries, and a trustee of the Ohio Legal Center. Other memberships included the American and Ohio Bar Associations, the American Arbitration Association, and the International Association of Philosophy of Law and Social Philosophy. His lifelong list of such activities indicates his faith in the possibility of improving the social matrix in which we live. In 1966, he wrote, "Hopefully, by communication, reflection and understanding, we will find our way to even greater social heights" ("Natural Rights: Conflict and Consequence," *Ohio State Law Journal* 27:590 [Fall 1966]).

His belief in social improvement by means of established, orderly processes, but with imagination, is in turn a clue to Pollack's nature in his day-to-day relations with friends and relatives. In his funeral eulogy, his brother emphasized his kindliness and his dedication to truth, the "idealist who strives for perfection." A law professor saw in him "the clarity and intensity of his sense of and sensitivity to human values" (both are quoted in Robert E. Mathews, "In Memory of Ervin Harold Pollack," *Law Library Journal* 66:113 [1973]). Another friend remembers him best as "courageous, humorous, proud, and undaunted" (Dee, above).

Pollack himself drew a message from the life of Miles Oscar Price (q.v.; see Pollack's "Miles Oscar Price," *Law Library Journal* 62:16 [February 1969]). We in turn may draw that same lesson from his: "Achievements are best attained through effort purposefully directed; the full bounty of life's riches is acquired through selfless dedication to others."

Biographical listings and obituaries—*A Biographical Directory of Librarians in the United States and Canada*, 5th ed.; *Biographical Directory of Law Librarians in the United States and Canada*, 2nd ed.; *Who Was Who in America* V (1969-1973); *Who's Who in Library Service*, 3rd ed., 4th ed.; *Who's Who in the Midwest*, 13th ed. (1972-1973). **Books and articles about the biographee**—Dee, Mathew F. "In Memory of Ervin H. Pollack." *Law Library Journal* 65:469 (1972); Mathews, Robert E. "In Memory of Ervin Harold Pollack." *Law Library Journal* 66:113 (1973).

—ROY M. MERSKY
—LEWIS C. BRANSCOMB

POOLE, REUBEN BROOKS (1834-1895)

Reuben Brooks Poole was born at Sandy Bay (now Rockport), Massachusetts, on April 5, 1834, the son of Nathaniel and Abigail H. Brooks Pool. He changed the spelling of his name around 1885 because, according to his brother, he disliked the sight of his name on "Pool and Billiards" signs. After attending the Kimball Union Academy in Meriden, New Hampshire, the Phillips Academy in Andover, Massachusetts, and the University Grammar School in Providence, he enrolled in Brown University and received a Bachelor of Arts degree in 1857.

After graduation, he returned to Rockport to teach school for a year, then moved to Philadelphia to teach in the House of Refuge. In 1861 and 1862, he worked for the New England Society, caring for soldiers in Philadelphia. In 1863, he moved to New York City to become a reporter for the *New York Tribune*.

In January 1865, Reuben Poole became librarian of the New York City Young Men's Christian Association, a position that included additional responsibility for evening classes, the reception and reading rooms, the gymnasium, and the distribution of reading materials to army and navy posts. He had found his vocation. During the next thirty years, he became the leading spokesman for YMCA libraries, an active member of library organizations, and a frequent contributor to library and YMCA periodicals.

A series of seven articles published by Poole in the *Watchman* in 1877-1878 provided a comprehensive manual for YMCA librarians and indicated both his devotion to the institution and his strong belief in the ameliorative value of wholesome reading. "While the library will be a place of interest to nearly every member, to some it will be the *most* attractive feature of the institution, and may be the bait by which not a few are won to Christ" (*Watchman* 3:6 [June 1, 1877]). In papers read before the International Conference of the Railroad Department of the YMCA in 1879 and 1882, he developed useful guides for library management and selecting books on railroad literature. In 1891, he was sent to Washington to speak to the annual meeting of the United States Christian Commission on the distribution of reading materials to military installations.

Poole was one of the librarians who received and responded to Melvil Dewey's (q.v.) original circular letter calling for the 1876 Conference of Librarians (Edward G. Holley, ed., *Raking the Historic Coals*, p. 60). A life member of the American Library Association (Number 36, 1876) and a participant in fourteen ALA conferences, he read papers at four conferences, served on numerous committees, and enjoyed the discussion and socializing of those leisurely meetings. The *Library Journal* reported that

Reuben Poole played second base in the 1887 conference ball game; William F. Poole (q.v.) was the pitcher.

Reuben Poole was one of the founders of the New York Library Club, was a member of the executive committee for eight years, and was twice elected president. Chairman of a committee to prepare a plan for a union list of periodicals, he was a frequent speaker at meetings of the Club. At the time of his death, he was president of the New York State Library Association.

His writings were largely eclectic; the range of topics included book binding standards, insurance of libraries, library cooperation, library management, and advocacy of the sheaf catalog that had been introduced at the YMCA Library on the recommendation of Robert Hoe. He contributed a long paper on "The Manuscript Age" (*Library Journal*, March, April 1893), and a series of nineteen articles on "How the Bible Was Transmitted to Us" (*Young Men's Era*, 1891-1892), but his real concerns seem to have been with improving bibliographical and reference services to readers. He was responsible for indexing sixty volumes for Poole's *Index* and urged the preparation of an index to portraits in 1888.

He was a life member of the YMCA and an active member of the Broadway Tabernacle, in which he served as a teacher and superintendent in the Chinese Sunday School. His wife, Frances E. Haskins Poole, died in December 1894, and there was one daughter, Mary B. Poole. Reuben Brooks Poole died of heart disease after a short illness at his home in New York City on April 5, 1895. The ALA memorial presented at the 1895 conference described him as a man "of quiet tastes, unassuming manners, profoundly interested in all religious manners and active and alert in everything pertaining to the interests of the organization he had served so long and well."

Biographical listings and obituaries—[Obituary]. Brown University. *Necrology, 1857*; [Obituary]. *Library Journal* 20:140 (April 1895), 20:212-13 (June 1895), and 20:50 (Dec. 1895); [Obituary]. *New York Times*, April 8, 1895, p. 2; [Obituary]. *Young Men's Era* 21:239 (April 11, 1895), with portrait. Books and articles about the biographee—Kraus, Joe W. "Libraries of the Young Men's Christian Associations in the Nineteenth Century." *Journal of Library History* 10:3-21 (Jan. 1975). Primary sources and archival materials—A bibliography of Reuben Poole's writings is on file with the YMCA Historical Library in New York.

—JOE W. KRAUS

POOLE, WILLIAM FREDERICK (1821-1894)

William Frederick Poole was born December 24, 1821, in Salem, Massachusetts, where his father, Ward Poole, in the family tradition, worked as a tanner. Ward's sons formed the generation that, while retaining the practical wisdom of their seventeenth century laboring forebears, moved up the social and economic ladder by taking advantage of new opportunities for education. Young Will attended the community's elementary school, but he was typical of his time in leaving school at the age of twelve to learn a trade. For the next five years, he worked as an apprentice in his cousin Edward Poole's jewelry shop in Keene, New Hampshire, as a helper on the farm near Worcester where Ward moved his family, as a clerk in a grain and provision store in Salem, and by age seventeen, as a teamster for the tannery. At that juncture, his mother, Eliza Wilder Poole, intervened in his life, precipitating a decisive change in its direction.

Many years later, Poole recounted to a friend the story of his mother's journey down from Worcester to persuade her son to leave his job as a laborer and return to school as preparation for college. Her earnest talk seems to have been convincing, for he persisted through three years of preparatory study at Leicester Academy, a year at Yale College that was ended by family financial difficulties, and three further years of work and saving before, in 1846, he was able to return to Yale to join the class of 1849 in their last three years of study. When Poole became a sophomore in 1846, he was almost 25 years old. Although he was destined to have one of the longest careers in nineteenth century librarianship, he came late to a life of learning.

At Yale College, learning was still in the mold of the classical curriculum, and classwork was narrowly restricted to textbook learning, whose mastery was demonstrated in daily recitations. Such an education did not require access to a library. Indeed, the students were allowed to use the college library only during their junior and senior years, and even then only if they paid a special fee. The narrow education reflected by these policies was on the verge of changing, but changes were already taking place in student life.

The major student agencies of expansion and change developed from a widely accepted conviction that educated men must be skilled in public speaking and debate. Yale's three student societies, the Calliopean, the Linonian, and the Brothers in Unity, had as their principal activity the mounting of orations and debates; and as a natural outgrowth of this enterprise, each society assembled a library of materials for the use of debaters. In the library of the Brothers in Unity, Poole was elected to serve during his junior year as assistant librarian and during his senior year as librarian, an experience that led him to his life's work. His salary for the work helped to pay his college expenses, but when he later called those years the "most profitable" he had spent in libraries, he was referring not to the money but to the experience he gained. With little precedent to guide them, the student librarians had the challenge of

improvising administrative and service arrangements to provide debate materials for their members as well as general reading matter for the whole college community.

The general pattern of service was from closed shelf collections, with readers customarily served during a thirty-minute period each day, presenting their requests for books selected from the printed catalog of the collection. For single monographs, this system worked reasonably well, but for composite works, such as collections of essays or periodical volumes, it was quite unsatisfactory. The difficulty in locating magazine articles was especially crippling, for fresh articles could be crucial to success in debate contests. To meet the need, John Edmands (q.v.), a previous Brothers librarian and, in later life, librarian of the Philadelphia Mercantile Library, published in January 1847 an eight-page leaflet entitled *Subjects for Debate, with References to Authorities*. The compilation was a bibliography arranged by topics most popular for debate, but it had no value as a guide to material on other subjects. Poole decided, during his year as assistant librarian, to prepare a true index to periodicals, so as to provide a key to material on all subjects.

This ambitious undertaking started the young librarian on a course that lasted during most of the rest of his life. The first index was simply a brief manuscript available in the Brothers Library, but its usefulness soon attracted students from all of the College. Thus, Poole decided to expand and publish his manuscript. Through the intervention of Henry Stevens, a former Brothers librarian then established as a London bookseller, Poole gained the backing of New York publisher George Palmer Putnam, and in July 1848, the volume appeared under the title *An Alphabetical Index to Subjects Treated in the Reviews and Other Periodicals to Which No Indexes Have Been Published*. The whole edition of 500 copies was sold almost immediately. Although only a small volume that selectively indexed 560 volumes of 31 different periodicals, it proved itself quite useful in its day, and as the first general index to periodicals it stands as a landmark of bibliographical history. The acclaim and rapid sale that greeted his first edition encouraged Poole to prepare a new, expanded edition. Even after graduation, he continued the enterprise, a delay in taking up a full-time occupation that seems to have been instrumental in permitting librarianship to capture him.

When Poole left Yale, he expected to become a lawyer, but first he devoted himself to finishing the new edition of the index. Even though set back in 1850 by the theft of his manuscript, he began again, but he was chosen in 1851 to fill a temporary vacancy as assistant librarian of the Boston Athenaeum before he completed the work. Even a short time spent in what was then one of the great libraries of the nation was enough to persuade the young man to seek permanent employment in a library and, as he said, to "pursue bibliography as a profession." In May 1852, he was elected librarian of the Mercantile Library Association of Boston. This institution served the clerks of business houses of Boston in ways similar to those of student society libraries. The Association provided facilities that could train young men for advancement in business careers, supply them with wholesome recreation, and develop in them a cultural background appropriate to the positions they hoped to attain in the world. Weekly literary meetings for oratory, discussion, and debate, public lectures by noted speakers, arrangements for instruction in bookkeeping, penmanship, and foreign languages, a newspaper reading room, and a substantial library collection were major features of the organization. At mid-century, the heavy demands for library service that were leading to the establishment of municipal public libraries made the social libraries popular and much-used institutions. Boston's Mercantile Library was one of the leaders.

As the principal full-time employee, Poole carried responsibilities for general oversight of the whole institution and performed many duties not strictly connected with the Library, such as maintaining records of membership and dues. During the years he served as librarian, he supervised the Association's move to handsome new quarters; refurnished, reorganized, and increased the collection; prepared and published a new printed library catalog; and, in general, administered the whole institution in accordance with the policies of the democratically elected Board of Directors, to whom he soon became especially valuable as an adviser. Poole thus made a place for himself in Boston, and the next four years confirmed him in his career and established him in his personal life.

The second edition of the index was published in 1853 by Charles B. Norton (q.v.) in a handsome volume of 521 pages. Hardly had the printing begun on that book before Poole started to prepare the catalog of the Mercantile Library. Using still another innovation to library practice, he was able to complete the work in the phenomenally brief time of six months. Instead of following one of the two previous bibliographical patterns by preparing a subject catalog with an author index or an author catalog with a subject index, he inaugurated the form of a dictionary catalog with author, title, and subject entries, all in a single alphabetical arrangement. The plan was frequently copied in the town libraries that were established during the last half of the nineteenth century, and the dictionary arrangement of American library catalogs owes much to the precedent that Poole established at the Mercantile Library.

Poole was still a young man, but he was already becoming familiar to librarians and to scholars. The new edition of his index prompted the *New York Times* to comment, "Henceforward Mr. Poole's name can never be pronounced without respect." At the world's first library conference, in September 1853, in New York, an advance copy of his index was displayed for the assembled librarians and literary men, who congratulated him personally and passed a formal resolution approving it. His diligent work won him a reputation abroad and, from the directors of the Mercantile Library Association, praise and an increase in salary.

His position secured, William Frederick Poole was married to Fanny Maria Gleason on November 22, 1854. In September 1855, their first children, twin daughters Alice and Helen, were born. With a burgeoning family, Poole naturally welcomed the Boston Athenaeum's offer, on the retirement of Charles Folsom in April 1856, of the position of librarian.

One of the largest and richest libraries of the nation, the Athenaeum was the private preserve of Boston's wealthy elite. Poole's earlier service there had satisfied both the proprietors and their venerable librarian, and in subsequent years, his accomplishments at the Mercantile Library had reinforced their good opinion. The new post then made him immediately one of the leading librarians of the country.

Poole satisfied the proprietors well during the next thirteen years. In contrast to the bold initiative and popular service appropriate at the Mercantile Library, his responsibilities at the Athenaeum demanded gradual adjustment to the developing needs of a settled institution with a conservative clientele. Changes were made with deliberation and with as little fanfare as possible. Pressing needs for increased space required moves of the collection, reclassification, and remodeling of the quarters at frequent intervals, yet the Athenaeum kept intact its dignified and quiet atmosphere. Nevertheless, during Poole's administration a fundamental reshaping of the institution took place. Located almost entirely on one floor in 1856, the Library occupied virtually all of three floors by 1868, connected by newly constructed interior staircases. The collection grew from about 60,000 volumes to about 80,000, enriched by important new materials, most notably an outstanding assemblage of Confederate newspapers, pamphlets, books, and other documents acquired as the fruit of an intensive campaign of gifts and purchases planned and marshalled by Poole. The staff grew substantially, from only one assistant librarian helped by two janitors in 1856 to seven assistants and one janitor in 1868. All in all, the Athenaeum developed under Poole's administration from simply an enlarged version of a gentleman's library to an operating institution of considerable size and complexity, with a specialized staff and extensive services. At the head of this institution, Poole employed, trained, and supervised employees who included the first woman known to work in an American library and librarians of such later prominence as Caroline M. Hewins (q.v.), pioneer of children's services, William I. Fletcher (q.v.), well known as a bibliographer and as librarian of Amherst College, and Charles Evans (q.v.), the compiler of the monumental *American Bibliography*. In all aspects of his work at the Athenaeum, Poole was notably successful, earning for himself over the years continuing approval from the proprietors in the tangible form of regular and substantial increases in his salary.

When he went to the Athenaeum, Poole, an established man of 34, settled with his wife and two children in a house in suburban Melrose. In 1868, there were five surviving children, including the last born, the only boy, named for his father. During these years, Poole had also published works on early New England history, thus laying the foundation of his reputation as a historian. Yet for no apparent reason, in February 1868, he asked the proprietors of the Athenaeum to recruit a successor, saying simply that he had in mind other employment, and when they delayed for ten months in finding a new man, he urgently renewed his request. Finally, at the end of the year, Charles A. Cutter (q.v.), recruited from the library at Harvard, took office at the Athenaeum. Poole set himself up in the city as a freelance "library agent."

This drastic decision has been the subject of considerable investigation by students of Poole's life. The best evidence suggests that Poole, perhaps spurred by the birth of his son, decided that the position at the Athenaeum would not satisfy his life's ambitions and energies. Ever venturesome, he now undertook to make his living by writing, by preparing and publishing a new edition of his index, and by serving as a consultant and commissioned buyer for some of the many libraries being established in the prosperous years following the Civil War.

During the next four years, Poole became involved in an official way with at least nine different libraries. His role was limited primarily to the selection of books for the Newton Public Library, the Easthampton Public Library, and Mount Holyoke Seminary (later College), all in Massachusetts; for the Fairbanks Library of St. Johnsbury, Vermont; for the Grosvenor Library of Buffalo, New York; and for the Indianapolis Public Library. He was commissioned to advise on the reorganization of the Naval Academy library in Annapolis, and he also served as active principal adviser in the formation of the Silas Bronson Library of Waterbury, Connecticut. His career then turned decisively toward public librarianship in

his service to the Cincinnati Public Library. Although the details and depth of Poole's involvement with the various libraries differed, a common feature was his use of the Athenaeum collection as a basis for his selection of books and his recommendation of former Athenaeum employees to serve the new institutions. Most notably, Fletcher became the librarian at the Bronson Library and Charles Evans at Indianapolis. Poole himself, after initial service as adviser, took the administrative responsibility of librarian of the Cincinnati Public Library.

Cincinnati's Library had barely survived since 1853 as the remnant of an abortive program to set up public libraries throughout Ohio under the authority of local school boards. Taxpayer opposition soon caused repeal of the library tax, but finally, in 1867, the state authorized a new library tax limited to large communities. Cincinnati's library supporters arranged for Poole's appointment as a consultant, with the initial understanding that he would devote only part of his time to Cincinnati and would remain only long enough to put the Library into proper operation. He continued to serve other libraries as adviser, and his family remained in Melrose even after he accepted full-time appointment as librarian early in 1871. Poole's move from Massachusetts to the Middle West took place gradually, but he dedicated himself energetically to setting the Cincinnati Public Library on its feet.

The Library advocates gave enthusiastic support. The Cincinnati School Board, as the parent body, provided funds and administrative experience and took steps to complete a permanent building. As construction proceeded, two catalogers from the former Athenaeum staff were working in Boston, on the basis of Cincinnati's accession book, to prepare a new catalog, which appeared in print soon after the new building was occupied in December 1870. Meanwhile, Poole was establishing the service organization. In something over a year, he took a faltering institution and turned it into an active, thriving library.

The new building contained on its three floors reading rooms and facilities for 200 seats, 300 current periodicals, and a book collection that grew in three months from 22,000 to 28,000 volumes. In March 1871, Cincinnati became the first large municipal library to open its reading room on Sundays. Very quickly the Public Library became a successful institution, already second only to Boston's in the nation. These positive results were the consequence of Poole's long experience, since he knew what books to buy, how to handle the business arrangements, how to arrange the collection, and how to provide the needed services. Soon a staff of thirteen full-time attendants served borrowers, who came in large numbers. Too, Poole encouraged the community's liberal tendencies by welcoming to the Library groups not always served by public libraries of the time, particularly children and businessmen. With an eye to establishing mutually beneficial relationships with the manufacturers in the city, he set up a special room for books concerning fine arts and decoration, pointing out the usefulness of such works to industrial designers. This department appears to have been the first subject department to have been established in an American public library.

Poole himself joined enthusiastically in the cultural life of Cincinnati, particularly through the Literary Club, and soon found a success and a prominence not easily available in the settled society of Boston. Late in 1873, however, to the dismay of many in Cincinnati, he announced that he had accepted an offer from Chicago. He now meant to do for that city what he had done for Cincinnati.

Chicago's move toward establishing its Public Library had been complicated but only momentarily delayed by the great fire of October 1871. By January 1, 1873, the reading room was opened with ceremony, and these early arrangements were only a beginning. The Library's board, determined to put the Library in full operation, offered Poole the position as librarian at a salary of $4,000, a full $1,000 increase from his Cincinnati pay. On January 2, 1874, he arrived in Chicago to begin work. Within a few months, the Library, its size increased by new books arriving at a rate above 1,000 volumes a week, moved into new rented quarters and, on May 1, 1874, began active service, including the loan of books in quantities greater than in any other public library of the country.

Poole now brought his family from Massachusetts and settled them in a house near the old University of Chicago. He soon undertook editorship of a literary review, *The Owl*, and at about the same time, became a charter member of the Chicago Literary Club, an organization that included many of the city's leaders. The prospects for the Chicago Public Library and its new librarian were bright.

These early favorable times were soon ended by political and economic changes. Hardly had Poole become settled into his new position before he faced problems of cutting expenditures to meet a sharply reduced budget. For the next few years, he must have questioned his wisdom in leaving the prosperity of Cincinnati, but his reports spoke only optimistically of the great opportunities for Chicago's Library, if adequate funds were provided. Using the available money to its fullest, he laid sound foundations for the prosperous years to come, and even with inadequate funds, the Chicago Public Library was a leader of the nation.

As the chief librarian of the Middle West, Poole was called upon in 1876 to join Justin Winsor (q.v.) of the Boston Public Library and Lloyd Pearsall

Smith (q.v.) of the Library Company of Philadelphia to form the organizing committee for a conference of librarians to be held in October in Philadelphia, in conjunction with the great exposition celebrating the centennial of the Declaration of Independence. This conference was being promoted by Frederick Leypoldt (q.v.) of *Publishers' Weekly* and its new companion periodical, *Library Journal*, and by a young assistant librarian of Amherst College, Melvil Dewey (q.v.). Poole, with a businesslike caution that has often since been misrepresented as opposition to the conference and the association that grew out of it, required evidence of the intentions and the responsibility of these promoters before lending his name to the project, but once assured, he gave the conference his full support. At the meeting in Philadelphia, he read a paper and was elected first-vice-president of the conference and of the American Library Association, which was formed at its conclusion. During the rest of his life, he faithfully attended every official conference of the Association, finding great satisfaction in the professional activities and in the warm friendships he made there. Winsor and Poole were respectively president and vice-president throughout the formative first ten years of the Association, and on Winsor's retirement, Poole was elected president for the next two terms.

In one of the significant professional actions of the Philadelphia meeting, the librarians agreed to band together to prepare a new edition of Poole's index to periodicals. Although the volume published in 1853 was still invaluable, coverage of the last 23 years was much needed. Indeed, many librarians had been making their own indexes each year. Poole himself had considered preparing a third edition, particularly at the time he left the Athenaeum, but had not completed one. Now he proposed to the librarians in Philadelphia that he coordinate a cooperative venture. Under the aegis of the Association, librarians from both the United States and England would index periodicals assigned to them, sending the entries to Poole in Chicago. He would consolidate the contributions into a manuscript and edit it with the assistance of his old associate, William I. Fletcher, now at the Watkinson Library in Hartford, Connecticut.

The plan worked well. Poole, as the chief editor and the only financial guarantor of the project, managed the affair, as he said, "with something of autocratic sway." During the next six years, the new edition occupied much of his attention. In manuscript, the work occupied more than 4,000 pages, and the final publication, printed in double columns, took more than 1,400 printed pages. When the volume appeared in December 1882, it contained 230,000 entries covering 6,205 volumes of 232 periodicals. A handsome royal octavo, the great third edition of *Poole's Index to Periodical Literature* was greeted with acclaim. Poole himself received, in June 1882, an LL.D. degree from Northwestern University, in recognition of his contributions to scholarship in both his library work and his indexing. The University was also honoring a neighbor, for Poole had recently moved his family to Evanston.

By 1880, the financial affairs of the Chicago Public Library had revived enough to allow the institution to fulfill its early promise. Now substantial increases in the collection each year permitted the Library to respond adequately to the heavy demands for its services. Although hampered by cramped and inconvenient quarters on the third and fourth floors of a downtown office building, the Library grew and multiplied its services. The collection grew from 7,000 volumes in 1873 to more than 60,000 in 1880 and then doubled to 120,000 volumes by 1887. The number of loans, reaching 400,000 during 1874-1875, had declined during the lean years of small purchases, but by 1886 had grown to 600,000 per year. As the city grew, delivery stations were established in shops in residential neighborhoods, where citizens could order books brought out from the Library. By 1887, eight delivery stations were operating. In part, the delivery stations served to relieve the pressures of space in the central building. Finally, in 1886, quarters made available in the new City Hall permitted the Library, for the first time in years, to offer its services in rooms befitting its place as a leader in the nation. In that year, the American Library Association held its annual meeting in Milwaukee, and most of those who attended stopped off in Chicago on the way to visit the Association's president in his newly occupied Library.

Poole was riding the crest of a wave of success. With the Chicago Public Library now operating at a great pace, he was unquestionably the first public librarian of the land, though a second term as president of the American Library Association that year was the last he agreed to accept. He was also a man of public stature as a scholar. Throughout his career, he had contributed to knowledge not only through the catalogs and indexes that grew from his work as a librarian but also, when time permitted, through scholarship in general. In early years, he had written on the side of the Merriams, successors to Noah Webster, in the controversy between the supporters of the two contending dictionaries of English, Worcester's and Webster's. Most particularly, however, he had concentrated his book reviewing and his original research upon American history, first upon the early days of New England and then upon the settlement of the West. Among the most important of his publications were a new edition, with an introduction, of Edward Johnson's *Wonder-Working Providence of Sion's Saviour in New England* (Andover, Mass., 1867), "Cotton Mather and Salem

Witchcraft" (*North American Review* 108:337-97 [April 1869]), and "The Ordinance of 1787 and Dr. Manasseh Cutler as an Agent in Its Formation" (*North American Review* 122:229-65 [April 1876]). His leading position as both a scholar and a librarian was behind the offer of appointment to one of the great library positions of the nation. The trustees of the Newberry estate asked him to take office as founding librarian of a new reference library to be established with the funds of a wealthy trust.

Already 65 years old, Poole may well have expected to complete his career in the Chicago Public Library, but the new challenge was an opportunity not to be declined. The Newberry Library had come into being almost by chance. Under the will of Walter Loomis Newberry, a pioneer Chicagoan who had made a fortune primarily in real estate, half of his estate was to go to found a library if both his daughters died without leaving children—an unlikely chance, but the unlikely had occurred. On the death of Newberry's widow in 1885, final settlement of the estate was made, and by July 1887, the trustees, E. W. Blatchford and William H. Bradley, could formally establish the library. They promptly offered the librarianship to Poole, who took office on August 1.

The new institution, although open to the public, was to function in a fashion complementary to the Public Library. Poole understood very well the mutually beneficial relationship between the Public Library, serving popular needs, and this new institution, which would be, he said, "the great reference library of the West." His threefold task, then, was to assemble for it an outstanding collection of scholarly works, to plan a building to house its books and services, and to recruit and organize a staff to administer and serve the institution.

Poole's whole life and career might have been planned to equip him for the new task. His years at the Athenaeum and his own scholarly achievements had given him a command of the bibliography of learning and a knowledge of great books and bookmaking. He began soundly by ordering from B. F. Stevens in London and from Otto Harrassowitz in Leipzig the great scholarly works that would form the basis of the library's bibliographical collection, the sources for the selection of the remainder of the collection. Aware of space limitations, Poole at first sought to buy only a working collection, but it was soon time to begin to acquire the fundamental scholarly sets, such as runs of the major periodicals and publications of the important learned societies of the world. Next came the great encyclopedias and other reference works, and then the important basic monographs of each subject. The collection was to be for working scholars and therefore not to concentrate upon bibliographical showpieces, but it was to be composed of sound books of substance and importance.

Encompassing virtually the whole of knowledge, the task was a formidable one. Moreover, although at first the two-million-dollar endowment seemed to provide unlimited funds, the trustees soon became apprehensive about the rate of purchase that Poole was recommending. The promise of some relief came in 1889 with the death of John Crerar, whose estate was to provide a second endowed public library for Chicago. As Poole had suggested as early as 1876, when the first word of the Newberry Library was heard, a division of fields of responsibility among the libraries would help them all, individually and collectively, to serve best the complex needs of Chicago's large and varied population. Leaving the Public Library to provide for the loan of books for popular reading and home use, the Crerar Library covered the fields of science and technology and the Newberry collected in literature, history, the arts, and the humanities.

During Poole's years, the collections were soundly and impressively established. In addition to the purchases of the basic scholarly sets, the Newberry took advantage of some special opportunities. With the purchase of the private library of Count Pio Resse, the Newberry became one of the foremost music libraries of the world. Then, in 1890, Poole's long-time friendship with Henry Probasco, a Public Library Board member in Cincinnati and a noted private book collector, resulted in the offer of Probasco's library. The Newberry thus was enabled to buy an extraordinary assemblage of books, including more than four hundred examples of three centuries of binding craftsmanship, eighty-eight rare Bibles, three of the four Shakespeare folios, both Audubon's *Birds* and his *Quadrupeds*, and other works of similar quality. All in all, during Poole's administration the Newberry acquired 120,000 books and 44,000 pamphlets at a cost close to a quarter of a million dollars. Impressive in itself, the collection laid the foundations for one of the notable libraries of the world.

The building to house the Library gave Poole the only opportunity of his career to plan a library from start to finish. He had made a specialty of library architecture, and his ideas were both unconventional and distinctively his own. His criticisms of library architecture over the years had produced in sum a proposal for a new sort of library building. He objected particularly to the copying of church architecture for libraries. The open hall surrounded by alcoves, especially when done on a large scale, produced a succession of galleries ascending around the nave to dizzying heights. Essentially a single, echoing space, these library buildings were noisy, difficult to

administer, and in case of fire, natural flues. Such monumental buildings, however, offered great attraction to architects interested in display and to donors interested in impressive memorials. Most librarians joined Poole in his criticisms but few endorsed his solution; the alternative that attracted most support was the bookstack that packed books in a separate low-ceilinged structure attached to what was essentially a second building for staff and readers, often including a great vaulted reading room that satisfied the lover of architectural display. Poole's solution was quite different.

With a remarkable awareness of the implications of the development of new structural materials, Poole argued for the use of iron beams in reading rooms, which could thus be made fifty feet wide without intervening structural columns. Ceiling heights would be limited to fifteen feet, a low height indeed at the time. The upper half of that space would be left free to allow the circulation of air and the penetration of light throughout the room. The lower half of the room, without structural walls, would be divided by free-standing bookshelves that could be moved about in response to changing needs of the library. A building of the sort that Poole proposed would also permit the allotment of space to subject reading rooms, with specialized collections served by librarians with strong subject preparation. Apparently growing out of a need to rationalize the use of a building, this plan of service also had become one of Poole's distinctive ideas. He was determined that his library be planned with a flexibility that would avoid age-old building problems and permit a subject-departmentalized service. This aim produced a substantial battle between the Newberry's librarian and the Newberry's architect.

Henry Ives Cobb had been engaged by the trustees to give the new building his exclusive attention. After travelling both in the United States and in Europe to see examples of library architecture, he drew up plans dominated by a bookstack and a monumental reading room. Poole was appalled. In a vigorous debate, carried out principally in a series of letters to the trustees, Cobb and Poole argued their cases. For a wonder, Poole's ideas won out and were incorporated in the building that Cobb finally designed and that stands today on West Walton Street.

In this building of pioneering design, the world's great works of scholarship were to be provided to readers in specialized subject departments. However, such a library demanded unusual qualifications in its staff. Among those Poole employed were a number with names that later became familiar. George Watson Cole (q.v.) became the great bibliographer and librarian of the Henry E. Huntington Library. Edwin Hatfield Anderson (q.v.) eventually headed the New York Public Library. Marilla Waite Freeman (q.v.)

POOLE POOLE

held a principal position in the Cleveland Public Library. William Stetson Merrill's (q.v.) *Code for Classifiers* became a standard work. Haakon Nyhuus returned to his native land to become known as the father of Norwegian librarianship. Charles Martel (q.v.) and J. C. M. Hanson (q.v.) are credited with being the chief designers of the Library of Congress Classification. Charles Evans returned to serve again under the chief who had introduced him to libraries. Yet, not even this impressive list exhausts the names of employees of unusually high qualification.

A staff of this quality was both expensive to employ and difficult to supervise. Poole's great strength as a developer of outstanding librarians lay in his capacity to inspire them and in his willingness to trust them, not in any inclination to instruct them in detail or to supervise them closely. Some, including one of the earliest recipients of an earned doctorate from the Johns Hopkins University, suspected that they were better qualified than their chief to administer the institution. These prima donnas posed no great threat to Poole in the early years, but after 1892, when a new, enlarged Board of Trustees took office, ominous signs began to appear, warnings Poole seemed not to see. The euphoric early days of unlimited funds were over. Construction costs of the new building and the large sums spent for the collections made the new trustees anxious. Strict economy became their watchword, and they called upon Poole to reduce the purchases of books. Without speaking of the matter to him directly, they were also inclined to believe that he was not sufficiently in control of the affairs of the Library. His means of administering the public libraries in Cincinnati and Chicago had been to rely primarily upon a trusted assistant librarian. His own work had taken the directions of developing the collections and of building relationships with groups outside the Library; he left the internal management very largely to the chief assistant librarian and to the independent responsibility and judgment of the staff. This loose control of the reins did not satisfy the hard-bitten businessmen and attorneys of the Board. Moreover, they saw little reason to employ an assistant librarian to relieve Poole of the need to run his own organization, particularly in a time of financial stringency. In 1893, they abolished the post, put the chief burden back upon Poole himself, and when he did not discharge the duties to their satisfaction, proposed to replace him with a new man, retaining Poole as consulting librarian at full pay for the first year and then at half salary.

Their decision came upon him as a crippling blow. Although there had been some danger signals, and even one very direct warning from an old friend on the Board, Poole seems not to have understood how

deeply the trustees' disapproval ran. Over the years, he had dealt with library trustees with great skill, usually winning them to his point of view. In this last great test, he had not understood in time. He set himself to win back their confidence by the vigor with which he took control, but apparently the shock and his 72 years were too much for him. He began to lose sleep and then came down with minor illnesses that rapidly progressed into serious complaints. He kept his courage and his surface cheerfulness, but soon he had an incapacitating fall that kept him at home. Finally, on March 1, 1894, he died.

At an impressive funeral held in Evanston, the honorary pallbearers included the presidents of Northwestern University and of the University of Chicago and twelve other distinguished citizens, only one of them, perhaps significantly, a member of the Newberry's Board. The funeral text was "Know ye not that there is a prince and a great man fallen this day in Israel?"

Among the librarians of the nineteenth century, Poole was indeed a prince and a great man. His 47 years as a librarian had traced the course of libraries in the United States. Beginning in social libraries, he served the oldest mercantile library association and the outstanding proprietary library before turning his eyes to the work of establishing on a sound basis two of the leading public libraries of the nation. After these notable services, he seized eagerly the opportunity to create from the very beginning a new research library to serve the scholars of the Middle West. As an accompaniment to his work, he compiled pioneering bibliographical works and wrote striking historical studies as direct contributions to the scholarship he served indirectly through the libraries he headed. His recognition of the potential of new construction materials led him to plan for the Newberry Library a complementary use of flexible space and subject departments that became dominant in library planning a half-century later.

An imaginative thinker and inspiring leader, William Frederick Poole was one of the great founding librarians of the United States. To his contemporary librarians, one of his outstanding achievements was his contribution in making librarianship a recognized and respected profession. He could make this contribution because he was a man of strength, scholarship, warmth, and dedication.

Biographical listings and obituaries—*Dictionary of American Biography* 15 (Carl B. Roden); Larned, J. N. "William Frederick Poole. In Memoriam. Action of the Executive Board [of ALA] Unanimously Adopted [Obituary]." *Library Journal* 19:92 (March 1894); *National Cyclopaedia of American Biography* 6; [Obituary]. *Chicago Tribune*, March 2, 1894; *Obituary Record of the Graduates of Yale University* (1894); *Who Was Who in America*, Historical Volume (1607-1896). **Books and articles about the biographee**—Chicago Literary Club. *In Memoriam William*

Frederick Poole. Chicago: The Club, 1894; Kessler, Sidney H. William Frederick Poole, Librarian-Historian." *Wilson Library Bulletin* 28:788-90 (May 1954); Newberry Library. Board of Trustees. *Memorial Sketch of Dr. William Frederick Poole.* Chicago: The Library, 1895; Roden, Carl B. "The Boston Years of Dr. W. F. Poole." In William Warner Bishop and Andrew Keogh, *Essays Offered to Herbert Putnam.* New Haven: Yale University Press, 1929, pp. 388-94; Williamson, William L. "An Early Use of Running Title and Signature Evidence in Analytical Bibliography." *Library Quarterly* 40:245-49 (April 1970); Williamson, William L. *William Frederick Poole and the Modern Library Movement.* New York: Columbia University Press, 1963. [Williamson's dissertation, on which this book is based, is available at the University of Chicago or on microfilm and contains exhaustive and detailed citation of all sources.] **Primary sources and archival materials**—The largest single body of material relating to Poole is at the Newberry Library, including correspondence received from 1887 to 1894, a memoir written by his son-in-law, Z. Swift Holbrook, and reminiscences by his office assistant, William Stetson Merrill. In addition, the author has recently deposited there copies of letters and other documents found in other locations. At the Boston Athenaeum, the Cincinnati Public Library, the Chicago Public Library, and the Newberry Library, the records of Poole's tenure remain, including letterpress books containing copies of much of his business correspondence. A few records of his student days remain in the Memorabilia Room of Yale University Library.

—WILLIAM LANDRAM WILLIAMSON

POWER, EFFIE LOUISE (1873-1969)

Effie Louise Power was born February 12, 1873, at Conneautville, Pennsylvania, the daughter of William Ellis and Frances Billings Power. Although a Pennsylvanian by birth, she spent a good part of her life in Cleveland. After obtaining a diploma from the Training School for Children's Librarians at the [Andrew] Carnegie [q.v.] Library in Pittsburgh in 1904, she acquired a teaching certificate at Columbia University in the summer of 1906. In 1934, Allegheny College awarded her an honorary A.M.

Power began her career in libraries in 1895 as an apprentice in the Cleveland Public Library, under the wing of William Howard Brett (q.v.), who was well known for endowing his associates with loving affection for their calling. After this beginning, she was for a brief period the school librarian of Cleveland Central High School but returned to the Public Library to take charge of the "Juvenile Alcove" under Brett's supervision and encouragement. In 1898, she opened the first real children's room, thus becoming the first children's librarian in the Cleveland system, where she remained until 1902.

From 1903 to 1908, Power was an instructor at the City Normal School in Cleveland, teaching courses in library use and in children's literature. In 1908, she returned to the Cleveland Public Library as the children's librarian, where she stayed for one year. In 1909, she joined the staff of the Carnegie Library in Pittsburgh as first assistant in the children's

department, a position she held until 1911. Then she left for St. Louis, where she was supervisor of work with children at the St. Louis Public Library. Returning to Pittsburgh, she was supervisor of the schools division of the Carnegie Library from 1914 to 1917, and from 1917 to 1920, she served as head of the Children's Department.

In 1920, Power again returned to Cleveland, and, until 1937, was director of work with children in the Cleveland Public Library, where she had originally initiated the children's work program. During this time, she also taught courses at Western Reserve University, as an instructor until 1925 and as an assistant professor from 1925 to 1929, specializing in work with children and storytelling. In 1918, she also embarked upon her supplemental career as lecturer and instructor in storytelling, work with children, and children's literature in various library schools throughout the country. During her career as lecturer in library schools in literally every section of the country, she was especially successful in developing cooperative programs between schools and public libraries.

During the 1920s, in cooperation with Western Reserve University, she was instrumental in transforming the Cleveland Public Library's training class in work with children into a graduate program leading to a master's degree. In the summer of 1926, Power introduced Cleveland's first "Book Caravan," a mobile library that was the forerunner of the modern bookmobile. Her efforts were always extended toward introducing children to the joys of library activities, at the same time developing in adults a desire to work with these same children.

In 1937, Power retired from the Cleveland Public Library. However, she was not ready to sit back and rest; when Columbia University beckoned, she joined the staff of the School of Library Service, staying until 1939.

Effie Power finally retired to Pompano Beach, Florida, where she became actively involved with that small city's Public Library. So great was the community's admiration for "Miss Effie" that when, in 1949, she was invited to celebrate her "golden jubilee" at the Cleveland Public Library, the entire Pompano community cooperated to provide her with a resounding send-off.

Power's professional and organizational involvements began as early as 1896 in the National Education Association and in the American Library Association in 1906, and were as numerous as the various facets of her professional life. She was president of the Library Department of NEA and also chaired the Children's Section of ALA in 1912-1913, and again in 1929-1930. From 1914 to 1919, she served on ALA's Council.

Always realizing that the problem of work with children had grown with great speed, and that training for this field had lagged behind, Effie Power did her utmost to correct that fault. She accomplished this by impressing her audiences with the fact that the educational period in a child's life was ever lengthening; this, in turn, afforded librarians a greater opportunity than ever before for active cooperation with the home, the school, and other agencies serving children.

She had very strong convictions as to what should be included in training courses for those who are to guide the reading habits and tastes of the world's children. Power knew that there was a demand for "real" librarians with administrative ability, scholarly appreciation of children's literature, and knowledge of child psychology—so that they might fill important positions in many kinds of libraries, for pursuing research in education, and for teaching fledgling librarians. She bent all of her efforts toward training this type of individual.

In 1928, she added to her many credits by appearing as a writer for children in collaboration with Mrs. Florence Everson, a Cleveland teacher. Their *Early Days in Ohio* (Dutton) was a successful attempt to reveal to children livelier aspects of pioneer life than had been evidenced in previous history books. The stories were tested in the classroom by Everson so they were especially pleasing to the children who subsequently read them. *Bag o' Tales* (Dutton, 1934); *Blue Caravan Tales* (Dutton, 1935); *Stories to Shorten the Road* (Dutton, 1936); and *From Umar's Pack* (Dutton, 1937) were among her other collections of stories for children. Among her professional publications were *How the Children of a Great City Get Their Books* (St. Louis Public Library, 1914), *Lists of Stories and Programs for Story Hours* (Wilson, 1925), *Children's Books for General Reading* (2nd edition; ALA, 1930), and numerous articles on technical subjects in library periodicals. She also edited lists of books for children's reading and handbooks on storytelling.

Both school and public librarians are equally indebted to the inspiration that Effie Power received from Brett and the inspiration she in turn kindled in the newer generations. Both of these dedicated individuals spent their professional lives working for quality in the training of children's librarians. The tenets they laid down for success in librarianship were: 1) a love for children; 2) a knowledge of children's books ("the right book to a child at the right time"); 3) an understanding of children and the educational process; and 4) a knowledge of library methods.

To accomplish this, Power advocated special training programs for children's librarians. She believed that a children's librarian could help to train children

for adult life, but that children must be permitted to remain children and enjoy the literature written especially for them. She further believed that children's librarians had a wider and more intimate contact with the family life of a city than any other group of library workers, and, therefore, could influence other librarians in their approach to patrons. Her philosophy dictated that children's librarians could offer other library workers (especially those working with new Americans) techniques in library instruction, story hours, reading clubs and close work with both large and small groups. She had an abiding faith in libraries as educational institutions, and she continually promoted this philosophy: "Many people, young and old, go to school in our libraries everyday. The only requirement is good behavior. Attendance is free and students need never graduate."

Another of Power's strong beliefs was that work with children in libraries had received its initial impetus from great administrators and that it must be carried on in that way. If the children's library movement was to keep pace with current educational movements, then administrators must be well grounded in efficient methods. Power stated that "to this end every library school training for public library work should include a definite presentation of children's department administrative procedure in its curriculum."

To accomplish this end, she favored developing recruiting publicity, continuing education for practicing librarians, and an awareness by library schools of the needs in the field. As a part of her professional commitment, she strove to establish equality in salary and status for children's librarians, as she believed that they had been sorely neglected in this respect.

Although her professional life led her down many paths, Effie Power's greatest love remained her desire to serve children, and she was happiest when serving them:

> Each day, I would go about the library and gather up travel, biography, history, and nature books either written for, or suited to, children and young people. I would arrange them on the counters of the children's alcove. Each day, they melted away like snow, exploding the theory that children wanted only fiction.

As much as Effie Power loved people, so did they love and respect her. She imbued young librarians with her spirit of friendliness and dedication. One of her former pupils, who has been away from Cleveland a good many years, still speaks of Effie as a "dear person; it was a joy to know her."

Effie Power died on October 8, 1969.

Biographical listings and obituaries—Howes, Durward, ed. *American Women.* Vol. II. Los Angeles: American Publications, Inc., 1937; *Who's Who in Library Service,* 1st ed., 2nd ed. **Books and articles about the biographee**—Bowker, R. R. "Some Children's Librarians." *Library Journal*

46:787-90 (Oct. 1, 1921); Cramer, C. H. *Open Shelves and Open Minds.* Cleveland: Case Western Reserve University, 1972; "Librarian Authors." *Library Journal* 54:901 (Nov. 1, 1929).

—REGINA F. BERNEIS

PRICE, MILES OSCAR (1890-1968)

Miles Oscar Price, librarian of the Columbia University Law School from 1929 to 1961, was probably the most influential and creative figure in law librarianship during that period. His role in shaping the development of modern law librarianship and the careers of many law librarians earned for him the designation "Dean of Law Librarians."

Miles Price was born in Plymouth, Indiana, on July 31, 1890, the son of Emanuel and Mary Jane Dickson Price. His mother died when he was just twelve years old, a loss that he felt deeply throughout his life. She had, though, instilled in him a strong desire for intellectual development and a deep regard for moral and ethical precepts. He was very conscious of that influence and prided himself on his Midwestern heritage and the traditional values associated with it. That background, and his personal struggle for education and advancement, developed lifelong attitudes that were an unusual mixture of political conservatism and pragmatic liberalism.

Under very difficult economic circumstances, Price worked his way through college, serving as a library assistant and earning a B.S. degree from the University of Chicago in 1914. He then worked as department chief in the University of Illinois Library for eight years and received his Bachelor of Library Science degree there in 1922. From 1922 to 1929, he was librarian of the U.S. Patent Office Library in Washington, D.C., a post that helped form his interest in law and his future career in law librarianship. In 1929, he assumed the prestigious librarianship of Columbia Law School, succeeding Frederick C. Hicks. The appointment was unusual in that Price lacked formal legal training. However, he studied law at Columbia while serving as its law librarian, and he was awarded the LL.B. degree with honors in 1938. He was admitted to practice law in New York State in 1940 and was appointed professor of law at Columbia Law School in 1956.

On January 3, 1915, Miles Price married Fannie Elliot, who survived him. They had two children: a son, Macy, who died in 1937, and a daughter, Mary.

During his long career, Miles Price was active in several library associations, often in leadership positions. He served on the Council of the American Library Association in 1924-1925 and from 1933 to 1937. He was a member of the Executive Board of the Special Libraries Association in 1930-1931 and was president of the District of Columbia Library

Association in 1924-1925. His activities in the American Association of Law Libraries were many and varied, and he served as its president in 1945-1946. He worked diligently to improve the status of law librarians within the legal community and to raise the quality of collections and services in law libraries.

Price's contributions to law librarianship were wide-ranging and were reflected in his work at the Columbia Law School Library, in his numerous published writings, and in his personal influence as a teacher, consultant, and colleague. He reshaped law library education, influenced cataloging and classification, acquisitions practices, reference work, and law library planning. He encouraged collection development in foreign and international law and interdisciplinary studies in law, fought for higher bibliographic standards, and recognized the importance of applying information science to law librarianship and computers to legal research. From his Patent Office experience, he was an expert in the field of intellectual property and influenced the early efforts for copyright law revision. His approach to librarianship was personal and pragmatic. As early as in his 1930-1931 report as Columbia law librarian, he wrote, "It has been my effort ... to use rules as guides, rather than as straitjackets, and to give patrons what they want with a minimum of fuss and a maximum of speed and common-sense."

A full list of his extensive publications appeared in a symposium to his memory in *Law Library Journal* (62:2-4 [1969]). Other contributions to that symposium discuss various aspects of his life, his personal attributes, and his professional achievements. His major writing was a detailed treatise on the sources and methods of legal research, *Effective Legal Research*, co-authored with Harry Bitner. The book, first published in 1953 and now in its third edition, was for many years the most respected and widely used text of its kind. The first edition has remained a standard reference tool by virtue of its copious historical notes and bibliographic appendices.

Although Price was a strong proponent of legal education as a preparation for administrative and public service work in law librarianship, he also recognized the essential contribution of those without law training. He believed deeply in the importance of rigorous training in legal bibliography for all who would work in law libraries, and his many educational activities were designed to that end. Price's six-week summer session course in legal bibliography and law library administration at the Columbia School of Library Service was first offered in 1937, and he continued teaching it until his retirement in 1961. It was the model for later courses at many other library schools and provided the bibliographic training for a generation of law librarians, many of whom were to become dominant figures in the profession. The course has been described as follows:

> Mr. Price was a dry lecturer and made little attempt to glamorize or dramatize his materials; the course was traditionally given in the very early morning in an atmosphere of sleepy heat and physical discomfort; the assignments were long and tedious, and the total work required made the course one of the most demanding in the library school. Despite these factors, it was for its many students a landmark in their professional development and an educational experience of the deepest importance.

Among the many librarians who were trained by Price, either by their work with him in the Columbia Law Library or through his library school course, were Harry Bitner (formerly librarian, Yale Law School and Cornell Law School), Morris L. Cohen (librarian, Harvard Law School), Frances Farmer (formerly librarian, University of Virginia Law School), Anthony P. Grech (librarian, Association of the Bar of the City of New York), Julius J. Marke (librarian, New York University Law School), the late Ervin H. Pollack (q.v.; formerly librarian, Ohio State University Law School), Meira G. Pimsleur (formerly acquisitions librarian, Columbia Law School), and Mortimer D. Schwartz (librarian, University of California at Davis Law School).

In 1954, Miles Price was awarded an Honorary Doctorate of Laws from Temple University, an unusual recognition and probably the only such award to a practicing law librarian. Following his retirement in 1961, he continued an active professional life—writing, speaking, and consulting. At an advanced age and plagued by serious illnesses, he undertook two major projects of enormous scope and importance in law librarianship, either of which would have taxed the stamina and courage of a younger person. From 1962 to 1964, he was an active consultant to the Library of Congress in the development of its Classification K (Law). Working at LC daily, he completed a large part of the KF (American Law) schedules and revitalized the project after its many years of delay and dispute. (Price had been, throughout his career, a prime advocate of the need for a modern classification of legal materials.) Then, during the years 1964 to 1967, he directed the Libraries Study Project of the Association of American Law Schools. That project involved the preparation of a comprehensive annotated bibliography of legal materials for every subject in the law school curriculum. The entries in the bibliography were also to be graded to aid small, medium-sized, and large libraries in their acquisitions programs. The work was begun and developed under Price's directorship and was completed, after his death, under Harry Bitner

and Meira G. Pimsleur. The project resulted in the publication of six looseleaf volumes containing 46 separate subject bibliographies, under the title *Law Books Recommended for Libraries* (South Hackensack, N.J.: Fred B. Rothman, 6 vols. looseleaf, 1967-1970; 4 vols. suppl., 1974-1975). The compilation is widely used for both reference and bibliographic work and is still a basic guide for law collection development. It received the Joseph L. Andrews Bibliographical Award for 1971.

Price's physical appearance was striking. He was well over six feet tall and lean, with broad shoulders carrying a strong-boned head, whose distinctive features were bristling eyebrows over piercingly intelligent eyes. His frequently gruff manner and raspy voice only briefly concealed from new acquaintances his warm personality and charm. He had a keen and often self-deprecating wit, a sharp and quick intelligence, and a deep sense of personal and professional pride. His varied non-professional interests included baseball, classical music, Shakespeare, and walking. He hiked extensively and every year, on the same day, he would circumambulate Manhattan Island by himself.

Miles Price's life and work, his many professional accomplishments (his modesty notwithstanding), and his willingness to give freely of himself, have made him a model for those who knew him and for future librarians to follow. He died in Maine on August 18, 1958, after a long illness. His portrait hangs in the Columbia Law School Library and a fine photograph appears in the *Law Library Journal* symposium issue referred to above.

Biographical listings and obituaries—*Biographical Directory of Law Librarians in the United States and Canada* (1964); *Contemporary Authors* 15; *Directory of Law Teachers*, 1939-1961; *Who Was Who in America* V (1969-1973); *Who's Who in Library Service*, 1st ed., 2nd ed., 3rd ed., 4th ed. Books and articles about the biographee—*Law Library Journal* 62:2-24 (Feb. 1969) [includes bibliography of Price's writings by Arthur J. Ruffier, and articles by Harry Bitner, Morris L. Cohen, Frances Farmer, Marian G. Gallagher, J. Myron Jacobstein, Mary W. Oliver and Lucille M. Elliott, Meira G. Pimsleur, and Ervin H. Pollack].

                                        —MEIRA G. PIMSLEUR
                                        —MORRIS L. COHEN

PRITCHARD, MARTHA CAROLINE (1882-1959)

Martha Caroline Pritchard was one of the pioneering leaders in the school library movement. She was born on May 2, 1882, in Newport, Rhode Island, to George A. and Martha C. Fernald Pritchard. Her early education was gained at the Wheaton Seminary in Norton, Massachusetts. She began her career as an assistant teacher at the Newport, Rhode Island, public schools (1902-1903) and then became a substitute and assistant at the Newport Public Library

(1906-1912). From 1913 to 1916, she was the first librarian at the White Plains, New York, High School.

While at White Plains, Pritchard attended the 1913 annual conference of the American Library Association held at Katerskill, New York, and became a member. At this conference, she also joined other school librarians in organizing a Normal and High School Librarians Round Table of ALA under the leadership of Mary E. Hall (q.v.). This Round Table became the ALA's School Libraries Section in December 1914.

Martha Caroline Pritchard received her initial library training at the New York Public Library School, from which she earned a diploma in 1914. During 1916-1917, she served as an assistant librarian at the New York State Normal and Training School at Geneseo while earning a diploma in library science from that school as well. From 1917 to 1919, she organized and administered the library at Bridgewater, Massachusetts, State Normal School and served as the first president of the New England School Library Association. In 1920, Teachers College of Columbia University awarded Pritchard the B.S. degree. Her M.A. in library science was awarded her by the Graduate Library School of the University of Chicago in 1935, following study there in 1928 and 1929-1930. Her thesis was a "Comparison of the Activities of Teachers and School Librarians with Relation to Children's Reading."

In September 1920, Pritchard became the librarian of the Detroit, Michigan, Teacher's College, and in the following summer, she taught 22 teachers who had been selected by their principals in the new platoon schools to learn librarianship. In the fall of 1922, each began work in a special library room in their schools, and they continued their studies in evening classes during the 1922-1923 academic year. In 1922, Pritchard also took on the role of supervising instructor in charge of elementary school librarians of Detroit. She served the College and city school librarians until 1926.

Martha Pritchard was very active professionally during this period. She became president of the National Council of Teachers of English Library Section for the 1918-1919 term. During 1919-1921, she chaired the School Librarians Section of ALA. She also served as president of the National Education Association Library Department during 1922-1923. Her published works during this period reflected her thinking and concern with the education program for school librarians, and she was constantly involved with ALA committees exploring aspects of library education for school librarians.

Her last and major pioneer endeavor was in Albany, New York. Dr. Abram R. Brubacher, president of New York State College for Teachers, invited her to organize and direct a department of librarianship to prepare librarians to work in the high schools and consolidated schools of the state. In September 1926, Pritchard began to develop a program that led to accreditation of the department by ALA in 1932.

Several theories were then current about the separate training of school librarians in a teachers' college; one was that all librarians should be trained together during the first year, then be given specialized instruction in a second year of work. In many colleges, courses in librarianship were given at the undergraduate level only. Pritchard felt strongly that a librarian must have a college degree and teaching experience and that "library training is a necessity." Her goal was realized when the group entering in 1936 consisted of graduate students with teaching or library experience. They took 36 hours of courses and did field work both in the Albany Public Library and in the College's Campus School library.

Pritchard wrote many professional articles. Two of these were included in Martha Wilson's *Selected Articles on School Library Experience* (H. W. Wilson, 1925): "The School Library, an Organ Vital to School Life" and "Pre-Vocational Course for High Schools." Other important articles were: "Recruiting for School Libraries" (*ALA Bulletin* 16:126-27 [1922]), "What Has Modern Education Done to Books?" (*Publishers' Weekly* 104:151-52 [1923]), "Instruction Problems in Libraries of Teacher-Training Institutions" (*Wilson Library Bulletin* 5:125-27 [1930]), and "The School Library Hour" (*Wilson Library Bulletin* 5:563-71 [1931]).

It is doubtful that any of her students realized she was such a pioneer in school library work. She was of average height, pleasingly plump, had unruly, fluffy white hair and blue eyes that sparkled behind her glasses when she was excited. A portrait may be found in the January 1, 1937, *Library Journal*, page 30.

To Pritchard's way of thinking, it was necessary that the library be as colorful and attractive as possible—more like a living room than a classroom. The librarian should be a host or hostess and on suitable occasions should have teas for teachers, parents, etc., as well as an occasional party for the student assistants. She reminded her students that they should never miss an opportunity to talk to parents about children's books and the importance of building home libraries. Before each graduation she gave a buffet supper in her apartment for the library department faculty, the graduating students, and the president of the College. At the conclusion, each student was given a copy of the "Librarian's Creed," and the entire group recited it in unison. At that moment, each student became a member of an ancient and honorable profession, proud of its heritage and anticipating his or her contribution to it in the future.

Pritchard knew each one of her students and followed their progress through the *Library School Alumni Letter* long after her retirement in 1941. On the twenty-fifth anniversary of the founding of the Library Department in 1951, the alumni founded a Martha Caroline Pritchard Scholarship for students desiring to become school librarians. Among the outstanding graduates of her school were Augusta Baker (New York Public Library children's librarian, author, speaker), Marcia Brown (author, illustrator), and Mary Helen Mahar (U.S. Office of Education).

The School Library Section of ALA invited her to attend the ALA Conference in San Francisco on July 3, 1947, to be honored as a member of the group of "Pioneer School Librarians." She attended and was given this citation:

> Martha Caroline Pritchard, friend, co-worker, and guide of many school librarians, for your understanding of the importance of the Normal School and Teachers College Library in school library development, for your early recognition of the possibilities of elementary school libraries, for your vision, accomplishments, and example in educating school librarians, the American Association of School Librarians honors you today and welcomes you as one of its honorary members.

After her retirement to Sierra Madre, California, Pritchard served for fifteen years as a member and secretary of the Sierra Madre Public Library Board of Trustees. A new library building was erected during that period, and the group called Friends of the Sierra Madre Public Library was organized on the initiative of the Library Board. On her retirement from the Board, she was made a life member and received a scroll of appreciation from the city council for her service to the city.

A lifelong member of Congregational churches, Martha C. Pritchard continued her devoted interest in church activities until her health failed. She died on February 3, 1959, at Sierra Madre, California.

Biographical listings and obituaries–[Obituary]. *Junior Libraries* 5:38 (May 1959); [Obituary]. *Library Journal* 84:1676 (May 15, 1959); [Obituary]. *Michigan Librarian* 25:34-35 (June 1959); *Who's Who in Library Service*, 1st ed. **Primary sources and archival materials**–The major source of personal correspondence, papers, etc., is the Archives, State University of New York at Albany.

—SUSAN SEABURY SMITH

PURDY, GEORGE FLINT (1905-1969)

George Flint Purdy was born September 2, 1905, in Mason City, Iowa, the son of George H. and Hattie Flint Purdy. Although the greater part of his life was to be spent in scholarly environments in the cities of New York, Chicago, and Detroit, he never repudiated or attempted to conceal his origins; on the contrary, he always maintained a strong emotional link to the

rural Iowa of his first 27 years. After attending public schools in Mason City, he went on to Iowa State Teachers' College and was graduated from there in 1925. During the next seven years, he taught and served as principal in public schools in Kelly and Calumet, Iowa. It was also during this period that he married Anna Breidinger, a fellow teacher.

The interest in and commitment to education established during these years was to continue throughout Purdy's life, but, in 1932, it was given a new focus when he entered the Columbia University School of Library Service in New York. Having secured his initial library degree from there in 1933, he accepted appointment as a research assistant at the University of Chicago Graduate Library School and began work on his Ph.D. During the course of his studies, he was also designated an American Library Association Fellow. In 1936, he was awarded his doctorate and, that same year, went to Detroit to head the library of the institution that during his tenure evolved into Wayne State University.

Purdy's appointment to Wayne in 1936 began a library career of service to his institution, his profession, and his community that lasted 33 years, until the very day of his death, September 26, 1969. In evidence of the unusual esteem in which he was held by the University, the main library building, which he planned and saw through to completion, now fittingly bears his name, and an award established in his honor is given annually to the librarian or faculty member who sustains Purdy's spiritual legacy by making an outstanding contribution to the University's library system.

Purdy's service to his profession at the national level is reflected in the variety of elective and appointive posts he held, including three terms on the ALA Council; long service as chairman of the Statistics Coordinating Committee; president of the Library Education Division of ALA in 1949-1950, and chairman of the Library Organization and Management Section of the Library Administration Division in 1969. He also served as chairman of the Board of Directors of the Center for Research Libraries in 1956-1957 (when it was known as the Midwest Inter-Library Corporation); and on the Board of Directors of the Association of Research Libraries, 1963-1967. And his ability to transmute his admittedly idealistic concept of library service into the tangible form of a library building caused him to be sought as a consultant in the planning of new academic libraries.

In his own state, he was elected president of the Michigan Library Association for the 1962-1963 term and also spent ten years as a member of the Michigan State Board for Libraries, serving as its chairman for two. While a member of the State Board, Flint Purdy was the major architect of a new legislative framework for Michigan public libraries, and for a state-wide, multi-type library network. This same concern for integrating the resources and services of all libraries in a kind of concentric regional pattern led him to direct the "Detroit Metropolitan Library Study," an intensive investigation of urban metropolitan library problems funded by the U.S. Office of Education in 1967-1969, the conclusions of which only began to be recognized some years after they were submitted.

Purdy's involvement and concern within his own academic community was no less. He taught occasional courses in library science at both the University of Illinois and Wayne State throughout his career; he was chairman of the editorial board of the Wayne State University Press from 1941 until his death; and he served a number of terms in the University's faculty senate.

This bare recital of offices and assignments does not give the true measure of the man, although it does indicate the range and direction of his concerns and the confidence and respect Purdy's peers and colleagues felt toward him. Notable as well was his ability to cause the clumsy and necessarily bureaucratic system he worked within to accept the ideals of librarianship and education. Purdy's ability to work for improvement and progress within the political realities of his environment was particularly manifested in his professional involvement in library affairs. His committee memberships and chairmanships showed a continuing concern with establishing norms and standards for library statistics, education, administration, and cooperation. These committee assignments, along with the many offices Purdy held in national, regional, and local library associations involved him in defining and confronting issues that could only be resolved in compromise, a resolution his intelligence and patience seldom failed to achieve.

Much of this work—deliberate, persistent, low-profile as it was—can be seen now to have been pioneer in conception and instrumental in shaping the present stature of the profession and its institutions. In an era when we seem to produce and consume statistics as naturally as we breathe, it is hard to comprehend that during the 1940s Purdy and a few colleagues struggled to convince librarians of the need for the regular reporting of standardized data, and even harder to believe that later they had to overcome some reluctance to allowing the federal government to collect and publish them. At a time when library interdependence is an accepted commonplace, it is startling to recall that in the 1950s Purdy was one of a small group of evangelists preaching the cause of the Midwest Inter-Library Corporation, now the firmly established Center for Research Libraries. And within his own institution, thirty years before the idea of faculty unions was accepted, he was already an active member and officer of a local American Federation of Teachers (AFT) chapter.

Flint Purdy belonged to that fortunate generation of librarians who practiced during what, in retrospect, is seen to have been the expansive era of higher education, and who could find room for growing talents and aspirations in a steadily enlarging environment. Like so many of that generation, he was firmly within the humanist tradition and never strayed far from that commitment either in his administrative tactics or in his relations with peers and colleagues and with those he encountered beyond the limits of the professional and academic world. If his identity tended to be submerged in the results of the communal projects he was associated with, his presence was always felt by his colleagues. He was a man who was serious of purpose but not solemn; persistent without nagging; forceful, yet not domineering; always a comfortable and productive person to work with, and, when occasion presented itself, a convivial companion. Even though intangible, these traits were imprinted to some degree on those who encountered him in the course of his career, and it is fair to say that Purdy's mark on his profession can best be measured in terms of his influence on people, especially on a following professional generation.

Biographical listings and obituaries—[Obituary]. *Library Journal* 95:119 (Jan. 15, 1970); [Obituary]. *Wilson Library Bulletin* 44:367 (Dec. 1969); *Who Was Who in America* V (1969-1973); *Who's Who in Library Service*, 2nd ed., 3rd ed., 4th ed. Primary sources and archival materials—Personnel and other records and files are at Wayne State University, Detroit.

—HOWARD A. SULLIVAN

PUTNAM, GEORGE HERBERT (1861-1955)

Herbert Putnam, librarian of the Minneapolis Athenaeum (1884-1887), the Minneapolis Public Library (1887-1891), the Boston Public Library (1895-1899), and Librarian of Congress (1899-1939), never served in a subordinate library position. He was always the chief librarian; moreover, he was so successful that each of the libraries he served now looks back to the Putnam administration as a crucial period in the shaping of the modern institution. While Putnam's best-known and most significant achievements took place at the Library of Congress, he was also a dominant figure in the American library movement—especially during the first half of his 40-year term as Librarian of Congress.

George Herbert Putnam was born in New York City on September 20, 1861. He was the sixth son and tenth child of George Palmer Putnam, founder of the Putnam publishing house, and Victorine Palmer Putnam. When Herbert was eleven years old, his father died, and an older brother, George Haven Putnam, assumed management of the family firm.

Young Herbert attended the private English and Classical School conducted by James H. Morse on upper Broadway. He entered Harvard in 1879, won several academic prizes, and received his B.A. in 1883, graduating *magna cum laude* and a member of Phi Beta Kappa. For the next year, Putnam attended Columbia University Law School, but then his friend and Harvard classmate Samuel Hill enticed him to Minneapolis and librarianship. Hill, a young and prosperous Minneapolis attorney, offered Putnam the job of librarian of the Minneapolis Athenaeum. Putnam decided to accept (and to pursue his legal studies independently), and the new librarian of the Minneapolis Athenaeum assumed his duties in October 1884.

Despite his lack of technical library training, Putnam responded quickly to the many problems facing the Athenaeum, modernizing its "antiquated methods," beginning a new cataloging system, and "opening up the alcoves to readers." In an account of Putnam's Minneapolis days, published in *Essays Offered to Herbert Putnam* (1929), Gratia A. Countryman (q.v.) notes that "not only were his methods new and thoroughgoing, but his courteous, genial manner created a new atmosphere." The librarian also continued his legal studies and was admitted to the Minnesota bar in 1885. On October 5, 1886, he married Charlotte Elizabeth Munroe of Cambridge, Massachusetts. They had two daughters, Shirley and Brenda.

Putnam worked toward the establishment of a public library in Minneapolis, and the city council authorized such an institution in 1885. It was agreed to merge the Athenaeum with the new Public Library and, in 1887, Putnam became librarian of the new Minneapolis Public Library, which was formally opened on December 16, 1889. Two years later, the serious illness of Mrs. Putnam's mother forced the Putnams to leave Minneapolis and settle in Massachusetts; his resignation was effective December 31, 1891. Under Putnam's leadership, the Minneapolis Public Library was off to a successful start; in 1939, a history of the institution stated that "the pattern for the development of the Library's services which Putnam laid out has been in large measure followed by his successors."

In 1892, Putnam was admitted to the Massachusetts bar, and, for the next three years, he practiced law with a Boston firm. A visit from Josiah Henry Benton, one of Boston's leading citizens and a trustee of the Boston Public Library, persuaded Putnam to return to librarianship. There had been "no solicitation nor appearance of candidacy" on Putnam's part, but on February 11, 1895, at the age of 33, he assumed the librarianship of the Boston Public Library, the largest public library in the United States. Moreover, only a few days earlier, the Boston Public

Library had moved into its magnificent new building on Copley Square. At the end of his first year, the Library trustees noted that the new librarian "has proved to be most competent and faithful in the discharge of his duties, which have been unusually difficult and trying."

Putnam's new position also propelled him into the activities of the American Library Association. In late 1896, along with several other librarians, most notably Melvil Dewey (q.v.), he represented the ALA at congressional hearings concerning the needs of the Library of Congress, its potential role as a national library, and the qualifications of its Librarian. The next year, he joined Dewey and Justin Winsor (q.v.) as the accredited American delegates to the International Conference of Librarians in London. In 1898, he became ALA president, filling out the unexpired term of the recently deceased Winsor; he occupied the same post in 1904.

In the 1896 hearings about the Library of Congress, Putnam advocated an expansion of the Library's national role once it occupied its spacious new building, and he also argued in favor of independence for the Librarian of Congress in administrative matters. Asked by the chairman of the Library Committee to define "library science," the Boston lawyer-librarian described it as consisting of

a certain knowledge of bibliography, of the process of book making, of the historical production of books, of the essentials which govern the cataloging of a book—making the book more useful after you have received it—of the questions of administration that enter into the mediation between the books and the readers—the reference use of the library.

On January 17, 1899, Librarian of Congress John Russell Young (q.v.) died, and Herbert Putnam was the ALA candidate to become his successor. The argument, as stated by ALA president William Coolidge Lane (q.v.), was that the Library of Congress should be directed by an experienced library administrator. Lane and his friends performed the herculean task of persuading not only President McKinley, but apparently also Putnam himself, of the wisdom of the appointment. After three months of political maneuvering, on April 5, 1899, Herbert Putnam became the eighth Librarian of Congress and took command of the largest library in the United States.

Putnam wasted little time in expanding the Library of Congress into the type of national library envisioned in his 1896 testimony before the Joint Committee of the Library. Ainsworth Rand Spofford (q.v.), Librarian of Congress from 1865 to 1897, had developed the Library's comprehensive Americana collections and provided Putnam with a monumental new building. While Spofford created a tradition of public service, Putnam established a systematic program of widespread service. In this effort, he had the full support of Congress, from whom Putnam expected and received generous annual appropriations. Putnam felt that a national library, rather than serving solely as a great national accumulation of books, should also actively serve other libraries. He succeeded in spectacular fashion, for within three years after he had taken office, the Library of Congress was the leader among American libraries. Putnam's philosophy was expressed in a July 1901 speech at the annual ALA meeting, held in Waukesha, Wisconsin: "If there is any way in which our National Library may 'reach out' from Washington, it should reach out."

Putnam's actions in 1901 were imaginative and decisive and were approved by both the Joint Library Committee and the professional library community. In that year, the first volume of a completely new classification scheme, based on the Library's own collections, was published; access to the Library was extended to "scientific investigators and duly qualified individuals" throughout the United States; an interlibrary loan system was inaugurated; the sale and distribution of Library of Congress printed cards began; the equivalent of a national union catalog was started; and finally, appended to his 1901 annual report was a 200-page "manual" describing the organization, facilities, collections, and operations of the Library, a description that set high standards for all other libraries. The 1901 annual report includes a full description of the new printed card service, an undertaking that had momentous impact on American library development in future years.

Recognized as a library "expert," Putnam enlisted the support of Congress and of Presidents in the expansion of the Library's collections and services. In a long letter to President Theodore Roosevelt on October 15, 1901, he explained:

A national library for the United States should mean in some respects much more than a national library in any other country has hitherto meant. . . . [The public libraries of the United States] look to the National Library for standards, for example, for leadership. It is now in a position to "standardize" library methods, to promote cooperation, to aid in the elimination of wasteful duplication, and to promote interchange of bibliographic service.

Thus prompted, in his first annual message to Congress, on December 3, 1901, Roosevelt called the Library of Congress "the one national library of the United States" and asked for additional congressional support for its activities. Roosevelt supported Putnam by deed as well. On March 9, 1903, for example, he approved an Executive Order that directed the

transfer of the records and papers of the Continental Congress and the personal papers of Washington, Madison, Monroe, Hamilton, and Franklin from the State Department to the Library of Congress. In 1905-1906, Putnam called and presided over the conference that led to the 1909 revision of the American copyright laws. In 1907, with remarkable foresight, he established the foundations of the Library's Slavic and Oriental collections through the acquisition of huge collections of Russian and Japanese books.

The Progressive Era was the age of efficiency and the scientific use of knowledge, and Putnam's establishment of a separate Legislative Reference Service at the Library of Congress was a direct result of the Progressive movement. The reference unit was created in 1914, and the next year, its functions were broadened in accordance with new language in the appropriations act: "to gather, classify, and make available in translations, indexes, digests, compilations, and bulletins, and otherwise, data for or bearing upon legislation, and to render such data available to Congress and committees and Members thereof."

During the next two decades, Putnam continued to expand the Library's national roles, through: 1) direction of the ALA's Library War Service Committee (1917-1919), which was headquartered at the Library; 2) establishment of the Library of Congress Trust Fund Board (1925), which enabled the Library to accept, hold, and invest gifts and bequests; 3) further development of the Library as a center for research and scholarship, largely through the creation of a series of "chairs" and consultantships for subject specialists; 4) the evolution of the Library as a national patron of the arts, due primarily to generous endowments enabling it to promote chamber music; 5) enhancement of the Library as a symbol of American democracy, a function that received widespread publicity when the Declaration of Independence and the Constitution were transferred to the Library in 1921.

When Herbert Putnam became Librarian in 1899, the Library's collection numbered approximately 900,000 volumes and the staff totalled 230. Forty years later, when Putnam retired and Archibald MacLeish assumed the post, the collection totalled over six million volumes and the staff numbered 1,300. Putnam's most significant achievement was described in a statement presented to him in 1939 by the American Council of Learned Societies "on behalf of the scholars of the United States":

For you, and the collaborators and associates whom you have chosen, have made the Library of Congress a national institution, the peer in all respects of its great prototypes, the British Museum and the Bibliotheque Nationale. You have made of it an indispensable instrument on the American continent for the promotion of learning and the increase of knowledge. Under your guidance it has exerted a profound and lasting influence upon libraries throughout the world.

Another indication of the esteem enjoyed by Putnam in the academic world is the list of his honorary degrees. In 1898, he received an honorary Litt.D. from Bowdoin College. In later years, he was awarded the same degree from Brown University (1914) and Princeton (1933). The honorary LL.D. was given him by Columbian [now George Washington] University (1903), the University of Illinois (1903), the University of Wisconsin (1904), Yale (1907), Williams (1911), Harvard (1929), and New York University (1930).

When Putnam retired and, on October 1, 1939, became Librarian Emeritus of Congress, his friends in the American Library Association paid him tribute:

Herbert Putnam is recognized and acknowledged by us all as the dean of our profession. . . . With rare skill, tact, and wisdom, Dr. Putnam has, over a period of two-score years, developed the Library of Congress from an establishment of only government significance to its present proud position as the world's largest bibliographical institution.

The Librarian Emeritus actively contributed to the Library of Congress until his death sixteen years later. In 1954, he told a *Washington Post* reporter who interviewed him on the fifty-fifth anniversary of his becoming Librarian of Congress that, at age 92, he still "gets up at 6 a.m., prepares his own breakfast, takes a trolley to Capitol Hill, maintains regular office hours, handles his mail, receives numerous visitors, and is available for consultation." While vacationing on Cape Cod in 1955, he fell and broke his hip; in the process of recovering, on August 14, 1955, at Woods Hole, Massachusetts, Herbert Putnam died of a coronary thrombosis.

Herbert Putnam was energetic, confident, and meticulous. David C. Mearns, in his memorial tribute (1956), evokes the image of the Librarian in his prime: "a little, red-headed man, in a high-backed chair, pipe in mouth, feet on hassock, brows arched, brown eyes flashing, mustachios bristling, and hands—those graceful, sophisticated, constantly moving hands—waving as he dictates to his secretary." Mearns also notes that Putnam was patrician to the point that some held "he was aloof, remote, detached, insensitive to his surroundings, disdainful of the petty preoccupations of lesser men." Apparently no associate at the Library of Congress ever called Putnam by his given name, and the Librarian's personal emotions were always indiscernible. Putnam was stern. He expected the highest standards of personal and professional conduct and frequently exercised his dismissal powers "for the good of the

service." Mearns notes that "to the staff, Herbert Putnam bore a relationship of the Great White Father to the aborigines of North America. He was venerated. He was endowed with extraordinary gifts." And "the staff's pride in him was inordinate":

pride in his urbanity, suavity, courage, understanding, prescience. There was pride in his wit; in his intellectual gaiety and exuberance. There was pride in his attraction for the learned men who sat at his Round Table in the Library's attic, or who hovered about his place at the Cosmos Club. There was pride in his eloquence, his idiom, the faultless style of his compositions. There was pride in his punctilio, in his sense of fitness and unfitness, in a tradition which first he made and then he served.

Herbert Putnam firmly convinced Congress that the Library of Congress was an institution worthy of generous support. He also gained the confidence of the American scholarly community and, at the same time, satisfied the demands of the professional library community. From the standpoint of the Library of Congress as an institution, this is Putnam's most lasting achievement: he established and defined a pattern of service to three divergent constituencies—Congress, scholars, and the professional librarians.

Putnam's last decade was not as fruitful or successful as those preceding it; the Annex building was completed, but Putnam insisted on maintaining personal control over all of the Library's diverse units, and the Library's effectiveness was thus impaired. As a result, a certain degree of administrative stagnation developed, as well as practical problems concerning cataloging backlogs and staff salaries and benefits. The principal accomplishment of Putnam's successor, Archibald MacLeish, was a thorough administrative reorganization of the Library. MacLeish's description of the Library of Congress as he came to it is a mixture of admiration and despair:

The Library of Congress in 1939 was not so much an organization in its own right as the lengthened shadow of a man—a man of great force, extraordinary abilities, and a personality which left its fortunate impress upon everything he touched. Only a man of Herbert Putnam's remarkable qualities could have administered an institution of the size of the Library of Congress by direct and personal supervision of all its operations, and only if his administration were based upon the intimate familiarities of forty years. . . . The principal difficulty with the old Library, from my point of view as the unexpected and unexpectant heir, was the fact that the whole fabric depended from the Librarian as the miraculous architecture of the paper wasp hangs from a single anchor.

Herbert Putnam considered library administration a full-time job and subordinated his personal life to the institution he served. In the interest of the

Library of Congress, he let it be known that he "avoided association with outside enterprises not directly contributing to it and reduced merely social relations to a minimum." He once expressed his "urgent concern that the personality to be considered significant is the personality of the institution itself, of which the staff, including myself, are merely components."

Putnam frequently addressed library groups and has many articles to his credit but, as J. Christian Bay (q.v.) has pointed out, he "left an inheritance of action rather than authorship." Putnam always declined to reminisce or to write his memoirs, declaring that his annual reports as Librarian of Congress contained everything that was worth preserving. In this sense, the autobiography of Herbert Putnam is found in the forty annual reports of the Librarian of Congress between 1899 and 1939.

Biographical listings and obituaries—Bay, J. Christian. "Herbert Putnam, 1861-1955." *Libri* 33:200-207 (1956); *Herbert Putnam, 1861-1955: A Memorial Tribute*. Washington, D.C.: The Library of Congress, 1956; *Who Was Who in America* III (1951-1960); *Who's Who in Library Service*, 1st ed., 2nd ed. Books and articles about the biographee—Mearns, David C. "Herbert Putnam: Librarian of the United States." In *An American Library History Reader*, selected by John David Marshall. Hamden, Conn.: The Shoe String Press, 1961, pp. 362-410; Solberg, Thorvald. "A Chapter in the Unwritten History of the Library of Congress: The Appointment of Herbert Putnam as Librarian." *Library Quarterly* 9:285-98 (July 1939). Primary sources and archival materials—*Essays Offered to Herbert Putnam by His Colleagues and Friends on His Thirtieth Anniversary as Librarian of Congress, 5 April 1929*. William Warner Bishop and Andrew Keogh, eds. New Haven: Yale University Press, 1929. Herbert Putnam's personal papers are in the Manuscript Division of the Library of Congress. His official correspondence is in the Library of Congress Archives.

—JOHN Y. COLE

QUIGLEY, MARGERY CLOSEY (1886-1968)

Margery Closey Quigley—author, teacher, and director of the Montclair Public Library for 29 years—was born in Los Angeles, on September 16, 1886, the daughter of Cyrus Edwards and Elizabeth Bryant Quigley. When she was twelve, her family moved to Alton, Illinois, just across the Mississippi River from St. Louis. There she attended experimental schools that undoubtedly helped to shape the progressive spirit characteristic of her later library career.

After graduation from Vassar College in 1908 (A.B.), Quigley began her library career in the St. Louis Public Library, where she served in 1909 and 1910 as an assistant in the Circulation and Stations Department and from 1911 to 1918 as a branch librarian. She served briefly, under the auspices of the American Library Association, at the base hospital library at Fort Riley, Kansas, before becoming chief librarian of the Endicott, New York,

Public Library in 1918. During her tenure at Endicott, Quigley attended the New York State Library School at Albany, which awarded her a Class A Librarian lifetime certificate in 1923. In 1924-1925, she served as president of the New York Library Association. At Endicott she met Mary E. Clark, who was to become her closest friend, her assistant director for the major portion of her long tenure at Montclair, and the collaborator with whom, under the pseudonym "Margery Clark" she published several books for children, including *Cook's Surprise* (1923) and *Poppy Seed Cakes* (1924).

From 1925 to 1927, Quigley served as branch librarian at the new Mount Pleasant Branch of the Washington, D.C., Public Library. Frederic G. Melcher (q.v.), then editor of *Publishers' Weekly* and a trustee of the Montclair Public Library, had observed her at ALA and other professional meetings. In 1927, he was instrumental in recruiting her as director of the Montclair Public Library.

During the three decades of her directorship at Montclair, from June 1, 1927, to October 1, 1956, Margery Quigley committed her extraordinary energies, plus a rare combination of idealism and pragmatism, to converting the Montclair Public Library into an institution of such excellence and dynamism that its example served to alter the very concept of a suburban library's role. While setting the highest standards of quality for the book collections and traditional library services, she introduced a spirit of experimentation that was to become the trademark of the Montclair Public Library. A home delivery service, using the facilities of Western Union, was begun in 1933. In 1938, she initiated a staff exchange program with foreign libraries. In 1940, she eliminated all overdue fines on children's books.

In addition to providing quality service and innovative programs, Quigley was also interested in improving the internal operations and working conditions of the Library. She frequently solicited the cooperation of Dr. Lillian Gilbreth, a famous time-and-motion expert and a trustee of the Library, in analyzing routines and work flows. With William Elder Marcus, Jr., then president of the Board of Trustees, she wrote *Portrait of a Library* (1936), which dealt with the development and administration of small and medium-sized public libraries. The book was well received and led, in 1940, to foundation support and the services of the internationally known filmmaker Hans Burger to produce the documentary film *Portrait of a Library*. This was distributed by the Museum of Modern Art and was shown throughout the world under the auspices of the U.S. Department of State. The book was especially influential in indicating how to handle the often difficult problem of the administrative relationships of the board of trustees to the librarian, library staff, and local government. It also indicated that a public library of that size could develop well-formulated personnel policies and programs.

Perhaps Quigley's best-known innovation was her work in designing electronic data processing techniques to be applied to library circulation and inventory procedures. She persuaded the International Business Machines Corporation not only to construct a library data processing system but also to build a laboratory annex to the Library in which experiments in the use of the system could be carried out. The work and the operation of the system were described in her article "Ten Years of IBM" (*Library Journal* 77:1152-57 [July 1952]). That system was the first example of the use of data processing equipment for circulation control in a public library, and it attracted much attention. Its ability to generate statistics resulted in substantial contributions to Bernard Berelson's *The Library's Public* and Watson Pierce's *Work Measurement in Public Libraries*. Since the system was supported by IBM as an experiment, its costs were never fully assessed; but IBM never fully pursued the idea. The result was that it was not copied elsewhere, had little effect on the development of library automation, and serves only as an interesting historical footnote.

Many years of effort finally brought, in 1955, the completion of a new main library building that was widely hailed for its pioneering architectural and functional innovations.

At the time of Quigley's death on April 17, 1968, Allan Angoff, editor of *Teaneck Points of Reference*, wrote that under her leadership "Montclair's public library was for years the most famous in New Jersey and the best known American suburban library in the world."

Margery Quigley's missionary zeal for librarianship was responsible for what she sometimes referred to as a parallel career. For more than twenty years, she taught "library publicity" at the Columbia University School of Library Service. She also taught that subject at various times in the library schools at Albany, Missouri, Pratt, and Rutgers. In addition, she wrote widely for mass circulation magazines as well as for professional journals. *Readers' Guide* and *Library Literature* cite over fifty of her articles.

Quigley was always active in state and national library activities. In the late 1930s and early 1940s, she was especially active in the American Library Association. She served on the Executive Board and as a member of the Council from 1935 to 1939 and ran unsuccessfully for the Council in 1942. During that same period, she served as well on a range of committees that indicate some of her varied interests: Annuities and Pensions; Conferences; Refugee Librarians; the Subcommittee on Library School Curricula of the Adult Education Board; Committee

Appointments; Nursing School Library; the Program Committee of the Adult Education Round Table; the Publicity Clinic; Cooperation with Commercial Organizations; the Subcommittee on Job Evaluation and Training of the Board of Education for Librarianship; the Board on Personnel Administration; and the Committee on Library Administration. In 1935, she was named as ALA's official representative to the World Federation of Education Associations meetings at Oxford and, in 1937, as one of the U.S. delegates to the World Congress of Universal Documentation in Paris.

In 1945, the New Jersey College of Women at Rutgers University awarded Margery C. Quigley an honorary Master of Arts degree for "her outstanding contributions to librarianship." Over her long career, especially at Montclair, Margery Quigley helped to shape in many significant ways the growth and development of public library service in the emerging American suburban community, and her work at Montclair often served as a model for other similar communities.

Biographical listings and obituaries—*American Women* II (1937-1938), III (1939-1940); [Obituary]. *Library Journal* 93:1961 (May 15, 1968); [Obituary]. *Montclair Times* 92:8 (April 18, 1968); [Obituary]. *New York Times* 117:47 (April 18, 1968); [Obituary]. *Wilson Library Bulletin* 42:875 (May 1968); *Who's Who in Library Service*, 1st ed., 2nd ed., 3rd ed.; *Who's Who in the East* I (1942-1943), II (1948). **Books and articles about the biographee**—Angoff, Allan. "Margery Quigley 1886-1968." *Teaneck Points of Reference* 3:3, 7-8 (May 1968); [Biographical article]. *Montclair Times* 80:1 (April 5, 1956); [Biographical article]. *Suburban Life* 16:36-39 (April 1946); Curley, Arthur. "Montclair Free Public Library." *Encyclopedia of Library and Information Science*. Allen Kent, Harold Lancour, and Jay E. Daily, eds. New York: Marcel Dekker, 1976. Vol. 18; Rebadavia, Consolacion. *Margery Closey Quigley: A Bibliography*. Montclair, N.J.: The Montclair Public Library, 1961. **Primary sources and archival materials**—Official files and records of the Montclair Public Library, Montclair, New Jersey (1927-1956).

—ARTHUR CURLEY

RANEY, McKENDREE LLEWELLYN (1877-1964)

M. Llewellyn Raney (he seldom used his first name) was born at Stanford, Kentucky, on February 28, 1877, the son of William Gabriel and Anne Josephine Jones Raney. At the age of twenty he received his B.A. from Centre College at Danville, Kentucky (1897). Thirty years later, his *alma mater* conferred upon him the honorary LL.D.

Like his contemporary William Warner Bishop (q.v.), Raney began his career as a teacher of Latin and Greek. First he taught at Centre College and then at Hogsett Military Academy, which was also located at Danville. Convinced that he needed graduate training, he enrolled at Johns Hopkins University, where he was a fellow in Greek from 1901 to 1903. In

1904, he received the degree of Doctor of Philosophy with a dissertation on "Case-Regimen of the Verbs of Hearing in Classical Greek from Homer to Demosthenes," reflecting the influence of one of his advisers, the great classical scholar Basil L. Gildersleeve. Raney was also elected to Phi Beta Kappa. Meanwhile, in 1903, he had married Catherine Placide Coulehan, with whom he enjoyed a marriage of more than sixty years. They had two children: a son, Llewellyn, and a daughter, Ruth.

In the same year as his marriage, an event occurred that was to determine the future course of Raney's career; Johns Hopkins' President Ira Remsen named him as assistant librarian to aid librarian Nicholas Murray in the administration of the growing library. Library schools were still an uncertain experiment, and Johns Hopkins University followed the prevailing academic practice of appointing a teaching member of the faculty as part-time librarian. However, on Murray's retirement five years later, Raney was promoted first to acting librarian, and then to librarian. His appointment was made on the recommendation of a faculty committee, and throughout his tenure Raney worked closely with the faculty.

For several years, Johns Hopkins had been struggling in cramped quarters in several buildings in downtown Baltimore. Library facilities were especially inadequate, and the situation was exacerbated by a fire in the same year that Raney became librarian. However, shortly afterward, President Remsen acquired the site for a new campus at Homewood in suburban Baltimore, and the library was assigned space in the greater part of Gilman Hall, the first building projected for the new campus. In cooperation with the University architect, Douglas Thomas, Raney was assigned the responsibility of designing a library that would house several hundred thousand volumes and yet preserve the intimacy of departmental libraries. With this in mind, Raney rejected the multitier steel stack, which had become almost universally popular with all libraries. Instead, he undertook to plan what he described as the first library apartment house. Gilman Hall Library was laid out in the form of a hollow square, with bookstacks on the inside, offices and seminar rooms on the outside, and a corridor between them. Books in the various subjects were shelved immediately opposite the departments concerned with them, with unusually generous working space provided for students in the bookstacks. As a result, students in a specific field, the books they needed, their professors, and their seminar rooms were grouped together to form an "apartment" on each floor. Closed stacks were eliminated, and the building was controlled at a single point. The plans of Raney and Thomas were approved, Gilman Hall was constructed during 1912-1914, and the Library moved into its new

expanded quarters in 1916. The significance of Raney's plan was that Gilman Hall became one of the first modular libraries—an idea more fully developed by Angus Snead Macdonald (q.v.) thirty years later.

Prior to the move to Gilman Hall, Raney made two important internal reforms in the Library. Following the publication of a code of cataloging rules in 1908, the old catalog entries were replaced by new typewritten headings on standard size cards. The other significant change was the adoption of the Library of Congress Classification in 1911, making the Library at Johns Hopkins one of the first academic libraries to adopt the new system.

In addition to Phi Beta Kappa, Raney maintained his professional and scholarly interests through memberships in the American Library Association and the Bibliographical Society of America. Following the entry of the United States into World War I, Raney was named the first spokesman for ALA overseas. After a survey of the field, his plan of book service to the armed forces of the nation on both land and sea was presented in person to General Pershing and Admiral Sims. It was accepted immediately, and proper tonnage was assigned. Later, Raney was assigned by the Department of State and the War Trade and Censorship Boards, on behalf of ALA, the task of arranging for educational institutions in America to receive appropriate enemy publications. His plan was also accepted by the British and French governments when presented at their foreign offices, and Raney was named director of ALA Overseas Service as part of ALA Library War Service. So successfully did this tonnage move, under government seal and his management, that, during the armistice, Raney was given complete power to examine shipments impounded in foreign harbors and admit or exclude them, according to his judgment. For this work, he received high praise in Washington. It is due to Raney's efforts in his wartime position that American universities owe the continuity of their German periodical files during this period (1917-1919).

After the war, Raney was chairman of the ALA Book Buying Committee for nine years (1920-1929). During the 1920s, he worked for the defeat of reactionary tariff legislation affecting book importations and libraries. Also during this decade, he inaugurated a long campaign to ward off attacks on the public's copyright privileges while endeavoring to have the United States qualify for membership in the International Copyright Union. Unfortunately, his efforts toward copyright reform yielded few results, and the controversy continued until the passage of a new copyright law in 1977.

In October 1927, Raney left Johns Hopkins to become the first full-time director of University Libraries at the University of Chicago. Like Johns Hopkins, Chicago had achieved a reputation as a pioneering university, emphasizing graduate study and research. Again, Raney's appointment was made on the strong recommendation of a faculty committee. At Chicago, Raney continued his policy of working in close cooperation with the faculty, availing himself not only of the Library Board, but also of a number of advisory committees. An outstanding example of this cooperation occurred in 1933, when Raney was asked to make a survey of the entire library collection as part of a survey of the University. Some two hundred teaching faculty joined the library staff in evaluating the University of Chicago collections, calling attention to deficiencies and pointing out directions for future growth. According to Guy R. Lyle, this survey was a pioneer in developing bibliographic checklists and procedures for ascertaining the periodical literature fundamental to each discipline.

At Chicago, Raney inaugurated two long-range policies. Under President William Rainey Harper, the creation of departmental libraries had been carried to an extreme, resulting in extensive duplication of reference materials and considerable inconvenience for students working in interdisciplinary areas. This situation had continued under the first director of libraries, Professor Ernest D. Burton, and the associate director, J. C. M. Hanson (q.v.). Meanwhile, Harper Memorial Library, which was opened in 1910 as the main library and general reference collection, had become badly overcrowded. Raney undertook to consolidate gradually many of the smaller departmental libraries into larger units, corresponding with the major divisions of the University curriculum. The Education, Lincoln, and Modern Poetry Libraries, which were planned and opened during Raney's administration, followed his concept of the library as an apartment house. Raney's ultimate ambition was a new, functional library building similar to Gilman Hall, which would incorporate most of the remaining departmental libraries and replace Harper as the central collection. Unfortunately, the long Depression of the 1930s put a halt to any major building construction, and the new central library building did not materialize until the Regenstein Library was opened in the 1970s. While working to centralize the Library, Raney worked hard to build up the total collection as well, which at his retirement amounted to more than one million volumes. At the same time, he did not neglect quality. One of his notable acquisitions was the private library of the great Lincoln collector and scholar, William E. Barton. The addresses delivered by Raney, Lloyd Lewis, Carl Sandburg, and William E. Dodd on this occasion were published under the title *If Lincoln Had Lived* (University of Chicago Press, 1935).

The second long-range policy that Raney introduced was the addition of subject specialists to the Library staff. Under Hanson, the catalog department at Chicago had reached a high degree of perfection. Without disparaging the importance of card catalogs and classification schemes as reference tools, Raney was convinced that equal reliance should be placed on subject specialists and bibliographers. Librarians already on the staff were encouraged to develop their own subject interests, and in some cases, members of the faculty were persuaded to shift from teaching to the Library staff. In other cases, subject specialists were brought in from the outside. Among the latter was Augustus F. Kuhlman, who had already won recognition as a sociologist before he served as Raney's associate director from 1929 to 1936.

However, the achievement for which Raney is best remembered is his introduction of microphotography to the library profession on a large scale. Before 1935, Harvard, Yale, the New York Public Library, and a few other libraries had experimented with microphotography (which originally meant only microfilms) on a small scale. Raney became impressed with the potential of this ingenious form for increasing resources for research, especially with its great economy of shelf space, while on a visit to eastern libraries in the autumn of 1935. Upon his return to Chicago, he prepared an exhibit of microfilms and microfilm projectors for the ALA midwinter meeting. This exhibit was followed by an all-day symposium conducted by the leaders in the field. With Raney as editor, the papers presented at this symposium were published by the Association under the title *Microphotography in Libraries* (1936). A second microphotography exhibit was held at the Richmond conference in 1936. At the same conference, the Committee on Photographic Reproduction of Library Materials was established, with Raney as chairman. During the autumn of the same year, the Rockefeller Foundation made a grant to the University of Chicago to equip a laboratory adequate to produce microfilms of a high quality and to demonstrate the value of such materials when made in quantity for more than one library.

Meanwhile, the American Committee on Intellectual Cooperation received an invitation to participate in the Paris International Exposition in 1937. The Committee decided to demonstrate the possibilities of microphotography as a means of promoting international intellectual cooperation. The ALA and the University of Chicago were asked to serve as joint sponsors of the exhibit, under Raney's direction. Another grant was made by the Rockefeller Foundation for the demonstration, which was held in the spring of 1937. A highlight was the filming of considerable parts of thirty files of periodicals from the period of the French Revolution; previously, these had not been available in American libraries.

As chairman of the Committee on Photographic Reproduction, Raney arranged a second symposium and an exhibit of equipment for the ALA 1937 conference in New York. The proceedings of this meeting were also edited by him and published. Another exhibit was held at the San Francisco Conference of 1939. The *Journal of Documentary Reproduction*, which began publication shortly afterward, was the logical successor to the two earlier publications.

Raney was also responsible for arranging an exhibit of microphotographic materials for the Tenth International Conference of Chemistry in Rome (1938), and for the provision of American papers for the sessions of the International Federation for Documentation at Oxford (1938) and at Zürich (1939). He extended further the range of his interests in the field through an exhibit and a paper before the Inter-American Bibliographical and Library Association at its 1940 meeting in Washington, as well as through numerous articles in professional journals. When Raney retired from Chicago in 1942, he had the satisfaction of knowing that in seven years (1935-1942), he had transformed a little-known activity into the technical highlight of the library profession. In both editions of their landmark book, *The University Library*, Louis Round Wilson and Maurice F. Tauber paid Raney a well-deserved tribute when they hailed him as the man responsible for the "dramatization of library interest in the development of microphotography."

In his last years at Chicago, Raney undertook on behalf of the Association of Research Libraries an exhaustive study of the H. W. Wilson [q.v.] Company's scale pricing system (1941). As a trustee of *Biological Abstracts* from 1938 to 1943, he helped save that valuable reference publication from suspension. Also, he became increasingly involved in controversies within ALA. In 1939, he was one of the few librarians who supported President Franklin D. Roosevelt's nomination of Archibald MacLeish as Librarian of Congress. This placed him in direct opposition to the official position of the Association. Moreover, throughout his career, Raney was critical of library schools as training grounds for future librarians. Pointing to his own experience as an illustration, Raney maintained that the best preparation for a future librarian was for a man or woman to obtain a graduate degree in one of the "basic disciplines"; then, upon reaching a fork in the road, he (or she) could decide whether to move into library administration and research or become a teacher. His convictions led him to decline the position of dean of the newly established Graduate Library School at Chicago. He continued to maintain a critical attitude toward the School, despite the conciliatory approach of Louis Round Wilson, who became the dean in

1932. However, Raney was willing to employ on his staff library school graduates whom he considered exceptionally well qualified or who had strong backgrounds in subject fields. Winifred VerNooy, a graduate of the New York State Library School who had joined Chicago's Library staff under Burton, stayed on with Raney to achieve an outstanding reputation as a reference librarian. Herman H. Fussler, a graduate of the University of North Carolina Library School, was appointed the first head of the Department of Photographic Reproduction (1936). Later, he advanced through the ranks to attain Raney's position of director of libraries (1948). Librarians whom Raney admired were Clement Walker Andrews (q.v.) at the John Crerar Library, who had been a chemist, and his friend Nathan Van Patten (q.v.) at Stanford University, who had a strong background in science and metallurgy.

Raney was a forthright, outspoken man who made no effort to conceal his views, no matter how unpopular they might be with his fellow librarians. His friend Theodore Wesley Koch (q.v.), at Northwestern University, described him as a man dominated by one idea at a time. However, this could be construed as a compliment. Once Raney seized upon a project and satisfied himself of its worth, he pursued it relentlessly. Along similar lines, his former associate director, A. F. Kuhlman, wrote in 1942:

Because of his complete absorption in the things he lived and fought for, few people really know him. Only his intimate friends have an appreciation of his true greatness: his keen and well disciplined mind, his appreciation of fine poetry, his great capacity for friendship, patience, charity and his complete devotion to the life of the spirit.

Raney retired as director of libraries at Chicago on October 1, 1942, and was succeeded by Ralph A. Beals (q.v.). Already the manpower draft and other wartime stringencies were being felt in the Chicago libraries in the months following the attack on Pearl Harbor. At that time, Kuhlman wrote:

It seems unthinkable that a man with the vitality and ability that Dr. Raney still possesses should retire now, in a world in which there is so much to be done in the realm in which he is so competent. Let us hope that he will be permitted to explore new frontiers, to initiate new movements and to contribute sane ideas and sound principles toward the solution of some of our perplexing library problems.

However, the remaining 22 years of Raney's life followed a placid course, in contrast to his earlier controversial positions. Following his retirement, Raney returned to Baltimore, where he and Mrs. Raney made their home. On December 20, 1944, he wrote a letter to President Roosevelt, recommending the appointment of Julian Boyd of

Princeton University to succeed MacLeish as Librarian of Congress. Otherwise, Raney's life in retirement was uneventful, and his death on March 26, 1964, at the age of 87, was virtually unnoticed in library publications. In view of his contributions as a pioneer in modular library planning and in library self-surveys, in planning book service to the armed forces in World War I, in preserving the continuity of receipt of German and other foreign publications during the same period, and as the foremost promoter of micro-photography for libraries, he has been strangely neglected by library historians.

Biographical listings and obituaries—[Obituary]. University of Chicago Libraries. *Library News and Announcements* 14:3 (Jan. 25, 1965); *Who Was Who in America* V (1969-1973); *Who's Who in Library Service*, 3rd ed. **Books and articles about the biographee**—[There is no full-length biography or book dealing with Raney. References to him must be found in periodical articles or chapters of books. The principal references are here listed.] French, John C. *A History of the University Founded by Johns Hopkins*. Baltimore: Johns Hopkins Press, 1946. [French was Raney's successor as librarian at Johns Hopkins]; Fussler, Herman H. *Photographic Reproduction for Libraries: A Study in Administrative Problems*. Chicago: University of Chicago Press, 1942; Koch, Theodore Wesley. *War Libraries and Allied Studies*. New York: G. E. Stechert & Company, 1918; Kuhlman, A. F. "McKendree Llewellyn Raney." *Illinois Libraries* 24:208-209 (Oct. 1942); Milum, Betty. "Choosing MacLeish's Successor: The Recurring Debate." *Journal of Library History, Philosophy & Comparative Librarianship* 12:86-109 (Spring 1977). [Contains reference to Raney's letter of December 20, 1944, endorsing Julian Boyd for Librarian of Congress]; Tauber, Maurice F., and Irlene R. Stephens, editors. *Library Surveys*. New York: Columbia University Press, 1967. [Contains Guy R. Lyle's estimate of 1933 library self-survey at University of Chicago]; Wilson, Louis Round, and Maurice F. Tauber. *The University Library: Its Organization, Administration and Functions*. Chicago: University of Chicago Press, 1945 (1st ed.), 1956 (2nd ed.) [Chapter 15 in each edition is relevant to Raney]. **Primary sources and archival materials**—Raney's reports as librarian of Johns Hopkins University are included in the reports of the president, published in the Johns Hopkins University *Circulars*, 1909-1927; Raney's reports as director of libraries at the University of Chicago are included in the *President's Reports* from 1928 until 1931, when they ceased publication.

—THOMAS S. HARDING

RATHBONE, JOSEPHINE ADAMS (1864-1941)

Josephine Adams Rathbone was born September 10, 1864, at Jamestown, New York, the daughter of Joshua Henry and Elizabeth Bacon Adams Rathbone. Her father, a physician, was from a New England family whose earliest American representative was John Rathbone, reported to have come from England in 1628 on the *Speedwell*. Her mother was from Georgia. She maintained throughout her life a blend of Yankee and Southern outlooks. Rathbone attended Wellesley College for one year (1882-1883) and the University of Michigan for two (1884-1885

and 1890-1891). She enrolled in the New York State Library School in 1891 and received the B.L.S. degree in 1893, having worked for one academic year (1892-1893) as assistant librarian at the Diocesan Lending Library, All Saints Cathedral, Albany.

In September 1893, she joined the institution to which she devoted the remaining 45 years of her professional life. Pratt Institute, a school for training in practical and vocational arts, was founded in Brooklyn in 1887 by Charles Pratt, one of John D. Rockefeller's original partners. The Pratt family was to maintain their interest in the Institute throughout the long association that Rathbone had with it. As assistant cataloger, she also helped train assistants for work in the Institute's Free Library. Although founded in 1890, it was reorganized in 1895 under the directorship of Mary Wright Plummer (q.v.); Rathbone became her assistant and later, in 1895, chief instructor. The relationship between the Library and Library School at Pratt was unusually close in terms of both physical quarters and the shared staff.

When Plummer was selected as director of the New York Public Library School in 1911, the trustees selected Edward F. Stevens to direct both the Library and the Library School. Rathbone received the title of vice-director and was in direct charge of the School. The two endured a strained relationship for the next quarter century, with the students and faculty looking to Rathbone for leadership and the trustees dealing with Stevens. This irritant was borne silently for the most part and probably with a good deal of restraint on Stevens's part.

Although the one-year curriculum at Pratt was patterned after that of Melvil Dewey's (q.v.) Albany school (where its faculty had been trained), it was a unique school. Students were admitted only upon successfully completing competitive entrance examinations. Formal education was not considered. Classes, limited to 25 students, took the same courses at the same time from instructors, many of whom were librarians in the Pratt Institute Free Library. Only one out of four applicants was accepted, and they then went through the vocationally oriented program under the personal supervision of Rathbone and her colleagues, with work experience in the Institute Library a normal requirement. As an alumnus remarked later, "No wonder Pratt turned out class after class of first-rate librarians who could do anything in a library."

The direction of the Library School claimed the greatest portion of Rathbone's life. Besides administering the School and taking personal responsibility for each student, she taught all the classes in book selection, fiction, reference work, bibliography, classification, and introductory survey/current problems of the profession. Rathbone also took placement seriously, and her interviews and evaluations were long remembered. She personally led her students in the annual spring trip to libraries in New England, Albany, and the Atlantic Seaboard.

Because of the unconventional nature of the Pratt School, Rathbone was particularly alarmed by the attempts to regularize education for librarianship taken by the Association of American Library Schools and, later, the American Library Association. She argued forcefully for the flexibility to allow schools such as her own to function under their founding documents. Her report to the Institute's trustees in 1924 reflected her frustration over C. C. Williamson's (q.v.) 1923 report and the foreseen aftermath; she concluded thus:

At present the Pratt Institute School of Library Science is designed to meet the existing requirements in the library field, ready when those requirements change to change with them. But true to the purposes of the Founder of Pratt Institute it will maintain the open door of opportunity to those who are worthy to enter, whether or not fortified with diplomas, degrees or other symbols of an educational caste erected by systems of standardization of things done rather than of capacities for the things to be done.

Clearly disheartened by the classification of her School as a "Junior Undergraduate Library School" by the ALA Board of Education for Librarianship, and ever conscious of the unique character of her beloved institution, she reported firmly to the trustees in 1927 that "the Pratt Library School ... continues as a vocational school, directing those who are especially adapted into a specific and greatly to be desired practical performance. As Pratt Institute is not a university, so its Library School is not a lecture course."

Josephine Rathbone's strong commitment to and personal involvement in the special program at Pratt did not prevent her from playing significant roles in professional associations. She was a founder of the Association of American Library Schools in 1915, writing the first defense for the organization in *Library Journal* (40:302-303 [May 1915]). In 1920-1921 and 1927-1928, she served as president. She held numerous ALA committee assignments, served on its Council for all but five years between 1912 and her death, and on its Executive Board in 1916-1919, 1922-1923, and 1931-1932. Her moment of glory was her year as ALA president in 1931-1932, during the depths of the Great Depression.

Rathbone's ALA presidential address was a challenge to librarians to fulfill the responsibilities placed upon them by the times. "Creative librarianship," she said, "is to know books and to understand the book needs of people, a task which cannot be appraised by the canons of art or measured by the instruments of

science." She pleaded that the "ideals upheld shall be those of an inner development; so that success shall not mean the accumulation of money, but the attainment of the good life, in which each man and woman has the leisure and the opportunity for the development of his innate tastes and aptitudes." In her peroration, she called upon her audience to make the library "a center from which shall radiate not only information but quickening impulses, dynamic forces, spiritual influences." This address was a statement of her professional creed.

Her written legacy is not large. She contributed to the ALA *Manual* (1911-1921), the *Cyclopedia of Education* (1911-1913), and edited "The Viewpoint Series" published by the ALA after World War I, contributing *Viewpoints in Travel* (1919) herself. Periodical articles included "Cooperation between Libraries and Schools: An Historical Sketch" (*Library Journal*, April 1901), "The Association of American Library Schools" (*Library Journal*, April 1916), "Some Aspects of Our Personal Life" (*Public Libraries*, February 1916), "Pratt Graduates in Library Work" (*Library Journal*, February 1929), "Creative Librarianship" (*ALA Bulletin*, May 1932). "Pioneers of the Library Profession" appeared posthumously in *Wilson Library Bulletin* (June 1949).

Several other affiliations added significance to her life. She was a member of the honorary American Library Institute and served in state and local organizations. Among them were the New York State Library Association (secretary, 1908), New York Library Club (president, 1918-1919; secretary, 1895-1897 and 1909-1910), the Long Island Library Association (president, 1912-1913), and the New York State Library School Association (secretary, 1895-1896). Her social clubs included The Cosmopolitan, Trail Riders of the Canadian Rockies, and the Adirondack Mountain Club.

The personal bearing and personality of Josephine Rathbone impressed itself on many generations of Pratt graduates and professional colleagues. Small in stature and well dressed, usually in tailored suits, she wore black-ribboned pince-nez eyeglasses that fell to the desk with regularity when she wriggled her nose to concentrate on a page. Always maintaining a discreet distance between herself and others, she would characteristically size up a person upon a first meeting with a penetrating gaze from head to toe. Her liberal outlook fashioned not only her philosophy of librarianship, but her personal life-style. This reflected itself in her broad interests in the theater, current political events, and literature. She firmly believed that librarians should concentrate primarily on being widely read and on knowing the needs of their clientele. She further enjoyed an active physical life, reflected in her travels, canoe trips, and mountain climbing. A run-down farm at New Russia (in upstate New York) was a refuge both for her and for select friends and provided ample opportunities for outdoor pursuits, such as tree planting.

In 1938, Rathbone retired to live with a cousin in Augusta, Georgia, her mother's home. Before she left Brooklyn at the age of 73, the Pratt graduates presented a fine portrait of her (done by Ivan G. Olinsky) to the Institute. The accompanying tribute included the following heartfelt words:

It is given to few teachers to inspire, uninterruptedly, the interest which you, Miss Rathbone, with your own boundless enthusiasm and unfailing zest, have been able to arouse alike in your pupils and your friends, and we love to feel that you have taken us into the circle of the latter, as well as the former. We rejoice that your portrait—we hope with your own quick smile—will remain in the classroom where we all have sat at your feet and where you have been an inspiration always.

Wayne Shirley (q.v.) remembered her final comment as she left the Library as, "I've had a ripping time!"

Her final three years were not stagnant. She bought a car and taught herself to drive, to the astonishment of her friends. She joined the local chapter of the Colonial Dames of America and the Philomathic Club and carried on the cultivated life she had thrived upon in the New York City area. She attended the Church of the Good Shepherd (Episcopal). Death came in Augusta on May 17, 1941, of coronary thrombosis. She was buried in Augusta in the Summerville Cemetery.

Biographical listings and obituaries—*American Women.* Los Angeles: American Publications, Inc., 1937; Hansen, Agnes C. "Josephine Adams Rathbone [Obituary]." *Library Journal* 66:509 (June 1, 1941) (portrait); Lydenberg, Harry M. "Josephine Adams Rathbone, 1864-1941 [Obituary]." *ALA Bulletin* 35:367-68 (June 1941) (portrait); *National Cyclopaedia of American Biography* D; *Notable American Women* (Joseph A. Boromé); [Obituary]. *New York Times,* May 19, 1941, p. 17 [portrait]; [Obituary]. In Pratt Institute. Library. *Report, 1940-41,* p. 18; *Who Was Who in America* I (1897-1942); *Who's Who in Library Service,* 1st ed. Books and articles about the biographee—Fenneman, Nordica. "Recollections of Josephine Adams Rathbone." *Wilson Library Bulletin* 23:773-74 (June 1949); "Josephine Adams Rathbone Retires." *Library Journal* 63:591 (Aug. 1938) (portrait); *New York State Library School Register, 1887-1926.* New York: New York State Library School Association, 1959; Shirley, Wayne. "Josephine Adams Rathbone." *Wilson Library Bulletin* 34:199-204 (Nov. 1959) (portrait). Primary sources and archival materials—Josephine Rathbone's public papers are divided among the archives of the organizations she served, notably Pratt Institute Library and Library School (Brooklyn) and the Association of American Library Schools (University of Illinois, Urbana). Her death certificate is in the Richmond County Health Department, Augusta, Georgia.

—DONALD G. DAVIS, JR.

RICE, PAUL NORTH (1888-1967)

Paul North Rice was born in Lowell, Massachusetts, on February 8, 1888, the son of Charles Francis and Miriam Jacobs Rice. He married Genevieve Briggs of Laporte, Indiana, on July 17, 1924. Their children were Charles B., Rachel, and Lenore. A second son, Horace, died in 1953 while an undergraduate at Colorado College in Colorado Springs.

Paul North Rice received his baccalaureate degree from Wesleyan University in 1910 and a certificate from the New York State Library School, Albany, in 1913. He was a member of Phi Beta Kappa, and Wesleyan University awarded him an honorary master's degree in 1935.

Rice was assistant reference librarian, Ohio State University, from 1911 to 1913. He then joined the staff of the reference department of the New York Public Library and served as reference assistant at the information desk (1914-1916), and as chief of stacks (1916-1917). He served in the United States Army (1917-1919), rising from private to second lieutenant. He then returned to the New York Public Library as chief of the Accessions Division and very shortly was promoted to chief of the Preparation Division (1920-1927).

Rice was head librarian of the Dayton (Ohio) Public Library (1927-1936), succeeding Electra Collins Doren (q.v.). In Dayton, he concentrated on improving the book collection, accelerating technical processes and increasing library use. Circulation, with some assist from widespread unemployment, rose from 651,336 in 1927 to 1,017,056 in 1931. Although he regarded the Dayton years as happy ones, economic conditions frustrated his dream of a new main library building and played a part in his decision to resign on January 31, 1936.

Rice returned to New York City as director of libraries of New York University (1936-1937), challenged by the prospect, as he put it, "of the building of a great new library" to replace the widely scattered university libraries. However, the new library was not to be until almost a quarter of a century later.

He was persuaded by former colleagues, presumably led by Harry Miller Lydenberg (q.v.), to return to the New York Public Library in 1938 as chief of the Reference Department, a post vacated by Keyes D. Metcalf. He filled this position with great distinction until his mandatory retirement in 1953.

Rice then took up service with his alma mater, as the Caleb T. Winchester librarian of the Olin Library at Wesleyan. He succeeded Fremont Rider (q.v.) of microcard fame in August 1953, and turned his formidable knowledge to putting technical processing on a current basis. After another mandatory retirement in 1956, Rice devoted his attention as librarian emeritus to compiling the ninth edition of the *Wesleyan Alumni Directory* (1961). He was trustee of the Russell Public Library (1954-1956) and of the Godfrey Genealogical Library, both of Middletown, Connecticut.

He was active professionally in state and national library matters as president of the Ohio Library Association (1930-1931), of the New York Library Association (1939-1940), and of the American Library Association (1947-1948). He served in the World War II Victory Book Campaign representing the ALA. Internationally, Rice contributed as executive secretary of the Association of Research Libraries (1942-1945), during which time he was instrumental in shaping the Farmington Plan. Perhaps his greatest achievement was formulating the plan for publication of the *Catalog of Books Represented by the Library of Congress Printed Cards* and then seeing to the completion of the project. He was also a fellow of the American Library Institute.

The finest tribute to Paul North Rice is that from Harry Miller Lydenberg at the time of Rice's retirement from the New York Public Library:

He is a friend and companion wherever you find him. Bring him a problem of daily life and you may be sure of welcome, of understanding, of sympathy, with comment and answer at the end based on his honest judgment, no matter whether they are what you hoped for or what you feared. Friends, acquaintances, all that touch him rate him as high as librarian as they do as a personality, a man showing his ideals and standards by his daily life and bearing. None will ask for himself anything better than that he may in time come somewhere near to matching his own performances with what he knows stands to the credit of Paul North Rice.

One hesitates simply to call Paul North Rice a gentleman of the old school, for he was much more than that. To countless younger men, including the writer, he was mentor, advocate, and friend. He was highly principled, yet humane. One of his favorite authors was Trollope, he had a photograph of Winston Churchill on his desk during World War II, and he was never a clean-desk man. He dealt with the desk problem in his usual directness. Shortly after his appointment, the Board minutes of the Dayton Public Library record authorization for the librarian to buy a roll-top desk. As chief of the Reference Department at the New York Public Library he sat at such a desk, piled high with book dealers' catalogs and much else. He knew exactly where everything was in those piles.

The following words from his inaugural address as ALA president in 1947 (*Bulletin of the American Library Association* 41:247 [August 1947]) are germane today:

If this war-torn world is to avoid another still more devastating and possibly a final war, nations must understand each other. Nothing contributes more to such intercultural understanding than does the printed page. Second only in importance to the writers who compose the message of the printed page, are the disseminators of these pages and we librarians play a vital part in such dissemination.

Following his death in Middletown, Connecticut, on April 16, 1967, the Executive Board of the American Library Association resolved that "in the death of Paul North Rice, the nation has lost an outstanding librarian whose career was devoted to creative librarianship ... [to which] he gave long and dedicated service."

Biographical listings and obituaries–*Current Biography* (1967); [Obituary]. *Library Journal* 92:2113 (June 1, 1967); *Who Was Who in America* IV (1961-1968); *Who's Who in Library Service*, 1st ed., 2nd ed., 3rd ed. Books and articles about the biographee–Lydenberg, Harry M. "Paul North Rice: The Man and the Librarian." *Bulletin of the New York Public Library* 57:389-91 (Aug. 1953); Faries, Elizabeth. *A Century of Service: History of the Dayton Public Library, Dayton, Ohio, 1847-1947.* Dayton, Ohio: Dayton Public Library, 1948; Kingery, Robert E. *The Dayton and Montgomery County Public Library and Its Precursors.* (Work in progress, 1977.) Primary sources and archival materials–Dayton Public Library, Dayton, Ohio. *Annual Reports* 1927-1935.

–ROBERT E. KINGERY

RICHARDSON, ERNEST CUSHING (1860-1939)

Ernest Cushing Richardson was born February 9, 1860, in the small New England town of Woburn, Massachusetts, the only son of James Cushing and Lydia Bartlett Taylor Richardson. As a boy he enjoyed baseball, ice skating, and reading in the Woburn Public Library, an early addiction he was never to overcome. Only sixteen years old when he enrolled at Amherst College, Richardson was five feet eight and one-half inches tall and weighed 141 pounds. Melvil Dewey (q.v.) was on the library staff during Richardson's first year at Amherst, but no written record of contact between the two has come to light. Amherst's librarian appointed Richardson as first assistant librarian in his senior year, and he was graduated with an A.B. and Phi Beta Kappa honors in 1880. The next three years he spent studying at Hartford Theological Seminary, where he was graduated in 1883 without taking a degree, since the Bachelor of Divinity had not yet been established. He was licensed to preach but never became a minister.

Richardson was granted the M.A. from Amherst, also in 1883, it being Amherst's custom at that time to confer this degree on certain of its graduates of at least three years standing who had spent a minimum of two years in professional or liberal studies. His honorary degrees included the Ph.D. from Washington and Jefferson College in 1888, when he was only 28, and the M.A. from Princeton University in 1896. During his long and varied professional career he was customarily referred to as "Dr. Richardson."

While at Hartford, Richardson first worked as a student assistant in the library and in 1882 was appointed assistant librarian (a year before he graduated). Then in 1884, following the first of many trips to Europe, he accepted the post of librarian with faculty rank at Hartford, succeeding Chester D. Hartranft, with whom he had worked earlier. His six years at Hartford were happy and productive. Funds for acquisitions were adequate, although not so generous for salaries. In addition to his full-time job as librarian, Richardson taught a course in bibliography, a facet of librarianship that was to become one of his principal interests and contributions to scholarship. He also developed a classification scheme for the Hartford collection. Richardson's work brought forth a resolution of the faculty on May 5, 1885 (quoted in faculty meeting minutes from Hartford, now in the Richardson Collection at Princeton):

> Resolved: that the faculty have observed with much satisfaction the fidelity and zeal of Mr. E. C. Richardson in the discharge of his duties as librarian, and that the way may be opened at no distant day for his appointment as an associate professor in connection with the library work.

"No distant day" turned out to be 1888, when Richardson was given a "dry" promotion—a raise in rank to associate professor but without salary increase. He was partly compensated by long vacations, which he spent largely in foreign travel purchasing books and studying manuscripts in 1884, 1888, 1889, and 1890.

Despite offers of better-paying positions, Richardson was loathe to leave Hartford, which had turned out to be a happy experience for him—and for Hartford. Yet the call in 1890 to the College of New Jersey, later known as Princeton University, at a salary of $3,000 (double that at Hartford) was irresistible. At age thirty, he had acquired three degrees including an honorary doctorate, had published one lengthy biography and numerous periodical articles, had worked extensively in the American Library Association, had enriched his experience through four European trips and had acquired a reputation as a young scholar.

Almost 35 of Ernest C. Richardson's 62 years of library work were spent at the Princeton Library, by far his longest official connection. Unhappily, a full measure of success eluded him and, when he left Princeton in 1925, he concluded the longest, bitterest controversy of his life.

He immediately plunged into the task of trying to improve library services through more adequate physical facilities, furnishings, book funds, bibliographic apparatus, and staff. His greatest success occurred in acquisitions, where he increased the book collection from 81,000 volumes in 1890 to approximately 450,000 in 1920, an increase in holdings of more than five-fold.

Richardsons' personal life was greatly and happily affected by his marriage in 1891 (shortly after going to Princeton) to Grace Duncan Ely. The Richardson's daughter and only child, Mary Ely, was born in 1900 but died in 1901. Thanks to his wife's money, Richardson was semi-independent of his salary for the rest of his life and with Mrs. Richardson was able to make at least sixteen extended visits to Europe during his long stay at Princeton. The president of Princeton, Woodrow Wilson, granted him the unusual privilege of being out of residence one semester each year on full salary, with the understanding that much of the time would be spent in Europe buying books and manuscripts for Princeton and working with librarians and scholars in international bibliographic cooperation. Probably no other librarian of his day had such an arrangement.

Classification and cataloging of library materials were two of Richardson's earliest and most enduring interests, beginning with his participation as a student assistant in applying the Dewey system to Amherst. At Princeton, he had the Richardson classification system, transforming the collection from a "fixed" to a "relative" location system, in operation by 1900. At the same time, he was chairman of the ALA's Committee on Cooperation, which was seriously studying the revolutionary possibility of the cooperative use of printed catalog cards.

On October 29, 1901, the Library of Congress issued a prospectus offering printed catalog cards for sale. Amherst was the first to subscribe, followed closely by Princeton. The fateful decision to adopt Library of Congress cards at Princeton came on a Sunday afternoon when the indefatigable Richardson brought together Woodrow Wilson, John L. Cadwallader, and Dr. John S. Billings (q.v.) of the New York Public Library (see Richardson's "The University Library in Its Cooperative Aspects" in *School and Society* 32:218 [1930]).

Early in his professional career, Richardson also became a very strong supporter of "short" or brief form cataloging. Being greatly concerned with both the quantitative increase in information and the improvement in methods of locating it, he felt it sufficient that a catalog card contain no more than enough information to identify the book and to locate it on the library shelves. He was one of the outstanding pioneers in a movement (which did not actually flower until years later) to reduce the amount of bibliographic detail in cataloging in order to realize very substantial savings in time and money. By 1920, the Princeton Library was cataloging six times as many titles by "short" cataloging as by the "full" cataloging method. But the time was not right, and he made few converts among his colleagues.

Related to his ideas on brief cataloging was Richardson's experimentation with the "title-a-bar" theory. With the help of a small linotype machine in the Princeton Library, he began to produce printed booklists, subject lists, and finally a catalog based on the shelflist of the entire Princeton collection. A basic ingredient of this interesting technique was the unalterable rule that every entry be restricted to one line. In 1904, he stated (in his *Annual Report*, October 12, 1904) that "the greatest administrative mistake of modern libraries in America is the failure to provide the comparatively inexpensive brief title printed catalog." He printed the official shelflist in six binders by this method and also used it in several of his books where extensive listing was involved. He was greatly disappointed when James T. Gerould (q.v.), his successor as director of the Princeton Library in 1920, discontinued the printed catalog in favor of bolstering the card catalog.

Always the student and always the teacher, Richardson continued his teaching of bibliography begun at Hartford Theological Seminary and added a course in paleography. He now held the rank and title of full professor. During his many trips abroad he studied hundreds of manuscripts relating to the early Christian fathers, St. Clement, and Jacapo da Varagine. As a result, his courses, some at the graduate level, were greatly enriched and he was encouraged to publish a number of articles and monographs in the field of manuscript studies. When relieved of his administrative duties at Princeton in 1920, Richardson formally continued to guide young minds in the study of bibliography and paleography, and he always lamented the fact that American library schools as compared with their European counterparts neglected scholarly training in paleography. His last teaching course, conducted at the Library of Congress from 1927 to 1929, was titled "Advanced Problems in Library Management" and included students from George Washington University as well as staff members of the Library of Congress.

During the first two decades of Richardson's stay at Princeton, things went well for the Library and for him, but, in 1913, financial support began a slow decline which was destined to continue until he gave up his administrative duties in 1920. A survey that he conducted in 1915 ("Some Business Aspects of the University Library," *Princeton Alumni Weekly*, April 21, 1915, pp. 675-76) showed that Princeton Library staff salaries were only 66 percent of the

average of those at 27 selected colleges and universities. By 1919, despite protests in letters and in annual reports, his staff was fewer by four or five people than it was in 1913.

To exacerbate the problem, the faculty demanded additional services. By 1920, the strain had reached a point where President John Grier Hibben felt obliged to appoint a committee of professors to investigate the work of the Library and to make appropriate recommendations. The committee made its study, reported that the Library had rendered good service considering the funds available to it, and recommended substantial increases in funds for both salaries and books. However, they also recommended appointment of an assistant or associate librarian and a thorough reorganization of the Library. The new position was filled by an assistant (Gerould), but the faculty's confidence in Richardson slowly weakened until the assistant really became the "librarian" (with administrative authority) while Richardson was made "director" and was left authority only for general policies, his teaching, and his work in bibliographical cooperation.

When Richardson and his wife returned from a European trip in May 1921, he was very upset to find that his cherished printed catalogs were being abandoned, the author and subject catalogs were being consolidated, and some classes of books were being reclassified from Richardson's system to that of the Library of Congress.

Richardson and Gerould argued bitterly, but the Trustee Library Committee upheld the latter. At this point, it was nearly all over but the shouting, and that was provided by Richardson, who in effect demanded that the administration choose between him and Gerould. By 1923, when the situation had grown intolerable, President Hibben, trying to be fair, urged Richardson to seek a formula that would restore peace. At Richardson's recommendation, the president appointed him both honorary director of the Library and research professor of bibliography. This left him with no library duties, only teaching responsibilities. When, in 1925, Herbert Putnam (q.v.), a long-time friend and colleague of Richardson, offered him the position of honorary consultant in bibliography and research at the Library of Congress without salary, Richardson accepted with alacrity.

It is difficult to determine after more than fifty years whether Richardson or the University should bear the greater responsibility for his painful separation after 35 years of service. It is quite clear, however, that neither was blameless. The University was unfair in not adhering to its contract with Richardson that his salary should always be equal to the maximum full professor's salary, in holding against him the European trips that had been fully approved by University President Woodrow Wilson, and in denying him full measure of due process during the bitter controversy over jurisdiction. But Richardson in part fomented his own troubles by insisting on pet ideas such as brief cataloging and "title-a-bar" schemes, by remaining unresponsive to the wishes of many of the faculty, by his insistence that the University choose between him and Gerould, and finally by his belligerent and somewhat irascible nature and unwillingness to compromise. Taking these and other facts into consideration, the final outcome was inevitable. Although Richardson retired from Princeton in 1925 without any personal grievances against any one individual, it is sad that his very substantial contributions should have ended on such an unhappy note.

So, at age 65, Richardson began a new phase in his professional life that was destined to bring him deep satisfaction and to constitute his single greatest contribution to librarianship and the research community worldwide—directorship of "Project B," which was essentially the development of bibliographic apparatus at the Library of Congress. For many years, Richardson had been engrossed in bibliographic problems and the goal of putting at least one copy of every book useful for research in a known location in the United States. George Schwegmann put it this way ("Ernest Cushing Richardson," *D.C. Libraries* 10:47 [1939]): "His chief enthusiasm was for cooperation among librarians and for the problems of organizing and developing materials for research. . . ." Richardson's background for the job was impressive: chairman of the ALA Committee on Bibliography (1922-1934); president of the American Library Institute (1915-1918); president of the American Library Association (1904-1905); councillor of the Bibliographical Society of America (1917-1937); chairman of the Bibliography Committee of the American Historical Society (1902-1915); and, for many years, America's most zealous advocate of the Brussels Institute and the Councilium Bibliographicum, both European-based.

The project began in September 1927 with Richardson as general director and Ernest Kletsch as executive director. Its two major goals, the first by far the more important, were substantial extension of the union catalog and expansion of the catalog of special collections of the Library of Congress. In 1927, the union catalog contained 1,500,000 titles on 1,960,000 cards. At project's end in 1932, there were 7,000,000 titles with 9,000,000 copies located in American libraries, and a grand total of approximately 15,000,000 volumes. Thus, the goal of 6,000,000 titles was more than reached. Less dramatic but quite useful was the listing of 4,884 special collections located on 20,000 cards in American libraries. "Project B" was an outstanding contribution to world scholarship and represented an important

step toward Richardson's long-sought goal of getting at least one copy of every research book into at least one American library, the very essence of the Farmington Plan, which in 1932 was still sixteen years in the future. Certainly, many hands and minds were responsible for these greatly improved bibliographic tools, but the vision was Richardson's, and its fulfillment during his lifetime was unapproached by any of his other projects.

"Project B" had been recommended by the ALA Committee on Bibliography and was a great success, but Richardson's experience on this Committee was destined to end unhappily. When the ALA Executive Board established the Committee in 1922, Richardson was named chairman because of his interest and extensive experience in bibliographic work. The Committee worked with foreign bibliographic enterprises as well as domestic, and it developed extremely ambitious projects based upon Richardson's great emphasis on the need for research books in known locations in American libraries. Funds to carry out programs were not readily available to Richardson's Committee and, when the Executive Board established the Cooperative Cataloging Committee in 1930 "to solicit funds for cooperative cataloging," Richardson bitterly resented it as competitive with and encroaching upon the duties of his Committee. Matters went from bad to worse as charges were followed by counter charges, not between the two committees, the personnel of which respected each other, but between Richardson and the Executive Board. By 1934, Richardson had failed to get funds for his Committee's two matured projects and to get the work of the Cooperative Cataloging Committee re-directed, so he resigned both as chairman and as a member of the Committee. In this unfortunate impasse, one sees some of the same factors that were present in Richardson's fight with the Princeton administration. In both instances, he dominated his staff or committee members, he failed to seek a compromise until it was too late, and he forced his opposition to an all-or-none final outcome. Again, there was bungling on both sides, but Richardson's views were sound. It is regrettable that his many years of very significant contribution to the work of ALA ended in frustration and unhappiness for him.

Richardson was a good scholar, as well as a bibliographer and librarian. His published works number approximately 25 books and more than 150 journal articles, pamphlets, chapters in books, prefaces, introductions, reviews, and reports. His most important published contribution to librarianship is *Classification, Theoretical and Practical* (1901; 2nd ed. 1912; 3rd ed. 1930). It sold well, and reviews on both sides of the Atlantic were uniformly favorable, as typified by one (*Public Libraries* 6:581 [1901]) that read in part, "no one has done more than he to give the thoro elucidation to many matters on which current thought is apt to be loose. All that he writes bears the hallmark of real scholarship and at the same time shows a genius for practicality." Unlike Dewey and Charles A. Cutter (q.v.), Richardson published his book with no intention of persuading other libraries to adopt his classification system. In fact, from time to time he advised libraries to adopt either the Dewey or Library of Congress schemes because, he pointed out, they were more generally in use than others and their practicality had been well tested. Richardson's book is deeply philosophical and intellectual, with his own classification scheme emerging almost incidentally at the end of the volume.

His *A Union World Catalog of Manuscript Books* (1933-1937) was a series in six parts designed to convince scholars, librarians, and educational foundations of the great need for and the appropriate methods of bringing the world's collections of manuscripts under firm bibliographic control. Richardson supplied the vision, but, as in so many instances, he could not convince others, and it remained for later scholars to implement his very sound ideas.

His other works include *General Library Cooperation and American Research Books* (1930), *Some Aspects of Cooperative Cataloging* (1934), and *Some Aspects of International Library Cooperation* (1928). His puckish humor found happy outlet in *The Beginnings of Libraries* (1914) and *Biblical Libraries* (1914), both delightful fantasies for librarians. He also wrote books and articles on ancient theological history and compiled checklists of collections of European history. Fortunately, he put into print almost every idea which his restless, fertile mind conceived; it may also be that he was more persuasive writing in support of his ideas than he was in arguing personally for them.

The sudden death of his wife in 1933 and his final defeat by the ALA Executive Board in 1934 came as twin blows to Richardson. His wife's companionship, devotion, and constant assistance had meant a great deal to him. He resigned from all ALA committees in 1934, and in 1935 and 1936, he resigned his membership in the American Library Institute and the Institut Français de Washington, respectively. He left the house in Princeton that had been home for the Richardsons for so many years and moved to his summer cottage, "High Pastures," near Old Lyme, Connecticut. His wife's niece and her family added to his happiness during this period by spending the summers with him. He seemed to find peace in this setting, and was free of bitterness and still optimistic that intellectual cooperation would be achieved domestically and internationally.

Even during his last years, Richardson's fertile mind and still energetic body continued to work. He delved into the financial affairs of his alma mater,

Amherst, served as a very active trustee of Hartford Theological Seminary, and made a triumphant one-day visit to his boyhood town of Woburn, Massachusetts, where he was hailed as a hometown hero by the local library and the newspapers. Just before his death of angina pectoris at age 79 on June 3, 1939, he was engaged in a study and evaluation of rare books.

Richardson's importance as a pioneer in librarianship in the United States has not been fully understood, and librarians generally are quite unaware of his very significant contributions in a number of areas. His contemporaries were absorbed, almost obsessed, with the mechanics of "fixed" versus "relative" location, book charging systems, and a myriad of necessary, but non-intellectual, aspects of the profession. By contrast, Richardson was a scholar-librarian and brought to librarianship the philosophy and viewpoint of a scholar. He did not excel in administration or in competitive relationships with professional colleagues, witness his controversies and defeats at Princeton and with the ALA Executive Board. His notions of new and better ways of achieving desirable goals were numerous and generally good, but he would have had much greater success had he been content to formulate plans and leave their execution to others. In some respects, the library profession had not caught up with Richardson, and his listeners did not always understand what he was trying to say or grasp its significance. As William W. Bishop (q.v.) put it ("Reminiscences of Princeton: 1902-1907," *Princeton University Library Chronicle* 8:156 [1947]), "He was a great man, but he lacked the ability to make his plans clear to a layman—or even to members of his own profession." Richardson recognized this problem himself and somewhat wistfully, perhaps, wrote to Melvil Dewey only a few months before Dewey's death (unpublished letter of July 15, 1931, in Richardson Collection at Princeton): "I often think over with renewed courage how often you put over matters in the old days despite the opposition—when you held the cards, as you usually did."

Although Richardson had no formal training in librarianship, he was interested in education in this field, taught bibliography at three institutions, and stressed the importance of the book sciences over the mechanics. His teaching and writings form a permanent contribution to library education in its earlier years in this country.

However, Richardson's greatest single contribution to librarianship and to scholarship was his work on "Project B"—transforming the National Union Catalog of the Library of Congress from an insignificant record of one and one-half million titles in 1927 into the magnificent bibliographical tool that listed and located seven million titles in sixteen million volumes in 1932. Beyond that, he advocated cooperative selection and acquisition of research library materials (later the Farmington Plan) and regional storage centers in Boston, New York, Washington, Chicago, and San Francisco. The subsequent rise of bibliographic centers in Philadelphia, Denver, and Seattle, and the Center for Research Libraries were the products of many people's efforts, but earlier than others, Richardson identified the problems, formulated solutions, published his ideas widely, made concrete contributions such as "Project B," and thereby left a rich, unsurpassed legacy in the area of research books. This is his greatest contribution and his soundest claim to library fame.

Biographical listings and obituaries—"Ernest Cushing Richardson 1860-1939: A Resolution of Appreciation." Bibliographical Society of America. *News Sheet* 55:4-5 (March 1, 1940); Esdaile, Arundell. "Obituary of Ernest Cushing Richardson." *Library Association Record*, Series 4, 6:446 (1939); Hartford Seminary Foundation. "Minute Adopted at the Meeting of the Board of Trustees, November 1, 1939." (Unpublished); *National Cyclopaedia of American Biography* 13; *The New Schaff-Herzog Encyclopedia of Religious Knowledge* 10; [Obituary]. *New York Herald Tribune*, June 3, 1939; [Obituary]. *Princeton Herald*, June 9(?), 1939; [Obituary]. *Washington (D.C.) Post*, June 4, 1939; Princeton University. "Minute Adopted by the University Faculty at Its Meeting Held October 2, 1939." (Unpublished); Sayers, W. C. Berwick. "Obituary of Ernest Cushing Richardson." *Library Association Record*, Series 4, 6:446-47 (1939); Schwegmann, George A., Jr. "Ernest Cushing Richardson." *D.C. Libraries* 10:46-47 (1939); U.S. Library of Congress. "Dr. Ernest Cushing Richardson." *Report of the Librarian of Congress*, 1939. Washington: Government Printing Office, 1940, pp. 341-42; Van Hoesen, Henry B. "Ernest Cushing Richardson, 1860-1939." *American Library Association Bulletin* 33:472, 520 (1939); *Who Was Who in America* I (1897-1942); *Who's Who in Library Service*, 1st ed. **Books and articles about the biographee**—Bishop, William Warner. "Reminiscences of Princeton: 1902-1907." *Princeton University Library Chronicle* 8:147-63 (1947); Branscomb, Lewis C. *A Bio-Bibliographical Study of Ernest Cushing Richardson, 1860-1939*. Ph.D. dissertation, the University of Chicago, 1954; Branscomb, Lewis C. "Ernest Cushing Richardson." In *Pioneering Leaders in Librarianship*, ed. by Emily Miller Danton. Chicago: American Library Association, 1953, pp. 141-52; Brick Row Book Shop, Inc. *The Books of an Old Librarian, Being the Books of Ernest Cushing Richardson, with Some Additions*. Special list Number 15. New York: Brick Row Book Shop, Inc., 1941; Hadidian, Dikran Y. "Ernest Cushing Richardson, 1860-1939." *College and Research Libraries* 33:122-26 (March 1972); Metcalf, Keyes D. "Card Production." *American Library Association Bulletin* 27:356 (1933); Murra, Kathrine O. "History of Some Attempt to Organize Bibliography Internationally." *Bibliographic Organization*, ed. by Jesse H. Shera and Margaret E. Egan. Chicago: University of Chicago Press, 1951, pp. 24-53; Wilson, L. R., and M. F. Tauber. "Ernest Cushing Richardson." In *The University Library*. Chicago: University of Chicago Press, 1945, pp. 498-99. **Primary sources and archival materials**—The preponderance of Richardson's manuscripts, letters, and other papers are in the Princeton University Library. Others are in the Library of Congress and the Hartford Seminary Foundation Library.

—LEWIS C. BRANSCOMB

RICHARDSON, HENRY HOBSON (1838-1886) *also* McKIM, CHARLES FOLLEN (1847-1909)

Henry Hobson Richardson was born on September 29, 1838, in Saint James Parish, Louisiana, the son of Henry and Catherine Richardson. A member of one of the state's wealthy families, Richardson received his education in the public and private schools of New Orleans, at the University of Louisiana, and at Harvard College. Richardson suffered from several physical disabilities during his life; he stuttered in his youth and, later in life, he was unusually large (although of medium height, he weighed more than 300 pounds). During his last years, Richardson had a full beard and mustache.

After he was graduated from Harvard in 1859, Richardson became the second American student (Richard Morris Hunt was the first) to study architecture at the École des Beaux-Arts in Paris. However, with the loss of his family's wealth in the American Civil War, Richardson was forced to combine employment with his studies. During his six years of study and work in Paris, he was associated with two of France's most important architects, Louis Andre and Theodore Labrouste. (Labrouste's brother Henri designed the first iron bookstack when planning the reading room for the Bibliothèque Nationale.)

In 1866, Richardson returned to the United States to establish his practice, first in New York and later in Brookline, Massachusetts. He was married to Julia Hayden in 1867; the couple had six children. Richardson is credited with being the first architect to establish a large-scale architectural firm next to his own home (in Brookline); Frank Lloyd Wright later adopted the same system of training young architects at Taliesin. From Richardson's office, a number of young men went on to establish important firms in the late nineteenth and early twentieth centuries: Charles McKim [see below], Stanford White, Charles Coolidge, George Shepley, and Charles Rutan.

During his twenty years of practice, Richardson designed churches, commercial buildings, homes for wealthy clients, governmental buildings, and libraries. Among his most noted buildings are Trinity Church in Boston, the New York State Capitol, Austin Hall at Harvard, the Allegheny County Courthouse in Pittsburgh, the Hay-Adams House in Washington, the Glessner House in Chicago, and the Marshall Field Wholesale Store in Chicago. The latter building was the forerunner of modern department stores and warehouses.

Richardson designed six library buildings between 1878 and 1886. Public libraries were built in four Massachusetts communities: Woburn, Malden, Quincy, and North Easton. He designed one academic library building at the University of Vermont, and the Howard Library in New Orleans was designed by Richardson, but was not built until after his death.

The library buildings that came from Richardson's drafting table were irregular masses of heavy stone, usually granite. His designs separated the reading room and book room functions of the library into separate parts of the building. Richardson liked to incorporate round or octagon-shaped wings into the library building, and some of his buildings also had towers. One of the distinctive features of a Richardson library was the low, round arches at the entrances. By modern standards, all of Richardson's libraries were small, with the library activities arranged on one floor.

Henry Richardson was the first formally trained American architect to study the type of structure needed for the emerging American institution, the community public library. Although his designs drew criticism from some members of the newly formed library profession, his designs did accurately reflect what donors and local committees wanted. His buildings served as museums, galleries, and community centers as well as libraries. Also, all of Richardson's library projects were privately funded projects in which he worked directly with the donor.

Hundreds of buildings were designed in the Richardson style by less skillful architects during the eighties and nineties in all parts of the East and the Midwest. The Richardson Romanesque style was used as well for post offices, courthouses, college buildings, commercial buildings, and homes, but it faded rapidly after the World's Columbian Exposition of 1893. After Richardson's death (at age 47 from Bright's Disease) on April 27, 1886, the firm of Shepley, Coolidge, and Rutan was formed as a successor. The present descendant firm in Boston is Shepley, Bulfinch, Richardson, and Abbott.

Richardson had a large influence on American architects and building style both during his lifetime and after his death. Charles McKim, Louis Sullivan, and Frank Lloyd Wright all acknowledged their debt to him. This influence is evident in Sullivan's Auditorium Building and his Transportation Building at the Columbian Exposition, in the Newberry Library by Henry Ives Cobb, and in the Chicago Public Library by the Shepley firm. Perhaps Richardson's most important influence in library architecture is seen in McKim's treatment of the Boston Public Library building in 1894.

Charles Follen McKim, nine years younger than Richardson, was born on August 24, 1847, in Chester County, Pennsylvania, to James and Sarah McKim, who were active abolitionists during the boy's early years. He entered the Lawrence Scientific School at Harvard in 1866, but stayed for only one year. He then went to France to study architecture in the École des Beaux Arts. After several years of study and travel, he returned to take a position as draftsman in Richardson's office, where he met William Mead and Stanford White. The three men would form the firm of McKim, Mead, and White in 1879. By the late 1880s, this association was established as one of the country's major architectural firms. Through his business and social connections, McKim received, in 1887, the commission to design the new Boston Public Library building to be located in Copley Square across the street from Trinity Church, a building McKim had worked on while in Richardson's office.

McKim's design for the Boston building incorporated several features used for the first time in a large public library: a monumental reading room across the front on the second floor, the separation of book storage from reading rooms, and a large central courtyard. The Library's exterior was influenced by three buildings: Richardson's Marshall Field Store in Chicago, Labrouste's Bibliothèque Sainte-Geneviève in Paris, and Alberti's San Francesco in Rimini, Italy. The Boston Public Library was thus one of the earliest examples of the Renaissance Revival style that McKim and others would promote during the decades before and after the turn of the century.

Not only was the Boston building an important commission for the McKim firm, it was a major event in the development of American architecture and librarianship. One of the first large public buildings in which the architect used the talents of major painters and sculptors to enhance the beauty of the interior, the Boston Public Library was also the first large public library in the world designed to house both scholarly research collections and popular circulating books. It remains today, ninety years after completion, a symbol of the public library and of the firm of McKim, Mead, and White.

Charles McKim was one of the architects of the World's Columbian Exposition in Chicago in 1893, where, along with Richard Hunt, he convinced the other architects to use the Renaissance style for the Court of Honor. His firm also designed one of the main buildings and the New York State building there. From 1894 until his death, McKim worked to establish an American Academy in Rome as a school of design dedicated to the styles he favored.

In 1901, President Theodore Roosevelt appointed McKim to the Washington Planning Commission, which developed plans for improving the Mall, the Capitol, and the Tidal Basin. McKim also worked on the restoration of the White House. With the success of the Boston Public Library and other designs, the firm received a number of major commissions around the turn of the century, and McKim was responsible for the Low Library at Columbia University and the Morgan Library.

After the completion of the Morgan Library and the murder of Stanford White in 1906, McKim was less active in the work of the firm. He died on September 14, 1909.

H. H. RICHARDSON

Biographical listings and obituaries–*Dictionary of American Biography* 15 (Talbot F. Hamlin). **Books and articles about the biographee**–Hitchcock, Henry-Russell. *The Architecture of H. H. Richardson and His Times.* Cambridge: Massachusetts Institute of Technology Press, 1966; O'Gorman, James F. *H. H. Richardson and His Office.* Cambridge: Harvard College Library, 1974; Van Rensselaer, Mariana G. *Henry Hobson Richardson and His Work.* Boston: Houghton Mifflin, 1888.

CHARLES F. McKIM

Biographical listings and obituaries–*Dictionary of American Biography* 12 (Charles Moore). **Books and articles about the biographee**–Butler, Alexander R. "McKim's Renaissance: A Study in the History of the American Architectural Profession." Ph.D. dissertation, Johns Hopkins University, 1953; Jordy, William H. *American Buildings and Their Architects.* Garden City, N.Y.: Doubleday, 1972; Moore, Charles. *The Life and Times of Charles Follen McKim.* Boston: Houghton Mifflin, 1929; Whitehill, Walter Muir. *Boston Public Library.* Cambridge: Harvard University Press, 1956.

–DONALD E. OEHLERTS

RIDER, ARTHUR FREMONT (1885-1962)

Arthur Fremont Rider was born in Trenton, New Jersey, on May 25, 1885, the son of George Arthur and Charlotte Elizabeth Meader Rider. During his childhood he lived in Middletown, Connecticut, for several years. In later life, he proudly remembered that when, as a small boy, he felt he had outgrown the town library, the Wesleyan University librarian, William James, allowed him to use the Wesleyan Library. Rider was graduated Phi Beta Kappa from Syracuse University (Ph.B.) in 1905 and later was honored by Syracuse with the L.H.D. in 1937. He then attended the New York State Library School (class of 1907) but left before graduation on the invitation of Melvil Dewey (q.v.), who was at that time leaving the School he had founded twenty years before. Rider worked for Dewey on a revision of the Decimal Classification at the Lake Placid Club. In his autobiography, Rider states that on arrival at the Club "he was introduced at their breakfast table to both of his future wives." On October 8, 1908, he married the niece of Dewey's first wife, Grace Godfrey of Milford, Massachusetts, who died in June 1950. Their son Leland was born in 1910 and their daughter Deirdre was born in 1913. Rider's second marriage (June 16, 1951) was to Marie Gallup Ambrose, Dewey's grandniece and daughter of the manager (who was also part owner with Dewey) of the Lake Placid Club. By this marriage, Rider acquired a step-son and a step-daughter.

Rider began an editorial career in 1907 as associate editor of *The Delineator*, became managing editor of *The New Idea Woman's Magazine* in 1908, and was editor of *Monthly Book Review* from 1909 to 1917. He was managing editor of *Publishers' Weekly* (1910-1917) and of *Library Journal* (1914-1917), while also editor of the *American Library Annual* (1912-1917), and *Information* (1915-1918), and working as well on the *Publishers' Trade List Annual.* During this period, he was president of the Rider Press (periodical printers, 1914-1932) publishing *International Military Digest* (1915-1918). He was also editor of *Business Digest* (1917-1921) and president of Cumulative Digest Corporation (publishers, 1917-1921). In addition, he had the energy and time to be vice president of the Arrow Publishing Corporation (1918-1922). He published in this interval a series of guide books to New York City (1916), Bermuda (1922), Washington (1923), and California (1925), each of which contains a prodigious fund of local information. The New York Public Library had six copies of his New York guide on the shelves of its Reference Department at the time of Rider's death. The Rider Press was his major concern for eighteen years, and he took great pride in its successful record of lucrative, timely, periodical and book publishing. He endured, not without struggle, exasperating dealings with unions and banks and also managed to contract operations to balance the effects of the Depression and the withdrawal of the R. R. Bowker [q.v.] Company's business.

In 1933, Rider began an active career as librarian of Wesleyan University. The offer of a permanent post in an academic institution that he respected, together with the opportunity of returning to Middletown, was more than a temptation at the peak of the Depression in New York City. He was the first to hold a chair of librarianship endowed through the philanthropy of Andrew Carnegie (q.v.), and he served as the Caleb T. Winchester librarian until his retirement in 1953. Wesleyan, as is its custom for non-Wesleyan graduates holding a tenured position as professor, awarded him an M.A. *ad eundum* in 1934 and, at his retirement, granted him the title of librarian emeritus.

Rider's seemingly abrupt change of career from printer-publisher to librarian had deep roots. His admiration for Melvil Dewey was a major factor, as testified in his laudatory biography, *Melvil Dewey* (ALA, 1944), in which he states (p. viii), "He remains the greatest man with whom I ever came into long-continued personal contact. Except for him I would never have entered the library profession. Except for him there would have been no library profession (in the form that we now know it) for me to enter!" Rider had continued his interest in classification while managing editor of *Publishers' Weekly*, contributing "Old Classifications—and the Excuse for New Ones" to the *Library Journal* (35:387-96 [September 1910]). Subsequently he proposed *A Tentative Decimal Classification and System of Subject Headings for the Literature of Business . . .* (Cumulative Digest Corp., 1924). He also maintained his concern for libraries through his business career as editor and printer of such Bowker publications as *Library Journal* and *Publishers' Weekly*.

At Wesleyan University, Rider was active in many areas, and the Olin Library profited in a number of respects. Over his 20-year librarianship, the book collection increased from 174,000 to 389,000 and, as corollaries, an addition to the book stack was built in 1938 and Rider's system of compact storage of books was inaugurated in 1945. While editor of the Friends of the Wesleyan Library periodical *About Books*, he published in the September 1940 issue (11, no. 1:1-11) "The Growth of American College and University Libraries—and of Wesleyan's." His statistics clearly indicated that college and university libraries doubled the size of their book collections every fifteen years. This caused some flurry in library circles and is still frequently quoted.

Compact Book Storage (Hadham Press, 1949) resulted from Rider's scheme for shelving less-used books on their fore-edges by size according to the dimension from spine to fore-edge. These books were bottom marked with the classification number surmounted by the size. Thus, each of sizes four to nine inches were shelved in a separate A to Z section, allowing, for example, as many as twelve shelves for four-inch books in a three-foot vertical section of stack, a 70 percent gain over the average seven shelves to a vertical section for normal book shelving. Books shelved thus were often placed in boxes to give more stability. Frequently, to fit books into a desired dimension, fore-edges were shaved by guillotine and, to achieve a smooth surface for inking the uneven base pages, leaves were bottom-cropped, leaving an ugly margin by the sewn spine. These outrages to the physical book became notorious and did much to counteract general acceptance of this basic plan (see F. J. Hill's review of *Compact Book Storage* in *Journal of Documentation* 7, No. 2:122-23 [June 1951]).

Rider's *Wesleyan Library Handbook* (Olin Library) went through four editions (1933, 1934, 1936, and 1942) and, in the process, became a model for numerous libraries and library schools, as was his *Staff Manual* (1941). His multiple order forms were sold by a library supply house as "Wesleyan Order System" forms. The "Wesleyan Book Truck" was for a time manufactured and sold by the Library Bureau, and Rider's portable book shelving, developed in wood locally, was manufactured in steel by Snead & Company (whose president was Angus Snead

Macdonald [q.v.]). For Wesleyan-held titles not in the Union Catalog of the Library of Congress, Wesleyan produced printed catalog cards in the mid-1930s, and these were also sent to regional catalogs and sold to subscribing libraries. In 1938-1939, Wesleyan distributed 24,000 printed catalog cards to 32 research libraries, but the war soon curtailed this project.

Wesleyan naturally became a participant in the Farmington Plan. At the Olin Library, Rider instituted a bindery that supported his "bulk acquisition" policy of buying entire libraries: three private libraries, stocks of two book stores and, with Harvard and the Boston Public Library, a portion of the Boston Society Library (that portion not merged with the Boston Athenaeum Collection). Rider figured this acquisition of 50,000 volumes was wholly financed by his wholesale disposition of 30,000 duplicates to dealers and librarians, thus acquiring 20,000 more or less desirable volumes for Wesleyan without cost. Duplicates and less desirable books were also made available to students and faculty in semi-annual "Dutch" book auctions, a custom that still continues.

Due to Rider's enthusiasm for building Wesleyan's library into a research collection, the many activities of the Friends of the Library, and Rider's skillful editing of the periodical *About Books* (generously distributed to Wesleyan alumni and many interested librarians), gifts to the library increased enormously. Rider estimated (conservatively, for once) that these gifts totalled over 100,000 volumes during his twenty years as librarian. He assessed their value at nearly $200,000. Almost all of these projects were pioneer adaptions to the library field and were followed with interest by librarians across the nation.

Fremont Rider was an early advocate of library cooperation and, during the 1930s, he was the leading spirit in an attempt to organize Connecticut Valley academic librarians to share the use of their book collections. Interestingly enough now in these days of computer-based data, his project apparently foundered upon his insistence for a yearly printed catalog of joint holdings. Undoubtedly, however, much of the ground work for the Hampshire Inter-Library Center was laid at this time.

Rider was an active member of national and regional library associations such as the American Library Association, the Association of College and Research Libraries, and the Connecticut Library Association. He spoke not only before library conventions and library schools but also before a wide variety of citizen groups intrigued by any one of his many projects. He was a member of the Acorn Club of Connecticut from 1939 and of the Middletown Rotary Club.

His pioneer thinking in regard to microreproduction of books led to the invention of microcards. It was his most important invention, but he refused to patent it as he wanted microcards to be widely used as an aid to scholarship. Inevitably a book followed: *The Scholar and the Future of the Research Library* (Hadham Press, 1944), which tied together his library and inventive interests. He had been successively involved with the Microcard Committee, the Microcard Corporation, and the Microcard Foundation, of which he happily served as chairman from 1945 until his death. Rider received the annual medal of the National Microfilm Association in 1961, "awarded in recognition of his achievements in the development of micro-opaque reproduction of textual materials."

While librarian at Wesleyan, he planned and, in 1951, had built the Godfrey Memorial Library, a non-circulating reference library for genealogical research. This incorporated, tax-free library is open to the public. Its primary function is the publication of his *American Genealogical-Biographical Index* (a revised and enlarged cumulation of a 1942-1952 publication), of which volume 100 (recently issued) brings the index to the letter "L." The Godfrey Library now contains some seven million cards on family names, indexing over 17,000 volumes of family histories, town directories, and biographies.

Given Rider's lifelong interest in classification and the ease with which he published, it was no surprise that, during his retirement, he had been working on the 1,217-page *Rider's International Classification for the Arrangement of Books on the Shelves of General Libraries* (Preliminary Edition, Middletown, Conn., 1961). It was for him an irresistible challenge to devise a major classification scheme, regardless of grueling work (never a deterrent to Rider). A few months before his death, in replying to one of the more charitable reviews, he admitted it was a task "too vast to be undertaken by any one individual." Although critics indicted his system as dated, derivative, and not practical for use, he must have been gratified to be complimented on "the wealth of wisdom in the preface." Nevertheless, this publication celebrates a fitting departure for "another of the library profession's all-time greats" (in the words of Karl Brown, who had worked with him on the 1930 edition of the *American Library Directory*).

Fremont Rider's eccentric *And Master of None, an Autobiography in the Third Person* (Godfrey Memorial Library, 1955) unblushingly chronicles his careers as editor, poet, publisher, short story writer, printer, economist, real estate developer, educational philanthropist, librarian-administrator, librarian-disseminator, dramatist, writer of non-fiction, inventor, architect, and genealogist. Of all of these, he was happiest in the library field where he was a mover and a shaker. He was a genius *manqué* of the profession, for his many inventions, innovations, and adaptions

have been transitional and we must be thankful for his role in the progression of librarianship. He was a man of singular purpose and enormous drive, not easy to work with and not likely to take note of opposition. His strong jaw and piercing blue eyes matched the energy of his walk and seemed to bespeak the originality and imagination of his approach to library concerns.

Fremont Rider died in Middletown, October 26, 1962, after a long illness. The memorial service at the North Congregational Church on October 31 was conducted by the Reverend Mr. R. A. Christie, who delivered a sermon written for the occasion by Rider the previous year.

Biographical listings and obituaries—"A. Fremont Rider [Obituary]." *Publishers' Weekly* 182:70 (Nov. 12, 1962); Brown, Karl. "Fremont Rider [Obituary]." *Library Journal* 87:4410-11 (Dec. 12, 1962); Colburn, Edwin B. "Fremont Rider [Obituary]." *Wilson Library Bulletin* 37:341 (Dec. 1962); Parker, Wyman W. "Fremont Rider [Obituary]." *College and Research Libraries* 24:73 (Jan. 1963); *Who Was Who in America* IV (1961-1968); *Who's Who in Library Service*, 1st ed., 2nd ed., 3rd ed. **Books and articles about the biographee**—"Fremont Rider Honored as Microcard Pioneer." *Publishers' Weekly* 180:25 (July 31, 1961); Lydenberg, Harry Miller. "An Account of Versatility." *Library Journal* 81, pt. 1:695-97 (March 15, 1956). **Primary sources and archival materials**—Rider's manuscripts and papers are in the Godfrey Library, Middletown, Connecticut. Many of his published books and some of his unpublished ephemera are in Olin Library of Wesleyan University.

—WYMAN W. PARKER

ROBINSON, OTIS HALL (1835-1912)

Otis Hall Robinson was born at Phelps, New York, on December 3, 1835. When he was quite young, his parents moved to the vicinity of Newark, where he received his grammar school education. Robinson also attended Benedict and Saterlee's Collegiate Institute in Rochester. After some experience in district school teaching and a year as principal of a graded school, he entered the University of Rochester in the fall of 1857; he received his B.A. degree in 1861. He also studied law, was admitted to the bar in 1863, and practiced in Rochester from 1863 to 1865.

In 1864, Robinson joined the faculty of the University of Rochester as a tutor in mathematics and began a formal relationship with that University that was to last the remainder of his life. He was also awarded the A.M. degree in 1864. He was promoted to assistant professor in 1867 and to professor of mathematics in 1869. In addition to his teaching duties, Robinson was appointed assistant librarian in 1866 and was named librarian in 1868. He added astronomy to his list of courses in 1872 and spent the summer of 1875 at Harvard studying observatory work. In 1878, he was appointed by the National Observatory to go to Wyoming Territory to observe the total eclipse of the sun. In 1884, when his work was expanded to cover the field of natural philosophy, his academic title became professor of mathematics and natural philosophy. Ottawa University conferred upon him an honorary Ph.D. degree in 1894. Throughout his career as a librarian, which ended in 1889, Robinson also had professorial duties.

As a librarian, Otis Robinson was a lover of system and order. He plunged into the business of organizing the library, doing all the work himself as he assumed responsibilities formerly held by student assistants. Not until 1870 did he have one student assistant. Although he was a part-time librarian, Robinson found time and energy to improve library techniques, promote student use of the library, become active in the fledgling American Library Association, and contribute papers to various library publications.

An early advocate of the library's place in the educational program, Robinson told his colleagues at the 1876 Conference that "somehow I reproach myself if a student gets to the end of his course without learning how to use the library. All that is taught in college amounts to very little; but if we can send students out self-reliant in their investigations, we have accomplished very much." To help students find materials, he created a looseleaf index to essays in books (comparable to the later ALA *Index*), a supplement to Poole's *Index to Periodical Literature*, and a card catalog for the library. He contributed three chapters to the U.S. Bureau of Education's *Public Libraries in the United States of America* (1876): one on college library administration, which is a landmark work in the history of academic libraries and can still be read with profit; one on indexing periodical and miscellaneous literature; and one on the titles of books. His view of the importance of the educational role of the library was similar to that of Justin Winsor (q.v.) at Harvard, and both were clearly in advance of their time. Robinson became ALA member number 10 at the 1876 Conference.

In January 1880, some three years after the 1876 *Report* appeared, Commissioner John Eaton (q.v.) published a small pamphlet in the USOE circular series called *College Libraries as Aids to Instruction*. The circular contained two essays, one by Winsor and one by Robinson. The latter expanded upon his previous views that library instruction was a vital part of the educational process. Robinson described library instruction on Saturday morning at the University of Rochester, where he had succeeded in getting at least half the faculty, a large number of students, and sometimes the president involved in library instruction. Robinson believed that it was the librarian's duty to administer his library so that everything it contained should be accessible to every reader, with as little inconvenience as possible. He worried less about how many books his library had or how much money he had to buy books than he did about the usefulness of the books, a spirit that guided his administration. He also was interested in developing the more scholarly use of books and libraries. He initiated classroom instruction in the use of books and libraries, and he and another professor made themselves available to talk about books with students and to help students make their selections. The two professors also contributed articles on the library to the student newspaper, writing about the arrangement and cataloging of the library and giving hints on book-buying and reading. Robinson's other major articles appeared in *Library Journal.*

As the initiator of the University of Rochester's first card catalog on the dictionary plan, Robinson enlisted the aid of another professor and several student assistants in his cataloging project. They wrote out all the cards for 9,560 volumes in 93 hours, completing the task in the summer of 1870 at a cost of $329 for labor and materials. These efforts seemed promising but, since there was no way to hold the cards in place, users were apt to "borrow" the cards to use as references. However, Robinson was inventive and devised a solution soon to become commonplace in all libraries. He punched holes in the lower left-hand corner of the card and inserted a stiff rod to hold the cards in place. He is not always given credit for this now widely used invention, for a French librarian, M. Pincon, also had experimented with the rods and holes. However, Robinson's scheme worked, because he was clever enough to make the holes larger than, rather than the same size as, the rod.

In 1877, Robinson saw the new $100,000 Sibley Library opened at the University of Rochester. One of the stipulations of Hiram Sibley's gift was that the Library would be open to Rochester citizens as well as the University community. This led to an article by Robinson in the College Library issue of *Library Journal* (1877) on "College Libraries as Semi-Public Libraries." In the next twelve years, the Library acquired 25,000 additional volumes. Robinson tried to increase hours of service, but not until 1890 was the Library open as much as five hours a day.

With a new building, expanding resources, and the burdens of scholarship and teaching, Robinson found it difficult to continue as University librarian. In a letter of resignation to the trustees in 1889 he wrote:

> For nearly twenty years I was an every day worker in the library, most of the time doing the work with little or no assistance. I often found myself devoting more care and strength to it than to my instruction. . . . I think that the man who does the work in the library should be the Librarian, and be charged with the management—under the President and Library Committee.

He had done as much as anyone in the American library profession to push the idea of the educational role of the college library.

Robinson continued to teach, and he occupied the chair of natural philosophy from 1891 to his retirement in 1903 because of failing health. In 1890, he travelled in Europe and, in 1905, visited the Pacific Coast.

Robinson was a member of Alpha Delta Phi fraternity, Phi Beta Kappa, and the American Association for the Advancement of Science. He had joined the Baptist church at the age of fourteen and for fifty years was an active member of Second Baptist Church in Rochester. He served twenty years as a deacon.

Otis Hall Robinson died on December 12, 1912. He was survived by his wife Sarah E. and two daughters, Flora and Louise.

Biographical listings and obituaries—[Obituary]. *Library Journal* 38:118 (Feb. 1913). **Books and articles about the biographee**—Hayes, Catherine D. "The History of the University of Rochester Libraries—120 Years." The University of Rochester *Library Bulletin* 25:68-74 (Spring 1970); Holley, Edward G. "Academic Libraries in 1876." *College and Research Libraries* 37:15-47 (Jan. 1976). **Primary sources and archival materials**—Other materials can be found in the Department of Rare Books, Manuscripts, and Archives, Rush Rhees Library, University of Rochester.

—EDWARD G. HOLLEY

RODEN, CARL BISMARCK (1871-1956)

Carl Bismarck Roden was born June 7, 1871, in Kansas City, Missouri, to Charles Ernst Ludwig and Louise Henrietta von Roden. Charles Roden, a grocer, moved the family to Chicago, seeking economic opportunity, when Carl was nine years of age. At age fifteen, Roden took (for $5.00 a week) a job as a page in the Chicago Public Library, which then occupied most of the third floor of City Hall. From his first date of employment with the Library until October 31, 1950, his date of retirement, he served an astonishing 64 years with that institution. During that period of time, he watched its growth from 220,736 volumes (in 1886) to over 2,500,000 (in 1950).

The young man had actually planned his career to be in law. In 1891, he completed the Chicago College of Law's course of study, and he was admitted to the Illinois bar in the same year. Yet, as he explained, "I did not enter the practice of law because I could not afford to risk quitting my job at the library. You see, I was supporting my parents."

Yet the great Library he loved held him. Whether through economic necessity or his much celebrated bibliophilia, Roden remained with the Library, becoming an assistant cataloger; then, in 1908, he became chief of the Catalog Division, acting librarian

the following year, and finally, in 1918, librarian. He held the position of chief librarian for 32 years, exactly half his career with the Library.

In appearance, Roden was extremely tall and large of frame. Repeatedly, his associates and colleagues, who commemorated his retirement in 1950, commented on the great size of the man, his determination, his character, and his intellect. A parallel thread runs through such descriptions—that he was shy, dignified, possessed of a highly subtle sense of humor, and not especially concerned with who got the credit for his innovations and creative ideas.

He was an avid collector of books, particularly on Chicago history, Americana (especially the old West), the Pennsylvania Dutch, and early printing and publication. Roden married twice: Harriette Amy Johnson in 1909, who died in 1919, and Lora A. Rich, a fellow employee of the CPL, in 1921. Throughout his tenure as chief librarian, he was to be seen patrolling the halls of the Library, immersed in a book, listening to symphonies, attending the weekly Saturday concerts, at virtually any time the Library was open. He was a fellow of the American Library Institute and a member of the Bibliographical Society of America (president, 1917-1918), the Illinois Library Association (president, 1905-1906), the Chicago Library Club (president, 1899-1900), and the Chicago Literary Club (president, 1926-1927). He also belonged to the Chicago Athletic Club, the City Club, the Cliff Dwellers Club, the University Club of Chicago, Rotary, the Caxton Club, and the Tavern Club.

Roden was not, by nature, assertive, but he was strong in defense of his convictions, and while soft-spoken, was extremely capable of firm and decisive action. One story runs that, in the 1920s, William Hale ("Big Bill") Thompson, Chicago's colorful (if unethical) mayor, was threatening violence to the royal nose of King George V of England, should the monarch have the temerity to visit Chicago. Pursuant to that grudge, and with an eye, perhaps, to Chicago's considerable German segment of the electorate, Thompson sent an agent around to the Library to root out and purge the shelves of "pro-British" books. Roden, advised of the man's presence, discovered him piling such "undesirable" literature on the floor for immediate removal. Looming over the representative of City Hall, Roden ordered the man out of the Library, never to return; he never did.

In 1927, Roden was elected president of the American Library Association. In his unofficial capacity as spokesman for American librarians, he visited the Library Association convention at Edinburgh in that year. It was in his travels in that year that his oratorical gift first received high praise. A glowing testimonial from his travelling companions attested to his enviable abilities as an orator. In fact, he is generally credited, and by a broad spectrum of his contemporaries, with having the felicitous gift of being able to use the right word at the right time, and to the right audience.

In addition to his continued success throughout his career as a speaker, Roden was a prolific writer on library matters. Writing that "bibliography speaks an international language," he encouraged the exchange of documents, literature, and personnel among libraries of all nations, believing that such commerce might aid in overcoming misunderstandings. His internationalism is clear, as he acquired speaking knowledge of Russian, German, French, Italian, and Spanish, despite the fact that his 1927 mission to Scotland and one subsequent week on the Continent were the extent of his foreign travel.

Carl Roden should largely be remembered and honored as a librarian who kept the patron's convenience in mind. He established "curb service" in the downtown library, due to his acute awareness of parking problems and the placement of the general circulating collection on the third and fourth floors of the massive structure. He insisted that his staff members consider themselves (and act) as educators: "It is my belief that the American library is on its way out unless it can show more satisfactory results than circulation. We must reorganize with a staff component to organize better educational opportunities."

Like his predecessor, Henry E. Legler (q.v.; director, 1909-1917), Roden believed strongly in extending services to the neighborhoods of Chicago, and under his influence, the Chicago Public Library brought its services and collections to the people. When Roden began working as a page, there were no branches. By 1918, when Legler left and Roden assumed leadership, there were 42. By the time of Roden's departure from active service in 1950, the number had climbed to 61. Throughout his long tenure in office, he continued Legler's policy by expanding the range of services offered by the Library. Currently, there are 73 branches, numerous substations, and several "floating branches," another Roden invention.

In 1936, upon the occasion of Roden's first completed half-century with the Library, Robert Maynard Hutchins, chancellor of the University of Chicago, toasted him thus: "No educator in this territory has had so wide and deep an influence as Mr. Roden. None deserves so well the gratitude of this community." Overstatement possibly, but a richly deserved testimonial in the view of Chicago's city officials. Although Roden himself was not a library school graduate, having literally risen through the ranks, he had taken the lead in a movement to bring the projected Graduate Library School to the University of Chicago in 1926. Ten years later

(1936), he sanctioned a survey of the Chicago Public Library by the enterprising new School. This survey, conducted by Carleton B. Joeckel (q.v.) and Leon Carnovsky (q.v.) of the Graduate Library School faculty, was later published as *The Metropolitan Public Library in Action* (University of Chicago Press, 1940) and became a landmark in public library surveys.

Praise for the man throughout the literature of library service is so uniform that one begins, at length, to suspect a hyperbolic conspiracy afoot, which some would call "professional backscratching." Detractors emerge, however, upon closer examination. Hints at Roden's sporadic abrasiveness and his occasional "devastating" disagreement with others can be found. All are couched in the record of his accomplishments so as to appear trivial when compared to his evident devotion to duty and love of learning.

However, during the late 1930s, some of the younger professional staff members became restive under what they considered to be Roden's conservative policies. They were especially critical of the slowness with which some of the survey recommendations were implemented. Some of the dissidents organized a library staff union affiliated with the State, County and Municipal Workers Union. Roden accepted the union's presence and discussed library problems freely with its officers. It reflects well on his fairness that a majority of the professional staff never joined the union and that no strike was ever threatened.

Adolph Kroch, a Chicago bookseller and founder of a dynasty in his own field, remembers Roden this way:

His punctilious, grandiose manners might have been mistaken for haughtiness but were merely characteristics of a wise man who enjoyed his prestige and the various honors bestowed upon him without showing them off. . . . Once you got to know him he was wonderful company. He talked entertainingly about the great in history and literature, disclosing profound knowledge of detailed characteristics gleaned from critical reading. He sailed under his own flag, expressing with gusto his own point of view.

Among Roden's foremost accomplishments was the realization, in 1916, of Legler's dream of regional branches, on the south, west, and north sides of the sprawling city. Such branches would operate in the vast extension network, as another link in the chain of localizing the Library, so that it was just down the street from everyman. Roden's regional concept attempted to bring the local patron together with the right materials; once in operation, it was termed, in Joeckel and Carnovsky's *The Metropolitan Public*

Library in Action, "Chicago's most original contribution to the pattern of American library service."

Carl Roden might have been remembered for another important contribution to librarianship. Between 1922 and 1930, the Chicago Public Library established and developed the most ambitious readers' advisor program in any American library. Had it not been for the Great Depression with its attendant severe cutbacks in funding and service, this might well have served as a model for all public libraries.

Subsequent to his retirement in 1950, Roden continued to read, devoting his working hours to writing. A prolific contributor to periodical literature, he remained a lucid, forceful commentator on the library scene far into his eighties. In his eighty-sixth year, following a stroke of paralysis, he died on October 25, 1956, in a nursing home in Palatine, Illinois. He was survived by his wife Lora and a daughter from his first marriage, Marian.

Upon his death, there was extensive discussion among his friends, co-workers, and family as to the type of memorial that would be most fitting. Perhaps the words of Leon Carnovsky, a longtime friend, express best the esteem in which he was held:

It will not be necessary to memorialize Carl Roden by naming a building or a room or a collection for him. These are all pleasant things, but they are trivial compared to the memorial he has created for himself through his service to his library, his city, and his profession.

Biographical listings and obituaries—*National Cyclopaedia of American Biography* C and 47; [Obituary]. *Illinois Libraries* 32:676-77 (Dec. 1950); [Obituary]. *Libri* 7:325-26 (1958); [Obituary]. *Library Journal* 75:2138-39 (Dec. 15, 1950); *Who Was Who in America* III (1951-1960). **Books and articles about the biographee**—[Biographical article]. Chicago Public Library *Staff News*, New Series, v. 3, no. 4 (April 1940); Chicago Public Library *Staff News*, New Series, v. 14, no. 3 (March 1951) [A *Festschrift* devoted entirely to Roden upon the occasion of his retirement after 64 years of service.] **Primary sources and archival materials**—Chicago Public Library. *Annual Reports*. 1917-1951.
                                    —BRUCE A. SHUMAN

ROORBACH, ORVILLE AUGUSTUS (1803-1861)

Orville Augustus Roorbach was born in Tivoli, Dutchess County, New York, on January 20, 1803. The descendant of Dutch farmers who settled in America in the eighteenth century, he spent his early boyhood on his father's farm and received his formal education in Albany, New York. In 1817, at the age of fourteen, he was apprenticed to Evert Duyckinck, a leading bookseller in New York City, and when Duyckinck retired in 1825, Roorbach bought much of his stock and became his successor. About 1830 he moved to Charleston, South Carolina, and, for perhaps eighteen years, was proprietor there of a book store called "At the Sign of the Red Bible," which was a

"famous resort for the literary people of that time" (Growoll, p. xl). (*Appleton's* puts the Charleston residency as from 1826 to 1845; Vol. V, p. 317.) While Roorbach was in South Carolina, he began systematically to compile a record of American books published since 1820. Working alone and in his spare time, at a distance from Boston, Philadelphia, and New York (the major publishing centers of the country), he did not make rapid progress.

He moved back to New York and was in charge of Wiley & Putnam's wholesale department until they dissolved their partnership. Following this, he joined George Palmer Putnam (father of Herbert Putnam [q.v.]), who established the publishing and bookselling house of G. P. Putnam in 1848. It was not until 1849, though, that the first volume of Roorbach's *Bibliotheca Americana–Catalogue of American Publications Including Reprints and Original Works from 1820 to 1848 Inclusive* was published, with the following imprint: New York: Orville A. Roorbach, for sale by G. P. Putnam. This work was intended to be a practical manual for the use of booksellers, listing as it did all American editions then on the market and printed since 1820. Price, size, binding style, and publisher were given. For out-of-print titles, size, publisher, and date of publication only were given.

Putnam published the first supplement in 1850, and in 1852, Roorbach (by then a book jobber) put the original work, the 1850 supplement, and the books of the previous two years into one volume listing over 24,000 titles, and published it himself (reprint, Peter Smith, 1939). This edition also listed the 486 periodicals being published in the United States in 1850. In 1855, Roorbach's son Orville A. Roorbach, Jr., published a supplement compiled by the senior Roorbach, including works published from October 1852 to May 1855. In 1858, Wiley & Halstead published addenda covering from May 1855 to March 1858 and, in 1861, Volume IV, covering from March 1858 to January 1861, was published. (The last three volumes were reprinted in one volume by Peter Smith in 1939.)

Roorbach's book jobbing and publishing business failed in 1857, and he was then employed at various times by several publishing houses—Dix and Edwards, Wiley & Halstead, D. Appleton and Co., and Harper and Bros. During this time, he also published a periodical for his customers—*The Bookseller's Medium and Publisher's Advertiser*—which came out on the first and fifteenth of every month from July 1858 to April 15, 1861. He was in Schenectady, New York, on business for one of the publishing firms when he was stricken with paralysis. He died in Schenectady on June 21, 1861, and was buried in Brooklyn's Greenwood Cemetery. Besides his son, he was survived by his wife and daughter living in Yonkers, New York.

Roorbach's *Bibliotheca Americana* concentrated on literature, history, and the arts; it omitted almanacs, newspapers, and assembly laws and proceedings. It listed approximately 42,000 titles for the forty-year period from 1820 to January 1861 and, as Growoll notes (p. xix), it "bristles with surprising errors and no less surprising omissions." In comparison, the *Checklist of American Imprints 1820-1831* (Scarecrow Press, 1964-1975) lists 52,408 titles for that eleven-year period alone. Roorbach only rarely included dates of publication and, since he intended his book solely as a tool for the book trade, he did not indicate what library, if any, held copies of the titles listed.

Five years after Roorbach's death, James Kelly began publishing his *American Catalogue of Books (Original and Reprints) Published in the United States from January 1861 to January 1871*, 2 vols. (1866-1871). Kelly had wanted this work to be a fifth volume of the *Bibliotheca Americana*, but Roorbach's son objected to this designation, so Kelly adopted the above title instead (Kelly, "Notice").

The Scarecrow Press *Checklist of American Imprints* does not give original price, size, or binding information as Roorbach does. It does, however, give pagination, publication date, and locations of copies of a title. So, for the period it covers, it now supersedes the *Bibliotheca Americana* for most purposes. Still, for more than 100 years, those looking for bibliographical information on a country-wide basis had to go first to the trade bibliography compiled by Roorbach, a bookseller-bibliographer working in his spare time in the mid-1800s.

Biographical listings and obituaries—*Appleton's Cyclopedia of American Biography* V (1888); *A Critical Dictionary of English Literature and British and American Authors II* (1878); [Obituary]. *American Publishers' Circular and Literary Gazette* 7, No. 26:1 (June 29, 1861). Books and articles about the biographee—Growoll, Adolph. *Book Trade Bibliography in the United States in the Nineteenth Century.* New York: Dibden Club, 1898; reprinted Burt Franklin, 1969.

—MARILYN L. HAAS

ROOT, AZARIAH SMITH (1862-1927)

Azariah Smith Root, son of Solomon Francis and Anna Smith Root, was born in Middlefield, Massachusetts, on February 3, 1862. He attended high school in Hinsdale and Pittsfield, Massachusetts, and received the Bachelor of Arts degree from Oberlin College in 1884. The following year he studied at Boston University Law School, then returned to Oberlin, where he worked as a cataloger in the College Library during the year 1885-1886. In 1886-1887, he was a student in the Harvard Law School. In 1887, he was appointed librarian of Oberlin College and, in 1890, was made professor of bibliography, appointments he

held until his death in 1927. He studied at the University of Göttingen in 1898-1899 and was a part-time member of the faculty of Western Reserve University's Library School from its inception in 1904 until the time of his death. He was a member of Phi Beta Kappa, the Bibliographical Society of America (president, 1909-1910 and 1923-1924), the Ohio Library Association (president, 1900-1901 and 1914-1915), the American Library Institute, the Bibliographical Society (London), the Gesellschaft für Typenkunde, and the Gutenberg Gesellschaft. In the American Library Association, he was president in 1921-1922. He married Anna May Metcalf, an Oberlin classmate, in 1887. They had one son, Francis Metcalf, and one daughter, Marion Metcalf Root.

Root's lifelong association with Oberlin began naturally when his father sent him to finish his preparatory education under the care of an uncle then serving on the Oberlin faculty. His father had other plans for his later education, but Azariah liked Oberlin and did so well that he was allowed to stay. Even at that age, he was loved and honored by his classmates, who sought his advice on all sorts of matters. Upon his graduation, he left Oberlin to enter Harvard Law School, but within a few months he was asked to return to catalog and classify the Library. He agreed and began "studying libraries two hours a day" before returning to Oberlin in July 1885 to begin work. By fall he was also teaching. In 1886, he again went to law school in the East. Shortly thereafter, the Oberlin faculty expressed "their great satisfaction with the manner in which he has performed the work of 'cataloging' the College Library," and on his twenty-fifth birthday elected him to the librarianship of Oberlin College. A compatriot said, "I . . . remember when he had his call to his life work in Oberlin. I think he asked no advice and we gave none; it was the natural and proper thing for him to undertake. We all felt the suitableness of the job for him and of him for the job." He assumed his new duties in April of 1887, and in the same month was married.

The influence of his family and their beliefs were reflected throughout his own life and work. His daughter states that "the Root, Smith, and Metcalf families were Baptists, of strong anti-slavery convictions, believers in and supporters of higher education and equal rights for men and women." During his long career, Root was active in church, civic and professional activities, and his actions reflected that background and upbringing. Intensely active in the First Church of Oberlin, he also preached at least once a year at each of Oberlin's Negro churches.

In Oberlin's civic affairs, he was equally active and influential. A major concern was a harmonious relationship between town and gown, the maintenance of which was due in large part to his personal efforts. He served on the Board of Commerce, as a director of the Telephone Company and of the Oberlin Mutual Benefit Association, on the Board of Health, as president of the Village Improvement Society, and for years as president of the Board of Education. It was from this latter post and as college librarian that he proposed and implemented the opening of the College Library to town citizenry and the inclusion of a high school reading room and children's room in the new library building donated by Andrew Carnegie (q.v.). This joint operation of college and public libraries survives today.

In 1903, Root outlined his ideas for that same new College Library building and later expanded it into a 23-page document, which Keyes Metcalf believes is the earliest extant library building program written by a librarian. The object of his program was to obtain a building that was mainly functional, rather than an "architectural masterpiece": "First and chiefest of all, it must be absolutely fireproof. Second—It is obvious that the building will have to be extremely simple in its exterior. Third—Economy of administration must also be kept in mind constantly." Of the partitions he wrote, "As far as possible I should like to have them independent of the structural organization of the building so that they could be shifted about, as the partitions in office buildings often are, to suit changing conditions."

In this and other matters, he was a man of vision and independent thought. In 1908, a

> careful list of all sets indexed in the "Poole" and other American indexes to general periodicals [was] prepared to be used as a basis for a contemplated union list of such periodicals in Ohio. It is hoped by this means to save the smaller libraries from the expense involved in collecting the less frequently used sets, to increase inter-library loans, and to relieve the larger libraries outside the state from the many calls upon their good nature and generosity.

In 1922, in his presidential address to the American Library Association, he advocated greater standardization of methods and routines, cooperative book lists, a clearinghouse for duplicate material, collective purchasing, and cooperative storage of little-used books. "The great need of American libraries today is that each library should think not in terms of itself and its own interests, but in the spirit and with the conception of library unity." He helped in guiding the direction that President Rutherford B. Hayes's library would take (advising his son Colonel Hayes regarding general policy, cataloging, books, and equipment to be purchased) and helped the librarians. Yet books and the library collection were his first love. Keyes Metcalf wrote,

> I think his greatest single accomplishment was building the Oberlin College Library from a collection of a handful of books into a library that was far and away the superior of any other college, as distinct from university, library in the country with the exception of Dartmouth which had had much larger funds available.... Perhaps even more important ..., he in some way or other contrived to make the library the real center of the college life.

One acquisition of which Root was especially proud was the Union Library Association Library, consisting of the combined libraries of both the men's and women's student societies. This collection was given to the College in 1908, the same year that the latter acquired its Carnegie library building. Root commented that the Union Library Association "was for many years the most important library connected with the institution, and up to the early 90's was easily more valuable than the College Library."

Root was more than librarian; he was also teacher, administrator, respected colleague, and friend. His services to the college were many. In 1908, he wrote that they had been

> mostly confined to the financial side of the work. I have been Chairman of the Budget Committee practically all the time for about fifteen years, and a member of the Prudential Committee [which coordinated operational matters] for the same length of time.... With a plant now worth perhaps two million dollars, and with invested funds to about the same amount, there is an immense amount of plain and rather hum-drum business which some one has to do, and a part of this ... has fallen to my lot.

He was vice-chairman of the General Faculty, College Faculty, and General Council, chairman of a fundraising campaign, and he served on numerous other committees. One trustee wrote after Root's death:

> He was such a broadminded man, so tolerant, so enthusiastic, so hard-working, so appreciative of big things and yet so willing to do the little things that must be done to keep matters going smoothly, that he combined an unusual number of rare qualities. I used to think of him somewhat as a Benjamin Franklin, for among other things he was very wise.

He was a teacher both at the College and at several library schools: Western Reserve (as noted), and summers at Columbia, the University of Michigan, and Pratt Institute. The New York Public Library School called him to serve as acting head for the year 1916-1917, following the death of Mary Wright Plummer (q.v.). His teaching was fresh and buoyant, learned but "absolutely unpedantic," according to William W. Bishop (q.v.), who also noted (*Papers of the Bibliographical Society of America* 22:66-68

[1928]) that Root's friends and colleagues all called him "Professor" Root as a sign of genuine respect for his abilities. His specialties were bibliography, the history of printing, and the history of illustration. During infrequent leaves, he conducted research abroad on Grolier bindings and Costeriana, pursuing the question of whether Coster preceded Gutenberg with printing. In order to do this latter work, he learned Dutch, and used the summer of 1926 to research archives in Haarlem. He influenced many students to pursue library careers, the most notable being Keyes D. Metcalf, younger brother of Mrs. Root.

Root was also highly involved in the development of library education in its growing stages. In 1918, C. C. Williamson (q.v.) consulted him (at the instigation of James Bertram [q.v.], secretary to Andrew Carnegie) concerning recommendations for a committee to investigate training for library work. This may have been partially a result of Root's 1917 ALA conference report on "The Library School of the Future" (*ALA Bulletin* 11:157-60 [July 1917]); certainly Bertram used Root's findings concerning the then-current state of library training as the basis for Appendix G to his 1918 "Memorandum" to the Carnegie Corporation on library training. More likely is that Root's expertise had been developed during his membership on the ALA Committee on Library Training. During his chairmanship (1908-1912), the Committee considered approaching the Carnegie Foundation for the Advancement of Teaching for the funds to survey library schools, but the idea was discouraged by Mary Wright Plummer, Root's successor as chairman. The data for the Committee's own studies were gathered through the assistance of Mary Eileen Ahern (q.v.), editor of *Public Libraries*, but the anticipated list of "approved" library schools was never issued. Rather, the Committee seems to have shifted responsibilities for library education standards to the newly formed American Association of Library Schools in 1915 (see Sarah K. Vann's *Training for Librarianship before 1923*, ALA, 1961).

Root's 1917 report, however, was highly optimistic concerning the need for trained librarians (although Vann has noted in *The Williamson Reports: A Study* [Scarecrow, 1971, p. 52] that he reported only on the "output of librarians" and not on the lack of training facilities). Indeed, Root's conclusion (p. 157) was that: "In all this there is nothing but hopefulness for the library schools; the more schools the better." In 1919, Root was appointed to the ALA Committee of Five, along with chairman Arthur Bostwick (q.v.), Linda Anne Eastman (q.v.), Carl Milam (q.v.), and Williamson. Their charge was to survey post-war developments, to consider standard-

ization, certification, and training, and to make recommendations ("Committee of Five: On a Library Survey," *ALA Bulletin* 13:32 [March 1919]). The "Report [of the Committee of Five], 1919" (*ALA Bulletin* 13:326-28 [July 1919]) recommended the creation of a national board of certification to investigate and certify schools and to correlate their activities. The resulting Committee of Nine on National Certification and Training (appointed in 1921) was chaired by Williamson.

Root also favored training librarians through correspondence schools as well as through more conventional means. Toward this end, he served as director of the American Correspondence School of Librarianship from its inception in 1923. Following Root's death in 1927, the School was, in 1928, transferred *in toto* to Columbia University's School of Library Service, under the direction of Williamson (see "In the Library World. New York," *Library Journal* 53:318 [April 1, 1928]).

Root was a man of immense size, weighing over 225 pounds but only five feet five inches tall, giving him a peculiarly rolling gait. He had an unusually retentive memory. Those who knew him characterize him best: he "was a picturesque person, always dressed in black and his clothes were apt to be decorated with bits of leather from book bindings. He was always smiling and entertaining. He was partly bald but had a funny little shock of hair standing up above his forehead." "He was always ready to give time and thought most generously, always kind and genial, always a loyal friend and co-laborer, and so wise a counselor that we trusted him." "Professor Root was as democratic and 'common' as any man who ever lived and his understanding of human life in all its phases was unusually correct and complete." "I suspect that 'Prof. Root' was probably the most useful and influential man on the College Faculty. He had knowledge, common sense and vision."

Azariah Smith Root died on October 2, 1927, in Oberlin.

Biographical listings and obituaries—*National Cyclopaedia of American Biography* 22; Oberlin College. *Alumni Necrology*, 1925-1930, p. 76; [Obituary]. *Oberlin Alumni Magazine* 24, no. 1:15-16 (Oct. 1927); *Who Was Who in America* I (1897-1942). **Books and articles about the biographee**—Bishop, William W. "Azariah Smith Root." *The Papers of the Bibliographical Society of America* 22:66-68 (1928); "Our Frontispiece: Azariah Smith Root." *Bulletin of Bibliography* 11:1 (Jan.-April 1920) [includes portrait]. **Primary sources and archival materials**—Hellman, Florence Selma. "Writings of Azariah Smith Root, 1862-1927." 9 leaves. 193-?; Root, Marion Metcalf. "Azariah Smith Root." 64 leaves. 1955?; Severance, Henry O. "Azariah Smith Root, 1862-1927." 24 leaves. 1941?; Root's papers are held at the Oberlin College Library.

—HERBERT F. JOHNSON

ROSE, ERNESTINE (1880-1961)

On a bright September morning in 1921, I came up out of the subway at 135th Street and Lenox into the beginnings of the Negro Renaissance. . . . I headed to . . . the Harlem Branch Library just up the street. There a warm and wonderful librarian, Miss Ernestine Rose, white, made newcomers feel welcome.

Thus begins a reminiscence of the Negro poet Langston Hughes. Ernestine Rose, a somewhat regal presence with her blond-grey hair done up in a coronet, likewise greeted many other figures on the Negro cultural scene in this time of ferment. The "great migration" of 1915-1919 had brought up from the South tens of thousands of Negroes to enter a labor force depleted of its immigrant populations because of World War I. Formerly a white middle-class area, Harlem now became the home of the largest concentration of Afro-Americans in the country, numbering some 300,000 by 1930. Ernestine Rose, having worked with immigrant groups as librarian at the Chatham Square (1908-1911) and Seward Park (1915-1917) Branches of the New York Public Library, and with Negro troops in Europe as part of the American Library Association's Library War Service (1918-1920), was the natural choice for the post of branch librarian at the New York Public Library's 135th Street Branch (renamed for writer Countee Cullen in 1951).

Ernestine Rose was born in Bridgehampton, New York, in 1880 to Stephen and Anna Chatfield Rose. She received her A.B. from Wesleyan University in 1902 and her B.L.S. from the New York State Library School in 1904. She served with the NYPL from 1905 (not the commonly accepted 1908) to 1942, except for the years she was assistant principal of the [Andrew] Carnegie [q.v.] Library School in Pittsburgh (1917-1918) and travelled with the Library War Service (1918-1920). From 1928 to 1947, she was instructor, and later associate professor, at Columbia University's School of Library Service.

Told by one of his teachers that the Negro had no history, Arthur A. Schomburg (q.v.), a Negro scholar born and educated in Puerto Rico, amassed a huge collection of books and manuscripts to prove the contrary. Schomburg and Rose, in the context of the burgeoning interest in Afro-American traditions, found themselves key figures in Harlem history. A Division of Negro Literature, History and Prints had been started at the NYPL's 135th Street Branch in 1925 to provide a non-circulating reference collection. In 1926, the Carnegie Foundation provided funds for the purchase of the Schomburg Collection, with Schomburg himself becoming the first curator in 1931.

The 135th Street Branch soon became a hub of community activity. In 1931, the American Association for Adult Education provided funds for a "Harlem experiment." Policies and plans were laid by Rose in concert with a committee representing all walks of life. Branch activities included a chorus of 160 voices, a family relations institute for local teachers and social workers, outdoor forums on current issues that attracted thousands of people, and get-togethers at neighborhood parks with young mothers. Literary and art workshops brought out the talents of men later famous. The most illustrious writers of the day, both black and white, attracted stand-up audiences. The Krigwa Players Little Negro Theatre, a resident company at the Library, won awards.

Women who worked with Ernestine Rose at the 135th Street Branch remember her with warmth. Jean Blackwell Hutson, curator of what is now the Schomburg Center for Research in Black Culture, was one of the "guinea pigs" in opening employment for Negroes in the city library system, and found Ernestine Rose easy to communicate with. Dorothy Homer (Rose's eventual successor) remembers how Rose canvassed branch after branch until she found one receptive to having a Negro behind the desk and thereby got Mrs. Homer placed.

Rose was active in the adult education movement, serving as chairman of the New York Library Association's Adult Education Committee and later on the ALA Adult Education Board. In the NYLA itself, she was vice-president in 1932 and president in 1934. Refusing to be drawn into controversies about just how large a role the library should play in the community, Rose said this "live and crackling power house for . . . self-education" should be used to its maximum, and that if a social agency later took on a task previously performed by the library, the latter could then give it up.

In 1939, Ernestine Rose presented the first Library Bill of Rights to the ALA, expressing the view that all races, nationalities, and political opinions be represented in library collections and that the library serve as "an institution to educate for democratic living" by means of cultural activities and discussions of questions of public interest. Rose also pressed ardently for a pension plan for NYPL librarians, which eventually came to pass. She retired in 1942.

Her major work, *The Public Library in American Life* (Columbia University Press, 1954), is a definitive historical study. Library services must be scaled to the users without conceding to "mediocrity," since the alert and intellectual mind, she maintained, transcends class and must be served. She was fond of the then current expressions: the library as "a people's university" and librarians as "professors of books." Rose was concerned that the first person greeting the potential user be trained and not apathetic.

Her book *Bridging the Gulf: Work with the Russian Jews and Other Newcomers* (Immigrant Publication Society, 1917) is a warm and detailed account of her experiences working with immigrants on the Lower East Side of Manhattan. She advocated the hiring of foreign-language-speaking staff and the stocking of books in those languages:

> Those who come to the library first at the call of a Yiddish or Hungarian book, are attracted by the "easy English" shelf, and later become regular readers of English.... Nearly one-third of the women in the Seward Park Mothers' Club have already taken out their own cards ... in a devouring desire to "get the English," which is winning away their children. So are they won to the library and the gulf is bridged.

Ernestine Rose was a pace-setter in the development of adult education in libraries, an important figure in the "Harlem renaissance," and a leader among and teacher of a generation of librarians. She died on March 28, 1961.

Biographical listings and obituaries–[Obituary]. *Library Journal* 86:2448 (July 1961); [Obituary]. *New York Library Association Bulletin* 9:36 (May 1961); [Obituary]. *Wilson Library Bulletin* 35:744 (June 1961); University of Wisconsin. *A Biographical and Bibliographical Directory of Women Librarians*. Madison: 1977; *Who's Who in Library Service*, 1st ed. Books and articles about the biographee–Monroe, Margaret Ellen. *Library Adult Education: The Biography of an Idea*. New York: Scarecrow Press, 1963 [Biographee's work in adult education is discussed herein].

—BERNICE SELDEN

ROTHROCK, MARY UTOPIA (1890-1976)

Mary Utopia Rothrock was born on September 19, 1890, in Trenton, Tennessee, the daughter of the Reverend Mr. John Thomas and Utopia Ada Herron Rothrock. She received a Bachelor of Science degree from Vanderbilt University in 1911 and a Master of Science degree the following year. From 1912 to 1914, she attended the New York State Library School at Albany, from which she received the Bachelor of Library Science degree in 1922. (Albany gave a certificate in 1914, followed up by a degree in 1922.) While attending the Library School, she also held the position of assistant in the New York State Library.

After receiving her library degree, Rothrock became head of the Circulation Department at Cossitt Library in Memphis. Two years later (1916), she became librarian at the Lawson McGhee Library in Knoxville and served in that position until 1934. She immediately became involved in the building of the new Lawson McGhee Library when she took the position and saw its completion and opening in 1917. During the next eighteen years, Rothrock developed a fine basic public library for Knoxville and began the

development of a branch system that would eventually serve both the city and the county. As a result of her efforts, in 1929, the Rosenwald Fund selected the Knoxville Library as one of nine in the country where funds for service to all the people of the county, rural and urban, Negro and white, were provided.

In 1934, she became supervisor of library services for the Tennessee Valley Authority, a position she held until 1948. She continued for three more years as a library consultant to TVA. In her TVA position, she encouraged a wide variety of cooperative relationships and promoted the first Southeastern States Library Cooperative Survey. From 1949 to 1955, she was librarian for Knox County, Tennessee. During her administration there, she reorganized the library and established it on a firm basis.

In 1941, Rothrock served as a member of the Advisory Committee on Libraries of the U.S. Office of Education. During her professional career, she was active in the American Library Association, having served in the following posts: member of the Editorial Committee (1924-1929 and 1932-1933); member of the Executive Board (1938-1942); Lending Section chairman (1922 and 1931); Library Extension Board (1933-1938); chairman of the Adult Education Round Table (1935-1936); member of the ALA Council (1932-1942); chairman of the Visual Methods Committee (1937-1940); chairman of the Audio-Visual Committee (1948-1949); chairman of the Joint Committee on Libraries and Educational Films (ALA-NEA) (1940-1942); chairman of National Defense Activities and Libraries (1941-1942); first vice president (1945-1946); Advisory Committee for the Public Library Inquiry (1947-1950); and president (1946-1947). Her presidential address, "Libraries in a New Era," was a plea for librarians to become more actively involved with technology and non-print media.

In addition to the American Library Association, Rothrock was active in other library and historical groups. She was a founder of the Southeastern Library Association (1920-1922) and served as its first president in 1922-1924. She was secretary-treasurer of the Tennessee Library Association (1916-1918) and twice president (1919-1920 and 1927-1928). In the East Tennessee Historical Society, she was secretary (1925-1928), treasurer (1929-1932), and twice president (1932 and 1937). She was also a member of the Society's Editorial Board (1929-1976). She served as a member of the Tennessee Historical Commission (1944-1967).

In 1938, Rothrock received the first Joseph W. Lippincott Award given by the American Library Association for "the most outstanding contribution to librarianship during 1935-36." The citation mentions specifically her "rare vision and intelligence shown in organizing regional library service and related adult education activities." As TVA librarian, she established libraries for workers and their families at dam construction sites. She also pushed for regional library development. In 1948, the University of Chattanooga conferred on her the honorary degree of Doctor of Letters. A few days before her death in 1976, the ALA Council selected her for its highest award, honorary membership.

Rothrock was the author of *Discovering Tennessee* and *This Is Tennessee*, which were adopted as textbooks for the state's schools. In 1946, she edited *French Broad-Holston Country: A History of Knox County, Tennessee*, which was published by the East Tennessee Historical Society. In 1959, she edited and published an annotated edition of Haywood's *Natural and Aboriginal History of Tennessee*, the state's first published history, which had been out of print for 136 years. In addition to these volumes, she contributed extensively to library and historical journals.

Rothrock was a fellow of the American Library Institute, a member of Delta Delta Delta Sorority, the Colonial Dames of America, the Presbyterian Church, and the Democratic Party.

She loved the mountains of her adopted East Tennessee home and spent many happy days there in her mountain cabin, and she also enjoyed trading in mountain real estate. Her rare combination of intelligence and charm made her equally a friend of unlettered mountain people and of leaders in many fields. Her friends and admirers were countless, and comments from two Southerners illustrate her contributions. Elizabeth Cole, consultant in the Division of Public Library Services in Georgia, has said, "She did originate the idea of regional library services which is a living and prospering idea that will stand as a monument to her great mind, her energetic, tenacious spirit, and her intelligent, logical vision." C. R. Graham, director of the Louisville Free Public Library, said, "I remember her best as a pleasant debater. She did not 'suffer fools gladly,' and one had to defend every single statement he made or be laughed into defeat. We called her 'the Best Man in the Library Profession.'" Known to her friends as "Topie," she encouraged many young people to enter the profession, and she was a leader in library development in the Southeast. She died in Knoxville on January 30, 1976. Her will directed that $10,000 be given to the Southeastern Library Association for a biennial award, and the McClung Historical Collection of the Knoxville-Knox County Public Library was made the residuary legatee of her estate ($285,000).

Biographical listings and obituaries—*Biographical Directory of Librarians in the United States and Canada*, 5th ed.; [Obituary]. *Knoxville Journal*, Jan. 31, 1976; [Obituary].

Knoxville News-Sentinel, Jan. 31, 1976; [Obituary]. *Nashville Tennessean*, Jan. 31, 1976; *Who's Who in America* 17-28 (1932/1933-1954/1955); *Who's Who in Library Service*, 1st ed., 2nd ed., 3rd ed.; *Who's Who of American Women* 1 (1958/1959). **Books and articles about the biographee**—"Consultant Named for Tennessee Project." *Library Journal* 58:995 (Dec. 1, 1933); Deaderick, Lucile. "Mary Utopia Rothrock—A Tribute." *Tennessee Librarian* 28:71-72 (Spring 1976); Harris, Helen M. "Tennessee's Letter Librarian." *Tennessee Librarian* 8:3-4 (Oct. 1955); "In Memory of Mary Rothrock, 1890-1976." *American Libraries* 7:442 (July-Aug. 1976); Johnson, James W. K. "Rothrock Story." *Tennessee Librarian* 8:73-75 (April 1956); Mills, Jesse C. "A Personal Tribute to Mary U. Rothrock." *Southeastern Librarian* 26:64-67 (Summer 1976); Suddarth, Emma. "Mary U. Rothrock." *Bulletin of Bibliography* 22:73-75 (Sept.-Dec. 1957). **Primary sources and archival materials**—Rothrock's papers and diaries are in the Calvin M. McClung Historical Collection, Knoxville-Knox County Public Library, 500 W. Church Ave., Knoxville, Tennessee 37902.

—LUCILE DEADERICK

RUDOLPH, ALEXANDER JOSEPH (c.1850-1917)

Alexander Joseph Rudolph was born in Austria, most likely near the middle of the nineteenth century. Very little is known of his early life except that he served in the Austrian army and eventually emigrated to San Francisco, possibly adopting the name Rudolph to conceal an earlier identity.

His first known contact with the American library profession was as an assistant to Frederick Beecher Perkins (q.v.) at the San Francisco Free Public Library in the 1880s. He continued there as the first assistant librarian under John Vance Cheney from 1887 to 1894, and, when Cheney went to the Newberry Library in Chicago in 1894, Rudolph went with him in the same role.

Rudolph's chief contribution to the library field was as an inventor of library technical devices related primarily to cataloging and book processing. His chief venture, which he called the Rudolph Continuous Indexer, was a mechanical method of displaying sheets of mounted catalog entries. The sheets of entries, each 16 inches long and containing room for 136 lines of compact type, were connected in the form of a linked belt. The sheets were placed in a cabinet, 42 inches high, and were drawn up over a drum to be viewed by the patron through a plate glass cover. As the patron cranked the belt to the desired entry, the unused sheets would pass down again into the cabinet into a hanging storage location below. He later produced a related device in which the sheets were simply held in an expandable binder.

Rudolph was convinced that his machine combined the best features of book and card catalogs. The catalog user could view a large number of entries at once, and the catalog could be kept up to date because single new entries (or whole sheets of new entries) could be easily inserted in their proper places.

Furthermore, Rudolph strongly felt that his device could reduce cataloging costs, first, because the mounting sheets could accommodate a variety of clipped and pasted entries—including those taken from existing printed catalogs—and second, because it made printed book catalogs unnecessary. The chief negative feature that he was never able to overcome, however, was the machine's tendency to tie up a much greater portion of the catalog by a single user than did card catalog drawers.

Rudolph first announced his invention to the American Library Association at its 1891 San Francisco meeting. His enthusiasm for the device as a panacea for cataloging caused many librarians to be wary of his claims. And during the next two years, when he failed to display the device because a patent had not yet been issued, the wariness of librarians turned to skepticism and criticism. Rudolph subsequently defended his invention (see his "Progressive Machine Index," *Nation* 55:125 [August 18, 1892]) and established a Chicago-based firm, the Rudolph Indexer Company, to manufacture and market it. By the time he presented it to the ALA at the World's Columbian Exposition in 1893, however, an important change had occurred in his plans. In order to make the device marketable and perhaps to bolster his claim that cataloging costs would be reduced, he prepared to add to his company a centralized cataloging bureau to supply the necessary catalog entries as well as the mechanical devices. It was the prospect of centralized cataloging that, in fact, aroused an enormous, positive interest among librarians at that later date. And when word spread that Rudolph was enlisting the services of Charles Ammi Cutter (q.v.) to head the cataloging bureau, librarians began making tacit commitments to purchase both the devices and the cataloging service. Unfortunately, however, Melvil Dewey's (q.v.) Library Bureau, which had initially stated that it did not plan to enter the centralized cataloging market, pre-empted that market in October 1893 by suddenly offering its own card cataloging service. Although he continued to market his expandable index books for a short time thereafter, Rudolph found his larger entrepreneurial dreams shattered by the Bureau.

During the late 1890s, Rudolph continued in his inclination for invention. He developed and publicized a blue-print process that held promise as a means of making book catalogs from card catalog entries (see his "Blue-Print Process for Printing Catalogs," *Library Journal* 24:102-105 [March 1899]). He worked on a process for removing stains from photo-prints (see his "Removing Stains from Prints," *Library Journal* 27:910 [October 1902]). He also developed an extensive and complex indexing system for the Newberry Library's genealogical collection (see his "Newberry Genealogical Index,"

Library Journal 24:53-55 [February 1899]) and a device for binding pamphlets, both of which employed his expandable index binders.

After an initial period of interest in them, Rudolph's inventions proved unacceptable—if not a bit eccentric—to the library profession. The Newberry Library itself gained a reputation for being a place where things were done "differently." Rudolph's own library career was closely tied to that of Cheney, who implicitly entrusted to him the technical administration of both the San Francisco and Newberry libraries. But Rudolph's overbearing and abrupt manner, characterized by rigidity and aristocratic authoritarianism, and further affected by bitterness related especially to his business failure, made it difficult for him to work with the Newberry staff. When Cheney retired in 1909, Rudolph soon ran afoul of the new administration and was dismissed. Eventually, all of his various inventions used there were discontinued. Between 1909 and 1917, he attempted market speculations, but these too failed. Despairing of his past and also of his failing health (he was going blind), Alexander J. Rudolph took his own life on August 16, 1917, in Chicago.

Biographical listings and obituaries—"Fearing Blindness, Veteran Librarian Ends Life in Hotel [Obituary]." *Chicago Herald*, Aug. 17, 1917; "Rudolph Kills Self in Hotel; Market Loser [Obituary]." *Chicago Daily Tribune*, Aug. 17, 1917. **Books and articles about the biographee**—Cutter, Charles A. [Editorial]. *Library Journal* 18:277-79 (Aug. 1893); Cutter, Charles A. "The Librarians at Chicago." *Nation* 57:150 (Aug. 31, 1893); Cutter, Charles A. "Librarians at San Francisco." *Nation* 53:329-30 (Oct. 29, 1891); Holley, Edward G. *Charles Evans, American Bibliographer*. Urbana: University of Illinois Press, 1963; Miksa, Francis L., ed. *Charles Ammi Cutter: Library Systematizer*. Littleton, Colo.: Libraries Unlimited, 1977; Miksa, Francis L. "Charles Ammi Cutter, Nineteenth Century Systematizer of Libraries." Ph.D. dissertation, University of Chicago, 1974. **Primary sources and archival materials**—Merrill, William Stetson. "Early Days at the Newberry Library: Reminiscences of Persons and Events." MS. Newberry Library; Volume of printed circulars and manuscript letters, Rudolph Indexer Company to William Richard Cutter, September and October 1893. Columbia University Library, Library of the School of Library Service; Letters between Charles A. Cutter and Melvil Dewey and between Charles A. Cutter and Richard R. Bowker concerning the Rudolph Indexer Company in 1893 will be found in the Columbia University Library, Melvil Dewey Papers and New York Public Library, Richard R. Bowker Papers.

FRANCIS L. MIKSA

RUSH, CHARLES EVERETT (1885-1958)

Charles Everett Rush was born March 23, 1885, on a farm near Fairmont, Indiana, to Nixon and Louisa Winslow Rush, both of whom were active in the Society of Friends (Quakers). Because of his small size, Rush decided early on a career other than farming. In an interview in the *Indianapolis News* of February 5, 1925, he stated:

Just what calling I would follow caused me a great deal of concern, and finally in desperation I turned to teaching; not that I wanted to teach, but it seemed a way out. Then suddenly it came over me that I would be a librarian. At that time I didn't even know there was such a vocation, but I knew I was going to be one anyway.

Following graduation from Fairmont Academy in 1902, Rush entered Earlham College. He helped to support himself by working as a library assistant in the college library, and during the summer of 1904, he took library courses at the University of Wisconsin. Graduating in 1905 with a bachelor of arts degree, he went back to the University of Wisconsin for advanced work. Rush enrolled at Melvil Dewey's (q.v.) New York State Library School in 1906 and helped finance his way by working as a cataloger in the Pruyn Private Library, and later as an assistant at the Newark (New Jersey) Public Library. It was during this period that Rush became acquainted with a fellow student, Lionne Adsit, whom he subsequently married (on September 7, 1910). They had three daughters, Alison Adsit, Frances Marie, and Myra Lionne.

Receiving his B.L.S. degree in 1908, Rush accepted the position of head librarian at the Jackson (Michigan) Public Library. He then went on to serve as head librarian of similar institutions in St. Joseph, Missouri (1910-1916) and Des Moines, Iowa (1916-1917). According to one biographer, Rush "made sound librarianship and Quaker fellowship unite in building first-class service for their community." He was an early believer in advertising the library's services.

In 1917, Rush went to Indianapolis as director of that city's library system. He immediately set about reorganizing the library and helped to develop it into one of the leading public libraries in the country. He established a Business Branch, a Teachers' Library, a library in the Riley Hospital for children, and a Readers' Advisory Service, primarily for out-of-work young people.

Rush was contacted to serve with the Library War Service effort of the American Library Association, and served from April to October 1918, first as a library organizer at Camp Humphreys, Virginia. Later, he was in charge of publicity at the War Service Headquarters in Washington, D.C.

Rush returned to Indianapolis and remained in that city until 1928, when he accepted the position of director of libraries and professor of education in the Teachers College of Columbia University. In 1930, that institution sent Rush to Europe to study various methods of bibliographic research at some of the major libraries there.

The 1930s were a very busy period for Rush. He served as vice-president of the American Library Association, became associate librarian at Yale University (1931-1938), served as an informal advisor on library services for the [Andrew] Carnegie [q.v.] Corporation, and, in 1936, again journeyed to Europe, this time as a U.S. delegate to the International Library Committee which met in Warsaw.

In 1938, Rush was chosen from forty possible candidates to succeed Linda Anne Eastman (q.v.) as librarian of the Cleveland Public Library. His stay in Cleveland was relatively short, however, and was marred by disagreements with the Library Board over administrative matters. However, the political situation in Cleveland brought forth strong support for Rush in the library press. When the position of librarian at the University of North Carolina became available in 1941, Rush resigned his position in Cleveland in order that he might "find harmony and professional opportunity" in this new position.

At the University of North Carolina, Rush served as both director of libraries and chairman of the library division. Here he was to remain for the rest of his professional career, and under his administration the library prospered, increasing its book stock, expanding the staff, and constructing an addition to the main building. Rush retired on June 30, 1954, ending nearly fifty years of library service.

In 1939, the *Cleveland Plain Dealer* made the following comment about Rush:

... an excellent disciplinarian, very prompt and expects others to be the same; ... is inordinately neat, imperturbable, smokes his pipe continually and for amusement enjoys camping, being an expert angler, going in for the casting and wading school of trout fishing.

Over the years, Rush contributed many articles to professional literature, both in journals and books. Among the topics covered in his earlier articles were reading for boys and girls, reference work, library administration, and adult education. He was especially interested in the library's role in this latter field, and he became a leader in the adult education movement. He was among the first librarians to take an interest in microphotography, establishing a microphotographic laboratory at Yale. He also chaired the first Board of Editors for the *Journal of Documentary Reproduction*. The books that he wrote or contributed to were: *Modern Aladdins and Their Magic: The Science of Things around Us* (1926) written in collaboration with Amy Winslow; "Microphotography in the Yale University Library," in *Microphotography for Libraries* (1936); "Foreign Situation in Microphotography," in *Microphotography for Libraries, 1937* (1937); and "Librarian of the Future," in *Library of Tomorrow* (1939), edited by Emily Danton. He also contributed a tribute to Andrew Keogh (q.v.), "There Is Honor in One's Own Country," in *Papers in Honor of Andrew Keogh*

(1938). In 1945, he edited *Library Resources of the University of North Carolina*, which was published in connection with the University's sesquicentennial celebration and to which he contributed "Co-operative Facilities in Research and Service."

Rush was a member of many professional, literary, civic, and educational associations, among which were the American Library Association (serving on its Council from 1915 to 1920 and from 1922 to 1927, and as vice-president in 1931-1932), the Missouri Library Association (president, 1912-1913), the Indiana Library Association (president, 1918-1919), the American Association for Adult Education (of which he was a charter member and vice-president, 1939), the Bibliographical Society of America, the National Council of Boy Scouts, the Grolier Club, the Indianapolis Literary Club, and the Rotary Club.

Over the years, Rush was presented with various awards, including an honorary M.A. from Yale University (1931) and an honorary Litt.D. from Earlham College at the fiftieth class reunion of his graduating class (1955).

Charles E. Rush died on January 31, 1958, in his adopted state of North Carolina, and was survived by his wife and three daughters.

Biographical listings and obituaries—*National Cyclopaedia of American Biography* 46; *Register of the New York State Library School* (1959); *Who's Who in Library Service*, 1st ed., 2nd ed., 3rd ed. **Books and articles about the biographee**—[Biographical article]. *Cleveland Plain Dealer*, July 23, 1939, p. 4A; [Biographical article]. *College and Research Libraries* 15:465-66 (Oct. 1954); [Biographical article]. *Indianapolis News*, Feb. 5, 1925, p. 33; [Biographical article]. *Library Journal* 63:496-97 (June 15, 1938); [Biographical article]. *Southeastern Librarian* 4:93-94 (Fall 1954); Winslow, Amy. "Charles Everett Rush." *Bulletin of Bibliography* 18:193-94 (Jan.-April 1946); Witmer, Eleanor M. "Charles E. Rush: Friend." *Library Service News* 7:33-34 (Aug. 1938). **Primary sources and archival materials**—Papers dealing with Charles E. Rush are held in the Indianapolis Public Library Archives.

—ROBERT L. LOGSDON

SABIN, JOSEPH (1821-1881)

Though neither an American by birth nor a librarian by training, Joseph Sabin made a significant contribution to American librarianship and to the study of Americana through the conception and production of his *Bibliotheca Americana, a Dictionary of Books Relating to America*. Frederick R. Goff called this book "the most important single bibliography relating to America that has ever been compiled." Although he did not live to see its completion, Sabin planned and worked on it for the last 25 years of his life and, on his death-bed, expressed the desire to live to finish it. So enormous a task had he undertaken, however, that the book was not completed until over fifty years after his death. In the

book's Prospectus (1866), Sabin reveals both his doubts and his dedication to the project he had begun:

> Had the magnitude and extreme difficulty of the undertaking been presented to my mind in full proportion at the outset, I should never have attempted it; and, indeed, I may remark, that I have more than once determined upon its abandonment; but a deep sense of its importance, however imperfectly it may be executed, and a strong partiality for bibliographical pursuits, have stimulated me to continue my labor, until the work has attained such a degree of completeness as to justify its publication, and render its conclusion a task of comparative ease; and I now present this volume as a fair specimen of what the work is intended to be, and respectfully invite for it a candid examination.

Sabin's interest in and knowledge of books developed early in his life. Born in December 1821, in Braunston, Northamptonshire (near Oxford), England, he attended the Oxford common schools, then was apprenticed to Charles Richards, an Oxford book dealer. Sabin began as a bookbinder, but Richards, recognizing his enthusiasm for and interest in books, transferred him to the salesroom after only a few months. Sabin thus gained extensive knowledge of books and prints, and he was soon well known and respected by the customers who frequented the shop. After three years as assistant salesman, he became general manager of Richards's and thus had the opportunity to buy as well as sell books.

While Sabin was at Richards's store, his responsibilities included the preparation of catalogs of libraries for sale, and this work prompted his interest in the auction trade. When his seven years of indenture ended in 1842, he formed a partnership with a Mr. Winterborn, son of an Oxford architect and builder, and opened a book store and auction house. Two years later, he married his partner's sister.

Before leaving Richards's, Sabin developed what was to be a lifelong interest in temperance. While at Oxford he wrote articles and made several public speeches in support of temperance. According to W. L. Andrews, "he practiced what he preached—water pure and simple was his exclusive beverage, and he eschewed tobacco in all its forms." So strong was his devotion to the cause that it was said that on his death-bed he objected to taking the brandy he had overheard his physician prescribe. One other notable event of Sabin's years at Oxford was the anonymous publication of "The Thirty-nine Articles of the Church of England, with Scriptural Proofs and References" (done anonymously lest his own lack of scholarly training and reputation inhibit its use by others).

In 1848, after four fairly successful years as a bookseller, Sabin sold his business to move to the United States. Goff remarks that his reasons for doing so are not known, but, before leaving England, Sabin had purchased several hundred acres of land in Texas, perhaps with the intention of becoming a farmer. According to the *New York Times* obituary (June 6, 1881), however, Sabin discovered when he reached the United States that the land "was in much the same condition as Martin Chuzzlewit's Eden investment, and he never went near it."

With his wife and two sons, Frank and Joseph, Sabin sailed on the ship *West Point* and arrived in New York on July 3, 1848. Unable to find suitable employment there, he left after a few days for Philadelphia and resumed his career as a bookseller. His first position was in the publishing house of George S. Appleton as general assistant and salesman, where he put to use not only his sales ability but also his early training as a book binder by introducing Appleton to the use of full and half calf and morocco bindings, previously unknown in the United States. Appleton, impressed with Sabin's knowledge of books, soon gave him increasing responsibilities in all aspects of the business.

After two years in Philadelphia, Sabin returned to New York and accepted a position with Cooley & Kesse, book auctioneers at Dey Street and Broadway, where his duties consisted primarily of the preparation of sales catalogs. The firm was sold to Lyman & Rawdon soon after Sabin arrived, but he was retained as cataloger. The first important catalog that Sabin prepared while at Lyman & Rawdon was that of the library of Dr. Samuel Farmar Jarvis (item 74683 in his *Dictionary*). Consisting primarily of theological works, it was called "the finest collection of books which up to that time had been sold at auction in this country." A subsequent dispute over payment for his work ultimately led to his leaving the firm. The description of the incident in the *New York Times* reveals both his concern with his work and his strong sense of his own worth:

To make the catalogue, which was a very complete one, Mr. Sabin was obliged to work a great deal overtime, and when he presented a bill to his employers, they objected to paying it. He was a high-spirited man, and refused to deliver the manuscript to the printer till his bill was paid. The result was that he received his money, but as an offset, the firm on the 1st of January, 1852, proposed to reduce his salary. He at once threw up his position, and was engaged at a higher salary by the rival house of Bangs Brothers, No. 13 Parkrow.

Sabin remained with Bangs Brothers for the next five years as cataloger. One of his most significant tasks was the preparation in 1856 of the catalog of the library of Mr. E. B. Corwin, one of the first

collections to consist almost entirely of Americana. According to the *New York Times* obituary, cataloging this collection first stimulated Sabin's interest in Americana and suggested to him the idea of compiling his *Dictionary*.

Sabin's next two ventures in business were in the rare book trade. In 1856, he opened a store on Canal Street in New York that proved to be only moderately successful. Consequently, after a year, he sold the business and returned to Philadelphia to rejoin his family. His shop at No. 27 South Sixth Street prospered until the outbreak of the Civil War, which resulted in the loss of his Southern clientele, until that time his most profitable customers.

In 1861, Sabin returned permanently to New York. He first formed a partnership with H. A. Jennings and opened an auction house under the name of J. Sabin and Co. After a few years, finding business dull, Sabin decided to leave the auction trade and deal exclusively in rare books. Thus, according to Andrews, he "purchased for $9000 the stock and good-will of Michael Noonan, a genial and popular Irishman who had built up quite a respectable business in second-hand and new books." First at 84 and then at 64 Nassau Street, called by Andrews "the 'Rialto' of the old book trade, and the place where book hunters did most love to congregate," Sabin's business thrived as his reputation in the book world grew. Brayton Ives, a collector of Americana, reveals (in the introduction to the catalog of his first auction sale) the excitement of the rare book trade of which Sabin was the center:

In those days Mr. Sabin's shop in Nassau Street was the favorite resort of book-collectors, and one could meet several of them there nearly every afternoon. The arrival of a box from London, containing new importations of books, was always an occasion of interest, and usually gave rise to keen competition for the privilege of making the first selections. Mr. Sabin was an enthusiastic student of Americana, and I was soon instilled with the same feeling. [Cited in Goff]

Sabin's reputation as an expert bibliographer and bibliopolist was worldwide. Active not only here, Sabin travelled regularly to Europe to attend all of the major book sales, making thirty trips within twenty years.

In addition to managing his book store (which also carried prints), Sabin continued to produce auction catalogs, including those of the Waltonian library of Dr. Bethune, the libraries of John Allen, Andrew Wright, Edwin Forrest, and John E. Wright, and the Menzies collection, which, according to its description in the *Dictionary*, was "the finest library ever sold in the United States." Although only 21 of Sabin's catalogs are listed in the *Dictionary*, he is reputed to have compiled over 150, the largest collections of which are now at the New York Public Library and the Library of Congress.

When the Menzies collection came on the auction block, Sabin both prepared the catalog and acted as auctioneer, realizing through the sale nearly $50,000. The *New York Times* (November 20, 1876) describes not only Sabin's bibliographic expertise but also his talent as an auctioneer:

> Mr. Sabin's reputation as a bibliographer is unequalled, and no one could spend an hour in the auction room without noticing that the auctioneer was a man of rare wit, and had a profound knowledge of books. He kept the audience in a roar of laughter and interspersed his remarks with remarkably free sarcasm about public men, dead and alive.

The highlight of Sabin's career as auctioneer (although he had almost entirely given that activity up by then to work on the *Dictionary*) was the sale of the library of George Brinley of Hartford. Goff calls this "the most complete and the most imaginative of all the contemporary public and private collections" of works relating to American history. In addition to its vast collection of Americana, the library included as well a copy of the Gutenberg Bible—the first ever sold at auction in the United States. Sabin lived to serve as auctioneer for only three of the five Brinley sales. In April 1881, he agreed to undertake the third, but did so against the advice of his physician. In doing so, he may have hastened his death, which came two months later. (Sabin did not, however, compile the catalog of the collection, which was done by James H. Trumbull, executor of the estate, and Frank B. Gay.)

Another of Sabin's occupations was the publication from 1869 to 1877 of the *American Bibliopolist*. "Dedicated to the fraternity of book lovers," the journal listed the recent acquisitions of J. Sabin & Sons, but it contained as well a variety of articles of interest to those in the book trade. In a detailed analysis of the first issue of the *American Bibliopolist*, Goff discusses the prefatory articles describing the sales of the libraries of A. A. Smets of Savannah, Captain Townsend of Albany, and Mr. Bruce of New York. He notes that other sections of the journal contain price lists of books recently published in the United States and in England, lists of books wanted, and a special catalog of books "in various departments of literature" that were available from Sabin's stock. Included also were advertisements of other book dealers and auctioneers and advertisements for Sabin's own publications, including both the *Dictionary* and his series of reprints of rare Americana (items 74696-74698 in his *Dictionary*). (His work on the *Dictionary* had shown him which items were in need of reprinting.)

Sabin's greatest accomplishment is his *Bibliotheca Americana, a Dictionary of Books Relating to America, from Its Discovery to the Present Time*. He states in his Prospectus (in Volume I) that before the publication of the first volume in 1867, he had spent fifteen years collecting material for the *Dictionary* and nearly four more years in classifying and arranging it. Andrews called the *Dictionary* Sabin's "old man of the sea," noting that Sabin spent all of his free time working on it: "Early morning hours, the small hours of the night, and stolen moments in cars and on shipboard were devoted to it." So great and all-consuming a burden was it for him that a friend suggested after his death that a most fitting epitaph would be "Killed by a Dictionary."

Sabin notes in his Prospectus that, in an effort to be as complete and accurate as possible in his compilation of the *Dictionary*, he himself examined all of the titles to which he had access. For those that were unavailable, he consulted printed library catalogs, bibliographies, and occasionally booksellers' catalogs—according to Sabin, "a less trustworthy source." Such a remark from the compiler of so many "bookseller's catalogs" may be considered partly tongue-in-cheek, but it reflects as well his knowledge of the inadequacy of many others he had encountered. Goff, describing an article by Sabin in the *American Bibliopolist* in which he discusses the catalog of the library of A. A. Smets, observes:

> Mr. Sabin was well aware of the exacting requirements of a book auction catalog . . . and he is most straight-forward in his criticism of this shoddy work. As he so succinctly expressed himself: "The Catalogue was made out by an amateur whose verdancy is only equalled by his ignorance, assumption, and redundance."

Although Sabin had little tolerance of ignorance that feigned knowledge, he was a great admirer of genuine learning, and he gratefully accepted the assistance of those who could help him in the compilation of the *Dictionary* and in his other endeavors. In his Prospectus, he freely acknowledged the fact that errors and omissions would occur in his work, and he solicited the help of any whose specialized knowledge might aid him. In the preface to his *Bibliography of Bibliography* (1877), he acknowledged both his appreciation for the assistance of Charles A. Cutter (q.v.) in compiling the bibliography and his admiration for the man's learning: "When librarians in general can approach his standard of library intelligence, there will cease to be that plentiful lack of knowledge by which some of them are now distinguished." Andrews, in two anecdotes about Sabin, shows both the pride and the seriousness that he brought to his work:

... In 1864 he catalogued the collection of the old Scotch antiquarian, John Allen, of pleasant memory. The title on the cover of this catalogue was awkwardly constructed, and, not being willing to father it, he signed himself as "Compiler of this catalogue, *the cover excepted*."

Among the one hundred and fifty or more libraries which Mr. Sabin is said to have catalogued was that of the Shakespearean scholar Richard Grant White, who remarked, as the result of his observations, that if anybody thought that bibliography was an easy subject he should serve an apprenticeship under Joseph Sabin.

Despite Sabin's demand for high quality and his great concern for his own work, his *Dictionary* was not, initially, universally well received. The managing editor of *Publishers' Weekly*, Mr. Adolf Growoll, considered the first volumes no more than a "finding list" for booksellers. He did, though, admit improvement in the later volumes, which he thought "attained somewhat to the dignity of a bibliography." Goff, in examining the correspondence between Growoll and Henry Harrisse (q.v.; compiler of the *Bibliotheca Americana Vetustissima*), discovered that, when asked by Growoll for his opinion of Sabin's *Dictionary*, Harrisse responded sharply, "I can only say that I have a very poor opinion of Sabin's first 12 or 13 vols., and of Mr. Sabin himself!" Goff modifies the remark by saying that Harrisse was generally a man with whom few got along well. He notes as well that Sabin himself may have brought about this hostility by selling the *Bibliotheca Americana Vetustissima* at less than the published price and by advertising it in the *American Bibliopolist* without mentioning the name of its compiler.

Since the publication of the first volume of Sabin's *Dictionary*, both the work and its compiler have grown in stature. In "The Final 'Statement' " of the final volume, the members of the editorial staff that directed its completion (Wilberforce Eames [q.v.] and R. W. G. Vail [q.v.]) point out that its increasing importance is related to the recognition of American history as a legitimate field of academic study. When Sabin began the work, however, that discipline had not yet assumed importance, and the value of the *Dictionary* as a source for historical research was not yet evident.

By 1881, Sabin had published twelve volumes of the *Dictionary* and had ready for publication another volume, which brought the work to the word "Pennsylvania." On June 5, however, after several weeks of illness, Sabin died. Funeral services were held the next day in his home at No. 3 Weirfield Avenue, Brooklyn; and he was buried in the Cypress Hills Cemetery.

Sabin's *Dictionary* has remained, as he wished, his greatest monument. Through his own efforts, and with the assistance of scholars and librarians throughout the country, Sabin attempted to produce as complete and accurate a work as possible. Despite the errors and omissions inevitable in so large an undertaking, an appropriate defense of Sabin's *Dictionary* can be taken from Samuel Johnson's preface to his own dictionary: "when it shall be found that much is omitted, let it not be forgotten that much likewise is performed."

Biographical listings and obituaries–*Dictionary of American Biography* 16 (Herman H. B. Meyer); [Obituary]. *New York Times*, June 6, 1881. (Also obituaries in New York *Sun*, *World*, *Tribune* and *Commercial Advertiser*, same date); [Obituary]. *Publishers' Weekly*, June 11, 1881; *Who Was Who in America*, Historical Volume (1607-1896). **Books and articles about the biographee**–Andrews, W. L. "Joseph Sabin." *Bookman* 1:381-83 (July 1895); Goff, Frederick R. "Joseph Sabin, Bibliographer (1821-1881)." *Inter-American Review of Bibliography* 12:39-53 (Jan.-June 1962). [Also issued separately by N. Israel, Amsterdam, 1963]; [Introductory material]. In Joseph Sabin. *Bibliotheca Americana, a Dictionary of Books Relating to America, from Its Discovery to the Present Time*. New York: Bibliographical Society of America, 1936, Vols. 1, 29 [Vol. 1 contains Sabin's Prospectus, and Vol. 29 contains contributions by Wilberforce Eames, R. W. G. Vail, and others]. **Primary sources and archival materials**–Information concerning Sabin is in the introductions to catalogs compiled by him. The two largest collections of these may be found in the New York Public Library and the Library of Congress.

—SANDRA ROSCOE

ST. JOHN, FRANCIS REGIS (1908-1971)

Francis Regis St. John was born in Northampton, Massachusetts, on June 16, 1908, to Edward Bernhard and Mary Elizabeth Shaughnessy St. John. As a boy and teenager, he worked for the Forbes Library (the local public library) in Northampton from 1919 to 1925. St. John worked himself up from page to desk assistant at Forbes while attending Northampton High School. He then worked in the library at Amherst College as a desk assistant before enrolling in the college for a degree in botany. There he was eventually advanced to student assistant in the Library and completed his A.B. degree in 1931.

In that year, St. John took three steps that were to shape his future course: he took a job as stack supervisor in the New York Public Library, enrolled in the Columbia University School of Library Service, and married Helen Florence McLeod (also from Northampton) on December 26, 1931. Receiving his B.L.S. from Columbia in 1932, he was then promoted to desk supervisor of the main reading room, which position he held from 1933 to 1934. From 1934 to 1939, he worked as a general assistant in the Preparations Division and the director's office. In 1939, with war breaking out in Europe, St. John joined the

Enoch Pratt Free Library in Baltimore, Maryland, as assistant director to the public-service-oriented Joseph L. Wheeler (q.v.).

The New York Public Library summoned St. John back in 1941 to be chief of the Circulation Department, which position was responsible for the branch libraries. Then the United States went to war and, from 1943 to 1945, St. John was acting librarian and then assistant to the director of the U.S. Army Medical Library from 1943 to 1945. He advanced from lieutenant to captain and was awarded the Legion of Merit for his reorganization of the Library.

Resigning from the New York Public Library in 1947, St. John became director of library services for the U.S. Veteran's Administration until he was called back to New York City to become chief librarian of the Brooklyn Public Library in 1949. To the Brooklyn Public Library, he brought a new vision of modern public librarianship, one that was pragmatic, administratively oriented, and professional. He actively recruited blacks to professional positions long before there was a civil rights act. He developed training programs for staff and responded to the community with meaningful service. Along the way, he attracted a cadre of professional librarians with expertise to carry out superior programs.

St. John served on the Councils of the American Library Association and the New York Library Association, as well as on the New York State Regents Library Advisory Committee, the Committee on Public Library Services, the New York State Commissioner of Education's Committee on Reference and Research Library Resources, and as a founding member of the National Book Committee. In these organizations, he helped implement certification of librarians in New York state, develop coordinated systems, establish a state aid program, promote reference and the work of the Research Resources Councils in New York state, and prepare reports concerning the accreditation of library schools.

St. John was a contributor to professional publications from 1942 until 1965. His paper "In-Service Training" was included in *Personnel Administration in Libraries: Papers Presented before the Library Institute at the University of Chicago, August 27-September 1, 1945* (ed. by Lowell Martin; University of Chicago Press, 1946). His report on *Internship in the Library Profession* was presented to the ALA Board of Education for Librarianship in 1938. Many of his articles were the result of his library surveys, but he also wrote on "Service for Senior Citizens" (*Wilson Library Bulletin*, March 1953) and prepared a report on his "Survey of Library Service for the Blind" (American Foundation for the Blind, 1957).

His most famous and controversial program in Brooklyn was the establishment of the District

Library Plan in 1959, when the shortage of professional librarians threatened to deny service to many deserving communities. St. John's plan called for the management of many centers by administrative personnel while professional services were supplied from a central district library.

After 15 years, and the death of his mentor and president of the Board of Trustees, Henry J. Davenport, St. John retired from the Brooklyn Public Library and established a consulting firm in 1964. He did surveys for the state of Oklahoma; Brookline, Massachusetts; Ontario; Mid-York Library System, Utica, New York; Winchester, Virginia; and Texas, among others. He closed out his firm in 1967 and returned to New England to become librarian at St. Anselm's College in Manchester, New Hampshire. He died there on July 19, 1971, at the age of 63.

Biographical listings and obituaries—*Biographical Record 1821-1939*. Amherst College, Amherst, Mass., 1939; *Directory of Library Consultants* (1969); "Francis R. St. John Dies at 63: Ex-Chief Librarian in Brooklyn [Obituary]." *New York Times*, July 23, 1971; [Obituary]. *American Libraries* 2:921 (Oct. 1971); [Obituary]. *Library Journal* 96:2725 (Sept. 15, 1971); *Who Was Who in America* V (1969-1973); *Who's Who in Library Service*, 1st ed., 2nd ed., 3rd ed., 4th ed. **Books and articles about the biographee**—"Francis R. St. John Named Research Associate in Columbia University's School of Library Services." *Library Journal* 89:596 (Feb. 1, 1964); "Francis R. St. John Will Be Retiring as Head of the Brooklyn Public Library at the End of This Year." *Wilson Library Bulletin* 38:327 (Nov. 1963); "Librarian of Brooklyn Public Library." *Publishers' Weekly* 155:1521 (April 2, 1949); "New V.A. Libraries Head." *Library Journal* 70:1208 (Dec. 15, 1945).

—MILTON S. BYAM

SANDERS, MINERVA AMANDA LEWIS (1837-1912)

Minerva Amanda Lewis was born in Marblehead, Massachusetts, the third and youngest child of Robert Girdler and Almira Amanda Armington Lewis, on February 11, 1837. Little is recorded of her early life. She may have attended a young ladies' boarding school, but her formal training did not include higher education. As a young woman she married Samuel Sanders, a man much older than herself, who died in 1863. Up until that time, she may have been a teacher.

In 1852, the library association of Pawtucket, Rhode Island, had established a subscription library for the use of share-owning subscribers, and, secondarily, as a public convenience and a help in general education. By the nation's one hundredth birthday, the idea of free public libraries was spreading, and the members of the subscription library board offered its 4,000 volumes to the town for the free use of all citizens. As Sanders had taken over the direction of the subscription library about three months earlier, she was offered, and accepted, the job of town librarian in 1876. She was to serve in that capacity for 34 years, until ill health forced her retirement in 1910.

She is credited with excellent stewardship of the Pawtucket Free Library, but most importantly, with several significant innovations. As Pawtucket was a manufacturing town, Sanders set out to attract to the Library the textile workers and their families, especially the children, whose leisure-time wanderings on the streets concerned her greatly. Her early work with children motivated her to pioneer and champion open stacks and free access for children, this in a profession in which closed stacks were theretofore considered a fact of life. Always sensitive to community needs, Sanders believed that a library should serve as an educational and cultural center for the town, furthering vocational education and promoting self-improvement and personal growth.

She petitioned her Board of Trustees to give her sufficient clerical assistance to free her "to mingle with the people, to learn their habits and tastes, and to direct their reading (especially of the young)" ("The Possibilities of Public Libraries in Manufacturing Communities," *Library Journal* 12:398 [1887]). To attract patrons, she made the Library a bright and cheerful place, with clearly labeled books on open shelves. Criticism of her open-shelves policy arose from members of the community who feared theft or mutilation of books or worried about "indiscriminate consultation" of books. She replied in her 1893 *Pawtucket Library Report* that "the educating influences on people in the handling and examining of books" was an advantage that outweighed possible misuse; thus, browsing was permitted to those who found the catalog to be an insuperable obstacle to use of the Library.

Sanders broke another tradition by opening a Sunday Reading Room in the United States in 1890. She had proposed this idea in a paper at the 1887 American Library Association conference, but was unable to open the Library on Sundays until three years later. The public's response demonstrated that these extra hours were needed. As she pointed out, many poorer families could not even afford newspapers and had no other source of educational materials; their only access to reading materials was through the Library.

Another innovation was the formal establishment of children's services in 1876. While not the first library to admit children, the Pawtucket Free Library was the first to offer continuous services to children. Through Sanders' advocacy, others followed her example. To attract children, she sawed legs off tables and chairs, hung pictures that also circulated, and arranged books and magazines on tables within reach of even the smallest of them. She also prepared book lists and gave much personal guidance in helping children select books. Because there were few books to choose from, she encouraged children to check out "adult" material. To those who objected to granting children rights to using the entire library, she replied, "We are too much inclined to think that wisdom in the selection of books is a product of maturity; we could give many illustrations to the contrary. There is a keen discrimination in some of these young minds. . . ." (*Pawtucket Library Report*).

Sanders continued to fight for children's access to the stacks, but in her investigations of children's services in public libraries in 1887, she became discouraged, noting that the prevailing attitude seemed to be "children and dogs not allowed!" Her concern for what children read led to her "Report on Reading for the Young," presented at the 1902 American Library Association conference (and printed in *Library Journal* 15:58-64 [1890]). She deplored children's literature of the "saintly, die-young-and-go-to-heaven-sure kind with a moral guideboard for a frontispiece and a tombstone for a finis," the kind presenting heroes whose "sole motive is ambition, and whose every thought and action is impelled by a vision ever before him of the judge's bench or the White House." Rather, she sought books to stimulate children's imagination and perception, works that would lead them to reading well-written, enriching literature as adults.

As an extension of services to children, Sanders set up a close relationship with the schools, encouraging teachers of elementary and high schools to bring in classes; she then instructed students in library use. She also sent book collections to teachers willing to circulate them to students. She believed that the library was an essential part of education and that teachers should make

> libraries the fountain of supply, not alone for the good of the pupil, but for their personal advantage in the saving of time and mental friction, as well as for the infinitely better results that will be secured in their work. Also by becoming conversant with its resources, of educational value, they can the more effectively help those committed to their charge to use it freely and intelligently; that from childhood to youth, and on to middle life and old age, the public library may be their amusement, instructor, companion and friend ("The Relation of the Public Library to the School," *Library Journal* 14:85 [1889]).

Local history collections in public libraries were another special service that Sanders championed. Visualizing them as more than a resource for journalists or antiquarians, she encouraged students to use the Rhode Island Collection to investigate their community, that they might increase both local pride and self-understanding (see her article "The Value of Local History in a Public Library," *Library Journal* 20 [December 1895]).

Above the personal goodwill she had generated through her activities in the Young Men's Christian Association, Woman's Board of State Institutions, and other civic groups, Sanders used several innovative public relations methods. In 1896, every house in Pawtucket received a placard which said "Consult the Public Library for anything you want to know." Bookmarks with advertising for a local merchant on one side and "When in Doubt Consult the Public Library" on the other were placed in patrons' books as they were checked out. Those who did come into the Library seeking information found a reference department that had the reputation of being the best in the state and a librarian whose motto was "Let us exhaust our references" (*Library Journal* 12:397 [1887]).

An energetic participant in ALA, although as an institutional representative and not as a personal member, Minerva Sanders was a well-known personality at the annual convention. She was elected to the ALA Council in 1904. Known affectionately as "Mawtucket of Pawtucket" throughout the state (except to children, who called her "Auntie Sanders"), she vigorously entered into debates and frequently contributed papers. Three of her more notable papers reprinted in *Library Journal* were: "Possibilities of Public Libraries in Manufacturing Communities" (12:395-400 [Sept.-Oct. 1887]), "The Relation of the Public Library to the School" (14:79-83 [March 1889]), and "Report on Reading for the Young" (15:58-64 [1890]).

Minerva Sanders' concern for the welfare of the community and her sensitivity to individual reading needs, both educational and recreational, led her to pioneer innovative and community-oriented library service much in advance of her time. She championed two basic truths of library service: that the best way to reach readers is through "persistent, enthusiastic personal interest and attention to the individual needs" (*Library Journal* 15:64 [1890]) and that community needs determine the library's services and collections.

In 1902, she had the pleasure of moving her collection to the new Deborah Cook Sayles Memorial Library, which she had planned for Pawtucket's clientele. Sanders is quoted as saying, "I never enjoyed three years as much as I did those while the library was building" (in Elva S. Smith [q.v.], "Minerva Sanders," *Pioneering Leaders in Librarianship*, ed. Emily M. Danton. ALA, 1953, p. 155). Upon her retirement in 1910, her long and devoted service was acknowledged by the trustees of the Library, who conferred upon her the title of librarian emeritus, the first time in the history of the state that a woman had been thus honored. She died almost two years later, on March 20, 1912, at the age of 74,

able to point proudly to several by then commonplace library practices that she had inaugurated and developed. This fact is, no doubt, her greatest tribute, and serves as her memorial.

Biographical listings and obituaries—[Obituary]. *ALA Bulletin* 6:447 (Sept. 1912); *Public Libraries* 17:176 (May 1912). **Books and articles about the biographee**—Long, Harriet G. *Public Library Service to Children: Foundation and Development.* Metuchen, N.J.: Scarecrow Press, 1969, pp. 88-89; Peacock, Joseph. "'Mawtucket' of Pawtucket." *Library Journal* 40:792-94 (Nov. 1915); Rider, Sidney S. "What I Saw in the Free Library in Pawtucket." *Library Journal* 14:40-41 (Jan.-Feb. 1889); Smith, Elva S. "Minerva Sanders." In *Pioneering Leaders in Librarianship*, ed. by Emily Miller Danton. Boston: Gregg Press, 1972, pp. 153-65.

—MARGO SASSÉ

SAVORD, CATHERINE RUTH (1894-1966)

Catherine Ruth Savord was born November 2, 1894, in Sandusky, Ohio, the daughter of Alexander J. and Jennie Kelly Savord. She was graduated from the local high school in June 1912, but severe physical and economic problems prevented her from proceeding at once to a higher education program. She concentrated on resolving these during the following year to prepare for admission to the Western Reserve University School of Library Science (now Case Western Reserve University School of Library Science) in Cleveland, Ohio.

Standards for admission to the School involved a rigid entrance examination, conferences with the dean, some experience in a library, and a good past record. One of her sponsors, Louise Allen Colton, a teacher at Sandusky (Ohio) High School, wrote, "She is an unusually clear, quick thinker, grasping both details and important principles with extreme readiness and speaking her thoughts clearly, concisely and fluently. Though of strong personal feeling she was quite self controlled" (quoted from her 1913 letter to the dean in the Savord archives at CWRU). Ruth Savord was well qualified in all respects, was admitted to the School, and was graduated in 1914.

Her professional career began as an assistant cataloger in the Cleveland Public Library (1914-1916), followed by a year of additional training at the University of Illinois Graduate School of Library Science, from which she was graduated in 1917. A brief war-time service as assistant chief clerk in the United States War Department, Office of Military Aeronautics, Radio Division, was followed by an appointment in the Newark (New Jersey) Public Library as first assistant in its catalog department. These experiences in cataloging, with their requirements for accuracy, imagination, and innovation, sharpened her native ability and became the perfect foundation for the bibliographic work in which she excelled and for which she was internationally recognized by scholars in the fields of social science and international politics.

Savord's introduction to the special library field occurred in 1920, when she was appointed organizer and librarian of the Frick Art Museum in New York City. Her duties included an extensive examination of art works in European museums for identification and cataloging. She left the Museum in 1924 to become librarian of the General Education Board, a Rockefeller corporation closely associated with the Rockefeller Foundation in New York. This library was established to develop, organize, and put to use documentation for information needed in selecting recipients and projects for grants in several specific educational areas: Negro, medical, and public education; cooperation with colleges and universities; and special surveys or studies. She remained there until 1929.

A brief period as reference assistant in the library of Batten, Barton, Durstine and Osborn, Inc. (an advertising agency in New York) gave her new insights into the details of information needed in advertising. Her correspondence with Dean Alice S. Tyler (q.v.) contains an amusing letter explaining the nature of an advertising agency's library requests and how often they had to be answered verbally by telephone, seldom by bibliographies. It was a new idea at that time—instant information provided for the conduct of business, activating the Special Libraries Association's slogan, "Putting Knowledge to Work."

In 1930, Savord accepted the invitation to organize and administer a library for the Council on Foreign Relations. It was to become her great life work, and for the next thirty years she made her unique contribution to librarianship in three areas: 1) establishing a special library and information service for a prestigious organization influential in international affairs, 2) participating so actively in the work of the Special Libraries Association as to become known as "Miss S.L.A.," and 3) sharing the results of her experience in promoting education and training for special librarianship.

Development of the library at the Council on Foreign Relations proceeded with dispatch, and the collection was put to use immediately. Savord was noteworthy both in preparing bibliographies and in acquiring, on a worldwide basis, materials concerning political and economic matters. Scholars and editors compiling the Council's annual publication *The United States in World Affairs* (e.g., Walter Lippman, Whitney Hunt Shepardson, W. O. Scroggs, and others, as well as William Leonard Langer and Hamilton Fish Armstrong, who edited the decennial *World Affairs Bibliography*) always included a special tribute to

Savord for her expertise in providing the bibliographies for their comprehensive volumes.

Shortly after starting her work at the Council, she realized the need for a directory of other organizations in the same general field. Thus, in 1931, she compiled the first *Directory of American Agencies Concerned with the Study of International Affairs*, with an introduction by Isaiah Bowman. Later editions carried the title *American Agencies Interested in International Affairs* (Council on World Affairs, 1942; 1942 rev. ed.; 1949; and 1955, compiled with Donald Wasson). This directory has become a standard "handbook" for anyone concerned with international affairs. Donald Wasson, who succeeded Savord as librarian of the Council, continued publishing revised editions of this directory; he acknowledged her foresight in his preface to the 1964 edition: "This volume owes much to Ruth Savord, former librarian of the Council, who originally conceived the idea of such a directory and who compiled the first four editions."

From October 1941 through July 1959, every issue of the quarterly journal *Foreign Affairs* carried her column "Source Material," which included a list of official government publications and communications of various countries, with addresses of where they could be obtained. Her competence in and knowledge of world affairs brought further recognition in 1945, when she was appointed a reference specialist in the International Secretariat at the United Nations organizing conference in San Francisco.

All during the time she was librarian of the Council, Ruth Savord was constructively active in the Special Libraries Association's work. She served on its committees, gave freely of her time, advice, and counsel, was editor of its official publication *Special Libraries* from 1931 to 1932, and held offices at the local chapter level in New York. She was elected president of the Association in 1934. Her presidential message to the Association included characteristic comments about her hopes and plans for it:

We want more members, but we do not want mere names—we want and need working members. Closely allied to membership is our appalling lack of knowledge of the abilities of our members. This is a waste of manpower that we, who like to think of ourselves as efficient, should deplore. We, as an Association, and the services we can offer are not known. We should be placing news stories in trade and general papers and in our local newspapers, thus educating prospective employers, which will inevitably result in the formation of new libraries when their value is appreciated. If we are successful in stimulating new libraries we must be prepared to suggest well-trained competent librarians to organize and administer them. Each of us should be a missionary not in urging indiscriminate additions to our ranks, but in a selective process of searching out the college student who is deciding on a career, the public librarian with a special library viewpoint, and by urging the library schools to offer suitable training.

Throughout her career, Savord continued to work with imagination and vigor for the constructive development of SLA and exhorted others to do the same, quoting, as a spur to such activities, a line from the preface of Sir Francis Bacon's *Maxims of the Law*: "I hold every man a debtor to his profession." She was a staunch friend to those on whom the mantle of directing the Association's work had fallen. Especially noteworthy was her continued concern with constitutional revision and the conduct of business according to recognized parliamentary procedure.

She was often called upon to address conferences at educational meetings. Her paper "Special Librarianship as a Career," first published by the Woman's College of the University of North Carolina's Institute of Women's Professional Relations in 1933, was revised several times and is considered a classic for the field. She contributed widely to professional journals, and wrote the "Special Library Looks Forward," a chapter in *The Library of Tomorrow*, edited by Emily Miller Danton (ALA, 1939).

She was a member of the American Library Association and also of several women's groups, including the American Women's Association, on whose executive board she served from 1937 to 1940.

With Eleanor Cavanaugh, librarian of Standard & Poor's in New York and a close friend and colleague who often had worked closely with Savord on numerous SLA projects, Savord was honored by SLA with its Professional Award in 1954. She was named to its Hall of Fame in 1960, when she retired.

After her retirement, she moved to Arizona, where she died on February 25, 1966.

Biographical listings and obituaries—"Ruth Savord Dies [Obituary]." *New York Times*, Feb. 27, 1966; *Who Was Who in America* IV (1961-1968); *Who's Who in Library Service*, 1st ed., 2nd ed., 3rd ed.; *Who's Who of American Women* 1 (1958-1959). Books and articles about the biographee—"Ruth Savord and Eleanor S. Cavanaugh, Joint Recipients of the S.L.A. Professional Award for 1954." *Special Libraries* 45:255 (July-Aug. 1955); "Ruth Savord: In Memoriam." *Special Libraries* 57:243 (April 1966); "Ruth Savord, Reference Consultant for Conference Library for the United Nations Conference on International Organizations (UNCIO)." In Doris Cruger Dale, *The United Nations Library*. Chicago: American Library Association, 1970, p. 23; "S.L.A. Professional Award and Hall of Fame." *Special Libraries* 51:385 (Sept. 1960); "Who's Who: Ruth Savord." *Special Libraries* 23:24 (Jan. 1932). Primary sources and archival materials—An extensive file of Savord's correspondence with Julia Whittlesey and with Alice S. Tyler, two deans at Western Reserve University School of Library

Science (now Case Western Reserve University School of Library Science), and other source data are contained in the archives of this School in Cleveland, Ohio.

—ROSE L. VORMELKER

SCHENK, RACHEL KATHERINE (1899-1973)

Rachel Katherine Schenk was born on February 24, 1899, the daughter of Carl John and Hermine Sulzener Schenk, Swiss immigrants who had settled in New Philadelphia, Ohio, near the site of the first town in Ohio. Because of the death of her father when she was five, her higher education was a product of her own efforts and of gradually accumulating credits by summer or part-time enrollment, initially at Wooster College and then at Kent State Normal College (now Kent State University).

After five years as a public school teacher in nearby towns, Schenk found her vocation as librarian of her home town library and became a protégé of Mary Elizabeth Downey, director of the Chautauqua, New York, School of Librarians, from which she received the diploma in 1926. While employed full time as assistant cataloger at Purdue University Library, Schenk earned her B.S. from Purdue (with distinction) in 1932. As circulation librarian in this library for twelve years, she was an influential figure, teaching library courses and in constant demand as a book reviewer. She earned her B.S. in L.S. from Columbia University School of Library Service in 1939 and her M.A. in L.S. from the Graduate Library School of the University of Chicago in 1945.

Rachel Schenk joined the faculty of the University of Wisconsin Library School in 1945 as an assistant professor, responsible for courses in cataloging and classification. At the death of George Allez in 1950, she became acting director and, in 1951, director of the Library School. Subsequently, she taught only library administration and the history of books and libraries.

In Wisconsin, the focus of library education expanded during the 1940s and 1950s from the traditional role of training public librarians to include more attention to the college and specialized level (with, however, a concomitant development in basic library education through extension channels). Largely because of the respect and the confidence that Rachel Schenk engendered, this change in focus was accomplished without alienating the many graduates who had been trained under the firm direction of Mary Emogene Hazeltine (q.v.), who now directed public libraries in the state. By 1955, the School's new master's program, which the faculty had built up under her direction, was accredited. She was promoted to associate professor in 1952 and to professor in 1959. Relinquishing the directorship in 1963, Schenk continued for two years as professor and director of placement. On the occasion of her retirement, her students honored her with a published *Festschrift.*

In her post-retirement second career as professor and acting director of the School of Library and Information Science at the University of Wisconsin-Milwaukee, Rachel Schenk shaped the program and planned the facilities of this new school, and she continued as part-time consultant until her final retirement in 1969. She died in Fort Atkinson, Wisconsin, on September 21, 1973.

As an administrator, Rachel Schenk was orderly, calm, objective in judgment, and always conscious of the human effect of her decisions. Her influence was personal rather than scholarly in the narrow sense, deriving partly from her personality and partly from her official position. For many years, when Madison's was the only accredited library program in the state, she was the voice of library education in Wisconsin. In one student's words, "not only did she appear to keep her finger firmly on the pulse of all that was going on in the library world but she buttonholed us so that we as students should be kept as current on these matters as she was."

Part of her leadership role in the library world of Wisconsin derived from Rachel Schenk's shrewd judgment of people. Her ability to evaluate students as well as employers, and to recognize human potential, made her particularly effective in placement. Part of her influence was due to her intellectual integrity, part to the warmth of her personality, and part to her concern for standards—which extended from the professional school and the profession at large to the individual and the deficiencies, intellectual or social, that might compromise a student's career.

Her professional commitments were extensive. She was an active member of the Association of American Library Schools, an officer and committee worker in the Library Education Division, and a member of a number of other divisions of the American Library Association. She was called on frequently for work with committees of the Wisconsin Library Association, especially those concerned with certification, professional and personnel problems, and adult education. The first "Citation of Merit" of the state association recognized these contributions.

Rachel Schenk had a natural authority, a warm and outgoing personality, and the ability to accept leadership without becoming arrogant. Her life-style was firmly established in the Swiss traditions of orderliness, practical good sense, canny judgment, and hospitality. Her first love in teaching was the course in history of books and libraries; her first aim in administration was to maintain quality while encouraging individuality; and the dominating elements in her personal life were people and, in her later years, travel. The Calvinist tradition from which

she sprang shaped her standards and her conduct, but it did not constrict her relish for living. She responded unabashedly to good food, good company, an apt quotation, an eccentric personality. She was the confidante and adviser of countless students and former students, many in leading positions throughout the nation. She was a tremendous source of professional and personal help to her colleagues on campus and in the state. Her own educational experience made her particularly sensitive to the needs of "late starters" and of students from other lands. With few pretensions to formal scholarship, she imparted to students her own admiration for the cultural and artistic heritage of their profession.

Biographical listings and obituaries—[Obituary]. *American Libraries* 4:663 (Dec. 1973); [Obituary]. *Library Journal* 99:19 (Jan. 1, 1974); [Obituary]. *Wilson Library Bulletin* 48:226 (Nov. 1973); [Obituary]. *Wisconsin Library Bulletin* 69:389 (Nov. 1973); *Who's Who in Library Service*, 1st ed., 2nd ed., 3rd ed., 4th ed.; *Who's Who in the Midwest* (1965-1966); *Who's Who of American Women*, 4th ed. (1966). **Books and articles about the biographee**—[Biographical sketch]. *Library Journal* 90:3253 (Aug. 1965); Crawford, Helen. "Rachel K. Schenk." *Bulletin of Bibliography* 23:145-46 (1962); Galiano, Blaise Marie. "Rachel Katherine Schenk." In *A Tribute to Rachel Katherine Schenk*. Madison, 1963, pp. 9-10; Henkle, Susan, ed. *A Tribute to Rachel Katherine Schenk, Director of the Library School, University of Wisconsin.* Madison, 1963. **Primary sources and archival materials**—Memorial resolution of the faculty of the University of Wisconsin on the death of Emeritus Professor Rachel Katherine Schenk. Faculty Document 168, 4 February 1974. The files of the Library School, University of Wisconsin, also contain material concerning Rachel Schenk.

—HELEN CRAWFORD

SCHOMBURG, ARTHUR ALFONSO (1874-1938)

Born on January 24, 1874, in San Juan, Puerto Rico, to Mary Joseph, a Negro laundress, and Carlos Schomburg, a German merchant, Arthur A. Schomburg was to become one of the first and foremost collectors and interpreters of materials relating to Negro history. By the time of his death on June 10, 1938, after a short illness, Schomburg had established himself and his collection as one of the primary sources for the study of that history. Although not a librarian, Schomburg pioneered in this field, and his long association with the New York Public Library did much to set the tone for later library interest and activity in the area that came to be called black studies.

Schomburg received his early education in Puerto Rico and St. Thomas, Virgin Islands. He attended school in St. Thomas. His immigration to New York in 1891 marked the end of his formal education. There, however, he worked for a period of time for the law firm of Pryor, Mellis, and Harris, doing clerical work and legal research. He was, for a period of time, secretary for Las Dos Antillas, a revolutionary party that sought independence for Cuba and Puerto Rico. In February 1906, Schomburg was employed as a messenger in the Bankers Trust Company, where his facility with language enabled him to become chief of the bank's foreign mailing section, a post he held until his retirement in December 1929. His initial interest in the materials of Negro history may have stemmed from his response to remarks made by a teacher in St. Thomas to the effect that Negroes had no history.

Married three times to Afro-American women (Elizabeth Hatcher, on June 30, 1895; Elizabeth Morrow Taylor, on March 12, 1902; and Elizabeth Green), Schomburg was the father of seven children. Although his earnings were never large, Schomburg managed both to support his growing family and to engage in his pursuit of Negro history. He became an enthusiastic and knowledgeable self-trained antiquarian, Africanist, historian, teacher, collector, curator, and librarian.

With John Edward Bruce he founded, in 1911, the Negro Society for Historical Research and served as its secretary-treasurer and librarian. In 1922, he was elected president of the American Negro Academy, another research society.

Schomburg became one of black America's leading bibliophiles as he purposefully collected books, manuscripts, documents, letters, paintings, and any other material he could identify that dealt with the history and culture of his race. As the scope and size of his vast private library grew, so too did its reputation. Items from his collection were loaned to schools, institutions, and organizations throughout the United States for exhibit. Often at his own expense, Schomburg travelled extensively to lecture to predominantly Negro audiences, exhorting them to collect and treasure evidences of their past history.

In 1926, a group of Harlem citizens organized by the Urban League persuaded the corporation established by Andrew Carnegie (q.v.) to purchase Schomburg's sizeable and unique collection for $10,000. It became the Schomburg Collection of the Negro Division of History and Literature at the 135th Street Branch of the New York Public Library. In that same year, he received the Harmon Foundation's bronze medal for the access he had already afforded the Negro community to his private library collection.

After retiring, Schomburg was appointed the first curator of the Negro Collection at Fisk University in Nashville, Tennessee. In January 1931, he left Fisk to become the first curator of his own collection at the New York Public Library, a position he held until his death.

He travelled extensively in the United States in pursuit of materials. In 1926, he embarked on a six-week tour of Europe to search for records of Negro contributions to European, American, and Caribbean society. On his return, he donated many rare items that he had acquired to the Schomburg Collection.

Physically Schomburg was short, with a fair olive complexion, fine brown hair, and languid brown eyes; he could easily have been mistaken for a person of Southern European heritage. While keenly resenting the persecution of Negroes, Arthur Schomburg nevertheless chose to identify himself proudly as a Puerto Rican of African descent—with the emphasis on African.

Schomburg was far more than a collector. Acknowledged by his peers as a "cultural missionary . . . , a maker of scholars . . . , incomparable benefactor of the social education of coming generations," Schomburg turned the Negro Collection at Harlem's 135th Street Branch Library into a mecca to which all were welcomed who sought his guidance and counsel. Deeply concerned about Harlem's younger generation, Schomburg encouraged them to use the Collection while guiding many toward a sounder appreciation of their heritage. Author James Baldwin and psychologist Kenneth Clark are only two of many prominent Afro-Americans whom Schomburg influenced. Clark, referring to Schomburg as one of his heroes, described him as "a rare person . . . wise and warm . . . incapable of condescension."

Schomburg's bibliographic skill in an area that had been ignored was called upon increasingly by scholars, writers, students, and the general library clientele. He was acclaimed and cited by them regularly for his generosity and helpfulness. Schomburg regularly contributed papers based on his research to conferences and was a steady writer for the leading Afro-American journals and newspapers. His article "Racial Identity: A Plea for the Establishment of a Chair of Negro History in Our Schools and Colleges" (1913) provided pioneer guidelines for modern black studies programs. In his article "The Negro Digs Up His Past" (1925), which appeared in Alain Locke's anthology *The New Negro*, Schomburg stated his belief that knowledge of the glories of the past could help instill a racial pride, which might in turn serve as an antidote for the prejudice and persecution the race as a whole had suffered.

In all of his endeavors, Schomburg showed his concern for identifying, preserving, and making known the materials related to Negro history and culture. His efforts in establishing this field as a legitimate area of scholarly research, culminating in the establishment of the Schomburg Collection at the New York Public Library, enabled him to identify, long before it was fashionable, an area of interest and activity that libraries were later to pursue vigorously. They do so on the base that Schomburg established.

Biographical listings and obituaries—Logan, Rayford, ed. *Dictionary of Negro Biography*. Washington, D.C.: Howard University Press, 1976; [Obituary]. *New York Times*, June 11, 1938, p. 15. **Books and articles about the biographee**—Sinnette, Elinor Des Verney. "Arthur Schomburg, Black Bibliophile and Curator: His Contribution to the Collection and Dissemination of Materials about Africans and Peoples of African Descent." Ph.D. dissertation, School of Library Service, Columbia University, 1977. **Primary sources and archival materials**—Additional material may be found in the Schomburg Center for Research in Black Culture, New York Public Library.

—ELINOR DES VERNEY SINNETTE

SCHWARTZ, JACOB, JR. (1846-19_ _)

Jacob Schwartz was born in New York City on March 13, 1846. Later, in some of his writings, he added the designation "Jr." to his name; otherwise, little is known of his personal life, though it is likely that he received some formal schooling. At the age of seventeen, he joined the staff of the Apprentices' Library, a branch of the General Society of Mechanics and Tradesmen of New York City. In 1871, when he was 25, he was appointed librarian, succeeding William Van Norden. He remained with the Library throughout his career and enmeshed himself completely in its affairs.

Shortly after becoming librarian, he issued his "System of Arranging and Numbering Books Used in the Apprentices' Library" (1872). Continuing the tradition begun by the Library in 1839, Schwartz edited an 1874 edition of the *Catalogue of the Apprentices' Library* (New York: Chatterton & Parker, Printers), arranged according to the system he had devised. He was one of three distinguished librarians (the other two being Stephen B. Noyes [q.v.] of the Mercantile Library, Brooklyn, New York, and John J. Bailey of the Public School Library, St. Louis, Missouri) invited by John Eaton (q.v.), U.S. commissioner of education, to describe their book catalogs for inclusion in *Public Libraries in the United States of America: Their History, Condition, and Management*. Special Report. Part I. (Washington: Government Printing Office, 1876). In his explanation (pp. 657-60), Schwartz identified the systematic arrangement as dividing "the whole field of knowledge into a system of classes or departments, with subdivisions in each, the place of each division being fixed according to its greater or less degree of dependence or relation to other classes." Thus, not only through the Apprentices' Library *Catalogue* but also through the 1876 Report, Schwartz's interest in, and application of, a systematic or classified arrangement became widely known.

Schwartz was also among those, including R. R. Bowker (q.v.), Charles A. Cutter (q.v.), Melvil Dewey (q.v.), and Justin Winsor (q.v.), who issued, in 1876, a

"Call for a Library Conference." He attended the Librarians' Conference, held in Philadelphia, which followed, and was recorded as member number 4 in the list of original members forming the American Library Association. Although Schwartz participated in the 1876 Conference, and several later ones, he seemed to be too engrossed in the administrative details of his library to be active in the Association. He was never elected to an office in it; he did serve, however, on the Executive Board of the New York Library Association (1885-1886) as it was being organized.

Through his writings rather than through his associational activities, then, Schwartz is remembered among nineteenth century librarians. Early issues of *Library Journal* report Schwartz's activities in the Apprentices' Library, such as the successful transfer of the collection (58,000 volumes) to a new building in two and one-half days, his designing of a charging system that introduced the joint use of a borrower's card and a book slip ("A 'Combined' Charging System," *Library Journal* 4:275-77 [July-August 1879]), his arranging fiction and juveniles on the shelves alphabetically by title rather than by author, and his coding of the sex of borrowers by using odd numbers for men and even numbers for women.

Not only was he innovative in his efforts to improve the Apprentices' Library, but he was alert to, and critical of, developments in the profession. His own basic rule for author entry—to "place under that form of name, whether real or assumed (literary), surname or title by which he [the author] is best known, and which is most frequently used in his writings"—was made in response to the 1877 report of the Co-operative Cataloguing Committee, with which he did not agree. Cutter, one of the Committee members, responded, in turn, that he preferred the use of the pseudonym as the exception rather than the rule. Because of Schwartz's preference for the classified arrangement, he criticized the alphabetical plan of William F. Poole's (q.v.) *Index* in 1878, although his name appeared later as a contributor in *Poole's Index to Periodical Literature, 1802-1881* (Boston: Houghton, 1891). Even Justin Winsor felt compelled to reply to an implied criticism in the preface of the 1881 edition of the *Catalogue of the Apprentices' Library*, for which Schwartz was responsible.

Schwartz's consuming interest, however, was his search for a system for classifying books. As early as 1871, he had been experimenting with a "Combined System" in which he embodied three arrangements: numerical, alphabetical, and classified. By using alphanumeric notation for his subject groupings, he subdivided his major headings numerically and then subarranged books by size under each of his headings. Within each size category, he distributed 1,000 numbers (0-999) according to his arithmetical assumption of number of titles to be classified in each.

Among those who knew of Schwartz's interest in classification was Dewey, who (on February 25, 1873) wrote to him inquiring about his scheme. Later, Dewey referred to the Apprentices' Library in his preface to *A Classification and Subject Index for Cataloguing and Arranging the Books and Pamphlets of a Library* (Amherst, Mass., 1876). There is little direct evidence of Schwartz's influence on Dewey, for Schwartz's scheme was far more complex in structure and notation than that of Dewey. Schwartz had demonstrated in his system, however, the concept of hierarchical relationships in subject analysis, the scattering of aspects of a subject throughout various classes and relating these aspects through an alphabetic index, and a flexible (rather than a fixed) location (shelf arrangement) through his book numbering scheme. Both preferred a classified system with an alphabetic index; however, in contrast to Dewey, who relied originally on size and acquisitional order for location within his classes, Schwartz integrated specific book numbers as a part of his system.

In 1878, following the publication of Schwartz's "A 'Combined' System for Arranging and Numbering" (*Library Journal* 3:6-10), Dewey openly rejected Schwartz's plan of book arrangement and was critical of his use of the law of probability in anticipating the "initials of authors of books not yet written." At the same time, Cutter, also concerned with book numbers, acknowledged his own indebtedness to Schwartz by noting that his book numbering system was "simply an application of the decimal system, already used in Mr. Dewey's class-notation, to Mr. Schwartz's idea of a table of letter-numbers."

In 1879, Schwartz issued his "Mnemonic System of Classification" (*Library Journal* 4:3-7), in which he developed further the use of the alphabet as a natural system of mnemonics. Schwartz's reliance on alphabetical sequence prompted Cutter to question whether mnemonic advantage in a classification could compensate for "incongruities in nomenclature." Dewey referred to it as a "mongrel classification." Throughout the year, both objections to and endorsements of Schwartz's ideas appeared in *Library Journal*. Because of the criticisms, Schwartz seems to have felt compelled or challenged to continue revising his system. Emphasizing that divisions should be proportionate to the number of books on a subject, he introduced, in 1882, "A New Classification and Notation" with an "Alphabetical Table for Authors" (*Library Journal* 7:148-66), in which mnemonic equivalency values for letter combinations were distributed among the four divisions of his 23 main departments (classes). Thus, Schwartz inextricably related his book notation to his divisional

arrangement within each class. Although the potential use of a part of Schwartz's scheme had been diminished, he revised his system once again in 1885, fifteen years after he had initiated his search, this time introducing into it a numeric key representing alphabetic values through which the notation could be interpreted (*Library Journal* 10:25-27, 77-78, 149-50, 174-75, 371-75). In this fourth and final revision, however, through his intransigent dependence on his alpha-mnemonic concept, Schwartz destroyed the logic, clarity, and, finally, any possible adoption of his system by others.

Although Schwartz was criticized again for his reliance on the mnemonic element in his scheme at the 1885 Conference of the American Library Association, he offered no further explanations of it as he had promised. Instead, following the publication of the second edition of Dewey's *Decimal Classification and Relativ Index* (Boston: Library Bureau, 1885), which had been revised and greatly enlarged, Schwartz, in association with Frederick B. Perkins (q.v.), made a disparaging attack on Dewey and his ideas (*Library Journal* 11:37-43, 68-74 [1886]). Because Dewey responded with an equal lack of restraint, the interchange polarized the differences between them.

Despite that confrontation, Schwartz was a guest lecturer, in 1887, at Dewey's School of Library Economy at Columbia College. In the same year, he dedicated a poem, partly humorous and partly satirical, entitled "Three Little Maids from the Library School," to Dewey (*Library Journal* 12:511).

Unrelated to his library affairs was Schwartz's interest in history, primarily in Jewish history. His major writing in this field, "The Pharaoh and the Date of the Exodus of the Hebrews" (*Theological Monthly* 1:145-46; 2:35-41, 129-32) was published in 1889. Following this publication, little was heard from Schwartz during the 1890s other than his paper, "An Indicator-Catalogue Charging System," for the Second International Library Conference held in London 1897 (International Library Conference, 2nd, London, 1897. *Transactions and Proceedings . . . July 13-16, 1897*. London: Printed for Members of the Conference, 1898, pp. 142-45). His views were reminiscent of his interest in, but differing from his 1879 idea of, a combined charging system; instead, he attempted to reconcile the salient features of the British "indicator" system with the use of a book card and a reader's or borrower's card.

The paper, read by Cutter since Schwartz did not attend the Conference, was the last creative idea advanced by Schwartz, for, in 1900, he resigned his position as librarian of the Apprentices' Library. No cause was given for his resignation nor was any acknowledgment made of his contributions to the Library or to the profession. No records concerning his long tenure as librarian have been found in the Library Department of the General Society of Mechanics and Tradesmen. Perhaps Schwartz anticipated such obscurity at the end of his career, for he had observed, in 1882, long before his resignation, that, while an indebtedness was not always acknowledged, his scheme of classification had "suggested all the systems of shelf-arrangement, devised since 1871." Such a statement obviously included Melvil Dewey. That self-evaluation serves as his best epitaph. His death date is unknown.

Books and articles about the biographee—Dewey, Melvil. "The Decimal Classification. A Reply to the 'Duet' [F. B. Perkins and Jacob Schwartz]." *Library Journal* 11:100-106 (April 1886), 132-39 (May 1886); Holley, Edward G. *Raking the Historic Coals: The A.L.A. Scrapbook.* Urbana, Ill.: Beta Phi Mu, 1967 (*passim*); LaMontagne, Leo E. *American Library Classification with Special Reference to the Library of Congress.* Hamden, Conn.: Shoe String Press, 1961 (*passim*); "Librarians." *Library Journal* 25:307 (June 1900); Miksa, Francis L., ed. *Charles Ammi Cutter: Library Systematizer.* Littleton, Colo.: Libraries Unlimited, 1977 (*passim*); U.S. Bureau of Education. *Public Libraries in the United States of America: Their History, Condition, and Management.* Special Report. Part I. Washington: Government Printing Office, 1876, pp. 936-38. Primary sources and archival materials—Schwartz's papers, if extant, have not yet been located. Letter from Melvil Dewey, February 24, 1873. In Dewey, Melvil. "Melvil Dewey Papers." Columbia University Libraries, Division of Special Collections, Rare Book and Manuscript Library.

—SARAH K. VANN

SCOGGIN, MARGARET CLARA (1905-1968)

Margaret Clara Scoggin was born on April 14, 1905, at Caruthersville, Missouri, the daughter of Alfred Polk and Margaret Ellen Bright Scoggin. After graduating as valedictorian with the highest grade average ever achieved at Columbia High School, she attended Radcliffe College, being elected to Phi Beta Kappa and graduating *magna cum laude* in 1926.

Considered a "pioneer" in young adult librarianship, Margaret Scoggin came to the field with a lifelong love of and association with books, but not the slightest intention of becoming a librarian. Her career began in 1926 as a summer replacement at a branch of the New York Public Library, where she gained the attention and respect of her co-workers and supervisors, including Mabel Williams. Williams, who was to encourage and influence Margaret Scoggin, was the superintendent of work with schools who had made early inroads into the new philosophy regarding reading and library service for the young adult. Following Williams's pattern, Margaret Scoggin used an innovative, creative approach to spark the interests of young patrons. Very early in her career, she realized the value of programming, clubs, student book reviewing, and the policy of "Let them read what interests them" to get the attention of young

people. As she moved from one branch of the New York Public Library to another, she was promoted to positions of increasing responsibility.

At this time, she realized her need for further training and, during a year's leave of absence in 1929, attended the School of Librarianship at the University of London. Upon her return, she was appointed school and reference librarian at the George Bruce Branch of the New York Public Library; at the same time, she joined the faculty of the Library's training school, where she taught until the program was discontinued in 1932, when it was transferred to Columbia University. Deciding to obtain her master's degree at the Columbia University School of Library Service, Scoggin fulfilled many of the requirements from 1938 to 1941, but being pressed for time and short on patience, she never did submit final work necessary for the degree.

With Mabel Williams's conviction that only Margaret Scoggin could effectively develop the first library solely for young adults, Scoggin was assigned to organize and direct the Nathan Straus Branch for Children and Young People. After a great deal of planning, the branch opened in 1940 (see her article "Nathan Straus Branch for Children and Young People," *Library Journal* 66:547-49 [June 15, 1941]). With its bright color schemes and carefully chosen collections, this well-lit, well-arranged branch became a model for similar young people's libraries all over the country. It became as well a training ground for personnel and a demonstration center for methods and techniques in this relatively new aspect of librarianship. One outstanding feature of the Library was *Circulatin' the News*, a book reviewing publication reflecting the views of its contributors, the young patrons.

In 1945, after appearing on "This Is Our Town," a radio program about New York City, Scoggin was invited to do a regular weekly show. Finally settling upon a format for the program that was a logical outgrowth of *Circulatin' the News*, she was to host the book reviewing show for fifteen years for the radio station and to continue it for another seven years under the auspices of the New York Public Library. Young students were her panelists, and the program achieved such popularity that it was recorded for re-broadcast all over the country and in the city's junior and senior high schools. "Teen-Age Book Talk" as the show became known in 1960, moved to television, and Margaret Scoggin, well experienced as a moderator, found still another career.

During her years at Nathan Straus, Scoggin was considered by Mabel Williams to be her protégé and, as retirement drew near for the older woman, she created the position of young people's specialist in 1950. This was to give Margaret Scoggin the final seasoning she would need to become the New York Public Library's superintendent of work with young people two years later, in 1952, a position she held until shortly before her death. Her retirement in 1967 marked the end of a 41-year career with the New York Public Library.

Margaret Scoggin's energy was boundless, and she was able to give her attention to many interests at one time. While developing her own career, she was willing to share her knowledge and experience with others and became active in numerous professional activities. She came to young adult librarianship in its infancy, yet she read a paper to librarians on the subject at an American Library Association conference as early as 1928. In 1937, she was secretary of the Young People's Reading Round Table and, in 1940, became chairman. In 1942, she was named an ALA Councilor. In 1949, because of her experience in organizing the renowned Nathan Straus Branch, she was sent by ALA and the Rockefeller Foundation to Munich, Germany, to assist Jella Lepman in the organization of the International Youth Library. Although her assignment was only to observe and advise, she stepped in, worked hard physically to help the librarians prepare for the opening, and developed programs to bring the young people in. As a sign of respect for her untiring efforts, the Children's Book Council has established a Margaret Scoggin Memorial Collection at the Library.

While in Europe, she also visited libraries in a number of countries and, upon her return to the United States, persuaded UNESCO to establish the Children's Book Fund and to include books in CARE packages. She wanted to give children all over the world the opportunity to have a glimpse of life in America. Margaret Scoggin's strong feelings regarding international relations led her to assume in 1950 the chairmanship of the ALA International Relations Committee, on which she had been very active.

In 1951-1952, the Children's and Young Adult Services Division of the New York Library Association was formed, and Margaret Scoggin became its first chairman.

Although in her young days she had been determined not to become a teacher, Scoggin did go on to teach librarianship in several schools of library science. She taught briefly at Pratt Institute in Brooklyn, New York, and at St. John's University, New York, where she taught from the 1940s through 1954. Her courses related not only to young adult work but also to the history of books and printing, which she loved as well. In 1952, she accepted an offer to institute a young adult course at Simmons College in Boston and flew there from New York once a week for one year. Aware of the dearth of qualified experts in the young adult field, she also realized the importance to the College and its students of establishing such a course.

In addition to her numerous articles in professional journals, from 1935 to 1940, her column "Books for Older Boys and Girls" was her continuous contribution to *Library Journal*; in 1940, this became "Books for Young People: Predominantly Adult Books," and, from 1944 to 1945, it was called "Books for Young Adults." Her contributions to *Horn Book* include "The War Years" (1944-1945) and "Outlook Tower" (1948-1967). Her success in knowing just what would interest young people is evident in her choice of stories from adult books for six anthologies she compiled: *Chucklebait, Lure of Danger, More Chucklebait, Edge of Danger, Battle Stations, Escapes & Rescues.* At the time of her death, Scoggin was co-editing an anthology of science fiction tales. In 1952, *Gateways to Readable Books*, designed for use with slow readers in high school, was published, co-edited by Scoggin, Ruth Strang, and Christine Gilbert.

At the height of her career, Margaret Scoggin's contributions to the library world were recognized by numerous awards. The first of these, in 1952, was the Women's National Book Association's Constance Lindsay Skinner Award for outstanding service in the world of books. In 1956, she received the Lane Bryant Award in recognition of her outstanding community service and the Marshall Field Award "in recognition of fundamental and imaginative contributions to the well being of children." Also recognizing her accomplishments in young adult reading, the Grolier Society gave her an award in 1960.

Friends and colleagues of Margaret Scoggin remember well her modest demeanor, contagious enthusiasm, and constant search for challenge. The tailored stern appearance of the tall, slim, brown-eyed, gray-haired librarian belied the boundless energy, intellectual brilliance, remarkable wit, and inner warmth that shone through when she was with "her" young people.

Several days before her death, the American Library Association presented her with a scroll that read in part:

Her ideas of library service for young adults have brought her authority and eminence in the field. Her simplicity and integrity of character have won her respect of young people throughout the world. Her wisdom and understanding and above all her sense of humor, have been guiding lights for her colleagues and associates. We honor Margaret Scoggin as one of our truly dedicated public servants.

Since her death on July 11, 1968, several memorial scholarships have been established, one by the NYLA and a one-time scholarship given to Simmons College by ALA. In 1970, the Scoggin Memorial Collections were established by the U.S. Section of the International Board on Books for Young People.

United States children's books of international interest are presented annually to repositories in parts of the world where publishing does not exist or is in a developing stage.

Biographical listings and obituaries—*Current Biography* (1952); [Obituary]. *Horn Book Magazine* 44:632+ (Oct. 1968); [Obituary]. *Library Journal* 93:3197 (Sept. 15, 1968); [Obituary]. *New York Times*, July 13, 1968, p. 27; *Who's Who in Library Service*, 2nd ed. **Books and articles about the biographee**—Lindquist, Jennie D. "A Tribute to Margaret Scoggin." *Horn Book Magazine* 28:85 (April 1952); Lowy, Beverly. "Margaret C. Scoggin (1905-1968): Her Professional Life and Work in Young Adult Librarianship." Master's thesis, Palmer Graduate Library School, Long Island University, 1970; "Margaret Scoggin." *Library Journal* 78:406 (March 1, 1952); "Margaret Scoggin Retires." *Wilson Library Bulletin* 42:880 (May 1968). **Primary sources and archival materials**—Clipping File, Nathan Straus Young Adult Library, Donnell Library Center, The New York Public Library; Columbia High School. "Official School Record of Margaret Clara Scoggin, 1918-1922." Columbia, Missouri; "History of the Nathan Straus Young Adult Library." New York: The New York Public Library, Office of Young Adult Service (Typewritten); "Margaret C. Scoggin Personal Papers 1915-1968"; The author also utilized personal interviews, among which those with Lillian Morrison (Feb. 20, 1970), Erna Obermeier (Feb. 6, 1970), Lillian Okun (March 2, 1970), and Sylvia Storch (Feb. 23, 1970) were most informative.

—BEVERLY LOWY

SEARS, MINNIE EARL (1873-1933)

Minnie Earl Sears was born in 1873 [the day is not known] in Lafayette, Indiana, daughter of Myron and Lydia Skinner Sears. She earned her B.S. (1891) and M.S. (1893) from Purdue University and received her B.L.S. from the University of Illinois in 1900. She served as head cataloger at the Bryn Mawr College Library (1903-1907), head cataloger at the University of Minnesota Library (1909-1914), and as first assistant of the Reference-Catalog Division of the New York Public Library (1914-1920). After twenty years of rich and varied experience in cataloging and administration, Sears joined the H. W. Wilson [q.v.] Company in 1923, and began that phase of her career during which she produced the works for which she is best remembered today. She taught at the Columbia University School of Library Service (1927-1931) and was successful in developing an advanced course in cataloging to be offered at the graduate level.

Although Sears saw herself primarily as a cataloger, her entire work reveals a strong interest in and concern for reference, bibliography, and literary research. In 1910, she published, in collaboration with Isadore Gilbert Mudge (q.v.), *The Thackery Dictionary*, and the two authors brought out their *George Eliot Dictionary* in 1924.

Author or co-author of a score of works, Sears is best remembered for her *List of Subject Headings for Small Libraries*, first published in 1923 and now in its

eleventh edition. The conception of this work is an example of Minnie Earl Sears's vision as well as her practicality and common sense, and its success probably far surpassed her modest hopes. It was almost immediately adopted as a text by cataloging teachers in library schools, and in the second edition (1926), the author added *See also* references in response to requests from the latter group. In the sixth edition, the title was changed to *Sears List of Subject Headings* "in recognition of the pioneering and fundamental contributions made by Miss Sears. . . ." Since the *List* was also used by medium-sized libraries, the phrase "for Small Libraries" was dropped. Barbara M. Westby ("Preface to the Tenth Edition," *Sears List of Subject Headings*, ed. Barbara M. Westby, 10th ed.; Wilson, 1972) notes also Sears's foresight in following the form of the Library of Congress subject headings, which could be added when her list should prove inadequate. "Practical Suggestions for the Beginner in Subject Heading Work" was added as a chapter to the third edition. It was also published as a monograph and has been translated into several languages.

Sears's name is associated with a number of important reference works and bibliographic tools in addition to her cataloging classic. The editor of the third (1925) and the fourth (1930) editions of the *Children's Catalog*, she completed as well the *Song Index* (1926), and she brought out the *Essay and General Literature Index* (1931-1933). She edited the American Library Association's *Standard Catalog for Public Libraries* (1927-1933) and the second edition of the ALA *Standard Catalog for High School Libraries* (1932). A number of these works have become standard aids in collection building, and they indicate her solid contribution to that aspect of library work as well as to cataloging and reference. By providing accurate cataloging copy in these compilations, Sears sought to combat wasteful duplication in cataloging and, in this respect, anticipated a number of trends in centralized and cooperative cataloging.

Sears was a member of ALA. She belonged also to the New York Library Association and the New York Library Club.

Sears was remembered by her friend and colleague Isadore Gilbert Mudge as a scholarly, meticulous worker whose "unusual power of organization" permitted her to plan, direct, and complete the many works she undertook ("Minnie Earl Sears 1873-1933," *Wilson Bulletin for Libraries* 8:290 [1934]). A senior H. W. Wilson executive, recalling his early days in the firm, described Sears as "a woman of considerable ability and strength of character, and so austere as to be rather formidable" (communication from Jamieson to the author). Mudge, however, found her "quiet and self-effacing," but a person of great energy and determination.

Seriously ill during the last two years of her life, Sears remained hard at work until a few days before her death on November 28, 1933, in New York.

Minnie Earl Sears's place in the annals of librarianship is secure. A number of her works are still in print and widely used. The fact that most have undergone considerable revision is evidence of Sears's breadth of vision—which included flexibility as well as precision. Through her associations with the New York Public Library, the H. W. Wilson Company, the Columbia University School of Library Service, and professional organizations, Sears was able to influence a large number of younger librarians, and the evidence is that she was an exemplary teacher in every sense of the word. Her works were widely known abroad, and perhaps the following words from the *Library Review*'s evaluation of the eighth edition of the *List* (1959, edited by Bertha M. Frick [q.v.]) best summarize the great respect that Sears enjoyed among her professional colleagues:

> The first edition of this standard work was published in 1923 under the editorship of Minnie Earl Sears, whose name has become legendary as an ultimate authority.... It is hardly necessary for us at this late date to describe a work that is in constant use in every worthwhile library throughout the world....

Biographical listings and obituaries—[Obituary]. *Library Association Record*, 4th Series. 1:57-58 (1934); *Who's Who in Library Service*, 1st ed. **Books and articles about the biographee**—Mudge, Isadore Gilbert. "Minnie Earl Sears, 1873-1933." *Wilson Bulletin for Librarians* 8:288-90 (1934); Westby, Barbara M. "Preface to the Tenth Edition." *Sears List of Subject Headings*. 10th ed., ed. by Barbara M. Westby. New York: Wilson, 1972.

—HARRY E. WHITMORE

SEYMOUR, EVELYN MAY (1857-1921)

Evelyn May Seymour, born on August 31, 1857, was one of four children of one of the influential families of Binghamton, New York. Her father, Louis Seymour, was an attorney and, later, a judge in Binghamton, a thriving, educationally progressive town. In her youth, Seymour showed talent as a pianist, but she abandoned her interest after recognizing, perhaps with too much modesty, her limitations. She attended Smith College, where, to meet admission requirements, she removed a deficiency in Greek in a remarkably short time. Graduating in the second class with a B.A. degree (1880), Seymour maintained an interest in the Association of Collegiate Alumnae for many years afterward.

Although she taught in the schools of St. Louis, Missouri, and of Englewood, New Jersey, after graduation, she continued her search for a more personally rewarding career. Eventually, when she heard

Melvil Dewey (q.v.) speak, she was captivated by his vigor, intensity, and firm conviction that librarianship offered career opportunities for college-educated women. Upon learning of his plans for a School of Library Economy at Columbia College, she eagerly sought admission. A member of the first class beginning January 5, 1887, she was, according to Dewey, "not only 1st to enter ... but 1st in ability, industry, and loyalty." Seymour's factual and terse notes of lectures for March 1887 indicate a comprehensive coverage of bibliographies in several languages (*School of Library Economy of Columbia College, 1887-1889; Documents for a History*. School of Library Economy, Columbia University, 1937, pp. 160-83). Since students were enmeshed in the crisis affecting Dewey following the establishment of the School, Seymour shared with her classmates uncertainty concerning their status. She was one of eleven who, on June 11, 1890, long after completing their studies, requested that President Seth Low of Columbia College grant them certificates of attendance "in accordance with the statement in the circular of information for 1887-88." Apparently each of them received a certificate on March 20, 1891, signed by President Low and indicating successful pursuit of prescribed courses and the passing of all required examinations.

While completing her studies at Columbia, Seymour helped organize the new Osterhout Free Library in Wilkes-Barre, Pennsylvania (1887-1888), under the direction of Hannah P. James (q.v.). While doing that, however, Seymour accepted a position as cataloger at Columbia College and, from that date until her death, her professional life was inextricably interwoven with that of Dewey, as was her personal life with that of the Dewey family.

After Dewey's resignation from Columbia in 1888, the Dewey family moved to Albany, where he assumed immediately his new dual responsibilities as secretary and treasurer of the Board of Regents of the University of the State of New York and as director of the State Library. He designed a demanding civil service examination, to be taken by those hoping to help him fulfill his plans for the Library; among those who passed the examination brilliantly was May Seymour, who accepted a position there as of April 1, 1890. That Seymour quickly followed Dewey to Albany reflected her loyalty to him through the Columbia crisis, her dependence on him, and her willingness to assume a subordinate, self-effacing, and ever-supportive role in furthering his views and plans.

Her first position at the State Library was as classifier; however, in 1891, according to Dewey's wish to create "one of the best educational libraries in the country," she became librarian (sub-librarian) of education, a position she held until 1906. In doing this, Seymour became more actively involved in demonstrating Dewey's conviction that "public libraries should be recognized as an essential part of the State system of education." She became increasingly indispensable to Dewey, who taught her his unique shorthand, which she wrote "so that it lookt like copper plate engraving." She imitated his simplified spelling. She assisted in the development of the Library School that Dewey was permitted to continue within the State Library and with which she was associated throughout the Dewey years in Albany. She was appointed also as an assistant to Dewey in his capacity as secretary to the Board of Regents and quickly broadened her grasp of the educational problems of New York State. According to Dewey (*Library Journal* 46:606 [1921]),

> her marvelous mind very quickly grasped the broader problems of the University, and no person, of several hundred on my staf during those seventeen years of re-organization helpt me more, not alone by loyal co-operation and servis, but in practical suggestions based on thoro study and most unusual breadth of comprehension of the great educational problems of the Empire State.

One of her special assignments was assisting Dewey in planning the New York State educational exhibit for the World's Columbian Exposition, held in Chicago in 1893. She served with Theresa West Elmendorf (q.v.) as one of the two associate editors (with Dewey as editor) of the 1904 *A.L.A. Catalog.* He entrusted her with the execution of the plans and noted that "her rare skill and devotion to this work have added much to its practical value" (*A.L.A. Catalog. 8,000 Volumes for a Popular Library, with Notes. 1904.* Prepared by the New York State Library and the Library of Congress, under the auspices of the American Library Association Publishing Board). He later identified the *Catalog* as a "monument to her ability and industry."

While at Albany, Seymour also assumed a major responsibility in editing editions 4, 5, and 6 of Dewey's Decimal Classification, published respectively in 1891, 1894, and 1899. She was also involved in the preparation of the first abridged edition, which appeared in *Library Notes* (4, no. 13-14:1-192 [January-April 1895]).

May Seymour was devoted to the Dewey family and, sympathetic with their need to be away from Albany during the hay fever season, shared their enthusiasm in founding the Lake Placid Club in the Adirondacks, where she spent her summers as well. Often while the Deweys were there and Seymour was in Albany, she assumed responsibilities delegated to her in his absence.

Following Dewey's resignation as state librarian, Seymour apparently had planned to remain at the State Library. However, his successor, Edwin H. Anderson (q.v.), seeking to eradicate evidences of Dewey's influence, requested her resignation, to be effective on March 1, 1906. Among the reasons given by Anderson for her dismissal were 1) that her "close association and sympathy with the previous administration" disqualified her "for usefulness under the new" and 2) that he was unwilling to have her involved in any classification activities at the State Library because of her "close identification with the Decimal Classification."

Seymour obligingly resigned; her decision was for her, as Dewey's had been for him, an introduction to a life far removed from the daily activities of the library world. The indignity that she had suffered was assuaged by an invitation from the Deweys to come to the Lake Placid Club. She became a close member of the Dewey family, living with them at the Cedars (the Dewey family cottage), as Dewey stated, "like an own sister, and yet more efficient than any salaried officer." He identified her as "the most activ co-founder" next to himself and Mrs. Dewey, for she had participated while in Albany in decisions made during the formative years of the Club. She, with Katharine L. Sharp (q.v.) and the Deweys, including their son, Godfrey, became known as the "Cedars Five."

Seymour's interest in music furthered the Club's reputation for offering "the best music of any American resort." She was responsible, also, for developing the Club Library and for the printery. Her major work, however, with the assistance of Dorkas Fellows (q.v.), was the continuing publication of the Decimal Classification: Edition 7 (792p.) in 1911, Edition 8 (850p.) in 1913, Edition 9 (856p.) in 1915, and Edition 10 (940p.) in 1919. She also edited the second edition of the *Abridged Decimal Classification and Relativ Index* (1915) and had completed the third edition, revised, and the *Outline*, both of which were published in 1921, shortly after her death. Edition 7 was the first edition edited by her to bear the imprint of Forest Press, Lake Placid Club. While a major criticism of Seymour's lengthy editorship of the Classification has concerned her reluctance to expand old or develop new subjects (often because of her concern for detail and her perfectionism), her efforts undoubtedly insured its continuity.

Dewey sent her as an emissary to Brussels to discuss, with Paul Otlet and Henri La Fontaine of the Office International de Bibliographie, matters relating to the Decimal Classification and to the Classification Décimale (Universal Decimal Classification). In Edition 11, which Seymour had been editing at the time of her death, Dewey acknowledged gratefully that

> for 32 years every item of work on new editions past thru her hands. For each edition she did all editorial and much constructiv work, secured expert cooperation, cald attention to faults or

SEYMOUR   SHARP

omissions, and sought the best availabl compromize where doctors disagreed, devoting to this vast labor rare skolarly industry and a loyalty for which no words of thanks can be adequate. She shared my faith in its immense usefulness, did the hardest work, and deservs the gratitude of all who profit by this invaluabl laborsaver. I often askt that her name appear on the title-paje of the book to which she gave so much, but she persistently refuzed.

Seymour was instrumental as well in the creation of the Lake Placid Club Education Foundation. Not only did she participate in and revise the plan for the Foundation, she was also "warmly and actively interested" in it. So great was her belief in the Foundation, chartered in 1922 after her death, that she directed that the income from her property, after the demise of immediate relatives, be used "to further . . . [its] hy ideals." As a memorial to Seymour, Dewey transferred to the Foundation "all copyryts and control of all editions" of the Classification.

Seymour was engrossed both in the Foundation plans and in the Decimal Classification at the time of her death on June 14, 1921. She died of pneumonia in New York City, where she had gone for some special dentistry. A tribute from the New York State Library, read at a memorial service for Seymour at the Lake Placid Club, stated that "the library world has lost one of its keenest minds and strongest characters."

She was thorough, meticulous, punctilious, exacting, "frank in criticism or needed correction"; her "impatience of inaccuracy, or mental sloppiness or indolence . . . made her a terror to the incompetent." Dewey praised her for her intellectual curiosity, her scholarship, and her fearlessness, both intellectual and physical. She was referred to as a "specialist in omniscience." These traits, evident both in her editing of the Classification and in her Club activities, endeared her to few, but those who knew her "found bak of that somewhat prim exterior and the critical mind, a welth of qualities of which they had litl dreamd."

One who knew little of May Seymour wrote at the time of her death: "Poor dear Miss Seymour earnest, honest, quietly humorus—the most generous 'exact' personality I ever knew." But she was not "poor Miss Seymour"; she found fulfillment in her life at the Lake Placid Club furthering Dewey's aims and revising the Classification. Henri La Fontaine assessed her as being "the soul of the D C." Indeed, her monument is her editorship of the Classification.

Biographical listings and obituaries—Dewey, Melvil. "May Seymour, August 31, 1857-June 14, 1921 [Obituary]." *Library Journal* 46:606-607 (July 1921); [Obituary]. *Public Libraries* 26:385 (1921). **Books and articles about the biographee**—Bidlack, Russell E. " 'The Coming Catalogue.' " *Library Quarterly* 27:137-60 (1957); Comaromi, John P. *The Eighteen Editions of the Dewey Decimal Classification.* Albany: Forest Press, 1976; Dawe, George Grosvenor. *Melvil Dewey: Seer, Inspirer, Doer, 1851-1931.* Biografic compilation. Club ed. Lake Placid Club, N.Y.: Melvil Dewey Biografy, 1932; Dewey, Melvil. *Decimal Classification and Relativ Index for Libraries and Personal Use, In Arranjing for Immediate Reference, Books, Pamflets, Clippings, Pictures, Manuscript Notes and Other Material.* Ed. 11, rev. and enl. Lake Placid Club, N.Y.: Forest Press, 1922; "Memorial Service for May Seymour. Full Report of Meeting at the Club on Anniversary of Her Birth." Reprinted from the *Lake Placid News*, Sept. 16, 1921; New York (State) Library School. *Handbook of New York State Library School Including Summer Courses and Library Training.* In New York (State) Library. *86th Annual Report, 1893.* Albany: University of the State of New York, 1904 [its Bulletin 82; Library School 15]; New York State Library School Association. *New York State Library School Register, 1887-1926.* James I. Wyer Memorial Edition [6th ed.]. New York, 1959. **Primary sources and archival materials**—Conversations with Dr. Godfrey Dewey and Deo B. Colburn, Lake Placid Club, New York; fragmentary correspondence of May Seymour, Lake Placid Club; letter from May Seymour to Nicholas Murray Butler, President, Columbia University, 3 February 1906, and other data. In Melvil Dewey, "Melvil Dewey Papers." Columbia University Libraries, Division of Special Collections, Rare Book and Manuscript Library.

—SARAH K. VANN

SHARP, KATHARINE LUCINDA (1865-1914)

Katharine Lucinda Sharp was born on May 21, 1865, at Elgin, Illinois, the daughter of John W. and Phebe Thompson Sharp. She received a diploma from the progressive Elgin Academy in Elgin, Illinois, in 1880, and a Bachelor of Philosophy degree from Northwestern University in 1885. For two years (1886-1888), she taught Latin, French, and German at the Elgin Academy but, in October of 1888, she became assistant librarian of the Scoville Institute in Oak Park, Illinois. The reasons for her decision to enter librarianship at that time are not completely clear, but she was strongly influenced by the professional concerns of the field of librarianship and a family tradition that supported involvement in a service occupation.

After a single year's experience in the Scoville Institute Library, Sharp was convinced that she needed additional specialized education and thereupon took the step that was to play a key role in her future. In the fall of 1889, she applied for admission to the newly established New York State Library School at Albany. In addition to her bachelor's degree, she had also completed requirements for the Master of Philosophy degree at Northwestern, and her superior academic credentials brought her ready acceptance; she was admitted to the second Albany class and began her studies under Melvil Dewey's (q.v.) supervision in the fall of 1890. From the outset, she was described by Dewey and his faculty as "so easily first" in a renowned class. In addition to her academic studies, she gained cataloging experience in Wheaton, Illinois, and Xenia, Ohio. Her work at Albany won her several academic awards, and, prior to receipt of the Bachelor of Library Science degree in 1892, she was selected to coordinate and administer the Comparative Library Exhibit at the World's Columbian Exposition held in Chicago in 1893. More important, however, was Dewey's recommendation of her as "the best man in America to start the [Armour Institute] library and library school." The Reverend Frank W. Gunsaulus, president of the new Institute, accepted Dewey's commendation and, in September of 1893, Katharine Sharp became director of the Library and the Department of Library Economy at the Armour Institute. The Library class was the first such school in the Midwest and only the fourth in the United States.

The first Armour Institute class began study in the fall of 1893 under difficult conditions and, throughout its existence, it was hampered by a lack of resources and space as well as a dearth of qualified staff. But the personality and ability of Katharine Sharp almost single-handedly won the admiration and respect of students and colleagues alike. She admitted only those few young women whose qualifications were higher than those of the typical high school graduate. The library classes were, to a great degree, directed by the vocational and technical emphases of the Institute, but Sharp continued to set high standards and ideals for the students. She modelled the curriculum on the first-year program of the Albany School and produced trained library assistants under trying circumstances. Every possible library and educational experience in the Chicago area was utilized in order to broaden the students' opportunities. As a result, during the years of the school's existence in Chicago, Sharp established her own reputation as a librarian and teacher. In addition, she became active in some of the "extra-curricular" library concerns that were to mark her professional career, among which were the Chicago Library Club, library extension classes around the state and the Midwest, the organization of the Illinois State Library Association, and the initiation and direction of a library summer school program in Wisconsin.

By the end of four years, Katharine Sharp had developed the Armour program to a point at which its future under the inherent limitations of the Armour Institute's vocational goals had to be considered. She had successfully added a second year of preparation and matriculated 58 students who were, for the most part, enhancing the Department of Library Economy's reputation. Sharp wanted more; she wanted a recognized degree program, not merely a certificate of accomplishment. Her summer school teaching at Madison, Wisconsin, brought an offer from that university to transfer the Armour program and, coincidentally, President Andrew Draper of the

University of Illinois also offered a home and a formal educational framework to the library class. In June 1897, Katharine Sharp, then only 32 years old, was appointed head librarian, director of the Library School and professor of library economy at the University of Illinois. Her selection of Illinois over Wisconsin was motivated largely by her personal philosophy that teachers of library courses must also be practicing librarians. At the University of Illinois, she could serve as director of both the Library and the Library School; at Wisconsin, she would have been only the director of the school.

Sharp's role as head librarian was a major challenge and, eventually, a major headache. Prior to her arrival on campus, librarians had been selected for reasons other than their professional training and experience. As a result, the University Library was lacking in organization, direction, and qualified staff. Although she arrived shortly after completion of a spacious building, she found that it was, typically, a library designed by someone who did not know what a library building should be. Not surprisingly, promises of extra staff failed to materialize, and this, coupled with her supervision of students within the library classes, made her early years times of stress. Illnesses and resignations of her staff were to plague Sharp for many years, yet her ability to see and solve the essential problems quickly brought results. She spared no effort in promoting the Library and, behind the scenes, set into motion significant organizational steps including systematized procedures for book selection and acquisition, an organized reference service and, under the direction of Margaret Mann (q.v.), a recataloging of a large portion of the collection. Sharp was especially concerned about the extension of library services and the modernization of library procedures through the use of consistent, accurate, and professional techniques. Because she believed that the efficient administrator was an efficient businessman, she carefully directed the economic aspects of library administration. Through her efforts, for the first time, the librarian was able to report what the Library owned, where it was located, and what should be obtained in the coming years.

Sharp's commitment to service and to the library user was emphasized in her attempts to make materials accessible. Collections were developed where needed; rules were secondary to demand. The reference department reflected her concern for the accessibility of information and the availability of professional staff for information services. Her interest in the library user extended into the community, where she helped to establish specialized book collections in both Champaign and Urbana as well as to staff the collections with willing library students. During the same years, she played an active role in regional and national library associations; she was president of the

Illinois Library Association (1903), a councilor of the American Library Association (1895-1905) and twice ALA vice-president (1898, 1907). She was also a fellow of the American Library Institute.

Despite her priority interest in the Library School over the Library directorship, her ten years at Illinois provided the base from which the outstanding University of Illinois research library developed. In a letter to Melvil Dewey (September 21, 1914; Sharp-Dewey Correspondence, University of Illinois Archives), her successor, F. K. W. Drury (q.v.), commented,

> As the librarian of the University of Illinois library, she had a far-seeing judgment which those who followed after have realized. There was no need to undo any piece of work that she had authorized, and the foundation laid by her was firm and stedfast. She builded for the future. . . .

At the same time that Sharp was shaping the University of Illinois Library, she was playing an even more significant role in strengthening acceptance of the value of formal education for librarians. The School's transfer to Illinois brought identification of the library program as an acceptable discipline that could lead to a bachelor's degree. Throughout her tenure at Illinois, she advocated the development of a graduate program but was denied this ultimate recognition, although by 1903, students who enrolled in the library classes had at least three years of undergraduate preparation prior to entrance in the Illinois State Library School.

Melvil Dewey's concepts and aims for library education were mirrored in Katharine Sharp's, and she brought to Illinois his plans and interests. She also, however, was continually interested in experimentation and innovation. The curriculum was expanded from the cataloging, classification, and administration basics to include public documents, library extension, research methods, and contemporary concerns. During Sharp's ten years at Illinois, the staff of the Library School and the University Library grew from three to fifteen. The Library increased in size from 37,000 to 96,000 volumes, with much of the preparation and servicing of the collection provided by Library School students who worked under the close supervision of the staff. Throughout this period, Katharine Sharp's reputation continued to grow; more and more she was admired as a librarian who not only served but lived her profession. Members of the Pacific Northwest Library Association wrote to Melvil Dewey (September 1914; Sharp-Dewey Correspondence) that

> Miss Sharp inspired us with the dignity of our profession and the willing self-sacrifice necessary for the service we are to render. We learned from her the indefinable something she called "library spirit" and the real memorial will always be in the

expression of that spirit by her students in libraries from the Atlantic to the Pacific.

The years of dedication and sacrifice took their heavy toll and, by the early 1900s, Katharine Sharp had fallen prey to her own inability to judge her capacity to handle the increasing demands of the two positions she held. Never physically strong after a bout with typhoid in Chicago, she often drained her strength by long hours and extra duties. A philosophical difference with the new University president, Edmund James, about the importance of the Library School vis-à-vis the Library, plus the unexpected death of both her father and half-brother, brought her to the brink of exhaustion and frustration. A timely offer from Melvil Dewey to serve as vice-president of the Lake Placid Club came, and, in April 1907, she wrote a letter to the chairman of the class of 1907 (Sharp Papers, University of Illinois Archives) in which she told the Library School students:

> You and I shall be graduating together. While I am leaving active library work, for a time at least, I am not leaving the library school, for that is a part of me and wherever I may live its interests will be vital to me. I have felt for some time that the pressure of administrative duties was preventing me from doing what I wished to do for the school. I have felt still more that it was crushing the human element out of my life.

In recognition of her service, the University awarded her an honorary master's degree in 1907.

No one expected that Sharp would not return to the field once her physical and emotional equilibrium had been restored. However, in the beautiful Adirondack Mountains, working and living with people whom she loved as her second family, she found, for the first time in her life, a complete existence that allowed her personal as well as professional happiness. That life was abruptly shattered on June 1, 1914, when she died at the age of 49 after suffering a massive concussion of the brain in an automobile accident. A special memorial service was held at Lake Placid, and her body was returned to Dundee, Illinois, where she was buried beside her parents. The University of Illinois Senate recognized her loss to both the School and the profession in a memorial Minute (Minutes of the University Senate; June 3, 1914, III, p. 167):

> As the founder of the Library School at Armour Institute, which on her appointment here became a part of this university, she made a notable contribution to the advancement of her chosen profession. Her administration of the University Library was marked by high ideals and great ability and secured for her a distinguished place among the librarians of the country.

Katharine Sharp was elected to membership in many social, literary, and scholarly organizations: Kappa Kappa Gamma (which she served as national president), Phi Beta Kappa, and the Bibliographical Society of America, in addition to the already mentioned professional library associations. Her writings are not numerous but include ten articles on various aspects of library work and one extensive volume on libraries in the state of Illinois: *Illinois Libraries* (1906-1907). (The work on Illinois libraries earned her the M.L.S. degree from Albany in 1906.) She made no attempt to communicate formally beyond the obvious reports of current activities and library concerns. What she wrote and spoke was prepared for practical reference, to summarize and consolidate what she had accomplished or thought.

The period in which Katharine Sharp lived and worked was not known for its concern about a philosophy of librarianship. If she made any real assertion or defense of library science, it was to emphasize the educational significance of the library and her vision of the power of books and libraries to shape the material, intellectual, and moral advancement of the people. That she was able to do this at a time when formal education for librarianship was not a common reality, when women as leaders were neither recognized nor accepted, when the profession lacked any definition of its purpose, attests to her powerful personality and dynamic administrative ability. Tall, regal, dignified, a woman above reproach, she brought to the profession a leadership that embodied all that was the best in librarianship at the turn of the century.

Biographical listings and obituaries—*Dictionary of American Biography* 17 (George B. Utley); New York State Library School *Register, 1887-1926*; *Notable American Women, 1607-1950* 3 (Rose B. Phelps); [Obituary]. *ALA Bulletin* 8:502 (Sept. 1914); [Obituary]. *ALA Bulletin* 9:212 (July 1915); [Obituary]. *Library Journal* 39:564, 567 (July 1914); [Obituary]. *Public Libraries* 19:513-14 (July 1914); University of Illinois *Annual Register*, 1898-1908; *Who Was Who in America* I (1897-1942); *Woman's Who's Who of America* 1914-1915. Books and articles about the biographee—Grotzinger, Laurel. *The Power and the Dignity: Librarianship and Katharine Sharp*. New York: Scarecrow Press, 1966; Howe, Harriet. "Katharine Lucinda Sharp, 1865-1914." In *Pioneering Leaders in Librarianship*, ed. by Emily Miller Danton. Chicago: American Library Association, 1953; Simpson, Frances. *Katharine L. Sharp, an Appreciation*. Chicago, 1914; Westermann, May Cynthia. "Katharine Lucinda Sharp, 1894-96." In *The History of Kappa Kappa Gamma Fraternity, 1870-1930*, by Florence B. Roth and May C. Westermann. Columbus, Ohio: The Fraternity, 1932. Primary sources and archival materials—The Sharp Papers are located in the University of Illinois Archives and the Melvil Dewey Papers are at Columbia University.

—LAUREL A. GROTZINGER

SHAW, CHARLES BUNSEN (1894-1962)

Charles Bunsen Shaw was born in Toledo, Ohio, on June 5, 1894, the son of Hubert Grover and Elizabeth Ann de Quedville Shaw. After graduating from Clark University with a baccalaureate degree in 1914, he received the A.M. degree from Clark (1915). In 1920, he earned a certificate in librarianship at the New York Library School at Albany. Clark University conferred upon him an honorary L.H.D. degree in 1947.

Shaw's interests in college were music, Keats, and tennis. He studied voice lessons in college and sang in local churches to help pay his college tuition. He has been described as having a natural love for people and a taste for simple pleasures, including an avid interest in baseball, and he was endowed with a quick turn of humor. He was married to Dorothy Joslyn on June 25, 1918. Three children were born to this union: Robert Joslyn, Charles Richard, and Dorothy.

Charles Shaw's professional career began in 1916 at the University of Maine as an instructor of English. In 1917-1918, he taught English at Goucher College. Journeying to North Carolina, he became associate professor and librarian at the Woman's College of the University of North Carolina (Greensboro). In 1927, he was appointed librarian at Swarthmore College and remained in that post until his death on January 28, 1962. A recognized scholar, Shaw was in demand as an adjunct professor at library schools. He taught in the summer session at Columbia University in 1930; for thirty summers (1932-1961) he served on the Library School faculty of the University of Michigan. For a period of ten years (1937-1947), he taught during the spring semester at the Library School of Drexel University.

Charles Bunsen Shaw was a man of many talents. His literary skills are reflected in the numerous articles that he wrote reflecting his great love for literature. Three of these titles include "Down the World with Marna" (*The South Atlantic Quarterly*, January 1922), "Bacon Wrote Shakespeare" (*The South Atlantic Quarterly*, October 24, 1924), and "This Fellow of Infinite Jest" (*Poet Lore*, Summer 1929). His most popular literary output was a book of essays that he edited entitled *American Essays*, first issued by New American Library in 1948 (with a fourth printing published in 1955).

However, it is as an academic librarian that Shaw made his greatest contribution. Among his most significant journal articles are "Bibliographical Instruction for Students" (*Library Journal*, April 1, 1928), "China's Christian Libraries" (*Library Journal*, February 15, 1950), "The Postwar Role of Libraries" (*College and Research Libraries*, December 1943), "Special Collections in the College Library" (*College and Research Libraries*, November 1957), "The Librarian and Scholarship" (*Library Journal*, June 1, 1932), and "Library Cooperation between Bryn Mawr, Haverford and Swarthmore" (*The Haverford Review*, Summer 1942). Among his monographs in librarianship are *American Painters* (Woman's College, 1927), *A Reading List of Biographies* (Woman's College, 1922), and *A List of Books for College Libraries* (American Library Association, 1931, and a supplement, 1940).

Shaw will be long remembered for his *A List of Books for College Libraries*, for it was the first comprehensive selection tool that academic librarians could rely on for collection building. The Shaw list was widely acclaimed. Helen Haines (q.v.) indicated in her *Living with Books* that "the selection itself represents an 'evaluation' that offers indispensable guidance in building up any college collection." While Shaw was a notable bookman, he did not rely only upon his own knowledge of books for this formidable list. More than 200 college professors, librarians, and other scholars assisted him in the selection, including his faculty colleagues at Swarthmore. Dean Hunt of Swarthmore stated that

> this was the genius of the man for he sensed that, since the professors were in the classroom engaged in teaching, they were in a better position to assess their instructional, research, and teaching resources' needs, therefore, he went to the fount of learning, the faculty, in spite of the fact that he was an excellent bibliophile and was aware of what was being published at the time.

Shaw was pleased with the favorable reaction that his list received throughout the country. His wife reports that "he received a great many letters of praise for it." She then tells the story that "we were out to dinner one night and somebody after hearing his name said are you any relation to the Shaw List?"

Charles Bunsen Shaw was motivated to enter librarianship, according to his wife, by "nobody but himself. As a matter of fact he was influenced not to become a librarian." Continuing, Mrs. Shaw revealed that "it was Louis Round Wilson . . . who discouraged him, so he went into teaching. He found out that what he really wanted to do was to be a librarian."

Following his graduation from the New York State Library School, Shaw was invited to the Woman's College of the University of North Carolina, Greensboro, to build a new library. His tenure of seven years as librarian was marked by several accomplishments in the development of academic library service. In addition to his responsibility as librarian, he was active in the University community. He sang with University and church groups in the community and participated in several dramas on campus, often playing the male lead. He also chaired the committee that brought distinguished lecturers to the campus, and at the same time, he found time to engage in scholarly research and writing.

In 1927, Shaw was invited by President Aydelotte to become the librarian of Swarthmore College and supervise construction of a new library building for the College. Mrs. Shaw notes that "he served under three presidents, all of whom he liked very much." His achievements and contributions to librarianship were made during his tenure as librarian at Swarthmore. He developed the Swarthmore College Library to the status of one of the great undergraduate libraries of the country. He had planned to retire at the end of the 1962 academic year. In anticipation of his retirement, he prepared notes for the last annual report that he did not live to write; his successor states in the 1961-1962 *Annual Report* that:

> Mr. Shaw noted as important milestones during his tenure: the addition of a wing for the Friends Historical Library in 1928; the reclassification of the book collection from the Dewey Decimal to the Library of Congress system, a procedure which required twelve years to complete, 1931-1943; the establishment of reference service in 1932; the addition of a book stack in 1935; the merging of four of our science departmental libraries to form the du Pont Science Library in 1960; a current library budget four times the size of the 1927 budget. The notes continue with a list of matters in which he felt pride: the size of the book collection and the annual appropriation; the size and calibre of the staff; the development of special collections; the number of hours the library is open; the reference service to the college community. The notes conclude with his regrets: an inadequate library building; continued existence of departmental libraries; the failure to enlarge the Wells Wordsworth and Wells Thomson collections; the status of the professional staff; too little bibliographical instruction; the Librarian office-bound rather than student-serving.

Charles Bunsen Shaw's years at Swarthmore were years of great achievement. One of his colleagues, Dr. John M. Moore, professor emeritus of philosophy and religion, gives this glowing account of his work at Swarthmore:

> He made the library as useful and accessible as possible to both students and his colleagues on the faculty. He was always helpful with bibliographical information and references, and he was always eager to experiment with different ways of handling problems like special reserves. He was particularly interested in the Honors program, since he realized that this required students to make use of the library and its resources more extensively than undergraduates are usually expected to do.

Although Shaw did not achieve all that he desired, the foregoing account of his work at Swarthmore indicates his many accomplishments. Mrs. Shaw indicated that there were two major goals that he had established that he did not accomplish at Swarthmore. She said that "he was disappointed in not being able to build a new library and also his failure to obtain faculty status for the librarians. He felt strongly about faculty status, for nearly everyone on the staff had advanced degrees, and he thought they should be recognized; he said the librarians without faculty status were neither fish nor fowl."

Librarian Emeritus Martha A. Connor, his successor, speaks about his other disappointment:

It was rather sad that when Charles Shaw came to Swarthmore from Woman's College, North Carolina, he was asked to come as quickly as he could in order to consult with an architect for a new building. Thirty-three years later, when he died, there was still no new building in sight, though the old building had been enlarged by the erection of a temporary stack structure. Then, several months after Charles died, an alumnus donated the money for a new building and we went ahead with planning and building it.

Shaw was astute enough to know that academic libraries are overwhelmingly dependent upon human resources for their effective functioning. Therefore, he was genuinely concerned about maintaining good relationships with the staff and trying to establish better working conditions. While not successful in obtaining faculty status for his staff, he maintained relations with them that Connor was to describe:

Charles was a very kind, considerate person. He knew each person on his staff as an individual and, in his quiet manner, was always friendly. Yet he was reserved, too. One could not say he was an outgoing person; he made the effort to know each staff-member. I think that each member of his staff felt that he was a dependable friend. His staff had great respect for him, too, and admired his scholarliness.

Besides being greatly admired by his library staff, Shaw was also held in high esteem by his colleagues on campus. Professor James Sorber declares:

He was an uncommonly scholarly librarian who was admired by all of his colleagues. Moreover, he laid down a solid foundation for a very good library in all fields, and I think that the spirit has continued. The faculty was constantly challenged to contribute to the growth of the collection because of the fine work that Charles had established.

Dean Emeritus Everett Hunt unequivocally believes that the work of Shaw brought recognition to Swarthmore. He says:

While he wanted to develop the Swarthmore College Library, he was equally ambitious for libraries all over the country. As a scholar he had a feeling that librarians ought to be scholars. . . . He was a scholar and did a great deal of writing; of course, he wanted to develop his own scholarship to enhance the prestige of librarians. He succeeded

John Russell Hayes as librarian. Hayes was a Quaker poet, and he was an amateur librarian. Charles Shaw represented the first professional librarian employed by the college. . . . Although his scholarship was prodigous, he was a very modest man who was loved by all of his colleagues. Because of his national prominence he brought national recognition to Swarthmore.

A man of varied interests and talents, Shaw was particularly interested in the work of private presses. He had a press of his own and exchanged printed items with other persons. He also gave a series of lectures on private presses, these sponsored by the Cooper Foundation. His own printing work was always well designed.

Shaw was not content to work only at Swarthmore, for he was very active in numerous local and national professional organizations. He was president of the Swarthmore Public Library Board for five years (1943-1948). He served as consultant to the [Andrew] Carnegie [q.v.] Corporation. He was a life member of the American Library Association and a member of the College Library Advisory Board of the Association of College and Reference Libraries (later the Association of College and Research Libraries) from 1933 to 1936. He was vice-president of the Pennsylvania Library Association (1937-1938), president of the Philadelphia Metropolitan Library Council (1941-1942), and a member of the Bibliographical Society of America; during his tenure in North Carolina, he served as president of the North Carolina Library Association. In 1943-1944, he served as president of the Association of College and Reference Libraries. World War II was coming to a close, and Shaw, a devout Quaker with an abiding faith in the uniqueness and importance of academic libraries, used his office as president of ACRL ("Message from President Shaw," *College and Research Libraries* 4:275 [1943]) to discuss the use of academic libraries in promoting peace:

Libraries, which have splendidly demonstrated their particular uses in war, are primarily instruments for the preservation and widening of the ways of peace. . . .

The academic libraries of the country are a vital potentiality in the struggle against future wars. To these libraries, for their information and their inspiration, come both many of the intellectual leaders of the republic and, in their formative years, the bulk of the more responsible rank and file who are the components of our democracy. It is not completely unrealistic or arrogant to think that, in Maine-like political tradition, as our libraries go, so goes the country. If librarians provide and disseminate the factual knowledge and expressions of the spirit on which nonviolent settlement of differences may be based, we have fertilized and nourished, to the extent of our professional abilities, the ever living and almost universal human hope that wars may cease.

Shaw was frequently called upon to serve as a consultant, doing work for sixteen American college libraries, including a library once directed by this writer. In 1947-1948, he was sent to China under the auspices of the United Board for Christian Colleges in China as a consultant and adviser to thirteen colleges and universities on library problems. He was appalled at the conditions of the libraries and the hardships of deprivation and war endured by the librarians and students. His account of this visit reveals again and again Shaw's love for people and libraries and, above all, his faith in the future. His report on his China trip ("China's Christian Libraries," *Library Journal* 75:245 [1950]) ends on this note:

Great nations and great libraries grow together; and in the years that lie ahead great libraries will develop in the great nation of China. What America's bibliothetical share in repaying our cultural debt is to be in the next decade or quarter-century, or some time after 2000 A.D. is a question at present to be answered by hope and patience rather than by prophecy.

Charles Bunsen Shaw—librarian, scholar, man of letters, teacher, printer—made a definite contribution to American librarianship. He died on January 28, 1962.

Biographical listings and obituaries—*National Cyclopaedia of American Biography* 46; New York State Library School *Register 1887-1926*, James I. Wyer Memorial Edition. New York, 1959; [Obituary]. *College and Research Libraries* 23:245 (May 1962); [Obituary]. *Library Journal* 87:1111 (March 15, 1962); [Obituary]. *New York Times*, January 30, 1962; *Who Was Who in America* III (1961-1968); *Who's Who in Library Service*, 1st ed., 2nd ed., 3rd ed. **Primary sources and archival materials**—Interview with Everett Lee Hunt, dean emeritus, Swarthmore College, Sept. 21, 1974; interview with Mrs. Dorothy J. Shaw, Sept. 21, 1974; interview with James D. Sorber, Sept. 21, 1974; letter to the author from Martha A. Connor, Sept. 21, 1974; letter to the author from John M. Moore, March 28, 1974; letter to the author from James D. Sorber, March 17, 1974; Swarthmore College, *Annual Report of the Librarian, 1961-62.* Shaw's papers are held by his widow (Mrs. Dorothy J. Shaw) in Swarthmore, Pennsylvania.

—E. J. JOSEY

SHAW, RALPH ROBERT (1907-1972)

Ralph Shaw, by choice a librarian, could equally well be called an administrator, bibliographer, businessman, consultant, critic, editor, educator, executive, inventor, organization official, publisher, scholar, and translator. Shaw's many interests and accomplishments were a result of his enormous energy and his driving ambition to succeed, and he thus became a major intellectual force who did much

to shape the dimensions of mid-twentieth century librarianship. He was also the most controversial library figure of his time, always ready to challenge those people whose ideas he thought were leading others astray. Perhaps the thing that he valued above all else was intelligence. He had no patience with slowness; action was his strong suit. He always believed that it was more important to get things done, even if it meant accepting a certain amount of error, than to plan forever and never accomplish anything.

Ralph Shaw was born on May 18, 1907, in Detroit, Michigan, to Max and Pauline Sandburg Shapiro. His parents were both Austrian and his father was in the real estate business. Early in Ralph's life, the family moved to Cleveland, where he began his career in librarianship by working as a page in the Cleveland Public Library in 1923. Upon graduating from Glenville High School, he enrolled in Adelbert College at Western Reserve University, where he received his B.A. degree (1928).

On November 27, 1929, he was married to Viola Susan Leff, who, until her death in March 1968, was to be an invaluable aid to Shaw. On February 5, 1969, he was married to Mary McChesney Andrews. He had no children. On October 14, 1972, after a long bout with cancer, Ralph Shaw died in a nursing home in Honolulu, where he had, characteristically, been working almost up to the day of his death.

While a student at Western Reserve, Shaw worked as an assistant to Mildred Stewart in the Department of Science and Technology at the Cleveland Public Library; he attributed much of his interest in and success as a science librarian to the training he received from her.

In 1928, Shaw went to New York to enroll as a student in the Columbia University School of Library Service. He received his B.S. in L.S. (1929) and his M.S. (1931) both from that School. His master's thesis, "Engineering Books Available in America prior to 1930" (1933), was indicative of the combined interest in science and bibliography that was to be one feature of much of his career. In 1928-1929, he worked as a general assistant at the New York Public Library and, from 1929 to 1936, he was the senior assistant and chief bibliographer at the Engineering Societies Library under Harrison W. Craver (q.v.), another person to whom Shaw attributed much of his success.

During this time, he translated Georg Schneider's *Theory and History of Bibliography* from German into English, doing much of the work while riding the subway to and from work. That book was published in 1934, as the first volume of the Columbia University Studies in Library Service series. In his last days, he was to translate, also from German, Richard

Muther's *German Book Illustration of the Gothic Period and the Early Renaissance (1460-1530)* (1972).

Although Shaw began to develop his interest in the scientific management of libraries while in New York, he found full range for the application of that interest when he became librarian of the Gary, Indiana, Public Library in 1936. There he expanded and improved library service to the community, winning the Distinguished Service Award of the United States Junior Chamber of Commerce in 1938. At Gary, he instituted a number of innovations based on his interest in scientific management, including transaction charging and the use of photography in circulation control, which resulted in his inventing and patenting the Photocharger. Mobile book stations were another typical Shaw endeavor. Rather than buy several expensive bookmobiles that would sit stationary for most of the day, he purchased a truck cab and three trailers; he and his staff would race around the city shuttling the trailers to the places where they were to provide service. His article on "The Influence of Sloping Shelves on Book Circulation" (1938) shows his careful attention to detail.

While at Gary, he enrolled in the Ph.D. program of the Graduate Library School, then headed by Louis Round Wilson, at the University of Chicago. As always, Shaw was the gadfly who provoked discussion and took delight in challenging at every opportunity not just his fellow students but the faculty and guest speakers as well. Work on his degree was delayed, but he did complete his dissertation, which was published in revised form as *Literary Property in the United States.* He was awarded the Ph.D. in 1950. Copyright represented another of Shaw's many interests, and it is characteristic of his primary concern that, despite his later role as a major publisher, in his dissertation, he very strongly took the side of authors. In the last article he was to write, *"Williams and Wilkins v. the U.S.:* A Review of the Commissioner's Report" (1972), he also dealt with the copyright issue, defending in that article the interests of librarians.

In 1940, Shaw succeeded Claribel Ruth Barnett as librarian at the U.S. Department of Agriculture. Under his leadership (fourteen years, except for a brief period of service in the Army Air Force and the Army Medical Department in 1944-1945), the Library was transformed into a major national resource that was subsequently to become the National Agricultural Library. His particular interest in the role of bibliography in scientific development was demonstrated in many ways during those years, but in no way more strongly than in the planning and production of the *Bibliography of Agriculture,* which quickly became a major international bibliographic tool. He continued to demonstrate his interest in scientific management and especially in the development and use of machines to assist in the handling of routine clerical operations. At this time, he invented and patented the Photoclerk and constructed the Rapid Selector, patenting the coding system used in that machine. Largely due to mechanical problems, the Rapid Selector, designed to use encoded microfilm for the subject analysis and retrieval of information, never achieved the success that Shaw envisaged for it (later work along the same lines was done by Eastman Kodak and IBM). Largely for his work with machines, Shaw became the first recipient of the Melvil Dewey [q.v.] Award from the American Library Association in 1953. Overall, he was able to improve greatly the Library's service at reduced cost and, in the process, made the USDA Library a real service, not just to the staff of that Department but to the agricultural and scientific community at large. For his service to that community, he won the Superior Service Award of the USDA in 1949.

During this same period, Shaw took on many additional assignments and became an internationally known and respected figure in librarianship. He began a lifetime of consulting and advising on a broad scope of national and international library and bibliographic activities. These services were to include: member of the Advisory Committee for the *Handbook of Latin American Studies* (1944-1954); member of the Advisory Board of the *United States Quarterly Book List* (1944-1954); advisor to the Food and Agriculture Organization (1947); chief delegate to the Royal Society's Scientific Information Conference (1948); consultant to the International Cooperation Administration to India (1957); member of the Board of Expert Examiners of the U.S. Civil Service Commission (1946-1961); member of the United States National Committee for the International Federation of Documentation (1960-1972); science consultant to the U.S. Supreme Commander, General Headquarters, Tokyo (1947); consultant to the preparatory commission for UNESCO; member of the International Advisory Committee on Bibliography, UNESCO (1953-1961); and member of the Scientific Information Council of the National Science Foundation (1964-1966). Shaw served as a consultant on major library organizational studies for the United Nations, the U.S. Department of State, the U.S. Veterans Administration, the American Medical Association, the city of Toronto, and the Brooklyn and Queens, New York, public libraries. His expertise carried him on major assignments involving the provision of library and/or bibliographical services to Canada, England, India, Japan, the Philippines, and, through his long service to the Inter-American Institute of Agricultural Science, a large part of Latin America.

In 1950, Shaw founded the Scarecrow Press. A keen student of publishing, Shaw concluded that there was a profitable market for books, especially in librarianship, if they could be economically produced. He proved that, with the use of offset production from typescript and a minimum of editorial work, books in librarianship and other fields could be produced in runs as small as 500 and, without subsidy, could be sold at a profit for both the author and the publisher. Since its establishment, Scarecrow Press has produced over 1,000 titles. While initially it was almost traditional for reviewers to decry the poor physical appearance and the typographical errors to be found in Scarecrow books, and at times to lament the intellectual quality and lack of editing, Scarecrow is now recognized as an important press which produces works of high quality. Unquestionably, the output as a whole has been of very great value and includes a significant number of important works.

Another of Shaw's innovations was mini-print, the publication of material in book format but in a reduced type size that requires no magnification to be read. Initially envisaged as a regular publication program for new material, mini-print became far more significant as a means of reprinting and inexpensively making available lengthy bibliographic and reference works.

Shaw ran Scarecrow himself, with assistance from Viola, until it became too complex for him to manage. As always, feeling that those who did the work should have as much responsibility as possible, he sold a controlling interest in Scarecrow to Albert Daub in 1955. It remained an independently owned firm, in which Shaw retained an active editorial interest, until 1968. At that time it was purchased outright by the Grolier Educational Corporation with the understanding that the management, including Shaw's role in editorial direction, would remain essentially unchanged except for the selection of an eventual successor to Shaw, which was accomplished with the appointment of Eric Moon as president in 1969. In 1970, Shaw became director for research and development of Grolier.

After moving to Hawaii in 1964, Shaw was to start another publishing venture, founding the Nokaoi Press. His intention at that time was to capitalize on the growing tourist market in Hawaii by publishing children's books with a local flavor that could be sold to tourists. Only one title was published and his idea never succeeded, largely because he was unable to obtain the necessary access to distribution outlets.

Shaw had taught bibliography at the Columbia University School of Library Service in the summers of 1936 and 1937, but it was while he was at USDA that his interest in library education began to develop. He created a course on the use of scientific management in libraries, the first of its kind, which he taught while serving on the faculty of the USDA Graduate School (1949-1953) and as a visiting

professor in the library schools at Columbia (1951) and Western Reserve (1953). In 1954, he left the USDA Library to join the newly established Graduate School of Library Service at Rutgers University, under the direction of Lowell Martin as dean. At Rutgers, he helped develop a strong program and curriculum with a solid, theoretical base. He organized and taught courses in bibliography, documentation, and scientific management. From 1959 to 1961, he served as dean and was largely responsible for establishing a strong Ph.D. program in the School.

Shortly after its establishment in 1956, the Council on Library Resources, under the direction of Verner W. Clapp (q.v.), decided that in order to establish its priorities for funding research, a major study of the current state of library activities that would point the way to needed research was called for. In late 1957, a two-year grant of $100,000 was awarded to Rutgers and Shaw. Under his leadership a number of people were commissioned to undertake a series of exhaustive bibliographic studies on cataloging and classification, classification systems, subject headings, gifts and exchanges, training of laymen in the use of the library, bibliographical services, charging systems, library buildings, shelving, storage warehouses, notched cards, aperture cards, punched cards, electronic searching, coding, production and use of microforms, reading devices and microimages, and full-size photocopying. The results were published in a series called "The State of the Library Art" (1960-1961). Of uneven quality, the series received mixed reviews, and little evidence exists that the Council on Library Resources was guided by the results. Also, the project suffered from the lack of strong editorial control by Shaw who, in his usual fashion, felt that once he had found competent people to do the work, the job was done.

As a student of bibliography, Shaw was aware of the fact that a major gap had been left in American national bibliography when Charles Evans's (q.v.) work ceased with 1800, rather than going up to 1820 as originally intended. As chairman of the American Library Association's Committee on Bibliography from 1954 to 1956, Shaw was involved in discussions concerning that gap with representatives of the American Historical Association. Undoubtedly because of Shaw's practicality, it was concluded that something was better than nothing and that a checklist could be produced from a variety of existing secondary sources. After unsuccessfully seeking financial support from foundations, Shaw organized a volunteer effort and, with an imprint file of 20,000 items loaned by the American Antiquarian Society, the project was begun. Between 1958 and 1966, a series of volumes entitled *American Bibliography: A Preliminary Checklist for 1801-1819* and listing over 50,000 items appeared under the editorship of Shaw and Richard Shoemaker (q.v.), who had joined the project as a volunteer and soon became the chief contributor. Subsequently continued by Shoemaker beyond 1820 to improve on the deficiencies of existing bibliographic coverage, the project continues, under other hands, with the eventual expectation that it will extend to 1875. While viewed as a preliminary checklist based on previous listings (including the massive files of the American Imprints Inventory) and subject to correction and revision, *American Bibliography* had proved to be remarkably accurate and, even with its few errors and omissions, is a major bibliographic tool of unquestionable value.

Impatient with the duties and demands of administration at Rutgers, Shaw resigned as dean in 1961, but from 1961 to 1964, he served as a distinguished service professor in the Library School there. Unable to resist new challenges, however, he left Rutgers in 1964 to become at first professor of library service and assistant to the president for libraries, and later dean of library activities, at the University of Hawaii. There he greatly strengthened the University Library by, among other things, planning a new building, reclassifying the collections from Dewey to LC, and establishing separate undergraduate and research libraries. He also established and got accredited the Graduate School of Library Studies. He did these things largely by securing the necessary commitments from the University and by hiring a quality staff and faculty. He served in that capacity until 1968, stepping down at that time to become a professor in the library school but retiring the next year to become professor emeritus.

Shaw maintained a long and active involvement with library associations. He was, at the appropriate times, a member of the New York, Indiana, District of Columbia, New Jersey, and Hawaii library associations. He served as president of the associations in Indiana (1938-1939) and New Jersey (1962-1963). He was a member of the Special Libraries Association from 1932 until his death and also belonged for many years to the American Documentation Institute, later the American Society for Information Science. In the early 1950s, he was especially active in the American Documentation Institute, serving on the Auditing Committee (1951-1952), and as an associate editor of *American Documentation* from its founding in 1950 to 1957.

However, the American Library Association represented Shaw's most active interest. Shaw joined ALA in 1929 and remained a member until, for his long and active service, he was elected an honorary member in 1971. In the early 1930s, Shaw was one of the charter members of the Junior Members Round Table. His first official duties were as a member of the Committee on Library Terminology from 1934 to 1937. At the 1936 ALA conference in Richmond, he

organized and, with help from a number of others, produced five issues of an informal conference newsletter, *Louder Please*. In 1935, he wrote a provocative article, "The American Library Association—Today and Tomorrow" which, when published in the *ALA Bulletin*, drew considerable response. In that article, Shaw first addressed concerns about ALA's relevance to its members that were to be constant themes of his relationship with the Association over the next 25 years. Shaw was appointed to the Constitution and By-Laws Committee in 1936 and served on that Committee, which worked closely with the Third Activities Committee, through 1940. The revision of the Constitution and By-Laws produced by that Committee, and adopted by the membership in 1940, first provided for the establishment of the divisions, created the system for election to the Council by the divisions that prevailed for many years, and first established a sliding dues structure based on salary levels.

Until just after his term as president of ALA (1956-1957), Shaw served in numerous capacities, including the Library Equipment and Appliances Committee (1937-1938); the Publicity Committee, later the Public Relations Committee (1937-1941); the Jury on Awards (1938-1940); the ALA Council (elected for a five-year term and served from 1940 to 1944, presumably resigning at the time of his military service); chairman of a joint committee with the Institute of Food Technologists (1941-1943); the Subcommittee to Study the Use of Punched Card Procedures in Libraries of the Library Equipment and Appliance Committee (1944-1946); the Subcommittee on Civil Service Relations of the Board on Personnel Administration (1945-1947); as chairman of the Fourth Activities Committee (1947-1949); as chairman of a Committee on the Relations of the Divisions to ALA (1947-1949); as chairman of the Committee for Bibliography (1953-1956); and on the Steering Committee on the Implementation of the Management Survey (1955-1956).

He served as well on a number of committees for the Association of College and Reference Libraries (later the Association of College and Research Libraries) during his long membership in that group, including the Committee on Publications (1942-1944, chairman, 1943-1944); the Research Planning Committee (1950-1954); the Nominating Committee (1953-1954); and the Committee on Relationships with Learned Societies (1954-1956).

In addition, he served as ALA's representative to a number of other associations or groups, including the Panel on Libraries of the U.S. National Commission for UNESCO (1949-1952); the Panel on UNESCO (1958-1960); the American Documentation Institute (1952-1954); the U.S. Committee for the United Nations (1956-1957); and the Council of National

Library Associations (1955-1957), a service he was later to perform (1960-1965) for the American Association of Library Schools.

In 1955, Shaw was elected first vice-president and president-elect of ALA, defeating Charles Gosnell. He served as first vice-president in 1955-1956 and as president the following year. In those capacities, and as immediate past president (1957-1958), he served on a number of committees, including Boards and Committees (1955-1956), Budget (1955-1957), Program (1955-1956), Conference Program (1956-1957, chairman), Organization (1956-1957), and Program Evaluation and Budget (1957-1958, chairman).

While he automatically became a member of the ALA Council as a past president, Shaw's service to ALA diminished greatly after his term as president. He continued to serve for a time, however, on groups relating to publishers and publishing, including the Committee on Relations with Publishers (later the American Book Publishers Council—ALA Committee on Reading Development; 1955-1958, chairman 1956-1957) and the Committee to the American Textbook Publishers Institute (1957-1963). His final official service to ALA came as a member of the Advisory Committee for the Library of the Future, Century 21, Project (1961-1963), and the New York World's Fair Library Exhibit Exploratory Committee, later the New York World's Fair Advisory Committee (1962-1966).

Despite his best efforts over a long period of time in many capacities, Shaw was never able to shape the Association to be the kind of clearly organized and efficient professional group that he thought that it could and should be. He was especially concerned as president that the lines of responsibility between the various divisions of the Association were not being defined clearly enough to allow those entities to speak on certain matters for the Association.

Shaw made numerous contributions to the literature of librarianship. He wrote over one hundred articles, reviews, books, contributions to symposia, surveys, or parts of books on a range of topics that covered acquisitions, automation, bibliography, classification, copyright, machines, microfilm, personnel administration, public relations, Russian publications, and the use of literature by scientists, as well as, in almost everything he wrote, the basic goals and philosophy of librarianship. Among his major works not already mentioned were *The Use of Photography for Clerical Routines* (1953), *The International Activities of ALA* (1946), and two challenging articles on automation that drew much criticism but remain as classic statements of Shaw's position: "From Fright to Frankenstein" (*D.C. Libraries*, 1953) and "The Form and the Substance" (1965). While mistakenly viewed by some as a conservative retreat from his early advocacy of machines, both pieces represented

his belief that people cannot "solve all of our problems with machines they have not yet thought about" and that it is necessary to "distinguish between the word and the deed; between the science and the folklore of our field." He also contributed an essay on "Electronic Storage and Searching" to an important series, "Freeing the Mind," that appeared in the *Times Literary Supplement* (1962).

Shaw was a strong critic of the value of library meetings; he had a standing offer of $1,000 to anyone who could prove that he had learned something from a speech at a meeting that could not be found in print just as readily. Yet, at the same time, he attended meetings inveterately and was in much demand as a speaker because of his sharp wit and provocative ideas.

His personal interests were as diverse as his professional interests and he brought to them the same intensity. He actively participated in a wide range of games and sports, including boating, cards—especially bridge and poker—fishing, flying, and golf. His passion for jokes was unmatched, and he once even suggested that he liked to read. Shaw was 5' 9" tall and weighed about 162 pounds at the peak of his career. His brown hair became thinner as he grew older, and his brown eyes were sometimes masked by horn-rimmed glasses hung over his prominent ears. Not the most immaculate dresser, he often appeared in a rumpled corduroy suit with a large bow tie. Perhaps his most notable characteristic was the wide grin that crossed his face to show his delight in either a joke or a brilliant intellectual idea. Because of his outspokenness, people did not always like him and sometimes found him difficult to deal with. Yet his straightforwardness and integrity earned him respect, as did his loyalty to people and ideas to which he became attached.

Ralph Shaw's impress on American librarianship was enormous. It was reflected in several ways that will carry his influence on for many years. As a teacher, he educated and influenced a significant number of students who have themselves become leaders; as an administrator, he helped shape and direct many professional careers; as a publisher, he founded a press whose works continue to make information available; as an inventory, he produced a number of machines that helped make possible much of the sophisticated use of technology in libraries; as a library manager and educator, he helped introduce to the profession the concept of using scientific management and other rigorous techniques for the investigation of library problems; as a bibliographer, he supervised the production of one of the major scientific and one of the major retrospective national bibliographies; as an outspoken critic of the improper use of machines and of false claims for the accomplishments of machines, his challenges helped lay the foundation for the more intelligent use of machines; as a person, his strong and controversial ideas left a lasting mark on many members of the profession.

Yet there was still another facet to Shaw's personality; he was a master at creating, or adapting, aphorisms. His skill at doing this was legendary and resulted in a number of sayings that are now a part of the folklore of librarianship and are already widely quoted with no indication and no knowledge of their source. None is more widely used, or more likely to endure, than his indictment of the poor quality of much of professional library literature, which he dismissed as being mainly articles on "how I run my library good."

Biographical listings and obituaries–*Current Biography* (1972); [Obituary]. *American Libraries* 4:16 (Jan. 1973); [Obituary]. *Library Journal* 97:3847 (Dec. 1, 1972); [Obituary]. *Library Resources and Technical Services* 17:267 (Spring 1973); [Obituary]. *New York Times*, Oct. 16, 1972; [Obituary]. *Publishers Weekly* 202:27 (Nov. 6, 1972); [Obituary]. *Special Libraries* 63:590 (Dec. 1972); *Who Was Who in America* V (1969-1973); *Who's Who in Library Service*, 1st ed., 2nd ed., 3rd ed., 4th ed. **Books and articles about the biographee**–"ALA Honors Ralph R. Shaw." *AB Bookman's Weekly* 48:9 (July 5-12, 1971); [Biographical sketch]. *ALA Bulletin* 49:364 (July-Aug. 1955); [Biographical sketch]. *College and Research Libraries* 25:513 (Nov. 1964); [Biographical sketch]. *Library Quarterly* 25:398-99 (Oct. 1955); [Biographical sketch]. *Special Libraries* 43:185 (May-June 1952); Duker, S. "Ralph Shaw." *Reference Quarterly* 12:305 (Spring 1973); Gaver, Mary V. "Ralph Shaw at Rutgers." *Wilson Library Bulletin* 47:478-80 (Feb. 1973); "Honoring Dr. Ralph R. Shaw." *Special Libraries* 45:352 (Oct. 1954); McDonough, Roger H. "Ralph R. Shaw, 1907-1972." *Library Journal* 97:3952 (Dec. 1972); "New Jersey Library Association Resolution for Ralph R. Shaw." *New Jersey Libraries* 5:2 (Dec. 1972); "Radical Turned Revisionist?" *Antiquarian Bookman* 35:738 (Feb. 22, 1965); Stevens, Norman D., ed. *Essays for Ralph Shaw*. Metuchen, N.J.: Scarecrow Press, 1975; Tauber, Maurice. "Our Frontispiece: Ralph Robert Shaw." *Bulletin of Bibliography* 23:193-95 (1962); Tauber, Maurice. "Ralph R. Shaw: The Library Innovator." *Information* 3:273-76 (1971); West, S. L. "Ralph R. Shaw: The Hawaiian Years." *Hawaii Library Association Journal* 30:47-50 (Dec. 1973).

–NORMAN D. STEVENS

SHEDLOCK, MARIE L. (1854-1935)

Marie Shedlock was born of English parents at Boulogne on May 5, 1854, and died in January 1935. Her father was an engineer engaged in the construction of railroads in France, but the family returned to England when Marie was six. Eight years later, she and one of her sisters went back to France to attend school. Marie remained in Versailles for three years before completing her education in Germany.

Marie Shedlock was just 21 when she began teaching at Notting Hill, an English public school for girls. Twenty-five years later, she gave up teaching, determined to become a professional storyteller. She

had made her storytelling debut ten years before at Steinway Hall, London, and, for many years, had entertained at evening parties by telling stories in French and English.

At the age of 46, she arrived in New York with a letter of introduction to a woman who later organized a series of public recitals for her. Mary Wright Plummer (q.v.), director of the Pratt Institute Library and Library School, attended one of them and invited Shedlock to tell stories for the teachers and students at Pratt. Anne Carroll Moore (q.v.), then head of the Children's Library at Pratt, listened "enthralled" to the program that Shedlock presented and arranged for her to return to Pratt on January 31, 1903, to tell stories to children. "Is she a Fairy, Miss Moore, or just a lady?" a little girl asked. And so Marie Shedlock became the fairy godmother of storytelling in America, often appearing in a long cloak wearing the peaked hat of a fairy godmother and carrying a wand. Portraits reveal a handsome woman with dark-browed eyes made more compelling by her abundant white hair. Although she was "diminutive," those who heard her recall her sense of presence and her charming voice. Others who knew her well attest to her strongly held values, whimsical sense of humor, friendliness, and generosity with her gift of storytelling.

The first of Marie Shedlock's American tours lasted seven years and included leading universities, teachers' colleges, and libraries. Anna Cogswell Tyler, a student in the Pratt Library School, heard Shedlock tell Hans Christian Andersen's "The Nightingale" and discovered her own vocation as a storyteller, one she fulfilled as the first supervisor of storytelling at the New York Public Library. For this reason, Anne Carroll Moore declared that "storytelling in the New York Public Library has its roots in Miss Shedlock's rendering of 'The Nightingale' twenty-five years ago."

Shedlock returned to London in 1907 to share her American experiences with teachers in England. In the years that followed, she published a collection of Buddha tales, *Eastern Stories and Legends*, and her classic work, *The Art of the Story-Teller* (1915).

In 1915, at the urging of Anne Carroll Moore and many of the American storytellers she had inspired to enter the profession, Marie Shedlock undertook a second tour of the United States. Ruth Sawyer, who was to become America's foremost storyteller, heard Shedlock telling the tales of Andersen at Columbia University. Recalling the event in the May 1934 *Horn Book*, she said that she vowed that day to become a storyteller: "If story-telling can be an art like this I will make it my art."

The second tour lasted for five years. Two years after Shedlock's return to London, the American Committee for Devastated France arranged for her to spend a month telling stories in the libraries established in the French villages.

To mark her eightieth birthday in May 1934, children from the United States, Canada, and France sent tributes of affection to the "Fairy Godmother" in London. "The most glorious birthday of my life," she wrote, "was made completely happy by the cable sent by the children's librarians from the Montreal meeting of the American Library Association." She died the following January (the date is uncertain).

Marie Shedlock was not a librarian, but she made a major contribution to library service to children. She established storytelling as an art, motivated some listeners to become professional storytellers, and made other listeners realize the value of storytelling as a means of introducing children to their literary heritage. The director of the New York Public Library, Edwin H. Anderson (q.v.), writing in the May 1934 *Horn Book*, concluded that "she really started the art of storytelling as it is now practiced more or less perfectly in most of the public libraries in this country, and began a new movement in library work which has been a boon to millions of people throughout the land."

Books and articles about the biographee–[Biographical sketch]. *Library Journal* 60:434-35 (May 15, 1935); Hill, Ruth A. "Story-Telling around the World; A Symposium, Part I: United States." *Library Journal* 65:285-89 (April 1, 1940); Moore, Anne Carroll. Foreword to *The Art of the Story-Teller*, by Marie Shedlock. New York: Dover Publications, 1951; Moore, Anne Carroll. *My Roads to Childhood*. Boston: The Horn Book, Inc., 1961; Moore, Anne Carroll. "Our Fairy Godmother Marie L. Shedlock." *The Horn Book* 10:137-67 (May 1934) [Includes twenty pages of tributes to Marie Shedlock]; Sayers, Frances Clarke. *Anne Carroll Moore*. New York: Atheneum, 1972. Primary sources and archival materials–Unpublished notes of Anne Carroll Moore at the New York Public Library, some of which concern Shedlock.

MARY E. KINGSBURY

SHERMAN, CLARENCE EDGAR (1887-1974)

Clarence Edgar Sherman was born in Brooklyn, New York, on January 14, 1887, the son of James Horze and Josephine Estelle Hamer Sherman. The family soon moved west to Cincinnati and later to Brockton, Massachusetts, where Sherman attended public schools until two years before his graduation from Williston Academy, Easthampton, Massachusetts, in 1907. He received a B.S. degree from Trinity College, Hartford, Connecticut, in 1911, and the next year completed the course at the New York State Library School at Albany. Later came honorary degrees from Trinity College (M.A., 1941), Brown University (L.H.D., 1952) and the University of Rhode Island (Litt.D., 1957).

Sherman's first position was as assistant librarian of the Amherst College Library from 1912 to 1917.

During this period he married Inez B. Copeland and subsequently had four children: Stuart Capen, Carolyn, Louise Copeland, and Richard Dana. He moved to the Lynn, Massachusetts, Public Library in 1917 and remained there until 1922, when he accepted a post at Providence, Rhode Island, Public Library as assistant librarian under William E. Foster (q.v.). In 1928, Sherman became associate librarian, and upon Foster's retirement in 1930, he assumed the post of librarian.

Clarence Sherman's association with the Providence Public Library spanned 35 years, during which it grew to be the second largest public library in New England, with a book stock that had doubled to well over half a million volumes and circulation of more than a million volumes annually. Three years before his retirement in 1957, the long-awaited $1,950,000 addition to the central building was completed and dedicated. The modern structure more than doubled available space, providing handsome new quarters for five library departments, an exhibition hall, auditorium, meeting rooms, and offices, plus six floors of stacks with shelf space for 350,000 books. It was an addition for which need had first been expressed in 1919, but the plans had been set aside in favor of branch library construction. During the nine years preceding the new building's dedication on January 12, 1954, Sherman's organizational and promotional abilities, as well as his perseverance and tact, guided the building program from the vote on the bond issue, through legal and political snags, inflation, and a steel strike, to a successful completion.

In an interview some years earlier (*Providence Journal*, August 10, 1947), Sherman had listed the achievements that he considered to be highlights of his first 25 years in Providence–the city-wide survey that led to establishing a modern system of branch library buildings; the improvement in personnel standards brought about by organizing and conducting library training classes; and the implementation of possibly the first comprehensive stack storage plan, which cleared crowded shelves of little-used materials, housed them in a separate building, and continued to guarantee control and access. In addition, he spoke of the establishment of a business branch and the organization of neighborhood advisory committees to provide for community participation at the local level. For, he said, "The best library is the library in which books are most carefully selected, which is well organized and operated, and which best meets local needs and standards."

The impact of Sherman's achievements reached well beyond the local community, for he was a frequent contributor to library journals, and, at various times, a lecturer at Rhode Island College of Education, Simmons College, Pratt Institute, and Columbia University. An active member of such

professional organizations as the Rhode Island and
American Library Associations, he became president
of the former (1925-1927) and second vice-president
of the latter (1942-1943). In the late 1930s, he
helped to found the New England Library Association and became the first chairman of its Executive
Committee. His deep interest in books, as well as
what the reporter in the previously cited interview
described as his lively, alert, urbane personality, led
to membership in the Grolier Club (New York), the
Club of Odd Volumes and the Society of Printers
(Boston), and the Art Club (Providence). He was a
member of the Bibliographical Society of America
and the American Institute of Graphic Arts, served on
the board of the Victory Book Campaign, and often
acted as a judge for printing and publishing awards.
His own publications include "John Masefield: A
Contribution toward a Bibliography" (*Bulletin of
Bibliography* 8:6, 158-60 [April 1915], "The Library
Budget" (in *Current Problems in Public Library
Finance*, ed. by Carl Vitz; Chicago: ALA, 1933), *The
Providence Public Library: An Experiment in En-
lightenment* (Providence, 1937), "The Definition of
Library Objectives" and "The Role of the Board in
Library Administration" (in *Current Issues in Library
Administration*, ed. by Carleton B. Joeckel [q.v.];
University of Chicago Press, 1939).

Sherman also played an active role in community
affairs. He was a trustee of several local educational
and financial institutions and a fellow of Trinity
College; he served as president of the Young Men's
Christian Association (1938-1940), the Players
(1943-1946), and the Rhode Island Historical Society
(1961-1963), and was appointed to government
advisory bodies at both the city and state levels.

Brown University, in awarding him the degree of
Doctor of Humane Letters, cited his "practical vision,
energetic promotion and perceptive management"
which "brought nearer to realization the democratic
ideal of a well-informed public." The University of
Rhode Island, in its Doctor of Letters citation,
described him as a "lifelong craftsman of free and
enlightened minds." His death occurred seventeen
years after his retirement, on February 13, 1974.

Biographical listings and obituaries—[Obituary]. *Library
Journal* 99:1265 (May 1, 1974); *Who's Who in Library
Service*, 1st ed., 2nd ed., 3rd ed. Books and articles about
the biographee—[Biographical sketch]. *Library Journal*
72:1289 (Sept. 15, 1947); [Biographical sketch]. *Reader's
Guide to Books* (Providence Public Library) 14:1 (July
1946); Carroll, Charles. *Rhode Island: Three Centuries of
Democracy*. New York: Lewis Historical Publishing Co.,
1932. Primary sources and archival materials—The Providence Public Library in its Rhode Island Index lists local
newspaper articles about Sherman's activities from 1922 to
1974, as well as periodical articles by and about him. His
correspondence and other papers are retained in the Library's
archives.

—VIRGINIA M. ADAMS

SHIPTON, CLIFFORD KENYON (1902-1973)

Clifford Kenyon Shipton—librarian, archivist, his-
torian—was born in Pittsfield, Massachusetts, on
August 5, 1902, the son of George Marsden and Edith
May Kenyon Shipton. He was graduated from
Harvard College in 1926 and earned an M.A. from the
same institution in 1927. After teaching history at
Brown University for two years, Shipton returned to
Harvard to work for his doctorate under Samuel Eliot
Morison, and it was the latter who induced Shipton
to undertake the continuation of John L. Sibley's
(q.v.) series *Sibley's Harvard Graduates*. Shipton's
doctoral dissertation became the fourth volume in
that series and his Ph.D. degree was awarded in 1933.
He served briefly as director of the WPA Writer's
Project for Massachusetts and, in 1938, became
custodian of the Harvard University Archives, a position he continued to hold, usually on a part-time
basis, until his retirement in 1969.

One of Shipton's closest friends and associates has
written,

Like Caesar's Gaul, Ted Shipton's professional
career can be divided into three parts: as librarian
and later director of the American Antiquarian
Society in Worcester, Mass.; as custodian of the
Harvard University Archives; and as Sibley Editor
of this [Massachusetts Historical] Society. To each
of these three careers he gave greatly of himself,
and he has left a lasting mark on these institutions
he served so well.

Appointed librarian of the American Antiquarian
Society in 1940, Shipton became its director in 1959,
a position he held until his retirement in 1967. For
the previous half century, the Society's chief drive
had been in terms of acquisitions or bibliographical
description. Shipton rededicated the Society to historical scholarship. Under his leadership, the collections of monographic literature were organized and a
new emphasis was placed upon imprints more recent
than 1820.

During these years, Shipton continued his own
interest in historical scholarship. *Roger Conant, a
Founder of Massachusetts* (Cambridge: Harvard University Press, 1944) and *Isaiah Thomas, Printer,
Patriot and Philanthropist, 1749-1831* (Rochester,
N.Y.: The Printing House of Leo Hart, 1948) were
significant contributions to our understanding of
Colonial life. The *National Index of American
Imprints through 1800; The Short-Title Evans* (Worcester, Mass.: American Antiquarian Society & Barre
Publishers, 1969, 2 vols.) was soon recognized as a
work of major importance to reference librarians,
scholars of the seventeenth and eighteenth centuries,
and all students of printing history. The following
statement from the introduction indicates the careful
manner in which Shipton always worked: "In the
course of this revision we have looked carefully at

every item, making sure that it is a separate work and not part of a larger one, that the title, the subject, the place of publication, the printer and the date are correct. . . ." *New England Life in the 18th Century; Representative Biographies from "Sibley's Harvard Graduates"* (Cambridge: Belknap Press of Harvard University Press, 1963) was further evidence of the breadth of his scholarship and the variety of his professional interest.

Shipton's truly great contribution to historical literature, and the one for which he will always be remembered, was fourteen volumes of *Sibley's Harvard Graduates: Biographical Sketches of Those Who Attended Harvard College*, published over the years by The Massachusetts Historical Society. Writing to his classmates on the occasion of their twenty-fifth anniversary, Ted Shipton referred to this work in these words: "It is fascinating work which leaves me bored with bridge and golf. I am beginning to be concerned with the fact that I am not likely to live long enough to carry the series to the class of 1800, my goal." On the last day of his life, he was making a final check on the seventeenth volume.

In the early 1930s, not a single genuine college archives existed in the United States. Harley P. Holden, Shipton's successor at the Harvard Archives, has written, "When Clifford K. Shipton came to the Harvard Archives in the 1930s, it was a small and largely unrecognized collection; when he left in 1969, it was the largest and richest in content of any university archives in the world." Holden also wrote, "Clifford K. Shipton's influence as an archivist was felt far beyond Harvard." A founding member of the Society of American Archivists, Shipton became its president in 1967.

While at the American Antiquarian Society, Shipton was responsible for the completion of Charles Evans's (q.v.) *American Bibliography*, and he was a prime mover, with the Readex Microprint Corporation, in "reproducing in microprint the full text of every non-serial item listed by Evans, or turned up subsequent to the printing of Evans' volume, a gathering together of nearly 40,000 items."

The day after receiving his M.A., Shipton married Dorothy Boyd MacKillop, who was to be his research aide for many years. They were the parents of three children: Ann Boyd, Nathaniel Niles, and George MacKay. Shipton was a diligent and an indefatigable scholar, yet always a vibrant, warm personality, a man whose home and family life was close and rich, who loved to garden and camp and hike, a man never too busy to help a young scholar, and tireless in his service to his community and the larger world of scholarship. Officer, committee member, director, or editor of dozens of organizations, he was always a penetrating scholar whose influence was, and will

continue to be, great. Recipient of many honors, including honorary degrees of D. Litt. (Harvard, 1964; Clark University, 1969), Ted Shipton was a great scholar and a tireless librarian and archivist. He died on December 4, 1973.

Biographical listings and obituaries–*A Biographical Directory of Librarians in the United States and Canada*, 5th ed.; [Obituary]. *College and Research Library News*, No. 6:143 (June 1974); [Obituary]. *New York Times*, Dec. 6, 1973; [Obituary]. *Wilson Library Bulletin* 48:539 (March 1974); *Who Was Who in America* VI (1974-1976); *Who's Who in Library Service*, 2nd ed., 4th ed. **Books and articles about the biographee**–[Biographical sketch]. *Harvard Librarian* 10, no. 2; [Biographical sketch]. *Newsletter* of the American Antiquarian Society, Jan. 1974; Holden, H. P. "Deaths: Clifford K. Shipton." *American Archivist* 37:513-18 (July 1974); "President, Society of American Archivists, 1967-1968." *American Archivist* 31:2 (Jan. 1968). **Primary sources and archival materials**–A wide variety of primary materials are available in the Harvard University Archives and at the American Antiquarian Society.

                                          —RALPH ADAMS BROWN

SHIRLEY, WILLIAM WAYNE (1900-1973)

William Wayne Shirley was born on January 12, 1900, in Franklin, New Hampshire, the son of Barron and Harriet Smith Shirley. His father died in 1906, and shortly thereafter his mother—left with three small children to support—was appointed librarian of Franklin Public Library, a position she held for 35 years. Although he did not receive his degree in librarianship until the age of 28, Wayne Shirley liked to recall in later years that he began his library career by stamping books at the age of seven in his mother's library. He attended Phillips Academy, Andover (class of 1918) and received the B.S. degree from Dartmouth College (class of 1922). For several years after graduation from college, he pursued a career in the business world. In 1928, he received the B.L.S. degree from Pratt Institute Library School, Brooklyn, where one of his teachers was Josephine Adams Rathbone (q.v.). He married Dorothy Bruce in 1929.

Wayne Shirley's career as a librarian spans a period of just over four decades, during which he held a number of responsible positions and made several contributions to his profession. He was assistant in the Economics Division, New York Public Library (1928-1929); librarian of the University of New Hampshire (1929-1932); first assistant in the Economics Division, New York Public Library (1932-1934); head of the Science-Technology Department, Pratt Institute Library (1934-1938); librarian and dean of the Library School at Pratt Institute (1938-1955); secretary of Pratt Institute (1940-1955); librarian of Finch College, New York City (1955-1962), and librarian of Wentworth Institute, Boston (1962-1969).

Shirley was quite active in the work of professional organizations at the national, state, and local levels. In 1946, he founded (with Louis Shores) the American Library Association's American Library History Round Table, and he served as ALHRT chairman for twenty years (1946-1966). He was a director of the ALA Library Education Division (1948-1950); president of the Association of American Library Schools (1951); a member of the library advisory board of *Collier's Encyclopedia* (1946-1973); and a member of the editorial advisory board of the *Journal of Library History* (1966-1968). He was president of the New Hampshire Library Association (1932) and president of the College and University Section of the New York Library Association (1960-1961).

Shirley was a friendly, sociable person. He founded the Melvil Dui Chowder and Marching Association in 1954; from that date until 1962, he was the "Worthy Scribe" of this Manhattan-based organization for men from the world of libraries, publishing, and bookselling. In 1938, he was elected to membership in the Rembrandt Club of Brooklyn, a group of business and professional men interested in the promotion and encouragement of the arts. He served as secretary of this club for a number of years (1944-1948; 1955-1962).

Wayne Shirley wrote for the library press from time to time. His articles were thoughtful, often witty and graceful, never dull. He contributed to Louis Shores's *Challenges to Librarianship* (1953), was co-editor of *Books—Libraries—Librarians* (1955), and co-author of the foreword and a contributor to *An American Library History Reader* (1961).

In 1962, he moved to the town of Durham in his native state, New Hampshire. After retirement from the Wentworth Institute in Boston, he was elected to a term (1969-1970) in the New Hampshire General Court. He also took an active interest in local community affairs. Wayne Shirley died suddenly on December 25, 1973; his ashes were scattered on the New Hampshire land he loved so well.

To his fellow librarians, students, and friends, Wayne Shirley was an unfailing source of encouragement and sound advice. A bookman in the old-fashioned and best sense of the word, he was a man with a keen wit and a sly sense of humor who had a deep belief in intellectual responsibility. Louis Shores wrote in the *Journal of Library History* (October 1974) that Shirley had a "courageous commitment to constants in an age of perpetual celebration of change."

Biographical listings and obituaries—*A Biographical Directory of Librarians of the United States and Canada*, 5th ed.; [Obituary]. *Wilson Library Bulletin* 48:457 (Feb. 1974); *Who's Who in America* 35 (1968-1969); *Who's Who in Library Service*, 1st ed., 2nd ed., 3rd ed., 4th ed. **Books and articles about the biographee**—Marshall, John David. "As I Remember Wayne Shirley." *Journal of Library History*

9:293 (Oct. 1974); Rush, N. Orwin. "Wayne Shirley, 1900-1973: An Appreciation." *Journal of Library History* 9:294-95 (Oct. 1974); Shores, Louis. "Wayne Shirley: In Memoriam." *Journal of Library History* 9:291-92 (Oct. 1974); "Wayne Shirley." *College and Research Libraries* 16:416 (Oct. 1955) [contains a small portrait].

—JOHN DAVID MARSHALL

SHOEMAKER, RICHARD HESTON (1907-1970)

Born in Cynwyd (a Main Line suburb of Philadelphia, Pennsylvania), on April 5, 1907, to Richard Martin Shoemaker, Jr., and Susan Evans Lodge Heston Shoemaker, Richard H. was brought up in a cultured milieu that gave him a lifelong love of books and reading. His father was first a jeweler, then a member of a brokerage firm. The family fell on hard times during the Great Depression, but Shoemaker had grown up with music, art, and summers at Cape May. He attended the University of Pennsylvania, receiving an A.B. in English literature (1935); he had taken time out for saving money and getting experience in banking. He was married in 1936 to Helen Louise Rose and they had one son, Richard Martin.

Shoemaker, thinking of joining the Episcopal clergy, had studied for a year in a seminary in Alexandria, Virginia, but then decided on librarianship as a career. In 1938, he was graduated with a B.S. from the School of Library Service of Columbia University; he took a job as cataloger at Temple University in that same year. He was next in charge of the Work Projects Administration cataloging project at the Mercantile Library of Philadelphia. In 1939, he went to Washington and Lee University as chief of the cataloging department. He did graduate work there as well, receiving an M.A. in English literature (1941). In 1940, he was made assistant librarian, in 1944, librarian. Foster Mohrhardt (q.v.; University librarian at Washington and Lee, 1938-1946) has commented on the efficient business measures that Shoemaker brought to library procedures there.

In 1947, Shoemaker left Washington and Lee to become librarian of the Newark Colleges of Rutgers University. This meant that he had direct responsibility for the general library, named after John Cotton Dana (q.v.), with supervisory authority over the law and pharmacy libraries. In 1959, at the invitation of the new dean, Ralph Shaw (q.v.), Shoemaker became professor of library service at Rutgers, where he remained until his death. His teaching included such courses as bibliography, the social functions of libraries, building collections, and research libraries. He was to have received an honorary doctorate from Susquehanna University later in the spring of the year he died. In 1971, the first annual Richard H. Shoemaker Lecture, established by his fellow faculty members, was given at Rutgers by Sir Frank Francis, formerly director and principal librarian of the British Museum.

Shoemaker belonged to several organizations: the American Library Association, the New Jersey Library Association, the Archons of Colophon, the Bibliographical Society of America, the University of Virginia Bibliographical Society, the American Association of University Professors, and the American Civil Liberties Union. He was not a prolific writer. Apart from several book reviews, his writings include a description of the Propaganda and Promotion Archives at Washington and Lee for the *Wilson Library Bulletin* (April 1942), an article on reclassifying the John Cotton Dana Library for the *Journal of Cataloging and Classification* (Winter 1949), an article on book catalogs for *Library Resources and Technical Services* (Summer 1960), and an essay on general bibliography for *Library Trends* (January 1967). In 1958, he was an [Andrew] Carnegie [q.v.] fellow in library administration, out of which came a study of the effect of cataloging-in-source on the Princeton University Library; this was printed in *Studies in Library Administration Problems* (Rutgers Graduate School of Library Service, 1960).

Shoemaker's major contribution to librarianship lies in his work as a bibliographer. With Ralph R. Shaw, he compiled the pioneering *American Bibliography: A Preliminary Checklist 1801-1819*, which appeared from 1958 to 1963 in volumes covering a year each, with corrections, author index, and title index coming out later. The need for the Shaw and Shoemaker bibliography arose from the fact that Charles Evans (q.v.) had been unable to complete his monumental *American Bibliography*, which he had intended to cover chronologically all books, pamphlets, periodicals, and broadsides printed in the United States up to 1820, the year that Orville Roorbach's (q.v.) *Bibliotheca Americana* begins. Evans's work was completed by Clifford K. Shipton (q.v.) through 1800, but for the years 1801 through 1819, a gap remained in United States national retrospective bibliography. The American Library Association's Committee on Bibliography, together with the American Historical Association, sought to close the gap, but they were unable to obtain foundation funding. The work thus had to be done on a volunteer basis and it was then, as Shaw, the prime mover, has described in the preface to the first volume, that "Mr. Shoemaker entered the scene ... as one of the volunteers to check the New York Public Library inventory, and undertook the work with such zeal and industry that he soon became a full partner in the undertaking, as indicated by the title page."

The resulting volumes were published by Shaw's own Scarecrow Press, photo-lithographically reproduced from typewriter composition. The compilers worked from many different secondary sources, the most important of which were slips at the American Antiquarian Society and the WPA imprint inventory files at the Library of Congress. Checking these slips against the books themselves would have been too lengthy a project; thus, not only are the lists incomplete, but there are also bibliographical ghosts and other inaccuracies. Nor is there a wealth of bibliographical detail: long titles are shortened and only concise imprint and collation statements are given. However, these shortcuts, deliberately taken by the compilers, are overshadowed by the fact that the work—with addenda, 51,960 entries—was actually done. Shaw and Shoemaker had made a major contribution to the study of our national history and to bibliographic control.

Shoemaker decided that he would continue the work alone to 1830 because the Roorbach bibliography was so faulty and incomplete. The *Checklist of American Imprints 1820-1829* was published by Scarecrow from 1964 to 1971, and, in 1972, the volume for 1830 appeared, with Gayle Cooper, who had worked with Shoemaker in his last year, as the compiler. (An 1831 volume came out in 1975, compiled by Scott and Carol Bruntjen. Other volumes are planned, to help correct the inadequacies of American national bibliography before 1876.) Thus, Shoemaker's contribution has continued after his death in the work of others.

His influence lives on as well in the inspiration he gave his students. Paul Shaner Dunkin (q.v.), a Rutgers colleague of Shoemaker's, has described what he represented in the profession and in the School:

They say Dick was a loving and loveable man and an inspiring teacher; and so he was. But Dick was also a man of iron and passion. For a decade he fought the losing fight for humanism in a profession rushing to give way to sociology, statistics, documentation, information science, and the computer. He pounded my desk and snorted that the deadly tables and graphs in a doctoral candidate's dissertation proved only obvious banalities. In one committee he tried (in vain) to bring history and substance into the empty solemnity of the social functions course; in another committee he fought (in vain) what he considered the undeserved promotion of a colleague. As chairman of a committee to nominate a new dean he worked tirelessly to get democratic consideration of every faculty member's ideas and to find the candidate best for the School—a thankless job at the best. He worked for causes before they were popular: intellectual freedom in libraries; student representation in School government; an end to Viet Nam.

Benjamin Weintraub, another Rutgers colleague, has written that "Professor Shoemaker was more than a dedicated scholar and inspiring teacher. He was a man of compassion who lived what he preached." He favorably impressed members of the book trade as well. Sol and Mary Ann Malkin wrote in the *AB Bookman's Weekly* at the time of his death: "Dick was one of those rare souls in the library teaching industry who felt deeply and preached wholeheartedly that bibliography was basic to librarianship." Here again is the theme that he was not afraid to go against current trends, to think for himself, and to fight for the principles he believed in.

In appearance, Shoemaker was of medium height, slim, conservatively dressed, with thinning white hair, a small moustache, and dark-framed glasses. According to some, he had an "El Greco" face. He has been described as a "gentleman of the old school" who read classical Greek, and he was as well a man of strong opinions, a superb administrator, a leader in academic politics. As a teacher, he was known for his honesty, sound knowledge, and clear perception. Students liked and respected him; he returned their regard by maintaining his own sympathy for young people and their ideas. Mrs. Shoemaker recalls his prodigious memory for music, among other things, and his mechanical ability.

As for the lasting importance of his work, Edwin Wolf II has said: "Richard Heston Shoemaker will be remembered as long as anyone buys, sells, catalogues or studies any American imprint between 1801 and 1830."

Biographical listings and obituaries—*Biographical Directory of Librarians in the United States and Canada*, 5th ed.; [Obituary]. *AB Bookman's Weekly* 45:1549 (May 4-11, 1970); [Obituary]. *Library Journal* 95:1435 (April 15, 1970); *Who Was Who in America* V (1969-1973); *Who's Who in Library Service*, 2nd ed., 3rd ed., 4th ed. Books and articles about the biographee—Dunkin, Paul S. "Richard Heston Shoemaker: The Library School Years." In Sir Frank Francis, *Bibliographical Information in Manuscript Collections*. New Brunswick, N.J.: Rutgers University Graduate School of Library Service, 1972, pp. ii-iii; Mohrhardt, Foster E. [Biographical sketch]. *College and Research Libraries* 9:82 (Jan. 1948); Wolf, Edwin, II. "Richard Heston Shoemaker, 1907-1970." In Sir Frank Francis, *Bibliographical Information in Manuscript Collections*. New Brunswick, N.J.: Rutgers University Graduate School of Library Service, 1972, pp. iv-ix. (Reprinted in M. Frances Cooper. *A Checklist of American Imprints 1820-1829: Title Index.* Metuchen, N.J.: Scarecrow Press, 1972.) Primary sources and archival materials—Both Mrs. Shoemaker and Benjamin Weintraub state that Shoemaker left no papers.

—SUSAN OTIS THOMPSON

SIBLEY, JOHN LANGDON (1804-1885)

John Langdon Sibley was born in Union, Maine, on December 29, 1804, the eldest son of Dr. Jonathan and Peris Morse Sibley. After several years of preparation at Exeter, Sibley entered Harvard in 1821, supporting himself by giving instruction in sacred music and working in the Harvard Library. He particularly enjoyed his work in the Library, where he labored under the watchful eyes of the famous bookman Joseph Green Cogswell (q.v.) and his colleague Charles Folsom. Shortly after his graduation in 1825, Sibley was offered full-time employment in the Library at $150 a year. He eagerly accepted the job, but his salary was diverted by the University administration a year later in order to increase the amount available for the salary of the new librarian, Benjamin Peirce, who succeeded Folsom in 1826.

Unemployed, and unable to find a position in any other library, Sibley pursued his studies in the Harvard Divinity School, graduating in 1828. He was ordained in the following May and served with the Reverend Jonathan Newell in a Unitarian church at Stow, Massachusetts, becoming pastor when Newell died in 1829. Sibley remained at Stow until 1833, but was never satisfied with the ministry and finally resigned to return to Cambridge. He took a room at Divinity Hall, gave occasional assistance to the Library, and edited for four years the *American Magazine of Useful and Entertaining Knowledge*, an illustrated monthly that was a financial failure.

In March 1841, the Harvard Library was moved from its cramped quarters in Harvard Hall to the newly completed Gore Hall. Sibley was employed only temporarily to assist in the process of moving the collection, but, because the size of the new building seemed to warrant a second full-time employee, he was appointed assistant librarian. Thus began his 36 years in the service of the Harvard University Library. In 1856, he was appointed librarian, to succeed Thaddeus William Harris; shortly before this, he had won a difficult fight with Louis Agassiz, who resented Sibley's attempts to curb the intemperate demands of young faculty members bent on liberalizing use policies in the Library.

Scholars, writing from the comfortable and well-stocked libraries of the twentieth century, have frequently laughed at Sibley, viewing him as a cantankerous old book-hoarder intent on protecting his treasures from the profane touch of disrespectful users. But viewed more realistically in the context of the general intellectual milieu of the early nineteenth century, and more specifically within the context of the history of higher education during that period, Sibley emerges as one of the more progressive academic librarians of the day. Certainly he was fascinated by books and the gathering of them. At the beginning of his term of service in the Library, the collection size stood at about 41,000 volumes and the annual income was less than $300; when he retired in 1877, the number of books had increased to 164,000 and he had increased library support to the income from an invested $170,000. Sibley himself recalled that his aggressive and voracious acquisition policy earned him the reputation of being a "sturdy beggar."

While he shall always be remembered for his efforts to enlarge and develop the Library's collections, it should also be remembered that he proposed many new ideas, some of which, as Clifford K. Shipton (q.v.) has noted, were "simply too advanced for his generation." One such proposal made to the Harvard Corporation in 1847 called for the appointment of "A Builder Up of the Library" or "Professor of Bibliography," who would lecture on books and bibliography in hopes of stimulating the book collecting interests of the students; perhaps they would one day become valuable friends and supporters of the Library. This new appointee, remarkably similar to modern-day subject bibliographers, would also correspond with authors and other potential donors and would handle book orders to prevent duplication and provide balance in the collection. While the Corporation chose to ignore Sibley's suggestion, it is obvious that Sibley himself filled the position of "Builder Up of the Library" with remarkable success. Indeed, his public relations campaign with the Alumni Association was so successful that he estimated one in every fifteen graduates was contributing at least one book a year to the Library.

When Gore Hall was completed, the building was deemed adequate to house the Library for the rest of the century, but due to the energetic efforts of Sibley, it was soon bulging with books. Since the president, Charles William Eliot, refused to permit Sibley to sell duplicates, the librarian nearly doubled the capacity of Gore Hall by the use of movable shelving. President Eliot and the architect angrily protested that the new shelving was a blight upon a once attractive building, a complaint that Sibley coldly silenced with a question, "For what was the library built—for books or for looks?"

The rapid growth in the collection soon forced the librarian to see to his catalogs, and, by 1861, the Harvard public card catalog in two parts—subject and author—was begun. Sibley also introduced a detailed catalog for newspapers, and prepared for students a seven-page guide to the use of the catalog. Sibley also pioneered in employing female assistants, at first using them to "clean small books" at a salary of six cents per hour. Soon, women, mainly because of the neatness of their handwriting, were helping with the cataloging work. In 1875, Anne Hutchins was appointed cataloger at a salary of $700 per year and is reputed to have "written" some 75,000 cards that year.

In 1863, because of printers' prices, Sibley bought a press and other equipment and commenced printing in the Library. He introduced the "Harvard College Library" letterhead in 1871. His interest in printing probably proceeded from his own experience as editor of twelve triennial catalogs (1842-1875) and one quinquennial catalog (1880) of Harvard. In addition, for twenty years (1850-1870), he also edited the annual catalogs and for fifteen years prepared the necrology issued at commencement time. In 1851, he published a history of his home town, and he was a contributor to the publications of the Massachusetts Historical Society as well.

Sibley's most ambitious work was the *Biographical Sketches of the Graduates of Harvard University.* He published three volumes (respectively in 1873, 1881, and 1885) covering graduates through the class of 1689. After the life of each graduate there is a full bibliography. One noted scholar remarked that "it is impossible to overestimate the worth of these volumes." *Sibley's Harvard Graduates*, as the volumes came to be known, were continued through volume 17 (through 1771) by Clifford K. Shipton.

The end of Sibley's administration was marked by clashes with the Library Committee and faculty over Library policy, especially the liberalization of hours, which Sibley opposed due to lack of staff and funds. Additionally, there was the problem of missing books and theft and Sibley's unbending enforcement of Library rules and regulations. Sibley was particularly unpopular with the administration as a result of his aggressive campaign for a new library building. Asked to write a "sketch" of Gore Hall for *The Harvard Book*, a commemorative volume intended chiefly for the members of the class of 1874, he closed his essay with scathing comments on the suitability of Gore Hall as a library. Sibley felt that "the immediate want is a convenient fire-proof edifice with hollow walls, so built as to admit of indefinite enlargement." However, he was thwarted by President Eliot's decision simply to make improvements in and enlarge Gore Hall.

In 1877, after a fruitful but stormy career, Sibley resigned. He had occupied his new office in the enlarged Gore Hall for less than six months, turning over administration of the Library to Justin Winsor (q.v.) on August 31. Sibley's final annual report, written with much difficulty because of failing eyesight, ends with these words: "I cannot divorce myself and go forth as a stranger from what has been the home of my heart so long. The Library will continue to be like an old home as long as I live." This was a typically candid but unusually sentimental reflection from the strong-willed and pugnacious librarian who directed the nation's greatest university library during its formative years.

After his retirement, Sibley continued to work as much as his tired eyes would permit, and he spent many happy hours with his wife Charlotte Augusta, daughter of merchant Samuel Cook, to whom he had been married in 1866. A generous man, he donated over $15,000 to Exeter Academy in his later years. He died after a long illness on December 9, 1885, in Cambridge.

Biographical listings and obituaries—*Dictionary of American Biography* 17 (Alfred C. Potter); *National Cyclopaedia of American Biography* 11; *Who Was Who in America*, Historical Volume (1607-1896). **Books and articles about the biographee**—*The Harvard Book*. Collected and edited by F. O. Vaille and H. A. Clark. Cambridge: Welch, Bigelow and Company, 1875; Peabody, Andrew P. *Harvard Reminiscences*. Boston: Ticknor and Co., 1888, pp. 146-54; Potter, Alfred Claghorn, and Charles K. Bolton. *The Librarians of Harvard College*. Cambridge: Library of Harvard University, 1897, pp. 39-42; Shipton, Clifford K. "John Langdon Sibley, Librarian." *Harvard Library Bulletin* 9:236-61 (1955). Reprinted in John David Marshall, ed. *An American Library History Reader*. Hamden, Conn.: Shoestring Press, 1961, pp. 161-89. **Primary sources and archival materials**—Sibley's library journal and his private journal, along with other very valuable manuscripts, are located in the Harvard University Library.

—MICHAEL H. HARRIS
—SISTER DEBORAH HARMELING

SMITH, CHARLES WESLEY (1877-1956)

Charles Wesley Smith was a librarian at the University of Washington for all of his 42-year career. During that time, he saw the Library grow from a minor collection of 20,000 volumes to one worthy of a great university at 600,000 volumes. More than any other single individual, he was responsible for developing the superb collection of Pacific Northwest Americana, one of the finest assets of the University of Washington Library. He contributed significantly to the literature of library science, and he left behind a reputation of excellence in library service and bibliography that is still esteemed today.

Smith was born in Elizabeth City, North Carolina, on June 20, 1877, to Charles W. and Hester Bourne Smith. He attended the University of Illinois, obtaining his A.B. from that institution in 1903 and his B.L.S. in 1905. He came to the University of Washington immediately after his graduation to assume his duties as assistant librarian. In 1913, he was promoted to the rank of associate librarian and, in 1929, was made head librarian, a rank he held until his retirement in 1947. Concurrently he also held the rank of associate professor in the University of Washington's School of Library Science from 1913 to 1926 and professor from 1926 to 1947.

One of the great projects of Smith's career was the development of the Pacific Northwest Collection. He had a keen interest in bibliography, and this he put to use when he first published his *Checklist of Books and Pamphlets Relating to the History of the Pacific Northwest* (1909). He followed this up in 1921 with *Pacific Northwest Americana: A Checklist of Books and Pamphlets Relating to the History of the Pacific*

Northwest, a third edition of which was published in 1950. With the publication of the first checklist, Smith set out to acquire systematically as many of the items on the list as he could, and he continued this policy during his entire career at the University.

As part of his administration of the Pacific Northwest Collection, Charles Wesley Smith devised a classification scheme that was unique. He felt that the regular [Melvil] Dewey [q.v.] Decimal system was not adequate to handle such a specialized collection. The result was *Expansion of the Dewey Decimal Classification for the History of the Pacific Northwest* (1908), a supplement to the Dewey system designed for use with collections dealing with old Oregon.

In 1923, Smith was sent to Europe for the summer by the University in order to purchase items for the Library. When he returned, he brought with him 9,000 books and 10,000 pamphlets covering a wide range of subjects. As another result of this trip, he had established contacts with a large number of book dealers that later proved beneficial to the University Library.

Smith was instrumental in forming the Pacific Northwest Library Association in 1909. He was a member of the Committee on Bibliography of that organization and, in 1936, writing in the *P.N.L.A. Quarterly*, he first issued a call for the establishment of the Pacific Northwest Bibliographic Center. He proposed the Center as a means of cutting expensive competition for resources among libraries in the Northwest. His efforts finally culminated, in 1940, with a grant from the [Andrew] Carnegie [q.v.] Corporation of $35,000 and the creation of a Work Projects Administration project, in the establishment of the Center. It continues to flourish to this day.

Smith was also active in the other affairs of PNLA. He actually formed the Bibliography Committee in 1917. He was president of the organization in 1919-1920 and continued to be a member until his retirement. He was also a member of the American Library Association, the Bibliographical Society of America, and the American Historical Association, and was a fellow of the American Library Institute. He published numerous articles concerning the Pacific Northwest Collection and the development of specialized collections, and he prepared bibliographies on individuals important to the Pacific Northwest. He also was business manager of the *Washington Historical Quarterly* from 1913 to 1935.

Upon his retirement from the University, he was appointed professor and librarian emeritus and bibliographic consultant by the Board of Regents, posts in which he was active until just before his death. Charles Wesley Smith died on July 5, 1956.

Biographical listings and obituaries—"Charles Wesley Smith [Obituary]." *Wilson Library Bulletin* 31:36 (Sept. 1956); "Dr. C. W. Smith, Librarian, Dies." *Seattle Post*

Intelligencer, July 6, 1956, p. 27; "Necrology." *Library Journal* 81:1972 (Sept. 15, 1956); *Who's Who in America* 26 (1950-1951); *Who's Who in Library Service*, 1st ed., 2nd ed., 3rd ed. **Books and articles about the biographee—** Bauer, Harry C. "Charles Wesley Smith." *College and Research Libraries* 17:515-16 (Nov. 1956); "C. W. Smith Gets Many Bargains during Summer Trip to Europe." *University of Washington Daily*, Dec. 13, 1923, p. 1; Conover, C. T. "Just Cogitating." *Seattle Times*, Dec. 6, 1951, p. 26; Gershevsky, Ruth Hale. "Charles W. Smith, 1877-1956: An Affectionate Tribute." *P.N.L.A. Quarterly* 20:156-57 (July 1956); McDonald, Lucille. "University's Research Hub." *Seattle Times*, Magazine Section, Sept. 28, 1947, p. 5; Sneddon, James O. "Professor Emeritus." *Washington Alumnus* 43, no. 1:7-8+ (Fall 1952). **Primary sources and archival materials—**Smith's papers are held by the University of Washington's records center, and the Library maintains a miscellaneous clipping file about him (see the article by Harry C. Bauer, especially).

—ANDREW F. JOHNSON

SMITH, ELVA SOPHRONIA (1871-1965)

Elva Sophronia Smith was born on April 28, 1871, at Burke Hollow, Vermont, the daughter of Franklin Horatio and Harriet Louisa Powers Smith. Shortly thereafter, the family moved to Lyndonville, Vermont, where Franklin Smith became a successful merchant. He later helped to found South Pasadena, California, and made and lost a fortune in real estate there before he died in 1889. Elva Smith graduated in 1888 from the Lyndon Institute, Lyndon Center, Vermont. She taught for one term in a country school near West Burke, Vermont, and, in 1890, was graduated from the Johnson Vermont State Normal School (now Johnson State College). During the year 1890-1891, she was teaching in district and town schools near West Burke, Vermont, while living with her grandparents. During both summers, she worked as a waitress for the Raymond Hotel System. In the winter of 1891 she had the same job in a Raymond Hotel in Pasadena, California, where she lived with her sisters, who had moved to South Pasadena about the time of their father's death.

From September 1892 until June 1898, Elva Smith taught in California public schools, her first assignment (1892-1893) being one in Lone Pine, to which she travelled by stage coach. Other assignments were in South Pasadena (1893-1897) and San Jacinto (1897-1898). She stood first in a class of 27 students who took the examination for the California teaching certificate at Los Angeles in 1895. Her first formal study in librarianship came in a Los Angeles Public Library training class, from which she earned a certificate dated September 5, 1899. During 1900-1901, she was the private tutor of a family of children in Long Beach, California.

In 1901, she moved to Pittsburgh, Pennsylvania, where her great contribution to children's literature and library service to children was to be made. The Training School for Children's Librarians had just opened in the [Andrew] Carnegie [q.v.] Library of Pittsburgh under the leadership of Frances Jenkins Olcott (q.v.). Elva Smith earned the diploma for the two-year program, graduating with the first class (1903). At the same time, she was gaining practical experience, since the school was in the Library building and students worked closely with the Boys' and Girls' Department. During the years that followed, Elva Smith filled a dual role as instructor (later associate professor) in the Carnegie Library School and as assistant cataloger (eventually head) of the Boys' and Girls' Department. From 1904 until her retirement in 1944, she taught book selection for children, history of children's literature, cataloging of children's books, bibliography, and development of children's library work. She lived at the Schenley Hotel, a fine one in those days, and conveniently only a block away from the central Carnegie Library of Pittsburgh. During summers, even after her retirement, she frequently taught courses at Pennsylvania State College in literature for children and young people, in storytelling, and in library work for children. During other summers, she travelled extensively in Europe and South America, always making connections and forming friendships with children's librarians, authors, and anyone else who could extend her knowledge of children's literature on the international scale.

To the end of her life Elva Smith read and wrote voluminously. Besides numerous articles for journals, her contributions to children's literature were almost a score of collections of stories, poems, history and legends, a number of them with Alice I. Hazeltine as co-editor. She made a special study of *Subject Headings for Children's Books*, which with *Cataloging of Children's Books* was published by the American Library Association in 1933. In 1937, ALA also published her *History of Children's Literature*, a landmark in the field and clear evidence of the depth and scope of her knowledge. This is a syllabus with selected bibliographies for the Anglo-Saxon period through the late nineteenth century. It has been an invaluable guide for teachers and for librarians who need help in building collections representative of the types of literature covered in the study. Many scholars have paid tribute to the value of Elva Smith's *History of Children's Literature*.

Elva Smith contributed greatly to the Carnegie Library School's reputation for leadership in the field of work with children. During her forty years as a teacher there, she influenced students who later attained prominence both in the United States and abroad. According to her nephew, Dr. George E. P. Smith, Jr., "her ninetieth birthday, April 28, 1961, was a great celebration, with cards, letters, and gifts from former students and associates all over the world and letters of congratulations from many notable figures, local and national."

A lesser-known aspect of Elva Smith's work was her development, with Frances Jenkins Olcott, of a notable collection of historical children's books; this became an important part of Carnegie Library School's resources and eventually was transferred with the School itself to the University of Pittsburgh's Graduate School of Library and Information Sciences. Elva Smith described briefly in her *History of Children's Literature* how "the Carnegie Library School, then known as the Training School for Children's Librarians, had the good fortune to obtain from Mr. Charles Welsh, a former member of the firm of Griffith, Farran, & Co., a small but choice collection of early children's books, representing chiefly the period between 1760 and 1835." (Perhaps the earliest book in the collection is a third edition of *Robinson Crusoe*, 1719.) The acquisition of these books by a library school made possible the development of an outstanding course in the history of children's literature. Under Elva Smith's guidance and initiative, the collection grew by gift and by purchase to 1,000 volumes and by 1975 had reached 5,000, a unique resource for a library school.

Elva Sophronia Smith was a lady in the best sense of the word, modest, unassuming, and self-critical. For even a short informal article, she re-wrote tirelessly, trying for perfection. But under the reserve and scrupulosity, her colleagues knew there was an inner sparkle. In an article entitled "Forty Years of Library School Education" in *The Carnegie Magazine* (Vol. 4, No. 4; September 1941), Victor C. Showers of the Reference Department, Carnegie Library of Pittsburgh, wrote,

Elva S. Smith, head of the boys and girls department here, has today the same buoyant enthusiasm, sense of humor, and youthful ideas that she had when she was graduated from the School with its first class. Beside these personal qualities, the fact that she has meanwhile become a national authority on children's literature seems almost incidental to those who know her.

Elva Smith's broad interests are evidenced by her membership in many clubs and associations. These included the American Library Association, for which she was chairman or member of numerous committees relating to work with children. She was on the ALA Council (1926-1930) and was very active in the formative period of the Children's Library Association (later the Children's Services Division). She was a founding member of the Carnegie Library School Association and served as first president (1921-1928). For the National Congress of Parents and Teachers she served as associate chairman of the Committee on Home Education, in charge of children's reading (1934-1938). She was a member of

the Pittsburgh Chapters of the Authors' Club, Better Magazine Council, the Foreign Policy Association, the Drama League, the National Travel Club, and an honorary member of the Eugene Field Society.

In June 1945, after her retirement, Elva Smith moved from Pittsburgh to Concord, New Hampshire, where she lived with her older sister, spending her winters in Winter Park, Florida. She died on October 26, 1965, in Concord, New Hampshire, and was buried in the family lot at Lyndon Cemetery, Lyndon Center, Vermont.

In her will, Elva Smith established a scholarship covering full tuition in the Carnegie Library School (now the Graduate School of Library and Information Sciences) to be given annually to a student "especially preparing for Library Service to Children Through Public Libraries." In her memory, Dr. George E. P. Smith, Jr., representing both himself and his father (Elva Smith's brother George) has added an endowment to the original bequest.

Biographical listings and obituaries—*Leaders in Education: A Biographical Directory*, 1st ed. (1932), 2nd ed. (1941), 3rd ed. (1948); *Who Was Who in America* V (1969-1973); *Who's Who among North American Authors* 11 (1938); *Who's Who in American Education*, 8th ed. Robert C. Cook Co., 1937, 1938; *Who's Who in Pennsylvania*. Philadelphia: Institute for Research in Biography, 1938; *Woman's Who's Who*. Larken, Roosevelt & Larkin, Ltd., 1941-1942. **Books and articles about the biographee**—"Elva Sophronia Smith Bequest to Vermont Public Library." *Wilson Library Bulletin* 44:18 (Sept. 1969); "Former Librarian's Will Enriches Vermont Libraries." *Library Journal* 94:3396 (Oct. 1, 1969); Munn, Ralph. [Biographical sketch]. *Library Journal* 69:1015 (Nov. 15, 1944); "Who's Who in the ALA." *ALA Bulletin* 24:253-54 (1930).

—MARGARET HODGES

SMITH, LLOYD PEARSALL (1822-1886)

" . . . a devourer of literature from his youth up, consumed by an insatiable thirst for knowledge, and interested in a wide range of subjects. A knowledge of the outsides of books is not sufficient. A librarian should be not only a walking catalogue, but a living cyclopedia." When Lloyd P. Smith cited these as necessary qualifications for a librarian in 1876, he was outlining his own goals. That he achieved them is reflected in the words of George M. Abbot, his assistant at the Library Company of Philadelphia for almost 25 years.

[Smith] was a man of learning, and as a reader was omnivorous; . . . everything that came his way was eagerly perused. With an excellent memory, all his reading seemed to remain with him, and he was thus possessed of a fund of information which was of the highest use to those who sought his help. His delight was in research and it was with a real pleasure that he gave his assistance to the many students and inquirers who came to the library.

The son of John Jay and Rachel Collins Pearsall Smith, Lloyd Pearsall Smith was born in Philadelphia on February 6, 1822. Smith's interest in libraries was fostered early, for, as the son of the librarian of the Philadelphia Library Company, he spent much of his childhood in the Library. In 1837, at the age of fourteen, he was graduated from Harvard College and began his career with the counting house of Walm & Leaming, a Philadelphia importing firm. Here he became an expert bookkeeper and accountant. On October 13, 1844, he married Hannah E. Jones, the daughter of Isaac C. Jones, an East India merchant. They adopted a daughter.

With the exception of a short time in business in New Orleans, Smith was a lifelong Philadelphia resident. In addition to his duties at Walm & Leaming, he took an early interest in publishing and editing. From 1845 to 1846, he published *Smith's Weekly Volume*, a successor of *Waldie's Select Circulating Library*, a publication edited by his father. At the same time, Smith also published *The Medical Library* and, in 1847, *A Plan of the District of Spring Garden, Philadelphia.*

In 1848, Smith began a formal association with the Library Company that was to last the rest of his life. The will of James Logan, one of the early benefactors of Philadelphia, gave members of the Smith family, his direct descendants, preference for appointment to the librarianship. Librarians thus appointed were given the title "hereditary librarian." Lloyd Smith, in this line, was appointed assistant librarian on December 7, 1848, and succeeded to the librarianship in February 1851, upon his father's resignation. Smith also served as treasurer and trustee of the Library.

By 1876, the Library Company had almost 1,000 members and over 100,000 volumes, including 11,000 in the Loganian Library. As a reflection of the conservative nature and stability of the institution, Smith noted in an article in the U.S. Bureau of Education's *Public Librarianship in the United States*:

Rotation in office has not yet invaded this venerable institution. It has happened more than once in its history that directors have held office for over fifty years, and during the last ninety years there have been only four librarians and five secretaries. Since 1750 the Loganian Library has had but six librarians.

Although open to the public, both the Library Company and the Loganian Library were more valuable to the scholar than to the general reader. Smith himself once acknowledged that the history of the Loganian Library might be described as "the greatest good for the smallest number." He remarked that the department of manuscripts contained examples of Hebrew, Arabic, Abyssinian, Siamese, Burmese, Greek, and Latin, and the collection of

incunabula in the Loganian Library contained works of the earliest printers in Germany, England, Venice, and Rome. He felt, though, that the strength of both libraries was in their collections of rare Americana.

Conservative though he was, Smith recognized the need for and took an active interest in public, tax-supported libraries. "Sooner or later," he wrote in *Library Journal* (July 1881),

the Middle and Southern States will be forced to follow the example of their more Northern brethren. . . . The present is an opportune time for Pennsylvania to act, and no better way of celebrating the two-hundredth anniversary of the landing of William Penn could be found than to establish a free public library in the city of Philadelphia.

Smith did not believe in open shelves; he advocated locked cases for all books with the exception of recent fiction and commonly used reference books. Open shelves would, he thought, "lead to disorder and make it impossible to say with promptitude and certainty whether a particular book is or is not 'in.' " Locked cases were intended not to impede but to facilitate service by allowing the librarian to have better control over the collection and to be able to provide books desired by patrons without delay. "It is not sufficient to find a book sooner or later. You want it sooner. . . . 'What thou doest, do quickly' is the unspoken address of everyone who approaches the desk of a public library."

On one occasion, however, Smith did make an exception, which he later recounted:

I recollect many years ago being touched by the fondness for books of a young man in shabby apparel, who came day after day to our library to read books which only a person of cultivation and taste would ask for. My heart warmed to the poor scholar, and at last I allowed him to have a key and open the cases himself. Alas for human nature! My poor scholar cut some plates out of Jameson's "Beauties of Charles II," and carried off in his coat-tail pocket three or four small books.

Smith added that the thefts were soon detected, the young man was arrested, and he was sentenced to six months in prison. When Smith later visited him, the young man advised him, "Always . . . keep [your] eyes skinned." Although Smith accepted this, he modified it by adding that "liberality and kindness proceeding from sympathy with souls thirsting for knowledge are better than suspicion. It is better that a few books should be stolen than that the visitor to a public library should feel he is looked on as a thief." He thought that if all library visitors were treated as gentlemen, they would behave as guests in a gentleman's house.

Smith's belief in the virtue of kindness and liberality had practical as well as philanthropic dimensions. He pointed out that the hospitality a man receives in a library may be reciprocated in the form of donations of books or money. He noted that Dr. James Rush left the Library Company a million dollars because of the pleasure he received from its books and the "readiness and civility" with which he received them.

Smith also took an active role in the formation and development of the American Library Association. He had already delivered a paper describing his classified index to the Library Company's catalog at the first national conference of librarians held in New York in 1853. In 1876, he was one of the first to respond to the call for another library conference. Smith, who served with Justin Winsor (q.v.) and William F. Poole (q.v.) on the committee that organized the conference, acted as conference host. An active member of the American Library Association, Smith served as vice-president and was a member of the Executive Board and a councillor. He was also a member of the committee formed to assist in the planning of a building for the Library of Congress. Up to his death in 1886, he had attended every conference but one since the formation of the Association.

In 1877, Smith attended the conference of librarians held in London that marked the formation of the Library Association, and he was elected one of the vice-presidents. In 1878 he was invited—with Winsor, Poole, Charles A. Cutter (q.v.), and Melvil Dewey (q.v.), among others—to become an honorary member of the United Kingdom Association. Smith enjoyed attending conferences and took advantage of them to advance the profession as a whole and to improve his own Library. He credited the Conference of 1853 with giving him the idea of a card catalog, and at a later conference, was much impressed with Dewey's classification system. Throughout his career, he exhibited an interest in cataloging and classification; at the 1882 Cincinnati conference, he delivered a paper, "On the Classification of Books." Smith's own classification system was considered by S. Austin Allibone and H. J. Dennis to be one of the best then in existence. As administrator of his own Library, Smith was known for the prudence, care, and constant concern he gave to its welfare and increased usefulness. His long-time assistant recalled that their last conversation, the day before Smith's death, was about its affairs.

Although Smith had been ill for several months, his death on July 2, 1886, was a surprise and a shock to his friends in the American Library Association, who had expected him to attend. Chief among them was William F. Poole, then ALA president, who had known him since their days as young men attending the 1853 Conference of Librarians. Poole included in his presidential address a graceful tribute to Smith:

A more lovely spirit and genial companion never lived. His sonorous laugh was something to be remembered. He was a fine classical scholar, and Latin to him was almost vernacular. He loved to think and talk and write in Latin, and his letters were often half, and sometimes wholly in Latin. His mind had a mediaeval tinge which led him to take delight in the monkish Latin of the middle ages. . . . He believed in what is old, rather than what is new, and in this respect was a typical Philadelphian.

To the profession of librarianship Lloyd Pearsall Smith devoted both his time and his talent and was acknowledged by all who knew him to be one of the foremost men in his field.

Biographical listings and obituaries—*Dictionary of American Biography* 17 (Joseph Jackson); [Obituary]. *Public Ledger*. Philadelphia, Pa., July 3, 1886; *Who Was Who in America*, Historical Volume (1607-1896). **Books and articles about the biographee**—Abbott, George M. *A Short History of the Library Company of Philadelphia* (1913); Abbott, George M. "Some Recollections of Lloyd P. Smith." *Library Journal* 12:545-46 (1887); Green, Samuel Swett. *The Public Library Movement in the United States, 1853-1898*. Boston: Boston Book Company, 1913; Holley, Edward G. *Raking the Historic Coals: The A.L.A. Scrapbook of 1876*. Beta Phi Mu, 1967; Scharf, J. T., and Thompson Wescott. *History of Philadelphia* (1884), Vol. II, p. 1185.

—SANDRA ROSCOE

SOLBERG, THORVALD (1852-1949)

Thorvald Solberg, the first register of copyrights, was born in Manitowoc, Wisconsin, on April 22, 1852, the eldest of six children of immigrant Norwegian parents. After graduating from the public schools of Manitowoc, he served an apprenticeship in the bookshop of a neighbor and travelled with him when he relocated in Knoxville, Tennessee. In 1872, Solberg journeyed north and found employment at the bookstore of James Campbell in Boston, but then rejoined his family who had moved to Omaha. Working for booksellers there and in Detroit, Solberg had by this time acquired what was to become a lifelong appreciation and knowledge of books and bibliography.

While in Knoxville, Solberg met many people in the intellectual set who were to play important roles in his life. He became the protégé of Dr. Josiah Curtis of Boston, a naturalist, and befriended novelist and playwright Frances Hodgson Burnett, creator of Little Lord Fauntleroy. A visitor to his bookshop, Mary Adelaide Nourse of Lynn, Massachusetts, became Mrs. Solberg on August 1, 1880. The Solbergs shared common interests in literature, civic matters, and travel. They had no children.

At the suggestion of Dr. Curtis, a friend of Librarian of Congress Ainsworth Rand Spofford (q.v.),

SOLBERG

Solberg applied for a position at the Library of Congress, where he began work on May 1, 1876. With the exception of a hiatus of eight years, he served at that institution until his seventy-eighth birthday in 1930. In these early years, Solberg worked chiefly as a cataloger in the Law Library, but he also assisted Spofford in receiving and caring for the works deposited under the copyright law. The Library, at this time located in the west central wing of the Capitol, was already beginning to feel the strains imposed by the greatly increased receipt of books and other materials required by provisions of the revised Copyright Law of 1870. Solberg commented, on assuming his duties, that

> under Mr. Spofford's peculiar method of administration, or rather because of the lack of much of any method, I had to find work for myself and I fell on a terrible mass (mess) of pamphlets and after some months had some 80,000 of them alphabetically arranged and tied up in bundles, and some thousands cataloged, bound and placed on the shelves.

Unlike his mentor, Solberg was the master of efficiency and orderliness—traits that were to be the hallmark of his administrative style.

Solberg's interest in the field of copyright and his compilations of a catalog of books and periodical contributions on this subject prompted Charles C. Soule of the Boston Book Company to arrange for Solberg to take a six-month leave of absence in 1887 to visit European cities and gather bibliographic data on foreign codes and annual law enactments. He was so successful that Soule persuaded him to leave the Library in 1889 to make annual visits to Great Britain for the Boston Book Company, gathering for American libraries sets of journals indexed in [William F.] Poole's [q.v.] *Index to Periodicals.* Although Solberg found the travel abroad stimulating and interesting, the work was so strenuous that he suffered complete physical exhaustion in 1892 and needed four years to rest and recover.

The Balearic Islands were chosen as the site of his recuperation. Solberg and his wife took up residence in an old monastery at Valdemosa, Majorca, in 1893, and thus they began their lifelong passion for and interest in these Mediterranean islands. Solberg collected a large number of books on the Balearics and published a bibliography for the Bibliographical Society of America, "Some Notes on the Balearic Islands," in 1929. In addition, he befriended Archduke Ludwig Salvator of Austria and worked on a bibliography, never published, of the Archduke's writings. Travel became an important part of Solberg's life and was to him the primary means for balancing the rigorous schedule he set for himself at the Library of Congress.

In 1897, the Library of Congress was reorganized and the Legislative Appropriation Act of February 19, 1897, authorized a copyright department, to be headed by a register of copyrights. Recognized as one of the nation's leading authorities on copyright matters, and having fully recovered from his physical collapse, Solberg was urged by librarians and publishers to apply for the new position. His application was presented through Senator Henry Cabot Lodge and was accompanied by a carefully written statement of his conceptions of the newly created office and its proper administration. Solberg was interviewed by President William McKinley and by the new Librarian of Congress, John Russell Young (q.v.), and took office on July 1, 1897.

Solberg was immediately confronted with a chaotic backlog of unregistered copyright receipts. Commenting on his first year as register, he noted, "In every direction the business was months and even years in arrears and there was practically no working organization.... It meant work daytime and nighttime." Utilizing his substantial organizational skills, Solberg was able to assemble an efficient working staff, help direct the move of the collections from the Capitol to the new building across the street, and, with the help of auditors from the Treasury Department, put into effect a suitable method of bookkeeping and accounting. During these hectic early years, Solberg was also called upon to assist in plans for reorganizing the entire Library and was appointed to the Librarian's committee to select qualified persons to fill a greatly increased number of new positions.

By 1903, Solberg felt that he had put the Copyright Office into sufficiently good working order and began to suggest improved copyright legislation. Although the 1870 revised law had been amended twelve times, it was generally accepted that copyright laws needed a major revision. At the suggestion of the Senate Committee on Copyrights, Librarian of Congress Herbert Putnam (q.v.) invited representatives of some thirty organizations concerned with revision to meet with him and the register of copyrights in a series of conferences held in 1905 and 1906. Solberg played a major role in organizing the conferences, recording opposing views, and drafting proposed legislation. The two most controversial issues that developed were the use of copyrighted music on mechanical instruments, such as piano rolls and phonograph records, and the importation by public libraries of books printed abroad. Finally, after numerous drafts and congressional action on several bills and their amendments, a new copyright law was enacted on March 4, 1909. The copyright law, Title 17 of the United States Code, was from then on basically the Act of 1909 with a number of amendments until passage of Public Law 94-553 in 1976, which amended the old Title 17 in its entirety, effective January 1, 1978.

With the passage of the Copyright Act of 1909, Solberg and the Copyright Office had a tremendous task in the "preparation of entirely new record books, new application blanks, new circulars of instruction—practically altogether new machinery of administration," as well as "a tremendous amount of correspondence to be answered." After initiation of the new system, Solberg needed another complete rest and took a long vacation at a friend's house in Dublin, New Hampshire.

During the years of his service as register of copyrights, Solberg was particularly concerned with establishing better copyright relations between the United States and other countries. He attended the sessions of the International Copyright Congress in Barcelona in 1893, Antwerp in 1894, Dresden in 1895, and, after becoming register, was the official United States delegate to the Congresses in Paris in 1900 and 1925, Berlin in 1908, Luxembourg in 1910, and Rome in 1928. One of Solberg's major disappointments was that the United States never adhered to the International Copyright Convention, known also as the Berne Convention, to which most European and other foreign countries were parties. He was especially concerned that the United States had long discriminated against the authors of the United Kingdom. Primarily because of his support of the rights of British authors, Solberg became friend and correspondent with George Bernard Shaw, drama critic and Ibsen translator William Archer, and other important literary figures of the day.

Solberg supported many of the numerous bills to permit adherence to the Berne Convention and, even after his retirement, testified several times before Congress for their passage. He implored librarians and others to appeal to their Congressmen to support this legislation. His article "Copyright and Librarians" (*Library Quarterly* 4:315-28 [April 1934]) is a good example of his efforts in his later years to effect improved international relations in the field of copyright. This statute follows the general approach urged by Solberg in that its terms are nearly enough in consonance with the principles of the Berne Convention that it may now be possible for the United States to join the Berne Union if it chooses to do so.

Throughout his career, Solberg took a keen interest in the affairs of American librarianship in general. He was one of the earliest members of the American Library Association and was a close friend of Charles A. Cutter (q.v.), J. C. M. Hanson (q.v.), David Hutchenson, William Coolidge Lane (q.v.), and Richard R. Bowker (q.v.). In 1899, Solberg and these men played a leading role in securing the

appointment of Herbert Putnam as Librarian of Congress, as described in Solberg's article "Chapter in the Unwritten History of the Library of Congress from January 17 to April 5, 1899" (*Library Quarterly* 9:285-98 [July 1939]).

Thorvald Solberg died on July 15, 1949, at the age of 97. Visitors to his home on Glenn Echo Heights in Maryland remarked that even in his last years his eyes sparkled and he showed signs of the vigor of his early days. Solberg's 46 years of service spanned the period of the most significant expansion of the Library of Congress, and he played an important role in setting the high standards that that institution has sought to maintain ever since. Although not all Solberg's associates, especially in the later years, were able to work comfortably with a man whose perceptions of life had been formed in the nineteenth century, a colleague and close personal friend, Richard Crosby De Wolf, wrote to Solberg:

> ... your example of painstaking thoroughness, persistency and industry in business, broadminded kindness in your dealings with your subordinates, cheerfulness and humor in your general attitude toward life, have helped and inspired me.

Biographical listings and obituaries—[Obituary]. *Library Journal* 74:1082 (Aug. 1949); [Obituary]. *Publishers' Weekly* 156:579 (Aug. 6, 1949); *Who Was Who in America* II (1943-1950). **Books and articles about the biographee**—Baensch, Emil. "Thorvald Solberg, Register of Copyrights." *The Wisconsin Magazine* 6:39-40 (Feb. 1928); Hanson, James C. M. "Thorvald Solberg, the First Register of Copyrights." *Scandinavia: A Monthly Magazine* (Grand Forks, N.D.) 1:75-78 (Feb. 1924); "A Popular Librarian." *The Publishers' Circular* (London), no. 1628:272 (Sept. 11, 1897); Robinson, Lee Lamar. "Expert Workers for Uncle Sam; LX: Thorvald Solberg." *Washington Post*, May 6, 1924, p. 6; Solberg, Thorvald. "Thorvald Solberg: An Autobiographical Sketch." *Town & Country Review* (London) (Sept. 1937), 4p.; "Thorvald Solberg, Register of Copyrights." *Publishers' Weekly* 101:1223-24 (April 29, 1922). **Primary sources and archival materials**—The personal papers of Thorvald Solberg are located in the Manuscript Division of the Library of Congress. Contained in twelve boxes, they consist of material on copyright matters, personal correspondence, copies of speeches and articles, and a manuscript, "Notes for an Autobiography."

—WILLIAM J. SITTIG

SONNECK, OSCAR GEORGE THEODORE (1873-1928)

Oscar George Theodore Sonneck was born in Lafayette, New Jersey—which later became part of Jersey City—on October 6, 1873, the son of George C. and Julia Meyne Sonneck. Sonneck's father died while Sonneck was a child, so Mrs. Sonneck took the boy to Germany, where she was employed as head of the household of a wealthy, widowed banker in Frankfurt-am-Main. Sonneck was thus raised as a son in the banker's home, where he had every advantage. He was educated in the Kieler Gelehrtenschule

(1883-1889) and the Kaiser Friedrich Gymnasium in Frankfurt (1889-1893). He attended the University of Heidelberg for one semester (1893) and then studied at the University of Munich (1893-1897), which he left without taking the examinations for a degree. Olin Downes described him in the *New York Times* (November 11, 1928) as "a student, but one that accommodated himself poorly to academic systems, also despising, at that time, academic degrees."

During his student days, Sonneck considered "*belles lettres* his calling and had ambitions to become a poet" (Otto Kinkeldey [q.v.], p. 26). He actually published two volumes of poetry (1895 and 1898), but gradually his interest in music prevailed. After he left the University of Munich, he studied privately for a year to improve his technical musical skills.

Sonneck spent the year 1899 engaged in research in Italian libraries. About the turn of the century, he returned to the United States, where he began his research into America's musical history. He spent two and one-half years travelling among some twenty libraries along the East Coast, devoting his full time to research. From that period ultimately came four books: *A Bibliography of Early Secular American Music* (1905); *Francis Hopkinson, the First American Poet-Composer (1737-1791) and James Lyon, Patriot, Preacher, Psalmodist (1735-1794), Two Studies in Early American Music* (1905); *Early Concert-Life in America (1731-1800)* (1907); and *Early Opera in America* (1915). Sonneck published the first two himself because no publishers could be found for American musical studies:

> He determined to attempt for his native land a kind of investigation which his historical studies in Europe had revealed to him as a necessary first step toward the establishment of a true record of a national or a local music history.... The young American musical Columbus found only one regular source that covered any appreciable period of time—the ordinary weekly and later daily newspapers [Kinkeldey, p. 26].

Indeed, Sonneck spent so much time in newspaper departments that the staff of the newspaper department at the Library of Congress thought he was writing a history of the American press. When they discovered he was actually a well-trained musical scholar, they suggested he visit Herbert Putnam (q.v.), Librarian of Congress, who was just at that time wrestling with the future of the newly formed Music Division. Putnam perceived LC's duty to music as the development of a

> collection on the scholarly side, and ... a scholarly conduct of it.

> But for both of these the indispensable, indeed the prerequisite, was the *man* with the adequate learning and the necessary qualities. The combination

required was complicated. He must be a specialist in the subject matter, thoroughly grounded through studies abroad; yet he must, if possible, have some familiarity with our American ways, some sympathies, some faith in what we might do in Music—some appreciation of what we had already done. He must be familiar with the technique of Music as an art, yet prefer to pursue it as a science: the history of it, the theory, the philosophy, even the bibliography. He must be young, for the task would be long; and personally industrious, for his staff would be small. And he must have the urge to gather and interpret for the benefit of others, which is the requisite in a library [Putnam, p. 2].

Little wonder that Putnam later felt that Providence had sent Sonneck into his office. Sonneck came, not in search of a position, but to offer the manuscript of his "Bibliography of Early Secular American Music" for publication by the Library of Congress. Although Putnam was unable to accept that offer, he countered by asking Sonneck to become chief of the Music Division. On August 1, 1902, Sonneck formally assumed his duties, but he had already spent the summer preparing a classification of music and literature on music in response to Putnam's request. According to his memo to Putnam (dated October 31, 1902), Sonneck based his proposed classification on published literature; typed music schedules of American libraries that had been collected by the Music Division; European schemes, eleven of which he critiqued; the systems used by music publishers; and his personal experience. On December 16, 1902, after several conferences and some modification to effect conformity with the overall LC Classification, Putnam approved Sonneck's proposal. The scheme was tested for two years and published: U.S. Library of Congress. Music Division. *Classification. Music and Books on Music. M: Music. ML: Literature of Music. MT: Musical Instruction and Study. Adopted December, 1902; As in Force April, 1904* (Washington: Government Printing Office, 1904). A revised edition was published in 1917; together with an addendum of "Additions and Changes ..." in subsequent printings, it is the version used now in many American libraries.

Sonneck appraised the Music Division in 1902 as "an accumulation of music ... rather than a collection; and most assuredly not a 'musical library' in any organic sense!" (*Library Journal* 40:587 [August 1915]). To begin his systematic development of the music collection, he prepared lists of the books and compositions listed in Hugo Riemann's *Musiklexikon* that were not in the LC collections; these desiderata lists he sent to European dealers for bids and supply. After those initial glaring gaps were filled, he embarked on a five-year plan of purchases to achieve "a reasonably comprehensive collection of material that bears in any direction on music in America, and more particularly on American music." The goal of his plans was to "ultimately release the American scholar of the necessity of consulting European libraries, except for research not bearing directly or indirectly on music in America as a reflex of music in Europe." [The quotations are from Sonneck's article in the *Proceedings* of the Music Teachers' National Association, 3:260-87 (1908), which is America's first published guide to building a music library—complete with considered judgments on collection development, acquisition procedures, technical services, and readers services. Its value remains undiminished.]

Together with his carefully articulated role of LC vis-à-vis European libraries, Sonneck stressed the importance of buying current imprints "now"; of scores over performance parts for a reference and research library; of original scores rather than arrangements—except piano/vocal scores; of transcripts, contemporary manuscripts, or photographic reproductions of otherwise unavailable works; and of collecting American autographs comprehensively. He considered want lists to be an active implementation of collection policy, while waiting for items to appear in dealers' catalogs was merely passive. Want lists in the hands of "reliable and energetic dealers" resulted in lower prices because of savings in clerical labor, correspondence, and time; they were also a hedge against unexpected acquisition monies: "We are ready . . . at a moment's notice."

Sonneck's concept of systematic collection development more than doubled the LC music collections during his fifteen-year tenure; and rather than consisting solely of copyright deposits, some nine-tenths of which he considered to be trash, they included approximately 82,500 items that he had purchased. When he resigned on September 5, 1917, he considered the collection to be "surpassed as a general international collection perhaps by Berlin alone" [Königliche Bibliothek] , while in musical Americana LC's superiority was "absolute" (*Report of the Librarian of Congress*, 1917, p. 66).

America's entry into the First World War distressed Sonneck. On the one hand his heart bled for Germany, where his mother still lived, but he was also a patriotic American. The circumstances made him uncomfortable in the nation's capital, so he accepted Rudolph Schirmer's offer to become director of the Publication Department of G. Schirmer, the New York music publisher, where he could continue his work for the advancement of American music. In 1921, he became vice-president of G. Schirmer, a position he retained until his untimely death in 1928.

Sonneck edited *The Musical Quarterly*, America's first magazine designed as a contribution to the cause of music in America rather than as a commercial enterprise, from its inception (volume 1, 1915) until his death. In 1919, he was a leader in the formation of the Society for the Publication of American Music, which has sponsored an ongoing series of contemporary American music publications since 1919-1920.

When the pianist Harold Bauer founded the Beethoven Association of New York in 1918, Sonneck became secretary, librarian, and historian. As librarian he gathered an outstanding collection of Beethoveniana, which was deposited in the New York Public Library when the Association was dissolved in 1940. Sonneck was the U.S. delegate to the Beethoven Centenary in Vienna (1927), representing the Beethoven Association. He also published three Beethoven studies in honor of the Centenary: *Beethoven, Impressions of Contemporaries* (1926); *Beethoven Letters in America; Fac-similes with Commentary* (1927); and *The Riddle of the Immortal Beloved: A Supplement to Thayer's "Life of Beethoven"* (1927).

Altogether, Sonneck published nineteen books, two volumes of poetry, innumerable articles, and a group of musical compositions, and he edited *The Musical Quarterly* from 1915 to 1928. Perhaps his most important publications for librarians, in addition to *Class M*, are his catalogs of portions of the Music Division of the Library of Congress: *Dramatic Music (Class M 1500, 1510, 1520). Catalogue of Full Scores* (Washington: Government Printing Office, 1908); *Orchestral Music (Class M 1000-1268) Catalogue. Scores . . .* (Washington: Government Printing Office, 1912); *Catalogue of Early Books on Music (before 1800)* by Julia Gregory . . . under the Direction of O. G. Sonneck . . . (Washington: Government Printing Office, 1913); *Catalogue of Opera Librettos Printed before 1800 . . .* (Washington: Government Printing Office, 1914); and his *Bibliography of Early American Secular Music* (1905; updated by William Treat Upton in 1945). Sonneck considered published catalogs of LC's holdings as a method of advertising the development of the collection, especially in Europe; as a way to apprise American scholars of LC's resources; and as bibliographies of permanent reference value. The catalogs of first editions of Stephen Foster (1915) and Edward MacDowell (1917), the four American studies which resulted from his pre-LC research years in the United States, and his research into the origins of American patriotic songs—undertaken at the request of the Librarian of Congress—were the beginnings of bibliographic and musicological studies of American music.

Sonneck staunchly, energetically, and aggressively advocated music in libraries—all libraries. A 1917 essay included seven arguments in support of that belief, three of which may be interpreted as his philosophy of librarianship:

> That a librarian ought not to content himself with giving the public what it happens to want, but ought to help create a demand for what the public needs; . . . that no self-respecting library can afford to be without certain cultural documents, whether they be consulted frequently or seldom. . . . [and] that the needs of one solitary scholarly specialist should weigh with librarians just as heavily as the wants of a hundred "general" and generally superficial and unproductive readers.

> After all, it is not the frequency of use that counts, but the use to which a book is put ["Music in Libraries," *The Art World* II (1917); reprinted in his *Miscellaneous Studies in the History of Music* (New York: Macmillan, 1921), pp. 287-95; and excerpted in *Music Departments of Libraries*, see below].

As an activity of the Music Teachers' National Association committee on the history of music and libraries, Sonneck prepared a questionnaire that was sent by the U.S. Bureau of Education to 2,849 libraries in 1917-1918 to discover the strengths and frequency of music collections in American libraries. The summary of the findings (Music Teachers' National Association. *Music Departments of Libraries*. U.S. Bureau of Education. Bulletin No. 33. Washington: Government Printing Office, 1921) is the first appraisal of "the condition and resources of the music sections of public and school libraries, containing 5,000 volumes or over, throughout the United States" (p. 5).

Sonneck's influence remains profound, extending to the present time. His classification, the model procedures he instituted at the Library of Congress Music Division, the importance of his studies in American music, his emphasis on published bibliographies and catalogs, and his recognition of the need for and appropriateness of American music and musical literature for American libraries combine to lend substance to a perception of Oscar George Theodore Sonneck as the father of American music librarianship.

The American composer Frank Patterson, whose friendship with Sonneck began during their student days in Munich, wrote of him:

> The fact is that he was an interminable worker. I have never known anyone who was so irresistibly energetic as he was in his work and so entirely lacking in any energy in the field of play. Since his tragic end I have tried my best to think back to our student days and to recall what pleasures he indulged in, and I must acknowledge that I can think of none. I have an idea that Sonneck simply wore himself out with work. . . .

Herbert Putnam found him neither

> . . . physically robust nor temperamentally sanguine or buoyant. He had not the stolidity of nerves which takes with equanimity the inconveniences and annoyances of life. They harassed him. . . .

> So he worked always under obstacles within himself, or at least without the aid of that physical buoyancy and that natural optimism which tonic many men to great accomplishment. And if, in spite of this handicap, he achieved greatly, it was because his conscience forced him on and through. His intense seriousness meant for him personally many deprivations; but it meant in his work that unflagging industry, dogged thoroughness, and persistence toward perfection that not merely reared those monuments of him at Washington, but have influenced wholesomely the standards and canons of an entire profession [p. 3].

Carl Engel, who succeeded him both at LC and at G. Schirmer's, wrote that

> On many, Oscar Sonneck was apt to make the impression of being forbiddingly sedate and short. Occasionally, he appeared irritable and could irritate. He seemed to look on life through the blue glasses of pessimism. . . . Some of us affectionately called him "Oscar Gloom." But there was another side to the man. He had a lively sense of humor; he enjoyed gaiety; he was not merely patient but he possessed unlimited enthusiasm; he believed in beauty and serenity as the supreme comforts of the soul [p. 150].

The dichotomy between pessimism, gloom, harassment by the petty annoyances of life and humor, gaiety, enthusiasm is difficult to resolve. Thus provoked, H. Wiley Hitchcock "determined to turn to Sonneck [himself] . . . in search of his personality, and especially that element of wit and humor claimed for him." The result is a charming portrait of the intellectual at play while he worked!

On November 9, 1904, Sonneck was married to Marie Elisabeth Ames, who survived him; no children were born of the marriage. Oscar George Theodore Sonneck died on October 30, 1928.

Biographical listings and obituaries—*Dictionary of American Biography* 17 (Carl Engel); Downes, Olin. "A Scholar's Passing; The Unique Contribution of Oscar G. Sonneck to the History of American Music." *New York Times*, Nov. 11, 1928, Theatre Section, p. 8 [includes portrait]; Engel, Carl. "A Postscript." *Musical Quarterly* 15:149-51 (1929); Kinkeldey, Otto. "A Notable Scholar Passes On; Oscar G. T. Sonneck, Musicologist and Editor, Enjoyed a Brilliant Career." *Musical America* 48:18 (Nov. 10, 1928) [includes portrait]; Putnam, Herbert. "Remarks . . . at the Funeral Services, November 1st, 1928 [for] O.G. Sonneck." *Musical Quarterly* 15:1-4 (Jan. 1929); *Who Was Who in America* I (1897-1942). **Books and articles about the biographee**—Engel, Carl. "O. G. Sonneck, ein Charakterbild." *Studien zur Musikgeschichte. Festschrift für Guido Adler zum 75.*

Geburtstag. Wien: Universal, 1930, pp. 216-20; Hitchcock, H. Wiley. *After 100 [!] Years: The Editorial Side of Sonneck. In Memoriam Oscar George Theodore Sonneck, 1873-1928. With . . . His Writing and Musical Compositions, a Bibliography* by Irving Lowens. Washington: Library of Congress, 1975; Kinkeldey, Otto. "Oscar George Theodore Sonneck (1873-1928)." *Notes* 11:25-32 (Dec. 1953); [Patterson, Frank]. "Personal Recollections of Oscar G. Sonneck." *Musical Courier* 97:8 (Nov. 15, 1928). **Primary sources and archival materials**—Sonneck's papers are in the Music Division of the Library of Congress.

                                        —CAROL JUNE BRADLEY

SPOFFORD, AINSWORTH RAND (1825-1908)

Ainsworth Rand Spofford was born in Gilmanton, New Hampshire, on September 12, 1825, the sixth child of the Reverend Mr. Luke Spofford and Greta Rand Spofford. Ainsworth's father, a Presbyterian pastor, served eight different congregations in New Hampshire and Massachusetts between the time of his son's birth and his boyhood, which was spent in Chilmark, Massachusetts, on Martha's Vineyard. Young Ainsworth was tutored at home, but poor health prevented him from attending Amherst; many years later, in 1882, that institution awarded him an honorary LL.D. degree. Adverse conditions on Martha's Vineyard, which resulted in the deaths of an older brother and sister, forced the Spofford family to leave the island in 1845. Spofford travelled to Cincinnati, then the commercial and the publishing center of the West, where he quickly found employment with bookseller and publisher Elizabeth D. Truman, the widow of William T. Truman, an early publisher of the *McGuffey Readers.*

In 1849, Spofford was the principal organizer of the Literary Club of Cincinnati, a group of young men who pledged themselves to debate the political and literary issues of the day. The slavery question dominated, and Spofford fervently argued the abolitionist cause. In 1851, Mrs. Truman made him a partner in the business, and through his efforts, Truman & Spofford became Cincinnati's leading importer of the books of the New England transcendentalists. Furthermore, beginning with Emerson's 1850 trip, Spofford was responsible for arranging the lecture tours that brought Ralph Waldo Emerson, Theodore Parker, and Bronson Alcott west for the first time. On September 15, 1852, the young entrepreneur married Sarah Partridge, formerly of Franklin, Massachusetts, and they had three children: Charles, Henry, and Florence.

In the late 1850s, Truman & Spofford found itself in financial trouble. In 1859, the firm failed, but Spofford had already embarked on a new career: associate editor and chief editorial writer for the city's leading newspaper, the *Cincinnati Daily Commercial.* In 1861, the *Commercial* sent Spofford to Washington to report on President Abraham Lincoln's

inauguration, a trip that soon led to Spofford's acceptance of the position of assistant librarian of Congress. He held that post from September 1861 until December 31, 1864, when Lincoln appointed him Librarian of Congress. Spofford served as Librarian until July 1, 1897, when he willingly stepped aside to assume the duties of chief assistant librarian in the administration of a new Librarian of Congress, John Russell Young (q.v.). He continued as chief assistant under Herbert Putnam (q.v.), who took office as Librarian of Congress in April 1899. Still in the service of the institution he joined in 1861, Ainsworth Rand Spofford died on August 11, 1908.

During his 32 years as Librarian, Spofford transformed the Library of Congress from a small legislative library in the Capitol into a separate institution of national significance. During his administration, the Library became the largest and most comprehensive American library and assumed a national role that it has never relinquished. In all, Ainsworth Rand Spofford successfully revived the idea of an American national library and provided his successors at the Library of Congress with the collections and the spacious building necessary for the creation of a truly modern national library.

His Cincinnati experience was an important reason for Spofford's later success at the Library of Congress. At Truman & Spofford, he had developed his lifelong talent for book selection and acquisition, had enhanced his knowledge of bookbinding, and had become familiar with the copyright laws. His twice-yearly book-buying trips to Boston kept him in touch with literary and publishing developments on the East Coast. Through his activities at the Literary Club, which he considered to be the "most valuable part" of his education, Spofford widened his intellectual horizons and increased his self-confidence. His closest friends were always fellow Literary Club members, and two of them, Reuben H. Stephenson and Rutherford B. Hayes, were of special importance to his Library of Congress career. Stephenson, librarian of the Young Men's Mercantile Library of Cincinnati, was indirectly responsible for Spofford's going to the Library of Congress; in 1861, when in Washington, D.C., Spofford paid a visit to Stephenson's brother, Librarian of Congress John G. Stephenson (q.v.)—who persuaded his Cincinnati visitor to begin work as assistant librarian of Congress. As a congressman from 1865 to 1867, Rutherford B. Hayes served as chairman of the Joint Committee on the Library and worked closely with his old Literary Club friend, Librarian of Congress Spofford, during the important first stages of Spofford's national library efforts. Hayes offered similar encouragement after he became President of the United States.

Spofford's extensive knowledge of the booktrade and his helpfulness to individual members of Congress quickly impressed all the members of the Joint Committee. They endorsed his efforts to expand the Library and willingly turned over direction of most of the Library's affairs to their efficient and energetic Librarian. In promoting the legislation that resulted in the Library's relatively sudden emergence into an institution of national importance, Spofford skillfully combined nationalistic rhetoric and flattery with sound, practical arguments. He also took advantage of a favorable post-Civil War political and intellectual atmosphere, in which a resurgent nationalism encouraged the growth of new federal agencies and American cultural institutions.

Between 1865 and 1870, Librarian Spofford obtained the passage of six legislative acts that made the Library of Congress the largest library in the United States and ensured its future national importance. The measures were: 1) an appropriation expanding the Library's rooms in the Capitol, approved in early 1865; 2) the copyright law amendment of 1865, which brought copyright deposits into the Library's collections; 3) the Smithsonian deposit of 1866, which transferred the 40,000-volume library of the Smithsonian Institution to the Library of Congress; 4) the appropriation of $100,000 for the purchase of Peter Force's unparalleled private library of Americana; 5) an 1867 resolution providing for new international exchange arrangements; and 6) the copyright law of 1870, centralizing all U.S. copyright registration and deposit activities at the Library. The copyright law stipulated that two copies of all copyrighted books, maps, prints, photographs, and pieces of music be deposited by their authors in the Library of Congress as a condition of copyright. The future growth of the Library's Americana collections was thereby guaranteed, without substantial cost to the Library.

The dramatic expansion of the Library's collections led to another of Spofford's principal achievements: the construction of a new Library of Congress building, separate from the Capitol. Spofford's administration between 1871 and 1897 was dominated by the unceasing flow of copyright deposits into the overcrowded Library, and by the Librarian's continual efforts to gain approval for a new building. Shelf space in the Library ran out in 1875, which led Spofford to warn that unless Congress authorized a new building before long, he would be presiding over "the greatest chaos in America." By 1877, more than 70,000 books were "piled on the floor in all directions." As a consequence—and to the dismay of librarians around the United States—other Library of Congress activities suffered. For example, publication of the Library's alphabetical catalog was abandoned in 1880. A proposed index to government documents was left uncompleted, and even cataloging itself slowly came to a halt.

But Spofford's 25-year struggle to obtain a separate Library building was successful. Its construction supervised by Bernard R. Green (q.v.), that structure—located directly across the east plaza from the Capitol and completed in 1897—was itself a national monument. The Main Building of the Library of Congress, in its day the "largest, costliest, and safest" library building in the world, enhanced the Library's national character and permanently ensured its national role. In late 1896, the impending move into that building precipitated congressional hearings about the Library and its organization. Spofford played a dominant part in these hearings, as well as in the subsequent reorganization of the Library, which was incorporated into the Legislative Appropriations Act for 1897 (approved February 19, 1897).

Spofford felt that the functions of a legislative and a national library were complementary, that the Library of Congress belonged to the American people and should serve both the citizenry and its elected representatives. Moreover, in his collection-building efforts, he often quoted Thomas Jefferson's (q.v.) statement that "there is no subject to which a member of Congress may not have occasion to refer." Infused with a strong sense of patriotism, Spofford wanted the American national library to surpass the great national libraries of Europe—which were also his models. He argued that the American national library should be a permanent, comprehensive collection of the country's literature, "representing the complete product of the American mind in every department of science and literature." In his view, that library should also be a unique institution and not part of any library system. This was one reason he operated quite independently from the American library movement and, after 1876, from the American Library Association.

Ainsworth Spofford was a self-educated, old-fashioned bookman who loved classical literature and had a remarkable memory for books, authors, and facts. He was industrious, fair-minded, and, above all, enthusiastic. His reputation as a reliable source of information for official and unofficial Washington made him a well-known figure in the nation's capital. Among librarians, Spofford was a conservative; his personal interests centered on acquisitions, on bibliography, and on serving as a "reader's advisor"—not on the cooperative, technically oriented activities that preoccupied most young librarians of his day. He was respected by all, even though his formal, somewhat abstract manner was not always understood or appreciated. In 1886, the Washington correspondent of the *Cleveland Leader* described the Librarian of Congress:

He is a curious looking man. As dark as a Spaniard, he has black hair and whiskers, mixed with gray. His eyes are jet, and with his short, lithe, wiry frame, every atom of which is muscle, he is the busiest man in the Capitol building. He can dictate as well as most men can write, and his ordinary conversation, which is usually slow and measured, would not look badly in print.

Another portrait of Spofford comes from the pen of his friend and successor, Herbert Putnam:

A figure of absorption and of labor; quaint indeed in mode and expression, yet efficient; immersed in the trivial, yet himself by no means trivial, imparting to it the dignity that comes of intense seriousness and complete sincerity. Grave in the task of infinite detail upon a mass of infinite dimension; grave, but never dour. Cheerful rather, even buoyant. Disdaining the frivolous as a waste of time; yet appreciating humor, and even responsive to jest.... A circulation free and abundant; the palate of a child; and a digestion unafraid.

Spofford was a prolific essayist, editor, and compiler, an inveterate and almost compulsive popularizer of knowledge. The primary purpose of his many compilations was to select and summarize what he felt was the "best" or most useful information, whether it be statistical facts or literary essays. In 1876, the Librarian of Congress contributed articles on the following subjects to the Office of Education compilation (under the direction of John Eaton [q.v.]) *Public Libraries in the United States*: binding and preservation of books, periodical literature and society publications, works of reference for libraries, library bibliography, and "Library of Congress, or National Library." His annual *American Almanac and Treasury of Facts, Statistical, Financial, and Political*, published from 1878 through 1889, exemplifies his reference works. Other typical, multi-volume compilations edited by Spofford included *The Library of Choice Literature: Prose and Poetry, Selected from the Most Admired Authors* (Philadelphia: Gebbie & Co., several editions, 1882-1888) and *The Library of Historic Characters and Famous Events of All Nations and All Ages* (several publishers and editions, 1894-1900). Finally, both the professional and personal interests of Ainsworth Rand Spofford were probably most accurately described in the formidable title of his *A Book for All Readers, Designed as an Aid to the Collection, Use, and Preservation of Books and Formation of Public Libraries* (G. P. Putnam's Sons, 1900).

Throughout his life, Spofford actively participated in local cultural societies. As mentioned before, in 1849, he was the principal organizer of the Literary Club of Cincinnati. In Washington, he was an active member of the Washington Literary Society and played a major role in the establishment of three important organizations: the Columbia Historical Society (1894), the District of Columbia Library Association (1894), and, in 1897, a library school at

Columbian College (now George Washington University).

Spofford was an important figure in the early history of American librarianship, not only because of his accomplishments at the Library of Congress, but also because his advice about all aspects of library operations was sought within the fledgling profession. By 1876, when the American Library Association was founded, Spofford already was an experienced and widely admired librarian. At the ALA organizational meeting in Philadelphia, then, Spofford was flattered when an Illinois librarian urged that a new cooperative book index be undertaken in order to have the equivalent of a "printed Spofford in every library." But President Justin Winsor's (q.v.) introduction for Spofford summarized the opinion of the audience: "We have laid aside some of the best for last; let us now listen to the official father of us all, the national keeper of our books, the Librarian of Congress."

Biographical listings and obituaries—*Dictionary of American Biography* 17 (William A. Slade); *National Cyclopaedia of American Biography* 6; [Obituary]. *New York Daily Tribune*, Aug. 13, 1908; [Obituary]. *Washington Evening Star*, Aug. 12 and 13, 1908; *Who Was Who in America* I (1897-1942). **Books and articles about the biographee**—*Ainsworth Rand Spofford, 1825-1908; A Memorial Meeting at the Library of Congress, November 12, 1908*. New York: The Webster Press, 1909; Cole, John Y. "Ainsworth Rand Spofford." *Quarterly Journal of the Library of Congress* 33:93-115 (April 1976); Cole, John Y., ed. *Ainsworth Rand Spofford: Bookman and Librarian*. Littleton, Colo.: Libraries Unlimited, 1975; Cole, John Y. "A National Monument for a National Library: Ainsworth Rand Spofford and the New Library of Congress, 1871-1897." *Records of the Columbia Historical Society of Washington, D.C., 1971-1972*. Washington: Published by the Society, 1973, pp. 468-507; Ford, Worthington C. "An Old-Fashioned Librarian, The Late A. R. Spofford." *Library Journal* 33:356-58 (Sept. 1908); Hollis, Carroll. "A New England Outpost: As Revealed in Some Unpublished Letters of Emerson, Parker, and Alcott to Ainsworth Spofford." *New England Quarterly* 38:65-85 (March 1965); Putnam, Herbert. "Ainsworth Rand Spofford: A Librarian Past." *The Independent* 65:1149-55 (Nov. 19, 1908). **Primary sources and archival materials**—Spofford's personal papers are in the Manuscript Division, Library of Congress; his official correspondence is in the Library of Congress Archives.

—JOHN Y. COLE

STALLMANN, ESTHER LAVERNE (1903-1969)

Esther Laverne Stallmann, daughter of John Hermann and Laura A. Hubbard Stallmann, was born September 29, 1903, at Martinsville, Indiana. Following graduation from her home town high school in 1921, she attended Indiana University, receiving the A.B. degree in social sciences with Phi Beta Kappa honors in 1924, and an A.M. degree in 1926. In 1927, she was awarded the B.S. in library science from the University of Illinois, and, in 1942, the Ph.D. from the University of Chicago Graduate Library School, where she was the recipient of an [Andrew] Carnegie [q.v.] fellowship and three University of Chicago scholarship awards.

Stallmann was a teacher in the Martinsville High School (1925-1926), a public school librarian in Flint, Michigan (1927-1929), and reference librarian in the West Washington College of Education, Bellingham (1929-1931). From 1932 to 1934, she was on the faculty of the library school at George Peabody College for Teachers. In the years following, she taught library science at Syracuse University (1935); the University of Tennessee (1935-1937); and the New York State Teachers College, Albany (1939-1948), where she was a professor and head of the Department of Librarianship. She joined the faculty of the new library school at the University of Texas at Austin in 1949 and became, in 1954, one of about half a dozen women on the Texas faculty who held the rank of full professor during that decade.

Before 1949, Stallmann's main professional interests were school libraries and librarianship. The subjects of her doctoral dissertation and her publications in national library journals during this period reflect that school orientation. After 1949, presumably as a result of her involvement in library association activities and new teaching assignments, the focus of her interests shifted to public and academic libraries and, particularly, to education for librarianship. She was an executive board member of the Association of American Library Schools (1953-1956) and the Association's president (1958-1959). In ALA, she was a member of the Committee on Accreditation (1964-1969) and its chairman (1969). Her concern with library education at the national level resulted in her writing several papers: *Library Internships: History, Purpose and a Proposal* (Occasional Papers, No. 37. Urbana: University of Illinois Library School, 1954), which served as the definitive treatise on the topic for more than two decades; "The Cost of Instruction in A.L.A.-Accredited Library Schools, Fall, 1959" (in Association of American Library Schools, *Report of Meeting*, Chicago, 1958; *Report of Meeting*, Chicago, 1959); "Associations of Professional Schools: A Comparison" (*Journal of Education for Librarianship*, Summer 1960); and "Accreditation" (*Drexel Library Quarterly*, April 1967).

While secretary of the Southwestern Library Association (1956-1958), she called the first meeting of administrators and teachers in library education agencies in the six-state region, from which evolved the Association's first Committee on Library Education, which she chaired. In 1960, at her suggestion and under her direction, a graduate student compiled the first directory of library education personnel and programs in the Southwest; this directory became the prototype for a national directory later issued by the

Library Services Branch of the U.S. Office of Education.

For six years, beginning in 1958, Stallmann was chairman of the Texas Council on Library Education, composed of library science teachers and administrators. Under her leadership, the Council for the first time in its twenty-year history became a cohesive, active group devoting its full attention to improving the quality of education for librarianship in the state.

Twice in her years at Texas, she participated in state-wide studies of library education. In 1956-1957, at the instigation of the Texas Council on Library Education, she designed and supervised a series of student theses that determined the current state of library education and the demand for library personnel. In 1967-1968, she collaborated with Robert R. Douglass in making a survey and report that provided the Coordinating Board of the Texas College and University System with accurate and complete background information to be used in its consideration of a state plan for library education: *Recommendation for the Improvement of Education for Librarianship in Texas* (Austin: The University of Texas, 1968).

In 1949, Texas was among the states lacking comprehensive plans for library development. Stallmann resolutely set about the task of educating the library practitioners, citizens, and library school students as to the state's library needs and potentialities. She did this in part by writing numerous articles related to library development in Texas, most of which are to be found in the *Texas Library Journal*. Also, she furthered this goal of education and went a step farther as well by formulating development plans, as chairman (1962-1965) of the Texas Library Association's first standing committee for planning (its Library Development Committee). A "Skeletal Plan for State-Wide Library Development..." was based largely on her ideas, and it was she who presented it in final form (*Texas Libraries*, Summer 1963). This plan, widely distributed by the Texas State Library, was a flexible, long-range development proposal, a basic document for continuing library planning in the state. It was used by the Texas State Library in administering federal funds made available under the Library Services and Construction Act. Later, it served as the basis of the Texas Library Systems Act when this legislation was introduced in the State Legislature and passed in 1969.

Stallmann furthered library development in Texas indirectly through the research studies produced by her students—the topics for which were more often than not suggested by her. For example, one thesis contained recommendations that were accepted by a Texas Library Association committee in its formulation of a plan for reorganization of the Association. Three statistical studies, planned and directed by

Stallmann, provided information on public and academic library conditions in Texas that was used for Texas's First Governor's Conference on Libraries (1966). In all, she directed 117 theses and reports at the University of Texas, approximately two-thirds of which were concerned with libraries and librarianship in the state or region. The studies provided accurate historical and statistical information, available in organized and synthesized form from no other source, that was widely employed in library study and planning. As a consequence of these and similar studies, perhaps in no other state were library conditions so thoroughly documented for the period covered.

Stallmann was an extremely able, demanding teacher. The lasting effects of her work have been testified to repeatedly by graduates.

During her twenty years in Texas, she served as surveyor or building consultant for ten municipal and county libraries in the state. Whenever feasible, she sought to involve interested graduate students in surveys, thereby helping them to translate principles and theory into practical application in the field. One example will suffice: in the early 1950s she planned and directed a survey of the Houston Public Library that resulted in five studies, four of which were published and distributed widely. Stallmann also became known and respected in Texas as a consultant for planning new public library buildings and re-modelling existing ones. In fact, her knowledge of public library building requirements became so well recognized that on occasion she was asked to lecture to students in architecture and to judge the library plans they prepared.

The belief that no true democracy can flourish without free access to adequate library facilities and services by its citizens permeated Esther Stallmann's thinking and provided the main thrust in her teaching, writing, and all other aspects of her professional life. Hers was a keen and highly analytical mind; it was a creative mind, also, that constantly sought to identify practical problems in need of solution. She had little patience with subterfuge or evasion and believed in going directly to the heart of a matter with frankness, even bluntness, that on occasion was somewhat disconcerting to her listeners. She did not force her views on others, but, at the same time, she was never reluctant to express her opinion on professional matters or to provide information when clarification of an issue was indicated. Socially, she was unobtrusive, even shy, in manner. She was tall and slender, dignified, always meticulously groomed. She was a warm, friendly human being, generous to a fault, loyal, unselfish, and completely dedicated to her profession.

In 1968, former students, with the assistance of friends and colleagues from across the country,

established a lecture fund in her honor. The citation mentioned, among other things, her strong mental fibre and unimpeachable integrity. In 1969, she was the recipient of the Beta Phi Mu Award for her service to library education, presented each year by the Teachers Section of the American Library Association's Library Education Division.

Esther Laverne Stallmann died on March 19, 1969, at Austin, Texas, after a long illness diagnosed as cranial arteritis, and is buried at Martinsville, Indiana.

Biographical listings and obituaries—*Directory of American Scholars*, 3rd ed. (1957); *Leaders in Education*, 3rd ed. (1948); [Obituary]. *Texas Library Journal* 45:105 (Summer 1969); *Who's Who in Library Service*, 2nd ed., 3rd ed., 4th ed. Primary sources and archival materials—Texas. University of Texas at Austin. *Documents and Minutes of the General Faculty.* "Report of the Memorial Resolution Committee for Esther Laverne Stallmann." November, 1971, pp. 10374-77 [Contains complete bibliography of her writings]; Information is also contained in the Official Files of the Graduate School of Library Science, University of Texas at Austin.

—ROBERT R. DOUGLASS

STARKS, SAMUEL W. (1865?-1908)

S. W. Starks, West Virginia state librarian, 1901-1906, was the first Negro to be named to that post in any state. Many state librarians at that time did not have library training, but were political appointees or worked up to the position from a department in state government. This was apparently true of Starks. Governor A. B. White appointed him West Virginia state librarian in 1901, and four years later, Governor Dawson reappointed him. The post of state librarian was considered to be a major appointment of a black person in any of the states of the Union.

Conflicting information exists regarding the birth date of Samuel Starks. One source indicates that he was born on March 11, 1866. Thomas E. Posey (in *Negro Citizens of West Virginia*), gives his birth date as April 5, 1865. However, there seems to be agreement that he was born in Charleston, South Carolina, where he was educated in the schools of his home town. At the age of sixteen, he entered the service of Kanawho and Ohio Railroad as messenger boy and later held the position of chief telegraph operator. He worked for a number of railroads and took courses in business at Chicago's Bryant and Stratton Business College.

Starks was active in a number of Negro business ventures in Ohio and West Virginia and was a member and leader in Negro fraternal circles. Posey, describing Starks's business and fraternal ventures, indicates that

he later operated a grocery store on Capitol Street. He served sixteen years as Grand Chancellor of the Knights of Pythias, was president of the Pythian Mutual Investment Association, and also president of the Pythian Temple and Sanitarium Commission which owned property in Chicago valued at $150,000.00. He headed the Republican political campaign for Negroes in [West Virginia] several times, and along with Christopher Payne was one of the outstanding political leaders of his day. Politics took a great deal of his time, and he was instrumental in beating back forces in West Virginia that were trying to institute segregation in public conveyances in 1900.

During Starks's tenure as state librarian, the librarian's responsibilities included those of the registrar of copyrights and the chief documents clerk. Starks appointed an assistant, J. Arthur Jackson, also a Negro, as a messenger. In 1917, Jackson became assistant state librarian, and, in 1921, he became state librarian, the second Afro-American to hold the position in West Virginia.

Starks's historical significance rests on the fact that he was the first Afro-American to become a state librarian. However, he is best remembered in the annals of the history of West Virginia for being a state librarian and a political figure. Samuel W. Starks died in 1908 (the date is not known).

Biographical listings and obituaries—Posey, Thomas E. *Negro Citizen of West Virginia*. Institute, W. Va.: Press of West Virginia State College, 1934, pp. 39-40. **Books and articles about the biographee**—[Biographical sketch]. *The Colored American* 9:1 (April 13, 1910); Jackson, Wallace V. "Some Pioneer Negro Library Workers." *Library Journal* 64:215-17 (March 15, 1939).

—CASPER LeROY JORDAN

STEARNS, LUTIE EUGENIA (1866-1943)

On September 13, 1866, Lutie Eugenia Stearns was born in Staughton, Massachusetts, the youngest of eleven children of Dr. Isaac Holden and Catherine Guild Stearns. In 1871, she accompanied her parents to Wisconsin, when her father became superintendent of the Soldiers' Home in Wauwautosa; in 1876, he entered general practice, but later abandoned the family to return to Massachusetts. After graduating from the Milwaukee State Normal School in 1886, she took a teaching position in the public schools there to support the family. She became well known for her use of the Milwaukee Public Library as a source for supplementary reading for her pupils; every Thursday she took three pupils to the Library to get several market-baskets of books for her classes. She later gained a national reputation among librarians and teachers. In 1888, the Milwaukee Public Library Board hired her as head of the Circulation Department, with the mission to stimulate other teachers to make similar use of the Library. For the next six years, she was a constant visitor in the Milwaukee schools, exhorting a greater use of the Library. Her success was evident: by 1894, school

circulation increased substantially, to almost 100,000 volumes per year.

During the same years, Stearns developed an interest in the problems of public library promotion and development in Wisconsin, and a sympathetic Library Board allowed her to spend increasing amounts of time aiding the establishment of public libraries in the cities and villages of the state. Such work convinced her of the need for a state library agency, and she was instrumental, with Frank Hutchins (q.v.), in the establishment of the Wisconsin Free Library Commission in 1895. She was appointed secretary, a position without administrative responsibility; upon reorganization of the Commission in 1897, Hutchins became secretary and Stearns became librarian. Later, in 1903, she was head of the Commission's Traveling Library Department, a post she held until 1914.

During its first two decades, the Free Library Commission's executive officers were held close to their duties in Madison, and it fell to Lutie Stearns to carry the public library message to the cities and villages of Wisconsin. Along with the message, she carried the books of the Traveling Library (in boxes of fifty and one hundred each) to farmers' homes, crossroads stores, and country post offices. By buggy and stage and sleigh, by daycoach and caboose, she travelled the length and breadth of Wisconsin, wearing out five bearskin coats, and, in the end, also her faith that libraries and librarians could bring about the reforms she believed necessary to the good health and order of American society. In 1914, she resigned from the Commission, partly owing to policy disagreements with its secretary, Matthew Dudgeon (q.v.), but principally for personal reasons. Her job was becoming routine, especially as the need for travelling libraries declined; her own interests were broadening, and she sought greater opportunity for expression of her ideas about them.

As she put it, she went "free lance" on the lecture circuit, speaking in behalf of a variety of causes: women's rights, industrial reform, the League of Nations, peace, education, and prohibition. She was especially active in the Federation of Women's Clubs and the Women's International League for Peace and Freedom. In 1928, she toured Europe, investigating conditions there as a member of the American Seminar for International Relations. From 1932 to 1935, she wrote a Sunday column for the Milwaukee *Journal*, "As a Woman Sees It." She never lost her interest in librarianship, and continued to speak and write on library matters, often to the discomfiture of her erstwhile colleagues. In 1935, her health began to fail, forcing her withdrawal from public activity, and she died of cancer on Christmas Day, 1943, after a long illness. Her last public appearance probably was at the 1942 meeting of the Wisconsin Library Association, where she was the honored guest.

Lutie Stearns was an ebullient and outspoken reformer. She claimed shyness, and suffered from a serious stammer, but refused to let those conditions prevent her participation in public affairs: "I felt that I had something to say that might be of help, and I determined that my difficulty in speaking should not be an impediment." In her youth and early middle years, she held a strong belief that public libraries and librarians could be effective agents for the improvement of America. When she could no longer sustain that belief, she turned to the discussion of issues and problems, dealing with the audiences she wished to reach and speaking directly on the problems she thought important. From 1914 to 1932, she lectured in 38 states, returning repeatedly to many of them. For the 18th Amendment, she took to the stump in Wisconsin, speaking in 65 cities and villages there. She campaigned for the 19th Amendment in Iowa, Missouri, Texas, and Wisconsin. In Missouri, she also conducted League of Women Voters citizenship classes for women.

Stearns described her political attitude as radical rather than liberal—agreeing with Heywood Hale Broun that "a liberal is a man who has just left the room when the fighting begins"—and, whatever her cause, she preferred to be in the room where the fighting was. Still, her radicalism was not offensive to established authority; in 1922, Governor Blaine appointed her to a five-year term on the State Normal School Board of Regents, and she was the resident regent for the Milwaukee Normal School, closely involved with its affairs.

By 1932, the progress of the Great Depression had caused a serious reduction in her income from lecturing, and this led her to become a columnist for the *Milwaukee Journal.* Disappointment in her causes also was a factor: the peace for which she worked already was evidently doomed; the repeal of Prohibition was imminent; and the enfranchisement of women had not fulfilled the promises of its advocates. This last was "one of the greatest disappointments" in Stearns's career: "Women rushed into politics without knowing a plank in a platform from a planked whitefish," and they proved to be no more intelligent or virtuous than men in politics.

It was a man's world in which Lutie Stearns lived and worked, and she resented it. Her feminist beliefs were summed up on the frontispiece of a bibliography she published, *Books of Interest and Consolation to Spinsters*: "What is man that we should be mindful of him?" There was a codicil on the endpiece: "I'd rather not be married, and be sorry I wasn't, than be married and be sorry I was." She exulted in the role, and she was a formidable advocate of it.

Nor was she able to accept a quiet life for librarians. In her work for the ·Free Library Com-

mission, she was a forceful advocate of the librarian's mission to use the public library as an instrument through which adults could help themselves to meet the manifold problems of modern society. After she left the Commission, she spoke and wrote frequently on that subject, and she denounced public librarians for their complacency and timid loyalty to the established order. In 1931, in "Tomorrow Is Just Another Day" (*Library Journal*, 1931), she foresaw an ultimate reckoning: "someday the citizens are going to rise up and take the library situation into their own hands." From that rising would come a new service: "Librarians will spend but little time in their offices, and will be out day and night among the people, getting their points of view and responding in fullest measure to their wishes."

Biographical listings and obituaries—*Dictionary of Wisconsin Biography*. Madison, 1960; [Obituary]. *Library Journal* 69:79 (Jan. 15, 1944); 69:213 (March 1, 1944); [Obituary]. *Milwaukee Journal*, Dec. 26, 1943; [Obituary]. *New York Times*, Dec. 27, 1943; *Notable American Women 1607-1950* 3; *Who Was Who in America* V (1969-1973). **Books and articles about the biographee**—[Biographical sketch]. *Library Journal* 76:471 (March 15, 1951); "Hutchins and Stearns: Ideas and Energy; Wisconsin Library Leaders, 1891-1914." *Wisconsin Library Bulletin* 71:72-73 (March 1975); "Resignation of Miss Stearns." *Public Libraries* 19:344 (Oct. 1914); Tannenbaum, Earl. "The Library Career of Lutie E. Stearns." *Wisconsin Magazine of History* 39:159-65 (1955-1956). **Primary sources and archival materials**—Stearns, Lutie E. "My Seventy-Five Years." *Wisconsin Magazine of History* 42:211-18, 282-87 (1958-1959), and 43:97-105 (1959-1960).

—JOHN CALVIN COLSON

STEINER, BERNARD CHRISTIAN (1867-1926)

Trained to be a lawyer and historian, Bernard Christian Steiner also followed his father's footsteps as librarian and teacher. Born in Guilford, Connecticut, on August 13, 1867, he was the son of Lewis Henry and Sarah Smith Steiner. He was educated at Frederick Academy and Guilford Institute and entered Yale in 1884, taking his A.B. in 1888 and his A.M. in 1890. He received his Ph.D. in history from Johns Hopkins in 1891 and an LL.B. from the University of Maryland in 1894. Dickinson College awarded him an honorary Litt.D. in 1923. He began a teaching career at Williams College in 1891. The death of Lewis Steiner in February of the following year led to Bernard Steiner's appointment as librarian of the Enoch Pratt Free Library in Baltimore, where he served the remaining 34 years of his life. Yet, his position as librarian did not keep him from academic pursuits. An instructor in history at Johns Hopkins from 1893 to 1911, he took on the additional obligations of dean and professor of constitutional law at Baltimore University (1897-1900), and dean and professor of public law at the Baltimore Law School (1900-1904). A member of the American Historical Society, the Connecticut Historical

Association, and the Maryland Historical Society, Steiner also edited the archives of Maryland in 1900 and 1916-1926. His extensive writings include many articles in historical journals, a three-part series on the history of early Maryland (1903-1911), and biographies of James McHenry (1907), Reverdy Johnson (1914), Henry Barnard (1919), and Roger B. Taney (1922).

Steiner's scholarship colored his approach to librarianship. Terming the library "the continuation school of the people," he broadened and institutionalized ideas brought to Enoch Pratt Free Library by his father, the first librarian of that institution, in 1884. With a focus on the educational needs of the public, Steiner concentrated his collection on scholarly, technical, and classic works, tolerating some light fiction but preferring to serve an elite cadre of thinking people and raise up the general public by their mental bootstraps. So convinced was he that the average man was eager to make use of the accumulated store of human knowledge if it were available that, despite limited funds, he was able to increase the library system from six to twenty-five branches, making classic and scholarly works available to citizens throughout Baltimore. A public clamor arose for more popular books, greater accessibility to the stacks, and a librarian who would devote his full time to the library; but Steiner stuck to his philosophical guns, retaining full selection control and offering open shelves only in certain rooms, although some of the branches maintained an open stack policy. In his efforts to uplift the public mind, Steiner circulated boxes of carefully selected books to public schools and other institutions and offered a series of public lectures at the main library. He also instituted a circulating Braille collection.

Steiner was a stern and unbending taskmaster whose height, beard, and fierce demeanor daunted many staff members. Though burdened by his self-imposed non-library activities, he refused to delegate tasks, personally undertaking selection and weeding duties and keeping a close eye on activities in the branches. He maintained membership in the American Library Institute and the American Library Association, serving on many committees and as a councillor (1909-1910). He took a great interest in the proposed copyright bill that became law in 1909. As president of the Library Copyright League (1906-1910), he fought successfully for rights of importation of foreign books in sufficient numbers to insure availability to scholars of this country.

Steiner was strongly religious and took an active part in the First Presbyterian Church, serving as an elder and as a delegate to the General Assembly of the Presbyterian Church of the United States in

1920-1921. He was also an active supporter of the Young Men's Christian Association and the Maryland Bible Society.

Steiner married Ethel Simes Mulligan of Yonkers, New York, on November 7, 1912. They had two sons. At the height of his activity in librarianship and historical scholarship, Bernard Steiner died of a heart attack on January 12, 1926, at his home in Baltimore.

Biographical listings and obituaries—"Bernard Steiner [Obituary]." American Antiquarian Society. *Proceedings*, n.s. 36:21-22 (April 1926); Bostwick, Arthur. "In Memoriam." *Library Journal* 51:145-46 (Feb. 1, 1926); *Dictionary of American Biography* 9 (James H. Phalen [Lewis Henry Steiner]; Lawrence Wroth [Bernard Christian Steiner]). Books and articles about the biographee—Hart, Richard H. *A Brief Account of the Careers of Lewis Henry Steiner and His Son Bernard Christian Steiner*. Baltimore: Enoch Pratt Free Library, 1936 [contains portrait and list of works]; Kalisch, Philip A. *The Enoch Pratt Free Library: A Social History*. Metuchen, N.J.: Scarecrow Press, 1969.
                                        —MICHAEL B. WESSELLS

STEPHENSON, JOHN GOULD (1828-1883)

John Gould Stephenson served as Librarian of Congress from May 21, 1861, until his resignation, effective December 31, 1864. A political appointee of President Abraham Lincoln, Stephenson was a physician and Republican partisan from Terre Haute, Indiana, who, as Librarian of Congress, apparently spent as much time serving the Union Army as he did supervising the Library. Shortly after assuming office, Stephenson hired Ainsworth Rand Spofford (q.v.), a Cincinnati bookseller and journalist, as assistant librarian; for all practical purposes the eager assistant librarian—with Stephenson's consent and knowledge—was in charge of the Library during the rest of Stephenson's term of office. On December 31, 1864, Spofford was appointed Librarian and held the post for the next 32 years. The consensus among historians of the Library of Congress seems to be that John G. Stephenson "did the Library of Congress neither harm nor good during his administration."

John Gould Stephenson was born in Lancaster, New Hampshire, on March 1, 1828, the sixth child of Reuben and Mary King Stephenson. Reuben Stephenson was a prominent Lancaster citizen and one of the incorporators of the Lancaster Academy, where John attended school. From the Academy, Stephenson went to the New Hampshire Medical Institution and then to Castleton Medical College, where he received a doctorate in medicine on November 23, 1849. About 1851, the young Dr. Stephenson migrated west to Terre Haute and, a few years later, he became active in the newly formed Republican Party. He was one of Lincoln's earliest supporters for the presidential nomination, and after Lincoln's nomination and election, Stephenson launched a determined campaign to become Librarian of Congress. His reasons for pursuing this particular post, rather than an appointment to another agency, remain obscure.

The Lincoln papers at the Library of Congress contain numerous letters from Indiana citizens and officials urging Stephenson's appointment as Librarian, including endorsements from Senator Henry S. Lane and the soon-to-be secretary of the interior, Caleb B. Smith. On May 7, 1861, the candidate himself was in Washington and wrote to Lincoln, informing the President that he had been "an earnest and continuous laborer in the Cause that triumphed in your election." After listing his political endorsements, Stephenson noted that his "pecuniary condition" would be "greatly relieved by you granting the application." Lincoln complied and, on May 24, 1861, appointed John G. Stephenson to be the fifth Librarian of Congress. His predecessor, John Silva Meehan (q.v.), who had served as Librarian since 1829, accepted the change gracefully and even nonchalantly, simply informing the chairman of the congressional Joint Library Committee (in a letter dated May 28, 1861) that "Mr. John G. Stephenson of Indiana will begin duties on first day of June next."

Less than four months later, Stephenson acquired the services of Spofford, an experienced bookman, as assistant librarian. Describing Stephenson to a friend in May 1862, Spofford characterized the Librarian as "a thorough good fellow, liberal, high-minded, & active, but with no special knowledge of books." By September of 1862, however, relations between Stephenson and Spofford were less congenial. Upset by the Librarian's dismissal of another assistant, Spofford threatened to quit unless he received a promise of full support from Stephenson in the future. As Spofford described the situation to his friend Henry B. Blackwell:

> I have made it a condition of retaining my post that I am to be subjected to no hasty deprivation of support—that no appointments or removals shall be made without my approval. While I conceive that Stephenson has in this instance disappointed the confidence I had always reposed, still his uniformly generous treatment of me & his readiness to repair the past by doing whatever I should advise, leave me willing to continue association with him.

The headstrong assistant librarian clearly was responsible for the major accomplishments of the Library of Congress during Stephenson's term of office: the compilation of two lengthy manuscript reports critical of the Library's condition and urging

Congress to authorize improvements; successful lobbying for a $160,000 appropriation to expand the Library's rooms; the inauguration of more comprehensive and efficient book-buying procedures; and, in September 1864, publication of the 1,200-page *Alphabetical Catalogue of the Library of Congress: Authors*, the first complete author catalog in the Library's history. Nevertheless, Stephenson undoubtedly lent his support and approval to Spofford's efforts.

Probably less is known about John G. Stephenson than about any other Librarian of Congress. In the summer of 1861, he served as a volunteer surgeon for members of the 19th Indiana Regiment, who were in a temporary hospital set up in the Patent Office building. For the rest of his career, however, the jobs he held were more political than medical in their nature. According to his own account, in 1863 he served with the Army of the Potomac, not as a surgeon but as "a volunteer aide de camp with my militia rank of Colonel, participating in the battles of Fitzhugh Crossing, Chancellorsville, and Gettysburg." He received a commendation for his performance at Gettysburg. William Dawson Johnston, in his *History of the Library of Congress 1800-1864* (Government Printing Office, 1904), states that Stephenson was "interested in speculations created by the war," citing as evidence a June 8, 1872, resolution paying the Library's London book agent $1,480, "of which sum he was unjustly defrauded by the conduct of the Librarian in 1863." Despite the harsh wording of the resolution, it is not clear whether war speculations or technical problems involving methods of payment prompted the congressional action.

Following his resignation as Librarian of Congress (in 1864), Stephenson kept his legal residence in Washington and apparently held several political jobs, even though his record of employment is unclear. On November 16, 1881, nearly seventeen years after he left the Library, he was appointed as a medical reviewer at the Pension Office. John G. Stephenson died on November 11, 1883, and is buried in an unmarked grave in the Congressional Cemetery in Washington, D.C.

Biographical listings and obituaries–[Obituary]. *Washington Evening Star*, Nov. 12, 1883; [Obituary]. *Washington Post*, Nov. 12, 1883. **Books and articles about the biographee**–Carter, Constance. "John G. Stephenson: Largely Known and Much Liked." *Quarterly Journal of the Library of Congress* 33:71-91 (April 1976); Cole, John Y. "A Congenial Intellectual Occupation." *Manuscripts* 26:246-53 (Fall 1974); Johnston, William D. *History of the Library of Congress 1800-1864*. Washington: Government Printing Office, 1904; Mearns, David C. *The Story Up to Now: The Library of Congress, 1800-1946*. Washington: Government Printing Office, 1947; Wood, Richard C. "Librarian-in-Arms: The Career of John G. Stephenson." *Library Quarterly* 14:263-69 (Oct. 1949). **Primary sources and archival materials**–

Material relating to Stephenson's family is in the Lancaster, New Hampshire, Historical Society. Stephenson's letterbooks while Librarian of Congress, as well as the two unpublished annual reports prepared during his administration, are in the Library of Congress Archives. Spofford's correspondence concerning Stephenson is in the National Woman Suffrage Association Archives, Library of Congress. There is a personnel file for Stephenson in Record Group 84, Office of the Secretary of the Interior, National Archives and Records Service.

–JOHN Y. COLE

STEVENSON, BURTON EGBERT (1872-1962)

Burton Egbert Stevenson was born November 9, 1872, of uncertain parentage in Chillicothe, Ohio, a small county-seat town located about fifty miles southwest of Columbus, where he spent the greater part of his ninety years. He was graduated from the local high school at the age of seventeen and attended Princeton University from 1890 to 1893, but he left without completing his degree. Returning to his home town, Stevenson went to work as a police reporter for the *Chillicothe Leader* and became city editor of the *Chillicothe Daily News*. On June 12, 1895, he married a brilliant and articulate local girl, Elizabeth Shepard Butler, who was serving as assistant librarian at the Chillicothe Public Library. They had no children, but one of the happy results of their marriage was Stevenson's introduction to the world of librarianship.

He had never intended to become a librarian but, when the position of librarian of the Chillicothe Public Library was offered to him in 1899, he accepted because he felt that it would be the ideal place to write novels in his spare time. "I thought I wouldn't stay very long," he recalled in later years, "but I found I could do my work there." Indeed, his first novel, *At Odds with the Regent*, was published by Lippincott in 1901. But Stevenson became interested in library work, so he remained on the job until his retirement in 1957—some 58 years after he had reluctantly accepted the position. When he first became librarian, Stevenson was expected to work from 9:00 a.m. until 9:00 p.m. daily for a salary of $50 a month. The novels he wrote during his first several years at the Library were intended to help supplement his income. These included *A Soldier of Virginia* (1901), *The Heritage* (1902), *Tommy Remington's Battle* (1902), *The Holladay Case* (1902), *The Marathon Mystery* (1904), and *Cadets of Gascony* (1904).

One might suspect that Stevenson was spending most of his time writing novels, but such was not the case. During his first years at the Library, he cataloged more than 7,000 books, and his careful method of indexing prepared the way for the detailed cross-indexed anthologies that were to become his

best-known legacies to the library field. His first anthology was *Days and Deeds: A Book of Verse* (1906), published while Stevenson was on a temporary leave of absence to the Logan Construction Company, a local automobile manufacturer. Its sequel, *Days and Deeds: Prose*, appeared the following year. Meanwhile, other novels were published: *The Girl with the Blue Sailor* and *Affairs of State* (1906), *The Young Train Dispatcher* and *That Affair at Elizabeth* (1907), *The Quest for the Rose of Sharon* (1909), and *The Path of Honor* (1910). Following his first trip to Europe, Stevenson wrote *The Spell of Holland* in 1911, the same year that saw the publication of *Favorite Poems in English*.

The first of Stevenson's great "Home" books, which became standard reference works, was *The Home Book of Verse* (1912). More novels followed: *The Mystery of the Boule Cabinet* and *The Young Apprentice* (both in 1912), *The Gloved Hand* (1913), *The Destroyer* (1913), *The Girl from Alsace* (1915), and another travel book, *The Charm of Ireland* (1913).

At the time of the American entry into World War I in 1917, Burton E. Stevenson, at age 45, had made no enduring contribution to either literature or librarianship. His books were popular but nonetheless ephemeral products not destined to take their place in our national literature. His tenure as librarian of a small public library in central Ohio was an unlikely appointment to place him in the front ranks of American librarianship. Nevertheless, by coincidence, Stevenson found himself in a position to organize a pioneer book service that would capture the imagination of both government officials and the American Library Association, that would take him to Paris, and that would eventually lead to the founding of the American Library in Paris. The accident that made this possible was the government's decision to locate a huge U.S. Army training center at Camp Sherman, on the outskirts of Chillicothe. During the summer of 1917, Stevenson organized a book service for the men stationed at Camp Sherman, and, with the help of the commandant, opened library collections in all the welfare centers at the Camp. A permanent library headquarters was later built there.

This ingenious project, carried out by volunteers working under Stevenson's direction, caught the attention of the federal government, and Herbert Putnam (q.v.), Librarian of Congress, was dispatched to Chillicothe to evaluate Stevenson's efforts. Immediately a plan for military library service was drawn up, and Stevenson was called to Washington to coordinate a national plan for collecting books. At the conclusion of the campaign, the War Department asked him to go to France to direct the Army Library Service in Paris, and, in March 1918, Stevenson and his wife sailed for France. During the next nine months, more than 3,000,000 books and magazines were distributed to American troops.

Following the Armistice, Stevenson had the idea of a permanent library in Paris that would serve as a center of information about American life and culture. He persuaded the American Library Association to appropriate a $25,000 endowment to finance his experiment. The books and equipment at his headquarters at 10 Rue de l'Élysée became the nucleus of the American Library in Paris, which was incorporated as a private nonprofit corporation on May 20, 1920. Satisfied that his new enterprise would survive without him, Stevenson returned to his native Chillicothe to resume his position as librarian and to continue his writing. This time, however, he returned home as a rather famous man and an important figure in the library world.

He was glad to be home, for, among other things, he always maintained that he could never write anyplace except in his home town. More books followed: *The Kingmakers* (1922), *Storm Center* (1924) and two more anthologies, *Famous Single Poems* (1923) and the *Home Book of Modern Verse* (1925). In an interview he gave several years after this well-known anthology had appeared, Stevenson explained how he worked up his information on thousands of index cards and managed the entire task himself without benefit of assistant editors or staff. But his scholarly pursuits were interrupted in late 1925 when he was asked to resume the directorship of the American Library in Paris. When he sailed to France in December, Stevenson expected to be gone for two years; he stayed nearly five.

During these years, Stevenson successfully persuaded private donors and foundations to contribute to the Library's endowment, enlarged the book collection, and extended its services throughout Europe. An arrangement with the French government permitted books to be mailed anywhere in France without cost. A similar arrangement was made with foreign embassies in Paris to extend this service to their own countries. A library school was also opened and, by 1928, some 25 international students were studying the techniques of American library service under Stevenson's supervision.

In June 1930, he resigned his post at the American Library and returned home to Chillicothe, where he resumed his writing and his work at the public library. Two novels appeared in 1932, *The House Next Door* and *The Mystery of the Villa Aurelia*, and, in 1934, his best-known compendium was published, *The Home Book of Quotations*. "I am not a real scholar," he said in a 1937 interview. "My only special virtue is, I guess, what you would call industry." Stevenson modestly reported that this anthology represented seven years of work without a

vacation, interrupted only by his service in Paris and the writing of novels for recreation.

During the years of World War II, Stevenson worked on *The Home Book of Proverbs, Maxims, and Familiar Phrases*, which was published in 1948 after nearly nine years of work. He was reported to be "as eager for the issuance of this book as he was to see his first news item printed when he was a cub on the Chillicothe newspapers." The capstone of his career was the *Home Book of Bible Quotations* (1948) and the *Home Book of Shakespeare Quotations* (1953). He finally retired from his position as librarian of the Chillicothe Public Library in 1957, at the age of 85.

Even as an elderly man, Stevenson was impressive. Although he was not tall, he had an air of dignity created by a full head of white hair and large dark eyebrows. He was also known for his waspish humor, his sometimes cantankerous manner, and his generous spirit. Since he had been orphaned early in life, he always took a keen interest in underprivileged children. The bulk of his estate, valued at more than one million dollars at the time of his death in 1962, was left to "The Burton E. Stevenson Endowment for Children" to provide scholarships and financial aid for underprivileged children in Chillicothe and Ross County. But this was just one of his legacies. A more permanent one is the great library in Paris that remains the continuation of his ideals, and the several shelf feet of books that have become a part of standard public library collections. If the life of Burton E. Stevenson can be summarized, it might best be done with one of his favorite quotations from Emerson: "The high prize of life, the crowning fortune of man, is to be born with a bias to some pursuit which finds him in employment and happiness." He died at Chillicothe, Ohio, on May 13, 1962, a few months short of his ninetieth birthday.

Biographical listings and obituaries—[Obituary]. *Ohio Library Association Bulletin*, July 1962; [Obituary]. *Wilson Library Bulletin*, Sept. 1962; *Twentieth Century Authors*. Stanley J. Kunitz, ed. (1942 ed.; 1955 ed.); *Who Was Who in America* IV (1961-1968). **Books and articles about the biographee**—Bone, Larry Earl. "The American Library in Paris." *American Libraries* 1:279-82 (March 1970); Davis, Walter L. "A Chair on the Boulevard: Meet Mr. Stevenson." *Cleveland Plain Dealer*, Dec. 29, 1928; Goulder, Grace. "Burton Stevenson, Chillicothe's Author-Librarian." *Cleveland Plain Dealer*, Feb. 26, 1950; Rigney, Eugene D. "Burton E. Stevenson." In William Coyle, ed., *Ohio Authors and Their Books*. Cleveland: World Publishing, 1962; Vince, Thomas L. "The Legacy of Burton E. Stevenson." *Journal of Library History* 9:73-82 (Jan. 1974); Walley, Harold R. "Librarian to a Nation." *Princeton Alumni Weekly*, Sept. 24, 1937, pp. 27-29; Weed, John Merrill. "A Very Bookish Man." *Columbus Dispatch*, May 12, 1974. **Primary sources and archival materials**—Papers of Burton Stevenson relating to the Army Library Service and the American Library in Paris are at the Library of Congress, along with Stevenson's correspondence with literary figures and publishers. Some collateral material is also on file at the American Library Association archives at the University of Illinois. Stevenson's unsorted literary manuscripts are at the McKell Library, Ross County Historical Society, Chillicothe, Ohio, and his public library records and scrapbooks are at the Public Library of Chillicothe and Ross County, Ohio.

—THOMAS L. VINCE

STROHM, ADAM JULIUS (1870-1951)

Adam Julius Strohm was born in Venersberg, Sweden, on February 16, 1870, the son of John and Ida Wettervik Strohm. He was married to Cecilia McConnel of Winnetka, Illinois, in 1902, and they had two children, Harriet and John G. Adam Strohm received the B.A. degree at the University of Upsala in 1888, a B.L.S. from the Library School of the University of Illinois in 1900, and an honorary LL.D. degree from Wayne State University on June 12, 1941. He was library assistant at the University of Illinois (1899-1900), librarian of the Armour Institute of Technology in Chicago (1900-1901), and of the Public Library of Trenton, New Jersey (1901-1911). In 1911, he became assistant to the librarian of the Detroit Public Library. In 1913 he became acting head and, also in 1913, librarian, of the Detroit Public Library. In 1930, he was elected president of the American Library Association. After retirement from Detroit in 1941, he served as acting Wayne County Library librarian from June 22, 1944, to December 31, 1945.

Adam Strohm came into the library field at a crucial time in the history of free public libraries, when they were about to reach out into a broader field of service. He is credited with leading the Detroit Public Library into the modern age of library service. Under his direction the city library system grew from the old, outmoded building in downtown Detroit with nine branches to a palatial Italian Renaissance building in the new cultural center with twenty-two branches. When, during a mayoral campaign, the new Public Library building was made an issue, some charging that money could be saved by substituting cheaper materials, Adam Strohm was ready with his usual eloquence, "A building should be [a] dignified and proper self expression of its purpose and of the spirit within; the revelation of one's self is largely by the 'front' we make; our modes of expression, our taste revealed and good manners practiced in public and private."

Strohm's vision of the type of service a library should supply had equal impact. Feeling that such an institution should be more than a mere repository for books, he was an early advocate of publicizing the library as a service to the public. He maintained that no unnecessary restrictions should be placed on the use of books, required no deposit or surety for withdrawing books, did away with railings and gates, and, wherever possible, made more books available

and within reach of readers. He believed that the public library's function was to encourage the public to come to it with problems and inquiries, that the library should be a source of information to the average citizen, and that it should be a sort of neighborhood club house. Many pamphlets and circulars were printed and distributed to acquaint the public with this new aspect of the Detroit Public Library's role, and Strohm may be considered a pioneer in advancing many of the ideas that are now a part of the philosophy of modern libraries. He had an antipathy for statistics as a measure of service, maintaining that cost accounting was not applicable to libraries. He strove for quality in both the materials presented and the attendants, so he insisted on better training for librarians. He worked for this both within the American Library Association and in the Detroit system, providing training classes for librarians and encouraging additional education for the staff.

Strohm's activities in the American Library Association brought him recognition as a generator of ideas in the library field. His activities as chairman of the Board of Education for Librarianship (1924-1928), which involved visiting training institutions and setting up criteria for educating librarians, gave him added prominence. The visits, as he reported, were "purposeful tours, with the day's work and movement responsibly planned." The report leaves no doubt that both the five members of the Board and the library schools they visited were kept well aware of their mission. Unfortunately, Adam Strohm's year in office as president of the ALA was marked by financial crisis. Thus, his energies were mostly directed toward increasing membership and raising funds to form an endowment (to replace funds no longer forthcoming from other sources). The drive was successful, but it may have prevented him from moving in other, more creative areas. In 1935, he was appointed ALA's delegate to the Second International Library and Bibliographic Congress in Spain.

Among Adam Strohm's publications were *Bibliography of Cooperative Cataloging and the Printing of Catalog Cards with Incidental References to International Bibliography and the Universal Catalog (1850-1902)*, with Torstein Jahr (reprinted from the *Report of the Librarian of Congress*, Washington, 1903) and *Wayne County Library, The First Twenty, 1920-1940* (the author, 1942). He began a journal, *Library Service*, published by the Detroit Public Library from 1917 to 1939, of which he was editor and chief contributor. He also wrote many articles and speeches, two of which are "The Detroit Public Library—A Municipal Temple of All Faiths," in *Architecture* (44, no. 1:203-205 [1921]) and an English translation of the dedication preface of Peter

Kalm's *Travels*, published in *Pennsylvania Magazine of History and Biography* (36:17-29).

Adam Strohm was a complex man, combining a certain noblesse with a love for the democratic traditions of his adopted country. A brisk, abrupt manner covered a dry humor that appears in his personal correspondence; his austere manner probably resulted from his essential honesty and hatred of sham and hypocrisy. His tendency toward scholarly pursuits contrasts with his love of the out-of-doors and physical activity, including curling in winter and golf in the summer. He maintained a summer home in northern Michigan and practiced ecology before it was popular. His severe aspect and gruffness of speech (increased by a heavy accent) had a frightening effect on many subordinates, but those who could stand up to him found him quite ready to negotiate his most autocratic decisions. His baronial aspect was strengthened by his well-tailored clothing and his good physique. Although of average height, he seemed taller, probably because of his erect posture and bearing. He had high standards and did not easily accept less than perfection. Many stories were told of his hot temper, but the staff was aware that he tried to be fair and had been known to apologize if he later decided he was wrong. Also, the employees of the Library were of great concern to him, as was exhibited on several occasions when he was on vacation in his summer home north of Detroit. Upon learning that the temperatures in Detroit had reached a certain unbearable height, he would telephone the Library to order that workers who could be spared should go home.

Strohm was a firm believer in equal rights for women, and he publicly stated that women should have the vote. He carried out his beliefs in personnel policies, requiring young men in library work to work up through the ranks rather than placing them in high positions at the start, a common practice in public libraries.

Considered rather an idealist and a dreamer by his fellow workers, Adam Strohm also got practical results. In one of his articles written for the *Detroit Saturday Night* Book Number (November 27, 1915), he puts some of his philosophy into words:

The restless rush of modern life is inimical to the contemplative mood in which alone the companionship of good books can be sought with profit. The fact is, much harm has been done by this quite prevalent idea that every unoccupied moment is wasted, and that it is a crime to sit and dream a while. To be always doing and never thinking is the greatest mistake in the world; those who have done fine deeds in almost any sphere, from the arts to engineering and commerce, are aware that it pays to let the mind lie fallow and

the memorable idea often comes when the brain ceases from planning and accepts the quiet hour as a grateful gift.

Adam J. Strohm died in Fletcher, North Carolina, on October 30, 1951.

Biographical listings and obituaries—"Adam Strohm—a Memorial." *The Michigan Librarian*, Dec. 1951, p. 9; [Obituary]. *Detroit Free Press*, Oct. 31, 1951; [Obituary]. *Detroit News*, Oct. 31, 1951; *Who Was Who in America* V (1969-1973); *Who's Who in Library Service*, 1st ed., 2nd ed. **Books and articles about the biographee**—"Adam Strohm." *Michigan Librarian* (June 1941), pp. 4-6; Albinson, Grace. "Detroit's Popular Librarian." *The American Swedish Monthly* (June 1941); [Biographical sketch]. *Bulletin of Bibliography* 15, no. 1:1-2 (May-Aug. 1933); Burton, Clarence M. *The City of Detroit, Michigan, 1701-1922*. Detroit, 1922, v. III, p. 155; "Who's Who in the ALA: The New President." *ALA Bulletin* 24:281-82 (July 1930); Woodford, Frank B. *Parnassus on Main Street: A History of the Detroit Public Library*. Detroit: Wayne State University Press, 1965. **Primary sources and archival materials**—The Adam Julius Strohm Papers, 1919-1947 (six boxes), are in the Burton Historical Collection of the Detroit Public Library.

—ALICE C. DALLIGAN

SWEM, EARL GREGG (1870-1965)

Researchers in Virginiana have reason to be grateful to Earl Gregg Swem, the foremost bibliographer of Old Dominion materials. The son of Edward Lawrence and Emmeline Luse Swem, he was born in Belle Plaine, Iowa, on December 29, 1870. After his preliminary education, he attended Lafayette College in Easton, Pennsylvania, taking an A.B. in 1893, and an A.M. in 1896. He was awarded honorary doctorates by Lafayette in 1926, Hampden-Sydney College in 1925, and the College of William and Mary in 1941.

A library career spanning 75 years began in 1887, when he worked as a high school student at the Iowa Masonic Library in Cedar Rapids, Iowa. After spending his immediate post-graduate years teaching in a New York preparatory school, Swem took a course in library methods offered by the Wisconsin State Library Commission; he was employed at the John Crerar Library in Chicago in 1899. He then served as cataloger and indexer for the Superintendent of Documents Library in Washington, D.C., from 1900 to 1901, when he returned to Chicago to the library of the Armour Institute (predecessor to the Illinois Institute of Technology). In 1903, he accepted the job of chief of the Catalog Division in the Copyright Office at the Library of Congress, serving until 1907.

Swem's connection with Virginia bibliography began with his twelve years as assistant librarian at the Virginia State Library from 1907 to 1919. Responding to the needs of researchers and legislators, Swem compiled nearly forty finding lists and bibliographies of books, manuscript materials, and historical records housed at the State Library. These include *A Bibliography of the Conventions and Constitutions of Virginia* (1910), *Maps Relating to Virginia in the Virginia State Library* (1914), *A Register of the General Assembly of Virginia, 1776-1918* (1918), and the three-volume *Bibliography of Virginia* (1915-1919), which gave rise to the expression "not in Swem" as denoting an extremely rare piece of material.

When Dr. J. A. C. Chandler became president of the College of William and Mary in 1919, he invited Swem to take the post of librarian. Serving until 1944, Swem built the William and Mary library collection from 25,000 books and 20,000 manuscripts to more than 240,000 books and approximately 400,000 manuscripts. He directed much energy toward the acquisition and care of both private and public papers of Virginians, travelling around the state and encouraging gifts and bequests through numerous articles in learned journals. His constant theme was that Virginia materials belonged in Virginia repositories, and success crowned his efforts.

On taking his position at William and Mary, Swem took immediate steps to establish greater rapport with patrons. He opened the stacks to both students and the public, taking the view that materials were for use. He offered lectures in library orientation for all students and specific library instruction for library assistants. He was managing editor of the *William and Mary Quarterly*, second series (1921-1943), was a member of the Board of Editors for the third series, served on advisory boards of the Historians of Colonial Williamsburg, the Institute of Early American History and Culture, the Williamsburg Restoration's committee for historical documents, and was honorary advisor to the National Park Service. In honor of his services in building up the William and Mary library collection and the status of historical research throughout the area, the new library of the College of William and Mary (dedicated in February 1966) was designated the Earl Gregg Swem Library.

In 1931, Swem took a leave of absence from his library work to compile his *magnum opus*, the *Virginia Historical Index* (1934-1936). Virginia's seven major historical publications, a total of 120 periodical volumes, are here indexed by name, place, and subject with copious cross references. Data for three centuries of Virginia history can now be located quickly and precisely. The work is a unique and invaluable treasure trove for historians of Virginia.

Swem was active in professional organizations, maintaining membership in the American Library Association, the American Library Institute, the American Antiquarian Society, the Virginia Historical Society, the Bibliographical Society of America (of which he was president in 1937-1938), the Virginia

Library Association (which he served as president in 1927-1928), the Society of American Archivists, and others.

Following his retirement from the College of William and Mary in 1944, Swem served as librarian emeritus and remained active in his bibliographic studies, penning numerous articles and prefaces. In 1957, he edited a series of 23 booklets commemorating the three hundred fiftieth anniversary of the first successful English colony at Jamestown. He personally presented a set to the visiting Queen Elizabeth II of England. In 1961, Swem moved to Louisville, Kentucky, but he maintained ties with Virginia and Virginiana until his death at age 94 on April 14, 1965. He was survived by his wife, Lilia Slaughter Hansbrough Swem, whom he had married in 1907, and by their one son.

Biographical listings and obituaries–[Obituary]. *College and Research Libraries* 26:352 (July 1965); [Obituary]. *Library Journal* 90:2526 (June 1, 1965); *Who's Who in Library Service*, 1st ed., 2nd ed., 3rd ed. **Books and articles about the biographee**–"Birthday of a Bibliographer." *Library Journal* 86:774 (Feb. 15, 1961); "Earl Gregg Swem." American Antiquarian Society. *Proceedings*, n.s. 75:220-22 (Oct. 1965); Servies, James A. *Earl Gregg Swem: A Bibliography*. Williamsburg, Va.: The College of William and Mary, 1960; Servies, James A. "Dr. Swem's Fiftieth Anniversary." *Virginia Librarian* 4:29-31 (Jan. 1958).

—MICHAEL B. WESSELLS

TAUBE, MORTIMER (1910-1965)

Mortimer Taube was born in Jersey City, New Jersey, December 6, 1910, the son of Solomon and Bertha Solosko Taube. From 1927 to 1930, he was a student at Rutgers University, but he eventually received his B.A. degree from the University of Chicago in 1933, where he was also elected to membership in Phi Beta Kappa. He studied at Harvard during 1931-1932 and received his doctorate from the University of California at Berkeley in 1935. Philosophy was his academic major. In 1936, he received the certificate from the School of Librarianship of the same university. On March 23, 1939, he was married to Bernice Schwartzman; they had three children: Susan Rose, Donald, and Deborah.

Taube was a teaching fellow in philosophy at the University of California at Berkeley (1932-1935), circulation librarian at Mills College (1936-1937), and cataloger at Rutgers University Library (1938-1940). In 1940, he moved to Duke University to become head of acquisitions, remaining there until 1944, when he went to the Library of Congress, first as assistant chief of general reference and bibliography; in 1945, he was appointed assistant director of acquisitions. He headed the Library's mission to Europe in 1946 to acquire foreign materials and was also head of the Library's Science and Technology Project from 1947 to 1949. From 1949 to 1958, he served as a consultant in science documentation and was a member of the Research and Development Board of the Department of Defense in 1948. He was deputy chief of the Technical Information Service of the Atomic Energy Commission (1949-1952) and a member of the Surgeon General's Committee on Medical Indexing. He served as a consultant to UNESCO's Committee on Bibliography (1950-1953).

In 1952, he founded Documentation Inc., and was chairman of its Board from that time until his death. He also served for brief periods as adjunct professor on the faculties of the Graduate Library School of the University of Chicago and the School of Library Service at Columbia University. In 1952-1953, he was editor of *American Documentation*, and he was the first recipient of the Special Libraries Association award for distinguished contributions to special librarianship in 1952.

Taube was the author of a number of books (in addition to many articles in library and other professional journals): *Causation, Freedom, and Determinism* (1936); a manual for bibliographers at the Library of Congress (1944) with Helen Conover; a series of five little volumes on coordinate indexing (1953-1959); and *Information Storage and Retrieval: Theory, Systems, and Devices* (1958). Probably his best-known work was *Computers and Common Sense: The Myth of the Thinking Machines* (1961), which was very favorably reviewed.

Taube died suddenly on September 3, 1965, after a severe heart attack following an excursion on his private boat.

Mortimer Taube's contribution to and influence upon librarianship are difficult to evaluate after so short an historical perspective—viewed, as it must be, against the background of controversy, dogmatism, and polemics that characterized the documentation movement in the 1950s and 1960s. In a number of ways, he can be regarded as the Melvil Dewey (q.v.) of mid-twentieth century American librarianship. That he was an extremely shrewd and successful businessman is evident from his having built Documentation Inc. into a multi-million dollar industry, and at his death, he was a wealthy man. But he was much more than an entrepreneur, or one who saw librarianship as ripe for economic exploitation. Unlike Dewey, he was a dedicated intellectual, a scholar with substantial academic capabilities. Though he characterized himself as a documentalist, he was very proud of his professional library background and his ability to weld successfully conventional librarianship and the then-emerging information science. Though not the first to make use of coordinate indexing and uniterms, he gave both techniques wide currency and practical applicability in many conventional library situations.

He failed through his inability to perceive the inherent fallacy in the coordinating of terms that leads inevitably to confusion by coordinating "library" and "school" into signifying either "school library" or "library school." Thus, his system was subject to what the computer engineer knows as "noise" and "false drops." But eventually he did perceive his error in insisting both on uncontrolled vocabulary in indexing and on his belief that the terms used in a document being indexed were adequate for the subject indexing of that document. His personal slogan was "seek simplicity and distrust it," but he did not always distrust his own simple explanations. Of him, Maurice F. Tauber wrote in *Library Resources and Technical Services* (9:495-96 [Fall 1965]):

> He was among the gad-flies of the profession, irritating, and forcing the less energetic to think. He was sometimes impatient with his critics, yet he was always helpful without many people knowing of his many acts of kindness to colleagues, friends, and students. A pioneer thinker and synthesizer, he fought hard for his convictions.

Tauber might also have added that Mortimer Taube fought vigorously against the extreme beliefs of engineers that computers could solve all of our information retrieval problems. He did, at times, oversimplify the complex; but his systems and techniques for retrieving scientific and technical content of graphic records did work—worked better, often, than the underlying philosophy suggested it might. This fact leads to consideration of the possibility that the retrieval of recorded knowledge may not be as complex as some of us believe, and that that mysterious mechanism we call the brain may well be capable of filling in for itself the lacunae in any information retrieval system. Perhaps the simple is more trustworthy than we tend to believe.

Biographical listings and obituaries—[Obituary]. *Library Journal* 90:4041 (Oct. 1, 1965); [Obituary]. *Library of Congress Information Bulletin* 24:489-90 (Sept. 7, 1965); [Obituary]. *Medical Library Association Bulletin*, Oct. 1965, pp. 686-87; *Who Was Who in America* IV (1961-1968); *Who's Who in Library Service*, 2nd ed. **Books and articles about the biographee**—Tauber, Maurice F. "Mortimer Taube." *Library Resources and Technical Services* 9:495-96 (Fall 1965); White, H. S. "In Memoriam: Dr. Mortimer Taube." *Special Libraries* 56:603 (Oct. 1965).

—JESSE H. SHERA

THWAITES, REUBEN GOLD (1853-1913)

Reuben Gold Thwaites was born at Dorchester, Massachusetts, on May 15, 1853, shortly after his parents migrated from England. When he was thirteen, the family moved to a farm near Omro, Wisconsin, where he attended public school. Later, he moved to New Haven, Connecticut, working as a reporter while taking a few courses at Yale's Sheffield Scientific School.

Still in his early twenties, Thwaites returned to Wisconsin as a newspaper man, and, in 1876, became managing editor of the (Madison) *Wisconsin State Journal.* Six years later, he was married to Jessie Inwood Turville, who later bore his son Frederic. After two years as assistant secretary, Thwaites succeeded Lyman Copeland Draper (q.v.) as secretary of the State Historical Society of Wisconsin. From this base, he was to achieve eminence in three fields: as a librarian, as an historical editor and writer, and as a key figure in the evolution of the American historical society.

To the substantial general library that Draper had assembled, Thwaites brought order, system, and a new professionalism. Methodical collecting raised the annual accession rate from 2,000 to 10,000 titles, and Wisconsin newspapers, government documents, and the records of early Wisconsin settlers became areas of major emphasis. A card catalog replaced the triennial printed lists of new acquisitions. Also, the noted Commons-Ely collection on organized labor was begun.

As early as 1897, Thwaites began collecting the transcripts of European archival material significant to the history of the Upper Mississippi Valley. He was one of those in the American Historical Association who sparked the cooperative foreign archival guide and transcript programs of the turn of the century. Furthermore, he organized a cooperative program among the historical societies of the Upper Mississippi Valley to assist and supplement this work in the French archives and later in Washington. In 1907, he was able to persuade the legislature to designate by law the State Historical Society of Wisconsin as the state's official archival agency. Under his leadership, the Society became one of the country's major resource centers for the study of American—particularly western American—history.

Intellectually, Thwaites was deeply influenced by the Progressive movement, which for the generation of Robert M. LaFollette, Sr., dominated Wisconsin public thinking. This was throughout much of the country a period of unquestioning faith in the perfectability of mankind through education, the social gospel, and the extension of political democracy.

Thwaites thus regarded the library as a great resource, not just for the scholar, but for educating the "masses." He was active in the development of libraries donated by Andrew Carnegie (q.v.) in Wisconsin, a founding member of the Wisconsin Library Association (1891), a long-time member of the Wisconsin Free Library Commission (1895), and a crusader for the Commission's travelling library (1896). He also advocated open stacks, children's rooms, rooms for the blind, interlibrary loans, and

philanthropic support to augment limited public funds. Member number 756 of the American Library Association, he attended sixteen of its national conventions, served on its Council, and was a charter member of the American Library Institute. He was ALA president 1899-1900.

As an editor, Thwaites produced 170 volumes, the most notable being the *Jesuit Relations* (73v., 1896-1901), *Early Western Travels* (32v., 1904-1907), and *The Original Journals of the Lewis and Clark Expedition* (8v., 1904-1905). He also wrote fifteen books, the more serious of them centering on Wisconsin and the early West. He contributed volumes to both the American Nation and American Commonwealth series, and he wrote the semicentennial history of the University of Wisconsin. He also published some eighty articles, pamphlets, and reports, and seven *Handbooks* and seventy *Bulletins of Information* of the State Historical Society.

But Thwaites's major contribution was his impact on the democratization of the state and local historical society. Collecting, preserving, editing and writing—at which Thwaites excelled—had been the traditional activities of the historical society. To them, he added the popular dimension.

Believing that local history was essential background for intelligent citizenship, he enlisted everyone he could in what became a grand design. He got the Federation of Women's Clubs and the state Archaeological Society to mark significant sites. He got the legislature to establish a Civil War History Commission to observe the fiftieth anniversary of the War and to publish ten volumes of source material. He persuaded the Sons of the American Revolution (Wisconsin) to finance three volumes of Draper Manuscripts on the Revolution, editing both sets of volumes himself. He built a broad, state-wide membership and a state-wide Board, and had the annual meetings held at various cities around the state. For the fiftieth anniversary of Wisconsin statehood (1898), he proposed an elaborate scheme to put industry, agriculture, schools, and women to work on various aspects of Wisconsin history, but the outbreak of the Spanish-American War aborted his plans.

Thwaites regarded the historical museum—well organized and well lighted, telling a story with attractive labels—as an educational vehicle less sophisticated than the research library but much more attractive to the public. He tied special exhibits to Madison convention dates, circulated exhibits to schools, and encouraged pageants and observances of historical anniversaries to stimulate public interest in history. He sponsored the founding of local societies, auxiliary to the state society. He accepted the state's first historic site and fought alongside the Women's Clubs to preserve the first Territorial capitol.

He carried the doctrine of public education and public participation from coast to coast, speaking, writing, and working with his fellow librarians, historians, and historical society colleagues. Within the American Historical Association, he launched the Conference of Historical Societies, which became the American Association for State and Local History in 1941. No part of Thwaites's program seems to have been unique or original; rather, it was eclectically developed from ideas generated elsewhere. But in tying the many pieces together, he built what his friend Frederick Jackson Turner recognized as "a new type of state historical society," the Progressive or Western type of society. By 1910, his example had been widely copied throughout the West, and today his influence is felt by nearly every historical society in the country.

Thwaites died suddenly on October 22, 1913. Librarians had awarded him their two highest honors. Historians had elected him president of the Mississippi Valley Historical Association (now the Organization of American Historians). The University of Wisconsin had conferred on him an honorary LL.D. At the time of his death, he was called by the *Wisconsin State Journal* the best-known man in Wisconsin outside of political life.

Biographical listings and obituaries—*Dictionary of American Biography* 9 (Louise Phelps Kellogg); *Dictionary of Wisconsin Biography*. Madison, 1960; Legler, Henry E., Charles H. Gould, and Victor H. Paltsits. "Reuben Gold Thwaites." *A.L.A. Bulletin* 8:128-29 (1914); *National Cyclopaedia of American Biography* 10; [Obituary]. *Wisconsin State Journal*, Oct. 14, 1913; Turner, Frederick J. *Reuben Gold Thwaites: A Memorial Address*. Madison, Wisc., 1914; *Who Was Who in America* I (1897-1942). **Books and articles about the biographee**—Lord, Clifford L., and Carl Ubellohde. *Clio's Servant: The State Historical Society of Wisconsin, 1846-1954*. Madison, 1967, Chaps. 6-10; Lord, Clifford L. "Reuben Gold Thwaites." *Wisconsin Magazine of History* 47:3-11 (Autumn 1963). **Primary sources and archival materials**—The Reuben Gold Thwaites papers are held by the State Historical Society of Wisconsin. Other papers are in the Administrative Files (Series 27/1/3) in the State Historical Society of Wisconsin Archives.

—CLIFFORD L. LORD

TICKNOR, GEORGE (1791-1871)

George Ticknor was born on August 1, 1791, to Elisha and Elizabeth Billings Curtis Ticknor. George's father was a prominent, if not overly wealthy, member of Boston society who sent his son to Dartmouth College at an early age. Later, he arranged to have George tutored in the classics by Dr. John Sylvester Gardiner, the acknowledged master of Latin and Greek in Boston. After several years of deliberate study, followed by several less serious years of work on the law, young Ticknor made the fateful decision to abandon the legal profession, and he simultaneously dismissed the idea of a career in politics as his

friends, Joseph Story, Daniel Webster, and Edward Everett had chosen. He also rejected the idea of a career in business, embracing instead a life of writing and research—"a life of letters"—and, as a preliminary to his career, went abroad for nearly four years of study, mostly at Göttingen.

Returning to Boston in 1819, Ticknor became the Abiel Smith Professor of the French and Spanish Languages and Literatures at Harvard. He held this post until 1835, when (with his fortunes bolstered by his wife's inheritance) he resigned to devote himself to research and writing, especially on his monumental *History of Spanish Literature* (1849, 3 vols.). From his impressive home on Boston's Beacon Hill, Ticknor ruled over the city's intellectual life and was looked to as one of the leading arbiters of intellectual and social affairs in the country. He was awarded LL.D. degrees by Harvard and Brown in 1850 and by Dartmouth in 1858.

In the 1850s, Ticknor, like his patrician friends, was growing more and more concerned about the tumultuous and riotous nature of the times. He was especially concerned with the flood of rough and generally unlettered Irish immigrants into Boston. As the Standing Committee of the Boston Public Library reported in 1852, these new residents of Boston were not well educated, and thought "little of moral and intellectual culture." The *Report* concluded with the anxious query, "Where is the remedy for this influx of ignorance?"

George Ticknor felt that one means of uplifting the masses while ensuring the stability of the Republic would be to establish a public library that would be as popular as possible. The idea was to assimilate the "masses to our national character, and bring them in willing subjection to our own institutions." As a result he argued forcefully and inflexibly for the "popularization" of the Boston Public Library. The Library, he argued, would be the "crowning glory" of Boston's fine educational system, and it would "differ from all free libraries yet attempted; I mean one in which any popular books, tending to moral and intellectual improvement, should be furnished in such numbers of copies that many persons, if they desired it, could be reading the same work at the same time." One of his greatest legacies to the library profession is the 1852 *Report* of the Trustees of the Boston Public Library, written by Ticknor and his friend Edward Everett. The final portion of the famous *Report* is still considered one of the most articulate and influential statements ever penned on public library philosophy. Upon publication, this *Report* caught the attention of Joshua Bates, a wealthy financier and partner in the firm of Baring Brothers of London. After reading it, Bates decided to give Boston $50,000 to purchase books once the city fathers had provided a suitable library building.

The Library opened in 1854, with 12,000 volumes housed in two rooms.

All through the fifties, Ticknor took an active part in the operation of the Library, always alert that his original intent to make the Library as popular as possible not be subverted by less optimistic trustees or librarians. In 1856, he himself went abroad to purchase books for the Library in the European book centers and, in 1860, he donated some 2,500 volumes from his magnificent Spanish collection to the Library.

Ticknor retained his interest in the Boston Public Library until his death on January 26, 1871, having served actively on the Board of Trustees for thirteen years. While he was frustrated to find that the "middling sorts" were not frequenting the Library as often as he had hoped, he never lost his faith in it as one means of social control and mass education. His authorship of the 1852 *Report* and his highly influential efforts to make the public library as popular as possible easily place him at the very head of any list of "significant trustees" in American public library history.

Biographical listings and obituaries—*Dictionary of American Biography* 18 (Jeremiah D. M. Ford); *National Cyclopaedia of American Biography* 6; *Who Was Who in America*, Historical Volume (1607-1896). **Books and articles about the biographee**—Harris, Michael H. *The Role of the Public Library in American History: A Speculative Essay*. Occasional Papers. Urbana: Graduate Library School, University of Illinois, 1975; Harris, Michael H., and Gerard Spiegler. "Ticknor, Everett, and the Common Man: The Fear of Societal Instability as the Motivation for the Founding of the Boston Public Library." *Libri* 24:249-76 (1974); Shera, Jesse. *Foundations of the Public Library: The Origins of the Public Library Movement in New England, 1629-1855*. Chicago: University of Chicago Press, 1949; Tyack, David B. *George Ticknor and the Boston Brahmins*. Cambridge: Harvard University Press, 1967 [Contains a full bibliography of works by and about Ticknor] ; Wadlin, Horace G. *The Public Library of the City of Boston: A History*. Boston: published by the Trustees, 1911; Whitehill, Walter Muir. *The Boston Public Library: A Centennial History*. Cambridge: Harvard University Press, 1956. **Primary sources and archival materials**—The most important collection of Ticknor letters is located in the Archives of the Dartmouth College Library. Especially pertinent to his library activities are the collections at the Rare Books Room of the Boston Public Library, which focus on his efforts to create the Boston Public Library, and the Houghton Library at Harvard, which focus on his activities at that institution. A smaller collection of useful materials is housed in the Massachusetts Historical Society Library. Ticknor's *Life, Letters, and Journals...*, ed. George S. Hilliard, Mrs. Anna Eliot Ticknor, and Miss Anna Eliot Ticknor, was published in two volumes (Boston: J. R. Osgood and Co., 1876).

—MICHAEL H. HARRIS

TILTON, EDWARD LIPPINCOTT (1861-1933)

Edward Lippincott Tilton, the son of Benjamin and Mary Tilton, was born on October 19, 1861, in New York City. Tilton was married to Mary Eastman Bigelow on June 5, 1901. They had two children, Mary Elizabeth and Charles Edward; the son followed his father in the architectural profession.

Tilton obtained his early education in private schools in Mount Vernon and Chappaqua, New York. After receiving private tutoring in architecture, he entered the offices of McKim, Mead, and White [re Charles F. McKim, see H. H. Richardson]. In 1887, Tilton went to Paris to study at the École des Beaux-Arts for three years. Upon his return to the United States he again joined the McKim firm, together with William A. Boring, one of his fellow students at the École. In 1891 Boring and Tilton formed a partnership and began an independent practice.

In 1894, Tilton went to Greece for a year to assist in the excavation and restoration of the Argive Heraeum, an experience that was the beginning of his lifelong interest in archaeology. He became a fellow of the American Institute of Architects, a fellow of the Archaeological Institute of America, one of the organizers of the Society of Beaux-Arts Architects, and a member of the American Library Association. Tilton was a member of the Society of Friends (Quakers).

Tilton's first exposure to library architecture probably came while he was working for Charles McKim in 1890 and 1891. At that time, the McKim firm was designing and constructing the Copley Square building for the Boston Public Library. After forming their partnership, Boring and Tilton submitted designs in the architectural competitions for both the [Andrew] Carnegie [q.v.] Library of Pittsburgh in 1892 and the Milwaukee Public Library in 1893, although neither design won the commission. In the 1890s, the firm was selected to design the immigration facilities on Ellis Island, a project that brought the young architects recognition and a gold medal at the Paris Exposition.

After 1900, Tilton began to specialize in library architecture, with designs for library buildings at Juniata College; Mount Vernon, New York; Winston-Salem, North Carolina; Bayonne, New Jersey; and Warren, Ohio. Several of these buildings were constructed with funds provided by Andrew Carnegie, thus beginning a long association between Tilton and the Carnegie library programs. Prior to 1910, Tilton designed branch library buildings at Cleveland and Philadelphia, and a Carnegie building in Sulphur Springs, Texas.

The turning point in Tilton's career as a library building planner came in 1907, when he received the commission to design a new library for the City Library Association in Springfield, Massachusetts. By 1912, when the building was completed, Tilton, the trustees, and the librarian, Hiller C. Wellman (q.v.), had planned and supervised the construction of one of the best public library buildings of the early twentieth century. The Springfield building served as a model for a series of public libraries, including those at Wilmington and the Enoch Pratt Free Library in Baltimore. The Springfield building was the first in which Tilton planned a main floor that was free of permanent partitions and walls. This so-called "open plan" was the first step in a succession of library designs that evolved into the modular libraries of the 1940s and 1950s. Tilton placed the bookstacks underneath the main reading rooms, rather than at the rear of the building, as had been the common practice previously.

From 1912 to the start of World War I, Tilton planned library buildings for Somerville, Massachusetts; Elizabeth, New Jersey; Sioux City, Iowa; Manchester, New Hampshire; and the University of Notre Dame. During this period, Tilton also became active as a library planning consultant, especially for the Carnegie Corporation.

During World War I, he served as a volunteer architect for the Library War Service program of the American Library Association. With the support of the Carnegie Corporation, Tilton designed and supervised the construction of sixty libraries and thirty theaters for military posts.

Boring left the partnership with Tilton to become dean of the School of Architecture at Columbia University in 1915, and Tilton formed a partnership with Alfred Morton Githens (q.v.) at some time between 1916 and 1919. During the 1920s, the firm was responsible for planning a number of public and academic library buildings, including those for George Peabody College; Wilmington, Delaware; Highland Park, Michigan; a branch in Providence, Rhode Island; Emory University; the Welch Medical Library at Johns Hopkins University; and Girard College. Tilton and Githens were awarded a gold medal in 1925 for their Wilmington building.

In 1929, Tilton and Githens were appointed consulting architects to assist Joseph Wheeler (q.v.) in planning the Enoch Pratt Free Library building in Baltimore. The Enoch Pratt building, the largest project with which Tilton was associated, incorporated the major features of the Springfield, Somerville, and Wilmington buildings: open main floors and bookstacks below the reading rooms. These features of the Pratt Library and the subject department plan of its main floor were widely copied after 1933, as was the street-level entrance.

Tilton and Githens also designed art galleries in Manchester, New Hampshire, and Springfield, Massachusetts. At the time of his death, the firm was planning a natural history museum in Springfield, a post office in Manchester, a library at Girard College,

and the Bergen County building in New Jersey. These projects were completed by Githens.

A number of contributions to the literature of architecture and librarianship came from Tilton's pen. He wrote an article on Greek architecture for the *Dictionary of Architecture*, edited by Russell Sturgis (1901), and the chapter on the architecture of the Argive Heraeum in *The Argive Heraeum*, edited by Charles Waldstein (1902). In 1907 Tilton wrote a series on the designs of small libraries for the *Inland Architect*; a similar article appeared in *Public Libraries* in 1912. Tilton's article on "Scientific Library Planning" was published in *Library Journal* (September 1912). In this article, Tilton first used the term "module" to describe the interior of a library that was an open space set off by a series of columns. Two of his major contributions were "Library Planning" in *Architectural Forum* (December 1927) and "Library Planning and Design" in the same journal (June 1932). Tilton also wrote an article entitled "School Libraries" in *Library Journal* (March 15, 1930) and the chapter "College Library Planning" in the *American School and University* (1933). He was also a frequent speaker at state and national conferences.

A number of letters praising Tilton's library designs are included in the Carnegie Corporation correspondence, particularly in regard to the Springfield building. William H. Brett (q.v.), librarian of the Cleveland Public Library, wrote in a letter of May 5, 1911, to James Bertram (q.v.), Carnegie's secretary, that "I would rather have Mr. Tilton build than any one else." Tilton was one of the few architects who was able to translate into practice some of the ideas concerning library design expressed by John Cotton Dana (q.v.), Hiller Wellman, Sam Foss, and others. Through Tilton, many of the features of the modern library building were passed on to Alfred Githens, Joseph Wheeler, and Angus Snead Macdonald (q.v.): open and flexible interiors, free-standing shelving, and the use of bookstacks for infrequently used materials. Several of Tilton's major library buildings are still in use with few alterations to the exteriors.

Tilton died on January 5, 1933, just as the Enoch Pratt Free Library was being completed and occupied.

Biographical listings and obituaries—*Dictionary of American Biography* 9 (Talcot F. Hamlin); *National Cyclopaedia of American Biography* A; [Obituary]. *New York Times*, Jan. 6, 1933, p. 19; *Who Was Who in America* I (1897-1942). **Primary sources and archival materials**—Carnegie Corporation of New York, Carnegie Library Correspondence. The file contains letters from Tilton to James Bertram, and from Bertram to Tilton about plans for numerous Carnegie library buildings.

—DONALD E. OEHLERTS

TITCOMB, MARY LEMIST (1857-1932)

Mary Lemist Titcomb was born in 1857, in Farmingham, New Hampshire. Her parents, George Alfred and Mary Elizabeth Lemist Titcomb, had one other daughter and four sons. Young Mary was taught at home by her mother for several years, but later was graduated from the Robinson Female Seminary in Exeter, New Hampshire, the town where she grew up. She did not seriously consider a career until after the death of her father and the marriage of her brothers, when she began to seek some kind of work to keep herself occupied. After considering nursing as a possible vocation, an article in her church paper persuaded her to pursue librarianship as a career.

Since formal training was not available to her at the time, she began her informal library education as an unpaid assistant in the Concord, Massachusetts, Public Library. Her second position was that of cataloger in the Free Library of Rutland, Vermont, where she later became librarian in chief. She then became secretary for the Vermont Library Commission, one of the first two women to hold state office in Vermont. This post was followed by twelve years as a library organizer for Vermont, during which Mary Titcomb travelled throughout the state organizing new libraries and assisting in reorganizing established ones.

In 1900, the community of Hagerstown, Maryland, had begun construction of its first public library and sought a librarian to administer it. (The library became the Washington County Free Library, one of the first two county libraries in the United States.) When Mary Titcomb, a New Englander, was hired as director, support of her appointment was not unanimous. Many townspeople felt that a local resident should have been chosen for the post, and one local citizen echoed a general concern when he complained that "a foreigner should be brought here, when there were so many local persons who were well able to do that job."

The controversy was brief, however, for the new library thrived under Titcomb's guidance. In her attempt to make books available to the widely dispersed residents of the county, she set up small collections of books in churches, schools, and other public places. Each collection consisted of about fifty books, and users had the privilege of requesting additional titles through these deposit stations. Although, after three years, the number of deposit stations had grown to 66, many people in remote sections of the county remained unserved by the Library.

To remedy this problem, Titcomb conceived the idea of a "book wagon," which would transport books to all corners of Washington County. The book wagon, designed by Mary Titcomb herself, had shelf space for about 200 volumes on the outside and

inside storage spaces for cases of books; it was drawn by two horses. In her discussion of the service at the American Library Association Conference at Bretton Woods in 1909, she reported that no better method had been devised for delivering library services to the back country. "The book," she said, "goes to the man. We do not wait for the man to come to the book." In fact, Mary Titcomb had designed the first book wagon ever used in the United States, an idea quickly emulated by libraries throughout the nation.

Active in the ALA, Mary Titcomb served as a member of the ALA Council, as chairman of the Training Class Section, and as second vice-president of ALA in 1915. During World War I, she acted as state chairman of the American Library Association Library War Service campaign. At home in Hagerstown, she saw that her Library provided books and activities for the education of the community concerning the Great War. "It is only as the library can enter into the war work of the community," she later told the 1918 Conference of ALA, "that it can justify its right to existence in war time." Later in the War, she received military orders to visit Fort Leavenworth to make recommendations concerning library facilities there, and she took a leave of absence from her duties in Hagerstown to do so. After spending three months at Fort Leavenworth, she travelled to Charleston, South Carolina, to administer the book collection at the 6th Naval District, remaining there for ten months.

Another of Mary Titcomb's projects was the inauguration of training classes for librarians. The Washington County Free Library Training Class first met in 1924 to provide, in Titcomb's words (quoted in *Pioneering Leaders*):

elementary training in Library methods to girls with a high school education or its equivalent, and who are judged to be good library material, and to afford them an opportunity to get into the ranks of library workers in subordinate positions. This gives the girl who by reason of lack of education, or perhaps lack of means, cannot enter a Library School, an opportunity to become a self-supporting person and through evening courses, summer courses, etc., in time acquire sufficient credits for entrance to a Library School.

The most noteworthy aspect of these efforts was that they emanated from so small a library, for most training classes of that day were provided in larger urban libraries. Titcomb's classes continued until 1931.

Those who first met Mary Titcomb in her professional role as librarian often referred to the "frost" in her manner, or to her "New England temperament." As her neighbors grew to know her, however, they realized that she was a charming and fun-loving woman who entertained graciously in her home, the

"Library House." Described as a "short person with a rather plumpish figure," she wore clothes of dark blue or grey and was never seen on the street without her white gloves and hat. These were the styles of her time, though, and she was noted for being current with the latest fashions.

In 1926, the library world joined Hagerstown in celebrating Mary Titcomb's quarter century of service at the Washington County Free Library. In honor of the occasion, she received letters from every state in the nation and from all over the world. Her friends in Hagerstown presented her with a gift of money and a silver pitcher lengthily inscribed with an expression of their respect and affection. She later commented, "After twenty-five years I felt I really belonged to Hagerstown." Five years after this celebration, Mary Titcomb became seriously ill, and she died on June 5, 1932.

Biographical listings and obituaries—*Who Was Who in America* I (1897-1942). **Books and articles about the biographee**—Holzapfel, Mary Louise. *The Washington County Free Library 1901-1951.* Hagerstown, 1951; Wilkinson, Mary S. "Mary L. Titcomb." In Emily Miller Danton, ed., *Pioneering Leaders in Librarianship.* Chicago: American Library Association, 1953; Willis, K. T. "Mary Lemist Titcomb." *Library Journal* 57:874 (Oct. 15, 1932). **Primary sources and archival materials**—Transcripts of speeches delivered in honor of Mary Titcomb are held by the Washington County Free Library in Hagerstown, Maryland.

—JUDITH BRAUNAGEL

TOMPKINS, MIRIAM DOWNING (1892-1954)

Miriam Downing Tompkins was born in Kalispell, Montana, on April 2, 1892, the daughter of John A. B. and Therese La Due Tompkins. Having received her early education in Milwaukee and elsewhere in Wisconsin, she attended the Milwaukee State Teachers College (now the University of Wisconsin-Milwaukee) from 1910 to 1912. In 1916, she received her B.A. from the University of Wisconsin in Madison and her M.A. from the same university in 1917. In 1919, she became director of the training class for the Milwaukee Public Library. After a short period of teaching in one of the Milwaukee high schools, she returned to the Library in 1923 as chief of adult education.

Tompkins's major contribution to librarianship was her emphasis on the human element in library service and the importance of the individual patron. She was among the first to initiate special programs, particularly in adult education, book selection, and services to labor. Her belief that the public library was the most significant agency for adult education was evident throughout her work at the Milwaukee Public Library.

Her pioneering work with labor unions began with a request for these services from the county central labor body. A school for union members—The

Milwaukee Worker's College—had been organized, and the leadership of the school, realizing the importance of reading, requested help from the Library in encouraging the use of library materials. At Miriam Tompkins's instigation, a room at the central Library was provided for the use of these classes and a librarian was assigned to meet the needs of the students.

In order to determine these needs, Tompkins enrolled in a class in economics and labor problems. She also realized that before much headway could be made, those enrolled would have to be taught how to use the Library. With the full cooperation of the Library administration and the Milwaukee area labor leadership, classes visited the various departments in the Library for instruction. More immediately, when course instructors mentioned certain books, these were brought directly to the class. This service brought to Tompkins's attention the lack of available, readable books in the subjects most wanted—economics, labor history and problems, collective bargaining, etc.; she thus focused much of her attention on searching for these necessary materials.

The Milwaukee Worker's College was governed by a Board of Trustees under the direction of the Federated Trade's Council, the Milwaukee County central labor body. Three students were selected by their fellow students to represent them on the Board, and Tompkins was accepted so fully that she was elected to the Board of Trustees as one of the student representatives.

As she became acquainted with the labor leadership, she requested and was granted credentials for two members of the Library staff to visit the unions to inform them of services available through the Library. (Credentials were rarely given to non-union members.) Additionally, a letter from the Council was sent to each of its affiliated unions, requesting permission for the Library's representatives to address them, so these representatives were greeted cordially wherever they went. A librarian attended all meetings of the Council with a collection of books—recreational as well as those of special interest—and if delegates requested specific reading recommendations, the librarian worked closely with the readers' advisor in planning reading programs for them. Inquiries from individual unions requesting service were met by a librarian being assigned to visit the union meetings with a collection of books. In several cases, at the request of the union, collections were deposited in the place of employment, with the cooperation of management.

Although the American Federation of Labor rarely published articles by non-unionists in the *American Federationist* (their official periodical), Miriam Tompkins was asked to write an article that was published in the April 1927 issue under the title: "The Library and Workers' Education."

Tompkins was also one of the pioneers in the library adult education movement. The Adult Education Department at the Milwaukee Public Library offered three services: information service, group service, and readers' advisory service. The information service consisted of an index of all adult educational agencies in the community. A card catalog, revised twice a year, listed both by name of agency and by subject all available information. The group service was organized to assist adult agencies in the community, and the readers' advisory service was designed for the individual who wanted help in systematic reading. The readers' advisory service was very popular, since, after consultation between the patron and the readers' advisor, personalized reading lists were planned and the books were made easily available to the patron. When applicable, the American Library Association "Reading with a Purpose" pamphlets and their recommendations were used. Many years after the service was discontinued, patrons who had used it commented on how much they had appreciated it and how it had benefitted them. This service has been described in several articles written by Tompkins (*Wisconsin Library Bulletin* 19:460-62 [1923], *Wisconsin Library Bulletin* 24:30-32 [1928], *ALA Bulletin* 39:259-65 [September 1945], *NJ Library Bulletin* 14:113-23 [September 1946], and others). As she worked more and more with patrons whose reading ability varied a great deal, Tompkins realized the need for readable books in many subjects, a fact reflected in her article "What Is a Readable Book?" (*ALA Booklist* 3:195-97 [March 1934]).

While attending the Graduate Library School at the University of Chicago in 1930 on a grant from the [Andrew] Carnegie [q.v.] Foundation, she worked with Douglas Waples and Ralph Tyler on their study of the interests of groups and problems in adult reading that culminated in the book *What People Want to Read About*. Through her initiative, members of the Milwaukee Public Library staff helped in the study by having patrons at some of the industrial plants, the post office, the police department, and other agencies keep reading diaries. These staff members filled out questionnaires and in other ways helped determine what people needed in the way of reading materials.

After her year at the Graduate Library School, Miriam Tompkins returned to the Milwaukee Public Library for a short time and was then appointed to the faculty of the Library School of Emory University. Here again she showed her pioneering spirit by a new approach to the teaching of book selection. Her emphasis was always on the needs of the individual reader and his background, rather than on maintaining a balanced book collection. This approach made the lack of readable materials in many subjects readily evident.

In 1935, she left Emory for a year's further study at Yale. She then accepted a teaching position at the School of Library Service at Columbia University, where she was teaching at the time of her death. At Columbia, Tompkins taught courses in fundamentals of library service and in the reading interests and habits of adults. Her emphasis was, as usual, on the human aspect of library service and the importance of the individual as a person, not just as a library patron.

Miriam Tompkins was, in 1929, a delegate to the International Conference on Adult Education in Cambridge, England. In 1950, under a Fulbright grant, she made a survey of public library services in New Zealand. An active member of the American Library Association, she served on the Board of Education for Librarianship, the Adult Education Board, and many committees. She also was active in the American Association for Adult Education and served on many committees of that organization. She belonged as well to the New York Library Association and the American Association of University Women.

Tompkins had varied interests, particularly in travel, music, art, and the theater. One of her disappointments was the communist take-over of China, which prevented her from making a planned trip to that country.

Sigrid Edge, a close friend, wrote (*Bulletin of Bibliography* 18, No. 2:25 [September-December 1943]):

> When the history of the library's role in Adult Education is written, the name of Miriam Tompkins will appear early and often in the record. Although not a member of the first ALA committee which in 1925 set forth the adult educational aims of public libraries, she has been largely responsible for the interpretation and direction of those aims.

Matthew S. Dudgeon (q.v.), Milwaukee city librarian, wrote (in a letter now in her personnel file there) about Miriam Tompkins that

> I know of no one in the library profession who, by training, experience, professional achievements and standards, intellectual abilities and personal qualities, is better fitted to function effectively upon a library school staff. She is a most inspiring teacher and a wise and thoughtful advisor of those students with whom she comes in contact.

All of these professional qualities, combined with a great deal of personal charm and attractiveness, made her indeed an inspiration to those who were fortunate enough to know her. She died on March 2, 1954.

Biographical listings and obituaries–[Obituary]. *College and Research Libraries* 15:232 (April 1954); [Obituary].

Library Journal 79:612 (April 1, 1954), 79:998-1000 (June 1, 1954); [Obituary]. *Wilson Library Bulletin* 28:742-43 (May 1954), 28:841 (June 1954); *Who's Who in Library Service*, 1st ed., 2nd ed. **Books and articles about the biographee**—Edge, Sigrid A. "Miriam Tompkins." *Bulletin of Bibliography* 18:25-26 (Sept.-Dec. 1943). **Primary sources and archival materials**—Letter from Matthew S. Dudgeon, city librarian, Milwaukee—Miriam Tompkins Personnel File at Milwaukee Public Library.

—RUTH SHAPIRO

TUCKER, HAROLD WALTON (1915-1973)

Harold Walton Tucker was a prominent public library administrator who made notable contributions to librarianship in the area of social responsibilities. He was born in Waco, Texas, on March 24, 1915, to Earl M. (Sr.) and Martha Frances Chambers Tucker. He earned an A.B. degree from Rice University (1936), a B.S.L.S. from the University of Illinois library school (1938), and an M.A. from the University of Chicago Graduate Library School (1941).

His professional work experience was interrupted twice by military service. He began as reference assistant at the Enoch Pratt Free Library in Baltimore (1938-1940), then became head of the Technology Section of the Dayton, Ohio, Public Library (1940-1942). Harold Tucker served in the U.S. Army from July 1942 to February 1946 in the Medical Service Corps, rising in rank from private to captain. From 1946 to 1947, he was assistant librarian at the Gary, Indiana, Public Library. He was associate director of the St. Louis County Public Library (1947-1950), then returned to serve as city librarian of Gary (1950-1954). However, he was recalled into the Army during the Korean War, assigned to the Medical Library in Washington (1951-1952).

Tucker became director of the Queens Borough Public Library in 1954. During his almost twenty years at Queens he worked constantly to integrate the Library fully into the life of the community, and he creatively channelled the considerable talents of his staff to meet the educational and social needs of the borough. Under his direction, the Library developed innovative programs designed to reach the dramatically different economic and cultural groups of the two million citizens of Queens. Largely due to Tucker's tireless efforts, Queens now boasts a major reference and research center in Jamaica. This Central Library opened in 1966. During his administration, twelve new library buildings and nine major rental facilities were opened; eleven existing branches were expanded or rehabilitated, and seventeen additional new facilities were planned.

As chairman of the American Library Association's World's Fair Committee, Tucker was instrumental in gaining the support and cooperation which made possible "Library U.S.A.," one of the most popular attractions at the New York World's Fair during 1964 and 1965.

In the area of social responsibilities, however, Tucker made some of his greatest contributions to librarianship in general, and to the people of Queens in particular. Long before the concept of the "Great Society" was popularized by President Lyndon Johnson, Tucker was devising ways in which his Library could give meaningful assistance to the disadvantaged in Queens. In 1963, he was appointed chairman of the ALA Advisory Committee for the study of "Access to Libraries" undertaken by International Research, Inc. The study was designed particularly to examine racial segregation in Southern libraries, but it unearthed an appalling inequality of access in Northern libraries as well.

Harold Tucker made certain that Queens was in the forefront of efforts to remedy this situation. He put the study's findings to good use in justifying the building of sorely needed branch libraries in deprived districts of Queens. Then, armed with the 1960 U.S. Census showing that, in Queens, pockets of severe economic and cultural deprivation existed where parents were passing on a cultural lag to their children, he conceived "Operation Head Start"—picture book programs to give 3-to-5-year-olds an entry to reading. This program served as a catalyst for many others throughout the nation. From this beginning grew such outreach programs as the "Library-Go-Round," a motor vehicle that brought the picture book program to inner-city areas; the "Tell-a-Tale Trailer" to provide programs for school-age children during summer; and the "Library-in-Action," originally conceived to fill the needs of the borough's young people, but recently expanded to serve drug rehabilitation centers and the Long Island City House of Detention.

Under his guidance, Queens also sponsored the nation's first "community action" library, the Langston Hughes Library & Cultural Center in Corona-East Elmhurst. Involving the community in every step of its planning and providing leadership with unique restraint, Tucker matched the store-front library to the people's need.

He was a member of the ALA legislative committee that successfully mustered support for federal legislation to assist urban libraries. This culminated in passage, under the sponsorship of Congressman John E. Fogarty (q.v.), of the Library Services and Construction Act in 1964. As past president of the New York Library Association and chairman of its legislative committee, Tucker made a major contribution in effecting improved New York state legislation for libraries.

In spite of his many professional commitments, Harold Tucker was very actively involved in community organizations. He was a Trustee of

Jamaica Hospital, past president of the Rotary Club of Jamaica, and a member of both the Board of Managers of the Queens Central Young Men's Christian Association and the Jamaica Chamber of Commerce's Committee for the Development of Human Resources. He also contributed to professional library journals and served as a consultant to other public libraries.

In 1969, he was doubly honored by Queens citizens. He received a Brotherhood Award from the National Conference of Christians and Jews and was designated "Man of the Year" by the Central Queens YMCA.

Harold Tucker was married to Madlyn Hayward and they had three children. He died on April 4, 1973, after a brief illness, at the age of 58.

Biographical listings and obituaries–*Biographical Directory of Librarians in the United States and Canada*, 5th ed.; [Obituary]. *American Libraries* 4:349 (June 1973); [Obituary]. *Library Journal* 98:1435 (May 1, 1973); [Obituary]. *New York Times*, April 6, 1973, p. 44; [Obituary]. *Wilson Library Bulletin* 47:737 (May 1973); *Who's Who in Library Service*, 2nd ed., 3rd ed., 4th ed. Books and articles about the biographee–[Biographical sketch]. *Library Journal* 79:94 (May 15, 1954); [Biographical sketch]. *New York Library Association Bulletin* 11:67-68 (May 1963); "Mr. Harold W. Tucker Took Office as President of the New York Library Association." *New York Library Association Bulletin* 12:135 (Nov. 1964). Primary sources and archival materials–The Queens Borough Public Library holds material pertinent to Tucker and his administration.

–JOHN SOLOMITA

TYLER, ALICE SARAH (1859-1944)

Alice Sarah Tyler was born in Decatur, Illinois, on April 27, 1859. Her parents, John William (a Disciples of Christ minister) and Sarah Roney Tyler, had emigrated from Fayette County, Kentucky, as pioneer settlers on a farm about five miles east of Decatur. Alice Tyler was the youngest of their eleven children, and was actually the last of a family of fourteen, since her father had three children by a former marriage.

Alice Tyler was educated in Decatur schools and, as frequently happens with the last daughter in a large family, she remained at home with her aging parents until they died, her father in 1888, and her mother in 1892. She was not "home-bound," however, and she became interested in what was beginning to be a new profession–librarianship. She read extensively after completing her public school education, preparing herself to take a position as library assistant in the Decatur Public Library in 1887. She remained there until after her mother's death, and in 1893 (when 34 years old), entered the first class at the Library School (run by Katharine L. Sharp [q.v.]) at the Armour Institute in Chicago (the progenitor of the University of Illinois Library School).

After completion of the one-year course at Armour, Tyler received her library certificate (1894) and was invited by William Howard Brett (q.v.) to become head cataloger of the Cleveland Public Library. She was that Library's first professionally trained assistant, and her gifts for organization and practical management showed early in her career. She believed in efficiency and in using the latest aids and equipment in promoting this. She almost at once asked for two typewriters to improve the work of her catalogers at a time when some librarians felt such equipment was either a desecration of the proper library atmosphere or promoted lower quality workmanship. However, Alice Tyler recognized the distinction between unskilled "hand" work and the effective use of new resources. In her annual report for the year ending in August 1899, she unequivocally stated that "untrained and inexperienced helpers in the Catalog Department are a positive detriment rather than a help" and insisted on trained or better qualified staff members.

She was actively interested in Brett's development of special training courses in 1896 and gave lectures at the Summer School established by him. Her first formal teaching experience came at this time, and her lectures were primarily on accessions and on making shelf lists.

Tyler remained in Cleveland until 1900, when she accepted an invitation from Johnson Brigham, state librarian of Iowa and president of the newly organized Iowa State Library Commission, to become the Commission's first secretary. Even before leaving Cleveland, she began making plans for her new position and wrote to Brigham of her ideas concerning the promotion of library development in the state, the need for office help, and the desirability of careful, long-range planning.

The duties outlined for the Iowa Library Commission were "to give advice and counsel to all free and public school libraries in the state, to establish and organize new libraries, to improve those already established and to cooperate with the trustees of the State Library in developing the travelling library system." Tyler entered energetically into this second phase of her career and soon became a leader in library extension work of all sorts. She was an adviser of trustees, a prodder of holders of local and state purse-strings, and a publicizer of libraries and good library service to the citizens of Iowa.

For thirteen productive years, Alice Tyler devoted much of her energy and ability to inspiring others to all kinds of library development in Iowa. In the *Bulletin* of the Commission and in the *Library Journal*, her name appeared again and again in connection with the public addresses she gave, the dedication ceremonies she attended, the progress reports she made. She wrote numerous papers and spoke at many state and national library meetings on such varied topics as the "Form of Library Organization for a Small Town Making a Library Beginning," "A Modification of Subject Entries for Card Catalogs," "Necessary Steps in the Erection of a Library Building," "The Library as a Social Center," and "Advertising the Library."

During the thirteen years that Tyler was secretary of the Iowa Library Commission, the number of free public libraries in Iowa increased from 41 to 114, and centers receiving travelling book collections increased from 90 to over 700. Additionally, she was editor of the *Bulletin of the Iowa Library Commission* (later to become the *Iowa Library Quarterly*). She also helped to establish a summer course for training librarians at the State University of Iowa, and was its director from 1901 to 1912. During summers, she lectured on general library subjects, including statistics and reports, book selection and buying, library architecture and interior arrangement, library administration, and methods of popularizing a library. In 1906, the Iowa Library Commission undertook a new program of systematic development of institutional libraries throughout the state, with Tyler the guiding hand behind this development as well.

Alice Tyler believed firmly that among the responsibilities of any professional worker was that of active participation in professional organizations. She was secretary of the first Executive Committee of the League of Library Commissions, which was organized in 1904 to make possible cooperative work in connection with booklists, handbooks, and other printed matter needed by all state library commissions. She became its president in 1906-1907. In 1909-1910, she was second vice-president of the American Library Association and presided at one of the general meetings of the thirty-second annual meeting of the Association. She was also elected to its General Executive Board. In 1909, she was also honored by being elected to membership in the American Library Institute, which consisted of one hundred library leaders selected by the American Library Association.

In 1913, Tyler was invited to return to Cleveland to become director of the Library School at Western Reserve University, and, though she was most reluctant to give up her active library work, she felt that there was great need to improve the education and training of more professional librarians. Many tributes and expressions of regret at her leaving appeared in Iowa newspapers as well as in professional journals, and handsome farewell gifts and entertainments quite overwhelmed her before her departure for Ohio.

The Library School of Western Reserve University was founded in 1903 through the efforts of William Howard Brett (q.v.) and Charles Franklin Thwing; it was supported by a substantial gift from Andrew Carnegie (q.v.). Tyler had become, in 1906, a visiting lecturer on library administration and extension topics, so she was already quite well acquainted with the School. Julia M. Whittlesey had retired in 1911 as director, and Bessie Sargent-Smith, of the Cleveland Public Library, had filled in as acting director in 1912. There was some hesitation on Tyler's part, because she had never worked in an academic atmosphere and she was not sure she could be as effective in developing a small, struggling school as she was in public work; but with much encouragement from Thwing, the president of the University, she accepted the offer.

At the beginning of Tyler's directorship, the School had an enrollment of only nineteen regular and sixteen special students and gave no graduate courses. Entrance was achieved by passing very comprehensive examinations, and students received certificates after successfully completing the one-year course. A full college degree was not required. By 1929, when she retired, the graduating class numbered 76, and two degrees were available. A "combined" four-year course with the College for Women of the University (later Flora Stone Mather College), begun in 1915, gave a Bachelor of Science degree from the College; and a fifth-year B.S. in L.S. was given to those who came to the School with a baccalaureate degree.

Many changes and modernizations were made in the Western Reserve library science curriculum during Tyler's directorship. Her wide practical experience in the active library world made her very aware of the "bread and butter" kinds of training needed, but she also was aware of the need for improvement of the intellectual content of the courses taught. She also began to encourage men as well as women to enter the profession by way of a formal course of study.

In 1924, the name of the School was changed to the School of Library Science and non-credit courses were offered in the summers from 1924 to 1928. In 1925, the University recognized Tyler's extensive and tireless efforts by giving her the title of dean and professor of library science. In 1927, the School was accredited by the Board of Education of the American Library Association both as a graduate and as a junior undergraduate school.

Tyler was an outstanding library school director during a period of active ferment and growth in library education fields. She was an inspiring lecturer, full of vigor and positive idealism, but, at the same time, could give a down-to-earth flavor to her lectures. She seemed to know all the important people of the library world and would characterize them vividly to her students. Indeed, many of these leaders came to the School to give lectures and share their expertise.

Alice Tyler was a very handsome woman, with snow-white hair in her later years, carefully selected clothes, and a dignified, relaxed, yet assured manner at all times. Her ability to express herself well in public made her a model whom many of her fellow workers and students tried to emulate. Very conscious of the value of instruction in public speaking, she introduced it as an elective into the curriculum, with a leading member of the Cleveland Playhouse staff as instructor.

She encouraged her students to become members of professional groups and to contribute by service, writing, committee work, and other activities beyond their daily jobs; she took great pains to take students with her to conventions and smaller meetings and to introduce them personally to many of the leaders of the library world. In the last month before her retirement, she escorted almost the whole class of 1929 to Washington to the American Library Association conference and took care to see that the students met as many "celebrities" as possible.

Outside of the School of Library Science, Tyler set a superb example of professional involvement, and many honors came to her. She was elected president of the Ohio Library Association (1916-1917), and of the Association of American Library Schools (1917-1919). In 1920, she was elected the third woman president of the American Library Association, and she served with distinction. She had been a member of many committees before that time, and continued to contribute to committee work, to write, and to speak at many library meetings until well after her retirement. In addition, she was founder and first president of the Cleveland Library Club (1922-1923), a charter member of the Women's City Club, a long-time member of the Daughters of the American Revolution, and a director of the Adult Education Association, as well as a member of the Citizens' League of Cleveland, the Unitarian Club, and other organizations.

In 1929, when the School of Library Science celebrated its twenty-fifth anniversary, Alice Tyler retired. Alumni of the School contributed to a sizeable fund to be presented to her for travel, an avocation of which she was very fond. Over three hundred alumni and students attended her retirement dinner, and she received numerous letters of congratulation, mixed, of course, with regrets. The relief from active administrative work then left her with time for the many other professional and non-professional interests that she enjoyed. She was still much in demand as a speaker and library consultant, and she continued to contribute to library periodicals until 1938. Her last paper ("In Reply to 'The Weaker Sex?' " *Library Journal* 63:294 [April 15, 1938]) was a staunch defense of women as heads of large libraries.

One of the first things Tyler did after retirement was to sign up for a course in Greek civilization at Cleveland College and to strengthen a long-time interest in reading translations of the old Greek philosophers. Her hobbies, besides travel, consisted of collecting rare book-plates, especially early American ones, and cat figurines, of which she accumulated over 500.

In October 1938, she broke her hip in a fall, and, although this cut down her outside activity, it in no way slowed her mental ability. Alice Sarah Tyler died just eleven days before her eighty-fifth birthday, on April 18, 1944, and was buried in Decatur. Only one sister of the original fourteen young Tylers survived her.

Tyler's own philosophy of librarianship was expressed in a talk to the Iowa State Library Commission in 1927, when she said,

> The ultimate goal in library work is after all elusive.... Certainly our real goal is not toward an external end; it must be in the realm of mind and spirit. If one can phrase a practical end for the elusive quest, it might be: Helping people to use their minds; Stimulating people to think!

Alumni and friends established a generous memorial scholarship at the School in her name, and many students have been aided in their professional training through this gift. In 1951, she was named as one of the forty early leaders of the American library world selected by the *Library Journal* with the help of many librarians ("A Library Hall of Fame," *Library Journal* 76:466-72 [March 15, 1951]).

At the time of Tyler's death, Linda Anne Eastman (q.v.), then retired as head of the Cleveland Public Library, wrote in the *American Library Association Bulletin* (38:260 [July 1944]):

> One thinks of the keen, alert mind, the clear thinking, the administrative ability, the courage of conviction and steadfastness of purpose, the integrity, the graciousness of manner, the social consciousness, kindliness, and never-failing human sympathy, the saving sense of humor, the talent for friendship.

An obituary in the *Cleveland Plain Dealer* for April 20, 1944, said,

> Descendant of two American presidents, James Monroe and John Tyler, member of a family which was among the pioneers who gradually made their way from Virginia to establish American civilization in the territories of the old Northwest, Miss Tyler fused the best traditions of her ancestors into a career which was at once that of an intellectual patrician and pioneer and humble servant of her fellows.

Biographical listings and obituaries—*Current Biography* (1944); *National Cyclopaedia of American Biography* 33; *Notable American Women, 1607-1950* (Helen M. Focke);

[Obituary]. *Cleveland News*, April 18, 1944, p. 15; *Who Was Who in America* V (1969-1973); *Who's Who in Library Service*, 1st ed.; *Women of Ohio: A Record of Their Achievements in the History of the State.* Sponsored by the Ohio Newspaper Women's Association. S. J. Clarke Publ., [1939], Vol. 2. **Books and articles about the biographee**—Eastman, Linda A. "Alice S. Tyler, 1859-1944." *ALA Bulletin* 38:260 (July 1944); "Library Alumni of Western Reserve University to Honor Miss Alice Tyler." *Cleveland Press*, April 1, 1938, p. 15; "A Library Hall of Fame." *Library Journal* 76:471-72 (March 15, 1951); Parker, Addison. "Alice S. Tyler 1859-1944." *Iowa Library Quarterly* 14:213-15 (July 1944); "Portrait and Sketch [of Alice Sarah Tyler]." *Bulletin of Bibliography and Dramatic Index* 13:61 (1927); Scott, Cora Richardson. "Alice Sarah Tyler." In *Pioneering Leaders in Librarianship*, ed. by Emily Miller Danton. Chicago: American Library Association, 1953, pp. 188-96 [taken largely from author's thesis prepared for Western Reserve University, School of Library Science, 1951].

—HELEN M. FOCKE

UTLEY, GEORGE BURWELL (1876-1946)

George Burwell Utley was born on December 3, 1876, in Hartford, Connecticut, to George Tyler and Harriet Ella Burwell Utley. He was of proud Yankee stock, the Utleys having emigrated from Yorkshire, England, in the mid-seventeenth century. His father was a businessman and secretary of the Connecticut Railroad Commission in Hartford; his mother's lineage could also be traced to the early pioneering years in Connecticut. She died when George was yet a child, and the boy was raised by his maternal aunts on their homeplace in Pleasant Valley. He always felt a strong attachment to "Burwell Heights," and it was to become his permanent home after his retirement in 1942.

While attending Vermont Academy at Saxton's River near Brattleboro, Utley met Lou Mabel Gilbert, the daughter of Hamilton Smith Gilbert, a farmer of Fairfield, Vermont. She was to become his wife, but not until he had attended Colgate University for one year and then, having transferred, received his Ph.B. from Brown in 1899. Although he was elected to Phi Beta Kappa, and throughout his lifetime regarded as a scholarly person, Utley's formal education ended with the baccalaureate. In 1923, however, Brown University bestowed on him an honorary A.M.

Upon graduation, Utley would have liked to teach English literature, but since jobs were scarce, he began working for an insurance company in Hartford. At this time, the job of assistant librarian was offered to him by Frank B. Gay of the Watkinson Library in Hartford. A special library, the Watkinson had a strong collection in Americana; it appealed to Utley's scholarly instincts, and he served there for two years.

In 1901, Utley (a Baptist) accepted an offer to head the Maryland Diocesan Library of the Episcopal Church in Baltimore; also, he was married to Lou Gilbert on September 4. Lou was his constant

companion through 45 years of marriage, and the Utleys were a familiar sight to those who attended American Library Association conferences on a regular basis. A matter of some pride to him was his attendance at some 38 or 40 conferences, and his wife accompanied him to most of them. An account of his first conference (1903) appeared in the *Wilson Library Bulletin* (November 1944).

George Utley was to remain at the Diocesan Library for four years and, while there, he researched his first book, *The Life and Times of Thomas John Claggett, First Bishop of Maryland* (published by Lakeside Press some eight years later in 1913). The letters, diaries, and journals were, of course, housed in the archives of the Diocesan Library, and he worked on the book in leisurely fashion. In the preface, he made it clear that he was less interested in theological doctrines than in the material picture of the rather ordinary gentleman and his time.

In 1905, Utley accepted his first and only public library position—in Jacksonville, Florida, a community of 35,000 people at the time. Jacksonville was the recipient of a $50,000 grant from Andrew Carnegie (q.v.) and was in a position to establish the first tax-supported public library in the state. The records from this period support the description of Utley provided later by colleagues, friends, and acquaintances: a bookish, scholarly man, but one at all times friendly, warm, receptive, and guided by humanitarian impulses. An illustration of his character is found in the Florida History Collection of the Jacksonville Public Library in his two-year correspondence with W. M. Seaver of *Publishers' Weekly* concerning an anticipated Richard R. Bowker (q.v.) publishing effort, "Bibliography of State Publications." Seaver was not able to find any Florida official to cooperate, so he appealed to Utley out of desperation. From July 1906 to the middle of 1908, Utley showed Seaver every kindness and endeavored to help him accomplish his task in a variety of ways. These efforts produced neither reward nor recognition but appear to be characteristic of Utley's helpful nature.

Also apparent from the records is the fact that he was a fine administrator, a resourceful, energetic individual who in his quiet and friendly manner saw to it that progress was made. The "experiment" in Jacksonville, as he referred to it in the beginning, was definitely successful as witnessed by the steady growth of the Library despite a shortage of funds. Also, the public had become receptive to such new policies as Sunday and holiday hours and the extension of borrowing privileges to children under twelve.

In 1910, the ALA needed a successor to Chalmers Hadley (q.v.) to step into the important and demanding job of secretary, the executive officer of the organization. Utley, now in his mid-thirties, had come to the attention of the Executive Board as a progressive individual, and the job was offered to him following an interview. It was with regret that he left Jacksonville in 1911, the *Florida Times Union* of January 24 reporting the "sincere congratulations of a host of friends"; but he was eager to respond to the challenges in this key position. Joseph Wheeler (q.v.) succeeded him in Jacksonville and referred to him in the annual report of 1911: "In five years, he brought the library to a place in the front rank of the libraries in cities of this size, having 9,000 active card holders, and an annual circulation of over 100,000 volumes."

Utley was to remain with ALA for nine years, the longest term since Melvil Dewey's (q.v.) original fourteen-year tenure from 1876 to 1890. Among his responsibilities, as reported at the time, were editing official publications and reports of various boards, handling correspondence, and travelling and delivering addresses before state associations. During this time, he performed yeoman service in organizing the headquarters in Chicago on a sound basis. His stay in Chicago was interrupted temporarily by the American entry into World War I, when he assumed additional responsibility as executive secretary of the ALA Library War Service Committee from 1917 to 1919, which required that he reside in Washington and work with Herbert Putnam (q.v.) at the Library of Congress. This proved to be an enormous task involving the planning and supervision of a program that supplied libraries and librarians to armed forces overseas centers and training camps. It was a highly successful operation for which Utley must be given much of the credit.

When the War was over and he was able to resume his duties in Chicago, Utley resumed work on some personal activities that had been set aside. One of these was his book on the first Conference of Librarians in 1853, a subject in which he had become interested through his association with Arthur Hastings Grant, the son of Seth Hastings Grant, the secretary of the Conference. Grant had given him his father's personal papers, and Utley felt that the event was worthy of publication. In 1920, however, another factor intervened and *The Librarians' Conference of 1853* was to become a retirement activity some 23 years later.

At this time, Edward Ryerson, the president of the Board of Trustees of the Newberry Library offered Utley the position of director. He readily accepted. The March 15, 1920, issue of *Library Journal* laments his departure from ALA and identifies him as "one of the ablest officials whom the association has had." Further reference is made to his executive ability, agreeable manner, effective voice, and abounding patience.

Utley's directorship of Newberry was his final position, and he held it until 1942, falling just two

and a half years short of his goal of a quarter century. His accomplishments were noteworthy in developing the Library's size, value, and readership; he also established many contacts with scholars, thus helping countless others in their professional pursuits. At first there was opposition from some members of the Library staff, but by 1930, Utley was firmly in control. As the size of the staff increased from 33 to 45 persons, he added some 180,000 volumes to the collection, many of which were real treasures. Growth was especially extensive in American history, English and American literature, music, and genealogy during these years, thus establishing a pattern of growth integral to Newberry's present identity.

While at Newberry, Utley was honored on several occasions in addition to the above-mentioned honorary A.M. In 1922, he was decorated by the Italian King with the Order of the Crown of Italy in appreciation of Utley's exhibition of the Library's Dante collection. (We can only conjecture on the reaction of the Connecticut Yankee, always a Republican politically, to this royal recognition.) In 1930, he was chosen by the American Booksellers Association as one of the Committee of Ten authorized to select books for the White House Library. Upon his retirement, he was the first Newberry librarian designated librarian emeritus, an honor bestowed upon him September 1, 1942.

During his lifetime, Utley belonged to numerous organizations, clubs, and societies and apparently served a number of them in an active manner. Elected president of ALA for the 1922-1923 term, he retained membership on the Executive Board for several years. He served as president of the Illinois Library Association (1924-1925) and was president of the American Library Institute (1937-1939). In addition, he was president of the Geographic Society of Chicago (1929-1931) and the Writers Guild of Chicago (1935-1937).

A paper presented in 1926 to the Chicago Literary Club (a group which some ten years later he also served as president) became his second major publication; *Fifty Years of the American Library Association* was published by the organization in official recognition of its semi-centennial. In addition to this book, many articles by Utley appeared in professional library periodicals, and a few in history publications, such as "Origin of the County Names in Florida" in the *Florida Historical Society Quarterly* (October 1908). Several of his addresses and papers were printed, and he contributed ten articles to the *Dictionary of American Biography*.

After his retirement in 1942, George Utley resumed work on what was to be his last major publication, *The Librarians' Conference of 1853*. Due to his breadth of interest, however, it was still a leisurely pursuit and time was given to the task only when it was available. Gardening was his favorite recreation, and he never lost his interest in reading, Robert Louis Stevenson's works being his personal favorites. His stamp collection received much attention at this time, and his automobile was another source of fascination to him.

As a result, Utley never really completed the book, which lacked some twelve pages at the time of his death in 1946. His nephew Gilbert H. Doane actually finished the manuscript, finally published by ALA in 1951. The Utleys' last years together evidently were quite enjoyable, as they would entertain frequent visitors at their Pleasant Valley home, then would journey to Winter Park, Florida, for the winter. It was while planning his Florida trip that George B. Utley died on October 4, 1946, in Pleasant Valley. Not yet seventy, he was the victim of a coronary while preparing his garden for the winter months ahead.

George Utley combined a natural administrative capability with bookish and humanitarian instincts. That he was systematic and organized in his thinking was apparent in his efficient guidance of the Jacksonville "experiment," his executive direction of ALA, and his management of collection development at Newberry. His personal qualities were also apparent in his staff relations both at Jacksonville and at Newberry, and the warmth and respect accorded him by his colleagues at ALA. He saw in the library a vehicle by which every workingman, student, businessman, and professional could be enlightened. In a 1908 article from the *Jacksonville Metropolis*, he stated the purpose of the library as "above all things, gradually, to raise the intellectual and moral tone of the community by means of great thoughts from master minds." His fidelity to these ideals and his effective action in their behalf are the elements that render him a notable figure in librarianship.

Biographical listings and obituaries—*Current Biography* (1946); *Dictionary of American Biography*, 4th Suppl. (Joseph A. Boromé); *National Cyclopaedia of American Biography* 33; *Who Was Who in America* II (1943-1950); *Who's Who in Library Service*, 1st ed., 2nd ed. **Books and articles about the biographee**—Doane, G. H. [Biographical sketch in foreword to] George B. Utley, *The Librarians' Conference of 1853*. Chicago: American Library Association, 1951; Hadley, Chalmers. "George Burwell Utley." *ALA Bulletin* 40:429-30 (Nov. 1946); Skogh, H. M. "George Burwell Utley." *Illinois Libraries* 24:210 (Oct. 1942). **Primary sources and archival materials**—Utley's papers are in the Newberry Library and the Jacksonville Public Library, Florida History Collection.

—RON BLAZEK

UTLEY, HENRY MUNSON (1836-1917)

Henry Munson Utley was born on August 5, 1836, in Plymouth, Michigan, to Hiram and Jane Sands Utley. He was married in 1864 to Kate Lilly Burr, and they had three daughters: Irene, Jane, and Frances. He was graduated from the University of Michigan, receiving his A.B. degree in 1861 and his A.M. degree in 1870. His early career was in journalism. From 1861 to 1866, he was a reporter for the *Detroit Free Press*; from 1866 to 1881, he was on the staff of the *Detroit Post* and its successor, the *Detroit Post Tribune*, where he served as city editor. From 1881 to 1885, he was secretary of the Detroit Board of Education.

In 1885, Henry M. Utley was appointed librarian of the Detroit Public Library. This appointment was a political one; except for a scholarly and literary background and the knowledge of municipal affairs that his newspaper career had given him, he had little obvious qualification for the post. *Library Journal* (August 1885) quoted the *Detroit Sunday News* as expressing misgivings about his ability to do much with the problems of the Library so long as the Detroit Library Commission tried to run things, thereby making the librarian no more than its lieutenant. Librarianship, it said, had become a profession, and the successful operation of a library required a strong librarian.

However, Utley's first duty as librarian was (according to the *Annual Report* for 1912, p. 22) "assignment to represent the Library at the conference of the American Library Association" at its Lake George meeting in 1885. There he met the leading librarians of the day, among them Justin Winsor (q.v.), William Frederick Poole (q.v.), Melvil Dewey (q.v.), Charles Ammi Cutter (q.v.), and others, and thus began his education in librarianship. He was a regular attendant at ALA conferences from that time on, and he became active in the work of the Association. He served on committees, on the Council, as recorder, and was elected president for the 1894-1895 term, presiding over the conference in Denver in 1895. He also encouraged his staff to attend professional meetings. In 1891, he helped to organize the Michigan Library Association and at its first meeting (in Detroit in September of that year), he was elected president. He held that office continuously until 1904.

During his tenure as librarian, the city of Detroit experienced great growth, while the Library experienced, in Utley's words (in the *Annual Report* for 1912, p. 22), a "marked and unexpected change in the institution and the character of its work [which] amounts to a revolution.... This was not merely an expansion along previously well defined lines, it was radical and fundamental in its quality and characteristics." The Dewey Decimal Classification was adopted in 1886, and the books were renumbered. The children's room was established in 1896 and soon was a very busy place. Sunday opening was begun in 1886 and was popular. (It was noted that the clergy, instead of disapproving of Sunday opening, actually commended it.) The reference department was organized and was soon serving people from surrounding communities as well as the residents of Detroit. In 1887, electric lights were introduced in the reading room and were found to be very satisfactory. Branch libraries were established, beginning in 1900, and new buildings were built, the first in 1906. (When it was suggested that outlying stations be put into operation where people could order books and have them delivered the following day for pick-up, Utley agreed that the idea was a good one; however, he said that in the long run it would not be in the interests of the best library service, because the help and guidance of the librarian would not be available. He felt that full-time branches were a better solution.)

The decade between 1901 and 1910 saw controversy in the city over the acceptance of an Andrew Carnegie (q.v.) grant for building branches and a new central building. The City Council was unwilling for years to accept Carnegie's terms, and some Council members expressed strong objections to receiving what they termed "blood money," referring to the early labor difficulties in Carnegie's company. The building of branches with Carnegie funds began only at the end of Utley's tenure. Collections of books were placed in factories so that workers would have access to them. Telephone service was inaugurated between the main library and branches, and motor trucks were used to deliver books to the branch libraries. The collection increased 250 percent between 1885 and 1912, and circulation was seven times as great.

Utley was the author of several books, among them *Michigan as a Province, Territory and State, the Twenty-sixth Member of the Federal Union* (1906), v. 1 and v. 4; and *The Class of Sixty-one, University of Michigan* (1902), with Byron McCutcheon. He also wrote many magazine articles as well as contributing to library periodicals. Indeed, he published articles from the first year of his appointment until after his retirement, with subjects covering the entire spectrum of public library operation. Included in the list were articles on the reclassification of books, the use of Library of Congress cards, newspaper volumes in a library, the relationship of the public library to the public school, library architecture, library legislation, and an item on the collection and registration of fines. He reported as well on the policy and methods of selecting books in the Detroit Public Library, describing an approval arrangement with a local book dealer who supplied copies of books for examination in the fields he knew the Library was interested in, and specific titles the Library requested. He reported with pride that the Library had acquired all the periodicals indexed in Poole's *Index*. His other interests included copyright revision, and the relations of Library trustees to their Library.

Utley's letters from vacation spots to his secretary reveal his direct control over details of the Library operation that would be unthinkable in a later period. In response to her inquiries, he wrote instructions regarding accounts and the payment of bills, and he also expressed a lively interest in the staff and its activities.

At the time of his retirement from active operation of the Library in 1912, Henry Utley was made librarian emeritus. *Public Libraries* (17:415 [1912]), reporting his retirement with regret, described him:

A gentle man, yet strong and decided in personality, a man of hopeful outlook on the progress of the world, a man with a conscientious attitude toward his work, both from within and without, a dependable man when hard tasks were to be performed, he has stood for many years in the Middle-West as a very present help in the forward movement that has gone on for the past 20 years. He has seen the Detroit library grow under his management from a small, insignificant collection of books to one of the great systems of the country, and to become an effective and much appreciated institution in Detroit.

At the time of his death on February 16, 1917, the Detroit Library Commission adopted a resolution (which appeared in the *Proceedings* dated February 15, 1917, p. 21); it said in part,

Coming to the work in middle age, with a wide experience in literary and educational activities, he entered, with quiet enthusiasm upon the task of bringing this library into line with the modern methods that were then arousing the library world. . . . He guided with a conservative hand the fortunes of the institution entrusted to him, from its small beginnings to its larger place in the life of the community.

The ALA also adopted a memorial resolution (*ALA Bulletin* 11:332 [1917]) at its 1917 annual conference that referred to his contributions to the Detroit Public Library, to the Association, and to the Michigan Library Association and that closed as follows:

With the rapid, almost revolutionary changes in public service and educational standards of our day, the record and contribution of the individual may soon be forgotten, but the rugged figure of Mr. Utley as he appeared among us—his kindly personality—will long be treasured among those who came to know his reserved yet lovable nature. He was one of the "old guard," and in paying tribute to his memory, we honor one whose sympathy and tolerance with human society in all its variations never faltered, and one whose career was singularly free from egotisms and self-exploitations.

His name survives in Detroit on a branch library constructed while he was librarian and in bronze letters in the lobby of the Main Library in a list of former directors. His work survives in the very foundations of a great library system.

Biographical listings and obituaries—*National Cyclopaedia of American Biography* 17; [Obituary]. *Library Journal* 42:190 (March 1917), 42:627 (Aug. 1917); [Obituary]. *Public Libraries* 22:106 (March 1917); *Who Was Who in America* I (1897-1942). **Books and articles about the biographee**—"Mr. H. M. Utley's Retirement." *Public Libraries* 17:415-16 (Dec. 1912); Strohm, Adam J., Frank P. Hill, and Mary C. Spencer. "Henry Munson Utley." *ALA Bulletin* 11:332 (1947); Woodford, Frank B. *Parnassus on Main Street.* Detroit, Wayne State University Press, 1963. **Primary sources and archival materials**—Letters and reports of, and papers about, Henry M. Utley are in the Detroit Public Library.

—FLORENCE RAY TUCKER

VAIL, ROBERT WILLIAM GLENROIE (1890-1966)

Robert William Glenroie Vail was born in the small town of Victor, New York, not far from Rochester, on March 26, 1890, to James Gardner and Mary Elizabeth Boughton Vail. Proximity to Ithaca may have influenced him in his choice of Cornell University for his undergraduate work. His class book refers to him as "Noah" and "Glen," and the caption accompanying his photograph indicated that "he is good natured, big-hearted and likes the acquaintance of antiques and relics." There seems to be a bit of prophecy here. He was graduated in 1914 with an A.B. degree. After graduation, his interest in librarianship brought him to New York City, where he attended the Library School of the New York Public Library during the years 1915 and 1916. While there he came under the influence of two distinguished librarians: Wilberforce Eames (q.v.), the doyen of American bibliographers, and Victor H. Paltsits (q.v.), who became Eames's successor as chief of the American History Division.

World War I interrupted Vail's apprenticeship and, for six months, he served as a private in the United States Army; most of his service appears to have been spent at Fort Totten, New York. Following his discharge, he was lured to the West to become librarian of the Minnesota Historical Society. Little published evidence exists of Vail's contribution to the Society other than a few paragraphs devoted to the growth and use of its Library, and the perennial problems of cataloging that appear in the biennial reports of the Society for the years 1919-1920 and 1921-1922. In June 1921, Vail returned to New York to accept a position with the Roosevelt Memorial Association.

His bibliographical training undoubtedly led to his joining the staff of the Association as librarian. At that time, the Association was engaged in publishing the collected works of Theodore Roosevelt, to be published in 24 volumes during the years 1923 to 1926. The bibliographical notes appearing in Volumes XII, XIV-XXII, and XXIV are Vail's contribution. He also compiled a complete bibliography of the writings of Theodore Roosevelt (presumably never published) and published a number of articles and privately printed booklets on Roosevelt.

In 1919, Vail returned to the New York Public Library. While employed there he frequently contributed articles to the *Bulletin* of that institution. Two in particular are cited for mention here, namely "A Message to Garcia: A Bibliographical Puzzle" (February 1930), and "*The Ulster County Gazette* and Its Illegitimate Offspring" (April 1930), both popular and helpful articles for which reference librarians everywhere must be grateful. Once and for all time, he settled the puzzling bibliographical details of both publications. During this period, Vail also assumed the joint editorship of the final sections of Joseph Sabin's (q.v.) *Dictionary of Books Relating to America.* With his staff, he saw the work to completion in 1936. The entries for which Vail was responsible run from numbers 84,556 to 106,413, some 21,000 entries. For this contribution alone, his name looms large in the annals of American bibliography.

During his editorship, Vail left New York once more to assume the librarianship of the American Antiquarian Society at Worcester, Massachusetts, where he remained until January 1940. During his tenure of office, he prepared annually a detailed report of the yearly accessions and found time to deliver lectures and prepare numerous articles for publication in the Society's *Proceedings*, including bibliographical studies devoted to Simeon Ide (a pioneer printer of Windsor, Vermont), Benjamin Gomez (New York's earliest Jewish bookseller), and Susanna H. Rowson (the author of *Charlotte Temple*, "the most popular romance of its generation"). In 1934, he contributed "Random Notes on the History of the American Circus," a subject that interested him for many years.

Perhaps his major contribution during this period was *A Guide to the Resources of the American Antiquarian Society* (1937). An appreciation of Vail's services to the Society, written by Clarence S. Brigham (q.v.), the director of the Society, stated:

> His tenure of office at the American Antiquarian Society has added much to the prestige of the institution. With a wide knowledge of library administration, a familiarity with American history and literature, and a notable ability in the field of bibliography, he helped to spread the importance of the Society's collections throughout the country.

Vail left Worcester to become state librarian of the New York State Library, where he remained for four years. The demands of this executive position did not permit him to devote much time to bibliographical pursuits, and it necessitated his resignation as permanent secretary of the Bibliographical Society of America, an appointment he had accepted in 1938. In 1944, he was elected president of the Bibliographical Society, the same year marking his return to New York City as director of the New-York Historical Society, where he remained until his retirement in 1960.

Two of his major works appeared during these busy sixteen years, *The Voice of the Old Frontier* and *Knickerbocker Birthday.* The former is essentially a bibliography of 1,300 entries consisting of books and pamphlets relating to the American frontier for the years 1542 to 1800. (This work is based on the lectures he gave in 1945-1946 as holder of the University of Pennsylvania's fellowship in bibliography, founded by Dr. A. S. W. Rosenbach.) In reviewing it, Professor Allan Nevins stated: "Mr. Vail has given to us one of the most valuable books of reference in American history published in many years." *Knickerbocker Birthday* is a detailed account of the New-York Historical Society covering 150 years of its existence (1804-1954).

After his retirement, Vail took up residence in Albuquerque, New Mexico, where he died on June 21, 1966. Marie Rogers Vail, to whom he had been married on June 1, 1918, survived him, as did two children, Robert W. and Elizabeth.

As a bibliophile, Vail collected for all the institutions he served. As a collector, he was insatiable, and his annual reports to the institutions he served testify to his discriminating taste and the understanding of the books, journals, and pamphlets for which he was personally responsible or which came to his personal attention. He loved his job, and through his special contributions, each institution grew in stature and importance. Vail's scholarship was recognized through the honorary degrees he received and the award of the gold medal from the New-York Historical Society. The citation at the time he received his Doctor of Letters degree from Dickinson College in 1951 read in part: "In the highest tradition of your profession you have made the materials of American history available to students and interpreters of American life and thought."

Similarly when Clark University conferred on him the degree of Doctor of Humane Letters, the citation read:

> He is by scholarly acclaim one of the nation's foremost bibliographers. He walks confidently where other bibliographers often fear to tread—by way of illustration, the insuperable task of completing Sabin's *Dictionary of Books Relating to America.* As author his enthusiasm lends to subjects abstruse and recondite an excitement akin

to drama. It is a delight to talk with him of old illustrations, the early American painters, the early collectors of American art. He is compact of old-time knowledge. It is a delight to visit the fine Renaissance building of the New-York Historical Society where he so ably and graciously presides and where ancient objects are so well preserved and so happily displayed. It is as though age renewed itself perennially.

Glen Vail left an indelible mark on American bibliographical scholarship. His several enduring contributions to the study of American history and literature place all students of American history in his debt. Large in frame and known as "Hercules" to some of his intimate friends, he was a bibliographical giant. This modest, genial, and generous man responded, when he received the gold medal of the New-York Historical Society on March 30, 1960, in a manner so typical of him:

> It is with deep gratitude that I accept from the Officers and Trustees of our Society its Gold Medal for Achievement in History. No honor could have surprised or pleased me more but I receive it in trust for all of the other little-known historians and bibliographers who, generally without recognition, prepare the tools which make easier the work of the more distinguished craftsmen.

In these few phrases, he wrote his own epitaph.

Biographical listings and obituaries—*Current Biography* (1966); [Obituary]. *Antiquarian Bookman* 38:64 (July 4-11, 1966); [Obituary]. *Library Journal* 91:3682 (Aug. 1966); [Obituary]. *The New York Times,* June 23, 1966; [Shipton, Clifford K.] [Obituary]. *Proceedings of the American Antiquarian Society* (Worcester, Mass.) 76, Part 2:224-27 (1966); *Who Was Who in America* IV (1961-1968); *Who's Who in Library Service,* 2nd ed., 3rd ed.   **Books and articles about the biographee**—[Biographical sketch]. *College and Research Libraries* 6:250-51 (June 1945); Goff, Frederick R. "R. W. G. Vail: A Bibliographical Appreciation." *Inter-American Review of Bibliography* 17, No. 3:281-98 (July-Sept. 1967) [bibliography, pp. 290-98].

—FREDERICK R. GOFF

VAN HOESEN, HENRY BARTLETT (1885-1965)

Henry Bartlett Van Hoesen, son of Henry I. and Alice Peck Van Hoesen, was born in Truxton, Cortland County, New York, on December 25, 1885. He attended public schools and, in 1905, was graduated from Hobart College (Geneva, New York) with honors and election to Phi Beta Kappa. He continued classical studies at Princeton University, earning the master's degree (1906) and the Ph.D. (1912). As a travelling fellow, he studied (1907-1908) at what was then known as the American School of Classical Studies in Rome (after January 1913, the American Academy absorbed the American School of Classical Studies in Rome); he studied also at Munich

University (1908-1909). In 1914, when he was teaching at Western Reserve University, he was married to Ruth Hutchinson, then dean of women there. Van Hoesen's father was a Princeton graduate and a country doctor; Ruth's father was a professor of Greek at the University of Minnesota. The children were Alice, Martha, and Drusilla.

On his return from study abroad, Van Hoesen served as instructor of classical studies at Princeton (1909-1911) and at Western Reserve (1912-1915); he then returned to Princeton as curator of manuscripts and rare books. From 1916 to 1928, he was assistant librarian, at first with particular responsibility for classification and cataloging in addition to his curator's duties but, later, taking part in general library administration. However, in 1920, when James T. Gerould (q.v.) was appointed librarian, Van Hoesen was relieved of administering the Order and Circulation departments and given more time for graduate instruction in papyrology, paleography, and bibliography.

He left Princeton in 1928 to become associate librarian of Brown University, and, after the retirement of Harry L. Koopman (q.v.), he began active duty as Brown's librarian in September 1930. Except for summer teaching at library schools in Chicago (1929 and 1931) and Columbia (1933), and a leave in 1946-1947 to serve as visiting professor at Columbia, he devoted himself to the dual role of librarian and John Hay Professor of Bibliography at Brown, retiring in 1950.

His major publications in classical studies are *Roman Cursive Writing* (Princeton University Press, 1915), an expansion of his dissertation, and, with his colleague A. C. Johnson, volume 1 of *Papyri in the Princeton University Collections* (Johns Hopkins University Studies in Archaeology, no. 10, 1931). After retirement, he assisted Otto Neugebauer, professor of the history of mathematics at Brown, in producing *Greek Horoscopes* (Memoirs of the American Philosophical Society, v. 48, 1959), with Greek text of most of the papyri and English translations of all the horoscopes. The scholarly interest that brought him into librarianship was never completely abandoned.

As bibliographer, Van Hoesen, with Frank K. Walter (q.v.) of the University of Minnesota, will be remembered for *Bibliography, Practical, Enumerative, Historical: An Introductory Manual* . . . (N.Y., Scribner, 1928; reprinted 1937 and again in 1971 by Burt Franklin). *Bibliography* is quite different from the popular, classified, annotated compilations of Alice B. Kroeger (q.v.) and Isadore Gilbert Mudge (q.v.). Its style is expository, like that of its European predecessors, Stein, Langlois, and Schneider, with titles and subject matters keyed to a bibliographical appendix of 77 closely printed pages. Perhaps the

severest disappointment of Van Hoesen's career was the rejection by the ALA and others of the manuscript of a new edition that was near completion in the late 1950s. The day of the specialist had arrived; general compilations of enumerative bibliography were suspect. Moreover, Mme. Louise Malclès had begun publication of her great *Sources du travail bibliographique.*

Soon after coming to Brown, Van Hoesen discovered President Manning's manuscript catalog of 607 volumes in the Library in 1782, and devoted most of a summer vacation to identifying and locating as many of them as he could. He found about 500, of which 102 were already in a Williams Table Collection. His account of the search for and description of some of the items was privately printed in 1938 in *Brown University Library . . . 1767-82.* Then in 1949, just before retiring, he started a small leaflet magazine, *Lincoln Annex*, to record contemporary references to Abraham Lincoln in diaries, letters, local histories, etc. He wrote that the title was borrowed from "a sort of purgatory of partly catalogued books known as the Lincoln Annex" of the McLellan Lincoln Collection.

Between 1929 and 1949, Van Hoesen wrote at least 38 reviews of works in the fields of papyrology, bibliography, and library administration, and contributed over a score of articles to journals. A characteristic article, one of two entitled "Perspective in Cataloging," appears in *College and Research Libraries* (1, no. 4 [Sept. 1940]). This article, seasoned with Van Hoesen humor, also exemplifies his patient continued concern with cataloging and scholars' complaints about its complexity.

Van Hoesen's administration at Brown coincided with the national crisis of the worst depression in United States history as well as World War II. Yet when he retired in 1950, Brown's president, Henry M. Wriston, a noted critic and champion of academic libraries, said in a report to the corporation: "With no qualities of showmanship at all, and without any appearance of the go-getter, Dr. Henry Van Hoesen has been one of the most progressive library administrators in the United States." In recent correspondence, Wriston wrote, "He was a remarkable man, with whom I enjoyed working."

In addition to the usual concerns of the academic libraries of his time—doubling holdings and providing space for them, developing "friends of the library" organizations, struggling to make the Works Progress Administration (later Work Projects Administration) useful, keeping the staffs intact, and during the War persuading foreign agents to collect and store books (at which Van Hoesen was unusually good)—Brown's librarian maintained progressive concerns about bibliography, cataloging, photographic reproduction, and library organization. He had been disappointed as chairman of the Bibliography Committee of the American Library Association in 1935-1936 in the bickering over the province of the Committee, and bitter in 1942-1943, when he felt that the Special Committee on International Cultural Relations (and especially its members William Warner Bishop [q.v.] and Milton Lord) were intent on usurping the functions of the Bibliography Committee (documentation for this may no longer exist). However, he continued to promote bibliographical activity by teaching, by encouraging it among his staff and faculty colleagues, and by collecting thousands of notices of new bibliographies for a new edition of *Bibliography*. His "Perspectives in Cataloging," mentioned above, are tinged with humor.

In 1918, *Library Journal* published his description of the Photostat machine at Princeton and an exhibit of its uses there, and the next year he read a paper about photographing manuscripts to the American Library Institute. After the War he experimented with microfilm and in March 1935, with a borrowed Leica, he produced film copies of symphony scores for projection in music classes to accompany recordings, a very successful venture. This and other successful film projects encouraged President Wriston to undertake the establishment of an independent, fully equipped photographic laboratory that, among other services, would provide film copies of articles abstracted in a new journal, *Mathematical Reviews*. So Brown, with a large grant from the Rockefeller Foundation, got its photographic laboratory, with its own building and staff, and a commitment to meet all of the photographic needs of the University.

While this activity was piloted through rough weather by President Wriston, Van Hoesen looked forward to another storm. In his annual report of 1936, he outlined a plan for a divisional organization of the Library that would absorb the eighteen departmental libraries in four divisions: humanities, social studies, physical sciences, and biological sciences. The new president approved and encouraged the plan, but adequate space was not available until 1939. Then, with an addition to the John Hay Library and construction of a new science laboratory, the plan was implemented, with unwavering support from President Wriston and great determination and diplomacy on the part of Van Hoesen. At about the same time, Ralph Ellsworth developed a divisional organization for a new University of Colorado Library and, a few years later, Frank Lundy reorganized the University of Nebraska Library into divisions responsible for all library functions, including cataloging; but Brown's reorganization was an extraordinary achievement for an academic library of its age and size. The University was doubly fortunate in progressive administrators.

In person, Van Hoesen resembled Abraham Lincoln enough for people to remark on it. He was lean, tall, dark, and craggy. In formal photographs, he usually looks sober or grim, probably because he hated the ordeal and perhaps because the lights hurt his eyes; his normal expression was an alert, lively sobriety. When amused, he grinned, slightly or widely according to the intensity of the stimulus. He was almost never without a pipe, frequently one that should have been discarded months before.

Van Hoesen's upstate New York Dutch heritage showed in his shrewd judgments, thriftiness, and his recreations: hiking, climbing, and vegetable gardening. His humor was witty, sometimes sharp and idiosyncratic. One day some roomers left windows open to a heavy rain shower, and Mrs. Van Hoesen, dismayed by the damage, asked Henry to speak to the tenants. When he found they were not in, he left a note: "Don't let it rain when you leave the windows open."

Van Hoesen's qualities as a man enhanced his ability as scholar and librarian and promoted a high degree of loyalty in the library staff. He was also a productive scholar, and he remained always the scholar's advocate (while some librarians forgot him among budgets, organizations, catalog cards, and politics). He died on January 6, 1965, in Providence, Rhode Island.

Biographical listings and obituaries—*Directory of American Scholars*, 3rd ed. (1957); Jonah, David A. "Memorial Minute." *Brown Alumni Monthly* 65, no. 7:59 [April 1965]; *Who Was Who in America* IV (1961-1968); *Who's Who in Library Service*, 1st ed., 2nd ed., 3rd ed. **Books and articles about the biographee**—Brigham, Herbert O. "Our Frontispiece: Henry Bartlett Van Hoesen." *Bulletin of Bibliography* 16, no. 6 [1938]; Gibson, Susan C. "Henry Bartlett Van Hoesen: Librarian of Brown University, 1930-1950 . . ." (Paper submitted in fulfillment of partial requirement for L.S. 305, University of Rhode Island, 1969; 34p.); Hathaway, Christine, and Philip Leslie. "A Tribute to Henry Bartlett Van Hoesen Upon the Completion of Twenty Years as Librarian. . . ." *Staff Bulletin*, John Hay Library, 11, no. 9 [June 1, 1950], 30p. [includes a chronological "preliminary list" of Van Hoesen's writings compiled by K. K. Moore, head cataloger]. **Primary sources and archival materials**—Collected writings, annual reports, miscellaneous biographical items and clippings are in the Archives, John Hay Library, Brown University, Providence, R.I. A few personal papers and photographs may be held by the daughters; consult Alice (Mrs. Horace Booth, Highland, Maryland 20777).

—H. GLENN BROWN

VAN NAME, ADDISON (1835-1922)

Addison Van Name was born in Chenango, New York (near Binghamton), on November 15, 1835, the son of Cornelius and Theodosia Ogden Van Name. His father was a farmer who also engaged in the lumber and transportation business, with interests in shipping on the canal. Van Name's ancestors were early settlers of New York, his father's family having emigrated from Holland and his mother's from England in the seventeenth century. After preparing at the Binghamton Academy and at Phillips Andover, Van Name entered Yale College in the fall of 1854.

At Yale, Van Name was an outstanding student. He was awarded scholarships for three years, elected to Phi Beta Kappa, and was graduated valedictorian of the class of 1858. Several of his 104 classmates became noted scholars, the most famous being the future physicist Josiah Willard Gibbs (1839-1903). Excelling also in Hebrew, Van Name was a favorite pupil of Gibbs, Sr., professor of sacred languages, and formed a close friendship with his son. Van Name, a "quiet, shy boy" according to the younger Gibbs's biographer, Muriel Rukeyser, became a part of the Gibbs family circle, and their comfortable home on the campus eventually became his lifelong residence. After graduation, Van Name spent several years in travel and study at the universities of Halle and Tübingen. In 1862, he was appointed to a tutorship at Yale and, from 1863 to 1866, served as an instructor in Hebrew in the Divinity School. He was licensed to preach in 1865, but he never made use of the license.

Upon the resignation of Daniel Coit Gilman (q.v.), Van Name was appointed librarian of Yale College in July 1865 and continued to serve until his retirement in 1905. During those forty years, Van Name built up the small college library of 44,500 volumes to a true university library, containing nearly half a million volumes and manuscripts. He consolidated the undergraduate libraries of the Linonian and Brothers-in-Unity societies with the main library and prepared a full card catalog of the entire library. Gilman had begun preparation of a dictionary catalog as early as 1857, but it was not finished. Shortly after he became librarian, Van Name undertook the preparation of an alphabetico-classified card catalog. By 1858, 21,000 cards had been prepared, and, by 1872, the catalog was in use by readers. While Van Name continued to expand the card catalog, he favored the compilation of subject bibliographies rather than detailed cataloging of each book. This belief brought him into conflict with Melvil Dewey (q.v.) at the 1887 annual meeting of the American Library Association, when Van Name delivered a paper titled "The Librarian's Duty to His Successor." Dewey expressed his disapproval, stating that librarians should preserve detailed records of their accumulated knowledge for the future. William F. Poole (q.v.) and William I. Fletcher (q.v.), however, agreed with Van Name that elaborate cataloging by an individual librarian was not an adequate substitute for cooperative subject bibliographies. Similarly, in the area of newspaper collecting, Van Name favored the acquisition of complete files of newspapers over "scrapping," the

customary collecting of clippings in files; he also opened a separate newspaper room. In 1890, Van Name began the reclassification of the Yale collection. Finding Dewey's scheme too limiting and Charles A. Cutter's (q.v.) too complicated, he adopted a modified version of John Edmands's (q.v.) scheme, which was a simplified version of Cutter's.

The growth and use of the Library was carefully documented by Van Name—in large ledgers that contain records of each item acquired and the name of every borrower; in reports and petitions of the librarian and the Library Committee, which reveal a constant struggle for increased funding by the University; and in a varied correspondence file (in many Western and Oriental languages) with booksellers and private collectors around the world. Under Van Name's direction, the Library acquired the Arabic manuscripts of Count Landbergh, the Chinese library of Samuel Wells Williams, the Edward E. Salisbury donation of Oriental books and manuscripts, as well as Van Name's own outstanding collection of Oriental literature.

Van Name was particularly noted for his linguistic achievements, especially in Oriental languages. In 1870, he published a treatise titled "Contributions to Creole Grammar," in the *Transactions of the American Philological Association.* In 1873, he contributed to the first session of the Congrès International des Orientalistes a review of the Marquis d'Hervey de Saint Denys's *Mémoire sur l'histoire ancienne du Japon*, and, in the same year, wrote the article in the *American Cyclopedia* on Arabic language and literature. Two years later, he contributed the article in *Johnson's Cyclopedia* on Chinese language and literature. He was also the author of the chapter on the history of the Yale Library in *Yale College: A Sketch of Its History* (1879). During his tenure as librarian of Yale, Van Name also served as librarian of the American Oriental Society and of the Connecticut Academy of Arts and Sciences.

In addition to scholarly and bibliographical societies, Van Name was a founder of the American Library Association. He served on the ALA Council (1882-1894) and, intermittently from 1876 through 1894, on the Committees of Permanent Organization and Nominations. In 1891, the *Library Journal* reported Van Name's election as first president of the Connecticut State Library Association. In his inaugural address, he stressed the importance of cooperative cataloging by cities and towns. He was especially interested in the improvement of small town libraries and served on the Branford, Connecticut, library board. Van Name believed that good local libraries were vital to the quality of civic life and the continuing education of the American public, particularly of immigrant groups.

To house adequately and protect the large scholarly collection that he had formed, Van Name planned and supervised the construction of two library buildings. Late in the 1880s, a Yale benefactor offered to donate a library in memory of his daughter. In planning for the Chittenden Library, Van Name surveyed new library buildings in 72 cities. His "Report on Library Architecture" was published in 1889 in the *Library Journal*, and Chittenden Library incorporated the latest advances and was completely fireproof. It featured the best lighting facilities, a glass roof, a ventilation system powered by electricity, and special shelving behind the delivery desk for the 25,000 books most in demand. The stacks had a capacity of 160,000 volumes, and service was facilitated by speaking tubes and a dumbwaiter. Adorning the main reading room, which accommodated ninety people, was a memorial window designed by Tiffany that cost $25,000. Although the building was a great improvement over the facilities provided by the old library (constructed in the 1840s), Van Name realized that a much larger building would eventually be needed. The Chittenden Library completed in 1890 was the first third of a building that would have a frontage of 350 feet and a capacity of at least 1,000,000 volumes.

The second stage of Van Name's building program was undertaken in 1905-1906, the year of his retirement. Again the nation was surveyed, and the latest improvements in commercial architecture were utilized, including an automatic book carrier similar to the electric carriers used in department stores, prismatic windows to gain maximum light as used in factories, traffic flow patterns like those used in railroad terminals, and the "telautograph" used in large hotels to duplicate handwritten orders on higher floors. The Linsly Library, which cost $300,000, featured a six-story, structural steel bookstack, with a capacity of 400,000 volumes. For the first time in the history of library construction, the stacks rested on steel pillars, thus allowing for thinner walls and wider window space.

In 1867, Van Name married Julia Gibbs, the sister of his classmate. The old Gibbs residence was renovated, and the Van Names occupied it with J. Willard Gibbs and his sister Anna. Julia died in 1916, leaving two sons and a daughter.

Engravings and photographs show little physical change in Van Name over the years, except for the full, flowing beard of his youth, which was gradually trimmed to a neat Van Dyke and was flecked with gray by the end of the century. Although Van Name left no known collection of personal papers, a record of his talent and accomplishments survives in the University archives, his letters found in the collections of his colleagues, and testimonials published at the time of his retirement and later at the time of his

death. In 1905, the Yale Corporation cited in particular "the unusual range of his interests," which resulted in a wide yet balanced acquisitions policy, "his remarkable memory, his rare judgment in purchasing so that the slender income of past years yielded results far beyond reasonable expectations, his uncommon linguistic attainments, [and] his unfailing courtesy and patience toward both the patrons and the staff of the Library." On the occasion of his eightieth birthday in 1915, the University commissioned the painting of his portrait by Sergeant Kendall so that Van Name would be "remembered with gratitude by the present and future generations as one of the builders of the modern University...." William Lyon Phelps said, in 1918, that Van Name was "probably the most skillful buyer of books on earth."

Van Name's eighteen years of retirement were spent in travel and research. In 1913, his *Catalogue of the William Loring Andrews Collection of Early Books* was published. When Van Name died on September 29, 1922, few people at the University remembered him, yet two articles appeared in the *Yale Alumni Weekly*. The lead editorial memorialized his many qualities, emphasizing that

> he was, however, above all else a great librarian and assembler of books at a time when such a profession was little understood and when buying obscure books for future users was an unpractised art. Yale to-day has one of the great scholarly libraries of the world, and it was very largely due to Professor Van Name that its foundations were so laid that this has proved to be the case.

Biographical listings and obituaries—*Dictionary of American Biography* 19 (Andrew Keogh); [Obituary]. *Journal of the American Oriental Society* 1923:151-52; [Obituary]. *New Haven Journal-Courier*, Oct. 3, 1923; [Obituary]. *New Haven Register*, Sept. 30, 1922; [Obituary]. *New York Times*, Sept. 30, 1922; *Obituary Record of Yale Graduates*, 1922-1923. New Haven, 1923; [Obituary]. *Yale Alumni Weekly* 32:61, 67 (Oct. 6, 1922) [reprinted in *Library Journal* 47:874 (Oct. 15, 1922)]; [Obituary]. *Yale Daily News*, Oct. 2, 1922; *Who Was Who in America* I (1897-1942); Yale College Class of 1858. *Biographical Record*, I-V (1865-1908). **Books and articles about the biographee**—Brough, Kenneth J. *Scholar's Workshop: Evolving Conceptions of Library Service*. Urbana: University of Illinois Press, 1953; Rukeyser, Muriel. *Willard Gibbs*. New York: Doubleday, 1942; Wheeler, Lynde Phelps. *Josiah Willard Gibbs*. New Haven: Yale University Press, 1952. **Primary sources and archival materials**—Basic sources are the records (including letters and reports) of the librarian and president, Yale University Archives, Yale University Library. Letters by and about Van Name are in Manuscripts and Archives (Sterling Memorial Library) and in the Beinecke Rare Book and Manuscript Library, Yale University. Van Name is also frequently noted and quoted in the *Proceedings* of annual conferences of the American Library Association published in *Library Journal*, 1876-1894.

—JUDITH A. SCHIFF

VAN PATTEN, NATHAN (1887-1956)

Nathan van Patten was born to John E. and Jennie Boughton van Patten on March 24, 1887, in Niskayuna (near Schenectady), New York. Even as a very small child, he showed the organizing instincts of a librarian, adding call numbers to his juvenilia and, at age ten, issuing a catalog of his private library, printed from rubber type line by line. He was graduated from the Union Classical Institute in 1907 and became a school teacher. His first efforts at publication during this period were two brief studies of genealogical interest and a revision of the *History of the City and County of Schenectady, New York* used by the public schools.

In 1917, van Patten became librarian of the Wolcott Gibbs Library of Chemistry at the College of the City of New York. In 1920, he moved to the Massachusetts Institute of Technology as a reference librarian and then as assistant librarian. During this period, he became an abstractor for *Chemical Abstracts*, an activity that he continued through 1928. In 1923, van Patten moved to Queen's University, Kingston, Canada, as chief librarian. During his sojourn in Canada, he also served as a lecturer in the library school at McGill University in Montreal. (After returning to the United States, van Patten maintained his contact with Canada as the honorary consultant in Canadiana at the Library of Congress.)

In 1927, van Patten made his last career move when he accepted the position of director of libraries at Stanford University, a position he held until 1947, when he became professor of bibliography. In 1952, he retired from this post but continued to serve as curator of the Memorial Library of Music at Stanford, the last major collection that he developed for Stanford. Van Patten also held lectureships in the Stanford Chemistry Department (1931-1952) and in the University of California School of Medicine, where he was a lecturer in medical history and bibliography. He also served as an advisor on the War Collection at the Yale University Library.

Van Patten's contributions to learned literary journals span such subjects as Arthur Machen, Bliss Carmen, Samuel Taylor Coleridge, Sir Walter Scott, and D. H. Lawrence. In library literature, he wrote on such diverse topics as cooperative cataloging, censorship, interlibrary loan fees, and training personnel. He also wrote on various scientific topics, the printing trade, and medical history. Van Patten founded the Arthur Machen Society and had an extensive collection of the Welsh novelist's works. He also collected bibliography and fine printing. His major monographic writings are *Bibliography of the Corrosion of Metals and Its Prevention* (1923), *Selective Bibliography of the Literature of Lubrication* (1926), *An Index to Bibliographies and Bibliographical Contributions Relating to the Work of American and British Authors (1923-1932)* (1934), *Printing in Greenland* (1939), and the *Catalogue of the Memorial Library of Music at Stanford University* (1950).

Nathan van Patten was married to Mabel Waite, and they had one daughter, Dolores. Van Patten passed away on March 17, 1956, after a brief illness.

Nathan van Patten was a bookman first, administrator second. A colleague of his, Edwin T. Coman, Jr., noted that the first time he met van Patten "he was walking ... with his nose buried in a book," and further described him as "one of those persons who is worthy to be called a bookman." Theodore Wesley Koch (q.v.), librarian of Northwestern University, described van Patten as one who

has tried consistently to bear in mind that libraries and librarians exist only because there are people who want to use libraries. Librarianship to him is more a matter of bibliographical scholarship placed at the service of library users than an undue concern about techniques, statistics, or salaries.

Lawrence Clark Powell wrote that van Patten wasn't "ignorant of the so-called science of administration: he just wasn't interested in the mechanics of running a library ... and he was critical of the library schools, which failed to recruit or to graduate the bookish librarians he esteemed."

In 1936, Nathan van Patten was the recipient of an honorary Litt.D. from Dartmouth College. The citation awarding this degree succinctly summed up the career and accomplishments of this Renaissance man:

From graduation at an historic eastern college to the director of libraries at a great western university, your career as librarian has marked you as a cosmopolitan, alike in the extra-ordinary breadth of your familiarity in diverse fields of knowledge. Distinguished in your chosen field as bibliographer and library administrator, and highly esteemed as a writer on technical subjects in this field, the range of your learning has made you also lecturer in chemistry, contributor to medical and chemical journals, authority on the literature of Latin America and specialist in the medical bibliography of these countries, exponent of the library's vital part in the educational system and author of learned papers in several languages and a wide variety of fields—literary, bibliographical, and scientific....

Van Patten was said to have had a well-developed sense of humor and never took himself or his professional colleagues "too seriously." In describing van Patten, Powell said, "There was nothing rapid about him. He was massively (and sometimes maddeningly) deliberate." Powell also commented that van Patten was "not an attractive personality on first meeting, he was shy and reserved and indifferent to small talk." Perhaps small talk about books was acceptable, for he "had a passion for books and bibliography, and when you were with him no other kind of conversation was possible . . . books were his labor and love. . . ."

Van Patten expressed his views on books and people quite succinctly, saying

By all means let's be efficient in technology, competent in administration, and yet very quiet about these things so that scholars and book collectors are not too much disturbed by them. . . .

These are the men who will build library buildings, fill them with books, and provide endowments from which better salaries can be paid, and all kinds of interesting gadgets provided for the amusement of those librarians who do not particularly care for books.

He was never seen without a cigarette dangling from his lips, with the ash growing longer and longer "while the slow stream of words came smoothly through a curtain of smoke." Powell described him as "generous to those who shared his bookish interest." Van Patten had befriended Powell while the latter was an employee of Jake Zeitlin's antiquarian bookshop and encouraged him during Powell's early years as a librarian.

Under Nathan van Patten's leadership, the Stanford University Library more than doubled in size. The Lane Medical Library enhanced its already fine collection of medical history works and two new collections, the Charlotte Ashley Felton Memorial Library (American and English literature) and the Sir Isaac Newton Collection (now the Frederick E. Brasch Collection on Sir Isaac Newton and the History of Scientific Thought), were developed. To this number must be added the Memorial Library of Music, van Patten's last effort. Raynard C. Swank, writing at van Patten's death, said, "His great contribution to Stanford was the building of the library collections. Dr. van Patten built for all time. Though few may remember, or give credit where it is due, all will benefit."

Biographical listings and obituaries—[Obituary]. *College and Research Libraries* 17:262 (May 1956); [Obituary]. *Library Association Record* 58:205 (May 1956); *Who Was Who in America* III (1951-1960); *Who's Who in Library Service*, 1st ed., 2nd ed. Books and articles about the biographee—Coman, Edwin T., Jr. "Nathan van Patten Retires." *College and Research Libraries* 13:390-91 (Oct. 1952); Powell, Lawrence Clark. "Nathan van Patten, 1887-1956." *Libri* 7:88-90 (1956). Primary sources and archival materials—Manuscript encomiums and a manuscript bibliography of van Patten's writings are in the Stanford University Archives. Manuscript essays written in his honor upon retirement by American and foreign scholars and librarians are held by Mrs. van Patten at the van Patten home at Stanford.

—RALPH W. HANSEN

VATTEMARE, NICOLAS-MARIE-ALEXANDRE (1796-1864)

Nicolas-Marie-Alexandre Vattemare was born in Paris on November 8, 1796, the son of a French advocate. A talented ventriloquist and impersonator, he renounced a theatrical career in order to promote his system of international literary and scientific exchange, which flourished in the United States between 1840 and the mid-1850s. Also a crusader for the free public library, he was instrumental in the founding of the Boston Public Library.

On the family estate near Lisieux, Normandy, young Alexandre first discovered his extraordinary power to "throw his voice" and to baffle his elders with mischievous pranks. Abandoning a promising future in medicine for ventriloquism in 1814, "Monsieur Alexandre" performed during the next fifteen years before thousands of distinguished admirers, including "twenty-eight kings and three emperors."

While appearing throughout Europe, Vattemare noted a vast amount of duplication in museums and libraries, as well as neglect and disuse of valuable materials. He was prompted to organize, in about 1825, an international exchange, which in four years' time, he later claimed, withdrew nearly two million volumes "from dust and oblivion." Having been urged by the Marquis de Lafayette and other prominent supporters, he came to the United States in October 1839; he then spent nineteen months in both the United States and Canada advancing his bibliographic schemes in more than fifty cities before the most influential people and institutions of the day, notably the U.S. Congress. The latter authorized the exchange of duplicates on July 20, 1840, under the direction of the Joint Committee on the Library.

Vattemare soon realized that a successful exchange depended on the availability of public libraries. Toward that end, while in Boston in the spring of 1841, he interested leading citizens in a plan for consolidating a number of its private libraries. What emerged instead was a tax-supported library (i.e., Boston Public Library), opened in 1854, made possible by enabling legislation in 1848, the "first official recognition by a state governing body of the principle of municipal library support." In the present building, the name of Alexandre Vattemare, along with eminent New Englanders, is inlaid in brass letters on the marble floor of the entrance as a memorial.

Ensconced in Paris in his Agence Centrale des Échanges Internationaux, Vattemare carried out his work, with funds from the French government and with some help from his son Hippolyte and son-in-law César Moreau. In the period 1840-1853, he won the support, also, of eighteen U.S. state legislatures, with Louisiana supplying the generous sum of

$3,000. During his second visit to the United States, from May 1847 to December 1850, Congress passed an act (in June 1848) giving the Joint Committee the right to establish agencies for exchange, naming Vattemare as official agent, and eventually allowing $1,500 for expenses. By 1853, when Vattemare submitted a report of his work to the Librarians' Convention in New York, there were enrolled 130 libraries and institutions, 74 of these in the United States. In addition to the "thousands" of books sent to the United States between 1841 and 1847, he claimed that a total of 61,011 items were sent between 1848 and 1851, and 30,655 of these were sent to the United States.

The system, however, lost favor. Appropriations in France were cut off in 1848; the U.S. Congress rescinded the law creating the exchange in 1852, and individual states gradually withdrew from the system. The exchange failed primarily because it was too ambitious an operation for one man. Officials in France and the United States complained of haphazard distribution, inappropriate materials, and lack of financial accounting. Another factor was the success of the Smithsonian Institution's International Exchange Service, in operation by 1850. Vattemare died in Paris on April 7, 1864.

Some of Vattemare's contemporaries considered him a charlatan, or at least an ambitious incompetent. However, many more have testified to the charm, zest, and oratorical skill he employed in singleminded devotion to the ideal of human brotherhood attainable through intercultural education. His own country named him a chevalier of the *Légion d'honneur.*

Biographical listings and obituaries–*Dictionary of American Biography* 19 (Elizabeth M. Richards); *Who Was Who in America*, Historical Volume (1607-1896). **Books and articles about the biographee**–Dargent, J. L. "Alexandre Vattemare." *Bulletin des Bibliothèques de France* 9:333-39 (Août 1964); Haraszti, Zoltan. "Alexandre Vattemare." *Boston Public Library Bulletin. More Books.*, 6th series, 2:257-66 (Nov. 1927); Richards, Elizabeth M. "Alexandre Vattemare and His System of International Exchanges." *Medical Library Association Bulletin* 32:413-48 (Oct. 1944) [Bibliography contains relevant congressional documents and manuscript references]; Utley, George B. *The Librarians' Conference of 1853.* Ed. by Gilbert H. Doane. Chicago: American Library Association, 1951; Whitehill, Walter Muir. *The Boston Public Library.* Cambridge: Harvard University Press, 1956.

–RUTH R. GAMBEE

VINTON, FREDERIC (1817-1890)

Frederic Vinton was born in Boston on October 9, 1817, the son of Josiah and Betsey Giles Vinton, and the descendant of a long line of Colonial forebears. He attended the Weymouth and Braintree academies and was graduated from Amherst College in 1837; Vinton then attended the divinity school at Yale and

the Andover Theological Seminary and was graduated from the latter in 1842.

After his marriage to Phoebe Clisbe in 1843, Vinton served as pastor to a church in St. Louis, Missouri, though he was never formally ordained to the ministry. Poor health forced his resignation in 1845, and he returned to New England, where he taught school until 1851, when a paralytic stroke changed the course of his life.

Following a lengthy recuperation, Vinton moved again to St. Louis to engage in literary work and to catalog a large private library belonging to his brother Alfred, a prominent St. Louis resident. The study through which he prepared himself for making the catalog determined his future career. In the introduction to the catalog, which he finished in 1854, he gave an account of the reading and planning he had done and included a translation of Brunet's introduction to the "Table Méthodique" of his *Manuel du Libraire.* The catalog itself has a classed arrangement under the broad headings of Brunet's system, but the subdivisions show considerable thought and flexibility on Vinton's part.

Following the death of his wife early in 1855, Vinton returned to Boston, where he taught school again for a year. He was married to Mary B. Curry in 1857.

In 1856 Vinton joined the staff of the Boston Public Library as assistant librarian, thereby launching a career that won him recognition as a literary librarian and an expert in subject cataloging. Under the direction of Edward Capen, the librarian, and (beginning in 1858) Superintendent Charles C. Jewett (q.v.), he assisted in producing the Library's printed catalogs of 1858, 1861, and 1865. In 1865, he moved to the Library of Congress as assistant librarian under Ainsworth Rand Spofford (q.v.). There he helped to prepare the *Catalogue of the Library of Congress: Index to Subjects* (1869) and was responsible for the annual volumes of the alphabetical catalog from 1867 to 1872.

In 1873, Vinton became the first full-time librarian of the College of New Jersey (now Princeton University). His administration there was noted for many accomplishments and for the sense of professionalism that he brought to the Library. Under him, the collection increased from 18,000 to 70,000 volumes and evolved from a very specialized and relatively unused collection into that of a well-rounded college library. Use of the Library by students, one of Vinton's greatest concerns, increased significantly. A card catalog was begun and, in 1884, the *Subject Catalogue of the Library of the College of New Jersey* was published.

While pursuing his career at Princeton, Vinton engaged also in literary, professional, and other activities. He wrote periodical articles on a wide variety of topics, but especially on subjects related to bibliography, church history, and missions. He was active in working with the poor as an expression of his own Christian endeavor. He also took an active part in the American Library Association—he was one of its founders in 1876—and related activities. He wrote for *Library Journal*. In 1876, he contributed two and possibly three separate chapters to the Bureau of Education's *Public Libraries in the United States of America . . . Special Report* (they appeared without his name), and he taught as a special lecturer in Melvil Dewey's (q.v.) School of Library Economy.

Vinton's most intense interest in librarianship was in catalog subject access to library materials, which grew out of his preparatory study for cataloging of his brother's library. Later, his work under Jewett in Boston exposed him to the dictionary concept which enabled him, still later, to offer counsel to Charles A. Cutter's (q.v.) exemplary work on the dictionary catalog for the Boston Athenaeum. His own later work favored the alphabetico-classed arrangement, especially in the Library of Congress 1869 volume, on which he worked with Stephen B. Noyes (q.v.; later of the Brooklyn Mercantile Library, and author of its alphabetico-classed catalog).

Vinton's proclivity for a classed catalog structure of some sort reflects his library philosophy. Education was for him a discipline involving rigorous and systematic inquiry, and, for that reason, he considered subject access to a library an absolute necessity. The arrangement of books and bibliographic access to them were to be based on a rigorously logical and consistent order, so that the apprehension of that order could become an aid to the library patron in the educational process. Because patrons did not easily learn such complex bibliographical structures, however, Vinton also felt, as a necessary concomitant, that the librarian had to work closely with patrons to bring them to a point of self-help. With his own wide reading and knowledge, he became an intellectual benefactor of students and a teacher of teachers. As a result of his library labors, he received an honorary Litt.D. from Amherst in 1886.

His concern for promoting greater use of the library by students places Vinton alongside Justin Winsor (q.v.), Reuben A. Guild (q.v.), and Otis H. Robinson (q.v.) as one of the college librarians who pioneered in service to readers. Yet, Vinton's courteous exercise of intellectual and personal fidelity toward his patrons was not without difficulties. The poor health of his early years continued with him and he often bore considerable physical pain. He remained at his post even so, almost to the end, and died on the first day of 1890.

Biographical listings and obituaries—*Dictionary of American Biography* 19 (James Thayer Gerould); *National Cyclopaedia of American Biography* 6. **Books and articles about the biographee**—Jerould, James Thayer. "An Early American Essay on Classification by Frederic Vinton." *Library Quarterly* 7:502-510 (Oct. 1937); "Frederick [sic] Vinton." *Library Journal* 15:179-80 (June 1890).

—FRANCIS L. MIKSA

WALKER, CAROLINE BURNITE (1875-1936)

The sources of Caroline Burnite Walker's sense of moral and social responsibility and the story of how that concern became translated into developing children's libraries are unknown. She was born on January 12, 1875, and the few other records that exist begin with her education at the Pratt Institute School of Library Science, where she was in the class of 1894. She received only As in her courses and listed her permanent address as Easton, Maryland. Her childhood, early education, the people, books, and ideas that most influenced her life were not recorded; her library work was done prior to her marriage.

Burnite left her first job as chief cataloger at the University for Catholic Women (1894-1896) in Brooklyn for the position of librarian at the Tome Institute in Port Deposit, Maryland (1896-1901). Here she first recognized the need for special library services and materials to attract children. During her career as a children's librarian, she helped define the objectives of children's library services—setting standards of book selection, creating an enthusiasm for storytelling, and developing the concept of guided reading. However, her strongest direct influence was on the children's librarians she trained at Cleveland Public Library.

Caroline Burnite was very much a part of the early twentieth-century reform movement that sought to develop healthy social institutions to promote strong moral character. Her personal beliefs coincided with these ideals, as Siri Andrews has noted:

Miss Burnite's whole concept of library work with children stemmed from her own deep sense of moral and social responsibility toward both the individual and society. What books and the library can do for the child as an individual and for the child as a member of the community are the justification for the existence of a library children's department and for its public support.

Reformist movements, child labor laws, and mass education all contributed to Caroline Burnite's remarkable success with children's services. In 1904, when she came to the Cleveland Public Library at the invitation of William Howard Brett (q.v.), a single service point existed for all children in Cleveland. In 1914, the *Cleveland Plain Dealer* reported that there were 453 distribution centers, that six out of ten children read library books in their homes, and that each reader averaged twenty books per year.

Before coming to Cleveland, Burnite had served under Frances Jenkins Olcott (q.v.) at the Carnegie Library of Pittsburgh and had taught in the training school for children's librarians. At Cleveland, she extended the work of Effie Power (q.v.) by establishing children's services in all of the branch libraries that Andrew Carnegie (q.v.) helped to build. She also moved the Library into the community; rather than wait for children to come to the Library, she sent books and librarians to where the children were.

Because many children had no access to a neighborhood library, Burnite established libraries in other institutions that served children—public schools, settlement houses, churches, synagogues, orphanages, and even in homes. (The Home Libraries were small book collections put in private homes in areas with no library service. A Library employee or volunteer visited the home once a week to circulate books, change the collection, and tell stories.) Story hours were another means of attracting children to the Library and inducing them to read books. Burnite believed that hearing a story had an even greater influence on children than reading it. Therefore, she wanted material to be selected carefully. She often used folk or traditional tales because she believed that folk literature embodied "the dreams and aspirations of mankind in the remote past" (*Public Libraries* 20:160) and transmitted fundamental moral values.

Story hours were one method of encouraging reading, but Burnite primarily stressed individual guidance. Her staff created "ladder lists" (sequential book lists) to guide children from simple books that related to their immediate experience to more complex ("adult") books. Another method was through reading clubs that adolescents organized and maintained themselves.

Underlying her principles of reading guidance was her intelligent and sensitive approach to book selection. This resulted in a set of standards that not only influenced what other librarians thought of as suitable material for children, but also encouraged publishers to offer books of the caliber she desired. Burnite noted that "directed moral instruction has little place in the making of character" (*Library Journal* 34:707 [1909]); rather, she believed that underlying values expressed through plot and characters would influence children's attitudes by glorifying certain concepts. Reading could thus influence children's development and could help compensate for a poor environment: "Children with social needs must have books with social values to meet those needs—right social contacts, true social perspective, traditions of family and race, loveliness of nature,

companionship of living things, right group association and group interests" (*ALA Bulletin* 7:282 [1913]).

In order to implement a successful children's program, Caroline Burnite needed a specially trained staff, but few institutions offered courses in children's work. Therefore, in 1909, she organized the Cleveland Public Library's Training Class for Children's Librarians. Under her direction, 81 librarians were trained in book selection, administration, work with adults in ethnic communities, outreach programs (such as work with schools), and storytelling. A student in the first training class described her as "a woman of strong, almost overwhelming personality, who nevertheless had the gift of bringing out the characteristic and individual traits of those under her." Burnite believed that to be a good librarian one must lead a rich, rewarding personal life; this also helped guard against the occupational hazard of talking only about children. So she introduced her students to plays, concerts, and even puppet shows in the Italian neighborhood. After she retired, the Training Class became part of the Library School at Western Reserve University.

Among the articles that Burnite published in professional journals, the following are considered to be her most important contributions: "The Beginnings of a Literature for Children" (*Library Journal* 31:107-112 [1906]), "The Standards of Selection of Children's Books" (*Library Journal* 36:161-66 [1911]), "Values in Library Work with Children" (*ALA Bulletin* 7:282-87 [1913]), "Sequences in Children's Reading" (*Public Libraries* 20:160-65 [1915]), and "Library Work with Children in War Time" (*Library Journal* 43:705-707 [1918]).

In 1919, Caroline Burnite was married to Robert Rastall Walker and retired to Easton, Maryland. However, she remained active by lecturing on children's librarianship and developing a correspondence course for librarians. She led a group that founded the Talbot County Free Library. The founders elected her the first president of the Library Board in 1925 and she kept the office until her death in 1936. Under her encouragement, the Library offered services to children both through its own collections and through services to the public schools. During the Depression, Caroline Walker served as the librarian from 1931 to 1936. After her death, the Library Board dedicated the children's room in the new building to her memory.

What has probably influenced the greatest number of people was her philosophy of librarianship as it related to children. As her colleague Annie Spencer Cutter described it, "She dignified the child as an individual and emphasized the strategic position which the children's librarian held in relation to the lives she touched and her resources in that relationship."

Caroline Burnite Walker died on November 2, 1936.

Books and articles about the biographee—Andrews, Siri. *Caroline Burnite Walker, a Pioneer in Library Work with Children.* Cleveland: Cleveland Public Library, 1950; Clark, Raymond B. "History of the Talbot County Free Library, Easton, Maryland, 1925-1962." M.S.L.S. thesis, Catholic University of America, 1963; Hatch, Bertha. "Caroline Burnite Walker." *Library Journal* 51:958-59 (Dec. 15, 1936). **Primary sources and archival materials**—Material concerning Caroline Burnite's tenure at the Cleveland Public Library is held at that institution.

—MARGO SASSÉ

WALTER, FRANK KELLER (1874-1945)

Frank Keller Walter was born on July 23, 1874, at Mount Pleasant, Pennsylvania, the son of Samuel A. and Elizabeth Keller Walter. He qualified as a teacher by attending the Westchester, Pennsylvania, State Normal School, graduating in 1894. He received his bachelor's degree from Haverford College in 1899, and his master's degree from the same college in 1900. While studying for his master's degree, he served as assistant professor of English and German. During 1903-1904, Walter was a special student at George Washington University, and at about this time, he decided to become a librarian. In 1906, he received his B.L.S. degree from the New York State Library School at Albany, and, upon graduation, became a reference assistant in the Brooklyn Public Library. He returned to the New York State Library School in 1907, where he was at first director's assistant, and, from 1908 to 1919, vice-director. In addition to his administrative duties at the New York State Library School, Walter was a teacher, and a successful one.

On June 22, 1907, at Westchester, he was married to S. Ruth McMichael. They had one son, Richard Keller, who died in childhood.

In 1919, he became librarian at the General Motors Corporation in Detroit, where he remained only one year. After leaving General Motors, he taught a semester at the University of Illinois Library School, and at the University of Michigan Library School in the summer of 1921. By this time, he had gained a national reputation as a library educator.

In the fall of 1921, Frank Walter was appointed librarian at the University of Minnesota, where he served until his retirement in 1943. At Minnesota, he was only the third librarian, having been preceded by William Watts Folwell (1869-1906) and James Thayer Gerould (q.v.; 1906-1921). Soon after his arrival in Minneapolis, Walter became involved in the construction of a new university library building, opened in 1924, which had been planned by Gerould.

As a librarian, Walter will probably be longest remembered for his work in developing the University of Minnesota Library into one of the important research libraries of the country, with, of course, the assistance of faculty and staff. He considered building the book collection to be his major responsibility as University librarian. His knowledge of and personal enthusiasm for books, both for their intellectual content and as physical objects, were of primary importance in achieving this aim, as well as in his success as a library school teacher and as an author on library subjects. He spent a considerable amount of his time reading and making selections from antiquarian book catalogs, for which he had a fondness and affection. For him, this was an essential part of his work and one of the most enjoyable parts. In addition to reading catalogs during the day, he often took several home, returning them next morning to the Acquisitions Department with titles checked for purchase. Constantly on the alert for bargains, and constantly reading catalogs and searching in bookstores, he became knowledgeable about book prices. In this work, his wide reading and knowledge of languages were also valuable.

Another of Walter's strong interests was bookbinding. He visited the University Library Bindery frequently, and often gave personal instructions on the binding of rare and important books, as well as on the treatment and care of those with interesting and unusual bindings.

In some areas of expenditure for the Library, he was at times thrifty to the point of frugality, but he was liberal in spending money for books. Although Walter sought increases from the University administration for other Library operations, and was reasonably successful, he was especially successful in securing book funds. The Library grew rapidly under his administration. From 1921 until his retirement in 1943, the book collection increased in size from about 250,000 to more than a million and a quarter volumes. In a survey published in the *Princeton Alumni Weekly* (February 1936), the University of Minnesota Library was rated third in growth among eighteen representative institutions. Shortly after Walter's retirement, Minnesota was ranked sixth among American research libraries in the number of volumes (according to the Association of Research Libraries statistical report for 1945-1946).

Walter also understood the importance of periodicals and newspapers in a research library and gave attention to acquiring back files. His interest in and understanding of the importance of periodicals had been signalled in the seven editions of his *Periodicals for Small and Medium Sized Libraries* (the first in 1913, the seventh in 1938). He believed that the holdings of a research library should not be limited to major authors but should include at least representative samples of minor authors: not only all of the works of Herman Melville, for example, but some of Mrs. E. D. E. N. Southworth.

Given his zeal for expanding the book collections, and given the attention he gave to his other areas of interest, personnel problems at the Library were somewhat slighted. He tended to be somewhat of a disciplinarian, although moderate rather than strict; communication with his staff was ordinarily on a one-to-one basis rather than in scheduled staff meetings.

In 1928, with the establishment of the Library School (originally the Division of Library Instruction) that he had strongly advocated, Walter added teaching in the School to his duties as director. Former students report almost unanimously that he was a fine teacher, knowledgeable in the subjects he taught, and able to bring them alive. His wide reading and retentive memory enabled him to illuminate a subject with quotations and stories, often humorous. He was a voluminous note taker, maintaining a card file, arranged by subject, which filled many drawers. Carl Vitz said that Walter's teaching method was to challenge students and to make them think.

Under his administration, the Library School relied largely on the staff of the University Library for teachers. This was due, in part, to an agreement with the University administration at the time of the founding of the School that, insofar as possible, it should be self-sustaining. From the School's beginning in 1928 until Walter's retirement in 1943, Lura Hutchinson was the only full-time faculty member. Walter was content that the courses were being taught by able, experienced librarians, and, although he did suggest to the University administration the need for additional full-time faculty, he seems, in general, to have accepted the idea that the School be self-supporting. Not until after his retirement were additional full-time faculty members appointed.

Not only was Walter dedicated to collecting books for the University of Minnesota Library, but book collecting was his strongest personal hobby. Both his office and his home were filled to overflowing with books, and his interests were completely book-centered. Among his special collecting interests were bibliography, publishing and printing, early children's books, humor (especially American), etiquette (mainly nineteenth and twentieth centuries), and book collecting. As mentioned earlier, he was also a constant reader of antiquarian catalogs, and in the course of selecting books for the University Library, he sometimes came across books of personal interest. From time to time he would ask to be notified if such a book was in the University Library, and if it were, he then felt free to order it for himself. Many of the books from his personal library (for example, his

etiquette collection) were acquired by the University Library.

Walter was active in local, state, and national library associations. He served on the Council of the American Library Association (1912-1917) and on its editorial committee (1924-1927). He was president of the New York Library Association (1915-1916). From 1919 to 1920, he was president of the Association of American Library Schools, having been an active member since its founding in 1915. Soon after he came to Minnesota, he was elected president of the Minnesota Library Association (1922-1923). He was secretary and treasurer of the American Library Institute (1930-1933) and a member of the Executive Board of the Bibliographical Society of America (1924-1928). He was a member of the Library Association of Great Britain, the Gutenberg Gesellschaft, and the Twin City Library Club. Phineas Windsor (q.v.) wrote that Walter was a welcome participant at library meetings, making perceptive, thought-provoking contributions to discussions.

As an author Walter made numerous contributions to the literature of librarianship; a conservative estimate indicates at least a hundred published items. While in his first position, reference assistant in the Brooklyn Public Library, he prepared *A Reading and Reference List on Costume* (Brooklyn Public Library, 1909). In 1911, volume one of *Modern Drama and Opera* was issued, followed in 1915 by volume two. His years at the University of Minnesota, beginning in 1921, were productive ones, with publications on many subjects. At the time of Walter's retirement in 1943, J. Christian Bay (q.v.) prepared a list of some 43 topics on which Walter had published journal articles; included are bookbinding, cataloging, library cooperation, hospital libraries, librarian authors, printing, periodicals, rare books, interlibrary loans, reference work, librarians' reading, library education, Sunday school libraries, and library schools.

Perhaps his most lasting publication is *Bibliography, Practical, Enumerative, Historical*, co-authored with Henry B. Van Hoesen (q.v.) and published in 1928. Although understandably in need of revision, it remains a useful work in its field and is currently available in a reprint edition. Also useful is his *Abbreviations and Technical Terms Used in Book Catalogs and in Bibliographies* (1919; reprinted, 1973). He had hoped to prepare a revised edition of this work and made numerous notes for such a revision, especially from antiquarian book catalogs. His *Periodicals for Small and Medium Sized Libraries* went through seven editions from 1913 to 1939. From the 1939 edition, the following comment on *The New Yorker* is an example of his writing style:

Very cleverly written and illustrated, consciously and deliberately "sophisticated" and cynical and with enough variations from scrupulous good taste to make many readers feel a pleasant thrill of vicarious wickedness. Will occasionally shock some readers but not a large proportion of most communities.

His *Library Printing* was published in 1913 and the *Library's Own Printing* in 1934. He edited and revised Mary Wright Plummer's (q.v.) *Training for Librarianship* in 1920 and 1923. With his retirement in 1943, Walter looked forward to completing a number of research and writing projects. By the time of his final illness in 1945, he had finished work on the "Jesuit Relations" part of *Jesuit Relations and Other Americana in the Library of James Ford Bell* at the University of Minnesota, although he did not live to see the final typed manuscript. He had also written much of a book-length manuscript on the history of the University of Minnesota Library, which remains unpublished.

Walter was of medium height with a tendency toward stoutness. Dignified and friendly in manner, he was modest, confident and poised. He possessed a rich vocabulary that he used skillfully. With rare exceptions, he was affable and mild-mannered. The Walters did not serve liquor in their home, and he was zealous in enforcing the no-smoking rule in the reading rooms of the University Library.

Frank K. Walter died on October 28, 1945. His contributions to the University of Minnesota were formally recognized in 1958, when the then main library was named the Frank K. Walter Library.

Biographical listings and obituaries—[Obituary]. *Minnesota Libraries* 14:383 (Dec. 1945); *Who Was Who in America* II (1943-1950); *Who's Who in Library Service*, 1st ed., 2nd ed. Books and articles about the biographee—Bay, J. Christian. "Frank K. Walter in Retrospect [with portrait]." *College and Research Libraries* 4:309-311 (Sept. 1943); Blegen, Theodore. "On the Retirement of Frank K. Walter." *Minnesota Libraries* 14:67-68 (Sept. 1943); Gray, James. *The University of Minnesota, 1851-1951.* Minneapolis: University of Minnesota Press, 1951, pp. 32-37; Russell, Harold. "Frank Keller Walter, 1874-1945." *Library Journal* 71:286 (Feb. 15, 1946); Vitz, Carl. "Frank K. Walter [with portrait]." *Bulletin of Bibliography* 18:97-99 (Sept. 1955); Windsor, Phineas. "Frank K. Walter [with portrait]." *Library Journal* 68:616 (Aug. 1943).

—RAYMOND H. SHOVE

WARREN, ALTHEA HESTER (1886-1958)

Althea Hester Warren was born December 18, 1886, in Waukegan, Illinois, the daughter of Lansing and Emma Newhall Blodgett Warren. She was graduated from the University of Chicago with a Ph.B. degree in 1908. She received the B.S.L.S. degree from the University of Wisconsin in 1911 and, in 1939, was awarded the honorary Litt.D. degree from Mills College.

Warren's first professional library position was in a branch of the Chicago Public Library in a slum section on the Northwest Side (1911-1912), where her work was largely with children of immigrant parents. In 1912, she was appointed librarian of the Sears Roebuck Branch of the Chicago Public Library, and she remained there until 1914.

In the fall of 1914, Warren moved to California to join her widowed mother in San Diego. In January 1915, she accepted a position in the San Diego Public Library and, in 1916, was made head librarian. She remained in this position until 1926.

During her period as librarian in San Diego, Warren demonstrated her belief in democratic administration. Staff members were drawn into all aspects of the Library's work and participated in a complete reorganization of the Library. Eugene Ferry Smith, president of the Board of Trustees, in his annual report for the year 1916, praised Warren's work: "Miss Warren, the new librarian, has shown splendid executive and administrative ability, and has met and handled the problems of reorganization in a manner highly satisfactory to the Board and this city can feel fortunate, indeed, in securing her services."

In the fall of 1925, Warren asked for a leave of absence because of her mother's illness and moved her, with a nurse, to Altadena, near Los Angeles. Soon after arriving in the Los Angeles area, she was offered and accepted, in 1926, the job of assistant city librarian in the Los Angeles Public Library, serving under Everett Perry. Her first assignment was to help move the Library collections from a rented building on Fifth and Broadway to a new building on Fifth and Flower. Other accomplishments during her first year as assistant librarian were a scientific study of book turnover, a survey of essentials in different areas of the book collections, and a salary proposal whose result was that salaries for branch librarians in Los Angeles were exceeded only by those of two other large public libraries in the United States. Nine branch libraries were completed in the year 1926-1927, bringing the total to 46.

Warren served as assistant city librarian for seven years and in 1933, after Perry's death, she was appointed to take his place. The appointment received the unanimous vote of the Board of Library Commissioners and the applause of the Library staff.

Warren came into the job at a time of drastic budget retrenchment in the city because of the Depression. She thus had to cope with problems of reduction of hours of service, cuts in personnel, and discontinuance of many services. However, she practiced economies that kept the Library in service, despite diminished resources.

She was especially interested in people and was known for her public relations efforts. In *The City Librarians of Los Angeles*, John Bruckman said, "Althea Warren had in abundance the rare gift of making people know that she was personally concerned with their achievements and problems, and she was able to convey that feeling because it was entirely sincere." Bruckman commented also on her book interests:

> Althea Warren was above all a book person. Good reading in all fields was her lifelong passion, and her literary knowledge was near unmatched. It is ironic that this woman of culture and sensitivity was forced by unyielding necessity to become a tough and skillful administrator.... [It] is the more remarkable that it was she who ably guided the library through two of its most difficult periods—that of the great depression and that of the second World War.

Warren served on numerous committees, lectured frequently at clubs and organizations, and participated in community and civic affairs. With the outbreak of World War II came added responsibility. Warren was asked by Charles H. Brown (q.v.), librarian of Iowa State College and president of the American Library Association, to become director of the Victory Book Campaign. In November 1941, she was given a four months' leave of absence to go to New York to do this. The purpose of the program was to collect millions of books for men in the armed services. The campaign was organized by states, with executive committees and workers in each locality. At the end of the first two months, the goal of five million volumes was already in sight and, by April 1942, this work had been completed to the point that Warren was able to return to her job in Los Angeles.

She returned to problems of shortage of personnel, book shortages, and lowered circulation. One of the first things she did was to extend the hours that the Los Angeles libraries were open to the public. Special war information programs were initiated, with special services for army personnel.

Warren was also active in the work of professional associations. Among the major offices she held was that of president of the California Library Association (1921-1922). In 1943, she was elected president of the American Library Association, the first Californian to attain this distinction. One of the tasks she undertook as president of ALA was to try to get the U.S. Congress to grant federal aid to libraries, and she spent considerable effort, energy, and travel time to and from Washington in this effort. She was also concerned about needed changes in the ALA organization, about discrimination against Negroes in the hotels of certain cities hosting ALA meetings, and about the fact that the presidency of ALA was confined to what she called "the elderly and pretentious in top positions."

Warren retired as city librarian of Los Angeles in the fall of 1947. Numerous tributes were paid to her when she retired. Mabel Gillis (q.v.), state librarian of

California, wrote about her in the *California Library Association Bulletin* (9:47-48 [December 1947]); she spoke especially about Warren as a book person, as a person with a keen sense of humor and with a special gift for friendship.

Soon after her retirement, Althea Warren was invited to teach in the Library School of the University of Southern California. This led to other similar invitations. In 1949-1950, she was a visiting professor in the Library School at the University of Michigan and, in 1950-1951, at the University of Wisconsin. After that she returned to teaching, on a part-time basis, at the University of Southern California and retired from this position in June 1957. Warren was ill with a malignant condition during the last year of her life and died on December 19, 1958.

Biographical listings and obituaries—*Current Biography* (1960); [Obituary]. *ALA Bulletin* 53:321-22 (April 1959); *Who Was Who in America* III (1951-1960); *Who's Who in Library Service*, 1st ed., 2nd ed., 3rd ed. **Books and articles about the biographee**—Boaz, Martha. *Fervent and Full of Gifts*. New York: Scarecrow Press, 1961; Bruckman, John D. *City Librarians of Los Angeles*. Los Angeles: Los Angeles Library Association, 1973, pp. 45-48; Gillis, M. R. "Althea Warren." *California Library Bulletin* 9:47-48 (Dec. 1947).

—MARTHA BOAZ

WATTERSTON, GEORGE (1783-1854)

The first full-time Librarian of Congress was born aboard a ship in New York harbor on October 23, 1783. George Watterston was the son of David Watterston, an emigrant master-builder who had left Jedburgh, Scotland, with his family in order to start a new life in New York City. Eight years later, lured by the opportunities afforded by the creation of the new federal city, the elder Watterston moved with his family to Washington, D.C. Young George was sent to school at Charlotte Hall in St. Mary's County, Maryland, where he received a good classical education. He was then attracted to the study of law, and later opened a law office in Hagerstown, Maryland. Law was not for him, however, for he soon began a literary career that continued throughout his life.

His growing distaste for the legal profession became apparent in his first novel, *The Lawyer, or Man as He Ought Not to Be* (1808), a psychological study of a thoroughly despicable character. He touched on a lighter theme for his next work, *The Child of Feeling: A Comedy in Five Acts* (1809), which was followed closely by a second novel, *Glencarn; or The Disappointments of Youth* (1810). The death of a rich uncle gave him an excuse to close his law office and travel to the West Indies to view his inheritance. He kept a journal of the trip and drew upon his experiences for his next literary endeavor, a poem entitled "The Wanderer in Jamaica" (1810), which he prefaced with a dedication to Dolley

Madison, wife of the President, as follows: "Madam, I have presumed to address this poetical effusion to you, from the reputation you have acquired of being desirous to promote the cause of general literature." Upon returning from his travels, Watterston opened a law office in Washington with Thomas Law. On October 26, 1811, he married Maria Shanley and established a home on Capitol Hill. They had eight children.

The 29-year-old Watterston, now an established inhabitant of the new District of Columbia, soon began his involvement with the political and social life of the city of his childhood; as a result, he soon became one of Washington's first civic and cultural leaders. In 1812, he became a candidate for the position of collector of the District of Columbia. The next year he was engaged as the editor of the *Washington City Gazette*, a Republican paper, the first of four newspaper editorships he was to hold throughout his life. The war with England raged around the city, and, in 1814, Watterston marched with Captain Benjamin Burch's company to meet the British at nearby Bladensburg. He returned to the city to find his own house pillaged, the nearby Capitol in ruins, and, of future importance to him. the fledgling Library of Congress within the Capitol building destroyed.

Prior to 1815, the clerk of the House of Representatives had the additional responsibility of caring for the Library of Congress. Patrick Magruder (q.v.), clerk of the House at that time, was discredited by those who thought he should have done something to save the Library before its destruction during the British occupation of the city. Because of the ill feeling that arose over this event, Magruder resigned his position on January 28, 1815. As a further consequence, it was determined that the position of Librarian should be distinct from the office of clerk of the House. Accordingly, on March 21, 1815, President Madison appointed George Watterston as the first full-time Librarian of Congress. While the legend persists that the dedication of his poem to Dolley Madison was responsible, the real reason was probably Watterston's unique position as Washington's only man of letters.

Watterston pursued his new duties with vigor. Indeed, he was responsible for all of the work in the Library, with the exception of the selection of materials, a pleasure reserved for the Joint Library Committee. Not until 1827 was he officially allowed to hire an assistant. Yet he approached his job with imagination and a vision as to what the Library should become, a vision that frequently clashed with the more practical realities posited by the Library Committee. His first job was to receive and arrange the library of Thomas Jefferson (q.v.), purchased in early 1815. The Library had been moved to temporary quarters in Blodgett's Hotel, where Watterston

arranged the wooden packing cases containing the Jefferson collection and began work on a catalog. On April 26, 1815, he wrote to Jefferson asking for the former President's "system of arrangement," which was based on the 44 "chapters" comprising Francis Bacon's table of knowledge. The Librarian decided to adopt the system in general, although he modified it by alphabetizing the books within chapters, rather than using the analytical or chronological subdivisions that Jefferson had devised.

In October 1815, Watterston's *Catalogue of the Library of the United States* went to press, with copies delivered to the Library Committee prior to December 4. Jefferson, when queried by the anxious Librarian as to how he liked the new arrangement within the chapters, replied mildly in a letter dated March 2, 1816, "Of course, you know, not so well as my own, yet I think it . . . may be more convenient to readers generally than mine. . . ." But the Library Committee members were distinctly unhappy. They did not consider the catalog to be of particular use to the members of Congress and, in their report of January 26, 1816, complained about its cost—a grand total of $1360.50 for 600 copies, "one third more than the annual appropriation made heretofore by Congress for the additional increase of the library, and more than one twentieth of the actual cost of our whole library." Despite the Committee's attitude, Jefferson's classification system as adapted by Watterston was used by the Library of Congress for the rest of the century.

The controversial title of the *Catalogue* was not mentioned in the Committee's report. Nevertheless, it does illustrate that Watterston wanted the Library to be more than just Congress's personal possession. Indeed, despite the Committee's concern with the "miscellanies" of the current collection, Watterston inserted a "Card" into the September 15, 1815, issue of *The National Intelligencer* asking "that American authors, engravers, and painters who are solicitous to preserve their respective productions as mementos of the taste of the times, would transmit to the Library a copy of such work as they may design for the public eye. . . ." The letter was issued from the "Library of the United States" and signed "George Watterston, Librarian of Congress." Later Librarians, of course, expanded upon Watterston's early ambitious attempts to build a truly national collection, in addition to a separate building. For on March 25, 1817, another letter written by the persistent Librarian argued for a new building for "the Library of the United States," the first of such dreams to haunt successive Librarians.

Watterston's desire for a building was thwarted, however, for on December 3, 1818, an act was approved that moved the Library to the north wing of the reconstructed Capitol. These quarters proved to be inadequate, and, in 1824, the Library was again moved, this time to the center reported in *The National Intelligencer* (August 28, 1823) to be "the most delightful part of the building, commanding a fascinating view of the most populous part of our city, and of the whole length of the Avenue that connects it with the other Public Offices, and the President's House." Fire was again to prove the Library's nemesis, however; on December 22, 1825, a blaze occurred that fortunately was quickly extinguished. The loss was not heavy, and nothing of consequence was destroyed; but Watterston urged that suitable precautions be taken to make the Library fireproof. Despite an official inquiry into the matter, no steps were taken. The Librarian's worst fears were later confirmed when, in 1851, fire again broke out, this time destroying two-thirds of the collection, including most of Jefferson's library.

Watterston's duties as Librarian did not deter his literary endeavors. Although he became more of an interpreter, critic, and journalist than an imaginative writer after his appointment, he did publish two more novels, which some critics think to be his most important creative works. In both *The L- - - Family in Washington; or a Winter in the Metropolis* (1822) and *The Wanderer in Washington* (1827), Watterston used Washington society for his setting, the first writer of fiction to do so. His interests were wide, and he contributed journalistic pieces to local papers on a variety of topics, including landscape gardening, local and national politics, music, education, and horticulture. In 1816, he became one of the founders of the Washington Botanical Society and, a year later, published a pamphlet on the history, culture, and uses of tobacco. Politics always intrigued him, and in the same year he assumed the editorship of a political paper (the *National Register*) for a time. Under his direction, the "splendid rooms" of the Library became a literary salon, where the leading men and women of letters gathered to read and discuss issues of the day. His critical pieces concerning his contemporaries were surprisingly accurate. At the same time, the Library received increasing support, mainly through the efforts of the Library Committee; on May 26, 1826, Congress raised the book budget to $5,000, a sum granted annually for many decades thereafter.

While his "boosting" of Washington brought him great local prominence, his avid participation in politics proved his downfall. In 1827, he began writing regularly for the *National Journal*, turning it into an organ for the Whig cause. His support of the Whigs and Henry Clay had continued unabated since 1818, when he published his *Letters from Washington, on the Constitution, Laws, and Public Characters of the United States*. Democratic President Andrew Jackson had no use for him in his new government and summarily dismissed him on May 28, 1829. Watterston was indignant. He stomped out of the Library carrying the record books with him. For the rest of his life, he attempted to regain his appointment, but it was a fruitless effort, even though the Whigs won the presidency twice in the next fifteen years. He finally expressed his contempt for the situation in 1850, when he rejected his party and became a Democrat.

Watterston's notorious contemporary Anne Royall, newspaperwoman and fellow writer, "was much struck with his gentlemanly appearance and manners." In her eyes, Watterston appeared as

a man of good size, neither spare nor robust; he is a fine figure and possessed of some personal beauty; his complexion fair, his countenance striking, shows genius and deep penetration, marked with gravity, though manly and commanding. A sweet serenity diffuses itself over his countenance, which no accident can ruffle; and under the veil of retiring modesty, discovers his blushing honors thick upon him.

He was charming and loyal to his friends, a realist who had to support himself largely by his writings. He had a happy home life, and maintained an affectionate interest in the activities of his children long after they had grown. Yet his behavior during the years he attempted to regain his position demonstrated that he was thin-skinned, outspoken to the point of being abusive, and filled—as historian David Mearns aptly described in "The Story Up to Now"—with "a sense of superiority" that caused him to become deeply embittered. Despite his futile attempts to regain his former job, he maintained a comfortable position and continued in his efforts to give Washington a place in the literature of the day. His success in this endeavor became apparent when *The Southern Literary Messenger*, to which Watterston had contributed many articles, dubbed him the "Metropolitan Author" after the appearance of the second of his Washington guidebooks, *A New Guide to Washington* (1842). (*A Picture of Washington* had appeared in 1840.)

In 1830, Watterston became the editor of the *National Journal*. Three years later, he began the movement to build the Washington Monument and remained as secretary of the Washington National Monument Society until his death, which occurred on February 4, 1854. Little mention was made of his passing. A notice of his death that appeared in *The National Intelligencer* on February 6, 1854, ironically made no mention of his years as Librarian and passed quickly over his literary achievements. Instead, it concentrated almost entirely on his activities with the Monument Society.

Although he is almost entirely forgotten now, George Watterston, the first full-time Librarian of

Congress, had a definite impact on the Library during his fourteen-year tenure. Starting with 6,500 volumes in 1815, the Library contained 15,000 volumes in 1829, placing it fourth among libraries in the United States. The book budget was increased from $1000 to $5000 to be provided on an annual basis. The Library had become a leading literary center in the new federal city, which was still trying to prove itself. Most important, perhaps, is the fact that George Watterston was the first of a number of distinguished Librarians who envisaged the Library of Congress as a national repository for American cultural history and have sought ever since to reach that objective.

Biographical listings and obituaries–*Appletons' Cyclopedia of American Biography* 6; *Dictionary of American Biography* 19 (Frederick William Ashley); *National Cyclopaedia of American Biography* 7; [Obituary]. *Daily Union*, Washington, D.C., Feb. 7, 1854; [Obituary]. *The National Intelligencer*, Washington, D.C., Feb. 6, 1854; *Who Was Who in America*, Historical Volume (1607-1896). **Books and articles about the biographee**–Johnston, William Dawson. *History of the Library of Congress*. Washington: Government Printing Office, 1904; Kennedy, Julia E. *George Watterston, Novelist, "Metropolitan Author," and Critic*. Washington: Catholic University of America, 1933; Matheson, William. "George Watterston, Advocate of the National Library." *Quarterly Journal of the Library of Congress* 32:370-88 (Oct. 1976); Mearns, David C. "The Story Up to Now." In *Annual Report of the Librarian of Congress*. Washington: Government Printing Office, 1947; Royall, Anne N. *Sketches of History, Life, and Manners in the United States*. New Haven, 1826. **Primary sources and archival materials**–The Watterston Papers in the Library of Congress consist of three bound volumes of letters and memoranda and two small manuscript volumes.

—NANCY E. GWINN

WEITENKAMPF, FRANK (1866-1962)

Frank Weitenkampf was born in New York City on August 13, 1866. Endowed with a keen mind and consuming interest in art, music, and languages, he was self-educated, with some private tutoring but little formal education. He attended night classes in drawing at Cooper Union for several years and later the Art Students League (1883-1885), hoping for a career as a political cartoonist. At age eighteen, he gave up this ambition; but his interest in caricature remained strong through his life, and he later devoted many articles to this subject, the first one written in 1887.

Weitenkampf joined the Astor Library (later part of the consolidated New York Public Library) as a "boy" (page) on March 1, 1881. From 1882 on, he also worked for the publishing firm of D. Appleton & Co., first in its Wholesale Department, later as a contributor of over 200 biographical sketches of artists, and some musicians, authors, and librarians, for its *Cyclopedia of American Biography*. At age eighteen, he had also become a member of the Literary Society at the famous old branch of the

Young Men's Christian Association, and then was its recording secretary. There he met writers, critics, and editors. In addition, he wrote the yearly report on Continental literature for *Appleton's Annual Cyclopedia* for eleven years. With incredible industry and zest to the very end of his long, productive life, Weitenkampf continued to write reviews and articles on art, music, and theatre for various newspapers and periodicals, using the pseudonym Frank White, or more often, Frank Linstow White in his earlier years.

In 1888, at the age of 22, he began to supply material for both a new edition of Phillips's *Dictionary of Biographical References* (Philadelphia, G. Gebbie & Co.) and the American supplement to the *Encyclopaedia Britannica* (vol. 4; Hubbard Bros., Philadelphia) by contributing articles on opera, organ, piano, painting, and sculpture, as well as biographies of some fifteen artists. Between December 1888 and February 1893, he worked on Appleton's *Medical Dictionary*, selecting medical terms, especially in French and German, from articles in periodicals. He translated from the French, compiled indexes for books published by various publishers, wrote articles for the *International Cyclopedia* and the *Library of Historical Characters & Famous Events*, and contributed Chapter XI, "The Fine Arts in New York City," to the *Memorial History of New York*, edited by James Grant Wilson. He contributed further to the *Dictionary of American Biography* and to the *Encyclopedia Americana*.

Weitenkampf gained the attention of the New York art world when he began to furnish art notes for the weekly publication *The Epoch* in April 1888. This work, which he continued until 1891, brought him into contact with artists, illustrators, and art critics. He also met artists in the Astor Library, where he helped them find source material for historical illustrations, and visits to exhibitions and artists' studios enlarged his horizon as well.

At the same time, Weitenkampf was active in New York's musical life, having begun as a choir boy in the 1870s. He continued until the late 1890s as a member of the Church Choral Society and of the Society of the Friends of Music.

His association and friendship with Samuel Putnam Avery, the New York art dealer and collector, brought a turning point in Weitenkampf's career as a librarian. He first met Avery in 1895, as a result of an article on lithography for artists written for the *Independent*. Avery asked Weitenkampf to prepare an annotated list of the finest prints in his (Avery's) collection, which then was printed as the catalog of an 1896 exhibition held at the Grolier Club on the centenary of the discovery of the process of lithography by Aloys Senefelder. Avery, in 1899, decided to present his notable collection of prints (mainly French etchings and lithographs) to the recently formed New York Public Library, thus establishing Manhattan's first print room. He further proposed that Weitenkampf, then chief of the Shelf Department at the Astor Library building, be curator of prints, to which position he was appointed in 1900.

After his appointment to this new position, Weitenkampf still divided his time between his former duty and that of the new at the Lenox Library building (where the Print Department was first installed until the Central Building was opened to the public). In 1910, Weitenkampf was appointed chief of the Art and Prints Division, a post he held until the Art Division became a separate unit under its own chief in 1923. He remained chief of the Prints Division until his retirement in 1942. During his 42 years as curator, Weitenkampf prepared nearly 300 exhibitions and also lectured on art at New York University, from which, in 1914, he received an honorary L.H.D.

Among the books written by Frank Weitenkampf during his tenure at the NYPL were: *How to Appreciate Prints* (Moffat, Yard & Co., 1908; revisions), *American Graphic Art* (Henry Holt and Co., 1912; revised and enlarged, Macmillan, 1924), *Famous Prints, Masterpieces of Graphic Art* . . . (C. Scribner's Sons, 1926), *The Quest of the Print* (C. Scribner's Sons, 1932), and *The Illustrated Book* (Harvard University Press, 1938). Several of them have been reprinted in recent years.

Most important for the New York Public Library, though, was his work in building up its art holdings. The Prints Division, under Weitenkampf's care, grew from modest beginnings to a center of national importance. His associations and friendships with artists and collectors and his devoted interest in the field of graphic art, led to the presentation of many handsome gifts to the collection. Not the least of his many contributions to the Division was the organization of an invaluable clipping file on printmakers and print subjects, a useful supplement to the printed sources. Under his philosophy, not a scrap of paper should be wasted if it could provide a bit of useful information or documentation in the interest of research.

In 1923, Frank Weitenkampf was married to Louise Suhl. They had no children.

Upon his retirement from the NYPL, as chief of the Prints Division, on June 30, 1942, Weitenkampf's was the longest term of service in the Library's history, over 61 years. His retirement did not stop his literary productivity, however. In 1944, he co-authored with historian Allan Nevins *A Century of Political Cartoons; Caricature in the United States from 1800 to 1900* (C. Scribner's Sons). Next, he produced the autobiographical *Manhattan Kaleidoscope* (Charles Scribner's Sons, 1947). His last major work was *Political Caricature in the United States in*

Separately Published Cartoons: An Annotated List (New York Public Library, 1953; reprint 1971).

Frank Weitenkampf left a double legacy to librarianship—his publications and the Prints Division of the New York Public Library. He died a few days past his ninety-sixth birthday, on August 23, 1962.

Biographical listings and obituaries—[Obituary]. *Antiquarian Bookman* 30:1666 (Nov. 5, 1962); [Obituary]. *Library Journal* 87:3419 (Oct. 1, 1962); [Obituary]. *Picturescope* 10:46-47 (Dec. 1962); [Obituary]. *Wilson Library Bulletin* 37:104+ (Oct. 1962). **Books and articles about the biographee**—Dain, Phyllis. *The New York Public Library: A History of Its Founding and Early Years.* New York: The New York Public Library, Astor, Lenox and Tilden Foundations, 1972 [especially Chapter IV, note 80, p. 388]. **Primary sources and archival materials**—Weitenkampf, Frank. *Manhattan Kaleidoscope.* New York: Charles Scribner's Sons, 1947; Papers relevant to Weitenkampf's tenure at the NYPL are held in that institution's MSS. and Archives Division.

—ELIZABETH E. ROTH

WELLMAN, HILLER CROWELL (1871-1956)

Hiller Crowell Wellman, whose ancestors date back to the seventeenth century, was born on March 2, 1871, in Boston, Massachusetts, the son of Joseph Hiller and Ellen Maria Crowell Wellman. The family lived in Massachusetts and in Westchester County, New York, where Wellman received his early schooling. He was graduated from the Brookline, Massachusetts, High School, then from Harvard College (1894), at which time he was elected to membership in Phi Beta Kappa. Wellman chose librarianship as a career not only because he was an avid reader and loved books but also because he was anxious to acquaint others with the joys and values of reading. This commitment was to characterize his long and successful career. At an early age he decided that the public library was a moving force in education, recreation, and information.

He secured his first position in the Boston Athenaeum, one of the best-known subscription libraries in the country. Although he found it satisfying to work with an excellent book collection, he desired wider experience. His record of service in the Athenaeum was rewarded by appointment, in 1896, as supervisor of branch libraries in the Boston Public Library (one of the country's largest), when he was 26 years old. Wellman was becoming active in local, regional, and state library clubs and associations as well as in the American Library Association. His charm and winning personality helped him become well known among educators, librarians, and those he served. He displayed such competence in the profession and such great enthusiasm for books, reading, and libraries that, in 1898, he became librarian of the Public Library in Brookline, Massachusetts, a suburban Boston community noted for its excellent school system and public library.

In September 1900, he married Emily Andem Whiston and they had a son, Bertram, and four daughters, three of whom (Constance, Margaret, and Ellen) survived.

The experience in Boston and Brookline provided Wellman opportunities to work with community groups, adult educators, and book leaders. Wellman, a discerning reader himself, had a flair for publicizing books and reading and for providing readers access to books through browsing at open shelves. This background and commitment proved to be the kind that the trustees of the City Library Association of Springfield, Massachusetts, were seeking when they appointed him librarian to succeed John Cotton Dana (q.v.) in 1902. The Association included not only a rapidly developing public library program, but also two art museums, a museum of science, and an historical society. During his 46 years of service in Springfield, Wellman helped build a cultural complex that continues to serve as a significant force for intellectual opportunity and advancement in its community.

Wellman began immediately to plan for expanded and improved library and information services in a city already dedicated to excellence in education, including a famous program of adult education. Indeed, this dedication was a major determinant in his decision to accept the Springfield position. One of his first tasks was the planning and construction of a new central library building that was to prove to be a landmark. It included street-level entrances and large open areas that integrated flexible arrangements of books and other library materials with attractive space for readers. Included also was a separate children's room with special sections for picture books, story hours, storage, and staff work space. The reference and art departments were planned to house all types of non-book materials. Springfield is credited with being among the first public libraries to lend recordings. Thus, imaginative service concepts were developed, including the design to accommodate them, an important principle seldom implemented in library building planning at the time. In addition, a major portion of the book collection was arranged on open shelves to give the public access to desired reading matter. The building was opened early in 1912 and attracted widespread attention as a marked improvement in library architecture, which also enhanced Wellman's prestige in the profession. A next priority was branch library service, which stemmed from his concept of "bringing libraries to people." Several additional branches were built as well as stations, deposits, and other outlets for books being established to foster their widest possible use and ease of access.

An evaluation of Wellman's accomplishments should include also his commitment to and success in working with the public schools. He had particular interest in complementing and supplementing their formal programs of instruction as well as in supporting adult education classes with appropriate materials. He served as president of the Springfield Adult Education Council, a powerful, successful organization that earned nationwide acclaim for its public forums, classes, and vocational opportunities. Wellman maintained that the public reacted positively to quality library service and proved his premise when Springfield residents increased their book borrowing from 2.6 per capita in 1900 to 15 per capita by 1931. He had faith in people and took a firm stand concerning their freedom to read and to choose their reading without censorship.

Wellman's presidential address to the 1915 American Library Association Conference (*ALA Bulletin* 9:93 [1915]) summed up his scholarly yet practical devotion to advancing the public library as a dynamic instrument of education:

> [W]hen we consider that not simply in preserving knowledge, but in diffusing it among the whole people, [the public library] has produced a condition of general enlightenment that has never before been known, ... it may not be immoderate to hope that this great art of printing will have an incalculable influence in deepening, strengthening, carrying higher, and prolonging this present wave of our civilization.... This, then, I conceive to be the great fundamental obligation of the public library—to make accessible to all men the best thought of mankind....

Wellman's achievements represent proof of his commitment.

Wellman received many honors in recognition of his devoted service to the people of Springfield: an honorary doctor of letters from Springfield's American International College, the coveted William Pynchon medal for public service, a fifteen-year term by gubernatorial appointment to the Massachusetts Board of Library Commissioners, and the presidency of the Massachusetts Library Association. He remained active following his retirement in 1948 by retaining the presidency of the Adult Education Council, by keeping up his reading, and by pursuing his two favorite sports, bridge and tennis, at both of which he excelled. He died at his home on February 3, 1956.

Biographical listings and obituaries—*Who Was Who in America* III (1951-1960); *Who's Who in Library Service*, 1st ed., 2nd ed. **Books and articles about the biographee**—[Biographical sketch]. *Bulletin of Bibliography and Dramatic Index* 11:153 (1922) [includes portrait]; [Biographical sketch]. *The City Library Bulletin*, Springfield, Mass., March 1956, pp. 35-36; Nov. 1957, p. 152; [Biographical sketch]. *Library Journal* 73:1360-61 (Oct. 1, 1948).

—JOHN A. HUMPHRY

WHEELER, JOSEPH LEWIS (1884-1970)

Joseph Lewis Wheeler was born on March 16, 1884, in Dorchester, Massachusetts, to George Stevens and Mary Jane Draffin Wheeler. His mother's parents were first-generation Irish immigrants, and his father's ancestors had been among the earliest Englishmen to migrate to the New World, arriving in Concord, Massachusetts, in the 1630s. Wheeler's roots were deep in New England and, although he spent most of his career outside that region, he periodically returned to New England and was to spend most of his retirement there.

After graduating from technical high school, Wheeler entered Brown University in the fall of 1902, determined to become a mechanical engineer. But, in his own words, "the Lord was looking after" him, and he got a two-and-one-half-hour job, six afternoons a week, in the Library. His supervisor, Harry L. Koopman (q.v.; whom Wheeler remembered as "a booklover, poet, fine administrator and loveable friend"), changed Wheeler's mind and, in January 1903, he changed courses to prepare for librarianship. In June 1904, Wheeler began working at an additional job three hours each evening in the art and industry departments of the Providence Public Library. Then, from 9:00 to 10:00 each night, he took over the reference room. His grades showed the time missed from studying, but the experience left Wheeler with the belief that he was primarily a reference librarian, a belief that persisted throughout his career and retirement.

Following receipt of his B.A. (1906), Wheeler stayed on at Brown for an additional year to earn his M.A. in political science (1907). At that point, he lacked money to go to library school, so he lived for a year with his aunt and uncle in Benson, Vermont, while he worked at a sawmill to earn money. During that year, he took some courses by examination from the New York State Library School at Albany and did so well that, the next year, he was able to complete the normal two-year course in but one, graduating with a B.L.S. in June 1909. (He would receive an honorary M.L.S. from Albany in 1924 and honorary Litt.D. degrees from Maryland in 1934 and Brown in 1936.)

Wheeler's first job following graduation was as assistant librarian in the District of Columbia Public Library (May 1909-February 1911). He was married to Mabel Archibald, a reference librarian in the District of Columbia Library, on October 10, 1910.

On March 1, 1911, Wheeler became librarian of the recently founded Jacksonville (Florida) Public Library. The Jacksonville experience, lasting but twenty months, was an unhappy and unsatisfactory one for the Wheelers other than for the birth of their first child, John Archibald. The hot, moist climate made them uncomfortable, and they were offended and frustrated by the racial prejudice that Wheeler described as "rampant and heartless, evident every hour of every day." The library position itself was "absorbing and the progress encouraging," but when an offer suddenly came from Los Angeles, the Wheelers did not hesitate to accept.

Wheeler began, in November 1912, as assistant librarian in the Los Angeles Public Library and would remain in that position until June 1915. His second child, Joseph Towne, was born in that city. Wheeler found the Los Angeles job challenging, and here his distinctive ideas about buildings, their location, and the role and mission of libraries began to appear. Among his first tasks was to find a new home for the Library, as the current lease was about to expire. The site Wheeler chose was in the heart of town, on the top three floors of a nine-story building. There "in the retail, pedestrian heart of a great city," he explained, "I saw further evidence that strategic location is a major factor in a public library's success." Once the new location was approved, Wheeler still found he had plenty to do. He not only supervised much of the planning and equipping of the new Main Library, he subsequently had the opportunity to plan several branches, experience that would serve him well in his later years as a director, consultant, and library surveyor. (See his paper "The Effective Location of Public Library Buildings" [University of Illinois Library School, Occasional Papers, no. 52 (1958)]. In 1967, a supplement appeared as *Occasional Papers*, no. 85, entitled, "A Reconsideration of the Strategic Location for Public Library Buildings.")

While Wheeler was still at the Los Angeles Public Library, Charles Green (chairman of the American Library Association committee to plan the library exhibit at the San Francisco World's Fair) asked Wheeler to plan, gather, and prepare material for the exhibit. This provided Wheeler with unique opportunities, especially in the contacts he was able to make all over the country through his correspondence in gathering materials. When the exhibit opened, Wheeler was asked to take charge and he agreed; his resignation at Los Angeles was undoubtedly made easier by Wheeler's reservations about his chief there, a man whom Wheeler described as "psychotic."

In the fall of 1915, Wheeler accepted the position of librarian at Youngstown, Ohio, "the City of Smoke and Steel." Youngstown was a new environment for him. He inherited an able staff, but finances, the book collection, and services were very backward in this industrial city. Wheeler's successful leadership was evident in the changes that followed. In his eleven-year term, circulation increased from 130,000 to 700,000 per year. The budget also grew, due in large part to two tax referenda that Wheeler actively promoted. Shortly before he left, moreover, in characteristic fashion, Joe Wheeler was building a small branch library in the center of town. (He also successfully promoted other branches.)

Two interruptions occurred in Wheeler's service in Youngstown. During World War I, from September 1917 to June 1918, Wheeler, like so many librarians, was on leave of absence with the ALA Library War Service in Washington. He was in charge of 32 regular camp libraries and book selection for all camps. He had a second leave (April 1921 through October 1922), spent in Benson, Vermont. Also in Youngstown, Robert Reid and Mary Bethel were born, rounding out the Wheeler family.

Early in 1926, Wheeler was offered and accepted the position of librarian of the Enoch Pratt Free Library in Baltimore, then a city of about 850,000. The situation was discouraging: with one exception, Baltimore stood lowest of large city libraries in public use and had the highest costs. The budget and book collection were "rolled so thin ... that the holes showed through the pancake"; salaries were "disgraceful"; and, of the 250-member staff, not a single one was a trained librarian and but four were college graduates. The spectacular changes that would characterize the Wheeler years (lasting until 1945) began immediately. Wheeler, for example, quickly denounced closed shelves at Pratt and promised to "pull ten thousand of the best books out of the stacks and place them on the open shelves" (Kalisch, *Enoch Pratt Free Library*, pp. 35-36). It was the attitude responsible for this and other pronouncements that had greatest impact. Wheeler was far-sighted but realistic, a hard-driving but personable leader who brought Pratt into the twentieth century. In 1925, circulation was 1,004,061; in 1929, it had increased to 2,491,174, an increase of over one hundred percent. Yet, between 1925 and 1928, the budget increased only from $288,000 to $304,000, a difference of but five and one-half percent. The key to this remarkable growth, it is obvious, lay in leadership.

Wheeler led. He fought for a badly needed new building, at times with considerable, intelligent help and, at other times, seemingly by himself. He demanded professionalization of his staff and, when enough products of professional schools proved unavailable, he started his own training school at Pratt. He encouraged his employees to join ALA and the Maryland Library Association. He enlisted the aid of Baltimore's leaders, like H. L. Mencken, in his campaigns and improved the image of the Library in the press and the public's eyes through intelligent and forceful publicity campaigns.

The results in the area of staffing were impressive. Wheeler actively recruited people who reflected his own image of the ideal librarian, and word soon got around that Wheeler was an ideal librarian (and boss) himself. Given that, and the significant changes he

was making in the Library, he quickly attracted talented individuals. If one among them stood above the others, it was probably Lucille Morsch (q.v.), who became director of cataloging at Pratt. Later, of course, she would become chief of descriptive cataloging at the Library of Congress. Others were of first rank as well. Harold Hamill went on to Kansas City and the Los Angeles Public Library. Richard Sealock would advance to Forest Press. Frances R. St. John (q.v.) went to the Army Medical Library and then to the Brooklyn Public Library. Amy Winslow moved to the Cuyahoga County Library and then back to Pratt as director.

Wheeler was personally responsible for much of the improvement. He understood issues and faced them squarely. In 1939, he hired a black professional staff member in the Southern city of Baltimore. He recruited men into what had been primarily a women's profession.

But above all was the concept or attitude that he personified and expected of others; he demanded it of his staff in particular. Indeed, Kalisch has concluded that, under Wheeler, "the name of the Pratt Library was synonymous with excellent service." The direction was unmistakable: young people were to have priority over adults; the staff was to be concerned with patrons rather than rules. Wheeler himself had little time for machines, computers, and what he would later call "McLuhanatics"—he emphasized books. His twenty-year service at Pratt was indeed, as Kalisch has termed it, revolutionary. In 1963, the Library cited him for leading it to its status as "one of the notable libraries of the world," as they dedicated the new auditorium to him.

Wheeler retired in March 1945. He was only 61, but he believed his health was failing, and the wartime death of his son Joe had dealt him a hard blow. But Joe Wheeler's retirement from Pratt was not a retirement from work and libraries. His revolution at Enoch Pratt had been, in fact, but one of the major accomplishments of his life. Before him lay his remarkable career as consultant and library surveyor.

His first assignment following his retirement was a study sponsored by the [Andrew] Carnegie [q.v.] Corporation on the status of education for librarianship (*Progress and Problems in Education for Librarianship*, Carnegie Corporation of New York, 1946). His selection for that survey reflected his long interest in education, for he had been a member of the ALA Board of Education for Librarianship from 1931 to 1936. In addition, both before and after the Carnegie study, he had lectured or taught in library schools throughout the country, among them Albany (New York State Library School), Columbia University, Western Reserve University (now Case Western Reserve), and Drexel Institute of Technology (now University).

Joe Wheeler had begun doing library surveys very early. His work selecting the site and planning the new Los Angeles Public Library should probably be considered his first such venture. But in the usual sense of the word, Wheeler had begun professional surveys in 1925, as a part of the Wisconsin "Better Cities" contest, and had continued that work, completing thirteen surveys by the time of his retirement from Pratt. From that time until his death 25 years later, Wheeler was the nation's busiest, best, and best known (and probably least expensive) library consultant and surveyor.

By 1960, he had completed well over one hundred surveys, doing as many as ten per year. Wheeler did so many surveys, it is obvious, because he was good—that is, demand for his services was high. The libraries he surveyed, moreover, were important ones: Albany, Jacksonville, Kansas City, Salt Lake City, Dallas, Atlanta, Roanoke, Champaign, San Diego, Princeton, Yonkers, Little Rock, University of Maryland, and Syracuse, among others. Outside of the United States, he served as consultant in Vancouver, B.C., and Mantanzas, Cuba. The effect of these surveys and, indeed, their legacy was two-fold. On one hand, they at times resulted in spectacular changes for individual libraries. In Dallas, his work evidently led to a reversal of public opinion and the building of a new library. Likewise, Champaign got a new library; others received less visible, but just as valuable changes. Like those of other consultants, however, Wheeler's surveys were uneven in quality and necessarily somewhat repetitive in content; some were received critically, among them that of the San Diego Public Library.

The surveys also led to Wheeler's book with Alfred Morton Githens (q.v.), *The American Public Library Building* (New York, 1941). That work forthrightly presented Wheeler's ideas about the concept of a building's shape and utilization and, in concert with the impact of Wheeler's surveys on individual libraries, has had an important and continuing effect on the design of library facilities.

After leaving Baltimore in 1945, Wheeler headquartered at the Bump Farm near Benson, Vermont. Not all of his time was spent doing surveys, and he was known in New England for his research and writing in local history. A wide audience appreciated his articles and letters—*Publishers Weekly*, the Rutland *Herald*, *Library Journal*, *The New York Times*, *Maryland Historical Magazine*, *Wilson Library Bulletin*—even Sherman Adams, President Eisenhower's special assistant—all had words from Joe Wheeler.

Because of his innovative leadership at Enoch Pratt, his energy and spirit, his publications, and his incisive and numerous surveys, as Professor Sarah Vann has pointed out, Wheeler's influence on libraries

and librarianship was widespread. She cites his receipt of the Joseph W. Lippincott Award for his involvement in professional activities as recognition of this pervasive influence. The Lippincott Award came in 1961 for distinguished service to the profession, and termed him a "pioneer in administrative methods, publicity, public relations, and staff participation in the development of programs." He was an early leader in the Special Libraries Association and an active force in other professional organizations. Most of his professional activity, however, was in the American Library Association. Although he was never president of the organization, he was first vice-president in 1926-1927, during the time he was in charge of the ALA exhibit at the Philadelphia World's Fair. He also served on numerous committees, the Council (1918-1923), and the Executive Board (1929-1933) throughout his long career. That was recognized in 1964 when he was made an honorary life member of the organization and identified as a "constructive force in American librarianship" and praised for his imagination, wisdom, and foresight. He was also president of the Ohio Library Association (1919-1920).

Wheeler was instrumental as well in projects where his name never appeared: both through his blunt, "stimulating skepticism" and his constructive views, Wheeler generated ideas, promoted projects, and challenged others to complete them. His name does not appear on the ALA Small Libraries Project, yet its conception was his. He was among those who recognized the need for such publications as *Industrial Arts Index* and *Library Literature*. He urged the creation of the Junior Members Round Table in ALA. The cause for which he was campaigning at the time of his death was "Cataloging in Source" (now Cataloging in Publication).

Wheeler wrote not only surveys, but well-conceived, well-executed books that have been reprinted. His *The Library and the Community* (ALA, 1924) appeared first; *My Maryland*, with Beta Kaessmann and Harold Manakee (Ginn, 1934) was a children's history text; *The American Public Library Building*, with Alfred Morton Githens (ALA, 1941; reprinted, 1947), was probably his best-known book; *Progress and Problems in Education for Librarianship* (Carnegie Corporation of New York, 1946), his Carnegie-sponsored study, went through three reprints. *Practical Administration of Public Libraries*, with Herbert Goldhor (Harper and Row, 1962), completed his major publications.

Wheeler was also an amateur historian, as shown by the Maryland history referred to above. With Mabel Wheeler, he wrote *The Mount Independence-Hubbardton 1776 Military Road*, which first appeared in the *Vermont History Magazine* (1959) and was later privately reprinted. A member of the

American Historical Association, he belonged as well to the Vermont and Maryland historical associations. In his later years, he became increasingly absorbed in genealogy, publishing records of the Archibald, Draffin, Towne, and Wheeler families. At the time of his death, he left unfinished a project for the American Association for State and Local History on which he had been working.

Among Wheeler's other memberships were the National Education Association, the American Society of Public Administrators, Rotary International, and the National Association for the Advancement of Colored People (NAACP).

Joe Wheeler died on December 4, 1970, in Rutland, Vermont, once again at home in New England. Although he was 86, his death seemed almost at mid-stride. His best epitaph, however, had been written on the editorial pages of the *Baltimore Sun* 25 years earlier, at his retirement: "He has builded so soundly that his work will long endure."

Biographical listings and obituaries—*A Biographical Directory of Librarians in the United States and Canada*, 5th ed.; *Directory of Library Consultants* (1969); *Directory of American Scholars* (1969); [Obituary]. *Library Journal* 96:585 (Feb. 15, 1971); [Obituary]. *New York Times*, Dec. 4, 1970, p. 50; [Obituary]. *Vermont Libraries* 1:2 (Dec. 1970); [Obituary]. *Wilson Library Bulletin* 45:527 (Feb. 1971); *Who's Who in America* 37 (1972-1973). **Books and articles about the biographee**—Bell, Marion V. "Joseph L. Wheeler: A Bibliography." *Bulletin of Bibliography* 23:127-31 (1961); Castagna, Edwin. *Three Who Met the Challenge: Joseph L. Wheeler, Lawrence Clark Powell, Frances Clarke Sayers.* Berkeley, Calif.: Peacock Press, 1965; Dennis, Donald D. "Profile: Joseph L. Wheeler." *Library Journal* 89:2941-43 (Aug. 1964); Edwards, Margaret A. "I Once Did See Joe Wheeler Plain." *Journal of Library History* 6:291-302 (1971); Ferguson, Charles W. "Joseph Lewis Wheeler." *Arkansas Libraries* 25:15-20 (Spring 1969); "Joseph L. Wheeler, 1884-1970 [editorial tribute]." *Library Resources and Technical Services* 15:5 (Winter 1970); Kalisch, Philip A. *The Enoch Pratt Free Library: A Social History.* Metuchen, N.J.: Scarecrow Press, Inc., 1969; "Three Tributes to Joseph L. Wheeler." *Library Journal* 70:283-85 (April 1, 1945) [by Harry M. Lydenberg, Charles H. Rush, and Francis R. St. John]. **Primary sources and archival materials**—Wheeler's papers are deposited in the School of Library Science, Florida State University. See Barbara Yates, "The Joseph L. Wheeler Papers." *Journal of Library History* 8:96-98 (April 1973).

—LEE H. WARNER

WILLIAMS, EDWARD CHRISTOPHER (1871-1929)

Edward Christopher Williams was born in Cleveland, Ohio, on February 11, 1871. He married Ethel Chesnutt, daughter of the Afro-American author Charles Waddell Chesnutt; they had one son, Charles. Williams attended the Cleveland public schools; he was graduated from Adelbert College of Western Reserve University, Phi Beta Kappa, as valedictorian (B.A., 1892) and the New York State Library School (1900). Williams also engaged in graduate study at

Columbia University. His professional positions were the following: first assistant librarian of Adelbert College at Western Reserve University (1892-1894); librarian of Hatch Library, Western Reserve University (1894-1898); University librarian, also a founder of and teacher in the Library School, Western Reserve University (1898-1909); principal of M Street School (now Dunbar High School), Washington, D.C. (1909-1916); librarian and teacher, Howard University (1916-1929). His publications include annual reports of the Library at Western Reserve University and the Library at Howard University; various articles in the *Howard University Record*; a novelette, "The Letters of David Carr," which appeared serially in *The Messenger* during the years 1925 and 1926; *A Sketch of the History and Present Conditions of the Library of Adelbert College* (1901); "The Value of the Study of Biography," in *The School Teacher* (1910); and various unpublished plays and literary works.

Edward Christopher Williams, an Afro-American, was a librarian, teacher, and scholar. As librarian at Western Reserve University he more than doubled the size of the collection, moved the collection into a new library building, and, within ten years, had obtained (through gifts and donations) a collection that outgrew it. The same ingenuity was applied to library procedures, and in suggesting a duplicating process, Williams wrote,

It is a matter of great regret to all librarians that the mere mechanical process of writing catalogue cards consumes so much time, and it is especially a source of aggravation when we consider how much of the work consists of mere repetition. There are two ways of overcoming this difficulty in some degree, one is the use of a duplicating process. . . .

Williams was a member of the committee that prepared the plan of organization for and persuaded Andrew Carnegie (q.v.) to finance the Library School of Western Reserve University. He was a member of its staff from its beginning, this in addition to his regular library job. William Howard Brett (q.v.), dean of the Library School at Western Reserve and librarian of the Cleveland Public Library, said, "Mr. Williams has unusual gifts as a teacher. He certainly has the facility of securing the attention of his classes and inspires an enthusiasm for study." Williams's student Ernest Reece, who later in life became a library educator, made this evaluation:

He was a man who always had something to give. A word to him on any subject invariably led to some fountain of incident or narrative or knowledge, leaving one enlightened and at the same time entertained. . . . And always he was reading or studying or observing, thereby accumulating the wherewithal for his continual outgiving.

As part of this accumulation of knowledge, Williams decided to attend the New York State Library School in Albany, where he completed the two-year course in one year. When he considered leaving Western Reserve University in 1909, Charles F. Thwing, the University's president, wrote,

> As a teacher he is apt, forceful, impressive, successful. Mr. Williams is also a good friend. In any place which he is willing to accept, Mr. Williams will give a good account of himself. If Mr. Williams should finally decide to retire from the two places which he holds in the University, he will bear with himself the respect and regard of each of his associates.

His successor as librarian, George F. Strong, wrote,

> In the short time I have served as Librarian, I have come to know that the importance and usefulness of our collection, unusual in proportion to its size, are largely due to Mr. Williams' wide and thorough knowledge of books, the pains which he took to advance the interests of the Library, and his active helpfulness to the faculty and students at the college.

William Howard Brett especially felt his loss: "The resignation of Mr. Williams as Librarian of Hatch Library took from the library school one of its ablest instructors and best friends."

No one knows why Williams left his successful position at Western Reserve to become principal of the M Street School, a Negro high school in Washington, D.C. After seven years there, he returned to library work as librarian at Howard University, where he also taught many classes. In his annual report of 1922 he writes,

> During the past year the Librarian has given three courses in Italian and one in French literature to the regular college classes, and three courses in Italian and one in Library Economy to the Evening Classes. As far as we can find out, the course in Dante given during the spring quarter is the first of its kind ever offered in a school for colored students. The elementary course in Library economy was given in response to a very insistent demand from the city, following the proposed opening of branches of the Public Library in the public school buildings.... It will be noted that for most of the year the librarians carried what is regarded in all institutions of the first grade as a full schedule of teaching hours ... he is sure that by so doing he has acquired a far better knowledge of the inner life of our university than he could have gotten by many years of study at second hand.

In addition to his various professional positions, Williams was active in many professional associations. He was a charter member of the Ohio Library Association and chairman of the committee that

drafted its constitution. In 1901-1902, he was its secretary and also the chairman of the College Section. He was a faithful member of the American Library Association and gave a talk on "Library Needs of Negro Institutions" to the College and Reference Section on May 30, 1928. Because of his unique position as one of the best-educated librarians of his time, he was frequently called upon to advise on library problems and library education. At the time of his death on December 29, 1929, he had taken a leave of absence from Howard University to study for his Ph.D. degree at Columbia, when he was 58 years old.

Biographical listings and obituaries—"Williams" [obituary]. *Crisis* 37:138 (April 1930). Books and articles about the biographee—Duncan, Anne McKay. "History of Howard University Library, 1867-1929." Master's thesis, Catholic University, 1951; Hundley, Mary Gibson. *The Dunbar Story, 1870-1955.* New York: Vantage Press, 1965; Josey, E. J. "Edward Christopher Williams: A Librarian's Librarian." *The Journal of Library History* 4:106-122 (April 1969) (includes references to primary source materials in the biographical study and in the footnotes); Porter, Dorothy B. "Phylon Profile IV: Edward Christopher Williams." *Phylon* 8:315-21 (Fourth Quarter 1947). Primary sources and archival materials—Letters of Edward Christopher Williams and his colleagues are held by the Moorland-Spingarn Research Center, Howard University, and the Office of the Case Western Reserve University Archivist.

—E. J. JOSEY

WILLIAMSON, CHARLES CLARENCE (1877-1965)

Charles Clarence Williamson was born in Salem, Ohio, on January 26, 1877, the eldest son of Clarence and Lizzie Mather Williamson. Charles, his brother Alfred, and his sister Mary (two and five years younger, respectively), were raised on a small farm in northeastern Ohio and attended a one-room country school. His father, a carpenter, worked a fifteen-acre farm to help supplement the family income, and Charles helped out with the farm chores. The parents taught the children to "be honest, truthful, kind but firm for what was right and to be industrious." Charles Williamson always appreciated the virtues of hard work, thrift, and self-reliance.

Charles was graduated on June 17, 1897, from the Salem (Ohio) High School as valedictorian. After graduation he taught for one year at the one-room country school in Mahoning County, Ohio. He decided to attend Ohio Wesleyan University, but stayed only one year. He returned to Salem in 1899 as a teacher, and, in the next year, he was principal and eighth grade teacher at the Columbia Street School. He wanted to return to college but was unable to afford it. In 1901, however, he was offered a position as secretary to President Charles F. Thwing of Western Reserve University, with the understanding that he would also work towards his bachelor's degree in economics at Adelbert College of that

University. Williamson was graduated, in June 1904, with a B.A. degree (magna cum laude) and was elected to Phi Beta Kappa.

He then decided to undertake graduate work in economics for his master's degree at Western Reserve, continuing as secretary to the president. However, in January 1905, he was offered a position by Richard T. Ely, professor of economics at the University of Wisconsin at Madison, to work as Ely's private secretary while pursuing a full program of study toward the doctorate, since Ely had advised, "I do not, however, recommend those to take the master's degree who expect to take the Ph.D." Williamson started to work at Wisconsin in the spring term of 1905 and, in addition to his usual duties as secretary, he was also involved in recommending economics books for purchase by the University Library. Before leaving Wisconsin, he wrote Ely, "I wish to thank you for giving me the opportunity of trying my hand at the difficult task of sifting the existing mass of economic literature. It has been invaluable to me and I trust of some value to the Library equipment."

In 1906, he transferred to Columbia University in New York City to complete work on the doctorate because he had been awarded a university fellowship in political economy. While at Wisconsin, he had been working on a paper dealing with the financial history of Cleveland, Ohio; he continued the research and writing at Columbia, and this eventually became his doctoral dissertation, "The Finances of Cleveland." The dissertation was accepted by the faculty of political science at Columbia University and he received the Ph.D. degree on June 12, 1907.

On June 22, 1907, he married Bertha Louise Torrey, whom he met when they both worked at Western Reserve. They had one child, Cornelia, who was born on August 15, 1913.

Williamson had studied under the leading economists of the day, was sincerely interested in this field, and wanted to make it his life's work. He had received a few job offers, including one from William Howard Brett (q.v.), then chief librarian of the Cleveland (Ohio) Public Library, asking Williamson to work there as a reference librarian and also attend library school. Williamson was tempted but answered, "For the present I am not ready to decide in favor of library work."

He received a letter, in February 1907, from President Martha Carey Thomas of Bryn Mawr College, indicating that Professor John B. Clark of Columbia had recommended him for the position of associate professor and head of the Economics Department; on March 25, 1907, President Thomas wrote him that he had been appointed to that position. Williamson was delighted with this opportunity and, in the fall of 1907, settled with his new bride on the beautiful Bryn Mawr campus. During his

early days there, he contracted typhoid fever, which left him extremely weak, and he obtained a "leave of absence" during the second semester of his first year. Things did not go well at Bryn Mawr in that he had a number of difficulties with President Thomas, who was a strong-willed and rather autocratic administrator. However, she commented that "his bibliographical knowledge in many economic fields is extraordinary, and his reading is also wide." Dissatisfied with conditions at Bryn Mawr, he made known to friends and former teachers that he was looking for a new position but continued at Bryn Mawr until June 1911.

Professor Edwin R. Seligman, one of Williamson's former teachers at Columbia, was approached by John Shaw Billings (q.v.), then director of the New York Public Library, for recommendations for a qualified person to head the Economics and Sociology Division soon to be opened in the new library building at Fifth Avenue and 42nd Street. Seligman, knowing that Williamson wanted to leave Bryn Mawr and aware of his knowledge of economic literature, recommended him to Billings, who offered him the position, which Williamson accepted on December 24, 1910. On June 1, 1911, he began full-time work as chief of this new division, working part-time from January to June 1911 to finish the academic year at Bryn Mawr. Ely congratulated him on this new position: "I am inclined to think that a satisfactory position in a great public library might prove the best thing after all." Williamson, extremely happy at the prospect, noted "Of all the changes I have made . . . this seems to me to be the best." With the move to the New York Public Library, Williamson stated, "I was definitely in my proper element." The Library had an "excellent professional staff and I was able to build up an interesting and worthwhile clientele for my department." At this point in his career, he still considered himself to be a "kind of special librarian." He continued in this position until 1914, feeling that in this work he was making an important contribution to the field of economics.

Williamson never attended library school and, in a letter of December 31, 1919, he commented on this to William F. Yust, then librarian of the Rochester (New York) Public Library, saying,

I came to library work from the teaching profession without the advantage of library school training. For some years I was inclined to question the necessity or value of such training for the particular kind of specialist work in which I had been interested, but experience of nearly ten years has thoroughly changed my attitude towards library school training.

By 1913, the establishment of the Municipal Reference Library of the City of New York had become a reality under the administration of the New

York Public Library. A librarian had been appointed but was dismissed, and the then director of the New York Public Library, Edwin H. Anderson (q.v.), turned to Williamson for help. Anderson knew of Williamson's interest in the field of municipal reference library services and asked him to assume the duties of municipal reference librarian, which he did on October 19, 1914. Williamson really did not want to leave the Economics Division and said that the change "was not of my choosing. . . . Mr. Anderson felt he needed me there and I never regretted that move. In many ways it broadened my library interest and helped to prepare me for the various tasks I was to undertake later." Williamson did a great deal to establish this Municipal Reference Library as a model for such libraries and was able to develop it into a highly efficient center for municipal reference services. While there, he started the publication *Municipal Reference Library Notes*, as well as being involved in the *Municipal Yearbook of the City of New York*. He also served as secretary of the Publications Committee for the *Minutes of the Common Council of the City of New York, 1784-1831*.

During this time, he also became associated with the Public Affairs Information Service, serving on the Advisory Board and being responsible for developing it into a major publication. Williamson "made available to the PAIS the printed resources of the Economics Division of the New York Public Library." John Fall, writing to Williamson in 1963, observed, "We cannot help but envy you your accomplishments, especially having been the person who made it possible for PAIS to emerge from a transient mimeographed Bulletin to an Index which is a brilliant and permanent record of our society." Williamson felt that his work with PAIS was "my most important achievement in the bibliographical field." He became interested in the work of the Special Libraries Association and served as its president from 1917 to 1918.

On May 1, 1918, he left the Municipal Reference Library to begin work as a statistician for the [Andrew] Carnegie [q.v.] Corporation of New York on their "Study of the Methods of Americanization." His reason for leaving was "based partly on personal grounds . . . and partly on certain political conditions in New York City which seem to threaten the usefulness of my present position." The Americanization Study was to examine existing methods by which Americanization was then being fostered. It took one year to complete, and Williamson was then prevailed upon by Anderson to return to his former position as chief of the Economics Division of the New York Public Library, "its scope and responsibilities to be much enlarged"; he continued there from 1919 to 1921. Keyes Metcalf felt that Williamson had made a major contribution to librarianship by his

work at the Economics Division which, under his direction, "stands without a peer in the library world." During this time, Williamson became better known in library circles as a result of his election as president of the New York Library Association for 1920-1921.

He also began to be known nationally as a result of three articles he wrote on library training for *Library Journal*: "The Need of a Plan for Library Development" (43:649-55 [September 1918]); "Efficiency in Library Management" (44:67-77 [February 1919]); and "Some Present-Day Aspects of Library Training" (44:563-68 [September 1919]). This last article was a reprint of an address that Williamson gave on June 26, 1919, at the American Library Association Convention at Asbury Park, New Jersey. He commented that his address had made a "deep impression on the immediate audience" and that he was "almost embarrassed by the seriousness with which my proposal was received by that audience."

These articles presented the seminal ideas that evolved into Williamson's Report of 1921 and 1923. He pointed out the confused state of library schools, the lack of conformity to standards, the multiplicity of training agencies, and the indefinite and fluctuating number of training classes—revealing a dismal picture of current library training. Although many librarians had long been aware of these conditions, Williamson brought them into focus. Adam Strohm (q.v.) summed up the attitude of many librarians, saying, "This matter of library training concerns us all. . . . Someone has said that Dr. Williamson tells us nothing new. Maybe not. Who does? But he has done *this*. He has vitalized the silent thoughts, the deep concerns, the earnest hopes of a good many of us. He has made the dormant fact alive. We are aroused."

Andrew Carnegie had donated millions of dollars to the building of libraries, but by 1917, these grants were discontinued, and the Carnegie Corporation of New York, which continued Carnegie's philanthropy, started to look at the problem of library training. In 1917, Alvin Johnson (q.v.) prepared a report for the Corporation that revealed a bleak picture of libraries providing inadequate service because of a lack of trained librarians and adequate funds. Through his previous work for the Corporation, Williamson was known as a person trained in the scientific method, and his writings revealed his growing interest in the problems of library training. Williamson stated that

Because of my previous interest in libraries the officers of the Corporation, notably the then secretary, Mr. James Bertram [q.v.], often discussed with me the problems the Corporation was facing in regard to its library buildings and its limited support of certain library schools. I believe the decision to ask me to make the study was based largely on these discussions no part of which was reduced to writing so as to find a place in my files.

In 1919, the Carnegie Corporation of New York "commissioned C. C. Williamson, a social scientist turned librarian, to make a field study of training for library service." The resulting document was the Williamson Report of 1921, entitled "Training for Library Work." Parts of this were published in 1923 under the title *Training for Library Service.* Both the unpublished and published reports have been reprinted in *The Williamson Reports of 1921 and 1923: Including Training for Library Work (1921) and Training for Library Service (1923)* (The Scarecrow Press, 1971).

Williamson undertook a survey of the then existing library schools following an orthodox research procedure in collecting data with questionnaires, interviews, and visits to the schools. Yet, it is important to understand that the Williamson Report was not intended to be a public document for the library world. The survey was sponsored, requested, and financed by, and prepared for the use of, the Carnegie Corporation as a document to provide the Corporation with needed data for its philanthropic work. However, the Report generated such interest that parts of it were made public in 1923.

The Williamson Report brought both criticism and praise. Some felt it was an unfair picture of existing conditions, while most were in agreement with his findings and recommendations. According to Frederick E. Keppel (q.v.), "apparently the Williamson Report has started something that won't stop in a hurry." Robert Leigh (q.v.) believed that the recommendations "became the major program for discussion and action regarding library education for the next quarter century. Much that he proposed was translated into practice during that period" and as a result a "distinctly different pattern of thinking for library education emerged." Williamson personally felt that increases in financial support by the Carnegie Corporation to American Library Association activities "could be interpreted as an outgrowth of my report." In 1943, he wrote to Louis Round Wilson, "In the library world I suppose the survey of the library schools which I undertook in 1920-1921 at the request of the Carnegie Corporation has had and may continue to have the most far-reaching results of anything I have ever done." However, in a 1955 letter to Sarah Vann, he stated that "the library training business was a side issue most of the time, never a part of my full-time job." This Report was his greatest contribution to librarianship.

In 1921, Williamson left library work to assume the position as director of information service of the Rockefeller Foundation. His major responsibility was for the Foundation's publicity, and the compilation,

editing, and publication of its reports, as well as the library, which was part of his department. He stated that "these years at the Rockefeller Foundation may seem like an interlude in my library work but I never regarded them as such."

The culmination of Williamson's professional career came with his appointment on May 1, 1926, as director of Columbia University Libraries and of the University's School of Library Service, where he was to remain for the next seventeen years, until his retirement in 1943. He was also named professor of library administration (without salary). One of the major problems at Columbia was felt immediately in his dual responsibility as director of both the Libraries and of the School of Library Service. In his seventeen years, he had to face the increasing complexities and demands of these two positions. He threatened to resign several times, but President Nicholas Murray Butler would not hear of it. Williamson stated, "it seems to be physically impossible for me to continue much longer with my present program of work." In spite of this heavy burden, his energy and zeal are reflected in what he was able to accomplish at Columbia. He did a great deal to expand the University Libraries, making Columbia one of the major research libraries of the world. He did this through a major reorganization, extensive development of the collections, and the building of South Hall, or, as it is called today, Butler Library. One of his major contributions was his organization and direction from 1929 to 1943 of the "Annual Conference of Eastern Librarians." Although he was a good organizer, he had one major weakness in that he tended to become involved in detail and found it difficult to delegate work. Williamson's work as a university librarian is important but will always be overshadowed by his influence and impact on library education.

He served as director of the School of Library Service from 1926 to 1930 and as dean from 1931 to 1943. As head of the School, he was able to put it on a sound graduate basis. Williamson realized, however, that his background in library education put him in a difficult situation regarding his own library school. In an address in 1926, he observed,

A few years ago I had the temerity to tell the library schools what they ought and ought not to do and to be. Not dreaming that I should ever have to prove that I was right in any particular. I could be as critical and as Utopian as I liked. Now, reflect on my predicament. Poetic justice you call it or fitting the punishment to the crime. For I have been maneuvered into a position where everybody can make the silencing challenge—"Put up or shut up."

The School officially opened on October 1, 1926, with the merger of the old New York State Library

School and the Library School of the New York Public Library into the reestablished School of Library Service at Columbia University. Williamson, in his brief address at the opening ceremonies, stated, "This is a notable step in the movement toward university status and organization for library training." In his career at Columbia, Williamson was responsible for the administration of a school that trained over 3,000 librarians, many of whom became leaders in the library profession. Williamson has been criticized because he did not devote sufficient time to the School, while others criticize him because he did not devote enough time to the University Libraries. Paul North Rice (q.v.) felt that the School of Library Service "will remain a monument to its first Dean." Keyes Metcalf also maintained that Williamson's contributions were many, but "building the largest Library School, even if it had predecessors, was no mean task, and by many will be considered his most important achievement. Of course, he was not a one achievement man."

During this time he received two important honors. In 1929, he was granted the degree of Litt.D. (*honoris causa*) at a special convocation at Columbia University. In the same year, he was named a "Chevalier of the Legion of Honor" by the French government for his work toward the publication of the printed catalog of the Bibliothèque Nationale.

Bertha Williamson died on September 16, 1939, after a long illness. On August 28, 1940, Charles Williamson was married to Genevieve Austen Hodge. They had no children.

He was a member of numerous professional groups and served on committees and in elected positions. His memberships included: American Library Association; Association of American Library Schools; American Library Institute; American Statistical Association; Manhattan Special Libraries Association; New York Library Association; Special Libraries Association; Bibliographical Society of America; New York Library Club; American Association of University Professors; American Economic Association; American Political Science Association; Academy of Political Science in the City of New York; National Municipal League; American Sociological Society; National Arts Club; American Humanist Association; Rationalist Press Association (London); American Council for Better Broadcasts; Phi Beta Kappa; Phi Gamma Delta; and Beta Phi Mu. He was president from 1929 to 1931 of the Association of American Library Schools, and a Board member, in 1933, of the American Library Institute. He ran for the elected office of vice-president (president-elect) of the American Library Association, in 1938, but was defeated by Ralph Munn (q.v.).

Williamson's published writing in librarianship is limited to *Training for Library Service*. However, he did edit other publications, as well as write periodical articles in the field of economics, bibliography, and librarianship. Some of the periodical literature consists of reprints of his talks and addresses. With Alice Jewett, he edited the first edition (1933) of *Who's Who in Library Service*; a second edition appeared in 1943. Williamson was also active as a consultant.

In 1941, he had decided to retire, but action was delayed. The Board of Trustees of Columbia University, on April 3, 1943, designated him the Libraries' director emeritus following his retirement from active service on June 30, 1943. When his retirement was announced, he received many letters that were bound in a "testimonial volume" given to him at a farewell reception.

Williamson's personality has been aptly described by Miles O. Price (q.v.), who stated that Williamson seemed "to inspire ... the same feeling that cats inspire in people: you either liked him very much indeed, or you didn't."

David Clift (q.v.) commented: "Williamson seemed somewhat aloof in his working relations, since there was very little, if any, of idle talk. Williamson was a retiring man. Many thought he found it difficult to unbend and be immediately, and openly pleasant about everything and to everybody."

Ernest J. Reece stated that Williamson had "an acute, analytical mind, which it gratified him to use; deliberate judgment; decision, determination and firmness; indefatigable in work, contented only when accomplishing something; interests wide-ranging; friendliness, consideration and attachment in dealing with people."

Alice Jewett observed:

He was a steady, diligent, relaxed worker, always in command of himself and of the work he was engaged in. His mind was phenomenally active and imaginative with a scientific grasp of the facts and problems involved in his various fields of interest. He was reserved but friendly, cooperative but firm in his convictions, persistent in his efforts to accomplish his purposes. ... He had an amazingly practical turn of mind, which was an advantage in putting his theories to practical work.

Williamson was an energetic, alert, rather wiry man. Strong and able to do heavy work, he was most skillful in the use of his hands. He always enjoyed the outdoors and took delight in hiking and working in his garden. Genevieve Williamson described him as a "tall, lean man, ... In the latter part of his life he was a strong and vigorous man with gray-white hair, bright blue eyes, a clear rosy complexion. His smile was bright and kindly." In retirement he remained active "associating himself with educational and political groups, as well as with interests of local garden clubs."

On June 21, 1956, he was elected a member of Beta Phi Mu (national library honor society). In 1964, this group gave him their annual award for "Distinguished Service to Education for Librarianship."

In October 1964, this author met Williamson several times at his home in Greenwich, Connecticut, and discussed with him plans for the writing of his biography as a doctoral dissertation. At that time, he was in good health and able to recall the events of his life and career. By Thanksgiving, he was not feeling well; after that time, his health declined rapidly. Not two months later, he was admitted to the Greenwich Hospital, where he died at 8:55 p.m. on January 11, 1965. Services were held in Hartford, Connecticut, with burial in the Village Cemetery at Weathersfield, Connecticut. At the age of 87, two weeks before his eighty-eighth birthday, Charles Clarence Williamson's long and fruitful career came to an end and with his death an era in library history ended.

Miles Price summed up Williamson's place eloquently: "He was a giant, with some of a giant's vices, but overwhelmingly, with a giant's virtues." If Melvil Dewey (q.v.) is the pioneer in library training, Charles Williamson is the synthesizer of modern library education. He came on the scene in American librarianship at the right time and was destined to have a major role in its development as a profession. He was a dominant figure in the historical development of librarianship and library education in the first half of the twentieth century in the United States.

Biographical listings and obituaries—"About People [Obituary]." *Library Journal* 90:612 (Feb. 1, 1965); "C. C. Williamson Dies at 88, Was Noted Librarian [Obituary]." *Greenwich Times*, Jan. 12, 1965, p. 2; "C. C. Williamson, Ran Libraries at Columbia [Obituary]." *New York Herald-Tribune*, Jan. 13, 1965, p. 14; "Charles C. Williamson [Obituary]." *New York Post*, Jan. 13, 1965, p. 33; "Charles C. Williamson, Dies at 88 [Obituary]." *The Hartford Courant*, Jan. 14, 1965, p. 4; "Charles Williamson, Educator, Librarian [Obituary]." *Newsday*, Jan. 13, 1965, p. 48; "Charles Williamson, 87, Dies: Directed Libraries at Columbia [Obituary]." *The New York Times*, Jan. 13, 1965, p. 25; "Dr. C. C. Williamson [Obituary]." *The Salem News*, Jan. 12, 1965, p. 8; *Leaders in Education*, 3rd ed. (1948); [Obituary]. *College and Research Libraries* 26:352 (July 1965); *Who Was Who in America with World Notables* IV (1961-1968); *Who's Who in Library Service*, 1st ed., 2nd ed. **Books and articles about the biographee**—"Beta Phi Mu Award." *Library Journal* 79:2938 (Aug. 1964); "Charles C. Williamson." *Wilson Library Bulletin* 4:210 (Jan. 1936); "Charles C. Williamson, 1877-1965." *Public Affairs Information Service Bulletin . . . 1965*; Crissey, Lucy M. "Charles C. Williamson, 1877-1965." *Library Service News* 26:1 (March 1965); "France Honors Dr. C. C. Williamson." *The New York Times*, Nov. 17, 1929, n.p.; Metcalf, Keyes D. "Charles C. Williamson." *Library Service News* 11:23-24 (Nov. 1943); "People: Charles Williamson." *Wilson Library Bulletin* 39:439 (Feb. 1965); Rankin, Rebecca B. "Dr. C. C. Williamson: In Memoriam." *Special Libraries* 56:120 (Feb. 1966); "Receipt of the Beta Phi Mu Award." *ALA Bulletin* 58:726 (Sept. 1964); "Receipt

of the Beta Phi Mu Award for Distinguished Service to Education for Librarianship." *Wilson Library Bulletin* 39:31 (Sept. 1964); Reece, Ernest J. "C. C. Williamson: A Record of Service to American Librarianship." *College and Research Libraries* 4:306-308 (Sept. 1943); Rice, Paul North. "Editorial Forum: C. C. Williamson." *Library Journal* 68:522 (June 15, 1943); Vann, Sarah K. *The Williamson Reports: A Study*. Metuchen, N.J.: The Scarecrow Press, 1971; Winckler, Paul A. "Charles Clarence Williamson (1877-1965): His Professional Life and Work in Librarianship and Library Education in the United States." Doctoral dissertation, New York University, 1968. **Primary sources and archival materials**—The "Williamson Papers" are located in the Special Collections Department of Columbia University in New York City.

—PAUL A. WINCKLER

WILSON, HALSEY WILLIAM (1868-1954)

For more than 53 of his 85 years, Halsey William Wilson presided over the bibliographic publishing firm that he founded and that bears his name. When he died at his home in Yorktown Heights, New York, on March 1, 1954, two years after his retirement as president of the H. W. Wilson Company, the library and book worlds mourned a man whose name was said (in a tribute that *Saturday Review* gave the firm on its fiftieth anniversary) to be "to bibliography what Webster is to dictionaries, Bartlett to quotations."

Born May 12, 1868, in Wilmington, Vermont, Halsey William Wilson was the son of John Thompson and Althea Dunnell Wilson. He married Justina Leavitt in 1895. Three years later, aided only by his wife, he published the first number of the *Cumulative Book Index*, which, along with the *Readers' Guide to Periodical Literature*, begun in 1901, was to dominate a new era in cumulative indexing on a large scale. In the next half century, he built *CBI* into a standard work of American national bibliography; applied his unique production techniques and the highest indexing standards to dozens of services covering both general and specialized subject areas; instituted a basis of payment for indexing and bibliographic work that enabled small libraries to afford needed services; and pioneered in union lists of library holdings, printed catalog-card sets, books for library practice, and professional, cooperative relationships between publishers and librarians. He brought to the financially hazardous field of bibliographic publishing a practical but imaginative business sense, building his subscriber list from some 300 in 1898 well toward the 100,000 libraries served by the firm 75 years later.

The Wilsons' only child did not survive infancy. When Justina Leavitt Wilson died in 1955, a year after her husband, their private estate passed by direction into a foundation, one that has made in his name many substantial grants to the library profession at large, particularly to benefit library recruitment and education.

As early as 1938, when the *New Yorker* magazine profiled him as the builder of a better "Mousetrap in the Bronx," referring to his efficient indexing and publishing set-up there, Wilson was receiving worldwide recognition. Professional honors, too, came to him, among them an honorary doctor of letters degree from Brown University (1939); the University of Minnesota's first Outstanding Achievement Medal (1948); special tributes from the American Library Association (honorary life membership) and Special Libraries Association on his fiftieth year of publishing (1948); and the American Library Association's Joseph W. Lippincott Award for special achievement in librarianship. This last-named honor was of particular note, for Wilson had neither earned a library degree nor worked as a professional in a library. While studying at the University of Minnesota, he had engaged in a series of odd jobs and enterprises, at first to make ends meet, but eventually with a singleness of purpose that prevented him from continuing his formal education. Toward the end of his career, however, when he had attended more than eighty national meetings of the American Library Association and hundreds of other professional library conferences, he remarked: "I sometimes wonder if all that is not equal to a year in library school."

Wilson's capacity for work, to become legendary among colleagues, was tested in his earliest childhood. Among his ancestors were Ann Hutchinson, Mary Dyer (the Quaker martyr), and Roger Williams, but he was a poor boy whose father was a tombstone cutter. Both parents died of tuberculosis before he was three, and he soon entered the world of hard work, doing farm chores for his grandparents in Massachusetts and later for an aunt and uncle in Iowa. He attended a Wisconsin boarding school (Beloit College), and, sporadically between 1885 and 1892 in Minneapolis, the University of Minnesota. There, he delivered newspapers, worked for a church, and, in 1889, borrowed $100 to form a bookselling firm with a young man named Henry S. Morris, who had run a bookstore on an Indian reservation. Selling textbooks to university faculty and students, the business prospered. After Morris was graduated, Wilson bought out his share, and, in the three years following his marriage, he built the enterprise into the best bookshop in the city.

At this point, he began to conceive of a new and better publishing record than those available, one that would enable him to "call the attention of those interested in particular lines of study to new books, reviews, and magazine articles in their subjects." *Publishers' Weekly* could help him from week to week, but when, according to an 1897 announcement, its cumulated semiannual record was to be discontinued, Wilson decided to publish his own monthly cumulation.

Several decisions had to be weighed carefully at the outset, among them, the most feasible type and format; the means of storing and handling the metal linotype slugs held for cumulations; the frequency of cumulation; and the most useful arrangement of entries. As a result of this initial thoroughness, several of the *CBI*'s early features endured for five decades and more. The first issue, sixteen pages, was dated February 1, 1898. Wilson himself delivered the full press run to the post office by streetcar.

Using his apartment as publishing office, Wilson worked on *CBI* business at night, while his wife edited by day. Soon, however, he rented a tiny office in the University Young Men's Christian Association building and hired as full-time editor an energetic young woman named Marion E. Potter, who went on to serve the company in various editorial capacities for 55 years. Potter's dedication to her lifetime employer was typical of many who grew up with the enterprise, for Wilson's enthusiasm was contagious, and his concern for his workers deep and paternal.

Although the first volume of *CBI* earned Wilson a number of congratulatory letters—such as that of a Pittsburgh bookseller who wrote, "It seems too good to be true"—it lost money, as did most of his bibliographic products for some fifteen years. But, increasingly, libraries as well as booksellers were finding them useful, and Wilson was now a victim of what he called "the bibliographic urge," a fascination with the challenges of keeping up bibliographically with the publishing output. "The malady is almost always financially fatal," he observed. Yet, without hesitation after *CBI* suffered a forty percent deficit its first year, he undertook a second major project, a cumulated list of American trade books in print that he called the *United States Catalog*; he issued it in 1899, then again in 1902. (By its fourth revision in 1928, however, the *Catalog* had grown to 190,000 in-print titles and become prohibitively expensive to produce. *CBI*, which had been published as a monthly and annual supplement to the *Catalog*, continued as the year-by-year record of English-language book publishing.) Further, he added *Readers' Guide* to *CBI* in 1901, at first as a supplement, but later, after consultation with librarians, as a separate available on a "service basis"—that is, priced according to a formula of use (a flat rate has been in effect since 1961).

The continued success of the bookstore kept him solvent, enabling him to incorporate the H. W. Wilson Company in 1903, sell preferred stock, and erect a handsome three-story company home across the street from the University of Minnesota.

Into this building, in 1905, he brought the *CBI*, *Readers' Guide*, *U.S. Catalog*, and a new, well-received undertaking, the *Book Review Digest*, which surveyed forty reviewing publications at the outset.

That same year, Wilson issued a five-year cumulation (1900-1904) of the *Readers' Guide*. Its dictionary arrangement, with uniform subject headings, had never before been achieved in an American periodical index.

The company grew fast now, with Wilson's life so inextricably bound to it that his story can almost be told in bibliographic outline: 1906—*Library Work* (a forerunner to *Library Literature* and the *Wilson Library Bulletin*); 1906—*Eclectic Library Catalog* (forerunner of *Abridged Readers' Guide*); 1907—*Readers' Guide Supplement* (forerunner to *International Index* and later the *Social Sciences and Humanities Index*); 1907—*Debaters' Handbook Series* (later the *Reference Shelf*); 1908—*Fiction Catalog*; 1909—*Children's Catalog*. In addition, he issued another *Readers' Guide* cumulation (1905-1909), the third revision of the *U.S. Catalog* (1912), and, as the unofficial University of Minnesota Press, dozens of general titles.

Much as Wilson enjoyed the expansion of his services, he eschewed the concept of corporate bigness ("If we ever feel big, it is only when thinking of our former littleness") and of the profit motive ("The company's uncompromising stand is always to put first its professional service rather than profit making"). Still, he believed that bibliographic publishing should be a self-supporting enterprise, and that it could be so only if each entrepreneur operated in a fairly exclusive area. "Competition," he said, "is likely to be the death rather than the life of the bibliographic trade, for it tolerates 'the good that is the enemy of the best' and draws away some support which is necessary to keep the 'best' up to its high standard." With this philosophy in mind, he made a gentleman's agreement in 1911 with Richard Rogers Bowker (q.v.), whose *Publishers' Weekly*, supplements to the *American Catalogue*, and certain other publications duplicated bibliographic work in some of the Wilson services. Bowker, whom Wilson termed a generous and helpful colleague, agreed to an arrangement affording each a greater specialization in the area he was to pre-empt for decades: Wilson in periodical indexing and English-language book bibliography, Bowker in booktrade guides and in-print bibliography.

In 1913, Wilson reluctantly sold his bookstore, packed the firm's equipment in a caravan of freight cars, and moved East to be nearer to both his major subscribers and the publishers from whom he received current books and periodicals.

After four years (1913-1917) in the New York suburb of White Plains (birthplace of *Industrial Arts Index*, *Agricultural Index*, and the *Wilson Bulletin for Librarians*), he settled his company on the East Bank of the Harlem River, Borough of the Bronx, New York City. To a five-story building on the site, he added, in 1929, an eight-story structure surmounted by a huge bronze book and on top of that a thirty-foot lighthouse, together towering some 250 feet above the river. The lighthouse, which Wilson characterized as representing the guidance his indexes gave to those seeking their way through the maze of books and periodicals, is the company symbol. Wilson raised a third adjoining building in 1938. (A fourth was completed in 1957.)

The 950 University Avenue site was an exciting one, within hearing distance of the cheers from the Polo Grounds, home of the New York Giants baseball team, just across the river. The working conditions were good, and the employees, though growing rapidly in number, were still a close-knit family. Their remarkable dedication and *esprit de corps* over the following decades helped account for the firm's great "Age of Indexing," during which Wilson created such enduring reference services as: *Education Index* (1929); *Art Index* (1929); *Vertical File Index* (1932); *Essay and General Literature Index* (1934); *Bibliographic Index* (1938); *Biography Index* (1946); *Play Index* (1949); and *Short Story Index* (1953). In addition, determined to help librarians with selection and cataloging as well as patrons with research, he followed *Children's Catalog* with *Standard Catalog for Public Libraries* (1918; later *Public Library Catalog*); *Standard Catalog for High School Libraries* (1926; later *Senior High School Library Catalog*); and *Fiction Catalog* (1942). Also of wide and long-lasting significance were *Sears List of Subject Headings*, prepared by Minnie Sears (q.v.) and first published in 1923 as *List of Subject Headings for Small Libraries*; the first *Union List of Serials in Libraries of the United States and Canada* (1927), produced on a non-profit, cooperative basis with the American Library Association and participating libraries; and printed catalog cards, first sold in 1938.

Wilson's concern, it should be stressed, was not to publish as many indexes as possible, but to create a system that would best organize the enormous amount of information in current literature. He approached this goal by hiring professional librarians and subject specialists to formulate subject headings—some indexes use as many as 100,000—and by standardizing as much as possible the mechanical aspects of production. He was proud of the expertise he gained through experience, and his eagerness to share it was evidenced by an expensive feasibility study—with no foreseeable financial gain for his own firm—of a continuing, cumulative supplement to the first *Library of Congress Catalog of Printed Cards*. The Library adopted his plan with some modifications, and a note of gratitude to Wilson appears in every supplement to the *National Union Catalog*. His professional interest in organizing information went beyond national or English-language publications, as in his call for a "Bibliographic League of Nations" at an international congress in 1929.

Though Wilson tied his life so closely to the firm's endeavors (as president until December 1952, then as Board chairman until illness claimed him in 1954), his character as a human being was spirited, diverse, and unforgettable to all who knew him. A robust, balding figure, with a closely trimmed moustache and round, merry features, he was as famous among friends for his puns, his sweet tooth, his debates over current affairs, and his spontaneous acts of generosity as he was for his publishing and bibliographic achievements. He was also capable of temper outbursts ("rare but devastating," recalls one colleague), a New England stubbornness, and "a righteous, satisfying grudge, though never for a mean or petty reason."

Wilson was a demanding employer with a puritanical work ethic, but he was also a progressive one. From the first, he put women into administrative positions, and he later instituted a pension system for older employees when pensions in American private industry were almost unknown. Other early company benefits included cumulative sick-pay and hospitalization. He made special efforts also to hire the physically handicapped. Howard Haycraft, who succeeded him as president of the firm, wrote: "Though he never took a vacation himself, it was characteristic that he believed in them for others."

Creighton Peet (in his *New Yorker* profile) was impressed with Wilson's work ethic, his devotion to his celebrated old rolltop desk, the symbolic ten-cent "better" mousetrap he kept nearby, and his lack of private office or personal secretary. But he was also taken by Wilson's sincerity, by his concept of the business as a public service, and by a love of humor that manifested itself in three collections of toastmasters' jokes (written under the pseudonym of Harold Workman Williams). Wilson also authored a delightful little handbook, *The Bookman's Reading and Tools* (1932).

Active in civic affairs of the Bronx Borough, he and the equally energetic Justina Wilson, a nationally prominent suffragette, lived in "Greenehold," a remodeled early Colonial house in Yorktown Heights, Westchester County, New York. In the mid-twenties, they bought a large tract of land in this area, and over the years sold acreage to employees and librarian friends, who established homes there.

The end came peacefully for Halsey William Wilson on the morning of March 1, 1954, and soon after, tributes poured in to the company from all parts of the world. None, however, could say more than one written to Wilson six years earlier by Paul North Rice (q.v.), then president of the American Library Association:

It is really incredible that one man could do so much. We take your various indexes and bibliographies for granted, but when we think of what American libraries would do without them, we realize it is no exaggeration to say that you have done more for libraries than any other living man.

Biographical listings and obituaries—*Current Biography* (1954); *Dictionary of American Biography*, Suppl. 5 (Phyllis Dain); "H. W. Wilson, Publisher of Index, Dead." *New York Herald-Tribune*, March 2, 1954; "Halsey W. Wilson, Publisher, Dead." *New York Times*, March 2, 1954; "Halsey William Wilson, May 12, 1868-March 1, 1954." *Wilson Library Bulletin* 28:665-68 (April 1954); *Who Was Who in America* III (1951-1960); *Who's Who in Library Service*, 1st ed. **Books and articles about the biographee**—[Articles on H. W. Wilson Co.]. *Wilson Library Bulletin* 22:783-808 (June 1948); Haycraft, H. "Mr. Wilson: An Informal Reminiscence [and other tributes]." 29:52-58 (Sept. 1954); Lawler, John. *The H. W. Wilson Company: Half a Century of Bibliographic Publishing.* Minneapolis: University of Minnesota Press, 1950; reprinted, Gregg, 1972 [Lawler interviewed Wilson and had access to company files]; Miller, Alvin. "Halsey W. Wilson: The Reader's Guide." *Minnesota Daily Ivory Tower Edition*, Jan. 17, 1955, pp. 8ff; Peet, Creighton. "A Mousetrap in the Bronx." *The New Yorker* 14, No. 37:25-28 (Oct. 29, 1938) [profile of H. W. Wilson]; Plotnik, Arthur. "H. W. Wilson." *Encyclopedia of Library and Information Science.* Allen Kent, Harold Lancour, Jay E. Daily, eds. New York: Marcel Dekker, 1973, Vol. 10; "Tributes to Mr. Wilson." *Wilson Library Bulletin* 28:668-69 (April 1954); Wilson, H. W., Co. *A Quarter Century of Cumulative Bibliography: Retrospect and Prospect.* New York: H. W. Wilson, 1923, 44p.; *Wilson Library Bulletin.* [During Mr. Wilson's lifetime, the *Bulletin* carried news and notes about the company in a regular feature called "The Lighthouse"]. **Primary sources and archival materials**—The H. W. Wilson Company has a limited amount of material concerning Wilson. See also, Halsey W. Wilson. *The Bookman's Reading and Tools.* New York: H. W. Wilson, 1932, 62p.; Halsey W. Wilson. "United We Go Forward." [Rome, Istituto Poligrafico dello Stato, 1932], 8p.; and Halsey W. Wilson. "Random Reminiscences." *Wilson Library Bulletin* 22:779-83 (June 1948).

—ARTHUR PLOTNIK

WINDSOR, PHINEAS LAWRENCE (1871-1965)

Phineas Lawrence Windsor was born on February 21, 1871, in the small town of Chenoa, Illinois, the son of John Alexander and Amy Arnold Windsor. He received the Ph.B. degree from Northwestern University in 1895. From 1897 to 1899, he was a student in the New York State Library School at Albany, then the leading professional school for librarians in the United States. Briefly tempted by the legal profession, he spent a year (1899-1900) in the Albany Law School.

In 1902, Phineas L. Windsor was married to Margaret Fursman Boynton of Lockport, New York, an alumna of Cornell University. Mrs. Windsor's strong inclinations toward science, unusual for a woman of her time, led her to become a candidate for the Ph.D. degree in systematic botany, embryology and entomology at Cornell in 1896-1897.

Windsor's father, John Alexander Windsor (a Methodist minister in the Central Illinois Conference for 34 years), had come to Illinois in 1857 from the old Windsor estate in Maryland. Despite the fact that members of the family were slave-holders, he himself was an ardent abolitionist. (The father's career is commemorated in a short unpublished biography by his son, entitled "A Central Illinois Methodist Minister, 1857-1891" [1944]). Phineas Windsor noted that his love of books originated with the large collection of historical and theological works in his father's library. His childhood was spent adjusting to new communities as the circuit-riding father moved his family from place to place. Money was scarce, and young Windsor hired out to farmers during the summer months. Later, he attributed his vigorous good health to the active outdoor life he had led during those formative years.

His interest in books and librarianship as a career was stimulated further by his serving as a student assistant in the Northwestern University Library. At the conclusion of his stay in Albany, Windsor accepted an appointment in the Library of Congress Copyright Office, under the direction of Thorvald Solberg (q.v.), register of copyrights, where he remained until 1903. This Washington experience was followed by six years as librarian of the University of Texas (1903-1909). Three daughters—Margaret, Mary Frances, and Elizabeth Arnold—were born to the Windsors during the years spent in Austin. Margaret and Elizabeth subsequently entered the library profession.

Though Windsor's sojourn in Texas was relatively brief, it was constructive and marked by keen interest in promoting statewide library service. He took the lead in drafting a bill creating the Texas Library Commission, and as secretary for three years of the newly formed Texas State Library Association, he edited a *Handbook of Texas Libraries* (1904). Also, the University of Texas Library's collections grew substantially during his term as librarian.

In 1909, he returned to his native state and began his long tenure as director of the Library and Library School at the University of Illinois, continuing until he reached mandatory retirement age in 1940. Under Windsor's leadership, the Library and Library School were brought to positions of eminence. The Library's collections grew ten-fold (from fewer than 150,000 volumes to more than 1,500,000 volumes), raising it to fifth place among American university libraries and first among state university libraries.

One type of material to which Windsor paid close attention was newspapers, especially papers representing Illinois communities large and small; American newspapers in foreign languages published for first- and second-generation immigrants ("to study and evaluate," as he remarked, "the contributions made

by various foreign elements to our culture"); and ephemeral papers issued in military camps during World War I and, later, for the Civilian Conservation Corps. Similarly, he is quoted as stating:

During my administration there have been consistent and systematic efforts made to collect in the library as much currently issued, more or less ephemeral literature from corporations, associations, government bureaus, societies, labor unions as possible because of my conviction that changing times will need this material even more than ordinary books published for sale.

Another field of special interest for Windsor was rare books, the history of printing, and well-designed contemporary books. He was principally responsible for choosing the early printers' devices (done in color on panels of tinted glass) inserted in the centers of the large windows of the main reading room at Illinois. His choice of these for decoration reflected his enthusiasm for the work of the original masters of the printing art.

The Library School also made conspicuous progress during the Windsor administration, notably in the direction of strengthening the curriculum and the faculty and in larger enrollments. Under his direction, the Illinois school, in 1926, became the second in the nation to offer a two-year graduate program for a master's degree in library science.

Physical facilities for the Library and Library School were much expanded during the Windsor years. In 1926, the two were moved from an outmoded, overcrowded, non-functional building (erected in 1897) to the first unit of the new central library building. Therein was introduced a novel concept—a building that could be added to almost indefinitely, with further units to be constructed as required to meet space needs of rapidly growing book collections, staff, and student enrollments. The soundness of the plan is demonstrated by the fact that six units have been added in the intervening years, and the building continues to be highly functional. (The success of the scheme was contingent upon the University's reserving the extensive area west of the original building for future expansion.) The Illinois building, which attracted wide attention in the 1920s and 1930s, influenced the planning of library buildings in universities elsewhere, and numerous librarians and architects visited the campus to inspect the building's unusual features. Another result was that Windsor was in demand as a building consultant, both in Illinois and in other states.

During World War I (1917-1918), he was on leave from the University to become assistant director of the American Library Association's Library War Service in Washington. His off-campus professional activities also involved him in the work of various associations. Nationally, he served as vice-president of the American Library Association (1923-1924), served three terms on the ALA Council (1909-1913, 1918-1923, and 1936-1941), and at various times was chairman of the Professional Training Section, the Committee on Standardization of Libraries and Certification of Librarians, the Committee on Code of Ethics, and the Finance Committee. He was the second president of the Association of College and Reference Libraries (1939-1940). He also served as president of the American Library Institute (1940-1942) and as vice-president of the Bibliographical Society of America. With several other prominent university librarians of the time, he was a leader in founding the Association of Research Libraries, in 1932. His interest in library education was shown by his election as president of the Association of American Library Schools for two terms (1921-1922 and 1934-1935). (He also served as president of AALS for the irregularly executed term of 1926-1927 and may have occupied the office for part of the preceding term as well; records for the period are somewhat scanty, but consult Donald G. Davis's "AALS: The Lost Years, 1925-1928," *Journal of Education for Librarianship* 17:98-105 [Fall 1976].)

On the state level, Phineas Windsor was president of the Illinois Library Association for two terms (1913 and 1935). He was a member of the Illinois State Library Advisory Committee from its establishment in 1935 until 1961 and served as its chairman for two extended terms (1935-1942 and 1948-1958). He assisted in drafting bills to improve library service in Illinois and used his considerable influence with state officials and legislators to secure their enactment. One such example is the legislation establishing the Illinois State Library's Extension Division. In 1944, he surveyed the library resources of the Kansas City area for the American Library Association. Recommendations based on that study led to the establishment in 1946 of the Linda Hall Library as a reference library emphasizing service in the fields of science and technology.

Beyond his normal administrative responsibilities on the Illinois campus, Windsor served on numerous committees concerned with determining the University's major policies and practices. Of special importance were the Budget Committee (of which he was one of three members for some years), charged with planning the biennial budget for the entire University, and the University Senate's famous Committee of Nine (during President Harry Chase's administration), which was responsible for making a thorough study of the organization and operation of the University preparatory to complete revision of the University statutes. Windsor's work on the latter committee strengthened the independence of the University and clarified the position of the Library within the institutional structure. The statutes relating to the Library's administration and management were widely adopted as models by other university libraries. As president of the local chapters of two honorary societies, Phi Beta Kappa and Phi Kappa Phi, Windsor also came into touch with many of the brightest students on the campus.

Civic activities outside the University were also primary concerns for Windsor. He was a member of the Wesley Methodist Church in Urbana for over fifty years, serving as steward and trustee of the congregation for much of that period. He helped to establish the Wesley Foundation and served as its treasurer for twenty years. He was a charter member of the Urbana Rotary Club (established in 1924) and served as its fifth president (1928-1929). His legal training and expertise in building matters were useful in his work as a director of the Commercial Savings and Loan Association of Urbana for 37 years. On the local level, too, he became involved in library affairs, serving for 26 years on the Board of Directors of the Urbana Free Library.

Recognition of Windsor's professional accomplishments came in the form of various honors. Columbia University conferred upon him the honorary degree of Doctor of Letters (1939). The citation, by President Nicholas Murray Butler, read, in part: "Phineas Lawrence Windsor . . . combining scholarship with thorough knowledge of scholarship's greatest laboratory, the library and its care." In 1945, he received the Northwestern University Alumni Association's Merit Award for "outstanding achievement," the citation for which noted that he was a "citizen of the highest type who has served untiringly in educational and civic capacities and has generously and unstintingly given of his knowledge without seeking personal recognition." In 1966, the Illinois State Library named its main reading and reference room the "Phineas Lawrence Windsor Reading Room." When he retired in 1940, contributions were received from several thousand alumni, former library staff members, friends, colleagues, and others for establishment of the "Phineas L. Windsor Lectures in Bibliography and Librarianship"; starting in 1949, and almost annually since, more than a score of distinguished librarians, bibliographers, authors, publishers, historians, scientists, and editors have presented lectures in this series, nearly all of which have been issued in book form.

Windsor himself was a doer rather than a writer, as he did not write with ease or with particular distinction. He wrote only a half-dozen minor articles, mainly in state journals, during the forty-plus years of his active career. To these, a complete bibliography would add several unpublished reports of library surveys. Two of his articles of general interest appeared in *Illinois Libraries*: "Books and the

Studious Life" (25:301-303 [October 1943]) and "On General Reading" (26:83-85 [February 1944]).

On the other hand, as the articles cited above might indicate, his friends knew him as an avid reader, eager to convert others to the satisfactions and values of reading. In a Phi Beta Kappa address presented in 1943, he took note of the idea then beginning to circulate that the present form of the book may eventually disappear, to be replaced by other media. He declared that "the book is after all likely to remain," because it is better than any other device for its purpose, and "notwithstanding the importance of the newer inventions and methods for the preservation of ideas and information, books as we know them are still of great potential value to most of us."

Phineas Windsor was described by colleagues closely associated with him as "good-humored, diplomatic, a good hiker and lover of the outdoors, who smoked big black pipes and Tampa cigars." He bought his first car about 1933, at age 62, and thereafter always drove Buicks, usually at high rates of speed. His success in staff relations inspired wits on the staff to claim that his initials PLW stood for "Placating Library Women." Tall, lean, erect in stature, and with a Vandyke beard, Windsor was a handsome, striking figure who easily stood out in a crowd.

Probably his greatest contribution to his chosen profession was the ability he convincingly demonstrated to bring a university's administration, faculty, and staff together in concerted action to create a great research library. Phineas Lawrence Windsor died on September 2, 1965, at the age of 94.

Biographical listings and obituaries–[Obituary]. *Illinois Libraries* 47:912 (Oct. 1965); [Obituary]. *Library Journal* 91:225 (Jan. 15, 1966); [Obituary]. *Texas Library Journal* 41:161 (Winter 1965); *Who Was Who in America* V (1969-1973); *Who's Who in Library Service*, 1st ed., 2nd ed., 3rd ed. **Books and articles about the biographee**–Bay, Jens C. "Phineas Lawrence Windsor." *Illinois Libraries* 24:212 (Oct. 1942); "Phineas Lawrence Windsor." [Columbia University] *Library Service News* 8:25-27 (Aug. 1939). **Primary sources and archival materials**–The Windsor papers for the long period of his association with the University of Illinois are in the University Archives, University of Illinois Library, Urbana. See also his article "Fifty Years." In *Fifty Years of Education for Librarianship: Papers Presented for the Celebration of the Fiftieth Anniversary of the University Library School.* Urbana: University of Illinois Press, 1943, pp. 33-37.

–ROBERT B. DOWNS

WING, DONALD GODDARD (1904-1972)

Donald Goddard Wing was born August 18, 1904, at Athol, Massachusetts, the son of Frank E. and Edith Smith Wing. He was graduated from Yale University in 1926, attended Trinity College (Cambridge University) as an affiliate student in 1926-1927, and received a master's degree in English from Harvard University in 1928. He earned his Ph.D. in English literature from Yale University in 1932. He was married to Charlotte Farquhar in 1930. They had two children, Robert and Cathya.

Wing joined the Yale Library staff in September 1928 in the Order Department. He was named assistant reference librarian in 1930. In 1939, he was made head of the Accessions Department and was appointed associate librarian in 1945. In 1965, his title was changed to associate librarian for the collections of the Library as well as research associate. In 1945, he was also made librarian of the Linonian and Brothers Library, an undergraduate "browsing room," which he "dearly loved to keep filled with a wide range of current books as well as old ones, so that undergraduates could find reading of interest and enjoyment in fields unrelated to their studies." During the period 1941 to 1960, Wing aided in and supervised the founding and development of the Library of Yale's Silliman College. In 1961, he served as consultant to the Syracuse University Library. He was granted a sabbatical leave in 1967 to work on the second edition of his *Short-Title Catalogue*–the first sabbatical leave awarded by Yale University to a librarian. With his retirement in 1970, Wing became emeritus associate librarian of Yale. He remained active at the Yale Library until his untimely death on October 8, 1972, barely two weeks after more than one hundred scholars and friends had gathered on September 27 in Yale's Sterling Library to honor him on the publication of the first volume of the second edition of "Wing"–the work that made his name familiar in every library in the English-speaking world.

Wing's contributions to library science are numerous, but he will be remembered best as the compiler of the "Wing" catalog of early English-language books. *The Short-Title Catalogue of Books Printed in England, Scotland, Ireland, Wales and British America and of English Books Printed in Other Countries, 1641-1700*–a continuation of Pollard and Redgrave's *Short-Title Catalogue of Books Printed in England, Scotland and Ireland and of English Books Printed Abroad, 1475-1640*–was immediately recognized as a bibliographic classic. It has since become familiar to every scholar and rare book handler and is indispensable for bibliographic research in the period covered.

Work on the *Short-Title Catalogue* began in 1933, shortly after Wing had received his doctorate. He had been working nights as a research assistant at the Yale Library ("mostly directing people to the men's room," as he said in an August 1972 interview in the *New York Times*) when he volunteered to catalog the Falconer Madan collection of rare books. In this work, he quickly discovered the lack of bibliographic ·

control over books published after 1640. His goal became to find every book, pamphlet, and broadside published in English in the last sixty years of the seventeenth century, Pollard and Redgrave having covered the period 1475-1640. Through correspondence with librarians, collectors, booksellers and scholars, he continued his searches beyond the Yale Library. In 1935, he received a Guggenheim Fellowship and leave from Yale to do research in British libraries for his bibliography. By that time, he had already 21 shoe boxes full of the paper slips on which individual entries were recorded. He returned with slips representing 90,000 titles. All of this he had done apart from his regular duties at Yale.

In the *Times* interview, Wing remarked that, when he began, he thought that his work would never be published and his slips would simply remain at Yale. But in the 1940s, scholars from several universities formed the Index Society, which sought to bring into existence research "tool-books" for scholars. Wing turned over his *Catalogue* to the Society and, in 1945, it was published in three volumes totaling 1,652 pages. Over the years, sales of the books have netted the Society $30,000, which has been used to finance other indexes. Wing had received nothing for his work beyond his regular librarian's salary, save great pleasure and extreme satisfaction.

However, that first edition was just a beginning. He then started work on a definitive second edition, which also totalled three volumes. Entries were given expanded, fuller imprints, and many new locations were added for those titles included in the first edition. Cross references, a weakness in the first edition, were increased for the convenience of the user. Of the 90,000 books included, Wing estimated that he had personally examined 70,000 and, therefore, could verify the information given.

Wing's *Catalogue* has been described as "a literary map of one of the most tangled periods in British history—the contentious times of Cromwell and the Commonwealth, the turbulent years of the Restoration, the quarrelsome period of the Popeish plot and the Whig Revolution." It has been acclaimed as "a prodigious feat of research and endurance—a life time of work by a single man that can be compared to Samuel Johnson's labors on his dictionary." Lawrence Clark Powell has described this "crusty, terse, direct, but also warm and very human man" as "a bibliographical genius," and his *Catalogue* as "an achievement of the highest order."

In order to reduce the problem of "ghosts" (entries representing books that someone had described but that failed to appear in any of the libraries examined), Wing compiled a work called *Gallery of Ghosts.* This was a listing of five thousand titles that could not be verified completely. Within six months after its publication, ten percent of the "ghosts" had been accounted for by contributors from throughout the world. Wing was extremely pleased over the response, and rightfully so; it demonstrated the carefulness and seriousness with which many librarians treated the identification of rare books. It was also an accolade for the long years that Wing devoted to the *Short-Title Catalogue.*

Wing also published reviews in a number of periodicals, including the *Yale Review* and the *Saturday Review of Literature.* He contributed to the *Festschrift* published in honor of A. S. W. Rosenbach's seventieth birthday (Philadelphia, 1946). In the last few years of his life, he was a consultant to the Editorial Board of the English Revolution (a series of British publications) and also to Library Resources, Inc., in regard to the lists of its "Library of English Literature."

He had been elected to membership in many distinguished literary and scholarly organizations: the Elizabethan Club at Yale, the Grolier Club, and the Bibliographical Societies of London, America, Cambridge, Oxford, and Edinburgh. He served as vice-president and president of the Faculty Club at Yale, and was a fellow of Yale's Silliman College. His interests included theatre, piano, tennis, and travel.

His was a dedicated career, one apparently little concerned with financial rewards. Work on the *Short-Title Catalogue* spanned almost thirty years in the two editions, yet his interest in its perfection never seemed to wane. As to why anyone would want to become involved in such a long-term project, Wing admitted, with tongue in cheek, that "only a fool would undertake such a project. But he has to be a particularly perservering fool to finish." The labor, he said, was made somewhat lighter by the realization that he was surrounded at Yale "by other fools even more perservering," busily engaged in similar projects dealing with Boswell, Walpole, and others. When asked about a continuation of his work beyond 1700, Wing admitted that he had little interest in the idea. "Something died with Dryden," he said, "and the following decades have always been less sympathetic to me." Willing to leave to others the challenge of such work, Wing stated, "I prefer to keep the new four-letter adjective pure. When booksellers offer Wing-period books I don't want to wonder what period."

Wing's contribution to the world of learning has been acclaimed by many, but the most eloquent praise has been made by Herman W. Liebert, then librarian of Yale's Beinecke Rare Book and Manuscript Library, who said in his memorial to Wing (printed in the *Yale University Library Gazette* of January 1973):

Don's work, done so quietly, so zealously, recently so bravely, and always alone, is one of the bright jewels in the crown of Yale's service to learning.

More than one of us here today has had the experience of visiting one of the universities throughout the world, of explaining that we came from Yale, and of being greeted with the slow dawn of comprehension—"Oh, yes. Wing's place." However, Liebert also knew and described the man Donald Wing, as well as the scholar:

> Yet another contradiction was the breadth of his interests, in spite of the sharp focus of his catalogue. The period 1641-1700 was but one band in the spectrum, and those who knew him only from his publication could not realize that, besides James Howell, Don assiduously collected, and also read, Henry James, Ronald Firbank, Marcel Proust, Edith Wharton, Ezra Pound, Ellen Glasgow, E. M. Forster, Andre Gide, and all the Sitwells.

> No man can be said to put you in mind of Donald Wing. He was that wonderful, extraordinary thing, an optimistic cynic, a gregarious misanthrope, a near-agnostic who had a lifelong love-affair with knowledge. He was, in short, a very amiable loner.

> Of the fact that he had a great capacity for friendship, this congregation is ample evidence. He did not suffer fools gladly, and many of us have felt the lash, when we came to him with an ill-formed or half-baked idea. But those who shared his love of learning always received, full measure and running over, his help, and advice and support.

Like many pioneers, though, Wing didn't understand why scholars were decanting superlatives over him. In the *New York Times* interview upon the forthcoming publication of the second edition of his *Catalogue*, Wing remarked: "It has been marvelous. I have actually been paid to read second-hand catalogues."

Biographical listings and obituaries—*Biographical Directory of Librarians in the United States and Canada*, 5th ed.; *New York Times Biographical Edition*, Aug. 1972, p. 1580; [Obituary]. *American Libraries* 3:1177 (Dec. 1972); [Obituary]. *Antiquarian Bookman Weekly* 51:1204 (Oct. 16, 1972); [Obituary]. *Library Journal* 97:3673 (Nov. 15, 1972); [Obituary]. *New York Times*, Oct. 11, 1972, p. 46; [Obituary]. *Wilson Library Bulletin* 47:230 (Nov. 1972); *Who's Who in Library Service*, 1st ed., 2nd ed., 3rd ed., 4th ed. **Books and articles about the biographee**—Liebert, Herman W. "In Memoriam." *Yale University Library Gazette* 47:134-36 (Jan. 1973); Munby, A. N. L., and N. Carol Evans. "Wing's STC." *The Book Collector*, Autumn 1974, pp. 388-93. **Primary sources and archival materials**—Wing, Donald G. "The Making of the Short-Title Catalogue, 1641-1700." *Bibliographical Society of America Papers* 45:59-69 (Jan.-March 1951); Wing, Donald G. "Wing on Wing." *Yale University Library Gazette* 44:1-7 (July 1969).

—KATHERINE CVELJO

WINSER, BEATRICE (1869-1947)

Beatrice Winser was born in Newark, New Jersey, on March 11, 1869, oldest child of Henry Jacob and Edith Cox Winser. Her father, a newspaperman, was appointed American consul to the German principality of Coburg, and Beatrice spent most of the first twelve years of her life in Germany, educated by private tutors, learning French, German, and English and developing an interest in books. In 1888, she attended Columbia College (later University), following the library course that later developed into the Albany Library School.

Upon completion of this course in 1889, she went to work at the newly established Newark Public Library as cataloger of French and German books. In 1894, she was appointed assistant to Frank P. Hill (q.v.), Newark's first librarian. Hill remained long enough to oversee the erection of the new main building, which opened its doors in March 1901, then Hill resigned to go to the Brooklyn Public Library. Winser was in charge for seven months, "perfectly capable of carrying on," as the Trustees said, but they preferred a man for the position and decided on John Cotton Dana (q.v.), who came from the Springfield, Massachusetts, Public Library to Newark in January 1902. From then until his death in 1929, John Cotton Dana and Beatrice Winser worked together for the advancement of library service in the city.

It was a remarkable partnership. Dana had many ideas for promoting library service to all segments of the population; Winser had the ability to carry out his ideas and attend to the day-to-day management of the Library. She would often walk around the building and visit the branches to observe whether improvements could be made. She kept in touch with the staff, noting strengths and weaknesses. Sometimes these visits resulted in immediate moving of furniture, and, at other times, transfers of staff. Winser oversaw the details of staffing, budgeting, and acquisitions, with Dana as ultimate authority.

Winser seconded him during the period of the organization of the Newark Museum. She became assistant director in 1915 and, a year later, a member of the Museum's Board of Trustees. Also in 1915, she was appointed to serve on the Newark Board of Education, the first woman to serve on any city agency. She was active in organizing and was twice president (1907-1908 and 1921-1922) of the New Jersey Library Association. A member of the American Library Association's Council of Fifty from 1909 to 1912 and again in 1930, she was second vice-president of the Association in 1931.

During World War I, the administration of the Newark Public Library faced problems from which many lessons were learned. The closing of branches, for instance, pointed out the need for city-owned structures. During the post-War period of expansion, Winser helped plan new branches, setting up extension services, running the new bookmobile, and overseeing acquisitions. As the 1920s wore on and Dana's health declined, Winser was in charge of both the Library and the Museum, while Dana was away recuperating or on a trip to buy books, prints, or museum objects.

After Dana's death in July, Winser was appointed librarian in August 1929. She also succeeded him as director of the Museum and maintained the close ties between the two institutions. At that time, she was one of four women to head a library in a city of over 400,000 population in the United States. Later, she was quoted in an interview in the *Newark Sunday Call* (March 29, 1936) as saying, "A woman can make good at whatever she wants to do. . . . I believe in women."

Unfortunately, the Depression set in as she was taking full charge, so she had to restrain her plans for wider service and renovation of the main building. However, she had preliminary studies made for the expansion of the building and acquired land behind the Library and north of the Museum to accommodate future services and collections. Physical deterioration of the main building necessitated shifting departments and leasing outside space. Winser seemed to enjoy moving things around, but she never lost sight of the ultimate need for more and better-arranged space—nor did she let the city administration forget the Library's needs. Budgets were cut, bookmobile service halted, hours of opening shortened, etc., and she fought to mitigate the problems. Library service was maintained at as high a level as possible by careful staffing and keeping the book budget flexible to provide for the city's current and future needs.

During this period, Winser was involved in the founding of Dana College, which became the University of Newark and which honored her with an LL.D. in 1937. (It is now the Newark campus of Rutgers University.) She was active in connection with the WPA agencies, some of which had headquarters in the Library, and she chaired the Art Division in 1935. In 1936, she was named one of the state's 25 outstanding women by the New Jersey Federation of Business and Professional Women's Clubs.

In 1936, acting on her belief in the library profession, Winser was prominent in taking exception to the appointment of Archibald MacLeish as Librarian of Congress. She conceded his abilities but deplored his lack of professional training and experience. Following her principles, as she had on the question of racism at the ALA Richmond Conference, she took ALA to task for acquiescing without adequate protest. She also protested attempts by customs officials to censor foreign books and publications. Fearing political control, she opposed federal aid to libraries.

The outbreak of World War II caused the quick transformation, in 1942, of the Newark Public Library's National Defense Center into a War Information Center to provide information and materials about new agencies, regulations, and appointments, as well as job training manuals to industries and groups in the city and surrounding areas. Borrowing privileges were extended to members of the armed services. Winser also headed the Wartime Council of Newark Libraries, which co-ordinated the work of the public and special libraries for wartime needs. She was active in book drives for camps and military installations. In addition, she set up a Paint and Clay Corner at Camp Kilmer, where Museum staff provided instructions and materials for drawing, painting, and modeling for the benefit of the soldiers at the camp.

In July 1942, Miss Winser announced her retirement as librarian as of September 1. At the same time, she brought to light a source of friction between herself and the Library Board of Trustees, charging interference in the administrative functions of the Library. She could have retired quietly, but, characteristically, she chose to air the difficulty so that her successor would not be unaware of what was, to her, a major problem. Although she retired from the Library, she continued to direct the Newark Museum until she left her unsalaried post at the end of May 1947. She did not live long to enjoy her leisure, as she died of heart disease on September 14, 1947. She is buried in the family plot in Greenwood Cemetery, Brooklyn.

Though Winser's main concerns were the library and museum fields, an incomplete listing of her memberships and the groups she supported shows her varied interests. She was on the Board of the World Center for Women's Archives; a member of the New Jersey Audubon Society; a fellow of the American Geographical Society; a supporter of the Bach Society of New Jersey; and she worked for the establishment of the New Jersey College for Women (now Douglass College of Rutgers University).

Beatrice Winser was not a large woman, but had a commanding presence which, along with her deep voice, could seem intimidating to those who did not know her. But the staff and others could depend on her sense of justice and her quick response to people. They remember her dedication to her work, her lively interest in the world; the deep dimple that belied the severe haircut and that came into play as she burst into laughter. She was full of zest for life, whether in the Library, the Museum, at her farm, or elsewhere.

As Marian Manley, librarian of the Business Library, wrote in *Library Journal* (October 15, 1947):

> Beatrice Winser as a courageous, gifted, constructive, inspiring public official, without consciousness of self, leaves a shining record. But it is Beatrice Winser, the invigorating, human, fearless, and understanding friend and chief whose influence cannot be measured. No one who worked with her—and their number is legion—could be untouched by that bracing, challenging ardor, which, while holding the highest standards, never lost response to the human side of life. No associates, from janitor to director, failed to find concerned, immediate help in time of need: no lighter moment went without her ringing laugh.

Biographical listings and obituaries—*Notable American Women* III (Katherine Coffey); [Obituary]. *New York Times*, Sept. 16, 1947; *Who Was Who in America* II (1943-1950). **Books and articles about the biographee**—[Editorial]. *New York Times*, Sept. 18, 1947; Heiderstadt, Dorothy. "Busiest Woman in Newark." *Wilson Library Bulletin* 16:478 (Feb. 1942); Jewell, Edward Alden. [Tribute]. *New York Times*, April 27, 1947; Manley, Marian C. "Beatrice Winser, Administrator and Friend." *Library Journal* 72:1481 (Oct. 15, 1947); Newark Museum. *Beatrice Winser, 1869-1947*. Newark Museum, 1948. **Primary sources and archival materials**—Some Dana papers are in the Woodstock, Vermont, Historical Society; correspondence, notes, etc., relating to Library and Museum matters are in the Dana Papers in the Newark Public Library and in the Winser file in the Newark Museum.

—JULIA SABINE

WINSHIP, GEORGE PARKER (1871-1952)

George Parker Winship, librarian and bibliographer, born on July 29, 1871, was the eldest of six children of Albert Ellis and Ella Rebecca Parker Winship. His father was a noted teacher, editor (of *The Journal of Education*), and clergyman. Winship went from Somerville High School to Harvard College (A.B., 1893; A.M., 1894), where his interest in American history took firm root. He also had an early attraction to libraries. Thus, after teaching history for two years, in 1895 he went to Providence, Rhode Island, at the recommendation of Justin Winsor (q.v.), to become librarian of the John Carter Brown private library, which was already outstanding in materials relating to America.

Brown had begun to collect Americana systematically in 1846 and, by 1874, when he died, the collection contained over 5,500 books on the Americas. His widow, Sophia Augusta Brown, shared her husband's keen interest in books and fostered a similar interest in their son, John Nicholas Brown, who assumed full control of acquisitions in 1890. The Browns and their part-time librarian, John Russell Bartlett, continued both to develop the collection and to answer the many inquiries of scholars. Because the scholarly demands on the library continued to

increase, however, Winship was appointed the full-time librarian. When Brown University accepted the collection in 1901 and opened a separate library for it in 1904, Winship was appointed librarian of the John Carter Brown Library.

When first appointed, Winship made a thorough inventory and evaluation of the collection. He used this intimate knowledge of the holdings to continue the practice of providing generous assistance to scholars and to continue the acquisition of primary materials on the Americas printed before 1801, as was decided in 1904. His vigorous pursuit of every kind of pertinent item increased the collection from 20,000 items, in 1904, to over 31,000 ten years later. Just as significant as the increase in numbers was the widening of the scope of the collection. Winship was able to see America from a European point of view and acquired books that set the New World within the context of European history.

As an undergraduate, Winship had been engaged in translating and editing; during his senior year he began studying the Spanish explorers, taking up Coronado's expedition to New Mexico and the Great Plains. This interest was further stimulated by trips to Mexico and New Mexico, as when he visited New Mexico on an expedition with the United States Bureau of Ethnology. The pursuit resulted in his first major publication, *The Coronado Expedition: 1540-1542* (1896). It was an excellent first work for the librarian because it required the use of those several skills—translation, textual criticism, and bibliography—which were invaluable to him in his later career.

Winship's next major work was his *Cabot Bibliography* (1900), which described the books relating to the voyages of John and Sebastian Cabot. It remains the standard bibliography on the Cabot books and is an excellent example of bibliographical method in Winship's time. He broke no new theoretical ground but described carefully the bibliographical and explorative history of each book. By having Henry N. Stevens supervise the proofreading, and by having the Chiswick Press do the printing, Winship carried on the tradition of outstanding nineteenth-century bibliographies of Americana. He was also able to satisfy his taste for fine printing, a taste that stayed with him throughout his life.

These two publications established his reputation as a bibliographer and librarian, and his experience in Providence was so attractive that he decided to remain a librarian rather than become the historian he had originally planned to be. Librarianship offered a wider canvas for his many talents. He was an ebullient and effective "promoter" of the John Carter Brown collection, frequently writing an essay or article about a particularly important acquisition, which was not an uncommon occurrence. Such enthusiasm strongly affected those who knew him and often influenced young people who subsequently had outstanding careers in bibliography and history, persons such as Margaret Bingham Stillwell and Walter Muir Whitehill. Enthusiasm for books and a love of writing about them were traits he retained throughout his career.

This energy and interest in all things bibliographic also engendered close relationships with bibliographers and scholars throughout the Americas and Europe. At the same time, Winship was closely tied to historical and educational institutions in Massachusetts. He became a corresponding member of the Colonial Society of Massachusetts in 1899 and of the Massachusetts Historical Society in 1905. In 1898, he became a non-resident member of the Club of Odd Volumes in Boston. Soon after his election to membership, and perhaps because of his interest in fine printing, the Club began to employ the best printers and typographers of the day to design and manufacture its publications.

In 1915, Winship was called back to Harvard as librarian of the Harry Elkins Widener Collection. The Collection had been formed by Widener during the years just before his death on the *Titanic* (1912). The Collection was provided with an attractive setting in the building that bore the collector's name when his mother decided to honor her son's memory by building a new library for Harvard. Because the Collection was to remain static by terms of the donation, Winship's duties were light. But instead of taking personal advantage of the situation, he turned his attention to all of the rare books in the Harvard Library. In 1926, he changed positions in the Harvard Library and was appointed assistant librarian for the Treasure Room. Winship developed cordial relationships with a wide variety of bibliographers and collectors, encouraging their interest in and donations to Harvard's collections. Having worked with private collectors, he recognized the great benefit that they and their collections could have on the development of a library, and his natural love for things New England, combined with a quick wit and humor, encouraged donations. However, realizing the general lack of knowledge about Harvard's rare books, Winship became the first editor of *Harvard Library Notes* (which first appeared in June 1920), through which he was able to publicly acknowledge the generosity of donors and publish articles about major holdings. He also turned to Harvard's own stacks, working diligently to insure the preservation of valuable and scarce books. His bibliographical training and experience made him keenly aware of the scholarly value of books, and it later became clear that Winship's sensitive and intelligent appreciation of rare books enabled Harvard to develop a program for

them that was started only decades later by other libraries.

Winship's pleasant relationship with faculty and alumni was matched by a genuine affection for undergraduates. Between 1915 and 1931, he offered a course called "History of the Printed Book" (Fine Arts 5e), which traced the historical development of printed books in terms of people and events, an approach that was successful in his published works. By this means he cultivated the collecting instincts of his students and promoted knowledge of the Harvard collections. One of the happiest results of his desire to share books with undergraduates was the formation of the John Barnard Associates, which also included alumni and faculty. Among the first members to join in 1927 was Arthur Amory Houghton, Jr., who afterward gave the Houghton Rare Book Library to Harvard.

George Parker Winship was married to Claire Bliven in 1912. They had two sons and a daughter.

Before and during his married life, Winship was engaged in a variety of private press activities, whereby he produced a wide range of materials, from Christmas cards to literary firsts. The "Sign of the George," as the press was called, provided a means for engaging his taste for fine printing, for gaining first-hand knowledge about the process of printing, and for issuing those biting pamphlets about New Englanders in whom Winship took great delight.

Winship published dozens of articles and newspaper accounts about printing history and book acquisitions, and many of them appeared as separate publications. His other books included his editing of *Sailors Narratives of Voyages along the New England Coast, 1524-1624* (Houghton, Mifflin & Company, 1905), *The John Carter Brown Library: A History* (John Carter Brown Library, 1914), and *Gutenberg to Plantin, a Outline of the Early History of Printing* (Harvard University Press, 1926). In 1940, he published a biography, *John Gutenberg* (Lakeside Press). Also in 1940, he published *Printing in the Fifteenth Century*, the result of the first lectures he gave as a Rosenbach fellow in bibliography. Lively and well-written, the book summarized the incunabular period for a non-specialist audience. Winship injected the same energy into the book as he had into teaching his courses, making it a fitting celebration for the quincentenary anniversary of printing by Johann Gutenberg.

Winship's next book, *The Cambridge Press: 1638-1692* (1945), the product of a second Rosenbach fellowship in 1941, showed the strength of his bibliographical and historical powers. He attacked the problem of the origin and history of the press boldly (as was necessary because of the poverty of evidence), relying on his deep knowledge of printing methods and publishing history to fill the gaps. Unlike *Printing*, the book was addressed to those who were familiar with the documents and events of the story. Winship's decision not to document carefully and to adopt a circuitous narrative style sometimes prevented a clear understanding of the book on the first reading; yet his thorough analysis of the political, technical, and publishing life of the press made it one of the earliest and best examples of history and bibliography being used in a thoroughly integrated way to describe an enterprise that had a rich cultural impact on its society.

Winship's last major book, *Daniel Berkeley Updike and The Merrymount Press* (1947), was a combined biography of Updike, history of the Press, and discussion of the design and production of the exquisite books the Press published. As in the writing of *The Cambridge Press*, Winship achieved a satisfying synthesis of events, persons, and technology for a well-written, enjoyable book.

Winship's bibliographical contributions were very much like his contributions to librarianship. He was able to work effectively in a variety of areas. No aspect of the history of the book and no area of rare book librarianship was unaffected by his thought and actions. His ability to be the highly successful generalist identifies him as one of America's first "professional" rare book librarians. Knowledgeable about books and about the care of books, a rare combination of extraordinary talents, George Parker Winship died on June 22, 1952.

Biographical listings and obituaries–*Dictionary of American Biography*, Suppl. 5 (Walter Muir Whitehill); "George Parker Winship." *School and Society* 76:14 (July 5, 1952), [Obituary]. *New York Times*, June 24, 1952, p. 29; Shipton, Clifford K. "George Parker Winship [Obituary]." *American Antiquarian Society Proceedings* 62, No. 2:117-20 (Oct. 1952); *Who's Who in Library Service*, 1st ed. **Books and articles about the biographee**–Stillwell, Margaret Bingham. *Librarians Are Human*. Boston: The Colonial Society of Massachusetts, 1973; Walton, C. E. "George Parker Winship." *Harvard Library Notes* 3:139-40 (May 1938); Whitehill, Walter Muir. "George Parker Winship." *Massachusetts Historical Society Proceedings* 71:366-75 (1953-1957) [reprinted in *Analecta Biographica: A Handful of New England Portraits*. Brattleboro, Vt., 1969]. **Primary sources and archival materials**–Winship, George Parker. "Recollections of a Private Printer." *The Colophon*. N.S. 3, No. 2:210-24 (Spring 1938) [autobiographical]. Papers and letters are held in the Brown University Archives and in the Harvard University Archives.

–PAUL S. KODA

WINSOR, JUSTIN (1831-1897)

Justin Winsor–librarian, editor, historian–was born on January 2, 1831, and reared in Boston, Massachusetts. He was the son of Nathaniel Winsor, Jr., a successful merchant shipper, and of Ann Thomas Howland Winsor, a fifth-generation descendant of *Mayflower* voyager John Howland. Young Justin attended the Latin Grammar School in Boston and, in the summers, gathered materials for his first historical work, *A History of the Town of Duxbury, Massachusetts, with Historical Registers* (1849). Published in Winsor's first year at Harvard College, the study grew out of its youthful author's love of local legends and ancestral traditions. In the course of his collegiate studies, he early demonstrated considerable disdain for the "dead hand" of the classical curriculum so common in that day. Growing increasingly bored and restless, Winsor withdrew from Harvard in his senior year (1852) to travel to France and Germany for two years of intensive language and literary study.

Upon his return home in 1854, he launched a vigorous, if rather undistinguished, career as poet, essayist, and literary critic. He pursued *belles-lettres* with great energy and tenacity for over ten years, but artistic fame eluded him in his every effort. On December 18, 1855, Justin Winsor was married to Caroline T. Barker, and they moved in with his father. They had a daughter, Constance.

In late 1866, he accepted an appointment to the Board of Trustees of the Boston Public Library. His reputation for energy and productivity, as well as his family's wealth, also led to his selection as chairman of the Library's examining committee. Winsor threw himself into this task with characteristic zeal and produced a report, in 1867, that would be hailed in future years as a masterwork of statistical analysis. Following Winsor's death, one commentator noted that, in the Examiner's Report, Winsor had demonstrated a remarkable facility for management and that he might well have succeeded in industry, for his administrative talents would have fitted him amply for commercial competition.

One year after Winsor wrote his landmark report, Superintendent Charles Coffin Jewett (q.v.) died unexpectedly, and the Boston Public Library's Board of Trustees called Winsor to assume temporary, then permanent, direction of the nation's premier public library. He quickly admitted that he had little experience to qualify him for the position, saying that it

> was by much the same process as in the New England seaboard towns, in the old times, a young man sometimes attained command of a ship without apprenticeship before the mast, by "crawling in through the cabin windows," that I got so conspicuous a place in the librarian's calling.

Inheriting an administration that "creaked a little," as Charles Ammi Cutter (q.v.) put it, Winsor set about with systematic and aggressive efforts to remedy the Library's shortcomings. In the next ten years, he pioneered in "getting books used," and focused the attention of the library world on Boston through his innovative promotion of popular fiction, reading guides, branch libraries, a shelflist with entries on cards, and Sunday opening. He also wrote masterful annual reports, filled with statistics and descriptions of practices at the Boston Public Library. These reports had wide currency, and Winsor's reputation grew accordingly.

When the American Library Association was founded in 1876, Winsor, instrumental in its formation, was chosen as its first president, a post he would hold for the period 1876-1885. He also helped in the founding of the *American Library Journal* (later *Library Journal*). He became the nation's foremost librarian, a man whose counsel was sought in nearly every matter of consequence in American librarianship. His correspondents included numerous contacts in foreign countries, and he earned the respect of leading European librarians. In 1877, he headed the American delegation to the first International Conference of Librarians, in London.

Also in 1877, he accepted a position at Harvard College, succeeding John L. Sibley (q.v.) as librarian, in which capacity he would serve for twenty years. Winsor removed to Cambridge partly because he had encountered difficulties with the Boston Board of Aldermen, which thought little of his professional status, and partly because he had long wished to secure a less demanding situation in which to pursue further historical research. At Harvard, he continued his emphasis on the application of library resources rather than their mere collection.

No one more fully approved of Charles W. Eliot's liberalization of the Harvard curriculum than did Winsor, who belatedly had received (in 1867) his bachelor's degree as a member of the class of 1853. Upon assuming the duties of librarian, Winsor was accorded the rank of professor, but his dislike of examinations and scholastic rankings deterred Harvard from offering and him from accepting frequent instructional assignments. Thus, he concentrated on his researches and on Library matters. He issued cards allowing students stack privileges, enlarged the reserve collection, reclassified books, unified various small libraries around the campus under the main Library, improved the physical aspects of the building (getting new furniture, improving air circulation, and installing electrical lighting in 1895), and gave instruction in the use of the Library. He also had published (in 1879) a union list of the serial publications of Boston-Cambridge area libraries, and he encouraged interlibrary loans as well.

Perfectly at home among the University's faculty, Winsor enjoyed a wide circle of friends. This was enriched by his memberships in the Massachusetts Historical Society, the Thursday and Saturday Evening literary clubs, and the Senate of Phi Beta Kappa. He shared his career with his family, both at home and in his travels.

Justin Winsor led the American library profession during the era of national industrialization with a measure of vitality and a singleness of purpose that were worthy of even the most successful barons of mechanical productivity and financial consolidation. Always a man of energy and system, he filled his years with literary and historical pursuits in such volume that none would deny him the peerage of Boston's Brahmin elite.

Yet Winsor's mixture of intellectual abilities and personal drives were unsuited to the life of leisure, grace, and ease that had characterized an earlier generation of American intellectuals. He lived in an age of industry and gave himself totally to each new endeavor, never holding back or wasting a moment. His compulsion for work and his thoroughness of organization set him apart in the unhurried world of nineteenth century librarianship. For Winsor, a library was not a literary retreat from reality, but a workshop for exploring, ordering, and promoting the creative forces of human progress. His libraries were not so much places or institutions, but processes, whereby a habit of producing was ignited by an explosive passion for knowledge and sustained by a missionary zeal for self-education.

In the field of historical inquiry, Winsor distinguished himself by advancing the medium of co-operative writing. He won acclaim for his editing of the four-volume *Memorial History of Boston* (1880-1881) and the eight-volume *Narrative and Critical History of America* (1886-1889). He had previously (1879) prepared the still useful *Reader's Handbook of the American Revolution*, a bibliographical manual. He followed the cooperative ventures with more works of his own, based on his cartographic studies: *Christopher Columbus* (1891), *Cartier de Frontenac* (1894), *The Mississippi Basin* (1895), and *The Westward Movement* (1897). Although his interest in maps was initially incidental, Winsor's researches soon absorbed him, and he became the leading American cartographer of his day, in addition to maintaining his scholarly and library-related reputation. In 1884, he chaired the organizational meeting of the American Historical Association, and, in 1886, that organization named him its president. For twenty years, Winsor successfully combined his scholarly activities with his duties as Harvard librarian, although from 1885 until his death, his principal interest was historical research and publication projects. He was in his own person the example of what he hoped the library experience would produce in others.

In 1897, Winsor was again elected president of the American Library Association, this time to lead the American delegation to the Second International Library Conference, held once more in London. Following his return and a brief illness, Justin Winsor died on October 22, 1897. His daughter Constance had died in 1895, and his wife and a granddaughter were his only survivors.

Biographical listings and obituaries—*Dictionary of American Biography* 20 (James Truslow Adams); [Obituary]. *Library Journal* 22:677 (Nov. 1897); [Obituary]. *New York Times*, Oct. 23, 1897, p. 7; *Who Was Who in America*, Historical Volume (1607-1896). **Books and articles about the biographee**—Boromé, Joseph. "The Life and Letters of Justin Winsor." Ph.D. dissertation, Columbia University, 1950 [contains an extensive bibliography of Winsor's works and of works about Winsor]; Brundin, Robert E. "Justin Winsor of Harvard and the Liberalizing of the College Library." *Journal of Library History* 10:57-70 (1975); Foster, William E. "Justin Winsor, 1831-1897." *Bulletin of Bibliography* 8:2-3 (1914); Lane, William C., and William A. Tillinghast. "Justin Winsor, Librarian and Historian—1831-1897." *Library Journal* 23:7-13 (1897); Scudder, Horace E. "Memoir of Justin Winsor." Massachusetts Historical Society *Proceedings*, 2nd Series, 12:457-82 (1899); Yust, William Frederick. *A Bibliography of Justin Winsor*. Cambridge: Harvard University Press, 1902. **Primary sources and archival materials**—The Winsor papers are located in the Massachusetts Historical Society (dealing mainly with his editing and historical activities), in the Harvard University Library (his activities as professor and librarian at Harvard), and in the Boston Public Library (his years as librarian of the BPL).

–WAYNE CUTLER
–MICHAEL H. HARRIS

WIRE, GEORGE EDWIN (1859-1936)

George Edwin Wire, one of the three founders of the American Association of Law Libraries, was born on February 6, 1859, in Dryden, Tompkins County, New York, about half-way between Albany and Buffalo. His parents were Thomas David Wire, a Methodist-Episcopal minister, and Nancy Bradley Cobb Wire. George was the youngest of three children, his two older brothers being Melville Cox and William Cobb.

The Reverend Mr. Wire served in several towns in the Northeast until he was superannuated (i.e., voluntarily resigned from parish work) in 1870. Seeking a quiet religious town where his sons could obtain a good education, Thomas Wire selected Evanston, Illinois, and the family purchased a farm south of Northwestern University. George was graduated from Evanston High School, attended the preparatory academy at Northwestern, and entered the Chicago Medical College (now Northwestern University Medical School) in 1881. While at the high school and academy, George worked part-time in both the Evanston Public Library and the library of the Garrett Biblical Institute.

George received his M.D. degree in 1883, but, rather than enter the practice of medicine, he returned to his family's home. In October 1885, he was appointed assistant librarian at the Northwestern University Library, then housed in University Hall.

This appointment, which carried a salary of $300 per year, made Wire one of the first paid full-time librarians on the Northwestern staff. Wire combined an interest in service with a meticulous attention to details. During his stay at Northwestern, the hours the Library was open were more than doubled (from 13 to 28 per week). He also developed a fixed location marking system. Wire was on good terms with the Evanston community as well; his annual report for 1886-1887 received almost a full-column news story in the *Evanston Index* (July 2, 1887).

However, realizing that he needed more education if he wished to make librarianship his career, Wire resigned from Northwestern in December 1887, moved to New York, and entered the Columbia College School of Library Economy, under the direction of Melvil Dewey (q.v.). Although he was graduated in 1889, Wire did not formally receive his B.L.S. until 1913, when the School was authorized to grant such degrees. Wire worked part-time in the College Library while he was a student; then, for a year after graduation, he was employed full-time in charge of the shelves.

Wire did not like living in New York, so he returned to Evanston at his first opportunity. This was in June 1890, when he became head of the medical department of the recently established Newberry Library (at $900 per year). During his five years at the Newberry, Wire built up and classified the collection and improved services. He was interested in binding and submitted a report on this subject in 1893 to the librarian, William Frederick Poole (q.v.). Wire's major contribution in this period was the development of Section Q (Medicine) of Charles Ammi Cutter's (q.v.) "7th Expansive Classification System." He also classified the collection at Northwestern's Medical School Library.

In 1895, Wire achieved the LL.B. degree from the Chicago Kent College of Law. Later that year, he resigned from the Newberry and spent the next two-and-a-half years in legal work. Early in 1898, he was appointed librarian of the Worcester County Law Library in Worcester, Massachusetts. The Library was in disarray when Wire took over, and he cataloged, classified, and reshelved the 19,000 volumes. As an outgrowth of this effort, he developed Section K (Law) of Cutter's classification system. This was the first major classification system in law, and, as Arthur Charpentier recently wrote (in "American Association of Law Libraries," *Encyclopedia of Library and Information Science*, vol. 1, p. 226), "George E. Wire ... developed a classification system which, with variations, is in use today in a good many libraries."

While at Worcester, Wire also produced a series of informative and sought-after annual reports. His work with the American Library Association (which he joined in 1884), especially with the Committee on

Subject Headings, also made him well known. In 1906, at Narragansett Pier, Wire, along with A. J. Small and Franklin O. Poole, founded the American Association of Law Libraries (AALL). Over the following three decades, Wire served on several committees and chaired those on binding and on memorials in state reports.

Public libraries were long another of Wire's major interests, and from 1904 to 1909, he was a director of the Free Public Library of Worcester. While in that post, he was active in the adoption of "a modern schedule of classified service for the library staff, which has been in use ever since" (Robert K. Shaw, "George Edwin Wire, 1859-1936," *Library Service News* 6:8 [October 1936]).

Wire wrote an excellent manual, *How to Start a Public Library*, which ALA published in 1900. It was reprinted in 1902, and a second edition appeared in 1913. Wire also wrote steadily, though not voluminously, for library and legal periodicals. In addition to his manual for public libraries, he wrote several articles on different aspects of law librarianship, many of which appeared in the *Law Library Journal*. Topics included binding, preservation, and history. He compiled several valuable indexes to legal series as well. Wire was also vigorous in his opposition to "hard sell" methods used by several booksellers who specialized in law books.

In 1929, at age seventy, Wire was retired. He remained active with special projects (e.g., classifying the Vignaud Collection at the University of Michigan), and with his work in both the AALL and the Wesley-Methodist-Episcopal Church.

In 1903, Wire had been married to Emma A. Clarke of Eliot, Maine, also a librarian; there were no children. Emma Wire died in 1937. George Edwin Wire succumbed, on February 23, 1936, to the heart trouble that had been bothering him for over a year.

Biographical listings and obituaries—"Dr. G. E. Wire, Librarian, Is Dead in East; Word of Former Evanston Man's Death in Worcester, Mass. Received Here." *Evanston Daily News Index*, March 3, 1936, p. 1; "Dr. George E. Wire." *Library Journal* 61:332 (April 15, 1936); [Obituary]. *Law Library Journal* 29:42 (April 1936); [Obituary]. *Massachusetts Library Association Bulletin* 26:31 (March 1936); *Who Was Who in America* III (1951-1960); *Who's Who in Library Service*, 1st ed. Books and articles about the biographee— Beatty, William K. "Medicine, Law, Librarianship: The Unique Contribution of George Edwin Wire" [as D. J. Davis Memorial Lecture on the History of Medicine]. In *Dedication Proceedings*, April 22, 1974, Library of the Health Sciences, University of Illinois at the Medical Center, pp. 37-48 [contains extensive bibliography (repeated in next reference), illustrations, and acknowledgments]; Beatty, William K. "Medicine, Law, Librarianship: The Unique Contribution of George Edwin Wire." *Law Library Journal* 68:82-91 (Feb. 1975); Charpentier, Arthur. "American Association of Law Libraries." *Encyclopedia of Library and Information Science*. Allen Kent, Harold Lancour, and Jay E. Daily, eds. New York: Marcel Dekker, 1968, vol. 1; Kirschner, Lydia E. "Memorial to George E. Wire, 1859-1936." National

Association of State Libraries *Proceedings and Papers* 39:49-50 (1936); Shaw, Robert K. "George Edwin Wire, 1859-1936." [Columbia University]. *Library Service News* 6:8 (Oct. 1936); Small, A. J. "Memorial to Dr. George E. Wire." *Law Library Journal* 29:112-13 (1936). Primary sources and archival materials—Letters and papers from and about Wire are held by the Archibald Church Library, Northwestern University Medical School, Chicago, Illinois, and in the William F. Poole papers and the Cataloguing Department Records in the Newberry Library, Chicago, Illinois. Letters and papers are held by the Wire family. Letters from Wire to Miss Sharp are in the Katharine L. Sharp [q.v.] Papers, University of Illinois Archives.

—WILLIAM K. BEATTY

WOODS, BILL MILTON (1924-1974)

Bill Milton Woods was born on May 24, 1924, in Pottawattamie County, Iowa. His bachelor's degree in geography from Peru, Nebraska, State College (1945) was followed by alternating graduate work in geography and library science while on the staffs of the University of Nebraska Library (1945-1946, 1947-1949) and the University of Illinois Library (1946-1947, 1949-1958). He obtained the B.S. in L.S. from Illinois in 1947 and the M.S. in L.S. in 1953. During his first Urbana stay, he met Janice Lovaine Thumm, a library school classmate who was originally from West Virginia, and was married to her a year later. They had three children: Suzanne Marie Kelley, David Owen, and Steven Alan.

Save for Woods's initial title as circulation assistant at Nebraska in 1945, he was by preference and title a university map librarian until becoming head of the Processing Section in the Map Division of the Library of Congress in 1958. He concurrently taught map librarianship at Illinois as an instructor, and later, as assistant professor. This interest continued throughout his life, and he taught a similar course at Drexel (1962, 1966, 1967, and 1968) and was an adjunct professor at the C. W. Post Center of Long Island University from 1972 until his death.

Woods's extremely active role in the Geography and Map Division of the Special Libraries Association led to his consideration by the SLA Board of Directors for the newly vacant position of SLA executive secretary in 1959, and to his subsequent selection. He proved to be a "natural" association staff head and soon had projected SLA and himself into the midst of inter-association activities in library science, documentation, and a variety of technical society forums.

The SLA Board recognized his aggressiveness and effectiveness on its behalf by appointing him executive director in 1963. He took this as encouragement to enter the international scene, based in part on his exposure as secretary-treasurer of the Council of National Library Associations (1962-1964) and as its chairman (1964-1967). He was also an organizer, secretary, and chairman of METRO (The New York

Metropolitan Reference and Research Library Agency, Inc.) during this period and a trustee until 1973. Many of his eighty-odd articles appeared in the leading library/information science periodicals during the decade of the 1960s.

During 1967, a state of coolness developed between Woods and SLA officialdom similar to that noticed for Carl Milam (q.v.) and ALA officialdom some time earlier, and it is as hard to explain. Woods responded by leaving SLA to become a consultant to the National Advisory Commission on Libraries for the summer of 1967. At about this time, the directors of Engineering Index, Inc., New York—the recognized leading abstracting and indexing service in engineering—were being encouraged by the National Science Foundation to re-examine its procedures with a view to extensive mechanization, if warranted. The EI Board included some individuals who had earlier worked closely with Woods in SLA matters and appreciated his forcefulness in "getting things done." They accordingly offered him the post of consultant (management planner) in September 1967, and he performed exceptionally. He subsequently became the Engineering Index executive director on March 11, 1968 (presiding over a staff of 85 indexers, abstractors and supporting persons), and served until ill health forced his retirement on March 25, 1973. An illustration of his continuing interest in geography during this period was the revision of his *Map Librarianship: A Selected Bibliography* and its publication by the New Jersey Library Association in 1970.

Upon assuming the EI post, Woods immediately became prominent in the affairs of the National Federation of (Science) Abstracting and Indexing Services, serving in each of its offices (as president, 1971-1972). He also became active in the American Society for Information Science in the metropolitan New York area as well as in a number of trade associations of exhibit executives and engineering society groups. Frequent trips to Washington followed as he accepted advisory group and working committee assignments. He saw standardization as a continuing urgent need from his earlier CNLA interests and became involved with such groups as the International Council of Scientific Union's Indexing and Abstracting Board (ICSU/AB) and the user groups of the newly emerging machine data base services in both Europe and the United States. He predicted that one day Engineering Index would have more overseas than domestic customers, and this became true recently.

Woods thrived on meetings, committee work, speeches, and cooperative professional ventures. Methodical in his scheduling, he informed friends of his "travel box score" with each year's Christmas card. His family knew that he enjoyed the personal contacts of meetings best, but they were able to share some of his other deep enthusiasms: genealogy, cartography, boating, folk music, cartophilately, local history, and everything Welsh. Also, each family member had a specific role to play in the hobby-filled vacations.

Bill Woods was a somewhat short, stocky person with a round cherubic face. His conservative manner of dress was consistent with EI's image among its clientele, although his later adoption of the modish longer hair style foretold some changes in image for both Woods and the organization itself.

While his usual intensity was coupled with friendliness, Woods's staff members were kept quite clear on what was expected of them and the exact schedule for accomplishment of those several tasks. The considerable personal loyalty in his groups only intensified as cancer began to make its inroads into his life in late 1972. Though forced to retire as Engineering Index executive director in March 1973, he continued to dictate memos and write voluminous notes on professional and publishing projects until his demise on May 1, 1974, at his East Northport, Long Island, New York home. Interment was at Center Ridge Cemetery, near Red Oak, Montgomery County, Iowa.

Professional colleagues saw him as "a good and kindly colleague and one of the most forward looking people in the library and information field" (Leslie Wilson, director, ASLIB [London]), "a warm hearted person" (Phyllis V. Parkins, executive director, BIOSIS), and full of "generous advice and support" (Stella Keenan, executive director, NFAIS). The present writer saw him as an effective administrator of and a benevolent despot with his respective staffs in the Special Libraries Association and Engineering Index, Inc. He was adept at facilitating the work of the elected officials at both organizations. Woods should be remembered, though, for helping to lead abstracting and indexing services from the paper-tape/typewriter stage of operation toward the universal computer-based typesetting/magnetic tape mode used today, and for encouraging "not-for-profits" and profit-making information organizations and jobbers to resolve differences to the benefit of the total community of information service users.

Honors received during his lifetime included various geographic awards, the SLA Geography and Map Division Honors Award, the certificates or scrolls of appreciation from Engineering Index, Inc. (1973) and National Federation of Abstracting and Indexing Services (1974). Similarly, the Special Libraries Association awarded him a scroll posthumously (1974). The numerous resolutions of appreciation and remembrance issued by the organizations that Bill Woods served so selflessly are held by Janice Woods.

Biographical listings and obituaries—*Biographical Directory of Librarians in the United States and Canada*, 5th ed.;

Current Biography (1966); [Obituary]. *New York Times*, May 3, 1974; [Obituary]. *News: Engineering Index, Inc.*, May 3, 1974; [Obituary]. *Notes and Comment, Engineering Index, Inc.* 1:1-3 (May 1974); *Who Was Who in America* VI (1974-1976); *Who's Who in Library Service*, 3rd ed., 4th ed. **Books and articles about the biographee**—[Biographical sketch]. *News: Engineering Index, Inc.*, March 26, 1973; McKenna, F. E. "Bill M. Woods: SLA Executive Director, 1959-1967." *Special Libraries* 58:538-39 (Sept. 1967); "Special Citation, 1974." *Picturescope* 22:38 (Summer 1974). **Primary sources and archival materials**—Correspondence files developed between Bill M. Woods and the author while they were respectively staff executive and elected official of Special Libraries Association and Engineering Index, Inc. (1959-1974); Official files, Engineering Index, Inc., 345 East 47th Street, New York, New York 10017 (1968-1974); Author's interviews with Janice Woods (1974 and 1975); Woods's extensive papers are held by Mrs. Woods in East Northport, Long Island, New York 11731.

—EUGENE B. JACKSON

WROTH, LAWRENCE COUNSELMAN (1884-1970)

For a good many years before the end of his long career, Lawrence Counselman Wroth was frequently called the dean of American bibliographers. This reputation was largely the result of his distinguished work as librarian of the John Carter Brown Library at Brown University, Providence, Rhode Island (1923-1957). However, his influence in the world of rare books extended beyond his own institution through consultantships at the Pierpont Morgan Library (beginning in 1937) and at the Library of Congress Rare Books Division (1943-1954), as well as through a large number of scholarly books and articles, many of which are still considered classics in their fields.

A native of Baltimore, he was born on January 14, 1884, the son of an Episcopal clergyman, the Reverend Mr. Peregrine Wroth, and his wife, the former Agusta Counselman. Wroth was graduated from Johns Hopkins University in 1905 and, in 1907, became librarian of the Maryland Diocesan Library. His strong interest in both early books and the history of his own state led to the publication of a number of articles and his first book, *Parson Weems, a Biographical and Critical Study* (1911). Five years later, Wroth became assistant librarian of the Enoch Pratt Free Library in Baltimore, where his duties included the administration of its branches.

His career was interrupted when he volunteered for military service the day after the declaration of war in March 1917. From private in the Maryland Field Artillery, he was promoted to first lieutenant and saw service in France. Following the Armistice, he attended classes at the Sorbonne before returning to Baltimore in 1919.

Wroth's first important bibliographical work, *A History of Printing in Colonial Maryland, 1686-1775* (1922), set a new standard for studies of American imprints, and its excellence made him the logical choice for appointment, in 1923, as librarian of the John Carter Brown Library. From that time on, his life was centered in Providence. He married Barbara Pease, of Burlington, Vermont, and they had three sons.

Wroth's scholarly interests expanded through the years to cover the entire field of the Library, a collection begun privately in the 1840s and constantly expanded after its acquisition by Brown University in 1900, with its focus on materials concerning the Western Hemisphere printed before 1800. In 1931, Wroth published *The Colonial Printer* (revised ed. 1938; reprinted 1964 and later), perhaps his most widely known work, which has been characterized by an eminent American historian as the best study of any Colonial industry. Other books and articles on a wide range of subjects followed, including: *An American Bookshelf 1755* (1934), based on lectures delivered in Philadelphia on the A. S. W. Rosenbach fellowship in bibliography; volume 3 of the *Catalogue of the John Carter Brown Library* (1931), covering its holdings for the years 1659-1674; *Roger Williams* (1937); *A History of the Printed Book, Being the Third Number of The Dolphin* (1938); *Some Reflections on the Book Arts in Early Mexico* (1945); *American Woodcuts and Engravings 1670-1800* (with Marion W. Adams, 1946); *Typographic Heritage, Selected Essays* (1949); *The Early Cartography of the Pacific* (1944); and *The Colonial Scene* (1950). For ten years (1937-1947), he contributed a biweekly column, "Notes for Bibliophiles," to the Sunday book review section of the *New York Herald-Tribune*. With George P. Winship (q.v.), Wroth edited *Bibliographical Essays: A Tribute to Wilberforce Eames* [q.v.] (Harvard University Press, 1924).

During the difficult years of the 1930s and World War II, when libraries in general suffered from the deterioration of their endowments, Wroth kept his institution intact and even strengthened it through his careful management of its resources and his astute collecting. In 1944, he was able to organize the Associates of the John Carter Brown Library, a group of the Library's friends, which began with 150 members contributing funds for the purchase of rare books. This organization has since grown to a membership, national and international, of more than five times that number. In connection with this activity, he wrote *The First Century of the John Carter Brown Library* (1946), and he enlarged the Library's annual reports, which he had developed into a series of concise, readable essays on the most important of the books acquired each year. In order to keep this useful information available, the entire series of annual reports was later re-published by the Library, with a comprehensive index.

Wroth received numerous honors, both before and after his retirement—honorary degrees from Brown, Yale, Michigan, and Washington College, Maryland; the medal of the American Institute of Graphic Arts (1948) and in 1957 the gold medal of the Bibliographical Society (London). In 1951, *Essays Honoring Lawrence C. Wroth* was published under the editorship of Frederick R. Goff. Wroth belonged to the American Library Association, the Bibliographical Society of America (president 1931-1933), the Bibliographical Society (London), the American Antiquarian Society, the historical societies of New York and Massachusetts, and the Society of Printers, among others. He was a member as well of the Club of Odd Volumes (Boston) and the Grolier Club (New York).

When he retired from the librarianship in 1957, Wroth continued to serve as research professor of American history on the Brown University faculty, and he was entrusted with the editorship of the University's bicentennial publications. The last ten years of his life, however, were for the most part devoted to his special interest in the early cartographic history of the Americas, and his research, sponsored by the Pierpont Morgan Library (to which he was a consultant from 1938 on), resulted in *The Voyages of Giovanni da Verrazzano 1524-1528*. This major work was published when Lawrence Counselman Wroth was in his eighty-seventh year, less than six months before his death on Christmas Day, 1970.

Biographical listings and obituaries—Black, Jeannette D. [Obituary]. *Terrae Incognitae* 4:125 (1972); *Contemporary Authors* 29; Lewis, Wilmarth S. [Obituary]. *The Walpole Society Note Book*, 1971, pp. 11-13; Swan, Bradford F. [Obituary]. *Proceedings of the American Antiquarian Society* 81:37-39 (part 1, 1971); Swan, Bradford F. [Obituary]. *The Providence Journal*, Dec. 26, 1970 (reprinted in *AB Bookman's Weekly*, Jan. 18, 1971); *Who's Who in America* 13-30 (1924-1959); *Who's Who in Library Service*, 1st ed., 2nd ed. Books and articles about the biographee— Adams, Thomas R. *Lawrence Counselman Wroth 1884-1970. The Memorial Minute Read before the Faculty of Brown University 9 February 1971 and a Handlist of an Exhibition of His Writings in the John Carter Brown Library of Brown University*. Providence, 1971; *Essays Honoring Lawrence C. Wroth* (Portland, 1951); especially "Introduction" by Wilmarth S. Lewis, pp. xix-xxi, and "A List of Published Writings of Lawrence C. Wroth to December 31, 1950," by Marion W. Adams and Jeannette D. Black, pp. 485-504; Goff, Frederick R. "Wroth of the JCB." *Brown Alumni Monthly*, May 1957, pp. 8-10; Matheson, William. "Seeking the Rare, the Important, the Valuable. The Rare Book Division." *Quarterly Journal of the Library of Congress* 30:211-27 (1973). Primary sources and archival materials—Correspondence (1923-1970) and manuscripts and proofs of his published books and articles are on file in the John Carter Brown Library, Brown University, Providence, Rhode Island 02912.

—JEANNETTE D. BLACK

WYER, JAMES INGERSOLL (1869-1955)

When James I. Wyer was appointed by the New York State Board of Regents to the position of director of the State Library in 1908, he took charge of a Library with a collection of over 900,000 items, one which ranked not only as the largest state library but also as the seventh largest library in the United States. Under the vigorous leadership of Melvil Dewey (q.v.; state librarian, 1880-1905), its reputation had been established as the most progressive of the state libraries—first to institute legislative reference service, travelling libraries, and service to the blind. Within less than three years, the disastrous Capitol fire of 1911 had reduced this great library to ashes. Wyer was to devote a major portion of his energies for the remainder of his professional career to restoring it to its former position of preeminence.

James Ingersoll Wyer was born at Red Wing, Minnesota, on May 14, 1869, the eldest son of James Ingersoll and Rosabel Shear Wyer. (His half-brother Malcolm G. Wyer [q.v.] would be born eight years later to the elder Wyer and his second wife.) Following his graduation from high school in Concordia, Kansas, young Wyer worked in banking at both Red Lake Falls and Concordia, Minnesota. In 1894, he was married to May Tyner. The following year, at the age of 26, he decided to undertake a career in librarianship, attending the University of Minnesota in preparation, and entering the New York State Library School at Albany in 1896 (after gaining his first working experience as an assistant at the Minneapolis Public Library). At Albany, he attended the school that Melvil Dewey had brought from Columbia just seven years before, studying under a faculty that included Dewey, Walter Stanley Biscoe (q.v.), and Florence Woodworth, and such visiting notables as John Cotton Dana (q.v.), Charles Ammi Cutter (q.v.), William H. Brett (q.v.), and Josephus N. Larned (q.v.). The two-year course was a demanding one, but Wyer found time to work as a library assistant in the State Library during his senior year. Upon his graduation in 1898, with a B.L.S., he accepted a position at the University of Nebraska, serving as librarian and professor of bibliography.

The seven years he spent in Nebraska clearly established his reputation in the profession: he was president of the Nebraska Library Association (1899-1901), president of the Nebraska Public Library Commission (1901-1905), and was elected secretary of the American Library Association in 1902, a post he held until 1909. While at Lincoln, he also taught library courses in Wisconsin, Minnesota, and Albany, published an expansion of the Dewey classification for agricultural literature, and wrote the first edition of his much-reprinted manual on government documents.

In January 1906, he accepted a position as reference librarian at the New York State Library and vice-director of the Library School, having been awarded the M.L.S. degree by the School in the previous year. Chalmers Hadley (q.v.), a student at the School that year, later remembered the new reference librarian as "a Wiry gentleman from the West and an extraordinary live one." For James Wyer, the return to Albany was the beginning of his life's work.

With the tragic Capitol fire of March 29, 1911, the task fell upon Wyer of building a great library from scratch. In a single night, nearly all of the collections, catalogs (the large classed public catalog was one of the few in the United States), indexes, correspondence, orders and exchange records, special bibliographies and publications in preparation, were destroyed. Wyer wrote in his 1911 annual report of the "round half million of books, three hundred thousand manuscripts, the costly apparatus of administration ... swept away in a few hot and disheartening hours." In the days and weeks that followed, a colleague described Wyer as the "top commander" of a staff "organized on military lines." A small but courageous group (notably Frank Tolman, Peter Nelson, A. J. F. Van Laer, Carl Vitz, and Joseph Gavit) working with I. N. Phelps Stokes (sent to Albany by the Board of Trustees of the New York Public Library) repeatedly entered the still-smouldering Capitol ruins to salvage a small portion of the manuscript, archive, and book collections.

The Library remained closed for nearly two years, its operations housed in six temporary locations around Albany, while Wyer directed the building of a new collection, the time-consuming work of cleaning and restoring salvaged materials, and the reconstruction of a catalog and other vital administrative records. All of the basic decisions needed to be made: the mission of the Library (Wyer wrote an important statement in 1911 on its purpose and scope, modestly titled *The New State Library—Book Purchases*), the classification scheme (it was decided to continue Dewey), and the nature of the catalog (a dictionary catalog was chosen to replace the classed one). Special acts of the Legislature made $550,000 available for book purchases. Library staff visited Chicago, Boston, Washington, Baltimore, Philadelphia, Annapolis, Richmond, and Princeton, searching out items from the duplicate collections of major libraries. When the Library moved into its spacious quarters in the new State Education Building in 1912-1913, Wyer was able to report 335,000 volumes on the shelves.

James Wyer believed in a strong state library, serving not only government but all the people of the state. Writing in the 1913 annual report, he described New York as having a "thoroughly organized State Library system," with a great central reference and lending collection available to supplement the resources of "12,000 registered libraries, schools and study clubs, which are thus in effect branches of the State Library." In his presidential address to the National Association of State Libraries (1914), he vigorously advocated three basic precepts: that the state library should provide statewide service, that it should be the coordinating agency for all of the library activities of the state, and that it should be recognized as "an expert and highly specialized service" directed by professionals.

Following the full reopening of the New York State Library in 1913, Wyer moved to expand and improve the statewide system of interlibrary loan. By 1921, he was able to report that there were three hundred cooperating institutions in the state, that interlibrary loan constituted over one-half of the Library's circulation, and that a new system of interlibrary loan forms, reports, reserves, and publicity had been instituted. At the same time, he sought to make the State Library a major resource for residents of the Capitol District, instituting Sunday opening in 1919 (he reported that over 13,000 people used the Library on Sundays during the next two years), and liberalizing the borrowers' regulations in 1922. His was a state library operated in the best traditions of the great American public libraries.

Despite this enlarged concept of service, Wyer was fated to direct the Library through the penurious 1920s, when governmental interest in libraries was at an ebb, as well as through the Great Depression of the 1930s. In his 1930 annual report, he pointed out that the size of his staff was exactly what it had been in 1912; he went on to say that "the trained staff of the State Library has never been large enough to make the books of most value and effect throughout the State." Even the acquisitions money promised by legislation at the time of the fire had never been fully appropriated, and, in 1933, the annual appropriation for books and binding was reduced from $67,000 to $39,000. All the more remarkable, then, was the rebuilding of the collections over the years, achieving both size and distinction in the subject areas of history, medicine, education, law, science and technology, and the social sciences.

From the beginning of his career, James Wyer had maintained a keen interest in library education and professional activities. While director of the New York State Library School (from 1908 until 1926, when the School was transferred to Columbia University), he also taught courses in advanced subject bibliography, American library history, and government documents. Wyer's contribution to the School was not merely perfunctory, as was attested many years later by Joseph L. Wheeler (q.v.), who had been a student there in 1909:

He was a guide, philosopher, and friend to all students who approached him, and things fell rather flat when he was not on the job. His ability to see into things and to get down to brass tacks in a hurry and his understanding of young people were great assets to the school.

Wyer's accomplishments as an educator were recognized in 1915 with his election to the presidency of the Association of American Library Schools, and again in 1919, when he was awarded an honorary Doctor of Pedagogy degree by the New York State College for Teachers.

A leader in professional associations, James Wyer served as president of the American Library Association (1910-1911), as president of the New York Library Association (1913-1914), and as chairman of the ALA Library War Service Committee (1917-1920), a group that raised $5,000,000 for camp libraries. He was a longtime active member of the Bibliographical Society of America. His hobbies included philately, in which he had an ardent and lifelong interest.

James Ingersoll Wyer influenced American and world librarianship chiefly through his continuing contributions, over more than a half century, to the professional literature. A prolific author, his articles, book reviews, and biographical sketches regularly appeared in *Library Journal*, *Library Quarterly*, and other professional periodicals, not only during his active career, but for a decade after his retirement. He was the author of chapters for the ALA *Manual of Library Economy* on both the college and university library and the state library, as well as on government documents, a field in which he was recognized as an authority by virtue of his frequently reissued manual on *U.S. Government Documents: Federal, State and City*. Fremont Rider (q.v.) has noted that Wyer's "keen interest in genealogy led to his publication of a number of significant contributions in this field."

By far his most significant and influential book, however, was *Reference Work: A Textbook for Students of Library Work and Librarians* (ALA, 1930), which remained the standard text in the field for more than twenty years. This first systematic book-length treatment of reference work was enormously influential in shaping the character of reference service in libraries of all types. Samuel Rothstein has termed James Wyer "the most ardent and convincing exponent of the 'liberal theory'" of reference service. Wyer's vision of what reference service should strive ideally to become was remarkably in advance of his time and was strikingly accurate as a prediction of the contemporary role of the library as a community information and referral center:

To *interpret* seems a much more exact and satisfying verb than to *aid*, to *help*, or to *assist*, in describing reference work. It connotes not merely less of mechanism and more of humanism: it suggests thoroughness (even in helping) as against superficiality; sympathetic as against perfunctory service; a colleague rather than a clerk; informed leadership rather than a steering committee; in a word, understanding. . . . Intelligent interpretation may require a confession that the library's own resources furnish nothing, and an offer to carry the inquiry to other libraries, persons, or institutions. . . .

The liberal, progressive, and enlightened theory of reference work will assume that every library desires to give the fullest possible attention to demands made on its reference service; that it will wish to find or to create ways and means to satisfy every questioner. . . . The only tenable, impregnable theory of reference work is that which frankly recognizes the library's obligation to give this unlimited service. . . . It is timid and inexcusable, as well as poor practical policy, for the library, created for precisely such service as is indicated above, better equipped and presumably more competent to render it than any other agency, to withhold its utmost service.

James I. Wyer, having retired from the New York State Library in 1938, resided in Salt Lake City until his death on November 1, 1955. His thirty years as director was the longest term of any librarian since the founding of that Library in 1818. They were years that witnessed many changes, touching the ascendent progressivism of Dewey at one end and the severe constraints of the Great Depression at the other. The most fitting tribute to the achievements of Wyer's career may be found in his own words, when, in the 1930 annual report, he noted that the State Library collections had passed the one-million mark, and he was able to say: "It is again, since its destruction in 1911, a noble library."

Biographical listings and obituaries—[Obituary]. *Bookmark* 15:75-76 (Dec. 1955); [Obituary]. *College and Research Libraries* 17:263 (May 1956); Rider, A. Fremont. "James Wyer." *Library Journal* 81:612 (March 1, 1956); *Who Was Who in America* III (1951-1960); *Who's Who in Library Service*, 1st ed., 2nd ed. **Books and articles about the biographee**—Brewster, Mary. "James Wyer." *New York Libraries* 16:102-103, 127 (Aug. 1938); Brown, Karl. "James Ingersoll Wyer, May 14, 1869-November 1, 1955—A Memoir and a List of His Writings." In New York State Library School Association *New York State Library School Register, 1887-1926*. New York: the Author, 1959; Roseberry, Cecil R. *For the Government and People of This State—A History of the New York State Library*. Albany: University of the State of New York, 1970, chaps. 15-18. **Primary sources and archival materials**—The annual report of the New York State Library that Wyer wrote for the years 1908 to 1938 (through 1919 called *Report of the Director*) provides invaluable source material, as do the *Journals of the Meetings of the Regents* of the University of the State of New York for the same period. Recollections of the early years in the Library School may be found in *The First Quarter Century* *of the New York State Library School, 1887-1912* (Albany: New York State Library School, 1912). A five-volume collection of Wyer's writings has been collected by the New York State Library under the binder's title of *Papers and Addresses.*

—PETER J. PAULSON

WYER, MALCOLM GLENN (1877-1965)

Malcolm Glenn Wyer was born in Concordia, Kansas, on August 21, 1877, the fourth child of James Ingersoll and Ellie Elizabeth Glenn Wyer. (Malcolm's half-brother James Ingersoll Wyer [q.v.] had been born eight years previously, to the elder Wyer and his first wife, Rosabel Shear Wyer.) The family moved back to Minnesota in 1881, and Malcolm was graduated from Minneapolis Central High School (1895) and from the University of Minnesota with an A.B. in classics (1899). Following a year spent working in his father's bank, he then returned to the University of Minnesota for his M.Litt. degree (1901); his thesis title was "Words from Latin into English through Old French." During these studies, he was an assistant in the Library (1900-1901) and also made the acquaintance of H. W. Wilson (q.v.), then manager of the bookstore serving the University community.

In the fall of 1901, Wyer entered the New York State Library School established at Albany by Melvil Dewey (q.v.), from which he received the B.L.S. (1903). He then spent a year as librarian at Colorado College (Colorado Springs), which introduced him to the Rocky Mountain region to which he would later return for the duration of his career. In 1904, Wyer headed to Iowa City to become acting librarian of the State University of Iowa (now the University of Iowa); he was made director in 1906. At the Library, he directed a consolidation of departmental collections and book budgets, resulting in a larger central fund from which to buy badly needed reference sets. He had the entire collection recataloged (which had not been done since an 1897 fire had destroyed forty percent of the original 50,000 volumes in addition to the card catalog). He also hired Harriet E. Howe (q.v.) as a cataloger in 1906, beginning a professional association that would be resumed when she responded to his call to the University of Denver School of Librarianship several years later.

Wyer's work was not confined to the Library during his tenure at Iowa, however. The Iowa Library Commission had founded a summer library training school (1901), and Wyer began teaching there in 1905. In 1906, he was made resident director of the program, thereby sealing a relationship between the University and the Commission regarding the school. In 1913, though, the University dissolved its affiliation with the Commission and assumed total control

of the School, with Wyer as director. Training was primarily for public librarians and was practical in nature, prefiguring Wyer's later arrangement at the University of Denver and the Denver Public Library.

Malcolm Wyer had been offered the post of librarian at the University of Nebraska (Lincoln) when his brother James vacated it in 1906, but had turned it down to continue the work barely started at Iowa City. In 1913, ready for a change, he was particularly attracted by Nebraska's renewed offer because of what he described (in *Books and People*, Old West Publishing Co., 1964, p. 22) as "much more informality in the campus and university life and greater intermingling of faculty and townspeople in the social life of the community." Also, since the Library at Nebraska was well organized and well stocked, he could devote himself to larger problems of library coordination. In particular, he sought to coordinate the services offered by five major libraries in Lincoln: the University of Nebraska, the Legislative Reference Bureau, the Nebraska Public Library Commission, the Nebraska Historical Society, and the Nebraska State Library. A plan was developed whereby the libraries involved would specialize services and exchange information but still retain their institutional autonomy. Although it failed to pass the legislature, it represented Wyer's philosophy of providing the best possible service through active cooperation on the part of libraries of all types.

His tenure at Nebraska was interrupted, in 1917, by a call from Herbert Putnam (q.v.), Librarian of Congress and director of the American Library Association's Library War Service Program. Wyer, given leave by the University, set up the library at Camp Logan (Houston, Texas), eating with the enlisted men for several weeks in order to discern their reading needs and tastes. He finished his work at Camp Logan in February 1918, but, in May of that year, was called by Putnam to be assistant director in charge of all libraries in large camps (15,000 personnel or more); eventually, he was administering 40 central and 1,500 branch libraries in a total of 44 camps.

Following the Armistice and his return to Nebraska, Malcolm Wyer became even more deeply involved in education for librarianship than he had been at Iowa. In 1920, ALA President Alice S. Tyler (q.v.) appointed him chairman of the ALA Library Training Committee. The Committee found that training for librarianship ranged from that offered by established library schools to informal instruction in individual libraries for only their own part-time assistants. Wyer's group was concerned with establishing standards for all library training, but ALA internal politics prevented action being taken on its recommendations until Council appointed (in 1923) a Temporary Library Training Board to set standards and to plan for ALA accreditation of library training programs. In 1924, this temporary committee was superseded by the permanent Board of Education for Librarianship, to which Wyer was appointed (1924-1930).

The year 1924 also saw the change in Wyer's career that was to be his final move, a change set in motion by the resignation of Chalmers Hadley (q.v.) as librarian of the Denver Public Library. Hadley recommended to Denver's Library Commission that they employ Wyer and to Wyer that he accept the offer; his recommendations were followed, and Wyer returned to Colorado to stay.

Public librarianship was not unfamiliar to him, given his experience with the Iowa and Nebraska library commissions. The primary challenge lay in Denver's position as the only major population center between Kansas City and California, a situation that afforded an opportunity for the DPL to assume leadership in developing library service for the vast Rocky Mountain region. In Colorado at the time, 44 public libraries served 63 counties, and over half of the 570,000 volumes reported held by those libraries were to be found in Denver. The facts that library service in the state was controlled by three distinct agencies (the Superintendent of Public Instruction, the Board of Library Commissioners, and the Travelling Library Commission) and that their total expenditures in 1928 did not exceed $4,650 indicated that much work was to be done if adequate regional library services were to be provided.

The library Wyer came to was housed in a building donated by Andrew Carnegie (q.v.) in 1910; its collection was stronger in current and popular materials than in those items deemed central to a strong reference collection. He thus turned to extra-library agencies (such as the Colorado Engineering Council, the Denver Art Museum, and the Allied Architects Association) to advise and help the Library strengthen its core collection. He unified scattered volumes in the Library into a new Fine Arts Department in 1926, again depending upon advice from non-library agencies (especially the Art Museum, on whose Board of Directors he sat). The Library's extensive Western History Collection had been started in 1904 as an informal grouping of books known as the "Colorado Collection," but under Wyer's guidance, it too became a separate department (now housed in its own quarters in the present DPL). To establish it, Wyer devised an agreement with the State Historical Society whereby the Society continued its acquisitions of strictly Colorado-related materials while the Library sought to acquire materials concerning the Rocky Mountain area and the West in general.

As has been noted, though, Wyer was interested in the regional services that the Denver Public Library might render in addition to its primary local responsibility. Thus, he headed the efforts that resulted in the creation of the Bibliographic Center for Research: Rocky Mountain Region. He later served as its president for ten years (1942-1952). His original intention was to have DPL establish its own strong bibliographical collections, but he soon modified this view to include the Library in partnership with college and university libraries in the region (including the University of Wyoming, Laramie), since no one institution could finance such a venture alone. Wyer was also able to use his previously developed contacts with Frederick Keppel (q.v.) of the Carnegie Corporation to secure an eventual total of $35,000 in grants, thereby giving the Bibliographic Center a strong financial footing. With these funds, the Center acquired a complete set of the Library of Congress catalogs as well as other essential, major bibliographical tools that previously had been unavailable to researchers in the Rocky Mountain area. The Center was housed in the Library, although totally independent of it, until its move in 1977 to separate quarters.

Probably as a result of his service on ALA committees concerned with education for librarianship, Wyer was particularly sensitive to the fact that no formal opportunities for library training existed between St. Louis and the Pacific Coast. The DPL had sponsored training classes (1893-1897) under John Cotton Dana (q.v.), but the only other training available in the region in the 1920s was training classes, again at the Library (after 1910), with summer schools also being offered (1918-1932) at Colorado A & M College (now Colorado State University; Fort Collins). ALA Secretary Carl H. Milam (q.v.) appointed a committee (George A. Works, Harrison W. Craver [q.v.], and Sydney B. Mitchell [q.v.]) that, in 1929, recommended the creation of a library school in Denver. This was done in affiliation with the University of Denver and financed in part by a series of grants from the Carnegie Corporation, so that, in 1931, the University of Denver School of Librarianship opened (after 1947 called the Graduate School of Librarianship); it was fully ALA-accredited by 1934. In a highly unusual arrangement, University officials persuaded the Library Commission that Wyer was the person to head the School, retaining at the same time the city librarianship. The only condition imposed by the Commission was that the Library remain his first priority.

In 1933, Wyer was to add a third title to this list, being simultaneously librarian of the Denver Public Library, dean of the University of Denver School of Librarianship, and director of the University of Denver Libraries. Since he had persuaded Harriet Howe to come to Denver (from the University of Chicago Graduate Library School) as director of the School, he was not responsible for day-to-day operations, but he was still deeply involved, as was to be expected. His appointment to the directorship of the University Libraries seemed only logical to the academic and civic officials concerned, especially given the paucity of funds brought on by the Great Depression. The fact that the man most interested in the totality of regional library service would be in positions whereby he could effect greater specialization and program coordination was also paramount, since it guaranteed cooperation (and the best use of limited funds) that otherwise might have been difficult to achieve.

The School was located in downtown Denver across the street from DPL, rather than on the University campus five miles away, an indication that its emphasis would be on public librarianship to meet regional needs for trained personnel. It also meant that the students had the largest "laboratory" in the area at their immediate disposal in order to learn and practice the mundane as well as theoretical aspects of their profession. Later, with more funds available to and greater demands made upon each institution, their coverage of previously specialized areas naturally began to overlap. Also, with the advent of more funds at the University, and with increased demands for academic librarians following World War II, the School was moved to the University of Denver campus in 1954, although Wyer had been successful in keeping it near DPL for many years longer than University officials would have liked. By then, however, the innovation by Wyer and Howe known as the "Denver Plan" had become a part of the curriculum (1947). Under this plan, the student's undergraduate work (with a defined core curriculum) was followed by a year of study leading to a master's degree (rather than a second bachelor's, as had previously been the case in library schools).

Yet, even with these responsibilities, Wyer was not content that Denver's libraries were fulfilling their potential as educational forces in the community. Toward this end, he started discussions in 1930 designed to lead to the creation of an adult education program for the city. In 1935, the Adult Education Center became a reality, located in, but still operationally independent of, the Denver Public Library (Wyer was on the Adult Education Council's Executive Committee until 1956). Again, Wyer's contacts with Keppel and the Carnegie Corporation were instrumental in gaining some financial backing. The result was an agency (presently housed outside of, but near, the Library) that still functions in many ways to promote the cause of adult education, a direct outgrowth of Malcolm Wyer's belief in the library as the agency best equipped to accomplish that end on a continuous basis.

Wyer was early a contributor to library literature (primarily on practical matters rather than on

theory), and he wrote for other periodicals and for newspapers occasionally as well. His first major project was an *Index of New York Governors' Messages, 1771-1901* (New York State Education Department, 1906). While in Iowa, he prepared *Bookplates in Iowa* (Torch Press, 1914) and wrote about Iowa library activities as well. He contributed the introduction to Douglas McMurtrie (q.v.) and Albert Allen's *Early Printing in Colorado . . .* (Hirschfeld Press, 1935) and wrote the article on Pike's Peak for the *Dictionary of American History* (Scribner's, 1940), on whose Advisory Council he also sat. His pamphlet *Western History Collection: Its Beginning and Growth* (DPL, 1950) presents that story from his unique vantage point. He also wrote survey reports of the libraries of the McCormick Theological Seminary, of Gary (Indiana) and Boulder (Colorado) and of the Linda Hall Library (Kansas City). His autobiography was published under the title *Books and People: Short Anecdotes from a Long Experience* (Old West Publishing Co., 1964).

Among the professional organizations to which Wyer belonged were the Iowa, Nebraska, and Colorado library associations, each of which he served as president (1910-1911, 1915-1917, and 1926-1927, respectively). In the American Library Association, he served on the previously named committees, on the Council (1917-1922, 1928), and twice as vice-president (1922-1923, 1928-1929). He was elected president of the Association for the 1936-1937 term. He was president of the Nebraska Public Library Commission (1918-1923) and of the Colorado Library Commission (1929-1933). He was also a member of the Bibliographical Society of America and the Bibliographical Society (London). Wyer's interest in the fine arts found partial expression in his work on the Executive Committee of the Central City (Colorado) Opera House Association (president, 1940), the Board of Directors of the Denver Civic Symphony Society, and the Board of Directors of the Colorado Springs Fine Arts Center.

The honors accorded Malcolm Wyer included a D.L.S. from the University of Nebraska (1931), an LL.D. from Colorado College (1938), and an LL.D. from the University of Denver (June 6, 1958). The University of Denver Alumni Association started the Malcolm G. Wyer Scholarship Fund on the occasion of his retirement from the School of Librarianship in 1948, and the University of Minnesota gave him its Alumni Achievement Award in 1951. An annual award given by the Adult Education Council of Denver beginning in 1960 was named the "Malcolm Glenn Wyer Award," and he was the first recipient.

In his method of retirement, Malcolm Wyer was also unusual, for he did not simply cease all of his library activities at once. He resigned his twin University of Denver posts in 1948 and was named dean emeritus (having served from 1931) and director emeritus (having served from 1933). Upon his retirement from the Denver Public Library three years later (his full term was 1924-1951), he was named librarian emeritus (the first in Denver's history). He remained with the Library as an active consultant during the construction of the new library building, and when it was completed, in 1956, the auditorium was named for him. This was also a period in which he performed other consulting services and spoke at library schools around the country, prompting Lawrence Clark Powell to note ("Readers' Voice," *Library Journal* 90:2182 [May 15, 1965]) that Wyer's was "an inspiring demonstration of undiminished intellectual interest and physical stamina."

Malcolm Glenn Wyer was married to Charlotte Spalding at Madeline Island, Wisconsin, on July 25, 1906. They were to have a daughter, Madeline, who would later graduate with the first class of the University of Denver School of Librarianship.

Following an illness of several months, Malcolm Glenn Wyer died on December 31, 1965. In its tribute to him, the (Denver) *Rocky Mountain News* ("He Still Remained a Bookman," January 4, 1966) noted that the "small, slim, erudite and quiet little man gave 41 years of his brilliant profession to Denver's Public Library" and that he demonstrated the "flexibility of librarianship at its best." Indeed, his highly successful efforts at achieving library coordination and regional service, combining public and academic librarianship, promoting adult education, and improving education for librarianship denote a unique vision and accomplishment. Yet, Malcolm Wyer also never lost sight of the idea most basic to all of his innovations and projects, as he wrote in *Books and People* (pp. 149-50):

> By all means, libraries should accept and utilize all inventions and mechanics that increase efficiency of library operation. But they should remember that these are not the library but the framework for the real library, which is today, as always, the collection of books with staff members who know books, who like people, and who are given definite time for the function of bringing books and people together.

Biographical listings and obituaries—[Obituary]. *Library Journal* 91:667 (Feb. 1, 1966); [Obituary]. *Mountain Plains Library Quarterly* 10:13 (Winter 1966); [Obituary]. *Wilson Library Bulletin* 40:490 (Feb. 1966); *Who Was Who in America* IV (1961-1968); *Who's Who in Colorado*. Centennial Anniversary Edition. Ed. by Daniel T. Valdes. Boulder: Who's Who in Colorado, Inc., 1958; *Who's Who in Library Service*, 1st ed., 2nd ed., 3rd ed. **Books and articles about the biographee**—Downs, Robert B. "Denver's Bibliographical Center." *Library Journal* 70:30 (Jan. 1, 1945); Gripton, Judith, and Lorraine Bangoura. "Dr. Malcolm Glenn Wyer, a Bio-Bibliography." Graduate School of Librarianship, University of Denver, 1966 [Contains chronologically arranged bibliography of works by and about Wyer, in addition to biographical sketch]; Killinger, M. W. "Malcolm Glenn Wyer." *ALA Bulletin* 60:383-84 (April 1966); Lancour, Harold. "The New Training Pattern Looks Good." *Library Journal* 73:685-87, 700 (May 1, 1948); "Richmond Conference." *Library Journal* 61:450+ (June 1, 1936); Thorne, Mildred. "The History of the State University of Iowa: The University Libraries." Master's thesis, The University of Iowa, 1943. **Primary sources and archival materials**—The *Annual Reports* of the State University of Iowa librarian (bound volume 1889-1922) and of the Iowa Library Commission, and the *Biennial Reports* of the Nebraska Public Library Commission (1914-1924), contain material concerning Wyer. The Denver Public Library and the University of Denver hold material for the years following 1924. Wyer's *Books and People: Short Anecdotes from a Long Experience* (Denver: Old West Publishing Co., 1964) is his autobiography.

—BOHDAN S. WYNAR
—KOERT C. LOOMIS, JR.

YONGE, ENA LAURA (1895-1971)

Ena Laura Yonge was born on April 1, 1895, in Bangalore, India, the daughter of English parents. She attended the American missionary school in India, leaving at the age of nine when her father, George Langford Yonge, died. His widow emigrated to New York City the following year with Ena and her sister Marjorie, and Ena completed her education at the Barnard School for Girls. Lacking academic degrees, she once observed that she learned her profession "through experience, observation and investigation, as there is not, and never has been, training for map curators."

Her lengthy and noteworthy career at the American Geographical Society in New York City started in January 1917, when she was hired as a typist and general assistant in the Map Department. Six months later, after returning from a short vacation, she discovered that she was the Department's sole employee, since both the curator and the assistant curator had resigned. At Yonge's request, Isaiah Bowman, the director of the Society, agreed to give her a year's trial as map curator. No further discussion of her appointment took place, and she retired some 45 years later, on December 31, 1962. Her designation as map curator emeritus followed shortly thereafter.

When Ena Yonge began working in 1917, the Geographical Society's Map Department collections numbered about 37,000 maps and 830 atlases. By 1962, the collections had grown to almost 280,000 maps and 4,000 atlases, forming a significant portion of the largest geographical library in the Western Hemisphere. Until 1939, Yonge's attentions were focused on the management of the Department, which she carried out alone except for occasional part-time help. During this period, she personally performed all of the reference services as well as the acquisition, cataloging, processing, and maintenance chores associated with the collections. "In the course-of time," wrote John Kirtland Wright in his history of the American Geographical Society, "she acquired a thorough mastery over her domain and an unquenchable urge to enlarge, and skill in the enlargement of, the collections under her charge."

The years following 1945 marked a decided change in Yonge's career. Not only was she granted additional staff to share the work of the Map Department, but she also became much more involved in professional matters apart from the American Geographical Society.

During the late 1940s, she joined the Association of American Geographers and was treasurer of the New York Metropolitan Division for several years. Having long been a member of the Society of Women Geographers, she served as chairman of its New York Group from 1958 to 1960. She was active in the formation of the New York City Group of the Special Library Association's Geography and Map Division, becoming the Group chairman in 1946 and, later on, serving as program chairman for a number of years. The SLA's national Geography and Map Division, officially created in 1944, elected her to serve as its national chairman from 1947 to 1949 and, in 1959, honored her for outstanding contributions to the special field of geography and map librarianship:

> For her help over the years to many young people learning to become good map librarians, for the organization and growth of the largest map collection in a society or association library in the Western Hemisphere, for her work as a consultant in establishing new libraries, and for her continuing service in a wide variety of capacities to the SLA.

Concurrent with her increasing involvement with such organizations, Yonge's earlier work learning the techniques of map librarianship, familiarizing herself with the collections, and providing scholarly reference services also enabled her to contribute gradually a wide variety of written material to her profession. In 1947, the American Geographical Society published the *Manual for the Classification and Cataloguing of Maps in the Society's Collection* prepared by Ena Yonge and Mary Elizabeth Hartzell, her assistant; a second edition was published in 1952. She was the invited editor of a special map issue of *Library Journal* in 1950 and was also the author of one of the articles. This issue was especially valuable because it came at a time when very little professional literature about map librarianship was available. Throughout the 1950s, she contributed frequently to the SLA Geography and Map Division *Bulletin* and, from 1957 to 1963, again by invitation, published a series of four extensive review articles on atlases for the *Geographical Review*.

Yonge's major work, *A Catalogue of Early Globes Made Prior to 1850 and Conserved in the United States*, represented more than ten years of research and was published in 1968 by the American Geographical Society. This listing resulted from the 1952 recommendation of the International Geographical Union's Commission on Ancient Maps that an "International Catalogue of Early Globes," published before 1850, be compiled. The American Geographical Society agreed to be responsible for the United States section, and the project was assigned to Yonge. As a tribute to her work after its publication, she was elected a corresponding member of the prestigious Coronelli Weltbund der Globusfreunde.

Yonge also became a tour leader and world traveller during the late 1950s, taking groups to visit cartographic institutions in South America, Western Europe, the Soviet Union, Spain, and Portugal. The first and third tours focused on international geographical meetings, with Yonge reading a paper in 1960 at the International Congress on the History of Discoveries.

Following her official retirement in 1962, she continued to work twice weekly at the American Geographical Society for the next five months. Long after the naming of the Society's atlas room as the "Ena L. Yonge Atlas Room" and her own designation as map curator emeritus, Yonge was involved actively in her profession. In addition to preparing the catalog of early globes, she served as a consultant to four map libraries and map publishers in Great Britain and also cataloged the Rucker Agee Map Collection at the Birmingham, Alabama, Public Library. Her death at her home in Florida on December 31, 1971, came exactly nine years after the date of her retirement.

Described by her colleagues as a born map curator, the energetic Yonge was devoted to the American Geographical Society and to map librarianship. Her personal interests were widely varied; her professional expertise, intelligent curiosity, and delightful personality enriched and enlivened the scholarly community for more than five decades. She was a pioneer in her field and not only helped to shape the careers of less experienced map librarians but also shaped the profession itself.

Biographical listings and obituaries—Felland, Nordis. "Ena L. Yonge 1895-1971 [obituary]." *Geographical Review* 62:414-17 (1972); Felland, Nordis. "Ena L. Yonge [obituary]." *Special Libraries* 63:489 (1972); LeGear, Clara E. "Ena Laura Yonge (1895-1971) [obituary]." *Imago Mundi* 25:85-86 (1971); "Miss Ena L. Yonge [obituary]." *Der Globusfreund*, No. 21-23:28 (1973); Ristow, Walter W. "Ena L. Yonge 1895-1971 [obituary]." Special Libraries Association. Geography and Map Division. *Bulletin*, No. 88:24-29 (1972). **Books and articles about the biographee**—LeGear, Clara E. "AGS Map Curator Retires." Special Libraries Association. Geography and Map Division. *Bulletin*, No. 51:13-14 (1963); Price, Jo-ann. "She Has Her Future All Mapped Out." *New York Herald Tribune*, May 26, 1963, p. 33. **Primary sources and archival materials**—Ena Yonge's biographical data and annual reports are at the

American Geographical Society, Broadway at 156th Street, New York City.

                            —NANCY M. KLINE

YOUNG, JOHN RUSSELL (1840-1899)

John Russell Young, future Librarian of Congress, was born on November 20, 1840, in County Tyrone, Ireland, the son of George and Eliza Rankin Young. Taken to the United States when less than a year old, Young began his formal schooling in Philadelphia and continued it in a high school in New Orleans, where he was sent following the death of his mother in 1851. His real education, however, like that of his better known contemporaries Samuel Clemens and William Dean Howells, took place in print shops and editorial offices, first in Philadelphia following his return to that city, and later in New York. He is said to have studied law in his late twenties, but he did not practice it professionally.

Young was married three times: to Rose Fitzpatrick on October 18, 1864; to Julia Coleman on April 25, 1882; and to Mary Dow Davids on November 18, 1890. The first two marriages ended tragically, Rose Fitzpatrick Young dying in 1881 of malaria contracted in California, Julia Coleman Young dying in Paris in 1883, while Young remained in Peking at his post as minister to China. Three children from his first marriage also died in childhood. The third Mrs. Young survived her husband, as did two sons, Russell Jewell Young from his second marriage, and Gordon Russell Young from his third.

John Young's success as a newspaperman came at an incredibly early age. He secured a position as copy boy with the *Philadelphia Press* at age sixteen, and less than five years later he was its managing editor. His abilities were immense, and he wrote well, if a little stiffly, for someone his age. He also had the knack of relieving his employers of routine management problems. And he was a prodigious worker. In the right place at the right time, Young rose in the editorial department of the *Press* in part because its editor-in-chief, John W. Forney, was much occupied with his duties in Washington as clerk of the Senate. Young also benefitted in national reputation from his having filed the first full and accurate account of the Union disaster at Bull Run in July 1861, to which he was an eyewitness. In addition to his service to Forney, Young during his Philadelphia years established the *Morning Post*, in which he maintained an interest for several years.

Following the Civil War, Young moved to New York, where he exceeded his Philadelphia success. He joined the staff of Horace Greeley's famous *New York Tribune* late in 1865 and became its managing editor six months later, aged 25. He served with distinction for three years, bringing about numerous changes, including an expanded overseas correspondent system to which he assigned George W. Smalley and for which he employed Henry M. Stanley. A special writer associated with the staff in this period was Samuel L. Clemens, whose sketches for *Innocents Abroad* were published in the *Tribune* (and two other newspapers) in 1867. The principal issue of these years, however, was the impeachment of Andrew Johnson, in favor of which Young wrote influential editorials. In his zeal on this issue, he exceeded Horace Greeley. Young differed from Greeley, however, concerning the 1868 Republican nominee. Young came to favor U.S. Grant, whereas Greeley favored Salmon P. Chase. Because of these differences, Greeley made no serious attempt to dissuade Young from resigning his position in 1869, following a dispute with the Associated Press in which Young thought his good name had been impugned.

Shortly after leaving the *Tribune*, Young helped to establish the American Press Association as a rival to the Associated Press, started a pro-Grant paper in New York (the short-lived *Evening Standard*), and also began to write for James Gordon Bennett's *New York Herald*. Throughout the 1870s, he was mostly in Europe as a representative of the *Herald*. After Grant left office, he sailed to England, where Young arranged a large press dinner in London for him. Urged by Grant to accompany him on his round-the-world progress, Young did so. The result was *Around the World with General Grant* (1879), a two-volume compilation of Young's dispatches to the *Herald*, embellished and enlarged. After Grant returned to the United States, he sought a suitable diplomatic post for Young. In a letter dated February 18, 1881, he recommended Young to President-elect Garfield as a potential minister to Japan: "The United States has a grand mission in the East and Mr. Young is the best equipped man in America to commence it."

It was not to be Garfield but his successor, Chester A. Arthur, who made Young's ministerial appointment, naming him minister to China (rather than Japan) on March 15, 1882. Young served with distinction until 1885, when Grover Cleveland replaced him with another appointee. Young was approached about a diplomatic appointment in 1889 (probably a return to China), but he had resumed his career in journalism and business and declined to be considered. After additional foreign residence, in the 1890s, he resettled in Philadelphia, where he edited the city's *Memorial History* and was active in the Union League, of which he had been the youngest of the founders in 1862. He was president of the League for two years, during which time he arranged the memorable gathering of Union and Confederate military heroes at Gettysburg in April 1893.

Young returned to government service as Librarian of Congress in mid-1897. He was appointed to the position by President McKinley on June 30 and confirmed by the Senate the same day, a fact that Young believed to be "unprecedented." He took the oath of office July 1.

Although Young's tenure was to be pitifully brief, his impact upon the Library was far-ranging. Unlike Ainsworth Rand Spofford (q.v.), his bookish but provincial predecessor, Young was a man of the world who had moved in the highest circles of journalism, politics, business, and diplomacy for more than thirty years. He was well known in Congress; his younger brother James, in fact, was a representative from Pennsylvania (and the "banner Republican") at the time of his appointment. John Young's business sense enabled him to supervise the restoration of some order in Copyright Office finances, which Spofford had muddled, and to deal effectively with the principal embarrassment that he inherited from his predecessor, the theft of some historic manuscripts by two staff members.

Young's immediate problems were controlled enlargement of the staff by more than 150 percent, movement of the collections into the spacious Main Building now ready for occupancy, and opening the building for use at the earliest possible date. Young achieved all these goals. He kept strict control over appointments, instituted a qualifying examination, and kept congressional sponsors at bay on patronage. (To Senator C. K. Davis, he wrote on September 7, 1898: "if I am *apparently* stubborn in answer to senators requests, it is not that I am *really* so—but unless we have competent people in what is a narrow and technical science, the Library as a useful institution will fall down.")

Among the "competent people" whom Young brought (or brought back) to principal positions on the staff were Thorvald Solberg (q.v.), who was to serve as register of copyrights for more than thirty years; J. C. M. Hanson (q.v.), who was in charge of the Catalogue Department for thirteen years before concluding his career at the University of Chicago; and Herbert Friedenwald, first chief of the Department of Manuscripts, who went on to become editor of the *American Jewish Yearbook* and a founder of the American Jewish Historical Society. Young also advanced staff members within the Library, such as the cartographer P. Lee Phillips. Spofford, of course, remained as his chief assistant, and, eighteen months later, succeeded Young *ad interim* before Herbert Putnam (q.v.) began his long association with the Library. To Senator A. O. Bacon, Young wrote (July 19, 1898) that he did not know whether his heads of departments (except for the law librarian) "had any politics. They are thoroughly trained in their work—and there I rested." A lesser or more

malleable man than Young would have been disastrous for the Library. His sturdy independence at a time of great expansion set a formidable precedent for his successors and strengthened the operation of a merit system for appointment and advancement in the national library.

In his second month as Librarian, Young instructed Spofford to devise "a special service for the blind" that would "go far towards the complete idea of a national library." Two weeks later, on September 2, 1897, Young called attention to the government's annual $10,000 contribution to the American Printing House for the Blind: "If this is so, I do not see why we should not make, at least, equitable claim for a copy of their publications." The "pavilion for the blind" was made part of Library operations when the Main Building opened for service in the fall of 1897; volunteers were engaged to read to the blind, and publishers were approached to contribute publications for this special service. In a few weeks, therefore, Young had anticipated many library services now organized at the Library within the Division for the Blind and Physically Handicapped.

In his first annual report as Librarian, written less than five months after assuming his office, Young called upon Congress to transfer to the Library the personal papers of early Presidents, which had been acquired by the government and housed at the Department of State. Like many of his initiatives, this one was effected several years later, in 1903.

To John Addison Porter, President McKinley's secretary, Young wrote on September 14, 1897, "There is chaos in the Library and each department has had to be reorganized from the ground up." Some of the problems were technical, and Young wrote often to John Shaw Billings (q.v.) and Melvil Dewey (q.v.) for their suggestions about solving them. Some of the problems were deficiencies in the collections, and Young made good use of his associations in government to solve them. He began to effect foreign exchange programs through his contacts in the diplomatic service. (He also wrote to an old friend, the Chinese ambassador, for assistance in cataloging Chinese books acquired with the Caleb Cushing Library.) He approached government agencies for cartographic and pictorial material officially prepared. He wrote to many newspapers and periodicals and, using the prestige and celebrity of the "new" Library of Congress, secured numerous gifts to the collections.

As an administrator, Young set an exacting standard. He insisted that all Library business be controlled in the office of the Librarian. He counteracted "a disposition on the part of some of the heads of Departments to open special lines of correspondence upon Library matters," but he gave his staff full support against unfounded criticism. In response to criticism of Solberg, Young wrote to Speaker of the House Joseph G. Cannon that Solberg was a "faithful, efficient government official," one who aroused criticism because he was "an exacting, conscientious man in charge of a monotonous department and bent upon having the government work done." Young resisted attempts of other agencies to secure assignments of space in the Library, even temporarily. (He did, however, offer Chief Justice Fuller the use of Library facilities for the Supreme Court.) He instituted a system of passes for security reasons. He thought the Library stacks should be as nearly closed as possible, and he severely limited borrowing privileges.

John Russell Young died on January 17, 1899, of Bright's disease, following a three-week illness that began with a serious fall on Christmas Eve. For eighteen months, he had devoted his energies to the position of Librarian of Congress. What course the Library might have taken under his continued leadership is a moot question. Obviously, however, no one of his predecessors or successors matched his achievements in a comparable period of service. Dignified and conscientious, Young set an independent tone for the Library that his successor, Herbert Putnam, put to good advantage.

A week after Young's death, his widow wrote a ten-page letter to President McKinley, urging him to select a new Librarian as well qualified in all respects as her husband had been. According to Mrs. Young, her husband "gave no one his confidence, he listened patiently to all, but he formed his own conclusions and governed absolutely according to his conscience." Although rather austere, like its subject, this statement may be taken as a satisfactory summary of John Russell Young as Librarian of Congress.

According to Alexander McClure, Young's "intimate acquaintance with eminent men exceeded that of any other one man in the entire country." Many of them attended his funeral, including Cabinet officers and the entire Chinese embassy staff as a mark of respect. One of those present, Young's long-time friend Henry Watterson, editor of the *Louisville Courier-Journal*, wrote that no one of Young's vast acquaintance did not regard him "in intellect and character as the peer of the best of his contemporaries." Walt Whitman, who knew Young off and on for his entire adult life, described Young as follows: "lymphatic—of course not thin: rather stout, brisk, compact—it might be said, a strong man." He thought Young resembled Edmund Gosse: "Combed, cleaned, polished, brushed, exact." But there was a difference. "Gosse is eminently scholar—all scholar: the university man: all refined, bookish, made up. Young . . . had more native grit."

Biographical listings and obituaries—*Dictionary of American Biography* 20 (Jeannette L. Berger); [Obituary]. *New York Times*, Jan. 18, 1899, p. 7; [Obituary]. *Washington Post*, Jan. 18, 1899, p. 2; *Who Was Who in America*, Historical Volume (1607-1896). **Books and articles about the biographee**—Broderick, John C. "John Russell Young: The Internationalist as Librarian." *Quarterly Journal of the Library of Congress* 33:116-49 (April 1976); Cummings, Amos J. "How Newspapers Are Made. The New York Tribune." *Packard's Monthly* 1:87-89 (Oct. 1868), 105-109 (Nov. 1868); Curti, Merle, and John Stalker. " 'The Flowery Flag Devils'—The American Image in China 1840-1900." *Proceedings of the American Philosophical Society* 96:663-90 (Dec. 1952); Dennett, Tyler. "American Choices in the Far East in 1882." *American Historical Review* 30:84-108 (Oct. 1924); "John Russell Young, 1841-1899, Librarian of Congress July 1, 1897-January 17, 1899. Biographical Sketch." *Report of the Librarian of Congress for . . . 1899*. Washington: Government Printing Office, 1899, Appendix I, pp. 17-18; Mearns, David C. *The Story Up to Now*. Washington: Library of Congress, 1947 [forms part of *Annual Report of the Librarian of Congress*, 1946]; Watterson, Henry. "John Russell Young." *The Washington Post*, Feb. 12, 1899, p. 21. **Primary sources and archival materials**—Library of Congress archives, Manuscript Division, Library of Congress; John Russell Young papers, Manuscript Division, Library of Congress; *Annual Report of the Librarian of Congress*, 1897, 1898. Washington: Government Printing Office, 1897, 1898.

—JOHN C. BRODERICK

Name Index

The name index, designed to show professional relationships within librarianship, accesses all citations to the biographees found throughout the *Dictionary*. Biographees' names and the pages on which their main sketches appear are shown in italics. The index also includes the names of people who were professionally associated with the biographees or who influenced their lives or careers. Family members generally are not listed although wives are included.